Contents

II European driving: cut through the confusion
IV Driving regulations
VIII Ski resorts
X Sights of Europe
XXIV European politics and economics

1 **Route planning maps**

1 Key to route planning map pages

24 **Road maps**

24 Key to road map pages · Distance table

201 **City plans and approach maps**

Alicante	C 201	Göteborg	C 210	Oslo	UC 219
Amsterdam	CU 202	Granada	C 210	Paris	CU 220
Antwerpen	C 201	Hamburg	CU 210	Praha	CU 222
Athina	UC 202	Helsinki	CU 211	Roma	CU 223
Barcelona	CU 203	İstanbul	U 211	Rotterdam	C 222
Basel	C 203	København	CU 212	Sankt Peterburg	U 222
Beograd	C 205	Köln Cologne	C 212	Sevilla	C 224
Berlin	CU 204	Lisboa	CU 213	Stockholm	CU 225
Bordeaux	CU 205	London	CU 213	Strasbourg	CU 224
Bruxelles	UC 205	Luxembourg	C 215	Stuttgart	C 224
Budapest	CU 206	Lyon	CU 215	Torino	UC 226
Dublin	CU 207	Madrid	UC 215	Venézia	C 226
Düsseldorf	CU 207	Málaga	C 216	Warszawa	CU 227
Edinburgh	C 207	Marseille	C 216	Wien	UC 227
Firenze Florence	C 209	Milano	CU 217	Zagreb	C 228
Frankfurt	C 209	Moskva	CU 218	Zürich	C 228
Genève Geneva	C 209	München	CU 218	C City street plan	
Génova Genoa	C 209	Nápoli	CU 219	U Urban area map	

229 **Index to road maps**

www.philips-maps.co.uk
First published in 2007 as *Philip's EasyRead Europe* by
Philip's, a division of Octopus Publishing Group Ltd
www.octopusbooks.co.uk
Endeavour House, 189 Shaftesbury Avenue,
London WC2H 8JY
An Hachette UK Company
www.hachette.co.uk
Third edition 2012,
First impression 2012

Ordnance Survey® This product includes mapping
data licensed from Ordnance
Survey®, with the permission of
the Controller of Her Majesty's Stationery Office © Crown
copyright 2012. All rights reserved. Licence number 100011710.

OS is a registered Trade Mark of the Northern Ireland
Department of Finance and Personnel.
This product includes mapping data licensed from
Ordnance Survey of Northern Ireland®, reproduced with the
permission of Land and Property Services under delegated
authority from the Controller of Her Majesty's Stationery Office,
© Crown Copyright 2012.

While every reasonable effort has been made to ensure that the
information compiled in this atlas is accurate, complete and
up-to-date at the time of publication, some of this information
is subject to change and the Publisher cannot guarantee its
correctness or completeness.

The information in this atlas is provided without any
representation or warranty, express or implied and the Publisher
cannot be held liable for any loss or damage due to any use
or reliance on the information in this atlas, nor for any errors,
omissions or subsequent changes in such information.

The representation in this atlas of any road, drive or track is not
evidence of the existence of a right of way.

The mapping on page 214 and the town plans of Edinburgh and
London are based on mapping data licenced from Ordnance
Survey with the permission of the Controller of Her Majesty's
Stationery Office, © Crown Copyright 2012. All rights reserved.
Licence number 100011710.

The maps of Ireland on pages 26 to 30 and the urban area map
and town plan of Dublin are based on Ordnance Survey Ireland by
permission of the Government Permit Number 8798 © Ordnance
Survey Ireland and Government of Ireland, and Land and Property
Services under delegated authority from the Controller of Her
Majesty's Stationery Office © Crown Copyright 2012
Permit Number 120078

Cartography by Philip's, Copyright © Philip's 2012

Photographic acknowledgements: Page II, marcutti /
iStockphoto.com • Page III, column 1 *Lya Cattel / iStockphoto.
com*; column 2 above *kelvinjay / iStockphoto.com*, below,
ollo/iStockphoto.com; columns 3 and 4 *Morten Normann
Almeland / iStockphoto.com*.

Printed in China

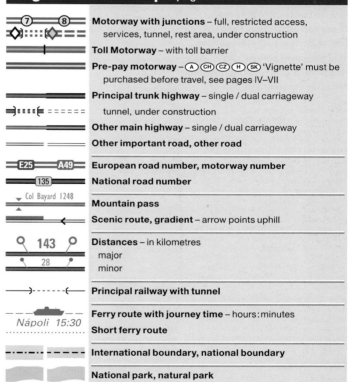

Legend to route planning maps pages 2–23

- Motorway with selected junctions
  tunnel, under construction
- Toll motorway, pre-pay motorway
- Main through route, other major road, other road
- **25** **56** European road number, motorway number
- **55** National road number
- 56 Distances – in kilometres
- International boundary, national boundary
- LE HAVRE Car ferry and destination
- 1089 Mountain pass, international airport, height in metres

Town – population

MOSKVA	5 million +	Gävle	50000–100000
BERLIN	2–5 million	Nybro	20000–50000
MINSK	1–2 million	Ikast	10000–20000
Oslo	500000–1million	Skjern	5000–10000
Århus	200000–500000	Lillesand	0–5000
Turku	100000–200000		

The green version of the symbol indicates towns
with Low Emission Zones

Legend to road maps pages 26–200

- **7** **8** Motorway with junctions – full, restricted access,
  services, tunnel, rest area, under construction
- Toll Motorway – with toll barrier
- Pre-pay motorway – Ⓐ CH CZ H SK 'Vignette' must be
  purchased before travel, see pages IV–VII
- Principal trunk highway – single / dual carriageway
  tunnel, under construction
- Other main highway – single / dual carriageway
- Other important road, other road
- E25 A49 European road number, motorway number
- 135 National road number
- Col Bayard 1248 Mountain pass
- Scenic route, gradient – arrow points uphill
- 143 Distances – in kilometres
  28 major / minor
- Principal railway with tunnel
- Nápoli 15:30 Ferry route with journey time – hours : minutes
- Short ferry route
- International boundary, national boundary
- National park, natural park

✈ Airport	⛷ Ski resort
Ancient monument	Theme park
Beach	⊙ World Heritage site
Castle or house	1754▲ Spot height
Cave	Sevilla World Heritage town
Other place of interest	Verona Town of tourist interest
Park or garden	■ ● City or town with Low Emission Zone
Religious building	

Scales

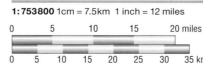

Pages 2–23

1:3200000 1cm = 32km 1 in = 50.51 miles

0 20 40 60 80 miles
0 20 40 60 80 100 120 140 km

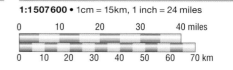

Pages 26–181

1:753800 1cm = 7.5km 1 inch = 12 miles

0 5 10 15 20 miles
0 5 10 15 20 25 30 35 km

Pages 182–200

1:1507600 • 1cm = 15km, 1 inch = 24 miles

0 10 20 30 40 miles
0 10 20 30 40 50 60 70 km

European driving:
cut through the confusion

Stay safe with GEM Motoring Assist

- Are you confused about European driving laws?
- Do you need advice about equipment requirements and which documents to take?
- Are you new to driving on the right-hand side?
- How will you know what speed limits apply?
- Who do you call if you have an accident or break down?

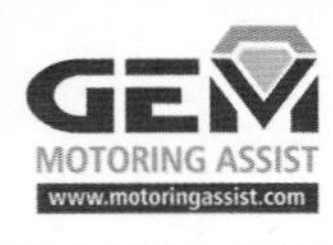

Around 8 million of us drive abroad while on holiday each year, yet research shows we tend to be reluctant to prepare for journeys and plan routes – and that 49% of us don't actually like getting behind the wheel abroad*. We're also unsure when it comes to carrying the right documents and equipment.

It's not easy getting to grips with the finer points of driving in other countries. Whether you have notched up thousands of miles of European driving or are preparing to make your first journey, the chances are you will encounter some road sign or legal requirement that will cause confusion.

What's more, 'driving in Europe' covers such a huge area. There are 27 countries in the European Union alone, each with its own set of road traffic laws and motoring customs. Driving in Europe can mean a spectacular and sunny coastal road that's within sight of Africa, or a snowy track amid the biting cold of the Arctic Circle, where the only others on the road are reindeer. Add to this some of the world's most congested cities, dense clusters of motorways (many with confusing numbers!) and a big variation in safety standards and attitudes to risk. No wonder we so often get lost, take wrong turnings or perhaps stop where we shouldn't!

Forewarned is forearmed, and it certainly pays to do a bit of research before you go, just to ensure you and your vehicle are up to the journey, your documents are in order and you're carrying the correct levels of equipment to keep the law enforcers happy.

BEFORE YOU GO

Some sensible planning will help make sure your European journey is enjoyable and – we hope – stress-free. So take some time before departure to ensure everything is in good shape – and that includes you, your travelling companions and your vehicle.

For you:

Try to become familiar with the driving laws of your holiday destination, including the local speed limits and which side of the road to drive on! You will be subject to these laws when driving abroad and if you are stopped by the police it is not an excuse to say that you were unaware of them. Police officers in many countries have the power to impose (and collect) substantial on-the-spot fines for motoring offences, whether you are a resident of that country or a visitor.

GEM Motoring Assist can link you direct with up-to-date information on driving in 27 European countries (including Norway and Switzerland, who are not members of the European Union).

For each country, you will find an attractive, downloadable three-page PDF document containing detailed information on driving facts, traffic laws, document and equipment requirements – and even a few simple emergency phrases to help you if you're in difficulty.
Go to www.motoringassist.com/europe
The Foreign and Commonwealth Office also gives country-specific travel advice (www.fco.gov.uk/travel) with information on driving.

Passports

Check everyone's passport to make sure they are all valid. Don't wait for your passport to expire. Unused time, rounded up to whole months (minimum one month, maximum nine months), will usually be added to your new passport.

New passports usually take two weeks to arrive. The Passport Office (0300 222 0000, www.ips.gov.uk) offers a faster service if you need a replacement passport urgently, but it'll cost a lot more.

Driving Licence

The new-style photocard driving licence is valid in all European Union countries. However, you must ensure you carry both parts: the credit card-size photocard and the paper licence. The previously used pink EU format UK licence is also valid, though it may not be recognized in some areas. So if you haven't already done so, now is the time to update your old licence. For more information, contact the DVLA (0300 790 6801, www.dvla.gov.uk)

Travel Insurance

Travel insurance is vital as it covers you against medical emergencies, accidents, thefts, cancellations and repatriation. Ask for details before buying any travel insurance policy. Find out what it covers you for, and to what value. More important, check what's not covered. One of the key benefits of GEM membership is the excellent discount you can get on travel insurance. For more details, please visit our website: www.motoringassist.com/philipsmaps

European Breakdown Cover

Don't risk letting a breakdown ruin your European trip. Ensure you purchase a policy that will cover you for roadside assistance, emergency repair and recovery of your vehicle to the UK, wherever in Europe you may be heading. Once again, GEM members enjoy a specially discounted rate. You'll find the details at www.motoringassist.com/philipsmaps

EHIC

The E111 medical treatment form is no longer valid. Instead, you need an EHIC card for everyone travelling. These are free and cover you for any medical treatment you may need during a trip to another EU country or Switzerland. However, do check at the time of requiring assistance that your EHIC will be accepted. Apply online (www.ehic.org.uk), by telephone (0845 606 2030) or complete an application form, available from a Post office. Allow up to 14 days for the cards to arrive.

For your vehicle:

Service

It makes sense to get your car serviced before you travel. As a minimum, ensure the tyres have plenty of tread left and that water and oil levels are checked and topped up if required. Check them regularly during your time away.

Vehicle Registration Document

Police in many countries can demand that you prove you have the right to be driving your car. That means you need to show the registration document, or a suitable letter of authorization if the registration document is not in your name. Remember you should never leave the registration document in the car.

Nationality plate

Your vehicle must display a nationality plate of an approved pattern, design and size.

MOT

If your car is more than three years old, make sure you take its current MOT test certificate with you.

Insurance

If you are planning a trip to Europe, you should find that your car insurance policy provides you with the minimum amount of cover you need. But it's important to contact your insurer before you go, to confirm exactly what level of cover you have and for how many days it will be valid.

Mechanical adjustments

Check the adjustments required for your headlights before you go. Beam deflectors are a legal requirement if you drive in Europe. They are generally sold at the ports, on ferries and in the Folkestone Eurotunnel terminal, but be warned – the instructions can be a little confusing! The alternative is to ask a local garage to do the job for you before you go. If you choose this, then make sure you shop around as prices for undertaking this very simple task vary enormously.

Equipment check-list

This check-list represents GEM's suggestions for what you should take with you in the car. Different countries have different rules about what's compulsory and these rules change from time to time. So it's important to check carefully before you set out. For country-by-country guidance, visit www.motoringassist.com/europe or see page IV of this atlas.

- Fire extinguisher
- First aid kit
- High-visibility jacket – one for each occupant
- Two warning triangles
- Replacement bulbs and fuses
- Spare spectacles (if worn) for each driver
- Snow chains for winter journeys
- Camera and notebook. Keep in your glove compartment and record any collisions or damage for insurance purposes (if it is safe).

Contact details

Make sure you have all relevant emergency helpline numbers with you, including emergency services, breakdown assistance, the local British consulate and your insurance company. There are links to embassies and consulates around the world from the Foreign Office website (www.fco.gov.uk). For information, the European emergency telephone number (our equivalent of 999) is 112.

MOTORWAY VIGNETTES

Some countries require you to purchase (and in some cases display) a vignette before using motorways.

In Austria you will need to purchase and display a vignette on the inside of your windscreen. Vignettes are available for purchase at border crossings and petrol stations. More details from www.austria.info

In the Czech Republic, you can buy a vignette at the border and also at petrol stations. Make sure you write your vehicle registration number on the vignette before displaying it. The roads without toll are indicated by a traffic sign saying 'Bez poplatku'. More details from www.motorway.cz

In Hungary a new e-vignette system was introduced at the beginning of 2008. It is therefore no longer necessary to display the vignette, though you should make doubly sure the information you give on your vehicle is accurate. Vignettes are sold at petrol stations throughout the country. Buy online at www.motorway.hu

In Slovakia, a vignette is also required to be purchased before using the motorways. This is sold in two kinds at the Slovak border and petrol stations. You will need to write your vehicle registration plate on the vignette before displaying it. More details from www.slovensko.com.

In Switzerland, you will need to purchase and display a 'vignette' before you use the motorway. You will need a separate vignette if you are towing a caravan. Purchase the Swiss vignette in advance from www.autobahnen.ch

TOP TIPS FOR STAYING SAFE

:ollisions abroad occur not just because
of poor driving conditions locally, but also
because we do not always take the same safety
precautions as we might expect to take at home,
for example by not wearing a seatbelt or by
drinking and driving.

1. Plan your route before you go. That includes the journey you make to reach your destination (with sufficient breaks built in) and any excursions or local journeys you make while you're there.

2. Remember that, wherever you drive, you will be subject to the same laws as local drivers. Claiming ignorance of these laws will not be accepted as an excuse.

3. Take extra care at junctions when you're driving on the 'right side' of the road. If driving in a family group, involve every member in a quick 'junction safety check' to help reduce the risk of a collision. Having everybody in the car call out a catchphrase such as 'DriLL DriLL DriLL' (Driver Look Left) on the approach to junctions and roundabouts is a small but potentially life-saving habit.

4. Take fatigue seriously. The excellent European motorway network means you can cover big distances with ease. But you must also make time for proper breaks (experts recommend a break of at least 15 minutes after every two hours of driving). If possible, share the driving and set strict daily limits to the number of driving hours.

5. Blood-alcohol limits across Europe are lower than those in the UK. The only exception is Malta, where the limit is the same (0.08%). Bear this in mind if you're flying to a holiday or business destination and plan to have a drink on the plane, as the combination of unfamiliar roads and alcohol in your bloodstream is not a safe one. It's also worth remembering that drivers who cause collisions because they were drinking are likely to find their insurance policy will not cover them.

6. Expect the unexpected. Styles of driving in your destination country are likely to be very different from those you know in the UK. Drive defensively and certainly don't get involved in any altercations on the road.

7. Don't overload your car while away, however tempting the local bargains may appear. Also, make sure you have good all-round visibility by ensuring you don't pile up items on the parcel shelf or boot, and keep your windscreen clear of dirt and dust.

8. Always wear a seatbelt and ensure everyone else on board wears one. Check specific regulations regarding the carriage of children: in some countries children under the age of 12 are not permitted to travel in the front of the car.

9. Don't use your mobile phone while driving. Even though laws on phone use while driving differ from country to country, the practice is just as dangerous wherever you are.

10. When you're exploring on foot, be wise to road safety as a pedestrian. You may get into trouble for 'jay-walking', so don't just wander across a road. Use a proper crossing, but remember that drivers may not stop for you! And don't forget that traffic closest to you approaches from the LEFT.

STOP AND GIVE WAY

Who has priority?

Make sure you keep a watchful eye on signs telling you who has priority on the road. Look for a yellow diamond sign, which tells you that traffic already on the road has priority. If you see the yellow diamond sign crossed out, then you must give way to traffic joining the road.

Priorité à droite

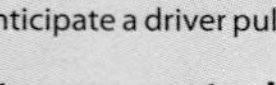

Despite the use of the yellow diamond signs, be aware that on some French roads (especially roundabouts in Paris), the traditional 'priorité à droite' practice is followed, even though it may no longer be legal. In theory these days, the rule no longer applies unless it is clearly signed. In practice, though, it makes sense to anticipate a driver pulling out in front of you, even though the priority may be yours.

Stop means stop!

If you come to a solid white line with an octagonal 'STOP' sign, then you must come to a complete stop. In other words your wheels must stop turning. Adherence to the 'STOP' sign is generally much more rigorously enforced in European countries than you may be used to here.

Headlight flash

Bear in mind that the practice of flashing headlights at a junction in France does not mean the same thing as it might in the UK. If another motorist flashes his headlights at you, he's telling you that he has priority and will be coming through in front of you!

FREQUENTLY ASKED QUESTIONS

Do I need to use dipped headlights all the time?

It's currently mandatory to use dipped headlights for daytime journeys in 14 of the 27 EU countries. Additionally, a European directive now requires all new cars to be fitted with daytime running lights, a move designed to improve the visibility of the car to other road users.

Do German motorways still not have speed limits?

Speed limits apply to around 30% of German motorways. A further 10% of motorways in Germany are subject to variable speed limits, determined by motorway control rooms. Across other stretches there is a recommended speed limit of 130km/h. It is worth remembering that whereas exceeding this limit is not an offence, the penalties for a high-speed driver being involved in an accident are considerably higher.

Why do European motorways all seem to have two numbers on the map and the road signs?

This is because the roads form the international network of 'E-roads'. In most countries maps and signs will have the European road number (shown in white on a green background) alongside the appropriate national road number. However, in Sweden and Belgium only the E-road number will be shown.

As a visitor to a country, rather than a resident, am I exempt from speeding fines?

No. Different countries have different mechanisms for dealing with traffic offences committed by non-resident drivers. If, for example, you are stopped for speeding, then expect to receive a fine which you can usually pay 'on the spot' by credit card. A number of bilateral agreements exist, allowing police to obtain non-resident driver details and issue penalties for offences recorded by automatic enforcement cameras.

Interestingly, 'foreign' drivers make up only about 5% of traffic on Europe's roads, yet they account for 15% of all speeding offences. Draft legislation was approved in Brussels at the end of 2010 for a full European cross-border enforcement directive to combat this problem. Other offences, such as non-wearing of seatbelts and crossing red traffic lights, are also expected to be included within the legislation.

If I hire a car in one country, am I allowed to take it into another country?

The issue is most likely to be with insurance, so check with the hiring company before setting off. Ask to see something in writing so you are sure that you are getting the right information. Often, when hiring, you will find you have only the minimum cover required for driving in the country where you hired the car. If you plan to take it into other countries, then make sure your insurance will cover you and purchase a top-up policy if necessary.

WORTH KNOWING

The following information is worth noting: In EU countries, if your car doesn't have a registration plate containing the GB euro-symbol, you will need a separate GB sticker.

Fuel is generally most expensive at motorway service areas and cheapest at supermarkets. However, these are usually shut on Sundays and Bank Holidays. So-called '24 hour' regional fuel stations in France seldom accept payment by UK credit card, so don't rely on them if your tank is running low during a night-time journey.

In non-EU countries the euro-plate is not valid anyway, so you will need the separate sticker as well.

Radar speed camera detectors are illegal in most European countries.

The insurance 'green card' is no longer required for journeys in Europe, but it is important to make sure you have contact details for your insurer in case of an accident or claim.

In Spain you must carry two warning triangles, plus a spare pair of glasses for every driver.

In Luxembourg, there are specific rules relating to how you fix a sat nav device to your windscreen. Get it wrong and you could be fined on the spot.

In Germany it is against the law to run out of fuel on the motorway. If you do run out, then you face an on-the-spot fine.

In France, if you are caught exceeding the speed limit by 50km/h, even on a first offence, you will face a term of imprisonment.

Norway and Sweden have particularly low blood-alcohol limits: just 0.01% and 0.02% respectively (compared to 0.08% in the UK).

In Slovakia, the blood-alcohol limit is zero.

In Hungary, the limit is also zero. If you are found to be drink-driving, your driving licence will be withdrawn by police officers on the spot.

Other laws and motoring advice to be aware of across Europe:

Austria New rules came into effect at the beginning of 2012, regarding giving way to emergency vehicles on highways, motorways and expressways. It is now compulsory to make a clear path for emergency vehicles ('Rettungsgasse') as soon as traffic on a two-, three- or four-lane road becomes congested and slow-moving or stationary. Bear in mind that you must do this whether or not there is an emergency vehicle approaching.

Belgium You will have to pay to use most public toilets – including those at motorway service stations. • You are not permitted to use cruise control on motorways when traffic is heavy. • There are also specific penalties for close-following on motorways. • Roadside drug-testing of drivers (using oral fluid testing devices) was introduced late in 2010 and now forms a regular part of any police controls.

Cyprus Recent changes to regulations have made the use of headlights mandatory for motorcycles on all journeys.

Denmark Cars towing caravans and trailers are prohibited from overtaking on motorways at certain times.

Finland If you hit an elk or deer, you must report the collision to the police. • Speeding fines are worked out according to your income. Access to a national database allows police at the roadside to establish a Finnish resident's income and number of dependants. Officers then impose a fine based on a specific number of days' income. A 'ticket calculator' on the Finnish Police website (www.poliisi.fi) allows you to work out the fine before committing the offence! The minimum speeding fine is 15 euros.

France As of 1 July 2012, any driver must be in possession of a valid breathalyser (displaying a 'BF' number), either electronic or chemical, to be shown to a police officer in case of control. The fine for failing to comply is €11.

As of 1 January 2013, all motorcycle riders and passengers must wear reflective clothing, measuring a minimum 150 square centimetres and worn on the upper part of the body. This must also be worn if they have had to stop at the side of the road.

- Jail terms for drivers caught at more than 50km/h above the speed limit – even first-time offenders.
- The banning of radar detectors, with fines of €1500 for anyone using them.
- Increased penalties for driving while using a mobile phone.

Germany Check your fuel contents regularly as it's an offence to run out of fuel on a German motorway. • It's also an offence to make rude signs to other road users.

Greece has Europe's highest accident rate in terms of the number of crashes per vehicle. Pay particular attention at traffic-light junctions, as red lights are frequently ignored. Since 2 April 2012 all drivers detected with more than 1.10 g/l of alcohol in blood, or more than 0.60mg/l in breath will be prosecuted for the offence.

Carrying a petrol can in a vehicle is forbidden.

Ireland The drink-drive limit was recently (28 October 2011) reduced from 0.8 mg per ml to 0.5. • Beware of rural three-lane roads, where the middle overtaking lane is used by traffic travelling in both directions. On wider rural roads it's the accepted practice for slower vehicles to pull over to let faster traffic through.

Italy Police can impound your vehicle if you cannot present the relevant ownership documents when requested. • You will need a red-and-white warning sign if you plan to use any rear-mounted luggage rack such as a bike rack. • Zero alcohol tolerance is now applied for drivers who have held a driving licence for less than three years, as well as to drivers aged 18 to 21, professional drivers, taxi drivers and truckers.

Norway Under new legislation, police officers can perform roadside drug impairment saliva tests. There are specific limits set for the presence of 20 common non-alcohol drugs. You'll find what amounts to a zero tolerance where drinking and driving is concerned. A blood-alcohol level of only 0.01% is permitted (compared to 0.08% in the UK). Speeding fines are high. For example, a driver caught at 25km/h over the 80km/h speed limit on a national road could expect a fine of around £600. • Portugal If you are towing a caravan, you must have a current inventory of the caravan's contents to show a police officer if requested.

Slovakia It is now mandatory to use dipped headlights on every road journey, regardless of the time of day, season or weather conditions.

Spain Motorway speed limits in Spain are 120km/h. • If you need glasses for driving, then the law requires you to carry a spare pair in the car. • It's compulsory to carry two warning triangles, spare bulbs for your car and reflective jackets.

Turkey Take great caution if you're driving at dusk. Many local drivers put off using their lights until it's properly dark, so you may find oncoming traffic very hard to spot. • During the time of Ramadan, many people will do without food and water between the hours of sunrise and sunset. This can seriously reduce levels of alertness, especially among people driving buses, trucks and taxis.

GEM MOTORING ASSIST

Since its foundation in 1932, GEM Motoring Assist has been at the forefront of road safety in the UK. Now one of the largest member-led road safety organisations, GEM provides a wide range of discounts and benefits for its 74,000+ members, including the UK's best-value range of breakdown recovery insurance products for motorists, motorcyclists and caravanners. GEM members also benefit from discounts on European breakdown cover and travel insurance, as well as enjoying free access to GEM's Accident Management Service, which provides free-of-charge legal help following any road traffic collision. Members receive *Good Motoring*, a free quarterly magazine, and access to an excellent line-up of road safety leaflets and web-based advice.

Why not make GEM Motoring Assist your one-stop shop for trouble-free motoring! Visit www.motoringassist.com/philipsmaps today.

Driving regulations

A national vehicle identification plate is always required when taking a vehicle abroad. It is important for your own safety and that of other drivers to fit headlamp converters or beam deflectors when taking a right-hand drive car to a country where driving is on the right (every country in Europe except the UK and Ireland). When the headlamps are dipped on a right-hand drive car, the lenses of the headlamps cause the beam to shine upwards to the left – and so, when driving on the right, into the eyes of oncoming motorists.

Where compulsory visibility vests should be kept in the passenger compartment and put on before exiting the vehicle in breakdowns or emergencies. All countries require that you carry a driving licence, green card/insurance documentation, registration document or hire certificate, and passport.

The penalties for infringements of regulations vary considerably from one country to another. In many countries the police have the right to impose on-the-spot fines (you should always request a receipt for any fine paid). Penalties can be severe for serious infringements, particularly for drinking when driving which in some countries can lead to immediate imprisonment. Insurance is important, and you may be forced to take out cover at the frontier if you cannot produce acceptable proof that you are insured. Please note that driving regulations often change.

Symbols

🛣 Motorway		△ Warning triangle	
⛙ Dual carriageway		✚ First aid kit	
⬟ Single carriageway		💡 Spare bulb kit	
🚗 Surfaced road		🧯 Fire extinguisher	
🚙 Unsurfaced / gravel road		🪖 Motorcycle helmet	
🏙 Urban area		⊖ Minimum driving age	
🕐 Speed limit in kilometres per hour (kph)		🖻 Additional documents required	
🎗 Seat belts		🖩 Mobile phones	
👤 Children		**LEZ** Low Emission Zone	
🍷 Blood alcohol level		★ Other information	

The publishers have made every effort to ensure that the information given here was correct at the time of going to press. No responsibility can be accepted for any errors or their consequences.

Andorra (AND)

🕐	🛣	⛙	⬟	🏙
	n/a	90	60/90	50

🎗 Compulsory

👤 Under 10 and below 150cm must travel in an EU-approved restraint system adapted to their size. If in front, any airbags must be deactivated.

🍷 0.05% △Compulsory ✚Recommended

💡 Compulsory 🧯Recommended

🪖 Compulsory for all riders ⊖18

🖻 International driving permit if driving licence has no photograph; green card recommended; third-party insurance

🖩 Not permitted whilst driving

★ Dipped headlights compulsory for motorcycles during day and for other vehicles during poor daytime visibility.

★ On-the-spot fines imposed

★ Visibility vests compulsory

★ Winter tyres recommended; snow chains compulsory in poor conditions or when indicated by signs

Austria (A)

🕐	🛣	⛙	⬟	🏙
	130	100	100	50
If towing trailer under 750kg / over 750 kg				
	100	100	100/80	50

🎗 Compulsory

👤 Under 12 and under 150cm cannot travel as a front or rear passenger unless they use a suitable child restraint; under 12 over 150cm must wear adult seat belt

🍷 0.049%; 0.01% if licence held less than 2 yrs

△ Compulsory

✚ Compulsory 💡Recommended

🧯 Recommended

🪖 Compulsory for all riders

⊖ 18 (16 for mopeds)

🖻 Third party insurance; photo identity if driving licence has no photograph

🖩 Only allowed with hands-free kit

LEZ On A12 motorway, non-compliant vehicles banned, certain substances banned, night-time restrictions, overtaking bans and speed limits on others. LEZ for Graz planned.

★ If you intend to drive on motorways or expressways, a motorway vignette must be purchased at the border. These are available for 10 days, 2 months or 1 year. Vehicles 3.5 tonnes and over must purchase an electronic tag.

★ Dipped headlights must be used during the day by all road users. Headlamp converters compulsory

★ Radar detectors prohibited

★ Snow chains recommended in winter. Winter tyres compulsory 1 Nov–15 Apr in poor driving conditions

★ Visibility vests compulsory

Belarus (BY)

🕐	🛣	⛙	⬟	🏙
	110	90	90	60*
If towing trailer under 750kg				
	90	70	70	

*In residential areas limit is 20 km/h · Vehicle towing another vehicle 50 kph limit · If full driving licence held for less than two years, must not exceed 70 kph

🎗 Compulsory in front seats, and rear seats if fitted

👤 Under 12 not allowed in front seat and must use appropriate child restraint

🍷 0.00% △ Compulsory ✚ Compulsory

💡 Recommended 🧯Compulsory

🪖 Compulsory for all riders ⊖18

🖻 Third party insurance; visa (ensure it's specific to driving); vehicle technical check stamp; international driving permit; health insurance for all visitors

🖩 Use prohibited

★ Belarus insurance and temporary vehicle import certificate must be purchased on entry, and driver must be registered

★ Dipped headlights compulsory in conditions of poor visibility, and when towing or being towed

★ Fees payable for driving on highways

★ Radar-detectors prohibited

★ Winter tyres and snow chains recommended

Belgium (B)

🕐	🛣	⛙	⬟	🏙
	120*	120*	90	50**
If towing trailer				
	90	90	60	50
Over 3.5 tonnes				
	90	90	60	50

*Minimum speed of 70kph may be applied in certain conditions on motorways and some dual carriageways **Near schools, hospitals and churches the limit may be 30kph

🎗 Compulsory

👤 All under 19s under 135 cm must wear an appropriate child restraint. Airbags must be deactivated if a rear-facing child seat is used in the front

🍷 0.05% △Compulsory ✚ Compulsory

💡 Recommended 🧯Compulsory

🪖 Compulsory for all riders ⊖18

🖻 Third party insurance

🖩 Only allowed with a hands-free kit

★ Cruise control is not permitted on motorways

★ Dipped headlights compulsory for motorcycles during day and other vehicles during poor daytime visibility

★ On-the-spot fines imposed

★ Radar detectors prohibited

★ Sticker indicating maximum recommended speed for winter tyres must be displayed on dashboard if using them

★ Visibility vest compulsory

Bosnia and Herzegovina (BIH)

🕐	🛣	⛙	⬟	🏙
	130	100	80	50

🎗 Compulsory if fitted

👤 Under 12 not allowed in front seat; under 5 must use appropriate child restraint

🍷 0.03% △ Compulsory ✚ Compulsory

💡 Compulsory 🧯 Compulsory ⊖ 18

🖻 Green card; visa; international driving permit third-party insurance

🖩 Prohibited

★ Dipped headlights compulsory for all vehicles at all times

★ GPS must have fixed speed camera function deactivated; radar detectors prohibited.

★ On-the-spot fines imposed

★ Visibility vest compulsory

★ Winter tyres compulsory 15 Nov-15 Apr; snow chains recommended

Bulgaria (BG)

🕐	🛣	⛙	⬟	🏙
	130	90	90	50
If towing trailer				
	100	70	70	50

🎗 Compulsory in front and rear seats

👤 Under 3s not permitted in vehicles with no child restraints; 3–10 year olds must sit in rear

🍷 0.05% △ Compulsory ✚ Compulsory

💡 Recommended 🧯 Compulsory

🪖 Compulsory for all riders ⊖18

🖻 Driving licence with translation or international driving permit, third party insurance

🖩 Only allowed with a hands-free kit

★ On-the-spot fines imposed

★ Dipped headlights recommended at all times; compulsory 1 Nov–1 Mar and for motorcycles.

★ Fee at border

★ GPS must have fixed speed camera function deactivated; radar detectors prohibited

★ Vignette system in operation, can be purchased from all border-crossing point and available annually, monthly and weekly. Write your vehicle registration number on the vignette before displaying it.

★ Visibility vest compulsory

Croatia (HR)

🕐	🛣	⛙	⬟	🏙
	130	110	90	50
Under 24				
	120	100	80	50
If towing				
	110	80	80	50

🎗 Compulsory if fitted

👤 Children 2–12 not permitted in front seats and must use appropriate child restraint. Under 2 permitted in front only in appropriate rear-facing seat with any airbags disabled

🍷 0.05%, 0.00% for drivers of vehicles over 3.5 tonnes and under-25s

△ Compulsory ✚ Compulsory

💡 Compulsory

🪖 Compulsory for all riders ⊖ 18

🖻 Documents: International driving permit third-party insurance/green card

🖩 Only allowed with hands-free kit

★ Dipped headlights compulsory late October - late March and during poor visibility; compulsory at all times for motorbikes

★ In winter, snow chains compulsory in the mountains; snow tyres required elsewhere; shovel

★ On-the-spot fines imposed

★ Radar detectors prohibited

★ Visibility vest compulsory

Czech Republic (CZ)

🕐	🛣	⛙	⬟	🏙
	130	130	90	50
If towing				
	80	80	80	50

🎗 Compulsory in front seats and, if fitted, in rear

👤 Children: Children under 36 kg and 150 c must use appropriate child restraint. Only front-facing child retraints are permitted in the front in vehicles with airbags fitted

🍷 0.00% △ Compulsory ✚Compulsory

💡 Compulsory 🧯 Compulsory

🪖 Compulsory for all riders

⊖ 18 (17 for motorcycles under 125 cc)

🖻 International driving permit; third-party insurance

🖩 Only allowed with a hands-free kit

LEZ Two-stage LEZ in Prague for vehicles ove 3.5 and 6 tonnes. Permit system.

★ On-the-spot fines imposed

★ Dipped headlights compulsory at all tim

★ GPS must have fixed speed camera function deactivated; radar detectors prohibited
★ Vignette needed for motorway driving, available for 1 year, 60 days, 15 days. Toll specific to lorries introduced 2006, those over 12 tonnes must buy an electronic tag
★ Visibility vest compulsory
★ Wearers of spectacles or contact lenses must carry a spare pair in their vehicle at all times
★ Winter tyres or snow chains compulsory between Nov and Apr

Denmark (DK)

🛣	🛤	⚠	🏭
130	80	80	50

If towing

	🛤	⚠	🏭
80	70	70	50

🔒 Compulsory front and rear
👶 Under 135cm must use appropriate child restraint; in front permitted only in an appropriate rear-facing seat with any airbags disabled.
🍷 0.05% △ Compulsory
🧰 Recommended 🔦 Recommended
🧯 Recommended
🏍 Compulsory for all riders ⊖ 17
🪪 Third party insurance
📱 Only allowed with a hands-free kit
Ⓩ Aalborg, Arhus, Copenhagen, Frederiksberg and Odense. Proofs of emissions compliance/compliant filter needed to obtain sticker. Non-compliant vehicles banned.
★ Dipped headlights must be used at all times
★ Radar detectors prohibited
★ Tolls apply on the Storebaeltsbroen and Oresundsbron bridges.
★ Visibility vest recommended

Estonia (EST)

🛣	🛤	⚠	🏭
n/a	90*	70	50

If full driving licence held for less than two years

	🛤	⚠	🏭
90	90	70	50

*In summer, the speed limit on some dual carriageways may be raised to 100/110 kph
🔒 Compulsory in front seats and if fitted in rear seats
👶 Under 12 not allowed in front seats; under 7 must have child safety seat in rear
🍷 0.02% △ 2 compulsory
🧰 Compulsory 🔦 Recommended
🧯 Compulsory
🏍 Compulsory for all riders ⊖ 18
🪪 International driving permit recommended; third-party insurance
📱 Only allowed with a hands-free kit
★ A toll system is in operation in Tallinn
★ Dipped headlights compulsory at all times
★ Winter tyres are compulsory Dec–Feb but illegal from May–Sep.

Finland (FIN)

🛣	🛤	⚠	🏭
120	100	80*	30/60

If towing

	🛤	⚠	🏭
80	80	80	30/60

*100 in summer • If towing a vehicle by rope, cable or rod, max speed limit 60 kph. Maximum of 80 kph for vans and lorries • Speed limits are often lowered in winter
🔒 Compulsory in front and rear
👶 Below 135 cm must use a child restraint or seat
🍷 0.05% △ Compulsory 🧰 Recommended
🧯 Recommended 🔦 Recommended
🏍 Compulsory for all riders
⊖ 18 (motorbikes below 125cc 16)
🪪 Third party insurance
📱 Only allowed with a hands-free kit
★ On-the-spot fines imposed

★ Dipped headlights must be used at all times
★ Radar-detectors are prohibited
★ Visibility vest compulsory
★ Winter tyres compulsory Dec–Feb

France (F)

🛣	🛤	⚠	🏭
130	110	90	50

On wet roads or if full driving licence held for less than 2 years

🛣	🛤	⚠	🏭
110	100	80	50

If towing below 3.5 tonnes gross / above 3.5 tonnes gross

🛣	🛤	⚠	🏭
110/90	100/90	90/80	50

50kph on all roads if fog reduces visibility to less than 50m • Licence will be lost and driver fined for exceeding speed limit by over 40kph
🔒 Compulsory in front seats and, if fitted, in rear
👶 Under 10 not allowed in front seats; in rear, if 4 or under, must have a child safety seat (rear facing if up to 9 months); if 5 to 10 must use an appropriate restraint system. Under 10 permitted in the front only if rear seats are fully occupied by other under 10s or there are no rear seat belts. In front if child is in rear-facing child seat, any airbags must be deactivated.
🍷 0.05%. If towing or with less than 2 years with full driving licence, 0.00% • All drivers/ motorcyclists must carry 2 unused breathalysers to French certification standards, showing an NF number.
△ Compulsory 🧰 Recommended
🔦 Recommended
🏍 Compulsory for all riders
⊖ 18 (16 for motorbikes under 80 cc)
📱 Use not permitted whilst driving
★ Dipped headlights compulsory in poor daytime visibility and at all times for motorcycles over 125cc
★ GPS must have fixed speed camera function deactivated; radar-detection equipment is prohibited
★ On-the-spot fines imposed
★ Tolls on motorways. Electronic tag needed if using automatic tolls.
★ Visibility vests must be worn at all times by motorcyclists and passengers; compulsory in other vehicles
★ Winter tyres - recommended. Carrying snow chains recommended in winter

Germany (D)

🛣	🛤	⚠	🏭
*	*	100	50

If towing

	🛤	⚠	🏭
80	80	80	50

*no limit, 130 kph recommended
🔒 Compulsory
👶 Under 150 cm and 12 or under must use an appropriate child seat or restraint. In front if child is in rear-facing child seat, airbags must be deactivated.
🍷 0.05%, 0.0% for drivers 21 or under or with less than two years full licence
△ Compulsory 🧰 Compulsory
🧯 Recommended 🔦 Recommended
🏍 Compulsory for all riders
⊖ 18 (motorbikes: 16 if under 50cc)
🪪 Third party insurance
📱 Use permitted only with hands-free kit – also applies to drivers of motorbikes and bicycles
Ⓛᴇᴢ More than 60 cities have or are planning LEZs. Proof of compliance needed to acquire sticker. Non-compliant vehicles banned.
★ GPS must have fixed speed camera function deactivated; radar detectors prohibited
★ Motorcyclists must use dipped headlights at all times; other vehicles must use dipped headlights during poor daytime visibility.

★ On-the-spot fines imposed
★ Tolls on autobahns for lorries
★ Winter tyres compulsory in all winter weather conditions; snow chains recommended

Greece (GR)

🛣	🛤	⚠	🏭
120	110	110	50

Motorbikes, and if towing

🛣	🛤	⚠	🏭
90	70	70	40

🔒 Compulsory in front seats and, if fitted, in rear
👶 Under 12 or below 135cm must use appropriate child restraint. In front if child is in rear-facing child seat, any airbags must be deactivated.
🍷 0.05%, 0.00% for drivers with less than 2 years' full licence and motorcyclists
△ Compulsory 🧰 Compulsory
🧯 Recommended 🔦 Compulsory
🏍 Compulsory for all riders ⊖ 17
🪪 Third party insurance
🗑 Not permitted.
★ Dipped headlights compulsory during poor daytime visibility and at all times for motorcycles
★ On-the-spot fines imposed
★ Radar-detection equipment is prohibited
★ Tolls on several newer motorways.

Hungary (H)

🛣	🛤	⚠	🏭
130	110	90	50

If towing

	🛤	⚠	🏭
80	70	70	50

🔒 Compulsory in front seats and if fitted in rear seats
👶 Under 150cm and over 3 must be seated in rear and use appropriate child restraint. Under 3 allowed in front only in rear-facing child seat with any airbags deactivated.
🍷 0.00% △ Compulsory
🧰 Compulsory 🔦 Compulsory
🧯 Recommended
🏍 Compulsory for all riders ⊖ 17
🪪 Third party insurance
📱 Only allowed with a hands-free kit
Ⓛᴇᴢ Budapest has vehicle restrictions on days with heavy dust and is planning an LEZ.
★ All motorways are toll and operate electronic vignette system with automatic number plate recognition, tickets are available for 4 days, 7 days, 1 month, 1 year
★ Dipped headlights are compulsory during daylight hours (cars exempted in built-up areas)
★ Electronic vignette system in use for tolls on several motorways
★ On-the-spot fines issued
★ Snow chains compulsory where conditions dictate
★ Visibility vest compulsory

Iceland (IS)

🛣	🛤	🚗	🚗⚠	🏭
n/a	90	80	50	

🔒 Compulsory in front and rear seats
👶 Under 12 or below 150cm not allowed in front seat and must use appropriate child restraint.
🍷 0.05% △ Compulsory
🧰 Compulsory 🔦 Compulsory
🧯 Compulsory 🏍 Compulsory for all riders
⊖ 18; 21 to drive a hire car; 25 to hire a jeep
🪪 Third party insurance
📱 Only allowed with a hands-free kit
★ Driving off marked roads is forbidden
★ Dipped headlights compulsory at all times
★ Highland roads are not suitable for ordinary cars
★ On-the-spot fines imposed
★ Winter tyres compulsory c.1 Nov–14 Apr (variable)

Ireland (IRL)

🛣	🛤	⚠	🏭
120	100	80	50

If towing

	🛤	⚠	🏭
80	80	80	50

🔒 Compulsory where fitted. Driver responsible for ensuring passengers under 17 comply
👶 Children 3 and under must be in a suitable child restraint system. Airbags must be deactivated if a rear-facing child seat is used in the front. Those under 150 cm and 36 kg must use appropriate child restraint in cars with seatbelts.
🍷 0.05%, 0.02% for novice and professional drivers
△ Compulsory 🧰 Recommended
🧯 Recommended 🔦 Recommended
🏍 Compulsory for all riders
⊖ 17 (16 for motorbikes up to 125cc; 18 for over 125cc; 18 for lorries; 21 bus/minibus)
🪪 Third party insurance; international driving permit for non-EU drivers
📱 Only allowed with a hands-free kit
★ Dipped headlights are compulsory during daylight hours
★ Driving is on the left
★ GPS must have fixed speed camera function deactivated; radar detectors prohibited
★ On-the-spot fines imposed
★ Dipped headlights compulsory for motorbikes at all times and in poor visibility for other vehicles
★ Tolls are being introduced on some motorways; the M50 Dublin has barrier-free tolling with number-plate recognition.

Italy (I)

🛣	🛤	⚠	🏭
130	110	90	50

If towing

	🛤	⚠	🏭
80	70	70	50

Less than three years with full licence

🛣	🛤	⚠	🏭
100	90	90	50

When wet

🛣	🛤	⚠	🏭
100	90	80	50

Some motorways with emergency lanes have speed limit of 150 kph
🔒 Compulsory in front seats and, if fitted, in rear
👶 Under 12 not allowed in front seats except in child safety seat; children under 3 must have special seat in the back
🍷 0.05%, but 0.00% for professional drivers or with less than 3 years full licence
△ Compulsory 🧰 Recommended
🧯 Compulsory 🔦 Recommended
🏍 Compulsory for all motorcyclists
⊖ 18 (14 for mopeds, 16 up to 125cc, 20 up to 350cc)
🪪 International Driving Licence unless you have photocard licence
📱 Only allowed with a hands-free kit
Ⓛᴇᴢ Most northern and several southern regions operate LEZs in winter. A22 motorway. Many towns and cities operate systems that restrict vehicle access. These vary greatly. Milan operates an experimental LEZ
★ Dipped headlights compulsory at all times for motorbikes and outside built-up areas or during poor visibility for other vehicles
★ On-the-spot fines imposed
★ Radar-detection equipment is prohibited
★ Tolls on motorways. Blue lanes accept credit cards; yellow lanes restricted to holders of Telepass pay-toll device.
★ Visibility vest compulsory
★ Snow chains compulsory 15 October–15 April

Kosovo (RKS)

⏱	🛣	⚏	⚏	🏘
	120	100	100	60

- Compulsory
- Under 12 must sit in rear seats
- 0.03%, 0.00% for professional, business and commercial drivers
- △ Compulsory Compulsory
- Compulsory Compulsory
- Compulsory
- 18 (16 for motorbikes less than 125 cc, 14 for mopeds)
- International driving permit, locally purchased third-party insurance - green card is not valid; passports must be carried at all times; documents stating reason for visit recommended.
- Only allowed with a hands-free kit
- ★ Winter tyres or snow chains compulsory in poor winter weather conditions
- ★ Dipped headlights compulsory at all times

Latvia (LV)

⏱	🛣	⚏	⚏	🏘
	90/100	90	90	50
If towing				
	90/100	90	90	50

In residential areas limit is 20kph • If full driving licence held for less than two years, must not exceed 80 kph

- Compulsory in front seats and if fitted in rear
- If under 12 years and 150cm must use child restraint in front and rear seats
- 0.05%, 0.02% with less than 2 years experience
- △ Compulsory Compulsory
- Recommended Compulsory
- Compulsory for all riders
- 18 (14 for mopeds, 16 up to 125cc, 21 up to 350cc)
- International driving permit if licence is not in accordance with Vienna Convention; third-party insurance
- Only allowed with hands-free kit
- ★ On-the-spot fines imposed
- ★ Dipped headlights must be used at all times all year round
- ★ Pedestrians have priority
- ★ Visibility vests compulsory
- ★ Winter tyres compulsory for vehicles up to 3.5 tonnes Dec–Feb, but illegal May–Sept

Lithuania (LT)

⏱	🛣	⚏	⚏	🏘
	130	110	90	50
If towing				
	n/a	70	70	50

In winter speed limits are reduced by 10–20 km/h

- Compulsory in front seats and if fitted in rear seats
- Under 12 not allowed in front seats unless in a child safety seat; under 3 must use appropriate child seat and sit in rear
- 0.04%, 0.02% for those with less than 2 years' full licence
- △ Compulsory Compulsory
- Recommended Compulsory
- Compulsory for all riders
- 18 (14 for mopeds)
- Visa for some non-EU citizens; green card if taking your own vehicle into the country; photographic proof of identity must be carried at all times; photographic licence or old-style licence with photo ID
- Only allowed with a hands-free kit
- ★ Dipped headlights must be used at all times
- ★ On-the-spot fines imposed
- ★ Visibility vest compulsory
- ★ Winter tyres compulsory 10 Nov–1 Apr

Luxembourg (L)

⏱	🛣	⚏	⚏	🏘
	130/110	90	90	50
If towing				
	90	75	75	50

If full driving licence held for less than two years, must not exceed 75 kph • In 20 km/h zones, pedestrians have right of way.

- Compulsory
- Children under 3 must use an appropriate restraint system. Airbags must be disabled if a rear-facing child seat is used in the front. Children 3 to 18 and / or under 150 cm must use a restraint system appropriate to their size. If over 36kg a seatbelt may be used in the back only
- 0.05%, 0.02 for young drivers, drivers with less than 2 years experience and drivers of taxis and commercial vehicles
- △ Compulsory Compulsory (buses)
- Compulsory
- Compulsory (buses, transport of dangerous goods)
- Compulsory 18
- Third party insurance
- Use permitted only with hands-free kit
- ★ Dipped headlights compulsory for motorcyclists and in poor visibility for other vehicles
- ★ On-the-spot fines imposed
- ★ Visibility vest compulsory
- ★ Winter tyres compulsory in winter weather

Macedonia (MK)

⏱	🛣	⚏	⚏	🏘
	120	100	60	60
Newly qualified drivers				
	100	80	60	60
If towing				
	80	70	50	50

- Compulsory in front seats; compulsory if fitted in rear seats
- Under 12 not allowed in front seats
- 0.05%, 0.00% for business, commercial and professional drivers and with less than 2 years experience
- △ Compulsory Compulsory
- Compulsory
- Recommended; compulsory for LPG vehicles
- Compulsory for all riders
- 18 (mopeds 16)
- International driving permit; visa
- Use not permitted whilst driving
- ★ Dipped headlights compulsory at all times
- ★ GPS must have fixed speed camera function deactivated; radar detectors prohibited
- ★ On-the-spot fines imposed
- ★ Tolls apply on many roads
- ★ Visibility vest must be kept in the passenger compartment and worn to leave the vehicle in the dark outside built-up areas
- ★ Winter tyres or snow chains compulsory 15 Nov–15 Mar

Moldova (MD)

⏱	🛣	⚏	⚏	🏘
	90	90	90	60
If towing or if licence held under 1 year				
	70	70	70	60

- Compulsory in front seats and, if fitted, in rear seats
- Under 12 not allowed in front seats
- 0.00% △ Compulsory
- Compulsory Recommended
- Compulsory Compulsory for all riders
- 18 (mopeds and motorbikes, 16; vehicles with more than eight passenger places, taxis or towing heavy vehicles, 21)
- International driving permit (preferred), third party insurance, visa
- Only allowed with hands-free kit

Montenegro (MNE)

⏱	🛣	⚏	⚏	🏘
	n/a	100	80	60

80kph speed limit if towing a caravan

- ★ Motorcyclists must use dipped headlights at all times
- ★ Winter tyres recommended Nov–Feb
- Compulsory in front and rear seats
- Under 12 not allowed in front seats
- 0.05% △ Compulsory
- Compulsory Compulsory
- Compulsory Compulsory
- 18 (16 for motorbikes less than 125cc; 14 for mopeds)
- International driving permit; visa; green card recommended
- Prohibited
- ★ An 'eco' tax vignette must be obtained when crossing the border and displayed in the upper right-hand corner of the windscreen
- ★ Dipped headlights must be used at all times
- ★ On-the-spot fines imposed
- ★ Tolls on some primary roads and in the Sozina tunnel between Lake Skadar and the sea
- ★ Visibility vest compulsory

Netherlands (NL)

⏱	🛣	⚏	⚏	🏘
	120/100	80/100	80/100	50

- Compulsory in front seats and, if fitted, rear
- Under 135cm must use appropriate child restraint; if no seat belts, under 3s not permitted in vehicle; rear-facing child seat permitted in the front only if airbags deactivated
- 0.05%, 0.02% with less than 5 years experience or moped riders under 24
- △ Recommended Recommended
- Recommended Recommended
- Compulsory 18
- Third party insurance
- Only allowed with a hands-free kit
- LEZ About 20 cities operate or are planning LEZs. Permit system/number plate recognition.
- ★ Dipped headlights compulsory for motorcycles
- ★ Radar-detection equipment is prohibited

Norway (N)

⏱	🛣	⚏	⚏	🏘
	90/100	80	80	30/50
If towing trailer with brakes				
	80	80	80	50
If towing trailer without brakes				
	60	60	60	50

- Compulsory in front seats and, if fitted, in rear
- Children less than 150cm tall must use appropriate child restraint. Children under 4 must use child safety seat or safety restraint (cot)
- 0.01% △ Compulsory
- Recommended Recommended
- Recommended Compulsory
- 18 (heavy vehicles 18/21)
- Only allowed with a hands-free kit
- LEZ Planned for Bergen, Oslo and Trondheim
- ★ On-the-spot fines imposed
- ★ At least 3mm of tread Oct–Mar; winter tyres Nov–Mar if in a hire car registered in Norway
- ★ Dipped headlights must be used at all times
- ★ Radar-detectors are prohibited
- ★ Tolls apply on some bridges, tunnels and access roads into Bergen, Oslo, Trondheim and Stavangar. Several use electronic fee collection only.
- ★ Visibility vest compulsory

Poland (PL)

⏱	🛣	⚏	⚏	🏘
Motor-vehicle only roads[1], under/over 3.5 tonnes				
	130[2]/80[2]	110/80	100/80	n/a
Motor-vehicle only roads[1] if towing				
	n/a	80	80	n/a
Other roads, under 3.5 tonnes				
	n/a	100	90	50/60[3]
Other roads, 3.5 tonnes or over				
	n/a	80	70	50/60[3]
Other roads, if towing				
	n/a	60	60	30

[1]Indicated by signs with white car on blue background. [2]Minimum speed 40 kph. [3]50 kph 05.00–23.00; 60 kph 23.00–05.00; 20 kph in marked residential areas

- Compulsory in front seats and, if fitted, in rear
- Under 12 not allowed in front seats unless in a child safety seat; in rear seats children under 12 and less than 150 cm must use child safety seat. Rear-facing child seats not permitted in vehicles with airbags.
- 0.02% △ Compulsory
- Recommended Recommended
- Compulsory
- Compulsory for all riders
- 18 (mopeds and motorbikes – 16)
- International permit (recommended); originals of insurance certificate and registration document must be carried, not photocopies
- Only allowed with a hands-free kit
- ★ On-the-spot fines imposed
- ★ Dipped headlights compulsory for all vehicles
- ★ Radar-detection equipment is prohibited

Portugal (P)

⏱	🛣	⚏	⚏	🏘
	120*	100	90	50
If towing				
	100*	90	80	50

*40kph minimum; 90kph maximum if licence held under 1 year

- Compulsory in front seats; compulsory if fitted in rear seats
- Under 12 and below 150cm must travel in the rear in an appropriate child restraint; rear-facing child seats permitted in front only if airbags deactivated
- 0.05% △ Compulsory
- Recommended Recommended
- Recommended
- Compulsory for all riders
- 18 (motorcycles under 50cc 17)
- MOT certificate for vehicles over three years old; letter of permission from the owner of any borrowed car; photographic proof of identity
- Only allowed with hands-free kit
- LEZ Lisbon operates a sticker system that is being extended
- ★ Dipped headlights compulsory for motorcycles, and for other vehicles in poor daytime visibility
- ★ Drivers with less than a year's experience should display a yellow 90 sticker obtainable from the ACP motoring club
- ★ On-the-spot fines imposed
- ★ Radar-detectors prohibited
- ★ Tolls on motorways; do not use green lanes, these are reserved for auto-payment users. Some motorways require an automatic toll device.
- ★ Visibility vest compulsory
- ★ Wearers of spectacles or contact lenses must carry a spare pair in their vehicle at all times

Romania (RO)

	🛣	🛤	🛤	🏘
Cars and motorcycles	120/130	100	90	50
Vans	110	90	80	50
Motorcycles	100	80	80	50

For motor vehicles with trailers or if full driving licence has been held for less than one year, speed limits are 20kph lower than those listed above •Jeep-like vehicles: 70kph outside built-up areas but 60kph in all areas if diesel

- Compulsory in front seats and, if fitted, in rear
- Under 12 not allowed in front seats
- 0.00% △ Compulsory 🔧 Compulsory
- Recommended 🦺 Compulsory
- Compulsory for all riders ⊖ 18
- Green card or locally bought insurance; photographic driving licence or international driving permit; registration certificate (if stay over 90 days)
- Only allowed with hands-free kit
★ Dipped headlights compulsory outside built-up areas, compulsory everywhere for motorcycles
★ Electronic road tax system; price depends on emissions category and length of stay
★ On-the-spot fines imposed
★ Tolls on motorways
★ Visibility vest compulsory
★ Winter tyres or snow chains compulsory in wintry weather

Russia (RUS)

	🛣	🛤	🛤	🏘
	110	90	90	60
If licence held for under 2 years	70	70	70	60

- Compulsory in front seats
- Under 12 permitted in front seat only in an appropriate child restraint
- 0.00% △ Compulsory 🔧 Compulsory
- Compulsory 🦺 Compulsory
- Compulsory ⊖ 18
- International driving licence with Russian translation; visa; green card should be endorsed for Russia (RUS)
- Only allowed with a hands-free kit
★ Dipped headlights compulsory during the day
★ On-the-spot fines imposed
★ Picking up hitchhikers is prohibited
★ Radar detectors/blockers prohibited
★ Road tax payable at the border

Serbia (SRB)

	🛣	🛤	🛤	🏘
	120	100	80	60

- Compulsory in front and rear seats
- Age 3–12 must be in rear seats and wear seat belt or appropriate child restraint; under 3 in rear-facing child seat permitted in front only if airbag deactivated
- 0.03% △ Compulsory 🔧 Compulsory
- Compulsory 🦺 Compulsory
- Compulsory
- 18 (16 for motorbikes less than 125cc; 14 for mopeds)
- International driving permit, third party insurance
- No legislation
★ 80km/h speed limit if towing a caravan
★ Dipped headlights compulsory
★ Radar detectors prohibited
★ Tolls on motorways and some primary roads
★ Visibility vest compulsory
★ Winter tyres or snow chains compulsory in poor winter weather conditions

Slovak Republic (SK)

🛣	🛤	🛤	🏘
130	90	90	60

- Compulsory in front seats and, if fitted, in rear
- Under 12 or below 150cm must be in rear in appropriate child restraint
- 0.0
- △ Compulsory 🔧 Compulsory
- Compulsory 🦺 Recommended
- Compulsory for motorcyclists
- 18 (15 for mopeds)
- International driving permit, proof of health insurance
- Only allowed with a hands-free kit
★ Dipped headlights compulsory at all times
★ On-the-spot fines imposed
★ Radar-detection equipment is prohibited
★ Tow rope recommended
★ Vignette required for motorways, car valid for 1 year, 30 days, 7 days; lorry vignettes carry a higher charge.
★ Visibility vests compulsory
★ Winter tyres compulsory

Slovenia (SLO)

	🛣	🛤	🛤	🏘
	130	100*	90*	50
If towing	80	80*	80*	50

*70kph in urban areas

- Compulsory in front seats and, if fitted, in rear
- Under 12 and below 150cm must use appropriate child restraint; babies must use child safety seat
- 0.05% △ Compulsory
- Compulsory 🦺 Compulsory
- Recommended
- Compulsory for all riders
- 18 (motorbikes up to 125cc – 16, up to 350cc – 18)
- International driving permit or photo licence; third-party insurance
- Only allowed with hands-free kit
★ At least 4mm of tread in winter; Snow chains or winter tyres compulsory 15 Nov–15 Mar
★ Dipped headlights must be used at all times
★ Vignettes valid for variety of periods compulsory for vehicles below 3.5 tonnes for toll roads. Write your vehicle registration number on the vignette before displaying it. For heavier vehicles electronic tolling system applies; several routes are cargo-traffic free during high tourist season.
★ Visibility vest compulsory

Spain (E)

	🛣	🛤	🛤	🏘
	110	100	90	50
If towing	80	80	70	50

- Compulsory in front seats and if fitted in rear seats
- Under 135cm and below 12 must use appropriate child restraint
- 0.05%, 0.03% if less than 2 years full licence or if vehicle is over 3.5 tonnes or carries more than 9 passengers
- △ Two compulsory (one for in front, one for behind)
- 🔧 Recommended
- Compulsory 🦺 Recommended
- Compulsory for all riders
- 18 (18/21 heavy vehicles; 18 for motorbikes over 125cc; 16 for motorbikes up to 125cc; 14 for mopeds up to 75cc)
- Third-party insurance, photo licence or older licence and international driving permit
- Only allowed with hands-free kit
★ Dipped headlights compulsory for motorcycles

★ Radar-detection equipment is prohibited
★ Snow chains recommended for mountainous areas in winter
★ Spare tyre compulsory
★ Tolls on motorways
★ Visibility vest compulsory
★ Wearers of spectacles or contact lenses must carry a spare pair in their vehicle at all times.

Sweden (S)

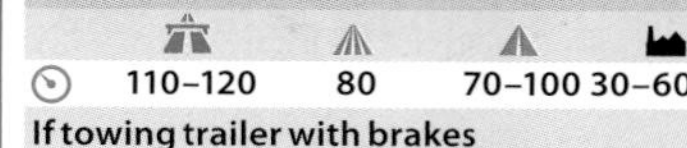

	🛣	🛤	🛤	🏘
	110–120	90	70–100	30–60
If towing trailer with brakes	80	80	70	50

- Compulsory in front and rear seats
- Under 16 or below 135cm must use appropriate child restraint; below 140cm may travel in front only if airbag deactivated; rear-facing child seat permitted only if airbag deactivated.
- 0.02% △ Compulsory
- 🔧 Recommended 🦺 Recommended
- Recommended
- Compulsory for all riders ⊖ 18
- Third-party insurance, photographic driving licence or old licence and photo ID
- No legislation
- LEZ Gothenberg, Helsingborg, Lund, Malmo, Mölndal and Stockholm have LEZs. Sticker system.
★ 1 Dec–31 Mar winter tyres, anti-freeze and shovel compulsory
★ Dipped headlights must be used at all times
★ On-the-spot fines imposed
★ Radar-detection equipment is prohibited

Switzerland (CH)

	🛣	🛤	🛤	🏘
	120	80	80	50/30
If towing up to 1 tonne / over 1 tonne	80		60/80	30/50

- Compulsory in front and, if fitted, in rear
- Up to 12 years and below 150 cm must use an appropriate child restraint
- 0.05%
- △ Compulsory
- 🔧 Recommended
- 🦺 Recommended
- Recommended
- Compulsory for all riders
- 18 (mopeds up to 50cc – 16)
- Third party insurance
- Only allowed with a hands-free kit
★ Dipped headlights recommended, compulsory in tunnels
★ GPS must have fixed speed camera function deactivated; radar detectors prohibited
★ Motorways are all toll and for vehicles below 3.5 tonnes a vignette must be purchased at the border. The vignette is valid for one calendar year. Vehicles over 3.5 tonnes must have an electronic tag for travel on any road.
★ On-the-spot fines imposed
★ Pedestrians have right of way
★ Picking up hitchhikers is prohibited on motorways and main roads
★ Wearers of spectacles or contact lenses must carry a spare pair in their vehicle at all times
★ Winter tyres recommended Nov–Mar; snow chains compulsory in designated areas in poor winter weather

Turkey (TR)

	🛣	🛤	🛤	🏘
	120	90	90	50
If towing	70	70	70	40

- Compulsory in front seats
- Under 150 cm and below 36kg must use suitable child restraint. If above 136 cm may sit in the back without child restraint.

Under 3s can only travel in the front in a rear facing seat if the airbag is deactivated. Children 3–12 may not travel in the front seat.
- 0.05%, 0.00% if towing
- △ Two compulsory (one in front, one behind)
- 🔧 Compulsory
- Compulsory
- Compulsory
- Compulsory for all riders ⊖ 18
- International driving permit advised; note that Turkey is in both Europe and Asia, green card/UK insurance that covers whole of Turkey or locally bought insurance
- Prohibited
★ Tow rope and tool kit must be carried
★ Several motorways, and the Bosphorus bridges are toll roads
★ On-the-spot fines imposed
★ Dipped headlights compulsory in daylight hours

Ukraine (UA)

	🛣	🛤	🛤	🏘
	130	90	90	60
If towing	80	80	80	60

Speed limit in pedestrian zone 20 kph

- Compulsory in front and rear seats
- Under 12 and below 145cm must sit in rear
- 0.02% - if use of medication can be proved. Otherwise 0.00%
- △ Compulsory
- 🔧 Compulsory
- Optional
- Compulsory
- Compulsory for all riders
- 18 cars; 16 motorbikes
- International driving permit; visa; International Registration Certificate recommended, third-party insurance or green card
- No legislation
★ A road tax is payable on entry to the country.
★ Tow rope and tool kit recommended
★ Winter tyres compulsory Nov–Apr in snowy conditions

United Kingdom (GB)

	🛣	🛤	🛤	🏘
	112	112	96	48
If towing	96	96	80	48

- Compulsory in front seats and if fitted in rear seats
- Under 3 not allowed in front seats except with appropriate restraint, and in rear must use child restraint if available; in front 3–12 or under 135cm must use appropriate child restraint, in rear must use appropriate child restraint (or seat belt if no child restraint is available, e.g. because two occupied restraints prevent fitting of a third).
- 0.08% (may change to 0.05% in Scotland)
- △ Recommended
- 🔧 Recommended
- Recommended
- Recommended
- Compulsory for all riders
- 17 (16 for mopeds)
- Only allowed with hands-free kit
- LEZ London's LEZ operates by number-plate recognition; non-compliant vehicles face hefty daily charges. Foreign-registered vehicles must register.
★ On-the-spot fines imposed
★ Driving is on the left
★ Smoking is banned in all commercial vehicles
★ Some toll motorways and bridges

Ski resorts

The resorts listed are popular ski centres, therefore road access to most is normally good and supported by road clearing during snow falls. However, mountain driving is never predictable and drivers should make sure they take suitable snow chains as well as emergency provisions and clothing. Listed for each resort are: the atlas page and grid square; the altitude; the number of lifts (the total for directly linked resorts); the season start and end dates; the nearest town (with its distance in km) and the telephone number of the local tourist information centre or ski centre ('00' prefix required for calls from the UK).

Andorra
Pyrenees

Pas de la Casa / Grau Roig 146 B2 2640m 66 lifts Dec–Apr •Andorra La Vella (30km) 🖳www.pasdelacasa-andorra.com *Access via Envalira Pass (2407m), highest in Pyrenees, snow chains essential.*

Austria
Alps

A 24-hour driving conditions information line is provided by the Tourist Office of Austria www.austria.info 0845 1011818

Bad Gastein 109 B4 1002m 51 lifts Dec–Mar •St Johann im Pongau (45km) ☎+43 6432 3393 0 🖳www.gastein.com

Bad Hofgastein 109 B4 860m 51 lifts Dec–Mar •St Johann im Pongau (40km) ☎+43 6432 3393260 🖳www.gastein.com/en/bad-hofgastein-austria

Bad Kleinkirchheim 109 C4 1100m 27 lifts Dec–Mar •Villach (35km) ☎+43 4240 8212 🖳www.badkleinkirchheim.at

Ehrwald 108 B1 1000m 13 lifts Dec–Apr •Imst (30km) ☎+43 512 5351 553 🖳www.tiscover.at/ehrwald

Innsbruck 108 B2 574m 78 lifts Dec–Apr •Innsbruck ☎+43 512 56 2000 🖳www.innsbruck-pauschalen.com *Motorway normally clear. The motorway through to Italy and through the Arlberg Tunnel are both toll roads.*

Ischgl 107 B5 1400m 44 lifts Dec–May •Landeck (25km) ☎+43 50990 100 🖳www.ischgl.com *Car entry to resort prohibited between 2200hrs and 0600hrs.*

Kaprun 109 B3 885m, 50 lifts Nov–Apr •Zell am See (10km) ☎+43 6542 770 🖳www.zellamsee-kaprun.com

Kirchberg in Tirol 109 B3 860m 60 lifts Nov–Apr •Kitzbühel (6km) ☎+43 5357 2000 🖳www.kitzbuehel-alpen.com *Easily reached from Munich International Airport (120 km)*

Kitzbühel (Brixen im Thale) 109 B3 800m 30 lifts Dec–Apr •Wörgl (40km) ☎+43 5357 2000 🖳www.kitzbuehel-alpen.com

Lech/Oberlech 107 B5 1450m 84 lifts Dec–Apr •Bludenz (50km) ☎+43 5583 21610 🖳www.lech-zuers.at *Roads normally cleared but keep chains accessible because of altitude.*

Mayrhofen 108 B2 630m 53 lifts Dec–Apr •Jenbach (35km) ☎+43 5285 6760 🖳www.mayrhofen.at *Chains rarely required.*

Obertauern 109 B4 1740m 26 lifts Dec–Apr •Radstadt (20km) ☎+43 6456 7252 🖳www.obertauern.com *Roads normally cleared but chain accessibility recommended. Camper vans and caravans not allowed; park these in Radstadt*

Saalbach Hinterglemm 109 B3 1003m 52 lifts Nov–Apr •Zell am See (19km) ☎+43 6541 680068 🖳www.saalbach.com *Both village centres are pedestrianised and there is a good ski bus service during the daytime*

St Anton am Arlberg 107 B5 1304m 80 lifts Dec–Apr •Innsbruck (104km) ☎+43 5446 22690 🖳www.stantonamarlberg.com

Schladming 109 B4 2708m 88 lifts Dec–Mar •Schladming ☎+43 36 87 233 10 🖳www.schladming-dachstein.at

Serfaus 108 B1 1427m 70 lifts Dec–Apr •Landeck (30km) ☎+43 5476 6239 🖳www.serfaus-fiss-ladis.at *Private vehicles banned from village, use world's only 'hover'-powered underground railway.*

Sölden 108 C2 1377m, 35 lifts Sep–Apr (glacier); Nov–Apr (main area) •Imst (50km) ☎+43 572 000 200 🖳www.soelden.com *Roads normally cleared but snow chains recommended because of altitude. The route from Italy and the south over the Timmelsjoch via Obergurgl is closed Oct–May and anyone arriving from the south should use the Brenner Pass motorway.*

Zell am See 109 B3 758m 50 lifts Dec–Mar •Zell am See ☎+43 6542 770 🖳www.zellamsee-kaprun.com *Low altitude, so good access and no mountain passes to cross.*

Zell im Zillertal (Zell am Ziller) 109 B3 580m 22 lifts Dec–Apr •Jenbach (25km) ☎+43 5282 2281 🖳www.zell.at *Snowfone +43 5282 716526.*

Zürs 107 B5 1720m 84 lifts Dec–Apr •Bludenz (30km) ☎+43 5583 2245 🖳www.lech-zuers.at *Roads normally cleared but keep chains accessible because of altitude. Village has garage with 24-hour self-service gas/petrol, breakdown service and wheel chains supply.*

France
Alps

Alpe d'Huez 118 B3 1860m 85 lifts Dec–Apr •Grenoble (63km) ☎+33 4 76 11 44 44 🖳www.alpedhuez.com *Snow chains may be required on access road to resort.*

Avoriaz 118 A3 2277m 35 lifts Dec–May •Morzine (14km) ☎+33 4 50 74 02 11 🖳www.avoriaz.com *Chains may be required for access road from Morzine. Car-free resort, park on edge of village. Horse-drawn sleigh service available.*

Chamonix-Mont-Blanc 119 B3 1035m 49 lifts Dec–Apr •Martigny (38km) ☎+33 4 50 53 00 24 🖳www.chamonix.com

Chamrousse 118 B2 1700m 26 lifts Dec–Apr •Grenoble (30km) ☎+33 4 76 89 92 65 🖳www.chamrousse.com *Roads normally cleared, keep chains accessible because of altitude.*

Châtel 119 A3 2200m 41 lifts Dec–Apr •Thonon-Les-Bains (35km) ☎+33 4 50 73 22 44 🖳http://info.chatel.com/english-version.html

Courchevel 118 B3 1850m 67 lifts Dec–Apr •Moûtiers (23km) ☎+33 4 79 08 00 29 🖳www.courchevel.com *Roads normally cleared but keep chains accessible. Traffic 'discouraged' within the four resort bases.*

Flaine 118 A3 1800m 26 lifts Dec–Apr •Cluses (25km) ☎+33 4 50 90 80 🖳www.flaine.com *Keep chains accessible for D6 from Cluses to Flaine. Car access for depositing luggage and passengers only. 1500-space car park outside resort. Near Sixt-Fer-á-Cheval.*

La Clusaz 118 B3 1100m 55 lifts Dec–Apr •Annecy (32km) 🖳www.laclusaz.com *Roads normally clear but keep chains accessible for final road from Annecy.*

La Plagne 118 B3 2100m 109 lifts Dec–Apr Moûtiers (32km) ☎+33 4 79 09 79 79 🖳www.la-plagne.com *Ten different centres up to 2100m altitude. Road access via Bozel, Landry or Aime normally cleared. Linked to Les Arcs by cablecar*

Les Arcs 119 B3 2600m 77 lifts Dec–May •Bourg-St-Maurice (15km) ☎+33 4 79 07 12 57 🖳www.lesarcs.com *Three base areas up to 2000 metres; keep chains accessible. Pay parking at edge of each base resort. Linked to La Plagne by cablecar*

Les Carroz d'Araches 118 A3 1140m 80 lifts Dec–Apr •Cluses (13km) ☎+33 4 50 90 00 04 🖳www.lescarroz.com

Les Deux-Alpes 118 C3 1650m 55 lifts Dec–Apr •Grenoble (75km) ☎+33 4 76 79 22 00 🖳www.les2alpes.com *Roads normally cleared, however snow chains recommended for D213 up from valley road (D1091).*

Les Gets 118 A3 1172m 52 lifts Dec–Apr •Cluses (18km) ☎+33 4 50 75 80 80 🖳www.lesgets.com

Les Ménuires 118 B3 1815m 40 lifts Dec–Apr •Moûtiers (27km) ☎+33 4 79 00 73 00 🖳www.lesmenuires.com *Keep chains accessible for D117 from Moûtiers.*

Les Sept Laux Prapoutel 118 B3 1350m, 24 lifts Dec–Apr •Grenoble (38km) ☎+33 4 76 08 17 86 🖳www.les7laux.com *Roads normally cleared, however keep chains accessible for mountain road up from the A41 motorway. Near St Sorlin d'Arves.*

Megève 118 B3 2350m 79 lifts Dec–Apr •Sallanches (12km) ☎+33 4 50 21 28 🖳www.megeve.com *Horse-drawn sleigh rides available.*

Méribel 118 B3 1400m 61 lifts Dec–May •Moûtiers (18km) ☎+33 4 79 08 60 01 🖳www.meribel.net *Keep chains accessible for 18km to resort on D90 from Moûtiers.*

Morzine 118 A3 1000m 67 lifts, Dec–Apr •Thonon-Les-Bains (30km) ☎+33 4 50 74 72 72 🖳www.morzine-avoriaz.com

Pra Loup 132 A2 1600m 53 lifts Dec–Apr •Barcelonnette (10km) ☎+33 4 92 84 10 04 🖳www.praloup.com *Roads normally cleared but chains accessibility recommended.*

Risoul 118 C3 1850m 52 lifts Dec–Apr •Briançon (40km) 🖳www.risoul.com *Keep chains accessible. Near Guillestre. Linked with Vars Les Claux*

St-Gervais Mont-Blanc 118 B3 850m 27 lifts Dec–Apr •Sallanches (10km) ☎+33 4 50 47 76 08 🖳www.st-gervais.com

Serre Chevalier 118 C3 1350m 77 lifts Dec–Apr •Briançon (10km) ☎+33 4 92 24 98 98 🖳www.serre-chevalier.com *Made up of 13 small villages along the valley road, which is normally cleared.*

Tignes 119 B3 2100m 47 lifts Jan–Dec •Bourg St Maurice (26km) ☎+33 4 79 40 04 40 🖳www.tignes.net *Keep chains accessible because of altitude*

Val d'Isère 119 B3 1850m 50 lifts Dec–Apr •Bourg-St-Maurice (30km) ☎+33 4 79 06 06 60 🖳www.valdisere.com *Roads normally cleared but keep chains accessible.*

Val Thorens 118 B3 2300m 29 lifts Dec–Apr •Moûtiers (37km) ☎+33 4 79 00 08 08 🖳www.valthorens.com *Chains essential – highest ski resort in Europe. Obligatory paid parking on edge of resort.*

Valloire 118 B3 1430m 34 lifts Dec–Apr •Modane (20km) ☎+33 4 79 59 03 96 🖳www.valloire.net *Road normally clear up to the Col du Galbier, to the south of the resort, which is closed from 1st November to 1st June. Linked to Valmeinier.*

Valmeinier 118 B3 2600m 34 lifts Dec–Apr •St Michel de Maurienne (47km) ☎+33 4 79 59 53 69 🖳www.valmeinier.com *Access from north on D1006 / D902. Col du Galbier, to the south of the resort closed from 1st November to 1st June. Linked to Valloire.*

Valmorel 118 B3 1400m 38 lifts Dec–Apr •Moûtiers (15km) ☎+33 4 79 09 85 55 🖳www.valmorel.com *Near St Jean-de-Belleville. Linked with ski areas of Doucy-Combelouvière and St François-Longchamp.*

Vars Les Claux 118 C3 1850m 52 lifts Dec–Apr •Briançon (40km) ☎+33 4 92 46 51 31 🖳www.vars-ski.com *Four base resorts up to 1850 metres. Keep chains accessible. Linked with Risoul.*

Villard de Lans 118 B2 1050m 28 lifts Dec–Apr •Grenoble (32km) ☎+33 4 76 95 10 38 🖳www.villarddelans.com

Pyrenees

Font-Romeu 146 B3 1800m 25 lifts Nov–Apr •Perpignan (87km) ☎+33 4 68 30 68 30 🖳www.font-romeu.fr *Roads normally cleared but keep chains accessible.*

Saint-Lary Soulan 145 B4 830m 31 lifts Dec–Mar •Tarbes (75km) ☎+33 5 62 39 50 81 🖳www.saintlary.com *Access roads constantly cleared of snow.*

Vosges

La Bresse-Hohneck 106 A1 900m 33 lifts Dec–Mar •Cornimont (6km) ☎+33 3 29 2 41 29 🖳www.labresse.net

Key to route planning map pages

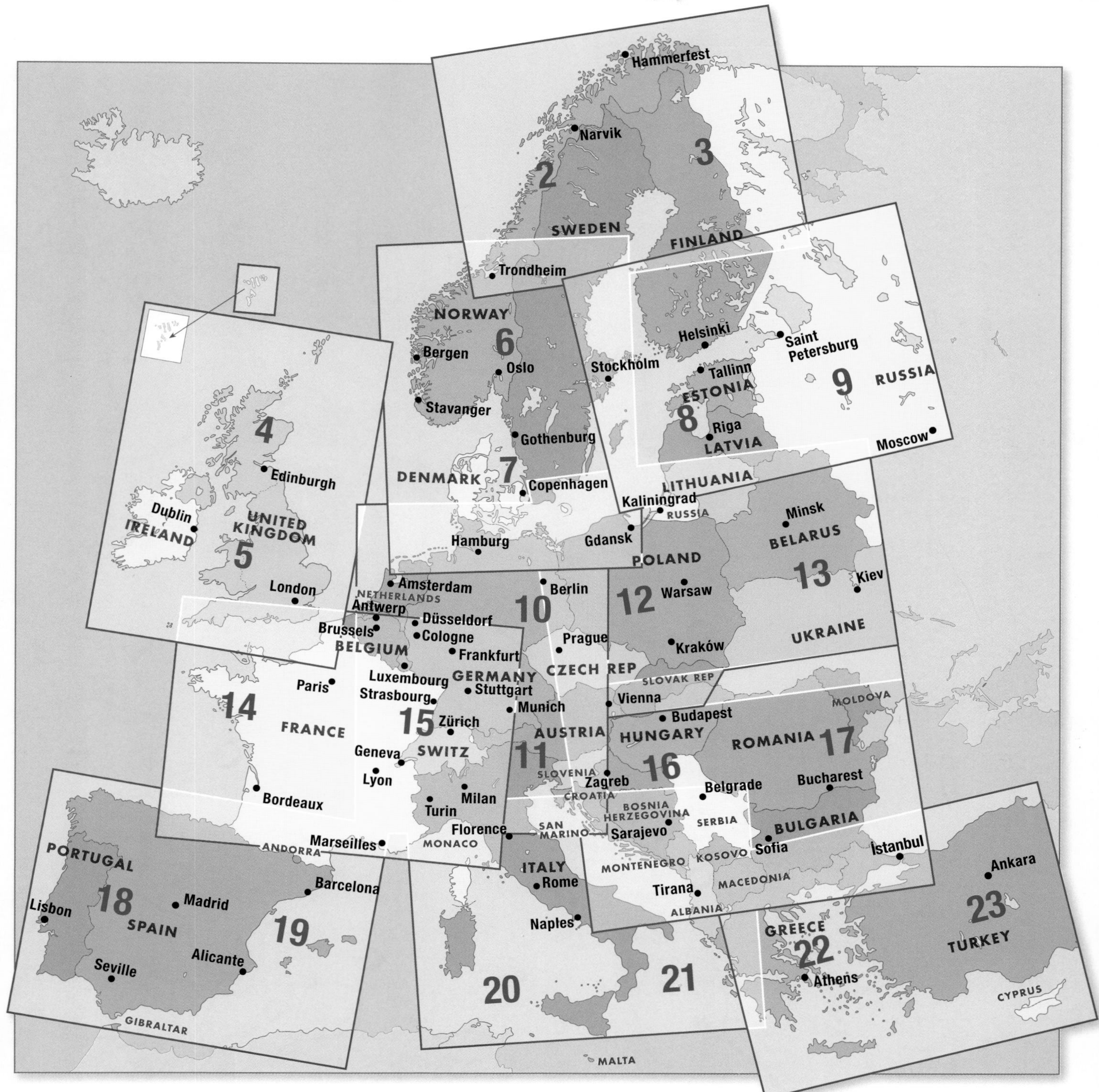

Hammerfest
Narvik
2
3
SWEDEN
FINLAND
Trondheim
NORWAY
6
Bergen
Oslo
Stavanger
Gothenburg
Helsinki
Saint Petersburg
Stockholm
Tallinn
ESTONIA
9
RUSSIA
8
Riga
LATVIA
Moscow
4
Edinburgh
DENMARK
7
Copenhagen
LITHUANIA
Kaliningrad
RUSSIA
Dublin
IRELAND
UNITED KINGDOM
5
London
Hamburg
Gdansk
Minsk
BELARUS
POLAND
Amsterdam
NETHERLANDS
Berlin
10
12
Warsaw
13
Kiev
Antwerp
Brussels
Düsseldorf
Cologne
BELGIUM
Frankfurt
Prague
Kraków
UKRAINE
Luxembourg
GERMANY
CZECH REP
SLOVAK REP
Paris
Strasbourg
Stuttgart
Munich
Vienna
MOLDOVA
14
FRANCE
15
Zürich
Budapest
AUSTRIA
HUNGARY
ROMANIA
17
Geneva
SWITZ
11
16
Lyon
SLOVENIA
Zagreb
Belgrade
Bucharest
Bordeaux
Milan
CROATIA
Turin
BOSNIA HERZEGOVINA
SERBIA
Florence
SAN MARINO
Sarajevo
BULGARIA
PORTUGAL
Marseilles
ANDORRA
MONACO
ITALY
MONTENEGRO
KOSOVO
Sofia
İstanbul
Ankara
Rome
Barcelona
Tirana
MACEDONIA
Lisbon
18
Madrid
SPAIN
19
Naples
ALBANIA
23
GREECE
TURKEY
22
Alicante
Seville
20
21
Athens
CYPRUS
GIBRALTAR
MALTA

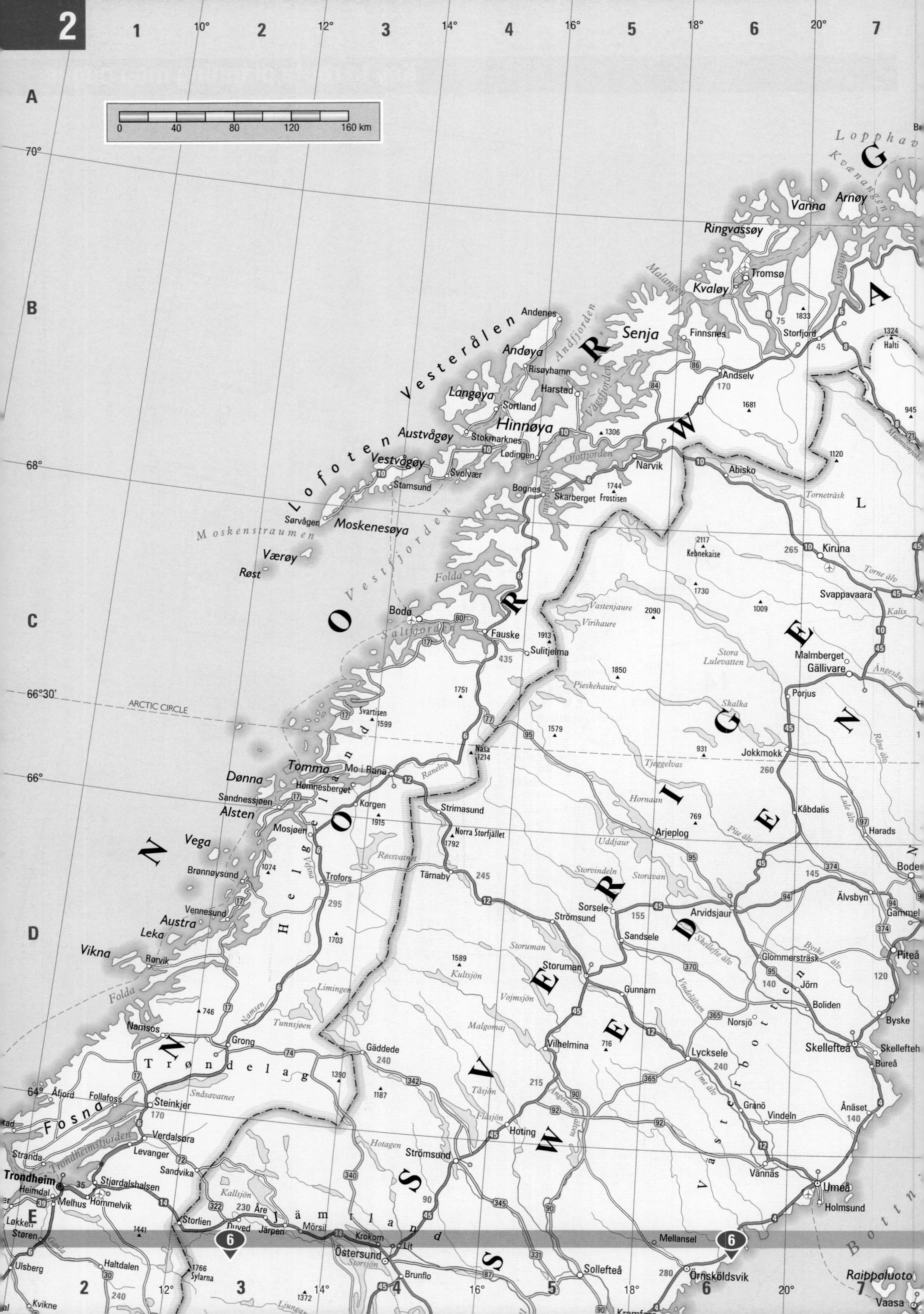

0 40 80 120 160 km
NORWEGEN
SWEDEN
Lofoten
Vesterålen
Helgeland
Trøndelag
Jämtland
Västerbotten
Loppha
Kvænangen
Vanna
Arnøy
Ringvassøy
Tromsø
Kvaløy
Malangen
Lyngen
Andenes
Senja
Andfjorden
Finnsnes
Storfjord
Halti
Andøya
Risøyhamn
Harstad
Andselv
Langøya
Sortland
Hinnøya
Austvågøy
Stokmarknes
Lødingen
Vestvågøy
Svolvær
Stamsund
Ofotfjorden
Narvik
Abisko
Bognes
Skarberget
Frostisen
Torneträsk
Sørvågen
Moskenesøya
Moskenstraumen
Værøy
Røst
Vestfjorden
Kebnekaise
Kiruna
Torne älv
Svappavaara
Folda
Bodø
Saltfjorden
Fauske
Sulitjelma
Vastenjaure
Virihaure
Kalix
Stora Lulevatten
Malmberget
Gällivare
Ängesån
Pieskehaure
ARCTIC CIRCLE
Svartisen
Skalka
Porjus
Nasa
Tjeggelvas
Jokkmokk
Råne älv
Tomma
Mo i Rana
Ranelva
Dønna
Hemnesberget
Hornaan
Sandnessjøen
Korgen
Alsten
Strimasund
Kåbdalis
Mosjøen
Norra Storfjället
Arjeplog
Lule älv
Harads
Vega
Uddjaur
Pite älv
Røssvatnet
Vefsna
Brønnøysund
Trofors
Tärnaby
Storvindeln
Storavan
Boden
Vennesund
Sorsele
Arvidsjaur
Älvsbyn
Gammel
Austra
Strömsund
Sandsele
Leka
Skellefte älv
Byske älv
Vikna
Rørvik
Storuman
Glommersträsk
Piteå
Kultsjön
Limingen
Jörn
Gunnarn
Vindelälven
Boliden
Vojmsjön
Namsen
Malgomaj
Norsjö
Byske
Namsos
Tunnsjøen
Grong
Vilhelmina
Lycksele
Skellefteå
Skellefteh
Gäddede
Bureå
Åfjord
Follafoss
Snåsavatnet
Tåsjön
Ume älv
Ångermanälven
Fosna
Steinkjer
Flåsjön
Granö
Vindeln
Ånäset
Verdalsøra
Hoting
Stranda
Trondheimsfjorden
Levanger
Hotagen
Sandvika
Trondheim
Stjørdalshalsen
Heimdal
Melhus
Hommelvik
Vännäs
Umeå
Kallsjön
Holmsund
Løkken
Støren
Storlien
Duved
Åre
Järpen
Mörsil
Krokom
Lit
Mellansel
Botten
Gaula
Ulsberg
Haltdalen
Sylarna
Östersund
Storsjön
Brunflo
Sollefteå
Örnsköldsvik
Raippaluoto
Vaasa
Kvikne
Ljungan
Kramfors

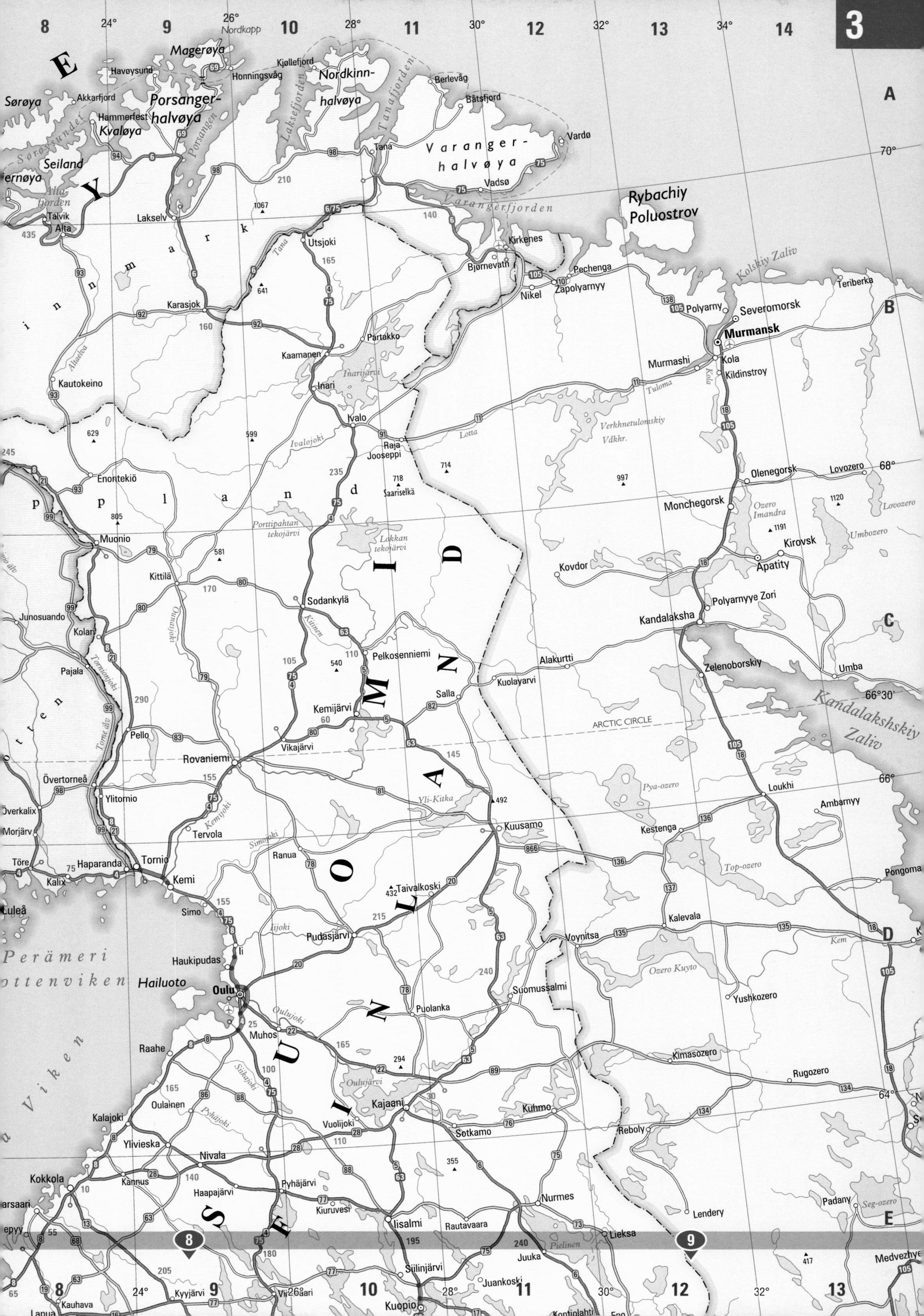
8
24°
9
26°
Nordkapp
10
28°
11
30°
12
32°
13
34°
14
A
B
C
D
E
70°
68°
66°30'
66°
64°
Magerøya
Havøysund
Honningsvåg
Kjøllefjord
Nordkinn-
halvøya
Berlevåg
Båtsfjord
Sørøya
Akkarfjord
Porsanger-
halvøya
Hammerfest
Kvaløya
Sørøysundet
Porsangen
Laksefjorden
Tanafjorden
Tana
Varanger-
halvøya
Vardø
Seiland
Vadsø
Varangerfjorden
Altafjorden
Talvik
Alta
Lakselv
Utsjoki
Kirkenes
Rybachiy
Poluostrov
Bjørnevatn
Pechenga
Zapolyarnyy
Nikel
Kolskiy Zaliv
Teriberka
Polyarny
Severomorsk
Murmansk
Karasjok
Partakko
Kaamanen
Kautokeino
Inarijärvi
Inari
Murmashi
Kola
Kildinstroy
Tuloma
Ivalo
Raja
Jooseppi
Ivalojoki
Lotta
Verkhnetulomskiy
Vdkhr.
Enontekiö
Saariselkä
Olenegorsk
Lovozero
Monchegorsk
Ozero
Imandra
Umbozero
Porttipahtan
tekojärvi
Lokkan
tekojärvi
Muonio
Kittilä
Kovdor
Kirovsk
Apatity
Sodankylä
Polyarnyye Zori
Kandalaksha
Junosuando
Kolari
Pajala
Pelkosenniemi
Alakurtti
Zelenoborskiy
Umba
Kuolayarvi
Salla
Kemijärvi
Kandalakshskiy
Zaliv
ARCTIC CIRCLE
Pello
Vikajärvi
Rovaniemi
Övertorneå
Ylitornio
Loukhi
Yli-Kitka
Ambarnyy
Pya-ozero
Överkalix
Morjärv
Tervola
Kuusamo
Kestenga
Ranua
Töre
Haparanda
Tornio
Kemi
Kalix
Top-ozero
Pongoma
Taivalkoski
Luleå
Simo
Kalevala
Pudasjärvi
Voynitsa
Kem
Perämeri
Bottenviken
Haukipudas
Ii
Hailuoto
Oulu
Ozero Kuyto
Suomussalmi
Yushkozero
Puolanka
Muhos
Oulujoki
Raahe
Kimasozero
Rugozero
Oulujärvi
Oulainen
Kajaani
Kuhmo
Kalajoki
Vuolijoki
Reboly
Sotkamo
Ylivieska
Nivala
Kokkola
Kannus
Haapajärvi
Pyhäjärvi
Kiuruvesi
Nurmes
Padany
Seg-ozero
Iisalmi
Rautavaara
Lendery
Lieksa
Pielinen
Juuka
Medvezh'ye
Siilinjärvi
Juankoski
Kyyjärvi
Kauhava
Kuopio
Kontiolahti
Lapua
F I N N M A R K
L A P P L A N D
M I D N O R R B O T T E N
E Y
S U O M I F I N L A N D

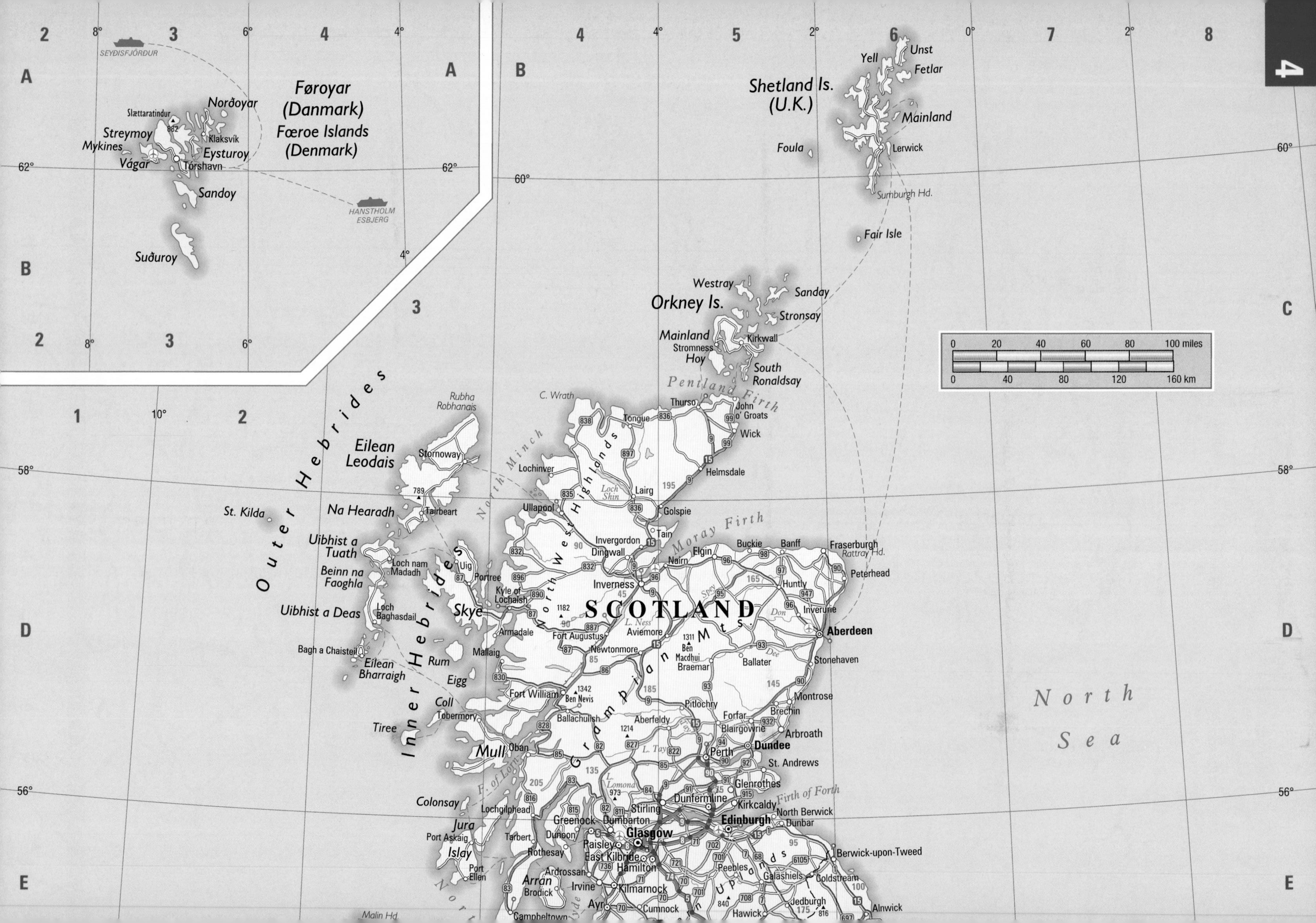
Føroyar
(Danmark)
Færoe Islands
(Denmark)
Seyðisfjørður
Slættaratindur
882
Norðoyar
Streymoy
Klaksvík
Mykines
Eysturoy
Vágar
Tórshavn
Sandoy
Hanstholm
Esbjerg
Suðuroy
Shetland Is.
(U.K.)
Unst
Yell
Fetlar
Mainland
Lerwick
Foula
Sumburgh Hd.
Fair Isle
Orkney Is.
Westray
Sanday
Stronsay
Mainland
Kirkwall
Stromness
Hoy
South
Ronaldsay
Pentland Firth
0 20 40 60 80 100 miles
0 40 80 120 160 km
Outer Hebrides
Eilean
Leodais
Rubha
Robhanais
Stornoway
St. Kilda
Na Hearadh
Tairbeart
789
Uibhist a
Tuath
Loch nam
Madadh
Beinn na
Faoghla
Uibhist a Deas
Loch
Baghasdail
Bagh a Chaisteil
Eilean
Bharraigh
Inner Hebrides
Uig
Portree
Skye
Rum
Eigg
Coll
Tobermory
Tiree
Mull
Colonsay
Jura
Port Askaig
Islay
Port
Ellen
Malin Hd.
C. Wrath
North Minch
Lochinver
Ullapool
Tongue
Thurso
John
o' Groats
Wick
Helmsdale
Lairg
Loch
Shin
Golspie
Tain
North West Highlands
Invergordon
Dingwall
Inverness
Moray Firth
Nairn
Elgin
Buckie
Banff
Fraserburgh
Rattray Hd.
Peterhead
Huntly
Inverurie
Aberdeen
Stonehaven
SCOTLAND
Grampian Mts.
Kyle of
Lochalsh
1182
Armadale
Mallaig
Fort Augustus
L. Ness
Aviemore
1311
Ben
Macdhui
Braemar
Ballater
Newtonmore
Fort William
1342
Ben Nevis
Ballachulish
Pitlochry
Aberfeldy
1214
L. Tay
Oban
F. of Lorn
Montrose
Brechin
Forfar
Blairgowrie
Arbroath
Dundee
Perth
St. Andrews
Glenrothes
L. Lomond
973
Stirling
Dunfermline
Kirkcaldy
Firth of Forth
North Berwick
Dunbar
Edinburgh
Lochgilphead
Greenock
Dumbarton
Glasgow
Dunoon
Tarbert
Rothesay
Paisley
East Kilbride
Hamilton
Ardrossan
Arran
Brodick
Irvine
Kilmarnock
Ayr
Cumnock
Campbeltown
Peebles
Galashiels
Coldstream
Berwick-upon-Tweed
Jedburgh
Hawick
Alnwick
840
816
Southern Uplands
North Sea
Spey
Dee
Don

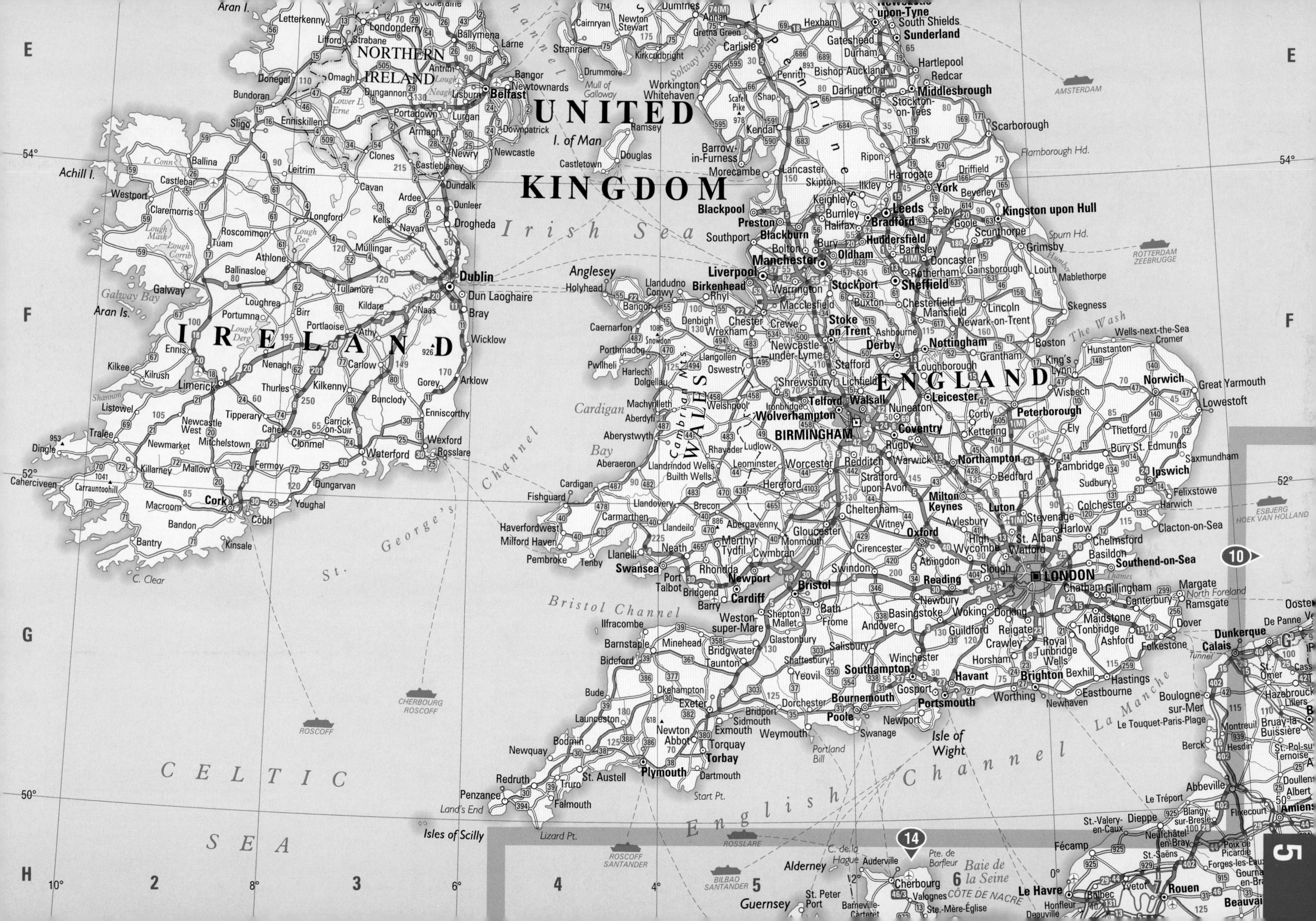

5
UNITED KINGDOM
IRELAND
NORTHERN IRELAND
ENGLAND
WALES
Irish Sea
CELTIC SEA
English Channel
La Manche
Bristol Channel
St. George's Channel
Cardigan Bay
The Wash
I. of Man
Anglesey
Isle of Wight
Isles of Scilly
Alderney
Guernsey
LONDON
BIRMINGHAM
Dublin
Belfast
Manchester
Liverpool
Leeds
Sheffield
Bristol
Cardiff
Cork
Limerick
Galway
Plymouth
Southampton
Portsmouth
Dover
Calais
Dunkerque
Cherbourg
Le Havre
Rouen
Amiens
AMSTERDAM
ROTTERDAM ZEEBRUGGE
ESBJERG HOEK VAN HOLLAND
CHERBOURG ROSCOFF
ROSCOFF
ROSCOFF SANTANDER
ROSSLARE
BILBAO SANTANDER

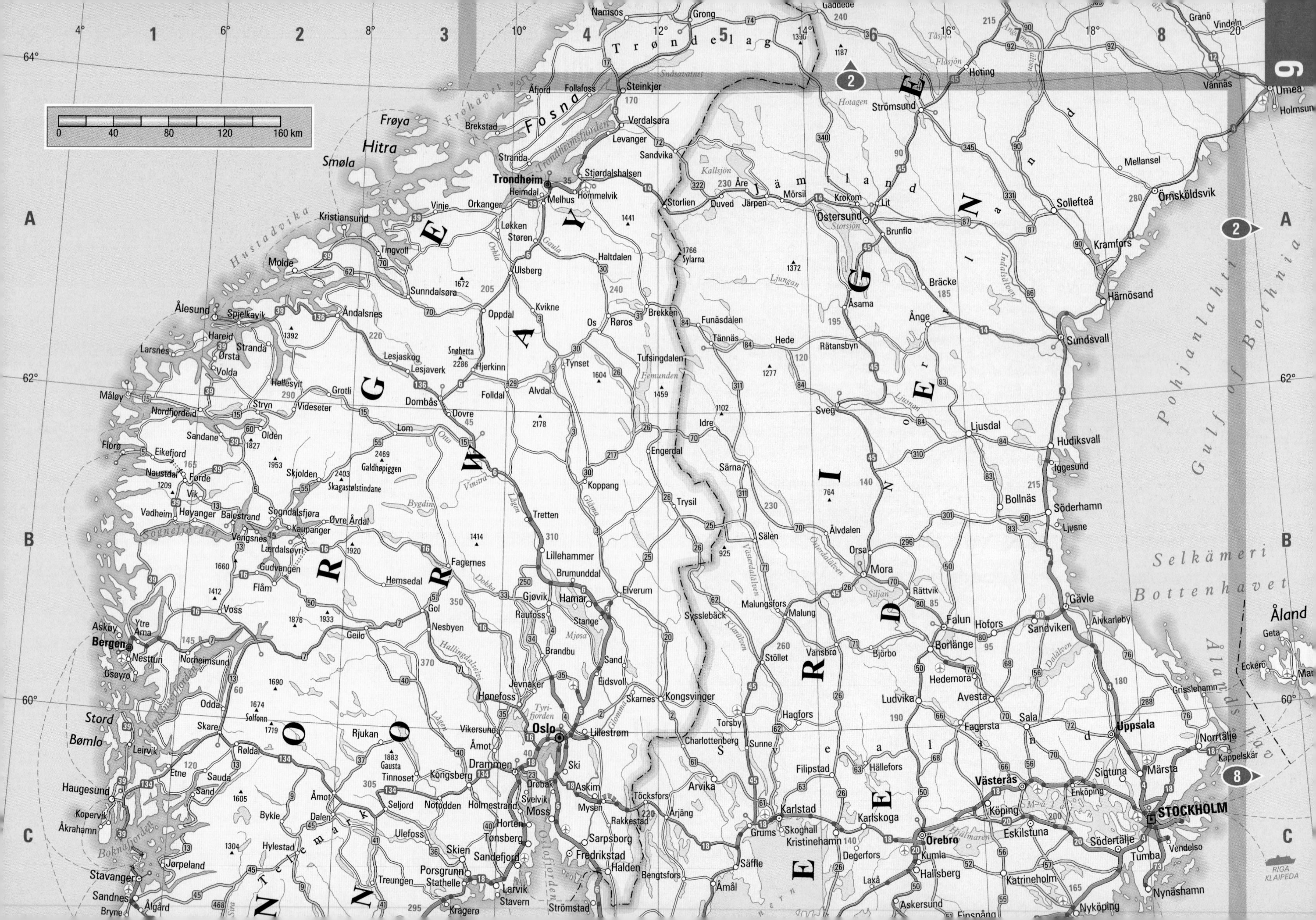
Trøndelag
Jämtland
Norrland
Svealand
Telemark
Gulf of Bothnia
Pohjanlahti
Selkämeri
Bottenhavet
Ålands hav
Åland
Fosna
Frøya
Hitra
Smøla
Stord
Bømlo
Hustadvika
Sognefjorden
Hardangerfjorden
Boknafjorden
Trondheimsfjorden
Oslofjorden
Mjøsa
Siljan
Storsjön
Femunden
Hjälmaren
Mälaren
STOCKHOLM
Oslo
Bergen
Trondheim
Stavanger
Uppsala
Västerås
Örebro
Gävle
Sundsvall
Östersund
Umeå
Härnösand
Örnsköldsvik
Sollefteå
Kramfors
Hudiksvall
Söderhamn
Bollnäs
Ljusdal
Falun
Borlänge
Mora
Karlstad
Lillehammer
Hamar
Gjøvik
Drammen
Ålesund
Molde
Kristiansund
Haugesund
Fredrikstad
Sarpsborg
Halden
Moss
Tønsberg
Larvik
Skien
Porsgrunn
Kongsberg
Røros
Oppdal
Dombås
Førde
Florø
Voss
Odda
Sandnes
Norrtälje
Södertälje
Nyköping
Eskilstuna
Köping
Sala
Avesta
Ludvika
Sveg
Strömsund
Steinkjer
Namsos
Grong
Hoting
Vännäs
Kongsvinger
Lillestrøm
Hønefoss
Elverum
Arvika
Kristinehamn
Karlskoga
Säffle
Åmål
Strömstad
Fagernes
Rjukan
Gausta
Galdhøpiggen
Snøhetta
0 40 80 120 160 km

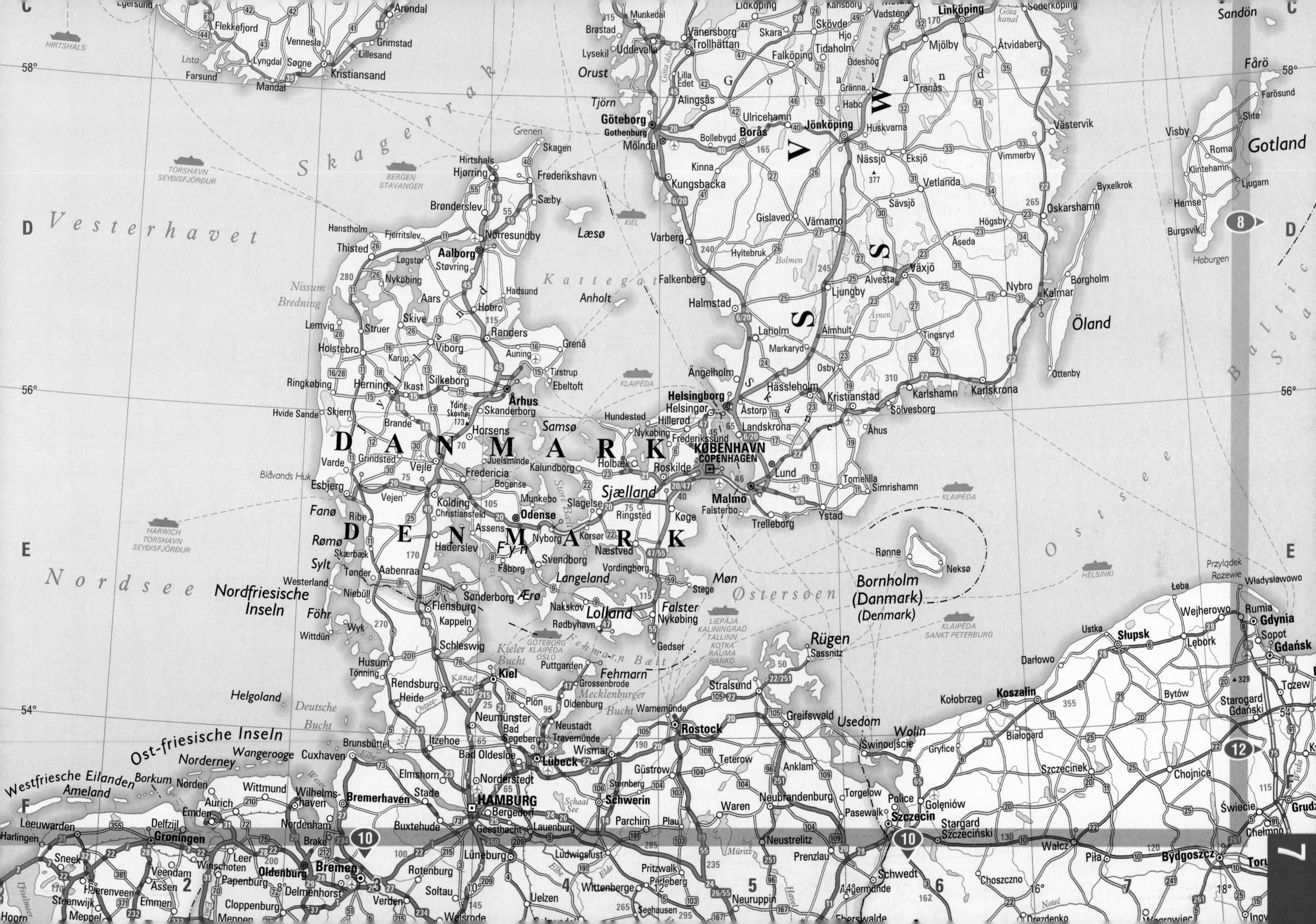

7
Skagerrak
Vesterhavet
Nordsee
Kattegat
Østersøen
Ostsee
Baltic Sea
DANMARK
DENMARK
SVERIGE
Gotland
Öland
Bornholm (Danmark) (Denmark)
Sjælland
Fyn
Lolland
Falster
Møn
Langeland
Ærø
Samsø
Anholt
Læsø
Fanø
Rømø
Sylt
Föhr
Fehmarn
Rügen
Usedom
Wolin
Helgoland
Nordfriesische Inseln
Ost-friesische Inseln
Westfriesche Eilanden
Deutsche Bucht
Kieler Bucht
Mecklenburger Bucht
Fehmarn Bælt
Store Bælt
Nissum Bredning
Blåvands Huk
Grenen
Göteborg
Gothenburg
Jönköping
Linköping
Borås
Halmstad
Helsingborg
Malmö
Lund
Kristianstad
Karlskrona
Kalmar
Växjö
Visby
Kristiansand
Arendal
Aalborg
Århus
Odense
KØBENHAVN
COPENHAGEN
Esbjerg
Kiel
Lübeck
HAMBURG
Bremen
Bremerhaven
Schwerin
Rostock
Stralsund
Szczecin
Koszalin
Słupsk
Gdynia
Gdańsk
Bydgoszcz
Groningen
Oldenburg
TORSHAVN SEYÐISFJÖRÐUR
BERGEN STAVANGER
HIRTSHALS
KIEL
KLAIPĖDA
HELSINKI
KLAIPEDA SANKT PETERBURG
HARWICH TORSHAVN SEYÐISFJÖRÐUR
GÖTEBORG KLAIPĖDA OSLO
LIEPĀJA KALININGRAD TALLINN KOTKA RAUMA HANKO
58°
56°
54°
16°
18°
10°
12°
C
D
E
F
2
3
4
5
6
7
8
10
12

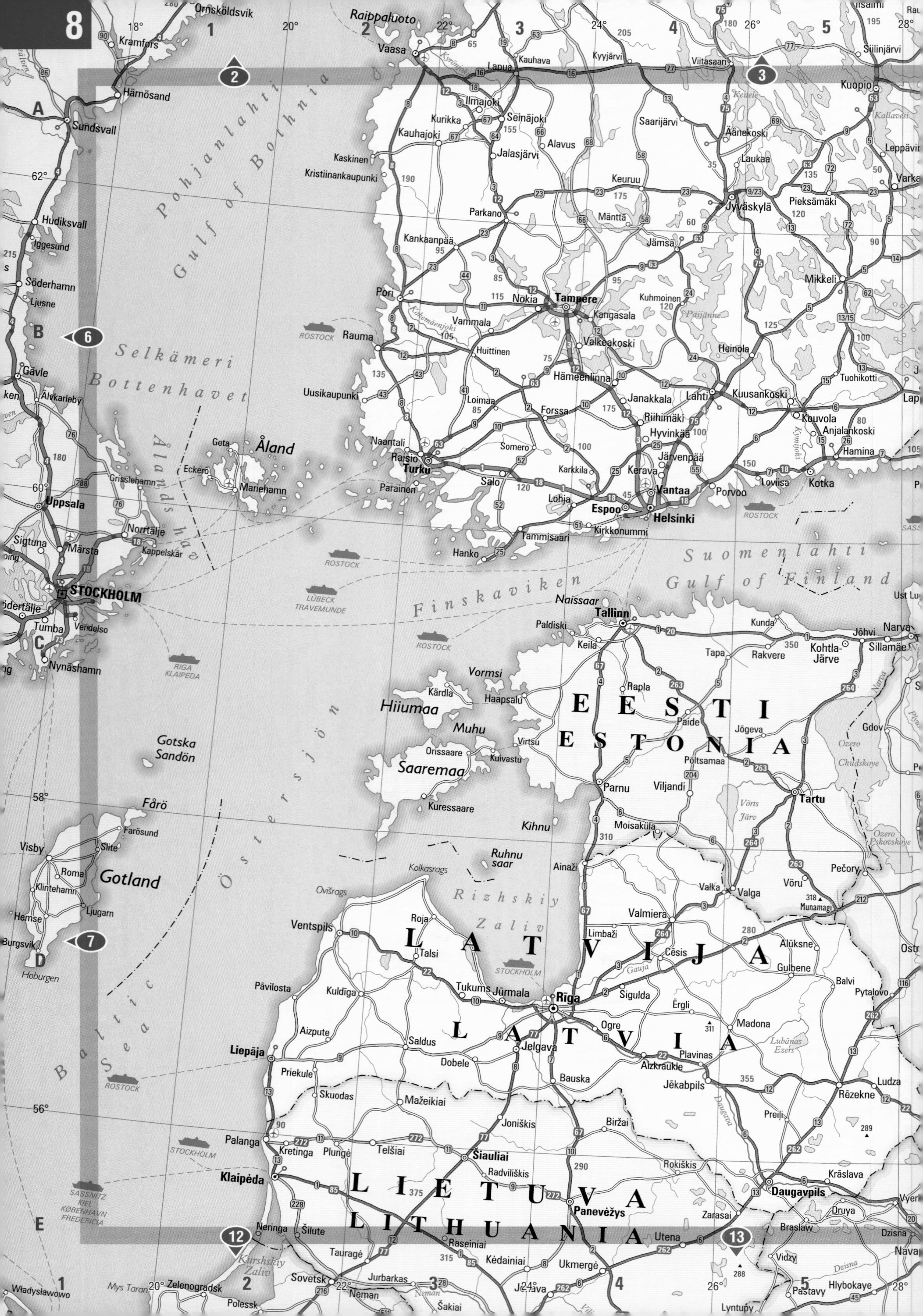
Örnsköldsvik
Kramfors
Härnösand
Sundsvall
Hudiksvall
Iggesund
Söderhamn
Ljusne
Gävle
Älvkarleby
Uppsala
Sigtuna
Märsta
Norrtälje
Kappelskär
Grisslehamn
STOCKHOLM
Södertälje
Tumba
Vendelso
Nynäshamn
Visby
Fårö
Farösund
Slite
Roma
Klintehamn
Ljugarn
Hemse
Burgsvik
Hoburgen
Gotland
Gotska Sandön
Pohjanlahti
Gulf of Bothnia
Selkämeri
Bottenhavet
Ålands hav
Åland
Geta
Eckerö
Mariehamn
Östersjön
Baltic Sea
Raippaluoto
Vaasa
Lapua
Kauhava
Kyyjärvi
Viitasaari
Siilinjärvi
Kuopio
Ilmajoki
Seinäjoki
Kurikka
Kauhajoki
Kaskinen
Kristiinankaupunki
Jalasjärvi
Alavus
Saarijärvi
Äänekoski
Laukaa
Leppävirta
Varkaus
Keuruu
Jyväskylä
Pieksämäki
Parkano
Mänttä
Kankaanpää
Jämsä
Mikkeli
Pori
Nokia
Tampere
Kangasala
Kuhmoinen
Päijänne
Rauma
Vammala
Huittinen
Valkeakoski
Heinola
Hämeenlinna
Tuohikotti
Uusikaupunki
Loimaa
Forssa
Janakkala
Lahti
Kuusankoski
Kouvola
Anjalankoski
Hamina
Riihimäki
Hyvinkää
Naantali
Raisio
Turku
Somero
Järvenpää
Kerava
Vantaa
Karkkila
Salo
Parainen
Lohja
Espoo
Helsinki
Porvoo
Loviisa
Kotka
Kirkkonummi
Tammisaari
Hanko
Suomenlahti
Gulf of Finland
Finskaviken
ROSTOCK
LÜBECK TRAVEMUNDE
RIGA KLAIPEDA
Naissaar
Tallinn
Paldiski
Keila
Kunda
Rakvere
Tapa
Kohtla-Järve
Jõhvi
Sillamäe
Narva
Vormsi
Kärdla
Hiiumaa
Haapsalu
Rapla
EESTI
ESTONIA
Paide
Jõgeva
Muhu
Orissaare
Kuivastu
Virtsu
Saaremaa
Põltsamaa
Kuressaare
Pärnu
Viljandi
Tartu
Võrts Järv
Ozero Chudskoye
Gdov
Kihnu
Moisaküla
Ruhnu saar
Ozero Pskovskoye
Ainaži
Pečory
Võru
Valka
Valga
Munamagi
Kolkasrags
Ovišrags
Rizhskiy Zaliv
Valmiera
Roja
Ventspils
Limbaži
Talsi
LATVIJA
Cēsis
Alūksne
Gauja
Gulbene
STOCKHOLM
Pāvilosta
Kuldīga
Tukums
Jūrmala
Rīga
Sigulda
Balvi
Pytalovo
Ērgli
Aizpute
Ogre
Madona
LATVIA
Liepāja
Saldus
Jelgava
Lubānas Ezers
Dobele
Aizkraukle
Plavinas
Priekule
Bauska
Jēkabpils
Rēzekne
Ludza
Skuodas
Mažeikiai
Daugava
Preiļi
Joniškis
Biržai
Palanga
Kretinga
Plungė
Telšiai
Šiauliai
Radviliškis
Klaipėda
Rokiškis
Krāslava
LIETUVA
LITHUANIA
Daugavpils
Panevėžys
Zarasai
Druya
Neringa
Šilute
Utena
Braslaw
Raseiniai
Tauragė
Kėdainiai
Ukmergė
Vidzy
Kurshskiy Zaliv
Sovetsk
Jurbarkas
Jonava
Zelenogradsk
Mys Taran
Neman
Šakiai
Polessk
Władysławowo
Hlybokaye
Pastavy
Lyntupy
Dzisna

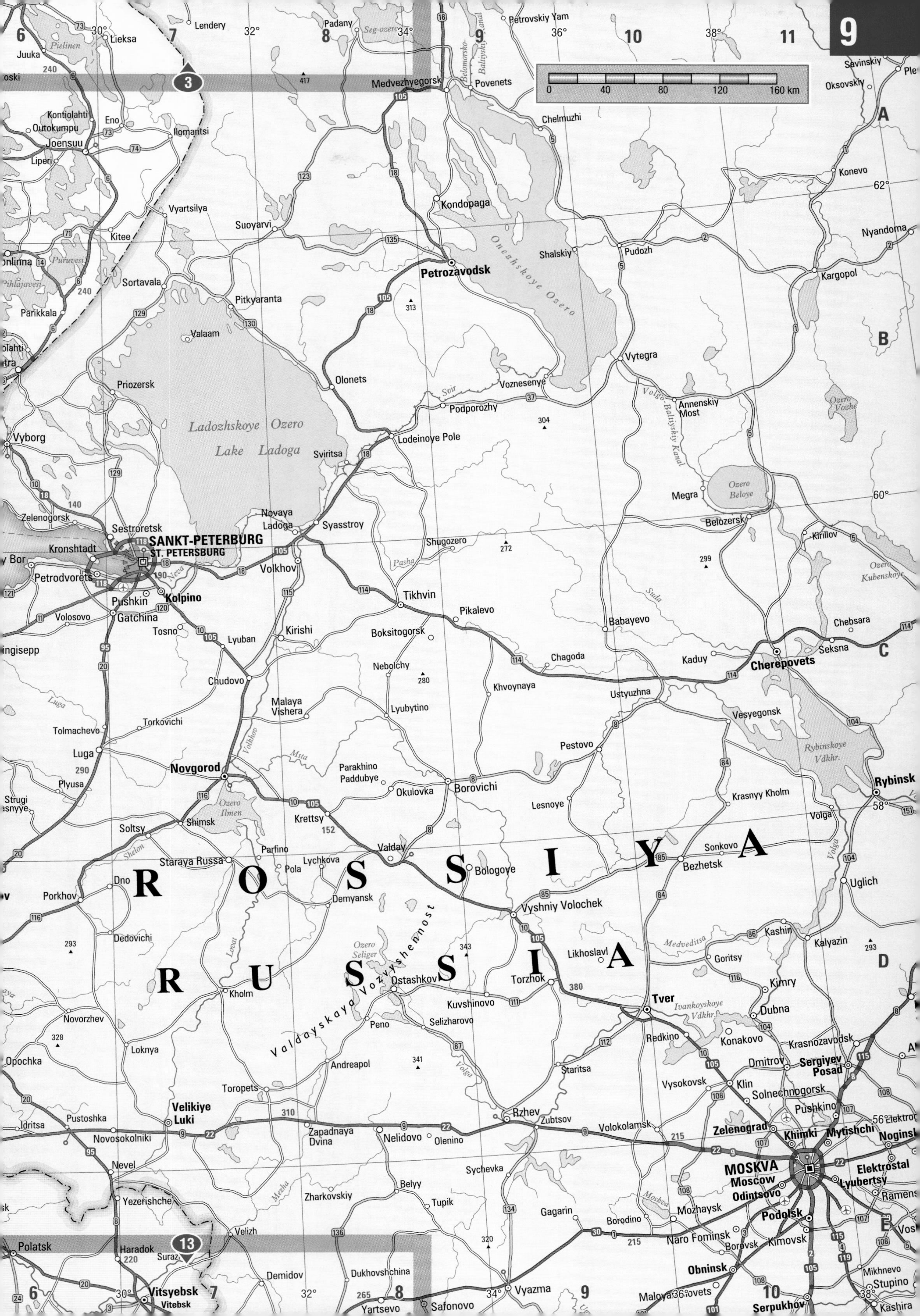
ROSSIYA
RUSSIA
SANKT-PETERBURG
ST. PETERSBURG
MOSKVA
Moscow
Ladozhskoye Ozero
Lake Ladoga
Onezhskoye Ozero
Rybinskoye Vdkhr.
Ozero Ilmen
Ozero Beloye
Ozero Seliger
Valdayskaya Vozvyshennost
Petrozavodsk
Novgorod
Tver
Cherepovets
Rybinsk
Vyborg
Kolpino
Pushkin
Gatchina
Petrodvorets
Kronshtadt
Sestroretsk
Zelenogorsk
Priozersk
Sortavala
Pitkyaranta
Olonets
Lodeinoye Pole
Podporozhy
Vytegra
Kargopol
Kondopaga
Medvezhyegorsk
Povenets
Suoyarvi
Volkhov
Kirishi
Tikhvin
Pikalevo
Boksitogorsk
Belozersk
Kirillov
Babayevo
Chagoda
Ustyuzhna
Vesyegonsk
Pestovo
Borovichi
Okulovka
Valday
Bologoye
Vyshniy Volochek
Torzhok
Likhoslavl
Bezhetsk
Kashin
Kalyazin
Uglich
Kimry
Dubna
Konakovo
Klin
Dmitrov
Sergiyev Posad
Solnechnogorsk
Zelenograd
Khimki
Mytishchi
Pushkino
Noginsk
Elektrostal
Lyubertsy
Odintsovo
Podolsk
Mozhaysk
Naro Fominsk
Obninsk
Serpukhov
Kashira
Stupino
Vyazma
Rzhev
Zubtsov
Staritsa
Volokolamsk
Gagarin
Nelidovo
Olenino
Velikiye Luki
Nevel
Toropets
Andreapol
Ostashkov
Peno
Selizharovo
Kuvshinovo
Kholm
Staraya Russa
Demyansk
Porkhov
Dno
Dedovichi
Soltsy
Shimsk
Luga
Plyusa
Tolmachevo
Chudovo
Lyuban
Tosno
Volosovo
Velizh
Vitsyebsk
Vitebsk
Haradok
Polatsk
Yartsevo
Safonovo
Demidov
Dukhovshchina
Belyy
Sychevka
Joensuu
Lieksa
Vyartsilya
Kitee
Parikkala
0 40 80 120 160 km

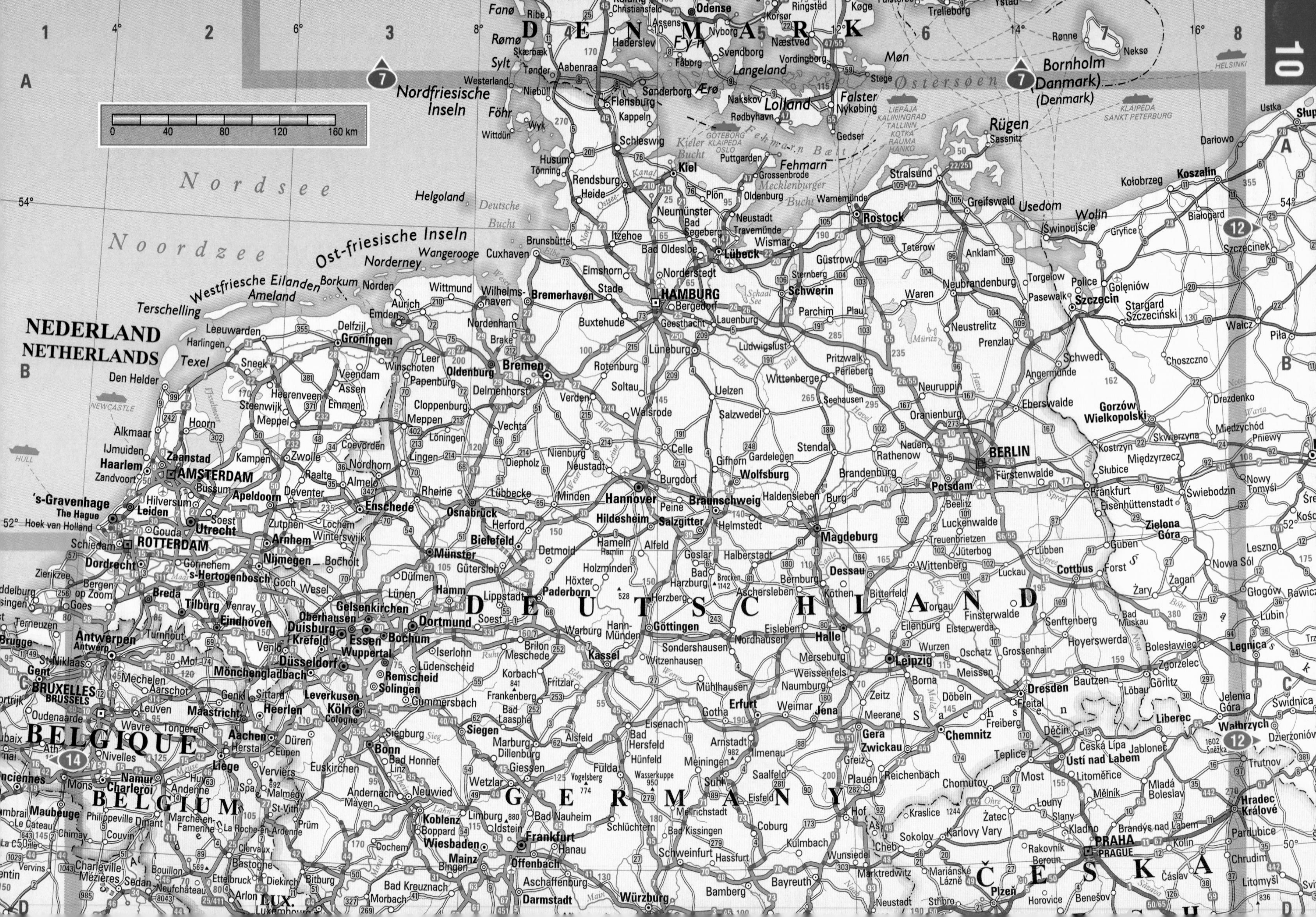

DENMARK
DEUTSCHLAND
GERMANY
NEDERLAND
NETHERLANDS
BELGIQUE
BELGIUM
ČESKÁ
LUX.
Nordsee
Noordzee
Østersøen
Nordfriesische Inseln
Ost-friesische Inseln
Westfriesche Eilanden
Bornholm (Danmark) (Denmark)
Rügen
BERLIN
HAMBURG
AMSTERDAM
ROTTERDAM
BRUXELLES BRUSSELS
PRAHA PRAGUE

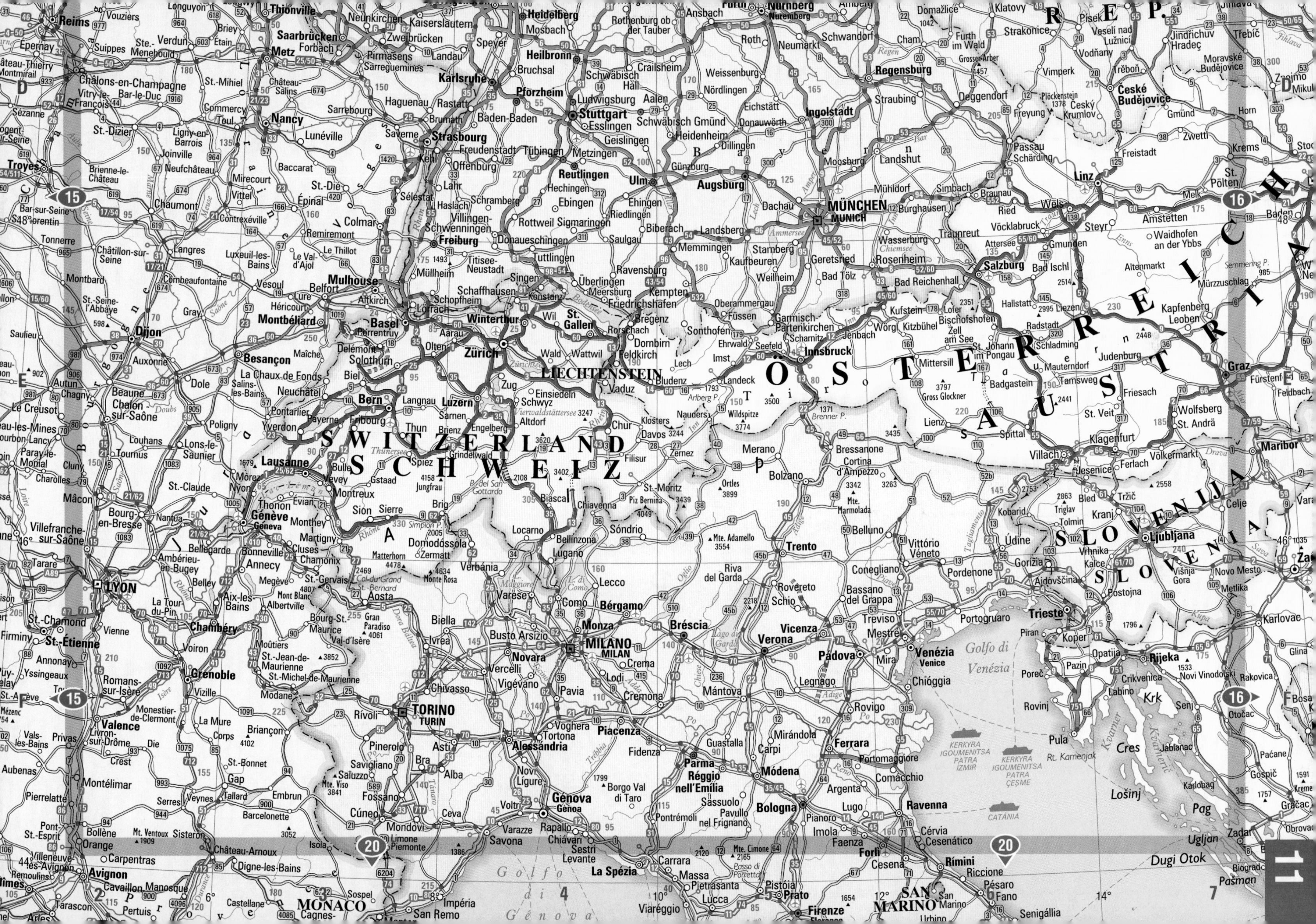
ÖSTERREICH
AUSTRIA
SWITZERLAND
SCHWEIZ
LIECHTENSTEIN
SLOVENIJA
SLOVENIA
SAN MARINO
MONACO
MÜNCHEN
MUNICH
MILANO
MILAN
TORINO
TURIN
Genève
Geneva
Lyon
Zürich
Bern
Basel
Innsbruck
Salzburg
Graz
Ljubljana
Venézia
Venice
Verona
Bologna
Firenze
Génova
Genoa
Grenoble
Dijon
Strasbourg
Stuttgart
Nürnberg
Regensburg
Linz
Trieste
Rijeka
Golfo di Venézia
Golfo di Génova

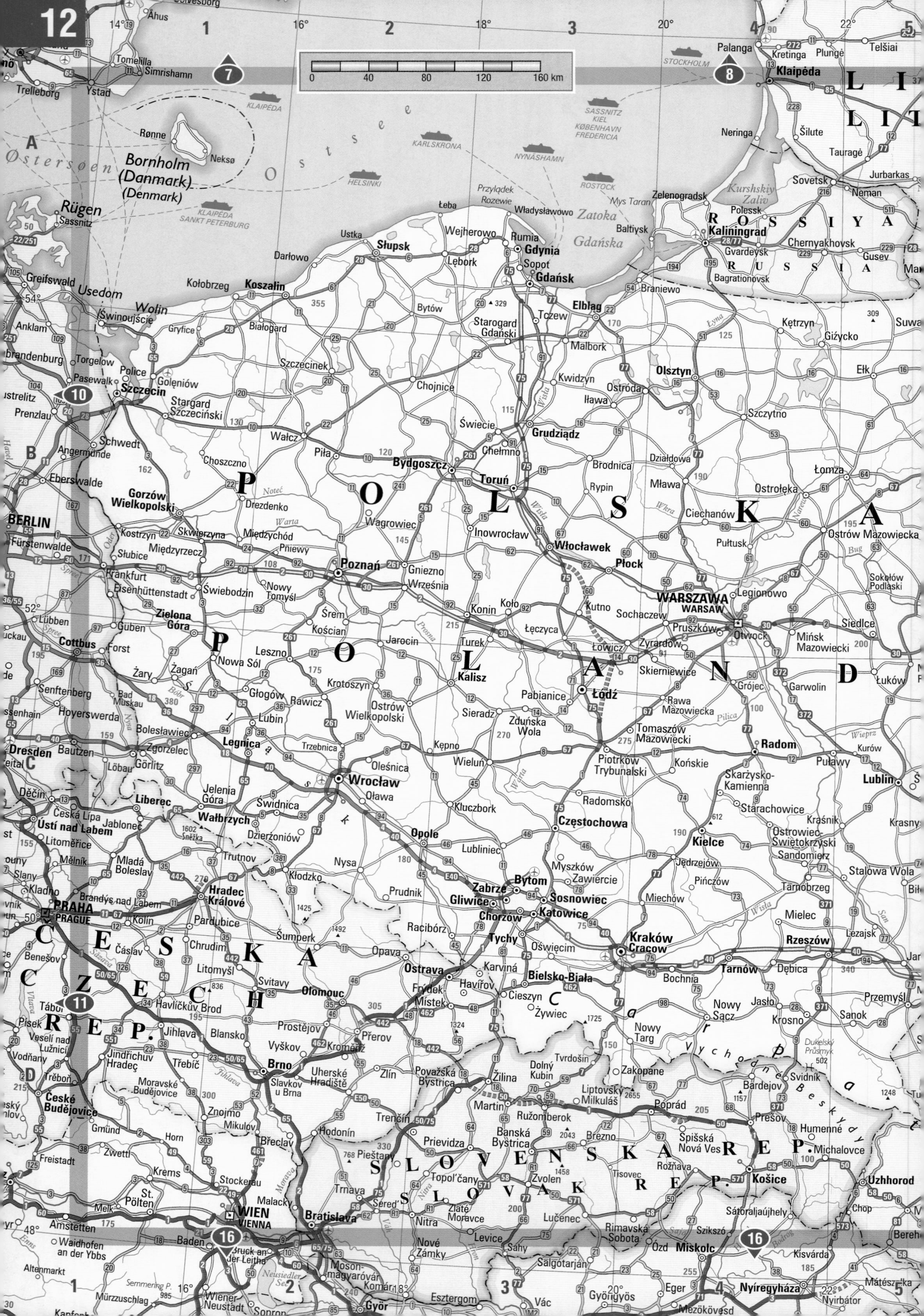

Åhus
Tomelilla
Simrishamn
Trelleborg
Ystad
Rønne
Nexø
Bornholm
(Danmark)
(Denmark)
Østersøen
Ostsee
Rügen
Sassnitz
KLAIPĖDA
KARLSKRONA
HELSINKI
NYNÄSHAMN
ROSTOCK
SASSNITZ
KIEL
KØBENHAVN
FREDERICIA
STOCKHOLM
KLAIPĖDA
SANKT PETERBURG
Palanga
Kretinga
Plungė
Telšiai
Klaipėda
Neringa
Šilutė
Tauragė
Jurbarkas
Sovetsk
Neman
Kurshskiy Zaliv
Zelenogradsk
Polessk
Kaliningrad
Gvardeysk
Chernyakhovsk
Gusev
Bagrationovsk
Baltiysk
ROSSIYA
RUSSIA
Mys Taran
Zatoka Gdańska
Przylądek Rozewie
Władysławowo
Łeba
Ustka
Słupsk
Wejherowo
Rumia
Gdynia
Sopot
Gdańsk
Lębork
Darłowo
Kołobrzeg
Koszalin
Bytów
Starogard Gdański
Tczew
Elbląg
Braniewo
Malbork
Greifswald
Usedom
Wolin
Świnoujście
Anklam
Gryfice
Białogard
Torgelow
Pasewalk
Police
Goleniów
Szczecin
Stargard Szczeciński
Prenzlau
Schwedt
Angermünde
Eberswalde
Szczecinek
Chojnice
Wałcz
Piła
Choszczno
Kwidzyn
Ostróda
Olsztyn
Iława
Grudziądz
Świecie
Chełmno
Bydgoszcz
Toruń
Brodnica
Rypin
Działdowo
Mława
Ciechanów
Szczytno
Kętrzyn
Giżycko
Ełk
Łomża
Ostrołęka
Ostrów Mazowiecka
Pułtusk
Gorzów Wielkopolski
Drezdenko
Noteć
Warta
Wągrowiec
Inowrocław
Włocławek
Płock
Kostrzyn
Skwierzyna
Międzychód
Pniewy
Międzyrzecz
Słubice
Frankfurt
Eisenhüttenstadt
Świebodzin
Nowy Tomyśl
Poznań
Gniezno
Września
Konin
Koło
Kutno
Łęczyca
Sochaczew
WARSZAWA
WARSAW
Legionowo
Pruszków
Otwock
Mińsk Mazowiecki
Siedlce
Sokołów Podlaski
BERLIN
Fürstenwalde
Lübben
Cottbus
Forst
Guben
Zielona Góra
Kościan
Śrem
Jarocin
Turek
Łowicz
Żyrardów
Skierniewice
Grójec
Garwolin
Łuków
Leszno
Nowa Sól
Żary
Żagań
Krotoszyn
Ostrów Wielkopolski
Kalisz
Sieradz
Zduńska Wola
Pabianice
Łódź
Rawa Mazowiecka
Tomaszów Mazowiecki
Radom
Kurów
Puławy
Lublin
Senftenberg
Hoyerswerda
Bad Muskau
Głogów
Rawicz
Lubin
Legnica
Bolesławiec
Zgorzelec
Görlitz
Bautzen
Dresden
Löbau
Trzebnica
Oleśnica
Kępno
Wieluń
Piotrków Trybunalski
Końskie
Skarżysko-Kamienna
Starachowice
Kraśnik
Radomsko
Wrocław
Oława
Kluczbork
Częstochowa
Kielce
Ostrowiec Świętokrzyski
Sandomierz
Stalowa Wola
Jelenia Góra
Liberec
Děčín
Česká Lípa
Jablonec
Ústí nad Labem
Litoměřice
Wałbrzych
Świdnica
Dzierżoniów
Śnieżka
Trutnov
Mladá Boleslav
Mělník
Slaný
Kladno
PRAHA
PRAGUE
Brandýs nad Labem
Hradec Králové
Pardubice
Kolín
Chrudim
Čáslav
Benešov
Kłodzko
Nysa
Opole
Lubliniec
Myszków
Zawiercie
Bytom
Zabrze
Gliwice
Chorzów
Sosnowiec
Katowice
Tychy
Oświęcim
Jędrzejów
Pińczów
Miechów
Kraków
Cracow
Tarnobrzeg
Mielec
Rzeszów
Leżajsk
Prudnik
Racibórz
Šumperk
Opava
Ostrava
Karviná
Havířov
Frýdek-Místek
Cieszyn
Bielsko-Biała
Żywiec
Bochnia
Tarnów
Dębica
Jasło
Krosno
Przemyśl
Sanok
Nowy Sącz
Nowy Targ
Zakopane
Litomyšl
Svitavy
Olomouc
Havlíčkův Brod
Tábor
Jihlava
Písek
Veselí nad Lužnicí
Vodňany
Jindřichův Hradec
Třebíč
Blansko
Prostějov
Přerov
Vyškov
Kroměříž
Brno
Slavkov u Brna
Uherské Hradiště
Zlín
Považská Bystrica
Žilina
Dolný Kubín
Tvrdošín
Liptovský Mikuláš
Martin
Ružomberok
Poprad
Bardejov
Svidník
Prešov
Humenné
Michalovce
Uzhhorod
Dukelský Průsmyk
Vychodné Beskydy
Karpaty
Třeboň
České Budějovice
Moravské Budějovice
Znojmo
Mikulov
Břeclav
Hodonín
Trenčín
Prievidza
Banská Bystrica
Brezno
Spišská Nová Ves
Rožňava
Košice
Gmünd
Horn
Zwettl
Freistadt
Krems
Stockerau
St. Pölten
Melk
Amstetten
Waidhofen an der Ybbs
Altenmarkt
Semmering P.
Mürzzuschlag
Wiener Neustadt
Baden
Bruck an der Leitha
WIEN
VIENNA
Malacky
Bratislava
Trnava
Piešťany
Sereď
Nitra
Zlaté Moravce
Topoľčany
Zvolen
Tisovec
Lučenec
Levice
Nové Zámky
Komárom
Esztergom
Győr
Mosonmagyaróvár
Neusiedler See
Šahy
Salgótarján
Vác
Gyöngyös
Eger
Rimavská Sobota
Ózd
Miskolc
Szikszó
Sátoraljaújhely
Chop
Kisvárda
Nyíregyháza
Nyírbátor
Mátészalka
Mezőkövesd
POLSKA
POLAND
ČESKÁ REP.
CZECH REP.
SLOVENSKÁ REP.
SLOVAK REP.
LIETUVA
Wisła
Pilica
Bug
Narew
Łyna
Wkra
Prosna
Odra
Nysa
Bóbr
Spree
Havel
Vltava
Morava
Dunaj
Sázava
Jihlava
Wieprz
San
Váh
Nitra
Hron
Enns
Sajó
Bodrog
0 40 80 120 160 km

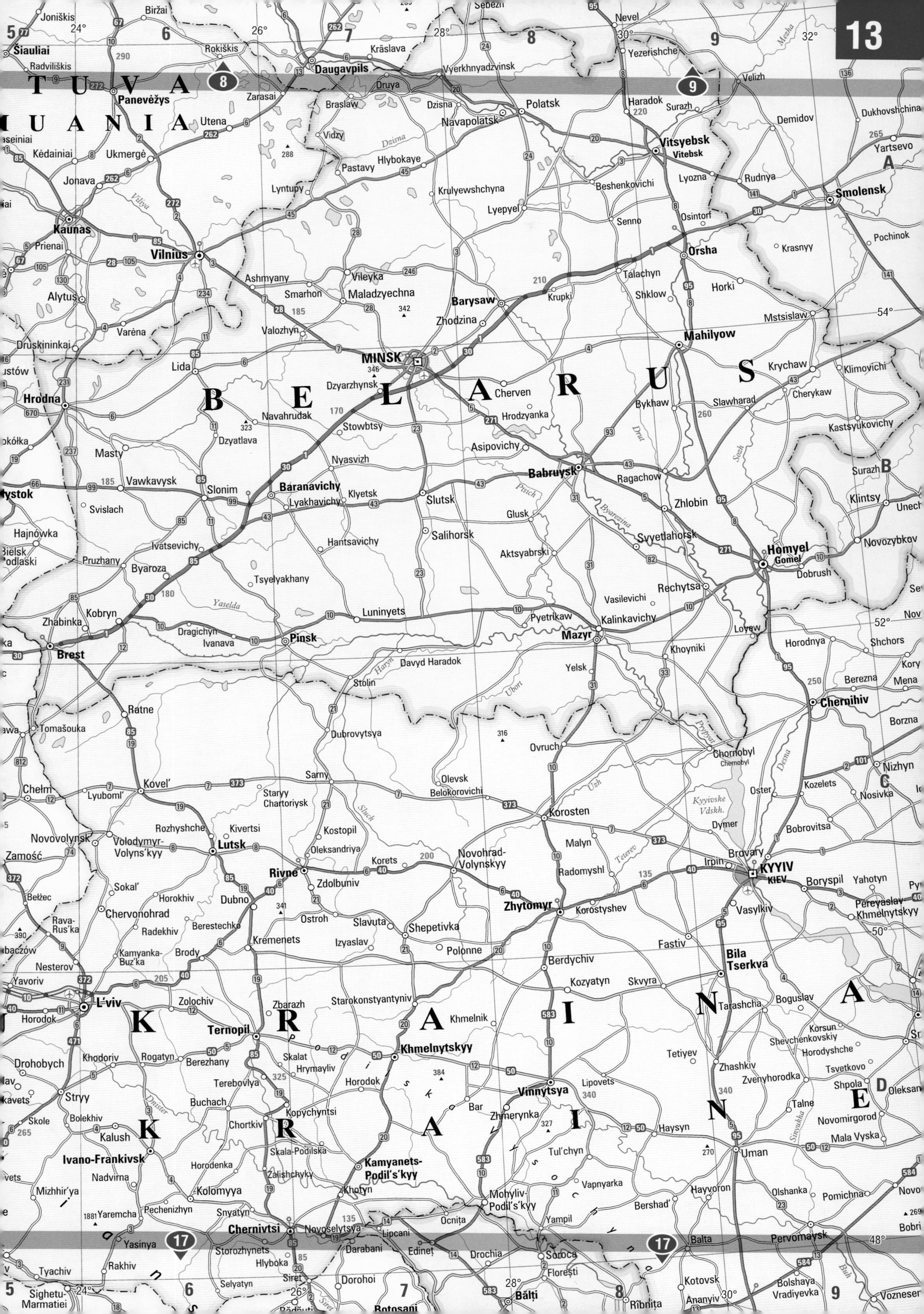
LITHUANIA
BELARUS
UKRAINA
Joniškis
Biržai
Šiauliai
Radviliškis
Rokiškis
Daugavpils
Krāslava
Sebezh
Nevel
Yezerishche
Vyerkhnyadzvinsk
Panevėžys
Zarasai
Druya
Braslaw
Dzisna
Polatsk
Navapolatsk
Haradok
Surazh
Velizh
Dukhovshchina
Demidov
Utena
Vidzy
Vitsyebsk
Vitebsk
Yartsevo
Kėdainiai
Ukmergė
Pastavy
Hlybokaye
Jonava
Lyntupy
Krulyewshchyna
Beshenkovichi
Lyozna
Rudnya
Smolensk
Lyepyel
Senno
Osintorf
Kaunas
Prienai
Vilnius
Orsha
Pochinok
Krasnyy
Ashmyany
Vileyka
Smarhon
Maladzyechna
Barysaw
Krupki
Talachyn
Shklow
Horki
Alytus
Zhodzina
Mstsislaw
Varėna
Valozhyn
Mahilyow
Druskininkai
MINSK
Krychaw
Klimovichi
Lida
Dzyarzhynsk
Cherven
Cherykaw
Hrodna
Navahrudak
Hrodzyanka
Bykhaw
Slawharad
Kastsyukovichi
Stowbtsy
Dzyatlava
Asipovichy
Masty
Nyasvizh
Surazh
Vawkavysk
Slonim
Baranavichy
Babruysk
Ragachow
Klyetsk
Lyakhavichy
Slutsk
Zhlobin
Klintsy
Svislach
Glusk
Hajnówka
Salihorsk
Svyetlahorsk
Hantsavichy
Novozybkov
Ivatsevichy
Aktsyabrski
Homyel
Gomel
Dobrush
Pruzhany
Byaroza
Tsyelyakhany
Rechytsa
Vasilevichi
Kobryn
Luninyets
Pyetrikaw
Kalinkavichy
Zhabinka
Dragichyn
Ivanava
Pinsk
Mazyr
Loyew
Brest
Khoyniki
Horodnya
Shchors
Davyd Haradok
Yelsk
Stolin
Berezna
Mena
Ratne
Chernihiv
Tomašouka
Dubrovytsya
Borzna
Ovruch
Chornobyl
Chernobyl
Sarny
Olevsk
Nizhyn
Chełm
Lyuboml'
Kovel'
Staryy Chartoriysk
Belokorovichi
Oster
Kozelets
Nosivka
Korosten
Kyyivske Vdskh.
Dymer
Rozhyshche
Kivertsi
Kostopil
Novovolynsk
Volodymyr-Volyns'kyy
Lutsk
Oleksandriya
Malyn
Bobrovitsa
Zamość
Rivne
Korets
Novohrad-Volynskyy
Radomyshl
Irpin
Brovary
KYYIV
KIEV
Boryspil
Yahotyn
Sokal'
Zdolbuniv
Bełżec
Horokhiv
Dubno
Zhytomyr
Korostyshev
Vasylkiv
Pereyaslav-Khmelnytskyy
Chervonohrad
Ostroh
Rava-Rus'ka
Radekhiv
Berestechko
Slavuta
Shepetivka
Kremenets
Izyaslav
Fastiv
Kamyanka-Buz'ka
Brody
Polonne
Bila Tserkva
Nesterov
Berdychiv
Yavoriv
Kozyatyn
Skvyra
L'viv
Zolochiv
Zbarazh
Starokonstyantyniv
Tarashcha
Boguslav
Horodok
Khmelnik
Ternopil
Korsun Shevchenkovskiy
Drohobych
Khodoriv
Rogatyn
Berezhany
Skalat
Hrymayliv
Khmelnytskyy
Horodyshche
Tetiyev
Zhashkiv
Tsvetkovo
Terebovlya
Horodok
Vinnytsya
Lipovets
Zvenyhorodka
Shpola
Oleksan
Stryy
Buchach
Bar
Talne
Skole
Bolekhiv
Kopychyntsi
Zhmerynka
Novomirgorod
Kalush
Chortkiv
Haysyn
Mala Vyska
Ivano-Frankivsk
Skala-Podilska
Tul'chyn
Uman
Horodenka
Kamyanets-Podil's'kyy
Mizhhir'ya
Nadvirna
Zalishchyky
Vapnyarka
Khotyn
Mohyliv-Podil's'kyy
Hayvoron
Olshanka
Pomichna
Kolomyya
Yaremcha
Pechenizhyn
Snyatyn
Bershad'
Ocnița
Yampil
Chernivtsi
Novoselytsya
Lipcani
Yasinya
Storozhynets
Darabani
Edineț
Drochia
Soroca
Balta
Pervomaysk
Hlyboka
Floresti
Kotovsk
Tyachiv
Rakhiv
Siret
Dorohoi
Bolshaya Vradiyevka
Sighetu-Marmatiei
Selyatyn
Bălți
Rîbnița
Ananyiv
Voznesen
Botoșani
Dzisna
Viliya
Yaselda
Pisich
Byarezina
Drut
Sozh
Horyn
Ubort
Prypyat
Desna
Uzh
Teterev
Sluch
Dnister
Sinyukha
Buh
Mezha
Podilska
Vysochyna
54°
52°
50°
48°
24°
26°
28°
30°
32°
5
6
7
8
9
A
B
C
D

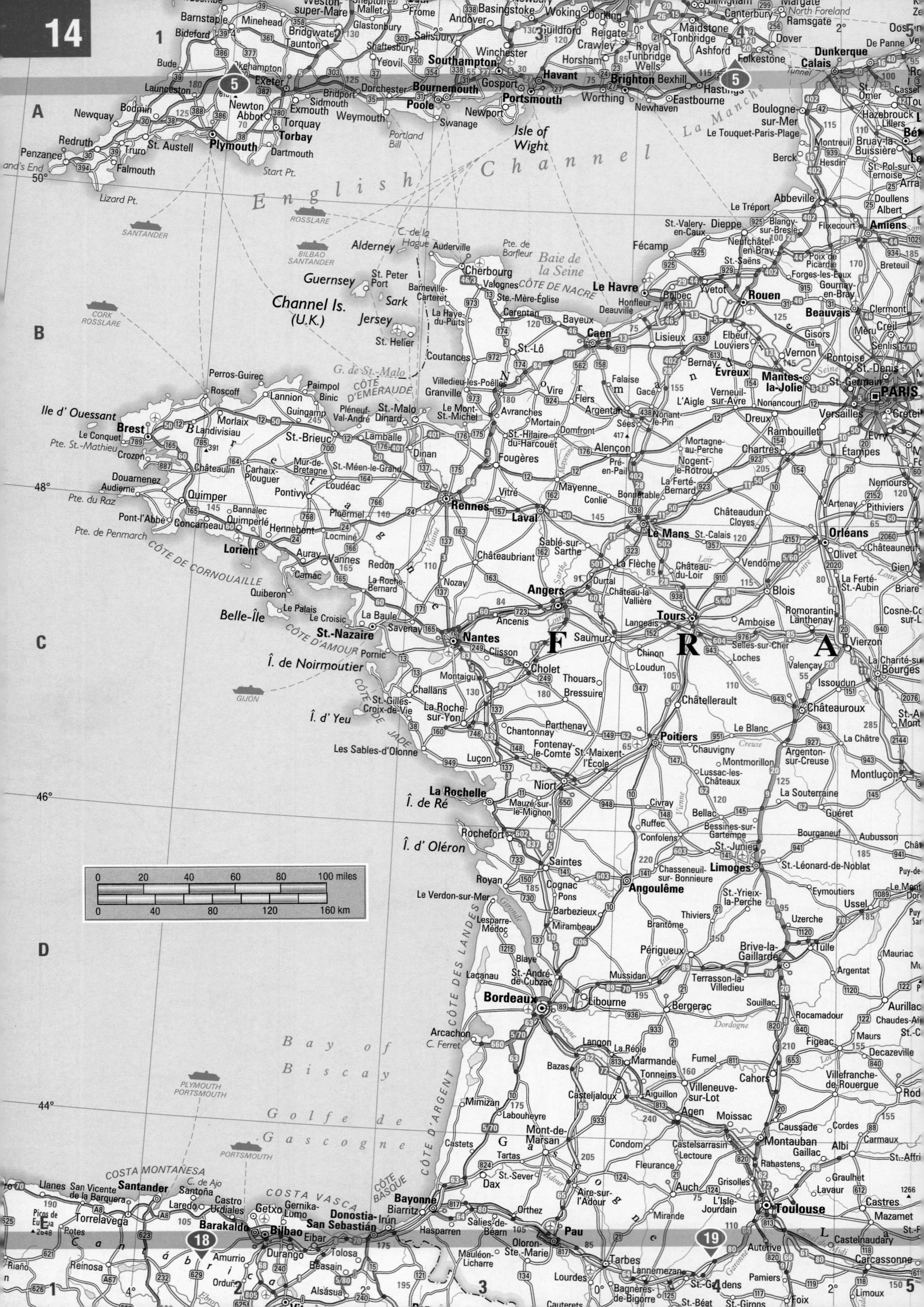
14
English Channel
La Manche
Channel Is. (U.K.)
Alderney
Guernsey
Sark
Jersey
St. Peter Port
St. Helier
Isle of Wight
Bay of Biscay
Golfe de Gascogne
FRANCE
Barnstaple
Bideford
Minehead
Bridgwater
Taunton
Weston-super-Mare
Glastonbury
Shaftesbury
Yeovil
Salisbury
Frome
Andover
Basingstoke
Woking
Dorking
Guildford
Reigate
Crawley
Horsham
Winchester
Southampton
Havant
Portsmouth
Gosport
Brighton
Worthing
Newhaven
Eastbourne
Hastings
Bexhill
Royal Tunbridge Wells
Tonbridge
Maidstone
Canterbury
Ashford
Folkestone
Dover
Ramsgate
Margate
North Foreland
Bude
Okehampton
Launceston
Exeter
Newton Abbot
Exmouth
Sidmouth
Torquay
Torbay
Dartmouth
Bridport
Dorchester
Weymouth
Bournemouth
Poole
Swanage
Portland Bill
Newport
Bodmin
Newquay
Redruth
Truro
St. Austell
Plymouth
Penzance
Land's End
Falmouth
Lizard Pt.
Start Pt.
Calais
Dunkerque
Boulogne-sur-Mer
Le Touquet-Paris-Plage
Berck
Montreuil
Hesdin
St.-Omer
Hazebrouck
Lillers
Bruay-la-Buissière
St.-Pol-sur-Ternoise
Arras
Doullens
Albert
Amiens
Abbeville
Le Tréport
Dieppe
St.-Valery-en-Caux
Fécamp
Yvetot
Bolbec
Le Havre
Honfleur
Deauville
Rouen
Elbeuf
Louviers
Neufchâtel-en-Bray
St.-Saëns
Forges-les-Eaux
Gournay-en-Bray
Poix de Picardie
Flixecourt
Breteuil
Beauvais
Clermont
Creil
Senlis
Méru
Gisors
Vernon
Pontoise
St.-Denis
St.-Germain
PARIS
Versailles
Mantes-la-Jolie
Évreux
Bernay
Lisieux
Caen
Bayeux
Cherbourg
Valognes
Ste.-Mère-Église
Carentan
St.-Lô
Barneville-Carteret
La Haye-du-Puits
Coutances
Granville
Villedieu-les-Poêles
Vire
Flers
Falaise
Argentan
Gacé
L'Aigle
Sées
Nonant-le-Pin
Verneuil-sur-Avre
Nonancourt
Dreux
Rambouillet
Chartres
Étampes
Évry
Nemours
Pithiviers
Artenay
Orléans
Olivet
Châteauneuf
Gien
La Ferté-St.-Aubin
Briare
Blois
Romorantin-Lanthenay
Vendôme
Châteaudun
Cloyes
St.-Calais
Le Mans
La Flèche
Château-du-Loir
Durtal
Château-la-Vallière
Tours
Amboise
Langeais
Chinon
Loudun
Loches
Selles-sur-Cher
Valençay
Vierzon
Bourges
Issoudun
Châteauroux
La Châtre
Le Blanc
Argenton-sur-Creuse
Montluçon
Guéret
La Souterraine
Aubusson
Bellac
Limoges
St.-Junien
St.-Léonard-de-Noblat
Eymoutiers
Ussel
Uzerche
Tulle
Brive-la-Gaillarde
Argentat
Mauriac
Aurillac
Figeac
Decazeville
Villefranche-de-Rouergue
Rodez
Cahors
Montauban
Caussade
Cordes
Albi
Carmaux
Gaillac
Rabastens
Graulhet
Lavaur
Castres
Mazamet
Castelnaudary
Carcassonne
Toulouse
Muret
Auterive
Pamiers
Foix
Limoux
St.-Gaudens
St.-Girons
Lannemezan
Tarbes
Lourdes
Bagnères-de-Bigorre
Pau
Oloron-Ste.-Marie
Orthez
Salies-de-Béarn
Mauléon-Licharre
Bayonne
Biarritz
Hasparren
Dax
St.-Sever
Aire-sur-l'Adour
Mont-de-Marsan
Tartas
Castets
Mimizan
Labouheyre
Auch
L'Isle-Jourdain
Mirande
Condom
Lectoure
Fleurance
Castelsarrasin
Moissac
Agen
Villeneuve-sur-Lot
Fumel
Aiguillon
Tonneins
Marmande
Casteljaloux
Bazas
La Réole
Langon
Bordeaux
Libourne
St.-André-de-Cubzac
Blaye
Lacanau
Lesparre-Médoc
Arcachon
C. Ferret
Bergerac
Périgueux
Mussidan
Terrasson-la-Villedieu
Souillac
Rocamadour
Brantôme
Thiviers
St.-Yrieix-la-Perche
Angoulême
Cognac
Pons
Barbezieux
Mirambeau
Saintes
Royan
Le Verdon-sur-Mer
Rochefort
La Rochelle
Î. de Ré
Î. d' Oléron
Niort
Mauzé-sur-le-Mignon
St.-Maixent-l'École
Fontenay-le-Comte
Luçon
Les Sables-d'Olonne
La Roche-sur-Yon
Challans
St.-Gilles-Croix-de-Vie
Î. d' Yeu
Î. de Noirmoutier
Pornic
Montaigu
Clisson
Cholet
Thouars
Bressuire
Parthenay
Chantonnay
Poitiers
Châtellerault
Chauvigny
Montmorillon
Lussac-les-Châteaux
Civray
Ruffec
Confolens
Chasseneuil-sur-Bonnieure
Saumur
Angers
Ancenis
Nantes
St.-Nazaire
La Baule
Le Croisic
Savenay
Belle-Île
Le Palais
Quiberon
Carnac
Auray
Vannes
Redon
La Roche-Bernard
Nozay
Châteaubriant
Rennes
Vitré
Laval
Mayenne
Sablé-sur-Sarthe
Fougères
Avranches
Mortain
Domfront
Alençon
Pré-en-Pail
Mortagne-au-Perche
Nogent-le-Rotrou
La Ferté-Bernard
Bonnétable
Conlie
Le Mont-St.-Michel
St.-Malo
Dinard
Dinan
Lamballe
St.-Brieuc
Pléneuf-Val-André
Paimpol
Binic
Guingamp
Lannion
Perros-Guirec
Roscoff
Morlaix
Landivisiau
Brest
Le Conquet
Ile d' Ouessant
Crozon
Châteaulin
Douarnenez
Audierne
Quimper
Pont-l'Abbé
Concarneau
Quimperlé
Bannalec
Lorient
Hennebont
Pontivy
Loudéac
Carhaix-Plouguer
Mûr-de-Bretagne
St.-Méen-le-Grand
Ploërmel
Locminé
Pte. St.-Mathieu
Pte. du Raz
Pte. de Penmarch
Côte de Cornouaille
Côte d'Amour
Côte de Jade
Côte d'Émeraude
Côte de Nacre
Côte des Landes
Côte d'Argent
Côte Basque
Baie de la Seine
G. de St.-Malo
C. de la Hague
Auderville
Pte. de Barfleur
Costa Montañesa
Costa Vasca
Santander
Santoña
C. de Ajo
Laredo
Castro Urdiales
Torrelavega
San Vicente de la Barquera
Llanes
Reinosa
Potes
Picos de Europa
Barakaldo
Bilbao
Getxo
Gernika-Lumo
Durango
Eibar
Amurrio
Orduña
Tolosa
Beasain
Alsasua
Donostia-San Sebastián
Irún
Rosslare
Santander
Bilbao
Cork
Gijón
Plymouth
Portsmouth
0 20 40 60 80 100 miles
0 40 80 120 160 km

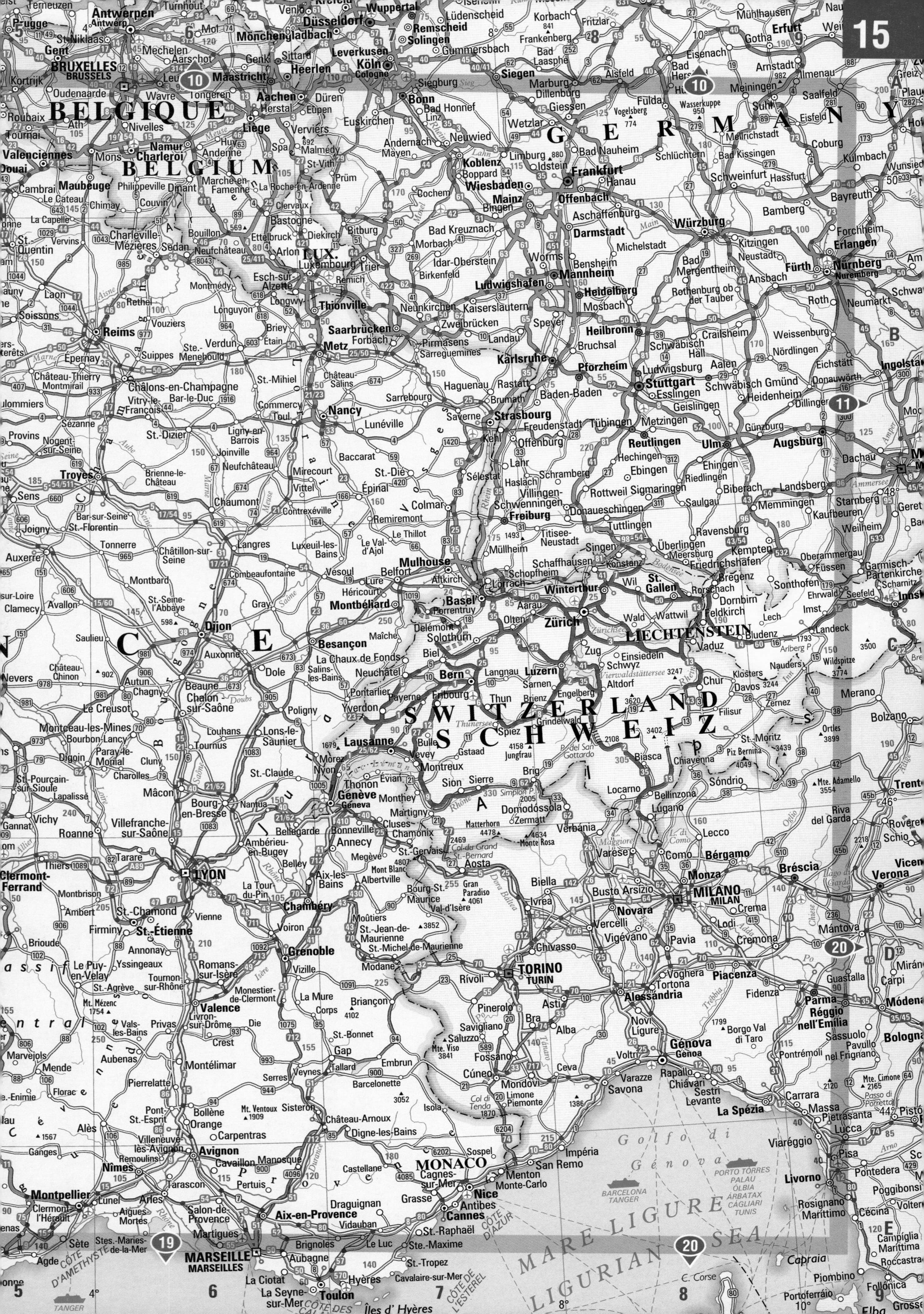
BELGIQUE
BELGIUM
GERMANY
SWITZERLAND
SCHWEIZ
LUX.
LIECHTENSTEIN
MONACO
MARE LIGURE
LIGURIAN SEA
Golfo di Génova
Antwerpen
Brugge
Gent
BRUXELLES
BRUSSELS
Mechelen
Kortrijk
Oudenaarde
Roubaix
Tournai
Valenciennes
Mons
Charleroi
Namur
Liège
Maastricht
Aachen
Heerlen
Sittard
Mönchengladbach
Düsseldorf
Wuppertal
Remscheid
Solingen
Leverkusen
Köln
Cologne
Gummersbach
Siegen
Siegburg
Bonn
Bad Honnef
Düren
Euskirchen
Verviers
Spa
Malmédy
St-Vith
Neuwied
Andernach
Mayen
Koblenz
Boppard
Wiesbaden
Mainz
Bingen
Frankfurt
Offenbach
Hanau
Limburg
Idstein
Bad Nauheim
Giessen
Wetzlar
Marburg
Dillenburg
Korbach
Frankenberg
Bad Laasphe
Alsfeld
Fulda
Bad Hersfeld
Eisenach
Gotha
Erfurt
Mühlhausen
Arnstadt
Ilmenau
Meiningen
Suhl
Saalfeld
Coburg
Kulmbach
Bayreuth
Bamberg
Schweinfurt
Hassfurt
Bad Kissingen
Schlüchtern
Aschaffenburg
Würzburg
Darmstadt
Michelstadt
Kitzingen
Neustadt
Erlangen
Forchheim
Fürth
Nürnberg
Nuremberg
Ansbach
Bad Mergentheim
Rothenburg ob der Tauber
Roth
Neumarkt
Weissenburg
Nördlingen
Eichstätt
Ingolstadt
Donauwörth
Dillingen
Augsburg
Ulm
Günzburg
Dachau
Landsberg
Memmingen
Kaufbeuren
Starnberg
Weilheim
Kempten
Füssen
Oberammergau
Garmisch-Partenkirchen
Sonthofen
Innsbruck
Bregenz
Dornbirn
Feldkirch
Bludenz
Vaduz
Landeck
Lech
Imst
Nauders
Davos
Klosters
Chur
St. Moritz
Merano
Bolzano
Trento
Worms
Mannheim
Ludwigshafen
Heidelberg
Mosbach
Bensheim
Speyer
Kaiserslautern
Neunkirchen
Zweibrücken
Landau
Pirmasens
Saarbrücken
Forbach
Sarreguemines
Karlsruhe
Bruchsal
Pforzheim
Heilbronn
Crailsheim
Schwäbisch Hall
Ludwigsburg
Stuttgart
Esslingen
Schwäbisch Gmünd
Aalen
Heidenheim
Geislingen
Baden-Baden
Rastatt
Freudenstadt
Tübingen
Reutlingen
Metzingen
Hechingen
Ebingen
Ehingen
Riedlingen
Biberach
Saulgau
Sigmaringen
Rottweil
Schramberg
Villingen-Schwenningen
Donaueschingen
Tuttlingen
Ravensburg
Friedrichshafen
Überlingen
Meersburg
Konstanz
Singen
Schaffhausen
Titisee-Neustadt
Freiburg
Müllheim
Lörrach
Offenburg
Lahr
Kehl
Strasbourg
Haguenau
Brumath
Saverne
Sélestat
Colmar
Mulhouse
Altkirch
Basel
Porrentruy
Delémont
Solothurn
Biel
Aarau
Olten
Winterthur
Zürich
St. Gallen
Wil
Rorschach
Zug
Einsiedeln
Schwyz
Altdorf
Luzern
Langnau
Sarnen
Bern
Fribourg
Thun
Interlaken
Brienz
Grindelwald
Spiez
Gstaad
Jungfrau
Neuchâtel
La Chaux-de-Fonds
Yverdon
Payerne
Lausanne
Vevey
Montreux
Morez
Nyon
Genève
Geneva
Thonon
Evian
Sion
Sierre
Brig
Martigny
Monthey
Zermatt
Matterhorn
Monte Rosa
Domodóssola
Biasca
Locarno
Bellinzona
Lugano
Chiavenna
Sóndrio
Verbánia
Varese
Como
Lecco
Bérgamo
Monza
MILANO
MILAN
Brescia
Verona
Mántova
Cremona
Lodi
Crema
Pavia
Vigévano
Novara
Busto Arsizio
Biella
Ivrea
Vercelli
Chivasso
Aosta
TORINO
TURIN
Rívoli
Pinerolo
Asti
Alba
Bra
Savigliano
Saluzzo
Fossano
Cúneo
Mondovì
Alessandria
Tortona
Voghera
Piacenza
Fidenza
Parma
Réggio nell'Emília
Módena
Sassuolo
Bologna
Guastalla
Carpi
Novi Lígure
Génova
Genoa
Savona
Varazze
Voltri
Rapallo
Chiávari
Sestri Levante
La Spézia
Carrara
Massa
Pietrasanta
Viaréggio
Lucca
Pisa
Livorno
Pontedera
Poggibonsi
Rosignano Maríttimo
Cécina
Volterra
Piombino
Follonica
Portoferráio
Elba
Capraia
Impéria
San Remo
Ventimiglia
Menton
Monte-Carlo
Nice
Antibes
Cannes
Cagnes-sur-Mer
Grasse
St.-Raphaël
Ste.-Maxime
St.-Tropez
Cavalaire-sur-Mer
Hyères
Toulon
La Seyne-sur-Mer
La Ciotat
Aubagne
MARSEILLE
MARSEILLES
Martigues
Aix-en-Provence
Salon-de-Provence
Arles
Nîmes
Montpellier
Sète
Agde
Lunel
Aigues-Mortes
Stes.-Maries-de-la-Mer
Tarascon
Avignon
Cavaillon
Carpentras
Orange
Bollène
Pont-St.-Esprit
Alès
Ganges
Villeneuve-lès-Avignon
Pertuis
Manosque
Digne-les-Bains
Sisteron
Château-Arnoux
Gap
Barcelonnette
Embrun
Briançon
Tallard
Veynes
Serres
Nyons
Montélimar
Pierrelatte
Aubenas
Privas
Crest
Die
Valence
Romans-sur-Isère
Tournon-sur-Rhône
Annonay
Vienne
St.-Chamond
St.-Étienne
Firminy
Le Puy-en-Velay
Yssingeaux
Brioude
Ambert
Montbrison
Thiers
Clermont-Ferrand
LYON
Villefranche-sur-Saône
Tarare
Roanne
Vichy
Gannat
Lapalisse
St.-Pourçain-sur-Sioule
Moulins
Digoin
Paray-le-Monial
Charolles
Cluny
Mâcon
Bourg-en-Bresse
Nantua
Bellegarde
Ambérieu-en-Bugey
Belley
La Tour-du-Pin
Chambéry
Aix-les-Bains
Annecy
Bonneville
Cluses
Chamonix
St.-Gervais
Megève
Albertville
Moûtiers
Bourg-St.-Maurice
Val-d'Isère
St.-Jean-de-Maurienne
St.-Michel-de-Maurienne
Modane
Grenoble
Voiron
Vizille
La Mure
Corps
Monestier-de-Clermont
Mont Blanc
Gran Paradiso
Mte. Viso
Mt. Ventoux
Mt. Mézenc
Montceau-les-Mines
Le Creusot
Bourbon-Lancy
Autun
Chagny
Beaune
Chalon-sur-Saône
Louhans
Tournus
Lons-le-Saunier
St.-Claude
Poligny
Pontarlier
Salins-les-Bains
Dole
Auxonne
Dijon
Besançon
Maîche
Montbéliard
Belfort
Héricourt
Lure
Vesoul
Gray
Luxeuil-les-Bains
Remiremont
Épinal
Vittel
Mirecourt
Contrexéville
Langres
Châtillon-sur-Seine
Chaumont
Neufchâteau
Joinville
St.-Dizier
Bar-le-Duc
Commercy
Toul
Nancy
Lunéville
Baccarat
St.-Dié
Sarrebourg
Château-Salins
Metz
Thionville
Longwy
Esch-sur-Alzette
Luxembourg
Arlon
Bastogne
Clervaux
Diekirch
Ettelbruck
Trier
Bitburg
Prüm
Cochem
Bad Kreuznach
Idar-Oberstein
Birkenfeld
Verdun
Étain
Briey
Longuyon
Montmédy
Sedan
Charleville-Mézières
Bouillon
Neufchâteau
Rethel
Reims
Laon
Soissons
St.-Quentin
Cambrai
Maubeuge
Le Cateau
La Capelle
Chimay
Couvin
Philippeville
Dinant
Marche-en-Famenne
La Roche-en-Ardenne
Vervins
Épernay
Château-Thierry
Châlons-en-Champagne
Vitry-le-François
Ste.-Menehould
St.-Mihiel
Sézanne
Provins
Nogent-sur-Seine
Troyes
Brienne-le-Château
Bar-sur-Seine
Sens
Joigny
St.-Florentin
Tonnerre
Auxerre
Montbard
Avallon
Clamecy
Saulieu
Château-Chinon
Nevers
Lake Geneva
Lac Léman
Bodensee
Zürichsee
Vierwaldstättersee
Thunersee
L. di Como
L. Maggiore
Côte d'Azur
Côte de l'Estérel
Côte d'Amethyste
Îles d'Hyères
Corse
BARCELONA TANGER
PORTO TORRES PALAU OLBIA ARBATAX CAGLIARI TUNIS
TANGER
Rhein
Rhône
Saône
Doubs
Loire
Allier
Isère
Durance
Po
Ticino
Adda
Oglio
Tanaro
Trebbia
Arno
Mosel
Main
Lahn
Sieg
Maas
Meuse
Marne
Aisne
Seine
Aube
Moselle
Inn
Lech
Iller
Donau
Eder
Werra
10
11
19
20
5
6
7
8
9
A
B
C
D
E

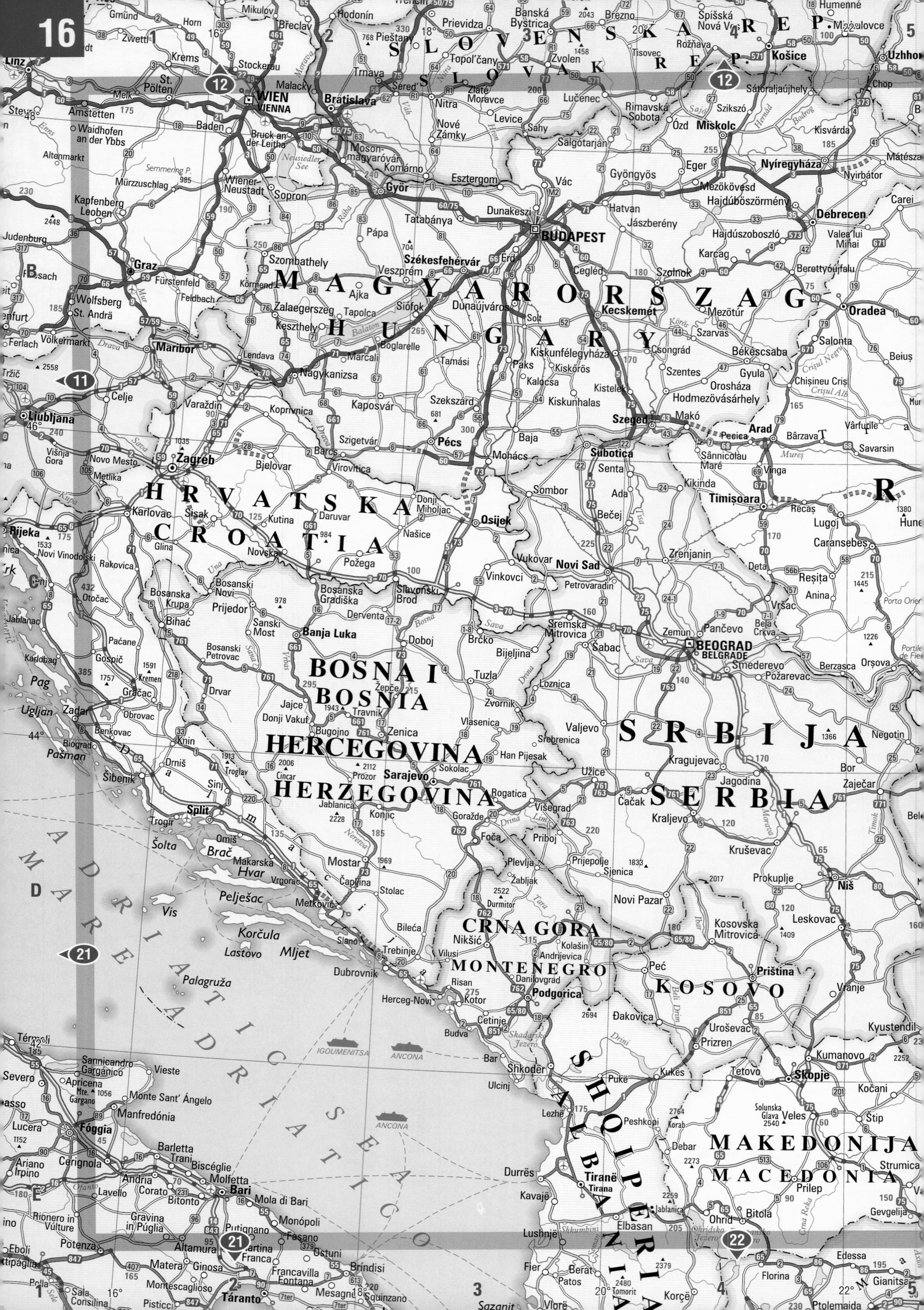
SLOVENSKÁ REP.
SLOVAK REP.
MAGYARORSZÁG
HUNGARY
HRVATSKA
CROATIA
BOSNA I HERCEGOVINA
BOSNIA HERZEGOVINA
SRBIJA
SERBIA
CRNA GORA
MONTENEGRO
KOSOVO
SHQIPERIA
ALBANIA
MAKEDONIJA
MACEDONIA
MARE ADRIATICO
ADRIATIC SEA
Linz
Gmünd
Horn
Zwettl
Krems
Stockerau
St. Pölten
Melk
Amstetten
Steyr
Waidhofen an der Ybbs
WIEN
VIENNA
Baden
Bruck an der Leitha
Mikulov
Břeclav
Hodonín
Malacky
Bratislava
Piešťany
Trnava
Sereď
Prievidza
Topoľčany
Nitra
Zlaté Moravce
Nové Zámky
Levice
Banská Bystrica
Zvolen
Brezno
Lučenec
Rimavská Sobota
Tisovec
Rožňava
Spišská Nová Ves
Košice
Michalovce
Uzhhorod
Sátoraljaújhely
Šahy
Salgótarján
Ózd
Miskolc
Szikszó
Kisvárda
Mátészalka
Nyíregyháza
Nyírbátor
Eger
Gyöngyös
Mezőkövesd
Hajdúböszörmény
Debrecen
Carei
Hatvan
Jászberény
Hajdúszoboszló
Valea lui Mihai
Karcag
Berettyóújfalu
Szolnok
Cegléd
Oradea
Mezőtúr
Szarvas
Salonta
Békéscsaba
Beiuș
Gyula
Chișineu Criș
Orosháza
Szentes
Csongrád
Kecskemét
Kiskunfélegyháza
Kiskőrös
Kalocsa
Kistelek
Kiskunhalas
Hodmezővásárhely
Makó
Szeged
Pecica
Arad
Bârzava
Vârfurile
Savarsin
Subotica
Senta
Sânnicolau Mare
Vinga
Kikinda
Timișoara
Recaș
Lugoj
Caransebeș
Reșița
Anina
Vršac
Bela Crkva
Pančevo
Zemun
BEOGRAD
BELGRADE
Smederevo
Požarevac
Berzasca
Orșova
Negotin
Bor
Zaječar
Semmering P.
Mürzzuschlag
Kapfenberg
Leoben
Judenburg
Graz
Fürstenfeld
Feldbach
Wolfsberg
St. Andrä
Völkermarkt
Ferlach
Tržič
Wiener-Neustadt
Sopron
Neusiedler See
Moson-magyaróvár
Komárno
Győr
Esztergom
Vác
Dunakeszi
BUDAPEST
Tatabánya
Pápa
Székesfehérvár
Érd
Szombathely
Körmend
Veszprém
Ajka
Siófok
Dunaújváros
Solt
Zalaegerszeg
Tapolca
Keszthely
Balaton
Boglarelle
Marcali
Tamási
Paks
Nagykanizsa
Kaposvár
Szekszárd
Lendava
Maribor
Celje
Ljubljana
Varaždin
Koprivnica
Szigetvár
Pécs
Mohács
Baja
Barcs
Virovitica
Bjelovar
Zagreb
Novo Mesto
Metlika
Karlovac
Sisak
Kutina
Daruvar
Donji Miholjac
Osijek
Našice
Požega
Novska
Rijeka
Novi Vinodolski
Rakovica
Otočac
Jablanac
Senj
Glina
Bosanski Novi
Bosanska Krupa
Prijedor
Bihać
Bosanska Gradiška
Slavonski Brod
Derventa
Sanski Most
Banja Luka
Doboj
Brčko
Bijeljina
Vinkovci
Vukovar
Novi Sad
Petrovaradin
Sombor
Bečej
Zrenjanin
Sremska Mitrovica
Šabac
Loznica
Tuzla
Zvornik
Vlasenica
Srebrenica
Valjevo
Han Pijesak
Kragujevac
Jagodina
Užice
Čačak
Kraljevo
Kruševac
Prokuplje
Niš
Leskovac
Vranje
Novi Pazar
Kosovska Mitrovica
Priština
Peć
Đakovica
Uroševac
Prizren
Kumanovo
Skopje
Tetovo
Kočani
Štip
Veles
Strumica
Prilep
Bitola
Gevgelija
Ohrid
Florina
Edessa
Gianitsa
Lipik
Gospić
Bosanski Petrovac
Kremen
Gračac
Drvar
Jajce
Donji Vakuf
Travnik
Žepče
Zenica
Bugojno
Sarajevo
Sokolac
Rogatica
Višegrad
Goražde
Foča
Priboj
Prijepolje
Pljevlja
Sjenica
Žabljak
Durmitor
Nikšić
Kolašin
Andrijevica
Danilovgrad
Podgorica
Cetinje
Budva
Bar
Ulcinj
Shkodër
Lezhë
Kukes
Pukë
Peshkopi
Debar
Tiranë
Tirana
Durrës
Kavajë
Elbasan
Lushnje
Fier
Patos
Berat
Tomorit
Korçë
Vlorë
Jablanica
Konjic
Prozor
Cincar
Mostar
Čapljina
Stolac
Bileća
Trebinje
Dubrovnik
Herceg-Novi
Risan
Kotor
Slano
Metković
Vrgorac
Makarska
Omiš
Split
Trogir
Sinj
Šibenik
Drniš
Knin
Obrovac
Benkovac
Biograd
Zadar
Pag
Ugljan
Pašman
Karlobag
Šolta
Brač
Hvar
Vis
Pelješac
Korčula
Lastovo
Mljet
Palagruža
IGOUMENITSA
ANCONA
Térmoli
Sannicandro Gargánico
Vieste
Apricena
Monte Sant' Ángelo
Manfredónia
Fóggia
Lucera
Barletta
Trani
Bisceglie
Molfetta
Cerignola
Andria
Corato
Bitonto
Bari
Mola di Bari
Monópoli
Gravina in Púglia
Altamura
Putignano
Fasano
Ostuni
Martina Franca
Matera
Ginosa
Francavilla Fontana
Bríndisi
Mesagne
Táranto
Squinzano
Montescaglioso
Potenza
Eboli
Rionero in Vúlture
Lavello
Sala Consilina
Pisticci

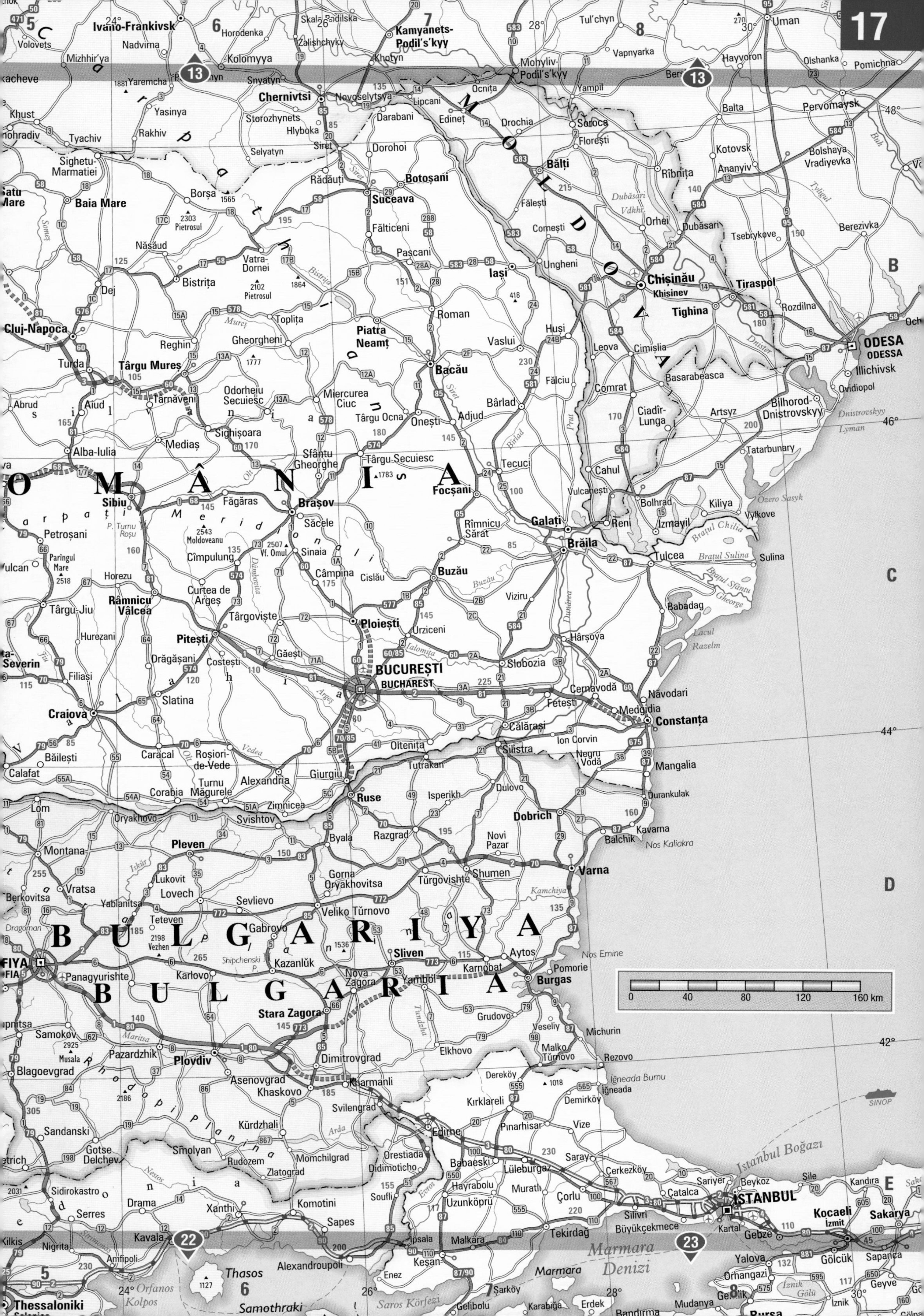

Ivano-Frankivsk
Nadvirna
Horodenka
Kolomyya
Kamyanets-Podil's'kyy
Khotyn
Tul'chyn
Vapnyarka
Mohyliv-Podil's'kyy
Uman
Hayvoron
Olshanka
Pomichna
Yampil
Snyatyn
Chernivtsi
Novoselytsya
Lipcani
Ocnița
Edineț
Drochia
Soroca
Florești
Balta
Pervomaysk
Khust
Yasinya
Storozhynets
Hlyboka
Darabani
Rakhiv
Tyachiv
Selyatyn
Siret
Dorohoi
Sighetu-Marmatiei
Satu Mare
Baia Mare
Borșa
Rădăuți
Botoșani
Suceava
Bălți
Kotovsk
Ananyiv
Bolshaya Vradiyevka
Ribnița
Fălești
Dubăsari
Orhei
Tsebrykove
Berezivka
Pietrosul
Năsăud
Fălticeni
Pașcani
Cornești
Ungheni
Vatra-Dornei
Bistrița
Dej
Iași
Chișinău
Khisinev
Tiraspol
Tighina
Rozdilna
Cluj-Napoca
Toplița
Roman
Piatra Neamț
Vaslui
Huși
Leova
Cimișlia
ODESA
Illichivsk
Ovidiopol
Turda
Reghin
Gheorgheni
Târgu Mureș
Bacău
Fălciu
Comrat
Basarabeasca
Bilhorod-Dnistrovskyy
Dnistrovskyy Lyman
Artsyz
Ciadîr-Lunga
Abrud
Aiud
Târnăveni
Odorheiu Secuiesc
Miercurea Ciuc
Târgu Ocna
Onești
Adjud
Bârlad
Sighișoara
Mediaș
Alba-Iulia
Sfântu Gheorghe
Târgu Secuiesc
Tecuci
Tatarbunary
Cahul
ROMÂNIA
Sibiu
Făgăras
Brașov
Focșani
Vulcanești
Bolhrad
Kiliya
Vylkove
Ozero Sasyk
Reni
Izmayil
Galați
Brăila
Petroșani
Săcele
Rîmnicu Sărat
Moldoveanu
Vf. Omul
Sinaia
Cîmpulung
Câmpina
Cislău
Buzău
Tulcea
Sulina
Brațul Chilia
Brațul Sulina
Brațul Sfântu Gheorghe
Horezu
Curtea de Argeș
Viziru
Babadag
Târgu-Jiu
Râmnicu Vâlcea
Târgoviște
Ploiești
Urziceni
Hârșova
Lacul Razelm
Hurezani
Pitești
Găești
Drăgășani
Costești
BUCUREȘTI
BUCHAREST
Slobozia
Severin
Filiași
Slatina
Cernavodă
Fetești
Năvodari
Medgidia
Constanța
Craiova
Călărași
Ion Corvin
Oltenița
Silistra
Negru Vodă
Mangalia
Băilești
Caracal
Roșiori-de-Vede
Tutrakan
Calafat
Giurgiu
Alexandria
Turnu Măgurele
Corabia
Zimnicea
Ruse
Isperikh
Dulovo
Durankulak
Dobrich
Lom
Oryakhovo
Svishtov
Byala
Razgrad
Novi Pazar
Kavarna
Balchik
Nos Kaliakra
Montana
Pleven
Lukovit
Lovech
Gorna Oryakhovitsa
Tŭrgovishte
Shumen
Varna
Berkovitsa
Vratsa
Yablanitsa
Sevlievo
Veliko Tŭrnovo
Teteven
Gabrovo
BULGARIYA
BULGARIA
Vezhen
Shipchenski P.
Kazanlŭk
Sliven
Aytos
Nos Emine
Pomorie
Karnobat
Burgas
SOFIYA
Panagyurishte
Karlovo
Nova Zagora
Yambol
Stara Zagora
Grudovo
Samokov
Musala
Pazardzhik
Plovdiv
Dimitrovgrad
Elkhovo
Malko Tŭrnovo
Michurin
Rezovo
Blagoevgrad
Asenovgrad
Khaskovo
Kharmanli
Dereköy
İğneada Burnu
İğneada
Kırklareli
Demirköy
Svilengrad
Kŭrdzhali
Sandanski
Edirne
Pınarhisar
Vize
Gotse Delchev
Smolyan
Rudozem
Momchilgrad
Zlatograd
Orestiada
Didimoticho
Babaeski
Lüleburgaz
Saray
Çerkezköy
İstanbul Boğazı
Sidirokastro
Drama
Xanthi
Komotini
Soufli
Hayrabolu
Uzunköprü
Muratlı
Çorlu
Çatalca
Sarıyer
Beykoz
Şile
Kandıra
İSTANBUL
Kocaeli
İzmit
Sakarya
Serres
Sapes
Silivri
Büyükçekmece
Kartal
Gebze
Kilkis
Nigrita
Kavala
Ipsala
Malkara
Tekirdağ
Marmara Denizi
Yalova
Gölcük
Sapanca
Amfipoli
Alexandroupoli
Thasos
Keşan
Enez
Marmara
Orhangazi
İznik Gölü
İznik
Geyve
Thessaloniki
Orfanos Kolpos
Samothraki
Saros Körfezi
Şarköy
Gelibolu
Karabiga
Erdek
Mudanya
Gemlik
Bursa
SINOP
0
40
80
120
160 km

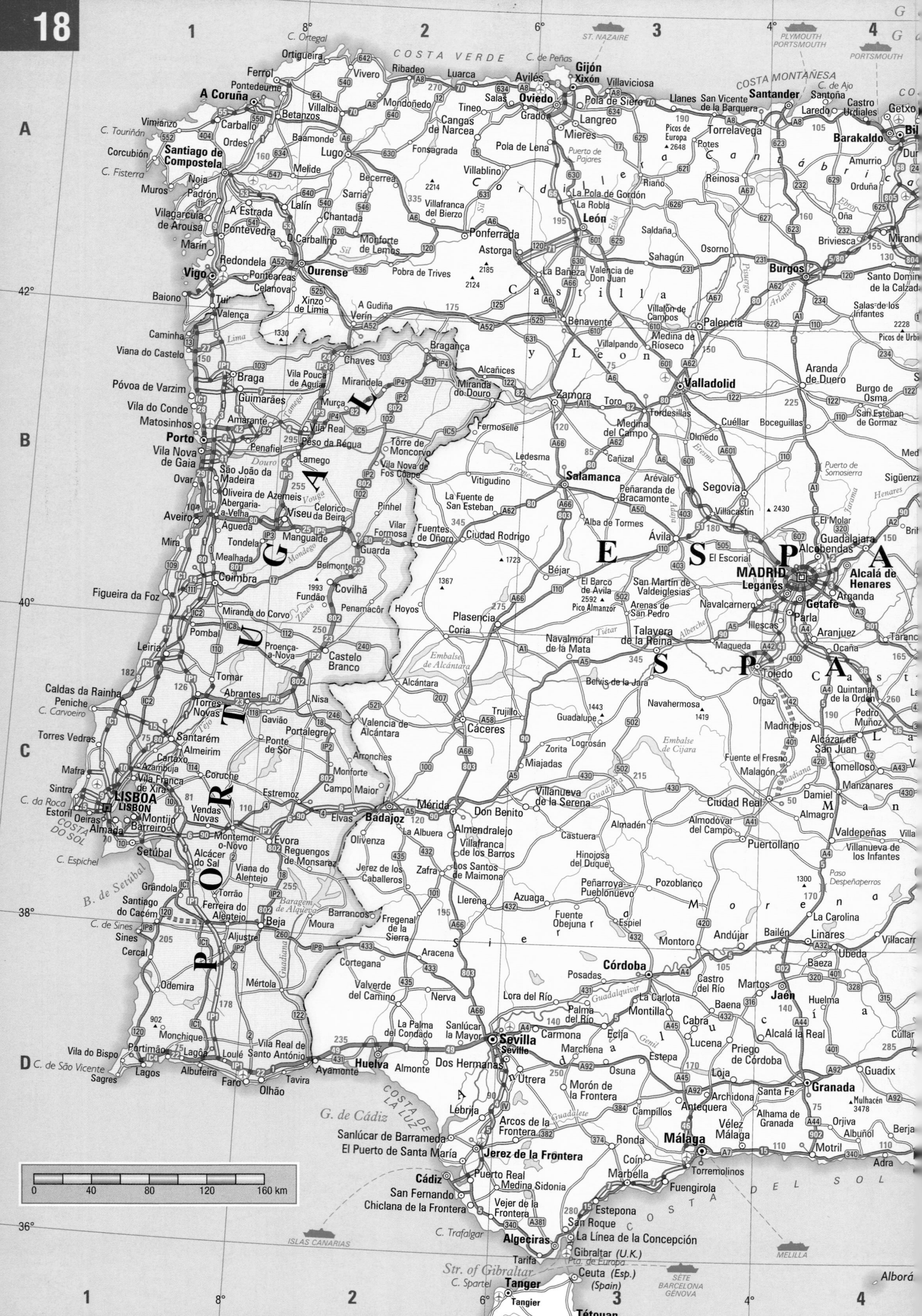
1
2
3
4
A
B
C
D
8°
6°
4°
42°
40°
38°
36°
COSTA VERDE
C. Ortegal
C. de Peñas
ST. NAZAIRE
PLYMOUTH
PORTSMOUTH
COSTA MONTAÑESA
C. de Ajo
Ortigueira
Ferrol
Vivero
Ribadeo
Luarca
Avilés
Gijón
Xixón
Villaviciosa
Pontedeume
A Coruña
Villalba
Mondoñedo
Tineo
Salas
Oviedo
Pola de Siero
Llanes
San Vicente de la Barquera
Santander
Santoña
Laredo
Castro Urdiales
Getxo
Betanzos
Grado
Langreo
Cangas de Narcea
Mieres
Picos de Europa
Torrelavega
Barakaldo
Vimianzo
C. Touriñán
Carballo
Ordes
Baamonde
Lugo
Fonsagrada
Pola de Lena
Puerto de Pajares
Potes
Corcubión
Santiago de Compostela
C. Fisterra
Melide
Villablino
Reinosa
Amurrio
Muros
Noia
Becerrea
Cordillera Cantábrica
Padrón
Sarriá
La Pola de Gordón
Riaño
Orduña
Vilagarcía de Arousa
A Estrada
Lalín
Chantada
Villafranca del Bierzo
La Robla
Oña
Pontevedra
León
Saldaña
Briviesca
Marín
O Carballino
Monforte de Lemos
Ponferrada
Astorga
Osorno
Miranda
Redondela
Ourense
Pobra de Trives
La Bañeza
Sahagún
Burgos
Vigo
Ponteareas
Celanova
Valencia de Don Juan
Santo Domingo de la Calzada
Baiona
Tui
Xinzo de Limia
Castilla y León
Valença
A Gudiña
Verín
Villalón de Campos
Salas de los Infantes
Caminha
Benavente
Palencia
Viana do Castelo
Bragança
Chaves
Villalpando
Medina de Rioseco
Picos de Urbión
Póvoa de Varzim
Braga
Vila Pouca de Aguiar
Mirandela
Alcañices
Miranda do Douro
Aranda de Duero
Valladolid
Guimarães
Zamora
Toro
Burgo de Osma
Vila do Conde
Murça
Tordesillas
Matosinhos
Amarante
Vila Real
Fermoselle
Medina del Campo
Cuéllar
Boceguillas
San Esteban de Gormaz
Porto
Penafiel
Peso da Régua
Torre de Moncorvo
Olmedo
Vila Nova de Gaia
Lamego
Ledesma
Cañizal
Ovar
São João da Madeira
Vila Nova de Fos Côa
Vitigudino
Salamanca
Arévalo
Puerto de Somosierra
Sigüenza
Oliveira de Azeméis
Peñaranda de Bracamonte
Segovia
Aveiro
Abergaria-a-Velha
Celorico da Beira
Pinhel
La Fuente de San Esteban
Viseu
Villacastín
Águeda
Mangualde
Vilar Formosa
Fuentes de Oñoro
Ciudad Rodrigo
Alba de Tormes
El Molar
Mira
Tondela
Guarda
Ávila
Guadalajara
Alcobendas
Mealhada
Belmonte
El Escorial
Coimbra
Béjar
MADRID
Leganés
Alcalá de Henares
Figueira da Foz
Fundão
Covilhã
El Barco de Ávila
San Martín de Valdeiglesias
Arganda
Penamacor
Hoyos
Pico Almanzor
Arenas de San Pedro
Navalcarnero
Getafe
Miranda do Corvo
Plasencia
Parla
Pombal
Coria
Talavera de la Reina
Illescas
Aranjuez
Tarancón
Leiria
Proença-a-Nova
Navalmoral de la Mata
Maqueda
Ocaña
Castelo Branco
Embalse de Alcántara
Toledo
Tomar
Alcántara
Belvís de la Jara
Quintanar de la Orden
Caldas da Rainha
Peniche
Abrantes
Nisa
Navahermosa
Orgaz
C. Carvoeiro
Torres Novas
Trujillo
Pedro Muñoz
Gavião
Valencia de Alcántara
Guadalupe
Madridejos
Torres Vedras
Santarém
Portalegre
Cáceres
Alcázar de San Juan
Almeirim
Ponte de Sor
Zorita
Logrosán
Embalse de Cijara
Cartaxo
Arronches
Fuente el Fresno
Tomelloso
Mafra
Azambuja
Coruche
Monforte
Miajadas
Malagón
Sintra
Vila Franca de Xira
Villanueva de la Serena
Manzanares
C. da Roca
LISBOA
LISBON
Estremoz
Campo Maior
Ciudad Real
Daimiel
Estoril
Oeiras
Vendas Novas
Elvas
Mérida
Don Benito
Almagro
Almada
Montijo
Badajoz
La Albuera
Almadén
Almodóvar del Campo
COSTA DO SOL
Barreiro
Montemor-o-Novo
Évora
Almendralejo
Castuera
Valdepeñas
Setúbal
Olivenza
Villafranca de los Barros
Puertollano
Villanueva de los Infantes
C. Espichel
Alcácer do Sal
Reguengos de Monsaraz
Jerez de los Caballeros
Zafra
Los Santos de Maimona
Hinojosa del Duque
Viana do Alentejo
Peñarroya-Pueblonuevo
Pozoblanco
Paso Despeñaperros
B. de Setúbal
Grândola
Torrão
Llerena
Azuaga
Sierra Morena
Santiago do Cacém
Ferreira do Alentejo
Barragem de Alqueva
Barrancos
Fregenal de la Sierra
Fuente Obejuna
Espiel
La Carolina
C. de Sines
Beja
Moura
Sines
Aljustrel
Linares
Villacarrillo
Cercal
Andújar
Bailén
Montoro
Úbeda
Aracena
Cortegana
Córdoba
Baeza
Posadas
Odemira
Mértola
Valverde del Camino
Castro del Río
Martos
Nerva
Lora del Río
La Carlota
Jaén
Palma del Río
Montilla
Huelma
Baena
Monchique
La Palma del Condado
Sanlúcar la Mayor
Carmona
Cabra
Alcalá la Real
Vila do Bispo
Portimão
Lagoa
Loulé
Vila Real de Santo António
Sevilla
Seville
Écija
Lucena
Cúllar
C. de São Vicente
Lagos
Albufeira
Faro
Olhão
Tavira
Ayamonte
Huelva
Almonte
Dos Hermanas
Marchena
Estepa
Priego de Córdoba
Sagres
Utrera
Osuna
Loja
Guadix
Morón de la Frontera
Archidona
Santa Fe
Granada
COSTA DE LA LUZ
G. de Cádiz
Lebrija
Antequera
Alhama de Granada
Mulhacén
Arcos de la Frontera
Campillos
Vélez Málaga
Orjiva
Sanlúcar de Barrameda
Ronda
Málaga
Albuñol
Berja
El Puerto de Santa María
Jerez de la Frontera
Coín
Motril
Adra
Cádiz
Puerto Real
Marbella
Torremolinos
San Fernando
Medina Sidonia
Fuengirola
COSTA DEL SOL
Chiclana de la Frontera
Vejer de la Frontera
Estepona
San Roque
La Línea de la Concepción
C. Trafalgar
Algeciras
Gibraltar (U.K.)
ISLAS CANARIAS
MELILLA
Tarifa
Pta. de Europa
Str. of Gibraltar
Ceuta (Esp.)
(Spain)
C. Spartel
Tanger
Tangier
SÈTE
BARCELONA
GÉNOVA
Tétouan
Alborán
PORTUGAL
ESPAÑA
ESPAÑA
Castilla - La Mancha
Andalucía
0
40
80
120
160 km

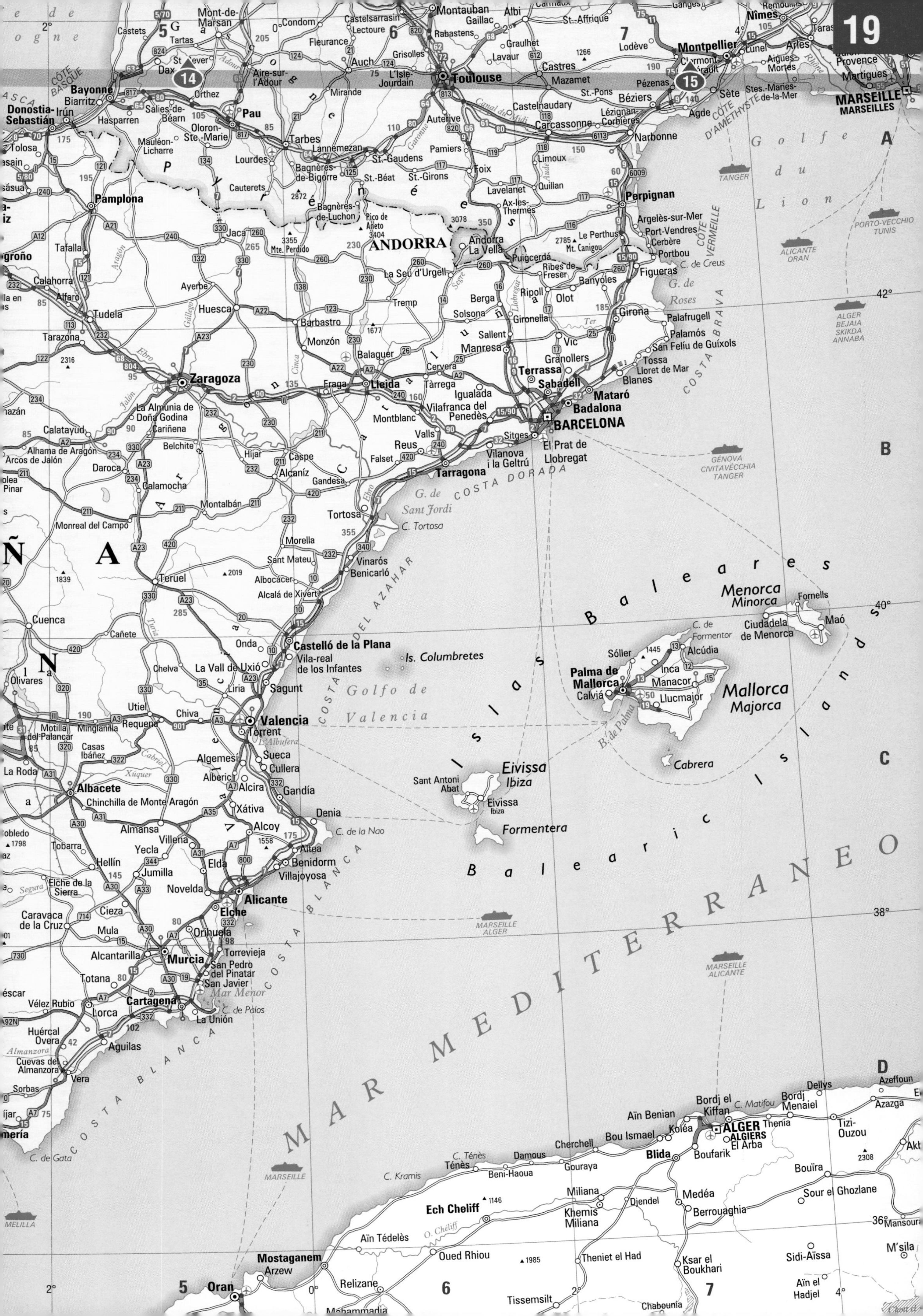

Mont-de-Marsan
Condom
Castelsarrasin
Montauban
Albi
Nîmes
Montpellier
Arles
Castets
Tartas
Lectoure
Fleurance
Rabastens
Gaillac
Graulhet
St.-Affrique
Lodève
Lunel
Aigues-Mortes
Martigues
Dax
Aire-sur-l'Adour
Auch
Grisolles
L'Isle-Jourdain
Toulouse
Lavaur
Castres
Mazamet
Pézenas
Clermont-l'Hérault
Sète
Stes.-Maries-de-la-Mer
MARSEILLE
MARSEILLES
Bayonne
Biarritz
Orthez
Mirande
Donostia-Sebastián
Irún
Hasparren
Salies-de-Béarn
Pau
Oloron-Ste.-Marie
Mauléon-Licharre
Tarbes
Lannemezan
St.-Gaudens
Lourdes
Bagnères-de-Bigorre
St.-Béat
St.-Girons
Pamiers
Foix
Autervie
Castelnaudary
Carcassonne
St.-Pons
Béziers
Lézignan-Corbières
Agde
Narbonne
Limoux
Quillan
Lavelanet
Ax-les-Thermes
Perpignan
Argelès-sur-Mer
Port-Vendres
Cerbère
Portbou
Le Perthus
Mt. Canigou
CÔTE BASQUE
CÔTE D'AMETHYSTE
CÔTE VERMEILLE
Golfe du Lion
TANGER
PORTO-VECCHIO
TUNIS
ALICANTE
ORAN
Tolosa
Pamplona
Cauterets
Bagnères-de-Luchon
Pico de Aneto
Jaca
Mte. Perdido
ANDORRA
Andorra La Vella
Puigcerdà
Ribes de Freser
Figueras
C. de Creus
G. de Roses
Tafalla
Logroño
Calahorra
Alfaro
Tudela
Tarazona
Ayerbe
Huesca
La Seu d'Urgell
Tremp
Berga
Ripoll
Olot
Banyoles
Girona
Palafrugell
Palamós
San Felíu de Guíxols
Tossa
Lloret de Mar
Blanes
COSTA BRAVA
ALGER
BEJAIA
SKIKDA
ANNABA
Barbastro
Monzón
Balaguer
Solsona
Sallent
Manresa
Vic
Granollers
Terrassa
Sabadell
Mataró
Badalona
BARCELONA
El Prat de Llobregat
Zaragoza
La Almunia de Doña Godina
Cariñena
Fraga
Lleida
Cervera
Tàrrega
Igualada
Vilafranca del Penedès
Montblanc
Valls
Reus
Falset
Tarragona
Sitges
Vilanova i la Geltrú
GÉNOVA
CIVITAVECCHIA
TANGER
Calatayud
Alhama de Aragón
Arcos de Jalón
Daroca
Belchite
Híjar
Caspe
Alcañiz
Gandesa
Calamocha
Montalbán
Tortosa
G. de Sant Jordi
C. Tortosa
COSTA DORADA
Monreal del Campo
Morella
Sant Mateu
Vinaròs
Benicarló
Teruel
Albocàcer
Alcalá de Xivert
COSTA DEL AZAHAR
Cuenca
Cañete
Onda
Castelló de la Plana
Vila-real de los Infantes
Is. Columbretes
Chelva
La Vall de Uxió
Liria
Sagunt
Golfo de Valencia
Utiel
Chiva
Requena
Valencia
Torrent
Minglanilla
Motilla del Palancar
Casas Ibáñez
Algemesí
Alberic
Alcira
Sueca
Cullera
Gandía
La Roda
Albacete
Chinchilla de Monte Aragón
Xàtiva
Almansa
Alcoy
Denia
C. de la Nao
Villena
Yecla
Elda
Altea
Benidorm
Villajoyosa
Tobarra
Hellín
Jumilla
Novelda
Alicante
Elche
Elche de la Sierra
Caravaca de la Cruz
Cieza
Mula
Orihuela
Torrevieja
Alcantarilla
Murcia
San Pedro del Pinatar
San Javier
Mar Menor
Totana
Cartagena
C. de Palos
La Unión
Vélez Rubio
Lorca
Huércal Overa
Aguilas
Cuevas del Almanzora
Vera
Sorbas
C. de Gata
COSTA BLANCA
MARSEILLE
ALGER
MARSEILLE
ALICANTE
MARSEILLE
MELILLA
Menorca
Minorca
Fornells
Ciudadela de Menorca
Maó
C. de Formentor
Sóller
Alcúdia
Palma de Mallorca
Inca
Manacor
Calviá
Llucmajor
Mallorca
Majorca
B. de Palma
Cabrera
Eivissa
Ibiza
Sant Antoni Abat
Formentera
Islas Baleares
Balearic Islands
MAR MEDITERRANEO
Dellys
Azeffoun
Bordj el Kiffan
Bordj Menaiel
C. Matifou
Azazga
Aïn Benian
ALGER
ALGIERS
Thenia
Tizi-Ouzou
Cherchell
Bou Ismael
Koléa
El Arba
Blida
Boufarik
C. Ténès
Ténès
Damous
Gouraya
Beni-Haoua
C. Kramis
Bouïra
Miliana
Djendel
Medéa
Sour el Ghozlane
Ech Cheliff
Khemis Miliana
Berrouaghia
Aïn Tédelès
O. Chéliff
Mansoura
M'sila
Mostaganem
Arzew
Oued Rhiou
Theniet el Had
Ksar el Boukhari
Sidi-Aïssa
Oran
Relizane
Tissemsilt
Chabounia
Aïn el Hadjel
Mohammadia

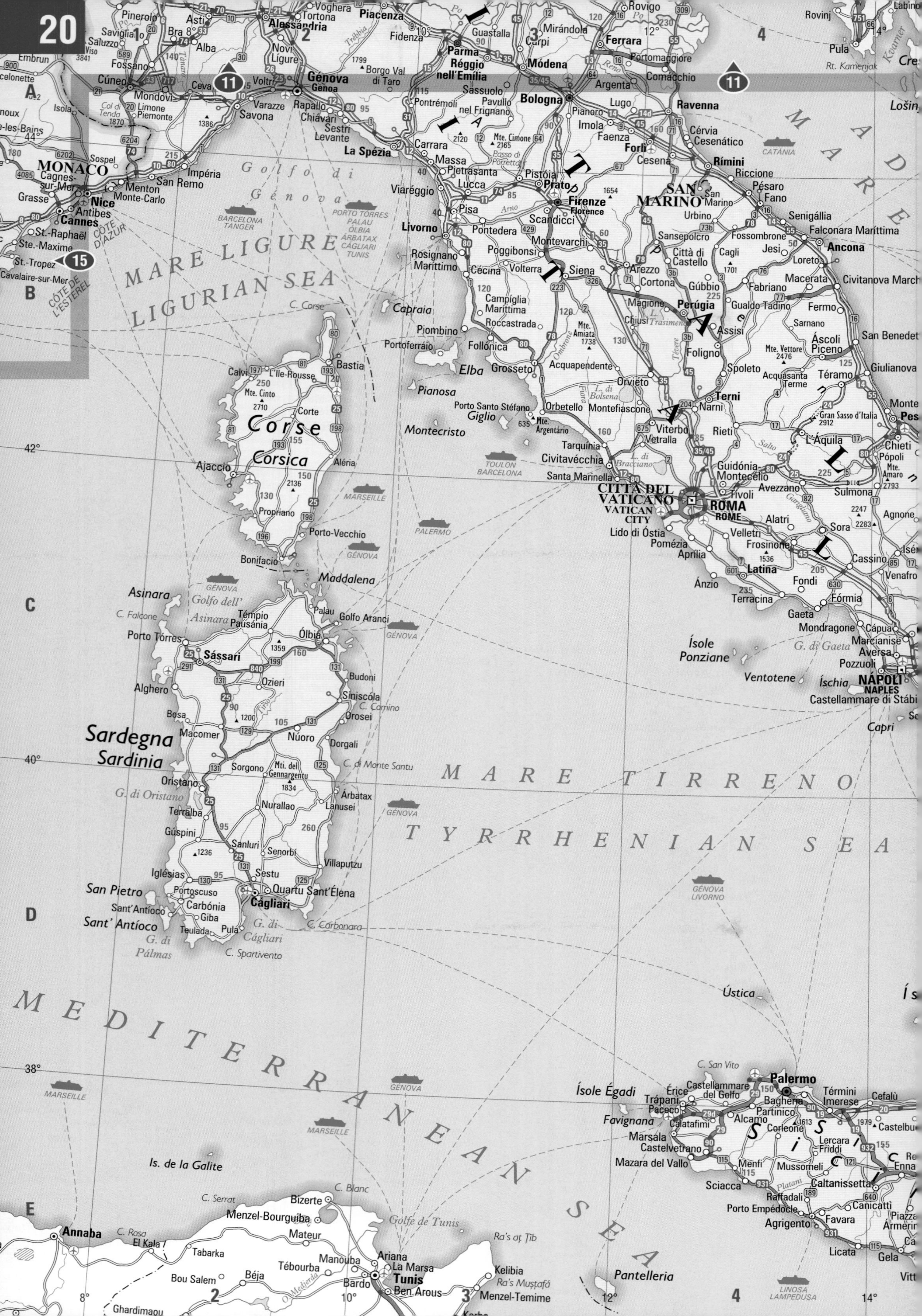
ITALIA
ITALY
MONACO
SAN MARINO
CITTÀ DEL VATICANO
VATICAN CITY
Corse
Corsica
Sardegna
Sardinia
MARE LIGURE
LIGURIAN SEA
Golfo di Génova
MARE TIRRENO
TYRRHENIAN SEA
MEDITERRANEAN SEA
MARE ADRIATICO
Pinerolo
Saviglia
Saluzzo
Asti
Bra
Alba
Alessándria
Novi Lígure
Voghera
Tortona
Piacenza
Fidenza
Fossano
Cúneo
Mondovì
Ceva
Limone Piemonte
Col di Tenda
Isola
Embrun
Barcelonnette
Sospel
Menton
Monte-Carlo
Nice
Antibes
Cannes
Grasse
Cagnes-sur-Mer
St.-Raphaël
Ste.-Maxime
St.-Tropez
Cavalaire-sur-Mer
Côte d'Azur
Côte de l'Esterel
Impéria
San Remo
Savona
Varazze
Voltri
Génova
Genoa
Rapallo
Chiávari
Sestri Levante
La Spézia
Carrara
Massa
Pietrasanta
Viaréggio
Lucca
Pisa
Livorno
Rosignano Maríttimo
Cécina
Pontedera
Poggibonsi
Volterra
Siena
Montevarchi
Scandicci
Firenze
Florence
Prato
Pistóia
Parma
Réggio nell'Emília
Módena
Sassuolo
Pavullo nel Frignano
Bologna
Guastalla
Mirándola
Carpi
Ferrara
Rovigo
Portomaggiore
Comácchio
Argenta
Lugo
Ravenna
Imola
Faenza
Forlì
Cervia
Cesenático
Cesena
Rímini
Riccione
Pésaro
Fano
Urbino
Sansepolcro
Città di Castello
Arezzo
Cortona
Gúbbio
Fossombrone
Senigállia
Falconara Maríttima
Ancona
Jesi
Loreto
Macerata
Civitanova Marche
Fabriano
Gualdo Tadino
Fermo
Sarnano
Áscoli Piceno
San Benedetto
Giulianova
Téramo
Perúgia
Magione
Chiusi
L. Trasimeno
Assisi
Foligno
Spoleto
Terni
Narni
Rieti
Orvieto
Montefiascone
L. di Bolsena
Viterbo
Vetralla
Tarquínia
Civitavécchia
Santa Marinella
L. di Bracciano
Guidónia-Montecélio
Tívoli
Avezzano
Sulmona
L'Áquila
Chieti
Pópoli
Pescara
Gran Sasso d'Italia
ROMA
ROME
Lido di Óstia
Pomézia
Aprília
Velletri
Frosinone
Alatri
Sora
Latina
Ánzio
Terracina
Fondi
Cassino
Venafro
Gaeta
Fórmia
Mondragone
Cápua
Marcianise
Aversa
Pozzuoli
NÁPOLI
NAPLES
Castellammare di Stábia
Capri
Íschia
Ventotene
Ísole Ponziane
G. di Gaeta
Campíglia Maríttima
Roccastrada
Piombino
Follónica
Grosseto
Acquapendente
Orbetello
Porto Santo Stéfano
Mte. Argentário
Capraia
Portoferráio
Elba
Pianosa
Giglio
Montecristo
Mte. Amiata
Mte. Cimone
Mte. Vettore
Passo di Porretta
Pontrémoli
Borgo Val di Taro
Bastia
Calvi
L'Île-Rousse
Mte. Cinto
Corte
Ajaccio
Aléria
Propriano
Porto-Vecchio
Bonifacio
C. Corse
Maddalena
Asinara
Golfo dell' Asinara
C. Falcone
Porto Torres
Sássari
Alghero
Tempio Pausánia
Palau
Golfo Aranci
Ólbia
Ozieri
Budoni
Siniscóla
C. Comino
Orosei
Bosa
Macomer
Núoro
Dorgali
Sorgono
Mti. del Gennargentu
C. di Monte Santu
Oristano
G. di Oristano
Terralba
Nurallao
Árbatax
Lanusei
Gúspini
Sanluri
Senorbì
Villaputzu
Iglésias
Sestu
Quartu Sant'Élena
Cágliari
San Pietro
Portoscuso
Carbónia
Giba
Sant'Antíoco
Teulada
Pula
G. di Pálmas
G. di Cágliari
C. Carbonara
C. Spartivento
Ústica
C. San Vito
Palermo
Érice
Castellammare del Golfo
Trápani
Paceco
Ísole Égadi
Favignana
Bagheria
Términi Imerese
Cefalù
Alcamo
Partinico
Corleone
Calatafimi
Marsala
Castelvetrano
Mazara del Vallo
Menfi
Sciacca
Lercara Friddi
Mussomeli
Caltanissetta
Raffadali
Canicattì
Porto Empédocle
Agrigento
Favara
Licata
Gela
Enna
Piazza Armerina
Sicilia
Pantelleria
Is. de la Galite
C. Serrat
C. Blanc
Bizerte
Menzel-Bourguiba
Mateur
Golfe de Tunis
Ra's aț Țib
Annaba
C. Rosa
El Kala
Tabarka
Béja
Tébourba
Manouba
Ariana
La Marsa
Tunis
Bardo
Ben Arous
Bou Salem
Ghardimaou
Kelibia
Ra's Muștafá
Menzel-Temime
Rovinj
Pula
Labin
Lošinj
Rt. Kamenjak
Kvarner
BARCELONA TANGER
PORTO TORRES PALAU ÓLBIA ÁRBATAX CÁGLIARI TUNIS
TOULON BARCELONA
MARSEILLE
PALERMO
GÉNOVA
GÉNOVA LIVORNO
CATÁNIA
LINOSA LAMPEDUSA
11
15
42°
40°
38°
44°
8°
10°
12°
14°
A
B
C
D
E
1
2
3
4

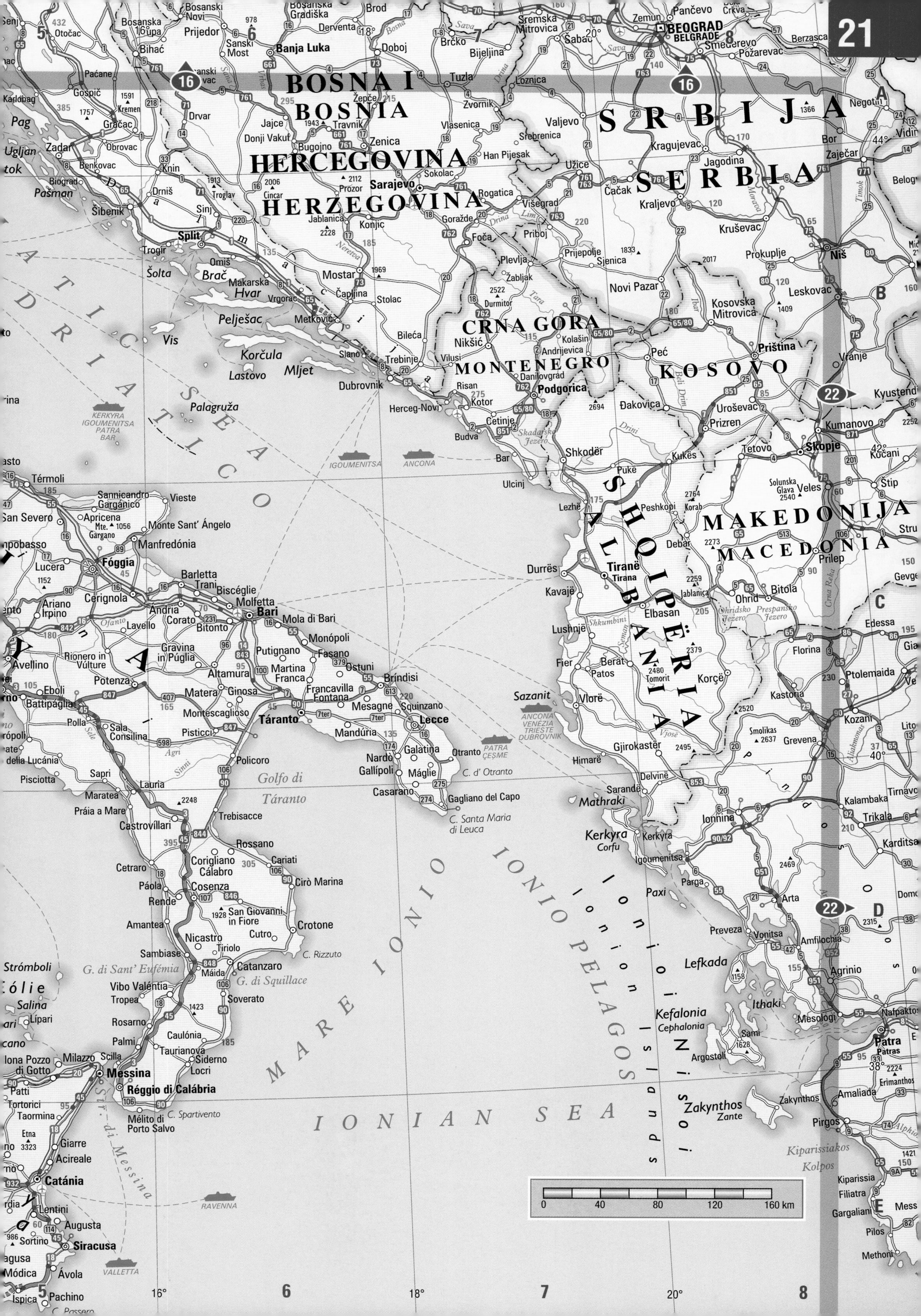

BOSNA I
BOSNIA
HERCEGOVINA
HERZEGOVINA
SRBIJA
SERBIA
CRNA GORA
MONTENEGRO
KOSOVO
SHQIPËRIA
ALBANIA
MAKEDONIJA
MACEDONIA
MARE IONIO
IONIO PELAGOS
IONIAN SEA
Ionioi Nisoi
Ionian Islands
Golfo di Táranto
G. di Sant' Eufémia
G. di Squillace
Str. di Messina
Kiparissiakos Kolpos
Senj
Otočac
Bosanski Novi
Bosanska Dubica
Prijedor
Bosanska Gradiška
Brod
Derventa
Sremska Mitrovica
Zemun
Pančevo
BEOGRAD
BELGRADE
Bihać
Sanski Most
Banja Luka
Doboj
Brčko
Šabac
Smederevo
Požarevac
Bijeljina
Berzasca
Paćane
Gospič
Tuzla
Loznica
Karlobag
Pag
Drvar
Kremen
Žepče
Zvornik
Negotin
Gračac
Jajce
Travnik
Vlasenica
Valjevo
Srebrenica
Donji Vakuf
Bugojno
Zenica
Ugljan
Zadar
Obrovac
Kragujevac
Bor
Zaječar
Benkovac
Han Pijesak
Jagodina
Knin
Sokolac
Užice
Biograd
Pašman
Drniš
Troglav
Cincar
Prozor
Sarajevo
Rogatica
Čačak
Šibenik
Sinj
Jablanica
Višegrad
Kraljevo
Konjic
Goražde
Priboj
Kruševac
Split
Trogir
Omiš
Šolta
Brač
Makarska
Hvar
Vrgorac
Mostar
Čapljina
Stolac
Foča
Pljevlja
Žabljak
Prijepolje
Sjenica
Prokuplje
Niš
Novi Pazar
Leskovac
Durmitor
Kosovska Mitrovica
Metković
Pelješac
Vis
Korčula
Lastovo
Mljet
Slano
Dubrovnik
Bileća
Trebinje
Nikšić
Vilusi
Kolašin
Andrijevica
Danilovgrad
Podgorica
Peć
Priština
Vranje
Kyustendil
Risan
Kotor
Herceg-Novi
Cetinje
Budva
Bar
Ulcinj
Đakovica
Uroševac
Prizren
Kumanovo
Skopje
Kočani
Tetovo
Shkodër
Kukës
Pukë
Lezhë
Peshkopi
Korab
Veles
Solunska Glava
Štip
Debar
Prilep
Durrës
Tiranë
Tirana
Kavajë
Jablanica
Ohrid
Bitola
Ohridsko Jezero
Prespansko Jezero
Elbasan
Lushnjë
Fier
Berat
Patos
Tomorit
Korçë
Edessa
Florina
Ptolemaida
Kastoria
Kozani
Vlorë
Sazanit
Gjirokastër
Smolikas
Grevena
Himarë
Delvinë
Sarandë
Mathraki
Ionnina
Kalambaka
Trikala
Kerkyra
Corfu
Igoumenitsa
Karditsa
Paxi
Parga
Arta
Preveza
Vonitsa
Amfilochia
Lefkada
Agrinio
Ithaki
Kefalonia
Cephalonia
Sami
Argostoli
Mesologi
Nafpaktos
Patra
Patras
Erimanthos
Amaliada
Zakynthos
Zante
Pirgos
Kiparissia
Filiatra
Gargaliani
Pilos
Methoni
Palagruža
KERKYRA IGOUMENITSA PATRA BAR
IGOUMENITSA
ANCONA
ANCONA VENEZIA TRIESTE DUBROVNIK
PATRA ÇEŞME
RAVENNA
VALLETTA
Térmoli
San Severo
Sannicandro Gargánico
Vieste
Apricena
Mte. Gargano
Monte Sant' Ángelo
Manfredónia
Campobasso
Lucera
Fóggia
Barletta
Trani
Bisceglie
Molfetta
Cerignola
Ariano Irpino
Andria
Corato
Bitonto
Bari
Mola di Bari
Lavello
Monópoli
Avellino
Rionero in Vúlture
Gravina in Púglia
Putignano
Fasano
Altamura
Martina Franca
Ostuni
Potenza
Bríndisi
Eboli
Battipáglia
Matera
Ginosa
Francavilla Fontana
Mesagne
Squinzano
Montescaglioso
Táranto
Lecce
Polla
Sala Consilina
Pisticci
Mandúria
Galatina
Otranto
Policoro
Nardò
Gallípoli
Máglie
C. d' Otranto
Sapri
Pisciotta
Lauria
Casarano
Gagliano del Capo
C. Santa Maria di Leuca
Maratea
Práia a Mare
Trebisacce
Castrovíllari
Rossano
Cetraro
Corigliano Cálabro
Cariati
Cirò Marina
Páola
Cosenza
Rende
San Giovanni in Fiore
Amantea
Crotone
Nicastro
Tiriolo
Cutro
Sambiase
Catanzaro
C. Rizzuto
Máida
Strómboli
Vibo Valéntia
Tropea
Soverato
Salina
Lipari
Rosarno
Palmi
Caulónia
Taurianova
Siderno
Locri
Milazzo
Scilla
Messina
Réggio di Calábria
Patti
Tortorici
Taormina
Mélito di Porto Salvo
C. Spartivento
Etna
Giarre
Acireale
Catánia
Lentini
Augusta
Sortino
Siracusa
Módica
Ávola
Ispica
Pachino
C. Passero
16°
18°
20°
6
7
8
A
B
C
D
E
0
40
80
120
160 km

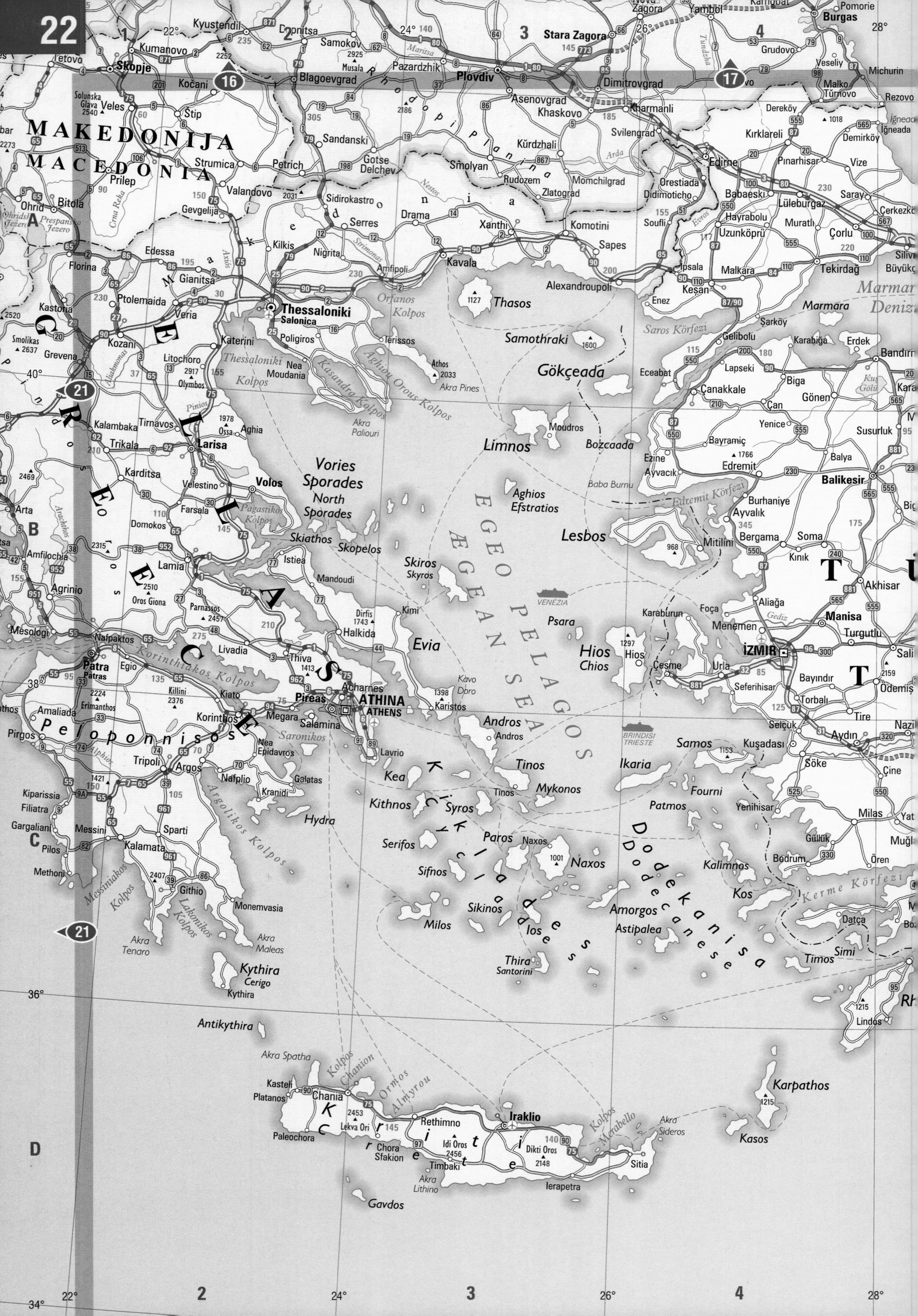
MAKEDONIJA
MACEDONIA
GREECE
ELLAS
Skopje
Kumanovo
Tetovo
Veles
Štip
Kočani
Strumica
Prilep
Bitola
Ohrid
Gevgelija
Valandovo
Kyustendil
Blagoevgrad
Sandanski
Petrich
Gotse Delchev
Samokov
Musala
Pazardzhik
Plovdiv
Asenovgrad
Khaskovo
Kharmanli
Dimitrovgrad
Stara Zagora
Nova Zagora
Yambol
Burgas
Pomorie
Grudovo
Malko Türnovo
Michurin
Rezovo
Smolyan
Kürdzhali
Momchilgrad
Zlatograd
Rudozem
Svilengrad
Rhodopi Planina
Makedonia
Edirne
Kırklareli
Vize
Saray
Lüleburgaz
Babaeski
Pınarhisar
Demirköy
İğneada
Çorlu
Muratlı
Tekirdağ
Uzunköprü
Hayrabolu
Malkara
Keşan
İpsala
Enez
Gelibolu
Şarköy
Marmara
Marmara Denizi
Saros Körfezi
Orestiada
Didimoticho
Soufli
Alexandroupoli
Komotini
Xanthi
Sapes
Kavala
Drama
Serres
Sidirokastro
Nigrita
Kilkis
Amfipoli
Thessaloniki
Salonica
Edessa
Florina
Gianitsa
Veria
Ptolemaida
Kozani
Kastoria
Grevena
Smolikas
Katerini
Olymbos
Litochoro
Poligiros
Nea Moudania
Ierissos
Athos
Akra Pines
Thessaloniki Kolpos
Kasandra Kolpos
Aghiou Orous Kolpos
Orfanos Kolpos
Akra Paliouri
Thasos
Samothraki
Gökçeada
Eceabat
Çanakkale
Lapseki
Biga
Gönen
Karabiga
Erdek
Bandırma
Çan
Yenice
Bayramiç
Ezine
Ayvacık
Edremit
Balya
Balıkesir
Susurluk
Burhaniye
Ayvalık
Bergama
Soma
Kınık
Akhisar
Manisa
Aliağa
Foça
Menemen
Turgutlu
İZMIR
Çeşme
Urla
Karaburun
Seferihisar
Torbalı
Bayındır
Ödemiş
Tire
Selçuk
Aydın
Kuşadası
Söke
Çine
Milas
Yenihisar
Güllük
Bodrum
Ören
Muğla
Datça
Kerme Körfezi
Edremit Körfezi
Baba Burnu
Bozcaada
Limnos
Moudros
Aghios Efstratios
Lesbos
Mitilini
Psara
Hios
Chios
Samos
Ikaria
Fourni
Patmos
Kalimnos
Kos
Simi
Timos
Lindos
Rh
Karpathos
Kasos
Akra Sideros
Dodekanisa
Dodecanese
Amorgos
Astipalea
Thira
Santorini
Ios
Sikinos
Milos
Naxos
Paros
Mykonos
Tinos
Andros
Syros
Serifos
Sifnos
Kithnos
Kea
Kiklades
Cyclades
Hydra
EGEO PELAGOS
AEGEAN SEA
VENEZIA
BRINDISI TRIESTE
Vories Sporades
North Sporades
Skiathos
Skopelos
Skiros
Skyros
Evia
Kimi
Halkida
Mandoudi
Istiea
Karistos
Kavo Doro
Dirfis
Lavrio
ATHINA
ATHENS
Pireas
Acharnes
Salamina
Megara
Thiva
Livadia
Parnassos
Oros Giona
Lamia
Agrinio
Amfilochia
Mesologi
Nafpaktos
Patra
Patras
Egio
Kiato
Korinthos
Korinthiakos Kolpos
Saronikos
Nea Epidavros
Galatas
Kranidi
Nafplio
Argos
Tripoli
Sparti
Kalamata
Messini
Pilos
Methoni
Gargaliani
Filiatra
Kiparissia
Pirgos
Amaliada
Erimanthos
Killini
Peloponnisos
Alphios
Githio
Monemvasia
Akra Maleas
Akra Tenaro
Messiniakos Kolpos
Lakonikos Kolpos
Argolikos Kolpos
Kythira
Cerigo
Antikythira
Larisa
Tirnavos
Kalambaka
Trikala
Karditsa
Farsala
Domokos
Velestino
Volos
Pagastikos Kolpos
Ossa
Aghia
Pinios
Arta
Arachthos
Pindos
Aliakmonas
Axios
Strimonas
Nestos
Arda
Evros
Tundzha
Maritsa
Crna Reka
Prespansko Jezero
Ohridsko Jezero
Akra Spatha
Kolpos Chanion
Ormos Almyrou
Kolpos Merabello
Kastelli
Platanos
Chania
Paleochora
Lefka Ori
Rethimno
Chora Sfakion
Idi Oros
Timbaki
Akra Lithino
Iraklio
Dikti Oros
Ierapetra
Sitia
Kriti
Gavdos
Kus Gölü
22°
24°
26°
28°
34°
36°
38°
40°
1
2
3
4
A
B
C
D
16
17
21
T
U

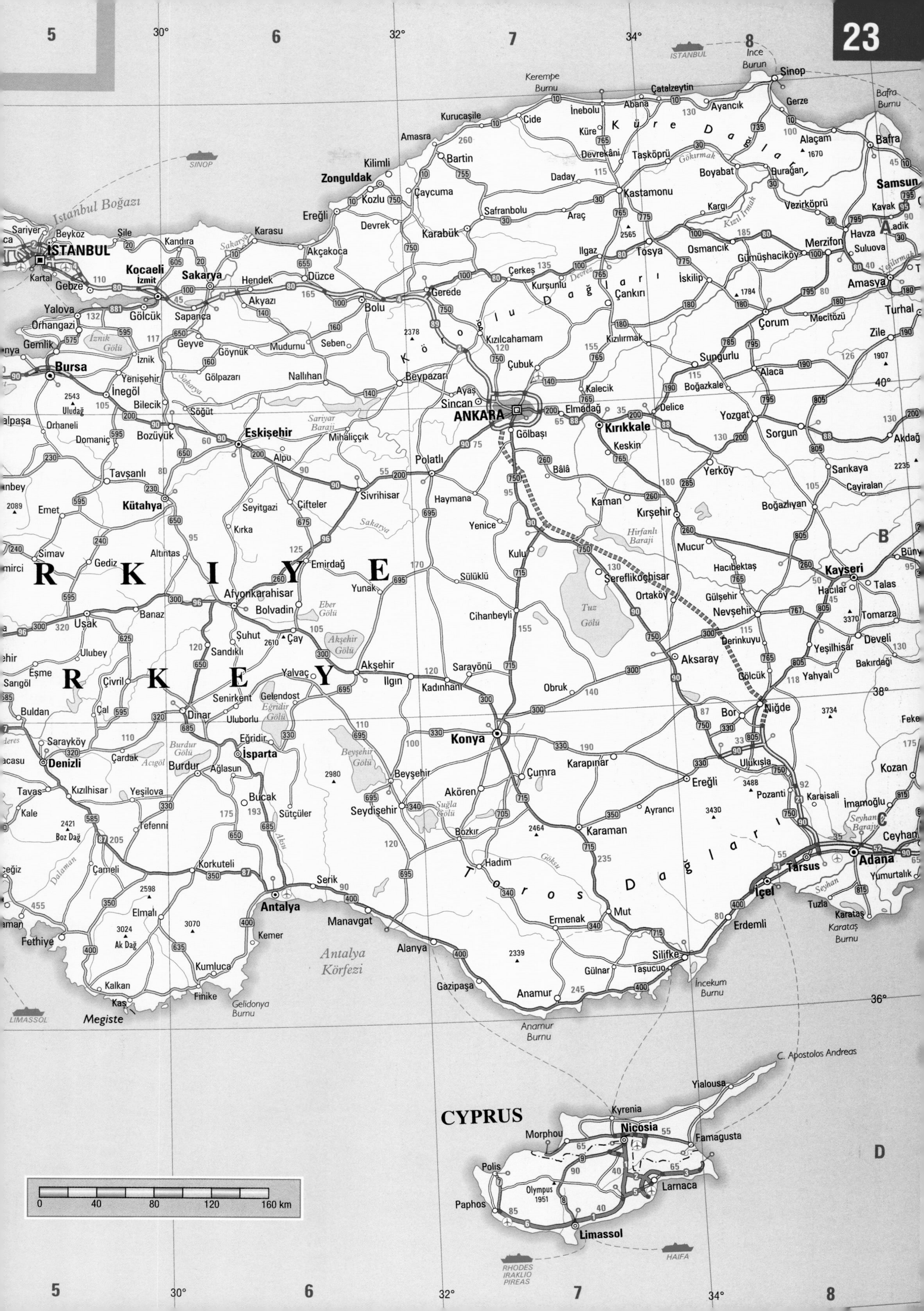
5
30°
6
32°
7
34°
8
Ince Burun
Sinop
Kerempe Burnu
Çatalzeytin
İnebolu
Abana
Ayancık
Gerze
Bafra Burnu
Kurucaşile
Cide
Küre
Küre Dağları
Amasra
Bartin
Devrekâni
Taşköprü
Alaçam
1670
Bafra
Kilimli
Zonguldak
Gökırmak
Boyabat
Daday
Kastamonu
Durağan
Samsun
Kozlu
Çaycuma
Ereğli
Devrek
Safranbolu
Kargı
Kızıl Irmak
Vezirköprü
Kavak
Karabük
Araç
2565
Havza
Ladik
Merzifon
Suluova
Sarıyer
Beykoz
Şile
Kandıra
Karasu
İstanbul Boğazı
İSTANBUL
Kartal
Gebze
Kocaeli İzmit
Sakarya
Akçakoca
Ilgaz
Tosya
Osmancık
Gümüşhaciköy
Düzce
Hendek
Çerkeş
Kurşunlu
Devrez
Çankırı
İskilip
1784
Amasya
Yeşilırmak
Yalova
Gölcük
Sapanca
Akyazı
Bolu
Gerede
Turhal
Orhangazi
İznik Gölü
Mecitözü
Çorum
Gemlik
Geyve
Göynük
Mudurnu
Seben
2378
Kızılcahamam
Köroğlu Dağları
Kızılırmak
Zile
İznik
Bursa
Yenişehir
Gölpazarı
Nallıhan
Çubuk
Sungurlu
1907
Alaca
İnegöl
Beypazarı
Ayaş
Kalecik
Boğazkale
40°
2543 Uludağ
Bilecik
Söğüt
Sincan
ANKARA
Elmadağ
Delice
Yozgat
Orhaneli
Sariyar Baraji
Kırıkkale
Sorgun
Akdağ
Domaniç
Bozüyük
Eskişehir
Mihaliççık
Gölbaşı
Keskin
Alpu
Polatlı
Bâlâ
Yerköy
Sarıkaya
2235
Tavşanlı
Çayıralan
Sivrihisar
Haymana
Kaman
Kırşehir
Boğazlıyan
2089
Emet
Kütahya
Seyitgazi
Çifteler
Yenice
Hirfanlı Baraji
Kırka
Sakarya
Mucur
B
Simav
Altıntaş
Emirdağ
Kulu
Gediz
Hacıbektaş
Kayseri
Talas
Şereflikoçhisar
Hacılar
Ortaköy
Gülşehir
Afyonkarahisar
Yunak
Sülüklü
Bolvadin
Eber Gölü
Nevşehir
Banaz
Cihanbeyli
Tuz Gölü
3370
Tomarza
Uşak
Derinkuyu
Develi
Şuhut
Çay
Akşehir Gölü
Aksaray
Yeşilhisar
2610
Sandıklı
Ulubey
Eşme
Sarıgöl
Akşehir
Sarayönü
Bakırdağı
Yalvaç
Ilgın
Çivril
Kadınhanı
Obruk
Gölcük
Yahyalı
Senirkent
Gelendost
38°
Buldan
Çal
Dinar
Eğridir Gölü
Uluborlu
Bor
Niğde
3734
Eğridir
Sarayköy
Konya
Burdur Gölü
Çardak
Acıgöl
Isparta
Denizli
Beyşehir Gölü
Burdur
Ağlasun
Karapınar
Kozan
Tavas
Kızılhisar
Yeşilova
Çumra
Ulukışla
2980
Beyşehir
Ereğli
Karaisali
Bucak
Akören
Pozanti
3488
İmamoğlu
Kale
Sütçüler
Seydişehir
Suğla Gölü
Ayrancı
3430
Seyhan Baraji
2421 Boz Dağ
Tefenni
Bozkır
2464
Karaman
C
Ceyhan
Aksu
Dalaman
Korkuteli
Hadım
Göksu
Tarsus
Adana
Çameli
Serik
Toros Dağları
Yumurtalık
İçel
Seyhan
2598
Elmalı
Antalya
Manavgat
Mut
Tuzla
Karataş
Karataş Burnu
3024 Ak Dağ
3070
Kemer
Ermenak
Erdemli
Fethiye
Antalya Körfezi
Alanya
2339
Silifke
Gülnar
Taşucu
Kumluca
Kalkan
Gazipaşa
Anamur
İncekum Burnu
Kaş
Finike
Gelidonya Burnu
36°
Megiste
LIMASSOL
Anamur Burnu
C. Apostolos Andreas
Yialousa
CYPRUS
Kyrenia
Morphou
Nicosia
Famagusta
D
Polis
Olympus 1951
Larnaca
Paphos
Limassol
HAIFA
RHODES IRAKLIO PIREAS
ISTANBUL
SINOP
TÜRKIYE
0
40
80
120
160 km
5
30°
6
32°
7
34°
8

Key to road map pages

● **Florence** **City plan**
 Firenze

□ **İstanbul** **City approach map**

■ **Milan** **City plan and approach map**
 Milano See pages 201–228 for city plans
 and approach maps

97 Map pages at 1:750 000

182 Map pages at 1:1 500 000

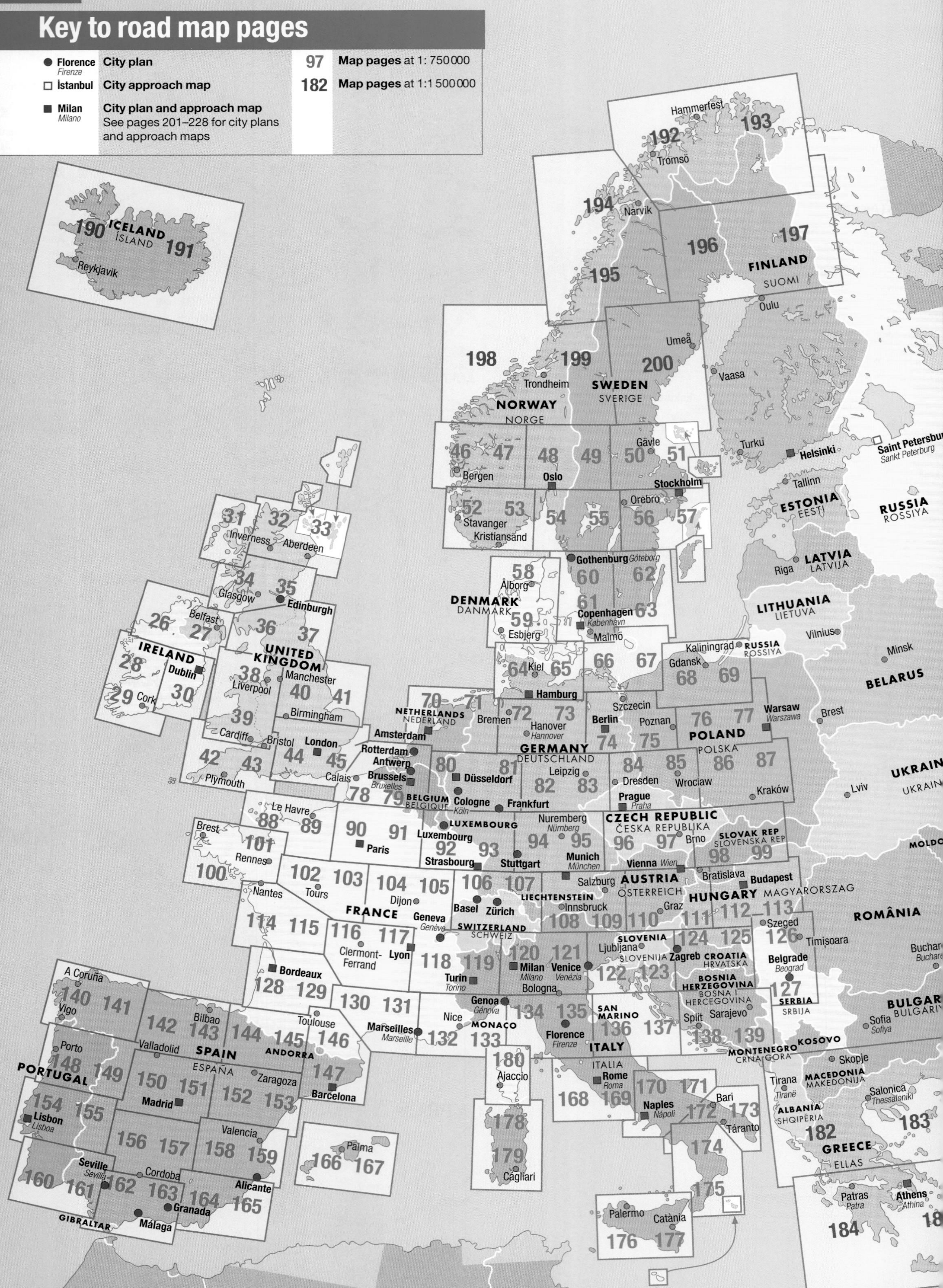

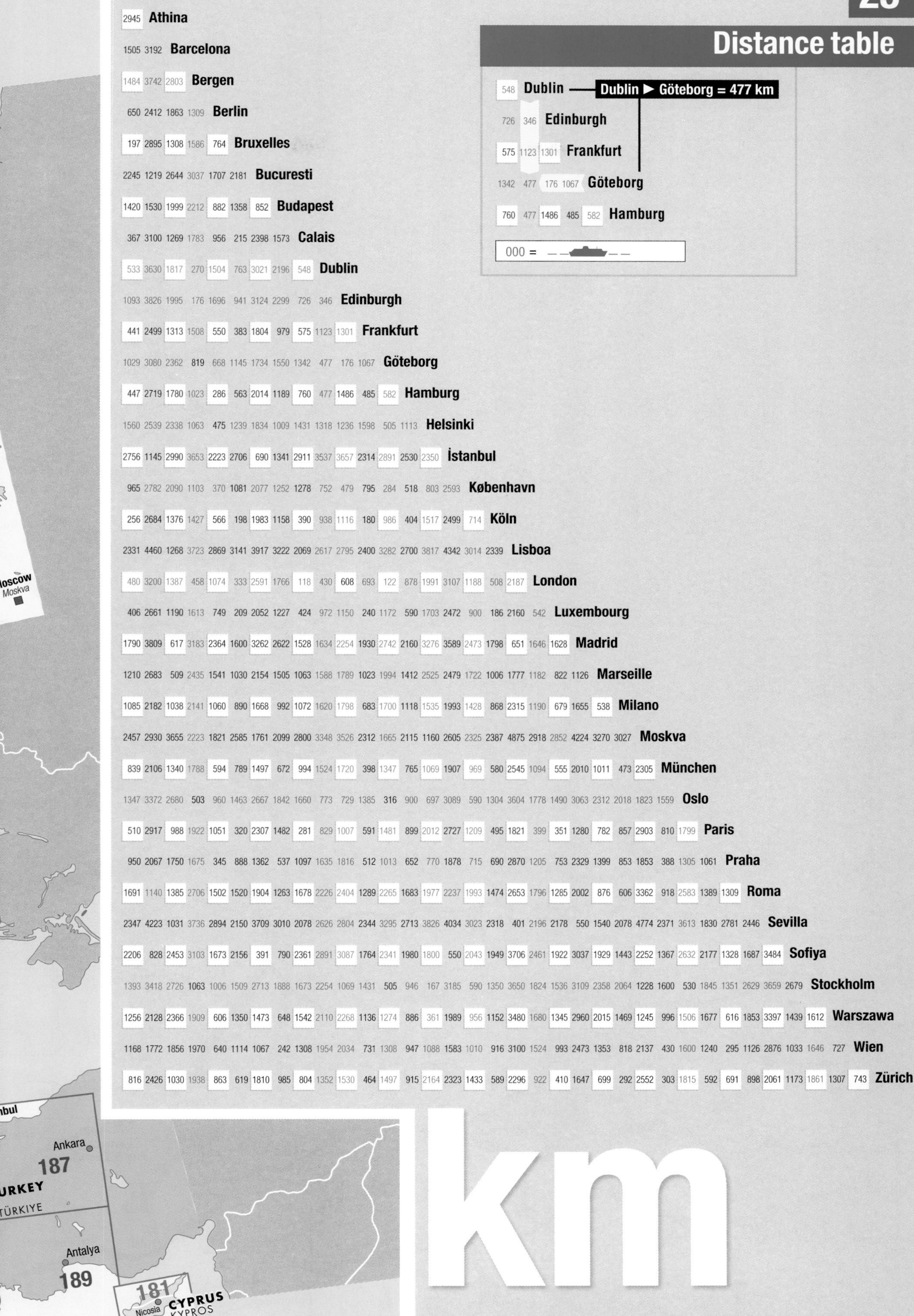

Distance table

Amsterdam

2945 **Athina**

1505 3192 **Barcelona**

1484 3742 2803 **Bergen**

650 2412 1863 1309 **Berlin**

197 2895 1308 1586 764 **Bruxelles**

2245 1219 2644 3037 1707 2181 **Bucuresti**

1420 1530 1999 2212 882 1358 852 **Budapest**

367 3100 1269 1783 956 215 2398 1573 **Calais**

533 3630 1817 270 1504 763 3021 2196 548 **Dublin**

1093 3826 1995 176 1696 941 3124 2299 726 346 **Edinburgh**

441 2499 1313 1508 550 383 1804 979 575 1123 1301 **Frankfurt**

1029 3080 2362 819 668 1145 1734 1550 1342 477 176 1067 **Göteborg**

447 2719 1780 1023 286 563 2014 1189 760 477 1486 485 582 **Hamburg**

1560 2539 2338 1063 475 1239 1834 1009 1431 1318 1236 1598 505 1113 **Helsinki**

2756 1145 2990 3653 2223 2706 690 1341 2911 3537 3657 2314 2891 2530 2350 **İstanbul**

965 2782 2090 1103 370 1081 2077 1252 1278 752 479 795 284 518 803 2593 **København**

256 2684 1376 1427 566 198 1983 1158 390 938 1116 180 986 404 1517 2499 714 **Köln**

2331 4460 1268 3723 2869 3141 3917 3222 2069 2617 2795 2400 3282 2700 3817 4342 3014 2339 **Lisboa**

480 3200 1387 458 1074 333 2591 1766 118 430 608 693 122 878 1991 3107 1188 508 2187 **London**

406 2661 1190 1613 749 209 2052 1227 424 972 1150 240 1172 590 1703 2472 900 186 2160 542 **Luxembourg**

1790 3809 617 3183 2364 1600 3262 2622 1528 1634 2254 1930 2742 2160 3276 3589 2473 1798 651 1646 1628 **Madrid**

1210 2683 509 2435 1541 1030 2154 1505 1063 1588 1789 1023 1994 1412 2525 2479 1722 1006 1777 1182 822 1126 **Marseille**

1085 2182 1038 2141 1060 890 1668 992 1072 1620 1798 683 1700 1118 1535 1993 1428 868 2315 1190 679 1655 538 **Milano**

2457 2930 3655 2223 1821 2585 1761 2099 2800 3348 3526 2312 1665 2115 1160 2605 2325 2387 4875 2918 2852 4224 3270 3027 **Moskva**

839 2106 1340 1788 594 789 1497 672 994 1524 1720 398 1347 765 1069 1907 969 580 2545 1094 555 2010 1011 473 2305 **München**

1347 3372 2680 503 960 1463 2667 1842 1660 773 729 1385 316 900 697 3089 590 1304 3604 1778 1490 3063 2312 2018 1823 1559 **Oslo**

510 2917 988 1922 1051 320 2307 1482 281 829 1007 591 1481 899 2012 2727 1209 495 1821 399 351 1280 782 857 2903 810 1799 **Paris**

950 2067 1750 1675 345 888 1362 537 1097 1635 1816 512 1013 652 770 1878 715 690 2870 1205 753 2329 1399 853 1853 388 1305 1061 **Praha**

1691 1140 1385 2706 1502 1520 1904 1263 1678 2226 2404 1289 2265 1683 1977 2237 1993 1474 2653 1796 1285 2002 876 606 3362 918 2583 1389 1309 **Roma**

2347 4223 1031 3736 2894 2150 3709 3010 2078 2626 2804 2344 3295 2713 3826 4034 3023 2318 401 2196 2178 550 1540 2078 4774 2371 3613 1830 2781 2446 **Sevilla**

2206 828 2453 3103 1673 2156 391 790 2361 2891 3087 1764 2341 1980 1800 550 2043 1949 3706 2461 1922 3037 1929 1443 2252 1367 2632 2177 1328 1687 3484 **Sofiya**

1393 3418 2726 1063 1006 1509 2713 1888 1673 2254 1069 1431 505 946 167 3185 590 1350 3650 1824 1536 3109 2358 2064 1228 1600 530 1845 1351 2629 3659 2679 **Stockholm**

1256 2128 2366 1909 606 1350 1473 648 1542 2110 2268 1136 1274 886 361 1989 956 1152 3480 1680 1345 2960 2015 1469 1245 996 1506 1677 616 1853 3397 1439 1612 **Warszawa**

1168 1772 1856 1970 640 1114 1067 242 1308 1954 2034 731 1308 947 1088 1583 1010 916 3100 1524 993 2473 1353 818 2137 430 1600 1240 295 1126 2876 1033 1646 727 **Wien**

816 2426 1030 1938 863 619 1810 985 804 1352 1530 464 1497 915 2164 2323 1433 589 2296 922 410 1647 699 292 2552 303 1815 592 691 898 2061 1173 1861 1307 743 **Zürich**

Legend:

548 **Dublin** — **Dublin ▶ Göteborg = 477 km**

726 346 **Edinburgh**

575 1123 1301 **Frankfurt**

1342 477 176 1067 **Göteborg**

760 477 1486 485 582 **Hamburg**

000 = ⛴

km

RUSSIA
ROSSIYA

Moscow
Moskva

Kiev
Kyyiv

UKRAINE
UKRAINA

MOLDOVA

İstanbul

Ankara

186 187

TURKEY
TÜRKIYE

İzmir

Antalya

188 189

181
Nicosia CYPRUS
KYPROS

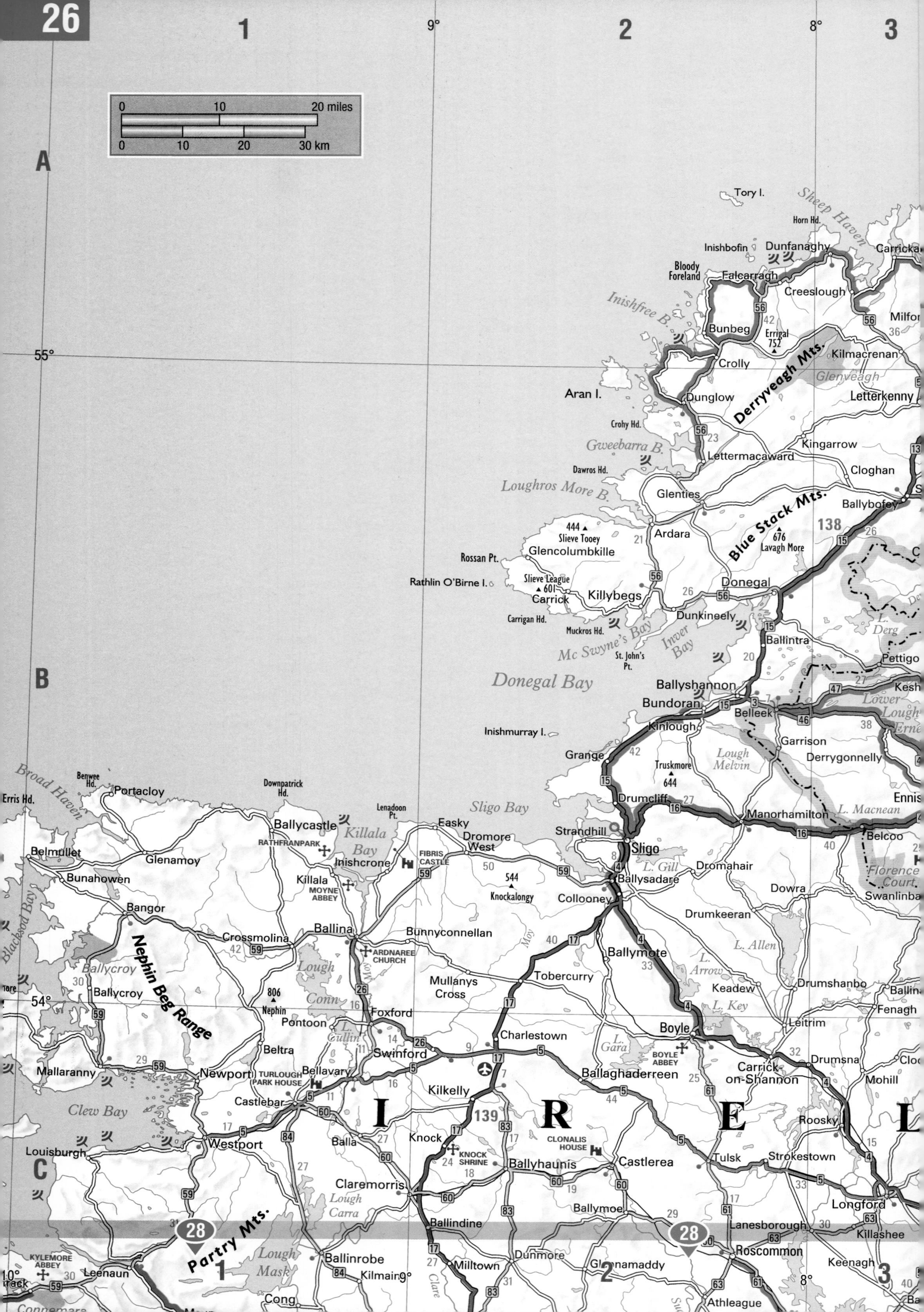
1
2
3
9°
8°
A
B
C
55°
54°
0 10 20 miles
0 10 20 30 km
Tory I.
Sheep Haven
Horn Hd.
Inishbofin
Dunfanaghy
Bloody Foreland
Falcarragh
Creeslough
Inishfree B.
Bunbeg
Errigal 752
Crolly
Derryveagh Mts.
Kilmacrenan
Glenveagh
Letterkenny
Aran I.
Dunglow
Crohy Hd.
Gweebarra B.
Lettermacaward
Kingarrow
Cloghan
Dawros Hd.
Loughros More B.
Glenties
Blue Stack Mts.
Ballybofey
444 Slieve Tooey
Ardara
138
676 Lavagh More
Rossan Pt.
Glencolumbkille
Rathlin O'Birne I.
Slieve League 601
Carrick
Killybegs
Donegal
Carrigan Hd.
Muckros Hd.
Dunkineely
Mc Swyne's Bay
St. John's Pt.
Inver Bay
Ballintra
L. Derg
Pettigo
Donegal Bay
Ballyshannon
Bundoran
Belleek
Lower Lough Erne
Kesh
Inishmurray I.
Kinlough
Garrison
Derrygonnelly
Grange
Truskmore 644
Lough Melvin
Drumcliff
Manorhamilton
L. Macnean
Ennis
Sligo Bay
Strandhill
Sligo
Belcoo
L. Gill
Dromahair
Ballysadare
Florence Court
Swanlinbar
Dowra
Collooney
Drumkeeran
Broad Haven
Benwee Hd.
Portacloy
Erris Hd.
Downpatrick Hd.
Lenadoon Pt.
Easky
Ballycastle
Killala Bay
Dromore West
Belmullet
Glenamoy
RATHFRANPARK
Inishcrone
FIBRIS CASTLE
544 Knockalongy
Bunahowen
Killala
MOYNE ABBEY
Blacksod Bay
Bangor
Nephin Beg Range
Crossmolina
Ballina
Bunnyconnellan
ARDNAREE CHURCH
Moy
L. Allen
Ballymote
Ballycroy
Lough Conn
806 Nephin
Mullanys Cross
Tobercurry
L. Arrow
Keadew
Drumshanbo
Pontoon
Foxford
L. Key
Fenagh
L. Cullin
Charlestown
Boyle
Leitrim
Beltra
Swinford
L. Gara
BOYLE ABBEY
Drumsna
Mallaranny
Newport
TURLOUGH PARK HOUSE
Bellavary
Kilkelly
Ballaghaderreen
Carrick-on-Shannon
Mohill
Castlebar
Clew Bay
I
R
E
L
139
Roosky
Louisburgh
Westport
Balla
Knock
CLONALIS HOUSE
KNOCK SHRINE
Ballyhaunis
Castlerea
Tulsk
Strokestown
Claremorris
Lough Carra
Ballymoe
Longford
Partry Mts.
Ballindine
Lanesborough
Killashee
28
KYLEMORE ABBEY
Leenaun
Lough Mask
Ballinrobe
Kilmaine
Milltown
Dunmore
Glenamaddy
Roscommon
Keenagh
Cong
Athleague
Connemara
Clare
10°

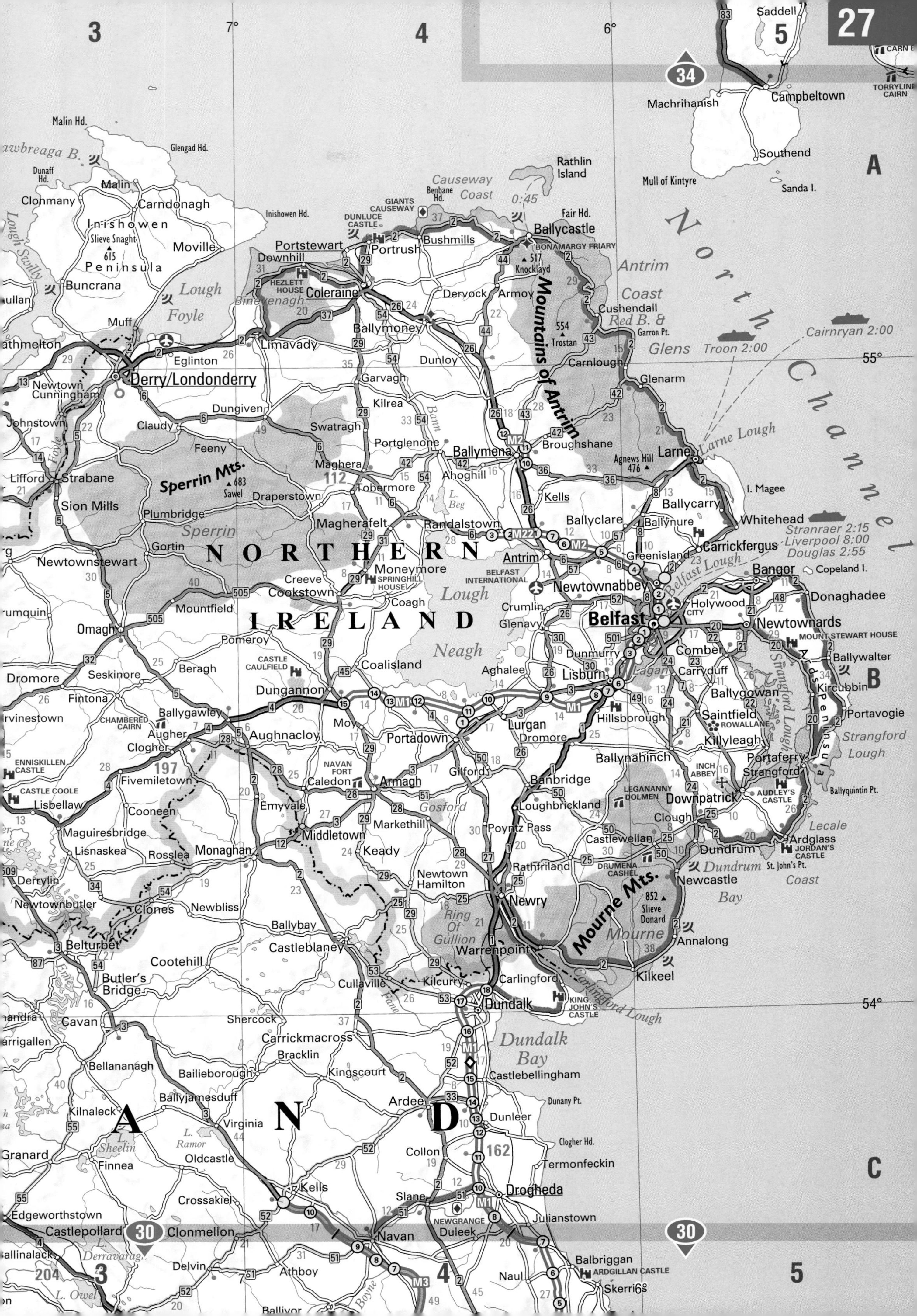
3
4
5
7°
6°
34
Saddell
Campbeltown
Machrihanish
Southend
Mull of Kintyre
Sanda I.
A
Rathlin Island
Causeway Coast
Benbane Hd.
GIANTS CAUSEWAY
DUNLUCE CASTLE
Fair Hd.
Ballycastle
BONAMARGY FRIARY
Knocklayd
North Channel
Malin Hd.
Glengad Hd.
Dunaff Hd.
Malin
Clonmany
Carndonagh
Inishowen
Slieve Snaght
Peninsula
Moville
Inishowen Hd.
Buncrana
Lough Swilly
Lough Foyle
Muff
Portstewart
Portrush
Bushmills
Downhill
HEZLETT HOUSE
Coleraine
Binevenagh
Dervock
Armoy
Mountains of Antrim
Antrim Coast
Cushendall
Red B. &
Garron Pt.
Glens
Troon 2:00
Cairnryan 2:00
Trostan
Carnlough
55°
Glenarm
Limavady
Eglinton
Derry/Londonderry
Newtown Cunningham
Ballymoney
Dunloy
Garvagh
Kilrea
Dungiven
Claudy
Johnstown
Foyle
Feeny
Swatragh
Portglenone
Bann
Ballymena
Broughshane
Agnews Hill
Larne
Larne Lough
Lifford
Strabane
Sperrin Mts.
Sawel
Maghera
Ahoghill
Tobermore
Draperstown
L. Beg
Kells
I. Magee
Ballycarry
Sion Mills
Plumbridge
Sperrin
Magherafelt
Randalstown
Ballyclare
Ballynure
Whitehead
Stranraer 2:15
Liverpool 8:00
Douglas 2:55
Gortin
NORTHERN
Antrim
Carrickfergus
Greenisland
Belfast Lough
Bangor
Copeland I.
Newtownstewart
Moneymore
SPRINGHILL HOUSE
BELFAST INTERNATIONAL
Newtownabbey
Donaghadee
Creeve
Cookstown
Lough
Holywood
CITY
Mountfield
Coagh
Crumlin
Belfast
Newtownards
Omagh
IRELAND
Glenavy
MOUNT STEWART HOUSE
Pomeroy
Neagh
Dunmurry
Comber
Ballywalter
CASTLE CAULFIELD
Beragh
Seskinore
Coalisland
Aghalee
Lisburn
Lagan
Carryduff
Ards Peninsula
Kircubbin
B
Dromore
Fintona
Dungannon
Ballygowan
Strangford Lough
Irvinestown
CHAMBERED CAIRN
Ballygawley
Augher
Clogher
Aughnacloy
Moy
Portadown
Lurgan
Dromore
Hillsborough
Saintfield
ROWALLANE
Portavogie
Killyleagh
Strangford Lough
ENNISKILLEN CASTLE
NAVAN FORT
Caledon
Armagh
Gilford
Ballynahinch
INCH ABBEY
Portaferry
Strangford
Fivemiletown
Banbridge
LEGANANNY DOLMEN
Downpatrick
AUDLEY'S CASTLE
Ballyquintin Pt.
CASTLE COOLE
Lisbellaw
Cooneen
Emyvale
Gosford
Loughbrickland
Clough
Lecale
Maguiresbridge
Middletown
Markethill
Poyntz Pass
Castlewellan
Ardglass
JORDAN'S CASTLE
Lisnaskea
Rosslea
Monaghan
Keady
Dundrum
Dundrum Bay
St. John's Pt.
Coast
Rathfriland
DRUMENA CASHEL
Newcastle
Derrylin
Newtown Hamilton
Newry
Mourne Mts.
Slieve Donard
Newtownbutler
Clones
Newbliss
Ring Of Gullion
Mourne
Ballybay
Annalong
Belturbet
Castleblaney
Warrenpoint
Kilkeel
Cootehill
Carlingford
Butler's Bridge
Cullaville
Kilcurry
Carlingford Lough
Fane
Dundalk
KING JOHN'S CASTLE
54°
Cavan
Shercock
Carrickmacross
Dundalk Bay
Bracklin
Bellananagh
Bailieborough
Kingscourt
Castlebellingham
Ballyjamesduff
Ardee
Dunany Pt.
Kilnaleck
A
N
D
Dunleer
Virginia
L. Sheelin
L. Ramor
Clogher Hd.
Granard
Finnea
Oldcastle
Collon
Termonfeckin
C
Kells
Slane
Drogheda
Crossakiel
NEWGRANGE
Julianstown
Edgeworthstown
Castlepollard
30
Clonmellon
Navan
Duleek
L. Derravaragh
Balbriggan
Delvin
Athboy
Naul
ARDGILLAN CASTLE
Skerries
L. Owel
Boyne
Ballivor
M1
M2
M3
M22

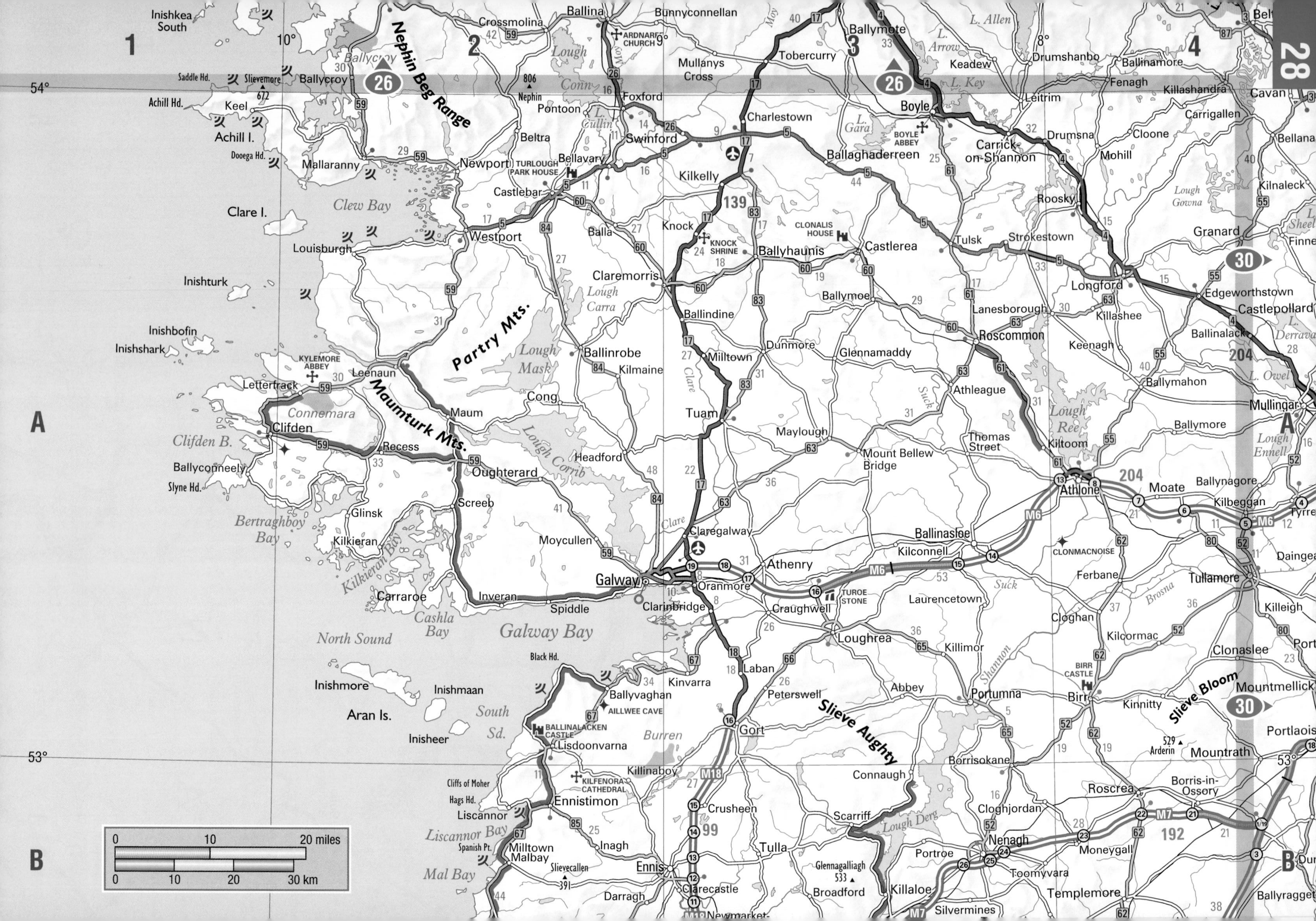

1
2
3
4
A
B
54°
53°
10°
8°
Inishkea South
Saddle Hd.
Slievemore
672
Achill Hd.
Keel
Achill I.
Dooega Hd.
Ballycroy
Nephin Beg Range
Mallaranny
Clare I.
Clew Bay
Louisburgh
Inishturk
Inishbofin
Inishshark
KYLEMORE ABBEY
Letterfrack
Leenaun
Connemara
Clifden
Clifden B.
Ballyconneely
Slyne Hd.
Bertraghboy Bay
Glinsk
Kilkieran
Kilkieran Bay
Carraroe
Cashla Bay
North Sound
Inishmore
Aran Is.
Inishmaan
Inisheer
South Sd.
Recess
Maumturk Mts.
Maum
Partry Mts.
Oughterard
Screeb
Inveran
Spiddle
Moycullen
Galway Bay
Galway
Black Hd.
Crossmolina
Ballina
Bunnyconnellan
ARDNAREE CHURCH
Mullanys Cross
Tobercurry
Ballymote
806
Nephin
Pontoon
L. Cullin
Conn
Lough
Foxford
Swinford
Beltra
Newport
TURLOUGH PARK HOUSE
Bellavary
Castlebar
Westport
Charlestown
Kilkelly
Knock
KNOCK SHRINE
Balla
Claremorris
Lough Carra
Lough Mask
Ballinrobe
Kilmaine
Cong
Lough Corrib
Headford
Ballindine
Milltown
Tuam
Clare
Claregalway
Oranmore
Clarinbridge
Ballyhaunis
CLONALIS HOUSE
Castlerea
Ballymoe
Dunmore
Glennamaddy
Maylough
Mount Bellew Bridge
Athleague
Roscommon
Lanesborough
Ballaghaderreen
L. Gara
BOYLE ABBEY
Boyle
L. Key
Keadew
L. Arrow
L. Allen
Drumshanbo
Leitrim
Carrick-on-Shannon
Drumsna
Cloone
Mohill
Ballinamore
Fenagh
Killashandra
Carrigallen
Cavan
Bellana
Kilnaleck
Lough Gowna
Granard
Rooskey
Tulsk
Strokestown
Longford
Killashee
Keenagh
Edgeworthstown
Castlepollard
Ballinalack
L. Derravaragh
L. Owel
Ballymahon
Mullingar
Ballymore
Lough Ennell
Lough Ree
Kiltoom
Thomas Street
Athlone
Moate
Ballynagore
Kilbeggan
Tyrrell
Daingean
Tullamore
CLONMACNOISE
Ferbane
Brosna
Killeigh
Cloghan
Kilcormac
Clonaslee
Portarlington
Mountmellick
Portlaoise
Slieve Bloom
Kinnitty
529
Arderin
Mountrath
Borris-in-Ossory
BIRR CASTLE
Birr
Roscrea
Moneygall
Templemore
Ballyragget
Durrow
Ballinasloe
Kilconnell
Athenry
Suck
Laurencetown
TUROE STONE
Craughwell
Loughrea
Killimor
Shannon
Portumna
Abbey
Slieve Aughty
Peterswell
Kinvarra
Laban
Ballyvaghan
AILLWEE CAVE
BALLINALACKEN CASTLE
Lisdoonvarna
Burren
Gort
Killinaboy
KILFENORA CATHEDRAL
Cliffs of Moher
Hags Hd.
Liscannor
Liscannor Bay
Spanish Pt.
Ennistimon
Milltown Malbay
Mal Bay
Slievecallen
391
Inagh
Ennis
Darragh
Clarecastle
Newmarket-
Crusheen
Tulla
Glennagalliagh
533
Broadford
Killaloe
Scarriff
Lough Derg
Connaugh
Borrisokane
Portroe
Cloghjordan
Nenagh
Toomyvara
Silvermines
139
99
192
204
30
26
0
10
20 miles
20
30 km

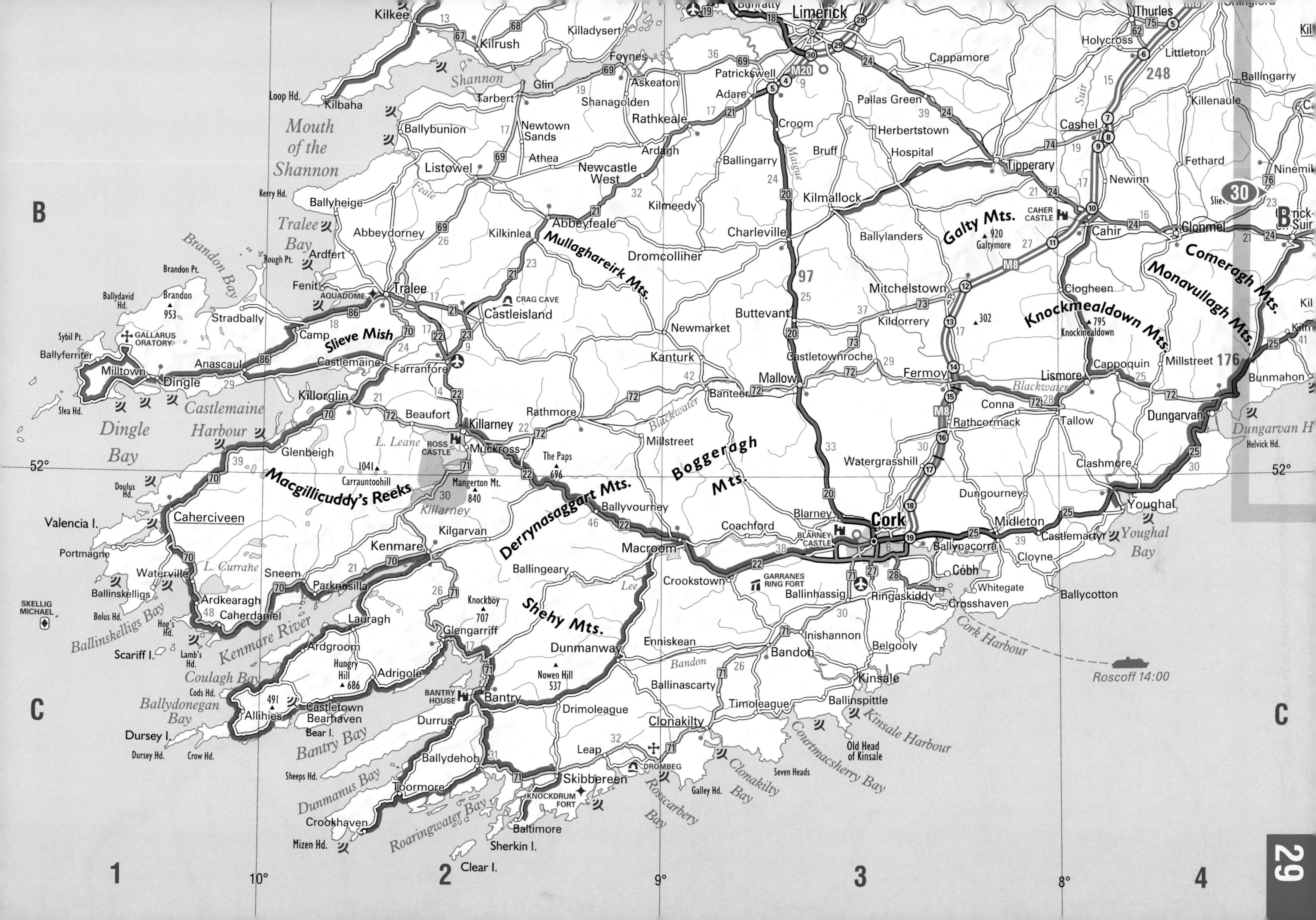
Limerick
Thurles
Kilkee
Kilrush
Killadysert
Foynes
Askeaton
Patrickswell
Adare
Shanagolden
Glin
Tarbert
Shannon
Loop Hd.
Kilbaha
Mouth of the Shannon
Ballybunion
Newtown Sands
Athea
Rathkeale
Ardagh
Listowel
Feale
Newcastle West
Kilmeedy
Ballingarry
Croom
Bruff
Maigue
Herbertstown
Hospital
Pallas Green
Cappamore
Holycross
Littleton
Ballingarry
Killenaule
Cashel
Suir
Fethard
Tipperary
Newinn
Ninemile
Kilmallock
Ballylanders
Galty Mts.
920 Galtymore
CAHER CASTLE
Cahir
Clonmel
Comeragh Mts.
Monavullagh Mts.
Knockmealdown Mts.
795 Knockmealdown
Clogheen
Cappoquin
Millstreet
Lismore
Dungarvan
Dungarvan H
Helvick Hd.
Bunmahon
Kerry Hd.
Ballyheige
Tralee Bay
Abbeydorney
Ardfert
Rough Pt.
Brandon Bay
Brandon Pt.
Brandon 953
Ballydavid Hd.
Fenit
AQUADOME
Tralee
Stradbally
GALLARUS ORATORY
Sybil Pt.
Ballyferriter
Milltown
Dingle
Anascaul
Camp
Slieve Mish
Castlemaine
Farranfore
Castleisland
CRAG CAVE
Kilkinlea
Abbeyfeale
Mullaghareirk Mts.
Dromcolliher
Charleville
Buttevant
Newmarket
Kanturk
Mallow
Banteer
Castletownroche
Kildorrery
Mitchelstown
302
Fermoy
Blackwater
Conna
Rathcormack
Tallow
Clashmore
Youghal
Youghal Bay
Slea Hd.
Dingle Bay
Castlemaine Harbour
Killorglin
Beaufort
Killarney
Rathmore
Millstreet
Boggeragh Mts.
Watergrasshill
Dungourney
Midleton
Castlemartyr
Cloyne
Ballycotton
Glenbeigh
L. Leane
ROSS CASTLE
Muckross
The Paps 696
1041 Carrauntoohill
Macgillicuddy's Reeks
Mangerton Mt. 840
Killarney
Derrynasaggart Mts.
Ballyvourney
Coachford
Blarney
BLARNEY CASTLE
Cork
Ballynacorra
Cóbh
Whitegate
Crosshaven
Ringaskiddy
Cork Harbour
Roscoff 14:00
Doulus Hd.
Valencia I.
Caherciveen
Portmagne
Kilgarvan
Kenmare
Macroom
Ballingeary
Lee
Crookstown
GARRANES RING FORT
Ballinhassig
Waterville
L. Currane
Sneem
Parknasilla
SKELLIG MICHAEL
Ballinskelligs
Bolus Hd.
Ballinskelligs Bay
Hog's Hd.
Ardkearagh
Caherdaniel
Kenmare River
Scariff I.
Lamb's Hd.
Lauragh
Knockboy 707
Glengarriff
Shehy Mts.
Dunmanway
Enniskean
Bandon
Inishannon
Belgooly
Kinsale
Ardgroom
Hungry Hill 686
Adrigole
Coulagh Bay
Cods Hd.
Ballydonegan Bay
491
Allihies
Castletown Bearhaven
Bear I.
Bantry Bay
BANTRY HOUSE
Bantry
Nowen Hill 537
Drimoleague
Ballinascarty
Timoleague
Clonakilty
Ballinspittle
Kinsale Harbour
Old Head of Kinsale
Courtmacsherry Bay
Dursey I.
Dursey Hd.
Crow Hd.
Durrus
Leap
DROMBEG
Clonakilty Bay
Seven Heads
Galley Hd.
Sheeps Hd.
Dunmanus Bay
Ballydehob
Toormore
Skibbereen
KNOCKDRUM FORT
Rosscarbery Bay
Crookhaven
Roaringwater Bay
Baltimore
Mizen Hd.
Sherkin I.
Clear I.
52°
10°
9°
8°
B
C
1
2
3
4

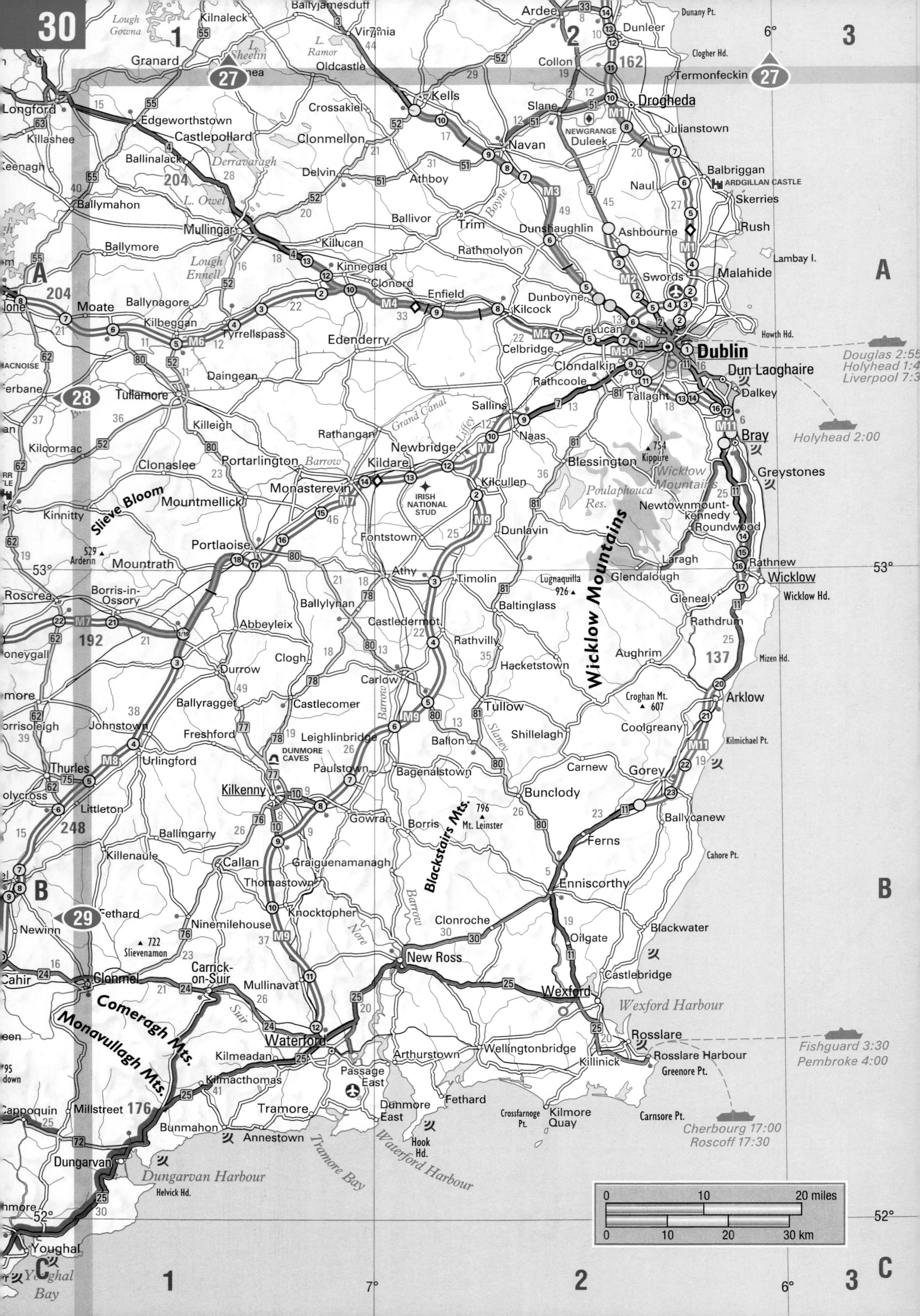
1
2
3
A
B
C
6°
7°
53°
52°
27
28
29
Lough Gowna
Kilnaleck
Ballyjamesduff
Virginia
L. Ramor
Ardee
Dunleer
Dunany Pt.
Clogher Hd.
Granard
L. Sheelin
Oldcastle
Collon
Termonfeckin
Longford
Edgeworthstown
Crossakiel
Kells
Slane
Drogheda
Killashee
Castlepollard
Clonmellon
NEWGRANGE
Duleek
Julianstown
Navan
L. Derravaragh
Ballinalack
Delvin
Athboy
Balbriggan
ARDGILLAN CASTLE
Naul
Skerries
L. Owel
Ballymahon
Ballivor
Trim
Boyne
Dunshaughlin
Ashbourne
Rush
Mullingar
Killucan
Rathmolyon
Ballymore
Lough Ennell
Kinnegad
Lambay I.
Swords
Malahide
Clonord
Enfield
Dunboyne
Moate
Ballynagore
Kilcock
Kilbeggan
Tyrrellspass
Edenderry
Lucan
Howth Hd.
Celbridge
Dublin
Dun Laoghaire
Clondalkin
Douglas 2:55
Holyhead 1:4
Liverpool 7:3
Daingean
Rathcoole
Tullamore
Tallaght
Dalkey
Sallins
Ferbane
Grand Canal
Bray
Holyhead 2:00
Killeigh
Rathangan
Liffey
Naas
Kilcormac
Newbridge
754 Kippure
Clonaslee
Portarlington
Barrow
Kildare
Blessington
Greystones
Wicklow Mountains
Kilcullen
Poulaphouca Res.
Slieve Bloom
Monasterevin
IRISH NATIONAL STUD
Mountmellick
Newtownmount-kennedy
Kinnitty
Roundwood
Dunlavin
Fontstown
Wicklow Mountains
Portlaoise
Laragh
529 Arderin
Mountrath
Rathnew
Glendalough
Athy
Timolin
Lugnaquilla 926
Wicklow
Roscrea
Borris-in-Ossory
Wicklow Hd.
Ballylynan
Baltinglass
Glenealy
Castledermot
Abbeyleix
Rathdrum
Rathvilly
Moneygall
Clogh
Aughrim
Mizen Hd.
Hacketstown
Durrow
Carlow
Croghan Mt. 607
Arklow
Ballyragget
Castlecomer
Tullow
Templemore
Johnstown
Coolgreany
Borrisoleigh
Freshford
Leighlinbridge
Shillelagh
Kilmichael Pt.
Ballon
Slaney
DUNMORE CAVES
Urlingford
Thurles
Paulstown
Carnew
Gorey
Bagenalstown
Holycross
Kilkenny
Bunclody
Littleton
Blackstairs Mts.
796 Mt. Leinster
Ballycanew
Gowran
Borris
Ballingarry
Ferns
Killenaule
Callan
Graiguenamanagh
Cahore Pt.
Thomastown
Enniscorthy
Fethard
Knocktopher
Nore
Clonroche
Newinn
Ninemilehouse
Blackwater
722 Slievenamon
Oilgate
New Ross
Castlebridge
Cahir
Clonmel
Carrick-on-Suir
Mullinavat
Wexford
Wexford Harbour
Comeragh Mts.
Suir
Monavullagh Mts.
Waterford
Rosslare
Fishguard 3:30
Pembroke 4:00
Kilmeadan
Arthurstown
Wellingtonbridge
Killinick
Rosslare Harbour
Passage East
Greenore Pt.
Kilmacthomas
Fethard
Cappoquin
Millstreet
Tramore
Dunmore East
Crossfarnoge Pt.
Kilmore Quay
Carnsore Pt.
Bunmahon
Annestown
Hook Hd.
Cherbourg 17:00
Roscoff 17:30
Tramore Bay
Waterford Harbour
Dungarvan
Dungarvan Harbour
Helvick Hd.
Youghal
Youghal Bay
0 10 20 miles
0 10 20 30 km

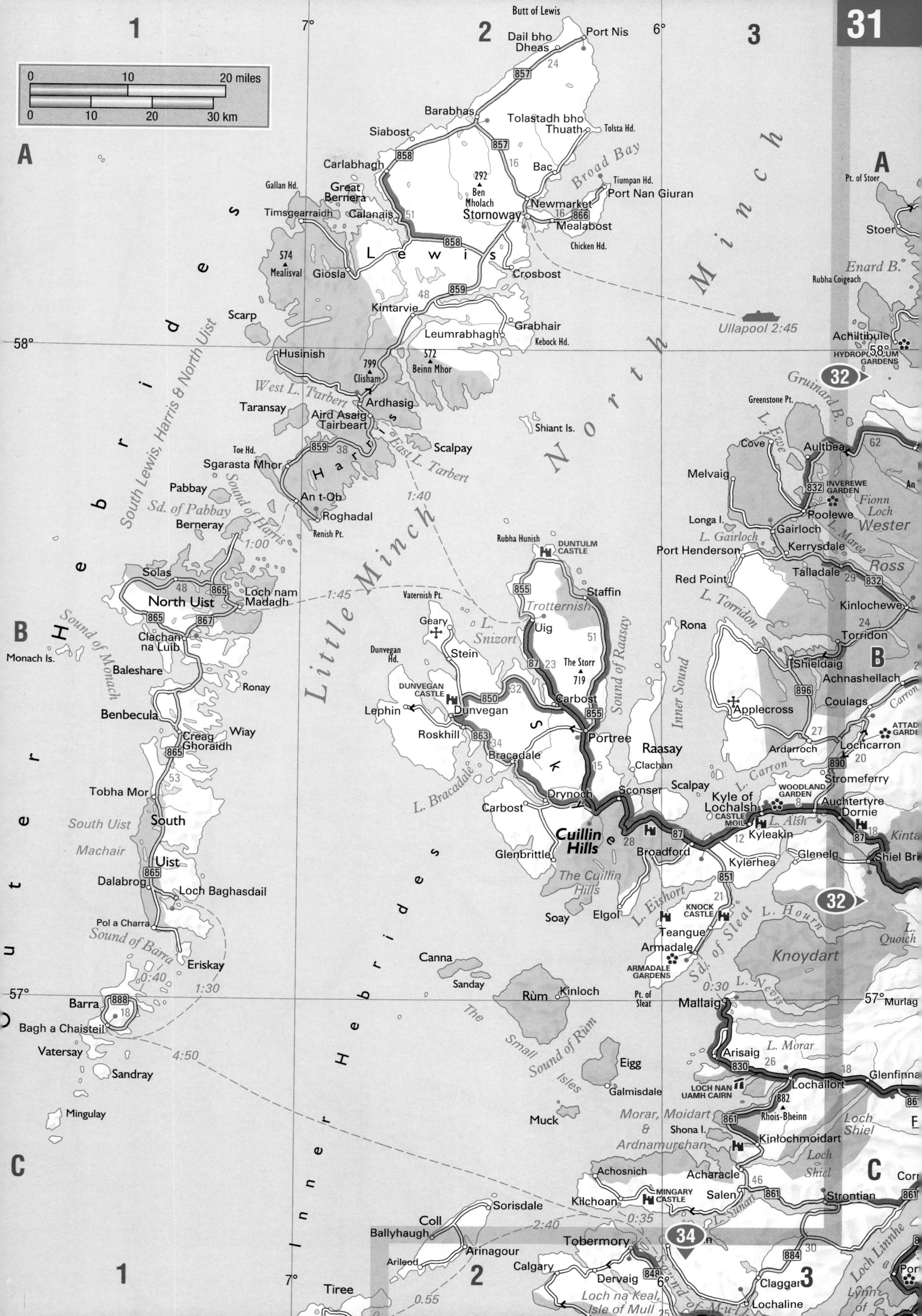

0 10 20 miles
0 10 20 30 km
Butt of Lewis
Port Nis
Dail bho Dheas
Barabhas
Siabost
Tolastadh bho Thuath
Tolsta Hd.
Carlabhagh
Broad Bay
Bac
Tiumpan Hd.
Port Nan Giuran
Gallan Hd.
Great Bernera
292 Ben Mholach
Newmarket
Timsgearraidh
Calanais
Stornoway
Mealabost
Chicken Hd.
Lewis
574 Mealisval
Giosla
Crosbost
Kintarvie
Scarp
Grabhair
Leumrabhagh
Kebock Hd.
Ullapool 2:45
North Minch
Husinish
799 Clisham
572 Beinn Mhor
West L. Tarbert
Ardhasig
Taransay
Aird Asaig
Tairbeart
Shiant Is.
Toe Hd.
Scalpay
Sgarasta Mhor
Harris
East L. Tarbert
Pabbay
Sound of Harris
An t-Ob
1:40
Sd. of Pabbay
Roghadal
Berneray
Renish Pt.
1:00
Little Minch
South Lewis, Harris & North Uist
Outer Hebrides
Solas
Loch nam Madadh
1:45
North Uist
Sound of Monach
Clachan na Luib
Monach Is.
Baleshare
Ronay
Benbecula
Wiay
Creag Ghoraidh
Tobha Mor
South Uist
South Uist Machair
Dalabrog
Loch Baghasdail
Pol a Charra
Sound of Barra
Eriskay
0:40
1:30
Barra
Bagh a Chaisteil
Vatersay
Sandray
4:50
Mingulay
Rubha Hunish
DUNTULM CASTLE
Staffin
Trotternish
Vaternish Pt.
Geary
L. Snizort
Uig
Dunvegan Hd.
Stein
The Storr 719
Sound of Raasay
DUNVEGAN CASTLE
Dunvegan
Lephin
Carbost
Portree
Roskhill
Bracadale
Raasay
Clachan
L. Bracadale
Skye
Carbost
Drynoch
Sconser
Scalpay
Cuillin Hills
Glenbrittle
Broadford
The Cuillin Hills
Soay
Elgol
L. Eishort
Rona
Inner Sound
Kyle of Lochalsh
CASTLE MOIL
Kyleakin
L. Alsh
Kylerhea
Glenelg
KNOCK CASTLE
Teangue
Armadale
ARMADALE GARDENS
Sd. of Sleat
Pt. of Sleat
Canna
Sanday
Rùm
Kinloch
The Small Isles
Sound of Rùm
Eigg
Galmisdale
Muck
Inner Hebrides
Mallaig
L. Nevis
Arisaig
L. Morar
LOCH NAN UAMH CAIRN
Lochailort
882 Rhois-Bheinn
Morar, Moidart & Ardnamurchan
Shona I.
Kinlochmoidart
Loch Shiel
Achosnich
Acharacle
Kilchoan
MINGARY CASTLE
Salen
L. Sunart
Strontian
0:35
Sorisdale
Coll
2:40
Ballyhaugh
Arinagour
Tobermory
Arileod
Calgary
Dervaig
Loch na Keal, Isle of Mull
Sound of Mull
Claggan
Lochaline
Loch Linnhe
Tiree
0.55
Pt. of Stoer
Stoer
Enard B.
Rubha Coigeach
Achiltibuie
HYDROPONICUM GARDENS
Gruinard B.
Greenstone Pt.
L. Ewe
Cove
Aultbea
Melvaig
INVEREWE GARDEN
Fionn Loch
Poolewe
Longa I.
Gairloch
L. Gairloch
L. Maree
Wester Ross
Port Henderson
Kerrysdale
Talladale
Red Point
L. Torridon
Kinlochewe
Torridon
Shieldaig
Achnashellach
Applecross
Coulags
Ardarroch
Lochcarron
L. Carron
Stromeferry
WOODLAND GARDEN
Auchtertyre
Dornie
Shiel Bridge
L. Hourn
Knoydart
L. Quoich
Glenfinnan
Murlag
0:30
58°
57°
7°
6°

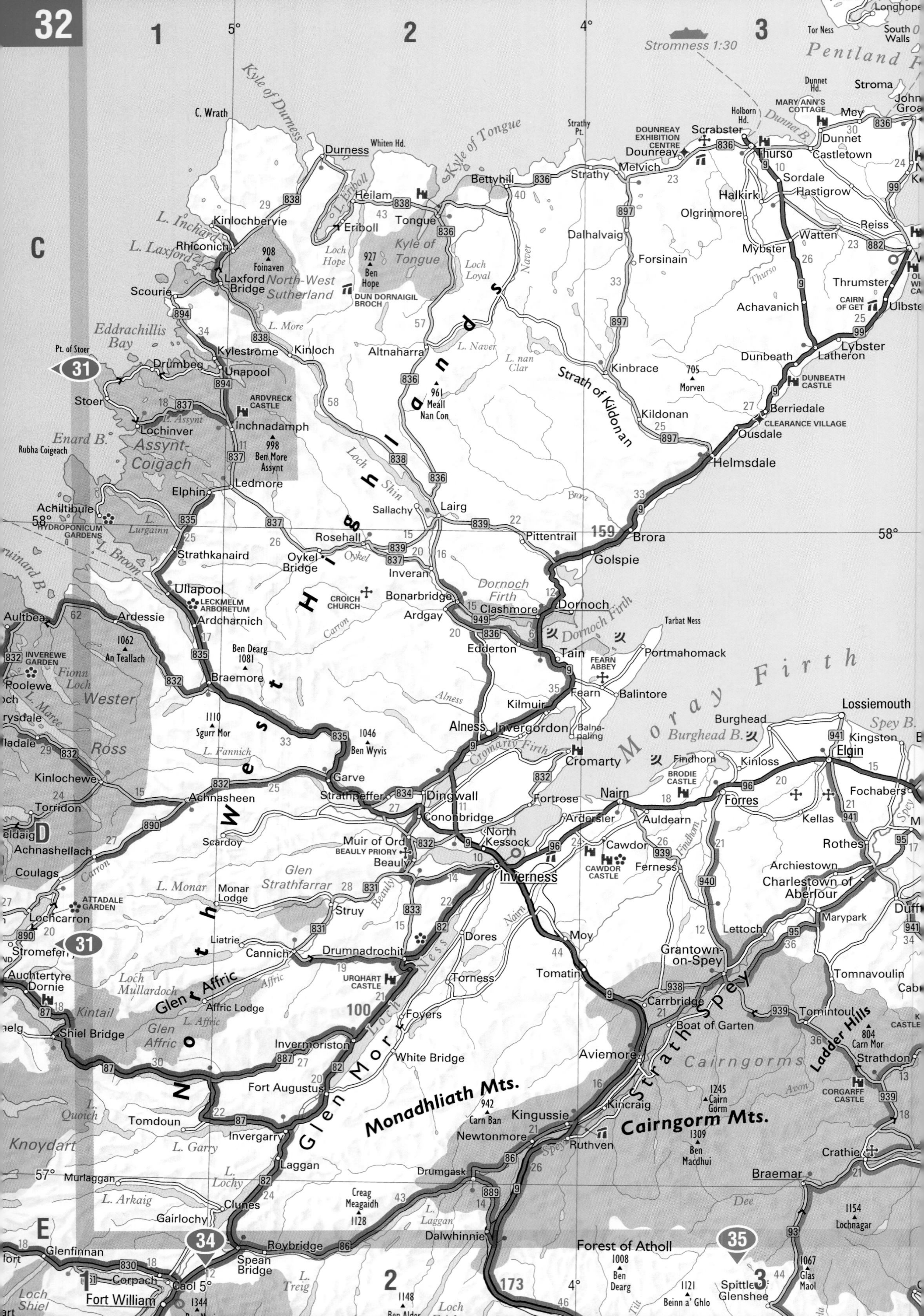

Stromness 1:30
Pentland F
C. Wrath
Kyle of Durness
Kyle of Tongue
Durness
Whiten Hd.
Bettyhill
Strathy
Melvich
Dounreay
DOUNREAY EXHIBITION CENTRE
Scrabster
Thurso
Dunnet
Castletown
Mey
Stroma
Dunnet Hd.
Holborn Hd.
MARY ANN'S COTTAGE
Dunnet B.
Kinlochbervie
L. Inchard
Rhiconich
L. Laxford
Laxford Bridge
Foinaven
North-West Sutherland
Scourie
Heilam
L. Eriboll
Eriboll
Tongue
Loch Hope
Ben Hope
DUN DORNAIGIL BROCH
Loch Loyal
Naver
Dalhalvaig
Forsinain
Halkirk
Olgrinmore
Sordale
Hastigrow
Mybster
Watten
Reiss
Thrumster
Achavanich
CAIRN OF GET
Ulbster
Lybster
Latheron
Dunbeath
DUNBEATH CASTLE
Eddrachillis Bay
Pt. of Stoer
Drumbeg
Kylestrome
Kinloch
L. More
Altnaharra
L. Naver
L. nan Clar
Kinbrace
Strath of Kildonan
Morven
Unapool
Stoer
ARDVRECK CASTLE
Inchnadamph
Lochinver
L. Assynt
Meall Nan Con
Kildonan
Berriedale
CLEARANCE VILLAGE
Ousdale
Helmsdale
Enard B.
Rubha Coigeach
Assynt-Coigach
Ben More Assynt
Loch Shin
Ledmore
Elphin
Achiltibuie
HYDROPONICUM GARDENS
L. Lurgainn
Sallachy
Lairg
Brora
Pittentrail
Golspie
58°
North West Highlands
Rosehall
Oykel
Oykel Bridge
Strathkanaird
L. Broom
Gruinard B.
Inveran
Dornoch Firth
Ullapool
LECKMELM ARBORETUM
CROICH CHURCH
Bonarbridge
Clashmore
Dornoch
Ardgay
Ardcharnich
Ardessie
Aultbea
An Teallach
INVEREWE GARDEN
Fionn Loch
Poolewe
Ben Dearg
Braemore
Carron
Edderton
Tain
Tarbat Ness
Portmahomack
FEARN ABBEY
Fearn
Balintore
Moray Firth
Wester Ross
L. Maree
Sgurr Mor
L. Fannich
Ben Wyvis
Alness
Kilmuir
Invergordon
Balnapaling
Burghead
Burghead B.
Lossiemouth
Spey B.
Kingston
Elgin
Kinloss
Findhorn
Cromarty Firth
Cromarty
Kinlochewe
Torridon
Garve
Achnasheen
Strathpeffer
Dingwall
Fortrose
Nairn
BRODIE CASTLE
Forres
Fochabers
Conon Bridge
Ardersier
Auldearn
Kellas
Achnashellach
Scardoy
Muir of Ord
BEAULY PRIORY
Beauly
North Kessock
Inverness
Cawdor
CAWDOR CASTLE
Ferness
Findhorn
Rothes
Archiestown
Charlestown of Aberlour
Coulags
L. Monar
Monar Lodge
Glen Strathfarrar
ATTADALE GARDEN
Lochcarron
Struy
Marypark
Stromeferry
Liatrie
Cannich
Drumnadrochit
Dores
Moy
Lettoch
Grantown-on-Spey
Auchtertyre
Dornie
Loch Mullardoch
Glen Affric
URQHART CASTLE
Torness
Tomatin
Tomnavoulin
Kintail
Affric Lodge
L. Affric
Foyers
Carrbridge
Boat of Garten
Tomintoul
Ladder Hills
Carn Mor
Shiel Bridge
Glen Affric
Invermoriston
Loch Ness
Strath Spey
Cairngorms
Strathdon
White Bridge
Aviemore
CORGARFF CASTLE
Avon
Fort Augustus
Monadhliath Mts.
Carn Ban
Kincraig
Cairn Gorm
L. Quoich
Tomdoun
Kingussie
Cairngorm Mts.
Glen Mor
Newtonmore
Ruthven
Ben Macdhui
Knoydart
Invergarry
L. Garry
Crathie
Laggan
Drumgask
Braemar
Murlaggan
57°
L. Lochy
L. Arkaig
Creag Meagaidh
Dee
Clunes
Gairlochy
L. Laggan
Lochnagar
Dalwhinnie
Glenfinnan
Roybridge
Forest of Atholl
Spean Bridge
Ben Dearg
Glas Maol
Corpach
Caol
Fort William
Ben Nevis
Loch Shiel
L. Treig
Ben Alder
Loch Ericht
Tilt
Beinn a' Ghlo
Spittle of Glenshee

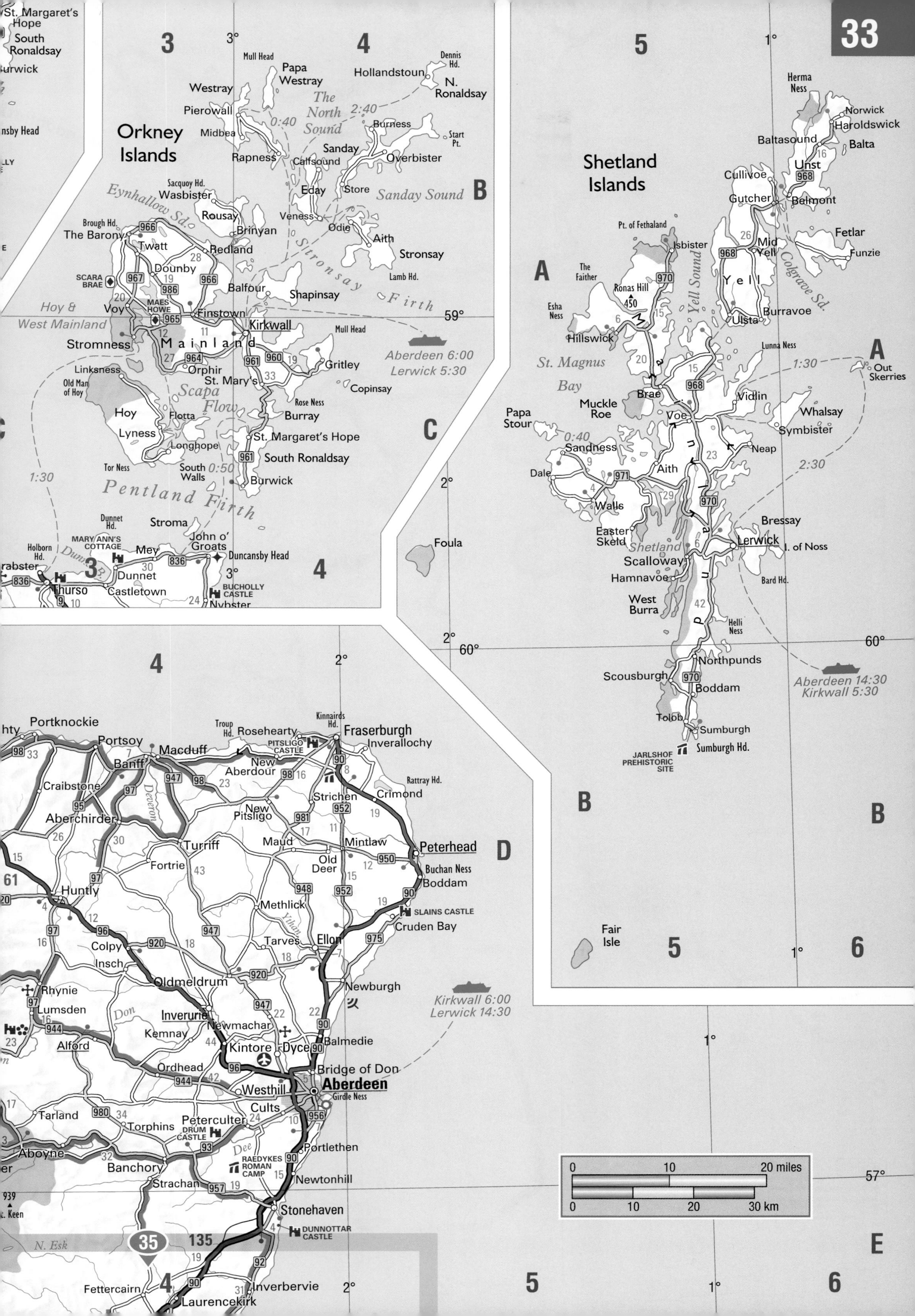

St. Margaret's
Hope
South
Ronaldsay
urwick

nsby Head

LY

E

Orkney Islands

Mull Head
Westray
Pierowall
Midbea
Rapness

Papa
Westray
The North Sound
0:40
2:40

Hollandstoun
Dennis Hd.
N. Ronaldsay
Burness
Start Pt.

Sacquoy Hd.
Wasbister
Rousay
Brinyan

Sanday
Calfsound
Eday
Veness
Ødie

Overbister
Store

B

Sanday Sound

Brough Hd.
The Barony
966
Twatt
Redland
967
986
Downby
966
20
Voy
MAES HOWE
965

Balfour
Shapinsay
Finstown
Kirkwall

Aith
Stronsay
Lamb Hd.

Stronsay Firth

59°

C

Mull Head
Gritley
Copinsay

Aberdeen 6:00
Lerwick 5:30

Stromness
27
964
Orphir
960
33
St. Mary's
19

Mainland
12
11

Linksness
Old Man of Hoy
Hoy
Lyness
Longhope

Flotta
Scapa Flow

Rose Ness
Burray
St. Margaret's Hope
South Ronaldsay

961

C

1:30
Tor Ness
Pentland Firth

South Walls
Burwick
0:50

Dunnet Hd.
Stroma

MARY ANN'S COTTAGE
Holborn Hd.
rabster
836
Mey
836
Dunnet
Castletown

John o'
Groats
Duncansby Head
BUCHOLLY CASTLE
Nybster

3

9
Thurso
10
24
30
4

Shetland Islands

Herma Ness
Norwick
Haroldswick
Balta
Baltasound
Unst
968
16

Pt. of Fethaland
Isbister
Cullivoe
Gutcher
Belmont
Mid Yell
Fetlar
Funzie

A
The Faither
Ronas Hill
450
6
Esha Ness
15
968
Yell
Ulsta
Burravoe

St. Magnus Bay
20
15
968
Brae
Lunna Ness
Out Skerries
1:30

A

Hillswick

Papa Stour
Muckle Roe
Voe
Vidlin
Whalsay
Symbister

Sandness
971
Aith
Neap
23
2:30

Dale
Walls
970

Easter Skeld
Shetland
Scalloway
Hamnavoe

Bressay
I. of Noss
Lerwick
Bard Hd.

West Burra
42
Helli Ness

2°
60°

Northpunds
Scousburgh
970
Boddam

Aberdeen 14:30
Kirkwall 5:30

2°
60°

Tolob
Sumburgh
Sumburgh Hd.
JARLSHOF PREHISTORIC SITE

B

(Mainland map)

4
2°

Portknockie
hty
Portsoy
98
33
Banff
Macduff
Craibstone
947
95
Aberchirder
97

Troup Hd.
Rosehearty
PITSLIGO CASTLE
New Aberdour
98
16
8

Kinnairds Hd.
Fraserburgh
Inverallochy

Strichen
981
952
New Pitsligo
17
11
Maud
19
Crimond

Rattray Hd.

B

15
26
30
Turriff
43
Fortrie
15
Old Deer
12
952
Mintlaw
950
Peterhead
Buchan Ness
Boddam

D

61
20
Huntly
97
12
Methlick
948
19
90
SLAINS CASTLE
Cruden Bay

97
96
Colpy
920
18
920
Tarves
975
Ellon

16
Insch
18
Oldmeldrum
Newburgh

Rhynie
97
Lumsden
16
944
944
Inverurie
Newmachar
22
22
Kemnay
Kintore
44
Dyce
90
Balmedie

Alford
23

Kirkwall 6:00
Lerwick 14:30

Ordhead
96
944
42
Westhill
Cults
Bridge of Don
Aberdeen
Girdle Ness

980
34
Torphins
DRUM CASTLE
Petercaster
93
24
10
956
Portlethen

Tarland
Rhynie

17

Aboyne
er
32
Banchory
Strachan
957
19

RAEDYKES ROMAN CAMP
15
Newtonhill

N. Esk
939
s. Keen

35
135
4
Fettercairn
19
Laurencekirk
90
92
Stonehaven
DUNNOTTAR CASTLE
Inverbervie
31

Fair Isle
5
1°
6

1°

0   10   20 miles
0   10   20   30 km

57°

E

5
1°
6

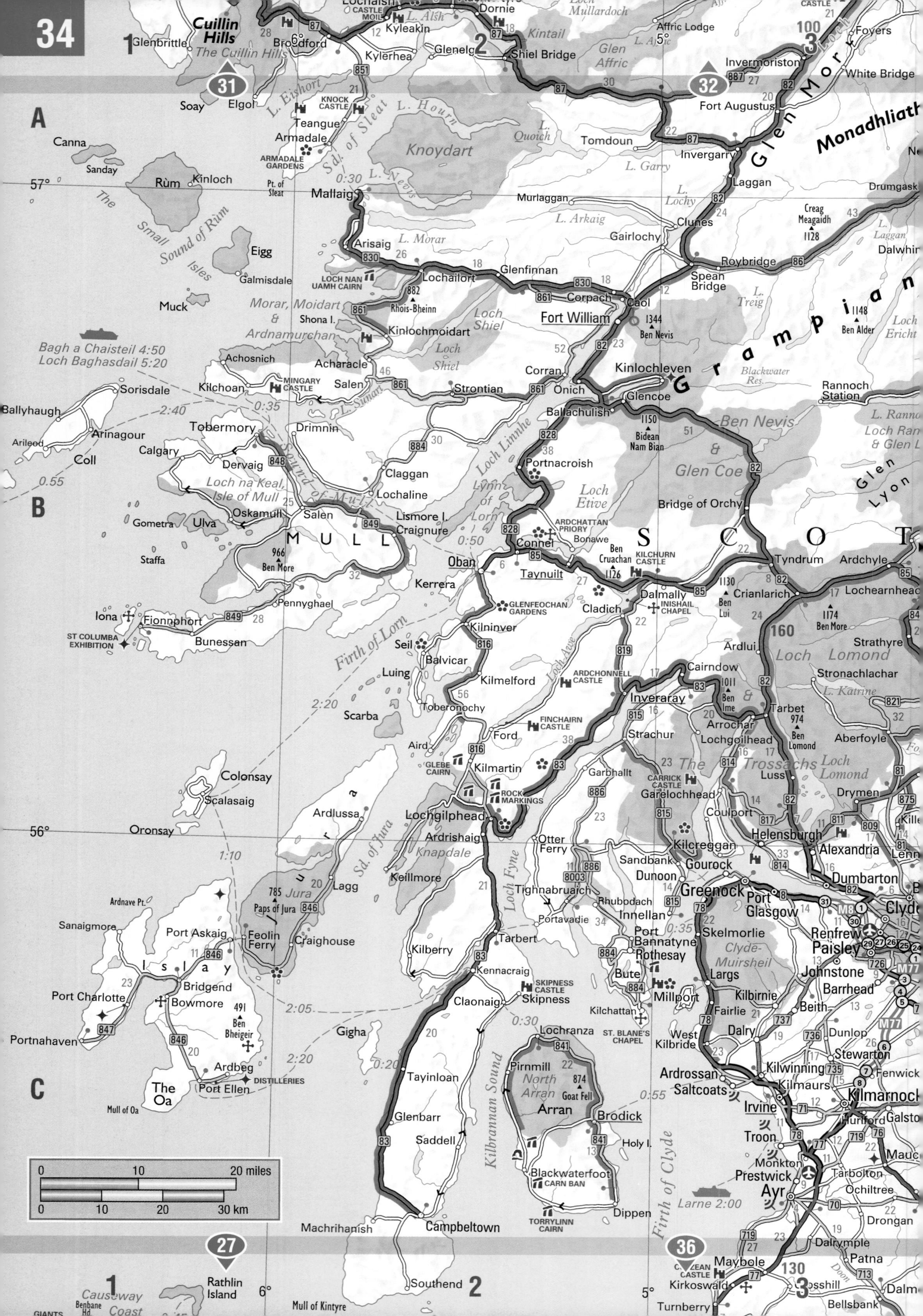

Cuillin Hills
The Cuillin Hills
Glenbrittle
Broadford
Kyleakin
Kylerhea
Dornie
Glenelg
Shiel Bridge
Kintail
L. Alsh
Loch Mullardoch
Glen Affric
Affric Lodge
L. Affric
Foyers
Invermoriston
White Bridge
Fort Augustus
Glen Mor
Loch Ness
Monadhliath
Soay
Elgol
L. Eishort
KNOCK CASTLE
Teangue
Armadale
ARMADALE GARDENS
Sd. of Sleat
L. Hourn
Knoydart
L. Quoich
Tomdoun
Invergarry
L. Garry
Laggan
Canna
Sanday
Rùm
Kinloch
The Small Isles
Sound of Rùm
Pt. of Sleat
Mallaig
L. Nevis
Murlaggan
L. Arkaig
L. Lochy
Clunes
Gairlochy
Creag Meagaidh
1128
L. Laggan
Drumgask
Dalwhinnie
Eigg
Galmisdale
Muck
Arisaig
L. Morar
LOCH NAN UAMH CAIRN
Lochailort
Glenfinnan
Corpach
Caol
Roybridge
Spean Bridge
L. Treig
Morar, Moidart & Ardnamurchan
Shona I.
882
Rhois-Bheinn
Kinlochmoidart
Loch Shiel
Fort William
1344
Ben Nevis
Grampian
1148
Ben Alder
Loch Ericht
Bagh a Chaisteil 4:50
Loch Baghasdail 5:20
Achosnich
Acharacle
Kilchoan
MINGARY CASTLE
Salen
L. Sunart
Strontian
Corran
Onich
Kinlochleven
Blackwater Res.
Rannoch Station
Glencoe
Ballachulish
Sorisdale
Ballyhaugh
Arinagour
Arileod
Coll
Tobermory
Drimnin
Calgary
Dervaig
Sound of Mull
Loch na Keal, Isle of Mull
Claggan
Lochaline
Loch Linnhe
Lynn of Lorn
1150
Bidean Nam Bian
Portnacroish
Ben Nevis & Glen Coe
Loch Etive
L. Rannoch
Loch Rannoch & Glen Lyon
Glen Lyon
Bridge of Orchy
Oskamull
Gometra
Ulva
Salen
Lismore I.
Craignure
MULL
ARDCHATTAN PRIORY
Bonawe
Connel
Ben Cruachan
1126
KILCHURN CASTLE
SCOTLAND
Tyndrum
Ardchyle
Staffa
966
Ben More
Oban
Taynuilt
Kerrera
Pennyghael
GLENFEOCHAN GARDENS
Cladich
Dalmally
INISHAIL CHAPEL
1130
Ben Lui
Crianlarich
Lochearnhead
1174
Ben More
Iona
Fionnphort
Bunessan
ST COLUMBA EXHIBITION
Firth of Lorn
Kilninver
Seil
Balvicar
Luing
Kilmelford
Loch Awe
ARDCHONNELL CASTLE
Ardlui
Loch Lomond
Strathyre
Stronachlachar
L. Katrine
Cairndow
1011
Ben Ime
Inveraray
Toberonochy
Scarba
FINCHAIRN CASTLE
Strachur
Arrochar
Tarbet
974
Ben Lomond
Aberfoyle
Lochgoilhead
Ford
Aird
GLEBE CAIRN
Kilmartin
Colonsay
Scalasaig
Garbhallt
The Trossachs
Loch Lomond
CARRICK CASTLE
Garelochhead
Luss
Drymen
ROCK MARKINGS
Lochgilphead
Ardlussa
Jura
Oronsay
Ardrishaig
Knapdale
Otter Ferry
Coulport
Helensburgh
Alexandria
Kilcreggan
Sandbank
Gourock
Dunoon
Dumbarton
Keillmore
Sd. of Jura
Loch Fyne
Tighnabruaich
Greenock
Port Glasgow
Ardnave Pt.
785
Paps of Jura
Lagg
Rhubodach
Innellan
Portavadie
Skelmorlie
Renfrew
Paisley
Clyde-Muirsheil
Sanaigmore
Port Askaig
Feolin Ferry
Craighouse
Tarbert
Port Bannatyne
Rothesay
Islay
Kilberry
Kennacraig
Bute
Largs
Johnstone
Barrhead
Bridgend
Port Charlotte
Bowmore
491
Ben Bheigeir
SKIPNESS CASTLE
Skipness
Claonaig
Millport
Kilchattan
Kilbirnie
Fairlie
Beith
Portnahaven
Gigha
Lochranza
ST. BLANE'S CHAPEL
West Kilbride
Dalry
Dunlop
Stewarton
Ardbeg
Port Ellen
The Oa
DISTILLERIES
Mull of Oa
Tayinloan
Pirnmill
North Arran
874
Goat Fell
Arran
Brodick
Kilbrannan Sound
Ardrossan
Saltcoats
Kilwinning
Kilmaurs
Fenwick
Kilmarnock
Irvine
Troon
Hurlford
Galston
Glenbarr
Saddell
Holy I.
Firth of Clyde
Monkton
Prestwick
Tarbolton
Ayr
Ochiltree
Blackwaterfoot
CARN BAN
Larne 2:00
Machrihanish
Campbeltown
TORRYLINN CAIRN
Dippen
Drongan
Dalrymple
Patna
Maybole
CULZEAN CASTLE
Kirkoswald
Crosshill
Southend
Mull of Kintyre
Rathlin Island
Causeway Coast
Benbane Hd.
GIANTS
Turnberry
Bellsbank
Doon
57°
56°
6°
5°
0 10 20 miles
0 10 20 30 km

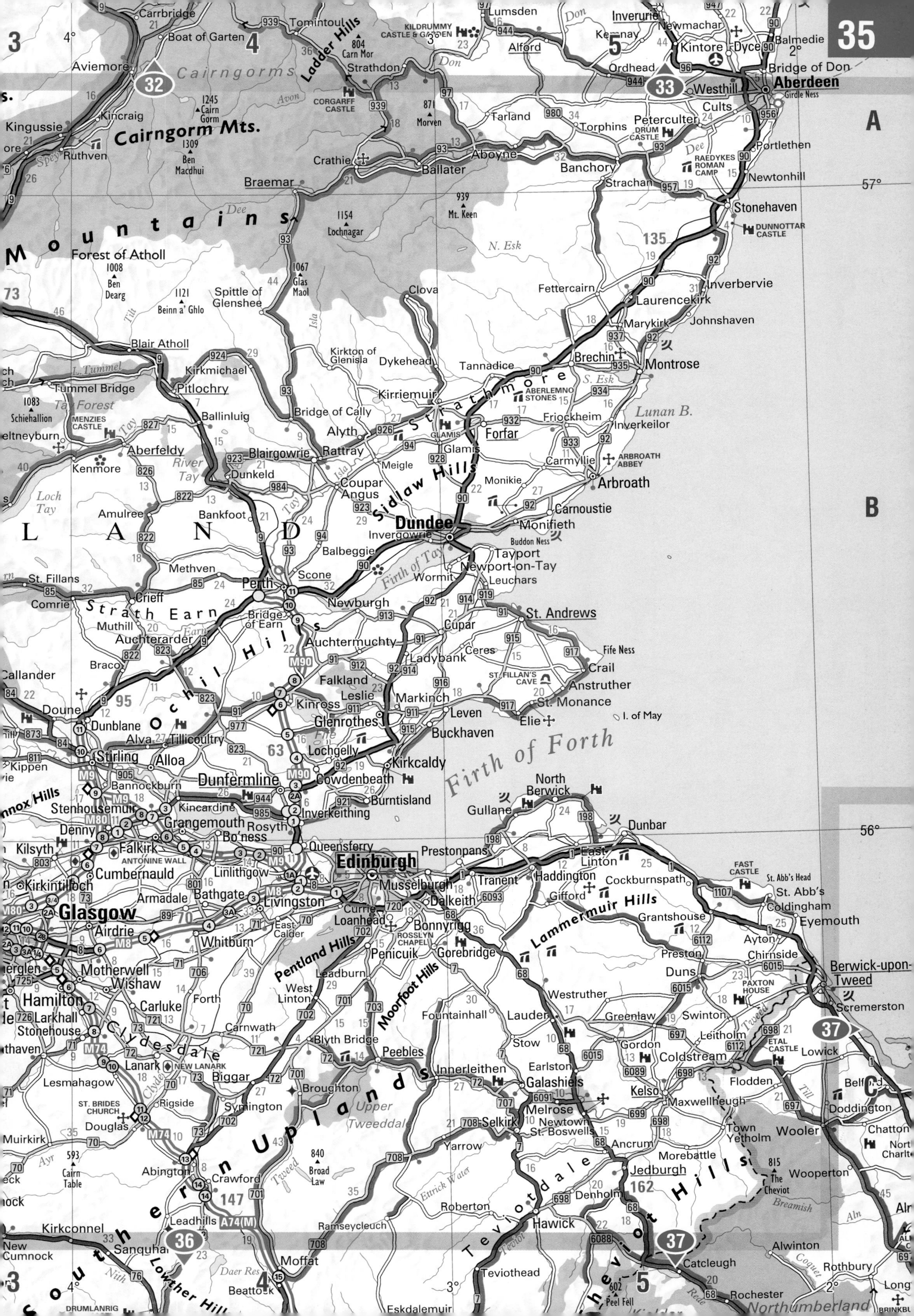
Carrbridge
Boat of Garten
Tomintoul
Ladder Hills
Lumsden
Inverurie
Kemnay
Newmachar
Kintore
Dyce
Balmedie
Aviemore
Cairngorms
Strathdon
Alford
Ordhead
Bridge of Don
Aberdeen
Girdle Ness
Westhill
Cults
Kingussie
Kincraig
Cairngorm Mts.
Corgarff Castle
Morven
Tarland
Torphins
Peterculter
Drum Castle
Portlethen
Ruthven
Ben Macdhui
Crathie
Ballater
Aboyne
Banchory
Raedykes Roman Camp
Newtonhill
Braemar
Strachan
Stonehaven
Dunnottar Castle
Mountains
Lochnagar
Mt. Keen
N. Esk
Forest of Atholl
Ben Dearg
Glas Maol
Spittle of Glenshee
Beinn a' Ghlo
Clova
Fettercairn
Inverbervie
Laurencekirk
Johnshaven
Marykirk
Blair Atholl
Kirkton of Glenisla
Dykehead
Tannadice
Brechin
Montrose
Kirkmichael
L. Tummel
Tummel Bridge
Pitlochry
Strathmore
S. Esk
Aberlemno Stones
Schiehallion
Tay Forest
Menzies Castle
Ballinluig
Bridge of Cally
Kirriemuir
Lunan B.
Alyth
Forfar
Friockheim
Inverkeilor
Kenmore
Aberfeldy
Blairgowrie
Rattray
Glamis
Arbroath Abbey
River Tay
Dunkeld
Meigle
Carmyllie
Arbroath
Loch Tay
Coupar Angus
Sidlaw Hills
Monikie
Carnoustie
Amulree
Bankfoot
Dundee
Monifieth
Invergowrie
Buddon Ness
Balbeggie
Tayport
Firth of Tay
Newport-on-Tay
Wormit
Leuchars
Methven
St. Fillans
Comrie
Crieff
Perth
Scone
Newburgh
Strath Earn
Bridge of Earn
Muthill
Auchterarder
Ochil Hills
Auchtermuchty
Cupar
St. Andrews
Ladybank
Ceres
Fife Ness
Crail
Callander
Braco
Falkland
St. Fillan's Cave
Anstruther
Kinross
Leslie
Markinch
St. Monance
Doune
Dunblane
Glenrothes
Leven
Elie
I. of May
Alva
Tillicoultry
Buckhaven
Firth of Forth
Stirling
Alloa
Lochgelly
Kirkcaldy
Kippen
Bannockburn
Dunfermline
Cowdenbeath
Burntisland
North Berwick
Stenhousemuir
Kincardine
Inverkeithing
Gullane
Denny
Grangemouth
Rosyth
Dunbar
Kilsyth
Falkirk
Bo'ness
Queensferry
Antonine Wall
Prestonpans
East Linton
Cumbernauld
Linlithgow
Edinburgh
Fast Castle
Kirkintilloch
Tranent
Haddington
Cockburnspath
St. Abb's Head
Armadale
Bathgate
Musselburgh
St. Abb's
Glasgow
Livingston
Currie
Dalkeith
Gifford
Coldingham
Airdrie
East Calder
Loanhead
Bonnyrigg
Lammermuir Hills
Grantshouse
Eyemouth
Whitburn
Rosslyn Chapel
Penicuik
Gorebridge
Ayton
Pentland Hills
Preston
Chirnside
Berwick-upon-Tweed
Motherwell
Wishaw
Leadburn
Moorfoot Hills
Duns
Paxton House
West Linton
Westruther
Hamilton
Carluke
Forth
Fountainhall
Lauder
Greenlaw
Swinton
Scremerston
Larkhall
Stonehouse
Clydesdale
Carnwath
Blyth Bridge
Stow
Gordon
Leitholm
Etal Castle
Lowick
Lanark
New Lanark
Peebles
Innerleithen
Earlston
Coldstream
Lesmahagow
Biggar
Broughton
Galashiels
Kelso
Flodden
Belford
St. Brides Church
Rigside
Symington
Upper Tweeddale
Melrose
Maxwellheugh
Doddington
Douglas
Selkirk
Newtown St. Boswells
Town Yetholm
Wooler
Chatton
Muirkirk
Yarrow
Ancrum
Morebattle
Cairn Table
Abington
Crawford
Broad Law
Teviotdale
Jedburgh
The Cheviot
Wooperton
Southern Uplands
Etrick Water
Denholm
Cheviot Hills
Breamish
Kirkconnel
Leadhills
Roberton
Hawick
New Cumnock
Sanquhar
Ramseycleuch
Alwinton
Moffat
Lowther Hills
Daer Res.
Teviothead
Catcleugh
Rothbury
Beattock
Peel Fell
Rochester
Drumlanrig
Eskdalemuir
Northumberland

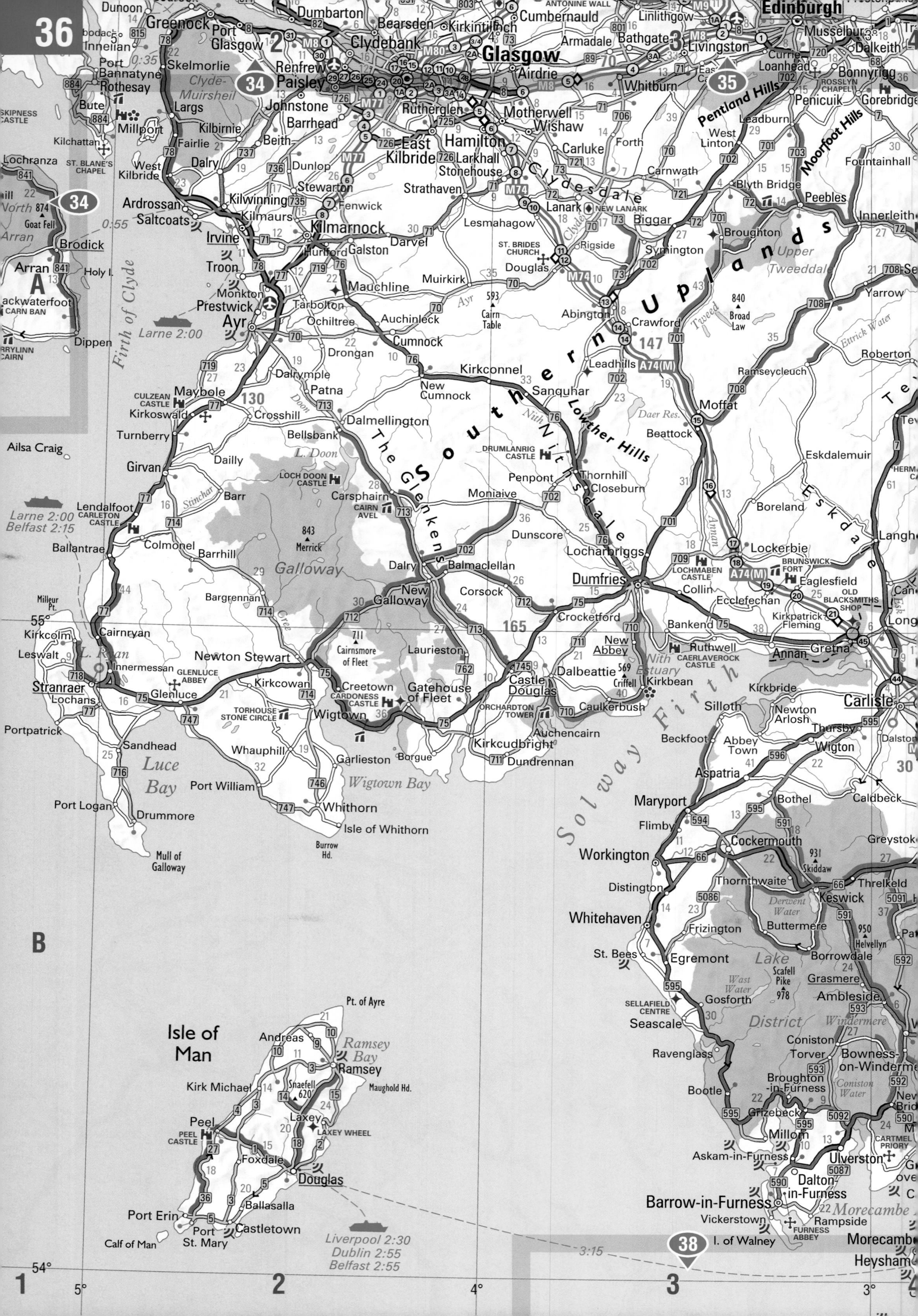
Dunoon
Greenock
Port Glasgow
Dumbarton
Bearsden
Kirkintilloch
Cumbernauld
ANTONINE WALL
Linlithgow
Edinburgh
Musselburgh
Dalkeith
Innellan
Clydebank
Glasgow
Armadale
Bathgate
Livingston
Currie
Loanhead
Bonnyrigg
Port Bannatyne
Skelmorlie
Renfrew
Paisley
Airdrie
Whitburn
ROSSLYN CHAPEL
Gorebridge
Rothesay
Clyde-Muirsheil
Johnstone
Rutherglen
Motherwell
Wishaw
Pentland Hills
Penicuik
SKIPNESS CASTLE
Bute
Largs
Barrhead
Leadburn
Millport
Kilbirnie
Fairlie
Beith
East Kilbride
Hamilton
Carluke
Forth
West Linton
Moorfoot Hills
Kilchattan
Lochranza
ST. BLANE'S CHAPEL
West Kilbride
Dalry
Dunlop
Larkhall
Stonehouse
Carnwath
Fountainhall
Stewarton
Strathaven
Clydesdale
Blyth Bridge
Peebles
North
Goat Fell
Arran
Ardrossan
Saltcoats
Kilwinning
Kilmaurs
Fenwick
Lanark
NEW LARKARK
Biggar
Innerleithen
Brodick
Irvine
Kilmarnock
Darvel
Lesmahagow
Broughton
Hurlford
Galston
ST. BRIDES CHURCH
Rigside
Symington
Upper Tweeddale
Holy I.
Troon
Douglas
Muirkirk
Mauchline
Southern Uplands
Yarrow
Blackwaterfoot
CARN BAN
Monkton
Prestwick
Tarbolton
Cairn Table
Abington
Broad Law
Crawford
Ayr
Ochiltree
Auchinleck
Tweed
Ettrick Water
Larne 2:00
Firth of Clyde
Dippen
Cumnock
Drongan
Roberton
Leadhills
Dalrymple
Kirkconnel
Ramseycleuch
CULZEAN CASTLE
Maybole
Patna
New Cumnock
Sanquhar
Lowther Hills
Moffat
Kirkoswald
Crosshill
Dalmellington
Daer Res.
Turnberry
Bellsbank
The Glenkens
Beattock
Ailsa Craig
L. Doon
DRUMLANRIG CASTLE
Eskdalemuir
Girvan
Dailly
LOCH DOON CASTLE
Thornhill
Nithsdale
Penpont
Closeburn
Carsphairn
Moniaive
Barr
Stinchar
CAIRN AVEL
Boreland
Eskdale
Larne 2:00
Belfast 2:15
Lendalfoot
CARLETON CASTLE
Merrick
Dunscore
Annan
Ballantrae
Colmonel
Barrhill
Lockerbie
Galloway
Dalry
Balmaclellan
Lochanbriggs
LOCHMABEN CASTLE
BRUNSWICK FORT
Eaglesfield
Dumfries
Collin
Milleur Pt.
Bargrennan
New Galloway
Corsock
Ecclefechan
OLD BLACKSMITHS SHOP
Crocketford
Bankend
Kirkpatrick Fleming
Kirkcolm
Cairnryan
Cairnsmore of Fleet
Laurieston
New Abbey
Annan
Gretna
Leswalt
L. Ryan
Newton Stewart
Ruthwell
Nith Estuary
CAERLAVEROCK CASTLE
Innermessan
GLENLUCE ABBEY
Dalbeattie
Criffell
Stranraer
Lochans
Glenluce
Kirkcowan
Creetown
Gatehouse of Fleet
CARDONESS CASTLE
Castle Douglas
Kirkbean
Kirkbride
Solway Firth
Silloth
Carlisle
Portpatrick
TORHOUSE STONE CIRCLE
Wigtown
ORCHARDTON TOWER
Caulkerbush
Newton Arlosh
Thursby
Sandhead
Auchencairn
Beckfoot
Abbey Town
Wigton
Dalston
Luce Bay
Whauphill
Garlieston
Borgue
Kirkcudbright
Dundrennan
Port William
Wigtown Bay
Aspatria
Port Logan
Drummore
Whithorn
Isle of Whithorn
Maryport
Bothel
Caldbeck
Flimby
Burrow Hd.
Mull of Galloway
Workington
Cockermouth
Skiddaw
Greystoke
Threlkeld
Distington
Thornthwaite
Keswick
Derwent Water
Whitehaven
Frizington
Buttermere
Helvellyn
St. Bees
Egremont
Lake District
Borrowdale
Wast Water
Scafell Pike
Grasmere
Ambleside
SELLAFIELD CENTRE
Gosforth
Seascale
Windermere
Pt. of Ayre
Isle of Man
Andreas
Ramsey Bay
Ramsey
Ravenglass
Coniston
Torver
Bowness-on-Windermere
Kirk Michael
Snaefell
Maughold Hd.
Broughton-in-Furness
Coniston Water
Bootle
Laxey
LAXEY WHEEL
Peel
PEEL CASTLE
Grizebeck
Millom
CARTMEL PRIORY
Foxdale
Askam-in-Furness
Ulverston
Douglas
Dalton-in-Furness
Ballasalla
Barrow-in-Furness
Morecambe
Port Erin
Port St. Mary
Castletown
Liverpool 2:30
Dublin 2:55
Belfast 2:55
Vickerstown
Rampside
FURNESS ABBEY
Calf of Man
I. of Walney
Heysham
Morecambe
34
35
38
A
B
1
2
3
5°
4°
3°
55°
54°

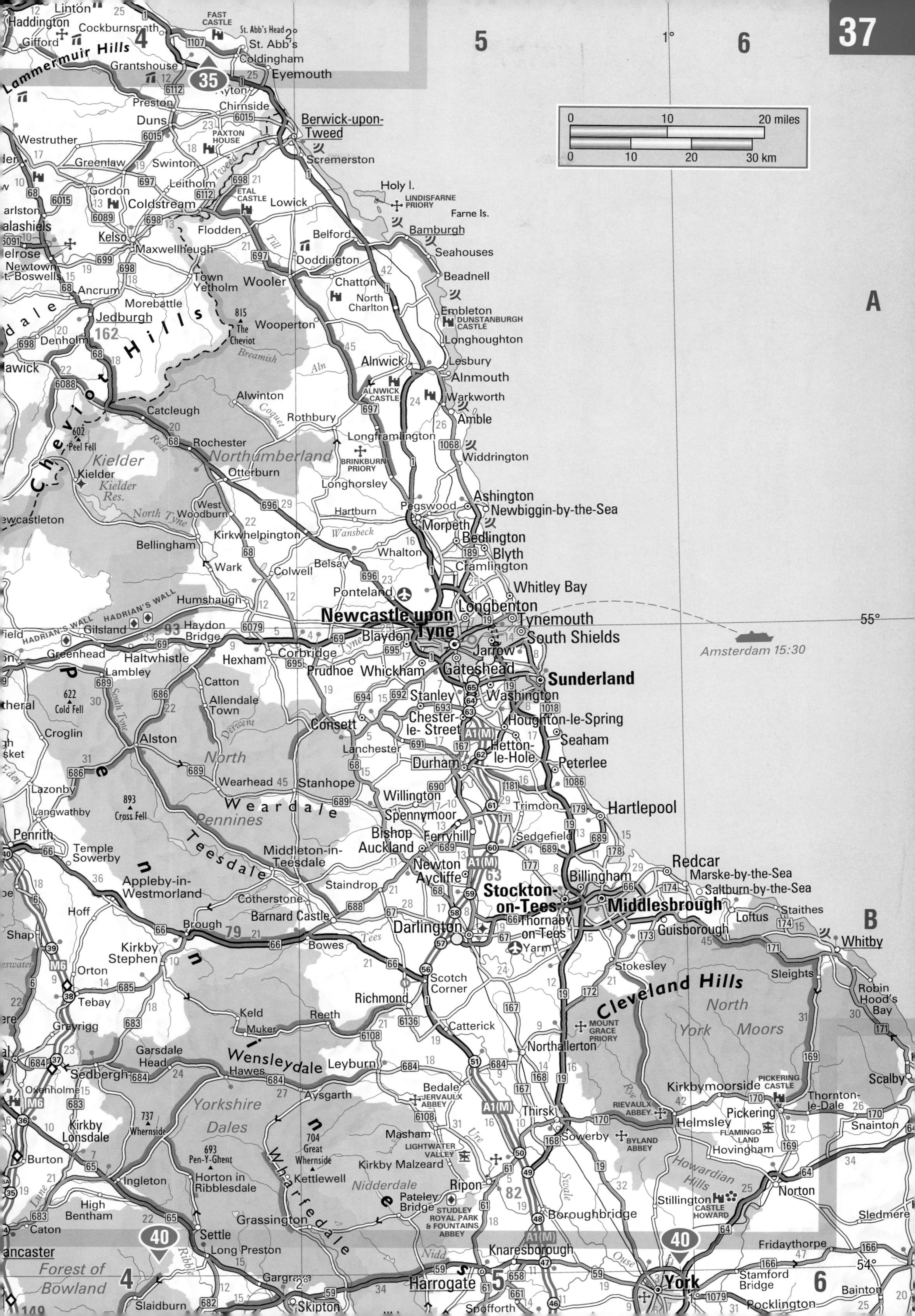
5
1°
6
0 10 20 miles
0 10 20 30 km
A
B
55°
54°
4
Linton
Haddington
Gifford
Cockburnspath
FAST CASTLE
St. Abb's Head
St. Abb's
Coldingham
Lammermuir Hills
Grantshouse
Eyemouth
Ayton
Preston
Chirnside
Duns
Berwick-upon-Tweed
PAXTON HOUSE
Westruther
Greenlaw
Swinton
Tweed
Scremerston
Gordon
Leitholm
ETAL CASTLE
Lowick
Holy I.
LINDISFARNE PRIORY
Farne Is.
Coldstream
Galashiels
Kelso
Flodden
Belford
Bamburgh
Melrose
Maxwellheugh
Till
Seahouses
Newtown St. Boswells
Doddington
Beadnell
Town Yetholm
Wooler
Chatton
Ancrum
Morebattle
North Charlton
Embleton
DUNSTANBURGH CASTLE
Jedburgh
Cheviot Hills
The Cheviot
Wooperton
Longhoughton
Denholm
Breamish
Aln
Alnwick
Lesbury
Hawick
ALNWICK CASTLE
Alnmouth
Alwinton
Coquet
Warkworth
Catcleugh
Rothbury
Amble
Peel Fell
Rochester
Longframlington
BRINKBURN PRIORY
Widdrington
Kielder
Northumberland
Otterburn
Kielder Res.
Longhorsley
Ashington
North Tyne
West Woodburn
Hartburn
Pegswood
Newbiggin-by-the-Sea
Newcastleton
Morpeth
Kirkwhelpington
Wansbeck
Bedlington
Bellingham
Whalton
Blyth
Wark
Colwell
Belsay
Cramlington
Whitley Bay
Ponteland
Humshaugh
HADRIAN'S WALL
Longbenton
Gilsland
Haydon Bridge
Newcastle upon Tyne
Tynemouth
South Shields
Greenhead
Haltwhistle
Hexham
Corbridge
Blaydon
Jarrow
Amsterdam 15:30
Lambley
Prudhoe
Whickham
Gateshead
Sunderland
Catton
Stanley
Washington
Cold Fell
Allendale Town
Chester-le-Street
Houghton-le-Spring
Croglin
Alston
Consett
Seaham
Derwent
Lanchester
Hetton-le-Hole
North
Durham
Peterlee
Eden
Wearhead
Stanhope
Lazonby
Weardale
Willington
Hartlepool
Cross Fell
Trimdon
Langwathby
Spennymoor
Pennines
Sedgefield
Penrith
Bishop Auckland
Ferryhill
Temple Sowerby
Middleton-in-Teesdale
Redcar
Teesdale
Newton Aycliffe
Marske-by-the-Sea
Billingham
Appleby-in-Westmorland
Staindrop
Stockton-on-Tees
Saltburn-by-the-Sea
Cotherstone
Middlesbrough
Staithes
Hoff
Barnard Castle
Thornaby on-Tees
Loftus
Brough
Darlington
Guisborough
Whitby
Shap
Kirkby Stephen
Bowes
Tees
Yarm
Stokesley
Orton
Scotch Corner
Sleights
Tebay
Richmond
Cleveland Hills
Robin Hood's Bay
North York Moors
Keld
Reeth
Grayrigg
Muker
Catterick
MOUNT GRACE PRIORY
Garsdale Head
Wensleydale
Leyburn
Northallerton
Sedbergh
Hawes
Bedale
Scalby
Oxenholme
Aysgarth
Kirkbymoorside
PICKERING CASTLE
Thornton-le-Dale
JERVAULX ABBEY
Yorkshire Dales
Rye
RIEVAULX ABBEY
Thirsk
Helmsley
Pickering
Kirkby Lonsdale
Whernside
Great Whernside
Masham
Sowerby
BYLAND ABBEY
FLAMINGO LAND
Snainton
Burton
Pen-Y-Ghent
LIGHTWATER VALLEY
Ure
Hovingham
Kirkby Malzeard
Ingleton
Horton in Ribblesdale
Kettlewell
Wharfedale
Nidderdale
Ripon
Howardian Hills
Lune
Swale
Norton
High Bentham
Pateley Bridge
STUDLEY ROYAL PARK & FOUNTAINS ABBEY
Stillington
CASTLE HOWARD
Boroughbridge
Sledmere
Caton
Settle
Grassington
Lancaster
Long Preston
Ribble
Nidd
Knaresborough
Ouse
Fridaythorpe
Forest of Bowland
Gargrave
Harrogate
York
Stamford Bridge
Slaidburn
Skipton
Spofforth
Pocklington
Bainton
M6
A1(M)
35
40
162
93
79
63
82

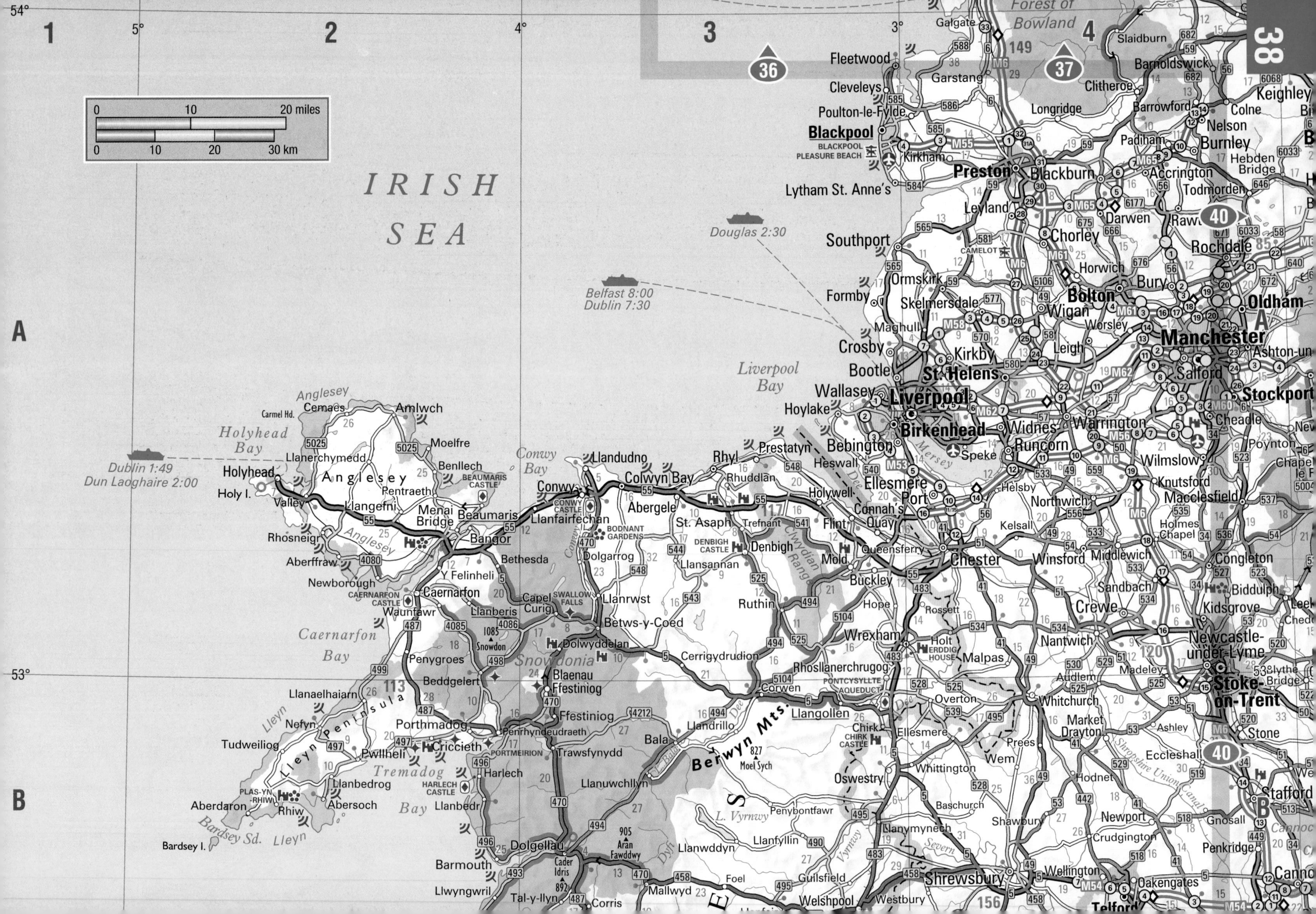

IRISH SEA
0 10 20 miles
0 10 20 30 km
Douglas 2:30
Belfast 8:00
Dublin 7:30
Dublin 1:49
Dun Laoghaire 2:00
Liverpool Bay
Holyhead Bay
Conwy Bay
Caernarfon Bay
Tremadog Bay
Bardsey Sd.
Forest of Bowland
Anglesey
Carmel Hd.
Cemaes
Amlwch
Moelfre
Benllech
Llanerchymedd
Pentraeth
Holyhead
Holy I.
Valley
Llangefni
Menai Bridge
Beaumaris
BEAUMARIS CASTLE
Rhosneigr
Aberffraw
Newborough
Bangor
Bethesda
Y Felinheli
Caernarfon
CAERNARFON CASTLE
Waunfawr
Llanberis
Snowdon
Penygroes
Beddgelert
Snowdonia
Llanaelhaiarn
Lleyn Peninsula
Nefyn
Tudweiliog
Pwllheli
Porthmadog
Criccieth
Llanbedrog
Abersoch
PLAS-YN-RHIW
Rhiw
Aberdaron
Bardsey I.
Lleyn
Penrhyndeudraeth
PORTMEIRION
Harlech
HARLECH CASTLE
Llanbedr
Barmouth
Dolgellau
Llwyngwril
Tal-y-llyn
Cader Idris
Corris
Mallwyd
Foel
Aran Fawddwy
Llanuwchllyn
Trawsfynydd
Ffestiniog
Blaenau Ffestiniog
Dolwyddelan
Capel Curig
SWALLOW FALLS
Betws-y-Coed
Llanrwst
Dolgarrog
Conwy
CONWY CASTLE
Llanfairfechan
Llandudno
Colwyn Bay
Abergele
BODNANT GARDENS
St. Asaph
Rhyl
Rhuddlan
Prestatyn
Trefnant
Denbigh
DENBIGH CASTLE
Llansannan
Ruthin
Cerrigydrudion
Clwydian Range
Bala
Llandrillo
Corwen
Berwyn Mts.
Moel Sych
Llangollen
Chirk
CHIRK CASTLE
Oswestry
L. Vyrnwy
Llanwddyn
Llanfyllin
Penybontfawr
Llanymynech
Guilsfield
Welshpool
Westbury
Shrewsbury
Baschurch
Whittington
Ellesmere
Overton
PONTCYSYLLTE AQUEDUCT
Rhosllanerchrugog
Wrexham
Holt
ERDDIG HOUSE
Rossett
Hope
Mold
Buckley
Flint
Holywell
Queensferry
Connah's Quay
Heswall
Hoylake
Wallasey
Birkenhead
Bebington
Ellesmere Port
Chester
Liverpool
Bootle
Crosby
Formby
Maghull
Southport
Ormskirk
Skelmersdale
St. Helens
Kirkby
Widnes
Runcorn
Speke
Helsby
Warrington
Wigan
Leigh
Bolton
Horwich
Chorley
Leyland
Preston
Blackpool
BLACKPOOL PLEASURE BEACH
Lytham St. Anne's
Kirkham
Poulton-le-Fylde
Cleveleys
Fleetwood
Garstang
Galgate
Longridge
Clitheroe
Slaidburn
Barnoldswick
Barrowford
Nelson
Colne
Burnley
Padiham
Accrington
Blackburn
Darwen
Hebden Bridge
Todmorden
Rochdale
Bury
Worsley
Manchester
Salford
Oldham
Ashton-under-Lyne
Stockport
Cheadle
Poynton
Wilmslow
Knutsford
Macclesfield
Holmes Chapel
Northwich
Kelsall
Winsford
Middlewich
Sandbach
Congleton
Biddulph
Kidsgrove
Crewe
Nantwich
Malpas
Audlem
Whitchurch
Market Drayton
Prees
Wem
Hodnet
Shawbury
Newport
Crudgington
Wellington
Telford
Oakengates
Madeley
Newcastle-under-Lyme
Stoke-on-Trent
Ashley
Stone
Eccleshall
Shropshire Union Canal
Stafford
Gnosall
Penkridge
Cannock
Keighley
CAMELOT
Dee
Mersey
Severn
Vyrnwy
Dyfi

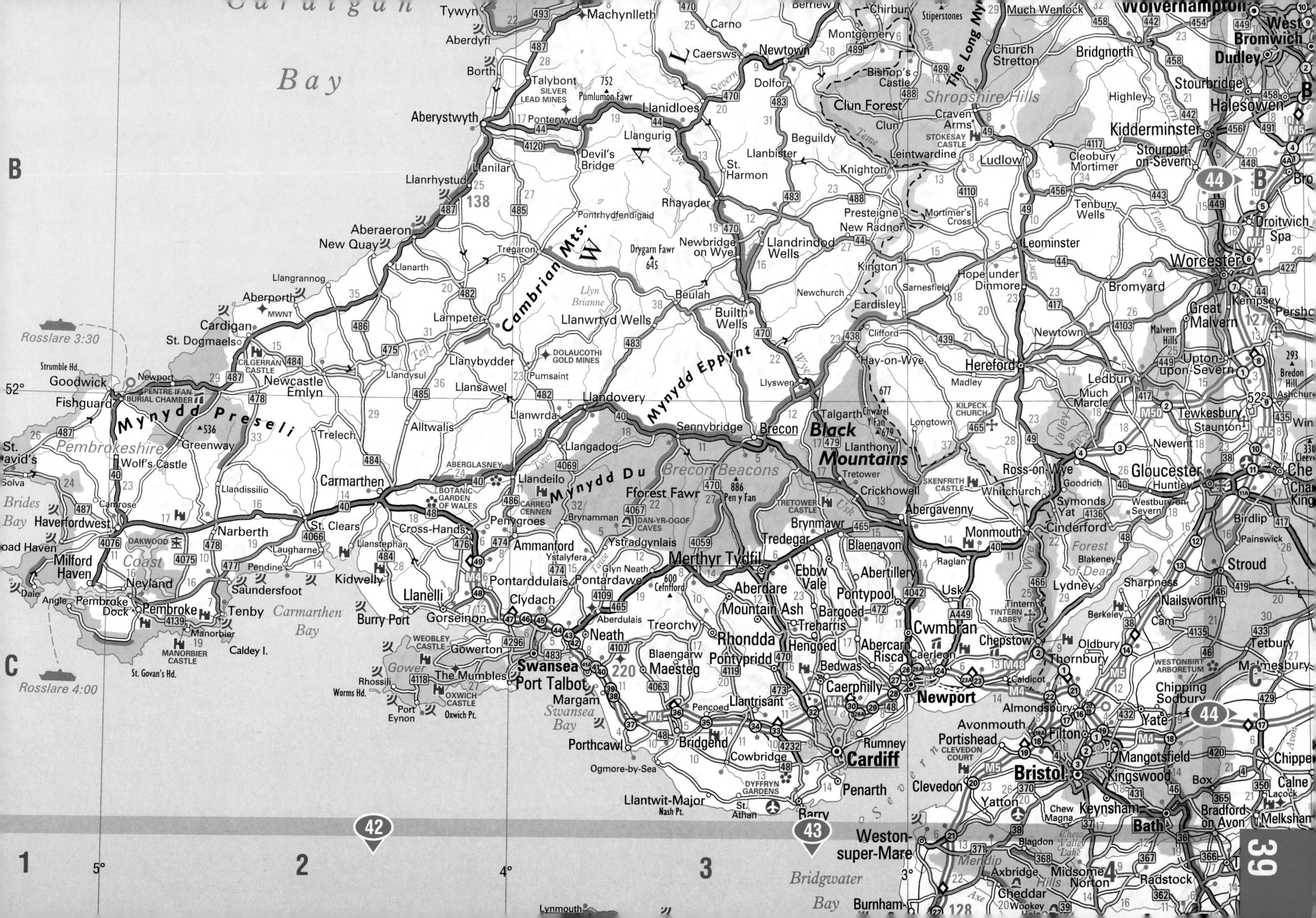

39
Bay
Rosslare 3:30
Rosslare 4:00
Bridgwater Bay
Carmarthen Bay
Swansea Bay
Mynydd Preseli
Cambrian Mts.
Mynydd Eppynt
Mynydd Du
Brecon Beacons
Black Mountains
Shropshire Hills
The Long Mynd
Clun Forest
Forest of Dean
Pembrokeshire Coast
Gower
Mendip Hills
Fishguard
Goodwick
Strumble Hd.
Newport
St. Davids
Solva
Haverfordwest
Milford Haven
Pembroke Dock
Pembroke
Neyland
Tenby
Saundersfoot
Caldey I.
St. Govan's Hd.
Cardigan
St. Dogmaels
Aberporth
New Quay
Aberaeron
Aberystwyth
Borth
Aberdyfi
Tywyn
Machynlleth
Llanidloes
Newtown
Carno
Caersws
Rhayader
Builth Wells
Llandrindod Wells
Lampeter
Llandovery
Carmarthen
St. Clears
Narberth
Kidwelly
Llanelli
Burry Port
Swansea
Port Talbot
Neath
Merthyr Tydfil
Aberdare
Rhondda
Pontypridd
Bridgend
Caerphilly
Cardiff
Penarth
Barry
Newport
Cwmbran
Pontypool
Abergavenny
Monmouth
Chepstow
Brecon
Hay-on-Wye
Hereford
Leominster
Ludlow
Ross-on-Wye
Gloucester
Stroud
Tewkesbury
Great Malvern
Worcester
Kidderminster
Bridgnorth
Stourbridge
Halesowen
Dudley
West Bromwich
Wolverhampton
Droitwich Spa
Bristol
Bath
Clevedon
Weston-super-Mare
Burnham-
Cheddar
Radstock
Chippenham
Calne
Melksham
Malmesbury
Tetbury
Yate
Chipping Sodbury

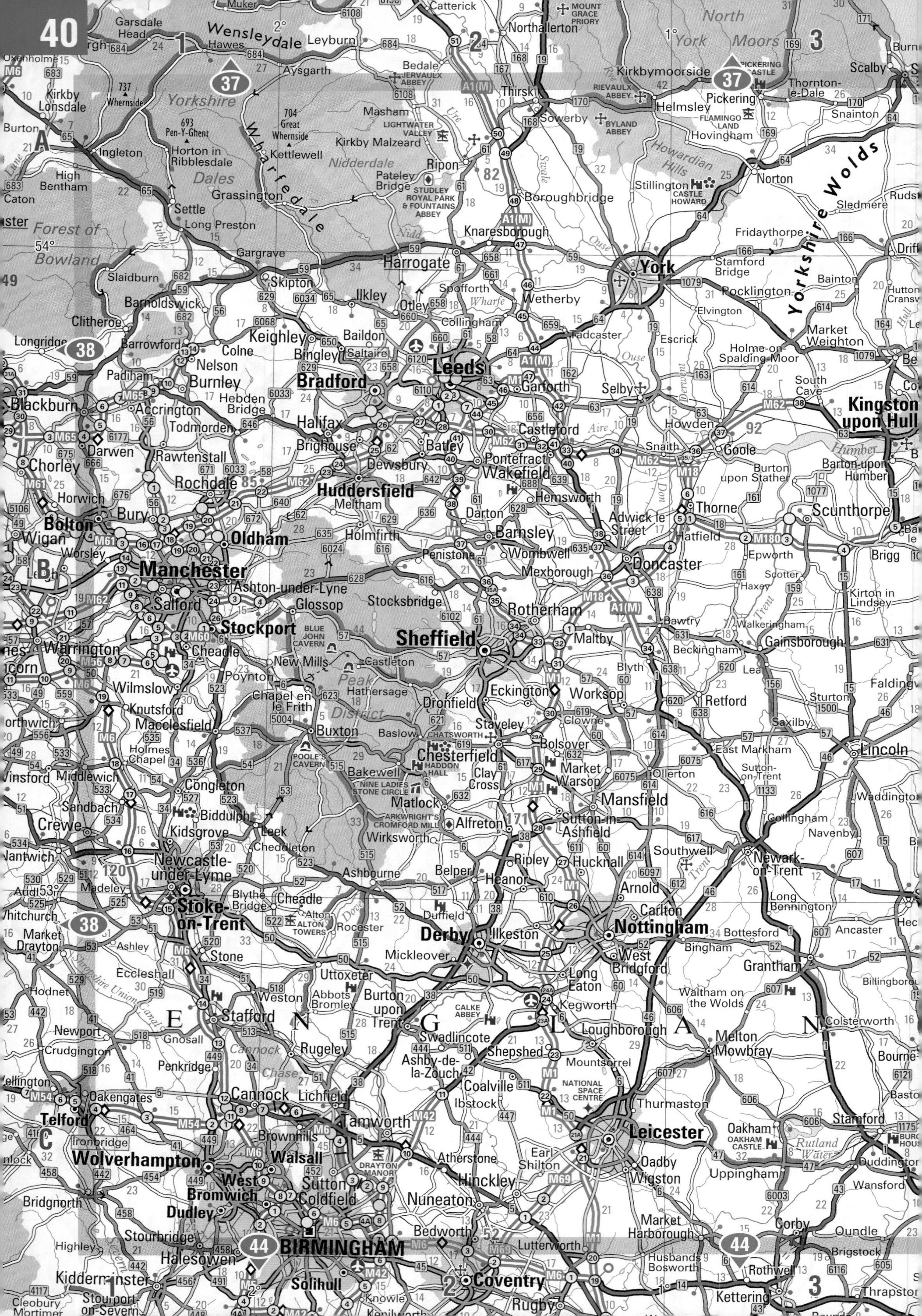
Garsdale Head
Wensleydale
Hawes
Leyburn
Catterick
Northallerton
MOUNT GRACE PRIORY
North York Moors
Oxenholme
Aysgarth
Bedale
JERVAULX ABBEY
Thirsk
Kirkbymoorside
RIEVAULX ABBEY
Helmsley
PICKERING CASTLE
Pickering
Thornton-le-Dale
Scalby
Kirkby Lonsdale
Whernside
Yorkshire
Masham
LIGHTWATER VALLEY
Sowerby
BYLAND ABBEY
FLAMINGO LAND
Hovingham
Snainton
Burton
Pen-Y-Ghent
Great Whernside
Kirkby Malzeard
Wharfedale
Ingleton
Horton in Ribblesdale
Kettlewell
Nidderdale
Ripon
Howardian Hills
High Bentham
Dales
Pateley Bridge
STUDLEY ROYAL PARK & FOUNTAINS ABBEY
Stillington
CASTLE HOWARD
Norton
Yorkshire Wolds
Caton
Grassington
Boroughbridge
Sledmere
Settle
Long Preston
Knaresborough
Fridaythorpe
Forest of Bowland
Gargrave
Harrogate
York
Stamford Bridge
Slaidburn
Skipton
Spofforth
Wetherby
Pocklington
Bainton
Barnoldswick
Ilkley
Otley
Collingham
Elvington
Clitheroe
Keighley
Baildon
Tadcaster
Escrick
Market Weighton
Longridge
Barrowford
Colne
Nelson
Bingley
Saltaire
Leeds
Holme-on-Spalding-Moor
Padiham
Burnley
Bradford
Garforth
Selby
South Cave
Blackburn
Accrington
Hebden Bridge
Halifax
Castleford
Howden
Kingston upon Hull
Todmorden
Brighouse
Batley
Snaith
Goole
Darwen
Rawtenstall
Dewsbury
Pontefract
Wakefield
Burton upon Stather
Barton-upon-Humber
Humber
Chorley
Rochdale
Huddersfield
Hemsworth
Horwich
Bury
Meltham
Darton
Adwick le Street
Thorne
Scunthorpe
Bolton
Oldham
Holmfirth
Barnsley
Hatfield
Wigan
Worsley
Penistone
Wombwell
Doncaster
Epworth
Brigg
Manchester
Mexborough
Ashton-under-Lyne
Glossop
Stocksbridge
Rotherham
Haxey
Scotter
Kirton in Lindsey
Salford
Stockport
BLUE JOHN CAVERN
Sheffield
Maltby
Bawtry
Walkeringham
Gainsborough
Warrington
Cheadle
New Mills
Castleton
Beckingham
Blyth
Wilmslow
Poynton
Peak District
Hathersage
Eckington
Worksop
Retford
Faldingworth
Knutsford
Chapel en le Frith
Dronfield
Clowne
Sturton
Northwich
Macclesfield
Buxton
Baslow
Staveley
CHATSWORTH
Saxilby
Holmes Chapel
POOLE'S CAVERN
Chesterfield
HADDON HALL
Bolsover
East Markham
Lincoln
Winsford
Middlewich
Bakewell
Clay Cross
Market Warsop
Ollerton
Sutton-on-Trent
Congleton
NINE LADIES STONE CIRCLE
Matlock
Mansfield
Waddington
Sandbach
Biddulph
ARKWRIGHT'S CROMFORD MILL
Alfreton
Sutton-in-Ashfield
Collingham
Navenby
Crewe
Kidsgrove
Leek
Wirksworth
Southwell
Nantwich
Cheddleton
Ripley
Hucknall
Newark-on-Trent
Newcastle-under-Lyme
Ashbourne
Belper
Heanor
Madeley
Blythe Bridge
Cheadle
Arnold
Long Bennington
Whitchurch
Stoke-on-Trent
Alton
ALTON TOWERS
Rocester
Duffield
Carlton
Market Drayton
Ashley
Derby
Ilkeston
Nottingham
Bottesford
Ancaster
Stone
Mickleover
West Bridgford
Bingham
Eccleshall
Uttoxeter
Grantham
Long Eaton
Shropshire Union Canal
Hodnet
Weston
Abbots Bromley
Burton upon Trent
CALKE ABBEY
Kegworth
Waltham on the Wolds
Billingborough
Newport
Gnosall
Stafford
Colsterworth
Crudgington
Cannock Chase
Rugeley
Swadlincote
Loughborough
Melton Mowbray
Bourne
Penkridge
Ashby-de-la-Zouch
Shepshed
Mountsorrel
Wellington
Oakengates
Cannock
Lichfield
Coalville
NATIONAL SPACE CENTRE
Ibstock
Thurmaston
Telford
Tamworth
Leicester
Oakham
OAKHAM CASTLE
Rutland Water
Stamford
Ironbridge
Brownhills
Walsall
Atherstone
Earl Shilton
Oadby
Uppingham
Duddington
Wolverhampton
DRAYTON MANOR
Wigston
Wansford
West Bromwich
Sutton Coldfield
Hinckley
Bridgnorth
Dudley
Nuneaton
Market Harborough
Corby
Oundle
Stourbridge
Bedworth
Highley
BIRMINGHAM
Lutterworth
Husbands Bosworth
Brigstock
Halesowen
Rothwell
Kidderminster
Solihull
Coventry
Stourport-on-Severn
Knowle
Rugby
Kettering
Thrapston
Cleobury Mortimer
ENGLAND

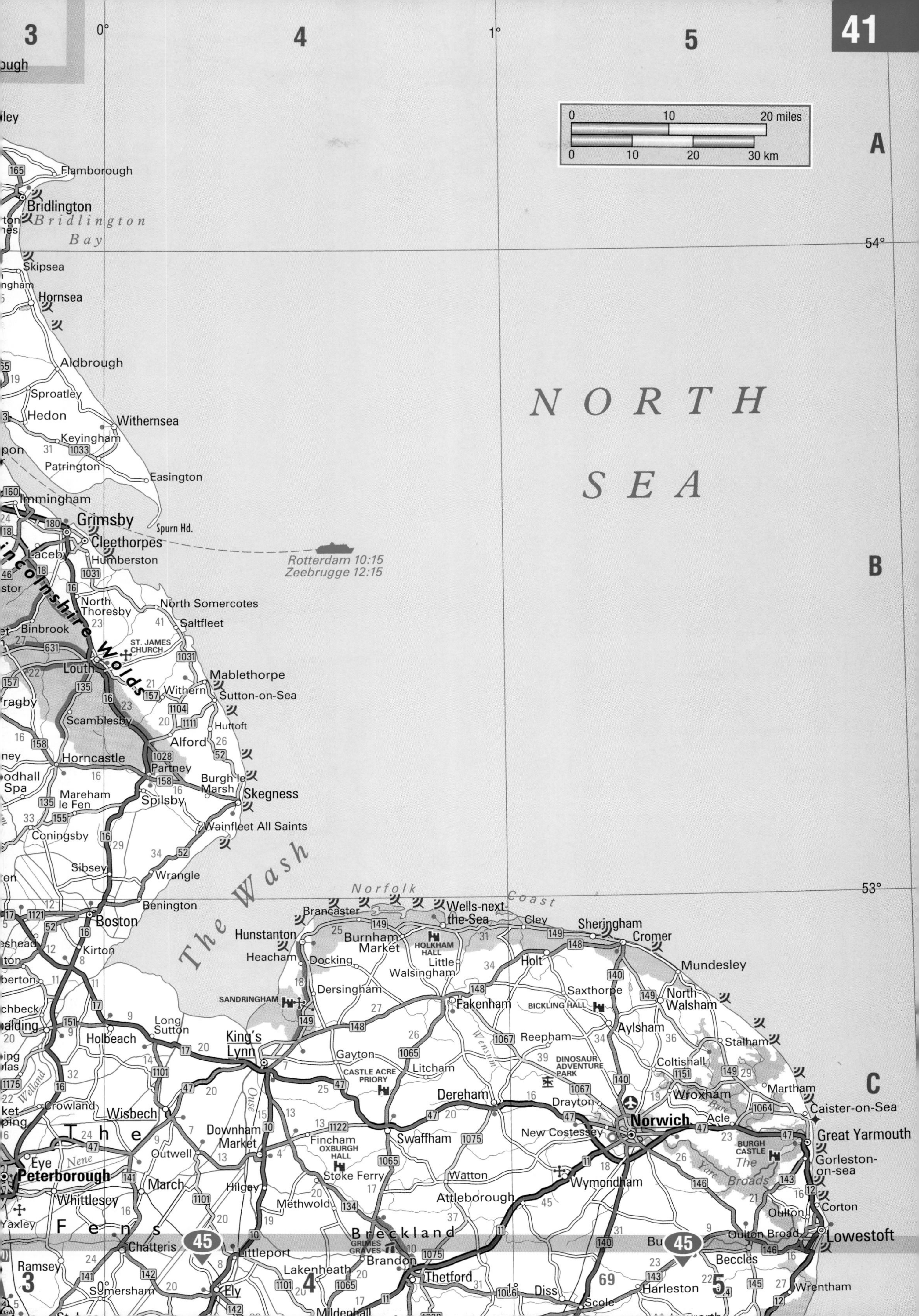

A

54°

NORTH

SEA

B

Bridlington
Bay

Flamborough
Bridlington
ton
ies

Skipsea
ngham
Hornsea
5

Aldbrough
19
Sproatley
Hedon
Withernsea
Keyingham
on
31   1033
Patrington
Easington
160
Immingham
24
18   180   Grimsby   Spurn Hd.
Laceby   Cleethorpes
46   Humberston
or   18   1031
16
North   North Somercotes
Thoresby   Saltfleet
Binbrook   23   41
et   27   ST. JAMES
631   CHURCH
Louth   1031
22
157   135   21   Mablethorpe
agby   16   157   Withern   Sutton-on-Sea
16   23   1104
158   Scamblesby   20   111   Huttoft
ney   1028   Alford   26
Horncastle   52
dhall   16   Partney   Burgh le
Spa   158   Marsh
Mareham   Spilsby   Skegness
135   le Fen   Wainfleet All Saints
33   155
Coningsby   16   29   34   52
Sibsey   Wrangle

Rotterdam 10:15
Zeebrugge 12:15

Norfolk   *Coast*
Benington   Wells-next-
17   1121   Brancaster   the-Sea   Cley   Sheringham
eshead   52   16   Boston   25   Burnham   149   149   Cromer
Kirton   Hunstanton   Market   HOLKHAM   31   148
Heacham   HALL   Little   Holt   Mundesley
17   Docking   Walsingham   34   140
151   9   Dersingham   148   Saxthorpe   North
ding   9   Long   SANDRINGHAM   27   Fakenham   BICKLING HALL   149   Walsham
as   Holbeach   Sutton   18   Reepham   34   36
17   149   1067   Aylsham   Stalham
175   14   1101   King's   148   39   Coltishall   149   29
22   16   47   Lynn   7   Gayton   26   DINOSAUR   1151   Wroxham   1064   Martham
Crowland   Wisbech   CASTLE ACRE   Litcham   ADVENTURE   140   19   Acle   Caister-on-Sea
47   PRIORY   1065   PARK   Wroxham
e   20   25   47   1067   Drayton   47   23   Norwich   47   Great Yarmouth
Eye   Downham   13   Dereham   New Costessey   BURGH   Gorleston-
Peterborough   141   Market   1122   Swaffham   1075   CASTLE   on-sea
Whittlesey   Outwell   4   Stoke Ferry   1065   26   *The*   143
March   13   20   Watton   146   *Broads*   16   12
Yaxley   16   Hilgay   Fincham   Wymondham   Corton
101   OXBURGH   17   Attleborough   45
The   Fens   Methwold   134   37   31   Oulton   146   Lowestoft
Ramsey   24   10   *Breckland*   11   140   Bu   45   Oulton Broad   Beccles
141   142   Chatteris   **45**   GRIMES   10   9   23   145   27   Wrentham
Somersham   20   Littleport   GRAVES   1075   **69**   143   22
4   Lakenheath   20   Brandon   Harleston   145
Ely   1101   1065   Thetford   31   Diss   Scole
142   Mildenhall   17   6

C

53°

The Wash

The

Ose

Nene

Welland

Wensum

Yare

Bure

Lincolnshire Wolds

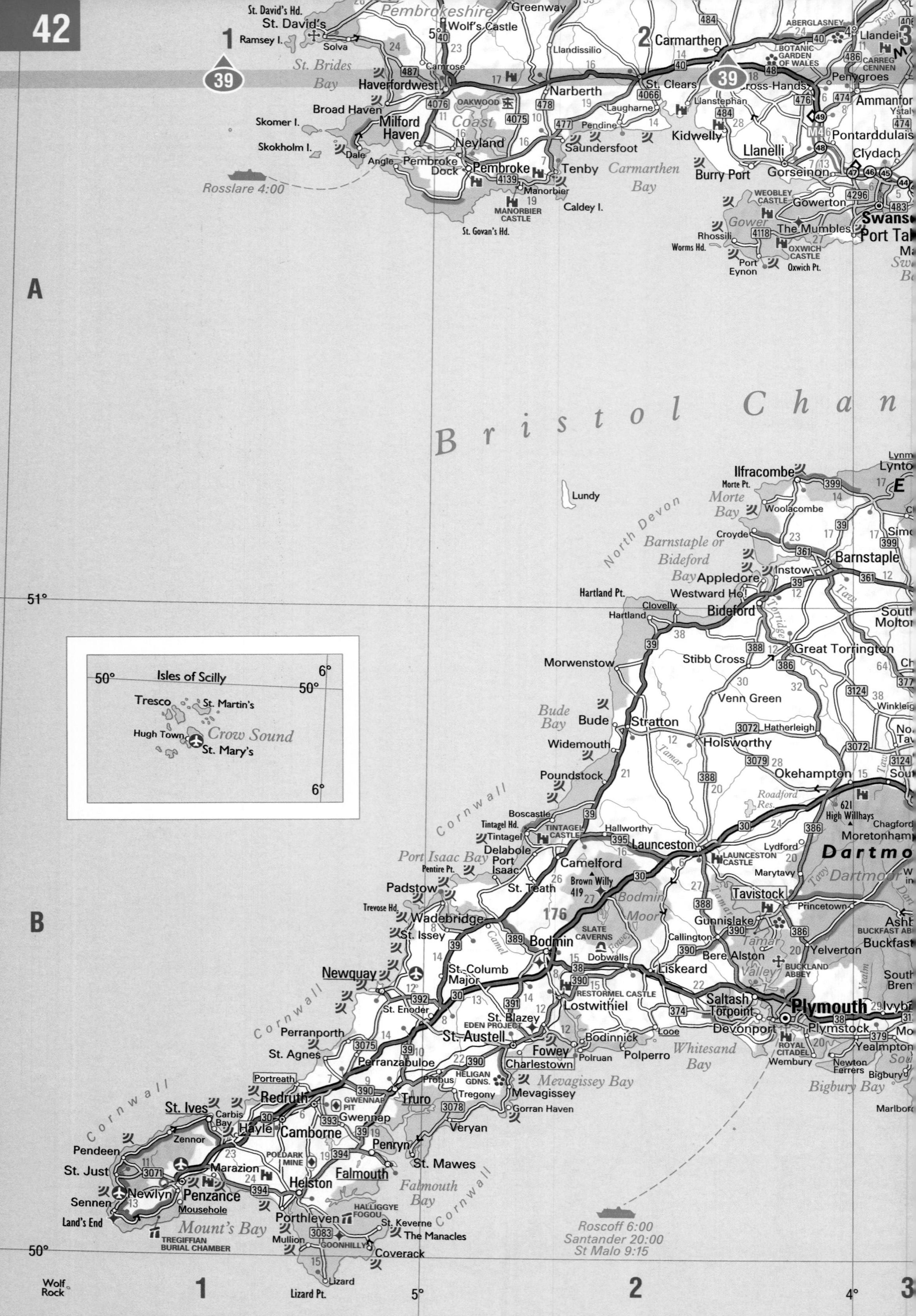
St. David's Hd.
St. David's
Ramsey I.
Solva
Pembrokeshire
Greenway
Wolf's Castle
Carmarthen
Llandissilio
Aberglasney
Botanic Garden of Wales
Carreg Cennen
Llandeilo
St. Brides Bay
Haverfordwest
Camrose
Narberth
St. Clears
Cross-Hands
Penygroes
Ammanford
Broad Haven
Oakwood
Laugharne
Llanstephan
Skomer I.
Milford Haven
Coast
Pendine
Kidwelly
Pontarddulais
Skokholm I.
Dale
Neyland
Saundersfoot
Llanelli
Clydach
Angle
Pembroke Dock
Pembroke
Tenby
Carmarthen Bay
Burry Port
Gorseinon
Rosslare 4:00
Manorbier
Manorbier Castle
Caldey I.
Weobley Castle
Gowerton
Gower
Swansea
St. Govan's Hd.
Rhossili
The Mumbles
Port Talbot
Worms Hd.
Oxwich Castle
Port Eynon
Oxwich Pt.
A
Bristol Channel
Lynmouth
Lynton
Ilfracombe
Morte Pt.
Morte Bay
Woolacombe
Lundy
North Devon
Croyde
Barnstaple or Bideford Bay
Barnstaple
Appledore
Instow
Westward Ho!
Hartland Pt.
51°
Clovelly
Bideford
Hartland
South Molton
Torridge
Great Torrington
Morwenstow
Stibb Cross
Venn Green
Winkleigh
Isles of Scilly
50°
6°
Tresco
St. Martin's
Hugh Town
Crow Sound
St. Mary's
Bude Bay
Bude
Stratton
Hatherleigh
Widemouth
Holsworthy
Tamar
Okehampton
Poundstock
Roadford Res.
Cornwall
Boscastle
High Willhays
Chagford
Tintagel Hd.
Tintagel
Tintagel Castle
Hallworthy
Moretonhampstead
Delabole
Launceston
Lydford
Launceston Castle
Dartmoor
Port Isaac Bay
Port Isaac
Camelford
Marytavy
Pentire Pt.
Brown Willy
Padstow
St. Teath
Bodmin Moor
Tavistock
Trevose Hd.
Wadebridge
Princetown
B
Gunnislake
Ashburton
St. Issey
Camel
Slate Caverns
Callington
Buckfast Abbey
Buckfastleigh
Bodmin
Bere Alston
Yelverton
Dobwalls
Buckland Abbey
Valley
Newquay
St. Columb Major
Liskeard
South Brent
Restormel Castle
Saltash
Plymouth
Ivybridge
St. Enoder
Lostwithiel
Torpoint
St. Blazey
Eden Project
Devonport
Plymstock
Perranporth
St. Austell
Looe
Bodinnick
Royal Citadel
Yealmpton
St. Agnes
Fowey
Polruan
Polperro
Whitesand Bay
Wembury
Newton Ferrers
Perranzabuloe
Charlestown
Bigbury
Portreath
Heligan Gdns.
Mevagissey Bay
Bigbury Bay
Probus
Redruth
Gwennap Pit
Truro
Tregony
Mevagissey
St. Ives
Carbis Bay
Gorran Haven
Marlborough
Hayle
Camborne
Gwennap
Veryan
Zennor
Pendeen
Poldark Mine
Penryn
St. Mawes
St. Just
Marazion
Falmouth
Newlyn
Penzance
Helston
Falmouth Bay
Sennen
Mousehole
Halliggye Fogou
Land's End
Porthleven
St. Keverne
Mount's Bay
The Manacles
Tregiffian Burial Chamber
Mullion
Goonhilly
Coverack
Roscoff 6:00
Santander 20:00
St Malo 9:15
Wolf Rock
1
Lizard
Lizard Pt.
5°
2
4°
3

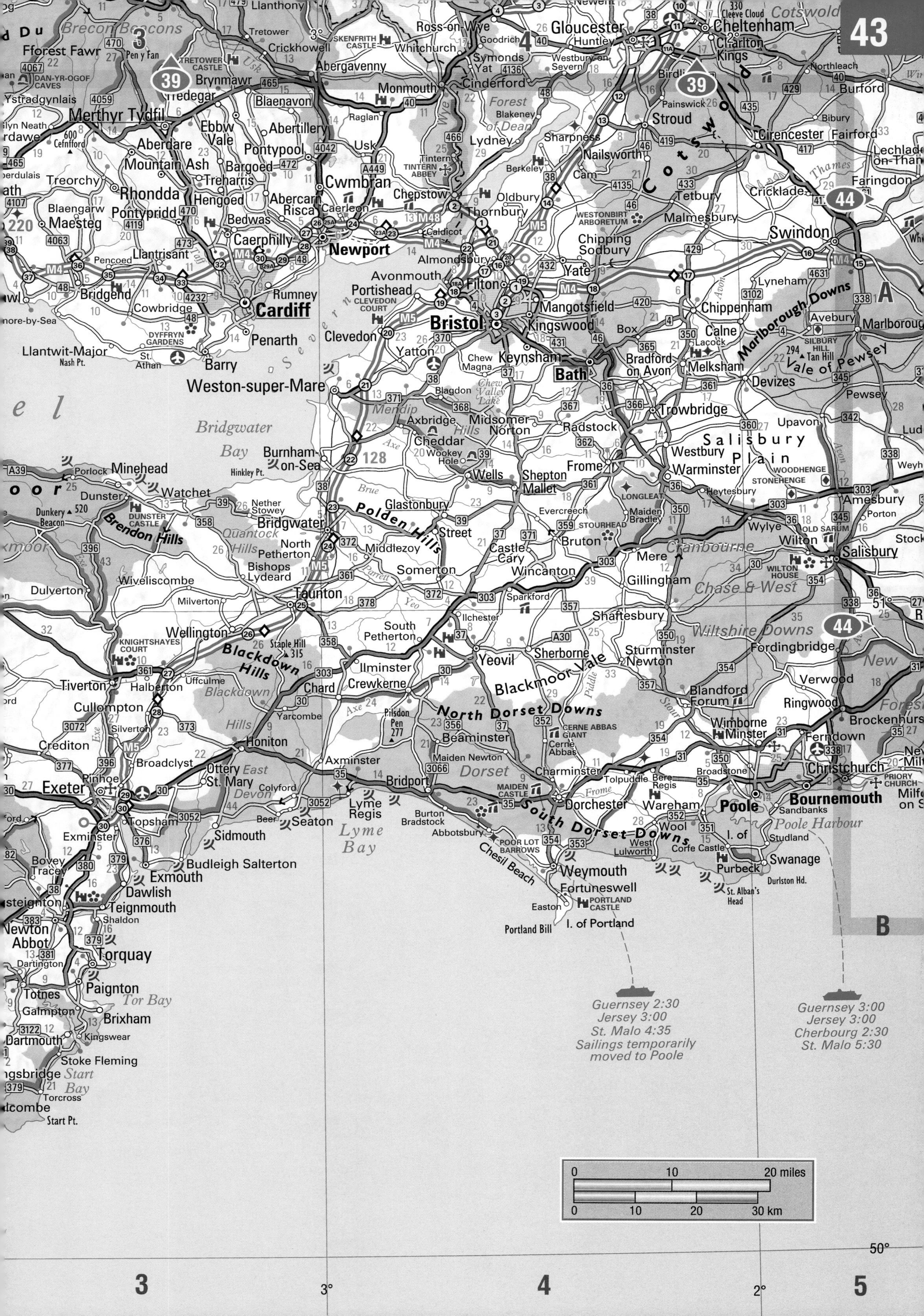
Brecon Beacons
Fforest Fawr
Llanthony
Tretower
Crickhowell
Abergavenny
Ross-on-Wye
Goodrich
Whitchurch
Symonds Yat
Gloucester
Huntley
Cheltenham
Charlton Kings
Cleeve Cloud
Cotswold
Northleach
Burford
Brynmawr
Tredegar
Blaenavon
Monmouth
Cinderford
Westbury-on-Severn
Forest of Dean
Blakeney
Painswick
Stroud
Bibury
Cirencester
Fairford
Lechlade on-Thames
Ystradgynlais
Merthyr Tydfil
Ebbw Vale
Abertillery
Raglan
Lydney
Sharpness
Nailsworth
Aberdare
Mountain Ash
Pontypool
Usk
Tintern Abbey
Berkeley
Cam
Tetbury
Cricklade
Faringdon
Treorchy
Rhondda
Treharris
Bargoed
Cwmbran
Chepstow
Oldbury
Thornbury
Westonbirt Arboretum
Malmesbury
Swindon
Blaengarw
Maesteg
Pontypridd
Hengoed
Abercarn
Risca
Caerleon
Bedwas
Caerphilly
Newport
Caldicot
Almondsbury
Chipping Sodbury
Yate
Llantrisant
Pencoed
Bridgend
Cowbridge
Rumney
Cardiff
Avonmouth
Portishead
Clevedon Court
Filton
Mangotsfield
Lyneham
Chippenham
Marlborough Downs
Avebury
Marlborough
Dyffryn Gardens
Penarth
Clevedon
Bristol
Kingswood
Box
Calne
Lacock
Silbury Hill
Tan Hill
Llantwit-Major
Nash Pt.
St. Athan
Barry
Yatton
Chew Magna
Keynsham
Bath
Bradford on Avon
Melksham
Vale of Pewsey
Devizes
Pewsey
Weston-super-Mare
Blagdon
Chew Valley Lake
Mendip Hills
Axbridge
Cheddar
Midsomer Norton
Radstock
Trowbridge
Upavon
Bridgwater Bay
Burnham-on-Sea
Hinkley Pt.
Wookey Hole
Wells
Shepton Mallet
Frome
Westbury
Warminster
Salisbury Plain
Woodhenge
Stonehenge
Heytesbury
Amesbury
Porton
Porlock
Minehead
Watchet
Dunster
Dunster Castle
Dunkery Beacon
Exmoor
Brendon Hills
Nether Stowey
Quantock Hills
Bridgwater
North Petherton
Glastonbury
Polden Hills
Street
Evercreech
Longleat
Maiden Bradley
Stourhead
Bruton
Wylye
Old Sarum
Wilton
Salisbury
Middlezoy
Castle Cary
Mere
Cranbourne Chase & West
Dulverton
Wiveliscombe
Bishops Lydeard
Somerton
Wincanton
Gillingham
Wilton House
Milverton
Taunton
Sparkford
Ilchester
Shaftesbury
Wiltshire Downs
Wellington
Knightshayes Court
Staple Hill
Blackdown Hills
South Petherton
Yeovil
Sherborne
Sturminster Newton
Fordingbridge
Tiverton
Halberton
Uffculme
Ilminster
Chard
Crewkerne
Blackmoor Vale
Blandford Forum
Verwood
Ringwood
Cullompton
Yarcombe
Pilsdon Pen
North Dorset Downs
Beaminster
Cerne Abbas Giant
Cerne Abbas
Wimborne Minster
Ferndown
Brockenhurst
Crediton
Silverton
Honiton
Maiden Newton
Broadclyst
Ottery St. Mary
East Devon
Axminster
Bridport
Dorset
Charminster
Tolpuddle
Bere Regis
Broadstone
Christchurch
Priory Church
Exeter
Pinhoe
Colyford
Lyme Regis
Maiden Castle
Dorchester
Wareham
Poole
Bournemouth
Sandbanks
Topsham
Beer
Seaton
Burton Bradstock
Abbotsbury
South Dorset Downs
Wool
I. of Purbeck
Poole Harbour
Studland
Exminster
Sidmouth
Lyme Bay
Chesil Beach
Poor Lot Barrows
West Lulworth
Corfe Castle
Swanage
Bovey Tracey
Budleigh Salterton
Exmouth
Weymouth
Fortuneswell
Durlston Hd.
Dawlish
Teignmouth
Shaldon
Easton
Portland Castle
St. Alban's Head
Newton Abbot
Portland Bill
I. of Portland
Torquay
Dartington
Totnes
Paignton
Tor Bay
Galmpton
Brixham
Kingswear
Dartmouth
Stoke Fleming
Start Bay
Torcross
Start Pt.
Guernsey 2:30
Jersey 3:00
St. Malo 4:35
Sailings temporarily moved to Poole
Guernsey 3:00
Jersey 3:00
Cherbourg 2:30
St. Malo 5:30
0 10 20 miles
0 10 20 30 km
50°
3°
2°
3
4
5
A
B

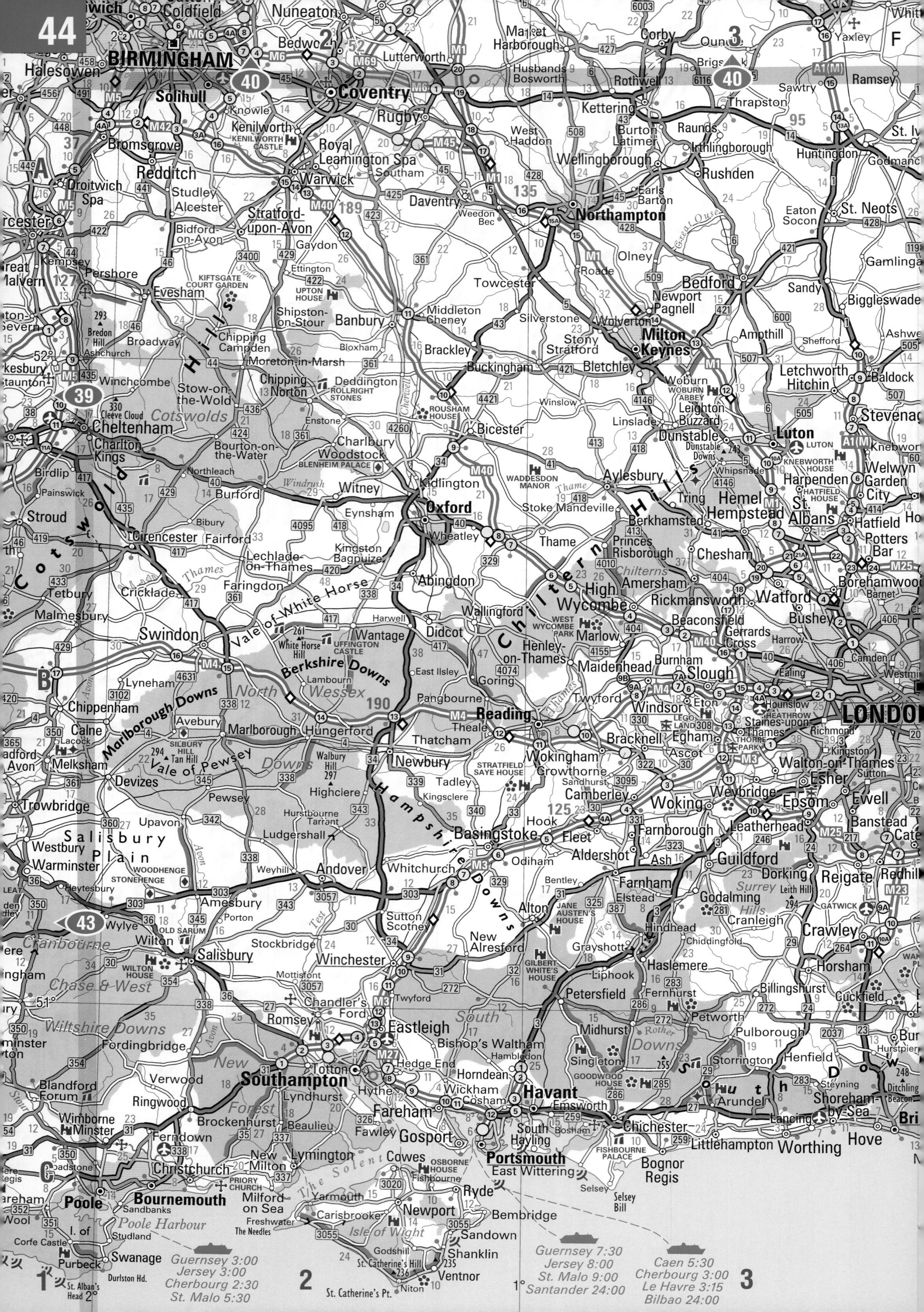
BIRMINGHAM
Coldfield
Nuneaton
Bedworth
Lutterworth
Market Harborough
Corby
Oundle
Yaxley
F
Halesowen
Solihull
Coventry
Husbands Bosworth
Rothwell
Sawtry
Ramsey
Knowle
Kenilworth
KENILWORTH CASTLE
Rugby
Kettering
Thrapston
Bromsgrove
Royal Leamington Spa
West Haddon
Burton Latimer
Raunds
Irthlingborough
Huntingdon
Godmanchester
Redditch
Southam
Warwick
Wellingborough
Rushden
Droitwich Spa
Studley
Alcester
Daventry
Northampton
Earls Barton
St. Neots
Eaton Socon
Worcester
Stratford-upon-Avon
Bidford-on-Avon
Weedon Bec
Gaydon
Great Ouse
Olney
Gamlingay
Great Malvern
Kempsey
Pershore
Evesham
KIFTSGATE COURT GARDEN
Ettington
UPTON HOUSE
Roade
Towcester
Bedford
Newport Pagnell
Sandy
Biggleswade
Tewkesbury
Bredon Hill
Broadway
Chipping Campden
Shipston-on-Stour
Banbury
Middleton Cheney
Silverstone
Wolverton
Milton Keynes
Ampthill
Shefford
Ashwell
Ashchurch
Bloxham
Brackley
Stony Stratford
Moreton-in-Marsh
Winchcombe
Chipping Norton
Deddington
ROLLRIGHT STONES
Buckingham
Bletchley
Woburn
WOBURN ABBEY
Letchworth
Hitchin
Baldock
Stow-on-the-Wold
Cleeve Cloud
Cotswolds
Cheltenham
ROUSHAM HOUSE
Winslow
Leighton Buzzard
Linslade
Stevenage
Charlton Kings
Bourton-on-the-Water
Enstone
Charlbury
Woodstock
BLENHEIM PALACE
Bicester
Dunstable
Dunstable Downs
Luton
LUTON
KNEBWORTH HOUSE
Whipsnade
Welwyn Garden City
Birdlip
Northleach
Painswick
Burford
Witney
Windrush
Kidlington
WADDESDON MANOR
Aylesbury
Thame
Tring
Harpenden
HATFIELD HOUSE
Stroud
Eynsham
Oxford
Stoke Mandeville
Berkhamsted
Hemel Hempstead
St. Albans
Hatfield
Bibury
Cirencester
Fairford
Wheatley
Princes Risborough
Chesham
Potters Bar
Cotswold Hills
Lechlade-on-Thames
Kingston Bagpuize
Thames
Chilterns
Amersham
Borehamwood
Tetbury
Cricklade
Faringdon
Abingdon
Chiltern Hills
High Wycombe
Rickmansworth
Watford
Barnet
Vale of White Horse
Malmesbury
Harwell
Wallingford
WEST WYCOMBE PARK
Marlow
Beaconsfield
Bushey
Swindon
White Horse Hill
UFFINGTON CASTLE
Wantage
Didcot
Henley-on-Thames
Gerrards Cross
Harrow
Camden
Berkshire Downs
East Ilsley
Maidenhead
Burnham
Slough
Ealing
Lyneham
Lambourn
Goring
North Wessex
Pangbourne
Twyford
Windsor
Eton
Hounslow
HEATHROW
LONDON
Chippenham
Marlborough Downs
Avebury
Reading
Theale
LEGOLAND
Egham
Staines-upon-Thames
Richmond
Calne
Lacock
SILBURY HILL
Marlborough
Hungerford
Thatcham
Bracknell
Ascot
THORPE PARK
Kingston
Melksham
Tan Hill
Vale of Pewsey
Walbury Hill
Newbury
Wokingham
Crowthorne
Walton-on-Thames
Esher
Sutton
Devizes
Downs
STRATFIELD SAYE HOUSE
Tadley
Sandhurst
Camberley
Ewell
Pewsey
Highclere
Kingsclere
Hampshire Downs
Woking
Weybridge
Epsom
Trowbridge
Hurstbourne Tarrant
Banstead
Upavon
Salisbury Plain
Ludgershall
Basingstoke
Hook
Fleet
Farnborough
Leatherhead
Westbury
Warminster
WOODHENGE
STONEHENGE
Weyhill
Andover
Whitchurch
Odiham
Aldershot
Ash
Guildford
Dorking
Reigate
Redhill
Heytesbury
Amesbury
Bentley
Farnham
Elstead
Godalming
Surrey Hills
Leith Hill
GATWICK
Alton
JANE AUSTEN'S HOUSE
Porton
Sutton Scotney
Wylye
Wilton
OLD SARUM
Hindhead
Cranleigh
Crawley
Cranborne
Stockbridge
New Alresford
Grayshott
Chiddingfold
Salisbury
WILTON HOUSE
Winchester
Haslemere
Horsham
Chase & West
Mottisfont
GILBERT WHITE'S HOUSE
Liphook
Billingshurst
Twyford
Petersfield
Fernhurst
Cuckfield
Chandler's Ford
Wiltshire Downs
Romsey
Eastleigh
South
Petworth
Fordingbridge
Bishop's Waltham
Hambledon
Midhurst
Rother
Pulborough
Burgess Hill
Hurstpierpoint
New
Hedge End
Horndean
Singleton
Storrington
Henfield
Totton
Southampton
GOODWOOD HOUSE
Verwood
Hythe
Wickham
Havant
South Downs
Ditchling Beacon
Steyning
Blandford Forum
Ringwood
Lyndhurst
Cosham
Emsworth
Arundel
Shoreham-by-Sea
New Forest
Brockenhurst
Beaulieu
Fareham
Chichester
Lancing
Wimborne Minster
Ferndown
Fawley
Gosport
South Hayling
Bosham
Littlehampton
Worthing
Hove
Brighton
New Milton
Lymington
Cowes
OSBORNE HOUSE
Portsmouth
FISHBOURNE PALACE
East Wittering
Bognor Regis
Christchurch
PRIORY CHURCH
The Solent
Fishbourne
Selsey
Selsey Bill
Poole
Bournemouth
Milford on Sea
Yarmouth
Ryde
Sandbanks
Carisbrooke
Newport
Bembridge
Wareham
Poole Harbour
Freshwater
The Needles
Isle of Wight
Sandown
I. of Purbeck
Studland
Corfe Castle
Godshill
Shanklin
Swanage
St. Catherine's Hill
Ventnor
Durlston Hd.
St. Alban's Head
St. Catherine's Pt.
Niton
Guernsey 3:00
Jersey 3:00
Cherbourg 2:30
St. Malo 5:30
Guernsey 7:30
Jersey 8:00
St. Malo 9:00
Santander 24:00
Caen 5:30
Cherbourg 3:00
Le Havre 3:15
Bilbao 24:00
1
2
3
A
B
C
40
39
43

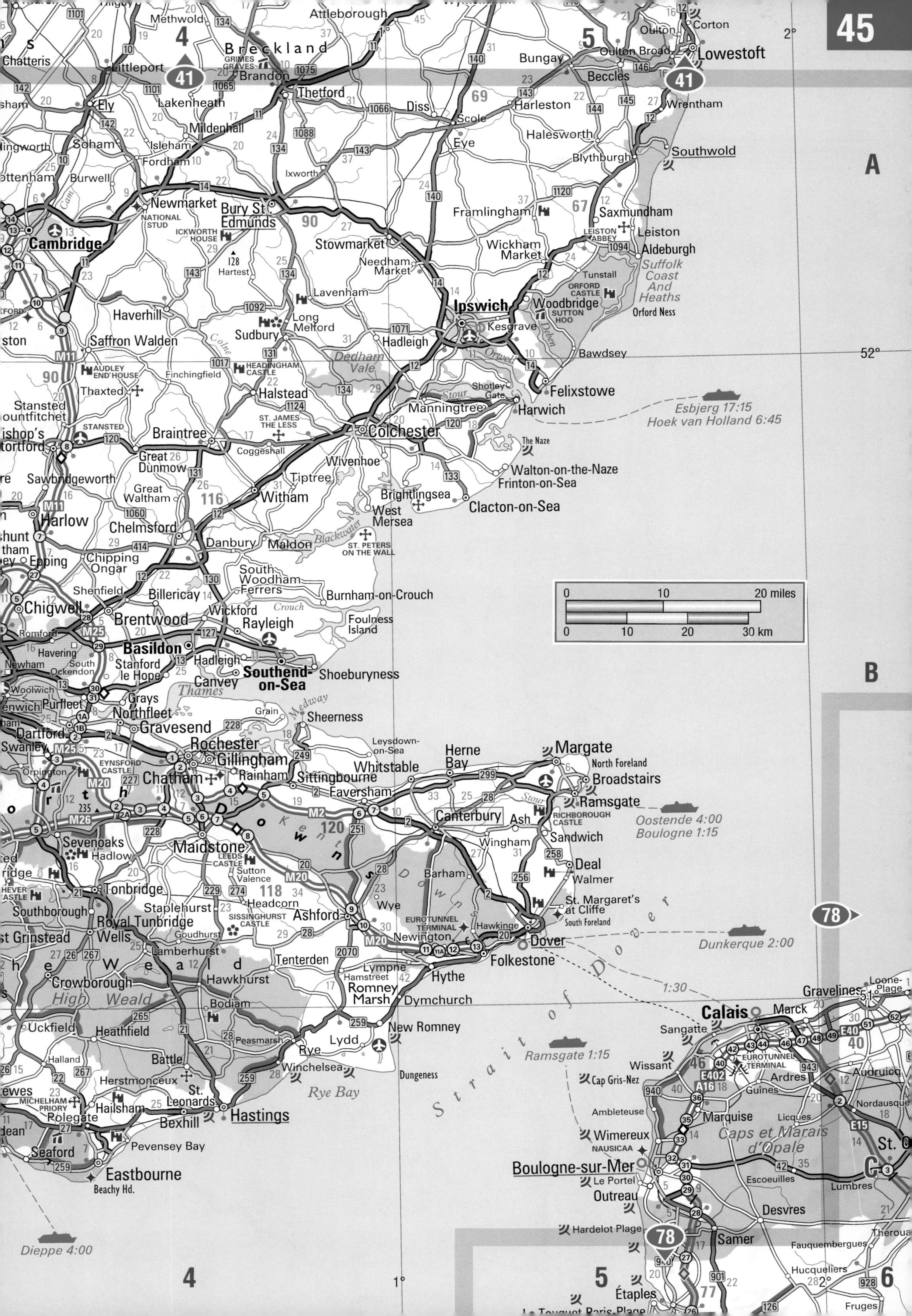
Attleborough
Methwold
Breckland
Chatteris
Littleport
Grimes Graves
Brandon
Thetford
Ely
Lakenheath
Mildenhall
Soham
Isleham
Fordham
Burwell
Newmarket
National Stud
Bury St Edmunds
Ickworth House
Cambridge
Hartest
Haverhill
Saffron Walden
Sudbury
Long Melford
Lavenham
Audley End House
Headingham Castle
Finchingfield
Thaxted
Halstead
Stansted Mountfitchet
Bishop's Stortford
Stansted
Braintree
Great Dunmow
Coggeshall
St. James the Less
Sawbridgeworth
Great Waltham
Witham
Harlow
Chelmsford
Epping
Chipping Ongar
Danbury
Maldon
Blackwater
St. Peters on the Wall
Shenfield
Billericay
South Woodham Ferrers
Burnham-on-Crouch
Crouch
Chigwell
Brentwood
Wickford
Rayleigh
Foulness Island
Romford
Havering
Basildon
Hadleigh
Newham
South Ockendon
Stanford le Hope
Canvey
Southend-on-Sea
Shoeburyness
Woolwich
Purfleet
Grays
Thames
Northfleet
Gravesend
Grain
Medway
Sheerness
Dartford
Swanley
Eynsford Castle
Rochester
Gillingham
Chatham
Rainham
Orpington
Sittingbourne
Leysdown-on-Sea
Whitstable
Herne Bay
Margate
North Foreland
Broadstairs
Ramsgate
Faversham
Stour
Canterbury
Ash
Richborough Castle
Sandwich
Wingham
Deal
Walmer
Sevenoaks
Hadlow
Maidstone
Leeds Castle
Sutton Valence
North Downs
Kent Downs
Barham
Tonbridge
Headcorn
Staplehurst
Southborough
Royal Tunbridge Wells
Sissinghurst Castle
Ashford
Wye
Eurotunnel Terminal
Hawkinge
St. Margaret's at Cliffe
South Foreland
East Grinstead
Goudhurst
Newington
Dover
Folkestone
Lamberhurst
Tenterden
Weald
Crowborough
Hawkhurst
Hamstreet
Lympne
Hythe
High Weald
Romney Marsh
Dymchurch
Bodiam
New Romney
Uckfield
Heathfield
Peasmarsh
Rye
Lydd
Battle
Winchelsea
Dungeness
Rye Bay
Halland
Herstmonceux
Lewes
Michelham Priory
Hailsham
St. Leonards
Hastings
Bexhill
Polegate
Seaford
Pevensey Bay
Eastbourne
Beachy Hd.
Dieppe 4:00
Oulton
Corton
Oulton Broad
Lowestoft
Bungay
Beccles
Harleston
Diss
Scole
Wrentham
Eye
Halesworth
Blythburgh
Southwold
Ixworth
Framlingham
Saxmundham
Leiston Abbey
Leiston
Aldeburgh
Stowmarket
Needham Market
Wickham Market
Suffolk Coast And Heaths
Tunstall
Orford Castle
Orford Ness
Woodbridge
Sutton Hoo
Ipswich
Kesgrave
Hadleigh
Deben
Orwell
Bawdsey
Dedham Vale
Felixstowe
Shotley Gate
Manningtree
Harwich
Esbjerg 17:15
Hoek van Holland 6:45
Colchester
The Naze
Wivenhoe
Walton-on-the-Naze
Frinton-on-Sea
Tiptree
Brightlingsea
West Mersea
Clacton-on-Sea
0 10 20 miles
0 10 20 30 km
Oostende 4:00
Boulogne 1:15
Dunkerque 2:00
Strait of Dover
Ramsgate 1:15
1:30
Gravelines
Loon-Plage
Calais
Marck
Sangatte
Eurotunnel Terminal
Wissant
Cap Gris-Nez
Ardres
Audruicq
Guînes
Nordausques
Ambleteuse
Marquise
Licques
Caps et Marais d'Opale
Wimereux
Nausicaa
St. Omer
Boulogne-sur-Mer
Le Portel
Escoeuilles
Lumbres
Outreau
Desvres
Hardelot Plage
Samer
Fauquembergues
Thérouanne
Hucqueliers
Étaples
Le Touquet Paris-Plage
Fruges
A
B
C
4
5
6
52°
1°
2°

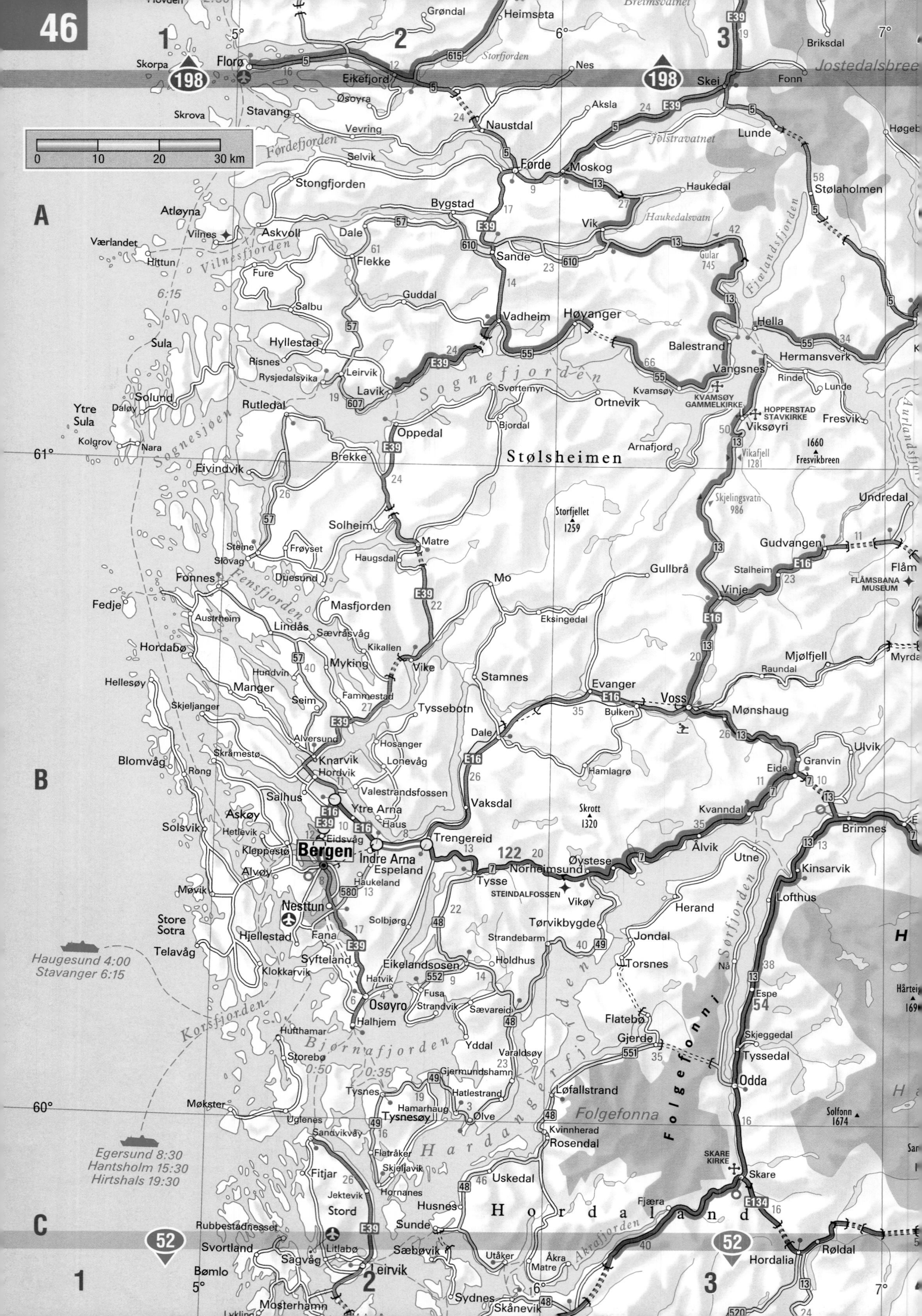

Florø
Skorpa
Skrova
198
Eikefjord
Grøndal
Heimseta
Storfjorden
Nes
Skei
Briksdal
Fonn
Jostedalsbree
Stavang
Øsoyra
Naustdal
Aksla
Jølstravatnet
Lunde
Høgeb
0 10 20 30 km
Førdefjorden
Vevring
Selvik
Førde
Moskog
Haukedal
Stølaholmen
Stongfjorden
Bygstad
Haukedalsvatn
Vik
Fjælandsfjorden
Atløyna
Vilnes
Askvoll
Dale
Værlandet
Hittun
Vilnesfjorden
Sande
Gular 745
Flekke
Fure
Guddal
Salbu
Vadheim
Høyanger
Hella
Balestrand
Hermansverk
Sula
Hyllestad
Risnes
Rysjedalsvika
Leirvik
Lavik
Sognefjorden
Vangsnes
Svortemyr
Rinde
Lunde
Solund
Ytre Sula
Daløy
Rutledal
Ortnevik
Kvamsøy
KVAMSØY GAMMELKIRKE
HOPPERSTAD STAVKIRKE
Viksøyri
Fresvik
Bjordal
Oppedal
Aurlandsfjo
Kolgrov
Nara
Sognesjøen
Arnafjord
1660 Fresvikbreen
Vikafjell 1281
61°
Brekke
Stølsheimen
Eivindvik
Skjelingsvatn 986
Undredal
Storfjellet 1259
Solheim
Matre
Gudvangen
Steine
Frøyset
Haugsdal
Stalheim
Flåm
Fonnes
Sløvåg
Duesund
Gullbrå
FLÅMSBANA MUSEUM
Fensfjorden
Mo
Fedje
Masfjorden
Vinje
Austrheim
Lindås
Eksingedal
Sævråsvåg
Kikallen
Mjølfjell
Myrdal
Hordabø
Myking
Raundal
Hundvin
Vike
Stamnes
Hellesøy
Manger
Evanger
Voss
Seim
Fammestad
Mønshaug
Skjeljanger
Tyssebotn
Bulken
Alversund
Dale
Ulvik
Hosanger
Skråmestø
Knarvik
Lonevåg
Granvin
Blomvåg
Rong
Hordvik
Hamlagrø
Eide
Valestrandsfossen
Salhus
Vaksdal
Askøy
Ytre Arna
Skrott 1320
Kvanndal
Solsvik
Hetlevik
Haus
Brimnes
Eidsvåg
Trengereid
122
Kleppestø
Bergen
Indre Arna
Norheimsund
Øystese
Ålvik
Utne
Espeland
Alvøy
Tysse
Kinsarvik
Haukeland
Møvik
STEINDALFOSSEN
Vikøy
Lofthus
Nesttun
Solbjørg
Herand
Store Sotra
Tørvikbygde
Sørfjorden
Fana
Hjellestad
Strandebarm
Jondal
Telavåg
Syfteland
Holdhus
Haugesund 4:00
Stavanger 6:15
Klokkarvik
Eikelandsosen
Torsnes
Hatvik
Nå
Fusa
Hårteig
Osøyro
Strandvik
Sævareid
Espe
Halhjem
Flatebø
Korsfjorden
Hufthamar
Bjørnafjorden
Yddal
Skjeggedal
Gjerde
Storebø
Varaldsøy
Tyssedal
Gjermundshamn
Folgefonni
Tysnes
Hatlestrand
Odda
Løfallstrand
Møkster
Hamarhaug
60°
Tysnesøy
Ølve
Folgefonna
Solfonn 1674
Uglenes
Kvinnherad
Sandvikvåg
Rosendal
Egersund 8:30
Hantsholm 15:30
Hirtshals 19:30
Flatråker
Hardangerfjorden
SKARE KIRKE
Skjeljavik
Fitjar
Skare
Uskedal
Hornanes
Jektevik
Husnes
Stord
Hordaland
Fjæra
Rubbestadnesset
Sunde
Akrafjorden
Svortland
Litlabø
Sæbøvik
Utåker
Røldal
Sagvåg
Åkra
Hordalia
Bømlo
Leirvik
Matre
Sydnes
Mosterhamn
Skånevik
Lykling
52

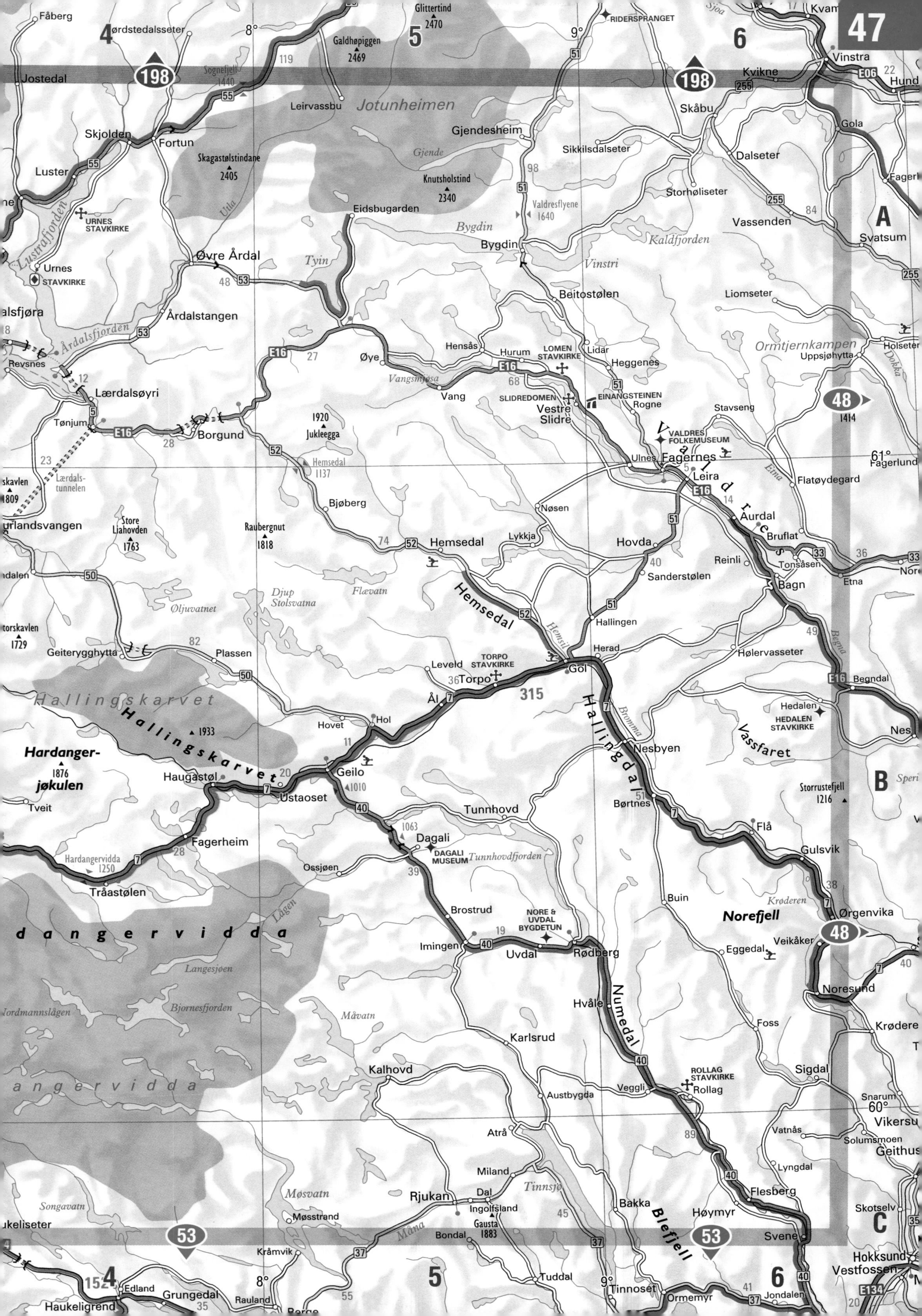

47
Fåberg
Ørdstedalsseter
Glittertind
2470
Galdhøpiggen
2469
Riderspranget
Sjoa
Kvam
Vinstra
Jostedal
Sognefjell
1440
Leirvassbu
Jotunheimen
Kvikne
Skåbu
Hund
Gola
Skjolden
Fortun
Gjendesheim
Gjende
Sikkilsdalseter
Dalseter
Luster
Skagastølstindane
2405
Knutsholstind
2340
Storhøliseter
Fagerli
Lustrafjorden
Urnes Stavkirke
Eidsbugarden
Utla
Valdresflyene
1640
Vassenden
Svatsum
Bygdin
Kaldfjorden
Urnes
Øvre Årdal
Tyin
Vinstri
Beitostølen
Liomseter
Årdalstangen
Årdalsfjorden
Ormtjernkampen
Holseter
Uppsjøhytta
Dokka
Revsnes
Hensås
Hurum
Lomen Stavkirke
Lidar
Heggenes
Øye
Vangsmjøsa
Lærdalsøyri
Vang
Slidredomen
Einangsteinen
Rogne
Vestre Slidre
Tønjum
Borgund
1920
Jukleegga
Stavseng
Valdres Folkemuseum
Valdres
Hemsedal
1137
Ulnes
Fagernes
Leira
61°
Fagerlund
Lærdals-tunnelen
Bjøberg
Etna
Flatøydegard
Nøsen
Aurdal
Store Liahovden
1763
Raubergnut
1818
Hemsedal
Lykkja
Hovda
Bruflat
Reinli
Tonsåsen
Etna
Sanderstølen
Bagn
Djup
Stolsvatna
Flævatn
Øljuvatnet
1729
Hallingen
Geiterygghytta
Plassen
Herad
Hølervasseter
Begna
Leveld
Torpo Stavkirke
Torpo
Gol
Hemsil
Begndal
Hallingskarvet
Ål
Hol
Hovet
1933
Hallingdal
Bromma
Hedalen
Hedalen Stavkirke
Vassfaret
Nes
Hardanger-jøkulen
1876
Haugastøl
Geilo
1010
Ustaoset
Nesbyen
Tveit
Tunnhovd
Børtnes
Storrustefjell
1216
1063
Dagali
Dagali Museum
Tunnhovdfjorden
Flå
Fagerheim
Hardangervidda
1250
Ossjøen
Gulsvik
Tråastølen
Lågen
Buin
Krøderen
Brostrud
Nore & Uvdal Bygdetun
Norefjell
Ørgenvika
Hardangervidda
Imingen
Uvdal
Rødberg
Veikåker
Eggedal
Langesjøen
Numedal
Noresund
Hvåle
Nordmannslågen
Bjornesfjorden
Måvatn
Foss
Krøderen
Karlsrud
Kalhovd
Rollag Stavkirke
Rollag
Sigdal
Veggli
Austbygda
Snarum
60°
Vikersund
Vatnås
Solumsmoen
Geithus
Atrå
Lyngdal
Miland
Tinnsjø
Møsvatn
Rjukan
Dal
Ingolfsland
Bakka
Blefjell
Flesberg
Høymyr
Skotselv
Songavatn
Møsstrand
Gausta
1883
Haukeliseter
Måna
Bondal
Svene
Kråmvik
Hokksund
Vestfossen
Edland
Tuddal
Grungedal
Rauland
Tinnoset
Ormemyr
Jondalen
Haukeligrend
8°
9°
4
5
6
A
B
C

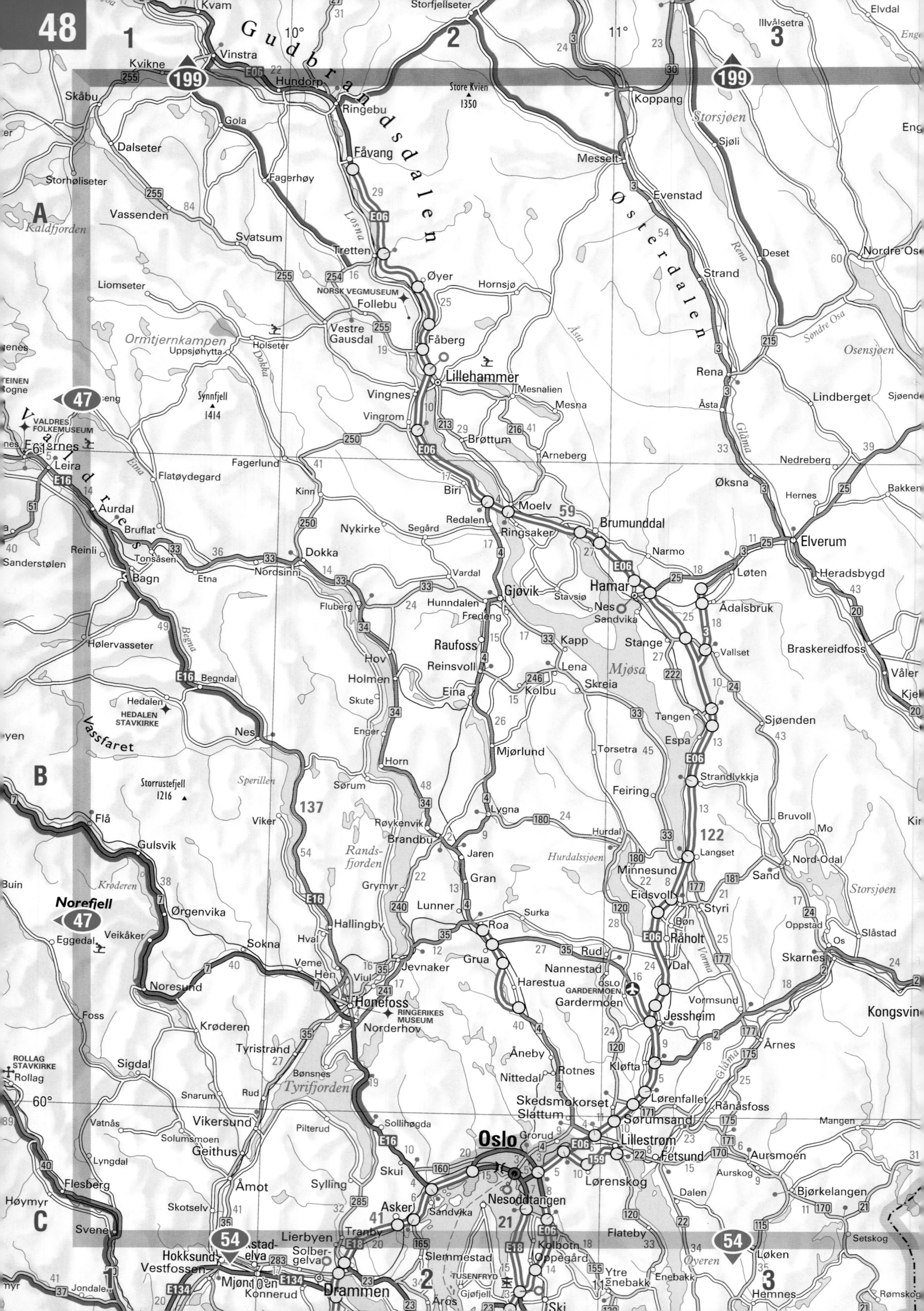

Gudbrandsdalen
Østerdalen
Valdres
Kvam
Storfjellseter
Elvdal
Illvålsetra
Kvikne
Vinstra
Hundorp
Ringebu
Store Kvien 1350
Koppang
Storsjøen
Sjøli
Skåbu
Gola
Dalseter
Fåvang
Messelt
Storhøliseter
Fagerhøy
Evenstad
Vassenden
Kaldfjorden
Losna
Svatsum
Tretten
Rena
Deset
Nordre Os
Strand
Øyer
Hornsjø
Liomseter
NORSK VEGMUSEUM
Follebu
Vestre Gausdal
Fåberg
Ormtjernkampen
Holseter
Uppsjøhytta
Dokka
Åsta
Søndre Osa
Osensjøen
Lillehammer
Mesnalien
Mesna
Vingnes
Vingrom
Synnfjell 1414
VALDRES FOLKEMUSEUM
Fagernes
Leira
Brøttum
Arneberg
Lindberget
Glåma
Nedreberg
Fagerlund
Flatøydegard
Eina
Biri
Moelv
Øksna
Hernes
Bakken
Aurdal
Kinn
Brumunddal
Redalen
Ringsaker
Nykirke
Segård
Bruflat
Reinli
Tonsåsen
Sanderstølen
Dokka
Nordsinni
Etna
Bagn
Narmo
Elverum
Vardal
Gjøvik
Hamar
Løten
Heradsbygd
Fluberg
Hunndalen
Fredeng
Stavsjø
Nes
Sandvika
Ådalsbruk
Raufoss
Kapp
Stange
Vallset
Hølervasseter
Begna
Hov
Reinsvoll
Lena
Mjøsa
Braskereidfoss
Våler
Holmen
Eina
Kolbu
Skreia
Begndal
Hedalen
HEDALEN STAVKIRKE
Skute
Tangen
Sjøenden
Vassfaret
Nes
Enger
Mjørlund
Torsetra
Espa
Horn
Strandlykkja
Storrustefjell 1216
Sperillen
Sørum
Feiring
Flå
Viker
Lygna
Hurdal
Bruvoll
Mo
Røykenvik
Brandbu
Randsfjorden
Jaren
Hurdalssjøen
Langset
Nord-Odal
Gulsvik
Gran
Minnesund
Sand
Buin
Krøderen
Grymyr
Eidsvoll
Storsjøen
Norefjell
Ørgenvika
Lunner
Surka
Styri
Eggedal
Veikåker
Hallingby
Roa
Bøn
Oppstad
Os
Slåstad
Sokna
Hval
Råholt
Vorma
Veme
Hen
Viul
Jevnaker
Grua
Rud
Nannestad
Dal
Skarnes
Noresund
Harestua
OSLO GARDERMOEN
Gardermoen
Vormsund
Kongsvinger
Hønefoss
RINGERIKES MUSEUM
Norderhov
Jessheim
Foss
Krøderen
Tyristrand
Åneby
Årnes
ROLLAG STAVKIRKE
Rollag
Sigdal
Bønsnes
Tyrifjorden
Kløfta
Nittedal
Rotnes
Snarum
Rud
Lørenfallet
Rånåsfoss
Skedsmokorset
Slattum
Sørumsand
Vikersund
Vatnås
Sollihøgda
Pilterud
Mangen
Solumsmoen
Geithus
Oslo
Grorud
Lillestrøm
Fetsund
Aursmoen
Lyngdal
Skui
Lørenskog
Aurskog
Flesberg
Åmot
Sylling
Nesoddtangen
Dalen
Bjørkelangen
Høymyr
Skotselv
Asker
Sandvika
Svene
Lierbyen
Tranby
Flateby
Setskog
Hokksund
Vestfossen
Åmot
Solbergelva
Slemmestad
Kolbotn
Oppegård
Ytre Enebakk
Enebakk
Øyeren
Løken
Mjøndalen
Konnerud
Drammen
TUSENFRYD
Gjøfjell
Ski
Hemnes
Jondalen
Røros
Rømskog

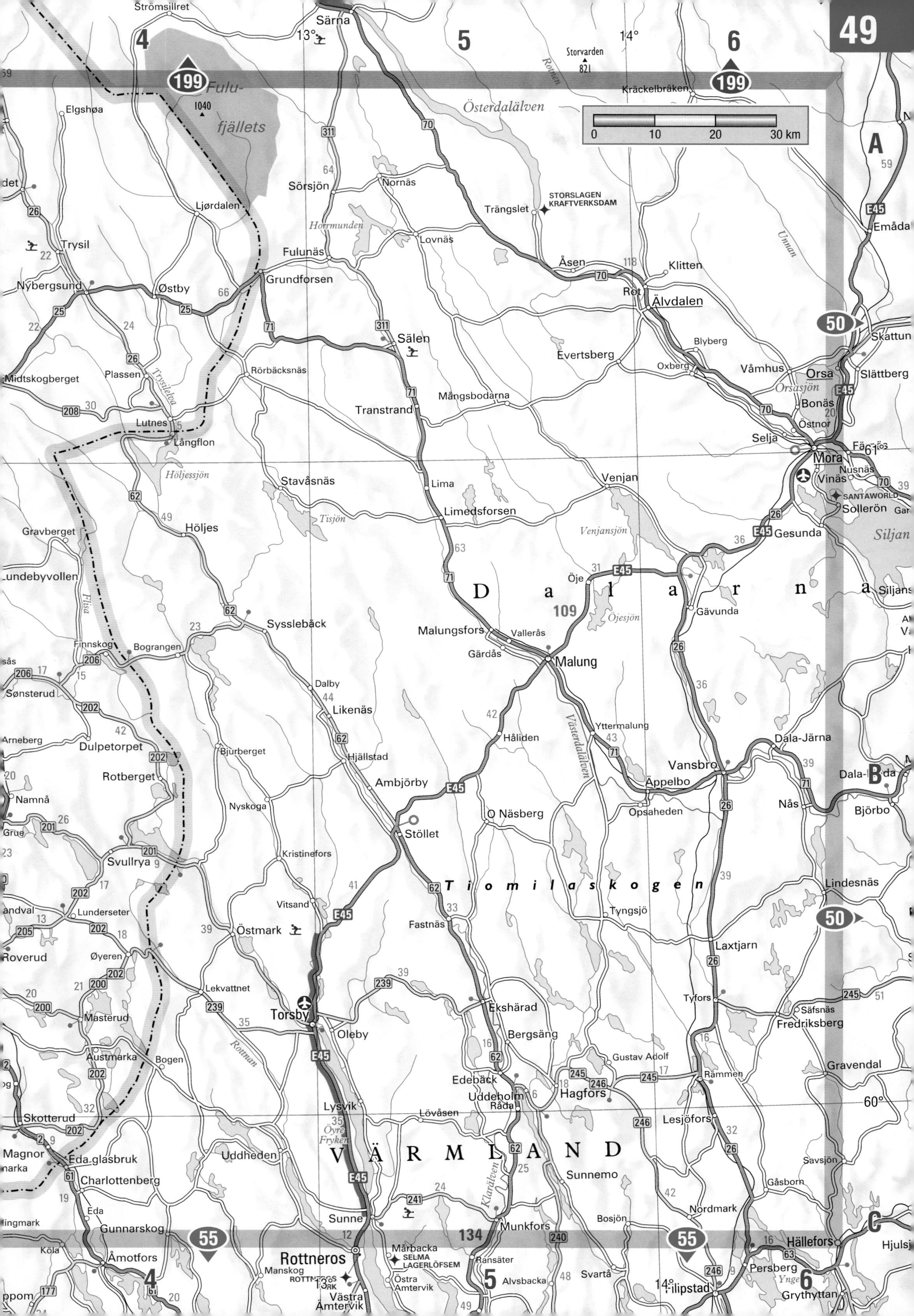
Särna
Strömsillret
Fulu-
fjällets
Storvarden 821
Österdalälven
0 10 20 30 km
Elgshøa
Sörsjön
Nornäs
Trängslet
STORSLAGEN KRAFTVERKSDAM
Ljørdalen
Trysil
Fulunäs
Lovnäs
Åsen
Klitten
Rot
Älvdalen
Nybergsund
Østby
Grundforsen
Sälen
Evertsberg
Blyberg
Oxberg
Våmhus
Orsa
Skattungbyn
Slättberg
Emåda
Midtskogberget
Plassen
Rörbäcksnäs
Mångsbodarna
Transtrand
Bonäs
Östnor
Selja
Mora
Nusnäs
Vinäs
SANTAWORLD
Sollerön
Gesunda
Siljan
Lutnes
Långflon
Höljessjön
Stavåsnäs
Lima
Venjan
Limedsforsen
Tisjön
Venjansjön
Gravberget
Höljes
Lundebyvollen
Öje
Ojesjön
Gävunda
Dalarna
Malungsfors
Vallerås
Gärdås
Malung
Sysslebäck
Finnskog
Bograngen
Sønsterud
Dalby
Likenäs
Yttermalung
Håliden
Västerdalälven
Dala-Järna
Vansbro
Äppelbo
Dala-Floda
Nås
Björbo
Arneberg
Dulpetorpet
Rotberget
Bjurberget
Hjällstad
Ambjörby
Namnå
Nyskoga
O Näsberg
Opsaheden
Grue
Stöllet
Svullrya
Kristinefors
Tiomilaskogen
Lindesnäs
Lunderseter
Vitsand
Fastnäs
Tyngsjö
Östmark
Roverud
Øyeren
Laxtjarn
Lekvattnet
Torsby
Ekshärad
Tyfors
Säfsnäs
Fredriksberg
Masterud
Oleby
Bergsäng
Rottnan
Austmarka
Bogen
Gustav Adolf
Rämmen
Gravendal
Edebäck
Hagfors
Uddeholm
Råda
Lysvik
Lövåsen
Lesjöfors
Skotterud
Övre Fryken
Magnor
Eda glasbruk
Uddheden
VÄRMLAND
Klarälven
Savsjön
Charlottenberg
Sunnemo
Gåsborn
Eda
Nordmark
Gunnarskog
Sunne
Munkfors
Bosjön
Hällefors
Köla
Mårbacka
SELMA LAGERLÖFSEM
Ransäter
Åmotfors
Rottneros
Manskog
ROTTNEROS PARK
Östra Amtervik
Alvsbacka
Svartå
Filipstad
Persberg
Yngen
Grythyttan
Västra Ämtervik
Hjulsjö
Unnan
Horrmunden
Trysilelva
Flisa

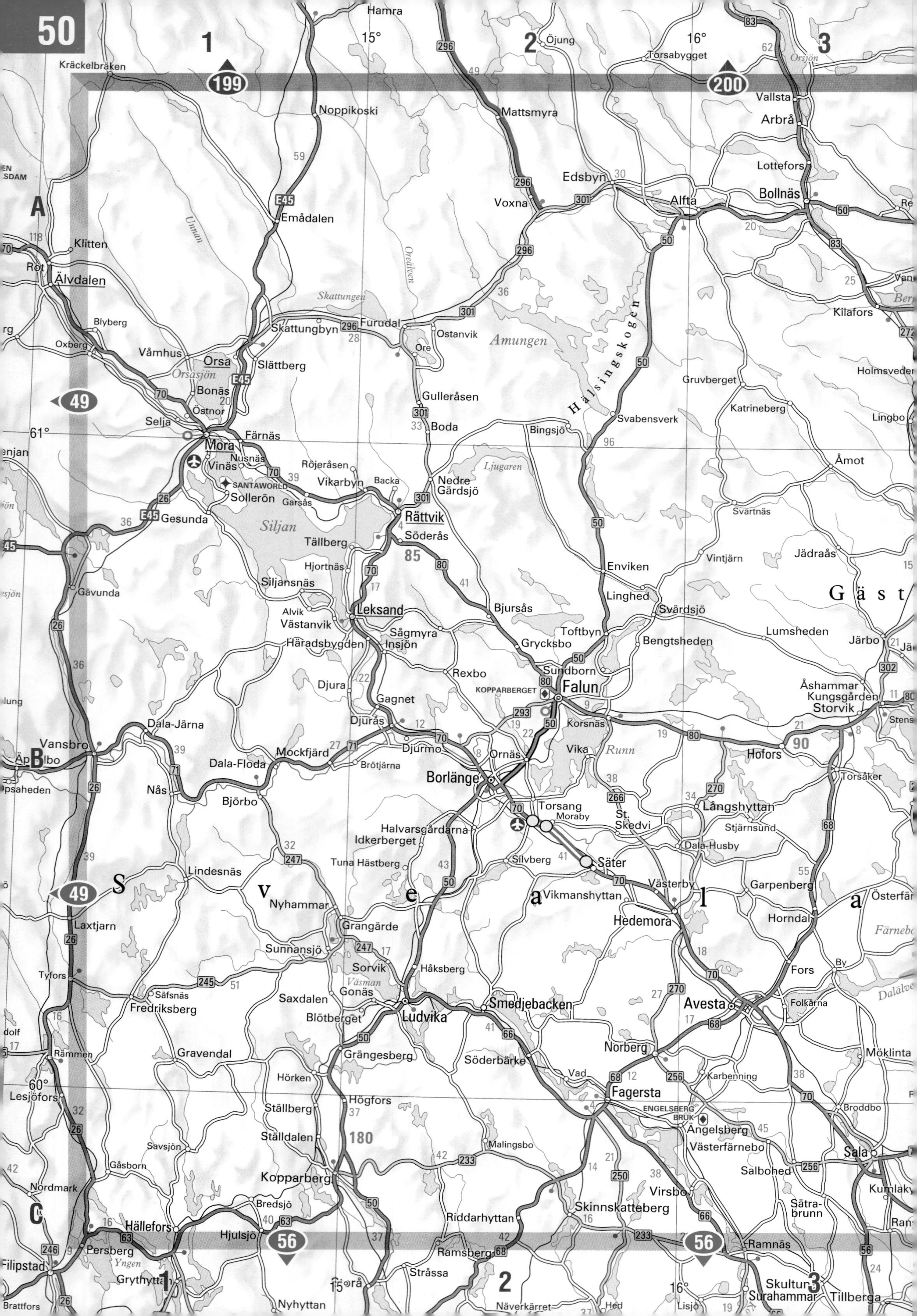

50
1
2
3
15°
16°
199
200
49
56
90
Hamra
Kräckelbräken
Öjung
Torsabygget
Orsjön
Noppikoski
Mattsmyra
Vallsta
Arbrå
Lottefors
Edsbyn
Voxna
Alfta
Bollnäs
Emådalen
Klitten
Rot
Älvdalen
Unnan
Orealven
Skattungen
Kilafors
Blyberg
Oxberg
Skattungbyn
Furudal
Ostanvik
Ore
Amungen
Hälsingskogen
Våmhus
Orsa
Orsasjön
Slättberg
Bonäs
Östnor
Gulleråsen
Gruvberget
Holmsveden
Katrineberg
Svabensverk
Lingbo
Selja
Färnäs
Mora
Boda
Bingsjö
61°
Vinäs
Nusnäs
Röjeråsen
Ljugaren
Åmot
SANTAWORLD
Vikarbyn
Backa
Nedre Gärdsjö
Sollerön
Garsås
Rättvik
Svartnäs
Gesunda
Siljan
Söderås
Tällberg
Hjortnäs
Vintjärn
Jädraås
Enviken
Gävunda
Siljansnäs
Linghed
Gäst
Alvik
Västanvik
Leksand
Bjursås
Svärdsjö
Lumsheden
Järbo
Sågmyra
Toftbyn
Bengtsheden
Häradsbygden
Insjön
Grycksbo
Sundborn
Rexbo
Djura
KOPPARBERGET
Falun
Åshammar
Kungsgården
Storvik
Gagnet
Djurås
Korsnäs
Dala-Järna
Djurmo
Vansbro
Mockfjärd
Ornäs
Vika
Runn
Hofors
Äppelbo
Dala-Floda
Brötjärna
Borlänge
Torsåker
Nås
Björbo
Torsang
Moraby
St. Skedvi
Långshyttan
Halvarsgårdarna
Idkerberget
Stjärnsund
Dala-Husby
Tuna Hästberg
Silvberg
Säter
Lindesnäs
Västerby
Garpenberg
Vikmanshyttan
Österfärnebo
Nyhammar
Hedemora
Horndal
Laxtjarn
Grangärde
Sunnansjö
Sorvik
Håksberg
Fors
Tyfors
Väsman
Gonäs
Säfsnäs
Fredriksberg
Saxdalen
Smedjebacken
Avesta
Folkärna
Dalälven
Blötberget
Ludvika
Rämmen
Gravendal
Grängesberg
Söderbärke
Norberg
Möklinta
Hörken
Vad
Karbenning
60°
Lesjöfors
Fagersta
Broddbo
Högfors
Ställberg
ENGELSBERG BRUK
Ängelsberg
Ställdalen
Västerfärnebo
Savsjön
Malingsbo
Sala
Gåsborn
Salbohed
Kopparberg
Kumlaby
Nordmark
Virsbo
Sätra-brunn
Bredsjö
Riddarhyttan
Skinnskatteberg
Hällefors
Hjulsjö
Ramsberg
Ramnäs
Persberg
Yngen
Filipstad
Grythyttan
Stråssa
Skultuna
Surahammar
Tillberga
Brattfors
Nyhyttan
Näverkärret
Hed
Lisjö
A
B
C
S v e a l a

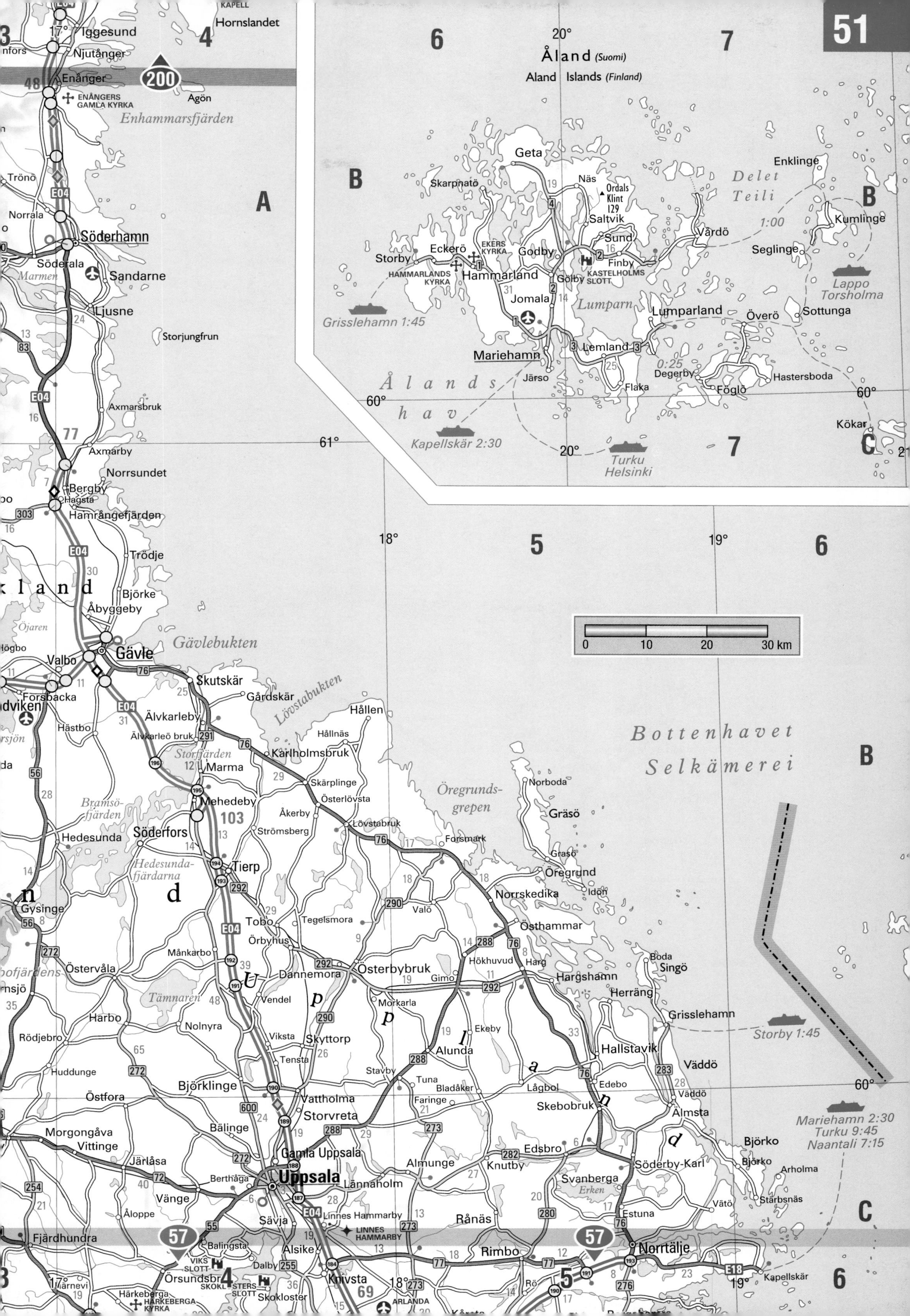

Åland (Suomi)
Aland Islands (Finland)
Geta
Skarpnatö
Näs
Ordals Klint 129
Saltvik
Delet
Teili
Enklinge
Kumlinge
Vårdö
Seglinge
Sund
Finby
Storby
Eckerö
EKERS KYRKA
Godby
HAMMARLANDS KYRKA
Hammarland
KASTELHOLMS SLOTT
Jomala
Lumparn
Lumparland
Överö
Sottunga
Lappo
Torsholma
Grisslehamn 1:45
Mariehamn
Lemland
Järso
Flaka
Degerby
Föglö
Hastersboda
Ålands hav
Kapellskär 2:30
Turku
Helsinki
Kökar
Iggesund
Hornslandet
Njutånger
Enånger
ENÅNGERS GAMLA KYRKA
Agön
Enhammarsfjärden
Trönö
Norrala
Söderhamn
Söderala
Sandarne
Marmen
Ljusne
Storjungfrun
Axmarsbruk
Axmarby
Norrsundet
Bergby
Hagsta
Hamrångefjärden
Trödje
Björke
Åbyggeby
Öjaren
Gävlebukten
Gävle
Valbo
Forsbacka
Skutskär
Gårdskär
Lövstabukten
Älvkarleby
Älvkarleö bruk
Hästbo
Hållen
Hållnäs
Karlholmsbruk
Storfjärden
Marma
Bottenhavet
Selkämerei
Skärplinge
Österlövsta
Öregrundsgrepen
Norboda
Gräsö
Bramsöfjärden
Mehedeby
Åkerby
Strömsberg
Lövstabruk
Hedesunda
Söderfors
Forsmark
Hedesundafjärdarna
Tierp
Öregrund
Norrskedika
Idön
Gysinge
Valö
Tobo
Tegelsmora
Östhammar
Örbyhus
Månkarbo
Hökhuvud
Harg
Boda
Singö
Östervåla
Dannemora
Österbybruk
Gimo
Hargshamn
Herräng
Vendel
Morkarla
Tämnaren
Grisslehamn
Storby 1:45
Harbo
Nolnyra
Ekeby
Rödjebro
Viksta
Skyttorp
Alunda
Hallstavik
Tensta
Väddö
Huddunge
Stavby
Tuna
Bladåker
Edebo
Lågbol
Björklinge
Skebobruk
Östfora
Vattholma
Faringe
Storvreta
Älmsta
Mariehamn 2:30
Turku 9:45
Naantali 7:15
Morgongåva
Bälinge
Björko
Vittinge
Gamla Uppsala
Almunge
Edsbro
Järlåsa
Knutby
Söderby-Karl
Arholma
Berthåga
Uppsala
Svanberga
Erken
Vänge
Lännaholm
Åloppe
Linnes Hammarby
Sävja
Vätö
Stärbsnäs
Rånäs
Estuna
Fjärdhundra
LINNES HAMMARBY
Balingsta
Alsike
Rimbo
Norrtälje
VIKS SLOTT
Dalby
Örsundsbro
Knivsta
Kapellskär
SKOKLOSTERS SLOTT
Skokloster
Härkeberga
HÄRKEBERGA KYRKA
Järnevi
ARLANDA
Rö
0 10 20 30 km

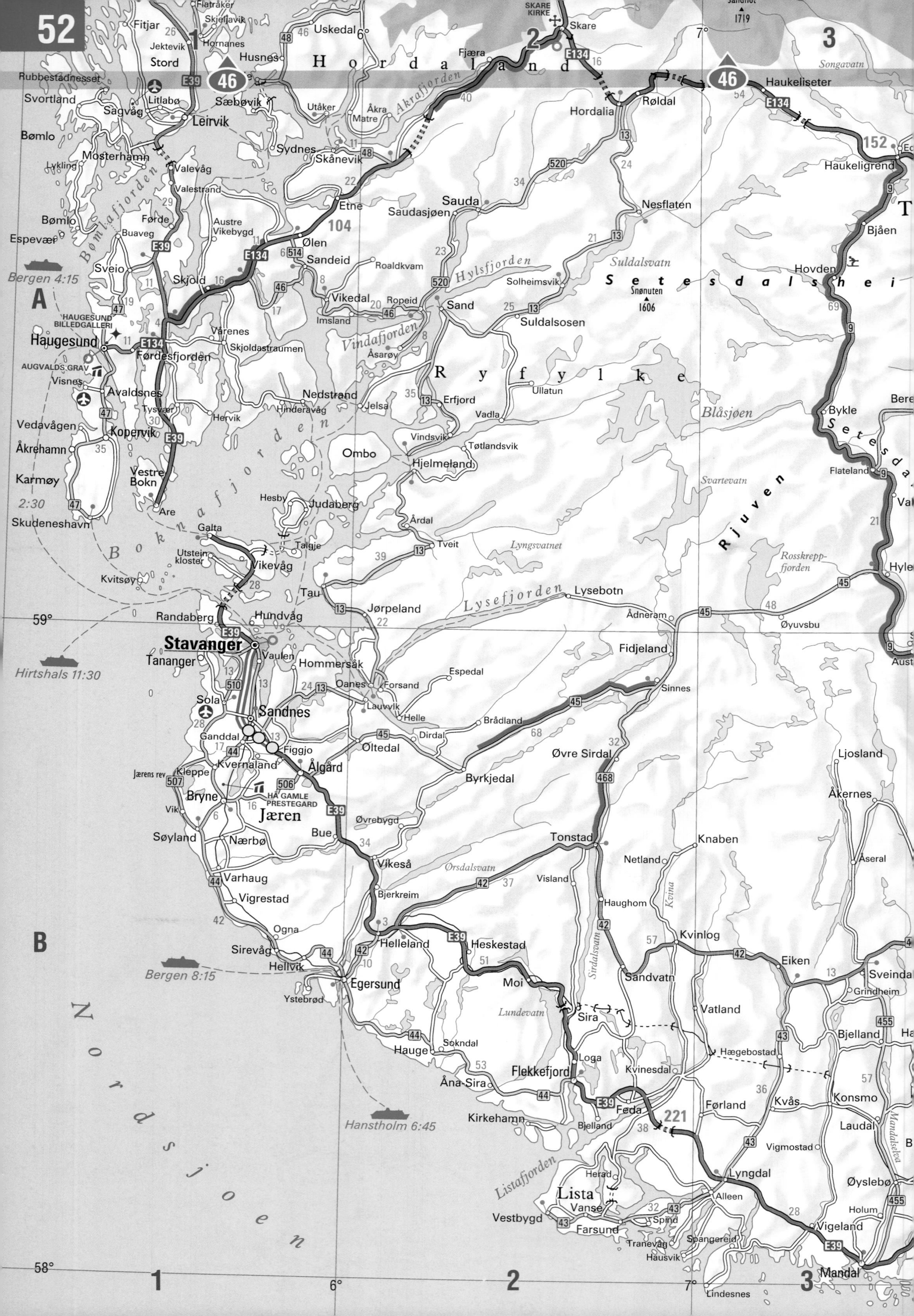
Hordaland
Fitjar
Flatråker
Skjeljavik
Hornanes
Jektevik
Stord
Husnes
Uskedal
Rubbestadnesset
Svortland
Sagvåg
Litlabø
Leirvik
Sæbøvik
Utåker
Åkra
Matre
Akrafjorden
Fjæra
Skare
SKARE KIRKE
1719
Songavatn
Haukeliseter
Røldal
Hordalia
Bømlo
Mosterhamn
Lykling
Valevåg
Sydnes
Skånevik
Valestrand
Bømlafjorden
Bømlo
Førde
Austre Vikebygd
Espevær
Buaveg
Etne
Sauda
Saudasjøen
Nesflaten
Haukeligrend
Bjåen
Hovden
Ølen
Sandeid
Roaldkvam
Bergen 4:15
Sveio
Skjold
Vikedal
Ropeid
Imsland
Sand
Hylsfjorden
Solheimsvik
Suldalsvatn
Setesdalsheii
Snønuten
1606
Suldalsosen
A
HAUGESUND BILLEDGALLERI
Haugesund
Vårenes
Skjoldastraumen
Førdesfjorden
Vindafjorden
Åsarøy
AUGVALDS GRAV
Visnes
Avaldsnes
Tysvær
Ryfylke
Ullatun
Nedstrand
Hinderavåg
Hervik
Jelsa
Erfjord
Vadla
Blåsjøen
Bykle
Setesdal
Vedavågen
Kopervik
Åkrehamn
Karmøy
Vestre Bokn
Ombo
Vindsvik
Tøtlandsvik
Hjelmeland
Svartevatn
Flateland
Boknafjorden
Hesby
Judaberg
Rjuven
2:30
Skudeneshavn
Are
Galta
Årdal
Tveit
Lyngsvatnet
Rossknepp-fjorden
Utstein kloster
Talgje
Vikevåg
Kvitsøy
Tau
Lysefjorden
Lysebotn
Hyle
Randaberg
Hundvåg
Jørpeland
Ådneram
Øyuvsbu
59°
Stavanger
Tananger
Vaulen
Hommersåk
Fidjeland
Hirtshals 11:30
Espedal
Forsand
Oanes
Sinnes
Sola
Lauvvik
Helle
Sandnes
Brådland
Dirdal
Ganddal
Figgjo
Oltedal
Øvre Sirdal
Ljosland
Jærens rev
Kleppe
Kvernaland
Ålgård
Byrkjedal
Bryne
HÅ GAMLE PRESTEGARD
Vik
Jæren
Åkernes
Øvrebygd
Søyland
Bue
Tonstad
Knaben
Nærbø
Vikeså
Ørsdalsvatn
Netland
Åseral
Varhaug
Visland
Bjerkreim
Haughom
Kvina
Vigrestad
Ogna
Sirdalsvatn
Kvinlog
B
Helleland
Heskestad
Sirevåg
Hellvik
Eiken
Sveindal
Bergen 8:15
Egersund
Moi
Sandvatn
Grindheim
Ystebrød
Lundevatn
Vatland
Sira
Nordsjøen
Hauge
Sokndal
Hægebostad
Bjelland
Loga
Kvinesdal
Flekkefjord
Åna-Sira
Konsmo
Kvås
Førland
Feda
Kirkehamn
Bjelland
Hanstholm 6:45
Laudal
Mandalselva
Vigmostad
Listafjorden
Herad
Lyngdal
Lista
Vanse
Alleen
Øyslebø
Vestbygd
Spind
Farsund
Holum
Vigeland
Tranevåg
Spangereid
Hausvik
Mandal
Lindesnes
58°
1
6°
2
7°
3

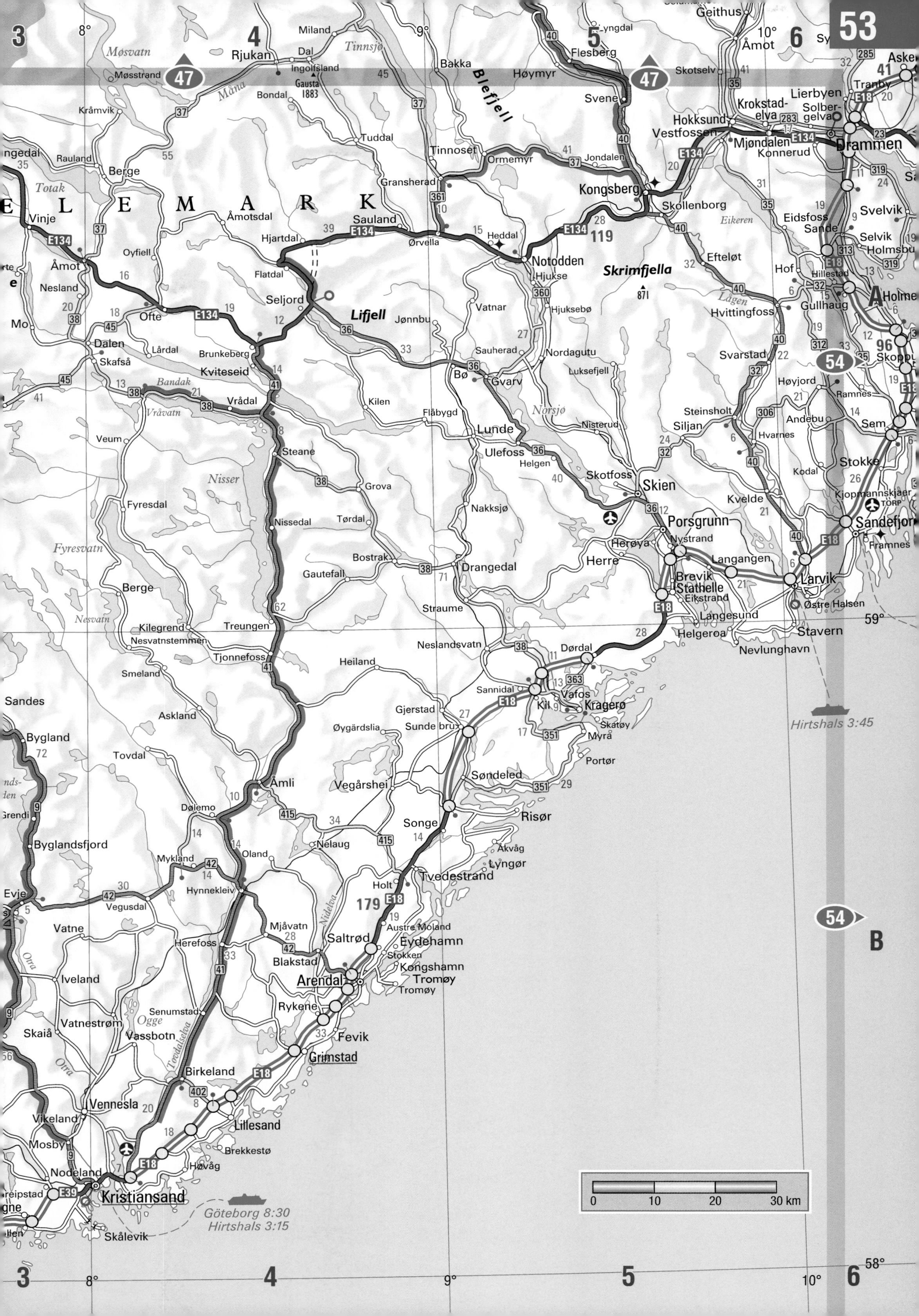

TELEMARK
Møsvatn
Rjukan
Dal
Miland
Tinnsjø
Ingolfsland
Gausta 1883
Møsstrand
Måna
Bondal
Kråmvik
Tuddal
Rauland
Berge
Totak
Vinje
Åmot
Oyfiell
Nesland
Mo
Åmotsdal
Hjartdal
Flatdal
Seljord
Lifjell
Ofte
Dalen
Skafså
Lårdal
Brunkeberg
Kviteseid
Bandak
Vrådal
Vråvatn
Veum
Steane
Nisser
Fyresdal
Fyresvatn
Nissedal
Tørdal
Grova
Berge
Nesvatn
Kilegrend
Nesvatnstemmen
Treungen
Tjonnefoss
Smeland
Sandes
Askland
Bygland
Tovdal
Åmli
Dølemo
Byglandsfjord
Mykland
Hynnekleiv
Evje
Vegusdal
Vatne
Herefoss
Mjåvatn
Iveland
Senumstad
Ogge
Vatnestrøm
Skaiå
Vassbotn
Birkeland
Vennesla
Vikeland
Mosby
Nodeland
Kristiansand
Skålevik
Lillesand
Brekkestø
Høvåg
Göteborg 8:30
Hirtshals 3:15
Grimstad
Fevik
Rykene
Arendal
Tromøy
Kongshamn
Stokken
Eydehamn
Austre Moland
Saltrød
Blakstad
Nidelva
Holt
Tvedestrand
Lyngør
Åkvåg
Nelaug
Oland
Songe
Risør
Vegårshei
Søndeled
Portør
Øygärdslia
Gjerstad
Sunde bru
Myra
Skatøy
Kragerø
Vafos
Kil
Sannidal
Dørdal
Neslandsvatn
Heiland
Straume
Drangedal
Gautefall
Bostrak
Nakksjø
Ulefoss
Helgen
Lunde
Flåbygd
Kilen
Bø
Gvarv
Sauherad
Jønnbu
Vatnar
Nordagutu
Luksefjell
Norsjø
Nisterud
Skotfoss
Skien
Porsgrunn
Herøya
Herre
Nystrand
Brevik
Stathelle
Eikstrand
Langesund
Helgeroa
Nevlunghavn
Stavern
Larvik
Østre Halsen
Langangen
Kvelde
Siljan
Steinsholt
Svarstad
Hvittingfoss
Efteløt
Lågen
Skrimfjella 871
Notodden
Hjukse
Hjuksebø
Heddal
Ørvella
Sauland
Gransherad
Tinnoset
Ormemyr
Bakka
Blefjell
Høymyr
Flesberg
Lyngdal
Svene
Jondalen
Kongsberg
Skollenborg
Eikeren
Geithus
Åmot
Skotselv
Hokksund
Vestfossen
Krokstad-elva
Mjøndalen
Konnerud
Solbergelva
Lierbyen
Tranby
Asker
Drammen
Svelvik
Eidsfoss
Sande
Selvik
Holmsbu
Hof
Hillestad
Gullhaug
Holme
Skopu
Høyjord
Ramnes
Andebu
Hvarnes
Sem
Stokke
Kodal
Kjopmannskjaer
TORP
Sandefjord
Framnes
Hirtshals 3:45
Sy
10°
9°
8°
58°
59°
3
4
5
6
A
B
47
54
96
119
179
E18
E39
E134
0 10 20 30 km

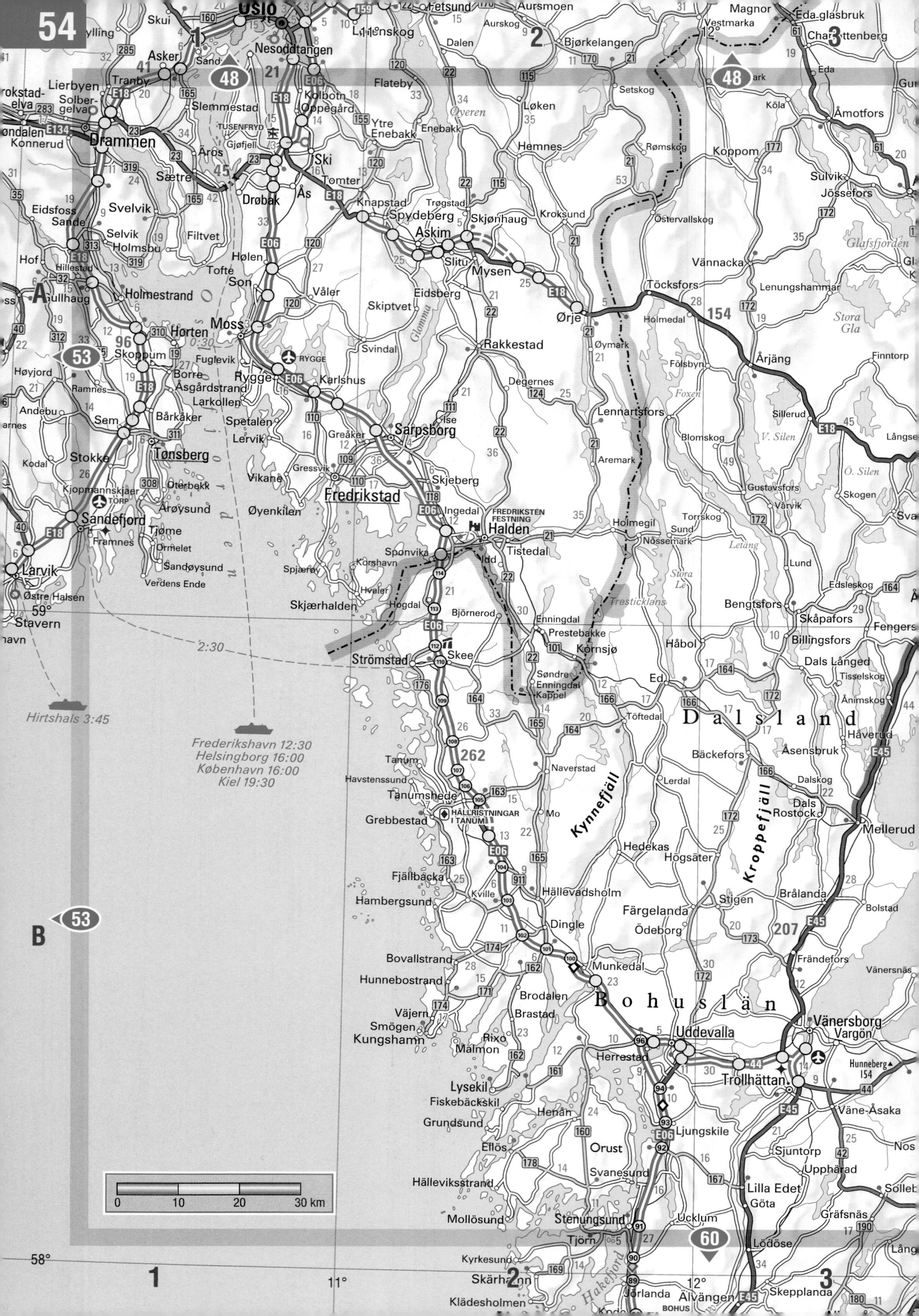
Oslo
Skui
Asker
Sandvika
Nesoddtangen
Lillestrøm
Fetsund
Aursmoen
Aurskog
Magnor
Vestmarka
Eda glasbruk
Charlottenberg
Eda
Lierbyen
Tranby
Drammenselva
Solbergelva
Slemmestad
Kolbotn
Oppegård
Flateby
Dalen
Bjørkelangen
Setskog
Øyeren
Løken
Køla
Åmotfors
Konnerud
Drammen
TUSENFRYD
Gjøfjell
Åros
Ytre Enebakk
Enebakk
Hemnes
Rømskog
Koppom
Sætre
Ski
Tomter
Sulvik
Jössefors
Eidsfoss
Sande
Svelvik
Drøbak
Ås
Knapstad
Trøgstad
Spydeberg
Skjønhaug
Kroksund
Östervallskog
Glafsfjorden
Selvik
Holmsbu
Filtvet
Askim
Hof
Hillestad
Hølen
Slitu
Mysen
Vännacka
Tofte
Son
Töcksfors
Lenungshammar
Gullhaug
Holmestrand
Våler
Eidsberg
Skiptvet
Glomma
Ørje
Holmedal
Stora Gla
Moss
Horten
Rakkestad
Øymark
Årjäng
Finntorp
Svindal
Høyjord
Skoppum
Fuglevik
Borre
Åsgårdstrand
Rygge
RYGGE
Karlshus
Fölsbyn
Ramnes
Larkollen
Degernes
Foxen
Andebu
Sem
Bårkåker
Spetalen
Lennartsfors
Sillerud
Lervik
Greåker
Sarpsborg
Ise
Blomskog
V. Silen
Långserud
Tønsberg
Gressvik
Aremark
Kodal
Stokke
Vikane
Skjeberg
Ö. Silen
Gustavsfors
Kjopmannskjaer
TORP
Oterbekk
Fredrikstad
Skogen
Vårvik
Årøysund
Øyenkilen
Ingedal
FREDRIKSTEN FESTNING
Torrskog
Sandefjord
Framnes
Tjøme
Halden
Holmegil
Sund
Nössemark
Svanskog
Ormelet
Sponvika
Tistedal
Letäng
Larvik
Sandøysund
Korshavn
Idd
Stora Le
Lund
Verdens Ende
Spjærøy
Hvaler
Tresticklan
Edsleskog
Østre Halsen
Skjærhalden
Hogdal
Bengtsfors
Stavern
Bjørnerod
Enningdal
Skåpafors
Prestebakke
Billingsfors
Fengersfors
Strömstad
Skee
Kornsjø
Håbol
Dals Långed
Søndre Enningdal
Kappel
Ed
Tisselskog
Hirtshals 3:45
Ånimskog
Töftedal
Dalsland
Håverud
Frederikshavn 12:30
Helsingborg 16:00
København 16:00
Kiel 19:30
Tanum
Bäckefors
Åsensbruk
Naverstad
Havstenssund
Lerdal
Dalskog
Tanumshede
Kynnefjäll
Dals Rostock
Grebbestad
HÄLLRISTNINGAR I TANUM
Mo
Kroppefjäll
Mellerud
Hedekas
Högsäter
Fjällbacka
Hällevadsholm
Brålanda
Hambergsund
Kville
Färgelanda
Stigen
Bolstad
Dingle
Ödeborg
Bovallstrand
Frändefors
Munkedal
Hunnebostrand
Vänersnäs
Brodalen
Bohuslän
Väjern
Brastad
Smögen
Kungshamn
Vänersborg
Vargön
Rixö
Uddevalla
Malmön
Herrestad
Hunneberg
Trollhättan
Lysekil
Fiskebäckskil
Henån
Väne-Åsaka
Grundsund
Ljungskile
Ellös
Orust
Sjuntorp
Upphärad
Svanesund
Hälleviksstrand
Lilla Edet
Göta
Mollösund
Stenungsund
Ucklum
Gräfsnäs
Tjörn
Lödöse
Kyrkesund
Skärhamn
Hakefjord
Jörlanda
Älvängen
Skepplanda
Klädesholmen
BOHUS
0
10
20
30 km
59°
58°
11°
12°
48
53
60
E18
E06
E45
1
2
3
A
B

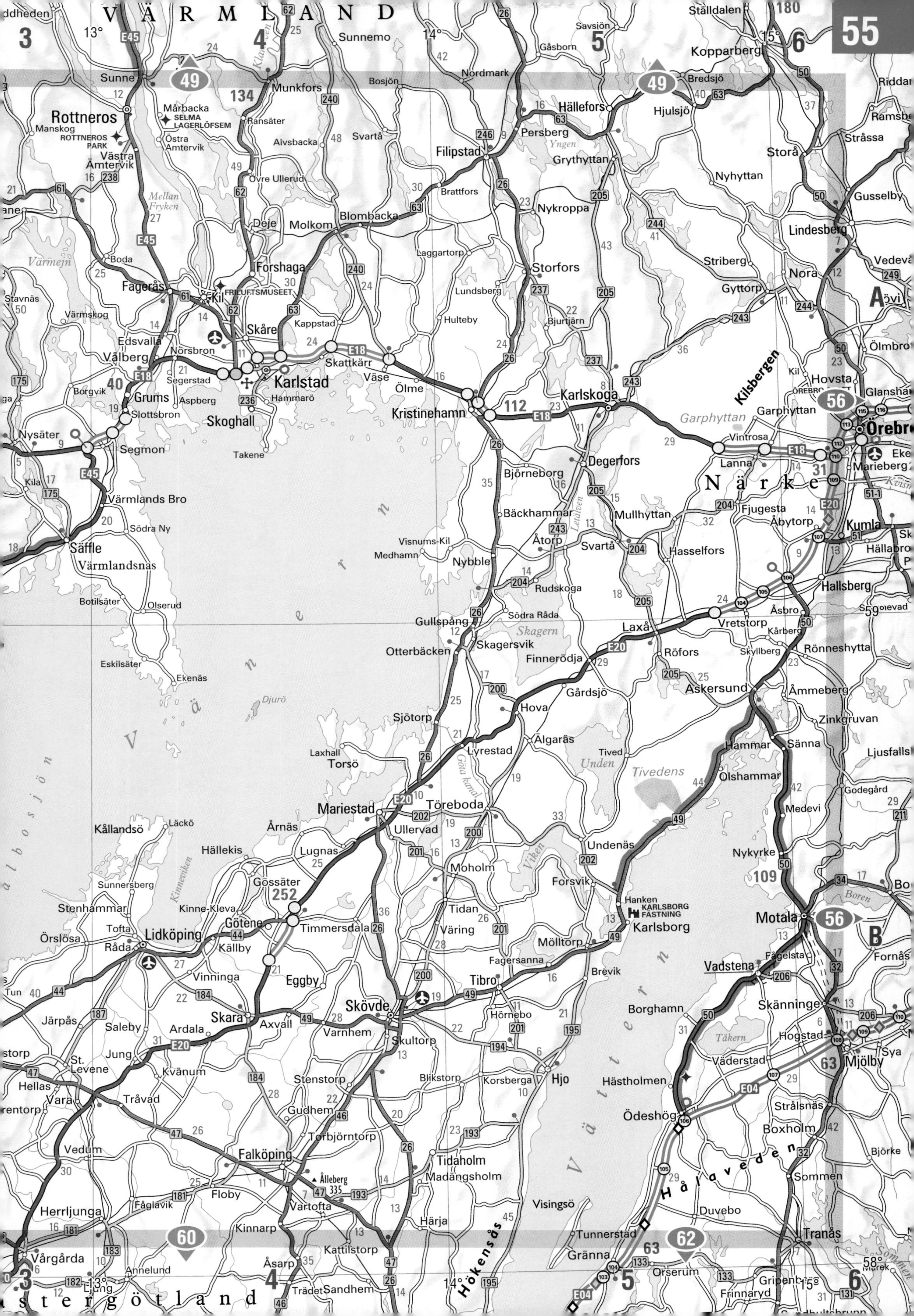
VÄRMLAND
Närke
Vänern
Vättern
Östergötland
Sunne
Rottneros
Manskog
Rottneros Park
Mårbacka
Selma Lagerlöfsem
Östra Ämtervik
Västra Ämtervik
Munkfors
Ransäter
Sunnemo
Bosjön
Alvsbacka
Svartå
Övre Ullerud
Mellan Fryken
Deje
Molkom
Blombacka
Forshaga
Kil
Friluftsmuseet
Fagerås
Boda
Värmeln
Stavnäs
Värmskog
Edsvalla
Vålberg
Nörsbron
Skåre
Kappstad
Skattkärr
Väse
Ölme
Karlstad
Segerstad
Aspberg
Hammarö
Skoghall
Takene
Grums
Borgvik
Slottsbron
Segmon
Nysäter
Kila
Värmlands Bro
Södra Ny
Säffle
Värmlandsnäs
Botilsäter
Olserud
Eskilsäter
Ekenäs
Djurö
Kristinehamn
Filipstad
Brattfors
Nordmark
Gåsborn
Savsjön
Ställdalen
Kopparberg
Bredsjö
Hjulsjö
Hällefors
Persberg
Yngen
Grythyttan
Nykroppa
Laggartorp
Storfors
Lundsberg
Hulteby
Bjurtjärn
Karlskoga
Degerfors
Björneborg
Bäckhammar
Visnums-Kil
Medhamn
Nybble
Åtorp
Svartå
Mullhyttan
Hasselfors
Rudskoga
Gullspång
Södra Råda
Skagern
Otterbäcken
Skagersvik
Finnerödja
Laxå
Röfors
Vretstorp
Åsbro
Kårberg
Skyllberg
Askersund
Gårdsjö
Hova
Älgarås
Tived
Unden
Tivedens
Sjötorp
Lyrestad
Göta kanal
Laxhall
Torsö
Mariestad
Töreboda
Ullervad
Årnäs
Lugnås
Hällekis
Kållandsö
Läckö
Sunnersberg
Kinneviken
Gössäter
Kinne-Kleva
Stenhammar
Götene
Timmersdala
Lidköping
Tofta
Örslösa
Råda
Källby
Vinninga
Eggby
Skara
Axvall
Ardala
Saleby
Järpås
Jung
St. Levene
Hellas
Vara
Kvänum
Tråvad
Vedum
Stenstorp
Gudhem
Torbjörntorp
Falköping
Ålleberg
Floby
Fåglavik
Vartofta
Herrljunga
Vårgårda
Annelund
Ljung
Kinnarp
Åsarp
Kattilstorp
Trädet
Sandhem
Skövde
Varnhem
Skultorp
Blikstorp
Tidaholm
Madängsholm
Härja
Hökensås
Moholm
Tidan
Väring
Fagersanna
Tibro
Hörnebo
Korsberga
Hjo
Mölltorp
Undenäs
Forsvik
Viken
Hanken
Karlsborg Fästning
Karlsborg
Brevik
Borghamn
Hästholmen
Ödeshög
Visingsö
Tunnerstad
Gränna
Orserum
Lindesberg
Storå
Stråssa
Nyhyttan
Gusselby
Striberg
Nora
Gyttorp
Kilsbergen
Hovsta
Garphyttan
Vintrosa
Lanna
Örebro
Marieberg
Fjugesta
Åbytorp
Kumla
Hallsberg
Rönneshytta
Ammeberg
Zinkgruvan
Hammar
Sänna
Olshammar
Medevi
Godegärd
Nykyrke
Motala
Boren
Fågelsta
Vadstena
Skänninge
Tåkern
Hogstad
Väderstad
Mjölby
Strålsnäs
Boxholm
Sommen
Hålaveden
Duvebo
Tranås
Gripenberg
Frinnaryd
Ljusfalls
Fornås
Bjorke
Sya
Riddar
Ramsberg
Vedevåg
Glanshammar
Ölmbro
Hällabro

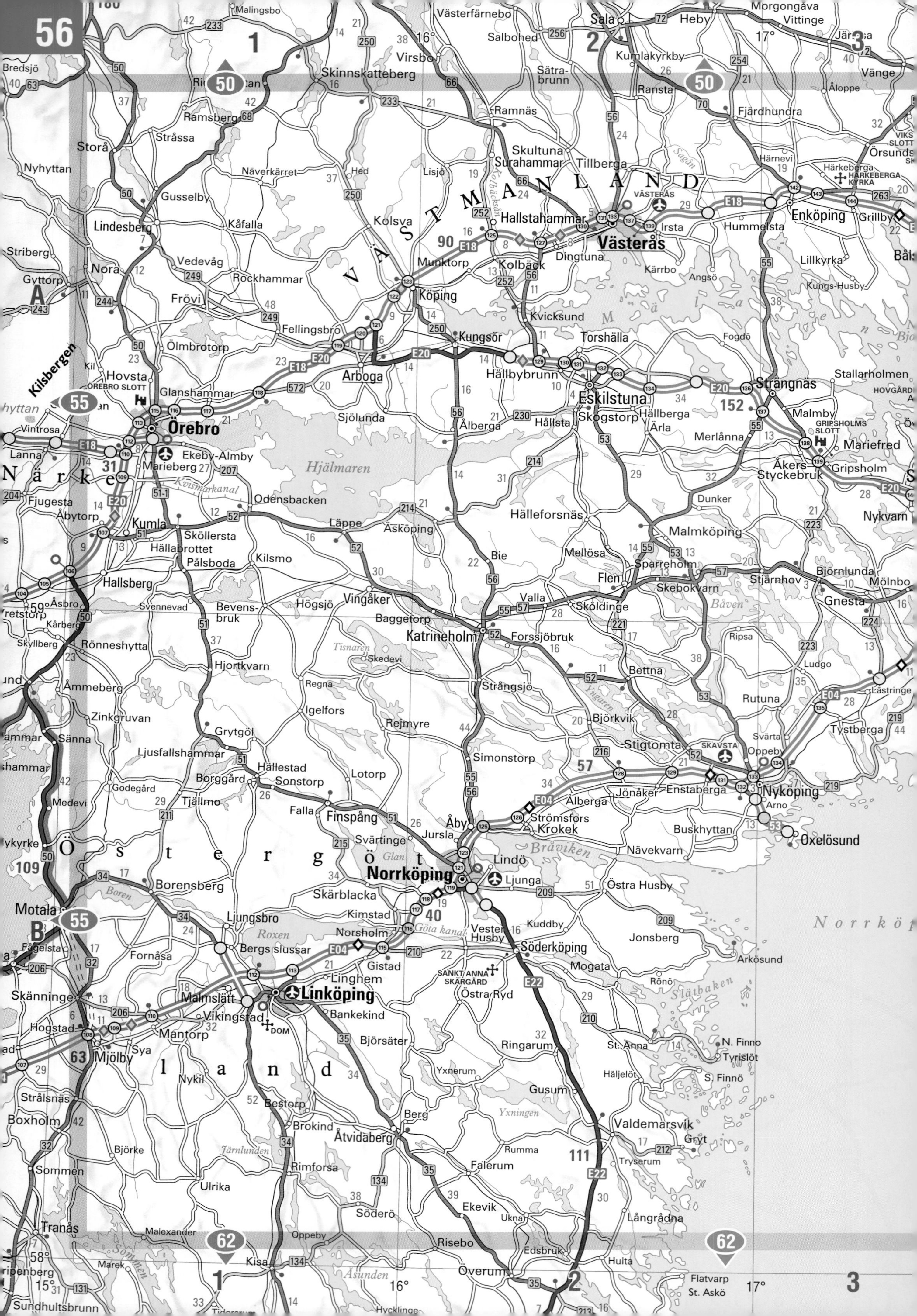

Malingsbo
Västerfärnebo
Sala
Heby
Morgongåva
Vittinge
Järlåsa
Salbohed
Virsbo
Kumlakyrkby
Vänge
Bredsjö
Skinnskatteberg
Sätra-brunn
Ransta
Åloppe
Fjärdhundra
Ramsberg
Ramnäs
Stråssa
Storå
Skultuna
Surahammar
Tillberga
Härnevi
Örsundsbro
Nyhyttan
Näverkärret
Hed
Lisjö
Härkeberga
HÄRKEBERGA KYRKA
VÄSTMANLAND
Gusselby
VÄSTERÅS
Lindesberg
Kåfalla
Kolsva
Hallstahammar
Västerås
Irsta
Hummelsta
Enköping
Grillby
Dingtuna
Striberg
Vedevåg
Munktorp
Kolbäck
Kärrbo
Angsö
Lillkyrka
Nora
Rockhammar
Gyttorp
Köping
Kungs-Husby
Frövi
Kvicksund
Mälaren
Fellingsbro
Kungsör
Torshälla
Fogdö
Ölmbrotorp
Kilsbergen
Hovsta
ÖREBRO SLOTT
Arboga
Hällbybrunn
Strängnäs
Stallarholmen
HOVGÅRDEN
Glanshammar
Eskilstuna
Sjölunda
Malmby
GRIPSHOLMS SLOTT
Vintrosa
Örebro
Ålberga
Hällsta
Skogstorp
Hällberga
Ärla
Merlånna
Mariefred
Lanna
Ekeby-Almby
Marieberg
Hjälmaren
Åkers Styckebruk
Gripsholm
Närke
Kvismarkanal
Odensbacken
Fjugesta
Åbytorp
Dunker
Hälleforsnäs
Nykvarn
Kumla
Läppe
Äsköping
Malmköping
Sköllersta
Hällabrottet
Pålsboda
Kilsmo
Bie
Mellösa
Sparreholm
Hallsberg
Flen
Stjärnhov
Björnlunda
Mölnbo
Skebokvarn
Åsbro
Svennevad
Bevens-bruk
Högsjö
Vingåker
Valla
Sköldinge
Gnesta
Båven
Kårberg
Baggetorp
Katrineholm
Forssjöbruk
Skyllberg
Rönneshytta
Tisnaren
Skedevi
Ripsa
Hjortkvarn
Bettna
Ludgo
Åmmeberg
Regna
Strångsjö
Yngaren
Rutuna
Lästringe
Zinkgruvan
Igelfors
Björkvik
Rejmyre
Tystberga
Grytgöl
Svärta
Sänna
Ljusfallshammar
Stigtomta
SKAVSTA
Oppeby
Simonstorp
Hällestad
Borggård
Sonstorp
Lotorp
Godegård
Jönåker
Enstaberga
Nyköping
Tjällmo
Ålberga
Medevi
Falla
Finspång
Strömsfors
Krokek
Arno
Åby
Jursla
Svärtinge
Buskhyttan
Oxelösund
Bråviken
Nävekvarn
Östergötland
Glan
Lindö
Borensberg
Boren
Norrköping
Ljunga
Skärblacka
Östra Husby
Motala
Kimstad
Ljungsbro
Kuddby
Roxen
Norsholm
Göta kanal
Vester-Husby
Norrköpingsbukten
Fågelsta
Fornåsa
Bergs slussar
Söderköping
Jonsberg
Gistad
Mogata
Arkösund
SANKT ANNA SKÄRGÅRD
Linghem
Skänninge
Malmslätt
Linköping
Östra Ryd
Rönö
Slätbaken
Vikingstad
Bankekind
Hogstad
DOM
Mantorp
Sya
Mjölby
Björsäter
Ringarum
St. Anna
N. Finnö
Tyrislöt
Nykil
Yxnerum
Häljelöt
S. Finnö
Strålsnäs
Bestorp
Gusum
Boxholm
Berg
Brokind
Åtvidaberg
Yxningen
Valdemarsvik
Gryt
Björke
Järnlunden
Rumma
Rimforsa
Tryserum
Sommen
Falerum
Ulrika
Ekevik
Söderö
Ukna
Långrådna
Tranås
Malexander
Oppeby
Risebo
Edsbruk
Hulta
Marek
Kisa
Åsunden
Överum
Flatvarp
St. Askö
Sundhultsbrunn
Tidersrum
Hycklinge

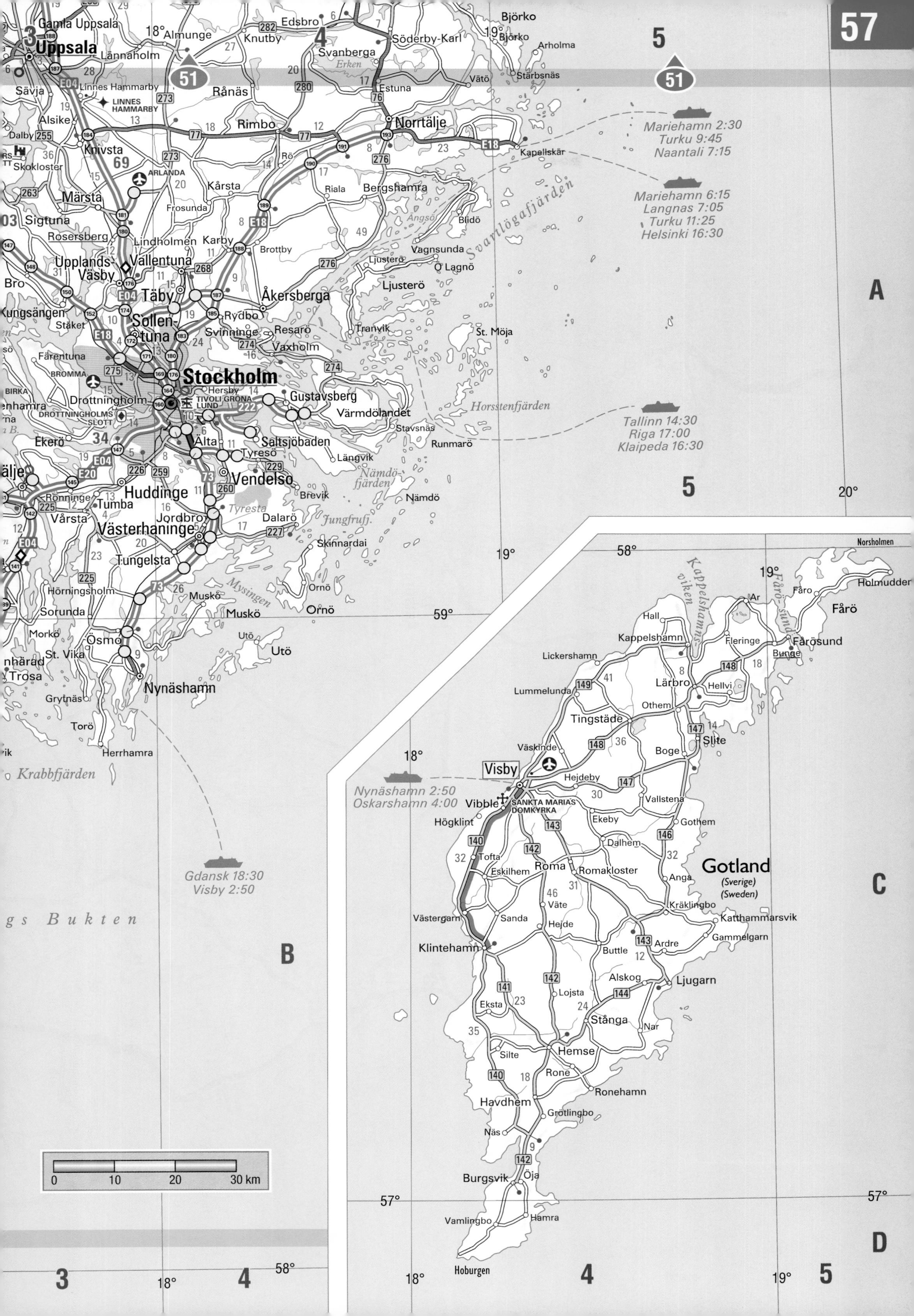
Gamla Uppsala
Uppsala
Lännaholm
Almunge
Knutby
Edsbro
Svanberga
Erken
Söderby-Karl
Björko
Arholma
Vätö
Stärbsnäs
Estuna
Sävja
Linnes Hammarby
LINNES HAMMARBY
Rånäs
Alsike
Rimbo
Norrtälje
Kapellskär
Mariehamn 2:30
Turku 9:45
Naantali 7:15
Dalby
Knivsta
Skokloster
ARLANDA
Kårsta
Riala
Bergshamra
Mariehamn 6:15
Langnas 7:05
Turku 11:25
Helsinki 16:30
Märsta
Frosunda
Sigtuna
Rosersberg
Lindholmen
Karby
Brottby
Ängsö
Blidö
Svartlögafjärden
Upplands-Väsby
Vallentuna
Vagnsunda
Ljusterö
Lagnö
Bro
Täby
Åkersberga
Kungsängen
Stäket
Sollentuna
Rydbo
Svinninge
Resarö
Vaxholm
Tranvik
St. Möja
Färentuna
BROMMA
Stockholm
Hersby
TIVOLI GRÖNA LUND
Gustavsberg
Värmdölandet
Horsstenfjärden
BIRKA
Drottningholm
DROTTNINGHOLMS SLOTT
Stavsnäs
Tallinn 14:30
Riga 17:00
Klaipeda 16:30
Ekerö
Älta
Saltsjöbaden
Runmarö
Tyresö
Längvik
Huddinge
Vendelsö
Nämdöfjärden
Brevik
Nämdö
Rönninge
Tumba
Vårsta
Jordbro
Tyresta
Dalarö
Jungfrufj.
Västerhaninge
Skinnardai
Tungelsta
Hörningsholm
Mysingen
Muskö
Ornö
Sorunda
59°
Morko
Ösmo
Utö
St. Vika
Trosa
Nynäshamn
Grytnäs
Torö
Herrhamra
Krabbfjärden
Gdansk 18:30
Visby 2:50
Bukten
B
0
10
20
30 km
3
4
18°
58°
20°
19°
A
5
C
D
Norsholmen
Holmudden
Kappelshamnsviken
Fårö-sund
Fårö
Ar
Hall
Kappelshamn
Fleringe
Fårösund
Bunge
Lickershamn
Lärbro
Hellvi
Lummelunda
Othem
Tingstäde
Slite
Väskinde
Boge
Visby
Hejdeby
Nynäshamn 2:50
Oskarshamn 4:00
Vibble
SANKTA MARIAS DOMKYRKA
Vallstena
Högklint
Ekeby
Gothem
Dalhem
Tofta
Roma
Romakloster
Gotland
(Sverige)
(Sweden)
Eskilhem
Anga
Väte
Kräklingbo
Västergarn
Sanda
Hejde
Katthammarsvik
Gammelgarn
Ardre
Klintehamn
Buttle
Alskog
Ljugarn
Lojsta
Eksta
Stånga
Nar
Hemse
Silte
Rone
Ronehamn
Havdhem
Grötlingbo
Näs
Burgsvik
Öja
57°
Vamlingbo
Hamra
Hoburgen

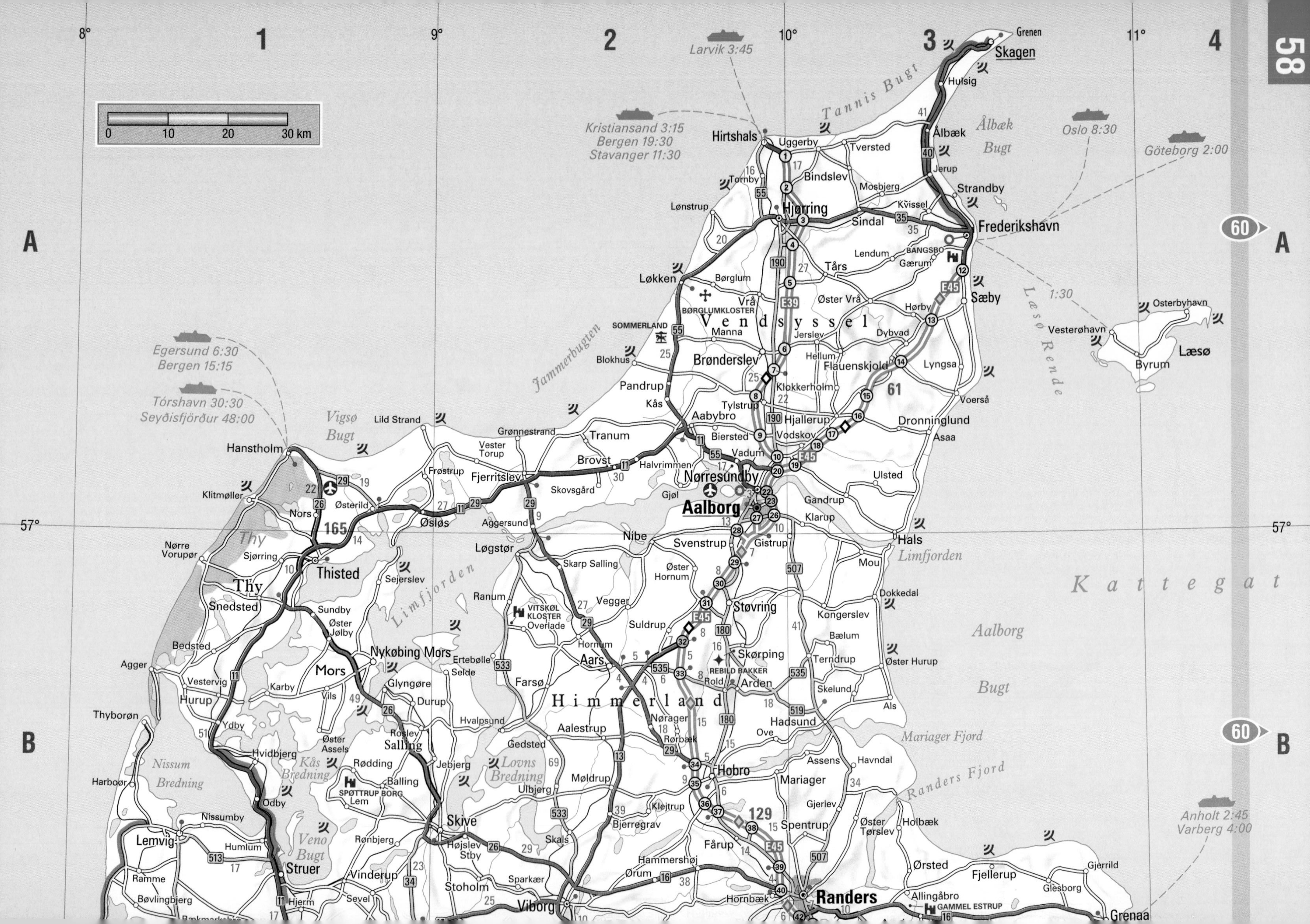

Skagen
Grenen
Hulsig
Ålbæk
Ålbæk Bugt
Tannis Bugt
Jerup
Strandby
Frederikshavn
Hirtshals
Uggerby
Tversted
Bindslev
Mosbjerg
Kvissel
Tornby
Hjørring
Sindal
Lønstrup
Lendum
Bangsbo
Gærum
Tårs
Sæby
Løkken
Børglum
Vrå
Børglumkloster
Øster Vrå
Hørby
Vendsyssel
Sommerland
Manna
Jerslev
Dybvad
Brønderslev
Hellum
Flauenskjold
Lyngsa
Klokkerholm
Blokhus
Pandrup
Kås
Tylstrup
Aabybro
Hjallerup
Dronninglund
Asaa
Voerså
Biersted
Vodskov
Vadum
Jammerbugten
Lild Strand
Vigsø Bugt
Grønnestrand
Tranum
Vester Torup
Brovst
Halvrimmen
Nørresundby
Aalborg
Gjøl
Ulsted
Gandrup
Klarup
Hals
Hanstholm
Frøstrup
Fjerritslev
Skovsgård
Klitmøller
Nors
Østerild
Øsløs
Aggersund
Nibe
Svenstrup
Gistrup
Mou
Limfjorden
Kattegat
Nørre Vorupør
Thy
Sjørring
Thisted
Sejerslev
Løgstør
Skarp Salling
Øster Hornum
Dokkedal
Ranum
Vitskøl Kloster
Overlade
Vegger
Støvring
Kongerslev
Snedsted
Sundby
Øster Jølby
Suldrup
Aalborg Bugt
Bedsted
Nykøbing Mors
Mors
Ertebølle
Selde
Hornum
Aars
Bælum
Terndrup
Øster Hurup
Skørping
Rebild Bakker
Agger
Vestervig
Hurup
Karby
Vils
Glyngøre
Durup
Farsø
Himmerland
Rold
Arden
Skelund
Als
Thyborøn
Ydby
Hvalpsund
Aalestrup
Nørager
Hadsund
Ove
Mariager Fjord
Øster Assels
Roslev
Salling
Gedsted
Rørbæk
Hvidbjerg
Nissum Bredning
Kås Bredning
Rødding
Lovns Bredning
Jebjerg
Møldrup
Hobro
Assens
Havndal
Harboør
Spøttrup Borg
Balling
Lem
Ulbjerg
Mariager
Randers Fjord
Odby
Kleitrup
Gjerlev
Nissumby
Skive
Bjerregrav
Spentrup
Øster Tørslev
Holbæk
Lemvig
Humlum
Veno Bugt
Rønbjerg
Højslev Stby
Skals
Fårup
Ørsted
Gjerrild
Struer
Hammershøj
Fjellerup
Ramme
Vinderup
Stoholm
Sparkær
Ørum
Allingåbro
Glesborg
Bøvlingbjerg
Hjerm
Sevel
Viborg
Hornbæk
Randers
Gammel Estrup
Grenaa
Osterbyhavn
Vesterøhavn
Læsø
Byrum
Læsø Rende
Larvik 3:45
Kristiansand 3:15
Bergen 19:30
Stavanger 11:30
Oslo 8:30
Göteborg 2:00
1:30
Egersund 6:30
Bergen 15:15
Tórshavn 30:30
Seyðisfjörður 48:00
Anholt 2:45
Varberg 4:00
0
10
20
30 km
8°
9°
10°
11°
57°
1
2
3
4
A
B
60
E45
E39

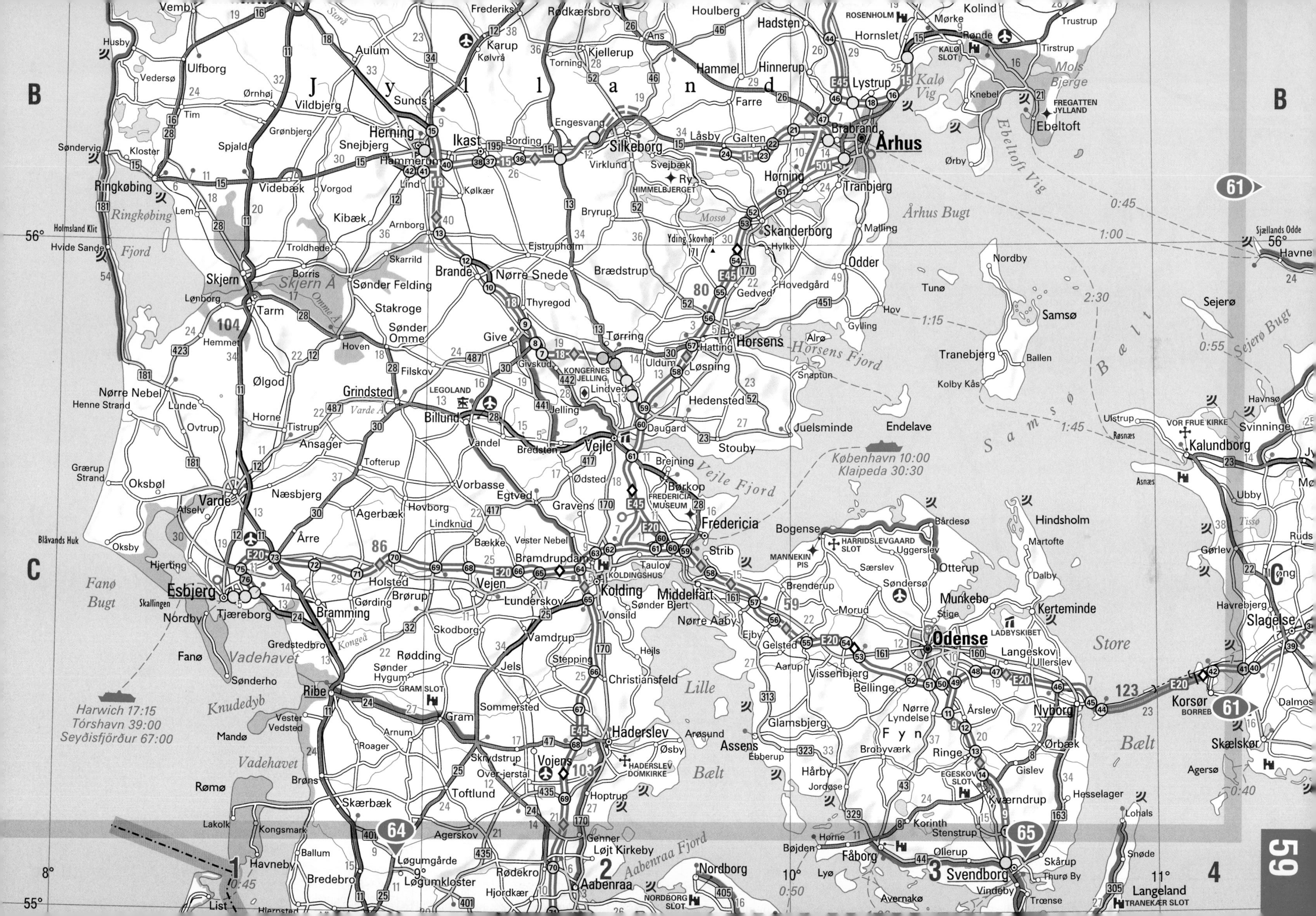
B
C
1
2
3
4
56°
55°
8°
9°
10°
11°
J y l l a n d
Fyn
Århus
Odense
Herning
Ikast
Silkeborg
Skanderborg
Horsens
Vejle
Fredericia
Kolding
Middelfart
Esbjerg
Varde
Ribe
Skjern
Ringkøbing
Billund
Grindsted
Brande
Haderslev
Aabenraa
Vojens
Christiansfeld
Assens
Fåborg
Svendborg
Nyborg
Kerteminde
Bogense
Korsør
Slagelse
Kalundborg
Ebeltoft
Odder
Hadsten
Hammel
Hinnerup
Lystrup
Hornslet
Brabrand
Hørning
Tranbjerg
Galten
Låsby
Farre
Engesvang
Kjellerup
Karup
Kølvrå
Aulum
Sunds
Vildbjerg
Snejbjerg
Hammerum
Ulfborg
Vedersø
Husby
Søndervig
Kloster
Spjald
Videbæk
Vorgod
Kibæk
Arnborg
Troldhede
Lem
Hvide Sande
Holmsland Klit
Tarm
Lønborg
Hemmet
Ølgod
Nørre Nebel
Henne Strand
Lunde
Ovtrup
Oksbøl
Oksby
Blåvands Huk
Hjerting
Nordby
Fanø
Sønderho
Tjæreborg
Bramming
Gørding
Holsted
Brørup
Vejen
Bramdrupdam
Lunderskov
Egtved
Vorbasse
Agerbæk
Nørre Snede
Thyregod
Give
Tørring
Uldum
Hedensted
Juelsminde
Gedved
Hovedgård
Ry
Bryrup
Brædstrup
Ejstrupholm
Sønder Felding
Stakroge
Sønder Omme
Hoven
Filskov
Legoland
Jelling
Kongernes Jelling
Lindved
Daugard
Stouby
Børkop
Brejning
Rødding
Sønder Hygum
Gram
Gram Slot
Skodborg
Vamdrup
Jels
Sommersted
Skrydstrup
Over-Jerstal
Toftlund
Skærbæk
Rømø
Mandø
Lakolk
Havneby
Kongsmark
Ballum
Bredebro
Løgumkloster
Løgumgårde
Agerskov
Rødekro
Hjordkær
Genner
Løjt Kirkeby
Hoptrup
Nordborg
Strib
Taulov
Sønder Bjert
Vonsild
Nørre Aaby
Ejby
Gelsted
Aarup
Vissenbjerg
Bellinge
Glamsbjerg
Hårby
Jordløse
Ebberup
Brobyværk
Ringe
Årslev
Nørre Lyndelse
Korinth
Stenstrup
Kværndrup
Ørbæk
Gislev
Hesselager
Langeskov
Ullerslev
Munkebo
Otterup
Søndersø
Særslev
Uggerslev
Morud
Brenderup
Dalby
Martofte
Hindsholm
Bårdesø
Samsø
Tranebjerg
Ballen
Nordby
Kolby Kås
Tunø
Endelave
Hov
Gylling
Alrø
Snaptun
Sejerø
Havnsø
Svinninge
Ulstrup
Røsnæs
Asnæs
Ubby
Gørlev
Havrebjerg
Skælskør
Agersø
Langeland
Lohals
Snøde
Skårup
Thurø By
Trønse
Vindeby
Avernakø
Lyø
Bøjden
Horne
Ollerup
Kattegat
Århus Bugt
Ebeltoft Vig
Kalø Vig
Mols Bjerge
Horsens Fjord
Vejle Fjord
Samsø Bælt
Sejerø Bugt
Store Bælt
Lille Bælt
Aabenraa Fjord
Ringkøbing Fjord
Skjern Å
Omme Å
Varde Å
Kongeå
Fanø Bugt
Vadehavet
Knudedyb
Mossø
Yding Skovhøj
København 10:00
Klaipeda 30:30
Harwich 17:15
Tórshavn 39:00
Seyðisfjörður 67:00
Rosenholm
Kalø Slot
Fregatten Jylland
Himmelbjerget
Fredericia Museum
Koldingshus
Mannekin Pis
Harridslevgaard Slot
Ladbyskibet
Egeskov Slot
Haderslev Domkirke
Nordborg Slot
Vor Frue Kirke
Tranekær Slot
Borreb
Sjællands Odde
E20
E45
61
64
65

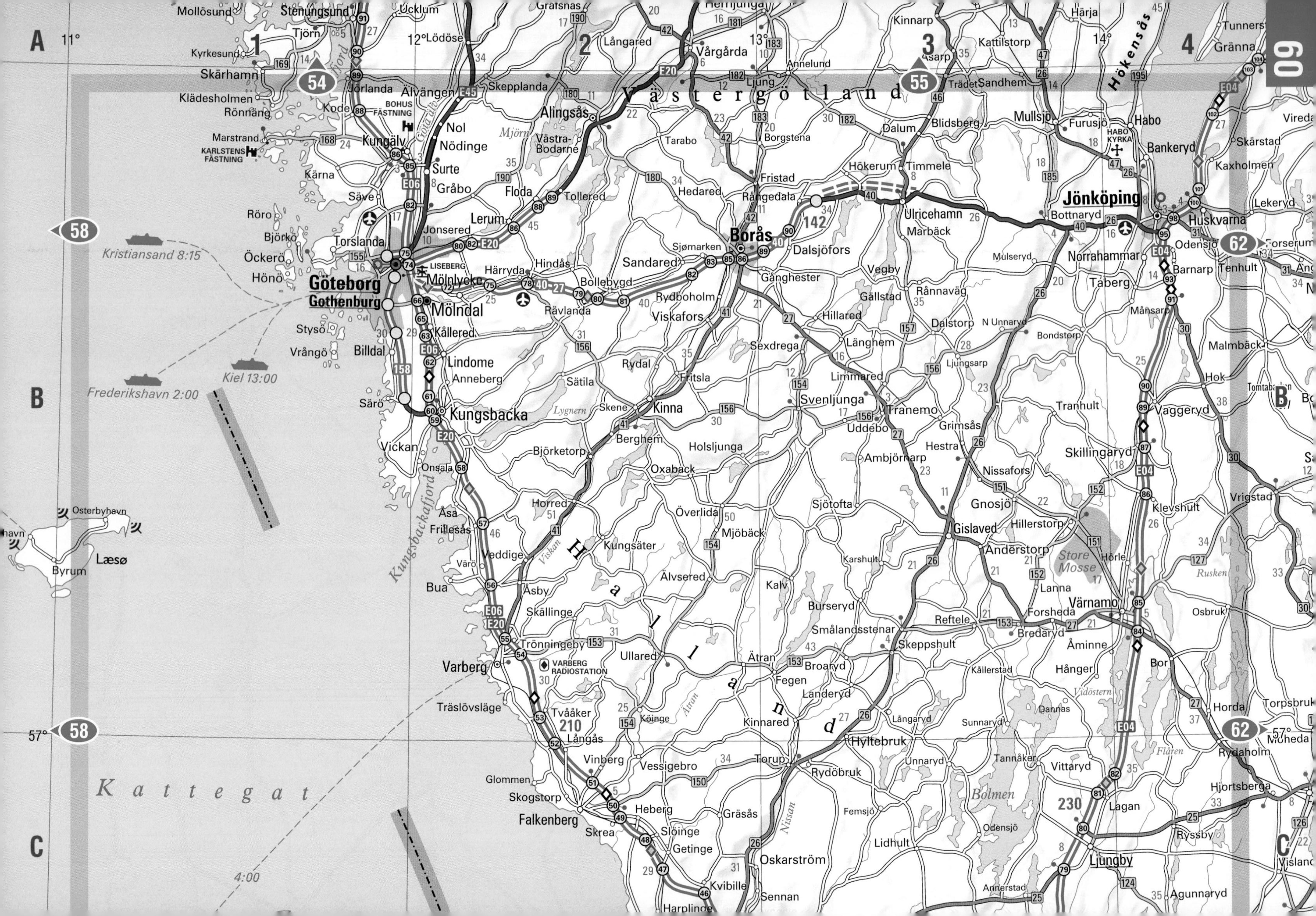
Västergötland
Halland
Kattegat
Göteborg
Gothenburg
Borås
Jönköping
Huskvarna
Varberg
Falkenberg
Kungsbacka
Mölndal
Alingsås
Kungälv
Lerum
Kinna
Ulricehamn
Gislaved
Värnamo
Ljungby
Hyltebruk
Vaggeryd
Skillingaryd
Svenljunga
Tranemo
Stenungsund
Tjörn
Mollösund
Kyrkesund
Skärhamn
Klädesholmen
Rönnäng
Marstrand
KARLSTENS FÄSTNING
BOHUS FÄSTNING
Kode
Jörlanda
Älvängen
Nol
Nödinge
Surte
Gråbo
Kärna
Säve
Röro
Björkö
Öckerö
Hönö
Torslanda
Styrsö
Vrångö
Billdal
Särö
Vickan
Onsala
Kållered
Lindome
Anneberg
Mölnlycke
LISEBERG
Jonsered
Härryda
Hindås
Bollebygd
Rävlanda
Sätila
Floda
Tollered
Västra-Bodarne
Skepplanda
Lödöse
Ucklum
Grafsnäs
Långared
Vårgårda
Annelund
Ljung
Tarabo
Borgstena
Fristad
Hedared
Sandared
Sjømarken
Rångedala
Dalsjöfors
Gånghester
Rydboholm
Viskafors
Rydal
Fritsla
Skene
Lygnern
Björketorp
Berghem
Holsljunga
Oxaback
Horred
Åsa
Frillesås
Veddige
Värö
Bua
Åsby
Kungsäter
Överlida
Mjöbäck
Älvsered
Skällinge
Trönningeby
VARBERG RADIOSTATION
Ullared
Träslövsläge
Tvååker
Långås
Köinge
Ätran
Fegen
Kinnared
Vinberg
Vessigebro
Glommen
Skogstorp
Heberg
Gräsås
Skrea
Slöinge
Getinge
Kvibille
Harplinge
Sennan
Oskarström
Torup
Rydöbruk
Femsjö
Lidhult
Nissan
Viskan
Kinnarp
Kattilstorp
Härja
Åsarp
Trädet
Sandhem
Mullsjö
Furusjö
Habo
HABO KYRKA
Bankeryd
Kaxholmen
Skärstad
Gränna
Tunnerstad
Vireda
Lekeryd
Forserum
Tenhult
Odensjö
Barnarp
Norrahammar
Taberg
Månsarp
Bottnaryd
Mulseryd
Dalum
Blidsberg
Hökerum
Timmele
Marbäck
Vegby
Rånnaväg
Gällstad
Hillared
Dalstorp
N Unnaryd
Bondstorp
Länghem
Sexdrega
Limmared
Ljungsarp
Uddebo
Grimsås
Hestra
Ambjörnarp
Nissafors
Sjötofta
Gnosjö
Hillerstorp
Anderstorp
Karshult
Kalv
Burseryd
Smålandsstenar
Skeppshult
Reftele
Broaryd
Landeryd
Långaryd
Kållerstad
Bredaryd
Forsheda
Lanna
Store Mosse
Hörle
Åminne
Hånger
Vidöstern
Dannäs
Sunnaryd
Tannåker
Unnaryd
Bolmen
Odensjö
Vittaryd
Lagan
Annerstad
Agunnaryd
Ryssby
Hjortsberga
Rydaholm
Moheda
Horda
Torpsbruk
Flåren
Bor
Osbruk
Rusken
Kleveshult
Vrigstad
Malmbäck
Hok
Tomtabacken
Hökensås
Läsø
Østerbyhavn
Byrum
Kristiansand 8:15
Frederikshavn 2:00
Kiel 13:00
4:00
11°
12°
13°
14°
57°
A
B
C
1
2
3
4
54
55
58
62
E20
E45
E06
E04

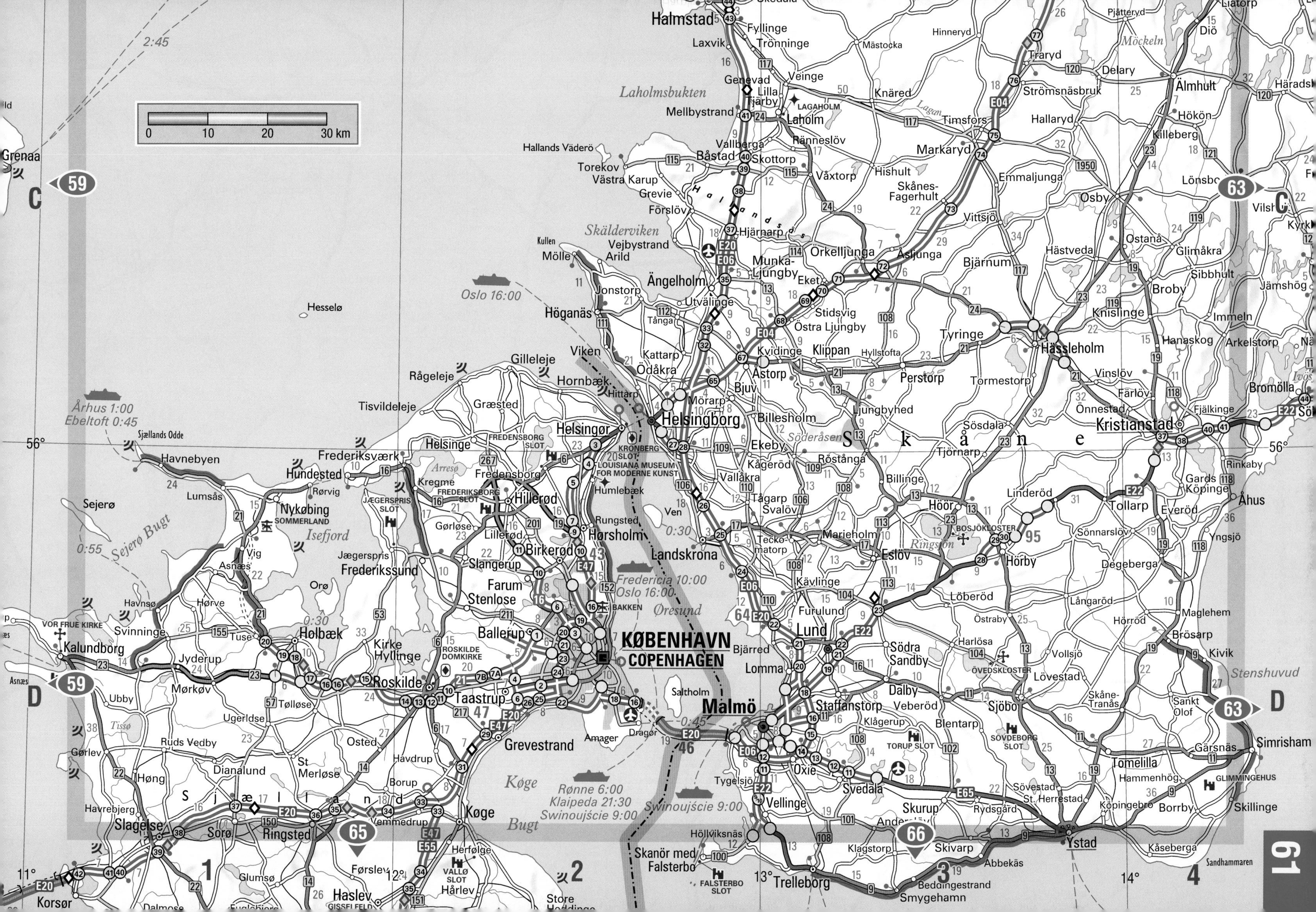

Halmstad
Laholmsbukten
Laholm
Båstad
Ängelholm
Höganäs
Helsingborg
Helsingør
KØBENHAVN
COPENHAGEN
Malmö
Lund
Landskrona
Trelleborg
Ystad
Kristianstad
Hässleholm
Simrishamn
Eslöv
Hörby
Sjöbo
Skurup
Svedala
Tomelilla
Åhus
Osby
Älmhult
Markaryd
Klippan
Åstorp
Perstorp
Höör
Hillerød
Roskilde
Køge
Holbæk
Kalundborg
Slagelse
Sorø
Ringsted
Korsør
Frederikssund
Frederiksværk
Hundested
Nykøbing
Tisvildeleje
Gilleleje
Hornbæk
Ballerup
Taastrup
Birkerød
Hørsholm
Grevestrand
Køge Bugt
Sejerø Bugt
Isefjord
Øresund
Skälderviken
Sejerø
Hesselø
Grenaa
Oslo 16:00
Fredericia 10:00
Oslo 16:00
Århus 1:00
Ebeltoft 0:45
Rønne 6:00
Klaipeda 21:30
Swinoujście 9:00
Skanör med Falsterbo
Smygehamn
Sandhammaren
Kullen
0
10
20
30 km

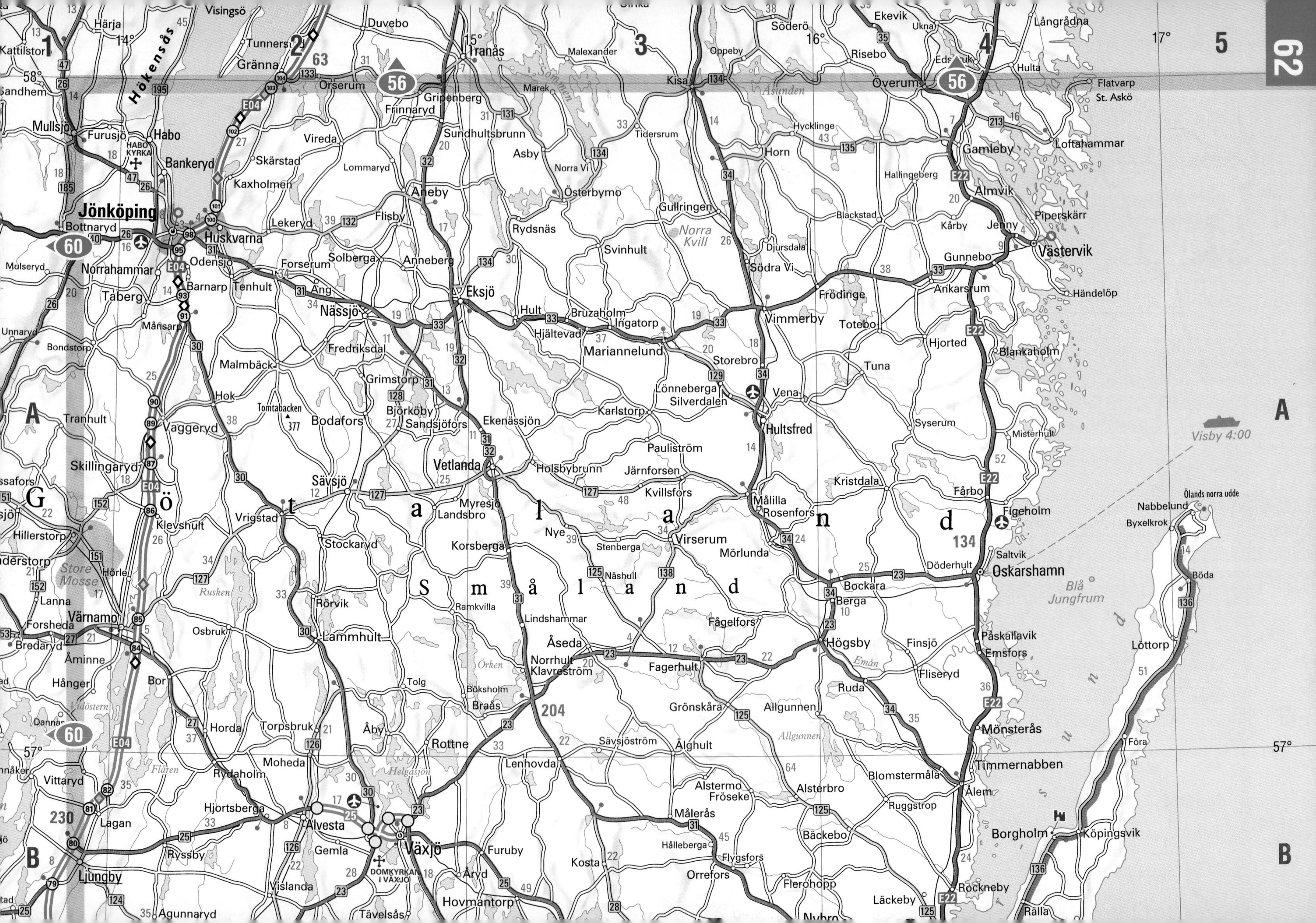

Jönköping
Huskvarna
Gränna
Tranås
Eksjö
Nässjö
Vetlanda
Vimmerby
Hultsfred
Västervik
Oskarshamn
Växjö
Alvesta
Värnamo
Ljungby
Borgholm
Småland
Visby 4:00
Blå Jungfrun
Ölands norra udde
Mönsterås
Kisa
Åseda
Högsby
Sävsjö

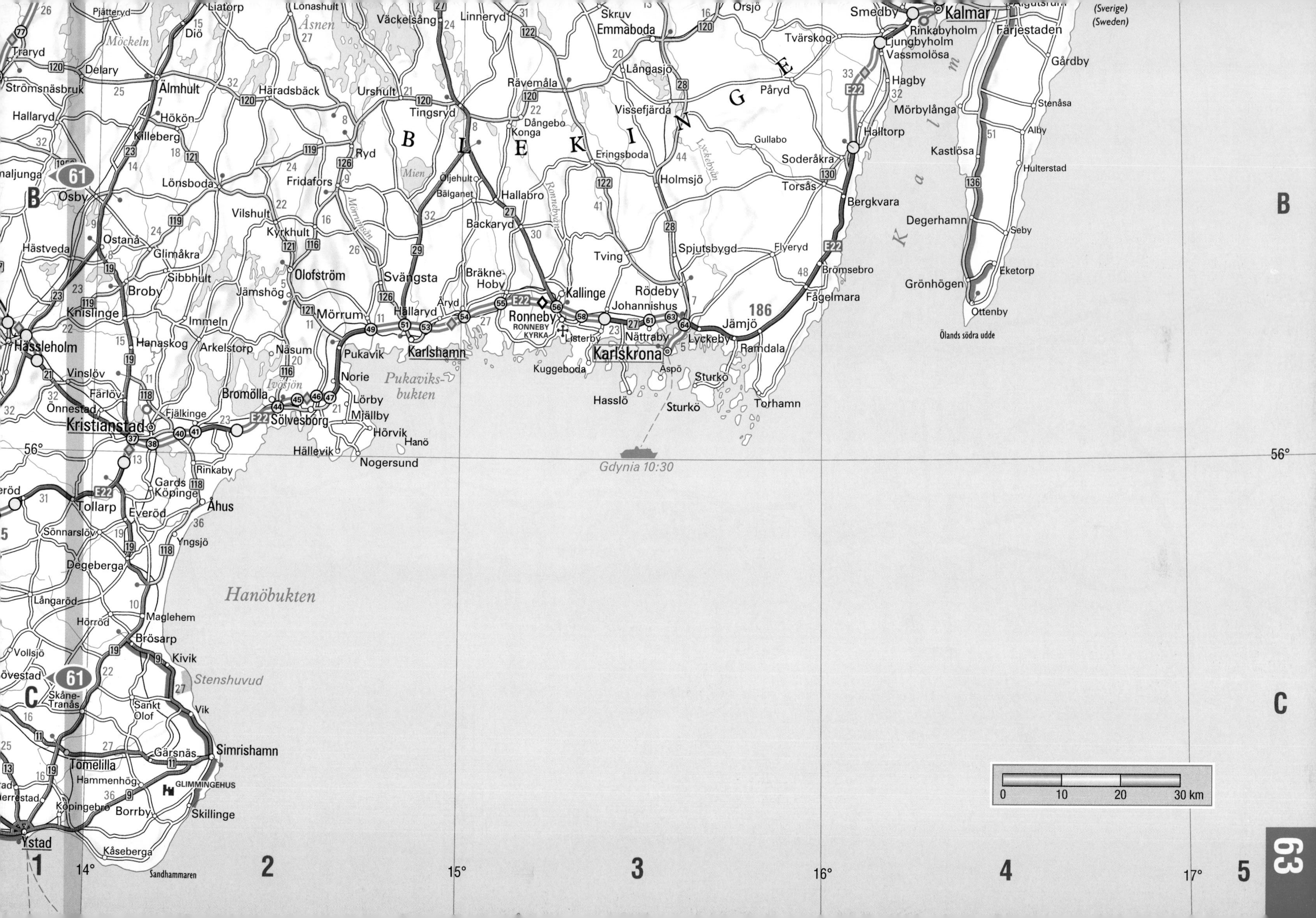

B

C

5

4

3

2

1

56°

17°

16°

15°

14°

(Sverige)
(Sweden)

Kalmar

30 km

20

10

0

Gårdby
Stenåsa
Alby
Hulterstad
Seby
Eketorp
Ottenby
Ölands södra udde

Färjestaden
Rinkabyholm
Ljungbyholm
Vassmolösa
Hagby
Mörbylånga
Halltorp
Kastlösa
Degerhamn
Grönhögen

Smedby

Öland

Kalmarsund

51
136
32
33
E22

Tvärskog
Orsjö
Påryd
Gullabo
Torsås
Söderåkra
Bergkvara
Brömsebro
Fågelmara

E22
130
48
E22

120
16
28
Långasjö
Visseljärda
Holmsjö
Spjutsbygd
Elveryd
Torhamn
186
Jämjö
Ramdala

Skruv
Emmaboda
Eringsboda
Rödeby
Johannishus
Nättraby
Lyckeby
Lyckebyån
Sturkö
Aspö
Sturkö

Lönashult
Lonsboda

122
44
41
28
7
5
63
64

Rävemåla
Dängebo
Konga
Tving
Kallinge
RONNEBY
KYRKA
Listerby
Kuggeboda
Hasslö

Gdynia 10:30

122
31
22
8
30
27
23
27
59
55

Linneryd
Väckelsång
Tingsryd
Urshult
Ryd
Ojehult
Bälganet
Bräkne-
Hoby
Bäckaryd
Hallabro
Ronneby
Asarum

E22
56
55

120
127
24
21
126
8
32
64

Mien
Mörrumsån
126
9
26
11
49

Mörrum
Svängsta
Hällaryd
Karlshamn
Pukavik
Norje
Lörby
Mjällby
Hörvik
Hanö
Nogersund

Hästveda
Härasbäck
Fridafors
Vilshult
Jämshög
Olofström
Näsum
Lersjön
Bromölla

119
24
22
16
121
5
120
116
47
46
45
44
21
E22

Pukaviks-
bukten

Hanöbukten

Stenshuvud

Simrishamn
Gislövshammar

Diö
Älmhult
Hökön
Killeberg
Lönsboda
Glimåkra
Sibbhult
Broby
Hanaskog
Arkelstorp
Fjälkinge
Gärds
Köpinge
Everöd
Åhus
Rinkaby
Ängsjö
Maglehem
Kivik
Brösarp
Sankt
Olof
Gärsnäs
Vik
Vitaby

61

120
15
18
121
32
24
119
19
118
13
37
38
40
41
118
9
118
36
10
27
9
19
22
27

Strömsnäsbruk
Hallaryd
Traryd
Delary
Osby
Visseltofta
Onnestad
Knislinge
Vinslöv
Färlöv
Kristianstad
Önnestad
Sönnarslöv
Degeberga
Hörröd
Långaröd
Övraby
Tollarp
Degeberga
Tomelilla
Hammenhög
Borrby
Skillinge
Kåseberga
Ystad

61

120
26
7
32
23
14
119
15
19
E22
31
118
19
22
16
11
25
19
13

Möckeln
Mörrumsån
Sandhammaren

Pjätteryd
Örkelljunga
Hässleholm
Sölvesborg
Hällevik
Skåne-
Tranås

56°

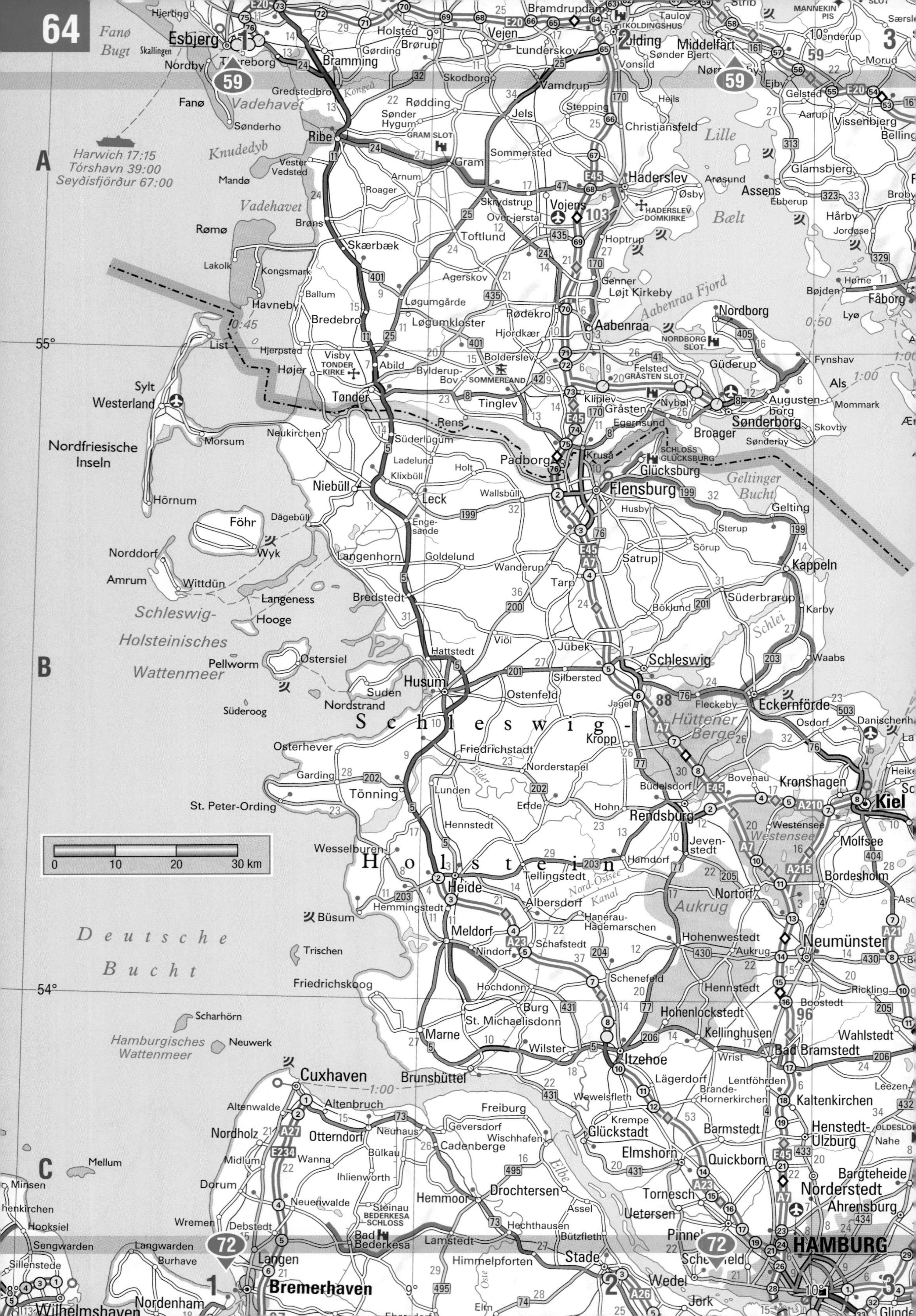
Fanø Bugt
Esbjerg
Skallingen
Nordby
Fanø
Vadehavet
Sønderho
Harwich 17:15
Tórshavn 39:00
Seyðisfjörður 67:00
Knudedyb
Mandø
Vester Vedsted
Rømø
Lakolk
Kongsmark
Havneby
List
0:45
Sylt
Westerland
Morsum
Nordfriesische Inseln
Hörnum
Föhr
Dägebüll
Wyk
Norddorf
Amrum
Wittdün
Langeness
Hooge
Schleswig-Holsteinisches Wattenmeer
Pellworm
Østersiel
Süderoog
Nordstrand
Suden
Hjerting
Bramming
Holsted
Gørding
Brørup
Vejen
Bramdrupdam
Kolding
Lunderskov
Taulov
Middelfart
Strib
Sønder Bjert
Vonsild
Skodborg
Vamdrup
Gredstedbro
Kongeå
Rødding
Sønder Hygum
Gram Slot
Gram
Ribe
Jels
Stepping
Christiansfeld
Sommersted
Haderslev
Haderslev Domkirke
Øsby
Arøsund
Arnum
Roager
Brøns
Skrydstrup
Vojens
Over-jerstal
Toftlund
Hoptrup
Skærbæk
Agerskov
Genner
Løjt Kirkeby
Ballum
Løgumgårde
Bredebro
Løgumkloster
Rødekro
Aabenraa
Aabenraa Fjord
Hjordkær
Hjerpsted
Visby
Tønder Kirke
Højer
Abild
Bolderslev
Bylderup-Bov
Sommerland
Tønder
Tinglev
Kliplev
Gråsten
Felsted
Gråsten Slot
Nybøl
Egernsund
Broager
Rens
Neukirchen
Süderlügum
Ladelund
Holt
Klixbüll
Niebüll
Padborg
Kruså
Schloss Glücksburg
Glücksburg
Leck
Wallsbüll
Flensburg
Enge-Sande
Husby
Langenhorn
Goldelund
Wanderup
Satrup
Sörup
Tarp
Bredstedt
Böklund
Viöl
Jübek
Hattstedt
Schleswig
Husum
Silberstedt
Ostenfeld
Jagel
Schleswig-Holstein
Kropp
Osterhever
Friedrichstadt
Garding
Tönning
Eider
Norderstapel
Lunden
Erfde
Hohn
St. Peter-Ording
Hennstedt
Wesselburen
Heide
Tellingstedt
Hemmingstedt
Albersdorf
Büsum
Meldorf
Schafstedt
Nindorf
Trischen
Deutsche Bucht
Friedrichskoog
Hochdonn
Burg
St. Michaelisdonn
Marne
Wilster
Scharhörn
Hamburgisches Wattenmeer
Neuwerk
Cuxhaven
Brunsbüttel
1:00
Altenwalde
Altenbruch
Nordholz
Otterndorf
Neuhaus
Geversdorf
Wischhafen
Freiburg
Cadenberge
Bülkau
Wanna
Midlum
Ihlienworth
Mellum
Minsen
Dorum
Neuenwalde
Steinau
Bederkesa Schloss
Hemmoor
Drochtersen
Wremen
Debstedt
Bad Bederkesa
Lamstedt
Hechthausen
Hooksiel
Sengwarden
Langwarden
Burhave
Sillenstede
Langen
Bremerhaven
Nordenham
Wilhelmshaven
Himmelpforten
Stade
Oste
Elm
Bützfleth
Assel
Elbe
Glückstadt
Krempe
Elmshorn
Wewelsfleth
Itzehoe
Lägerdorf
Kellinghusen
Wrist
Hohenlockstedt
Hennstedt
Schenefeld
Hohenwestedt
Aukrug
Nortorf
Hanerau-Hademarschen
Nord-Ostsee Kanal
Hamdorf
Rendsburg
Jevenstedt
Büdelsdorf
Hüttener Berge
Bovenau
Kronshagen
Kiel
Westensee
Molfsee
Bordesholm
Neumünster
Rickling
Boostedt
Bad Bramstedt
Wahlstedt
Lentföhrden
Brande-Hörnerkirchen
Kaltenkirchen
Leezen
Barmstedt
Henstedt-Ulzburg
Nahe
Quickborn
Bargteheide
Norderstedt
Ahrensburg
Tornesch
Uetersen
Pinneberg
Schenefeld
Wedel
Jork
Hamburg
Glinde
Eckernförde
Fleckeby
Osdorf
Danischenhagen
Waabs
Schlei
Karby
Süderbrarup
Kappeln
Sterup
Gelting
Geltinger Bucht
Sønderborg
Augustenborg
Skovby
Sønderby
Als
Mommark
Fynshav
Güderup
Nordborg
Nordborg Slot
0:50
1:00
Lyø
Fåborg
Bøjden
Hørne
Jordløse
Håarby
Ebberup
Assens
Glamsbjerg
Lille Bælt
Aarup
Vissenbjerg
Gelsted
Ejby
Nørre Aaby
Mannekin Pis
Særslev
Morud
Brobyværk
Belling
Kolding
Koldingshus
55°
54°
9°
10°
A
B
C
1
2
3
0
10
20
30 km

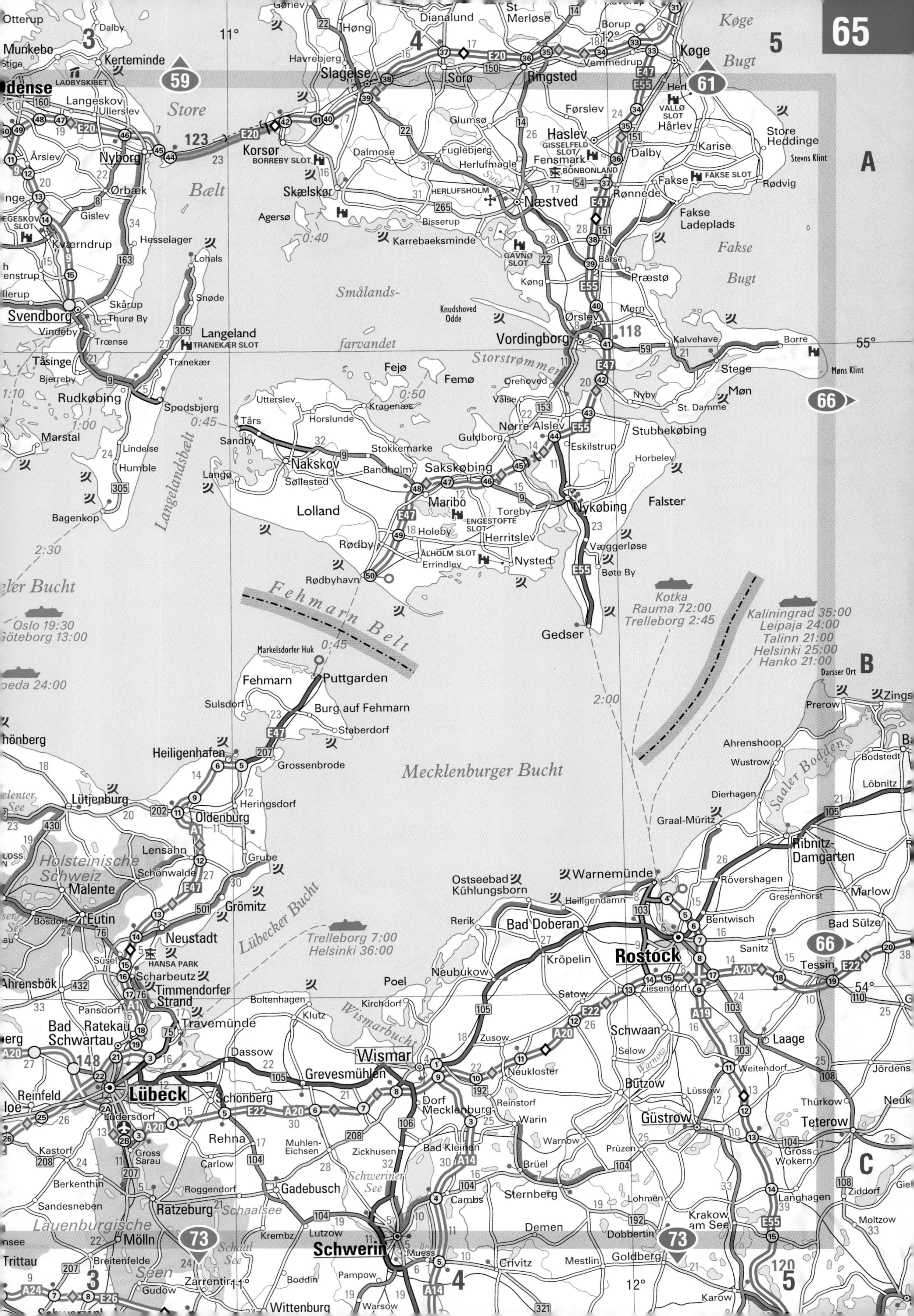

65
Otterup
Dalby
Munkebo
Kerteminde
Odense
Langeskov
Ullerslev
Nyborg
Årslev
Ørbæk
Gislev
Hesselager
Kværndrup
Svendborg
Skårup
Thurø By
Vindeby
Trœnse
Tåsinge
Bjerreby
Rudkøbing
Marstal
Langeland
Tranekær
Spodsbjerg
Lindelse
Humble
Bagenkop
Lohals
Snøde
Store
Bælt
Korsør
Skælskør
Agersø
Slagelse
Høng
Havrebjerg
Dianalund
Sorø
Ringsted
Merløse
Borup
Køge
Vemmedrup
Køge Bugt
Glumsø
Dalmose
Fuglebjerg
Herlufmagle
Næstved
Haslev
Fensmark
Førslev
Hårlev
Store Heddinge
Stevns Klint
Dalby
Karise
Fakse
Rødvig
Rønnede
Fakse Ladeplads
Fakse Bugt
Bisserup
Karrebaeksminde
Præstø
Kong
Mern
Smålands-
farvandet
Knudshoved Odde
Vordingborg
Ørslev
Kalvehave
Borre
Møns Klint
Stege
Møn
Nyby
St. Damme
Storstrømmen
Fejø
Femø
Orehoved
Vålse
Kragenæs
Utterslev
Horslunde
Tårs
Sandby
Langø
Nakskov
Søllested
Stokkemarke
Bandholm
Sakskøbing
Nørre Alslev
Guldborg
Eskilstrup
Stubbekøbing
Horbelev
Maribo
Toreby
Nykøbing
Falster
Lolland
Holeby
Herritslev
Rødby
Nysted
Errindlev
Vægerløse
Bøte By
Rødbyhavn
Gedser
Langelandsbælt
Fehmarn Belt
Kotka
Rauma 72:00
Trelleborg 2:45
Kaliningrad 35:00
Leipaja 24:00
Talinn 21:00
Helsinki 25:00
Hanko 21:00
Oslo 19:30
Göteborg 13:00
Markelsdorfer Huk
Fehmarn
Puttgarden
Burg auf Fehmarn
Sulsdorf
Staberdorf
Heiligenhafen
Grossenbrode
Mecklenburger Bucht
Lütjenburg
Oldenburg
Heringsdorf
Lensahn
Holsteinische Schweiz
Malente
Schönwalde
Grube
Eutin
Bösdorf
Grömitz
Neustadt
Lübecker Bucht
Trelleborg 7:00
Helsinki 36:00
Süsel
Scharbeutz
Timmendorfer Strand
Pansdorf
Ahrensbök
Bad Schwartau
Ratekau
Travemünde
Lübeck
Reinfeld
Ludersdorf
Kastorf
Gross Sarau
Berkenthin
Sandesneben
Ratzeburg
Lauenburgische Seen
Mölln
Trittau
Breitenfelde
Gudow
Zarrentin
Schönberg
Dassow
Rehna
Carlow
Roggendorf
Gadebusch
Grevesmühlen
Wismar
Poel
Boltenhagen
Klutz
Kirchdorf
Wismarbucht
Muhlen-Eichsen
Zickhusen
Schweriner See
Lutzow
Krembz
Schwerin
Pampow
Boddin
Wittenburg
Warsow
Muess
Dorf Mecklenburg
Bad Kleinen
Cambs
Neubukow
Rerik
Ostseebad Kühlungsborn
Heiligendamm
Bad Doberan
Kröpelin
Warnemünde
Rostock
Satow
Zusow
Neukloster
Reinstorf
Warin
Brüel
Sternberg
Crivitz
Demen
Mestlin
Dobbertin
Goldberg
Schwaan
Selow
Bützow
Güstrow
Lüssow
Prüzen
Lohmen
Krakow am See
Karow
Laage
Weitendorf
Bentwisch
Rövershagen
Gresenhorst
Marlow
Bad Sülze
Sanitz
Tessin
Ribnitz-Damgarten
Graal-Müritz
Dierhagen
Wustrow
Ahrenshoop
Prerow
Darsser Ort
Zingst
Bodstedt
Löbnitz
Saaler Bodden
Thürkow
Teterow
Gross Wokern
Zidorf
Langhagen
Moltzow
Jördens
11°
12°
55°
54°
59
61
66
73
A
B
C
3
4
5

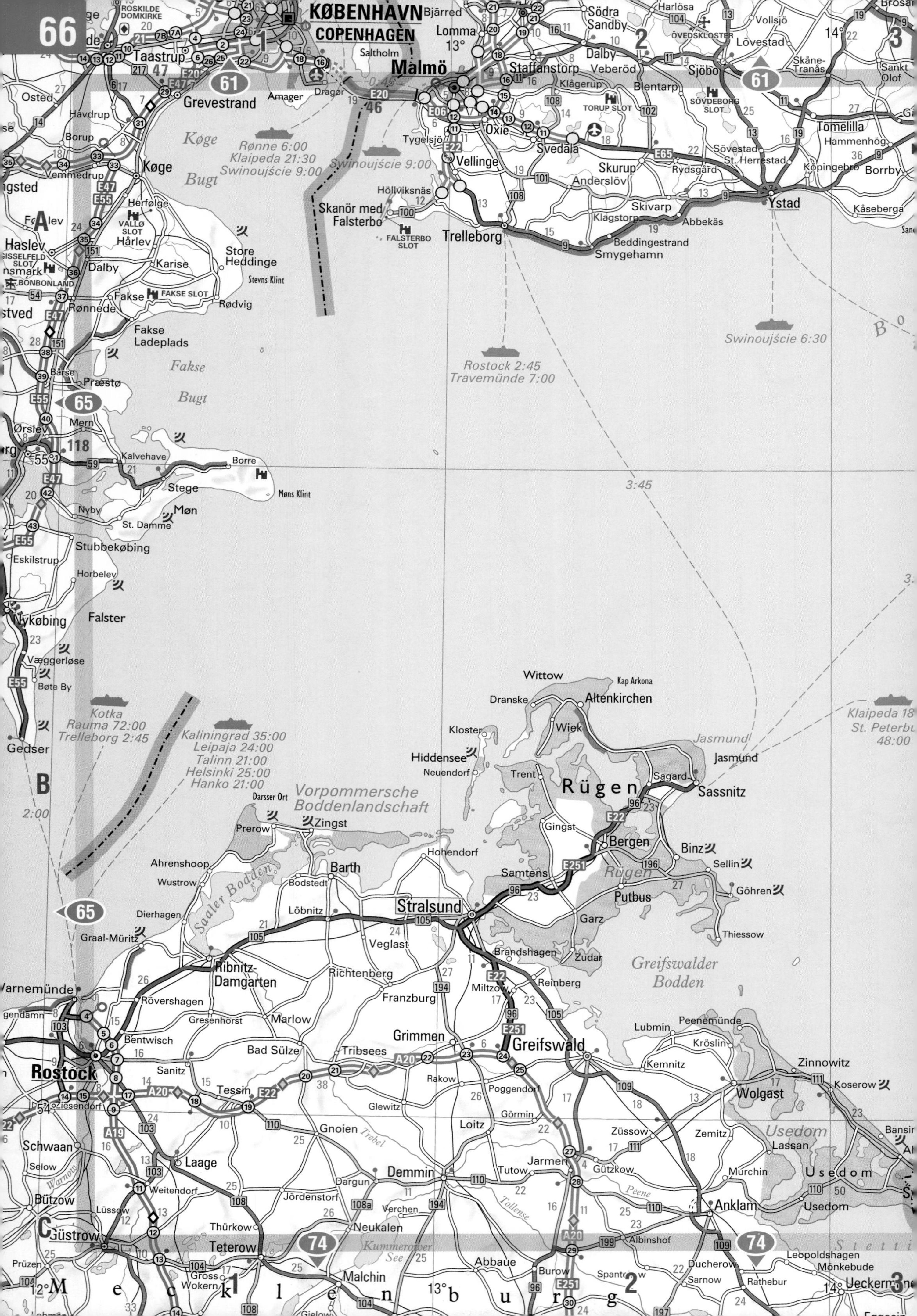
KØBENHAVN
COPENHAGEN
Malmö
Taastrup
Grevestrand
Køge
Køge Bugt
Rønne 6:00
Klaipeda 21:30
Swinoujście 9:00
Swinoujście 9:00
Lomma
Bjärred
Saltholm
Amager
Dragør
Tygelsjö
Vellinge
Höllviksnäs
Skanör med Falsterbo
FALSTERBO SLOT
Trelleborg
Staffanstorp
Södra Sandby
Dalby
Veberöd
Klågerup
TORUP SLOT
Oxie
Svedala
Skurup
Anderslöv
Blentarp
Sjöbo
Lövestad
Vollsjö
ÖVEDSKLOSTER
Harlösa
SÖVDEBORG SLOT
Sövestad
Rydsgård
Tomelilla
Hammenhög
St. Herrestad
Köpingebro
Borrby
Ystad
Kåseberga
Skivarp
Abbekäs
Klagstorp
Beddingestrand
Smygehamn
Skåne-Tranås
Sankt Olof
Osted
Havdrup
Borup
Vemmedrup
Herfølge
VALLØ SLOT
Hårlev
Haslev
GISSELFELD SLOT
BONBONLAND
Dalby
Karise
Store Heddinge
Stevns Klint
Fakse
FAKSE SLOT
Rødvig
Rønnede
Fakse Ladeplads
Fakse Bugt
Bårse
Præstø
Mern
Ørslev
Kalvehave
Stege
Borre
Møns Klint
Møn
Nyby
St. Damme
Stubbekøbing
Eskilstrup
Horbelev
Nykøbing
Falster
Væggerløse
Bøte By
Gedser
Swinoujście 6:30
Rostock 2:45
Travemünde 7:00
3:45
Kotka
Rauma 72:00
Trelleborg 2:45
Kaliningrad 35:00
Leipaja 24:00
Talinn 21:00
Helsinki 25:00
Hanko 21:00
2:00
Klaipeda 18
St. Peterbu
48:00
Wittow
Kap Arkona
Dranske
Altenkirchen
Kloster
Wiek
Hiddensee
Neuendorf
Jasmund
Trent
Rügen
Sagard
Sassnitz
Gingst
Bergen
Binz
Sellin
Samtens
Putbus
Göhren
Garz
Thiessow
Zudar
Brandshagen
Reinberg
Greifswalder Bodden
Darsser Ort
Vorpommersche Boddenlandschaft
Prerow
Zingst
Hohendorf
Ahrenshoop
Wustrow
Barth
Bodstedt
Saaler Bodden
Löbnitz
Stralsund
Dierhagen
Graal-Müritz
Veglast
Ribnitz-Damgarten
Richtenberg
Franzburg
Miltzow
Warnemünde
Rövershagen
Gresenhorst
Marlow
Bentwisch
Bad Sülze
Tribsees
Grimmen
Greifswald
Rostock
Sanitz
Tessin
Rakow
Poggendorf
Glewitz
Gnoien
Trebel
Görmin
Loitz
Lubmin
Peenemünde
Kröslin
Kemnitz
Zinnowitz
Koserow
Wolgast
Züssow
Zemitz
Usedom
Lassan
Bansin
Jarmen
Gützkow
Murchin
Anklam
Peene
Tollense
Schwaan
Selow
Laage
Warnow
Weitendorf
Bützow
Lüssow
Demmin
Dargun
Tutow
Jördenstorf
Verchen
Neukalen
Kummerower See
Güstrow
Thürkow
Teterow
Albinshof
Ducherow
Rathebur
Leopoldshagen
Mönkebude
Ueckerm
Sarnow
Spantekow
Prüzen
Gross Wokern
Malchin
Abbaue
Burow
Gielow
Mecklenburg
Stettin
Ziesendorf
Sandhagen

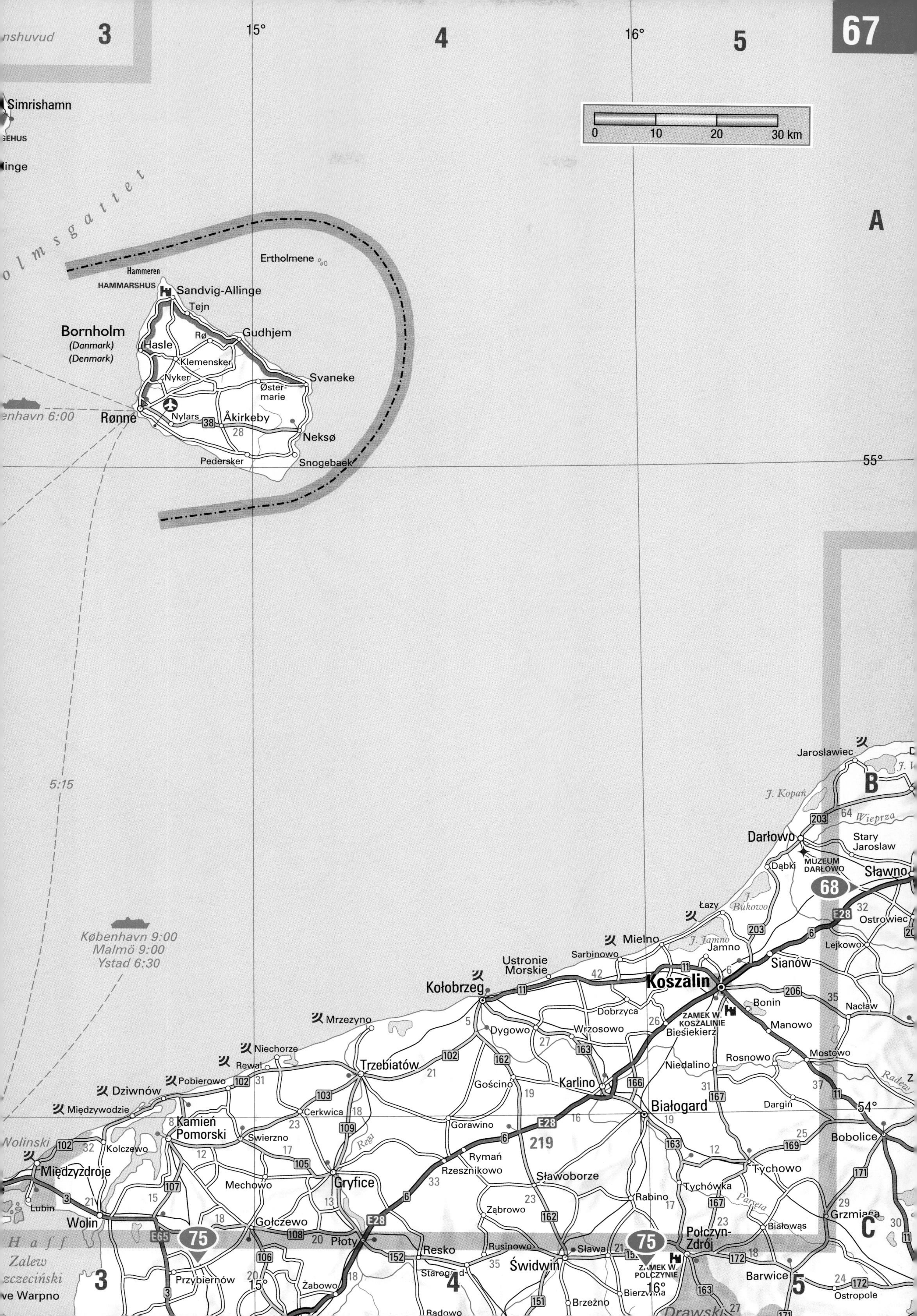

nshuvud   3   15°   4   16°   5

Simrishamn
GEHUS
linge

0   10   20   30 km

A

olmsgattet

Ertholmene

Hammeren
HAMMARSHUS   Sandvig-Allinge
Tejn

Bornholm
(Danmark)   Rø   Gudhjem
(Denmark)   Hasle
Klemensker   Svaneke
Nyker   Øster-
marie
enhavn 6:00   Rønne   Nylars   Åkirkeby
38   28   Neksø
Pedersker   Snogebaek

55°

5:15

København 9:00
Malmö 9:00
Ystad 6:30

Jaroslawiec
J. L

B
J. Kopań
203   64   Wieprza
Darłowo   Stary
Jaroslaw
Dąbki   MUZEUM
DARŁOWO   Sławno
68
Łazy   J.   32
Bukowo   E28   Ostrowiec
203   6   20
Mielno   J. Jamno
Jamno   Lejkowo
Ustronie   Sarbinowo   Sianów
Morskie   42   11
Kołobrzeg   Koszalin   206   35   Nacław
11   Dobrzyca   ZAMEK W   Bonin
Mrzezyno   5   Dygowo   26   KOSZALINIE   Manowo
Wrzosowo   163   Biesiekierz   Mostowo
Niechorze   102   162   Niedalino   Rosnowo   37   11   Radew
Rewał   31   Trzebiatów   Gościno   Karlino   31   167   Dargiń
Pobierowo   102   21   166   Białogard   54°
Dziwnów   103   Cerkwica   18   Gorawino   E28   16   19   163   25   Bobolice
Międzywodzie   109   Rega   6   219   12   169
Kamień   23   Swierzno   17   Rymań   Sławoborze   167   Tychowo   171
Wolinski   102   Pomorski   Reszkowo   33   Tychówka   Parseta   29   Grzmiaca
Międzyzdroje   32   Kolczewo   12   105   Rabino   17   167   30
Lubin   107   Mechowo   13   Gryfice   6   Ząbrowo   162   Białowąs   Barwice
Wolin   21   15   18   Gołczewo   E28   Resko   Rusinowo   Połczyn-   163   24   172
Haff   E65   75   108   20   Płoty   152   Sława   75   Zdrój   Ostropole
Zalew   106   Przybiernów   Żabowo   Starogard   Świdwin   ZAMEK W.   172
zczeciński   3   20   15°   4   151   16°   POLCZYNIE   5
ve Warpno   Radowo   Brzeżno   Bierzwica   171
Drawskis

54°

C

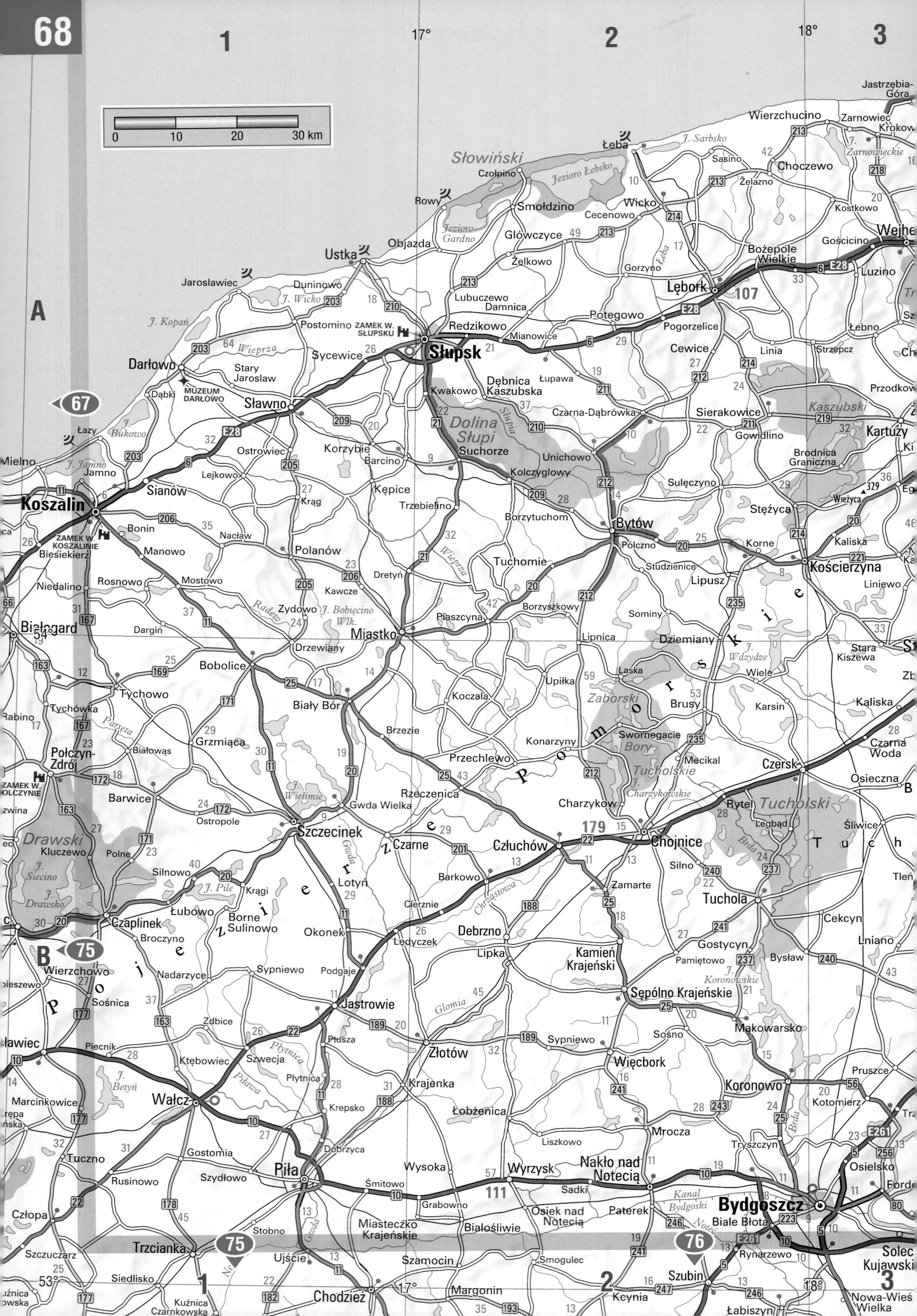

1
2
3
A
B
17°
18°
0 10 20 30 km
Słowiński
Jezioro Łebsko
Łeba
Wierzchucino
Jastrzębia-Góra
Żarnowiec
Krokowa
J. Sarbsko
Sasino
Choczewo
J. Żarnowieckie
Żelazno
Czołpino
Rowy
Smołdzino
Wicko
Cecenowo
Kostkowo
Gościcino
Wejherowo
Jezioro Gardno
Główczyce
Ustka
Objazda
Żelkowo
Gorzyno
Bożepole Wielkie
Luzino
Jarosławiec
Duninowo
J. Wicko
Lubuczewo
Damnica
Lębork
J. Kopań
Postomino
ZAMEK W. SŁUPSKU
Redzikowo
Potęgowo
Pogorzelice
Łebno
Mianowice
Darłowo
Wieprza
Sycewice
Słupsk
Cewice
Linia
Strzepcz
Stary Jarosław
Dębnica Kaszubska
Łupawa
Prodkowo
Dąbki
MUZEUM DARŁOWO
Sławno
Kwakowo
Kaszubski
J. Bukowo
Dolina Słupi
Czarna-Dąbrówka
Sierakowice
Gowidlino
Kartuzy
Łazy
Korzybie
Barcino
Brodnica Graniczna
Mielno
J. Jamno
Jamno
Ostrowiec
Suchorze
Unichowo
Lejkowo
Kolczyglowy
Sulęczyno
Koszalin
Sianów
Kępice
Krąg
Trzebielino
Borzytuchom
Stężyca
Wieżyca
Bonin
ZAMEK W. KOSZALINIE
Biesiekierz
Nacław
Bytów
Półczno
Korne
Kaliska
Manowo
Polanów
Tuchomie
Studzienice
Kościerzyna
Niedalino
Rosnowo
Mostowo
Kawcze
Dretyń
Lipusz
Liniewo
Radew
Żydowo
J. Bobięcino Wlk.
Borzyszkowy
Sominy
Białogard
Dargiń
Piaszczyna
Miastko
Lipnica
Dziemiany
Stara Kiszewa
Drzewiany
J. Wdzydze
Bobolice
Laska
Wiele
Tychowo
Upiłka
Koczała
Zaborski
Brusy
Karsin
Kaliska
Tychówka
Biały Bór
Parsęta
Grzmiąca
Brzezie
Swornegacie
Bory Tucholskie
Białowąs
Konarzyny
Mecikal
Czarna Woda
Połczyn-Zdrój
Przechlewo
Czersk
Osieczna
ZAMEK W. POŁCZYNIE
J. Charzykowskie
J. Wielimie
Rzeczenica
Barwice
Gwda Wielka
Charzykowy
Rytel
Tucholski
Ostropole
Szczecinek
Legbąd
Śliwice
Drawski
Czarne
Człuchów
Chojnice
Kluczewo
Polne
Gwda
J. Siecino
Silnowo
Lotyń
Silno
Tleń
J. Pile
Krągi
Barkowo
Zamarte
Tuchola
J. Drawsko
Łubowo
Chrząstowa
Czaplinek
Borne Sulinowo
Cierznie
Cekcyn
Okonek
Debrzno
Broczyno
Ledyczek
Gostycyn
Lniano
Lipka
Kamień Krajeński
Pamiętowo
Bysław
Wierzchowo
Nadarzyce
Sypniewo
Podgaje
J. Koronowskie
Sośnica
Sępólno Krajeńskie
Jastrowie
Glomia
Zdbice
Makowarsko
Ptusza
Sypniewo
Sośno
Piecnik
Złotów
Ktębowiec
Szwecja
Płytnica
Więcbork
J. Betyń
Pruszcz
Piława
Koronowo
Marcinkowice
Wałcz
Krajenka
Kotomierz
Krepsko
Łobżenica
Brda
Mrocza
Tuczno
Gostomia
Liszkowo
Dobrzyca
Tryszczyn
Osielsko
Rusinowo
Szydłowo
Wysoka
Wyrzysk
Nakło nad Notecią
Piła
Śmitowo
Sadki
Kanal Bydgoski
Bydgoszcz
Grabowno
Fordon
Człopa
Osiek nad Notecią
Paterek
Miasteczko Krajeńskie
Białośliwie
Stobno
Noteć
Białe Błota
Trzcianka
Solec Kujawski
Szczuczarz
Ujście
Szamocin
Smogulec
Rynarzewo
Siedlisko
Szubin
Chodzież
Margonin
Kcynia
Kuźnica Czarnkowska
Łabiszyn
Nowa-Wieś Wielka
Pojezierze Pomorskie
Tuchola

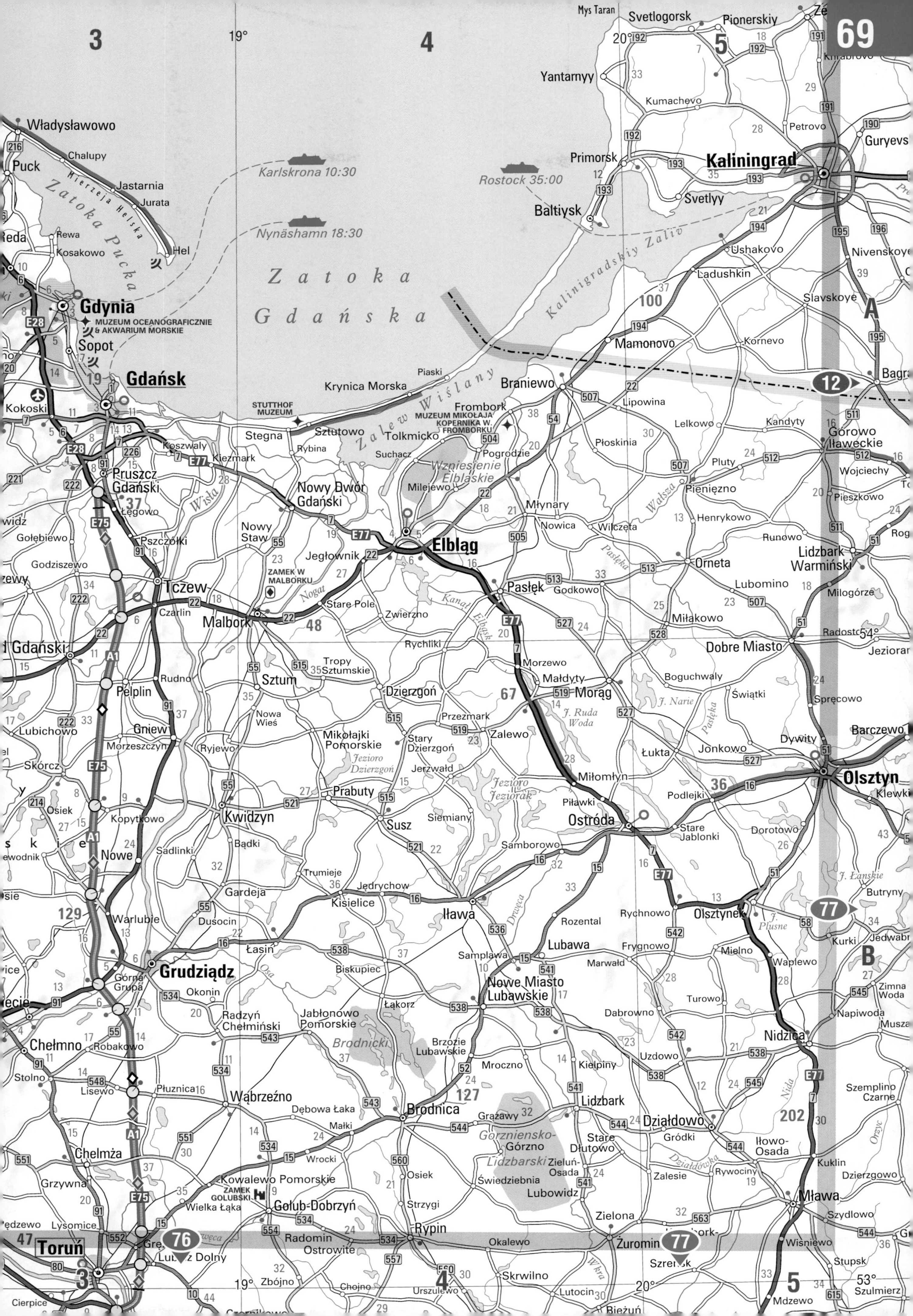
Zatoka Gdańska
Zatoka Pucka
Mierzeja Helska
Kalinigradskiy Zaliv
Zalew Wiślany
Karlskrona 10:30
Nynäshamn 18:30
Rostock 35:00
Gdynia
Gdańsk
Sopot
Kaliningrad
Elbląg
Olsztyn
Toruń
Grudziądz
Malbork
Tczew
Braniewo
Baltiysk
Svetlogorsk
Pionerskiy
Yantarnyy
Primorsk
Svetlyy
Mamonovo
Władysławowo
Puck
Hel
Jastarnia
Jurata
Chalupy
Reda
Rewa
Kosakowo
Kokoski
Pruszcz Gdański
Krynica Morska
Stegna
Frombork
Tolkmicko
Nowy Dwór Gdański
Pasłęk
Morąg
Ostróda
Iława
Kwidzyn
Sztum
Prabuty
Susz
Nowe Miasto Lubawskie
Brodnica
Lidzbark
Działdowo
Nidzica
Olsztynek
Mława
Rypin
Golub-Dobrzyń
Wąbrzeźno
Chełmno
Chełmża
Orneta
Dobre Miasto
Lidzbark Warmiński
Górowo Iławeckie
Pieniężno
Młynary
Dzierzgoń
Gniew
Pelplin
Nowe
Lubawa
Żuromin
STUTTHOF MUZEUM
MUZEUM OCEANOGRAFICZNIE & AKWARIUM MORSKIE
MUZEUM MIKOŁAJA KOPERNIKA W. FROMBORKU
ZAMEK W MALBORKU
ZAMEK GOLUBSKI
Wzniesienie Elbląskie
Brodnicki
Gorznienско-Lidzbarski
Jezioro Jeziorak
Jezioro Dzierzgoń
E28
E75
E77
A1
12
76
77
3
4
5
A
B
19°
20°
54°
53°

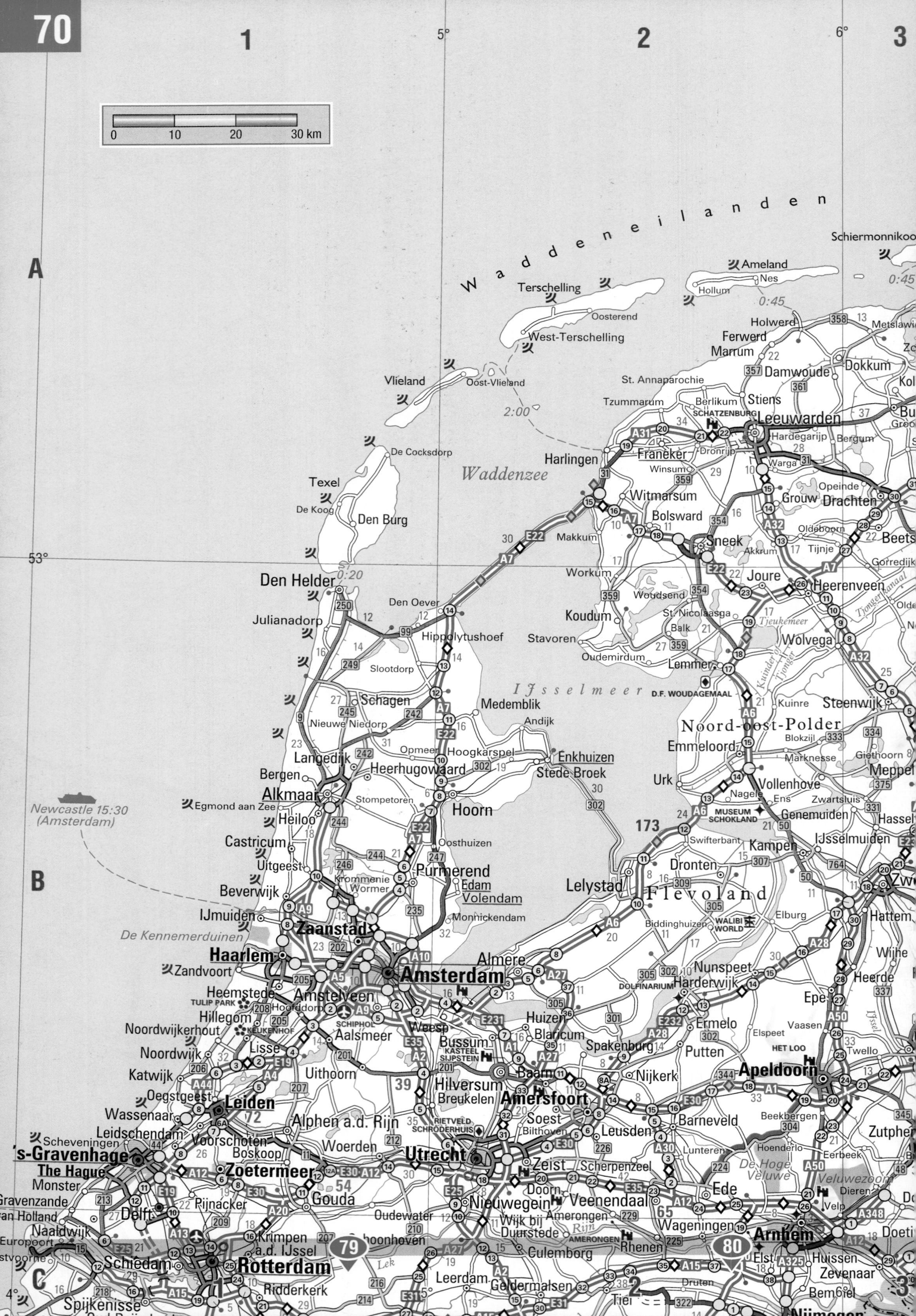
1
2
3
5°
6°
0 10 20 30 km
A
B
C
53°
4°
W a d d e n e i l a n d e n
Schiermonnikoog
Ameland
Nes
Hollum
0:45
Terschelling
Oosterend
West-Terschelling
Vlieland
Oost-Vlieland
2:00
De Cocksdorp
Texel
De Koog
Den Burg
Waddenzee
0:20
Den Helder
Julianadorp
Den Oever
Hippolytushoef
Slootdorp
Schagen
Nieuwe Niedorp
Medemblik
Andijk
Opmeer
Hoogkarspel
Enkhuizen
Stede Broek
Langedijk
Heerhugowaard
Bergen
Alkmaar
Stompetoren
Egmond aan Zee
Heiloo
Hoorn
Castricum
Uitgeest
Oosthuizen
Purmerend
Krommenie
Wormer
Edam
Volendam
Beverwijk
IJmuiden
Monnickendam
Zaanstad
De Kennemerduinen
Newcastle 15:30 (Amsterdam)
Haarlem
Zandvoort
Amsterdam
Almere
Heemstede
TULIP PARK
Amstelveen
Hoofddorp
Hillegom
KEUKENHOF
SCHIPHOL
Noordwijkerhout
Aalsmeer
Weesp
Lisse
Noordwijk
Katwijk
Uithoorn
Bussum
KASTEEL SIJPSTEIN
Hilversum
Breukelen
Oegstgeest
Leiden
Wassenaar
Leidschendam
Voorschoten
Scheveningen
's-Gravenhage
The Hague
Boskoop
Alphen a.d. Rijn
Woerden
RIETVELD SCHRÖDERHUIS
Utrecht
Zoetermeer
Gouda
Monster
Delft
Rijnacker
Naaldwijk
Europoort
Schiedam
Rotterdam
Krimpen a.d. IJssel
Schoonhoven
Oudewater
Nieuwegein
Spijkenisse
Ridderkerk
Leerdam
Geldermalsen
Culemborg
Tiel
Wijk bij Duurstede
Amerongen
AMERONGEN
Rhenen
Veenendaal
Doorn
Zeist
Scherpenzeel
Bilthoven
Soest
Baarn
Amersfoort
Leusden
Barneveld
Lunteren
Ede
Wageningen
Arnhem
Elst
Huissen
Zevenaar
Bemmel
Druten
Nijmegen
Lek
Rijn
Huizen
Blaricum
Spakenburg
Nijkerk
Putten
Ermelo
Harderwijk
DOLFINARIUM
Nunspeet
Elspeet
Vaasen
Epe
HET LOO
Apeldoorn
Twello
Beekbergen
Hoenderlo
Eerbeek
Zutphen
De Hoge Veluwe
Veluwezoom
Dieren
Velp
Doetinchem
Heerde
Wijhe
Hattem
Zwolle
Elburg
Biddinghuizen
WALIBI WORLD
Flevoland
Dronten
Lelystad
Swifterbant
Kampen
IJsselmuiden
Genemuiden
Hasselt
Zwartsluis
MUSEUM SCHOKLAND
Nagele
Ens
Vollenhove
Urk
Emmeloord
Marknesse
Noord-oost-Polder
Blokzijl
Giethoorn
Meppel
Kuinre
Steenwijk
D.F. WOUDAGEMAAL
IJsselmeer
Lemmer
Oudemirdum
Balk
St. Nicolaasga
Stavoren
Koudum
Woudsend
Tjeukemeer
Wolvega
Heerenveen
Joure
Workum
Makkum
Akkrum
Tijnje
Beetsterzwaag
Gorredijk
Oldeboorn
Sneek
Bolsward
Witmarsum
Harlingen
Franeker
Dronrijp
Winsum
Warga
Grouw
Opeinde
Drachten
Hardegarijp
Bergum
Leeuwarden
SCHATZENBURG
Berlikum
Stiens
Tzummarum
St. Annaparochie
Marrum
Ferwerd
Holwerd
Damwoude
Dokkum
Metslawier
Kollum
Buitenpost
Grootegast
Oldeberkoop
Tjongerkanaal
Kuinder of Tjonger
IJssel
173
39
54
65
72
79
80

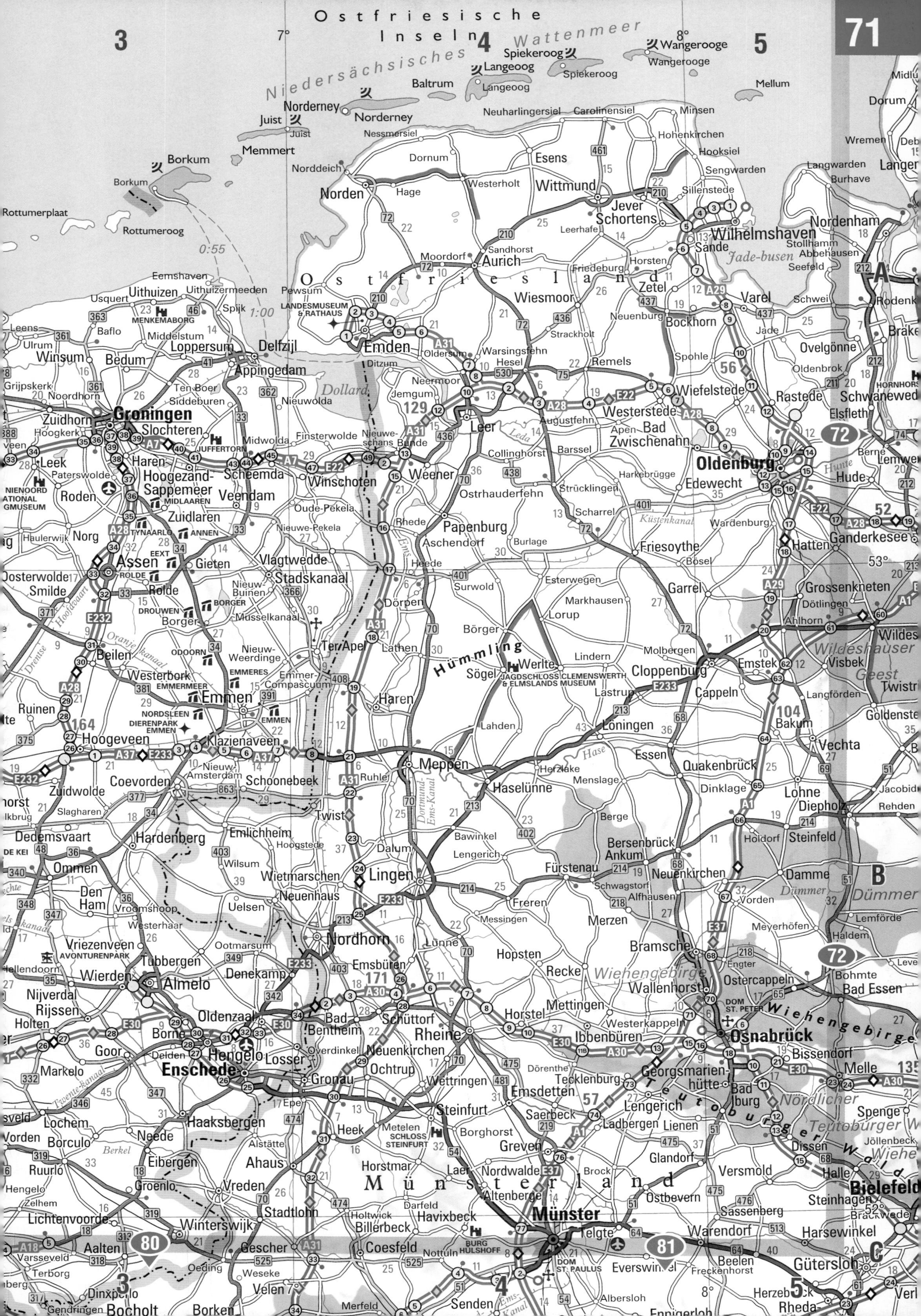
Ostfriesische Inseln
Niedersächsisches Wattenmeer
Borkum
Juist
Norderney
Baltrum
Langeoog
Spiekeroog
Wangerooge
Mellum
Memmert
Rottumerplaat
Rottumeroog
Norddeich
Norden
Hage
Dornum
Nessmersiel
Neuharlingersiel
Carolinensiel
Esens
Westerholt
Wittmund
Jever
Schortens
Minsen
Hohenkirchen
Hooksiel
Sengwarden
Sillenstede
Wilhelmshaven
Sande
Jade-busen
Nordenham
Stollhamm
Abbehausen
Seefeld
Langwarden
Burhave
Dorum
Wremen
Moordorf
Aurich
Sandhorst
Leerhafe
Friedeburg
Horsten
Ostfriesland
Wiesmoor
Zetel
Varel
Bockhorn
Neuenburg
Strackholt
Schweiburg
Rodenkirchen
Brake
Jade
Ovelgönne
Oldenbrok
Rastede
Elsfleth
Schwanewede
Pewsum
Landesmuseum & Rathaus
Emden
Ditzum
Oldersum
Warsingsfehn
Hesel
Remels
Spohle
Neermoor
Jemgum
Leer
Augustfehn
Apen
Bad Zwischenahn
Westerstede
Wiefelstede
Oldenburg
Hude
Dollard
Eemshaven
Uithuizen
Uithuizermeeden
Usquert
Menkemaborg
Spijk
Baflo
Middelstum
Loppersum
Delfzijl
Appingedam
Leens
Ulrum
Winsum
Bedum
Grijpskerk
Noordhorn
Ten Boer
Siddeburen
Nieuwolda
Zuidhorn
Groningen
Slochteren
Hoogkerk
Leek
Haren
Hoogezand-Sappemeer
Scheemda
Midwolda
Finsterwolde
Nieuweschans
Bunde
Winschoten
Weener
Collinghorst
Barssel
Harkebrügge
Edewecht
Roden
Paterswolde
Veendam
Oude-Pekela
Nieuwe-Pekela
Zuidlaren
Ostrhauderfehn
Strücklingen
Scharrel
Küstenkanal
Wardenburg
Hatten
Ganderkesee
Rhede
Papenburg
Aschendorf
Burlage
Friesoythe
Bösel
Norg
Assen
Gieten
Vlagtwedde
Stadskanaal
Heede
Surwold
Esterwegen
Garrel
Grossenkneten
Dötlingen
Ahlhorn
Wildeshausen
Wildeshauser Geest
Rolde
Smilde
Borger
Musselkanaal
Dörpen
Markhausen
Lorup
Börger
Beilen
Westerbork
Nieuw-Weerdinge
Ter Apel
Lathen
Hümmling
Sögel
Werlte
Lindern
Molbergen
Cloppenburg
Emstek
Visbek
Cappeln
Lastrup
Langförden
Emmen
Emmer-Compascuum
Haren
Lahden
Löningen
Bakum
Goldenstedt
Ruinen
Hoogeveen
Klazienaveen
Meppen
Essen
Quakenbrück
Vechta
Coevorden
Zuidwolde
Nieuw-Amsterdam
Schoonebeek
Ruhle
Haselünne
Herzlake
Menslage
Dinklage
Lohne
Diepholz
Twist
Slagharen
Dedemsvaart
Hardenberg
Emlichheim
Hoogstede
Dalum
Bawinkel
Berge
Bersenbrück
Ankum
Holdorf
Steinfeld
Ommen
Wilsum
Wietmarschen
Lingen
Lengerich
Fürstenau
Neuenkirchen
Damme
Dümmer
Den Ham
Vroomshoop
Uelsen
Neuenhaus
Freren
Schwagstorf
Alfhausen
Vorden
Westerhaar
Messingen
Merzen
Meyerhöfen
Lemförde
Haldem
Vriezenveen
Avonturenpark
Tubbergen
Ootmarsum
Nordhorn
Lünne
Hopsten
Bramsche
Engter
Wierden
Almelo
Denekamp
Emsbüren
Recke
Wiehengebirge
Ostercappeln
Bohmte
Bad Essen
Nijverdal
Rijssen
Oldenzaal
Bad Bentheim
Schüttorf
Horstel
Mettingen
Wallenhorst
Holten
Borne
Hengelo
Losser
Rheine
Westerkappeln
Ibbenbüren
Osnabrück
Goor
Delden
Enschede
Gronau
Overdinkel
Neuenkirchen
Ochtrup
Dörenthe
Tecklenburg
Georgsmarienhütte
Bissendorf
Melle
Markelo
Wettringen
Emsdetten
Bad Iburg
Teutoburger Wald
Lochem
Haaksbergen
Epe
Steinfurt
Saerbeck
Lengerich
Ladbergen
Lienen
Spenge
Borculo
Neede
Heek
Metelen
Schloss Steinfurt
Borghorst
Greven
Glandorf
Dissen
Jöllenbeck
Ruurlo
Eibergen
Alstätte
Ahaus
Horstmar
Laer
Nordwalde
Brock
Versmold
Halle
Bielefeld
Hengelo
Zelhem
Groenlo
Vreden
Münsterland
Altenberge
Ostbevern
Steinhagen
Lichtenvoorde
Winterswijk
Stadtlohn
Holtwick
Darfeld
Havixbeck
Münster
Telgte
Sassenberg
Brackwede
Aalten
Varsseveld
Gescher
Coesfeld
Billerbeck
Burg Hülshoff
Nottuln
Warendorf
Harsewinkel
Terborg
Oeding
Weseke
Velen
Everswinkel
Beelen
Freckenhorst
Gütersloh
Dinxperlo
Gendringen
Bocholt
Borken
Merfeld
Senden
Dom St. Paulus
Albersloh
Herzebrock
Rheda
Dortmund-Ems-Kanal
Ems
Hase
Hunte
Leda
Berkel
Twente-kanaal
Drentse Hoofdvaart
Oranjekanaal
Groningen
Sandhorst
Emstek
Nienoord
Juffertorn
Midlaren
Tynaarlo
Annen
Eext
Drouwen
Odoorn
Emmeres
Emmermeer
Nordsleen
Dierenpark Emmen
Jagdschloss Clemenswerth & Emslands Museum
Dom St. Peter
0:55
1:00
7°
8°
53°

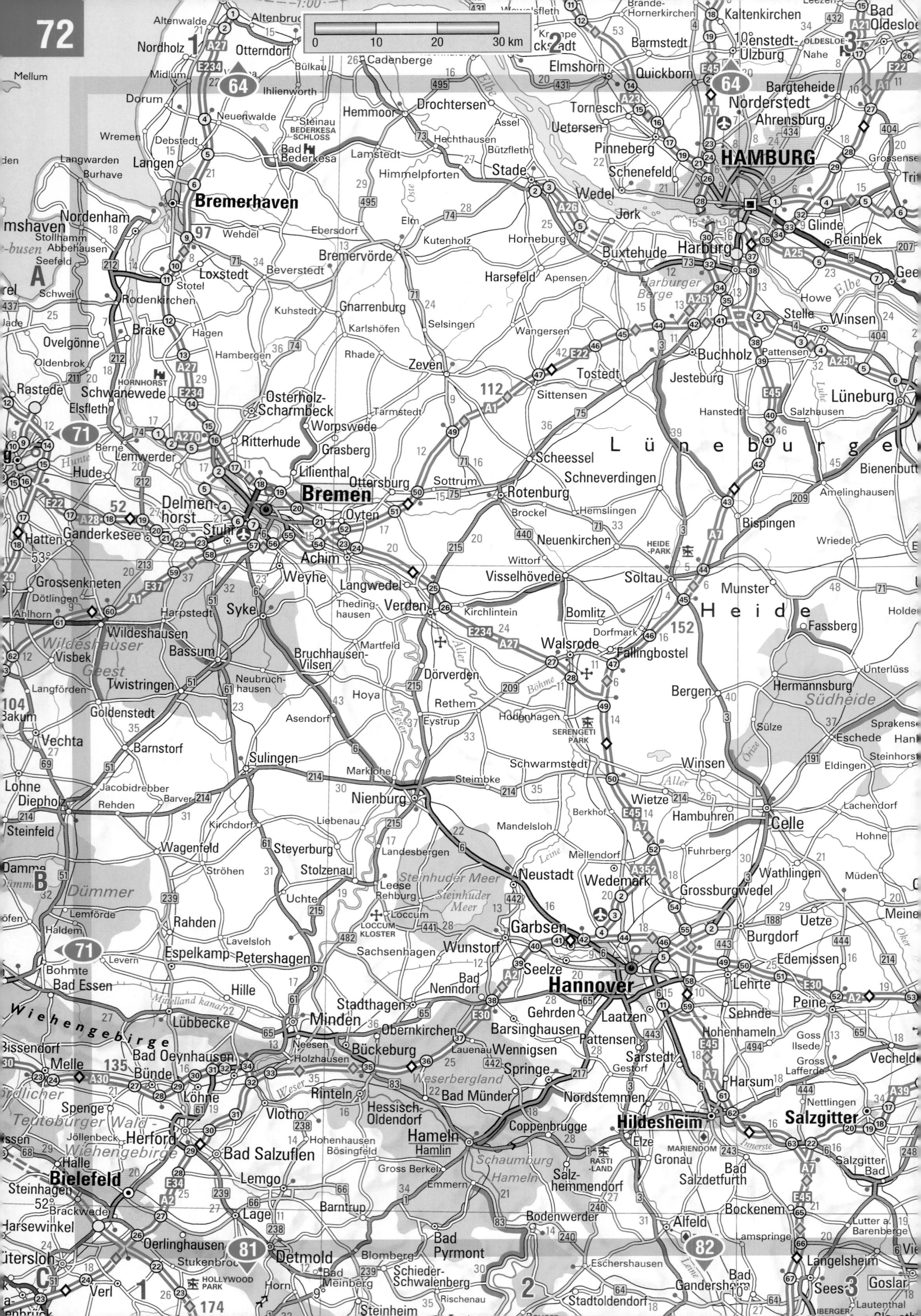

0 10 20 30 km
Altenwalde
Nordholz
Otterndorf
Cadenberge
Mellum
Midlum
Bülkau
Ihlienworth
Dorum
Neuenwalde
Wremen
Debstedt
Bad Bederkesa
Langen
Langwarden
Burhave
Bremerhaven
Nordenham
Stollhamm
Abbehausen
Seefeld
Loxstedt
Stotel
Beverstedt
Schwei
Rodenkirchen
Brake
Hagen
Ovelgönne
Oldenbrok
Hambergen
Rastede
Schwanewede
Elsfleth
Osterholz-Scharmbeck
Worpswede
Ritterhude
Berne
Lemwerder
Hude
Delmenhorst
Ganderkesee
Hatten
Stuhr
Bremen
Lilienthal
Grasberg
Ottersburg
Oyten
Achim
Weyhe
Hemmoor
Drochtersen
Hechthausen
Lamstedt
Himmelpforten
Stade
Bremervörde
Ebersdorf
Gnarrenburg
Kuhstedt
Karlshöfen
Selsingen
Rhade
Zeven
Tarmstedt
Sottrum
Rotenburg
Scheessel
Schneverdingen
Brockel
Hemslingen
Neuenkirchen
Visselhövede
Wittorf
Langwedel
Verden
Kirchlinteln
Thedinghausen
Syke
Bassum
Harpstedt
Wildeshausen
Visbek
Grossenkneten
Dötlingen
Ahlhorn
Twistringen
Neubruchhausen
Bruchhausen-Vilsen
Martfeld
Hoya
Dörverden
Rethem
Eystrup
Asendorf
Langförden
Goldenstedt
Bakum
Vechta
Barnstorf
Sulingen
Marklohe
Nienburg
Steimbke
Lohne
Diepholz
Jacobidrebber
Barver
Rehden
Steinfeld
Kirchdorf
Liebenau
Wagenfeld
Steyerburg
Landesbergen
Damme
Dümmer
Ströhen
Stolzenau
Leese
Rehburg
Uchte
Loccum
Lemförde
Haldem
Rahden
Lavelsloh
Espelkamp
Petershagen
Sachsenhagen
Wunstorf
Levern
Bohmte
Bad Essen
Hille
Bad Nenndorf
Stadthagen
Minden
Lübbecke
Wiehengebirge
Obernkirchen
Bückeburg
Neesen
Holzhausen
Bad Oeynhausen
Melle
Bünde
Löhne
Spenge
Vlotho
Rinteln
Hessisch-Oldendorf
Herford
Bad Salzuflen
Hohenhausen
Bösingfeld
Hameln
Bielefeld
Halle
Steinhagen
Brackwede
Lemgo
Lage
Barntrup
Harsewinkel
Oerlinghausen
Gütersloh
Stukenbrock
Detmold
Horn
Verl
Blomberg
Bad Meinberg
Schieder-Schwalenberg
Bad Pyrmont
Steinheim
Rischenau
Kaltenkirchen
Bad Oldesloe
Barmstedt
Henstedt-Ulzburg
Elmshorn
Quickborn
Bargteheide
Norderstedt
Tornesch
Uetersen
Ahrensburg
Pinneberg
HAMBURG
Schenefeld
Wedel
Jork
Glinde
Reinbek
Buxtehude
Harburg
Horneburg
Kutenholz
Harsefeld
Apensen
Harburger Berge
Howe
Stelle
Winsen
Wangersen
Buchholz
Pattensen
Tostedt
Jesteburg
Sittensen
Lüneburg
Hanstedt
Salzhausen
Lüneburger Heide
Bienenbüttel
Amelinghausen
Bispingen
Wriedel
Soltau
Munster
Bomlitz
Dorfmark
Fassberg
Walsrode
Fallingbostel
Unterlüss
Hermannsburg
Südheide
Bergen
Hodenhagen
Schwarmstedt
Winsen
Eschede
Eldingen
Wietze
Hambühren
Celle
Lachendorf
Berkhof
Mandelsloh
Mellendorf
Wedemark
Fuhrberg
Neustadt
Steinhuder Meer
Grossburgwedel
Wathlingen
Garbsen
Uetze
Burgdorf
Edemissen
Seelze
Hannover
Lehrte
Peine
Gehrden
Laatzen
Sehnde
Barsinghausen
Pattensen
Hohenhameln
Wennigsen
Sarstedt
Springe
Harsum
Bad Münder
Nordstemmen
Coppenbrügge
Hildesheim
Salzgitter
Elze
Gronau
Salzhemmendorf
Bad Salzdetfurth
Emmern
Bodenwerder
Bockenem
Alfeld
Lamspringe
Langelsheim
Eschershausen
Gandersheim
Stadtoldendorf
Seesen
Goslar

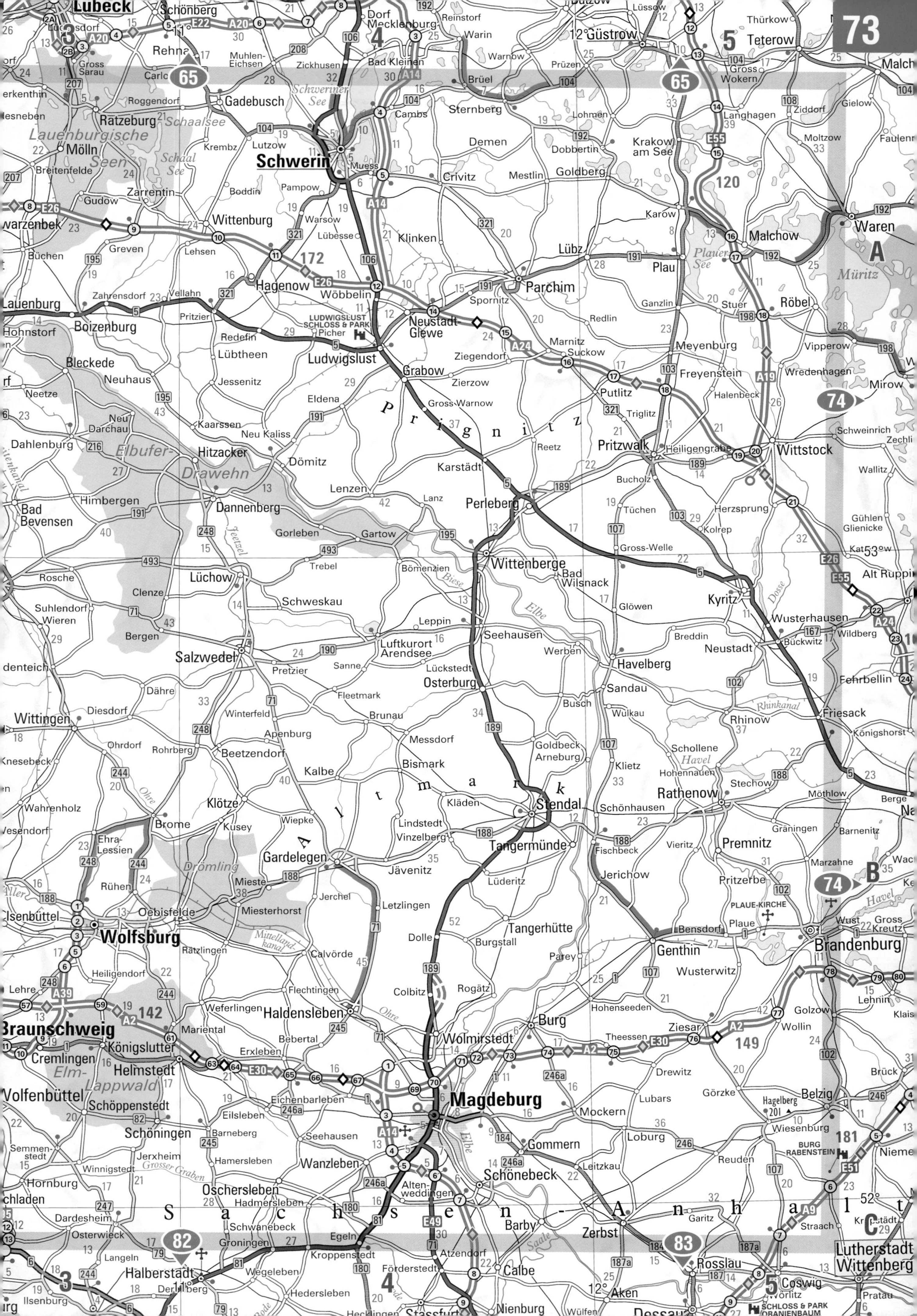
Lübeck
Schönberg
Dorf Mecklenburg
Reinstorf
Bützow
Lüssow
Thürkow
Güstrow
Teterow
Warin
Rehna
Mühlen-Eichsen
Zickhusen
Bad Kleinen
Warnow
Prüzen
Gross Wokern
Malchin
Gross Sarau
Carlow
Brüel
Schweriner See
Sternberg
Lohmen
Roggendorf
Gadebusch
Cambs
Langhagen
Ziddorf
Gielow
Ratzeburg
Schaalsee
Lauenburgische Seen
Krembz
Lutzow
Demen
Dobbertin
Krakow am See
Moltzow
Faulenrost
Mölln
Schwerin
Schaal See
Muess
Crivitz
Mestlin
Goldberg
Breitenfelde
Zarrentin
Boddin
Pampow
Gudow
Warsow
Karow
Schwarzenbek
Wittenburg
Lübesse
Klinken
Malchow
Waren
Büchen
Greven
Lehsen
Lübz
Plauer See
Plau
Müritz
Hagenow
Wöbbelin
Parchim
Lauenburg
Zahrensdorf
Vellahn
Pritzier
Spornitz
Ganzlin
Stuer
Röbel
Hohnstorf
Boizenburg
Ludwigslust Schloss & Park
Picher
Neustadt-Glewe
Redlin
Redefin
Lübtheen
Ludwigslust
Marnitz
Suckow
Meyenburg
Vipperow
Bleckede
Ziegendorf
Freyenstein
Wredenhagen
Neuhaus
Grabow
Zierzow
Putlitz
Halenbeck
Mirow
Neetze
Jessenitz
Gross Warnow
Triglitz
Eldena
Neu Darchau
Prignitz
Karrsen
Neu Kaliss
Dahlenburg
Hitzacker
Elbufer-Drawehn
Dömitz
Reetz
Pritzwalk
Heiligengrabe
Wittstock
Schweinrich
Zechlin
Karstädt
Bucholz
Wallitz
Lenzen
Lanz
Perleberg
Himbergen
Dannenberg
Tüchen
Herzsprung
Bad Bevensen
Kolrep
Gühlen Glienicke
Gorleben
Gartow
Jeetzel
Gross-Welle
Wittenberge
Trebel
Bömenzien
Bad Wilsnack
Alt Ruppin
Rosche
Lüchow
Biese
Clenze
Kyritz
Dosse
Suhlendorf
Wieren
Schweskau
Glöwen
Wusterhausen
Leppin
Elbe
Bergen
Seehausen
Breddin
Wildberg
Salzwedel
Luftkurort Arendsee
Werben
Neustadt
Bückwitz
Pretzier
Sanne
Lückstedt
Havelberg
Fehrbellin
Osterburg
Sandau
Dähre
Fleetmark
Busch
Wittingen
Diesdorf
Winterfeld
Brunau
Wulkau
Rhinkanal
Rhinow
Friesack
Apenburg
Messdorf
Königshorst
Ohrdorf
Rohrberg
Beetzendorf
Goldbeck
Arneburg
Schollene
Havel
Knesebeck
Bismark
Kalbe
Klietz
Hohennauen
Stechow
Altmark
Ohre
Klötze
Kläden
Stendal
Rathenow
Möthlow
Wahrenholz
Schönhausen
Brome
Kusey
Wiepke
Lindstedt
Vinzelberg
Gräningen
Barnewitz
Vesendorf
Tangermünde
Premnitz
Ehra-Lessien
Fischbeck
Vieritz
Gardelegen
Jävenitz
Marzahne
Drömling
Jerichow
Pritzerbe
Rühen
Mieste
Lüderitz
Jerchel
Letzlingen
Plaue-Kirche
Isenbüttel
Oebisfelde
Miesterhorst
Plaue
Wust
Gross Kreutz
Wolfsburg
Tangerhütte
Bensdorf
Mittellandkanal
Dolle
Burgstall
Genthin
Brandenburg
Rätzlingen
Calvörde
Parey
Heiligendorf
Wusterwitz
Lehnin
Lehre
Flechtingen
Colbitz
Rogätz
Klaistow
Golzow
Weferlingen
Haldensleben
Hohenseeden
Burg
Braunschweig
Mariental
Ziesar
Wollin
Königslutter
Bebertal
Wolmirstedt
Theessen
Cremlingen
Erxleben
Helmstedt
Elm-Lappwald
Drewitz
Brück
Wolfenbüttel
Schöppenstedt
Eichenbarleben
Magdeburg
Lubars
Görzke
Belzig
Hagelberg
Eilsleben
Mockern
Schöningen
Barneberg
Seehausen
Loburg
Wiesenburg
Semmenstedt
Jerxheim
Gommern
Burg Rabenstein
Niemegk
Winnigstedt
Grosser Graben
Hamersleben
Wanzleben
Reuden
Leitzkau
Hornburg
Schönebeck
Oschersleben
Altenweddingen
Schladen
Hadmersleben
Dardesheim
Sachsen-Anhalt
Barby
Zerbst
Garitz
Straach
Kropstädt
Osterwieck
Schwanebeck
Groningen
Egeln
Kroppenstedt
Atzendorf
Saale
Lutherstadt Wittenberg
Langeln
Halberstadt
Wegeleben
Förderstedt
Calbe
Rosslau
Coswig
Derenburg
Hedersleben
Aken
Wörlitz
Pratau
Ilsenburg
Hecklingen
Stassfurt
Nienburg
Wülfen
Dessau
Schloss & Park Oranienbaum

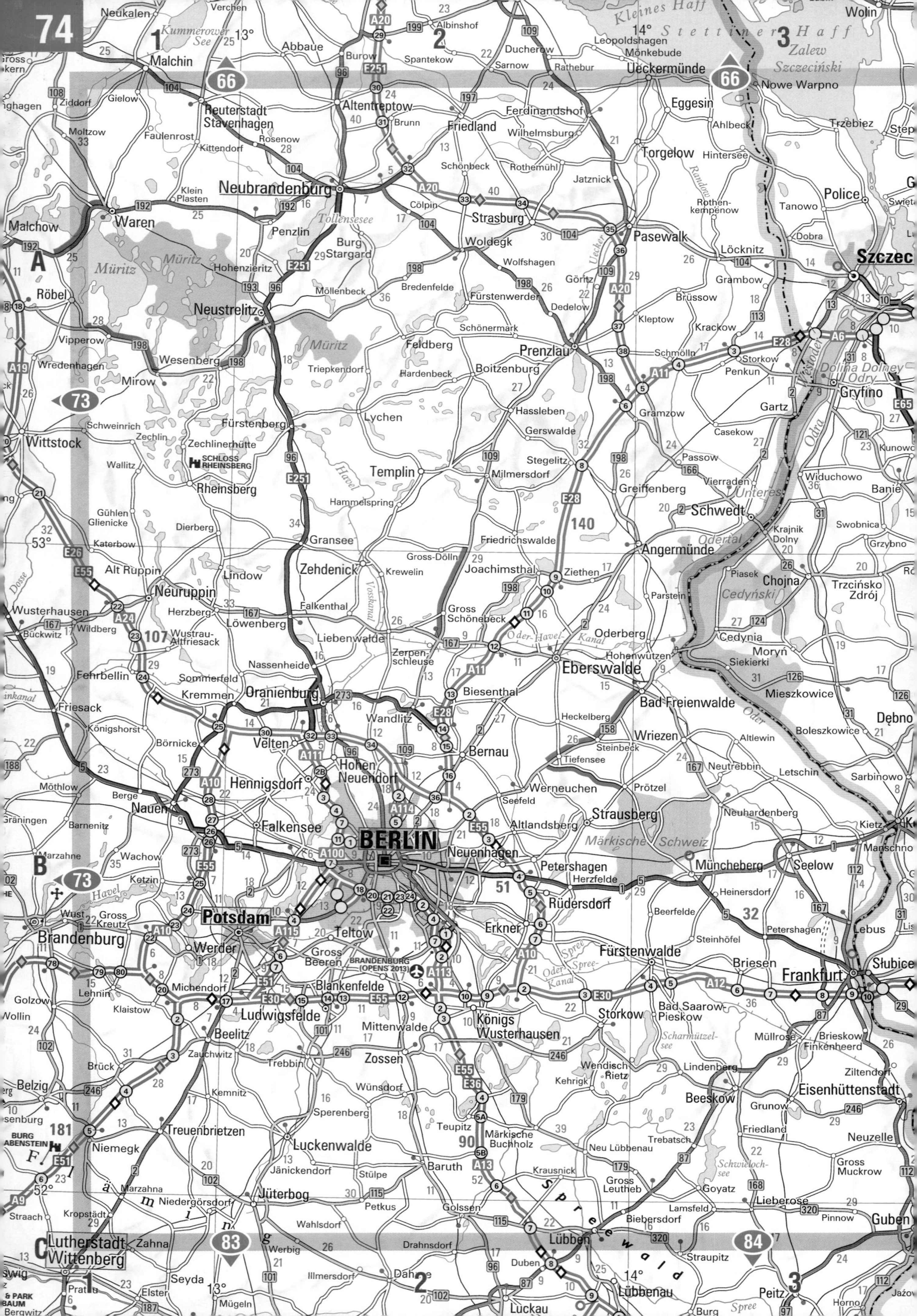
Neukalen
Verchen
Kummerower See
Malchin
Abbaue
Burow
Albinshof
Spantekow
Ducherow
Sarnow
Kleines Haff
Stettiner Haff
Zalew Szczeciński
Leopoldshagen
Mönkebude
Rathebur
Ueckermünde
Wolin
Nowe Warpno
Ziddorf
Gielow
Reuterstadt Stavenhagen
Altentreptow
Brunn
Friedland
Ferdinandshof
Wilhelmsburg
Eggesin
Ahlbeck
Trzebież
Moltzow
Faulenrost
Kittendorf
Rosenow
Schönbeck
Rothemühl
Torgelow
Hintersee
Jatznick
Neubrandenburg
Klein Plasten
Cölpin
Strasburg
Rothenkempenow
Police
Tanowo
Malchow
Waren
Penzlin
Tollensesee
Burg Stargard
Woldegk
Pasewalk
Löcknitz
Dobra
Szczecin
Müritz
Hohenzieritz
Wolfshagen
Görtz
Grambow
Röbel
Neustrelitz
Möllenbeck
Bredenfelde
Fürstenwerder
Dedelow
Brüssow
Kleptow
Krackow
Vipperow
Schönermark
Feldberg
Prenzlau
Schmölln
Storkow
Penkun
Wredenhagen
Wesenberg
Mirow
Triepkendorf
Hardenbeck
Boitzenburg
Gryfino
Dolina Dolnej Odry
Westoder
Odra
Gartz
Hassleben
Gramzow
Casekow
Schweinrich
Wittstock
Fürstenberg
Zechlin
Zechlinerhütte
Lychen
Gerswalde
Kunowo
Schloss Rheinsberg
Wallitz
Templin
Stegelitz
Milmersdorf
Passow
Vierraden
Widuchowo
Banie
Rheinsberg
Greiffenberg
Unteres Odertal
Schwedt
Hammelspring
Gühlen Glienicke
Dierberg
Krajnik Dolny
Swobnica
Gransee
Friedrichswalde
Grzybno
Katerbow
Gross-Dölln
Angermünde
Zehdenick
Krewelin
Joachimsthal
Ziethen
Piasek
Chojna
Trzcińsko Zdrój
Alt Ruppin
Lindow
Dosse
Neuruppin
Falkenthal
Vosskanal
Gross Schönebeck
Parstein
Cedyński
Wusterhausen
Herzberg
Löwenberg
Bückwitz
Wildberg
Wustrau-Altfriesack
Liebenwalde
Zerpenschleuse
Oder-Havel-Kanal
Oderberg
Cedynia
Moryń
Hohenwutzen
Siekierki
Nassenheide
Eberswalde
Fehrbellin
Sommerfeld
Kremmen
Oranienburg
Biesenthal
Bad Freienwalde
Mieszkowice
Friesack
Wandlitz
Heckelberg
Dębno
Königshorst
Börnicke
Velten
Wriezen
Altlewin
Boleszkowice
Hennigsdorf
Hohen Neuendorf
Bernau
Steinbeck
Tiefensee
Neutrebbin
Letschin
Sarbinowo
Möthlow
Berge
Nauen
Werneuchen
Prötzel
Seefeld
Gräningen
Barnenitz
Falkensee
Strausberg
Neuhardenberg
Altlandsberg
Kietz
Märkische Schweiz
Marzahne
Wachow
BERLIN
Neuenhagen
Manschnow
Petershagen
Müncheberg
Seelow
Ketzin
Havel
Herzfelde
Heinersdorf
Rüdersdorf
Wust
Gross Kreutz
Potsdam
Beerfelde
Brandenburg
Teltow
Erkner
Lebus
Werder
Steinhöfel
Gross Beeren
Brandenburg (opens 2013)
Fürstenwalde
Briesen
Słubice
Spree
Oder-Spree-Kanal
Frankfurt
Lehnin
Michendorf
Blankenfelde
Klaistow
Golzow
Wollin
Ludwigsfelde
Mittenwalde
Königs Wusterhausen
Storkow
Bad Saarow-Pieskow
Müllrose
Brieskow Finkenheerd
Beelitz
Zauchwitz
Zossen
Scharmützelsee
Trebbin
Wendisch Rietz
Lindenberg
Ziltendorf
Brück
Kehrigk
Belzig
Kemnitz
Wünsdorf
Beeskow
Eisenhüttenstadt
Grunow
Sperenberg
Teupitz
Märkische Buchholz
Trebatsch
Friedland
Neuzelle
Niemegk
Treuenbrietzen
Luckenwalde
Burg Rabenstein
Neu Lübbenau
Jänickendorf
Stülpe
Baruth
Krausnick
Schwielochsee
Gross Muckrow
Fläming
Marzahna
Niedergörsdorf
Jüterbog
Gross Leuthen
Goyatz
Petkus
Golssen
Lieberose
Strauch
Kropstädt
Wahlsdorf
Biebersdorf
Lamsfeld
Pinnow
Guben
Lutherstadt Wittenberg
Zahna
Werbig
Drahnsdorf
Lübben
Spreewald
Straupitz
Seyda
Illmersdorf
Dahme
Duben
Lübbenau
Peitz
Pratau
Elster
Mügeln
Luckau
Burg
Horno
Jaźow
Bergwitz

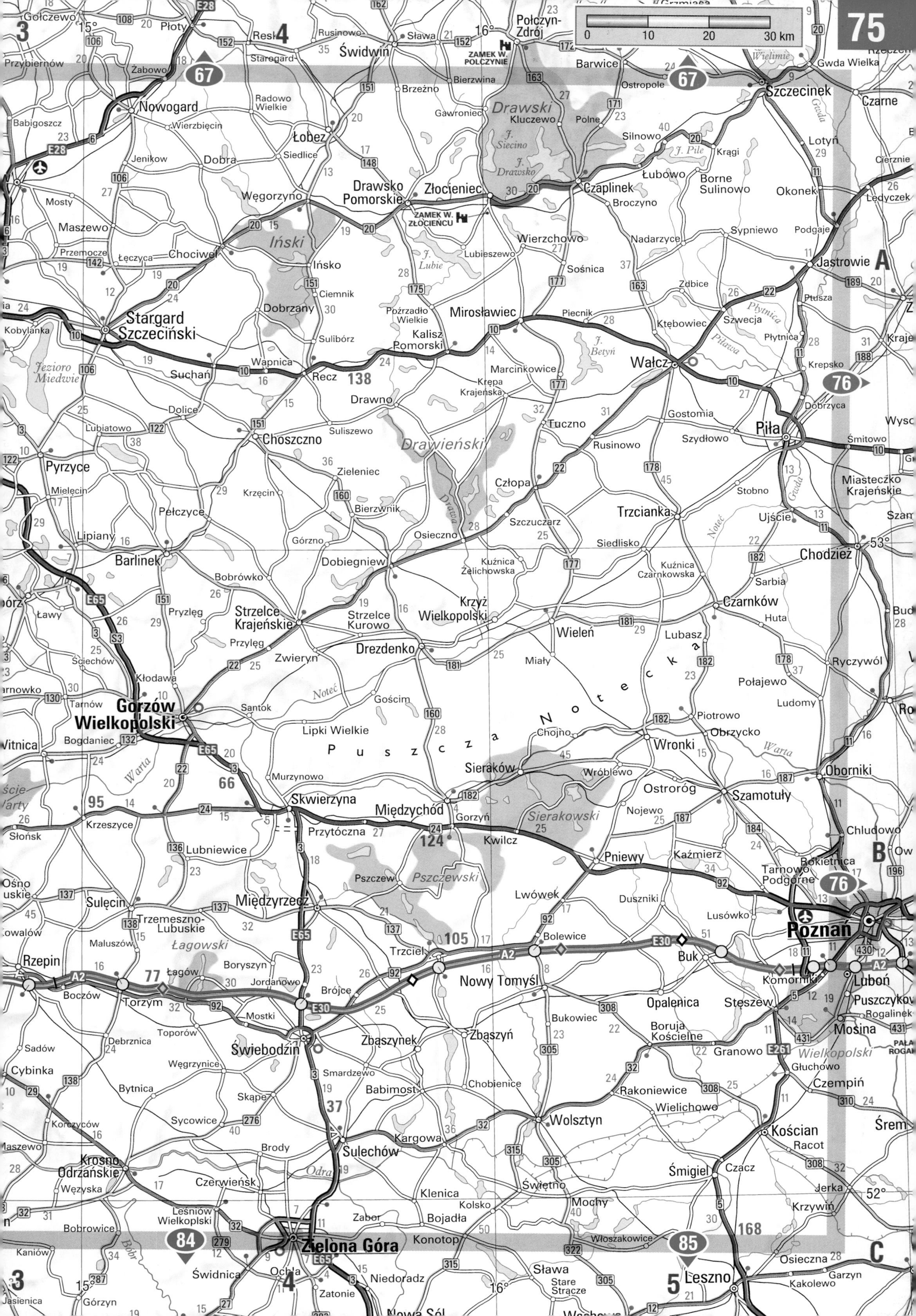

0 10 20 30 km
Gołczewo
Płoty
Resko
Świdwin
Sława
Połczyn-Zdrój
ZAMEK W. POŁCZYNIE
Barwice
Szczecinek
Gwda Wielka
Przybiernów
Żabowo
Starogard
Bierzwina
Ostropole
Czarne
Nowogard
Radowo Wielkie
Brzeżno
Gawroniec
Drawski
Kluczewo
Polne
Silnowo
Babigoszcz
Wierzbięcin
Łobez
J. Siecino
J. Drawsko
J. Pile
Krągi
Lotyń
Jenikow
Dobra
Siedlice
Łubowo
Borne Sulinowo
Okonek
Drawsko Pomorskie
Złocieniec
Czaplinek
Broczyno
Lędyczek
Mosty
Węgorzyno
ZAMEK W. ZŁOCIEŃCU
Maszewo
Iński
Wierzchowo
Nadarzyce
Sypniewo
Podgaje
Przemocze
Łęczyca
Chociwel
Ińsko
J. Lubie
Lubieszewo
Sośnica
Jastrowie
Ciemnik
Zdbice
Płusza
Stargard Szczeciński
Dobrzany
Pożrzadło Wielkie
Mirosławiec
Piecnik
Kłębowiec
Szwecja
Płytnica
Kobylanka
Kalisz Pomorski
Sulibórz
J. Betyń
Wałcz
Krepsko
Jezioro Miedwie
Suchań
Wapnica
Recz
Marcinkowice
Krępa Krajeńska
Drawno
Dolice
Tuczno
Gostomia
Dobrzyca
Lubiatowo
Choszczno
Suliszewo
Drawieński
Rusinowo
Szydłowo
Piła
Śmiłowo
Pyrzyce
Zieleniec
Człopa
Miasteczko Krajeńskie
Mielęcin
Krzęcin
Bierzwnik
Stobno
Pełczyce
Drawa
Szczuczarz
Trzcianka
Ujście
Lipiany
Górzno
Osieczno
Siedlisko
Chodzież
Barlinek
Dobiegniew
Kuźnica Żelichowska
Kuźnica Czarnkowska
Bobrówko
Sarbia
Krzyż Wielkopolski
Czarnków
Ławy
Przylęg
Strzelce Krajeńskie
Strzelce Kurowo
Huta
Przyłęg
Drezdenko
Wieleń
Lubasz
Ściechów
Zwierzyn
Miały
Ryczywół
Kłodawa
Noteć
Połajewo
Tarnów
Gościm
Ludomy
Gorzów Wielkopolski
Santok
Puszcza Notecka
Piotrowo
Lipki Wielkie
Chojno
Obrzycko
Bogdaniec
Wronki
Warta
Sieraków
Wróblewo
Oborniki
Murzynowo
Ostroróg
Skwierzyna
Międzychód
Szamotuły
Krzeszyce
Gorzyń
Nojewo
Słońsk
Przytóczna
Kwilcz
Sierakowski
Chludowo
Lubniewice
Pniewy
Kaźmierz
Rokietnica
Tarnowo Podgórne
Pszczew
Pszczewski
Sulęcin
Międzyrzecz
Lwówek
Duszniki
Lusówko
Poznań
Trzemeszno-Lubuskie
Maluszów
Łagowski
Bolewice
Rzepin
Boryszyn
Trzciel
Buk
Łagów
Jordanowo
Nowy Tomyśl
Komorniki
Luboń
Boczów
Torzym
Brójce
Opalenica
Stęszew
Puszczykowo
Rogalinek
Mostki
Bukowiec
Mosina
Toporów
Debrznica
Zbąszynek
Zbąszyń
Boruja Kościelne
Sadów
Świebodzin
Granowo
Wielkopolski
Cybinka
Węgrzynice
Smardzewo
Głuchowo
Bytnica
Chobienice
Rakoniewice
Czempiń
Babimost
Skąpe
Wielichowo
Korczyców
Sycowice
Wolsztyn
Kościan
Śrem
Kargowa
Racot
Brody
Sulechów
Krosno Odrzańskie
Odra
Śmigiel
Czacz
Węzyska
Czerwieńsk
Klenica
Święto
Jerka
Krzywiń
Mochy
Kolsko
Leśniów Wielkopolski
Zabór
Bojadła
Bobrowice
Konotop
Włoszakowice
Kaniów
Zielona Góra
Bóbr
Osieczna
Sława
Garzyn
Świdnica
Ochla
Niedoradz
Stare Strącze
Leszno
Kąkolewo
Jasienica
Górzyn
Zatonie
Nowa Sól
Wschowa
A
B
C
15°
16°
53°
52°

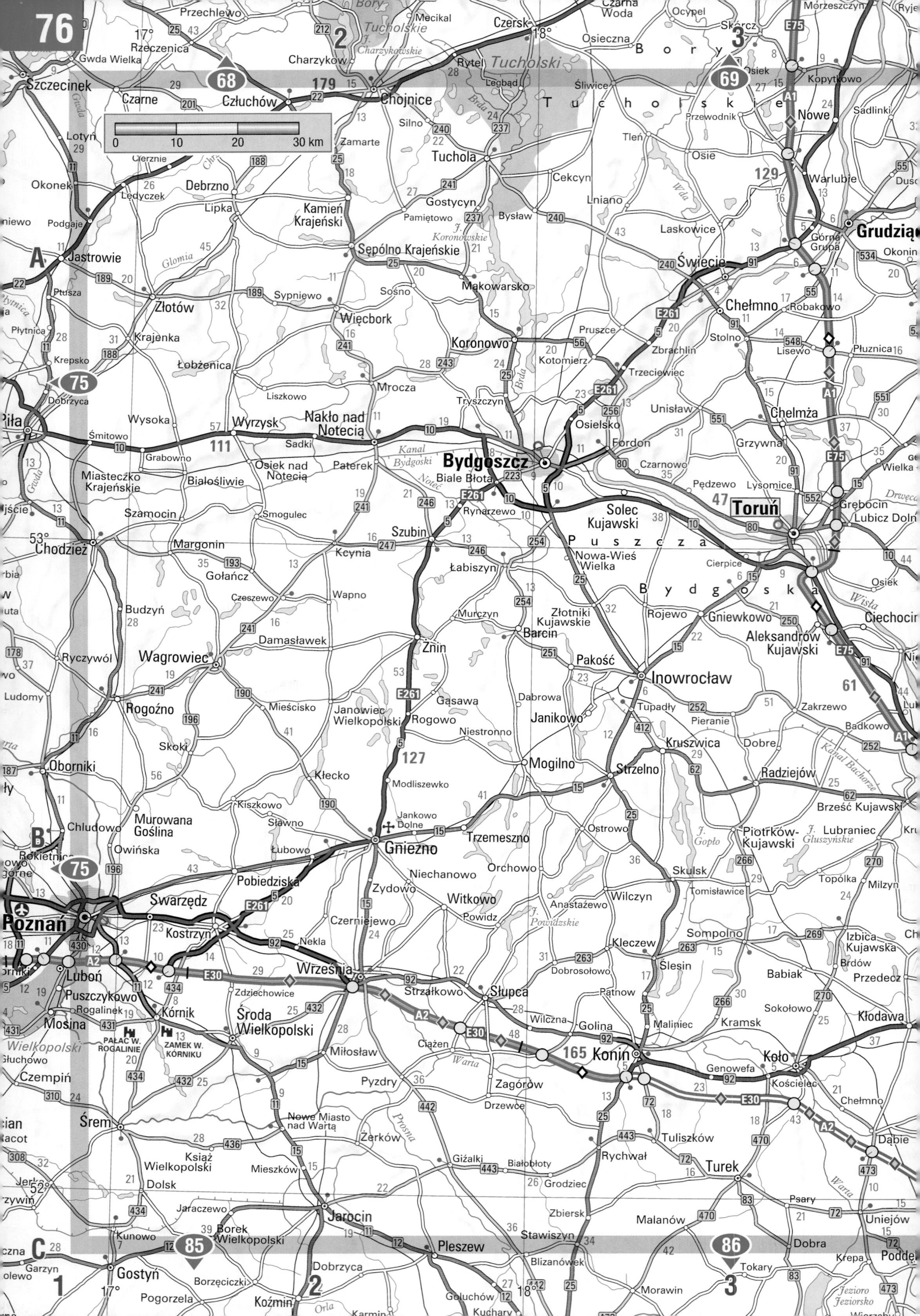

Przechlewo
Rzeczenica
Gwda Wielka
Szczecinek
Czarne
Człuchów
Chojnice
Charzykowy
Mecikal
Tucholskie
Bory
Czersk
Rytel
Czarna Woda
Osieczna
Ocypel
Skórcz
Mórzeszczyn
B o r y
T u c h o l s k i e
Legbąd
Śliwice
Osiek
Kopytkowo
Nowe
Przewodnik
Sadlinki
0
10
20
30 km
Lotyń
Zamarte
Silno
Tuchola
Tleń
Osie
Okonek
Debrzno
Lipka
Kamień Krajeński
Gostycyn
Cekcyn
Lniano
Warlubie
Pamiętowo
Bysław
Laskowice
Grudziądz
Górna Grupa
Jastrowie
Glomia
Sępólno Krajeńskie
Koronowskie
Świecie
Okonin
Podgaje
Mąkowarsko
Złotów
Sypniewo
Sośno
Więcbork
Chełmno
Robakowo
Krajenka
Koronowo
Pruszce
Płytnica
Krepsko
Łobżenica
Kotomierz
Zbrachlin
Stolno
Lisewo
Płużnica
Trzeciewiec
Mrocza
Liszkowo
Dobrzyca
Tryszczyn
Unisław
Chełmża
Piła
Wysoka
Wyrzysk
Nakło nad Notecią
Osielsko
Śmitowo
Sadki
Fordon
Grzywna
Grabowno
Kanał Bydgoski
Bydgoszcz
Czarnowo
Miasteczko Krajeńskie
Białośliwie
Osiek nad Notecią
Paterek
Białe Błota
Pędzewo
Łysomice
Szamocin
Smogulec
Rynarzewo
Solec Kujawski
Toruń
Grębocin
Lubicz Dolny
Chodzież
Margonin
Szubin
Kcynia
P u s z c z a
B y d g o s k a
Cierpice
Nowa-Wieś Wielka
Gołańcz
Łabiszyn
Osiek
Czeszewo
Wapno
Budzyń
Murczyn
Złotniki Kujawskie
Rojewo
Gniewkowo
Ciechocinek
Barcin
Aleksandrów Kujawski
Damasławek
Żnin
Wągrowiec
Ryczywół
Pakość
Inowrocław
Ludomy
Rogoźno
Mieścisko
Janowiec Wielkopolski
Gąsawa
Dąbrowa
Janikowo
Tupadły
Pieranie
Zakrzewo
Rogowo
Niestronno
Kruszwica
Badkowo
Skoki
Dobre
Kanał Bachorze
Oborniki
Kłecko
Mogilno
Strzelno
Radziejów
Modliszewko
Kiszkowo
Brześć Kujawski
Murowana Goślina
Jankowo Dolne
Chludowo
Sławno
Trzemeszno
Ostrowo
Piotrków-Kujawski
Lubraniec
Gopło
Głuszyńskie
Owińska
Gniezno
Łubowo
Rokietnica
Orchowo
Pobiedziska
Niechanowo
Skulsk
Topólka
Milzyn
Tomisławice
Zydowo
Swarzędz
Witkowo
Wilczyn
Poznań
Anastazewo
Powidz
Powidzkie
Czerniejewo
Kostrzyn
Sompolno
Izbica Kujawska
Nekla
Kleczew
Brdów
Luboń
Września
Ślesin
Babiak
Przedecz
Dobrosołowo
Zdziechowice
Strzałkowo
Słupca
Pątnow
Puszczykowo
Rogalinek
Kórnik
Środa Wielkopolski
Sokołowo
Kłodawa
Mosina
Wilczna
Golina
Maliniec
Kramsk
PAŁAC W. ROGALINIE
ZAMEK W. KÓRNIKU
Wielkopolski
Łuchowo
Miłosław
Ciążen
Konin
Koło
Warta
Czempiń
Genowefa
Kościelec
Pyzdry
Zagórów
Chełmno
Drzewce
Nowe Miasto nad Wartą
Śrem
Prosna
Żerków
Tuliszków
Dąbie
Książ Wielkopolski
Mieszków
Giżałki
Białobłoty
Rychwał
Turek
Dolsk
Grodziec
Jaraczewo
Psary
Jarocin
Zbiersk
Malanów
Uniejów
Kunowo
Borek Wielkopolski
Stawiszyn
Pleszew
Dobra
Gostyń
Garzyn
Dobrzyca
Blizanówek
Tokary
Krepa
Borzęciczki
Pogorzela
Koźmin
Gołuchów
Kuchary
Morawin
Jezioro Jeziorsko
Orla
Karmin
Piła
A
B
C
1
2
3
68
69
75
85
86
17°
18°
53°
52°
E30
E75
E261
A1
A2

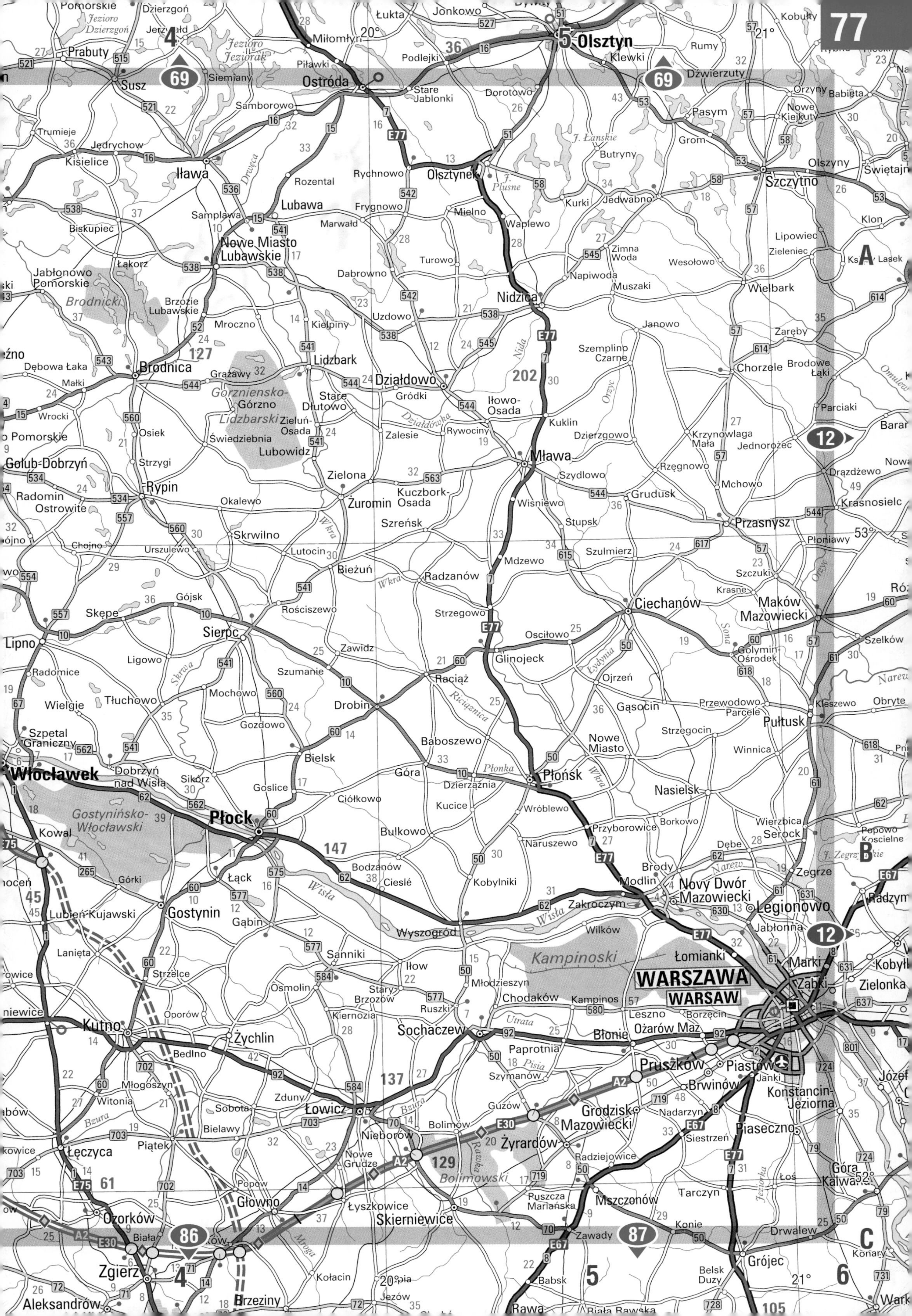

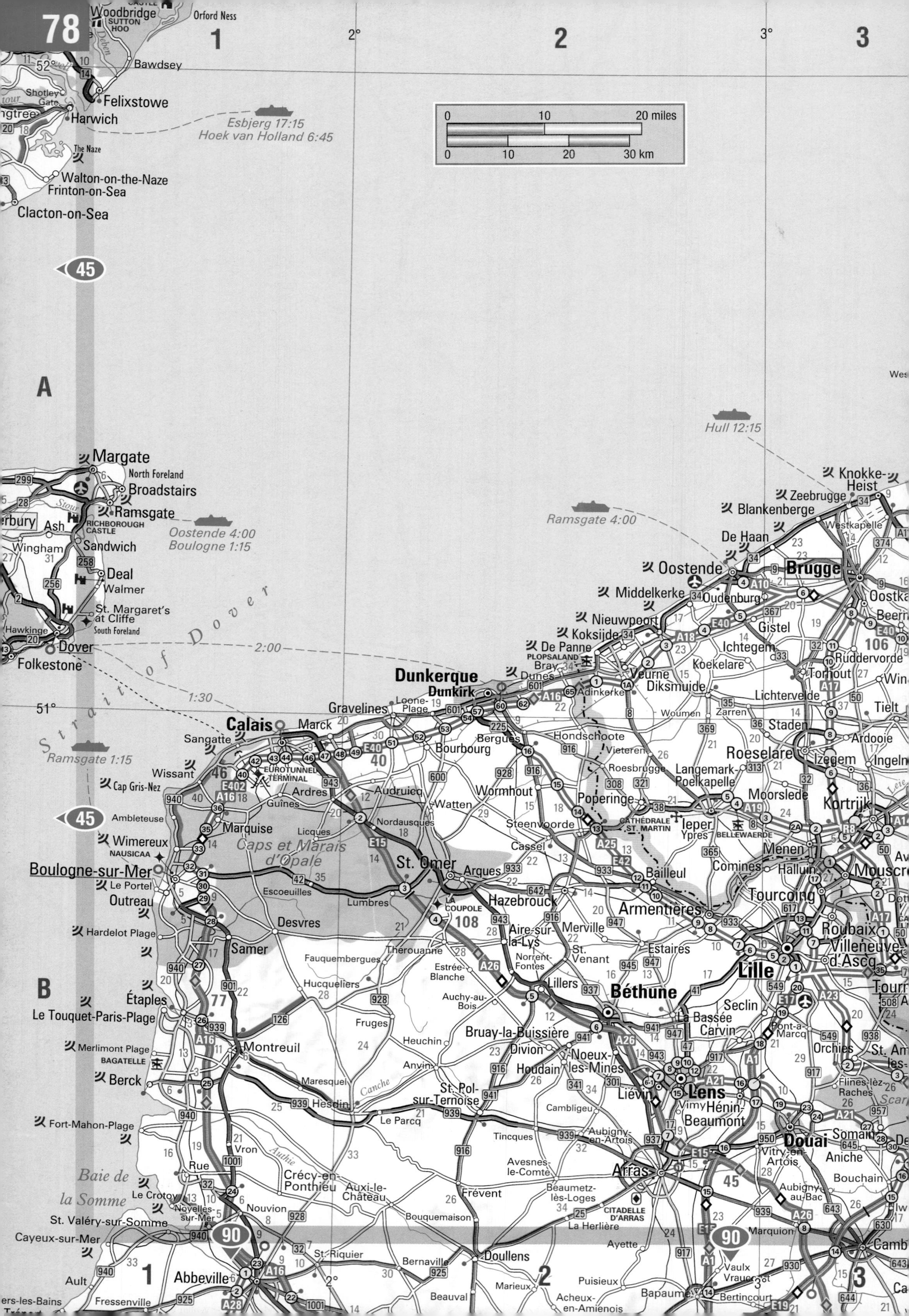

Woodbridge
Orford Ness
Sutton Hoo
Bawdsey
Felixstowe
Harwich
Shotley Gate
Esbjerg 17:15
Hoek van Holland 6:45
The Naze
Walton-on-the-Naze
Frinton-on-Sea
Clacton-on-Sea
0 10 20 miles
0 10 20 30 km
2°
3°
1
2
3
A
B
45
Margate
North Foreland
Broadstairs
Ramsgate
Richborough Castle
Sandwich
Ash
Wingham
Deal
Walmer
St. Margaret's at Cliffe
South Foreland
Hawkinge
Dover
Folkestone
Oostende 4:00
Boulogne 1:15
Strait of Dover
2:00
1:30
51°
Ramsgate 1:15
Hull 12:15
Ramsgate 4:00
Knokke-Heist
Zeebrugge
Blankenberge
Westkapelle
De Haan
Oostende
Brugge
Middelkerke
Oudenburg
Nieuwpoort
Gistel
Koksijde
De Panne
Plopsaland
Ichtegem
Koekelare
Torhout
Ruddervoorde
Bray-Dunes
Veurne
Diksmuide
Adinkerke
Lichtervelde
Tielt
Woumen
Zarren
Staden
Ardooie
Roeselare
Izegem
Langemark-Poelkapelle
Moorslede
Kortrijk
Dunkerque
Dunkirk
Gravelines
Loon-Plage
Calais
Sangatte
Marck
Bergues
Hondschoote
Vleteren
Roesbrugge
Bourbourg
Eurotunnel Terminal
Wissant
Cap Gris-Nez
Ardres
Audruicq
Guînes
Wormhout
Poperinge
Cathédrale St. Martin
Ieper
Ypres
Bellewaerde
Menen
Halluin
Mouscron
Watten
Nordausques
Steenvoorde
Ambleteuse
Marquise
Licques
Caps et Marais d'Opale
Wimereux
Nausicaa
Cassel
Boulogne-sur-Mer
Le Portel
Outreau
St. Omer
Arques
Bailleul
Comines
Tourcoing
Escoeuilles
Lumbres
Hazebrouck
La Coupole
Armentières
Roubaix
Villeneuve-d'Ascq
Hardelot Plage
Desvres
Aire-sur-la-Lys
Merville
Samer
Thérouanne
Fauquembergues
Estrée-Blanche
Norrent-Fontes
St. Venant
Estaires
Lille
Étaples
Le Touquet-Paris-Plage
Hucqueliers
Lillers
Béthune
Auchy-au-Bois
Seclin
La Bassée
Carvin
Fruges
Bruay-la-Buissière
Merlimont Plage
Bagatelle
Montreuil
Heuchin
Divion
Noeux-les-Mines
Houdain
Orchies
Berck
Anvin
Lens
Liévin
Vimy
Hénin-Beaumont
Flines-lez-Raches
Maresquel
Hesdin
Canche
St. Pol-sur-Ternoise
Le Parcq
Fort-Mahon-Plage
Cambligeu
Tincques
Aubigny-en-Artois
Douai
Somain
Vitry-en-Artois
Aniche
Vron
Authie
Baie de la Somme
Rue
Crécy-en-Ponthieu
Auxi-le-Château
Avesnes-le-Comte
Arras
Bouchain
Le Crotoy
Noyelles-sur-Mer
Frévent
Beaumetz-lès-Loges
Aubigny-au-Bac
Nouvion
Bouquemaison
Citadelle d'Arras
St. Valéry-sur-Somme
La Herlière
Marquion
Cayeux-sur-Mer
Ayette
Camb
St. Riquier
Doullens
Bernaville
Ault
Abbeville
Vaulx-Vraucourt
Fressenville
Beauval
Marieux
Puisieux
Acheux-en-Amienois
Bapaume
Bertincourt
90

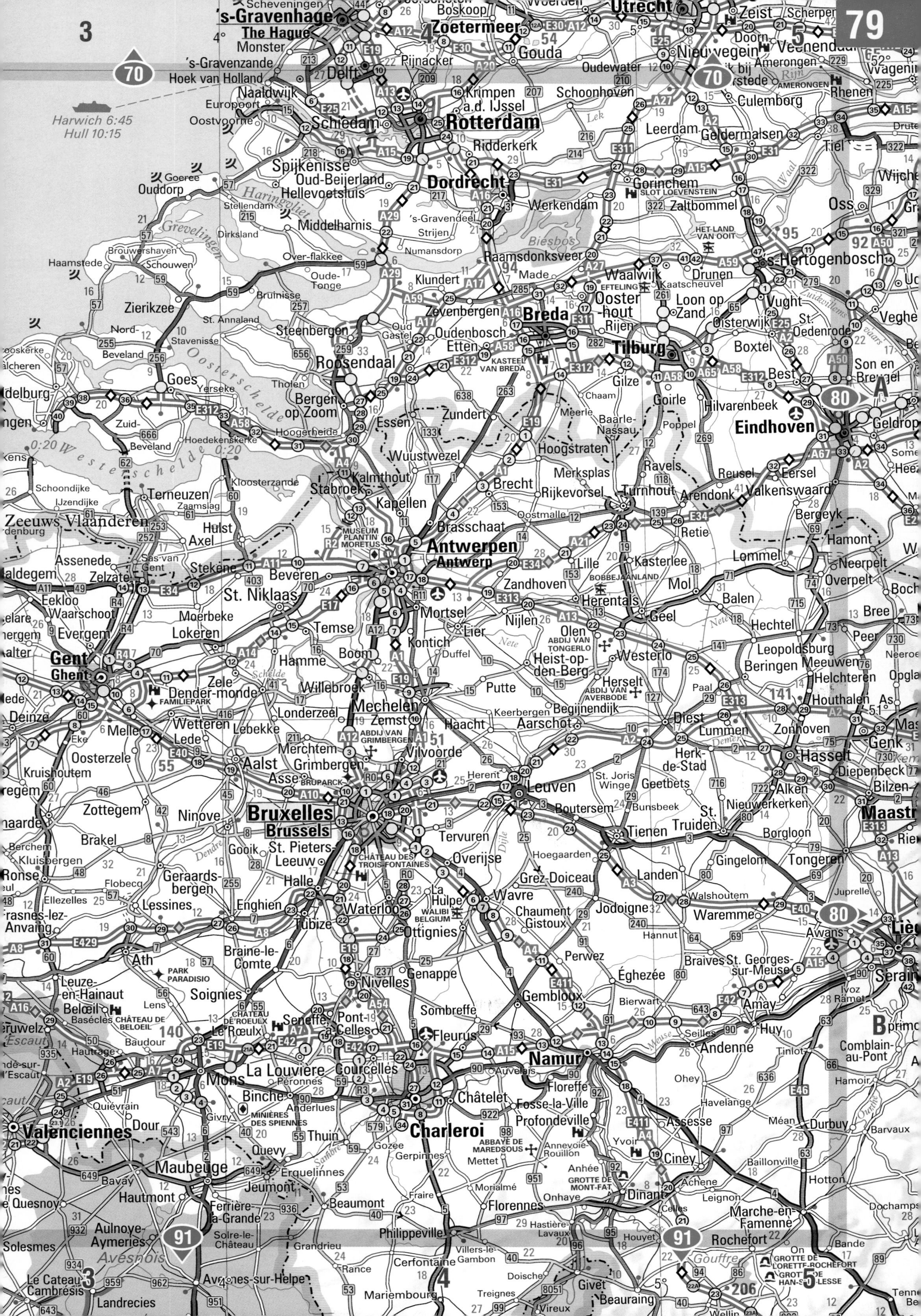
's-Gravenhage
The Hague
Scheveningen
Zoetermeer
Boskoop
Woerden
Utrecht
Zeist
Monster
's-Gravenzande
Hoek van Holland
Delft
Pijnacker
Gouda
Nieuwegein
Doorn
Veenendaal
Amerongen
Wageningen
Rhenen
Naaldwijk
Europoort
Oostvoorne
Schiedam
Rotterdam
Krimpen a.d. IJssel
Schoonhoven
Oudewater
Culemborg
Harwich 6:45
Hull 10:15
Ridderkerk
Leerdam
Geldermalsen
Tiel
Spijkenisse
Oud-Beijerland
Hellevoetsluis
Dordrecht
Gorinchem
Goeree
Ouddorp
Haringvliet
Stellendam
Middelharnis
'S-Gravendeel
Strijen
Werkendam
Zaltbommel
Slot Loevestein
Oss
Grevelingen
Dirksland
Brouwershaven
Haamstede
Schouwen
Over-flakkee
Numansdorp
Biesbos
Het Land van Ooit
Raamsdonksveer
Waalwijk
Drunen
's-Hertogenbosch
Oude-Tonge
Klundert
Made
Efteling
Kaatsheuvel
Bruinisse
Zierikzee
St. Annaland
Zevenbergen
Breda
Oosterhout
Loon op Zand
Vught
Steenbergen
Oud Gastel
Oudenbosch
Rijen
Oisterwijk
St. Oedenrode
Nord-Beveland
Stavenisse
Etten
Tilburg
Boxtel
Roosendaal
Kasteel van Breda
Gilze
Best
Son en Breugel
Goes
Yerseke
Tholen
Oosterschelde
Bergen op Zoom
Zundert
Chaam
Goirle
Hilvarenbeek
Eindhoven
Geldrop
Middelburg
Vlissingen
Zuid-Beveland
Hoogerheide
Hoedekenskerke
Essen
Meerle
Baarle-Nassau
Poppel
0:20
Westerschelde
Wuustwezel
Hoogstraten
Ravels
Reusel
Eersel
Kalmthout
Kloosterzande
Merksplas
Schoondijke
IJzendijke
Terneuzen
Zaamslag
Stabroek
Brecht
Rijkevorsel
Turnhout
Arendonk
Valkenswaard
Kapellen
Bergeyk
Zeeuws Vlaanderen
Hulst
Axel
Brasschaat
Oostmalle
Retie
Hamont
Museum Plantin Moretus
Antwerpen
Antwerp
Lille
Kasterlee
Lommel
Neerpelt
Overpelt
Assenede
Zelzate
Sas-van Gent
Stekene
Beveren
Zandhoven
Bobbejaanland
Mol
Maldegem
St. Niklaas
Herentals
Balen
Bree
Eekloo
Waarschoot
Moerbeke
Mortsel
Nijlen
Geel
Hechtel
Evergem
Lokeren
Temse
Lier
Kontich
Olen
Abdij van Tongerlo
Peer
Leopoldsburg
Gent
Ghent
Hamme
Boom
Duffel
Heist-op-den-Berg
Westerlo
Beringen
Meeuwen
Helchteren
Zele
Dendermonde
Familiepark
Willebroek
Putte
Herselt
Abdij van Averbode
Paal
Houthalen
Deinze
Melle
Wetteren
Lede
Lebekke
Londerzeel
Mechelen
Zemst
Keerbergen
Begijnendijk
Aarschot
Diest
Lummen
Zonhoven
Genk
Eke
Oosterzele
Merchtem
Abdij van Grimbergen
Vilvoorde
Haacht
Herk-de-Stad
Hasselt
Kruishoutem
Aalst
Grimbergen
Asse
Bruparck
Herent
Leuven
St. Joris Winge
Geetbets
Alken
Diepenbeck
Bilzen
Zottegem
Ninove
Bruxelles
Brussels
Boutersem
Bunsbeek
Nieuwerkerken
St. Truiden
Maastricht
Brakel
Gooik
St. Pieters-Leeuw
Tervuren
Tienen
Borgloon
Kluisbergen
Château des Trois-Fontaines
Overijse
Hoegaarden
Gingelom
Tongeren
Ronse
Flobecq
Geraards-bergen
Halle
La Hulpe
Grez-Doiceau
Landen
Ellezelles
Lessines
Enghien
Waterloo
Wavre
Jodoigne
Walshoutem
Waremme
Frasnes-lez-Anvaing
Tubize
Walibi Belgium
Ottignies
Chaumont Gistoux
Hannut
Awans
Liège
Ath
Braine-le-Comte
Perwez
Braives
St. Georges-sur-Meuse
Park Paradisio
Genappe
Éghezée
Seraing
Leuze-en-Hainaut
Soignies
Nivelles
Gembloux
Lens
Beloeil
Basècles
Château de Beloeil
Château de Roeulx
Le Roeulx
Seneffe
Pont-à-Celles
Sombreffe
Bierwart
Amay
Ivoz Ramet
Péruwelz
Escaut
Baudour
Fleurus
Huy
Seilles
Comblain-au-Pont
Hautrage
Mons
La Louvière
Courcelles
Auvelais
Namur
Andenne
Tinlot
Condé-sur-l'Escaut
Péronnes
Binche
Anderlues
Châtelet
Floreffe
Ohey
Hamoir
Quiévrain
Minières des Spiennes
Fosse-la-Ville
Havelange
Valenciennes
Dour
Givry
Thuin
Charleroi
Profondeville
Assesse
Méan
Durbuy
Barvaux
Abbaye de Maredsous
Annevoie-Rouillon
Yvoir
Ciney
Quevy
Gozee
Gerpinnes
Mettet
Baillonville
Maubeuge
Erquelinnes
Jeumont
Anhée
Grotte de Mont-Fat
Achene
Hotton
Bavay
Hautmont
Beaumont
Morialmé
Fraire
Florennes
Onhaye
Dinant
Leignon
Le Quesnoy
Ferrière-la-Grande
Marche-en-Famenne
Dochamps
Aulnoye-Aymeries
Solre-le-Château
Philippeville
Hastière-Lavaux
Houyet
Rochefort
Solesmes
Avesnois
Grandrieu
Villers-le-Gambon
Bande
Rance
Cerfontaine
Gouffre
Grotte de Lorette-Rochefort
Grotte de Han-sur-Lesse
Le Cateau-Cambrésis
Avesnes-sur-Helpe
Doische
Givet
Landrecies
Mariembourg
Treignes
Vireux
Beauraing
Wellin

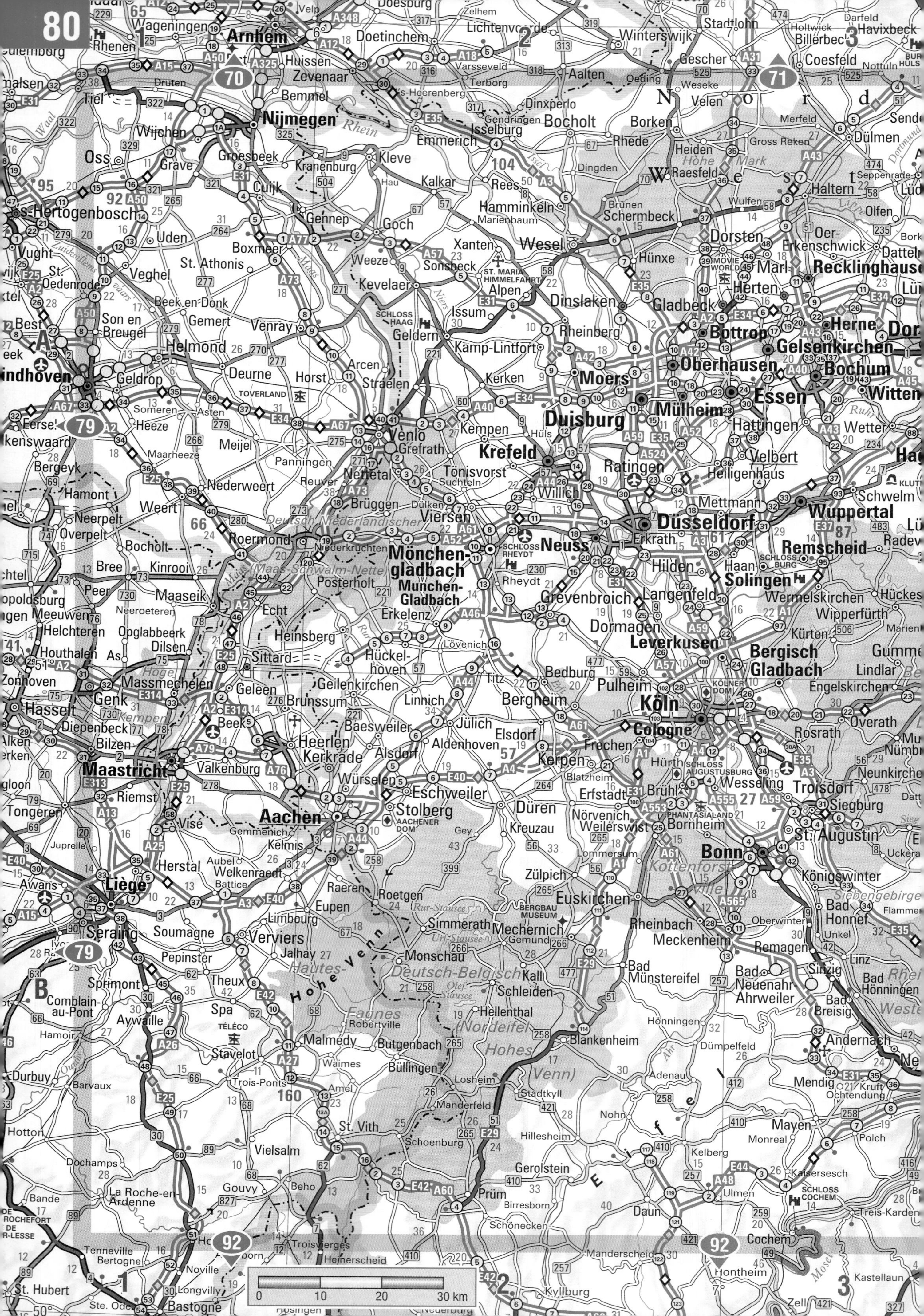
Arnhem
Wageningen
Rhenen
Doetinchem
Lichtenvoorde
Winterswijk
Stadtlohn
Havixbeck
Billerbeck
Coesfeld
Huissen
Zevenaar
Aalten
Gescher
Tiel
Nijmegen
Bemmel
Bocholt
Borken
Dülmen
Wijchen
Emmerich
Isselburg
Rhede
Oss
Grave
Groesbeek
Kranenburg
Kleve
Cuijk
Kalkar
Rees
Haltern
's-Hertogenbosch
Gennep
Goch
Hamminkeln
Schermbeck
Olfen
Vught
Uden
Boxmeer
Xanten
Wesel
Dorsten
Hünxe
Marl
Recklinghausen
St. Oedenrode
Veghel
St. Athonis
Weeze
Sonsbeck
Kevelaer
Alpen
Dinslaken
Gladbeck
Herten
Beek en Donk
Gemert
Issum
Best
Son en Breugel
Venray
Geldern
Rheinberg
Bottrop
Gelsenkirchen
Herne
Helmond
Kamp-Lintfort
Eindhoven
Geldrop
Deurne
Horst
Arcen
Straelen
Kerken
Moers
Oberhausen
Bochum
Essen
Witten
Mülheim
Duisburg
Hattingen
Wetter
Eersel
Heeze
Someren
Asten
Venlo
Kempen
Krefeld
Ratingen
Velbert
Valkenswaard
Maarheeze
Meijel
Panningen
Grefrath
Tönisvorst
Heiligenhaus
Bergeyk
Hamont
Nederweert
Weert
Reuver
Nettetal
Willich
Mettmann
Schwelm
Wuppertal
Brüggen
Viersen
Düsseldorf
Neerpelt
Overpelt
Roermond
Neuss
Erkrath
Remscheid
Bocholt
Bree
Kinrooi
Mönchengladbach
Hilden
Haan
Solingen
Peer
Maaseik
Posterholt
Munchen-Gladbach
Rheydt
Langenfeld
Meeuwen
Echt
Erkelenz
Grevenbroich
Wermelskirchen
Hückeswagen
Wipperfürth
Helchteren
Opglabbeek
Heinsberg
Dormagen
Leverkusen
Houthalen
Dilsen
Sittard
Hückelhoven
Lövenich
Bergisch Gladbach
Gummersbach
Zonhoven
Massmechelen
Geleen
Geilenkirchen
Bedburg
Pulheim
Lindlar
Engelskirchen
Genk
Hasselt
Brunssum
Linnich
Titz
Bergheim
Köln
Diepenbeek
Beek
Baesweiler
Jülich
Elsdorf
Overath
Bilzen
Heerlen
Kerkrade
Alsdorf
Aldenhoven
Frechen
Cologne
Rosrath
Maastricht
Valkenburg
Kerpen
Hürth
Wesseling
Troisdorf
Würselen
Eschweiler
Erftstadt
Brühl
Siegburg
Tongeren
Riemst
Aachen
Stolberg
Düren
Kreuzau
Weilerswist
Bornheim
St. Augustin
Visé
Gemmenich
Kelmis
Bonn
Herstal
Welkenraedt
Zülpich
Königswinter
Liège
Raeren
Roetgen
Euskirchen
Bad Honnef
Seraing
Soumagne
Limbourg
Eupen
Simmerath
Mechernich
Rheinbach
Meckenheim
Remagen
Verviers
Jalhay
Pepinster
Monschau
Kall
Bad Münstereifel
Bad Neuenahr-Ahrweiler
Sinzig
Linz
Bad Hönningen
Sprimont
Theux
Schleiden
Comblain-au-Pont
Spa
Hellenthal
Bad Breisig
Aywaille
Malmedy
Butgenbach
Blankenheim
Andernach
Hamoir
Stavelot
Büllingen
Durbuy
Trois-Ponts
Adenau
Mendig
Barvaux
Amel
Losheim
Stadtkyll
St. Vith
Hotton
Vielsalm
Schoenburg
Hillesheim
Mayen
Polch
Dochamps
Gerolstein
Kelberg
Kaisersesch
La Roche-en-Ardenne
Gouvy
Beho
Prüm
Birresborn
Ulmen
Daun
Treis-Karden
Tenneville
Bertogne
Houffalize
Troisvierges
Manderscheid
Cochem
Hontheim
St. Hubert
Longvilly
Bastogne
Kyllburg
Kastellaun
Zell
Hohe Venn
Eifel
Nordeifel
Kottenforst
Siebengebirge
0 10 20 30 km

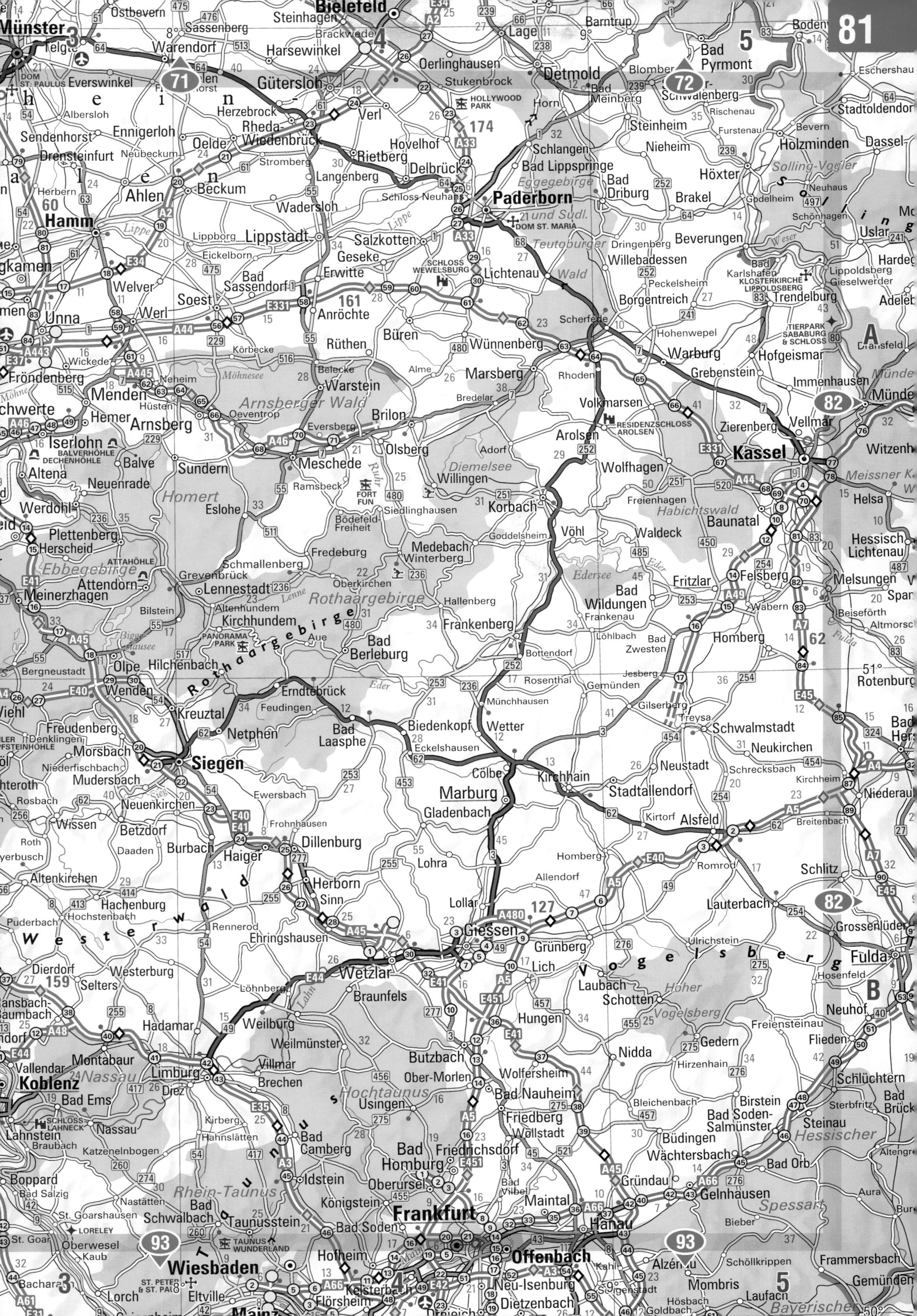
Münster
Ostbevern
Telgte
Warendorf
Sassenberg
Everswinkel
Albersloh
Sendenhorst
Drensteinfurt
Ennigerloh
Neubeckum
Oelde
Ahlen
Beckum
Hamm
Kamen
Unna
Werl
Welver
Soest
Bad Sassendorf
Lippstadt
Lippborg
Eickelborn
Bielefeld
Steinhagen
Brackwede
Harsewinkel
Gütersloh
Herzebrock
Rheda-Wiedenbrück
Stromberg
Verl
Rietberg
Langenberg
Wadersloh
Hovelhof
Delbrück
Schloss Neuhaus
Paderborn
Salzkotten
Geseke
Erwitte
Anröchte
Rüthen
Büren
Belecke
Warstein
Lichtenau
Schloss Wewelsburg
Wünnenberg
Lage
Oerlinghausen
Stukenbrock
Hollywood Park
Detmold
Bad Meinberg
Horn
Schlangen
Bad Lippspringe
Eggegebirge
Bad Driburg
Teutoburger Wald
Barntrup
Blomberg
Bad Pyrmont
Schwalenberg
Steinheim
Nieheim
Höxter
Brakel
Holzminden
Stadtoldendorf
Dassel
Solling-Vogler
Uslar
Beverungen
Dringenberg
Willebadessen
Borgentreich
Bad Karlshafen
Trendelburg
Lippoldsberg
Gieselwerder
Hofgeismar
Tierpark Sababurg & Schloss
Warburg
Scherfede
Hohenwepel
Grebenstein
Immenhausen
Münden
Vellmar
Kassel
Zierenberg
Wolfhagen
Volkmarsen
Arolsen
Residenzschloss Arolsen
Rhoden
Marsberg
Bredelar
Fröndenberg
Menden
Neheim
Hüsten
Möhnesee
Körbecke
Arnsberger Wald
Arnsberg
Oeventrop
Hemer
Schwerte
Iserlohn
Balverhöhle
Dechenhöhle
Balve
Altena
Neuenrade
Werdohl
Plettenberg
Herscheid
Sundern
Meschede
Eversberg
Brilon
Olsberg
Ramsbeck
Fort Fun
Homert
Eslohe
Willingen
Diemelsee
Adorf
Korbach
Siedlinghausen
Bödefeld-Freiheit
Medebach
Winterberg
Schmallenberg
Fredeburg
Grevenbrück
Lennestadt
Attendorn
Attahöhle
Ebbegebirge
Meinerzhagen
Altenhundem
Kirchhundem
Bilstein
Oberkirchen
Rothaargebirge
Panorama Park
Biggesee
Bad Berleburg
Aue
Olpe
Hilchenbach
Erndtebrück
Feudingen
Bergneustadt
Wenden
Gummersbach
Wiehl
Kreuztal
Netphen
Siegen
Freudenberg
Denklingen
Morsbach
Wissen
Betzdorf
Daaden
Burbach
Haiger
Dillenburg
Herborn
Sinn
Neunkirchen
Bad Laasphe
Biedenkopf
Eckelshausen
Hallenberg
Frankenberg
Goddelsheim
Vöhl
Edersee
Waldeck
Bad Wildungen
Frankenau
Löhlbach
Bad Zwesten
Fritzlar
Wabern
Felsberg
Melsungen
Baunatal
Habichtswald
Helsa
Hessisch Lichtenau
Witzenhausen
Meissner
Homberg
Bottendorf
Rosenthal
Gemünden
Jesberg
Münchhausen
Wetter
Gilserberg
Treysa
Schwalmstadt
Neukirchen
Schrecksbach
Neustadt
Kirchhain
Cölbe
Marburg
Stadtallendorf
Kirtorf
Alsfeld
Gladenbach
Lohra
Romrod
Lauterbach
Schlitz
Niederaula
Breitenbach
Rotenburg
Bad Hersfeld
Kirchheim
Allendorf
Lollar
Giessen
Grünberg
Lich
Laubach
Schotten
Hoher Vogelsberg
Vogelsberg
Ulrichstein
Fulda
Hosenfeld
Grossenlüder
Neuhof
Flieden
Freiensteinau
Gedern
Nidda
Hirzenhain
Schlüchtern
Steinau
Bad Brückenau
Birstein
Bad Soden-Salmünster
Bleichenbach
Büdingen
Wächtersbach
Bad Orb
Gelnhausen
Spessart
Hungen
Wolfersheim
Bad Nauheim
Friedberg
Wöllstadt
Butzbach
Ober-Morlen
Usingen
Hochtaunus
Wetzlar
Braunfels
Ehringshausen
Rennerod
Westerwald
Hachenburg
Altenkirchen
Dierdorf
Selters
Westerburg
Hadamar
Weilburg
Weilmünster
Löhnberg
Villmar
Limburg
Diez
Montabaur
Nassau
Koblenz
Vallendar
Bad Ems
Lahnstein
Braubach
Schloss Lahneck
Katzenelnbogen
Boppard
Bad Salzig
Nastätten
St. Goarshausen
St. Goar
Loreley
Oberwesel
Kaub
Bacharach
Lorch
Eltville
Wiesbaden
Mainz
Bad Schwalbach
Taunusstein
Taunus Wunderland
Rhein-Taunus
Idstein
Bad Camberg
Brechen
Kirberg
Königstein
Oberursel
Bad Homburg
Friedrichsdorf
Bad Vilbel
Maintal
Hanau
Frankfurt
Offenbach
Bad Soden
Hofheim
Kelsterbach
Flörsheim
Neu-Isenburg
Dietzenbach
Dreieich
Seligenstadt
Alzenau
Mombris
Schöllkrippen
Frammersbach
Gemünden
Laufach
Goldbach
Hösbach
Bayerischer
Gründau
Bieber
Aura
Altengronau

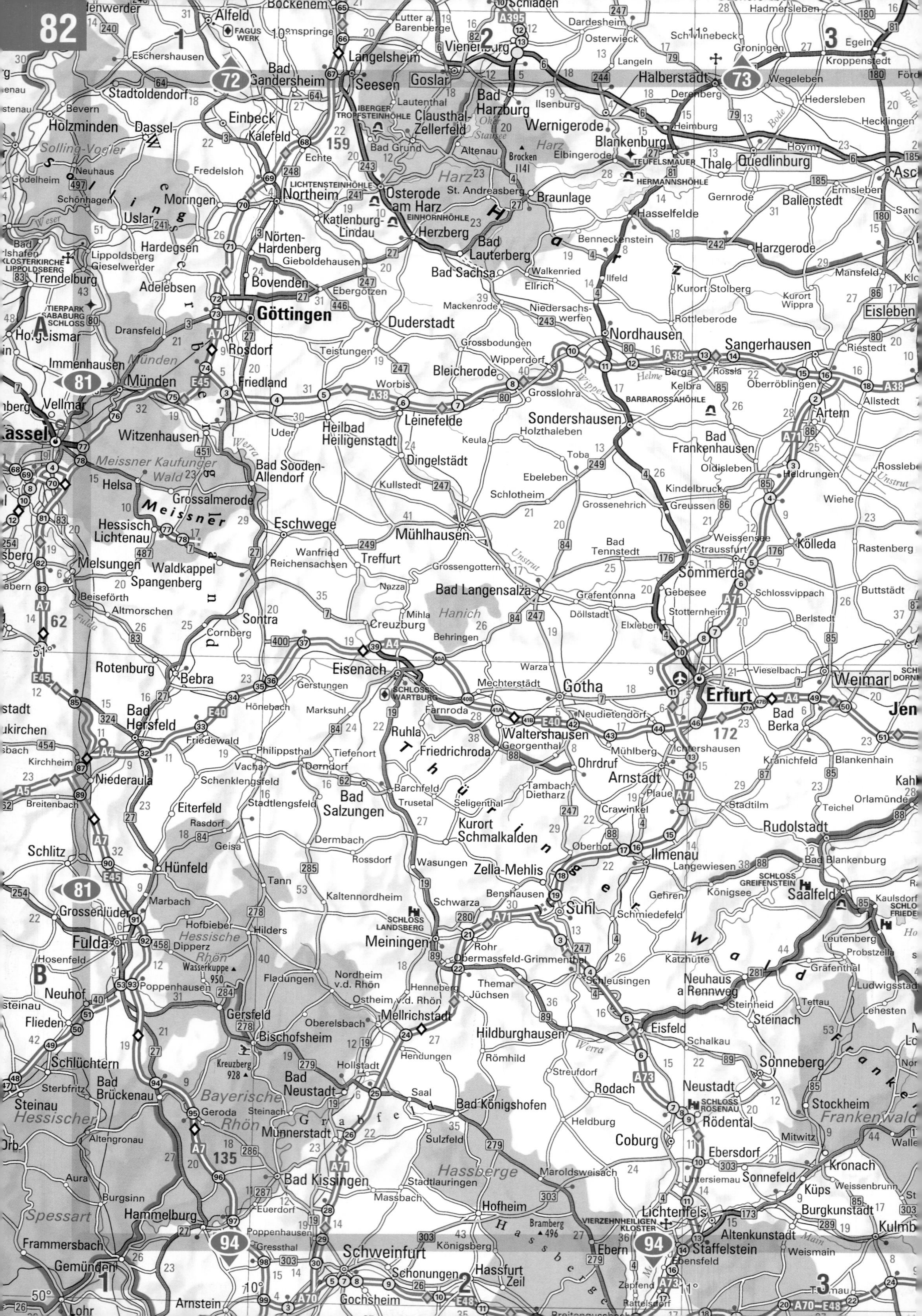
Alfeld
FAGUS WERK
Bockenem
Schladen
Dardesheim
Hadmersleben
Eschershausen
Bad Gandersheim
Langelsheim
Vienenburg
Osterwieck
Schwanebeck
Groningen
Egeln
Kroppenstedt
Stadtoldendorf
Seesen
Goslar
Halberstadt
Wegeleben
Bevern
Lautenthal
Bad Harzburg
Ilsenburg
Derenburg
Hedersleben
Holzminden
Dassel
Einbeck
IBERGER TROPFSTEINHÖHLE
Clausthal-Zellerfeld
Wernigerode
Heimburg
Hecklingen
Solling-Vogler
Kalefeld
Bad Grund
Oker Stausee
Blankenburg
Hoym
Neuhaus
Echte
Altenau
Brocken 1141
Harz
Elbingerode
TEUFELSMAUER
Thale
Quedlinburg
Godelheim
Fredelsloh
LICHTENSTEINHÖHLE
Osterode am Harz
St. Andreasberg
HERMANNSHÖHLE
Gernrode
Ballenstedt
Ermsleben
Schönhagen
Moringen
Northeim
Braunlage
Uslar
Katlenburg-Lindau
EINHORNHÖHLE
Herzberg
Hasselfelde
Bad Lauterberg
Benneckenstein
Harzgerode
Lippoldsberg
KLOSTERKIRCHE LIPPOLDSBERG
Gieselwerder
Hardegsen
Nörten-Hardenberg
Gieboldehausen
Bad Sachsa
Walkenried
Ellrich
Ilfeld
Mansfeld
Trendelburg
Adelebsen
Bovenden
Ebergötzen
Kurort Stolberg
Kurort Wippra
TIERPARK SABABURG SCHLOSS
Göttingen
Duderstadt
Mackenrode
Niedersachswerfen
Rottleberode
Eisleben
Hofgeismar
Dransfeld
Rosdorf
Nordhausen
Teistungen
Grossbodungen
Wipperdorf
Sangerhausen
Riestedt
Immenhausen
Münden
Friedland
Bleicherode
Worbis
Berga
Rossla
Kelbra
Oberröblingen
Vellmar
Grosslohra
BARBAROSSAHÖHLE
Allstedt
Kassel
Witzenhausen
Uder
Heilbad Heiligenstadt
Leinefelde
Sondershausen
Holzthaleben
Artern
Bad Frankenhausen
Keula
Meissner Kaufunger Wald
Bad Sooden-Allendorf
Dingelstädt
Toba
Oldisleben
Heldrungen
Helsa
Grossalmerode
Kullstedt
Ebeleben
Schlotheim
Kindelbruck
Greussen
Grossenehrich
Wiehe
Meissner
Hessisch Lichtenau
Eschwege
Mühlhausen
Bad Tennstedt
Weissensee
Kölleda
Melsungen
Waldkappel
Wanfried
Reichensachsen
Treffurt
Grossengottern
Unstrut
Straussfurt
Rastenberg
Spangenberg
Sömmerda
Gebesee
Schlossvippach
Buttstädt
Beiseförth
Altmorschen
Nazza
Bad Langensalza
Grafentonna
Sontra
Mihla
Hanich
Döllstadt
Stotternheim
Berlstedt
Cornberg
Creuzburg
Behringen
Elxleben
Rotenburg
Bebra
Eisenach
Warza
Vieselbach
Weimar
Gerstungen
SCHLOSS WARTBURG
Mechterstädt
Gotha
Erfurt
Bad Berka
Hönebach
Marksuhl
Farnroda
Neudietendorf
Bad Hersfeld
Friedewald
Ruhla
Waltershausen
Georgenthal
Mühlberg
Ichtershausen
Kirchheim
Philippsthal
Tiefenort
Friedrichroda
Kranichfeld
Blankenhain
Niederaula
Schenklengsfeld
Vacha
Dorndorf
Ohrdruf
Arnstadt
Barchfeld
Tambach-Dietharz
Breitenbach
Stadtlengsfeld
Bad Salzungen
Trusetal
Seligenthal
Plaue
Stadtilm
Orlamünde
Eiterfeld
Rasdorf
Crawinkel
Teichel
Kurort Schmalkalden
Rudolstadt
Dermbach
Thüringer Wald
Geisa
Oberhof
Ilmenau
Schlitz
Hünfeld
Rossdorf
Wasungen
Zella-Mehlis
Langewiesen
Bad Blankenburg
SCHLOSS GREIFENSTEIN
Tann
Kaltennordheim
Benshausen
Gehren
Königsee
Saalfeld
Marbach
Schwarza
Suhl
Schmiedefeld
Grossenlüder
SCHLOSS LANDSBERG
Hofbieber
Hilders
Fulda
Dipperz
Hessische Rhön
Meiningen
Rohr
Obermassfeld-Grimmenthal
Katzhütte
Leutenberg
Probstzella
Hosenfeld
Wasserkuppe 950
Fladungen
Nordheim v.d. Rhön
Henneberg
Themar
Schleusingen
Neuhaus a Rennweg
Gräfenthal
Ludwigsstadt
Neuhof
Poppenhausen
Ostheim v.d. Rhön
Jüchsen
Steinheid
Tettau
Lehesten
Flieden
Gersfeld
Oberelsbach
Mellrichstadt
Eisfeld
Steinach
Bischofsheim
Hildburghausen
Schalkau
Schlüchtern
Kreuzberg 928
Hendungen
Römhild
Sonneberg
Frankenwald
Hollstadt
Bad Neustadt
Streufdorf
Rodach
Neustadt
Bad Brückenau
Sterbfritz
Bayerische Rhön
Saal
Bad Königshofen
SCHLOSS ROSENAU
Stockheim
Steinau
Geroda
Grabfeld
Rödental
Heldburg
Mitwitz
Altengronau
Münnerstadt
Sulzfeld
Coburg
Ebersdorf
Kronach
Spessart
Bad Kissingen
Stadtlauringen
Hassberge
Maroldsweisach
Untersiemau
Sonnefeld
Küps
Aura
Burgsinn
Massbach
Hofheim
Lichtenfels
Weissenbrunn
Hammelburg
Euerdorf
Bramberg 496
VIERZEHNHEILIGEN KLOSTER
Burgkunstadt
Frammersbach
Poppenhausen
Altenkunstadt
Kulmbach
Gemünden
Gressthal
Schweinfurt
Königsberg
Ebern
Staffelstein
Weismain
Schonungen
Hassfurt
Zeil
Ebensfeld
Zapfendorf
Arnstein
Gochsheim
Rattelsdorf
Lohr

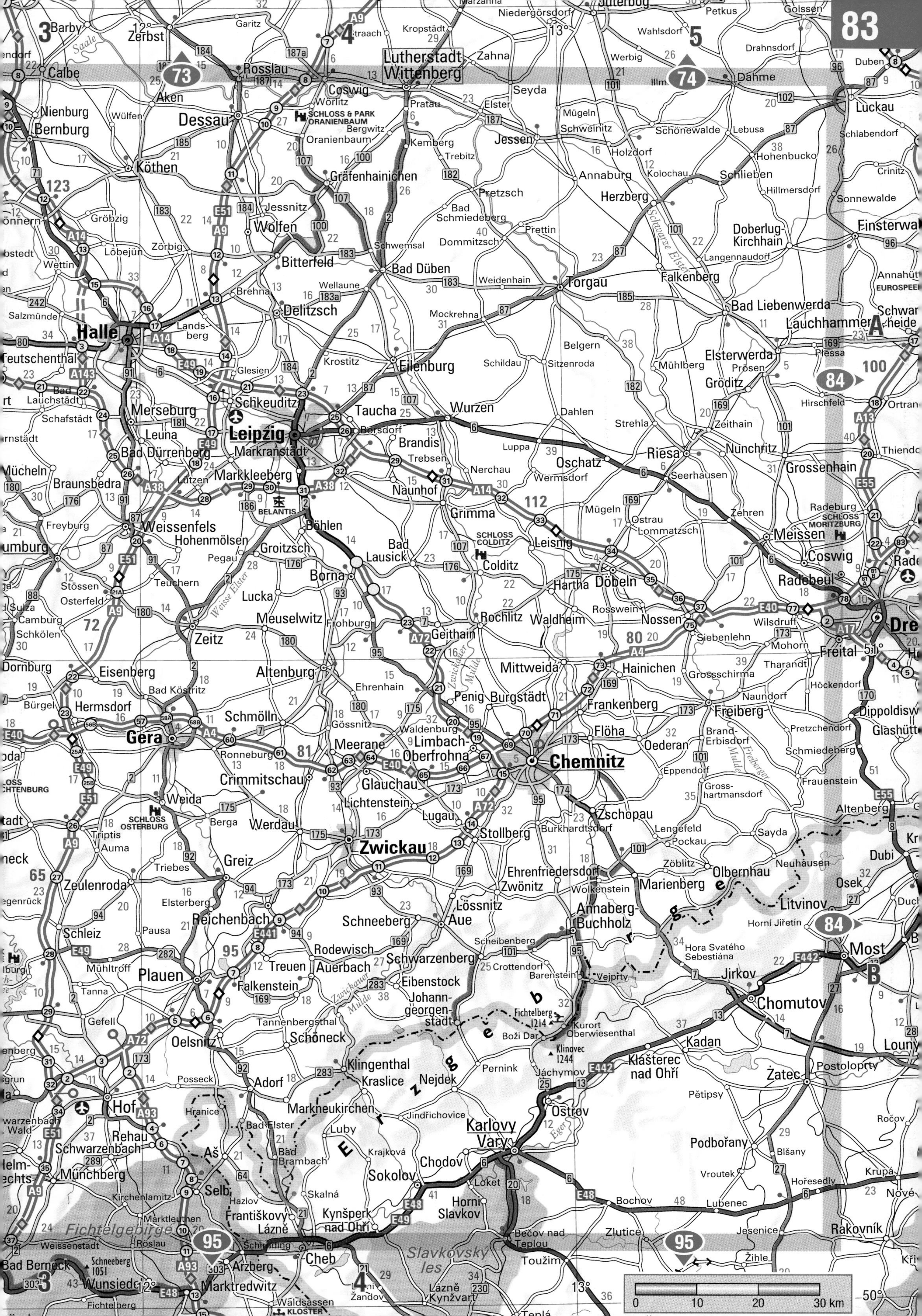
83
Barby
Zerbst
Calbe
Rosslau
Lutherstadt Wittenberg
Zahna
Coswig
Dessau
Aken
Nienburg
Bernburg
Köthen
Jessen
Kemberg
Gräfenhainichen
Oranienbaum
Schloss & Park Oranienbaum
Wolfen
Jessnitz
Bitterfeld
Bad Düben
Bad Schmiedeberg
Pretzsch
Prettin
Dommitzsch
Torgau
Annaburg
Herzberg
Schlieben
Luckau
Dahme
Doberlug-Kirchhain
Falkenberg
Finsterwalde
Bad Liebenwerda
Elsterwerda
Lauchhammer
Gröditz
Halle
Delitzsch
Brehna
Landsberg
Eilenburg
Schkeuditz
Merseburg
Leipzig
Markranstädt
Taucha
Wurzen
Brandis
Naunhof
Grimma
Bad Dürrenberg
Markkleeberg
Leuna
Lützen
Belantis
Weissenfels
Hohenmölsen
Böhlen
Groitzsch
Borna
Bad Lausick
Colditz
Schloss Colditz
Leisnig
Oschatz
Riesa
Strehla
Dahlen
Grossenhain
Meissen
Schloss Moritzburg
Radeburg
Coswig
Radebeul
Döbeln
Hartha
Waldheim
Rochlitz
Geithain
Nossen
Wilsdruff
Freital
Mittweida
Hainichen
Frankenberg
Freiberg
Burgstädt
Penig
Chemnitz
Flöha
Oederan
Zeitz
Meuselwitz
Altenburg
Eisenberg
Hermsdorf
Gera
Bad Köstritz
Schmölln
Ronneburg
Crimmitschau
Meerane
Glauchau
Limbach-Oberfrohna
Lichtenstein
Werdau
Zwickau
Weida
Schloss Osterburg
Greiz
Zeulenroda
Reichenbach
Stollberg
Zschopau
Marienberg
Olbernhau
Annaberg-Buchholz
Aue
Schneeberg
Schwarzenberg
Auerbach
Plauen
Falkenstein
Oelsnitz
Schöneck
Klingenthal
Kraslice
Adorf
Bad Elster
Markneukirchen
Johanngeorgenstadt
Fichtelberg 1214
Kurort Oberwiesenthal
Klínovec 1244
Jáchymov
Ostrov
Karlovy Vary
Chodov
Sokolov
Loket
Horní Slavkov
Kadaň
Klášterec nad Ohří
Chomutov
Jirkov
Most
Litvínov
Žatec
Postoloprty
Podbořany
Louny
Rakovník
Hof
Rehau
Schwarzenbach a. Wald
Münchberg
Selb
Aš
Marktredwitz
Arzberg
Cheb
Wunsiedel
Fichtelgebirge
Schneeberg 1051
Františkovy Lázně
Kynšperk nad Ohří
Bečov nad Teplou
Toužim
Slavkovský les
Erzgebirge
Zwickauer Mulde
Freiberger Mulde
Weisse Elster
Schwarze Elster
Saale
Eger
73
74
84
95
0 10 20 30 km
12°
13°
50°

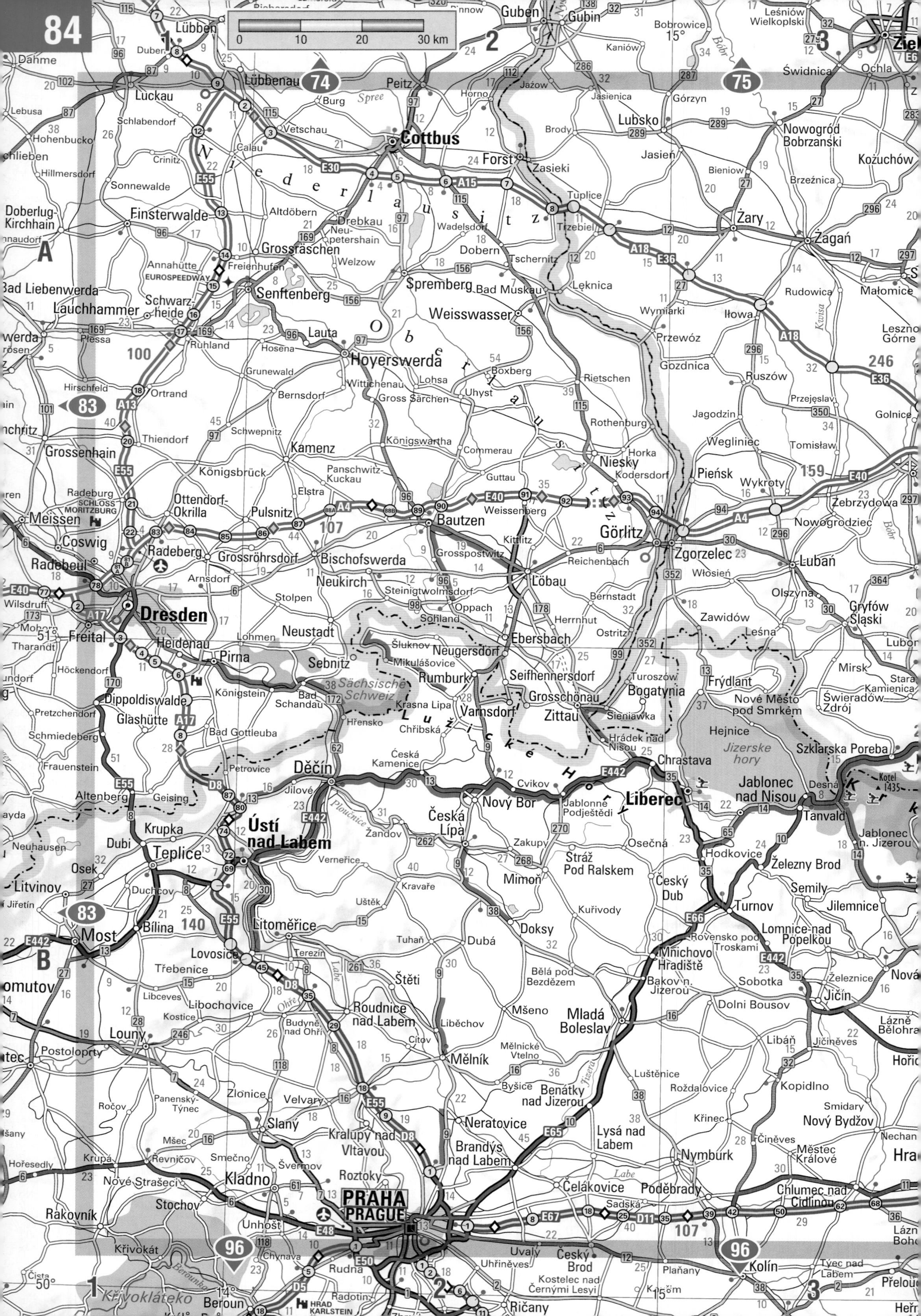
0 10 20 30 km
74
75
83
96
107
Lübben
Dahme
Duben
Lübbenau
Luckau
Lebusa
Schlabendorf
Hohenbucko
Crinitz
Calau
Vetschau
Burg
Spree
Peitz
Cottbus
Guben
Gubin
Bobrowice
Leśniów Wielkopolski
Zielona Góra
Świdnica
Ochla
Kaniów
Bóbr
Horno
Jaźow
Jasienica
Górzyn
Lubsko
Brody
Nowogród Bobrzański
Kożuchów
Forst
Zasieki
Jasień
Bieniow
Brzeźnica
Hillmersdorf
Sonnewalde
Niederlausitz
Doberlug-Kirchhain
Finsterwalde
Altdöbern
Drebkau
Neu-petershain
Welzow
Wadelsdorf
Dobern
Tschernitz
Tuplice
Trzebiel
Żary
Żagań
Annahütte
Freienhufen
EUROSPEEDWAY
Grossräschen
Spremberg
Bad Muskau
Łęknica
Rudowica
Małomice
Bad Liebenwerda
Lauchhammer
Schwarzheide
Senftenberg
Weisswasser
Wymiarki
Iłowa
Kwisa
Plessa
Ruhland
Hosena
Lauta
Hoyerswerda
Oberlausitz
Przewóz
Gozdnica
Leszno Górne
Grunewald
Boxberg
Rietschen
Ruszów
Hirschfeld
Ortrand
Bernsdorf
Wittichenau
Lohsa
Gross Särchen
Uhyst
Przejęsław
Golnice
Jagodzin
Rothenburg
Thiendorf
Schwepnitz
Kamenz
Königswartha
Commerau
Horka
Niesky
Węgliniec
Tomisław
Grossenhain
Königsbrück
Panschwitz-Kuckau
Guttau
Kodersdorf
Pieńsk
Wykroty
Radeburg
SCHLOSS MORITZBURG
Ottendorf-Okrilla
Elstra
Pulsnitz
Weissenberg
Bautzen
Görlitz
Zgorzelec
Zebrzydowa
Nowogrodziec
Meissen
Coswig
Radeberg
Grossröhrsdorf
Bischofswerda
Grosspostwitz
Kittlitz
Reichenbach
Lubań
Radebeul
Arnsdorf
Neukirch
Steinigtwolmsdorf
Löbau
Włosień
Olszyna
Wilsdruff
Dresden
Stolpen
Oppach
Bernstadt
Gryfów Śląski
Mohorn
Freital
Tharandt
Sohland
Herrnhut
Zawidów
Ostritz
Leśna
Lubomierz
Heidenau
Lohmen
Neustadt
Šluknov
Neugersdorf
Ebersbach
Pirna
Sebnitz
Mikulášovice
Höckendorf
Rumburk
Seifhennersdorf
Turoszów
Frýdlant
Mirsk
Stara Kamienica
Dippoldiswalde
Königstein
Bad Schandau
Sächsische Schweiz
Krasna Lipa
Varnsdorf
Grossschönau
Zittau
Bogatynia
Sieniawka
Nové Město pod Smrkem
Świeradów Zdrój
Pretzschendorf
Glashütte
Hřensko
Chřibská
Lužické Hory
Hejnice
Schmiedeberg
Bad Gottleuba
Hrádek nad Nisou
Jizerske hory
Szklarska Poreba
Frauenstein
Petrovice
Děčín
Česká Kamenice
Chrastava
Kotel 1435
Altenberg
Geising
Jílové
Cvikov
Nový Bor
Jablonné Podještědí
Liberec
Jablonec nad Nisou
Desná
Tanvald
Krupka
Ústí nad Labem
Ploučnice
Žandov
Česká Lípa
Zákupy
Osečná
Jablonec n. Jizerou
Neuhausen
Dubí
Teplice
Osek
Verneřice
Stráž Pod Ralskem
Hodkovice
Železný Brod
Litvínov
Duchcov
Kravaře
Mimoň
Český Dub
Semily
Jiřetín
Úštěk
Kuřivody
Turnov
Jilemnice
Most
Bílina
Litoměřice
Doksy
Lomnice nad Popelkou
Tuhaň
Dubá
Rovensko pod Troskami
Lovosice
Terezín
Mnichovo Hradiště
Třebenice
Labe
Štětí
Bělá pod Bezdězem
Bakov n. Jizerou
Sobotka
Železnice
Nová Paka
Chomutov
Libceves
Libochovice
Ohře
Jičín
Kostice
Roudnice nad Labem
Mšeno
Mladá Boleslav
Dolni Bousov
Louny
Budyně nad Ohří
Liběchov
Lázně Bělohrad
Postoloprty
Citov
Mělnické Vtelno
Libáň
Jičíněves
Hořice
Mělník
Jizera
Luštěnice
Roždalovice
Kopidlno
Byšice
Benátky nad Jizerou
Smidary
Nový Bydžov
Zlonice
Velvary
Panenský-Týnec
Ročov
Slaný
Neratovice
Křinec
Činěves
Mšec
Lysá nad Labem
Nechanice
Kralupy nad Vltavou
Brandýs nad Labem
Nymburk
Městec Králové
Hořesedly
Krupá
Řevničov
Smečno
Švermov
Hradec Králové
Roztoky
Nové Strašecí
Kladno
Čelákovice
Poděbrady
Chlumec nad Cidlinou
Stochov
PRAHA PRAGUE
Sadská
Rakovník
Unhošť
Lázně Bohdaneč
Křivoklát
Chýnava
Úvaly
Český Brod
Plaňany
Kolín
Týnec nad Labem
Přelouč
Uhříněves
Beroun
Rudná
Kostelec nad Černými Lesy
Radotín
HRAD KARLSTEIN
Kouřim
Říčany
Čistá
Berounka
Křivokláteko
Heřmanův Městec
15°
50°

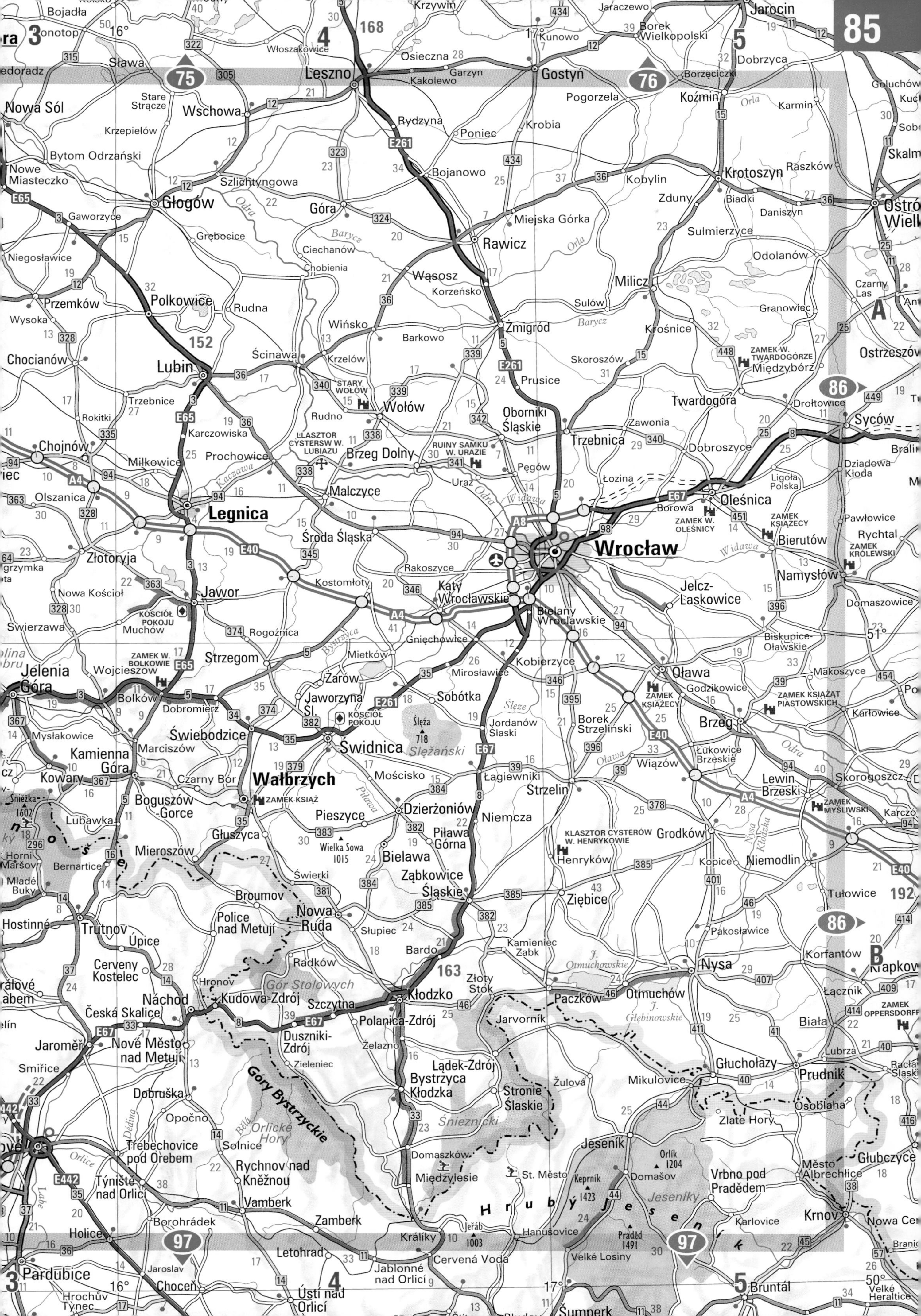

Bojadła
Konotop
Sława
Nowa Sól
Wschowa
Stare Strącze
Krzepielów
Bytom Odrzański
Nowe Miasteczko
Szlichtyngowa
Głogów
Gaworzyce
Grębocice
Niegosławice
Przemków
Wysoka
Polkowice
Rudna
Chocianów
Lubin
Trzebnice
Rokitki
Karczowiska
Chojnów
Miłkowice
Prochowice
Olszanica
Legnica
Złotoryja
Nowa Kościół
Jawor
Kościół Pokoju
Muchów
Swierzawa
Rogoźnica
Strzegom
Jelenia Góra
Wojcieszów
Zamek w. Bolkowie
Bolków
Dobromierz
Mysłakowice
Kamienna Góra
Marciszów
Świebodzice
Kowary
Czarny Bór
Wałbrzych
Zamek Książ
Boguszów-Gorce
Lubawka
Głuszyca
Mieroszów
Bernartice
Śnieżka 1602
Horní Maršov
Mladé Buky
Hostinné
Trutnov
Úpice
Cerveny Kostelec
Náchod
Česká Skalice
Jaroměř
Nové Město nad Metují
Smiřice
Dobruška
Opočno
Třebechovice pod Orebem
Týniště nad Orlicí
Holice
Borohrádek
Pardubice
Jaroslav
Choceň
Hrochův Týnec
Leszno
Włoszakowice
Osieczna
Kakolewo
Garzyn
Rydzyna
Poniec
Bojanowo
Góra
Ciechanów
Chobienia
Barycz
Odra
Rawicz
Wąsosz
Korzeńsko
Wińsko
Barkowo
Ścinawa
Krzelów
Stary Wołów
Wołów
Rudno
Llasztor Cystersw w. Lubiazu
Brzeg Dolny
Ruiny Samku w. Urazie
Uraz
Malczyce
Środa Śląska
Kostomłoty
Rakoszyce
Kąty Wrocławskie
Gniechowice
Mietków
Żarów
Jaworzyna Śl.
Kościół Pokoju
Świdnica
Mościsko
Pieszyce
Dzierżoniów
Piława Górna
Bielawa
Wielka Sowa 1015
Świerki
Broumov
Police nad Metují
Nowa Ruda
Słupiec
Ząbkowice Śląskie
Bardo
Radków
Hronov
Kudowa-Zdrój
Gór Stołowych
Szczytna
Kłodzko
Polanica-Zdrój
Duszniki-Zdrój
Zieleniec
Żelazno
Lądek-Zdrój
Bystrzyca Kłodzka
Góry Bystrzyckie
Orlické Hory
Solnice
Rychnov nad Kněžnou
Vamberk
Zamberk
Letohrad
Králíky
Jablonné nad Orlicí
Ústí nad Orlicí
Červená Voda
Domaszków
Międzylesie
Jeřáb 1003
Hanušovice
Ślęża 718
Ślężański
Sobótka
Mirosławice
Jordanów Śląski
Łagiewniki
Niemcza
Strzelin
Złoty Stok
Krzywiń
Gostyń
Kunowo
Jaraczewo
Borek Wielkopolski
Jarocin
Dobrzyca
Borzęciczki
Pogorzela
Krobia
Koźmin
Karmin
Kobylin
Krotoszyn
Raszków
Zduny
Biadki
Daniszyn
Miejska Górka
Sulmierzyce
Odolanów
Milicz
Sułów
Żmigród
Prusice
Skoroszów
Krośnice
Granowiec
Zamek w. Twardogórze
Międzybórz
Twardogóra
Drołtowice
Syców
Oborniki Śląskie
Trzebnica
Zawonia
Dobroszyce
Pęgów
Łozina
Borowa
Oleśnica
Zamek w. Oleśnicy
Ligoła Polska
Dziadowa Kłoda
Pawłowice
Zamek Książęcy
Bierutów
Rychtal
Zamek Królewski
Namysłów
Wrocław
Widawa
Jelcz-Laskowice
Bielany Wrocławskie
Kobierzyce
Biskupice-Oławskie
Makoszyce
Domaszowice
Oława
Zamek Książęcy
Godzikowice
Zamek Książąt Piastowskich
Karłowice
Borek Strzeliński
Brzeg
Łukowice Brzeskie
Wiązów
Lewin Brzeski
Skorogoszcz
Zamek Myśliwski
Karczów
Klasztor Cysterów w. Henrykowie
Henryków
Grodków
Kopice
Niemodlin
Tułowice
Ziębice
Pakosławice
Kamieniec Ząbk.
J. Otmuchowskie
Nysa
Korfantów
Krapkowice
Paczków
Otmuchów
J. Głębinowskie
Łącznik
Zamek Oppersdorff
Biała
Javorník
Głuchołazy
Prudnik
Żulová
Mikulovice
Stronie Śląskie
Śnieżnicki
Zlaté Hory
Osoblaha
Jeseník
St. Město
Kepřník 1423
Orlík 1204
Domašov
Vrbno pod Pradědem
Město Albrechtice
Głubczyce
Hrubý Jeseník
Jeseníky
Praděd 1491
Karlovice
Krnov
Nowa Cerekwia
Velké Losiny
Šumperk
Bruntál
Velké Heraltice

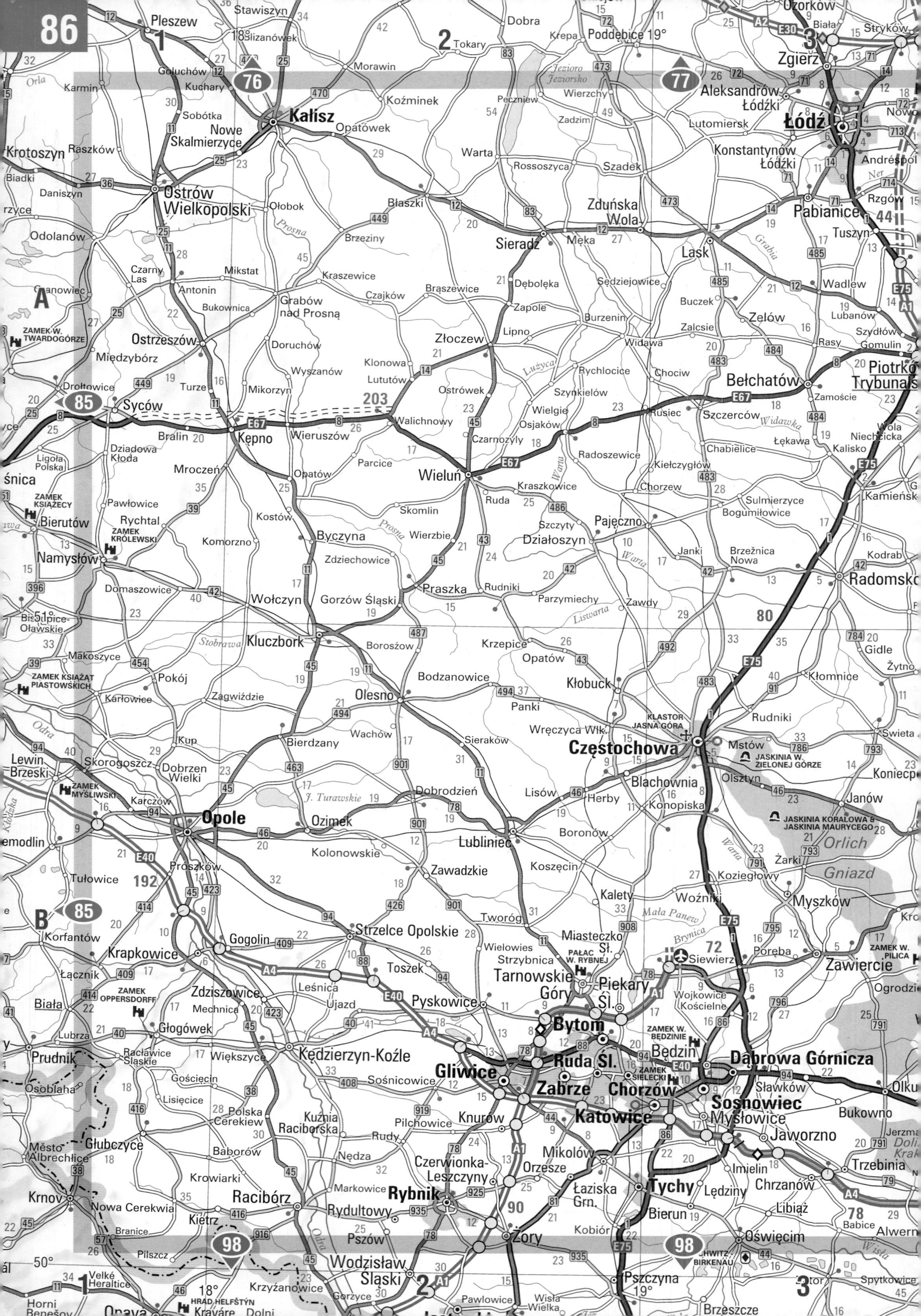
Pleszew
Stawiszyn
Blizanów
Tokary
Dobra
Krepa
Poddębice
Ozorków
Biała
Stryków
Zgierz
Gołuchów
Kuchary
76
Morawin
Jezioro Jeziorsko
77
Aleksandrów Łódzki
Karmin
Orla
Sobótka
Nowe Skalmierzyce
Kalisz
Koźminek
Opatówek
Pęczniew
Wierzchy
Zadzim
Lutomiersk
Łódź
Krotoszyn
Raszków
Warta
Rossoszyca
Szadek
Konstantynów Łódzki
Andrespol
Biadki
Daniszyn
Ostrów Wielkopolski
Ołobok
Błaszki
Zduńska Wola
Pabianice
Rzgów
Odolanów
Prosna
Brzeziny
Sieradz
Męka
Lask
Tuszyn
Grabia
Czarny Las
Mikstat
Kraszewice
Dębołęka
Sędziejowice
Wadlew
Granowiec
Antonin
Bukownica
Grabów nad Prosną
Czajków
Brąszewice
Zapole
Buczek
Zelów
Lubanów
A
ZAMEK W. TWARDOGÓRZE
Ostrzeszów
Doruchów
Złoczew
Lipno
Burzenin
Zalcsie
Widawa
Szydłów
Gomulin
Międzybórz
Klonowa
Lututów
Lużyca
Rychłocice
Chociw
Bełchatów
Piotrków Trybunalski
Drołtowice
Turze
Mikorzyn
Wyszanów
Ostrówek
Szynkielów
Zamoście
85
Syców
203
Wielgie
Rusiec
Szczerców
Bralin
Kępno
Wieruszów
Walichnowy
Osjaków
Czarnożyły
Widawka
Łękawa
Wola
Niechcicka
Kalisko
Ligota Polska
Dziadowa Kłoda
Mroczeń
Parcice
Opatów
Wieluń
Radoszewice
Chabielice
Kiełczygłów
Kamieńsk
śnica
ZAMEK KSIĄŻECY
Bierutów
Pawłowice
Rychtal
ZAMEK KRÓLEWSKI
Namysłów
Kostów
Skomlin
Ruda
Kraszkowice
Chorzew
Sulmierzyce
Bogumiłowice
Byczyna
Prosna
Wierzbie
Szczyty
Pajęczno
Działoszyn
Komorzno
Zdziechowice
Janki
Brzeźnica Nowa
Kodrab
Radomsko
Domaszowice
Wołczyn
Gorzów Śląski
Praszka
Rudniki
Parzymiechy
Zawdy
Liswarta
Bierutów
Bis. Sulpice-Oławskie
Stobrawa
Kluczbork
Boroszów
Krzepice
Opatów
Gidle
Żytno
Makoszyce
ZAMEK KSIĄŻĄT PIASTOWSKICH
Pokój
Bodzanowice
Panki
Kłobuck
Kłomnice
Karłowice
Zagwiździe
Olesno
Odra
Wachów
Bierdzany
Kup
Sieraków
Wręczyca Wlk.
KLASZTOR JASNA GÓRA
Częstochowa
Mstów
Rudniki
Święta
Lewin Brzeski
Skorogoszcz
Dobrzeń Wielki
JASKINIA W. ZIELONEJ GÓRZE
ZAMEK MYŚLIWSKI
Karczów
Dobrodzień
J. Turawskie
Lisów
Herby
Blachownia
Konopiska
Olsztyn
Koniecpol
Janów
Opole
Ozimek
Lubliniec
Boronów
JASKINIA KORALOWA & JASKINIA MAURYCEGO
Orlich
Niemodlin
Kolonowskie
Prószków
Zawadzkie
Koszęcin
Żarki
Tułowice
Koziegłowy
Gniazd
Kalety
Woźniki
Myszków
B
Korfantów
Gogolin
Strzelce Opolskie
Tworóg
Mała Panew
Miasteczko Śl.
Wielowies
Strzybnica
PAŁAC W. RYBNEJ
Brynica
Siewierz
Poręba
Zawiercie
ZAMEK W. PILICA
Krapkowice
Toszek
Tarnowskie Góry
Piekary Śl.
Łącznik
ZAMEK OPPERSDORFF
Zdzieszowice
Leśnica
Ujazd
Pyskowice
Wojkowice Kościelne
Ogrodzieniec
Biała
Mechnica
Głogówek
Bytom
ZAMEK W. BĘDZINIE
Prudnik
Lubrza
Racławice Śląskie
Większyce
Kędzierzyn-Koźle
Gliwice
Ruda Śl.
Będzin
Dąbrowa Górnicza
Osoblaha
Gościęcin
Sośnicowice
Zabrze
ZAMEK SIELECKI
Chorzów
Sławków
Olkusz
Lisięcice
Polska Cerekiew
Kuźnia Raciborska
Pilchowice
Knurów
Katowice
Sosnowiec
Mysłowice
Bukowno
Město Albrechtice
Głubczyce
Baborów
Rudy
Mikołów
Jaworzno
Jerzmanowice
Nędza
Czerwionka-Leszczyny
Orzesze
Imielin
Trzebinia
Krowiarki
Markowice
Rybnik
Łaziska Grn.
Tychy
Lędziny
Chrzanów
Krnov
Nowa Cerekwia
Racibórz
Kietrz
Rydułtowy
Bieruń
Libiąż
Babice
Alwernia
Branice
Pszów
Żory
Kobiór
Oświęcim
Wisła
Pilszcz
98
Wodzisław Śląski
SCHWITZ-BIRKENAU
Velké Heraltice
HRAD HELFŠTÝN
Krzyżanowice
Gorzyce
Pawłowice
Pszczyna
Spytkowice
Horní Benešov
Opava
Kravaře
Dolní
Wisła Wielka
Brzeszcze
1
2
3
50°
18°
19°

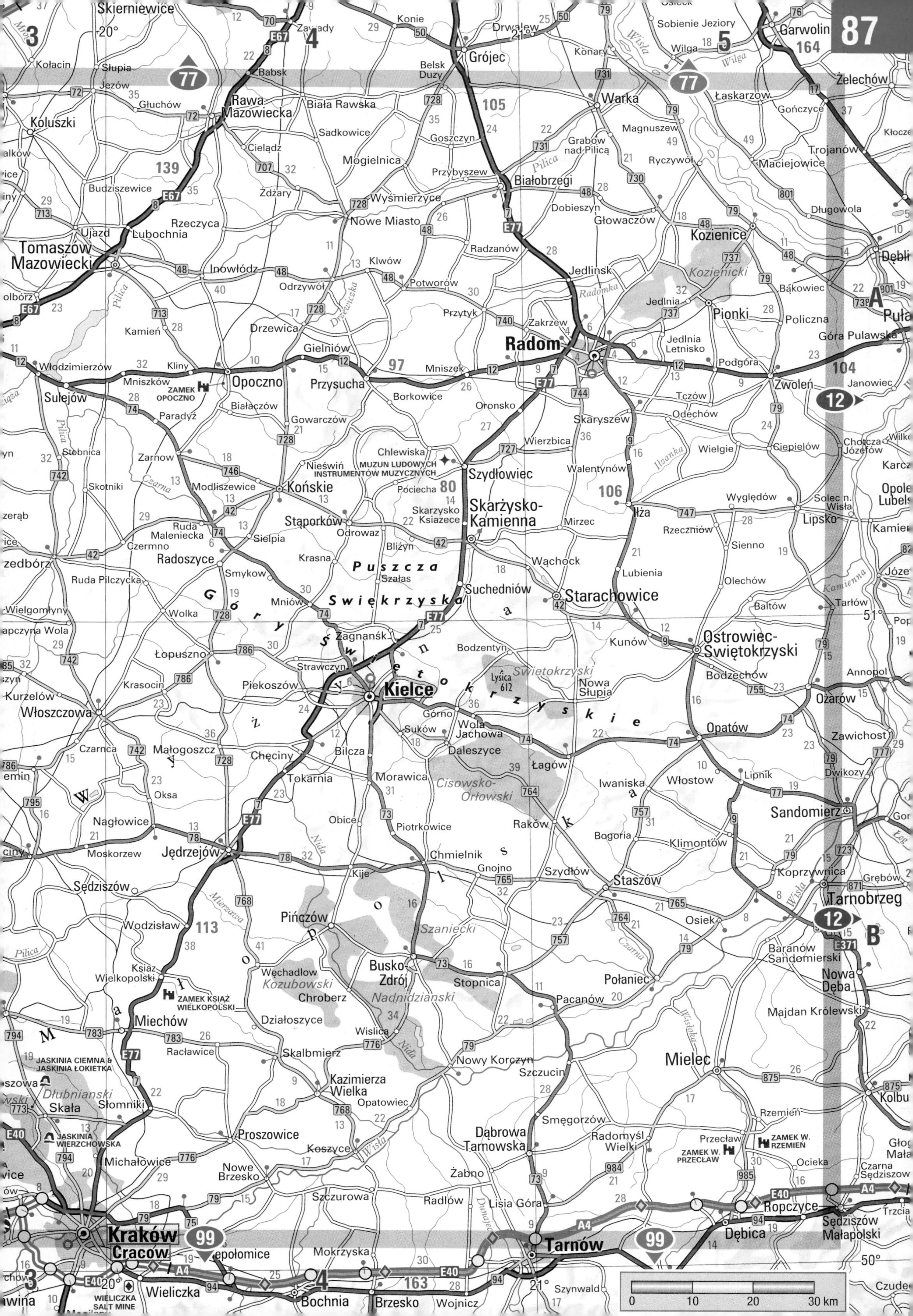
Skierniewice
Garwolin
Grójec
Warka
Rawa Mazowiecka
Koluszki
Tomaszów Mazowiecki
Białobrzegi
Kozienice
Dęblin
Radom
Pionki
Opoczno
Przysucha
Sulejów
Zwoleń
Końskie
Szydłowiec
Skarżysko-Kamienna
Stąporków
Iłża
Lipsko
Starachowice
Ostrowiec-Świętokrzyski
Włoszczowa
Kielce
Opatów
Jędrzejów
Sandomierz
Staszów
Tarnobrzeg
Pińczów
Busko-Zdrój
Miechów
Mielec
Dąbrowa Tarnowska
Kraków
Cracow
Wieliczka
Bochnia
Brzesko
Tarnów
Dębica
Ropczyce
Sędziszów Małopolski
Puszcza Świękrzyska
Góry Świętokrzyskie
Wyżyna Małopolska
0 10 20 30 km

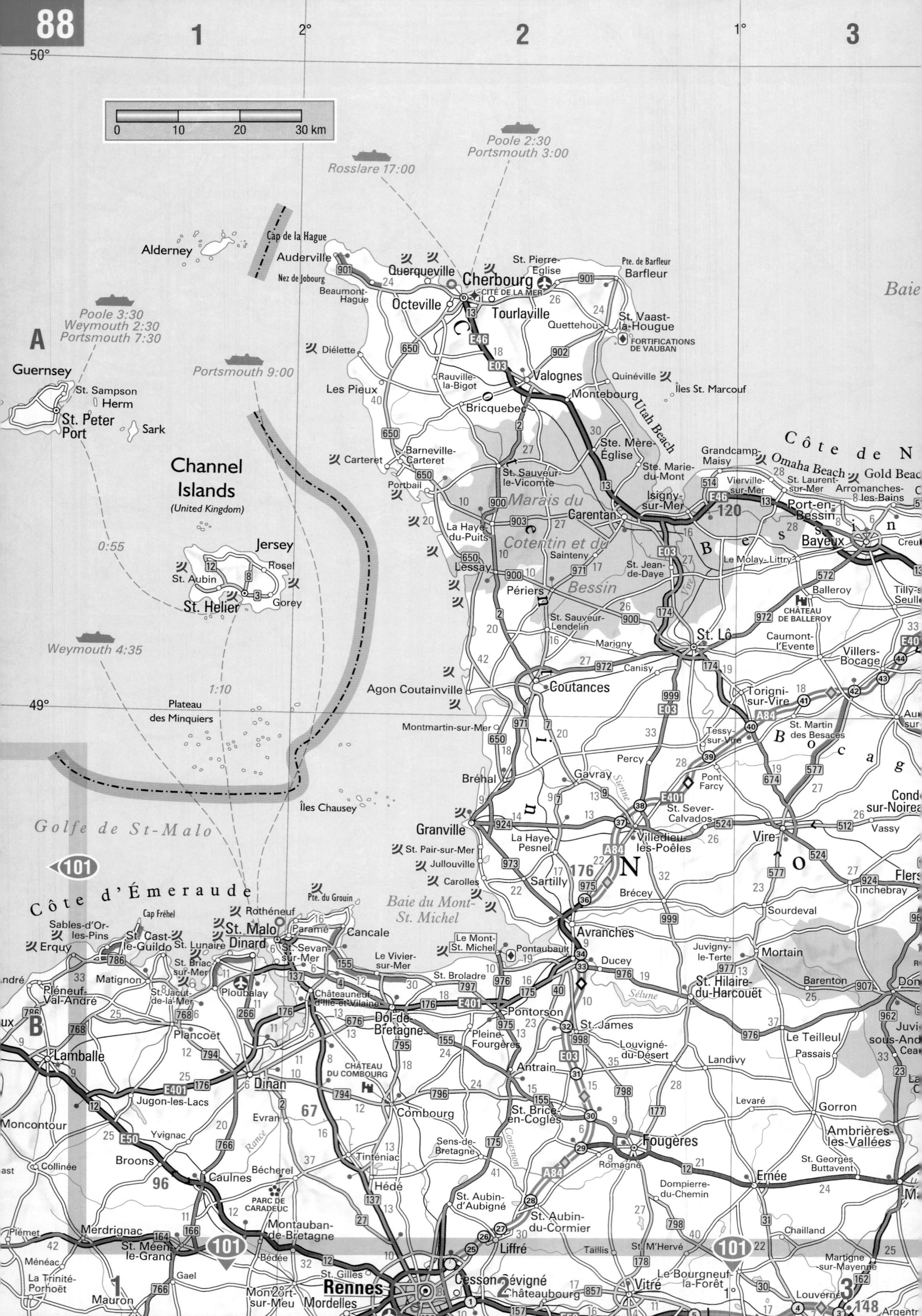
1
2
3
2°
1°
50°
49°
0
10
20
30 km
A
B
Poole 2:30
Portsmouth 3:00
Rosslare 17:00
Poole 3:30
Weymouth 2:30
Portsmouth 7:30
Portsmouth 9:00
Weymouth 4:35
0:55
1:10
Cap de la Hague
Alderney
Auderville
Nez de Jobourg
Beaumont-Hague
Querqueville
Cherbourg
Octeville
Tourlaville
CITÉ DE LA MER
St. Pierre-Église
Pte. de Barfleur
Barfleur
Quettehou
St. Vaast-la-Hougue
FORTIFICATIONS DE VAUBAN
Diélette
Valognes
Rauville-la-Bigot
Quinéville
Îles St. Marcouf
Les Pieux
Montebourg
Utah Beach
Bricquebec
Guernsey
St. Sampson
Herm
St. Peter Port
Sark
Channel Islands
(United Kingdom)
Carteret
Barneville-Carteret
Ste. Mère-Église
Portbail
St. Sauveur-le-Vicomte
Ste. Marie-du-Mont
Grandcamp-Maisy
Omaha Beach
Gold Beach
Côte de N
Vierville-sur-Mer
St. Laurent-sur-Mer
Arromanches-les-Bains
Isigny-sur-Mer
Port-en-Bessin
Bayeux
Marais du Cotentin et du Bessin
Carentan
La Haye-du-Puits
Sainteny
Jersey
Rosel
St. Aubin
St. Helier
Gorey
Lessay
Périers
St. Jean-de-Daye
Le Molay-Littry
Balleroy
CHÂTEAU DE BALLEROY
Tilly-s
Seulle
St. Sauveur-Lendelin
St. Lô
Marigny
Caumont-l'Evente
Villers-Bocage
Canisy
Agon Coutainville
Coutances
Torigni-sur-Vire
Plateau des Minquiers
Montmartin-sur-Mer
Tessy-sur-Vire
St. Martin des Besaces
Percy
Pont Farcy
Bréhal
Gavray
Sienne
St. Sever-Calvados
Cond sur-Noireau
Îles Chausey
Golfe de St-Malo
Granville
La Haye-Pesnel
Villedieu-les-Poêles
Vire
Vassy
St. Pair-sur-Mer
Jullouville
Carolles
Sartilly
Brécey
Flers
Tinchebray
Côte d'Émeraude
Pte. du Grouin
Baie du Mont-St. Michel
Sourdeval
Cap Fréhel
Rothéneuf
St. Malo
Paramé
Cancale
Le Mont-St. Michel
Avranches
Sables-d'Or-les-Pins
St. Cast-le-Guildo
St. Lunaire
Dinard
St. Servan-sur-Mer
Pontaubault
Juvigny-le-Tertre
Mortain
Erquy
St. Briac-sur-Mer
Le Vivier-sur-Mer
Ducey
Matignon
St. Broladre
Barenton
St. Hilaire-du-Harcouët
Pléneuf-Val-André
St. Jacut-de-la-Mer
Ploubalay
Châteauneuf-d'Ille-et-Vilaine
Sélune
Pontorson
Dol-de-Bretagne
Pleine-Fougères
St. James
Juvi sous-And
Plancoët
Le Teilleul
Louvigné-du-Désert
Passais
Lamballe
CHÂTEAU DU COMBOURG
Antrain
Landivy
Dinan
Jugon-les-Lacs
Levaré
Gorron
Moncontour
Evran
Combourg
St. Brice-en-Coglès
Yvignac
Rance
Sens-de-Bretagne
Couesnon
Fougères
Ambrières-les-Vallées
Broons
Tinténiac
Romagné
St. Georges Buttavent
Collinée
Bécherel
Caulnes
Ernée
Hédé
Dompierre-du-Chemin
PARC DE CARADEUC
St. Aubin-d'Aubigné
St. Aubin-du-Cormier
Plémet
Merdrignac
Montauban-de-Bretagne
Chailland
St. Méen-le-Grand
Liffré
Taillis
St. M'Hervé
Martigné-sur-Mayenne
Ménéac
Bédée
La Trinité-Porhoët
Gael
St. Gilles
Le Bourgneuf-la-Forêt
Rennes
Cesson Sévigné
Vitré
Mauron
Montfort-sur-Meu
Mordelles
Châteaubourg
Louverné
Argentr
Baie
Bocage
Normandie
E46
E03
E401
E50
A84
101
120
176
67
96
148

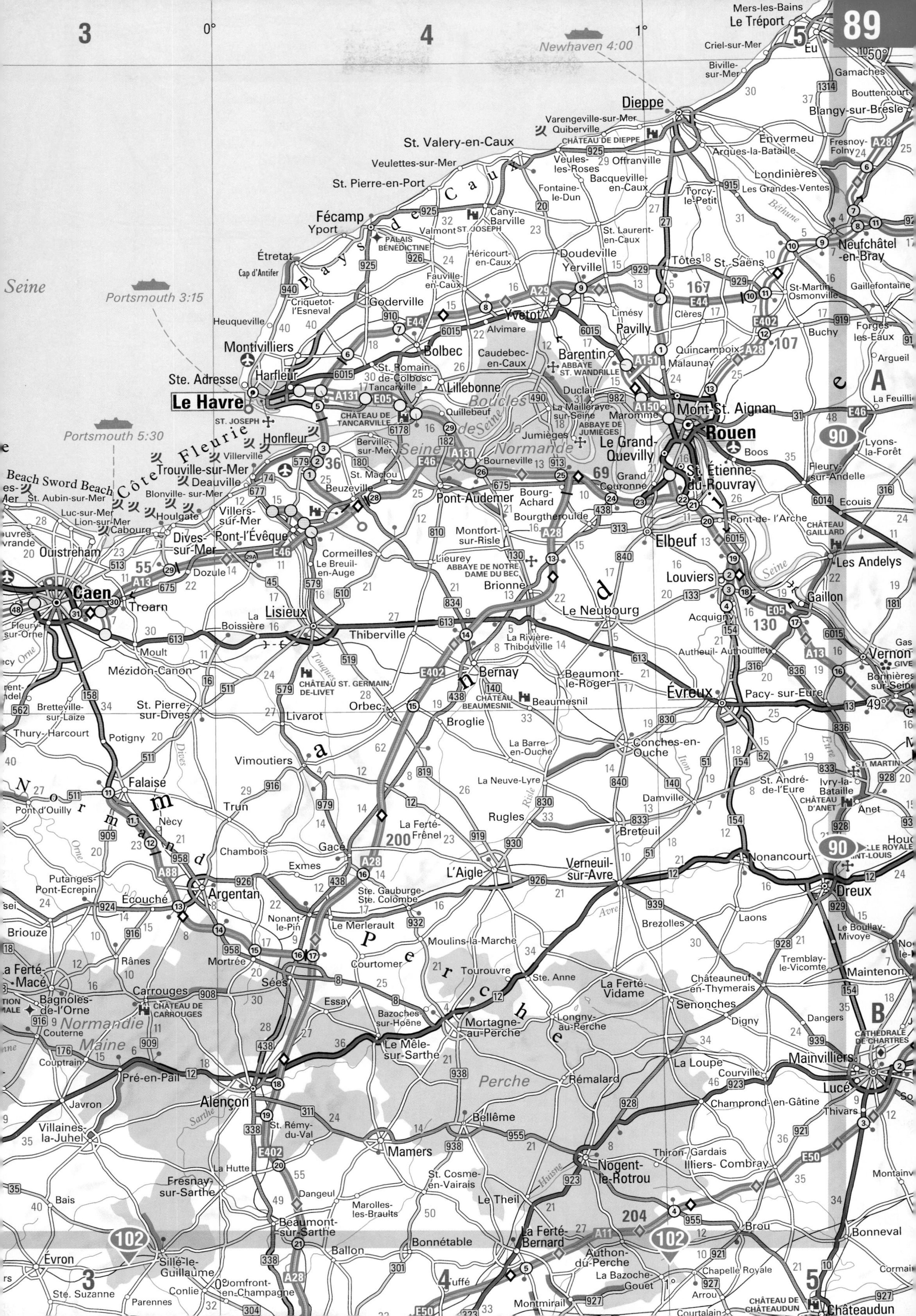

Newhaven 4:00
Portsmouth 3:15
Portsmouth 5:30
Seine
Mers-les-Bains
Le Tréport
Eu
Criel-sur-Mer
Biville-sur-Mer
Gamaches
Bouttencourt
Blangy-sur-Bresle
Dieppe
Varengeville-sur-Mer
Quiberville
CHÂTEAU DE DIEPPE
St. Valery-en-Caux
Envermeu
Arques-la-Bataille
Fresnoy-Folny
Veulettes-sur-Mer
Veules-les-Roses
Offranville
Bacqueville-en-Caux
Londinières
Les Grandes-Ventes
St. Pierre-en-Port
Fontaine-le-Dun
Torcy-le-Petit
Pays de Caux
Fécamp
Yport
Cany-Barville
Valmont
ST. JOSEPH
PALAIS BÉNÉDICTINE
St. Laurent-en-Caux
Neufchâtel-en-Bray
Étretat
Cap d'Antifer
Héricourt-en-Caux
Doudeville
Yerville
Tôtes
St. Saëns
Fauville-en-Caux
St-Martin-Osmonville
Gaillefontaine
Criquetot-l'Esneval
Goderville
Yvetot
Limésy
Pavilly
Clères
Buchy
Forges-les-Eaux
Heuqueville
Alvimare
Barentin
Quincampoix
Malaunay
Argueil
Montivilliers
Bolbec
Caudebec-en-Caux
ABBAYE ST. WANDRILLE
Ste. Adresse
Harfleur
St. Romain-de-Colbosc
Tancarville
Lillebonne
Duclair
La Feuillie
Le Havre
CHÂTEAU DE TANCARVILLE
Quillebeuf
Boucles de la Seine Normande
La Mailleraye-sur-Seine
ABBAYE DE JUMIÈGES
Jumièges
Maromme
Mont-St. Aignan
Rouen
Lyons-la-Forêt
ST. JOSEPH
Honfleur
Berville-sur-Mer
Le Grand-Quevilly
Boos
Côte Fleurie
Villerville
Trouville-sur-Mer
Deauville
St. Maclou
Bourneville
Grand Couronne
St. Étienne-du-Rouvray
Fleury-sur-Andelle
Beach Sword Beach
St. Aubin-sur-Mer
Luc-sur-Mer
Lion-sur-Mer
Blonville-sur-Mer
Beuzeville
Pont-Audemer
Bourg-Achard
Bourgtheroulde
Ecouis
Houlgate
Cabourg
Villers-sur-Mer
Dives-sur-Mer
Pont-l'Évêque
Cormeilles
Montfort-sur-Risle
Elbeuf
Pont-de-l'Arche
CHÂTEAU GAILLARD
Ouistreham
Dozule
Le Breuil-en-Auge
Lieurey
ABBAYE DE NOTRE DAME DU BEC
Brionne
Louviers
Les Andelys
Caen
Troarn
Lisieux
La Boissière
Le Neubourg
Gaillon
Fleury-sur-Orne
Thiberville
La Rivière-Thibouville
Acquigny
Vernon
Moult
Autheuil-Authouillet
Bonnières-sur-Seine
Mézidon-Canon
CHÂTEAU ST. GERMAIN-DE-LIVET
Bernay
Beaumont-le-Roger
Bretteville-sur-Laize
St. Pierre-sur-Dives
Orbec
CHÂTEAU BEAUMESNIL
Beaumesnil
Évreux
Pacy-sur-Eure
Livarot
Broglie
Thury-Harcourt
Potigny
La Barre-en-Ouche
Conches-en-Ouche
Vimoutiers
ST. MARTIN
Falaise
La Neuve-Lyre
St. André-de-l'Eure
Ivry-la-Bataille
CHÂTEAU D'ANET
Anet
Pont d'Ouilly
Trun
Damville
Nècy
Rugles
La Ferté-Frênel
Breteuil
Chambois
Gacé
Putanges-Pont-Ecrepin
Exmes
L'Aigle
Verneuil-sur-Avre
Nonancourt
Argentan
Ste. Gauburge-Ste. Colombe
Dreux
Écouché
Nonant-le-Pin
Le Merlerault
Briouze
Brezolles
Laons
Le Boullay-Mivoye
Moulins-la-Marche
Rânes
Mortrée
Tremblay-le-Vicomte
La Ferté-Macé
Courtomer
Tourouvre
Ste. Anne
Maintenon
Sées
Carrouges
CHÂTEAU DE CARROUGES
Bagnoles-de-l'Orne
La Ferté-Vidame
Châteauneuf-en-Thymerais
Essay
Senonches
Normandie Maine
Couterne
Bazoches-sur-Hoëne
Mortagne-au-Perche
Longny-au-Perche
Digny
Dangers
CATHÉDRALE DE CHARTRES
Le Mêle-sur-Sarthe
Couptrain
La Loupe
Mainvilliers
Pré-en-Pail
Perche
Rémalard
Courville
Lucé
Javron
Alençon
Champrond-en-Gâtine
Thivars
Bellême
Villaines-la-Juhel
St. Rémy-du-Val
Mamers
Thiron-Gardais
Illiers-Combray
Nogent-le-Rotrou
La Hutte
St. Cosme-en-Vairais
Montainv
Fresnay-sur-Sarthe
Bais
Dangeul
Le Theil
Marolles-les-Braults
Brou
Beaumont-sur-Sarthe
La Ferté-Bernard
Bonneval
Bonnétable
Authon-du-Perche
Evron
Ballon
Chapelle Royale
Sillé-le-Guillaume
La Bazoche-Gouet
Domfront-en-Champagne
Conlie
Tuffé
Ste. Suzanne
Parennes
Arrou
Montmirail
Courtalain
CHÂTEAU DE CHÂTEAUDUN
Châteaudun
Uiffé

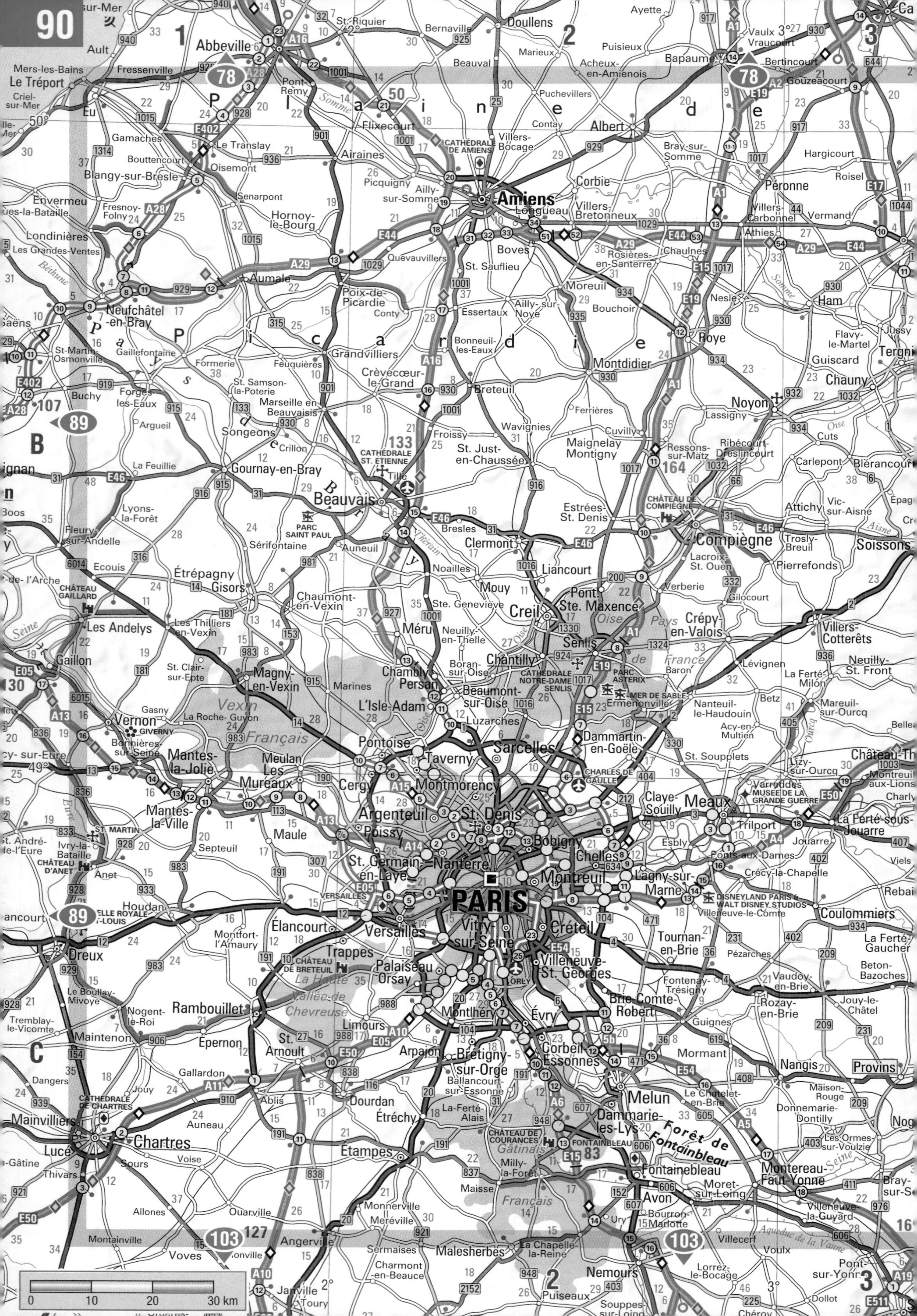
Abbeville
Doullens
Ayette
Bapaume
Vaulx Vraucourt
Bertincourt
Gouzeaucourt
Bernaville
Beauval
Marieux
Puisieux
Acheux-en-Amienois
St. Riquier
Ault
Mers-les-Bains
Le Tréport
Criel-sur-Mer
Fressenville
Pont-Remy
Eu
Flixecourt
Puchevillers
Contay
Albert
Villers-Bocage
Cathédrale de Amiens
Gamaches
Le Translay
Airaines
Bouttencourt
Oisemont
Blangy-sur-Bresle
Picquigny
Ailly-sur-Somme
Amiens
Corbie
Bray-sur-Somme
Hargicourt
Péronne
Roisel
Envermeu
Fresnoy-Folny
Senarpont
Hornoy-le-Bourg
Longueau
Villers-Bretonneux
Villers-Carbonnel
Vermand
Londinières
Les Grandes-Ventes
Boves
Rosières-en-Santerre
Chaulnes
Athies
Quevauvillers
St. Sauflieu
Aumale
Moreuil
Nesle
Ham
Neufchâtel-en-Bray
Poix-de-Picardie
Conty
Essertaux
Ailly-sur-Noye
Bouchoir
Roye
St-Martin-Osmonville
Gaillefontaine
Formerie
Feuquières
Grandvilliers
Bonneuil-les-Eaux
Montdidier
Flavy-le-Martel
Guiscard
Chauny
Buchy
Forges-les-Eaux
St. Samson-la-Poterie
Crèvecœur-le-Grand
Breteuil
Noyon
Lassigny
Marseille en Beauvaisis
Songeons
Argueil
Crillon
Ferrières
Wavignies
Cuvilly
Maignelay Montigny
Ressons-sur-Matz
Ribécourt-Dreslincourt
Cuts
Froissy
St. Just-en-Chaussée
Carlepont
Cathédrale St. Etienne
La Feuille
Gournay-en-Bray
Tillé
Beauvais
Attichy
Vic-sur-Aisne
Lyons-la-Forêt
Château de Compiègne
Estrées-St. Denis
Parc Saint Paul
Bresles
Compiègne
Trosly-Breuil
Soissons
Fleury-sur-Andelle
Sérifontaine
Auneuil
Clermont
Lacroix-St. Ouen
Pierrefonds
Ecouis
Étrépagny
Gisors
Noailles
Liancourt
Mouy
Verberie
Château Gaillard
Chaumont-en-Vexin
Ste. Geneviève
Creil
Pont-Ste. Maxence
Gilocourt
Les Andelys
Les Thilliers-en-Vexin
Méru
Neuilly-en-Thelle
Crépy-en-Valois
Villers-Cotterêts
Gaillon
St. Clair-sur-Epte
Magny-en-Vexin
Chambly
Persan
Boran-sur-Oise
Chantilly
Senlis
Cathédrale Notre-Dame Senlis
Parc Asterix
Mer de Sable
Ermenonville
Lévignen
La Ferté-Milon
Neuilly-St. Front
Vernon
Giverny
Gasny
La Roche-Guyon
Marines
Beaumont-sur-Oise
L'Isle-Adam
Luzarches
Nanteuil-le-Haudouin
Acy-en-Multien
Mareuil-sur-Ourcq
Bonnières-sur-Seine
Mantes-la-Jolie
Meulan
Les Mureaux
Pontoise
Taverny
Sarcelles
Dammartin-en-Goële
St. Soupplets
Lizy-sur-Ourcq
Château-Thierry
Charles de Gaulle
Cergy
Montmorency
Varreddes
Musée de la Grande Guerre
Mantes-la-Ville
Argenteuil
St. Denis
Claye-Souilly
Meaux
Trilport
La Ferté-sous-Jouarre
St. Martin
Poissy
Bobigny
Esbly
Jouarre
Maule
Ivry-la-Bataille
Château d'Anet
Anet
Septeuil
St. Germain-en-Laye
Nanterre
Chelles
Ponts-aux-Dames
Montreuil
Lagny-sur-Marne
Crécy-la-Chapelle
Disneyland Paris & Walt Disney Studios
Villeneuve-le-Comte
PARIS
Versailles
Houdan
Élancourt
Coulommiers
Montfort-l'Amaury
Vitry-sur-Seine
Créteil
Dreux
Trappes
Château de Breteuil
Tournan-en-Brie
Pézarches
La Ferté-Gaucher
Villeneuve-St. Georges
Palaiseau
Orsay
Orly
Beton-Bazoches
Le Boullay-Mivoye
Nogent-le-Roi
Rambouillet
Vallée de Chevreuse
Fontenay-Trésigny
Vaudoy-en-Brie
Jouy-le-Châtel
Brie-Comte-Robert
Rozay-en-Brie
Montlhéry
Évry
Tremblay-le-Vicomte
Maintenon
Epernon
Limours
St. Arnoult
Arpajon
Brétigny-sur-Orge
Corbeil-Essonnes
Guignes
Mormant
Nangis
Provins
Gallardon
Dangers
Jouy
Ballancourt-sur-Essonne
Melun
Le Châtelet-en-Brie
Maison-Rouge
Cathédrale de Chartres
Mainvilliers
Chartres
Lucé
Auneau
Ablis
Dourdan
Étréchy
La-Ferté-Alais
Dammarie-les-Lys
Donnemarie-Dontilly
Les Ormes-sur-Voulzie
Château de Courances
Gâtinais
Forêt de Fontainebleau
Fontainebleau
Étampes
Milly-la-Forêt
Montereau-Faut-Yonne
Sours
Voise
Thivars
Maisse
Moret-sur-Loing
Avon
Bourron-Marlotte
Ury
Bray-sur-Seine
Villeneuve-la-Guyard
Allones
Ouarville
Monnerville
Méréville
Montainville
Voves
Angerville
Sermaises
Malesherbes
La Chapelle-la-Reine
Villecerf
Voulx
Aqueduc de la Vanne
Charmont-en-Beauce
Nemours
Lorrez-le-Bocage
Pont-sur-Yonne
Janville
Toury
Puiseaux
Souppes-sur-Loing
Chéroy
Dollot
Somme
Oise
Seine
Marne
Aisne
Eure
Thérain
Ourcq
Béthune
Pays de Bray
Picardie
Plaine de Picardie
Vexin Français
Pays de France
La Haute Vallée de Chevreuse
0 10 20 30 km

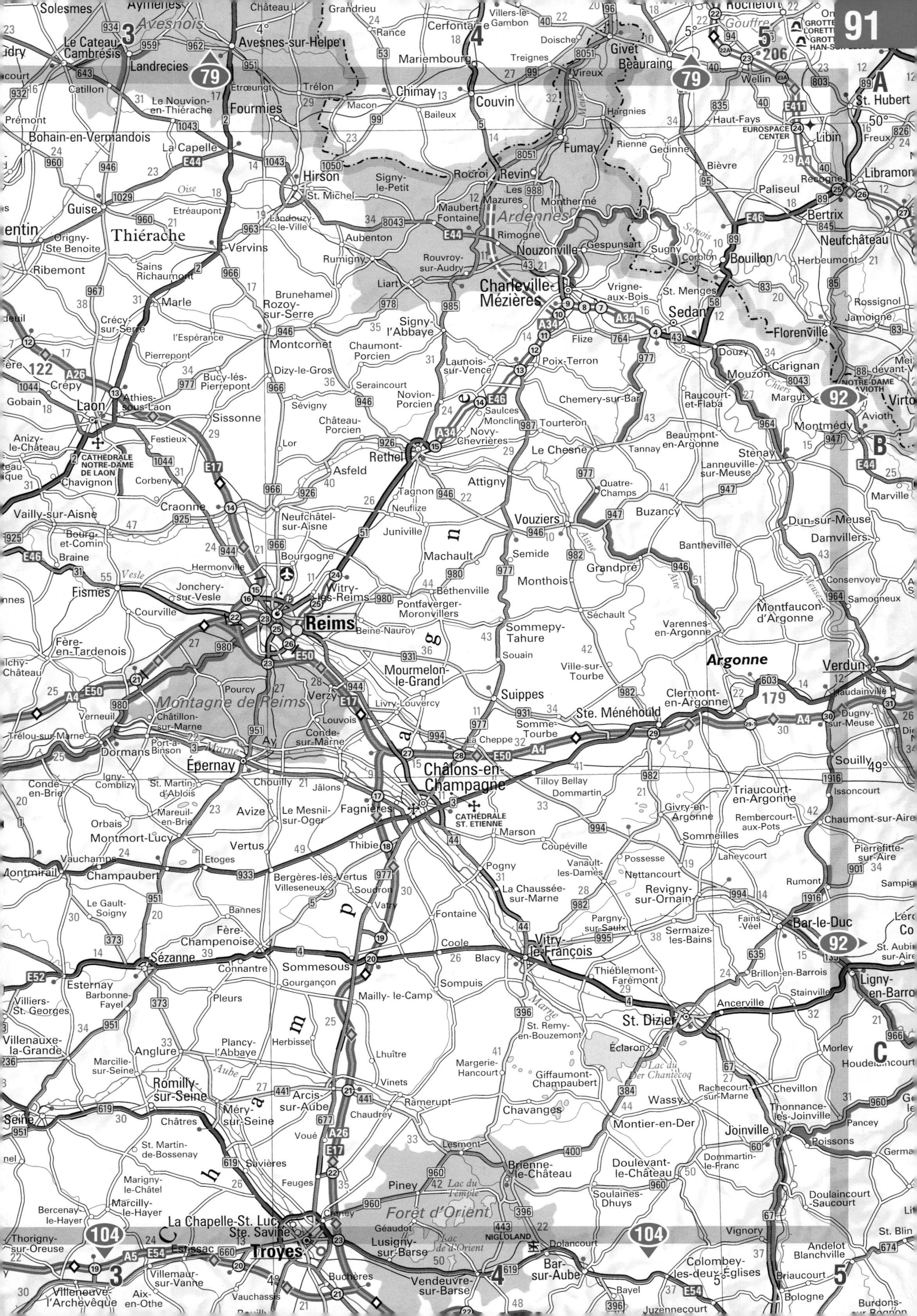
Solesmes
Avesnois
Le Cateau-Cambrésis
Landrecies
Avesnes-sur-Helpe
Grandrieu
Rance
Cerfontaine
Villers-le-Gambon
Doische
Givet
Beauraing
Rochefort
Gouffre
Mariembourg
Treignes
Vireux
Wellin
St. Hubert
Catillon
Le Nouvion-en-Thiérache
Étroeungt
Trélon
Chimay
Couvin
Hargnies
Haut-Fays
Eurospace Center
Libin
Prémont
Fourmies
Macon
Baileux
Freux
Bohain-en-Vermandois
La Capelle
Hirson
Signy-le-Petit
Rocroi
Revin
Fumay
Rienne
Gedinne
Bièvre
Libramont
Guise
Oise
St. Michel
Les Mazures
Monthermé
Maubert-Fontaine
Ardennes
Paliseul
Recogne
Bertrix
Etréaupont
Thiérache
Origny-Ste Benoite
Landouzy-le-Ville
Aubenton
Rimogne
Nouzonville
Gespunsart
Semois
Sugny
Corbion
Bouillon
Neufchâteau
Herbeumont
Ribemont
Vervins
Rumigny
Rouvroy-sur-Audry
Sains Richaumont
Liart
Brunehamel
Rozoy-sur-Serre
Charleville-Mézières
Vrigne-aux-Bois
St. Menges
Sedan
Rossignol
Jamoigne
Marle
Crécy-sur-Serre
l'Espérance
Montcornet
Signy-l'Abbaye
Chaumont-Porcien
Flize
Florenville
Pierrepont
Launois-sur-Vence
Poix-Terron
Douzy
Carignan
Mouzon
Chiers
Crépy
Bucy-lès-Pierrepont
Dizy-le-Gros
Seraincourt
Novion-Porcien
Raucourt-et-Flaba
Margut
Notre-Dame Avioth
Avioth
Gobain
Laon
Athies-sous-Laon
Sissonne
Sévigny
Château-Porcien
Saulces Monclin
Chemery-sur-Bar
Tourteron
Montmédy
Anizy-le-Château
Festieux
Cathédrale Notre-Dame de Laon
Lor
Rethel
Novy-Chevrières
Le Chesne
Tannay
Beaumont-en-Argonne
Stenay
Corbeny
Chavignon
Asfeld
Attigny
Lanneuville-sur-Meuse
Quatre-Champs
Marville
Craonne
Tagnon
Neuflize
Buzancy
Vailly-sur-Aisne
Neufchâtel-sur-Aisne
Juniville
Vouziers
Dun-sur-Meuse
Bourg-et-Comin
Braine
Bourgogne
Machault
Semide
Bantheville
Damvillers
Fismes
Vesle
Hermonville
Jonchery-sur-Vesle
Vitry-lès-Reims
Béthenville
Monthois
Grandpré
Aire
Consenvoye
Courville
Reims
Pontfaverger-Moronvilliers
Séchault
Montfaucon-d'Argonne
Samogneux
Fère-en-Tardenois
Beine-Nauroy
Sommepy-Tahure
Varennes-en-Argonne
Argonne
Souain
Ville-sur-Tourbe
Verdun
Haudainville
Mourmelon-le-Grand
Pourcy
Montagne de Reims
Verzy
Livry-Louvercy
Suippes
Clermont-en-Argonne
Verneuil
Châtillon-sur-Marne
Louvois
Ste. Ménehould
Dugny-sur-Meuse
Trélou-sur-Marne
Dormans
Port-à-Binson
Marne
Ay
Condé-sur-Marne
La Cheppe
Somme-Tourbe
Épernay
Châlons-en-Champagne
Souilly
Condé-en-Brie
Igny-Comblizy
St. Martin-d'Ablois
Chouilly
Jâlons
Tilloy Bellay
Dommartin
Triaucourt-en-Argonne
Issoncourt
Orbais
Mareuil-en-Brie
Avize
Le Mesnil-sur-Oger
Fagnières
Cathédrale St. Etienne
Marson
Givry-en-Argonne
Rembercourt-aux-Pots
Chaumont-sur-Aire
Montmort-Lucy
Vertus
Thibie
Coupéville
Sommeilles
Pierrefitte-sur-Aire
Vauchamps
Etoges
Possesse
Laheycourt
Montmirail
Champaubert
Bergères-lès-Vertus
Villeseneux
Pogny
Vanault-les-Dames
Nettancourt
Rumont
La Chaussée-sur-Marne
Soudron
Revigny-sur-Ornain
Le Gault-Soigny
Vatry
Fontaine
Pargny-sur-Saulx
Fains-Véel
Bar-le-Duc
Bannes
Sermaize-les-Bains
St. Aubin-sur-Aire
Fère-Champenoise
Coole
Vitry-le-François
Sézanne
Connantre
Sommesous
Blacy
Brillon-en-Barrois
Thiéblemont-Farémont
Ligny-en-Barrois
Esternay
Barbonne-Fayel
Gourgançon
Sompuis
Stainville
Villiers-St. Georges
Pleurs
Mailly-le-Camp
Ancerville
Villenauxe-la-Grande
St. Remy-en-Bouzemont
St. Dizier
Anglure
Plancy-l'Abbaye
Herbisse
Eclaron
Lac du Der Chantecoq
Morley
Marcilly-sur-Seine
Aube
Lhuître
Margerie-Hancourt
Giffaumont-Champaubert
Houdelaincourt
Romilly-sur-Seine
Vinets
Rachecourt-sur-Marne
Chevillon
Arcis-sur-Aube
Ramerupt
Wassy
Thonnance-lès-Joinville
Seine
Châtres
Méry-sur-Seine
Chaudrey
Chavanges
Montier-en-Der
Pancey
Joinville
Voué
Poissons
St. Martin-de-Bossenay
Lesmont
Savières
Brienne-le-Château
Doulevant-le-Château
Dommartin-le-Franc
Marigny-le-Châtel
Feuges
Piney
Lac du Temple
Soulaines-Dhuys
Doulaincourt-Saucourt
Marcilly-le-Hayer
Bercenay-le-Hayer
Creney
Forêt d'Orient
La Chapelle-St. Luc
Ste. Savine
Géraudot
Thorigny-sur-Oreuse
Estissac
Troyes
Lusigny-sur-Barse
Lac de d'Orient
Nigloland
Dolancourt
Vignory
St. Blin
Andelot Blanchville
Villemaur-sur-Vanne
Bar-sur-Aube
Colombey-les-deux-Églises
Briaucourt
Bréviandes
Buchères
Vendeuvre-sur-Barse
Villeneuve-l'Archevêque
Aix-en-Othe
Vauchassis
Bayel
Juzennecourt
Bologne
Burdons-sur-Rognon
Champagne
79
92
104
A
B
C
3
4
5

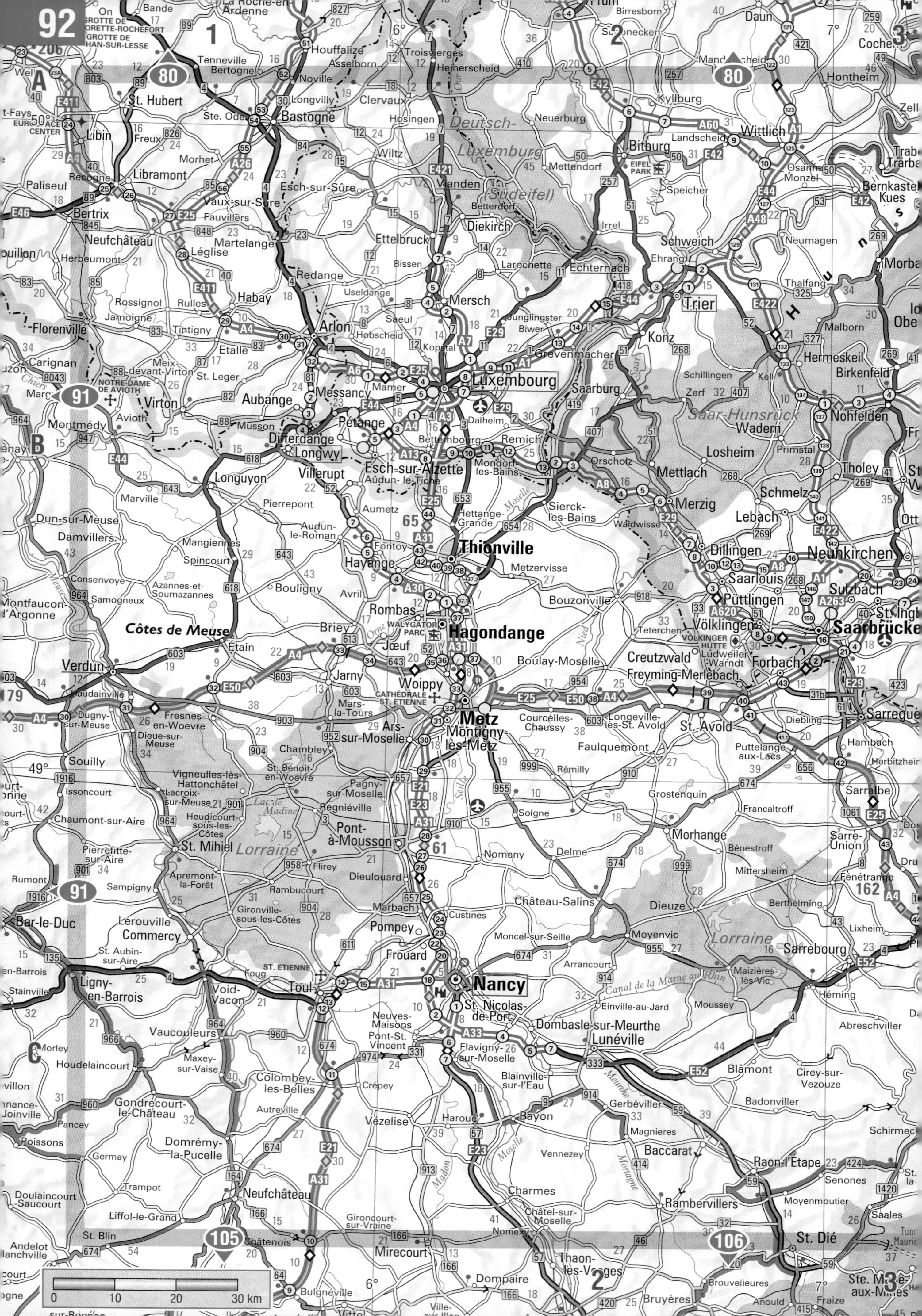
Houffalize
Tenneville
St. Hubert
Bastogne
Libin
Libramont
Bertrix
Neufchâteau
Florenville
Carignan
Virton
Arlon
Habay
Aubange
Messancy
Wiltz
Clervaux
Troisvierges
Vianden
Diekirch
Ettelbruck
Mersch
Echternach
Luxembourg
Deutsch-Luxemburg (Südeifel)
Bitburg
Wittlich
Trier
Schweich
Konz
Saarburg
Bernkastel-Kues
Hermeskeil
Nohfelden
Wadern
Losheim
Mettlach
Merzig
Lebach
Dillingen
Saarlouis
Neunkirchen
Völklingen
Saarbrücken
Forbach
Sarreguemines
Saar-Hunsrück
Hunsrück
Montmédy
Longwy
Differdange
Pétange
Esch-sur-Alzette
Villerupt
Longuyon
Thionville
Hayange
Hagondange
Rombas
Briey
Étain
Verdun
Côtes de Meuse
Metz
Montigny-lès-Metz
Woippy
Boulay-Moselle
Creutzwald
St. Avold
Faulquemont
Sarralbe
Sarre-Union
Morhange
Château-Salins
Dieuze
Sarrebourg
Lorraine
Pont-à-Mousson
St. Mihiel
Commercy
Bar-le-Duc
Ligny-en-Barrois
Toul
Nancy
Lunéville
Baccarat
Rambervillers
Raon-l'Étape
St. Dié
Charmes
Mirecourt
Neufchâteau
Vaucouleurs
Colombey-les-Belles
Vézelise
Dompaire
Thaon-les-Vosges
Bruyères
0 10 20 30 km

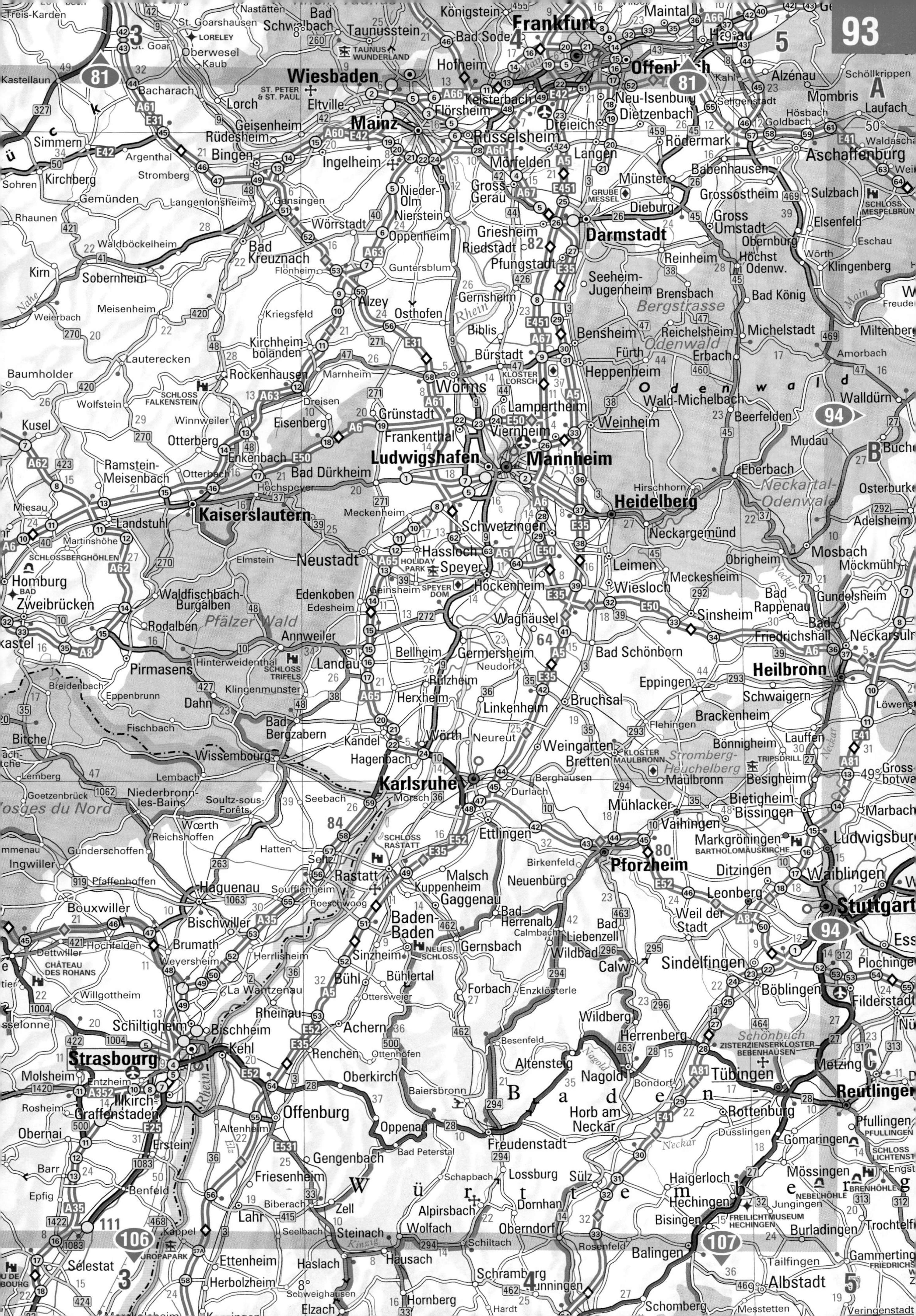

Frankfurt
Offenbach
Wiesbaden
Mainz
Rüsselsheim
Darmstadt
Aschaffenburg
Bingen
Rüdesheim
Bad Kreuznach
Alzey
Worms
Ludwigshafen
Mannheim
Heidelberg
Kaiserslautern
Neustadt
Speyer
Landau
Karlsruhe
Pforzheim
Heilbronn
Stuttgart
Baden-Baden
Rastatt
Offenburg
Strasbourg
Haguenau
Kehl
Tübingen
Reutlingen
Freudenstadt
Pirmasens
Zweibrücken
Homburg
Bad Dürkheim
Frankenthal
Viernheim
Weinheim
Bensheim
Heppenheim
Sinsheim
Bruchsal
Ettlingen
Böblingen
Sindelfingen
Ludwigsburg
Waiblingen
Leonberg
Herrenberg
Nagold
Calw
Rottenburg
Balingen
Albstadt
Lahr
Sélestat
Obernai
Bitche
Wissembourg
Kirn
Simmern
Kusel
Landstuhl
Rockenhausen
Kirchheimbolanden
Grünstadt
Hockenheim
Schwetzingen
Walldürn
Mosbach
Eberbach
Miltenberg
Odenwald
Pfälzer Wald
Bergstrasse
Baden
Württemberg
Rhein
Neckar
Main
Nahe
Kinzig
Nagold
81
94
106
107
3
4
5
A
B
C

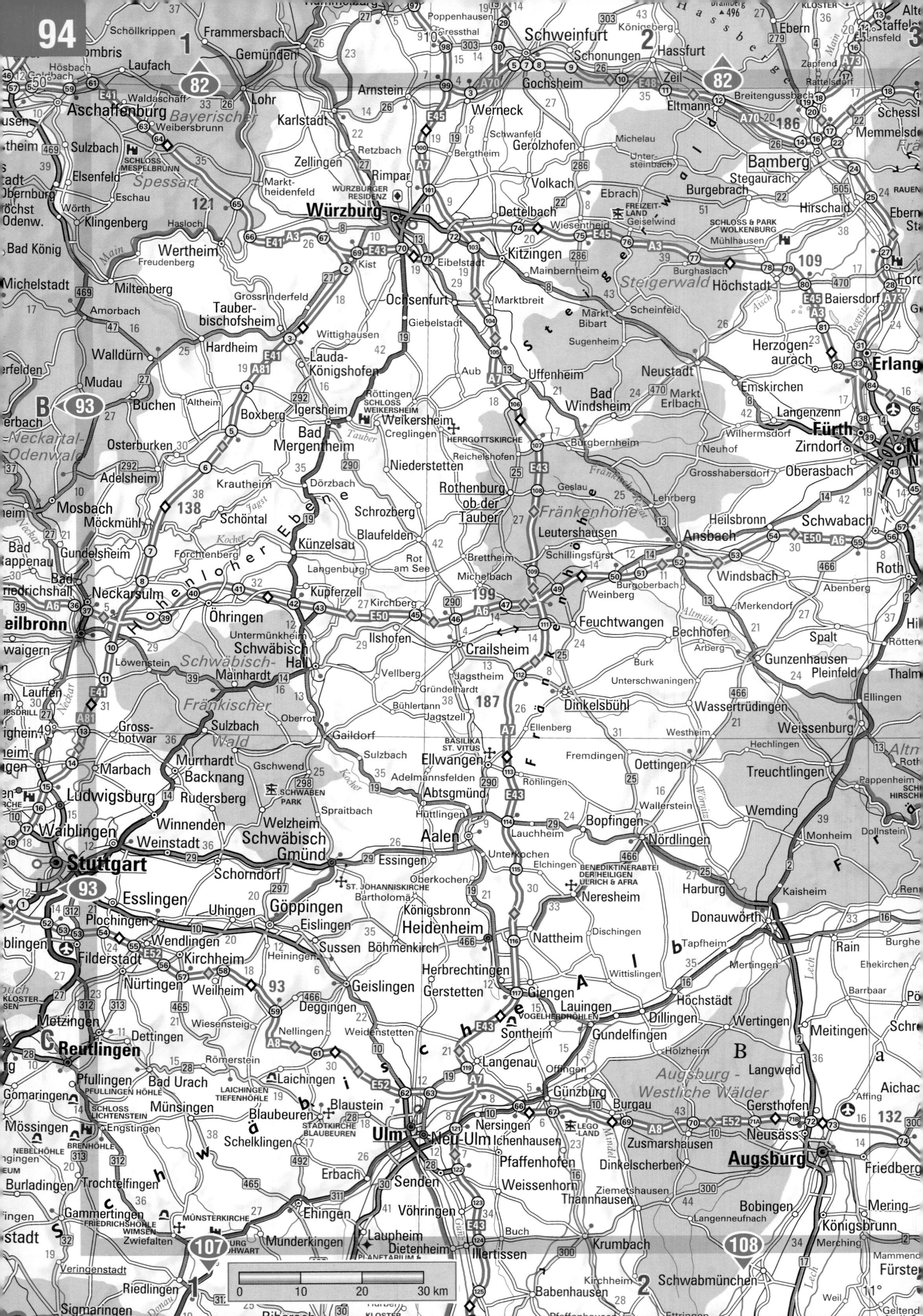

Schöllkrippen
Frammersbach
Gemünden
Poppenhausen
Gressthal
Schweinfurt
Königsberg
Hassfurt
Ebern
Staffelstein
Hösbach
Laufach
Lohr
Arnstein
Werneck
Gochsheim
Schonungen
Zeil
Eltmann
Breitengussbach
Rattelsdorf
Aschaffenburg
Waldaschaff
Bayerischer
Weibersbrunn
Karlstadt
Schwanfeld
Gerolzhofen
Michelau
Bamberg
Memmelsdorf
Sulzbach
SCHLOSS MESPELBRUNN
Spessart
Retzbach
Zellingen
Bergtheim
Unter-steinbach
Stegaurach
Elsenfeld
Obernburg
Höchst i. Odenw.
Wörth
Eschau
Rimpar
Markt-heidenfeld
WÜRZBURGER RESIDENZ
Volkach
Ebrach
Burgebrach
Hirschaid
Klingenberg
Hasloch
Würzburg
Dettelbach
FREIZEIT-LAND Geiselwind
Wiesentheid
SCHLOSS & PARK WOLKENBURG
Mühlhausen
Bad König
Wertheim
Freudenberg
Main
Kist
Eibelstadt
Kitzingen
Mainbernheim
Burghaslach
Steigerwald
Höchstadt
Forchheim
Michelstadt
Miltenberg
Grossrinderfeld
Ochsenfurt
Marktbreit
Scheinfeld
Baiersdorf
Amorbach
Tauber-bischofsheim
Giebelstadt
Markt Bibart
Wittighausen
Sugenheim
Herzogen-aurach
Walldürn
Hardheim
Lauda-Königshofen
Aub
Uffenheim
Neustadt
Emskirchen
Erlangen
Mudau
Buchen
Altheim
Boxberg
Igersheim
Röttingen
SCHLOSS WEIKERSHEIM
Weikersheim
Creglingen
HERRGOTTSKIRCHE
Bad Windsheim
Markt Erlbach
Langenzenn
Wilhermsdorf
Fürth
Zirndorf
Nürnberg
Neckartal-Odenwald
Osterburken
Bad Mergentheim
Tauber
Niederstetten
Reichelshofen
Burgbernheim
Neuhof
Oberasbach
Adelsheim
Krautheim
Dörzbach
Rothenburg ob der Tauber
Geslau
Grosshabersdorf
Frankenhöhe
Lehrberg
Mosbach
Möckmühl
Schöntal
Jagst
Schrozberg
Blaufelden
Leutershausen
Heilsbronn
Schwabach
Bad Rappenau
Gundelsheim
Kocher
Forchtenberg
Künzelsau
Rot am See
Brettheim
Schillingsfürst
Ansbach
Windsbach
Roth
Bad Friedrichshall
Neckarsulm
Langenburg
Kupferzell
Michelbach
Burgoberbach
Weinberg
Abenberg
Heilbronn
Öhringen
Kirchberg
Hohenloher Ebene
Merkendorf
Untermünkheim
Ilshofen
Feuchtwangen
Bechhofen
Altmühl
Spalt
Schwäbisch Hall
Crailsheim
Arberg
Burk
Gunzenhausen
Pleinfeld
Löwenstein
Schwäbisch-
Mainhardt
Vellberg
Jagstheim
Unterschwaningen
Lauffen
Fränkischer Wald
Gründelhardt
Bühlertann
Dinkelsbühl
Wassertrüdingen
Ellingen
Jagstzell
Oberrot
Ellenberg
Weissenburg
Gross-bottwar
Sulzbach
Gaildorf
Westheim
Hechlingen
Murrhardt
Gschwend
BASILIKA ST. VITUS
Ellwangen
Fremdingen
Oettingen
Treuchtlingen
Marbach
Backnang
Sulzbach
Adelmannsfelden
Röhlingen
Pappenheim
Ludwigsburg
Rudersberg
SCHWABEN PARK
Abtsgmünd
Wallerstein
Wörnitz
Wemding
Winnenden
Spraitbach
Hüttlingen
Welzheim
Bopfingen
Nördlingen
Monheim
Dollnstein
Waiblingen
Weinstadt
Schwäbisch Gmünd
Aalen
Lauchheim
Unterkochen
Elchingen
Stuttgart
Schorndorf
Essingen
BENEDIKTINERABTEI DER HEILIGEN ULRICH & AFRA
Neresheim
Harburg
Kaisheim
ST. JOHANNISKIRCHE
Oberkochen
Bartholomä
Esslingen
Göppingen
Königsbronn
Uhingen
Plochingen
Eislingen
Heidenheim
Dischingen
Donauwörth
Rain
Wendlingen
Sussen
Böhmenkirch
Nattheim
Tapfheim
Filderstadt
Kirchheim
Heiningen
Herbrechtingen
Mertingen
Nürtingen
Weilheim
Geislingen
Gerstetten
Giengen
Wittislingen
Höchstädt
KLOSTER DENKENDORF
Deggingen
Lauingen
Dillingen
Wertingen
Meitingen
Metzingen
Wiesensteig
VOGELHERDHÖHLEN
Sontheim
Gundelfingen
Dettingen
Nellingen
Weidenstetten
Reutlingen
Römerstein
Holzheim
Langenau
Offingen
Augsburg - Westliche Wälder
Langweid
Aichach
Pfullingen
Bad Urach
Laichingen
PFULLINGEN HÖHLE
LAICHINGEN TIEFENHÖHLE
Günzburg
Burgau
Gersthofen
Affing
Gomaringen
Münsingen
Blaustein
SCHLOSS LICHTENSTEIN
Blaubeuren
STADTKIRCHE BLAUBEUREN
Nersingen
LEGO LAND
Mössingen
Engstingen
Ulm
Neu-Ulm
Ichenhausen
Zusmarshausen
Neusäss
NEBELHÖHLE
BÄRENHÖHLE
Schelklingen
Pfaffenhofen
Augsburg
Burladingen
Trochtelfingen
Erbach
Senden
Weissenhorn
Dinkelscherben
Friedberg
Ziemetshausen
Thannhausen
Gammertingen
FRIEDRICHSHÖHLE WIMSEN
MÜNSTERKIRCHE ZWIEFALTEN
Ehingen
Vöhringen
Bobingen
Mering
Langenneufnach
Königsbrunn
Munderkingen
Laupheim
PLANETARIUM
Dietenheim
Illertissen
Buch
Krumbach
Merching
Veringenstadt
Riedlingen
Babenhausen
Kirchheim
Schwabmünchen
Sigmaringen
Schwäbische Alb
Frankenalb
Fränkische Rezat
Hassberge
Steigerwald
0
10
20
30 km

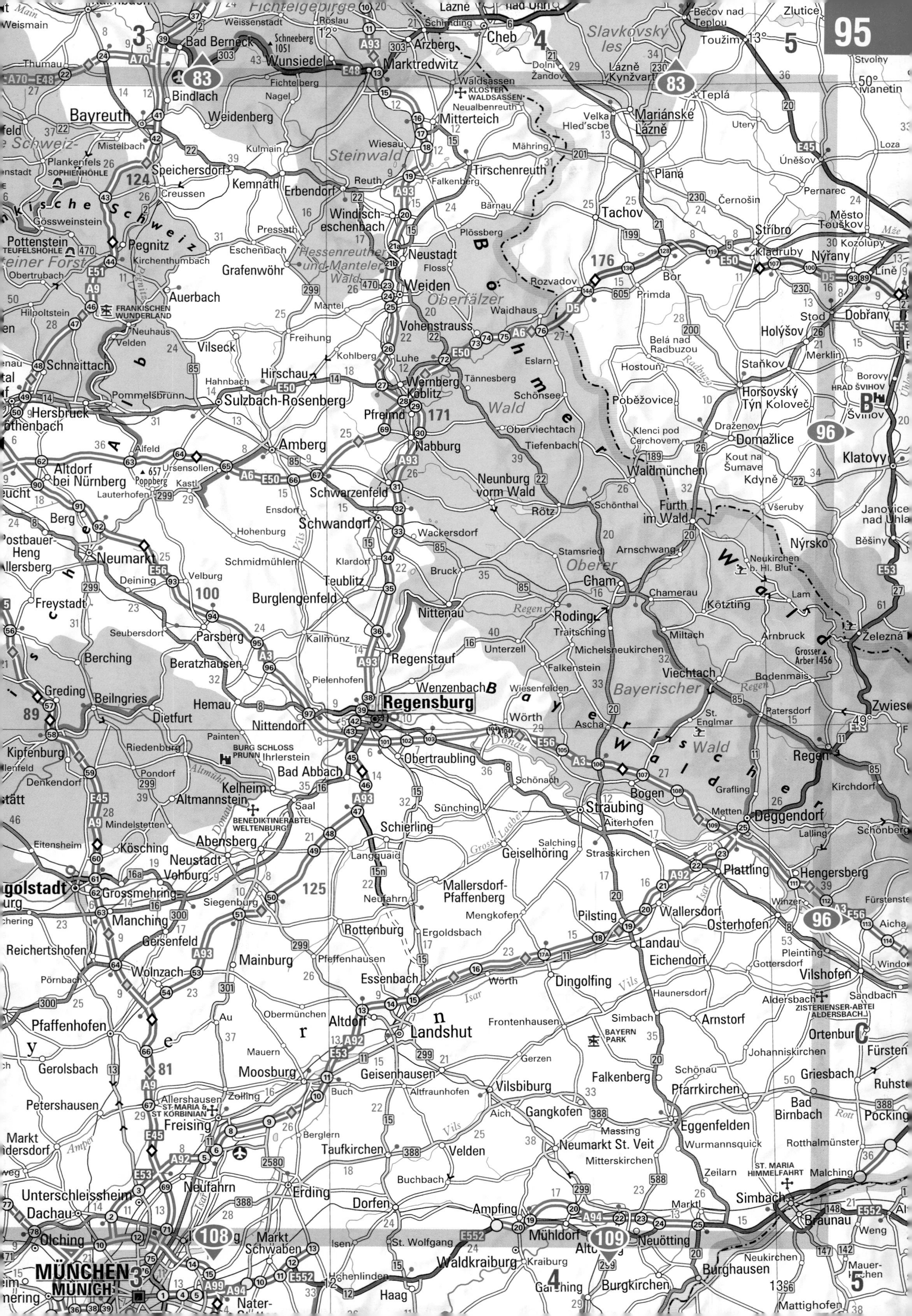

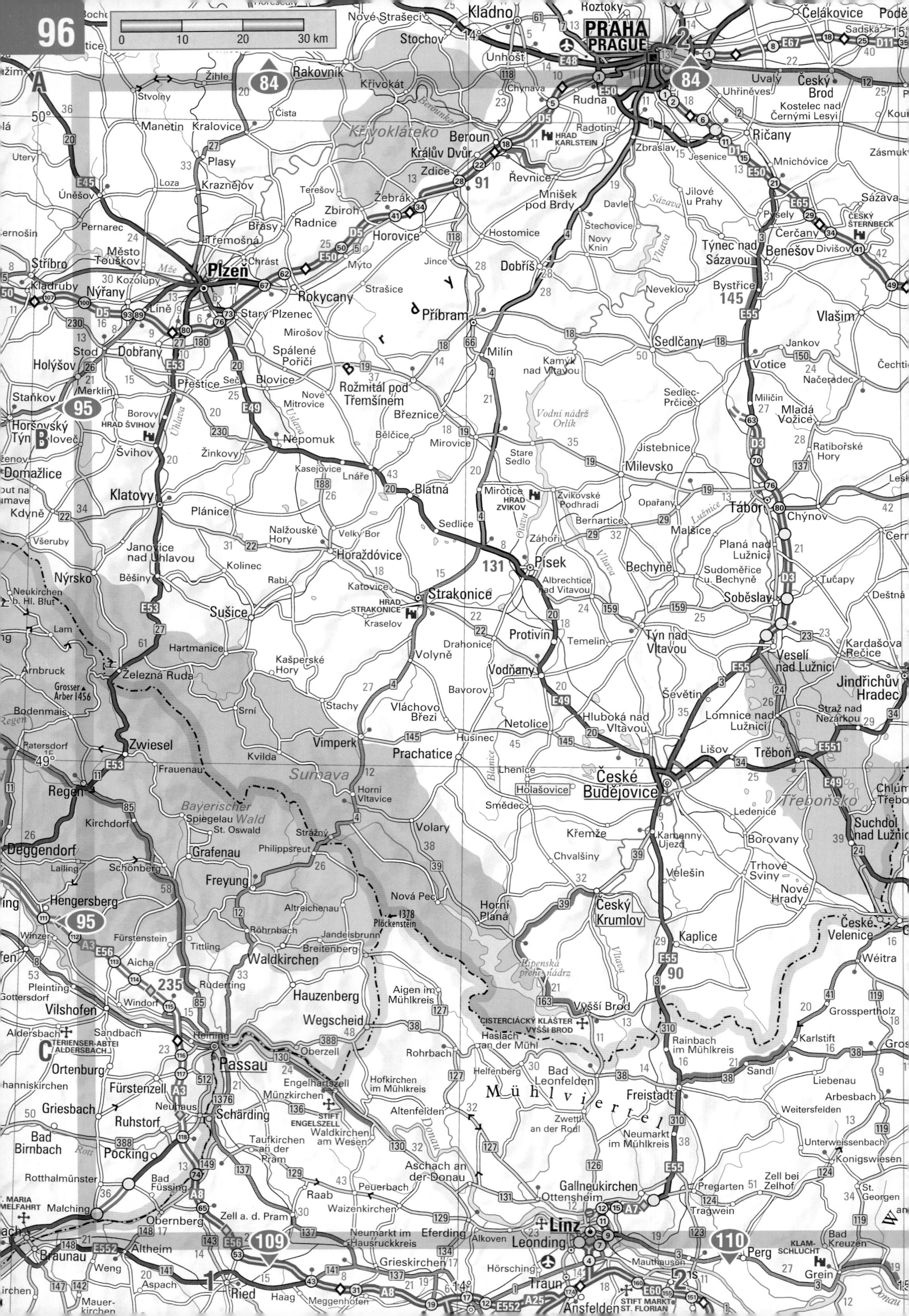
0
10
20
30 km
84
95
109
110
Kladno
Roztoky
PRAHA
PRAGUE
Čelákovice
Nové Strašecí
Stochov
Unhošť
Rakovník
Křivoklát
Chynava
Rudna
Uhříněves
Úvaly
Český Brod
Kostelec nad Černými Lesy
Sadská
Stvolny
Žihle
Čista
Manetín
Kralovice
Křivoklátsko
Beroun
Králův Dvůr
Zdice
HRAD KARLŠTEJN
Radotín
Zbraslav
Jesenice
Říčany
Mnichovice
Zásmuky
Plasy
Kaznějov
Loza
Úněšov
Utery
Terešov
Žebrák
Zbiroh
Radnice
Břasy
Třemošná
Hořovice
Řevnice
Mníšek pod Brdy
Davle
Jílové u Prahy
Sázava
Pyšely
Čerčany
ČESKÝ ŠTERNBECK
Štěchovice
Nový Knín
Týnec nad Sázavou
Benešov
Divišov
Hostomice
Pernarec
Stříbro
Město Touškov
Kladruby
Kozolupy
Nýřany
Plzeň
Chrást
Mýto
Jince
Dobříš
Rokycany
Strašice
Neveklov
Bystřice
Líně
Starý Plzenec
Příbram
Brdy
Vlašim
Mirošov
Spálené Poříčí
Milín
Sedlčany
Jankov
Votice
Čechtice
Holýšov
Stod
Dobřany
Přeštice
Seč
Blovice
Rožmitál pod Třemšínem
Kamýk nad Vltavou
Načeradec
Staňkov
Merklín
Nové Mitrovice
Sedlec-Prčice
Miličín
Mladá Vožice
Horšovský Týn
Borovy
HRAD ŠVIHOV
Březnice
Vodní nádrž Orlík
Bělčice
Mirovice
Nepomuk
Švihov
Žinkovy
Stare Sedlo
Jistebnice
Ratibořské Hory
Domažlice
Kasejovice
Lnáře
Milevsko
Klatovy
Blatná
Mirotice
HRAD ZVIKOV
Zvíkovské Podhradí
Opařany
Tábor
Kdyně
Plánice
Sedlice
Bernartice
Chýnov
Všeruby
Nalžovské Hory
Velký Bor
Záhoří
Malšice
Janovice nad Úhlavou
Horažďovice
Planá nad Lužnicí
Nýrsko
Kolinec
Písek
Bechyně
Sudoměřice u. Bechyně
Běšiny
Rabí
Katovice
Albrechtice nad Vltavou
Tučapy
Neukirchen b. Hl. Blut
Strakonice
HRAD STRAKONICE
Kraselov
Soběslav
Deštná
Sušice
Lam
Hartmanice
Drahonice
Protivín
Temelín
Týn nad Vltavou
Kardašova Řečice
Arnbruck
Kašperské Hory
Volyně
Vodňany
Veselí nad Lužnicí
Železná Ruda
Grosser Arber 1456
Bavorov
Ševětín
Jindřichův Hradec
Bodenmais
Srní
Stachy
Vlachovo Březí
Netolice
Hluboká nad Vltavou
Lomnice nad Lužnicí
Stráž nad Nežárkou
Zwiesel
Patersdorf
Vimperk
Husinec
Prachatice
Lišov
Třeboň
Kvilda
Frauenau
Šumava
Lhenice
České Budějovice
Holašovice
Regen
Horní Vltavice
Bayerischer Wald
Spiegelau
St. Oswald
Kirchdorf
Smědec
Třeboňsko
Chlum u Třeboně
Ledenice
Volary
Strážný
Křemže
Suchdol nad Lužnicí
Deggendorf
Grafenau
Philippsreut
Kamenný Újezd
Borovany
Chvalšiny
Lalling
Schönberg
Freyung
Velešín
Trhové Sviny
Nové Hrady
Hengersberg
Nová Pec
Horní Planá
Český Krumlov
Altreichenau
1378 Plöckenstein
Röhrnbach
Winzer
Fürstenstein
Jandelsbrunn
Kaplice
České Velenice
Tittling
Breitenberg
Aicha
Waldkirchen
Lipenská přehr. nádrž
Weitra
Ruderting
Pleinting
Gottersdorf
Hauzenberg
Aigen im Mühlkreis
Vyšší Brod
Grosspertholz
Vilshofen
Windorf
Wegscheid
CISTERCIÁCKÝ KLÁŠTER VYŠŠÍ BROD
Aldersbach
Sandbach
TERIENSER-ABTEI ALDERSBACH
Heining
Oberzell
Haslach an der Mühl
Rainbach im Mühlkreis
Karlstift
Ortenburg
Passau
Rohrbach
Sandl
Helfenberg
Bad Leonfelden
Liebenau
Fürstenzell
Engelhartszell
Hofkirchen im Mühlkreis
Mühlviertel
Freistadt
Arbesbach
Griesbach
Neuhaus
Münzkirchen
STIFT ENGELSZELL
Schärding
Altenfelden
Weitersfelden
Ruhstorf
Waldkirchen am Wesen
Zwettl an der Rodl
Neumarkt im Mühlkreis
Bad Birnbach
Pocking
Taufkirchen an der Pram
Donau
Unterweissenbach
Königswiesen
Rotthalmünster
Bad Füssing
Aschach an der Donau
Raab
Peuerbach
Gallneukirchen
Pregarten
Zell bei Zelhof
St. Georgen
Malching
Obernberg
Zell a. d. Pram
Waizenkirchen
Ottensheim
Tragwein
Neumarkt im Hausruckkreis
Eferding
Alkoven
Linz
Leonding
KLAM-SCHLUCHT
Bad Kreuzen
Braunau
Altheim
Grieskirchen
Hörsching
Mauthausen
Perg
Weng
Aspach
Grein
Ried
Haag
Meggenhofen
Traun
STIFT MARKT ST. FLORIAN
Ansfelden

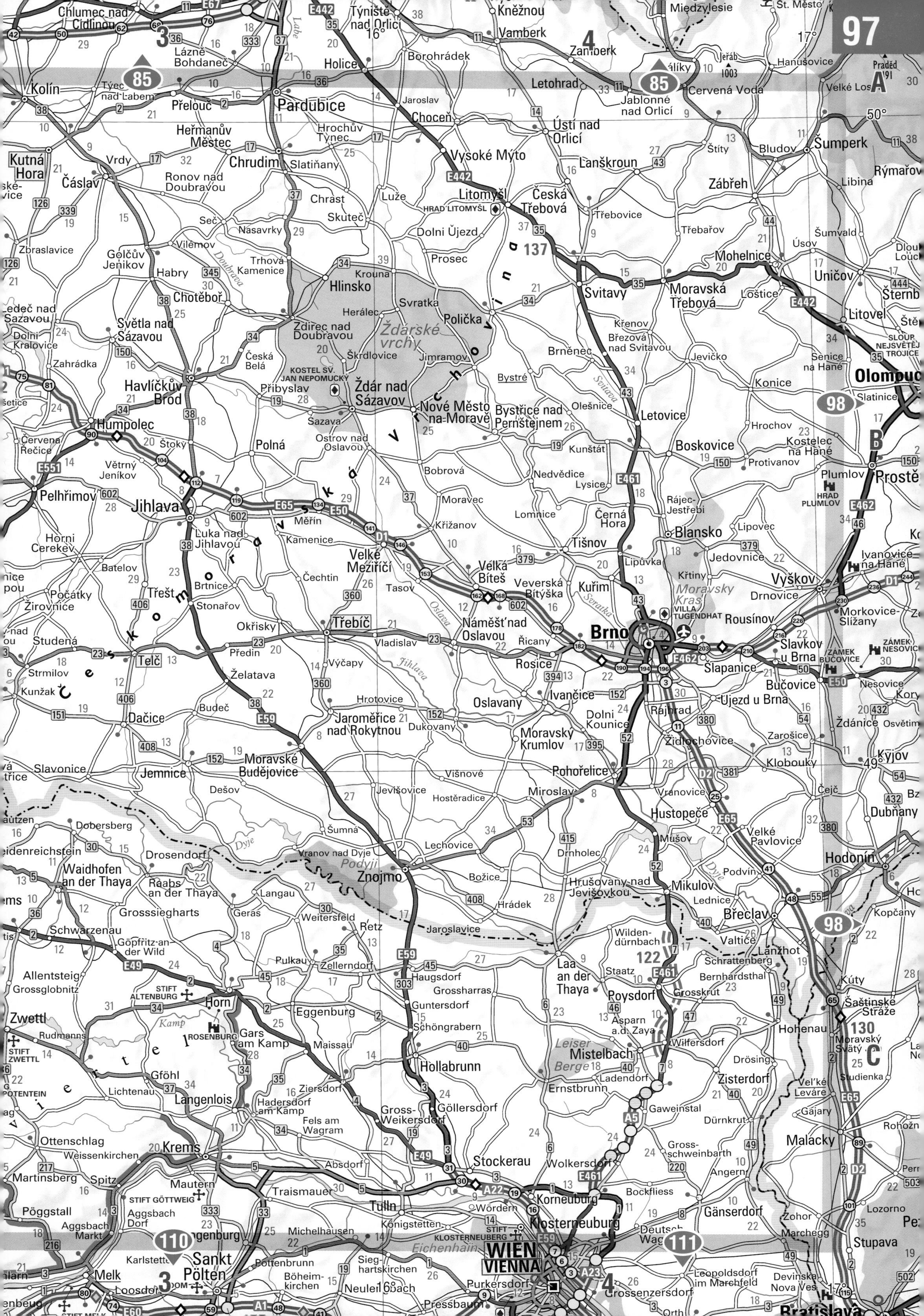
Pardubice
Hradec
Kolín
Kutná Hora
Čáslav
Chrudim
Litomyšl
Svitavy
Šumperk
Olomouc
Jihlava
Havlíčkův Brod
Žďár nad Sázavou
Třebíč
Brno
Znojmo
Mikulov
Břeclav
Hodonín
Vyškov
Telč
Dačice
Horn
Krems
Hollabrunn
Mistelbach
Stockerau
Tulln
Sankt Pölten
WIEN VIENNA
Malacky
Bratislava
Českomoravská vrchovina
Waldviertel
Žďárské vrchy
Moravský Kras
85
98
110
111
122
130
137

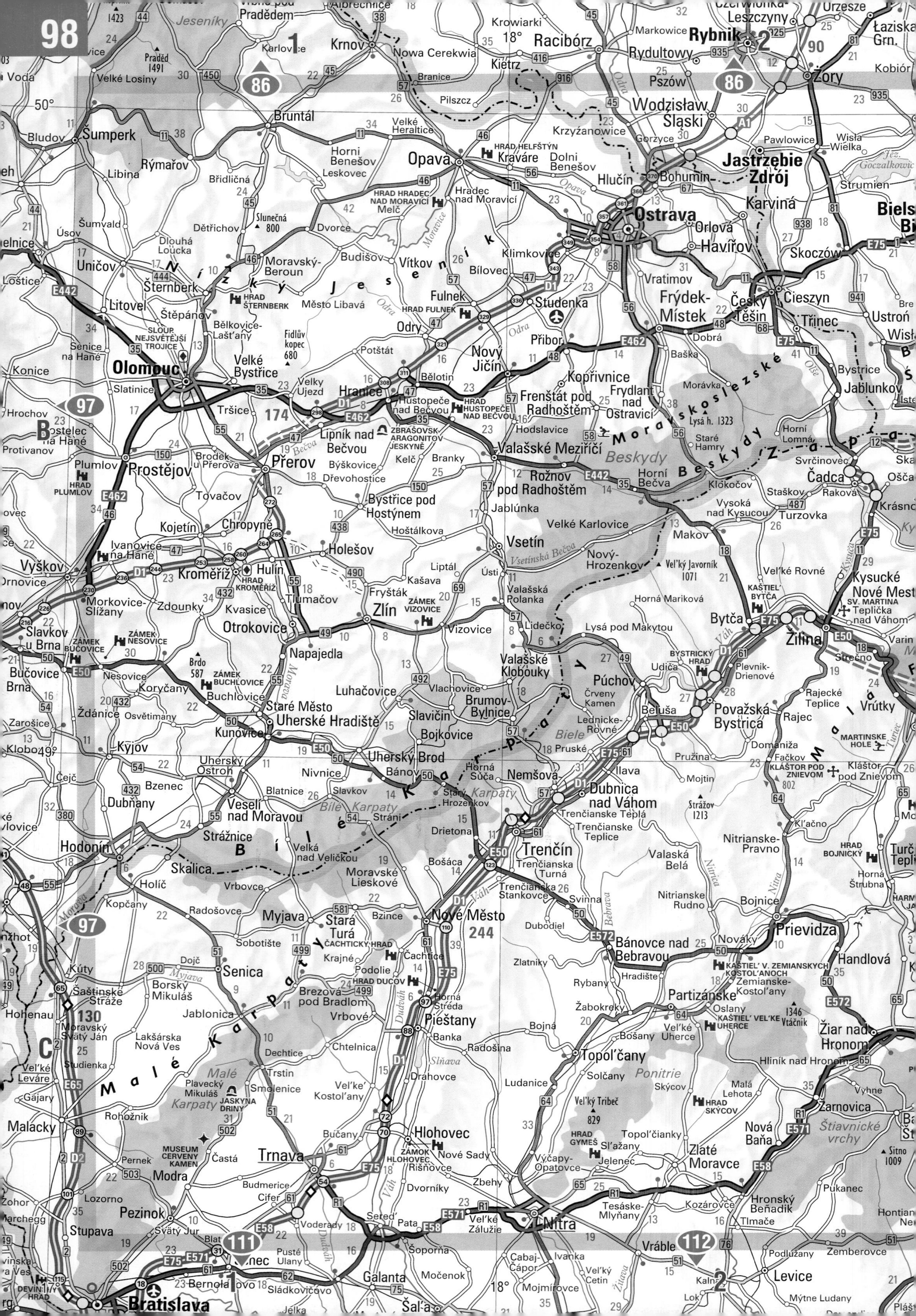
Jeseníky
Praděd 1491
Velké Losiny
Krnov
Nowa Cerekwia
Racibórz
Rybnik
Rydułtowy
Pszów
Wodzisław Śląski
Žory
86
Šumperk
Bruntál
Rýmařov
Opava
Kravaře
Hlučín
Bohumín
Jastrzębie Zdrój
Karviná
Ostrava
Orlová
Havířov
Skoczów
Nízký Jeseník
Šternberk
Uničov
Litovel
Olomouc
Studénka
Fulnek
Odry
Nový Jičín
Příbor
Frýdek-Místek
Český Těšín
Cieszyn
Třinec
Kopřivnice
Frenštát pod Radhoštěm
Frýdlant nad Ostravicí
Moravskoslezské Beskydy
Lysá h. 1323
Jablunkov
Hranice
Lipník nad Bečvou
Přerov
Prostějov
97
Valašské Meziříčí
Rožnov pod Radhoštěm
Čadca
Bystřice pod Hostýnem
Vsetín
Holešov
Kroměříž
Hulín
Vyškov
Zlín
Otrokovice
Vizovice
Bytča
Žilina
Slavkov u Brna
Bučovice
Napajedla
Valašské Klobouky
Púchov
Považská Bystrica
Uherské Hradiště
Staré Město
Kunovice
Uherský Brod
Kyjov
Veselí nad Moravou
Bílé Karpaty
Dubnica nad Váhom
Trenčín
Hodonín
Skalica
Strážnice
Prievidza
Nové Mesto
Myjava
Senica
Bánovce nad Bebravou
Handlová
Piešťany
Partizánske
Topoľčany
Malé Karpaty
Malacky
Hlohovec
Trnava
Zlaté Moravce
Nová Baňa
Žarnovica
Pezinok
Modra
Sereď
Nitra
Vráble
Levice
Galanta
Šaľa
Senec
Bratislava
111
112

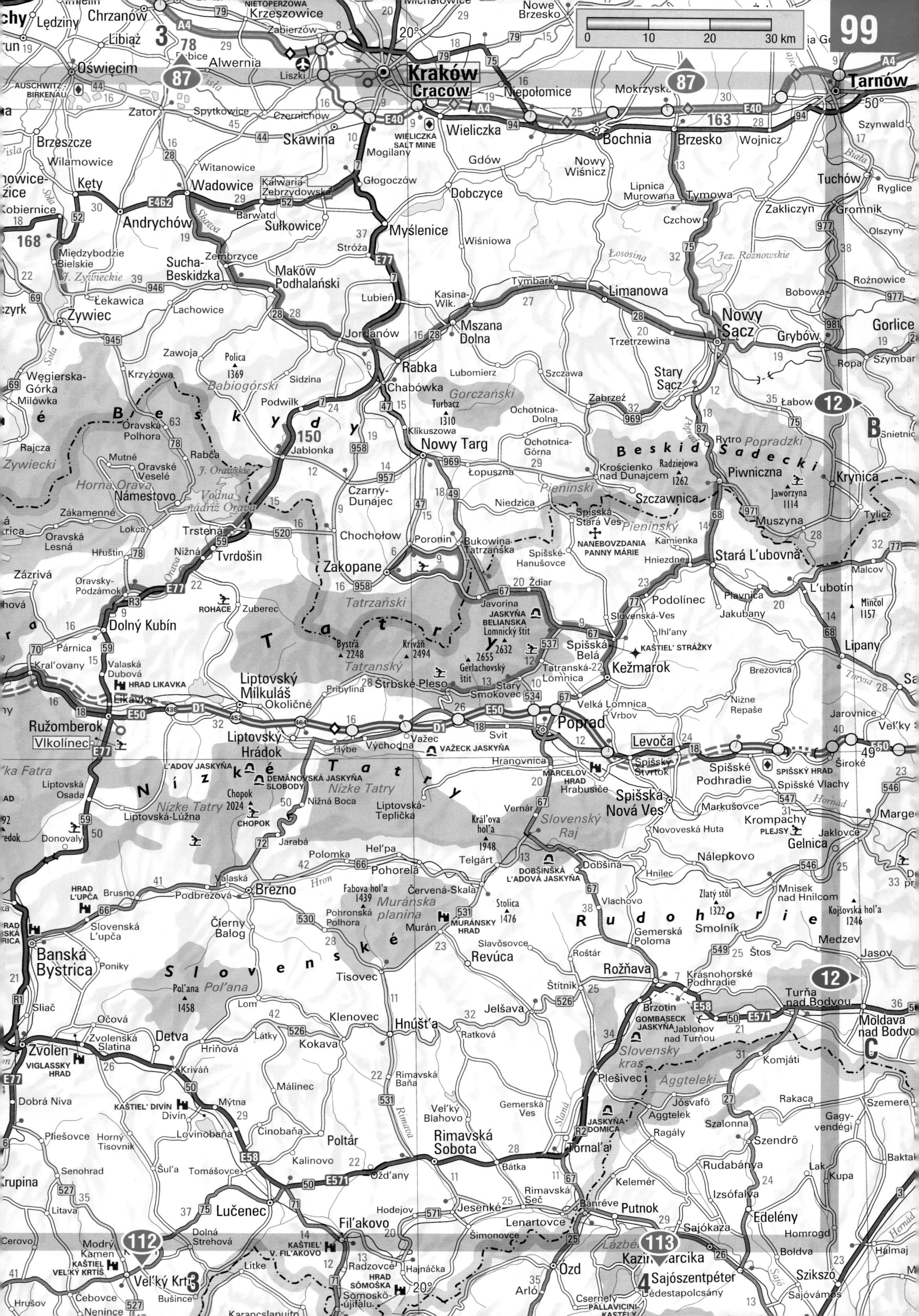

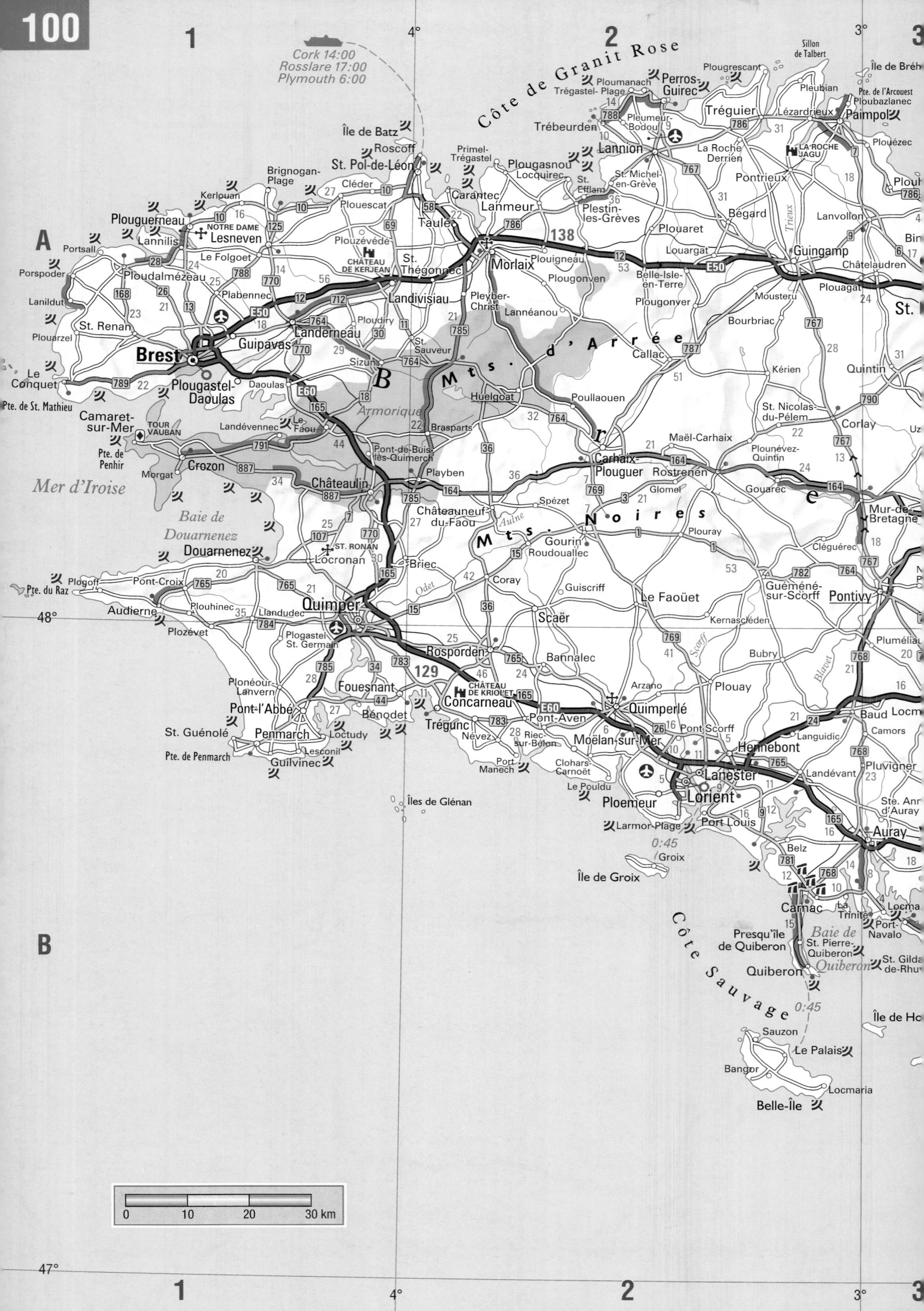

1   4°   2   3°   3

Cork 14:00
Rosslare 17:00
Plymouth 6:00

Côte de Granit Rose

Sillon de Talbert
Île de Bréhat

Plougrescant
Pleubian
Pte. de l'Arcouest
Ploumanac'h
Perros-Guirec
Trégastel-Plage
Pleumeur-Bodou
Tréguier
Lézardrieux
Plubazlanec
Paimpol
Plouézec
Île de Batz
Trébeurden
Lannion
La Roche Derrien
LA ROCHE JAGU
Roscoff
St. Efflam
St. Michel-en-Grève
Pontrieux
Brignogan-Plage
St. Pol-de-Léon
Plougasnou
Locquirec
Plestin-les-Grèves
Bégard
Lanvollon
Kerlouan
Cléder
Plouescat
Carantec
Lanmeur
Plouaret
Louargat
Guingamp
Châtelaudren
Plouguerneau
NOTRE DAME
Lesneven
Plouzévédé
Taulé
Morlaix
Plouigneau
Belle-Isle-en-Terre
Plougonven
Mousteru
Plouagat
Lannilis
Le Folgoet
CHÂTEAU DE KERJEAN
St. Thégonnec
Plougonver
Bourbriac
Portsall
Porspoder
Ploudalmézeau
Plabennec
Landivisiau
Pleyber-Christ
Lannéanou
Kérien
Quintin
St.
Lanildut
St. Renan
Guipavas
Landerneau
Ploudiry
St. Sauveur
Mts. d'Arrée
Callac
St. Nicolas-du-Pélem
Corlay
Plouarzel
BREST
Sizun
Huelgoat
Poullaouen
Maël-Carhaix
Plounévez-Quintin
Le Conquet
Plougastel-Daoulas
Daoulas
B
Armorique
Brasparts
Carhaix-Plouguer
Rostrenen
Gouarec
Mur-de-Bretagne
Pte. de St. Mathieu
Camaret-sur-Mer
TOUR VAUBAN
Landévennec
Le Faou
Pont-de-Buis-lès-Quimerch
Playben
Glomel
Cléguérec
Pte. de Penhir
Crozon
Châteaulin
Châteauneuf-du-Faou
Spézet
Mts. Noires
Plouray
Morgat
Mer d'Iroise
Baie de Douarnenez
St. RONAN
Briec
Gourin
Roudouallec
Guéméné-sur-Scorff
Pontivy
Douarnenez
Locronan
Coray
Guiscriff
Le Faouët
Pluméliau
Plogoff
Pte. du Raz
Pont-Croix
Plouhinec
Llandudec
Quimper
Coray
Scaër
Kernascléden
Bubry
Audierne
Plozévet
Plogastel St. Germain
Rosporden
Bannalec
Plouay
Languidic
Camors
Plonéour-Lanvern
Fouesnant
CHÂTEAU DE KÉRIOLET
Concarneau
Arzano
Quimperlé
Baud
Locm
Pont-l'Abbé
Bénodet
Tréguic
Pont-Aven
Moëlan-sur-Mer
Pont Scorff
Hennebont
Pluvigner
St. Guénolé
Penmarch
Loctudy
Névez
Riec-sur-Bélon
Landévant
Pte. de Penmarch
Lesconil
Port Manech
Clohars-Carnoët
Ploemeur
Lanester
Lorient
Ste. Anne d'Auray
Guilvinec
Le Pouldu
Auray
Îles de Glénan
Larmor-Plage
Port Louis
Belz
Groix
Île de Groix
Côte Sauvage
Carnac
Locma
La Trinité
Presqu'île de Quiberon
St. Pierre-Quiberon
Port-Navalo
Quiberon
Quiberon
St. Gildas-de-Rhuys
Baie de St. Pierre-Quiberon
Baie de Quiberon
Île de Ho
Sauzon
Le Palais
Bangor
Locmaria
Belle-Île

A

B

0   10   20   30 km

47°
48°

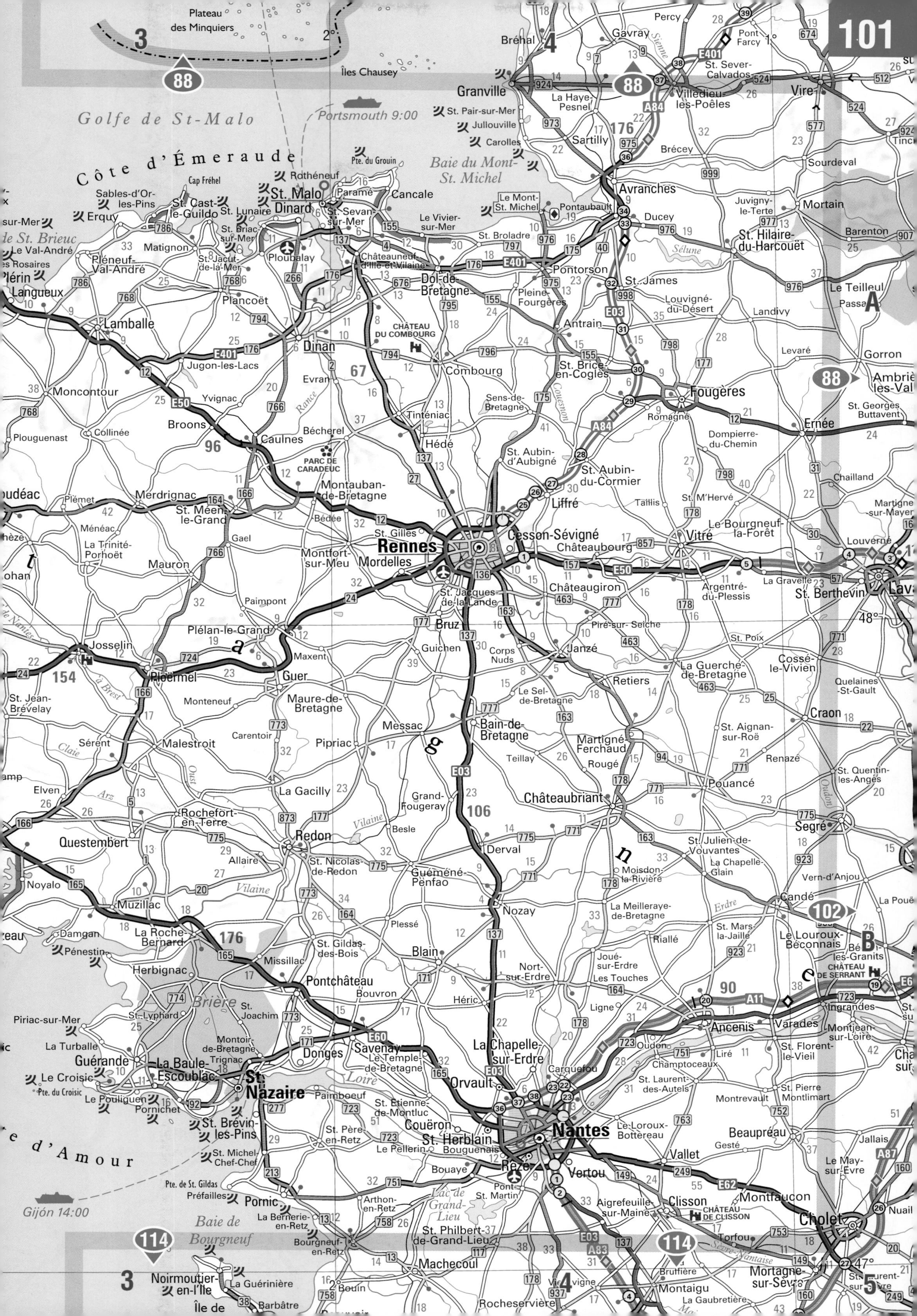
Plateau des Minquiers
Îles Chausey
Golfe de St-Malo
Portsmouth 9:00
Côte d'Émeraude
Cap Fréhel
Pte. du Grouin
Baie du Mont-St. Michel
Bréhal
Gavray
Percy
Pont Farcy
Granville
St. Pair-sur-Mer
Jullouville
Carolles
La Haye-Pesnel
Villedieu-les-Poêles
St. Sever-Calvados
Vire
Sartilly
Brécey
Sourdeval
Avranches
Juvigny-le-Tertre
Mortain
Ducey
Barenton
St. Hilaire-du-Harcouët
Sélune
Le Teilleul
Passais
Le Mont-St. Michel
Pontaubault
Rothéneuf
St. Malo
Paramé
Cancale
Dinard
St. Lunaire
St. Servan-sur-Mer
Le Vivier-sur-Mer
St. Broladre
Pontorson
Sables-d'Or-les-Pins
St. Cast-le-Guildo
Erquy
St. Briac-sur-Mer
Matignon
Ploubalay
St. Jacut-de-la-Mer
Pléneuf-Val-André
Le Val-André
Les Rosaires
Plérin
Langueux
Châteauneuf-d'Ille-et-Vilaine
Dol-de-Bretagne
Pleine-Fougères
St. James
Louvigné-du-Désert
Landivy
Plancoët
Lamballe
Dinan
CHÂTEAU DU COMBOURG
Antrain
Levaré
Gorron
Jugon-les-Lacs
Evran
Combourg
St. Brice-en-Coglès
Fougères
Ambrières-les-Vallées
Moncontour
Yvignac
Rance
Sens-de-Bretagne
Romagné
Couesnon
St. Georges-Buttavent
Broons
Tinténiac
Ernée
Plouguenast
Collinée
Caulnes
Bécherel
Hédé
Dompierre-du-Chemin
PARC DE CARADEUC
St. Aubin-d'Aubigné
St. Aubin-du-Cormier
Chailland
Loudéac
Merdrignac
Montauban-de-Bretagne
Liffré
Taillis
St. M'Hervé
Martigné-sur-Mayenne
Plémet
St. Méen-le-Grand
Ménéac
Bédée
St. Gilles
Rennes
Cesson-Sévigné
Châteaubourg
Vitré
Le Bourgneuf-la-Forêt
Louverné
La Trinité-Porhoët
Gael
Montfort-sur-Meu
Mordelles
Rohan
Mauron
Châteaugiron
Argentré-du-Plessis
La Gravelle
St. Berthevin
Laval
St. Jacques-de-la-Lande
Paimpont
Bruz
Piré-sur-Seiche
Josselin
Plélan-le-Grand
Maxent
Guichen
Corps Nuds
Janzé
St. Poix
Cossé-le-Vivien
Ploërmel
Guer
Retiers
La Guerche-de-Bretagne
Quelaines-St-Gault
St. Jean-Brévelay
Monteneuf
Maure-de-Bretagne
Le Sel-de-Bretagne
Craon
Messac
Bain-de-Bretagne
St. Aignan-sur-Roë
Sérent
Malestroit
Carentoir
Pipriac
Claie
Oust
Martigné-Ferchaud
Teillay
Rougé
Renazé
St. Quentin-les-Anges
Elven
Arz
La Gacilly
Grand-Fougeray
Châteaubriant
Pouancé
Oudon
Rochefort-en-Terre
Vilaine
Besle
Segré
Questembert
Redon
Derval
St. Julien-de-Vouvantes
Allaire
St. Nicolas-de-Redon
Guémené-Penfao
Moisdon-la-Rivière
La Chapelle-Glain
Vern-d'Anjou
Noyalo
Muzillac
Nozay
La Meilleraye-de-Bretagne
Candé
Erdre
La Pouëze
Damgan
La Roche-Bernard
Plessé
St. Gildas-des-Bois
St. Mars-la-Jaille
Riaillé
Le Louroux-Béconnais
Bécon-les-Granits
Pénestin
Herbignac
Missillac
Blain
Joué-sur-Erdre
Nort-sur-Erdre
Les Touches
CHÂTEAU DE SERRANT
Pontchâteau
Bouvron
Héric
Ligné
Ingrandes
Brière
St. Lyphard
St. Joachim
Varades
Ancenis
Montjean-sur-Loire
Piriac-sur-Mer
La Turballe
Montoir-de-Bretagne
Trignac
Donges
Savenay
Le Temple-de-Bretagne
La Chapelle-sur-Erdre
Oudon
Liré
St. Florent-le-Vieil
Guérande
La Baule-Escoublac
Le Croisic
Pte. du Croisic
Le Pouliguen
Pornichet
St. Nazaire
Loire
Paimboeuf
St. Etienne-de-Montluc
Orvault
Carquefou
Champtoceaux
St. Laurent-des-Autels
St. Pierre Montlimart
Montrevault
St. Brévin-les-Pins
St. Père-en-Retz
Couëron
St. Herblain
Nantes
Le Loroux-Bottereau
Beaupréau
Jallais
Côte d'Amour
St. Michel-Chef-Chef
Le Pellerin
Bouguenais
Rezé
Vertou
Vallet
Gesté
Bouaye
Le May-sur-Èvre
Pte. de St. Gildas
Préfailles
Pornic
Arthon-en-Retz
Lac de Grand-Lieu
Pont St. Martin
Aigrefeuille-sur-Maine
Clisson
CHÂTEAU DE CLISSON
Montfaucon
Cholet
Nuaillé
Gijón 14:00
Baie de Bourgneuf
La Bernerie-en-Retz
Bourgneuf-en-Retz
St. Philbert-de-Grand-Lieu
Torfou
Sèvre-Nantaise
Machecoul
Noirmoutier-en-l'Île
La Guérinière
Barbâtre
Île de
Bouin
Rocheservière
Vieillevigne
Montaigu
Boufféré
La Gaubretière
Mortagne-sur-Sèvre
St. Laurent-sur-Sèvre
88
102
114
90
96
106
154
176
67
48°
47°
2°
1°

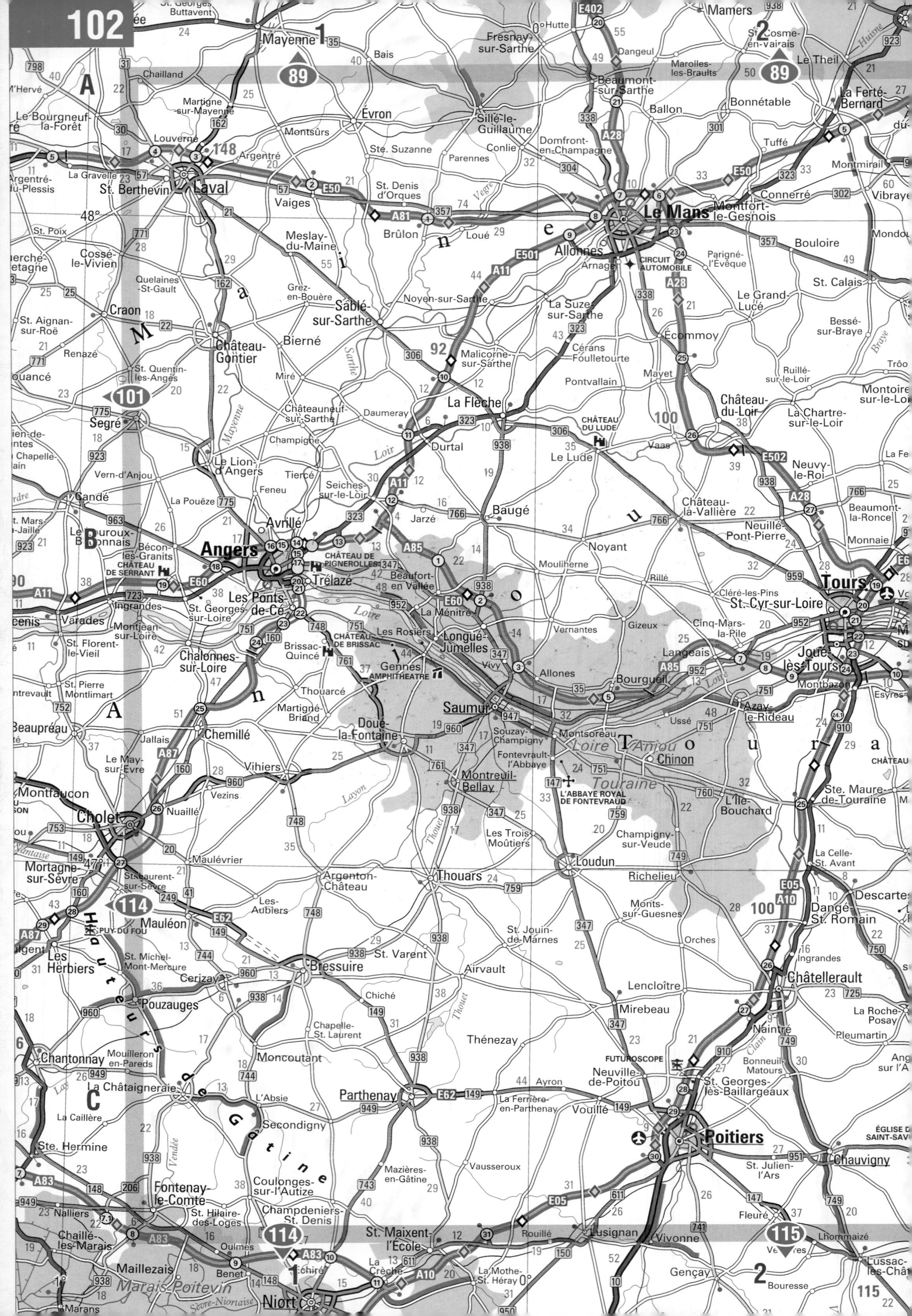

St. Georges-Buttavent
Mayenne
Bais
Fresnay-sur-Sarthe
Hutte
Mamers
Dangeul
St. Cosme-en-Vairais
Le Theil
89
Chailland
Marolles-les-Braults
Beaumont-sur-Sarthe
La Ferté-Bernard
Martigné-sur-Mayenne
Évron
Sillé-le-Guillaume
Ballon
Bonnétable
Le Bourgneuf-la-Forêt
Montsûrs
Conlie
Domfront-en-Champagne
Tuffé
Louverné
Argentré
Ste. Suzanne
Parennes
Montmirail
La Gravelle
St. Berthevin
Laval
Argentré-du-Plessis
Vaiges
St. Denis d'Orques
Connerré
Vibraye
Le Mans
Montfort-le-Gesnois
Brûlon
Loué
St. Poix
Meslay-du-Maine
Allonnes
Bouloire
Cossé-le-Vivien
Arnage
CIRCUIT AUTOMOBILE
Parigné-l'Évêque
Quelaines-St-Gault
Grez-en-Bouère
Sablé-sur-Sarthe
Noyen-sur-Sarthe
St. Calais
La Suze-sur-Sarthe
Le Grand-Lucé
Craon
St. Aignan-sur-Roë
Château-Gontier
Bierné
Écommoy
Bessé-sur-Braye
Renazé
St. Quentin-les-Anges
Malicorne-sur-Sarthe
Cérans Foulletourte
Mayet
Pontvallain
Ruillé-sur-le-Loir
Trôo
Miré
Montoire-sur-le-Loir
101
Segré
Châteauneuf-sur-Sarthe
Daumeray
La Flèche
Château-du-Loir
La Chartre-sur-le-Loir
CHÂTEAU DU LUDE
Champigné
Durtal
Le Lude
Vaas
Le Lion-d'Angers
Tiercé
Neuvy-le-Roi
Vern-d'Anjou
Seiches-sur-le-Loir
Feneu
Candé
La Pouëze
Baugé
Jarzé
Château-la-Vallière
Beaumont-la-Ronce
Neuillé-Pont-Pierre
Avrillé
Monnaie
Le Louroux-Béconnais
Bécon-les-Granits
Noyant
CHÂTEAU DE SERRANT
Angers
CHÂTEAU DE PIGNEROLLES
Mouliherne
Trélazé
Beaufort-en-Vallée
Rillé
Tours
Cléré-les-Pins
St. Cyr-sur-Loire
Ingrandes
St. Georges-sur-Loire
Les Ponts-de-Cé
La Ménitrée
Varades
Montjean-sur-Loire
Vernantes
Gizeux
Cinq-Mars-la-Pile
Les Rosiers
CHÂTEAU DE BRISSAC
Longué-Jumelles
St. Florent-le-Vieil
Brissac-Quincé
Langeais
Joué-lès-Tours
Chalonnes-sur-Loire
Gennes
AMPHITHÉATRE
Vivy
Allonnes
Bourgueil
Montbazon
St. Pierre Montlimart
Thouarcé
Saumur
Azay-le-Rideau
Beaupréau
Martigné-Briand
Doué-la-Fontaine
Souzay-Champigny
Montsoreau
Ussé
Chemillé
Jallais
Fontevrault-l'Abbaye
Loire Anjou Touraine
Chinon
Le May-sur-Èvre
Vihiers
Montreuil-Bellay
L'ABBAYE ROYAL DE FONTEVRAUD
Ste. Maure-de-Touraine
Montfaucon
Vezins
L'Île-Bouchard
Cholet
Nuaillé
Les Trois Moûtiers
Champigny-sur-Veude
Mortagne-sur-Sèvre
Maulévrier
Loudun
Richelieu
La Celle-St. Avant
Argenton-Château
Thouars
Descartes
St. Laurent-sur-Sèvre
114
Les Aubiers
Monts-sur-Guesnes
Dangé-St. Romain
Mauléon
PUY DU FOU
St. Jouin-de-Marnes
Les Herbiers
St. Michel-Mont-Mercure
St. Varent
Orches
Ingrandes
Bressuire
Cerizay
Airvault
Châtellerault
Pouzauges
Lencloître
Chiché
Mirebeau
La Roche-Posay
Chapelle-St. Laurent
Naintré
Thénezay
Pleumartin
Chantonnay
Mouilleron en-Pareds
Moncoutant
FUTUROSCOPE
Bonneuil-Matours
La Châtaigneraie
Neuville-de-Poitou
Ayron
St. Georges-lès-Baillargeaux
L'Absie
Parthenay
La Ferrière-en-Parthenay
Vouillé
La Caillère
Secondigny
Poitiers
Ste. Hermine
Hauteurs de Gâtine
St. Julien-l'Ars
Chauvigny
Vausseroux
Mazières-en-Gâtine
Fontenay-le-Comte
Coulonges-sur-l'Autize
Nalliers
St. Hilaire-des-Loges
Champdeniers-St. Denis
Fleuré
Chaillé-les-Marais
St. Maixent-l'École
Rouillé
Lusignan
Vivonne
115
Lhommaizé
Oulmes
Maillezais
Benet
La Crèche
La Mothe-St. Héray
Gençay
Lussac-les-Châteaux
Marais Poitevin
Sèvre-Niortaise
Niort
Bouresse
Marans

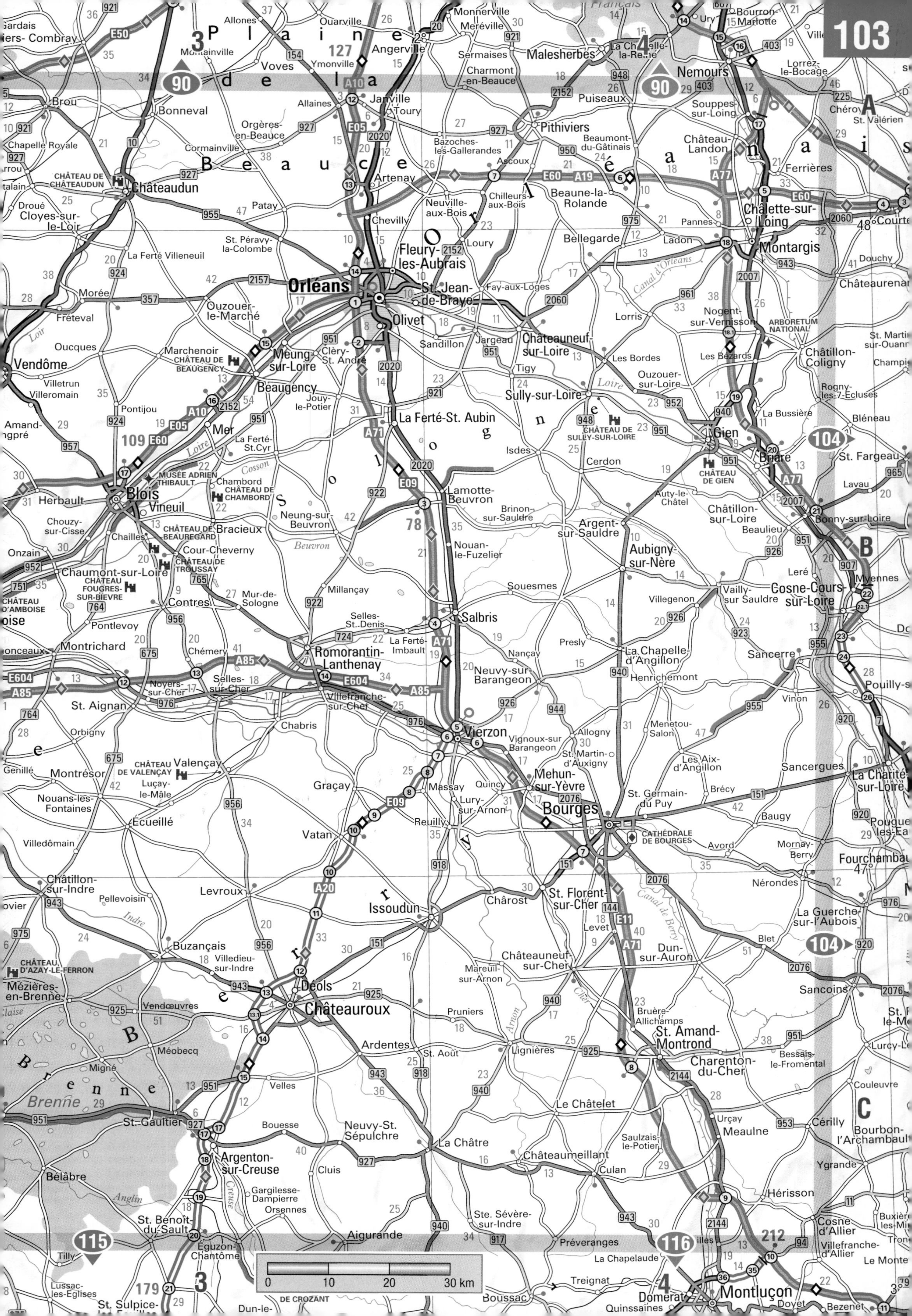
103
Plaine de la Beauce
Orléanais
Sologne
Berry
Brenne
Châteaudun
CHÂTEAU DE CHÂTEAUDUN
Brou
Bonneval
Cloyes-sur-le-Loir
Voves
Angerville
Janville
Toury
Artenay
Patay
Malesherbes
Pithiviers
Puiseaux
Nemours
Souppes-sur-Loing
Château-Landon
Ferrières
Châlette-sur-Loing
Montargis
Beaune-la-Rolande
Bellegarde
Orléans
Fleury-les-Aubrais
St. Jean-de-Braye
Olivet
Meung-sur-Loire
Beaugency
CHÂTEAU DE BEAUGENCY
Châteauneuf-sur-Loire
Jargeau
Sully-sur-Loire
CHÂTEAU DE SULLY-SUR-LOIRE
Lorris
Gien
CHÂTEAU DE GIEN
Briare
Châtillon-Coligny
ARBORETUM NATIONAL
Vendôme
Fréteval
Morée
Ouzouer-le-Marché
Mer
Blois
Vineuil
MUSÉE ADRIEN THIBAULT
Chambord
CHÂTEAU DE CHAMBORD
CHÂTEAU DE BEAUREGARD
Cour-Cheverny
CHÂTEAU DE TROUSSAY
Chaumont-sur-Loire
CHÂTEAU FOUGRES-SUR-BIEVRE
CHÂTEAU D'AMBOISE
Contres
Montrichard
St. Aignan
Selles-sur-Cher
Romorantin-Lanthenay
La Ferté-St. Aubin
Lamotte-Beuvron
Nouan-le-Fuzelier
Salbris
Argent-sur-Sauldre
Aubigny-sur-Nère
Cosne-Cours-sur-Loire
Sancerre
La Chapelle-d'Angillon
Henrichemont
Vierzon
Mehun-sur-Yèvre
Bourges
CATHÉDRALE DE BOURGES
La Charité-sur-Loire
CHÂTEAU DE VALENÇAY
Valençay
Montrésor
Écueillé
Graçay
Vatan
Issoudun
Levroux
Châtillon-sur-Indre
Buzançais
Châteauroux
Déols
CHÂTEAU D'AZAY-LE-FERRON
Mézières-en-Brenne
St. Florent-sur-Cher
Châteauneuf-sur-Cher
Dun-sur-Auron
St. Amand-Montrond
Sancoins
Lignières
La Châtre
Châteaumeillant
Le Châtelet
Argenton-sur-Creuse
St. Gaultier
St. Benoît-du-Sault
Éguzon-Chantôme
Aigurande
Montluçon
Domérat
Cérilly
Bourbon-l'Archambault
Cosne d'Allier
0 10 20 30 km
90
104
115
116
109

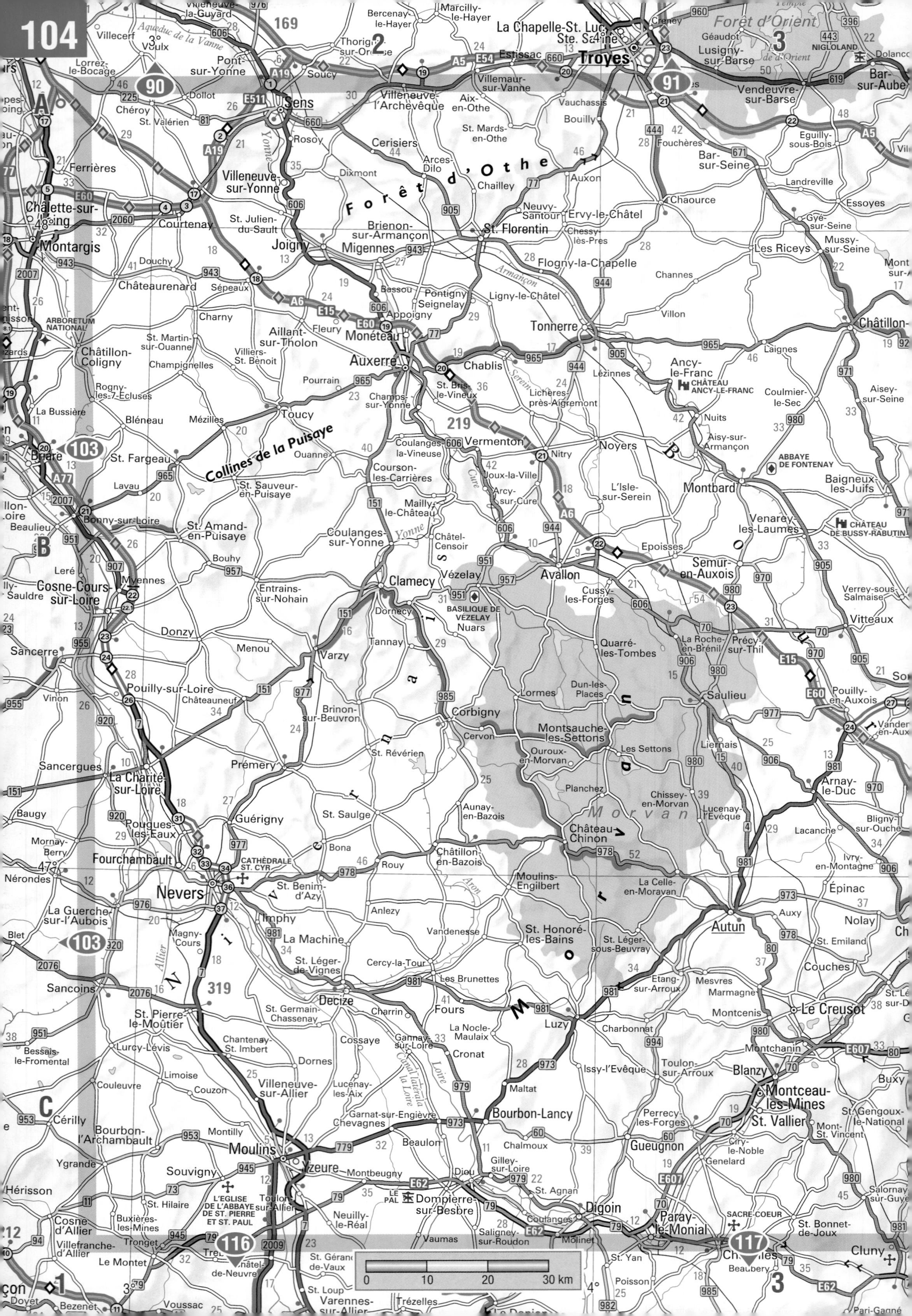

Troyes
La Chapelle-St. Luc
Ste. Savine
Forêt d'Orient
Géraudot
Lusigny-sur-Barse
Vendeuvre-sur-Barse
Bar-sur-Aube
Dolancourt
Nigloland
Estissac
Villemaur-sur-Vanne
Aix-en-Othe
Villeneuve-l'Archevêque
Bercenay-le-Hayer
Marcilly-le-Hayer
Thorigny-sur-Oreuse
Pont-sur-Yonne
Villeneuve-la-Guyard
Villecerf
Voulx
Lorrez-le-Bocage
Aqueduc de la Vanne
Soucy
Sens
Dollot
Chéroy
St. Valérien
Rosoy
Cerisiers
Arces-Dilo
Dixmont
St. Mards-en-Othe
Vauchassis
Bouilly
Fouchères
Bar-sur-Seine
Eguilly-sous-Bois
Landreville
Essoyes
Chaource
Gyé-sur-Seine
Mussy-sur-Seine
Les Riceys
Channes
Villon
Châtillon-sur-Seine
Laignes
Forêt d'Othe
Chailley
Auxon
Neuvy-Sautour
Ervy-le-Châtel
Chessy-les-Prés
St. Florentin
Flogny-la-Chapelle
Armançon
Brienon-sur-Armançon
Migennes
Joigny
St. Julien-du-Sault
Villeneuve-sur-Yonne
Courtenay
Ferrières
Châlette-sur-Loing
Montargis
Douchy
Châteaurenard
Sépeaux
Charny
Arboretum National
Châtillon-Coligny
St. Martin-sur-Ouanne
Champignelles
Villiers-St. Benoît
Aillant-sur-Tholon
Fleury
Bassou
Pontigny
Seignelay
Appoigny
Moneteau
Ligny-le-Châtel
Tonnerre
Auxerre
Chablis
St. Bris-le-Vineux
Champs-sur-Yonne
Pourrain
Toucy
Mézilles
Bléneau
Rogny-les-7-Écluses
La Bussière
Briare
St. Fargeau
Collines de la Puisaye
Ouanne
Lavau
St. Sauveur-en-Puisaye
Bonny-sur-Loire
Beaulieu
St. Amand-en-Puisaye
Bouhy
Léré
Cosne-Cours-sur-Loire
Myennes
Entrains-sur-Nohain
Donzy
Menou
Sancerre
Pouilly-sur-Loire
Châteauneuf
Vinon
Sancergues
La Charité-sur-Loire
Baugy
Rougues-les-Eaux
Guérigny
Prémery
Mornay-Berry
Fourchambault
Nérondes
Nevers
Cathédrale St. Cyr
La Guerche-sur-l'Aubois
Blet
Magny-Cours
Imphy
La Machine
Sancoins
St. Pierre-le-Moûtier
Allier
Lézinnes
Ancy-le-Franc
Château Ancy-le-Franc
Lichères-près-Aigremont
Serein
Nuits
Aisy-sur-Armançon
Coulmier-le-Sec
Aisey-sur-Seine
Abbaye de Fontenay
Montbard
Baigneux-les-Juifs
Vermenton
Coulanges-la-Vineuse
Courson-les-Carrières
Nitry
Noyers
Joux-la-Ville
Arcy-sur-Cure
Cure
L'Isle-sur-Serein
Mailly-le-Château
Coulanges-sur-Yonne
Yonne
Châtel-Censoir
Vézelay
Basilique de Vézelay
Avallon
Epoisses
Venarey-les-Laumes
Château de Bussy-Rabutin
Semur-en-Auxois
Verrey-sous-Salmaise
Vitteaux
Cussy-les-Forges
Clamecy
Dornecy
Nuars
Tannay
Varzy
Quarré-les-Tombes
La Roche-en-Brénil
Précy-sous-Thil
Saulieu
Pouilly-en-Auxois
Vandenesse-en-Auxois
Dun-les-Places
Lormes
Corbigny
Brinon-sur-Beuvron
Cervon
Montsauche-les-Settons
Ouroux-en-Morvan
Les Settons
Liernais
Arnay-le-Duc
St. Révérien
Planchez
Chissey-en-Morvan
Lucenay-l'Évêque
Morvan
Aunay-en-Bazois
St. Saulge
Bona
Châtillon-en-Bazois
Château-Chinon
Bligny-sur-Ouche
Lacanche
Ivry-en-Montagne
Rouy
St. Benin-d'Azy
Moulins-Engilbert
Aron
La Celle-en-Morvan
Épinac
Anlezy
Vandenesse
St. Honoré-les-Bains
St. Léger-sous-Beuvray
Autun
Auxy
Nolay
St. Emiland
Couches
St. Léger-des-Vignes
Cercy-la-Tour
Les Brunettes
Etang-sur-Arroux
Mesvres
Marmagne
Le Creusot
Montcenis
Decize
St. Germain-Chassenay
Charrin
Fours
La Nocle-Maulaix
Luzy
Charbonnat
Montchanin
Chantenay-St. Imbert
Lurcy-Lévis
Bessais-le-Fromental
Cossaye
Gannay-sur-Loire
Cronat
Dornes
Limoise
Couzon
Couleuvre
Villeneuve-sur-Allier
Lucenay-les-Aix
Canal latéral à la Loire
Loire
Maltat
Issy-l'Évêque
Toulon-sur-Arroux
Blanzy
Montceau-les-Mines
St. Vallier
Buxy
Cérilly
Bourbon-l'Archambault
Montilly
Garnat-sur-Engièvre
Chevagnes
Bourbon-Lancy
Perrecy-les-Forges
Mont-St. Vincent
St. Gengoux-le-National
Moulins
Yzeure
Beaulon
Chalmoux
Gueugnon
Cirry-le-Noble
Genelard
Ygrande
Souvigny
Montbeugny
Diou
Gilley-sur-Loire
St. Agnan
Hérisson
L'Eglise de l'Abbaye de St. Pierre et St. Paul
St. Hilaire
Toulon-sur-Allier
Le Pal
Dompierre-sur-Besbre
Neuilly-le-Réal
Digoin
Paray-le-Monial
Sacré-Coeur
Salornay-sur-Guye
Cosne-d'Allier
Buxières-les-Mines
Tronget
Villefranche-d'Allier
Vaumas
Saligny-sur-Roudon
Coulanges
Molinet
St. Bonnet-de-Joux
Le Montet
Châtel-de-Neuvre
St. Gérand-de-Vaux
St. Yan
Charolles
Beaubery
Cluny
St. Loup
Varennes-sur-Allier
Trézelles
Poisson
Voussac
Bezenet
Doyet
Pari-Gagné
0 10 20 30 km

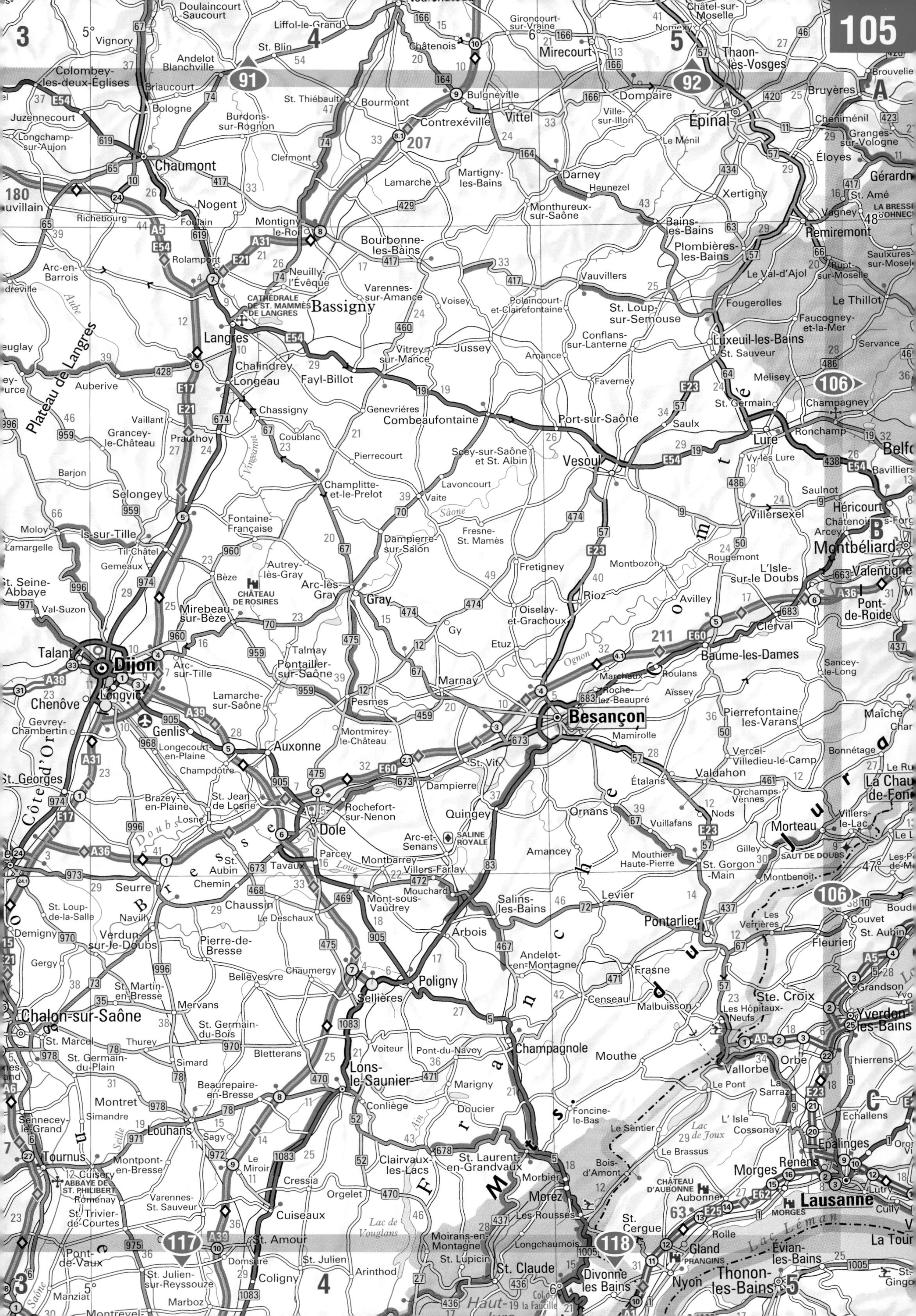

Doulaincourt-Saucourt
Vignory
Liffol-le-Grand
Gironcourt-sur-Vraine
Châtel-sur-Moselle
Nomexy
Thaon-les-Vosges
Mirecourt
Châtenois
Andelot Blanchville
St. Blin
Colombey-les-deux-Églises
Briaucourt
Bologne
St. Thiébault
Bourmont
Bulgnéville
Vittel
Contrexéville
Dompaire
Ville-sur-Illon
Épinal
Bruyères
Chenimeniл
Granges-sur-Vologne
Éloyes
Gérardmer
Juzennecourt
Longchamp-sur-Aujon
Burdons-sur-Rognon
Clefmont
Chaumont
Lamarche
Martigny-les-Bains
Darney
Le Ménil
Heunezel
Xertigny
St. Amé
Vagney
Remiremont
Nogent
Foulain
Richebourg
Montigny-le-Roi
Bourbonne-les-Bains
Monthureux-sur-Saône
Bains-les-Bains
Plombières-les-Bains
Saulxures-sur-Moselotte
Rupt-sur-Moselle
Le Val-d'Ajol
Rolampont
Arc-en-Barrois
Neuilly-l'Évêque
Varennes-sur-Amance
Vauvillers
Le Thillot
Fougerolles
Aube
Cathédrale de St. Mammès de Langres
Bassigny
Voisey
Polaincourt-et-Clairefontaine
St. Loup-sur-Semouse
Faucogney-et-la-Mer
Plateau de Langres
Langres
Conflans-sur-Lanterne
Luxeuil-les-Bains
St. Sauveur
Servance
Auberive
Chalindrey
Longeau
Fayl-Billot
Vitrey-sur-Mance
Jussey
Amance
Faverney
Melisey
Champagney
Chassigny
Genevriéres
Combeaufontaine
Port-sur-Saône
St. Germain
Ronchamp
Belfort
Vaillant
Grancey-le-Château
Prauthoy
Coublanc
Vingeanne
Saulx
Lure
Barjon
Pierrecourt
Scey-sur-Saône et St. Albin
Vesoul
Vy-lès-Lure
Bavilliers
Selongey
Champlitte-et-le-Prelot
Lavoncourt
Vaite
Saône
Saulnot
Héricourt
Villersexel
Moloy
Is-sur-Tille
Fontaine-Française
Fresne-St. Mamès
Dampierre-sur-Salon
Montbéliard
Lamargelle
Til-Châtel
Gemeaux
Bèze
Autrey-lès-Gray
Fretigney
Montbozon
Rougemont
L'Isle-sur-le-Doubs
Valentigney
St. Seine-l'Abbaye
Château de Rosires
Arc-lès-Gray
Gray
Rioz
Avilley
Pont-de-Roide
Val-Suzon
Mirebeau-sur-Bèze
Oiselay-et-Grachoux
Gy
Clerval
Talant
Dijon
Arc-sur-Tille
Talmay
Pontailler-sur-Saône
Etuz
Ognon
Baume-les-Dames
Sancey-le-Long
Chenôve
Longvic
Marnay
Marchaux
Roulans
Aïssey
Gevrey-Chambertin
Lamarche-sur-Saône
Pesmes
Roche-lez-Beaupré
Besançon
Maîche
Genlis
Longecourt-en-Plaine
Auxonne
Montmirey-le-Château
Mamirolle
Pierrefontaine-les-Varans
Champdôtre
St. Vit
Vercel-Villedieu-le-Camp
Bonnétage
St. Georges
Côte d'Or
Brazey-en-Plaine
St. Jean de Losne
Losne
Dampierre
Étalans
Valdahon
Orchamps-Vennes
La Chaux-de-Fonds
Rochefort-sur-Nenon
Dole
Quingey
Ornans
Nods
Morteau
Villers-le-Lac
Doubs
Bresse
Arc-et-Senans
Saline Royale
Vuillafans
Gilley
Saut de Doubs
St. Aubin
Tavaux
Parcey
Loue
Montbarrey
Villers-Farlay
Amancey
Mouthier-Haute-Pierre
St. Gorgon-Main
Montbenoît
Seurre
Chemin
Mouchard
Salins-les-Bains
Levier
St. Loup-de-la-Salle
Navilly
Chaussin
Mont-sous-Vaudrey
Le Deschaux
Pontarlier
Les Verrières
Couvet
Fleurier
Demigny
Verdun-sur-le-Doubs
Pierre-de-Bresse
Arbois
Andelot-en-Montagne
Frasne
St. Aubin
Gergy
Chaumergy
Bellevesvre
Poligny
Grandson
St. Martin-en-Bresse
Sellières
Censeau
Malbuisson
Ste. Croix
Yverdon-les-Bains
Chalon-sur-Saône
Mervans
Les Hôpitaux-Neufs
St. Marcel
St. Germain-du-Bois
Thurey
Bletterans
Champagnole
Mouthe
Orbe
St. Germain-du-Plain
Simard
Voiteur
Pont-du-Navoy
Lons-le-Saunier
Vallorbe
Thierrens
Montret
Beaurepaire-en-Bresse
Marigny
Le Pont
La Sarraz
Sennecey-le-Grand
Simandre
Conliège
Doucier
Foncine-le-Bas
L' Isle
Cossonay
Echallens
Louhans
Sagy
Seille
Ain
Le Sentier
Lac de Joux
Epalinges
Tournus
Montpont-en-Bresse
Le Miroir
Le Brassus
Cuisery
Abbaye de St. Philibert
Romenay
Clairvaux-les-Lacs
St. Laurent-en-Grandvaux
Bois-d'Amont
Morges
Renens
Cressia
Morbier
Château d'Aubonne
Aubonne
Lausanne
Varennes-St. Sauveur
Orgelet
Morez
Morges
Lutry
Cully
St. Trivier-de-Courtes
Cuiseaux
Lac de Vouglans
Les Rousses
St. Cergue
Rolle
Lac Léman
Pont-de-Vaux
St. Amour
Moirans-en-Montagne
Longchaumois
Gland
Prangins
Évian-les-Bains
La Tour
Domsure
St. Julien
St. Lupicin
Divonne les Bains
Nyon
Thonon-les-Bains
St. Julien-sur-Reyssouze
Coligny
Arinthod
St. Claude
Col de la Faucille
Manziat
Marboz
Montrevel
Haut-Jura
Monts Jura
Franche-Comté

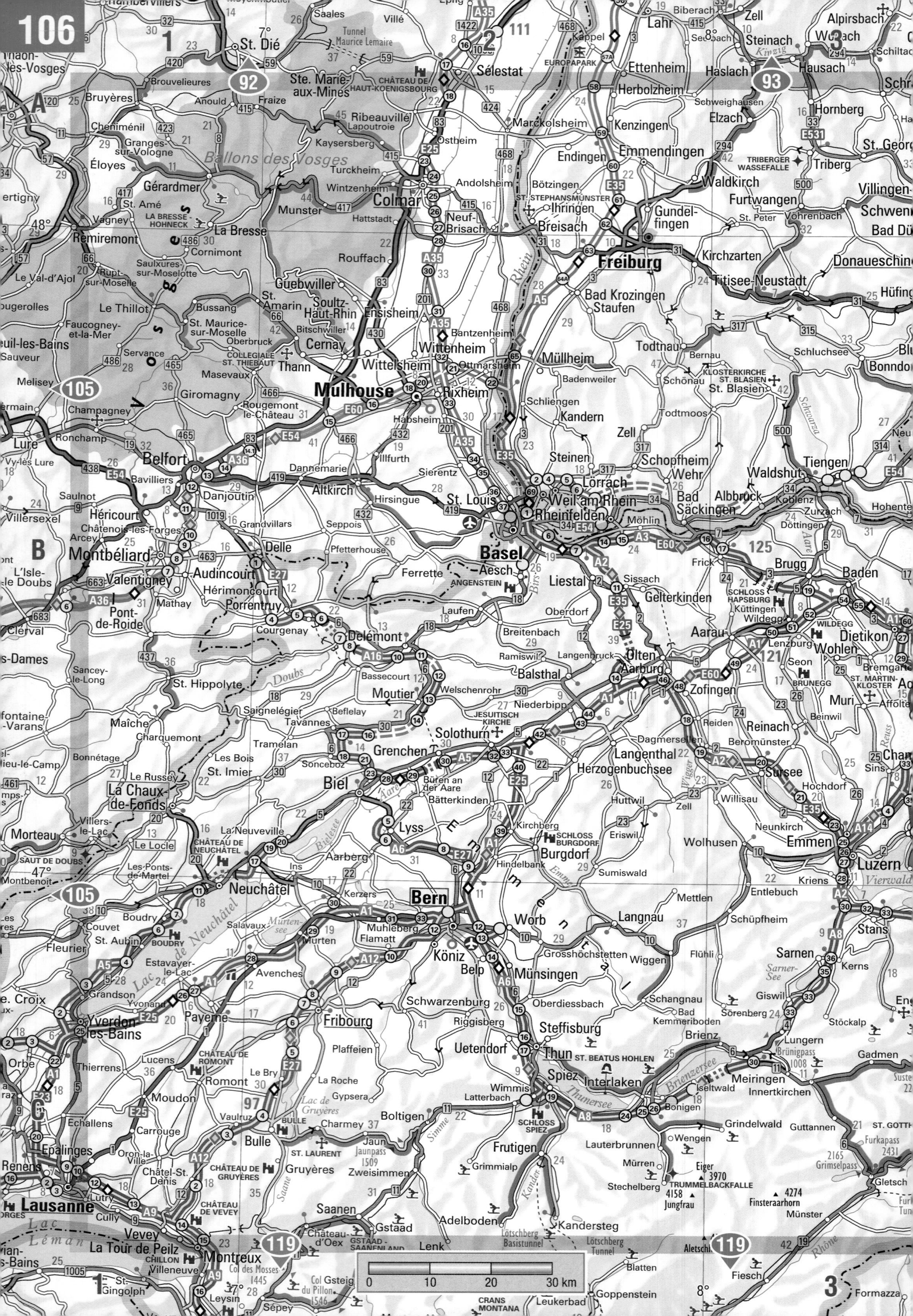
St. Dié
Saales
Villé
Tunnel Maurice Lemaire
Sélestat
Lahr
Biberach
Zell
Alpirsbach
Kappel
Europapark
Steinach
Wolfach
Schiltach
Thaon-les-Vosges
Brouvelieures
Ste. Marie-aux-Mines
Château de Haut-Koenigsbourg
Ettenheim
Haslach
Hausach
Bruyères
Anould
Fraize
Ribeauvillé
Lapoutroie
Herbolzheim
Schweighausen
Hornberg
Cheniménil
Granges-sur-Vologne
Kaysersberg
Ostheim
Marckolsheim
Kenzingen
Elzach
Éloyes
Ballons des Vosges
Turckheim
Endingen
Emmendingen
Triberger Wassefälle
Triberg
St. Georgen
Gérardmer
Wintzenheim
Andolsheim
Bötzingen
Waldkirch
Villingen-
St. Amé
Colmar
St. Stephansmünster
Ihringen
Gundelfingen
Furtwangen
Vagney
La Bresse-Hohneck
Munster
Hattstadt
Neuf-Brisach
Breisach
St. Peter
Vöhrenbach
Schwen
Remiremont
La Bresse
Cornimont
Bad Dü
Rouffach
Freiburg
Kirchzarten
Donaueschin
Le Val-d'Ajol
Rupt-sur-Moselle
Saulxures-sur-Moselotte
Guebwiller
Titisee-Neustadt
Hüfing
Plombières
Le Thillot
Bussang
St. Amarin
Soultz-Haut-Rhin
Ensisheim
Bad Krozingen
Staufen
Faucogney-et-la-Mer
St. Maurice-sur-Moselle
Bitschwiller
Bantzenheim
Todtnau
Luxeuil-les-Bains
Oberbruck
Cernay
Wittenheim
Bernau
Schluchsee
Sauveur
Servance
Collégiale St. Thiebaut
Thann
Wittelsheim
Ottmarsheim
Müllheim
Klosterkirche St. Blasien
Bonndo
Melisey
Masevaux
Badenweiler
Schönau
St. Blasien
Giromagny
Mulhouse
Rixheim
Schliengen
Champagney
Rougemont-le-Château
Habsheim
Kandern
Todtmoos
Lure
Ronchamp
Zell
Belfort
Illfurth
Steinen
Schopfheim
Tiengen
Vy-lès-Lure
Bavilliers
Dannemarie
Sierentz
Lörrach
Wehr
Waldshut
Danjoutin
Altkirch
St. Louis
Weil am Rhein
Bad Säckingen
Albbruck
Koblenz
Hohente
Saulnot
Héricourt
Hirsingue
Rheinfelden
Möhlin
Zurzach
Villersexel
Châtenois-les-Forges
Grandvillars
Seppois
Döttingen
Arcey
Montbéliard
Delle
Pfetterhouse
Basel
Frick
Brugg
Baden
L'Isle-sur-le Doubs
Valentigney
Audincourt
Hérimoncourt
Ferrette
Aesch
Angenstein
Liestal
Sissach
Schloss Habsburg
Küttingen
Wildegg
Gelterkinden
Pont-de-Roide
Mathay
Porrentruy
Courgenay
Laufen
Oberdorf
Clerval
Delémont
Breitenbach
Aarau
Dietikon
Lenzburg
Wohlen
Baume-les-Dames
Ramiswil
Langenbruck
Olten
Aarburg
Bremgarten
Sancey-le-Long
Bassecourt
Balsthal
Seon
Brunegg
St. Martin-Kloster
St. Hippolyte
Doubs
Welschenrohr
Zofingen
Moutier
Niederbipp
Muri
Affoltern
Saignelégier
Beflelay
Tavannes
Jesuitisch Kirche
Beinwil
Pierrefontaine-les-Varans
Maîche
Charquemont
Solothurn
Reiden
Reinach
Tramelan
Grenchen
Dagmersellen
Beromünster
Langenthal
Reuss
Bonnétage
Les Bois
Sonceboz
Herzogenbuchsee
Sursee
Sins
Cham
Orchamps
St. Imier
Le Russey
Büren an der Aare
Wigger
Hochdorf
La Chaux-de-Fonds
Biel
Bätterkinden
Huttwil
Zell
Willisau
Lyss
Kirchberg
Neunkirch
Morteau
Villers-le-Lac
Le Locle
La Neuveville
Schloss Burgdorf
Eriswil
Emmen
Wolhusen
Saut de Doubs
Château de Neuchâtel
Bielersee
Aarberg
Burgdorf
Hindelbank
Sumiswald
Emme
Les-Ponts-de-Martel
Luzern
Vierwald
Montbenoit
Ins
Kriens
Neuchâtel
Kerzers
Emmental
Entlebuch
Mettlen
Bern
Boudry
Langnau
Salavaux
Murtensee
Muhleberg
Flamatt
Worb
Schüpfheim
Stans
Couvet
St. Aubin
Murten
Lac de Neuchâtel
Fleurier
Estavayer-le-Lac
Köniz
Belp
Grosshöchstetten
Wiggen
Flühli
Sarnen
Kerns
Avenches
Münsingen
Sarnersee
Grandson
Yvonand
Payerne
Schwarzenburg
Oberdiessbach
Schangnau
Giswil
Ste. Croix
Yverdon-les-Bains
Fribourg
Riggisberg
Steffisburg
Bad Kemmeriboden
Sörenberg
Stöckalp
Lucens
Plaffeien
Brienz
Lungern
Orbe
Thierrens
Château de Romont
Uetendorf
Thun
St. Beatus Hohlen
Brünigpass
Gadmen
Romont
Le Bry
La Roche
Spiez
Interlaken
Brienzersee
Meiringen
Innertkirchen
Moudon
Gypsera
Wimmis
Iseltwald
Latterbach
Bönigen
Lac de Gruyères
Thunersee
Echallens
Vaulruz
Bulle
Boltigen
Schloss Spiez
Grindelwald
Guttannen
St. Gotthard
Carrouge
Charmey
Jaun
Jaunpass
Simme
Wengen
Furkapass
Epalinges
Oron-la-Ville
St. Laurent
Frutigen
Lauterbrunnen
Grimselpass
Renens
Château de Gruyères
Gruyères
Zweisimmen
Grimmialp
Mürren
Eiger
Trummelbackfalle
Gletsch
Châtel-St.-Denis
Saane
Kander
Stechelberg
Jungfrau
Finsteraarhorn
Lausanne
Lutry
Château de Vevey
Saanen
Adelboden
Kandersteg
Münster
Cully
Vevey
Gstaad
Lac Léman
La Tour de Peilz
Château-d'Oex
Gstaad Saanenland
Lenk
Lötschberg Basistunnel
Lötschberg Tunnel
Aletsch
Rhône
Évian-les-Bains
Chillon
Montreux
Villeneuve
Col des Mosses
Blatten
Fiesch
St.-Gingolph
Col Gsteig du Pillon
Leysin
Sépey
Crans Montana
Leukerbad
Goppenstein
Formazza
0
10
20
30 km

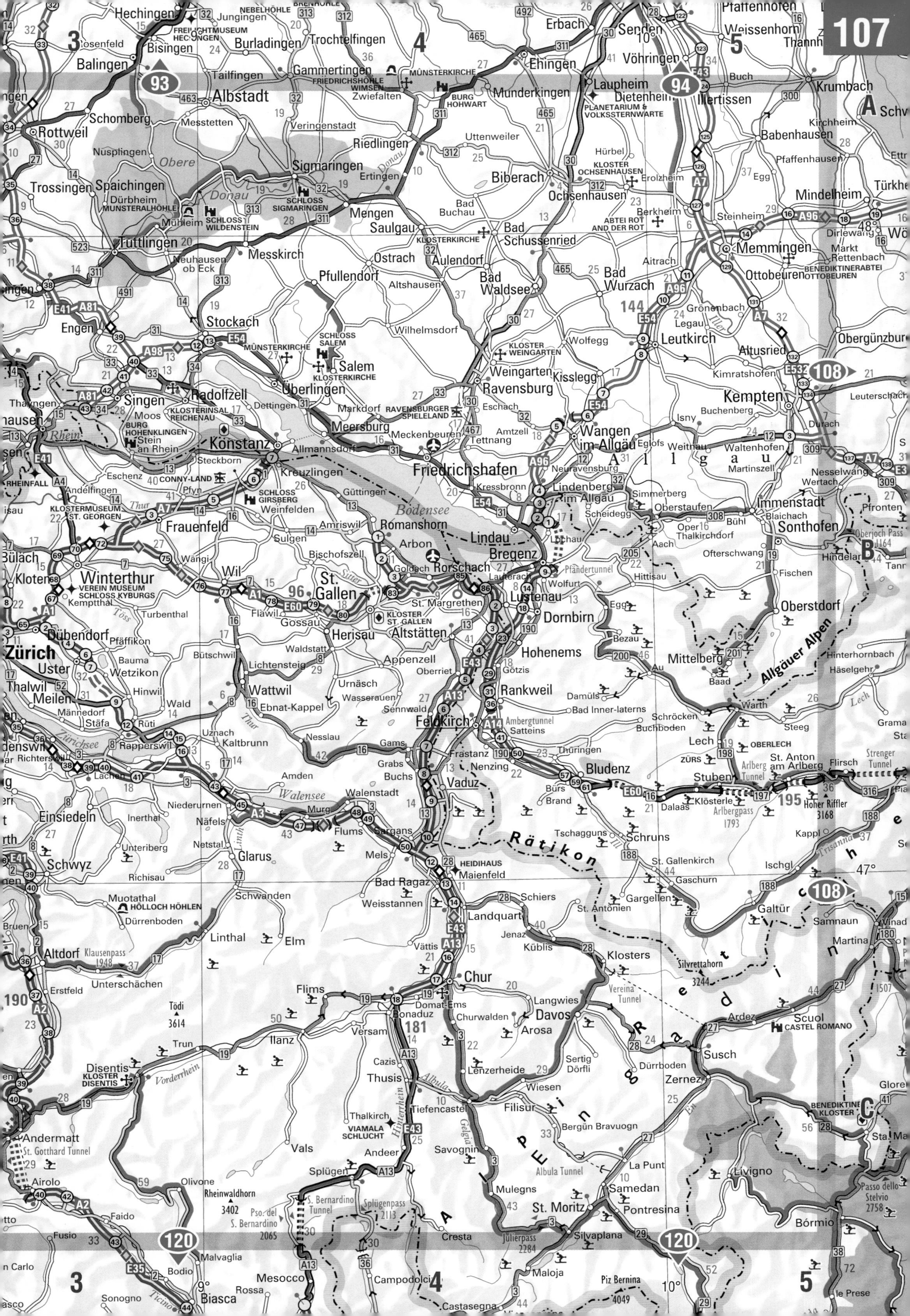

Hechingen
Bisingen
Balingen
Burladingen
Trochtelfingen
Gammertingen
Erbach
Senden
Weissenhorn
Vöhringen
Ehingen
Laupheim
Dietenheim
Illertissen
Krumbach
Albstadt
Tailfingen
Zwiefalten
Munderkingen
Rottweil
Schomberg
Messtetten
Veringenstadt
Riedlingen
Babenhausen
Uttenweiler
Trossingen
Spaichingen
Sigmaringen
Biberach
Ochsenhausen
Mindelheim
Donau
Mengen
Saulgau
Bad Schussenried
Memmingen
Tuttlingen
Messkirch
Ostrach
Aulendorf
Ottobeuren
Pfullendorf
Altshausen
Bad Waldsee
Bad Wurzach
Stockach
Engen
Salem
Wilhelmsdorf
Weingarten
Leutkirch
Altusried
Kisslegg
Ravensburg
Kempten
Singen
Radolfzell
Überlingen
Markdorf
Meersburg
Konstanz
Tettnang
Wangen im Allgäu
Isny
Friedrichshafen
Kreuzlingen
Allgäu
Frauenfeld
Weinfelden
Romanshorn
Bodensee
Lindau
Bregenz
Lindenberg im Allgäu
Oberstaufen
Immenstadt
Sonthofen
Winterthur
Wil
St. Gallen
Rorschach
Arbon
Lustenau
Dornbirn
Oberstdorf
Zürich
Uster
Dübendorf
Herisau
Altstätten
Appenzell
Hohenems
Mittelberg
Allgäuer Alpen
Wetzikon
Thalwil
Meilen
Lichtensteig
Wattwil
Rankweil
Feldkirch
Rapperswil
Kaltbrunn
Vaduz
Bludenz
Lech
St. Anton am Arlberg
Einsiedeln
Walensee
Glarus
Sargans
Schruns
Rätikon
Schwyz
Bad Ragaz
Maienfeld
Landquart
Klosters
Galtür
Altdorf
Linthal
Elm
Chur
Davos
Arosa
Scuol
Flims
Ilanz
Thusis
Lenzerheide
Susch
Zernez
Disentis
Andermatt
Tiefencastel
Bergün Bravuogn
Airolo
Splügen
Samedan
Pontresina
St. Moritz
Livigno
Silvaplana
Bormio
Maloja
Biasca
Mesocco
Piz Bernina
4049

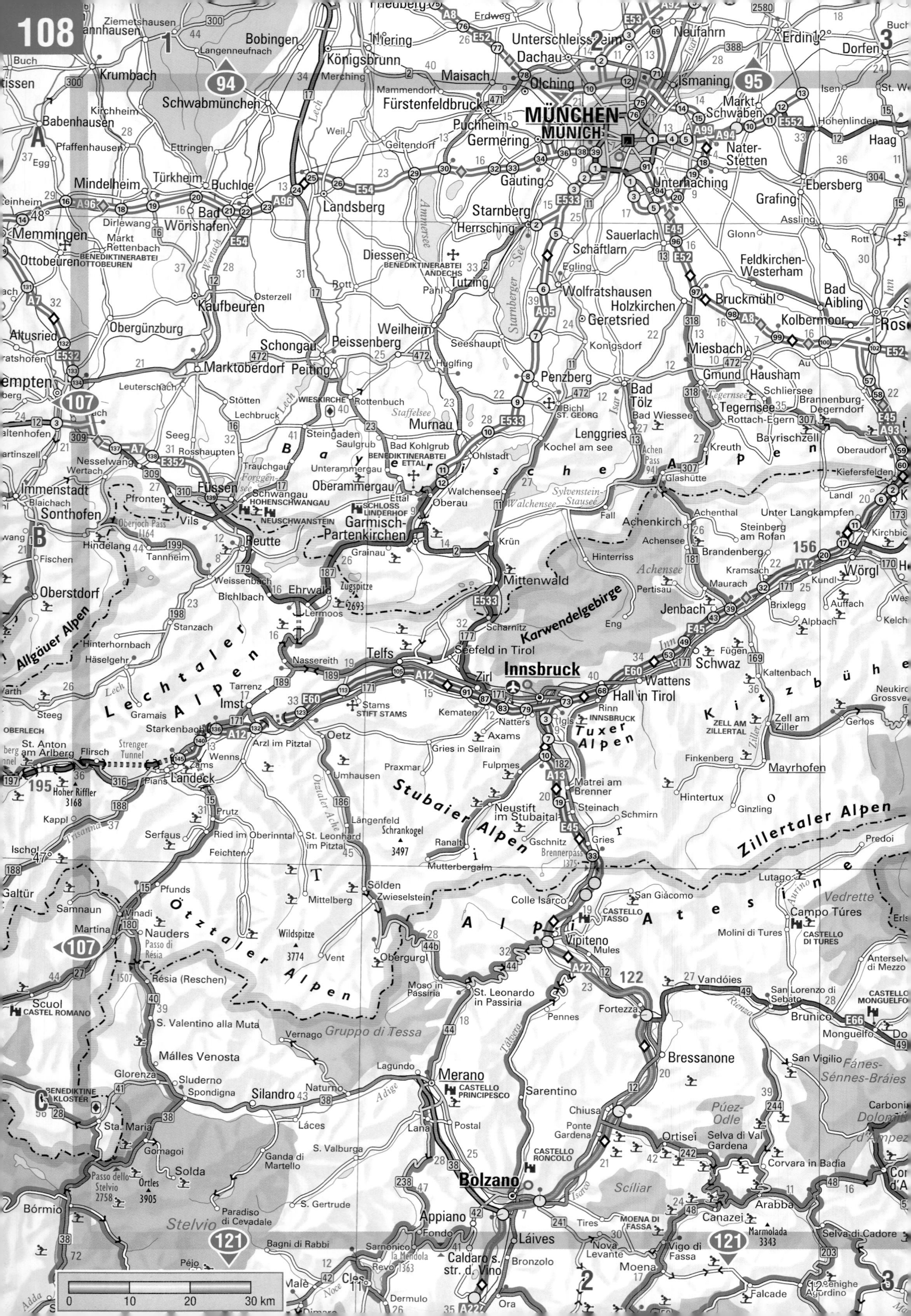

Ziemetshausen
Bobingen
Königsbrunn
Krumbach
Schwabmünchen
Babenhausen
Pfaffenhausen
Mindelheim
Türkheim
Buchloe
Bad Wörishofen
Memmingen
Ottobeuren
BENEDIKTINERABTEI OTTOBEUREN
Kaufbeuren
Obergünzburg
Marktoberdorf
Kempten
Altusried
Schongau
Peissenberg
Peiting
Landsberg
Ammersee
Diessen
BENEDIKTINERABTEI ANDECHS
Herrsching
Weilheim
Tutzing
Starnberg
Starnberger See
Gauting
Germering
Puchheim
Fürstenfeldbruck
Olching
Dachau
Maisach
Unterschleissheim
MÜNCHEN
MUNICH
Ismaning
Neufahrn
Erding
Dorfen
Markt Schwaben
Hohenlinden
Haag
Nater-Stetten
Unterhaching
Ebersberg
Grafing
Sauerlach
Schäftlarn
Wolfratshausen
Geretsried
Holzkirchen
Feldkirchen-Westerham
Bruckmühl
Bad Aibling
Kolbermoor
Miesbach
Gmund
Hausham
Tegernsee
Schliersee
Rottach-Egern
Bayrischzell
Brannenburg-Degerndorf
Oberaudorf
Kiefersfelden
Penzberg
Bad Tölz
Bad Wiessee
Lenggries
Kochel am see
Murnau
Staffelsee
Bad Kohlgrub
Oberammergau
BENEDIKTINERABTEI ETTAL
SCHLOSS LINDERHOF
Garmisch-Partenkirchen
Grainau
Zugspitze
2693
Mittenwald
Walchensee
Sylvenstein-Stausee
Achenkirch
Achensee
Füssen
HOHENSCHWANGAU
NEUSCHWANSTEIN
Pfronten
Nesselwang
Immenstadt
Sonthofen
Oberstdorf
Hindelang
Reutte
Tannheim
Ehrwald
Lermoos
Karwendelgebirge
Scharnitz
Seefeld in Tirol
Telfs
Nassereith
Imst
Zirl
Innsbruck
Hall in Tirol
Wattens
Schwaz
Jenbach
Wörgl
Kufstein
Allgäuer Alpen
Lechtaler Alpen
Bayerische Alpen
Kitzbüheler Alpen
Tuxer Alpen
Stubaier Alpen
Ötztaler Alpen
Zillertaler Alpen
Zell am Ziller
Mayrhofen
Landeck
St. Anton am Arlberg
Strenger Tunnel
Hoher Riffler
3168
Ischgl
Galtür
Serfaus
Prutz
Oetz
Umhausen
Längenfeld
Schrankogel
3497
Sölden
Obergurgl
Wildspitze
3774
Vent
Nauders
Resia (Reschen)
Passo di Résia
Matrei am Brenner
Steinach
Neustift im Stubaital
Brennerpass
1375
Gries
Colle Isarco
Vipiteno
CASTELLO TASSO
Alpi Atesine
Campo Túres
CASTELLO DI TURES
Brunico
Fortezza
Bressanone
Chiusa
Ortisei
Selva di Val Gardena
Corvara in Badia
Canazei
Marmolada
3343
Moena
Vigo di Fassa
Bolzano
CASTELLO RONCOLO
Merano
CASTELLO PRINCIPESCO
Lana
St. Leonardo in Passiria
Moso in Passíria
Gruppo di Tessa
Silandro
Naturno
Sluderno
Glorenza
Málles Venosta
S. Valentino alla Muta
CASTEL ROMANO
Scuol
BENEDIKTINE KLOSTER
Sta. Maria
Solda
Ortles
3905
Passo dello Stelvio
2758
Stelvio
Bórmio
Paradiso di Cevadale
Appiano
Caldaro s. str. d. Vino
Láives
Bronzolo
Ora
Sciliar
Fánes-Sénnes-Bráies
Dolomiti d'Ampezzo
Selva di Cadore
Cles
Malè
Péjo
Bagni di Rabbi
94
95
107
121
122
156
195
0
10
20
30 km

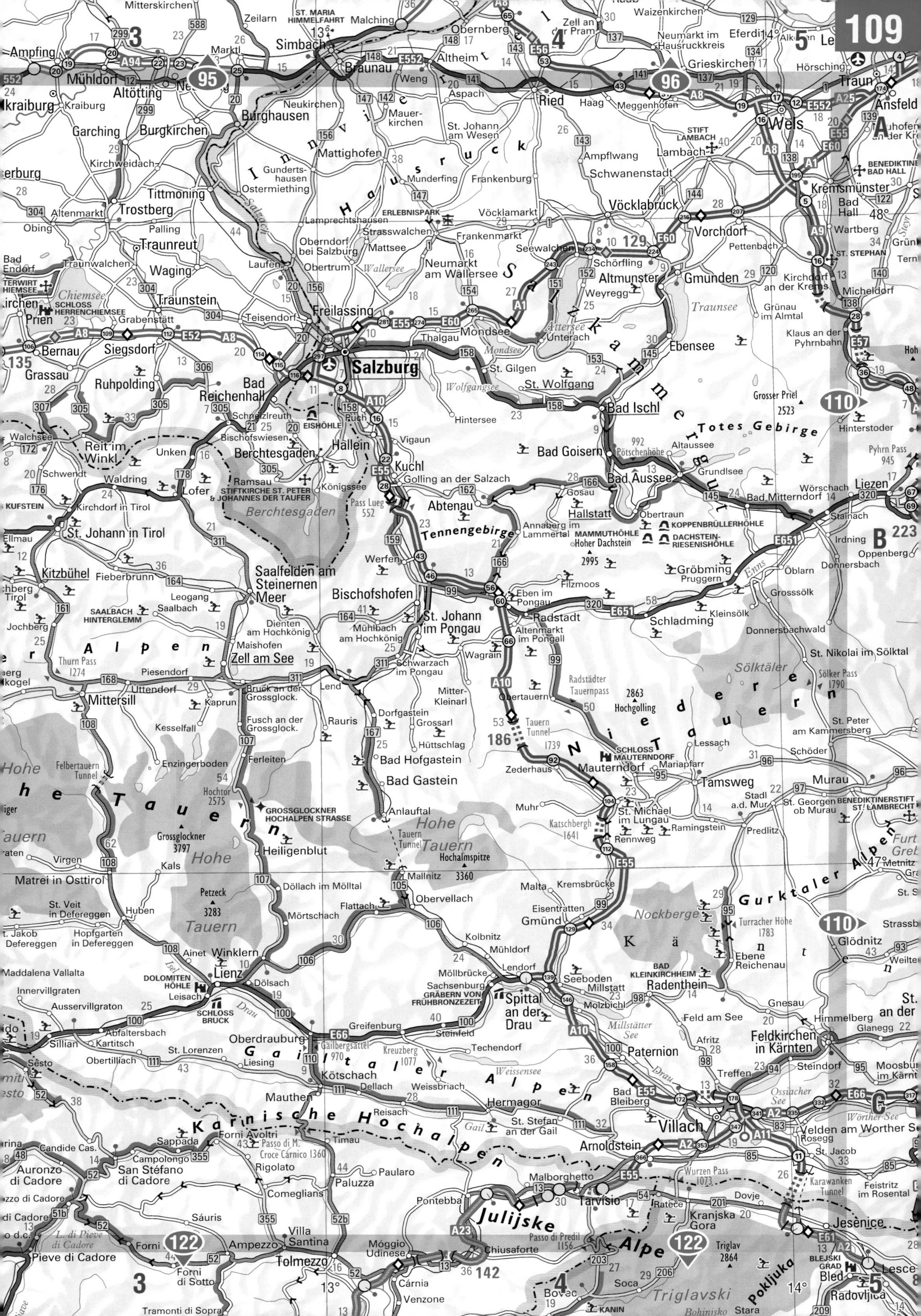

Salzburg
Braunau
Simbach
Burghausen
Mühldorf
Altötting
Ried
Wels
Grieskirchen
Traun
Ansfelden
Vöcklabruck
Gmunden
Kremsmünster
Vorchdorf
Traunstein
Freilassing
Bad Reichenhall
Berchtesgaden
Hallein
Mondsee
St. Gilgen
St. Wolfgang
Bad Ischl
Ebensee
Bad Goisern
Bad Aussee
Hallstatt
Liezen
Kitzbühel
St. Johann in Tirol
Saalfelden am Steinernen Meer
Bischofshofen
St. Johann im Pongau
Radstadt
Schladming
Zell am See
Mittersill
Bad Hofgastein
Bad Gastein
Tamsweg
Murau
Mauterndorf
Heiligenblut
Lienz
Spittal an der Drau
Villach
Feldkirchen in Kärnten
Hermagor
Tarvisio
Tolmezzo
Pieve di Cadore
Bled
Jesenice
Hohe Tauern
Niedere Tauern
Gurktaler Alpen
Karnische Hochalpen
Gailtaler Alpen
Salzkammergut
Hausruck
Totes Gebirge
Tennengebirge
Julijske Alpe
95
96
110
122

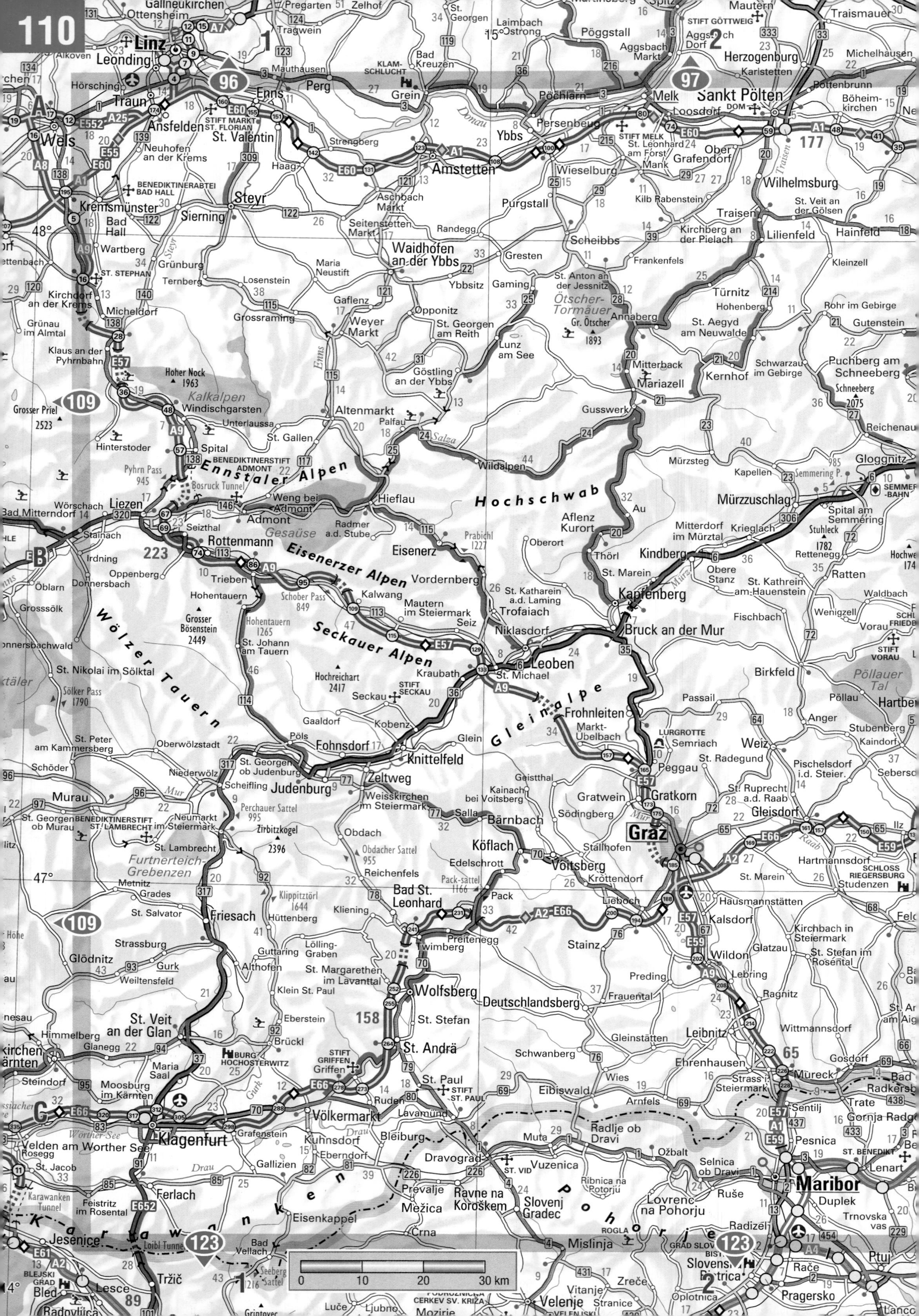

96
97
109
123
Linz
Leonding
Ottensheim
Gallneukirchen
Pregarten
Zelhof
Tragwein
Mauthausen
Hörsching
Traun
Ansfelden
Enns
St. Valentin
STIFT MARKT ST. FLORIAN
Perg
KLAM-SCHLUCHT
Grein
Bad Kreuzen
St. Georgen
Laimbach
Ostrong
Pöggstall
Aggsbach Markt
Aggsbach Dorf
STIFT GÖTTWEIG
Mautern
Traismauer
Herzogenburg
Karlstetten
Michelhausen
Pottenbrunn
Böheim-kirchen
Sankt Pölten
DOM
Loosdorf
Melk
STIFT MELK
Pöchlarn
Persenbeug
Ybbs
Donau
Amstetten
Strengberg
Haag
Wels
Neuhofen an der Krems
BENEDIKTINERABTEI BAD HALL
Kremsmünster
Bad Hall
Sierning
Steyr
Wieselburg
St. Leonhard am Forst
Mank
Ober Grafendorf
Wilhelmsburg
Traisen
St. Veit an der Gölsen
Hainfeld
Lilienfeld
Kirchberg an der Pielach
Kilb
Rabenstein
Purgstall
Scheibbs
Aschbach Markt
Seitenstetten Markt
Randegg
Waidhofen an der Ybbs
Gresten
Frankenfels
Kleinzell
Wartberg
Grünburg
ST. STEPHAN
Ternberg
Losenstein
Maria Neustift
Ybbsitz
Gaming
St. Anton an der Jessnitz
Ötscher-Tormäuer
Gr. Ötscher 1893
Annaberg
Türnitz
Hohenberg
St. Aegyd am Neuwalde
Rohr im Gebirge
Gutenstein
Kirchdorf an der Krems
Micheldorf
Grünau im Almtal
Klaus an der Pyhrnbahn
Grossraming
Gaflenz
Weyer Markt
Opponitz
St. Georgen am Reith
Lunz am See
Göstling an der Ybbs
Mitterback
Mariazell
Kernhof
Schwarzau im Gebirge
Puchberg am Schneeberg
Schneeberg 2075
Hoher Nock 1963
Kalkalpen
Windischgarsten
Grosser Priel 2523
Unterlaussa
Hinterstoder
Altenmarkt
Palfau
St. Gallen
Salza
Gusswerk
Reichenau
Spital
BENEDIKTINERSTIFT ADMONT
Pyhrn Pass 945
Bosruck Tunnel
Ennstaler Alpen
Wildalpen
Mürzsteg
Kapellen
Semmering P.
Gloggnitz
Hochschwab
Mürzzuschlag
Spital am Semmering
SEMMERING-BAHN
Liezen
Wörschach
Bad Mitterndorf
Stainach
Weng bei Admont
Admont
Gesäuse
Radmer a.d. Stube
Hieflau
Prabichl 1227
Au
Aflenz Kurort
Oberort
Mitterdorf im Mürztal
Krieglach
Stuhleck 1782
Seizthal
Rottenmann
Irdning
Oppenberg
Donnersbach
Öblarn
Trieben
Eisenerzer Alpen
Eisenerz
Vordernberg
Thörl
Kindberg
St. Marein
Obere Stanz
Rettenegg
Ratten
Kalwang
Schober Pass 849
Hohentauern
Grosser Bösenstein 2449
Grosssölk
Mautern im Steiermark
Seiz
St. Katharein a.d. Laming
Trofaiach
Kapfenberg
St. Kathrein am Hauenstein
Waldbach
Wenigzell
Fischbach
Vorau
STIFT VORAU
Wölzer Tauern
Hohentauern 1265
St. Johann am Tauern
Seckauer Alpen
Niklasdorf
Bruck an der Mur
Leoben
St. Michael
Kraubath
St. Nikolai im Sölktal
Sölker Pass 1790
Hochreichart 2417
STIFT SECKAU
Seckau
Birkfeld
Pöllauer Tal
Pöllau
Gleinalpe
Passail
Frohnleiten
Markt-Übelbach
LURGROTTE
Semriach
Anger
Stubenberg
Kaindorf
Gaaldorf
Kobenz
Pöls
Fohnsdorf
Glein
Knittelfeld
Weiz
St. Radegund
Pischelsdorf i.d. Steier.
St. Peter am Kammersberg
Oberwölzstadt
Schöder
Niederwölz
St. Georgen ob Judenburg
Scheifling
Judenburg
Zeltweg
Weisskirchen im Steiermark
Geistthal
Kainach bei Voitsberg
Gratwein
Peggau
Gratkorn
St. Ruprecht a.d. Raab
Gleisdorf
Murau
St. Georgen ob Murau
BENEDIKTINERSTIFT ST. LAMBRECHT
Neumarkt im Steiermark
Perchauer Sattel 995
Zirbitzkogel 2396
Salla
Bärnbach
Södingberg
Graz
Ilz
Raab
St. Lambrecht
Obdach
Köflach
Stallhofen
Furtnerteich-Grebenzen
Metnitz
Grades
St. Salvator
Obdacher Sattel 955
Reichenfels
Edelschrott
Voitsberg
Pack-sattel 1166
Pack
Krottendorf
Hartmannsdorf
SCHLOSS RIEGERSBURG
Studenzen
St. Marein
Friesach
Klippitztörl 1644
Hüttenberg
Bad St. Leonhard
Kliening
Lieboch
Hausmannstätten
Kalsdorf
Kirchbach in Steiermark
Strassburg
Lölling-Graben
Guttaring
Twimberg
Preitenegg
Stainz
Wildon
Glatzau
St. Stefan im Rosental
Glödnitz
Gurk
Weitensfeld
Althofen
St. Margarethen im Lavanttal
Klein St. Paul
Wolfsberg
Deutschlandsberg
Preding
Lebring
Ragnitz
St. Veit an der Glan
Eberstein
St. Stefan
Frauental
Wittmannsdorf
Himmelberg
Glanegg
Brückl
BURG HOCHOSTERWITZ
STIFT GRIFFEN
Griffen
St. Andrä
Gleinstätten
Leibnitz
Maria Saal
Schwanberg
Ehrenhausen
Gosdorf
Mureck
Bad Radkersburg
Steindorf
Moosburg im Kärnten
Ruden
St. Paul
STIFT ST. PAUL
Eibiswald
Wies
Arnfels
Strass i. Steiermark
Trate
Sentilj
Gornja Radgona
Velden am Worther See
Rosegg
Wörther-See
Klagenfurt
Grafenstein
Völkermarkt
Lavamünd
Drau
Kühnsdorf
Eberndorf
Bleiburg
Dravograd
Muta
Radlje ob Dravi
Ožbalt
Selnica ob Dravi
Pesnica
ST. BENEDIKT
Lenart
St. Jacob
Gallizien
ST. VID
Vuzenica
Ribnica na Pohorju
Ruše
Maribor
Duplek
Karawanken Tunnel
Feistritz im Rosental
Ferlach
Prevalje
Mežica
Ravne na Koroškem
Slovenj Gradec
Lovrenc na Pohorju
Pohorje
Karawanken
Eisenkappel
Črna
Radizel
Trnovska vas
Jesenice
Loibl Tunnel
Bad Vellach
Seeberg Sattel
Mislinja
ROGLA
GRAD SLOV. BIST.
Slovenska Bistrica
Rače
Ptuj
Pragersko
BLEJSKI GRAD
Bled
Lesce
Tržič
Radovljica
Velenje
Vitanje
Zreče
Stranice
Oplotnica
Luče
Ljubno
Mozirje
Gornji Grad
0 10 20 30 km
48°
47°
A
B
C
1
2

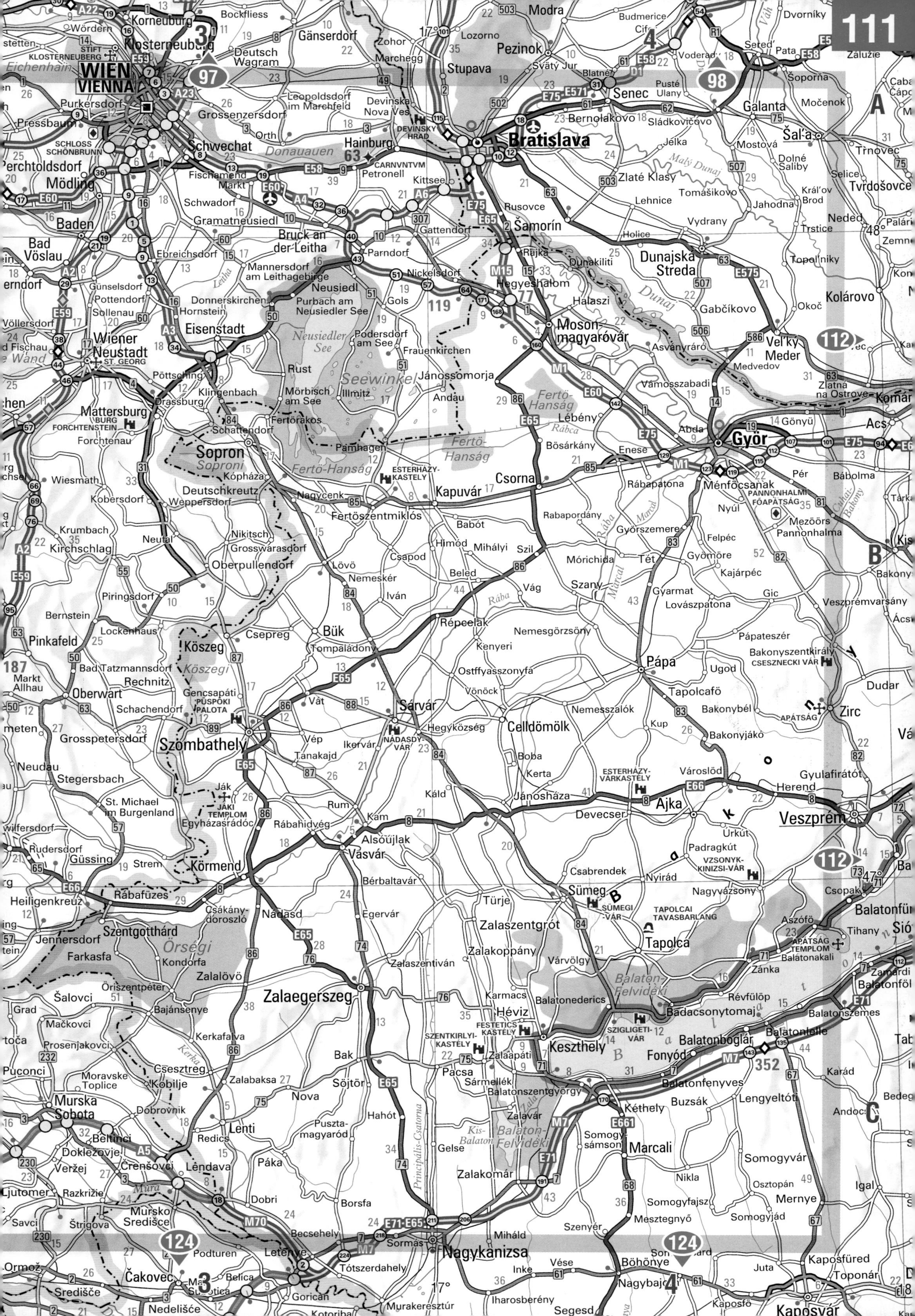

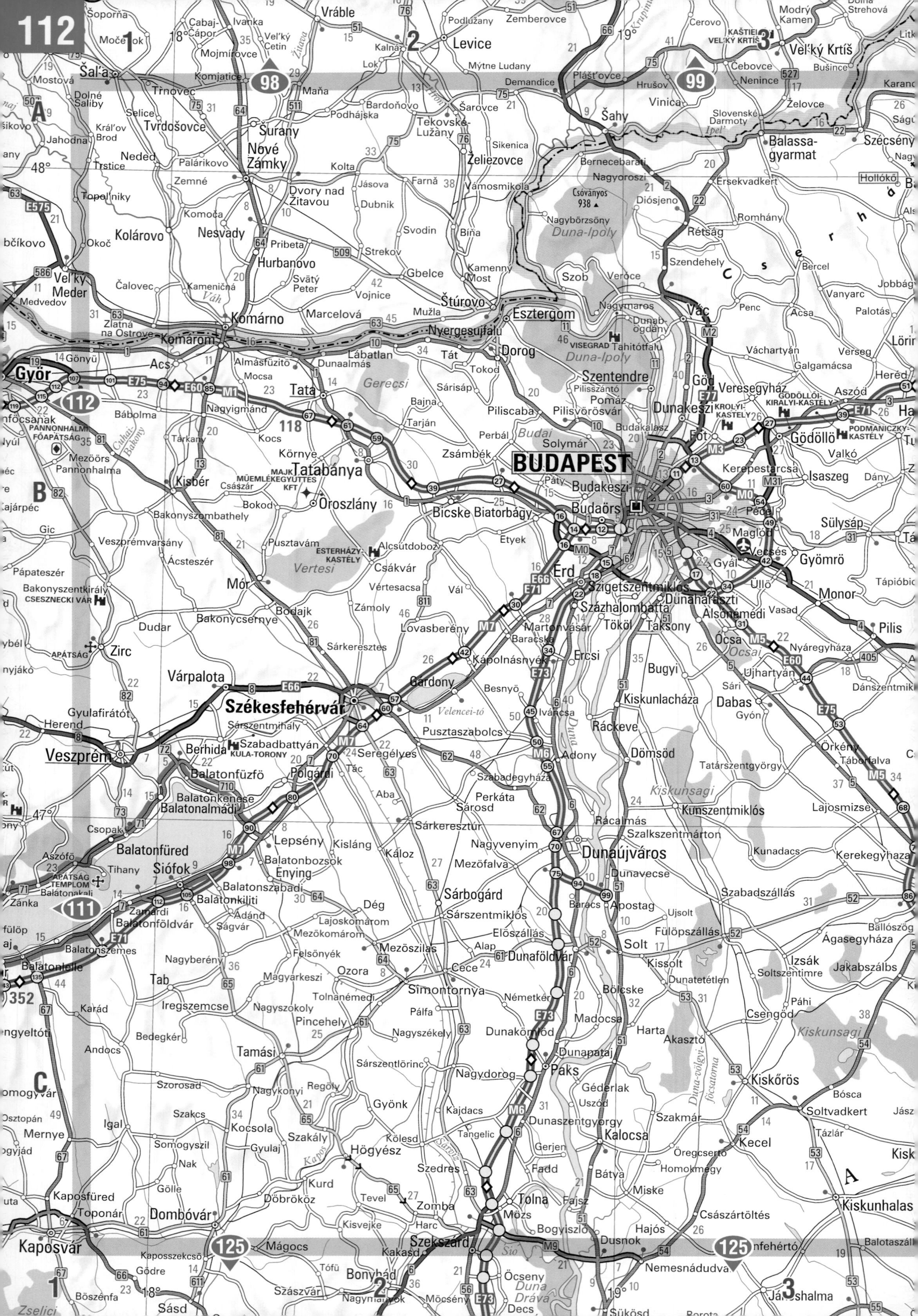
Šoporňa
Vráble
Podlužany
Zemberovce
Cerovo
Modrý Kameň
Dolná Strehová
Močenok
Cabaj-Čápor
Ivanka
Veľký Cetín
Kalná
Levice
KAŠTIEĽ VEĽKÝ KRTÍŠ
Veľký Krtíš
Mojmírovce
Lok
Mýtne Ludany
Čebovce
Šaľa
Mostová
Komjatice
98
Maňa
Demandice
Plášťovce
99
Nenince
Bušince
Dolné Saliby
Trnovec
Hrušov
Vinica
Želovce
Selice
Bardoňovo
Šarovce
Šahy
Slovenské Ďarmoty
Kráľov Brod
Tvrdošovce
Podhájska
Tekovské Lužany
Sikenica
Jahodná
Šurany
Ipeľ
Balassagyarmat
Szécsény
Neded
Nové Zámky
Želiezovce
Trstice
Palárikovo
Kolta
Bernecebaráti
Nagyoroszi
Hollókő
Zemné
Jásova
Farná
Vámosmikola
Érsekvadkert
Topoľníky
Dvory nad Žitavou
Dubník
Csóványos 938
Diósjenő
Komoča
Nagybörzsöny
Romhány
Kolárovo
Nesvady
Svodin
Bíňa
Duna-Ipoly
Rétság
Okoč
Pribeta
Strekov
Cserhát
Hurbanovo
Szendehely
Bercel
Veľký Meder
Čalovec
Kameničná
Svätý Peter
Gbelce
Kamenný Most
Szob
Verőce
Jobbágyi
Medvedov
Váh
Vojnice
Štúrovo
Vanyarc
Zlatná na Ostrove
Komárno
Marcelová
Mužla
Esztergom
Nagymaros
Vác
Penc
Acsa
Palotás
Komárom
Nyergesújfalu
Dunabogdány
Gönyű
Ács
Almásfüzitő
Lábatlan
Dunaalmás
Tát
Dorog
VISEGRAD
Tahitótfalu
Váchartyán
Verseg
Győr
Mocsa
Tokod
Gerecsi
Szentendre
Galgamácsa
Göd
Veresegyház
Heréd
112
Tata
Sárisáp
Pilisszántó
Pomáz
GÖDÖLLŐI-KIRÁLYI-KASTÉLY
Aszód
Bábolna
Nagyigmánd
Bajna
Piliscaba
Pilisvörösvár
Dunakeszi
KROLYI-KASTELY
Écsanak
PANNONHALMI FŐAPÁTSÁG
Tárkány
Kocs
Tarján
Budai
Budakalász
Fót
PODMANICZKY-KASTELY
Gödöllő
Cuhai-Bakony
Környe
Perbál
Solymár
Mezőörs
Pannonhalma
Tatabánya
Zsámbék
BUDAPEST
Kerepestarcsa
Valkó
Isaszeg
Kisbér
MŰEMLÉKEGYÜTTES MAJK KFT
Páty
Dány
Császár
Budakeszi
Bokod
Oroszlány
Bicske
Biatorbágy
Budaörs
Pécel
Sülysáp
Kajárpéc
Bakonyszombathely
Maglód
Gic
Veszprémvarsány
Pusztavám
Alcsútdoboz
ESTERHÁZY-KASTÉLY
Etyek
Vecsés
Gyömrő
Ácsteszér
Pápateszér
Vertesi
Csákvár
Gyál
Erd
Bakonyszentkirály
CSESZNECKI VÁR
Mór
Vértesacsa
Üllő
Tápióbicske
Szigetszentmiklós
Monor
Zámoly
Vál
Dunaharaszti
Bodajk
Százhalombatta
Dudar
Bakonycsernye
Lovasberény
Alsónémedi
Vasad
Martonvásár
Tököl
Taksony
Pilis
Sárkeresztes
Baracska
Ócsa
Zirc
APÁTSÁG
Kápolnásnyék
Ercsi
Nyáregyháza
Ocsai
Bugyi
Újhartyán
Várpalota
Gárdony
Besnyő
Sári
Dánszentmiklós
Székesfehérvár
Kiskunlacháza
Dabas
Gyulafirátót
Velencei-tó
Iváncsa
Gyón
Herend
Sárszentmihály
Pusztaszabolcs
Ráckeve
Szabadbattyán
KULA-TORONY
Berhida
Seregélyes
Adony
Dömsöd
Örkény
Veszprém
Tác
Táborfalva
Balatonfüzfő
Polgárdi
Szabadegyháza
Tatárszentgyörgy
Kiskunsagi
Balatonkenese
Balatonalmádi
Aba
Perkáta
Sárosd
Lajosmizse
Csopak
Sárkeresztúr
Rácalmás
Kunszentmiklós
Szalkszentmárton
Balatonfüred
Lepsény
Kisláng
Nagyvenyim
Dunaújváros
Kunadacs
Kerekegyháza
Aszófő
Tihany
Siófok
Balatonbozsok
Káloz
Mezőfalva
Enying
Dunavecse
APÁTSÁG TEMPLOM
Balatonszabadi
Sárbogárd
Szabadszállás
Balatonakali
Zánka
111
Zamárdi
Balatonkiliti
Adánd
Dég
Baracs
Apostag
Sárszentmiklós
Ujsolt
Balatonföldvár
Ságvár
Lajoskomárom
Mezőkomárom
Előszállás
Fülöpszállás
Ballószög
Fülöp
Balatonszemes
Mezőszilas
Alap
Solt
Ágasegyháza
Felsőnyék
Dunaföldvár
Kissolt
Izsák
Balatonlelle
Nagyberény
Cece
Soltszentimre
Jakabszállás
Tab
Magyarkeszi
Ozora
Dunatetétlen
352
Simontornya
Németkér
Bölcske
Karád
Iregszemcse
Nagyszokoly
Tolnanémedi
Páhi
Pálfa
Csengőd
Kiskunsagi
Pincehely
Madocsa
Andocs
Bedegkér
Nagyszékely
Dunakömlőd
Harta
Akasztó
Tamási
Dunapataj
Duna-völgyi-főcsatorna
Sárszentlőrinc
Somogyvár
Szorosad
Regöly
Nagydorog
Paks
Gédérlak
Kiskőrös
Nagykónyi
Uszód
Bócsa
Igal
Szakcs
Kocsola
Gyönk
Kajdacs
Szakmár
Soltvadkert
Osztopán
Mernye
Dunaszentgyörgy
Tázlár
Szakály
Tengelic
Kalocsa
Kecel
Somogyszil
Kölesd
Gerjen
Gyulaj
Kapos
Högyész
Sárvíz
Öregcsertő
Nak
Fadd
Homokmégy
Szedres
Gölle
Kurd
Bátya
Kaposfüred
Tevel
Döbrököz
Tolna
Fajsz
Miske
Kiskunhalas
Toponár
Dombóvár
Zomba
Mözs
Császártöltés
Kaposvár
Kisvejke
Harc
Bogyiszló
Hajós
Mágocs
125
Szekszárd
Dusnok
Kaposszekcső
Kakasd
Sió
Nemesnádudvar
Balotaszállás
Tófű
Bonyhád
Őcseny
Gödre
Szászvár
Mőcsény
Duna Dráva
Jánoshalma
Bőszénfa
Nagymányok
Zselici
Sásd
Decs
Sükösd
Rorota

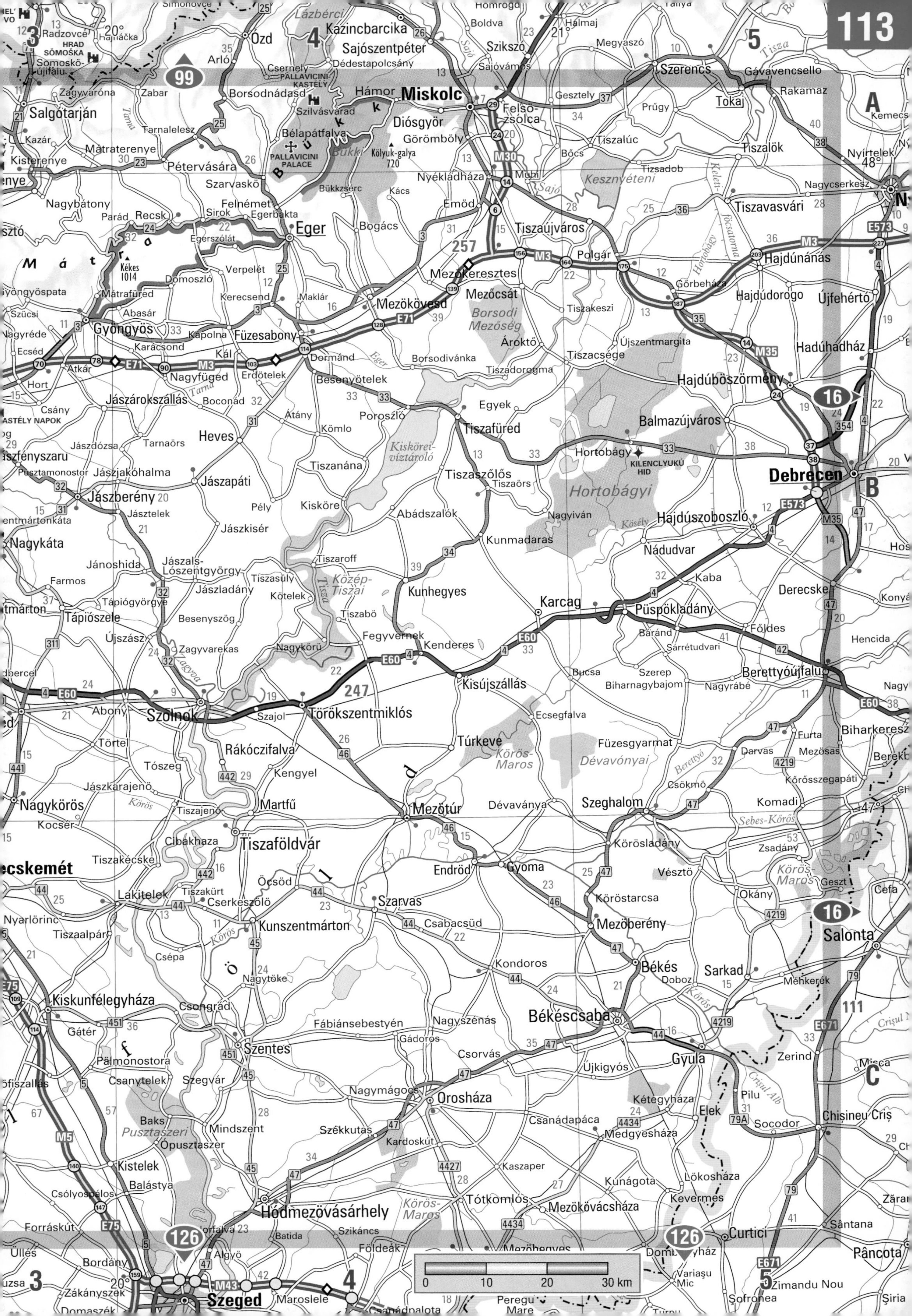

Ózd
Kazincbarcika
Sajószentpéter
Dédestapolcsány
Arló
Szikszó
Boldva
Halmaj
Megyaszó
Radzovce
Hajnáčka
HRAD SOMOŠKA
Somoskőújfalu
Zagyvaróna
Zabar
Salgótarján
Borsodnádasd
Hámor
Miskolc
Szilvásvárad
Felsőzsolca
Sajóvámos
Szerencs
Gávavencsello
Rakamaz
Tokaj
Gesztely
Prügy
Kemecse
Tarnalelesz
Diósgyör
Bélapátfalva
Görömböly
Bükk
Kólyuk-galya 720
PALLAVICINI PALACE
PALLAVICINI KASTÉLY
Kazár
Mátraterenye
Kisterenye
Pétervására
Szarvaskő
Tiszalúc
Bőcs
Tiszalök
Nyírtelek
Tiszadob
Kesznyétení
Nagycserkesz
Nagybátony
Parád
Recsk
Sirok
Felnémet
Egerbakta
Eger
Bükkszérc
Kács
Bogács
Nyékládháza
Muhi
Emőd
Tiszaújváros
Tiszavasvári
Hajdúnánás
Mátra
Kékes 1014
Egerszólát
Verpelét
Domoszló
Mátrafüred
Gyöngyöspata
Kerecsend
Maklár
Mezőkövesd
Mezőkeresztes
Mezőcsát
Polgár
Görbeháza
Hajdúdorog
Újfehértó
Szűcsi
Abasár
Nagyréde
Gyöngyös
Kápolna
Füzesabony
Borsodi Mezőség
Tiszakeszi
Ároktő
Újszentmargita
Ecséd
Karácsond
Kál
Dormánd
Borsodivánka
Tiszacsege
Hadúhadház
Atkár
Hort
Nagyfüged
Erdőtelek
Besenyőtelek
Tiszadorogma
Hajdúböszörmény
Csány
Jászárokszállás
Boconád
Poroszló
Egyek
Balmazújváros
Átány
Kömlo
Tiszafüred
Heves
Tarnaörs
Jászdózsa
Kiskörei-víztároló
Hortobágy
KILENCLYUKÚ HÍD
Jászfényszaru
Pusztamonostor
Jászjákóhalma
Tiszanána
Tiszaszőlős
Tiszaörs
Debrecen
Jászapáti
Jászberény
Jásztelek
Pély
Kisköre
Hortobágyi
Hajdúszoboszló
Abádszalók
Nagyiván
Kösély
Jászkisér
Nagykáta
Kunmadaras
Nádudvar
Jánoshida
Jászalsószentgyörgy
Tiszaroff
Farmos
Tiszasüly
Jászladány
Közép-Tiszai
Kunhegyes
Kaba
Derecske
Tápiógyörgye
Kötelek
Karcag
Püspökladány
Tápiószele
Besenyszög
Tiszabő
Fegyvernek
Báránd
Sárrétudvari
Földes
Újszász
Zagyvarekas
Nagykörű
Kenderes
Hencida
Bucsa
Szerep
Biharnagybajom
Nagyrábé
Berettyóújfalu
Kisújszállás
Abony
Szolnok
Szajol
Törökszentmiklós
Ecsegfalva
Törtel
Rákóczifalva
Túrkeve
Füzesgyarmat
Darvas
Furta
Mezősas
Biharkeresztes
Tószeg
Kengyel
Körös-Maros
Dévaványai
Kőrösszegapáti
Jászkarajenő
Nagykőrös
Tiszajenő
Martfű
Mezőtúr
Dévaványa
Szeghalom
Csökmő
Komadi
Kocsér
Cibakháza
Tiszaföldvár
Körösladány
Sebes-Körös
Zsadány
Kecskemét
Tiszakécske
Endrőd
Gyoma
Vésztő
Geszt
Öcsöd
Lakitelek
Tiszakürt
Cserkeszőlő
Szarvas
Köröstarcsa
Okány
Cefa
Nyárlőrinc
Tiszaalpár
Kunszentmárton
Csabacsüd
Mezőberény
Salonta
Csépa
Kondoros
Békés
Sarkad
Nagytőke
Doboz
Méhkerék
Kiskunfélegyháza
Csongrád
Nagyszénás
Békéscsaba
Gátér
Fábiánsebestyén
Gádoros
Szentes
Csorvás
Újkígyós
Gyula
Zerind
Pálmonostora
Csanytelek
Szegvár
Nagymágocs
Orosháza
Kétegyháza
Pilu
Misca
Baks
Pusztaszeri
Mindszent
Ópusztaszer
Székkutas
Csanádapáca
Medgyesháza
Elek
Socodor
Chișineu Criș
Kardoskút
Kistelek
Balástya
Kaszaper
Kunágota
Lőkösháza
Csólyospálos
Hódmezővásárhely
Tótkomlós
Mezőkovácsháza
Kevermes
Zărand
Forráskút
Batida
Szikáncs
Curtici
Sântana
Üllés
Bordány
Földeák
Algyő
Dombegyház
Pâncota
Zákányszék
Szeged
Maroslele
Variașu Mic
Zimandu Nou
Domaszék
Csanádpalota
Peregu Mare
Sofronea
Șiria
0 10 20 30 km

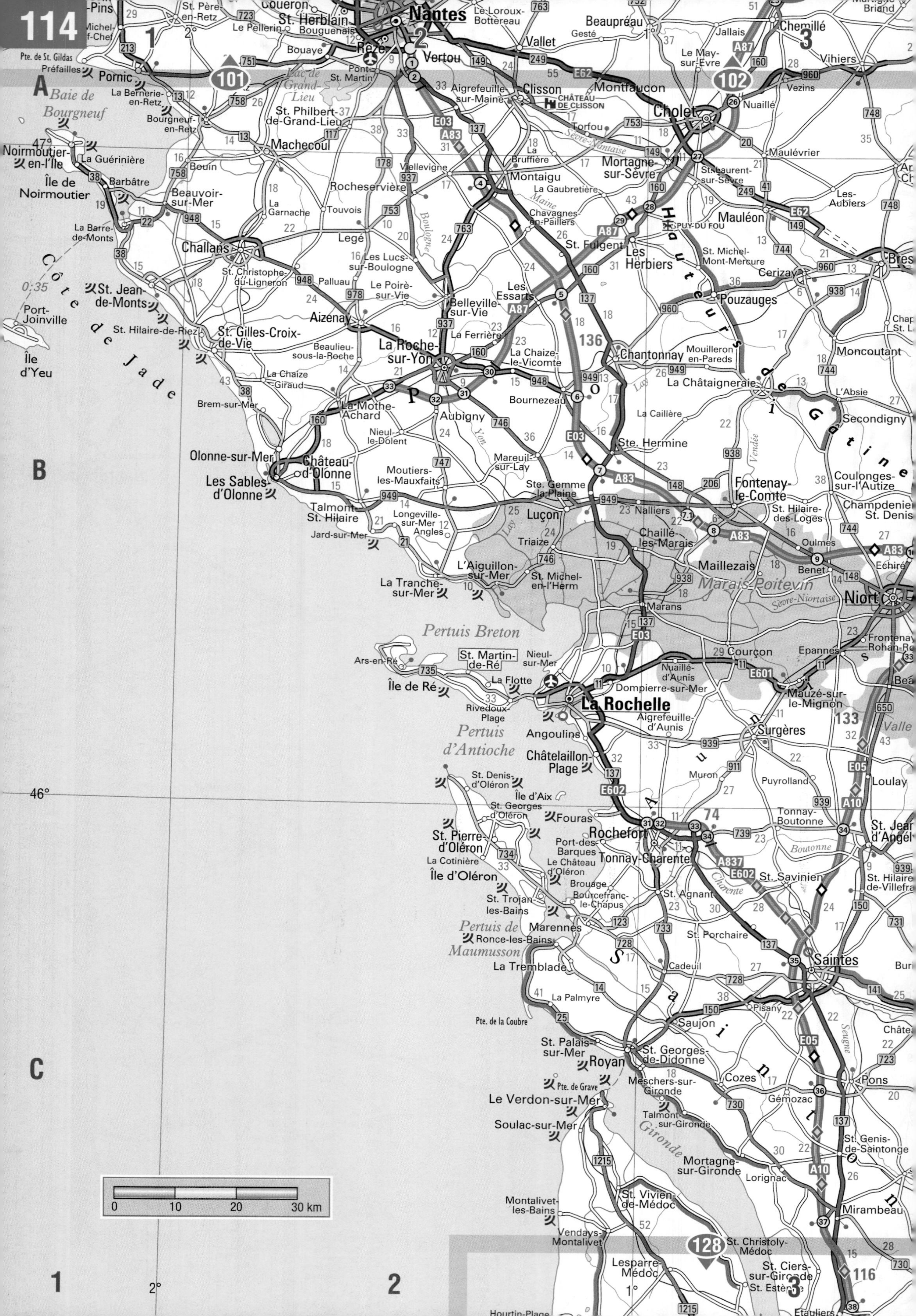
Nantes
St. Herblain
Rezé
Vertou
Bouguenais
Le Pellerin
Coueron
St. Père-en-Retz
Le Loroux-Bottereau
Vallet
Beaupréau
Chemillé
Jallais
Vihiers
Pornic
Préfailles
Pte. de St. Gildas
Baie de Bourgneuf
La Bernerie-en-Retz
Bourgneuf-en-Retz
Lac de Grand-Lieu
St. Philbert-de-Grand-Lieu
Aigrefeuille-sur-Maine
Clisson
CHÂTEAU DE CLISSON
Montfaucon
Cholet
Nuaillé
Vezins
Torfou
Machecoul
Noirmoutier-en-l'Île
La Guérinière
Île de Noirmoutier
Barbâtre
La Barre-de-Monts
Beauvoir-sur-Mer
Bouin
La Garnache
Rocheservière
Vieillevigne
Montaigu
La Bruffière
La Gaubretière
Mortagne-sur-Sèvre
St. Laurent-sur-Sèvre
Maulévrier
Les Aubiers
Mauléon
PUY-DU-FOU
Chavagnes-en-Paillers
St. Fulgent
Les Herbiers
Hauteurs de Gâtine
St. Michel-Mont-Mercure
Cerizay
Pouzauges
Challans
St. Christophe-du-Ligneron
Touvois
Legé
Les Lucs-sur-Boulogne
Palluau
Le Poiré-sur-Vie
Les Essarts
Belleville-sur-Vie
Aizenay
St. Jean-de-Monts
Côte de Jade
Port-Joinville
Île d'Yeu
St. Hilaire-de-Riez
St. Gilles-Croix-de-Vie
Beaulieu-sous-la-Roche
La Roche-sur-Yon
La Ferrière
La Chaize-le-Vicomte
Chantonnay
Mouilleron-en-Pareds
La Châtaigneraie
Moncoutant
L'Absie
Secondigny
La Chaize-Giraud
Brem-sur-Mer
La Mothe-Achard
Aubigny
Bournezeau
La Caillère
Nieul-le-Dolent
Ste. Hermine
Olonne-sur-Mer
Château-d'Olonne
Les Sables-d'Olonne
Moutiers-les-Mauxfaits
Mareuil-sur-Lay
Ste. Gemme-la-Plaine
Fontenay-le-Comte
Coulonges-sur-l'Autize
Talmont-St. Hilaire
Longeville-sur-Mer
Angles
Jard-sur-Mer
Luçon
Nalliers
St. Hilaire-des-Loges
Champdeniers-St. Denis
Triaize
Chaillé-les-Marais
Oulmes
L'Aiguillon-sur-Mer
St. Michel-en-l'Herm
Maillezais
Benet
Echiré
La Tranche-sur-Mer
Marais Poitevin
Sèvre-Niortaise
Niort
Marans
Pertuis Breton
Ars-en-Ré
St. Martin-de-Ré
Nieul-sur-Mer
Courçon
Epannes
Frontenay-Rohan-Rohan
Île de Ré
La Flotte
Rivedoux-Plage
Nuaillé-d'Aunis
Dompierre-sur-Mer
Mauzé-sur-le-Mignon
La Rochelle
Pertuis d'Antioche
Angoulins
Aigrefeuille-d'Aunis
Surgères
Châtelaillon-Plage
St. Denis-d'Oléron
Île d'Aix
Muron
Puyrolland
Loulay
St. Georges-d'Oléron
Fouras
Tonnay-Boutonne
St. Pierre-d'Oléron
Rochefort
Port-des-Barques
Le Château-d'Oléron
Tonnay-Charente
St. Jean-d'Angély
La Cotinière
Île d'Oléron
Brouage
Bourcefranc-le-Chapus
St. Agnant
St. Savinien
St. Hilaire-de-Villefranche
St. Trojan-les-Bains
Pertuis de Maumusson
Marennes
Ronce-les-Bains
St. Porchaire
La Tremblade
Cadeuil
Saintes
La Palmyre
Pte. de la Coubre
Pisany
Saujon
St. Palais-sur-Mer
Royan
St. Georges-de-Didonne
Meschers-sur-Gironde
Pte. de Grave
Le Verdon-sur-Mer
Cozes
Gémozac
Pons
Soulac-sur-Mer
Talmont-sur-Gironde
Gironde
Mortagne-sur-Gironde
St. Genis-de-Saintonge
Lorignac
Montalivet-les-Bains
St. Vivien-de-Médoc
Mirambeau
Vendays-Montalivet
St. Christoly-Médoc
Lesparre-Médoc
St. Ciers-sur-Gironde
St. Estèphe
Hourtin-Plage
Etauliers
Saintonge
Aunis
Poitou
47°
46°
2°
1°
0:35
0 10 20 30 km
A
B
C
1
2
3
101
102
128
116
133
136

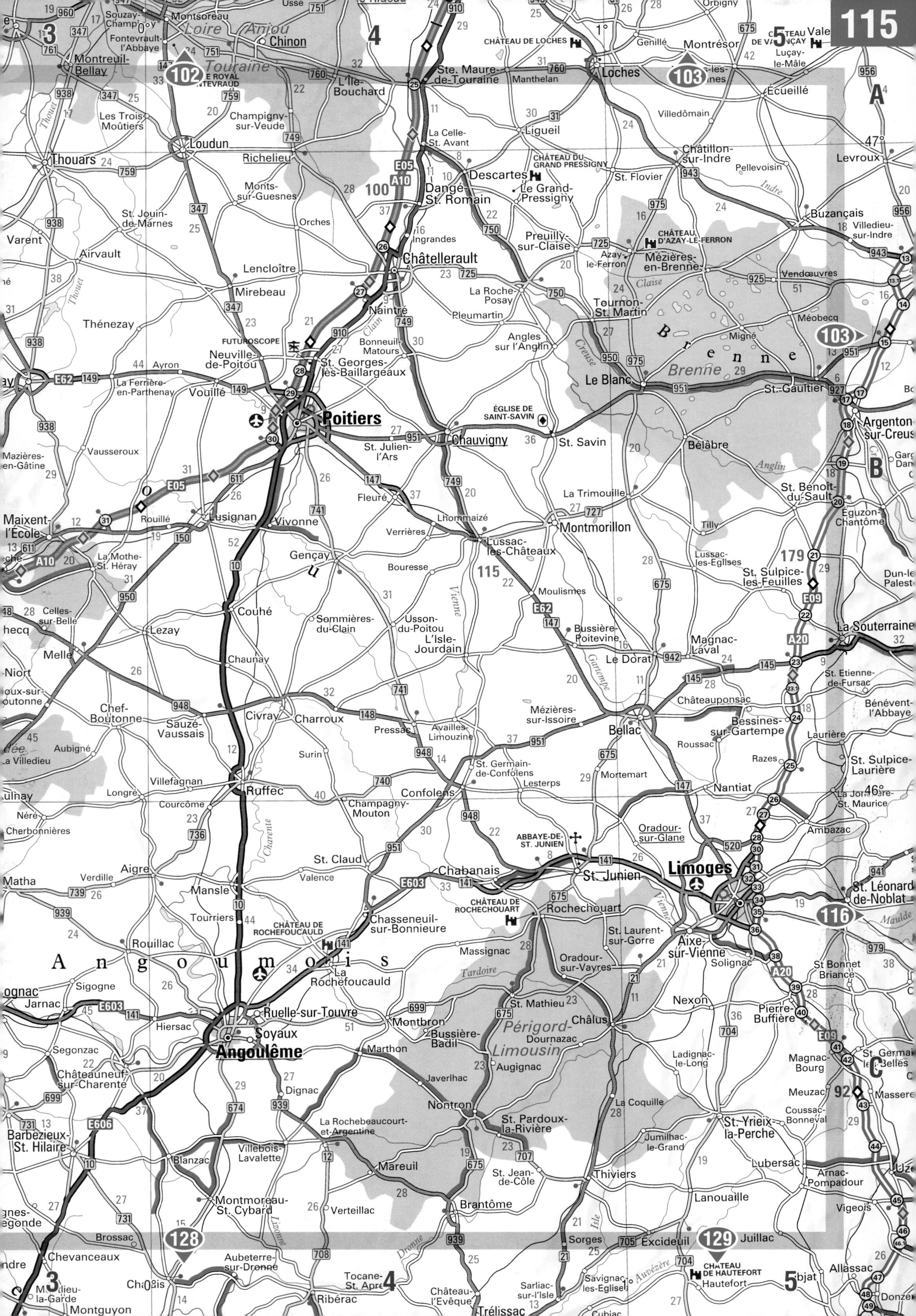

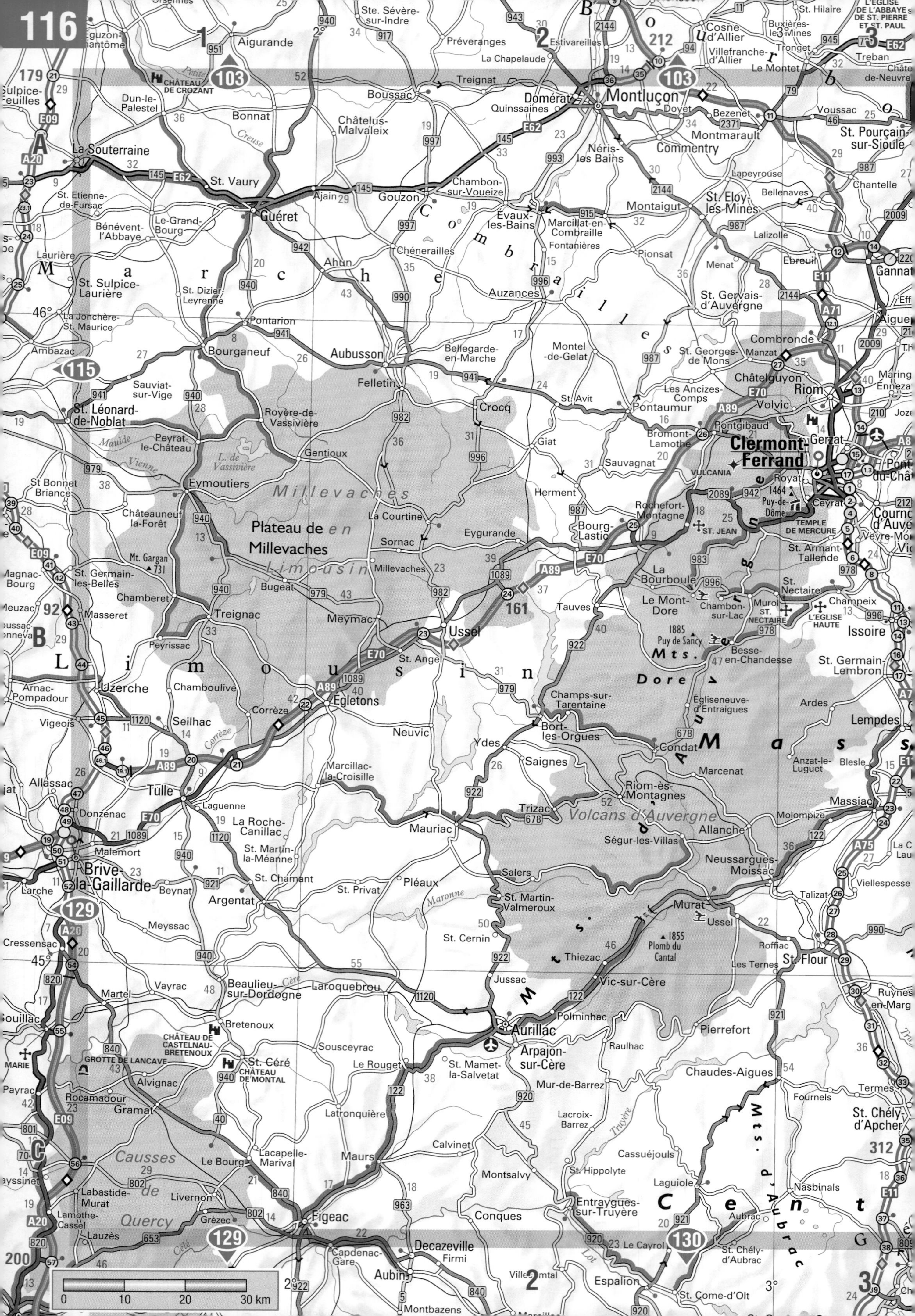
Aigurande
Guéret
Montluçon
Commentry
Néris-les Bains
La Souterraine
Bourganeuf
Aubusson
Felletin
Plateau de Millevaches
Millevaches
Limousin
Eymoutiers
St. Léonard-de-Noblat
Treignac
Meymac
Ussel
Uzerche
Egletons
Tulle
Brive-la-Gaillarde
Argentat
Mauriac
Bort-les-Orgues
Clermont-Ferrand
Riom
Volvic
Issoire
Besse-en-Chandesse
Le Mont-Dore
La Bourboule
Puy de Sancy
Mts. Dore
Massiac
St. Flour
Murat
Plomb du Cantal
Vic-sur-Cère
Aurillac
Arpajon-sur-Cère
Salers
Figeac
Decazeville
Espalion
Chaudes-Aigues
Laguiole
Rocamadour
Gramat
Causses de Quercy
Combrailles
Limousin
Marche
Volcans d'Auvergne
Monts d'Aubrac
0 10 20 30 km

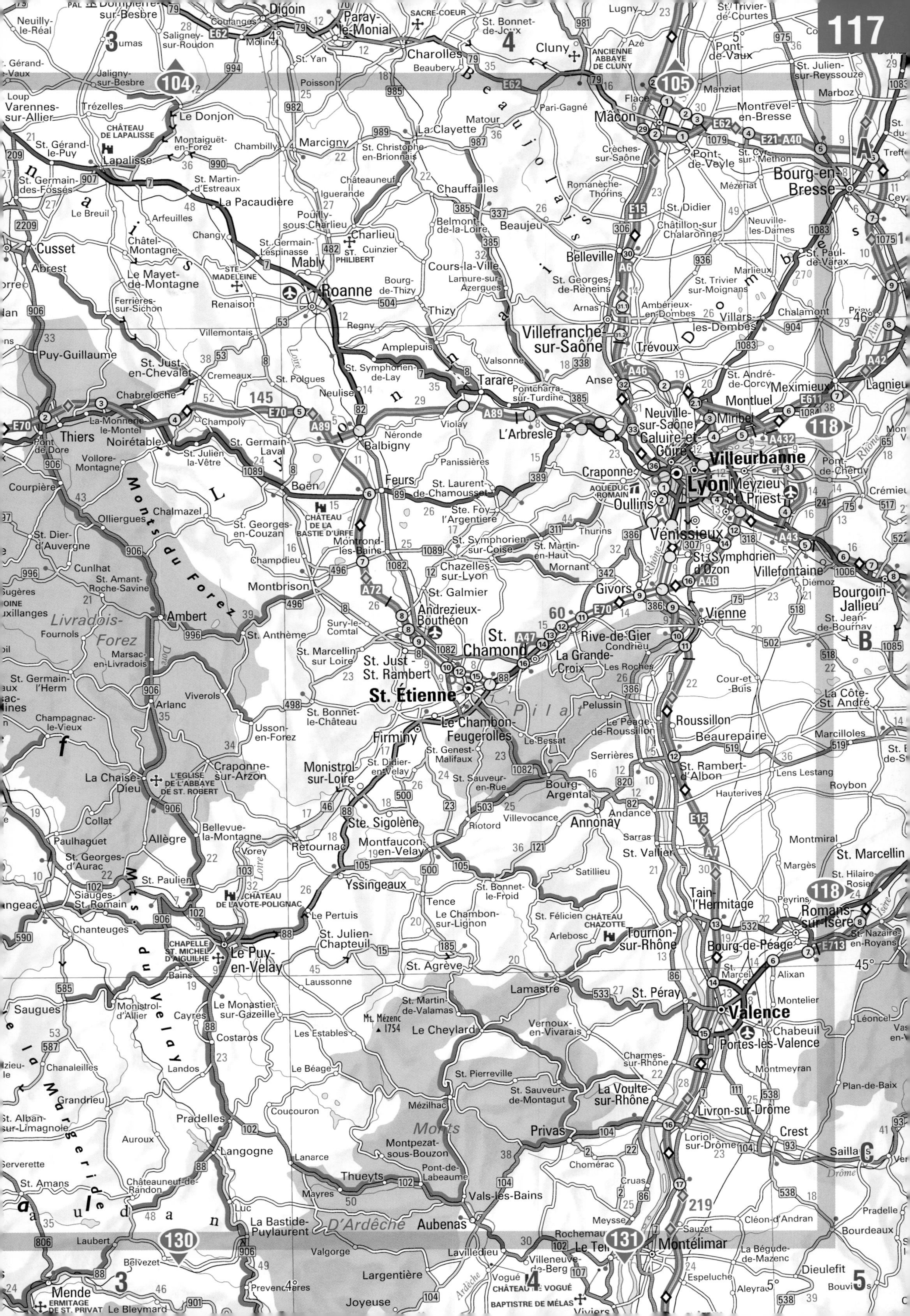

104
105
118
130
131
Digoin
Paray-le-Monial
Sacré-Coeur
Charolles
Cluny
Ancienne Abbaye de Cluny
Mâcon
Beaujolais
Dombes
Monts du Lyonnais
Monts du Forez
Livradois-Forez
Pilat
Monts du Velay
Monts de la Margeride
Mt. Mézenc 1754
Lapalisse
Château de Lapalisse
Le Donjon
Vichy
Cusset
Thiers
Roanne
Charlieu
Chauffailles
Beaujeu
Belleville
Villefranche-sur-Saône
Trévoux
Tarare
L'Arbresle
Bourg-en-Bresse
Montluel
Meximieux
Villeurbanne
Lyon
Caluire-et-Cuire
Oullins
Vénissieux
Givors
Vienne
Rive-de-Gier
St. Chamond
St. Étienne
Firminy
Montbrison
Feurs
Boën
Ambert
Noirétable
Craponne-sur-Arzon
La Chaise-Dieu
Yssingeaux
Le Puy-en-Velay
Annonay
Tournon-sur-Rhône
Tain-l'Hermitage
Romans-sur-Isère
Valence
Portes-lès-Valence
La Voulte-sur-Rhône
Privas
Crest
Livron-sur-Drôme
Montélimar
Aubenas
Vals-les-Bains
Le Cheylard
Lamastre
Langogne
Mende
Saugues
Bourgoin-Jallieu
Villefontaine
Roussillon
Beaurepaire
St. Marcellin
Château de La Bastie d'Urfé
Château de Lavoûte-Polignac
Château Chazotte
Château de Vogüé
Chapelle St. Michel d'Aiguilhe
L'Église de l'Abbaye de St. Robert
Aqueduc Romain
Ermitage de St. Privat
Baptistère de Mélas
E15
E62
E70
A6
A7
A46
A47
A72
A89
A43
A42
A432

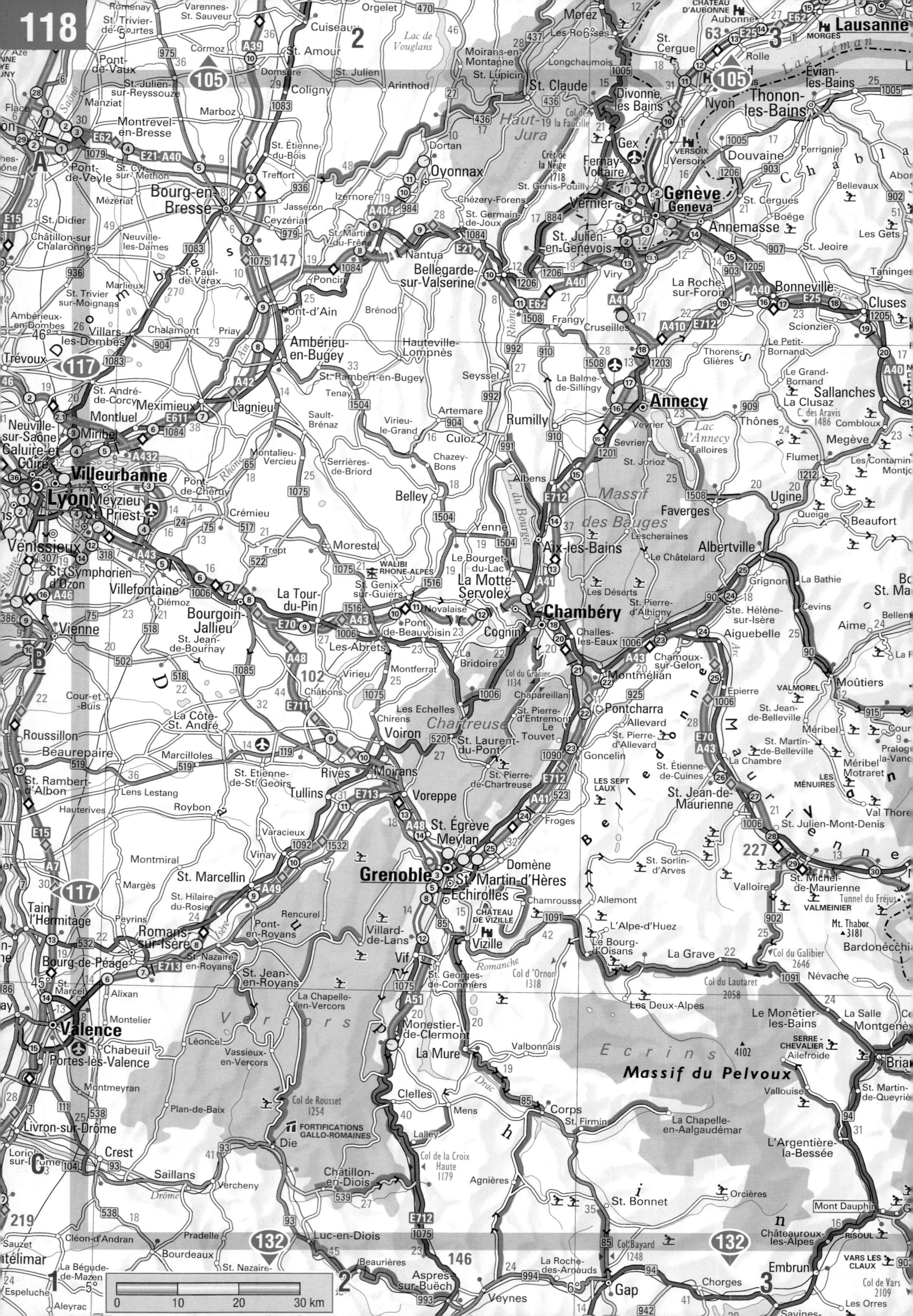

Romenay
Varennes-St. Sauveur
Orgelet
Morez
Château d'Aubonne
Aubonne
Lausanne
St. Trivier-de-Courtes
Cuiseaux
Lac de Vouglans
Les Rousses
St. Cergue
Morges
Lac Léman
Cormoz
St. Amour
Moirans-en-Montagne
Longchaumois
Rolle
Pont-de-Vaux
Domsure
St. Julien
St. Lupicin
Évian-les-Bains
St. Julien-sur-Reyssouze
Coligny
Arinthod
St. Claude
Divonne-les-Bains
Thonon-les-Bains
Manziat
Nyon
Marboz
Haut-Jura
Col de la Faucille
Montrevel-en-Bresse
St. Étienne-du-Bois
Dortan
Crêt de la Neige 1718
Gex
Versoix
Douvaine
Perrignier
Pont-de-Veyle
St. Cyr-sur-Menthon
Treffort
Oyonnax
Ferney-Voltaire
Chablais
St. Genis-Pouilly
Bellevaux
Mézériat
Bourg-en-Bresse
Izernore
Chézery-Forens
Genève
Geneva
St. Cergues
Jasseron
Ceyzériat
St. Germain-de-Joux
Vernier
Boëge
St. Didier
St. Martin-du-Frêne
Annemasse
Châtillon-sur-Chalaronne
Neuville-les-Dames
Nantua
St. Julien-en-Genevois
Les Gets
St. Jeoire
Dombes
St. Paul-de-Varax
Bellegarde-sur-Valserine
Viry
Taninges
Marlieux
Poncin
La Roche-sur-Foron
Bonneville
St. Trivier-sur-Moignans
Cluses
Pont-d'Ain
Brénod
Frangy
Cruseilles
Scionzier
Ambérieux-en-Dombes
Villars-les-Dombes
Chalamont
Priay
Ambérieu-en-Bugey
Hauteville-Lompnès
Thorens-Glières
Le Petit-Bornand
Trévoux
St. Rambert-en-Bugey
Seyssel
La Balme-de-Sillingy
Le Grand-Bornand
St. André-de-Corcy
Meximieux
Lagnieu
Tenay
Annecy
Sallanches
Montluel
Sault-Brénaz
Artemare
Rumilly
La Clusaz
Neuville-sur-Saône
Miribel
Virieu-le-Grand
Culoz
C. des Aravis 1486
Combloux
Caluire-et-Cuire
Veyrier
Thônes
Sevrier
Lac d'Annecy
Megève
Montalieu-Vercieu
Serrières-de-Briord
Chazey-Bons
St. Jorioz
Talloires
Flumet
Villeurbanne
Pont-de-Chéruy
Albens
Les Contamines-Montjoie
Lyon
Meyzieu
Belley
Massif des Bauges
Ugine
St. Priest
Crémieu
Faverges
Beaufort
L. du Bourget
Yenne
Lescheraines
Vénissieux
Trept
Morestel
Aix-les-Bains
Albertville
St. Symphorien-d'Ozon
Walibi Rhône-Alpes
Le Bourget-du-Lac
Le Châtelard
Villefontaine
La Tour-du-Pin
St. Genix-sur-Guiers
La Motte-Servolex
Grignon
La Bâthie
Diémoz
Les Déserts
St. Pierre-d'Albigny
Vienne
Bourgoin-Jallieu
Novalaise
Chambéry
Cevins
St. Jean-de-Bournay
Pont-de-Beauvoisin
Cognin
Challes-les-Eaux
Ste. Hélène-sur-Isère
Aime
Les Abrets
Aiguebelle
La Bridoire
Chamoux-sur-Gelon
Montmélian
Moûtiers
Cour-et-Buis
Virieu
Montferrat
Col du Granier 1134
Valmorel
Châbons
Chapareillan
Epierre
Pontcharra
Les Echelles
St. Jean-de-Belleville
Roussillon
La Côte-St. André
Chirens
Chartreuse
St. Pierre-d'Entremont
Allevard
Méribel
Voiron
St. Laurent-du-Pont
Le Touvet
St. Pierre-d'Allevard
St. Martin-de-Belleville
Beaurepaire
Marcilloles
Goncelin
La Chambre
St. Étienne-de-St. Geoirs
Rives
Moirans
St. Pierre-de-Chartreuse
St. Étienne-de-Cuines
Les Ménuires
St. Rambert-d'Albon
Lens Lestang
Tullins
Voreppe
Les Sept Laux
St. Jean-de-Maurienne
Belledonne
Maurienne
Hauterives
Roybon
Val Thorens
St. Égrève
Meylan
Froges
St. Julien-Mont-Denis
Varacieux
Domène
St. Sorlin-d'Arves
Montmiral
Vinay
Grenoble
St. Martin-d'Hères
St. Michel-de-Maurienne
St. Marcellin
Échirolles
Valloire
Tunnel du Fréjus
Margès
Chamrousse
Allemont
Valmeinier
St. Hilaire-du-Rosier
Rencurel
Château de Vizille
Tain-l'Hermitage
Peyrins
Pont-en-Royans
Villard-de-Lans
L'Alpe-d'Huez
Mt. Thabor 3181
Romans-sur-Isère
Vizille
Le Bourg-d'Oisans
Bardonècchia
Bourg-de-Péage
St. Nazaire-en-Royans
Vif
La Grave
Col du Galibier 2646
St. Jean-en-Royans
Romanche
Col d'Ornon 1318
Névache
St. Marcel
Alixan
St. Georges-de-Commiers
Col du Lautaret 2058
La Chapelle-en-Vercors
Montelier
Vercors
Monestier-de-Clermont
Les Deux-Alpes
Le Monêtier-les-Bains
Valence
Chabeuil
Léoncel
La Mure
Valbonnais
Écrins
Serre-Chevalier
Ailefroide
Portes-lès-Valence
Vassieux-en-Vercors
4102
Massif du Pelvoux
Briançon
Montmeyran
Drac
St. Martin-de-Queyrières
Vallouise
Col de Rousset 1254
Clelles
Mens
Corps
St. Firmin
Plan-de-Baix
Fortifications Gallo-Romaines
La Chapelle-en-Valgaudémar
Livron-sur-Drôme
Lalley
L'Argentière-la-Bessée
Die
Col de la Croix Haute 1179
Crest
Loriol-sur-Drôme
Saillans
Vercheny
Châtillon-en-Diois
Agnières
Orcières
Drôme
St. Bonnet
Mont Dauphin
Pradelle
Luc-en-Diois
Col Bayard 1248
Châteauroux-les-Alpes
Risoul
Sauzet
Cléon-d'Andran
Bourdeaux
Montélimar
La Bégude-de-Mazenc
St. Nazaire-le-Désert
Beaurières
La Roche-des-Arnauds
Vars les Claux
Embrun
Espeluche
Aspres-sur-Buëch
Chorges
Col de Vars 2109
Gap
Veynes
Aleyrac
Savines
Les Orres
0 10 20 30 km

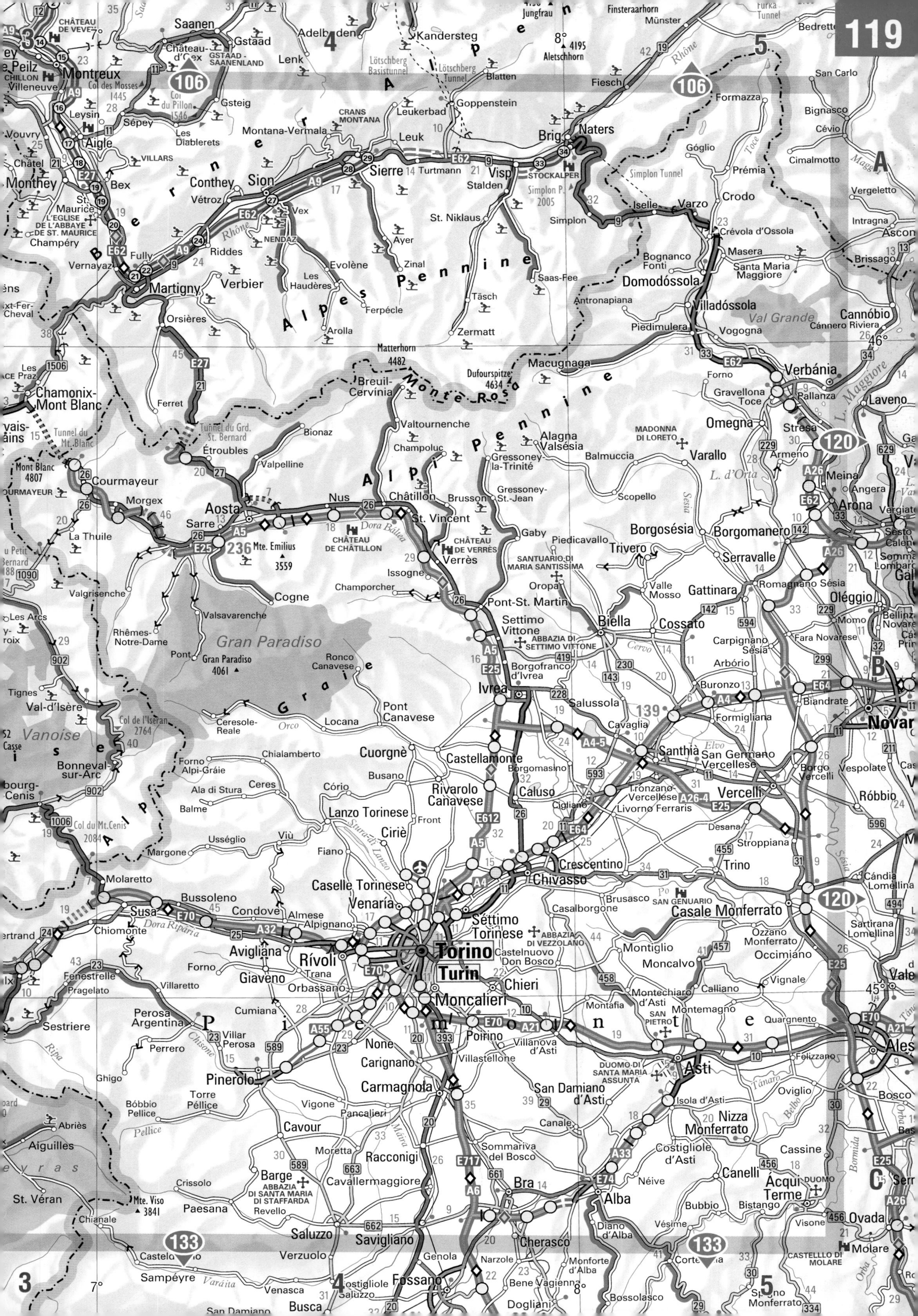
Montreux
Aigle
Monthey
Sion
Sierre
Visp
Brig
Naters
Martigny
Verbier
Zermatt
Matterhorn 4482
Monte Rosa
Dufourspitze 4634
Domodóssola
Verbània
Omegna
Chamonix-Mont Blanc
Mont Blanc 4807
Courmayeur
Aosta
Châtillon
St. Vincent
Gran Paradiso 4061
Ivrea
Biella
Vercelli
Novara
Torino
Turin
Moncalieri
Chieri
Asti
Alba
Bra
Pinerolo
Saluzzo
Savigliano
Fossano
Casale Monferrato
Alpes Pennine
Alpi Pennine
Berner Alpen
Alpi Graie
Piemonte
Simplon Tunnel
Tunnel du Mt. Blanc
Col du Mt. Cenis 2084
Col de l'Iseran 2764
Mte. Viso 3841
Lago Maggiore

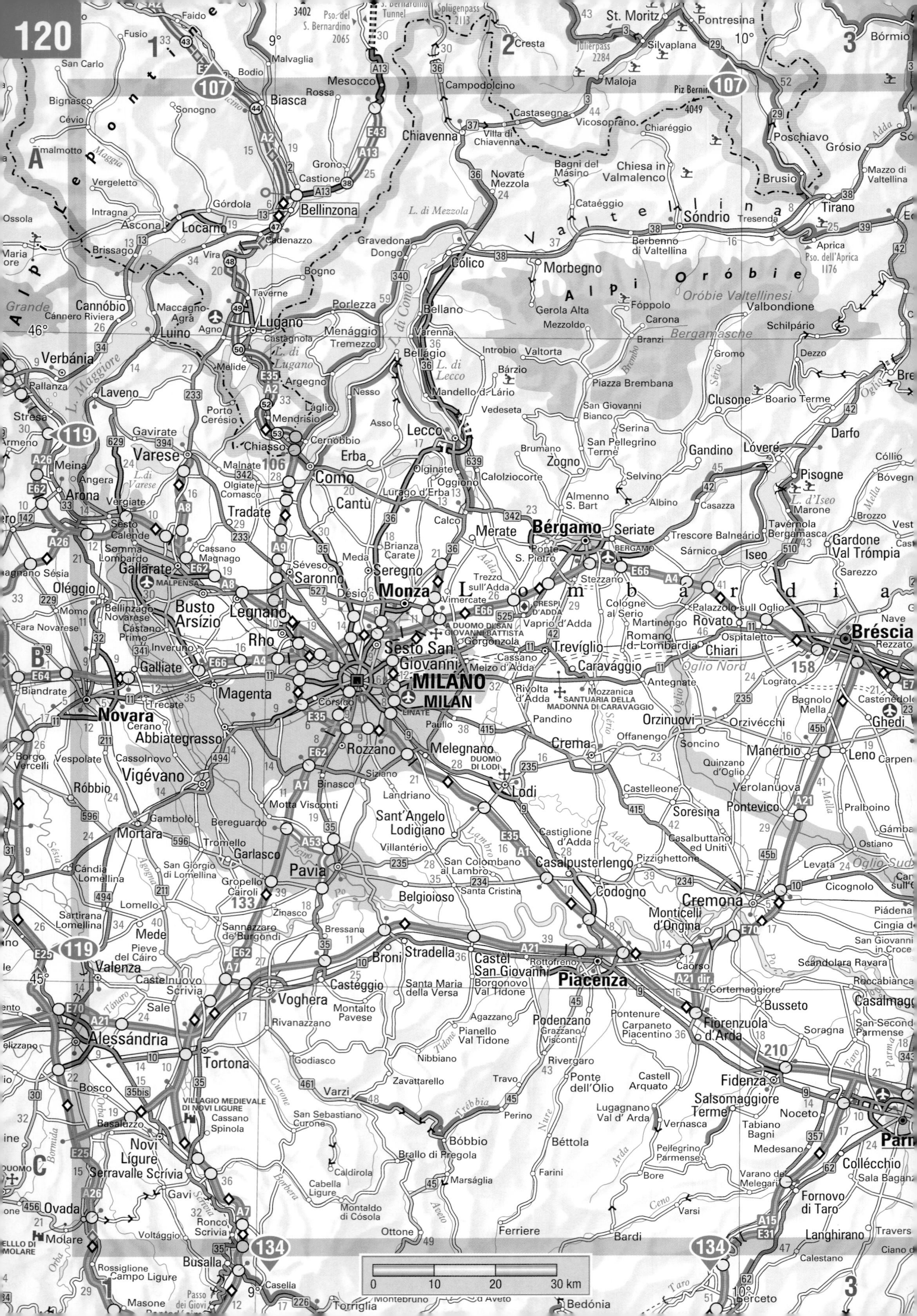

Faido
Fusio
Alpi Lepontine
9°
Malvaglia
Pso. del S. Bernardino 2065
S. Bernardino Tunnel
Splügenpass 2113
Cresta
St. Moritz
Pontresina
Silvaplana
Julierpass 2284
10°
Bórmio
San Carlo
Bodio
107
Mesocco
Campodolcino
Maloja
Piz Bernina 4049
Bignasco
Rossa
Biasca
Sonogno
Castasegna
Vicosoprano
Chiaréggio
Cévio
Chiavenna
Villa di Chiavenna
Poschiavo
Grósio
Maggia
Grono
Castione
Novate Mezzola
Bagni del Másino
Chiesa in Valmalenco
Brusio
Mazzo di Valtellina
Vergeletto
Górdola
Bellinzona
Locarno
Ascona
Intragna
Ossola
Cadenazzo
L. di Mezzola
Cataéggio
Valtellina
Sóndrio
Tresenda
Tirano
Aprica
Pso. dell'Aprica 1176
Brissago
Vira
Gravedona
Dongo
Berbenno di Valtellina
Bogno
Cólico
Morbegno
Alpi Oróbie
Oróbie Valtellinesi
Valbondione
Taverne
Fóppolo
Carona
Gerola Alta
Cannóbio
Cánnero Riviera
Maccagno-Agra
Agno
Lugano
Porlezza
Bellano
Mezzoldo
Bergamasche
Branzi
Schilpário
Luino
46°
Castagnola
L. di Lugano
Menággio
Tremezzo
L. di Como
Varenna
Introbio
Valtorta
Gromo
Dezzo
Verbánia
Pallanza
Melide
Argegno
Bellágio
L. di Lecco
Bárzio
Piazza Brembana
Stresa
Laveno
L. Maggiore
Porto Cerésio
Mendrisio
Láglio
Nesso
Mandello d. Lário
Clusone
Boario Terme
Vedeseta
San Giovanni Bianco
Serina
Armeno
119
Gavirate
Chiasso
Cernóbbio
Asso
Lecco
Brumano
San Pellegrino Terme
Darfo
Gandino
Lóvere
Meina
Varese
Malnate
106
Erba
Zogno
Angera
L. di Varese
Olgiate Comasco
Como
Olginate
Oggiono
Calolziocorte
Selvino
Pisogne
Cóllio
Bóvegno
Arona
Vergiate
Cantù
Lurago d'Erba
Almenno S. Bart
Albino
L. d'Iseo
Marone
Tradate
Calco
Merate
Bérgamo
Seriate
Casazza
Tavernola Bergamasca
Brozzo
Sesto Calende
Somma Lombardo
Cassano Magnago
Brianza Carate
Meda
Ponte S. Pietro
Trescore Balneário
Sárnico
Iseo
Gardone Val Trómpia
Gallarate
Malpensa
Séveso
Saronno
Seregno
Trezzo sull'Adda
Stezzano
Sarezzo
Oléggio
Busto Arsízio
Legnano
Désio
Monza
Vimercate
Crespi d'Adda
Lombardia
Cologne al Serio
Palazzolo sull'Oglio
Bellinzago Novarese
Momo
Fara Novarese
Castano Primo
Rho
A Duomo di San Giovanni Battista
Gorgonzola
Vaprio d'Adda
Martinengo
Rovato
Nave
Bréscia
Rezzato
Inveruno
Sesto San Giovanni
Cassano
Tréviglio
Romano d. Lombardia
Ospitaletto
Chiari
Galliate
Milano
Milan
Melzo d'Adda
Caravággio
Oglio Nord
158
Biandrate
Magenta
Trecate
Rivolta d'Adda
Santuario della Madonna di Caravaggio
Mozzanica
Antegnate
Lograto
Castenedolo
Novara
Córsico
Linate
Pandino
Orzinuovi
Orzivécchi
Bagnolo Mella
Ghedi
Borgo Vercelli
Cerano
Abbiategrasso
Paullo
Offanengo
Crema
Soncino
Manérbio
Leno
Vespolate
Cassolnovo
Rozzano
Melegnano
Duomo di Lodi
Quinzano d'Oglio
Vigévano
Róbbio
Binasco
Siziano
Lodi
Castelleone
Verolanuova
Motta Visconti
Landriano
Sant'Angelo Lodigiano
Soresina
Pontevico
Pralboino
Gambolò
Mortara
Bereguardo
Tromello
Garlasco
Villantério
Castiglione d'Adda
Casalbuttano ed Uniti
Ostiano
Gámbara
Cándia Lomellina
San Giórgio di Lomellina
Pavia
San Colombano al Lambro
Casalpusterlengo
Pizzighettone
Levata
Oglio Sud
Gropello Cairoli
133
Belgioioso
Santa Cristina
Codogno
Cremona
Cicognolo
Lomello
Zinasco
Sartirana Lomellina
Sannazzaro de' Burgondi
Bressana
Monticelli d'Ongina
Piádena
Cingia de'
Mede
Pieve del Cáiro
Broni
Stradella
Castel San Giovanni
Rottofreno
Piacenza
Caorso
San Giovanni in Croce
Scandolara Ravara
Valenza
45°
Castelnuovo Scrivia
Casteggio
Santa Maria della Versa
Borgonovo Val Tidone
Cortemaggiore
Roccabianca
Casalmaggiore
Sale
Voghera
Montalto Pavese
Busseto
Alessándria
Rivanazzano
Agazzano
Pianello Val Tidone
Podenzano
Grazzano Visconti
Pontenure
Carpaneto Piacentino
Fiorenzuola d'Arda
Soragna
San Secondo Parmense
Tortona
Godiasco
Nibbiano
Rivergaro
210
Bosco
Zavattarello
Travo
Ponte dell'Ólio
Castell Arquato
Fidenza
Villaggio medievale di Novi Ligure
Cassano Spinola
Varzi
Perino
Lugagnano Val d'Arda
Salsomaggiore Terme
Noceto
Basaluzzo
San Sebastiano Curone
Vernasca
Tabiano Bagni
Parma
Novi Lígure
Bóbbio
Béttola
Medesano
Serravalle Scrívia
Caldirola
Brallo di Pregola
Pellegrino Parmense
Colléchio
Cabella Ligure
Marságlia
Farini
Bore
Varano de' Melegari
Sala Baganza
Gavi
Ovada
Montaldo di Cósola
Varsi
Fornovo di Taro
Ronco Scrivia
Voltággio
Molare
Ottone
Ferriere
Bardi
Langhirano
Busalla
134
Rossiglione
Campo Ligure
Casella
Calestano
Masone
Passo dei Giovi
Torriglia
Bedónia
Berceto
0 10 20 30 km

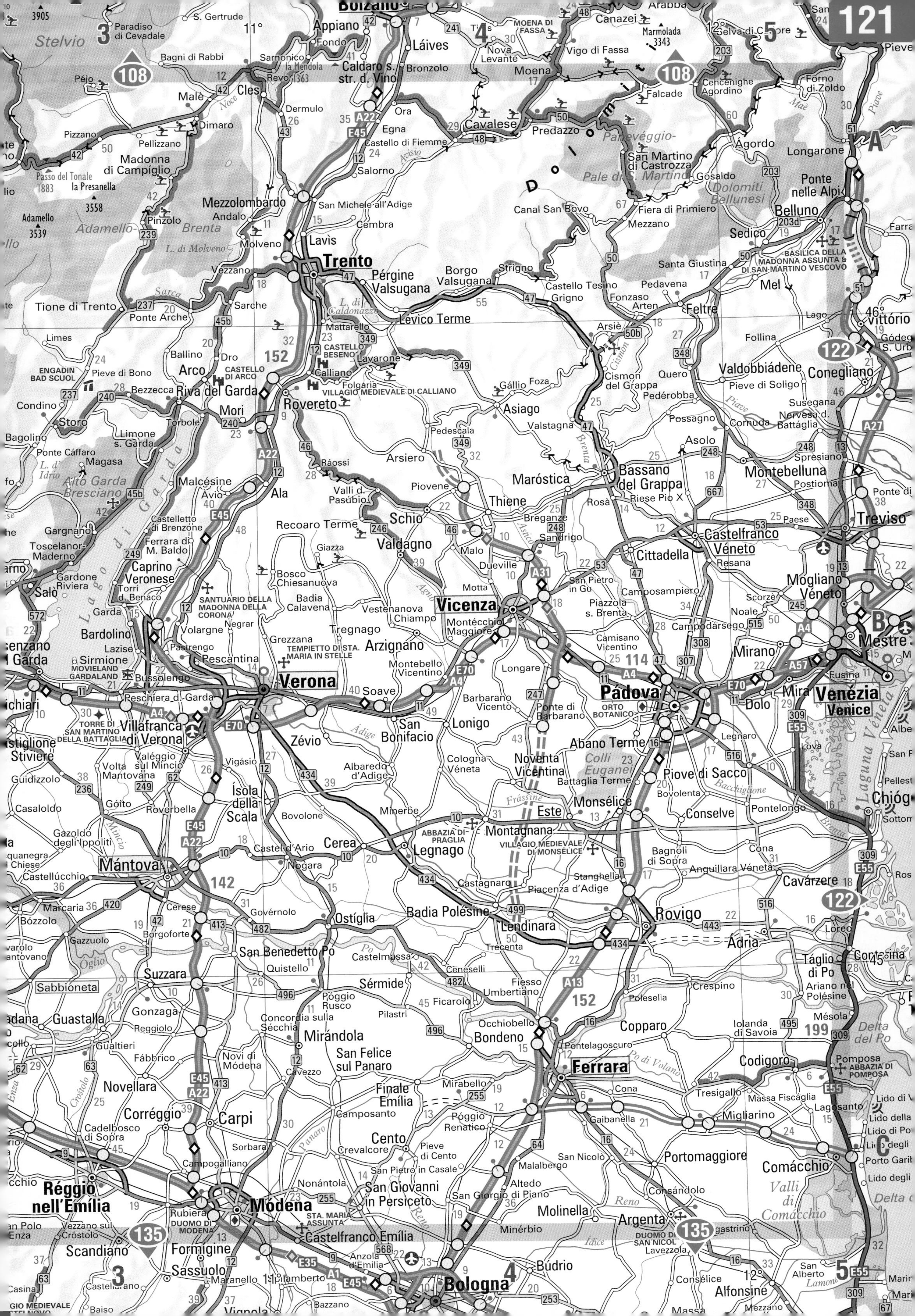

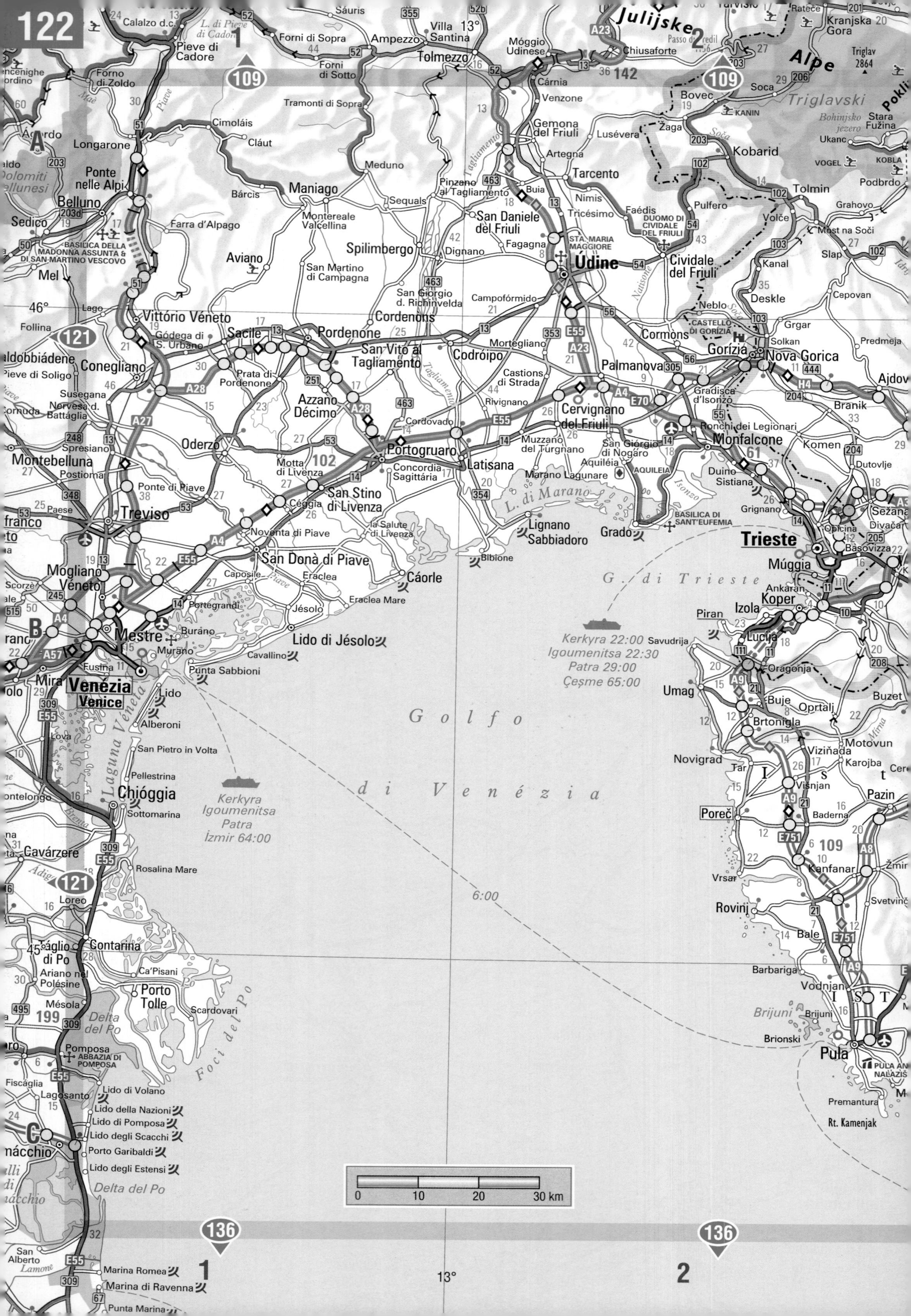

Údine
Trieste
Venézia
Venice
Golfo di Venézia
G. di Trieste
Julijske Alpe
Triglavski
Pordenone
Treviso
Mestre
Chióggia
Gorízia
Nova Gorica
Monfalcone
Koper
Izola
Piran
Umag
Novigrad
Poreč
Rovinj
Pula
Belluno
Vittório Véneto
Conegliano
Sacile
Cordenons
Codróipo
Palmanova
Cervignano del Friuli
Portogruaro
Latisana
Lignano Sabbiadoro
Grado
Cáorle
San Donà di Piave
Lido di Jésolo
Kerkyra 22:00
Igoumenitsa 22:30
Patra 29:00
Çeşme 65:00
Kerkyra
Igoumenitsa
Patra
İzmir 64:00
6:00
0 10 20 30 km

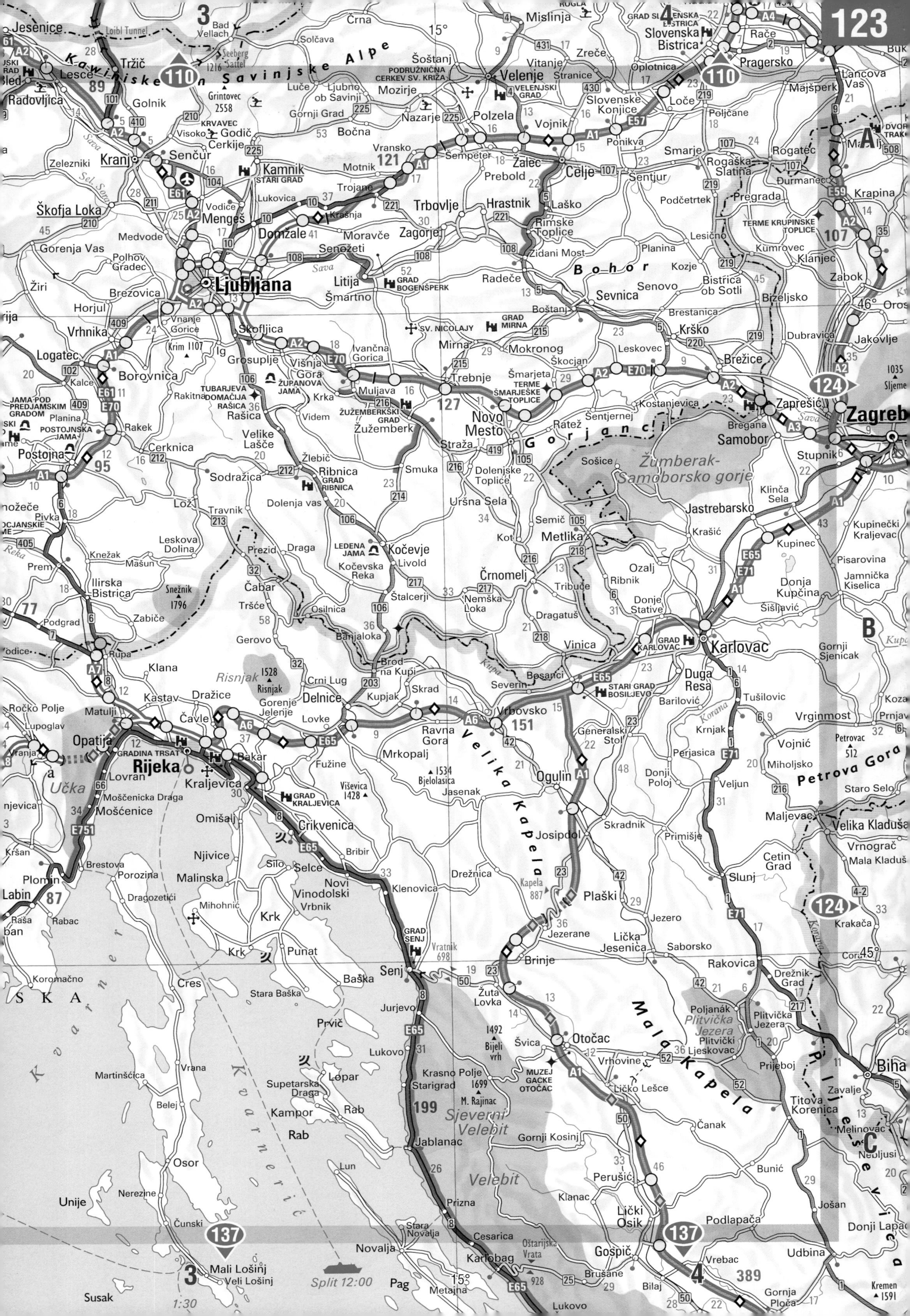

Jesenice
Loibl Tunnel
Bad Vellach
Seeberg Sattel
Kawinkske Savinjske Alpe
Tržič
Bled
Lesce
Radovljica
Golnik
Grintovec 2558
Solčava
Črna
Šoštanj
Mislinja
Velenje
Slovenska Bistrica
Pragersko
Rače
Zreče
Vitanje
Oplotnica
Luče
Ljubno ob Savinji
Mozirje
Gornji Grad
Bočna
Nazarje
Polzela
Vojnik
Slovenske Konjice
Loče
Poljčane
Majšperk
Lancova Vas
Ponikva
Kranj
Senčur
Cerklje
Kamnik
Zelezniki
Škofja Loka
Vodice
Mengeš
Medvode
Gorenja Vas
Polhov Gradec
Domžale
Lukovica
Trojane
Motnik
Vransko
Šempeter
Žalec
Celje
Šentjur
Šmarje
Rogaška Slatina
Rogatec
Ðurmanec
Krapina
Prebold
Trbovlje
Hrastnik
Zagorje
Moravče
Laško
Rimske Toplice
Zidani Most
Podčetrtek
Pregrada
Kumrovec
Klanjec
Zabok
Lesično
Planina
Kozje
Bohor
Senožeti
Litija
Šmartno
Radeče
Ljubljana
Žiri
Horjul
Brezovica
Vrhnika
Vnanje Gorice
Škofljica
Grosuplje
Sevnica
Senovo
Bistrica ob Sotli
Bizeljsko
Boštanj
Brestanica
Krško
Dubravica
Jakovlje
Logatec
Borovnica
Krim 1107
Ivančna Gorica
Višnja Gora
Mirna
Mokronog
Leskovec
Šentjernej
Brežice
Zaprešić
Zagreb
Samobor
Bregana
Kostanjevica
Trebnje
Šmarjeta
Škocjan
Novo Mesto
Muljava
Krka
Žužemberk
Postojna
Planina
Rakek
Cerknica
Rašica
Velike Lašče
Straža
Gorjanci
Žumberak-Samoborsko gorje
Stupnik
Sošice
Sodražica
Ribnica
Žlebič
Smuka
Dolenjske Toplice
Uršna Sela
Klinča Sela
Jastrebarsko
Lož
Travnik
Dolenja vas
Semič
Metlika
Krašić
Kupinec
Kupinečki Kraljevac
Pivka
Leskova Dolina
Prezid
Draga
Kočevje
Kočevska Reka
Livold
Kot
Ozalj
Ribnik
Pisarovina
Knežak
Mašun
Prem
Ilirska Bistrica
Snežnik 1796
Čabar
Tršće
Osilnica
Štalcerji
Črnomelj
Nemška Loka
Tribuče
Dragatuš
Donje Stative
Donja Kupčina
Jamnička Kiselica
Šišljavić
Podgrad
Zabiče
Gerovo
Banjaloka
Vinica
Karlovac
Gornji Sjenicak
Rupa
Klana
Risnjak
Risnjak 1528
Crni Lug
Brod na Kupi
Skrad
Severin
Bosanci
Stari Grad Bosiljevo
Duga Resa
Tušilovic
Barilović
Kastav
Dražice
Gorenje Jelenje
Delnice
Kupjak
Lovke
Ravna Gora
Vrbovsko
Generalski Stol
Krnjak
Vrginmost
Vojnić
Petrovac 512
Ročko Polje
Lupoglav
Matulji
Čavle
Opatija
Rijeka
Bakar
Kraljevica
Lovran
Učka
Mošćenicka Draga
Mošćenice
Fužine
Mrkopalj
Bjelolasica 1534
Višecica 1428
Jasenak
Velika Kapela
Ogulin
Perjasica
Donji Poloj
Veljun
Miholjsko
Petrova Gora
Staro Selo
Maljevac
Velika Kladuša
Vrnograč
Mala Kladuš
Omišalj
Crikvenica
Njivice
Malinska
Silo
Selce
Bribir
Novi Vinodolski
Vrbnik
Klenovica
Drežnica
Josipdol
Skradnik
Primišje
Cetin Grad
Slunj
Plomin
Labin
Brestova
Porozina
Dragozetići
Mihohnić
Krk
Kapela 887
Plaški
Jezero
Rabac
Raša
Jezerane
Lička Jesenica
Saborsko
Krakača
Punat
Senj
Vratnik 698
Brinje
Rakovica
Drežnik-Grad
Koromačno
Cres
Baška
Stara Baška
Jurjevo
Žuta Lovka
Poljanak
Plitvička Jezera
Plitvički Ljeskovac
Mala Kapela
Prvič
Lukovo
Bijeli vrh 1492
Švica
Otočac
Vrhovine
Prijeboj
Zavalje
Bihać
Kvarner
Kvarnerić
Vrana
Martinšćica
Lopar
Supetarska Draga
Krasno Polje
Starigrad
Muzej Gacke Otočac
Ličko Lešce
Belej
Kampor
Rab
Sjeverni Velebit
M. Rajinac
Jablanac
Gornji Kosinj
Čanak
Titova Korenica
Melinovac
Nebljusi
Osor
Lun
Velebit
Perušić
Bunić
Nerezine
Unije
Klanac
Prizna
Lički Osik
Čunski
Stara Novalja
Novalja
Cesarica
Oštarijska Vrata
Podlapača
Donji Lapac
Gospić
Udbina
Mali Lošinj
Veli Lošinj
Split 12:00
Karlobag
Brušane
Vrebac
Pag
Metajna
Susak
Bilaj
Lukovo
Gornja Ploča
Kremen 1591
Sljeme 1035

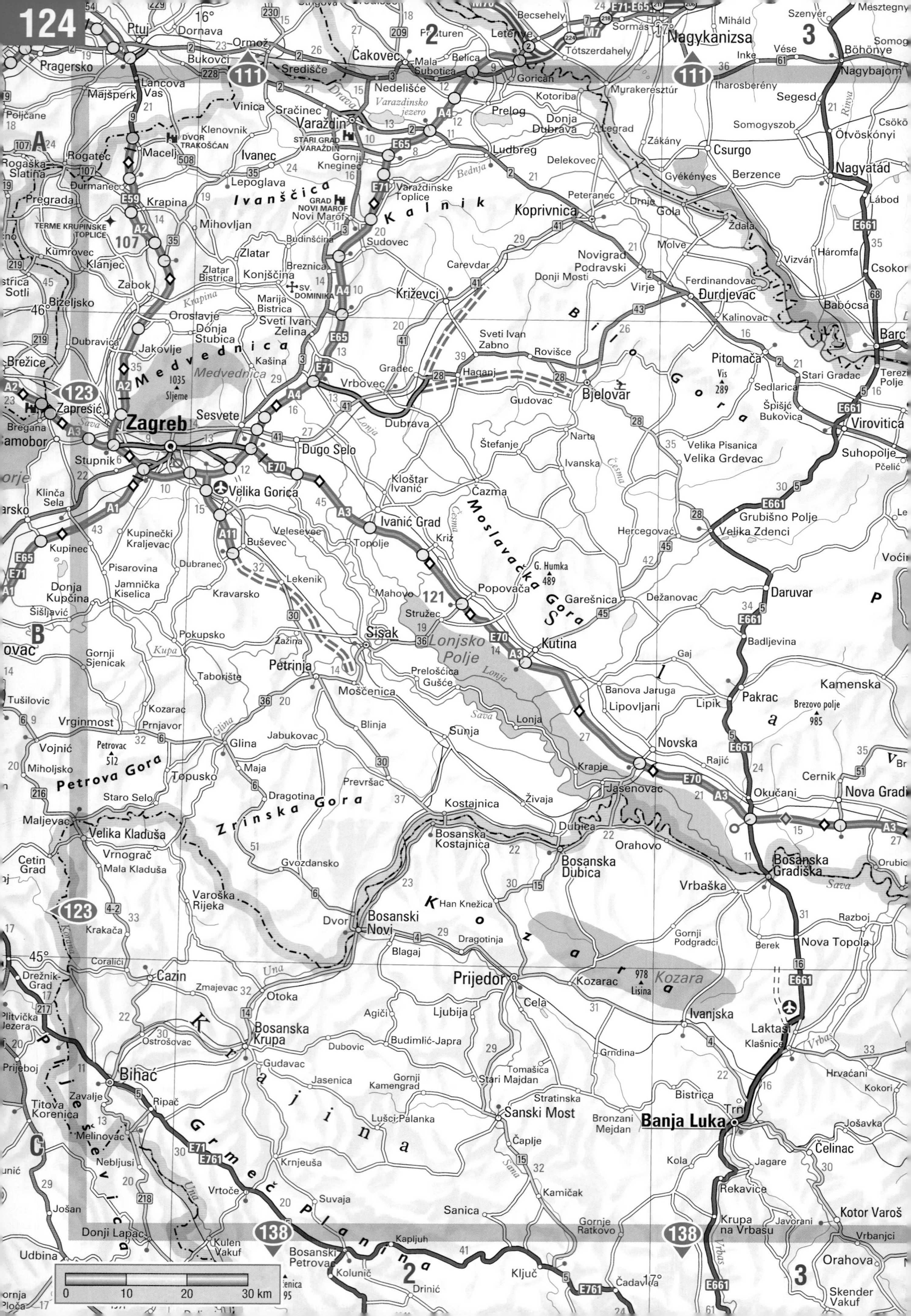
Zagreb
Varaždin
Čakovec
Koprivnica
Bjelovar
Sisak
Karlovac
Petrinja
Kutina
Novska
Daruvar
Virovitica
Nagykanizsa
Banja Luka
Prijedor
Bihać
Bosanski Novi
Bosanska Gradiška
Sanski Most
Medvednica
Kalnik
Ivanščica
Moslavačka Gora
Bilo Gora
Petrova Gora
Zrinska Gora
Kozara
Grmeč Planina
Lonjsko Polje
0 10 20 30 km

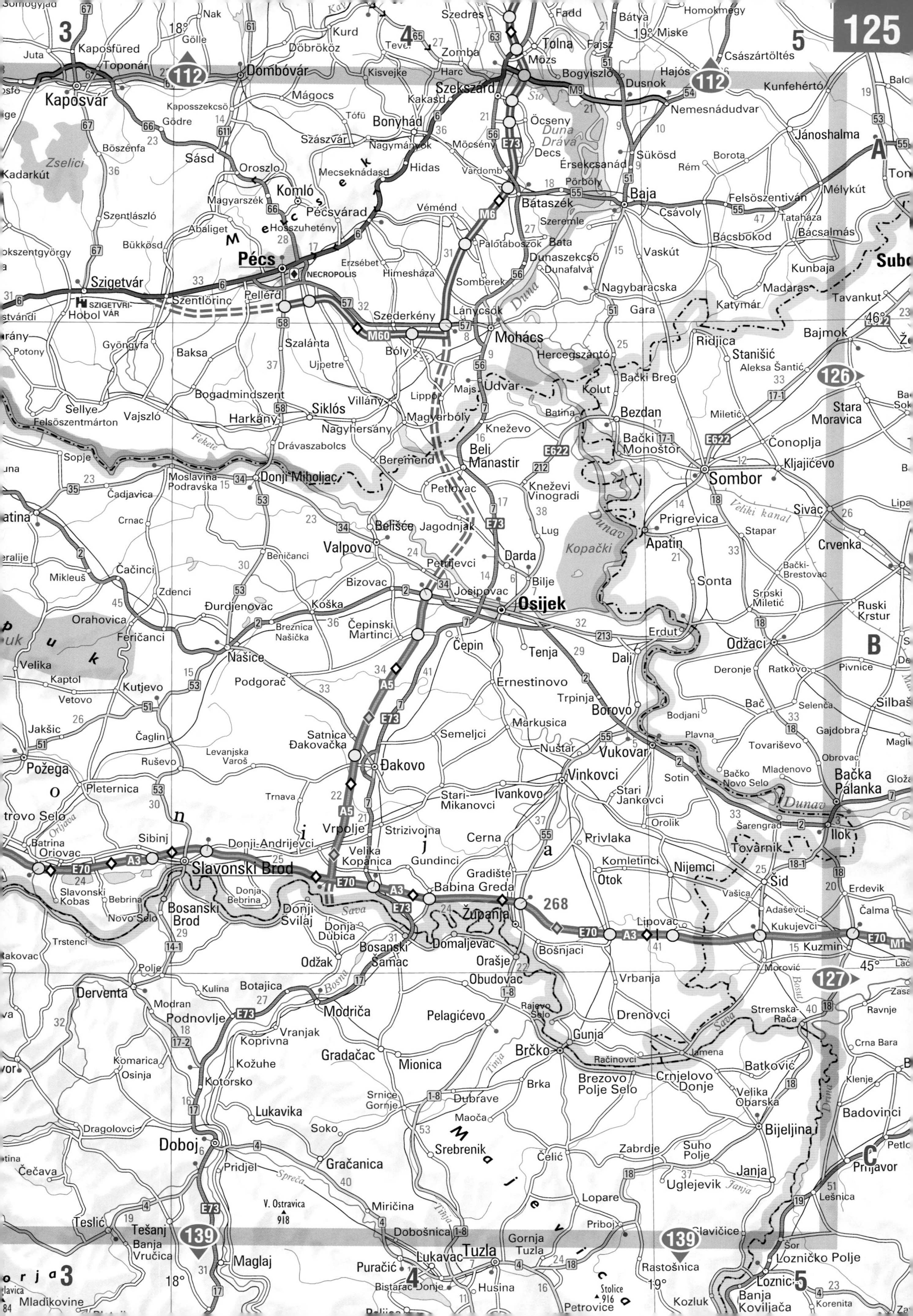

3
4
5
Kaposfüred
Nak
Gölle
Kurd
Döbrököz
Tevel
Zomba
Szedres
Fadd
Bátya
Homokmégy
Miske
Tolna
Mözs
Fajsz
Császártöltés
Juta
Toponár
Dombóvár
Kisvejke
Harc
Bogyiszló
Hajós
Dusnok
Kunfehértó
Kaposvár
Kaposszekcső
Mágocs
Kakasd
Szekszárd
Sió
Nemesnádudvar
Gödre
Tófű
Bonyhád
Öcseny
Duna
Dráva
Decs
Szászvár
Nagymányok
Mőcsény
Jánoshalma
Böszénfa
Zselici
Sásd
Süksöd
Borota
Rém
Érsekcsanád
Kadarkút
Oroszló
Mecseknádasd
Hidas
Várdomb
Pörböly
Komló
Magyarszék
Pécsvárad
Véménd
Bátaszék
Baja
Felsőszentiván
Mélykút
Szentlászló
Csávoly
Tataháza
Abaliget
Hosszúhetény
Szeremle
Bácsbokod
Bácsalmás
Bükkösd
Palotabozsok
Bata
Pécs
Erzsébet
Himesháza
Dunaszekcső
Vaskút
Dunafalva
Kunbaja
Szigetvár
NECROPOLIS
Somberek
Nagybaracska
Madaras
Szentlőrinc
Pellérd
Szigetvári vár
Hobol
Szederkény
Lánycsók
Gara
Katymár
Tavankut
Szalánta
Mohács
Ridjica
Bajmok
Gyöngyfa
Potony
Baksa
Újpetre
Bóly
Hercegszántó
Stanišić
Aleksa Šantić
Udvar
Bački Breg
Bogadmindszent
Lippó
Majs
Kolut
Sellye
Vajszló
Siklós
Villány
Batina
Bezdan
Miletić
Stara Moravica
Felsőszentmárton
Harkány
Nagyharsány
Magyarbóly
Kneževo
Bački Monoštor
Fekete
Drávaszabolcs
Beli Manastir
Čonoplja
Sopje
Beremend
Kljajićevo
Sombor
Moslavina Podravska
Donji Miholjac
Kneževi Vinogradi
Čadjavica
Petlovac
Crnac
Lug
Dunav
Prigrevica
Veliki kanal
Sivac
Stapar
Belišće
Jagodnjak
Apatin
Crvenka
Kopački
Valpovo
Beničanci
Darda
Mikleuš
Čačinci
Petrijevci
Bački-Brestovac
Bizovac
Bilje
Sonta
Zdenci
Josipovac
Srpski Miletić
Koška
Osijek
Orahovica
Đurdjenovac
Breznica Našička
Čepinski Martinci
Ruski Krstur
Feričanci
Čepin
Erdut
Odžaci
Našice
Tenja
Dalj
Velika
Deronje
Ratkovo
Pivnice
Kaptol
Podgorač
Ernestinovo
Kutjevo
Vetovo
Trpinja
Borovo
Bač
Selenča
Silbaš
Bodjani
Jakšic
Čaglin
Satnica Đakovačka
Semeljci
Markusica
Plavna
Gajdobra
Tovariševo
Levanjska Varoš
Nuštar
Vukovar
Požega
Ruševo
Đakovo
Vinkovci
Obrovac
Mladenovo
Bačko Novo Selo
Sotin
Bačka Palanka
Pleternica
Trnava
Stari Mikanovci
Ivankovo
Stari Jankovci
Orolik
Šarengrad
Ilok
Batrina
Sibinj
Vrpolje
Strizivojna
Cerna
Privlaka
Tovarnik
Oriovac
Donji-Andrijevci
Velika Kopanica
Gundinci
Komletinci
Nijemci
Slavonski Brod
Gradište
Otok
Šid
Erdevik
Slavonski Kobas
Bebrina
Donja Bebrina
Babina Greda
Županja
Vašica
Adaševci
Čalma
Bosanski Brod
Donji Svilaj
Novo Selo
Sava
Lipovac
Kukujevci
Donja Dubica
Domaljevac
Trstenci
Bosanski Šamac
Odžak
Orašje
Bošnjaci
Kuzmin
Polje
Obudovac
Vrbanja
Morović
Bosut
Kulina
Botajica
Derventa
Modriča
Pelagićevo
Rajevo Selo
Drenovci
Stremska-Rača
Ravnje
Modran
Podnovlje
Vranjak
Koprivna
Gunja
Crna Bara
Komarica
Osinja
Gradačac
Mionica
Brčko
Račinovci
Jamena
Batković
Kožuhe
Tinja
Kotorsko
Brka
Brezovo Polje Selo
Crnjelovo Donje
Klenje
Velika Obarska
Srnice Gornje
Dubrave
Lukavika
Maoča
Badovinci
Bijeljina
Dragolovci
Soko
Srebrenik
Majevica
Doboj
Gračanica
Čelić
Zabrdje
Suho Polje
Janja
Prnjavor
Pridjel
Spreča
Čečava
Uglejevik
Lešnica
V. Ostravica
918
Miričina
Lopare
Teslić
Tešanj
Priboj
Dobošnica
Slavičice
Banja Vručica
Gornja Tuzla
Sor
Tuzla
Rastošnica
Lozničko Polje
Maglaj
Puračić
Lukavac
Loznica
Bistarac Donje
Husina
Stolice
916
Kozluk
Banja Koviljača
Korenita
Mladikovine
Petrovice
18°
19°
45°
46°
112
126
127
139
268
E70
E73
A3
A5
M6
M60
E622
M9

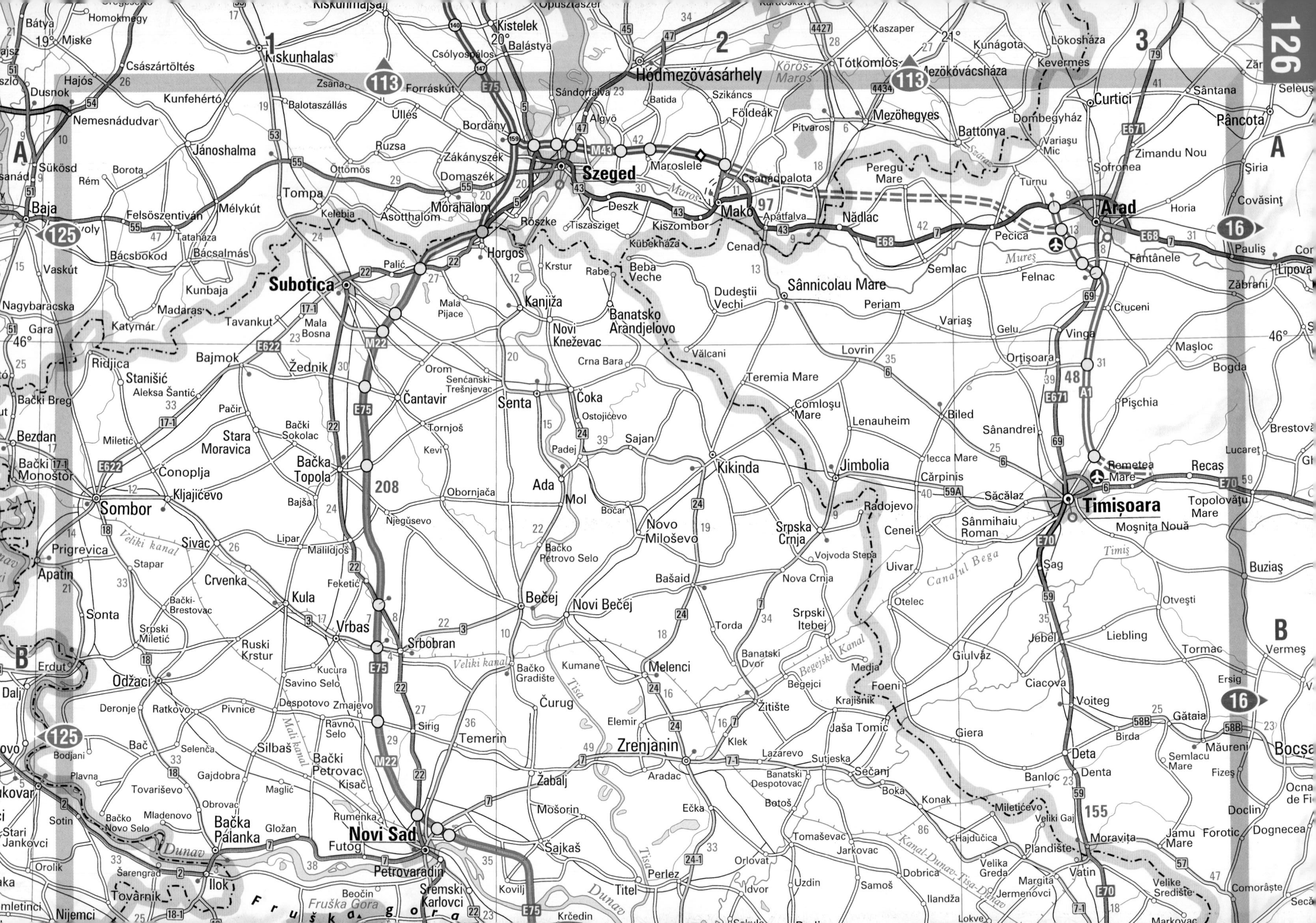

Kiskunhalas
Kistelek
Hódmezővásárhely
Tótkomlós
Mezőkovácsháza
Kunágota
Lőkösháza
Kevermes
Curtici
Pâncota
Baja
Jánoshalma
Mélykút
Tompa
Mórahalom
Szeged
Maroslele
Csanádpalota
Makó
Nădlac
Arad
Lipova
Mezőhegyes
Battonya
Subotica
Horgoš
Kanjiža
Senta
Čoka
Ada
Kikinda
Jimbolia
Sânnicolau Mare
Timişoara
Recaş
Buziaş
Sombor
Apatin
Kula
Vrbas
Srbobran
Bačka Topola
Bečej
Novi Bečej
Melenci
Zrenjanin
Temerin
Žabalj
Novi Sad
Petrovaradin
Sremski Karlovci
Titel
Bačka Palanka
Odžaci
Ilok
Vukovar
Deta
Moraviţa
Vršac
Dunav
Tisa
Mureş
Timiş
Fruška Gora
E68
E70
E75
E622
E671
M43
M22
16
113
125
155
208
97
48
46°
20°
21°
19°
1
2
3
A
B

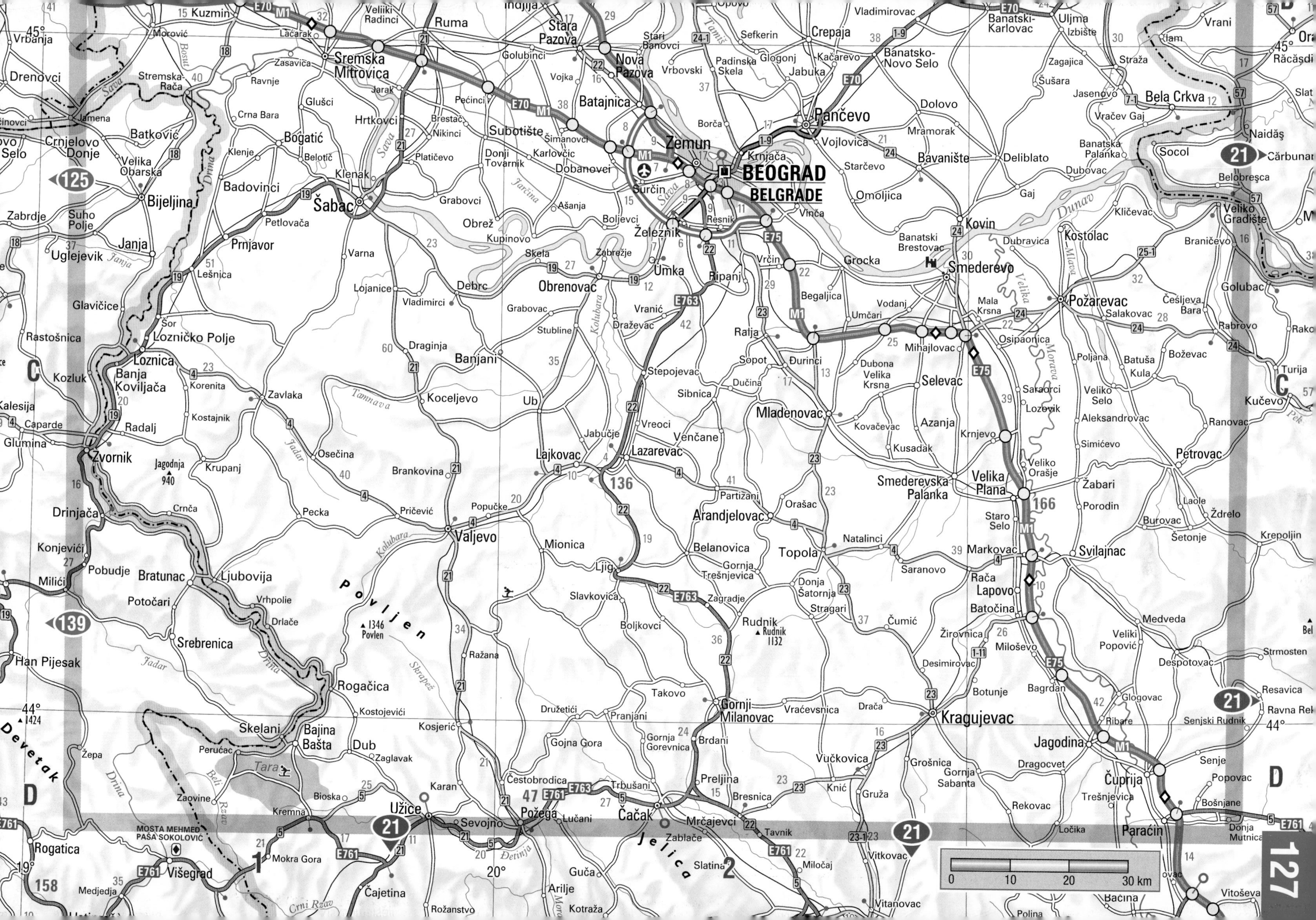
BEOGRAD
BELGRADE
Zemun
Pančevo
Smederevo
Požarevac
Kostolac
Kovin
Bela Crkva
Veliko Gradište
Golubac
Kučevo
Petrovac
Velika Plana
Smederevska Palanka
Svilajnac
Jagodina
Ćuprija
Paraćin
Kragujevac
Topola
Arandjelovac
Mladenovac
Lazarevac
Obrenovac
Valjevo
Gornji Milanovac
Čačak
Požega
Užice
Kosjerić
Bajina Bašta
Ljubovija
Loznica
Banja Koviljača
Zvornik
Bijeljina
Šabac
Sremska Mitrovica
Ruma
Stara Pazova
Nova Pazova
Batajnica
Surčin
Uglejevik
Bratunac
Srebrenica
Višegrad
Rogatica
Drina
Sava
Dunav
Velika Morava
Kolubara
Povljen
Jelica
Devetak
Tara
E70
E75
E763
E761
M1
0 10 20 30 km

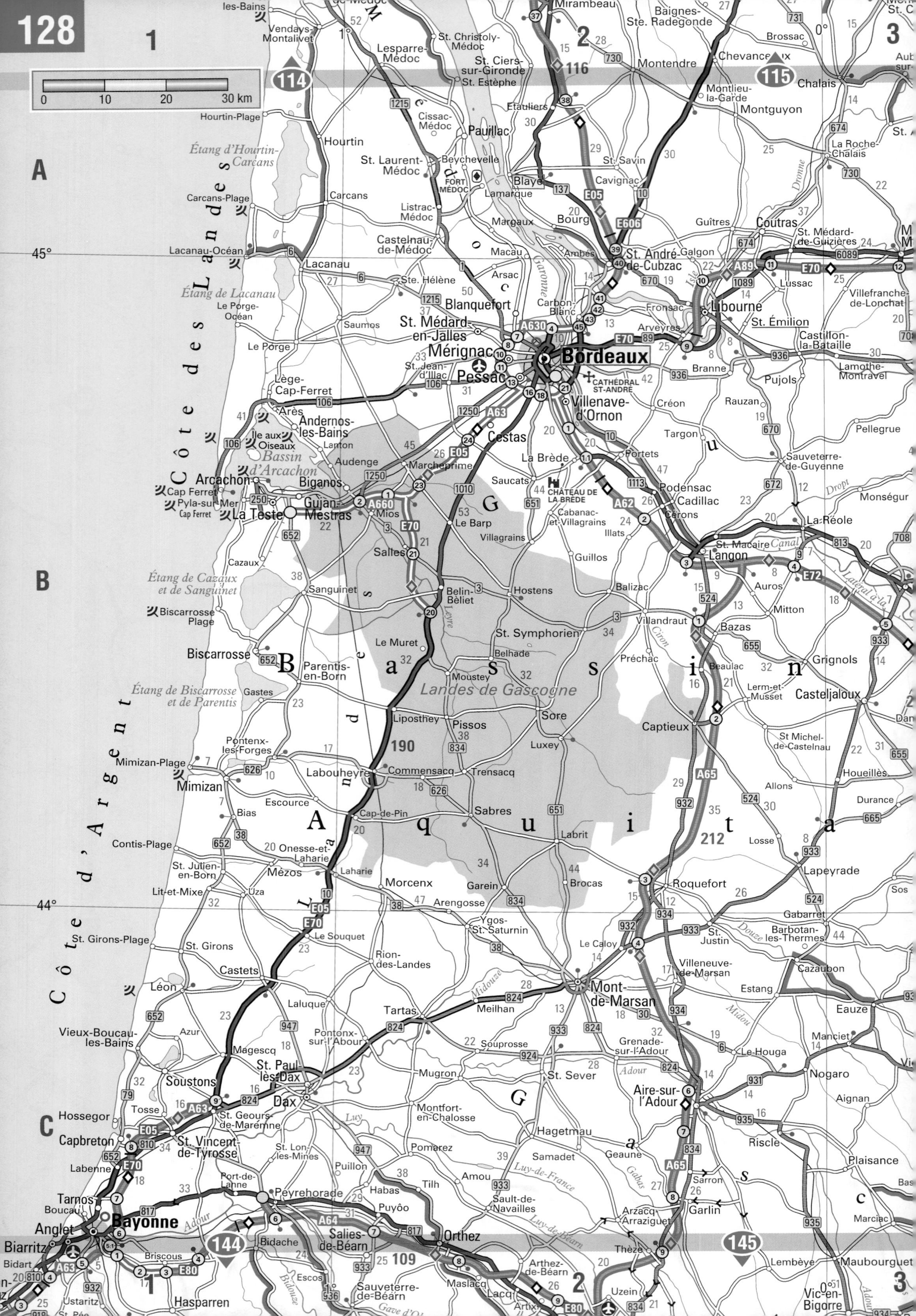

128
1
2
3
A
B
C
0
10
20
30 km
114
115
116
144
145
45°
44°
Bordeaux
Mérignac
Pessac
St. Médard-en-Jalles
Blanquefort
Villenave-d'Ornon
Cestas
La Brède
CHÂTEAU DE LA BRÈDE
CATHÉDRAL ST-ANDRÉ
Libourne
St. Émilion
St. André-de-Cubzac
Blaye
Bourg
Pauillac
FORT MÉDOC
Lesparre-Médoc
Hourtin
Carcans
Lacanau
Lacanau-Océan
Hourtin-Plage
Carcans-Plage
Étang d'Hourtin-Carcans
Étang de Lacanau
Le Porge
Lège-Cap-Ferret
Arès
Andernos-les-Bains
Bassin d'Arcachon
Arcachon
La Teste
Gujan-Mestras
Biganos
Cap Ferret
Pyla-sur-Mer
Étang de Cazaux et de Sanguinet
Biscarrosse
Biscarrosse Plage
Étang de Biscarrosse et de Parentis
Parentis-en-Born
Mimizan
Mimizan-Plage
Landes de Gascogne
Langon
Cadillac
Podensac
Bazas
La Réole
Casteljaloux
Captieux
Roquefort
Mont-de-Marsan
Tartas
Dax
St. Paul-lès-Dax
Soustons
Capbreton
Hossegor
Bayonne
Anglet
Biarritz
Peyrehorade
Orthez
Salies-de-Béarn
Sauveterre-de-Béarn
Hasparren
St. Sever
Aire-sur-l'Adour
Nogaro
Eauze
Riscle
Plaisance
Maubourguet
Vic-en-Bigorre
Garlin
Hagetmau
Morcenx
Labouheyre
Sabres
Pissos
Sore
Villandraut
Coutras
Côte des Landes
Côte d'Argent
Bassin
Aquitaine
Gascogne

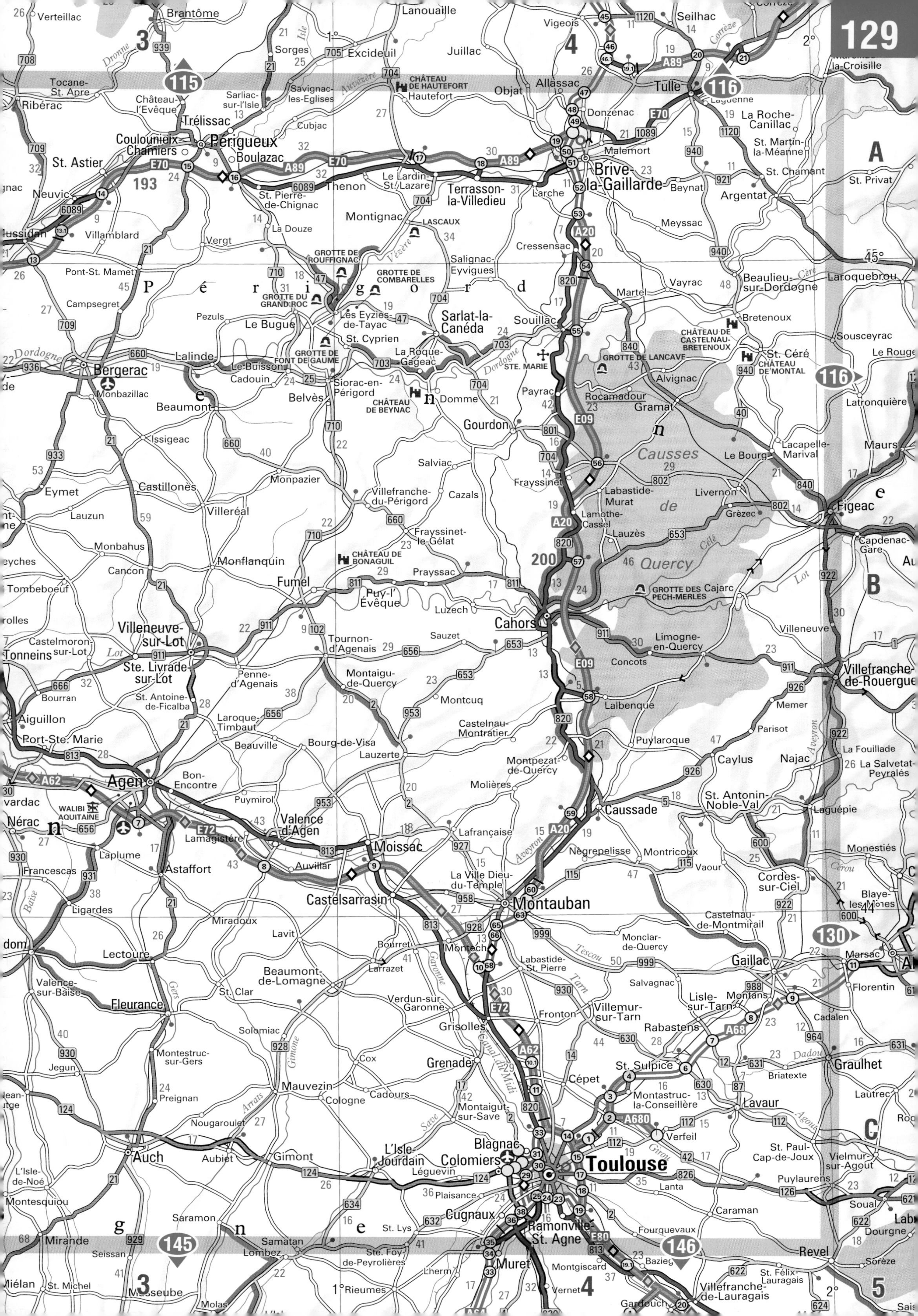
Verteillac
Brantôme
Lanouaille
Vigeois
Seilhac
Sorges
Excideuil
Juillac
Tocane-St. Apre
Ribérac
Château-l'Evêque
Sarliac-sur-l'Isle
Savignac-les-Eglises
CHÂTEAU DE HAUTEFORT
Hautefort
Objat
Allassac
Tulle
Laguenne
La Roche-Canillac
Trélissac
Coulounieix-Chamiers
Périgueux
Boulazac
Cubjac
Donzenac
St. Martin-la-Méanne
St. Astier
Neuvic
Le Lardin-St. Lazare
Terrasson-la-Villedieu
Larche
Malemort
Brive-la-Gaillarde
Beynat
Argentat
St. Chamant
St. Privat
Thenon
St. Pierre-de-Chignac
Montignac
LASCAUX
Mussidan
Villamblard
Vergt
La Douze
Meyssac
Cressensac
GROTTE DE ROUFFIGNAC
GROTTE DE COMBARELLES
Salignac-Eyvigues
Pont-St. Mamet
Martel
Vayrac
Beaulieu-sur-Dordogne
Laroquebrou
Campsegret
Périgord
GROTTE DU GRAND ROC
Les Eyzies-de-Tayac
Sarlat-la-Canéda
Souillac
Bretenoux
Pezuls
Le Bugue
St. Cyprien
CHÂTEAU DE CASTELNAU-BRETENOUX
Sousceyrac
Dordogne
Bergerac
Lalinde
Le Buisson
Cadouin
GROTTE DE FONT DE GAUME
La Roque-Gageac
STE. MARIE
GROTTE DE LANCAVE
St. Céré
CHÂTEAU DE MONTAL
Le Rouget
Monbazillac
Beaumont
Belvès
Siorac-en-Périgord
CHÂTEAU DE BEYNAC
Domme
Payrac
Rocamadour
Alvignac
Gramat
Latronquière
Issigeac
Gourdon
Causses
Lacapelle-Marival
Le Bourg
Maurs
Eymet
Castillonès
Monpazier
Salviac
Frayssinet
Labastide-Murat
Livernon
Villeréal
Villefranche-du-Périgord
Cazals
de
Figeac
Lauzun
Lamothe-Cassel
Grèzec
Capdenac-Gare
Monbahus
Frayssinet-le-Gélat
Lauzès
Célé
Quercy
Tombeboeuf
Cancon
Monflanquin
CHÂTEAU DE BONAGUIL
Prayssac
Fumel
Puy-l'Évêque
Luzech
GROTTE DES PECH-MERLES
Cajarc
Lot
Villeneuve-sur-Lot
Cahors
Villeneuve
Castelmoron-sur-Lot
Tonneins
Tournon-d'Agenais
Sauzet
Limogne-en-Quercy
Ste. Livrade-sur-Lot
Penne-d'Agenais
Concots
Villefranche-de-Rouergue
Montaigu-de-Quercy
Bourran
St. Antoine-de-Ficalba
Montcuq
Aiguillon
Laroque-Timbaut
Lalbenque
Memer
Port-Ste. Marie
Beauville
Bourg-de-Visa
Castelnau-Montratier
Puylaroque
Parisot
Lauzerte
La Fouillade
Caylus
Najac
La Salvetat-Peyralès
Agen
Bon-Encontre
Montpezat-de-Quercy
Molières
Puymirol
Caussade
St. Antonin-Noble-Val
Laguépie
WALIBI AQUITAINE
Nérac
Valence-d'Agen
Lamagistère
Moissac
Lafrançaise
Nègrepelisse
Montricoux
Vaour
Monestiés
Laplume
Francescas
Astaffort
Auvillar
La Ville Dieu-du-Temple
Cordes-sur-Ciel
Castelsarrasin
Montauban
Blaye-les-Mines
Ligardes
Castelnau-de-Montmirail
Miradoux
Lavit
Bourret
Montech
Monclar-de-Quercy
Lectoure
Larrazet
Labastide-St. Pierre
Gaillac
Marsac
Beaumont-de-Lomagne
Salvagnac
Florentin
Valence-sur-Baïse
St. Clar
Villemur-sur-Tarn
Lisle-sur-Tarn
Montans
Fleurance
Verdun-sur-Garonne
Grisolles
Fronton
Cadalen
Rabastens
Solomiac
Montestruc-sur-Gers
Cox
Grenade
Canal du Midi
St. Sulpice
Graulhet
Jegun
Cépet
Montastruc-la-Conseillère
Briatexte
Mauvezin
Cadours
Lavaur
Lautrec
Preignan
Cologne
Montaigut-sur-Save
Nougaroulet
Verfeil
Auch
Aubiet
Gimont
L'Isle-Jourdain
Blagnac
Colomiers
Toulouse
St. Paul-Cap-de-Joux
Vielmur-sur-Agout
L'Isle-de-Noé
Léguevin
Lanta
Puylaurens
Plaisance
Montesquiou
Saramon
Cugnaux
Caraman
Soual
Ramonville-St. Agne
Fourquevaux
Dourgne
Mirande
Seissan
Samatan
Lombez
St. Lys
Ste. Foy-de-Peyrolières
Muret
Revel
Sorèze
Montgiscard
Baziège
St. Félix-Lauragais
Miélan
St. Michel
Masseube
Rieumes
Lherm
Vernet
Villefranche-de-Lauragais
Gardouch
Molas
Garonne
Tarn
Aveyron
A20
A89
A62
A68
A680
E70
E72
E80
E09
115
116
130
145
146

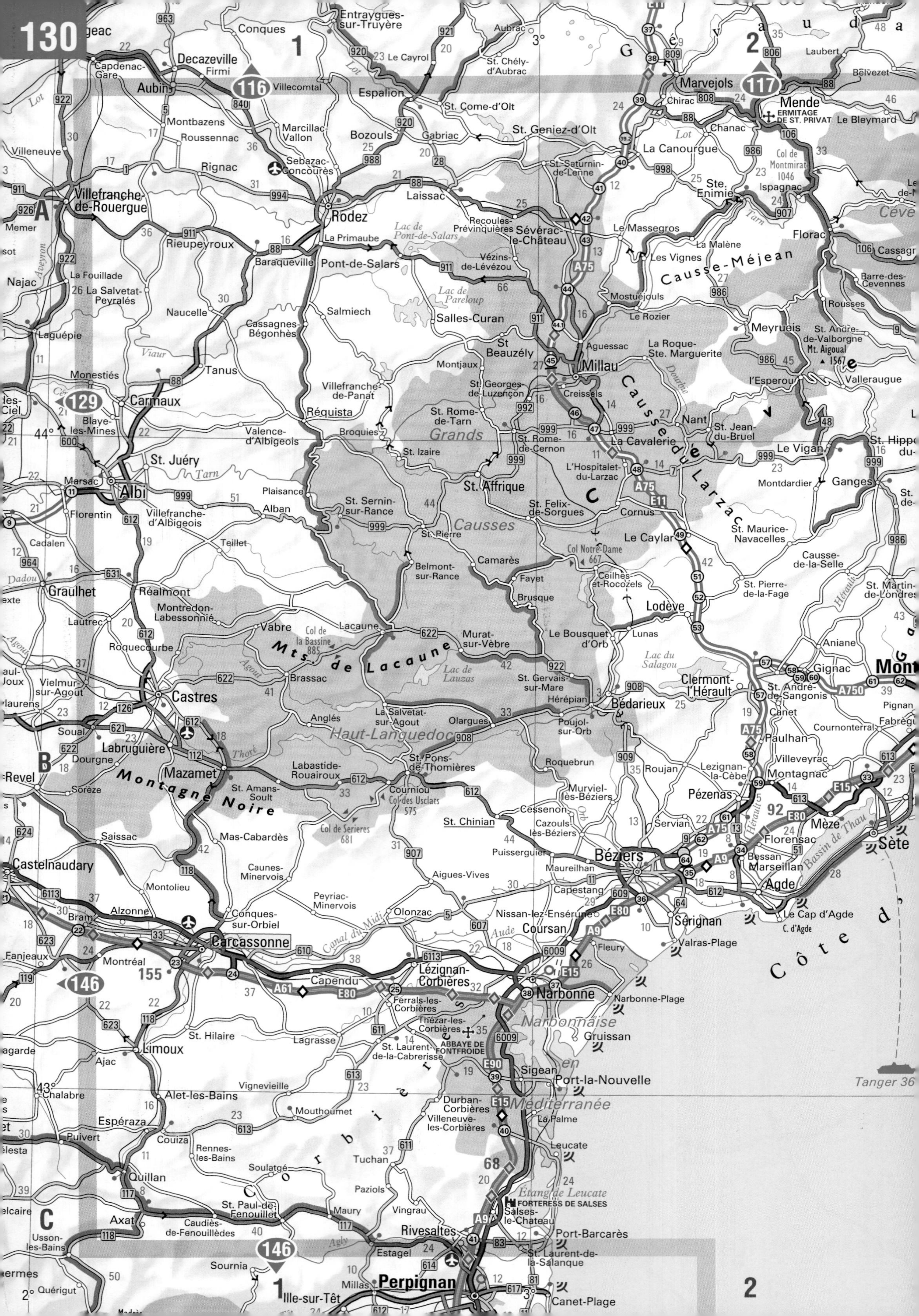
Conques
Entraygues-sur-Truyère
Decazeville
Firmi
Capdenac-Gare
Aubin
Villecomtal
Le Cayrol
Aubrac
St. Chély-d'Aubrac
Espalion
St. Come-d'Olt
Marvejols
Chirac
Mende
ERMITAGE DE ST. PRIVAT
Le Bleymard
Laubert
Bélvezet
Montbazens
Roussennac
Marcillac-Vallon
Bozouls
Gabriac
St. Geniez-d'Olt
Chanac
La Canourgue
Col de Montmirat 1046
Villeneuve
Rignac
Sebazac-Concourès
St. Saturnin-de-Lenne
Ste. Enimie
Ispagnac
Villefranche-de-Rouergue
Rodez
Laissac
Recoules-Prévinquières
Sévérac-le-Château
Le Massegros
Florac
Memer
La Primaube
Lac de Pont-de-Salars
Rieupeyroux
Baraqueville
Pont-de-Salars
Vézins-de-Lévézou
Les Vignes
La Malène
Causse-Méjean
Cassagnas
Najac
La Fouillade
La Salvetat-Peyralès
Barre-des-Cevennes
Lac de Pareloup
Mostuéjouls
Le Rozier
Naucelle
Salmiech
Salles-Curan
Rousses
Laguépie
Cassagnes-Bégonhès
St Beauzély
Aguessac
La Roque-Ste. Marguerite
Meyrueis
St. Andre-de-Valborgne
Mt. Aigoual 1567
Viaur
Tanus
Montjaux
Millau
Monestiés
St. Georges-de-Luzençon
Creissels
Villefranche-de-Panat
Causse du Larzac
L'Esperou
Valleraugue
Carmaux
Réquista
St. Rome-de-Tarn
Blaye-les-Mines
Valence-d'Albigeois
Broquiès
Grands
St. Rome-de-Cernon
Nant
St. Jean-du-Bruel
La Cavalerie
Le Vigan
St. Hippolyte-du-Fort
St. Juéry
St. Izaire
L'Hospitalet-du-Larzac
Tarn
Marsac
Albi
St. Affrique
Montdardier
Ganges
Plaisance
Florentin
Villefranche-d'Albigeois
Alban
St. Sernin-sur-Rance
Causses
St. Felix-de-Sorgues
Cornus
Cadalen
Teillet
St. Pierre
Le Caylar
St. Maurice-Navacelles
Col Notre-Dame 667
Belmont-sur-Rance
Camarès
Causse-de-la-Selle
Graulhet
Réalmont
Fayet
Ceilhes-et-Rocozels
St. Pierre-de-la-Fage
St. Martin-de-Londres
Montredon-Labessonnié
Brusque
Lodève
Lautrec
Vabre
Col de la Bassine 885
Lacaune
Murat-sur-Vèbre
Le Bousquet-d'Orb
Lunas
Roquecourbe
Mts. de Lacaune
Lac de Lauzas
Lac du Salagou
Aniane
Brassac
St. Gervais-sur-Mare
Clermont-l'Hérault
Gignac
Vielmur-sur-Agout
Castres
Hérépian
Bédarieux
St. André-de-Sangonis
Pignan
Anglés
La Salvetat-sur-Agout
Olargues
Poujol-sur-Orb
Canet
Soual
Labruguière
Haut-Languedoc
Paulhan
Cournonterral
Fabrègues
Dourgne
Thoré
Mazamet
Labastide-Rouairoux
St. Pons-de-Thomières
Roquebrun
Roujan
Lezignan-la-Cèbe
Villeveyrac
Revel
Montagne Noire
St. Amans-Soult
Courniou
Col des Usclats 575
Montagnac
Sorèze
Murviel-lès-Béziers
Pézenas
Mèze
Col de Serieres 681
St. Chinian
Cessenon
Cazouls-lès-Béziers
Servian
Florensac
Saissac
Mas-Cabardès
Bassin de Thau
Sète
Castelnaudary
Puisserguier
Béziers
Bessan
Marseillan
Caunes-Minervois
Aigues-Vives
Maureilhan
Agde
Montolieu
Capestang
Peyriac-Minervois
Bram
Alzonne
Conques-sur-Orbiel
Olonzac
Nissan-lez-Ensérune
Le Cap d'Agde
C. d'Agde
Sérignan
Canal du Midi
Carcassonne
Aude
Coursan
Valras-Plage
Fanjeaux
Montréal
Fleury
Côte d
Lézignan-Corbières
Capendu
Narbonne
Narbonne-Plage
Ferrals-les-Corbières
Narbonnaise
Thézar-les-Corbières
ABBAYE DE FONTFROIDE
Gruissan
St. Hilaire
Lagrasse
St. Laurent-de-la-Cabrerisse
Limoux
Lagarde
Ajac
Sigean
en
Port-la-Nouvelle
Tanger 36
Vignevieille
Chalabre
Alet-les-Bains
Méditerranée
Mouthoumet
Durban-Corbières
Villeneuve-les-Corbières
La Palme
Espéraza
Puivert
Couiza
Corbières
Leucate
Rennes-les-Bains
Tuchan
Quillan
Soulatgé
Étang de Leucate
Paziols
FORTERESS DE SALSES
Axat
St. Paul-de-Fenouillet
Maury
Vingrau
Salses-le-Château
Caudiès-de-Fenouillèdes
Rivesaltes
Port-Barcarès
Usson-les-Bains
Agly
Estagel
St. Laurent-de-la-Salanque
Sournia
Millas
Perpignan
Quérigut
Ille-sur-Têt
Canet-Plage

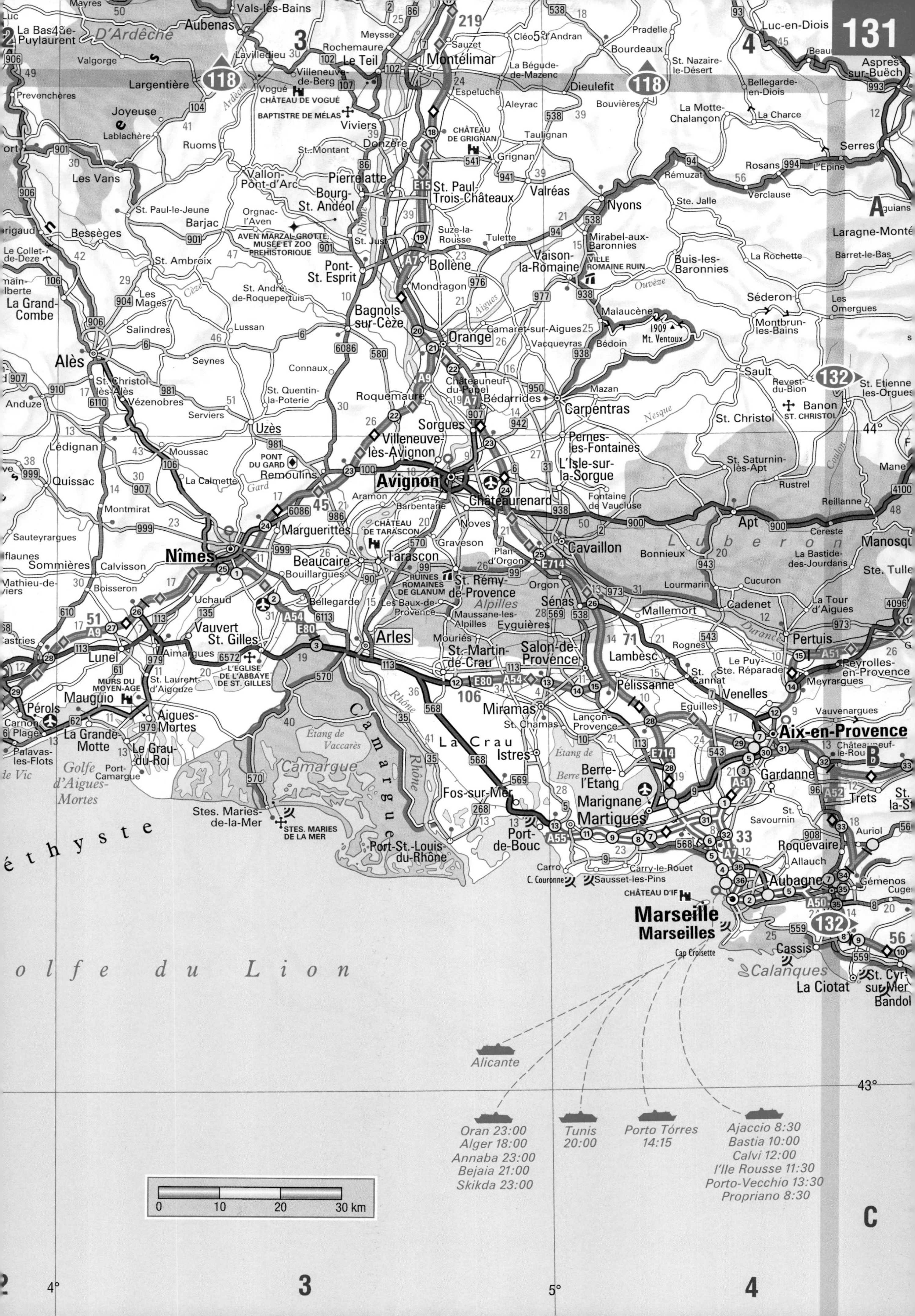

Aubenas
Vals-les-Bains
Montélimar
Le Teil
Largentière
Joyeuse
Les Vans
Viviers
Donzère
Pierrelatte
Bourg-St. Andéol
St. Paul-Trois-Châteaux
Grignan
Valréas
Nyons
Dieulefit
Bollène
Pont-St. Esprit
Bagnols-sur-Cèze
Orange
Vaison-la-Romaine
Mt. Ventoux
Carpentras
Alès
Uzès
Avignon
Villeneuve-lès-Avignon
Sorgues
Châteauneuf-du-Pape
L'Isle-sur-la-Sorgue
Cavaillon
Apt
Nîmes
Beaucaire
Tarascon
St. Rémy-de-Provence
Arles
Lunel
Vauvert
St. Gilles
Aigues-Mortes
La Grande-Motte
Le Grau-du-Roi
Camargue
Stes. Maries-de-la-Mer
Salon-de-Provence
Miramas
Istres
Fos-sur-Mer
Martigues
Marignane
Aix-en-Provence
Gardanne
Aubagne
Marseille
Marseilles
Cassis
La Ciotat
Pertuis
Manosque
Golfe du Lion
Alicante
Oran 23:00
Alger 18:00
Annaba 23:00
Bejaia 21:00
Skikda 23:00
Tunis
20:00
Porto Tórres
14:15
Ajaccio 8:30
Bastia 10:00
Calvi 12:00
l'Ile Rousse 11:30
Porto-Vecchio 13:30
Propriano 8:30
0
10
20
30 km

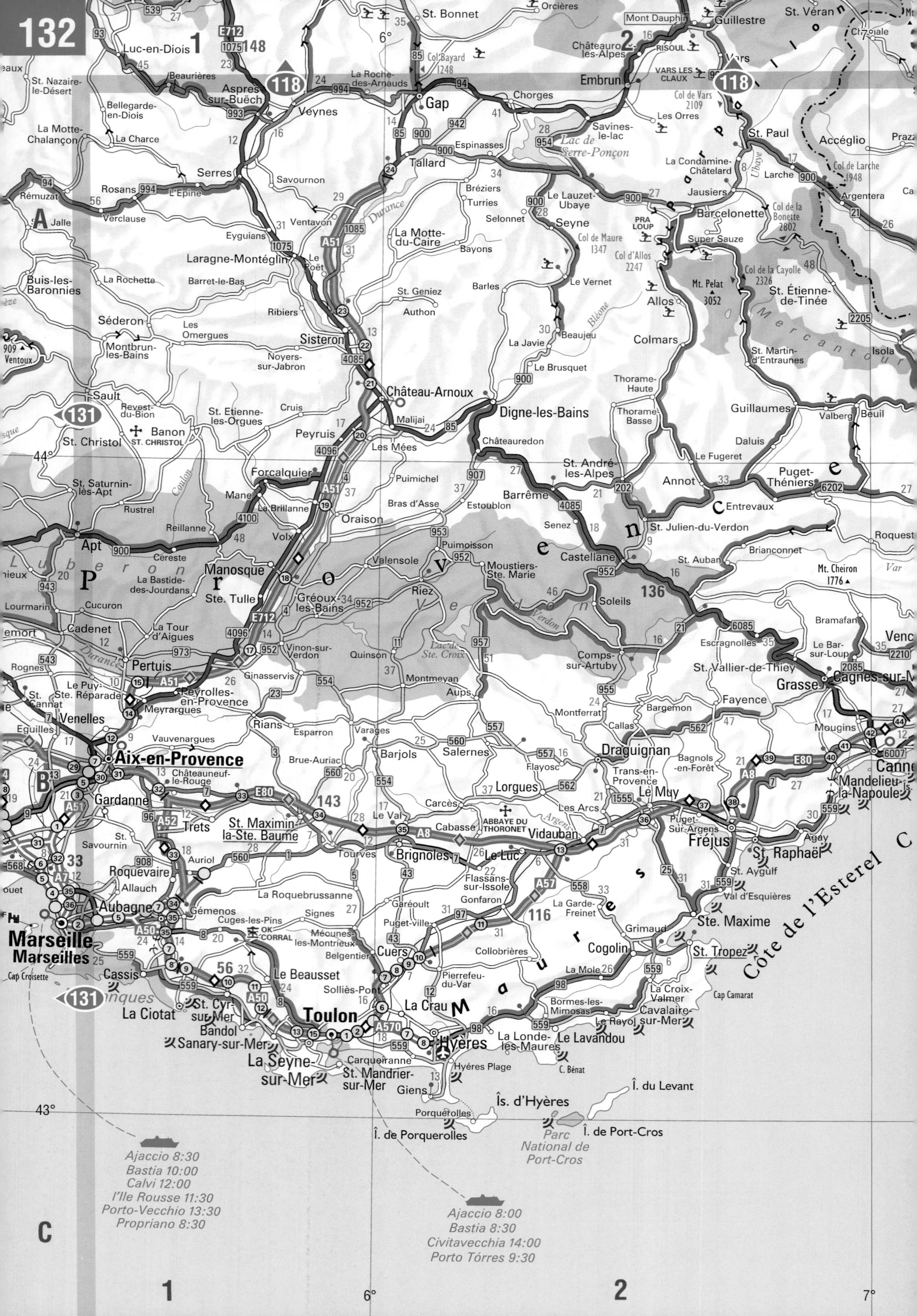

Luc-en-Diois
St. Bonnet
Orcières
Mont Dauphin
Guillestre
St. Véran
St. Nazaire-le-Désert
Beaurières
Aspres-sur-Buëch
La Roche-des-Arnauds
Gap
Col Bayard 1248
Châteauroux-les-Alpes
Embrun
RISOUL
VARS LES CLAUX
Vars
Col de Vars 2109
Bellegarde-en-Diois
Veynes
Chorges
Savines-le-lac
Les Orres
La Motte-Chalançon
La Charce
Espinasses
Lac de Serre-Ponçon
St. Paul
Accéglio
Tallard
La Condamine-Châtelard
Ubaye
Col de Larche 1948
Larche
Serres
Savournon
Rosans
L'Epine
Rémuzat
Bréziers
Turries
Le Lauzet-Ubaye
Jausiers
Argentera
Selonnet
Barcelonette
Col de la Bonette 2802
Verclause
Jalle
Ventavon
Durance
Seyne
PRA LOUP
Super Sauze
Eyguians
La Motte-du-Caire
Col de Maure 1347
Col d'Allos 2247
Laragne-Montéglin
Le Poët
Bayons
Le Vernet
Mt. Pelat 3052
Col de la Cayolle 2326
Buis-les-Baronnies
La Rochette
Barret-le-Bas
Barles
Allos
St. Étienne-de-Tinée
Ribiers
St. Geniez
Authon
Bléone
Séderon
Les Omergues
Sisteron
Beaujeu
Colmars
Mercantour
Montbrun-les-Bains
Ventoux
Noyers-sur-Jabron
La Javie
St. Martin-d'Entraunes
Isola
Le Brusquet
Thorame-Haute
Sault
Château-Arnoux
Revest-du-Bion
Cruis
Digne-les-Bains
Thorame-Basse
Guillaumes
Valberg
Beuil
St. Etienne-les-Orgues
Malijai
Banon
ST. CHRISTOL
St. Christol
Peyruis
Châteauredon
Daluis
44°
Les Mées
St. André-les-Alpes
Le Fuget
Forcalquier
Puimichel
Puget-Théniers
St. Saturnin-lès-Apt
Coulon
Mane
Barrême
Annot
Bras d'Asse
Estoublon
Entrevaux
Rustrel
La Brillanne
Oraison
Senez
St. Julien-du-Verdon
Reillanne
Apt
Volx
Puimoisson
Castellane
Roquest
Cereste
Valensole
St. Auban
Brianconnet
Luberon
Manosque
Moustiers-Ste. Marie
Mt. Cheiron 1776
Var
La Bastide-des-Jourdans
Provence
Lourmarin
Cucuron
Ste. Tulle
Gréoux-les-Bains
Riez
Soleils
Verdon
Bramafan
Cadenet
La Tour d'Aigues
Lac de Ste. Croix
Escragnolles
Le Bar-sur-Loup
Vence
Vinon-sur-Verdon
Quinson
Comps-sur-Artuby
Rognes
Pertuis
St. Vallier-de-Thiey
Grasse
Cagnes-sur-Mer
Le Puy-Ste. Réparade
Ginasservis
Montmeyan
Aups
St. Cannat
Peyrolles-en-Provence
Fayence
Meyrargues
Venelles
Montferrat
Bargemon
Eguilles
Rians
Esparron
Varages
Callas
Mougins
Vauvenargues
Aix-en-Provence
Brue-Auriac
Barjols
Salernes
Draguignan
Flayosc
Bagnols-en-Forêt
Cannes
Châteauneuf-le-Rouge
Trans-en-Provence
Mandelieu-la-Napoule
Gardanne
Lorgues
Le Muy
Trets
St. Maximin-la-Ste. Baume
Le Val
Carcès
Les Arcs
ABBAYE DU THORONET
Cabasse
Vidauban
Argens
Puget-sur-Argens
Fréjus
Agay
St. Savournin
Tourves
Brignoles
Le Luc
St. Raphaël
Auriol
Roquevaire
Allauch
Flassans-sur-Issole
St. Aygulf
Côte de l'Esterel
La Roquebrussanne
Gonfaron
La Garde-Freinet
Val d'Esquières
Aubagne
Gémenos
Signes
Garéoult
Puget-ville
Cuges-les-Pins
OK CORRAL
Méounes-les-Montrieux
Grimaud
Ste. Maxime
Marseille
Marseilles
Collobrières
Cogolin
St. Tropez
Belgentier
Cuers
Cap Croisette
Cassis
Le Beausset
Pierrefeu-du-Var
La Mole
Solliès-Pont
La Croix-Valmer
Cap Camarat
Calanques
La Ciotat
St. Cyr-sur-Mer
Bandol
Toulon
La Crau
Maures
Bormes-les-Mimosas
Cavalaire-sur-Mer
Le Rayol
Sanary-sur-Mer
Hyères
La Londe-les-Maures
Le Lavandou
La Seyne-sur-Mer
Carqueiranne
St. Mandrier-sur-Mer
Hyères Plage
C. Bénat
Giens
Î. du Levant
Îs. d'Hyères
43°
Porquerolles
Î. de Porquerolles
Î. de Port-Cros
Parc National de Port-Cros
Ajaccio 8:30
Bastia 10:00
Calvi 12:00
l'Ile Rousse 11:30
Porto-Vecchio 13:30
Propriano 8:30
Ajaccio 8:00
Bastia 8:30
Civitavecchia 14:00
Porto Tórres 9:30
6°
7°

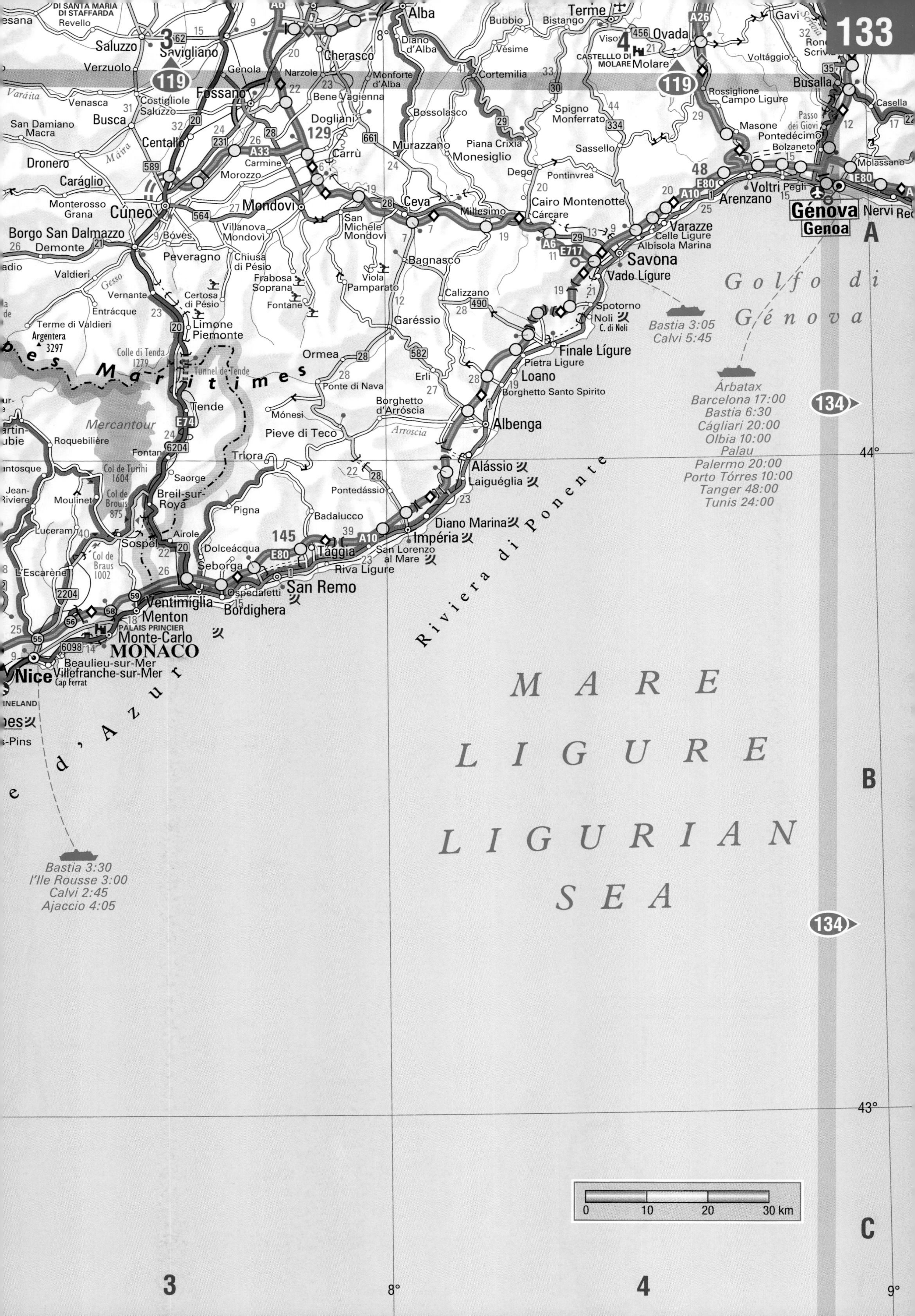

DI SANTA MARIA
DI STAFFARDA
Revello

Saluzzo
Verzuolo

Venasca
Busca

Costigliole
Saluzzo

Centallo

Caráglio

Monterosso
Grana

Borgo San Dalmazzo
Demonte

Valdieri

Terme di Valdieri
Argentera
3297

Roquebilière

Jean-
Rivière

Moulinet

Lucéram

L'Escarène

Col de Turini
1604

Col de
Brouis
875

Sospel

Col de
Braus
1002

Saorge

Breil-sur-
Roya

Airole

Seborga

Ventimiglia

Menton

Monte-Carlo
PALAIS PRINCIER
MONACO

Beaulieu-sur-Mer
Villefranche-sur-Mer
Cap Ferrat

Nice

Savigliano

Genola

Fossano

Cherasco

Narzole

Bene Vagienna

Dogliani

Carmine

Morozzo

Villanova
Mondoví

San Michéle
Mondoví

Mondoví

Bóves

Peveragno

Chiusa
di Pésio

Certosa
di Pésio

Frabosa
Soprana

Fontane

Limone
Piemonte

Tende

Tunnel de Tende

Ponte di Nava

Ormea

Triora

Pigna

Badalucco

Dolceácqua

Tággia

Ospedaletti

Bordighera

San Remo

Riva Ligure

San Lorenzo
al Mare

Impéria

Pontedássio

Diano Marina

Laiguéglia

Alássio

Pieve di Teco

Mónesi

Erli

Garéssio

Bagnasco

Viola
Pamparato

Calizzano

Borghetto
d'Arróscia

Albenga

Borghetto Santo Spirito

Loano

Pietra Ligure

Finale Lígure

C. di Noli

Noli

Spotorno

Vado Lígure

Savona

Alba

Bubbio
Bistango

Diano
d'Alba

Vésime

Cortemilia

Monforte
d'Alba

Bossolasco

Murazzano

Piana Crixia
Monesiglio

Spigno
Monferrato

Sassello

Dego

Pontinvrea

Cairo Montenotte
Cárcare

Millésimo

Ceva

Celle Lígure
Albisola Marina

Varazze

Arenzano

Voltri

Masone

Rossiglione
Campo Ligure

Pontedécimo

Bolzaneto

Génova
Genoa

Nervi

Terme
Viso

Ovada
Molare

CASTELLLO DI
MOLARE

Gavi

Voltággio

Passo
dei Giovi

Busalla

Casella

Molassano

Pegli

Golfo di
Génova

Bastia 3:05
Calvi 5:45

Árbatax
Barcelona 17:00
Bastia 6:30
Cágliari 20:00
Olbia 10:00
Palau
Palermo 20:00
Porto Tórres 10:00
Tanger 48:00
Tunis 24:00

Riviera di Ponente

MARE
LIGURE

LIGURIAN
SEA

Bastia 3:30
l'Ile Rousse 3:00
Calvi 2:45
Ajaccio 4:05

0   10   20   30 km

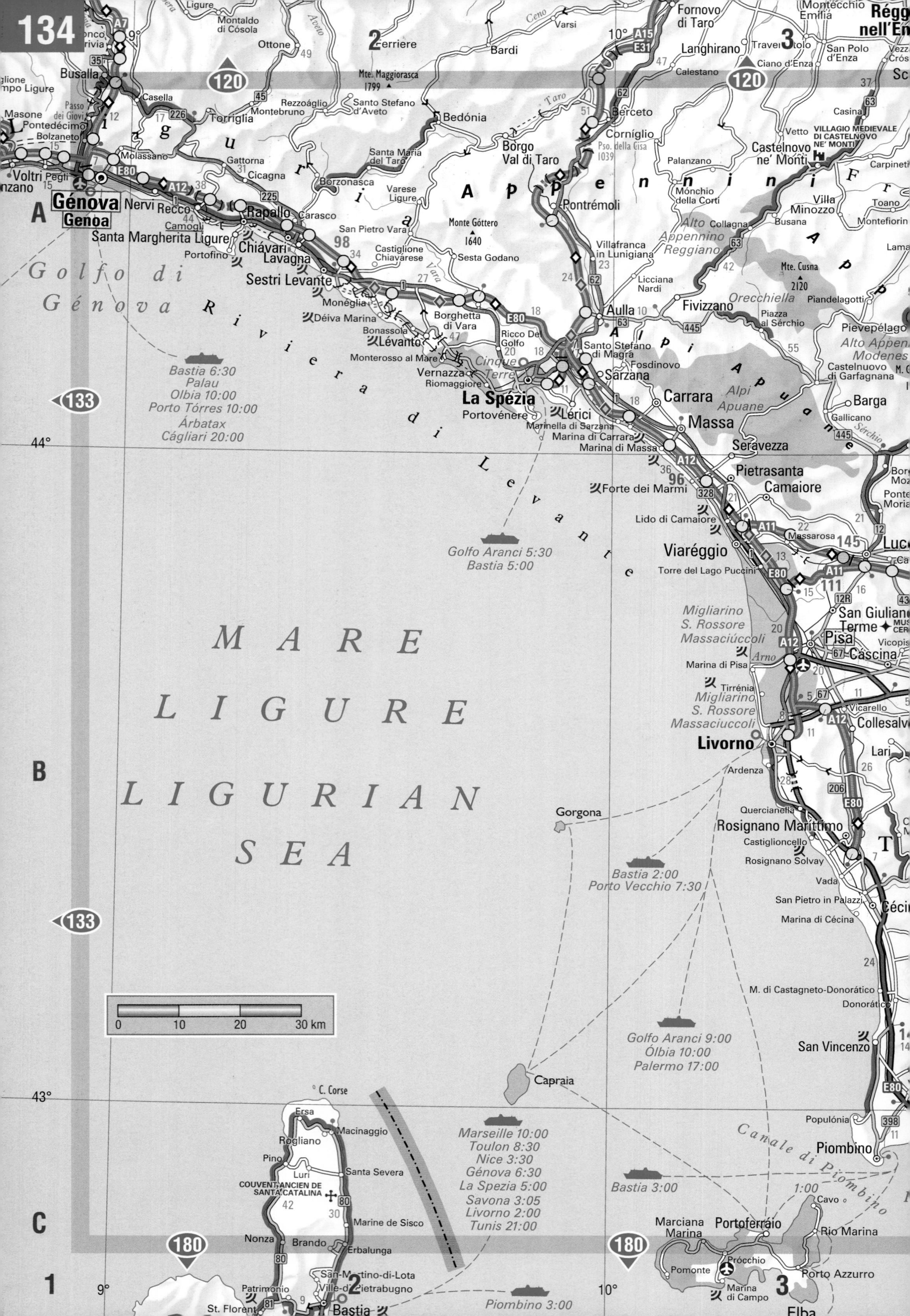
Génova
Genoa
Golfo di Génova
Riviera di Levante
MARE LIGURE
LIGURIAN SEA
La Spézia
Livorno
Pisa
Viaréggio
Massa
Carrara
Rapallo
Chiávari
Sestri Levante
Portofino
Santa Margherita Ligure
Cinque Terre
Appennino
Alpi Apuane
Gorgona
Capraia
Elba
Portoferráio
Piombino
Canale di Piombino
Bastia
C. Corse
Bastia 6:30
Palau
Olbia 10:00
Porto Tórres 10:00
Árbatax
Cágliari 20:00
Golfo Aranci 5:30
Bastia 5:00
Bastia 2:00
Porto Vecchio 7:30
Golfo Aranci 9:00
Ólbia 10:00
Palermo 17:00
Marseille 10:00
Toulon 8:30
Nice 3:30
Génova 6:30
La Spezia 5:00
Savona 3:05
Livorno 2:00
Tunis 21:00
Bastia 3:00
Piombino 3:00
0 10 20 30 km
120
133
180
44°
43°
9°
10°

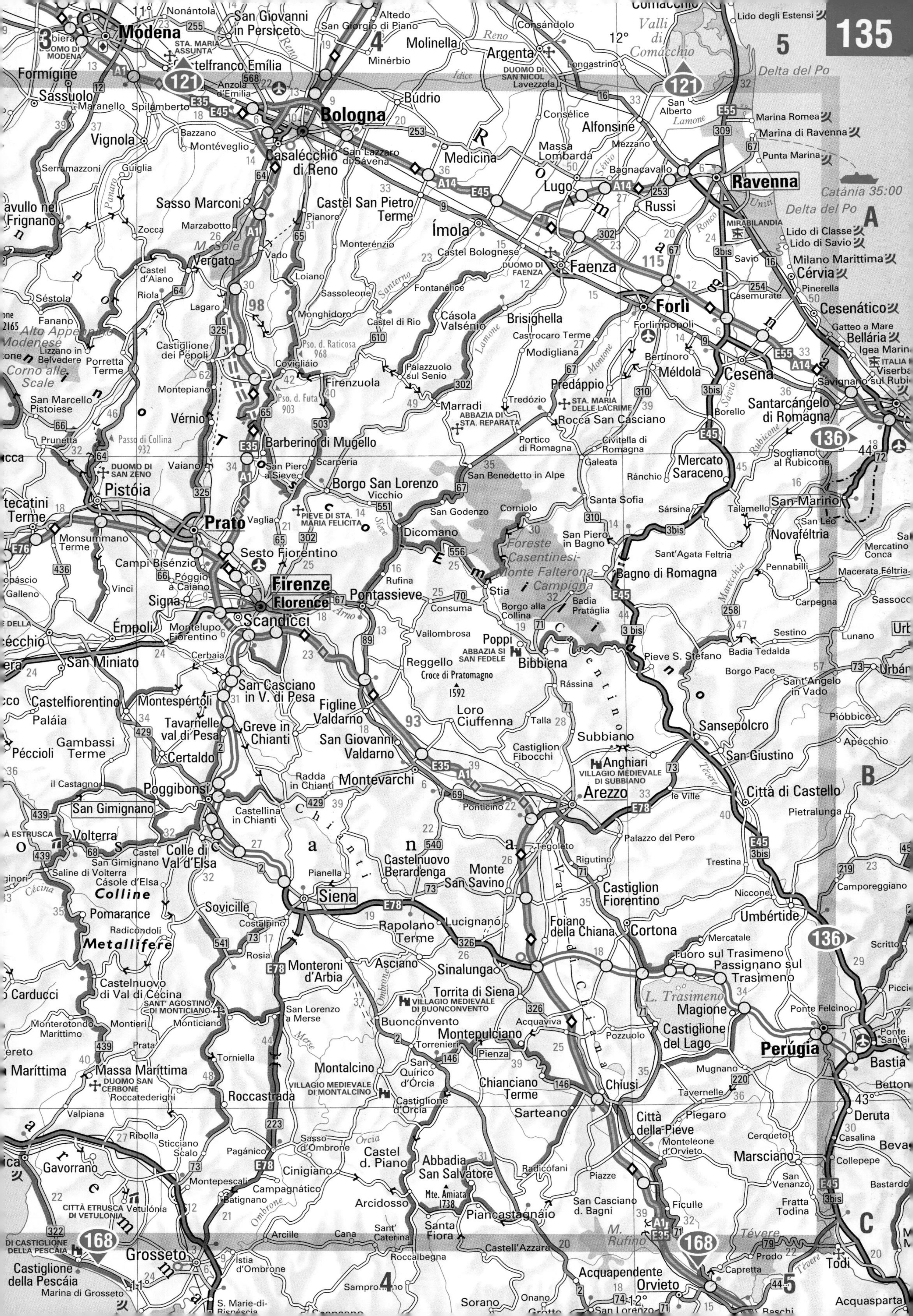
Módena
Bologna
Ravenna
Firenze
Florence
Prato
Pistóia
Siena
Arezzo
Perúgia
Forlì
Cesena
Faenza
Ímola
Lugo
Grosseto
Orvieto
San Marino
Delta del Po
Cesenático
Rímini
Empoli
Scandicci
Montevarchi
Cortona
Chiusi
Montepulciano
Montalcino
Poggibonsi
San Gimignano
Volterra
Colle di Val d'Elsa
Sansepolcro
Città di Castello
Bibbiena
Poppi
Borgo San Lorenzo
Sesto Fiorentino
Pontassieve
Castiglion Fiorentino
Magione
L. Trasimeno
Massa Maríttima
Follonica
Todi
Deruta
Marsciano
Chianciano Terme
Abbadia San Salvatore
Piancastagnáio
Acquapendente
Castiglione della Pescáia
Colline Metallifere
Forli
Chianti
Casentino
Catánia 35:00

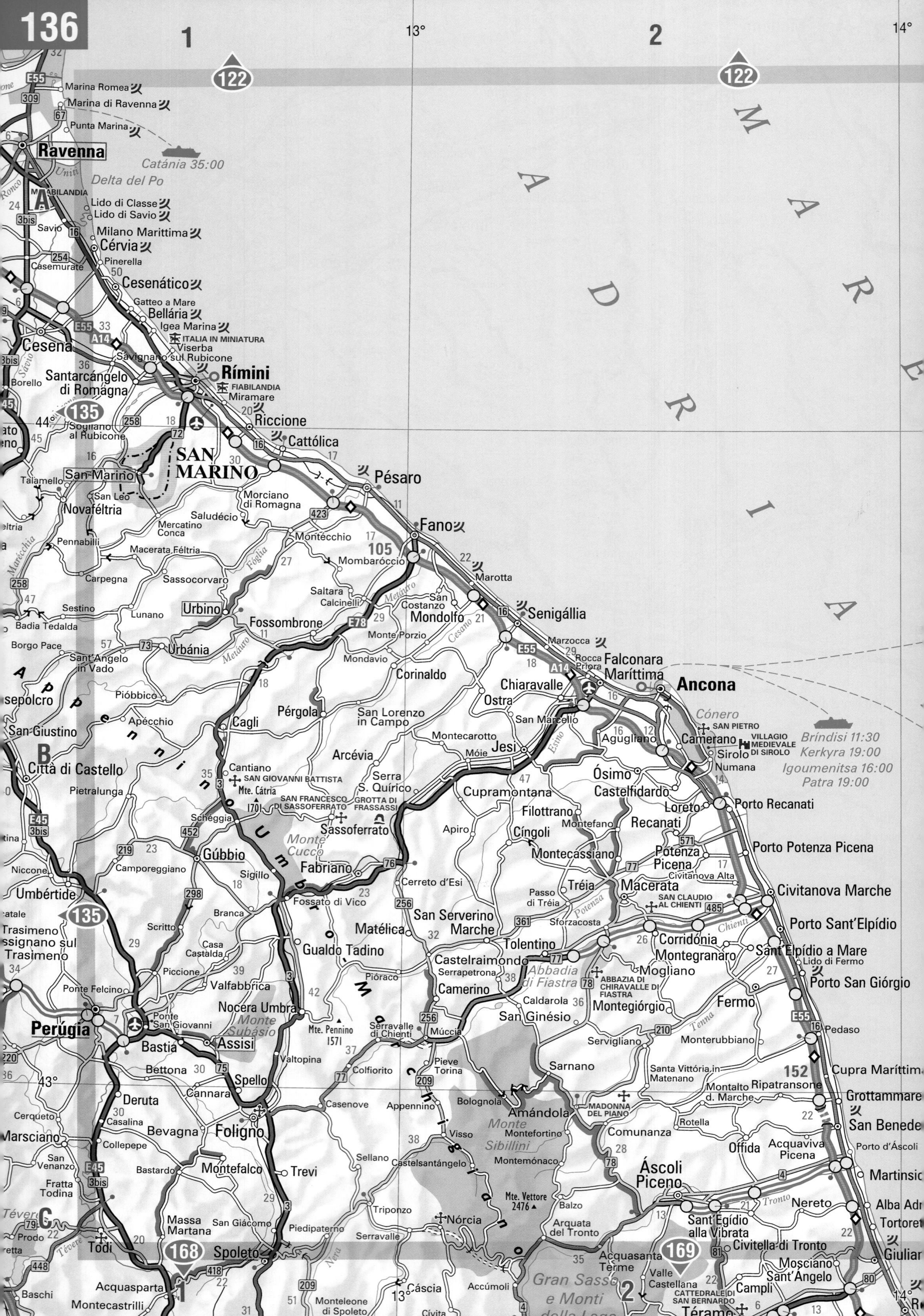
1
13°
2
14°
122
122
MARE ADRIATICO
Marina Romea
Marina di Ravenna
Punta Marina
Ravenna
Catánia 35:00
Delta del Po
MIRABILANDIA
Lido di Classe
Lido di Savio
Savio
Milano Marittima
Cérvia
Pinerella
Casemurate
Cesenático
Gatteo a Mare
Bellária
Igea Marina
ITALIA IN MINIATURA
Viserba
Cesena
Savignano sul Rubicone
Borello
Santarcángelo di Romagna
Rímini
FIABILANDIA
Miramare
135
Sogliano al Rubicone
Riccione
Cattólica
SAN MARINO
San Marino
Talamello
San Leo
Novaféltria
Pésaro
Morciano di Romagna
Saludécio
Mercatino Conca
Fano
Pennabilli
Montécchio
Macerata Féltria
105
Mombaróccio
Carpegna
Sassocorvaro
Marotta
Saltara
Calcinelli
San Costanzo
Sestino
Lunano
Urbino
Mondolfo
Senigállia
Badia Tedalda
Fossombrone
Monte Porzio
Borgo Pace
Sant'Angelo in Vado
Urbánia
Mondavio
Marzocca
Rocca Priora
Falconara Maríttima
Ancona
Corinaldo
Chiaravalle
Ostra
Sansepolcro
Pióbbico
Apécchio
Pérgola
San Lorenzo in Campo
San Marcello
Cónero
San Giustino
Cagli
Montecarotto
Móie
Jesi
Agugliano
SAN PIETRO
Camerano
VILLAGIO MEDIEVALE DI SIROLO
Sirolo
Numana
Bríndisi 11:30
Kerkyra 19:00
Igoumenitsa 16:00
Patra 19:00
Città di Castello
Arcévia
Cantiano
SAN GIOVANNI BATTISTA
Serra S. Quírico
Ósimo
Castelfidardo
Pietralunga
Mte. Cátria 1701
SAN FRANCESCO DI SASSOFERRATO
GROTTA DI FRASSASSI
Cupramontana
Loreto
Porto Recanati
Scheggia
Sassoferrato
Filottrano
Montefano
Recanati
Monte Cucco
Apiro
Cíngoli
Appennino Umbro-Marchigiano
Gúbbio
Camporeggiano
Montecassiano
Potenza Picena
Porto Potenza Picena
Fabriano
Civitanova Alta
Niccone
Sigillo
Cerreto d'Esi
Tréia
Macerata
Civitanova Marche
Umbértide
Fossato di Vico
Passo di Tréia
SAN CLAUDIO AL CHIENTI
Branca
San Severino Marche
Sforzacosta
Porto Sant'Elpídio
Trasimeno
Passignano sul Trasimeno
Scritto
Matélica
Tolentino
Corridónia
Sant'Elpídio a Mare
Casa Castalda
Gualdo Tadino
Castelraimondo
Montegranaro
Lido di Fermo
Piccione
Valfabbrica
Serrapetrona
Abbadia di Fiastra
ABBAZIA DI CHIARAVALLE DI FIASTRA
Mogliano
Porto San Giórgio
Ponte Felcino
Pióraco
Camerino
Caldarola
Montegiórgio
Fermo
Perúgia
Ponte San Giovanni
Nocera Umbra
Monte Subásio
Mte. Pennino 1571
Serravalle di Chienti
Múccia
San Ginésio
Pedaso
Bastia
Assisi
Servigliano
Monterubbiano
Valtopina
Pieve Torina
Sarnano
Santa Vittória in Matenano
152
Cupra Maríttima
Bettona
Spello
Colfiorito
Montalto d. Marche
Ripatransone
Deruta
Cannara
Bolognola
Amándola
MADONNA DEL PIANO
Grottammare
Cerqueto
Casalina
Casenove
Appennino
Monte Sibillini
Montefortino
Comunanza
Rotella
San Benedetto
Marsciano
Bevagna
Foligno
Visso
Offida
Acquaviva Picena
Porto d'Áscoli
Collepepe
Sellano
Castelsantángelo
Montemónaco
Martinsicuro
San Venanzo
Bastardo
Montefalco
Trevi
Áscoli Piceno
Fratta Todina
Mte. Vettore 2476
Balzo
Nereto
Alba Adriatica
Massa Martana
San Giácomo
Tripónzo
Nórcia
Sant'Egídio alla Vibrata
Tortoreto
Prodo
Todi
Piedipaterno
Serravalle
Arquata del Tronto
Civitella di Tronto
Giulianova
168
Spoleto
169
Acquasanta Terme
Mosciano Sant'Angelo
Baschi
Acquasparta
Montecastrilli
Cáscia
Accúmoli
Gran Sasso e Monti della Laga
Valle Castellana
CATTEDRALE DI SAN BERNARDO
Campli
Teramo
Monteleone di Spoleto
Cívita
43°
44°
E55
E45
E78
A14

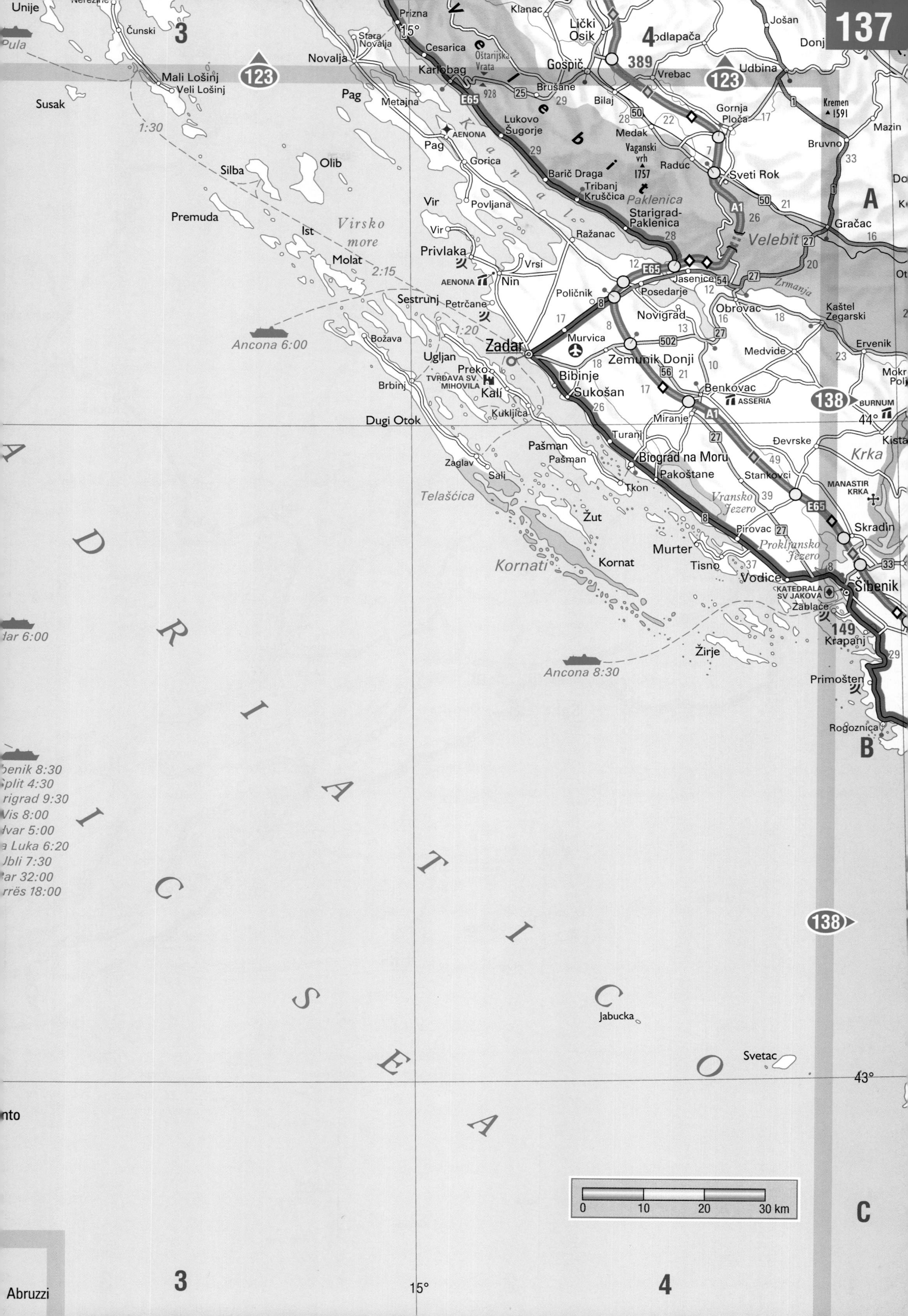
Unije
Čunski
3
Pula
Mali Lošinj
Veli Lošinj
Susak
123
1:30
Silba
Olib
Premuda
Ist
Molat
Virsko more
2:15
Ancona 6:00
Prizna
15°
Stara Novalja
Novalja
Cesarica
Karlobag
Pag
Metajna
AENONA
Gorica
Lukovo Šugorje
Velebit
Kanal
Oštarijska Vrata
928
25
Brušane
29
Klanac
Lički Osik
Gospić
4
Podlapača
389
Vrebac
Udbina
Jošan
Bilaj
Gornja Ploča
Kremen 1591
Mazin
Bruvno
50
22
28
17
Medak
Vaganski vrh 1757
Raduč
Sveti Rok
Barič Draga
Tribanj
Kruščica
Paklenica
Starigrad-Paklenica
Ražanac
A1
26
21
33
A
Gračac
Velebit
16
20
Vir
Povljana
Privlaka
Vrsi
AENONA
Nin
Sestrunj
Petrčane
1:20
Božava
Ugljan
Preko
TVRĐAVA SV. MIHOVILA
Kali
Brbinj
Zadar
Poličnik
Murvica
Zemunik Donji
Bibinje
Sukošan
E65
Jasenice
Posedarje
54
27
Zrmanja
Obrovac
Novigrad
502
Kaštel Zegarski
18
Ervenik
Medvide
23
56
Benkovac
ASSERIA
138
BURNUM
44°
Dugi Otok
Kukljica
Miranje
Turanj
Pašman
Biograd na Moru
Pakoštane
Đevrske
Krka
Zaglav
Sali
Tkon
Stankovci
Vransko Jezero
39
MANASTIR KRKA
Skradin
Telašćica
Žut
Pirovac
Prokljansko Jezero
Murter
Tisno
Kornati
Kornat
Vodice
KATEDRALA SV JAKOVA
Šibenik
Zablaće
149
Krapanj
Žirje
Ancona 8:30
Primošten
Rogoznica
B
Zadar 6:00
Šibenik 8:30
Split 4:30
Starigrad 9:30
Vis 8:00
Hvar 5:00
Vela Luka 6:20
Ubli 7:30
Bar 32:00
Durrës 18:00
ADRIATIC SEA
138
Jabucka
Svetac
43°
nto
0 10 20 30 km
C
Abruzzi
3
15°
4

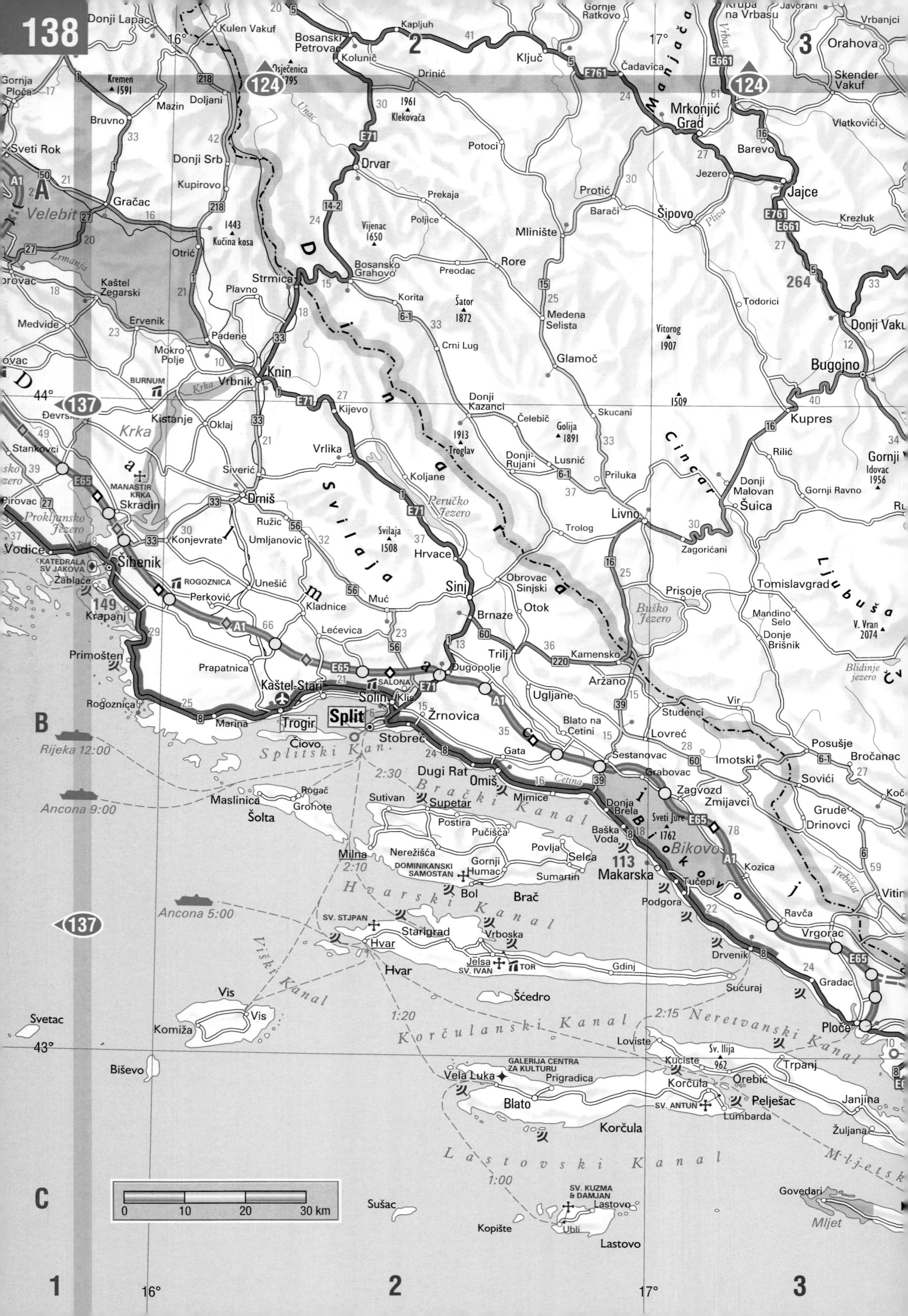
Donji Lapac
Kulen Vakuf
Bosanski Petrovac
Kapljuh
Kolunič
Drinić
Ključ
Gornje Ratkovo
Krupa na Vrbasu
Javorani
Vrbanjci
Orahova
Skender Vakuf
Manjača
Čadavica
Mrkonjić Grad
Barevo
Jezero
Jajce
Vlatkovići
Krezluk
Šipovo
Pliva
Protić
Barači
Mlinište
Potoci
Drvar
Klekovača
Osječenica
Unac
Kremen
Gornja Ploča
Mazin
Doljani
Bruvno
Sveti Rok
Donji Srb
Kupirovo
Gračac
Velebit
Zrmanja
Otrić
Kučina kosa
Prekaja
Poljice
Vijenac
Bosansko Grahovo
Preodac
Rore
Medena Selista
Korita
Šator
Crni Lug
Glamoč
Todorici
Vitorog
Donji Vakuf
Bugojno
Kupres
Kaštel Zegarski
Strmica
Plavno
Ervenik
Medvide
Padene
Mokro Polje
Knin
Vrbnik
BURNUM
Krka
Kistanje
Oklaj
Kijevo
Donji Kazanci
Čelebič
Golija
Skucani
Troglav
Vrlika
Koljane
Donji Rujani
Lusnić
Priluka
Cincar
Rilić
Gornji Idovac
Donji Malovan
Gornji Ravno
Šuica
Livno
Trolog
Zagorićani
Peručko Jezero
Dinara
Svilaja
Stankovci
Siverić
Drniš
MANASTIR KRKA
Skradin
Pirovac
Prokljansko Jezero
Ružic
Umljanovic
Konjevrate
Hrvace
Sinj
Vodice
KATEDRALA SV JAKOVA
Šibenik
Žablaće
ROGOZNICA
Unešić
Perković
Krapanj
Kladnice
Muć
Obrovac Sinjski
Otok
Brnaze
Prisoje
Buško Jezero
Tomislavgrad
Ljubuša
Mandino Selo
Donje Brišnik
V. Vran
Blidinje jezero
Primošten
Prapatnica
Lećevica
Dugopolje
Trilj
Kamensko
Aržano
Kaštel-Stari
SALONA
Solin
Klis
Rogoznica
Marina
Trogir
Split
Žrnovica
Ugljane
Blato na Cetini
Studenci
Vir
Lovreć
Posušje
Imotski
Bročanac
Sovići
Grude
Drinovci
Zagvozd
Zmijavci
Grabovac
Šestanovac
Rijeka 12:00
Ancona 9:00
Čiovo
Splitski Kan.
Stobreč
Dugi Rat
Omiš
Gata
Cetina
Mimice
Maslinica
Rogač
Grohote
Šolta
Sutivan
Supetar
Brački Kanal
Postira
Pučišća
Povlja
Selca
Donja Brela
Baška Voda
Sveti Jure
Biokovo
Makarska
Tučepi
Kozica
Podgora
Trebižat
Ravča
Vrgorac
Vitina
Milna
Nerežišća
DOMINIKANSKI SAMOSTAN
Gornji Humac
Sumartin
Bol
Brač
Hvarski Kanal
Ancona 5:00
SV. STJPAN
Starigrad
Vrboska
Hvar
Jelsa
SV. IVAN
TOR
Gdinj
Sućuraj
Drvenik
Gradac
Ploče
Viški Kanal
Vis
Komiža
Ščedro
Svetac
Korčulanski Kanal
Neretvanski Kanal
Loviste
Kuciste
Sv. Ilija
Trpanj
Orebić
Biševo
GALERIJA CENTRA ZA KULTURU
Vela Luka
Prigradica
Korčula
Blato
SV. ANTUN
Lumbarda
Pelješac
Janjina
Žuljana
Lastovski Kanal
Mljetski
Sušac
SV. KUZMA & DAMJAN
Lastovo
Ubli
Kopište
Govedari
Mljet
0 10 20 30 km
A
B
C
1
2
3
16°
17°
44°
43°
124
137
149
113
264

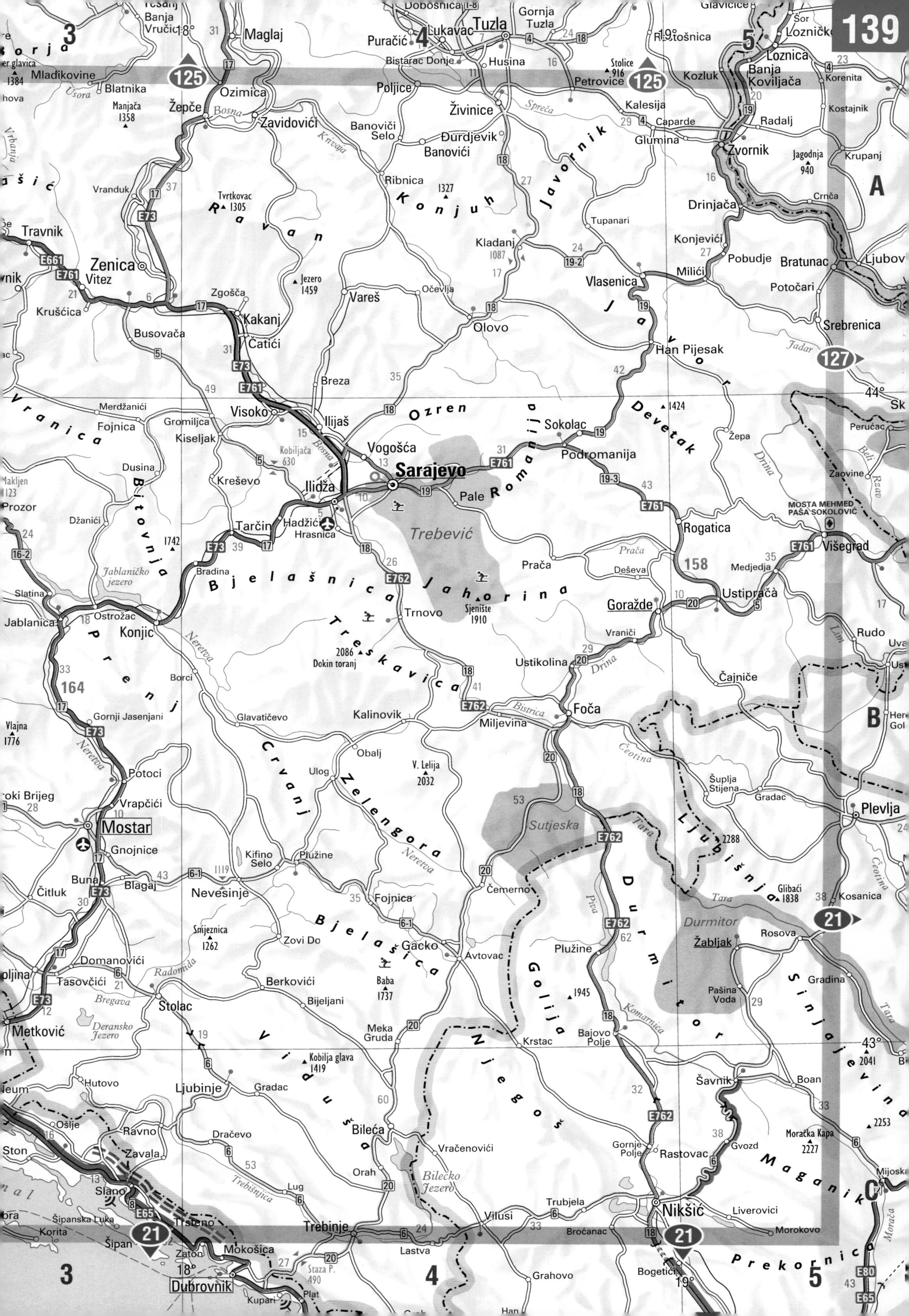
Banja Vručica
Maglaj
Puračić
Lukavac
Tuzla
Gornja Tuzla
Živinice
Husina
Bistarac Donje
Poljice
Petrovice
Stolice 916
Kozluk
Loznica
Banja Koviljača
Mladikovine
Blatnika
Manjača 1358
Ozimica
Žepče
Zavidovići
Banovići Selo
Đurđevik
Banovići
Kalesija
Caparde
Glumina
Radalj
Zvornik
Jagodnja 940
Krupanj
Vranduk
Tvrtkovac 1305
Ravan
Ribnica
1327
Konjuh
Javornik
Drinjača
Crnča
Tupanari
Konjevići
Pobudje
Bratunac
Ljubov
Travnik
Zenica
Vitez
Kladanj
1087
Vlasenica
Milići
Potočari
Kruščica
Zgošča
Jezero 1459
Vareš
Očevlja
Kakanj
Olovo
Srebrenica
Busovača
Čatići
Han Pijesak
Jadar
Javor
Breza
Devetak
1424
Merdžanići
Fojnica
Gromiljca
Kiseljak
Visoko
Ilijaš
Ozren
Sokolac
Romanija
Podromanija
Žepa
Perućac
Vranica
Dusina
Kobiljača 630
Vogošća
Sarajevo
Pale
Zaovine
Kreševo
Ilidža
Prozor
Bitovnja
Džanići
Tarčin
Hadžići
Hrasnica
Trebević
Rogatica
MOSTA MEHMED PAŠA SOKOLOVIĆ
Višegrad
1742
Jablaničko jezero
Bradina
Prača
Deševa
Medjedja
Bjelašnica
Jahorina
Slatina
Jablanica
Ostrožac
Konjic
Trnovo
Sjenište 1910
Goražde
Ustiprača
Prenj
Treskavica
2086 Dokin toranj
Vraniči
Rudo
Ustikolina
Drina
Lim
Borci
Čajniče
Neretva
Kalinovik
Miljevina
Bistrica
Foča
Gornji Jasenjani
Glavatičevo
Vlajna 1776
Obalj
Ćeotina
Crvanj
Potoci
Ulog
V. Lelija 2032
Zelengora
Šuplja Stijena
Gradac
Široki Brijeg
Vrapčići
Plevlja
Mostar
Sutjeska
Tara
Ljubišnja
2288
Gnojnice
Kifino Selo
Plužine
Buna
Blagaj
Nevesinje
Čemerno
Piva
Durmitor
Glibaći 1838
Kosanica
Čitluk
Fojnica
Snijeznica 1262
Zovi Do
Bjelašica
Gacko
Avtovac
Plužine
Žabljak
Rosova
Domanovići
Radomida
Golija
Gradina
Tasovčići
Berkovići
Baba 1737
1945
Pašina Voda
Sinjajevina
Čapljina
Bregava
Stolac
Bijeljani
Metković
Deransko Jezero
Meka Gruda
Krstac
Bajovo Polje
Komarnica
Vidusa
Njegoš
Kobilja glava 1419
2041
Hutovo
Ljubinje
Gradac
Šavnik
Boan
Neum
Ošlje
Ravno
Dračevo
Bileća
Vračenovići
Gornje Polje
Rastovac
Gvozd
Moračka Kapa 2227
2253
Ston
Zavala
Trebišnjica
Orah
Bilećko Jezero
Maganik
Mijoska
Slano
Lug
Trubjela
Nikšić
Liverovici
Šipanska Luka
Korita
Trsteno
Trebinje
Vilusi
Šipan
Zaton
Mokošica
Lastva
Broćanac
Morokovo
Staza P. 490
Grahovo
Bogetići
Prekornica
Morača
Dubrovnik
Kupari
Plat
A
B
C
3
4
5
18°
19°
43°
44°
125
127
21
158
164
E73
E761
E762
E661
E65
E80

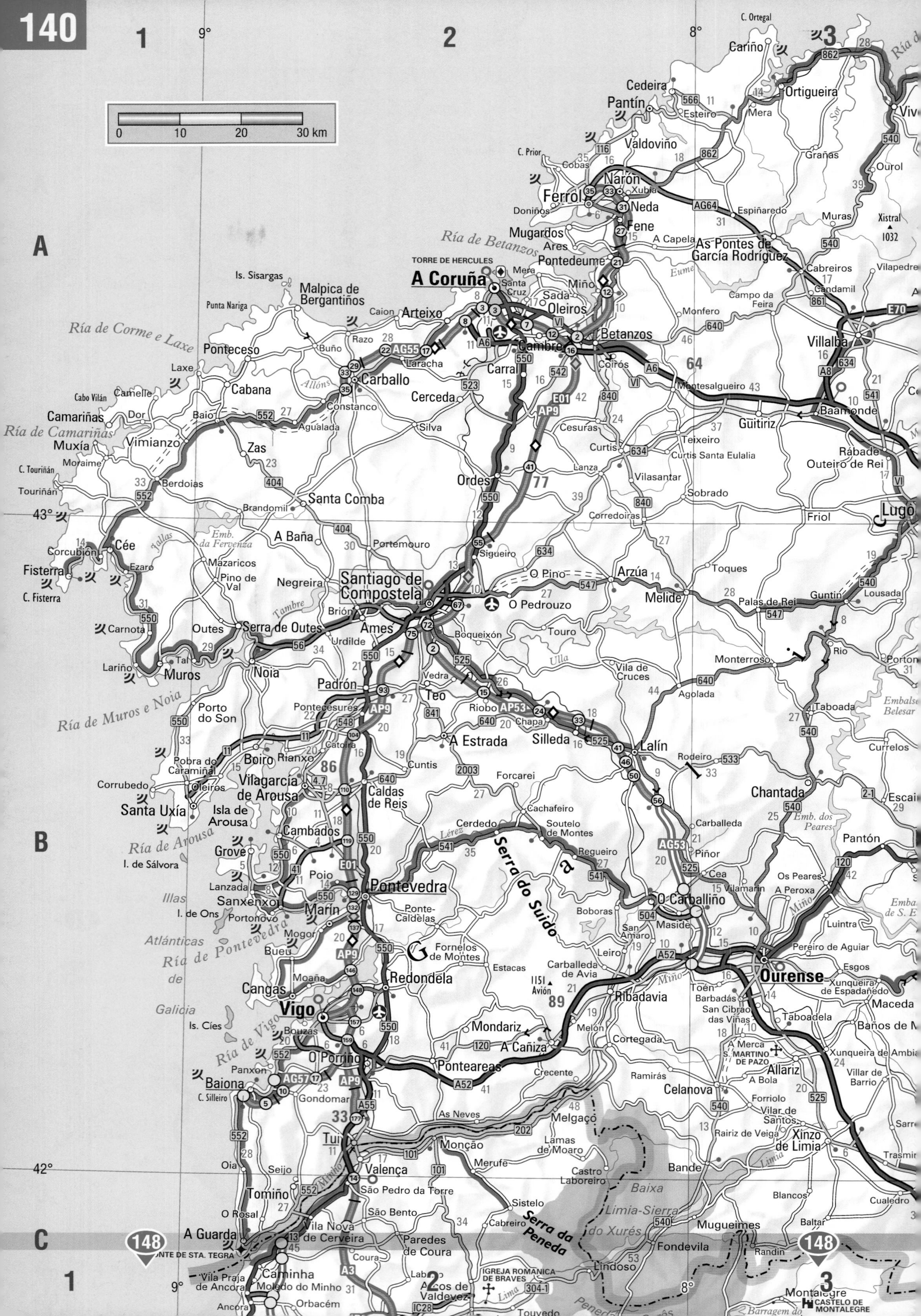

1
2
3
A
B
C
9°
8°
43°
42°
0 10 20 30 km
C. Ortegal
Cariño
Cedeira
Pantín
Ortigueira
Esteiro
Mera
Viveiro
Valdoviño
C. Prior
Cobas
Ferrol
Narón
Xubia
Neda
Fene
Doniños
Mugardos
Ares
Ría de Betanzos
A Capela
As Pontes de García Rodríguez
Espiñaredo
Muras
Xistral 1032
Ourol
Grañas
Eume
Pontedeume
Miño
TORRE DE HERCULES
A Coruña
Mera
Santa Cruz
Sada
Oleiros
Betanzos
Cambre
Carral
Coirós
Cabreiros
Candamil
Vilapedre
Campo da Feira
Monfero
Villalba
Montesalgueiro
Baamonde
Guitiriz
Rábade
Outeiro de Rei
Teixeiro
Curtis
Curtis Santa Eulalia
Cesuras
Lanza
Vilasantar
Sobrado
Corredoiras
Friol
Lugo
Is. Sisargas
Malpica de Bergantiños
Punta Nariga
Caion
Arteixo
Ría de Corme e Laxe
Ponteceso
Buño
Razo
Laracha
Laxe
Carballo
Cabana
Cabo Vilán
Camelle
Camariñas
Ría de Camariñas
Dor
Muxía
Vimianzo
Baio
Constanco
Agualada
Cerceda
Silva
Moraime
C. Touriñán
Touriñán
Zas
Berdoias
Ordes
Santa Comba
Brandomil
Allóns
Jallas
Emb. da Fervenza
A Baña
Portemouro
Sigüeiro
Corcubión
Cée
Ezaro
Fisterra
C. Fisterra
Mazaricos
Pino de Val
Negreira
Santiago de Compostela
O Pino
Arzúa
Melide
Toques
Palas de Rei
Guntín
Lousada
O Pedrouzo
Carnota
Outes
Serra de Outes
Tambre
Brión
Ames
Urdilde
Boqueixón
Touro
Ulla
Lariño
Tal
Muros
Noia
Padrón
Vedra
Teo
Vila de Cruces
Agolada
Monterroso
Rio
Portomarín
Ría de Muros e Noia
Porto do Son
Pontecesures
Riobo
Chapa
Silleda
Lalín
Rodeiro
Taboada
Embalse de Belesar
Pobra do Caramiñal
Boiro
Rianxo
Catoira
A Estrada
Cuntis
Forcarei
Chantada
Currelos
Corrubedo
Santa Uxía
Vilagarcía de Arousa
Oleiros
Caldas de Reis
Escairón
Isla de Arousa
Ría de Arousa
Cambados
Cerdedo
Lérez
Cachafeiro
Soutelo de Montes
Carballeda
Serra do Suido
Emb. dos Peares
Pantón
Grove
I. de Sálvora
Poio
Regueiro
Piñor
Os Peares
Lanzada
Sanxenxo
Pontevedra
Cea
Vilamarín
A Peroxa
Illas Atlánticas de Galicia
I. de Ons
Portonovo
Marín
Ponte-Caldelas
Boboras
O Carballiño
Maside
Emb. de S. Esteban
Luintra
Mogor
Ría de Pontevedra
San Amaro
Bueu
Fornelos de Montes
Leiro
Pereiro de Aguiar
Esgos
Moaña
Estacas
Carballeda de Avia
Miño
Ourense
Xunqueira de Espadañedo
Cangas
Redondela
1151 Avión
Ribadavia
Toén
Barbadás
San Cibrao das Viñas
Maceda
Vigo
Is. Cíes
Ría de Vigo
Bouzas
Mondariz
Melón
Taboadela
Baños de Molgas
Cortegada
A Cañiza
A Merca
S. MARTINO DE PAZO
Xunqueira de Ambía
Panxon
O Porriño
Ponteareas
Ramirás
Allariz
Villar de Barrio
Baiona
C. Silleiro
Gondomar
Crecente
Celanova
A Bola
Forriolo
Vilar de Santos
As Neves
Melgaço
Rairiz de Veiga
Xinzo de Limia
Sarreaus
Tui
Lamas de Moaro
Monção
Trasmiras
Valença
Merufe
Castro Laboreiro
Bande
Limia
Oia
Seijo
São Pedro da Torre
Baixa Limia-Sierra do Xurés
Tomiño
Sistelo
Blancos
Cualedro
O Rosal
São Bento
Cabreiro
Serra da Peneda
Mugueimes
Baltar
A Guarda
Vila Nova de Cerveira
Paredes de Coura
Fondevila
Randín
148
MONTE DE STA. TEGRA
Coura
Caminha
Lindoso
Vila Praia de Ancora
Moledo do Minho
Labruja
Arcos de Valdevez
IGREJA ROMANICA DE BRAVES
Lima
Montalegre
CASTELO DE MONTALEGRE
Orbacém
Ancora
Touvedo
Barragem do

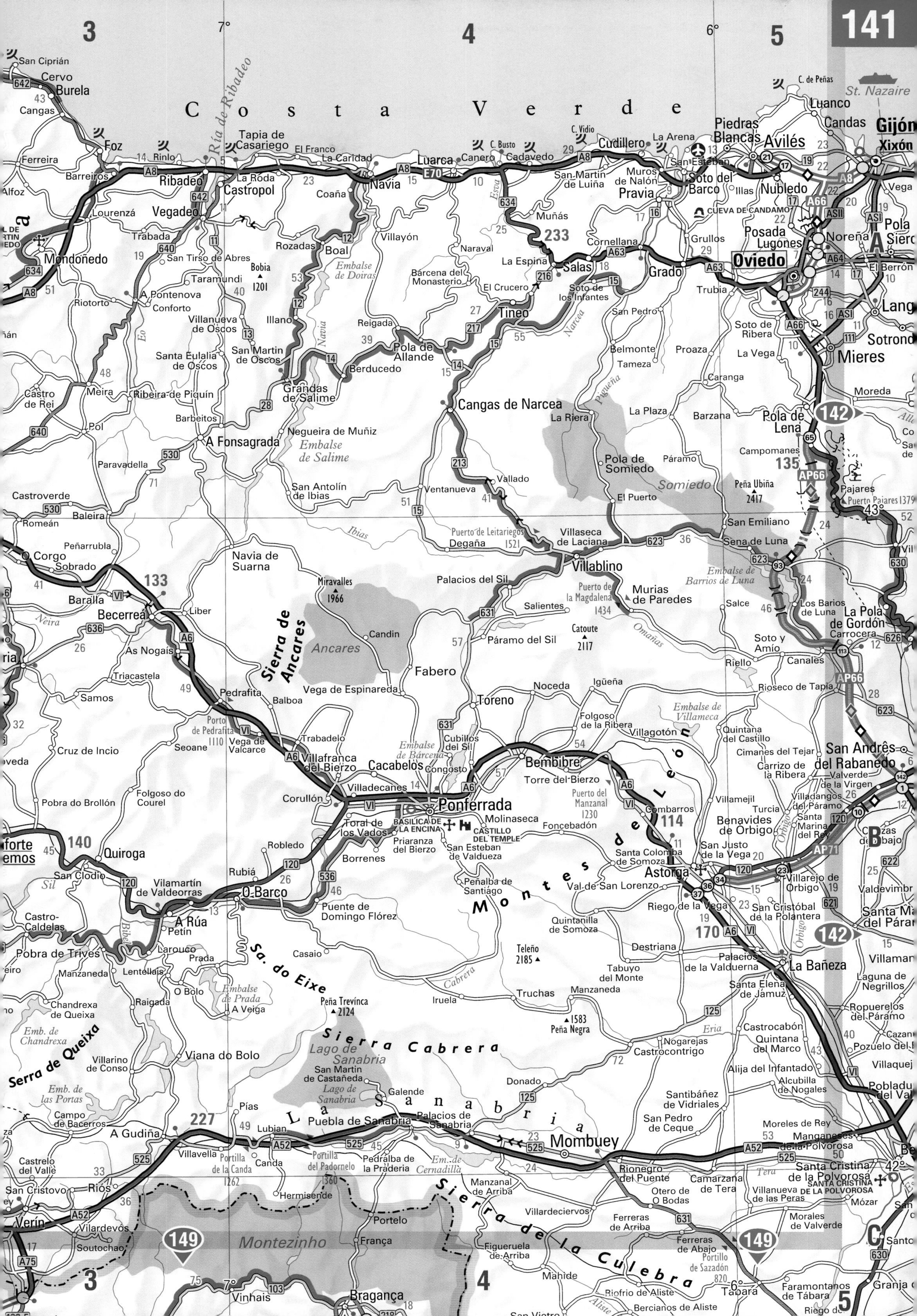
Costa Verde
Ría de Ribadeo
San Ciprián
Cervo
Burela
Cangas
Foz
Ferreira
Barreiros
Rinlo
Ribadeo
Tapia de Casariego
El Franco
La Caridad
Castropol
La Roda
Navia
Coaña
Luarca
Canero
C. Busto
Cadavedo
C. Vidio
Cudillero
La Arena
Piedras Blancas
Avilés
C. de Peñas
Luanco
Candas
St. Nazaire
Gijón
Xixón
San Esteban
Muros de Nalón
Soto del Barco
Pravia
San Martín de Luiña
Illas
Nubledo
Muñás
Cueva de Candamo
Posada
Lugones
Noreña
Pola Siero
Oviedo
El Berrón
Cornellana
Grullos
Grado
Trubia
Salas
La Espina
Soto de los Infantes
El Crucero
Tineo
Naraval
Bárcena del Monasterio
Villayón
Boal
Rozadas
Vegadeo
Lourenzá
Trabada
Mondoñedo
Alfoz
San Tirso de Abres
Taramundi
Bobia 1201
A Pontenova
Conforto
Riotorto
Villanueva de Oscos
San Martín de Oscos
Santa Eulalia de Oscos
Illano
Embalse de Doiras
Reigada
Pola de Allande
Berducedo
Grandas de Salime
Castro de Rei
Meira
Ribeira de Piquín
Barbeitos
Pol
A Fonsagrada
Negueira de Muñiz
Embalse de Salime
Paravadella
San Antolín de Ibias
Castroverde
Baleira
Romeán
Peñarrubla
O Corgo
Sobrado
Baralla
Becerreá
Liber
Navia de Suarna
As Nogais
Triacastela
Samos
Pedrafita
Balboa
Porto de Pedrafita 1110
Seoane
Vega de Valcarce
Trabadelo
Villafranca del Bierzo
Cruz de Incio
Pobra do Brollón
Folgoso do Courel
Corullón
Cacabelos
Villadecanes
Ponferrada
Basílica de la Encina
Castillo del Temple
Molinaseca
Toral de los Vados
Priaranza del Bierzo
San Esteban de Valdueza
Borrenes
Robledo
Rubiá
Quiroga
San Clodio
Vilamartín de Valdeorras
O Barco
A Rúa
Petín
Larouco
Castro-Caldelas
Pobra de Trives
Manzaneda
Lentellais
Prada
O Bolo
Raigada
Chandrexa de Queixa
Emb. de Chandrexa
Embalse de Prada
A Veiga
Serra de Queixa
Villarino de Conso
Viana do Bolo
Emb. de las Portas
Campo de Bacerros
A Gudiña
Castrelo del Valle
San Cristovo
Ríos
Verín
Vilardevós
Soutochao
Montezinho
Vinhais
Bragança
França
Portelo
Hermisende
Villavella
Portilla de la Canda 1262
Canda
Pías
Lubián
Portilla del Padornelo 1360
Pedralba de la Pradería
Puebla de Sanabria
Palacios de Sanabria
La Sanabria
Lago de Sanabria
San Martín de Castañeda
Galende
Peña Trevinca 2124
Sierra Cabrera
Sa. do Eixe
Casaio
Puente de Domingo Flórez
Iruela
Truchas
Manzaneda
Peña Negra 1583
Teleño 2185
Montes de León
Quintanilla de Somoza
Val de San Lorenzo
Peñalba de Santiago
Santa Colomba de Somoza
Foncebadón
Puerto del Manzanal 1230
Torre del Bierzo
Bembibre
Congosto
Embalse de Bárcena
Cubillos del Sil
Toreno
Fabero
Vega de Espinareda
Sierra de Ancares
Ancares
Candín
Miravalles 1966
Noceda
Igüeña
Folgoso de la Ribera
Villagotón
Embalse de Villameca
Combarros
Astorga
Riego de la Vega
Destriana
Tabuyo del Monte
Castrocontrigo
Nogarejas
Donado
Mombuey
Em. de Cernadilla
Manzanal de Arriba
Villardeciervos
Figueruela de Arriba
Sierra de la Culebra
Mahíde
Riofrío de Aliste
Bercianos de Aliste
Tábara
Faramontanos de Tábara
Ferreras de Arriba
Ferreras de Abajo
Portillo de Sazadón 820
Otero de Bodas
Rionegro del Puente
Camarzana de Tera
Santibáñez de Vidriales
San Pedro de Ceque
Alcubilla de Nogales
Alija del Infantado
Castrocabón
Quintana del Marco
Moreles de Rey
Manganeses de la Polvorosa
Santa Cristina de la Polvorosa
Villanueva de las Peras
Morales de Valverde
Mózar
Granja
Santo
La Bañeza
Palacios de la Valderuerna
Santa Elena de Jamuz
San Cristóbal de la Polantera
Villarejo de Órbigo
San Justo de la Vega
Benavides de Órbigo
Santa Marina del Rey
Turcia
Villamejil
Villadangos del Páramo
Valverde de la Virgen
San Andrés del Rabanedo
Carrizo de la Ribera
Cimanes del Tejar
Quintana del Castillo
Rioseco de Tapia
Riello
Canales
Soto y Amío
Carrocera
La Pola de Gordón
Los Barrios de Luna
Embalse de Barrios de Luna
Salce
Murias de Paredes
Puerto de la Magdalena 1434
Catoute 2117
Salientes
Páramo del Sil
Palacios del Sil
Villablino
Villaseca de Laciana
Puerto de Leitariegos 1521
Degaña
Ventanueva
Vallado
Cangas de Narcea
La Riera
Pola de Somiedo
Somiedo
El Puerto
Peña Ubiña 2417
San Emiliano
Sena de Luna
Pajares
Puerto Pajares 1379
Campomanes
Pola de Lena
Moreda
Barzana
La Plaza
Páramo
Caranga
La Vega
Proaza
Belmonte
Tameza
San Pedro
Soto de Ribera
Mieres
Sotrondio
Langreo
Valdevimbre
Santa María del Páramo
Laguna de Negrillos
Ropuerelos del Páramo
Pozuelo del Páramo
Villaquejida
Pobladura del Valle
Montes de León

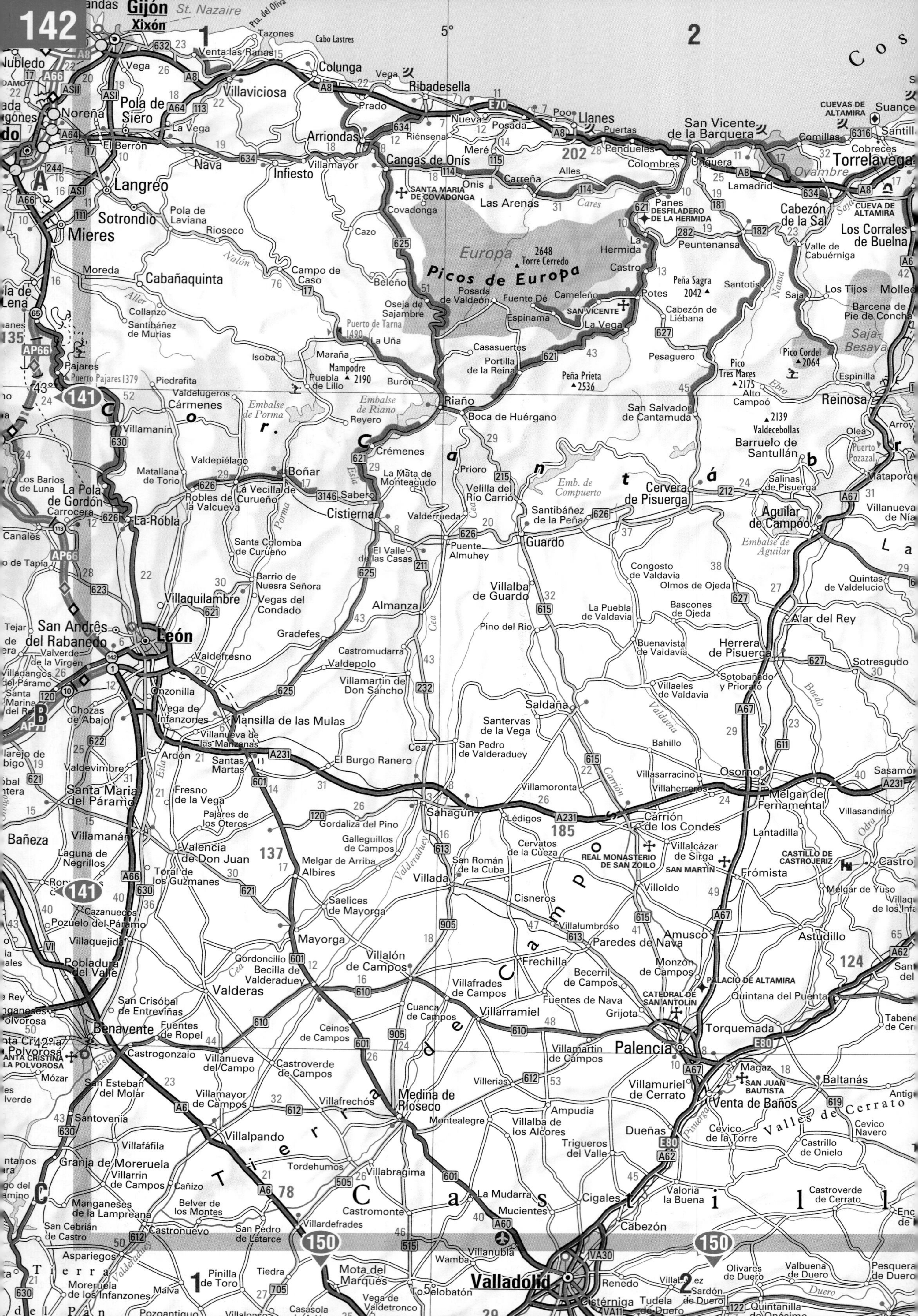
Gijón
Xixón
St. Nazaire
Pta. del Oliva
Tazones
Cabo Lastres
Venta las Ranas
Colunga
Vega
Ribadesella
Villaviciosa
Pola de Siero
Noreña
La Vega
El Berrón
Nava
Infiesto
Arriondas
Villamayor
Prado
Nueva
Riénsena
Posada
Poo
Llanes
Puertas
Pendueles
Colombres
San Vicente de la Barquera
Unquera
Comillas
Cobreces
Torrelavega
Oyambre
Suances
CUEVAS DE ALTAMIRA
Cangas de Onís
Meré
Onís
Carreña
Alles
Las Arenas
Cares
SANTA MARÍA DE COVADONGA
Covadonga
Langreo
Sotrondio
Mieres
Pola de Laviana
Rioseco
Nalón
Cazo
Panes
DESFILADERO DE LA HERMIDA
Hermida
Peuntenansa
Lamadrid
Cabezón de la Sal
CUEVA DE ALTAMIRA
Los Corrales de Buelna
Valle de Cabuérniga
Europa
2648 Torre Cerredo
Picos de Europa
Castro
Peña Sagra 2042
Santotis
Nansa
Saja
Los Tijos
Barcena de Pie de Concha
Saja-Besaya
Moreda
Cabañaquinta
Campo de Caso
Beleño
Posada de Valdeón
Fuente Dé
Cameleño
Potes
SAN VICENTE
Cabezón de Liébana
La Vega
Espinama
Aller
Collanzo
Santibáñez de Murias
Oseja de Sajambre
Puerto de Tarna 1490
La Uña
Isoba
Maraña
Mampodre 2190
Puebla de Lillo
Casasuertes
Portilla de la Reina
Peña Prieta 2536
Pesaguero
Pico Tres Mares 2175
Alto Campoó
Pico Cordel 2064
Espinilla
Reinosa
Ebro
Pajares
Puerto Pajares 1379
Piedrafita
Valdelugeros
Cármenes
Embalse de Porma
Burón
Embalse de Riano
Riaño
Boca de Huérgano
Reyero
San Salvador de Cantamuda
2139
Valdecebollas
Barruelo de Santullán
Olea
Puerto Pozazal
Arroyo
Villamanín
Cordillera Cantábrica
Valdepiélago
Crémenes
Matallana de Torio
Boñar
La Mata de Monteagudo
Prioro
Velilla del Río Carrió
Emb. de Compuerto
Cervera de Pisuerga
Salinas de Pisuerga
Mataporquera
Los Barios de Luna
La Pola de Gordón
Carrocera
La Robla
La Vecilla de Curueño
Robles de la Valcueva
Sabero
Esla
Cistierna
Valderrueda
Cea
Santibáñez de la Peña
Aguilar de Campóo
Villanueva de Nía
Canales
Santa Colomba de Curueño
Porma
El Valle de las Casas
Puente Almuhey
Guardo
Embalse de Aguilar
Congosto de Valdavia
Olmos de Ojeda
Quintanas de Valdelucio
Tapia
Barrio de Nuesra Señora
Vegas del Condado
Villaquilambre
Almanza
Villalba de Guardo
La Puebla de Valdavia
Bascones de Ojeda
Alar del Rey
Tejar
San Andrés del Rabanedo
León
Gradefes
Pino del Rio
Buenavista de Valdavia
Herrera de Pisuerga
Valverde de la Virgen
Villadangos
del Páramo
Santa Marina del Rey
Valdefresno
Castromudarra
Valdepolo
Villamartín de Don Sancho
Villaeles de Valdavia
Sotobañado y Priorato
Sotresgudo
Boedo
Chozas de Abajo
Onzonilla
Vega de Infanzones
Mansilla de las Mulas
Saldaña
Santervas de la Vega
Valdavia
Villanueva de las Manzanas
Ardón
Santas Martas
El Burgo Ranero
San Pedro de Valderaduey
Bahillo
Valdevimbre
Fresno de la Vega
Villasarracino
Villaherreros
Osorno
Melgar de Fernamental
Sasamón
Santa María del Páramo
Villamoronta
Carrión
Pajares de los Oteros
Gordaliza del Pino
Sahagún
Lédigos
Carrión de los Condes
Villasandino
Lantadilla
Odra
Bañeza
Villamañán
Laguna de Negrillos
Valencia de Don Juan
Galleguillos de Campos
Melgar de Arriba
Albires
Cervatos de la Cueza
REAL MONASTERIO DE SAN ZOILO
Villalcázar de Sirga
SAN MARTÍN
CASTILLO DE CASTROJERIZ
Castrojeriz
Frómista
Toral de los Guzmanes
San Román de la Cuba
Villada
Valderaduey
Villoldo
Melgar de Yuso
Villaquirán de los Infantes
Cazanuecos
Pozuelo del Páramo
Saelices de Mayorga
Cisneros
Villalumbroso
Amusco
Astudillo
Villaquejida
Mayorga
Paredes de Nava
Pobladura del Valle
Gordoncillo
Becilla de Valderaduey
Villalón de Campos
Frechilla
Monzón de Campos
Valderas
Villafrades de Campos
Becerril de Campos
PALACIO DE ALTAMIRA
Quintana del Puente
San Crisóbal de Entreviñas
Cuanca de Campos
Villarramiel
Fuentes de Nava
CATEDRAL DE SAN ANTOLÍN
Grijota
Benavente
Fuentes de Ropel
Ceinos de Campos
Torquemada
Tabanera de Cerrato
Santa Cristina de la Polvorosa
Castrogonzalo
Villanueva del Campo
Castroverde de Campos
Villamartín de Campos
Palencia
Mózar
San Esteban del Molar
Villerías
Villamuriel de Cerrato
Magaz
SAN JUAN BAUTISTA
Baltanás
Villamayor de Campos
Villafrechós
Medina de Ríoseco
Venta de Baños
Santovenia
Montealegre
Ampudia
Villalba de los Alcores
Dueñas
Pisuerga
Cevico de la Torre
Valles de Cerrato
Cevico Navero
Villalpando
Villafáfila
Trigueros del Valle
Castrillo de Onielo
Granja de Moreruela
Villarrin de Campos
Tordehumos
Cañizo
Villabrágima
Manganeses de la Lampreana
Belver de los Montes
La Mudarra
Cigales
Valoria la Buena
Castroverde de Cerrato
Tierra de Campos
Castilla
Castromonte
Mucientes
Villardefrades
San Cebrián de Castro
Castronuevo
San Pedro de Latarce
Cabezón
Aspariegos
Villanubla
Wamba
Tierra del Pan
Moreruela de los Infanzones
Pinilla de Toro
Tiedra
Mota del Marqués
Valladolid
Renedo
Villabáñez
Sardón de Duero
Olivares de Duero
Valbuena de Duero
Pesquera de Duero
Duero
Malva
Vega de Valdetronco
Torrelobatón
Cistérniga
Tudela de Duero
Quintanilla de Onésimo
Pozoantiguo
Villalonso
Casasola de Arión
5°
43°
42°
1
2
A
B
C
141
150
135
137
185
202
124
78
29
A8
A66
A64
AS I
AP66
A6
A60
A62
A67
A231
E70
E80
N-I
VI
VA30
VA11

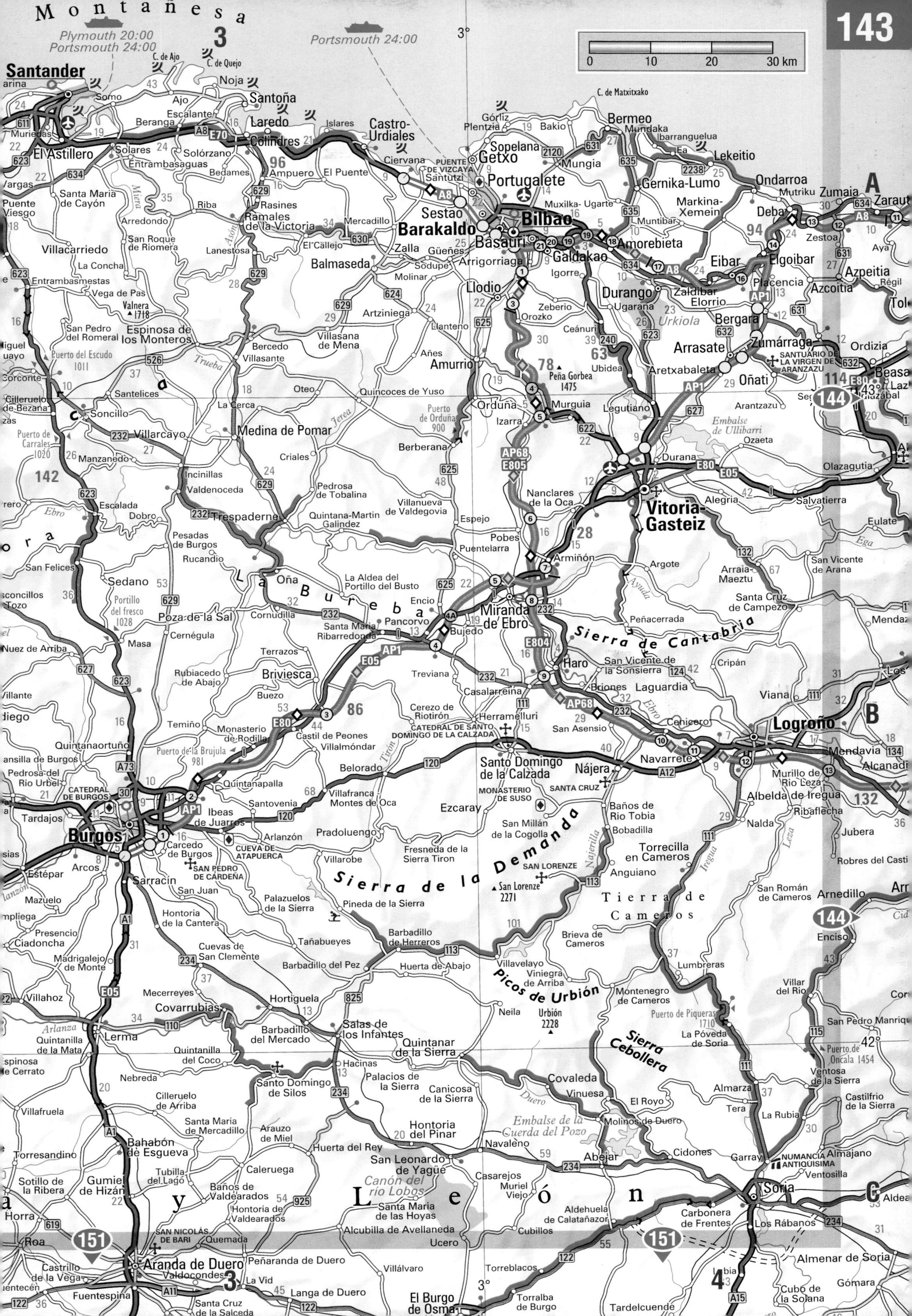

Montañesa
Plymouth 20:00
Portsmouth 24:00
Portsmouth 24:00
0 10 20 30 km
Santander
C. de Ajo
C. de Quejo
Noja
Santoña
Somo
Ajo
Escalante
Beranga
Laredo
Islares
Castro-Urdiales
Colindres
Muriedas
El Astillero
Solares
Entrambasaguas
Solórzano
Bedames
Ampuero
El Puente
Ciervana
Puente de Vizcaya
Santutzi
Getxo
Sopelana
Plentzia
Górliz
Bakio
Bermeo
Mundaka
Ibarranguelua
Ea
Lekeitio
Mungia
Portugalete
Sestao
Barakaldo
Bilbao
Basauri
Galdakao
Muxilka- Ugarte
Gernika-Lumo
Markina-Xemein
Ondarroa
Mutriku
Zumaia
Zarautz
Deba
Zestoa
Azpeitia
Aya
Régil
Amorebieta
Muntibar
Eibar
Elgoibar
Placencia
Azcoitia
Durango
Zaldibar
Elorrio
Igorre
Arrigorriaga
Zalla
Güeñes
Sodupe
Balmaseda
El Callejo
Molinar
Llodio
Zeberio
Orozko
Ugarana
Urkiola
Bergara
Arrasate
Zumárraga
Ordizia
Beasain
Lazkao
Oñati
Aretxabaleta
Santuario de la Virgen de Aranzazu
Arantzazu
Ceánuri
Ubidea
Peña Gorbea 1475
Artziniega
Llanteno
Villasana de Mena
Añes
Amurrio
Santa María de Cayón
Riba
Rasines
Ramales de la Victoria
Mercadillo
Arredondo
San Roque de Riomera
Lanestosa
Villacarriedo
La Concha
Entrambasmestas
Vega de Pas
Valnera 1718
Puente Viesgo
Vargas
San Pedro del Romeral
Espinosa de los Monteros
Bercedo
Villasante
Trueba
Puerto del Escudo 1011
Corconte
Cilleruelo de Bezana
Santelices
Soncillo
Oteo
Quincoces de Yuso
La Cerca
Medina de Pomar
Puerto de Orduña 900
Orduña
Izarra
Murguia
Legutiano
Berberana
Villarcayo
Manzanedo
Puerto de Carrales 1020
Criales
Incinillas
Valdenoceda
Pedrosa de Tobalina
Villanueva de Valdegovia
Trespaderne
Quintana-Martin Galindez
Espejo
Escalada
Dobro
Ebro
Embalse de Ullibarri
Ozaeta
Durana
Vitoria-Gasteiz
Nanclares de la Oca
Alegria
Salvatierra
Olazagutia
Eulate
Ega
Pobes
Puentelarra
Armiñón
Argote
Arraia-Maeztu
San Vicente de Arana
Pesadas de Burgos
Rucandio
San Felices
Sedano
Portillo del fresco 1028
La Aldea del Portillo del Busto
Oña
La Bureba
Encio
Pancorvo
Santa María Ribarredonda
Bujedo
Miranda de Ebro
Ayuda
Peñacerrada
Santa Cruz de Campezo
Mendaza
Sierra de Cantabria
Poza de la Sal
Cornudilla
Cernégula
Masa
Nuez de Arriba
Terrazos
Treviana
Haro
San Vicente de la Sonsierra
Briones
Laguardia
Cripán
Viana
Rubiacedo de Abajo
Briviesca
Buezo
Casalarreina
Cerezo de Riotirón
Herramelluri
Catedral de Santo Domingo de la Calzada
San Asensio
Cenicero
Logroño
Mendavia
Alcanadre
Temiño
Monasterio de Rodilla
Castil de Peones
Villalmóndar
Tirón
Quintanaortuño
Puerto de la Brujula 981
Pedrosa del Rio Urbel
Catedral de Burgos
Quintanapalla
Belorado
Santo Domingo de la Calzada
Nájera
Navarrete
Santa Cruz
Monasterio de Suso
Murillo de Río Leza
Albelda de Iregua
Ribafrecha
Nalda
Jubera
Tardajos
Burgos
Ibeas de Juarros
Santovenia
Villafranca Montes de Oca
Ezcaray
Baños de Rio Tobia
Bobadilla
Arlanzón
Pradoluengo
San Millán de la Cogolla
Carcedo de Burgos
Cueva de Atapuerca
Fresneda de la Sierra Tiron
Torrecilla en Cameros
Leza
Iregua
Robres del Castillo
Estépar
Arcos
San Pedro de Cardeña
Villarobe
Sierra de la Demanda
San Lorenzo
San Lorenzo 2271
Anguiano
Najerilla
Sarracín
San Juan
Mazuelo
Palazuelos de la Sierra
Pineda de la Sierra
Tierra de Cameros
San Román de Cameros
Arnedillo
Hontoria de la Cantera
Presencio
Ciadoncha
Tañabueyes
Barbadillo de Herreros
Brieva de Cameros
Enciso
Madrigalejo de Monte
Cuevas de San Clemente
Barbadillo del Pez
Huerta de Abajo
Villavelayo
Viniegra de Arriba
Picos de Urbión
Lumbreras
Villar del Rio
Montenegro de Cameros
Villahoz
Mecerreyes
Covarrubias
Hortiguela
Neila
Urbión 2228
Puerto de Piqueras 1710
Sierra Cebollera
La Póveda de Soria
San Pedro Manrique
Puerto de Oncala 1454
Lerma
Arlanza
Quintanilla de la Mata
Barbadillo del Mercado
Salas de los Infantes
Quintanar de la Sierra
Quintanilla del Coco
Hacinas
Palacios de la Sierra
Canicosa de la Sierra
Covaleda
Vinuesa
El Royo
Almarza
Ventosa de la Sierra
Castilfrio de la Sierra
Tera
La Rubia
Nebreda
Santo Domingo de Silos
Cilleruelo de Arriba
Villafruela
Santa Maria de Mercadillo
Arauzo de Miel
Hontoria del Pinar
Duero
Embalse de la Cuerda del Pozo
Molinos de Duero
Navaleno
Cidones
Garray
Numancia Antiquisima
Almajano
Ventosilla
Torresandino
Bahabón de Esgueva
Huerta del Rey
San Leonardo de Yagüe
Tubilla del Lago
Caleruega
Abejar
Sotillo de la Ribera
Gumiel de Hizán
Baños de Valdearados
Cañon del río Lobos
Casarejos
Muriel Viejo
Soria
Castilla y León
Santa Maria de las Hoyas
Hontoria de Valdearados
Aldehuela de Calatañazor
Carbonera de Frentes
Los Rábanos
Horra
Roa
San Nicolás de Bari
Quemada
Alcubilla de Avellaneda
Ucero
Cubillos
Almenar de Soria
Castrillo de la Vega
Aranda de Duero
Valdocondes
Peñaranda de Duero
Villálvaro
Torreblacos
La Vid
Langa de Duero
Fuentespina
Santa Cruz de la Salceda
El Burgo de Osma
Torralba de Burgo
Tardelcuende
Cubo de la Solana
Gómara

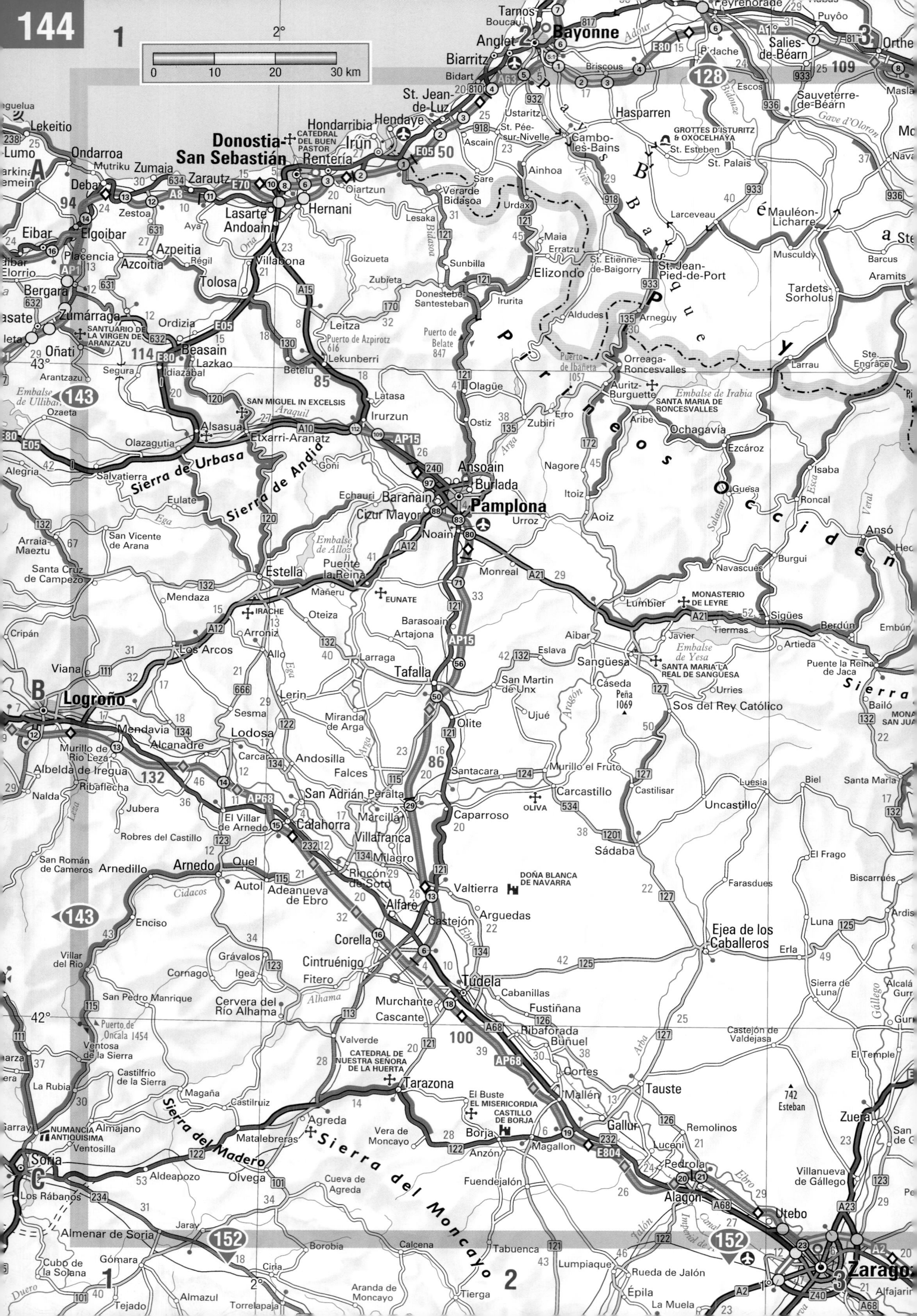
1
2°
0 10 20 30 km
Tarnos
Boucau
Bayonne
Anglet
Biarritz
Bidart
St. Jean-de-Luz
Hendaye
Hondarribia
Irún
Donostia-San Sebastián
CATEDRAL DEL BUEN PASTOR
Rentería
Oiartzun
Hernani
Lasarte
Andoain
Lekeitio
Ondarroa
Mutriku
Zumaia
Zarautz
Deba
Zestoa
Eibar
Elgoibar
Placencia
Azpeitia
Azcoitia
Régil
Tolosa
Villabona
Bergara
Zumárraga
Oñati
SANTUARIO DE LA VIRGEN DE ARANZAZU
Arantzazu
Ordizia
Beasain
Lazkao
Segura
Idiazábal
Embalse de Ullibarri
Ozaeta
SAN MIGUEL IN EXCELSIS
Alsasua
Olazagutia
Etxarri-Aranatz
Salvatierra
Alegría
Sierra de Urbasa
Sierra de Andía
Goñi
Eulate
Arraia-Maeztu
San Vicente de Arana
Santa Cruz de Campezo
Estella
Mendaza
IRACHE
Arroniz
Los Arcos
Viana
Logroño
Cripán
Allo
Oteiza
Mañeru
Puente la Reina
Embalse de Alloz
Echauri
Barañain
Cizur Mayor
Noain
Pamplona
Burlada
Ansoain
Ostiz
Olagüe
Latasa
Irurzun
Betelu
Lekunberri
Leitza
Puerto de Azpirotz 616
Goizueta
Zubieta
Donestebe-Santesteban
Puerto de Belate 847
Sunbilla
Lesaka
Verarde Bidasoa
Sare
Urdax
Ainhoa
Maia
Erratzu
Elizondo
Irurita
Ustaritz
St. Pée-sur-Nivelle
Ascain
Cambo-les-Bains
Hasparren
Briscous
Bidache
Peyrehorade
Puyôo
Salies-de-Béarn
Orthez
Sauveterre-de-Béarn
Escos
GROTTES D'ISTURITZ & OXOCELHAYA
St. Esteben
St. Palais
Larceveau
Mauléon-Licharre
Musculdy
Barcus
Aramits
Tardets-Sorholus
St. Etienne-de-Baigorry
St. Jean-Pied-de-Port
Aldudes
Arneguy
Puerto de Ibañeta 1057
Orreaga-Roncesvalles
Auritz-Burguette
SANTA MARIA DE RONCESVALLES
Embalse de Irabia
Aribe
Ochagavía
Ezcároz
Larrau
Ste. Engrâce
Isaba
Roncal
Guesa
Ansó
Burgui
Navascués
Erro
Zubiri
Nagore
Itoiz
Aoiz
Urroz
Monreal
EUNATE
Barasoain
Artajona
Larraga
Tafalla
Lumbier
MONASTERIO DE LEYRE
Sigües
Tiermas
Javier
Berdún
Embún
Aibar
Eslava
Sangüesa
Embalse de Yesa
SANTA MARIA LA REAL DE SANGÜESA
Urriés
Artieda
Puente la Reina de Jaca
Bailó
San Martin de Unx
Cáseda
Peña 1069
Sos del Rey Católico
Ujué
Olite
Lerin
Sesma
Miranda de Arga
Mendavia
Lodosa
Alcanadre
Murillo de Río Leza
Albelda de Iregua
Ribaflecha
Nalda
Jubera
Robres del Castillo
Carcar
Andosilla
Falces
Santacara
Murillo el Fruto
Carcastillo
Castilisar
Luesia
Biel
Santa María
Uncastillo
San Adrián
Peralta
Marcilla
Villafranca
Milagro
OLIVA
Caparroso
El Villar de Arnedo
Calahorra
Sádaba
El Frago
Biscarrués
San Román de Cameros
Arnedillo
Arnedo
Quel
Autol
Adeanueva de Ebro
Rincón de Soto
Alfaro
Valtierra
DOÑA BLANCA DE NAVARRA
Farasdues
Arguedas
Castejón
Enciso
Corella
Cintruénigo
Fitero
Ejea de los Caballeros
Luna
Erla
Villar del Río
Grávalos
Cornago
Igea
Tudela
Cabanillas
Fustiñana
Ribaforada
Buñuel
San Pedro Manrique
Cervera del Río Alhama
Murchante
Cascante
Sierra de Luna
Castejón de Valdejasa
El Temple
Puerto de Oncala 1454
Ventosa de la Sierra
Valverde
CATEDRAL DE NUESTRA SEÑORA DE LA HUERTA
Cortes
Castilfrío de la Sierra
La Rubia
Magaña
Tarazona
El Buste
EL MISERICORDIA
CASTILLO DE BORJA
Mallén
Tauste
742 Esteban
Castilruiz
Agreda
Vera de Moncayo
Borja
Gallur
Remolinos
Zuera
NUMANCIA ANTIQUISIMA
Almajano
Ventosilla
Matalebreras
Sierra del Madero
Sierra del Moncayo
Magallon
Anzón
Luceni
Pedrola
Soria
Aldeapozo
Olvega
Cueva de Agreda
Fuendejalón
Villanueva de Gállego
Los Rábanos
Alagón
Utebo
Almenar de Soria
Jaray
Borobia
Calcena
Tabuenca
Cubo de la Solana
Gómara
Ciria
Lumpiaque
Rueda de Jalón
Zaragoza
Almazul
Aranda de Moncayo
Tierga
Épila
La Muela
Tejado
Torrelapaja
Alfajarín
Pirineos Occidentales
Pays Basque
Ebro
Adour
42°
43°

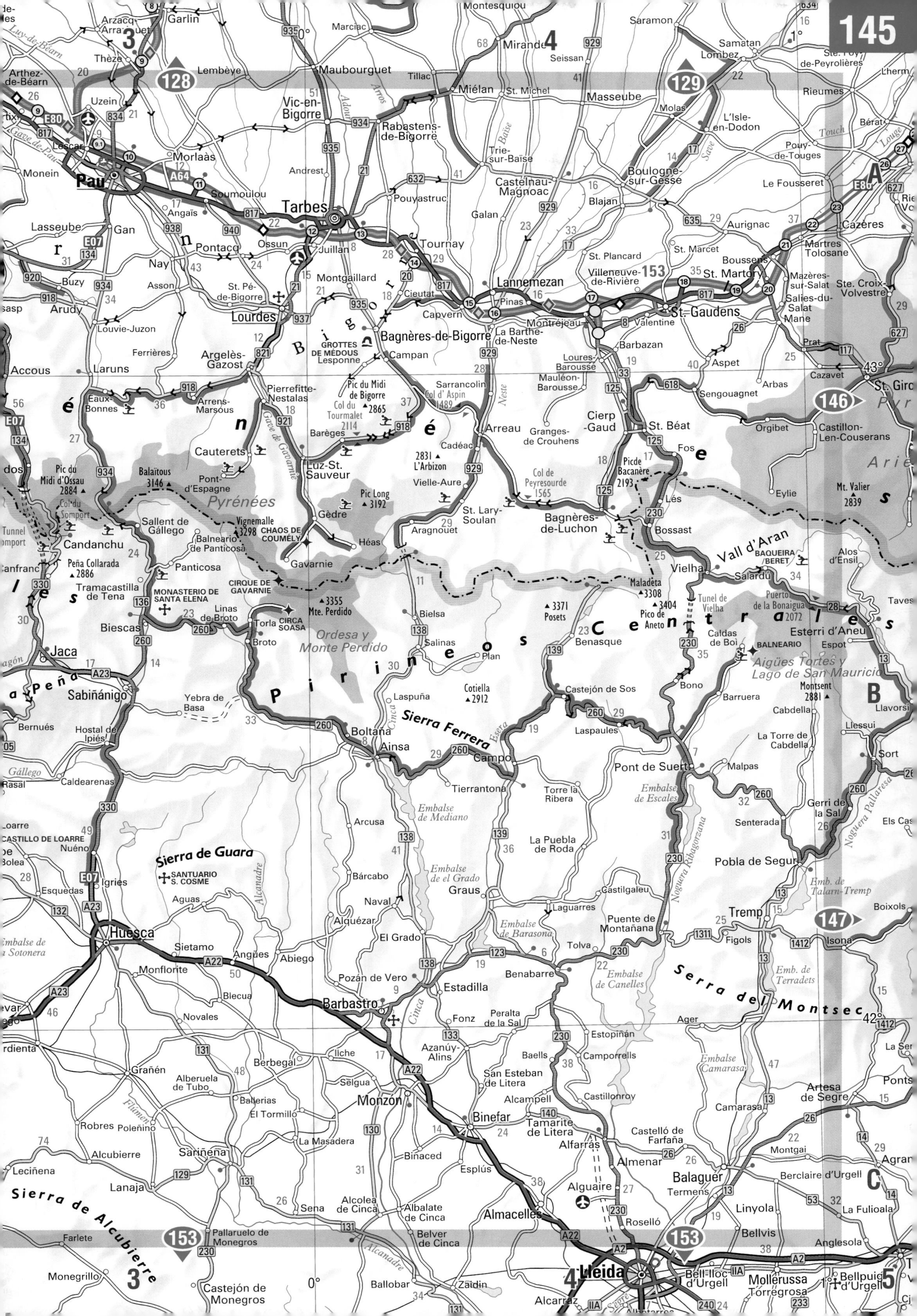
Garlin
Arzacq-Arraziguet
Montesquiou
Saramon
Marciac
Mirande
Seissan
Samatan
Lombez
Ste. Foy-de-Peyrolières
Thèze
Lembeye
Maubourguet
Tillac
Arthez-de-Béarn
Uzein
Vic-en-Bigorre
Miélan
St. Michel
Masseube
Molas
L'Isle-en-Dodon
L'herm
Rieumes
Bérat
Lescar
Rabastens-de-Bigorre
Trie-sur-Baïse
Pouy-de-Touges
Monein
Pau
Morlaàs
Andrest
Soumoulou
Castelnau-Magnoac
Boulogne-sur-Gesse
Le Fousseret
Angaïs
Tarbes
Pouyastruc
Galan
Blajan
Aurignac
Cazères
Lasseube
Gan
Ossun
Juillan
Tournay
St. Plancard
St. Marcet
Boussens
Martres Tolosane
Nay
Pontacq
Montgaillard
Villeneuve-de-Rivière
St. Martory
Mazères-sur-Salat
Ste. Croix-Volvestre
Buzy
Asson
St. Pé-de-Bigorre
Cieutat
Lannemezan
Pinas
Salies-du-Salat
Mane
Arudy
Lourdes
Capvern
Montréjeau
St. Gaudens
Valentine
Louvie-Juzon
Bagnères-de-Bigorre
La Barthe-de-Neste
Ferrières
Argelès-Gazost
GROTTES DE MÉDOUS
Lesponne
Campan
Barbazan
Prat
Accous
Laruns
Loures-Barousse
Aspet
Cazavet
St. Girons
Mauléon-Barousse
Arbas
Pierrefitte-Nestalas
Sarrancolin
Sengouagnet
Eaux-Bonnes
Arrens-Marsous
Pic du Midi de Bigorre
Col d'Aspin 1489
Col du Tourmalet 2114
2865
Arreau
Granges-de Crouhens
Cierp-Gaud
St. Béat
Orgibet
Castillon-Len-Couserans
Barèges
Cadéac
Cauterets
Luz-St. Sauveur
2831 L'Arbizon
Fos
Ariège
Pic du Midi d'Ossau 2884
Balaïtous 3146
Pont-d'Espagne
Vielle-Aure
Col de Peyresourde 1565
Pic de Bacanère 2193
Pyrénées
Pic Long 3192
Eylie
Mt. Valier 2839
Col du Somport
Tunnel Somport
Candanchu
Sallent de Gállego
Vignemalle 3298
CHAOS DE COUMÉLY
Gèdre
St. Lary-Soulan
Les
Bagnères-de-Luchon
Bossast
Aragnouet
Balneario de Panticosa
Héas
Canfranc
Peña Collarada 2886
Panticosa
Gavarnie
Vall d'Aran
BAQUEIRA /BERET
Alos d'Ensil
Vielha
Salardú
CIRQUE DE GAVARNIE
Tramacastilla de Tena
MONASTERIO DE SANTA ELENA
Maladeta 3308
3404 Pico de Aneto
Tunel de Vielha
Puerto de la Bonaigua 2072
Taves
Linas de Broto
Torla
CIRCA SOASA
3355 Mte. Perdido
Bielsa
3371 Posets
Esterri d'Aneu
Biescas
Broto
Salinas
Benasque
Caldas de Boì
BALNEARIO
Espot
Jaca
Ordesa y Monte Perdido
Plan
Aigües Tortes y Lago de San Mauricio
Sabiñánigo
Pirineos Centrales
Cotiella 2912
Castejón de Sos
Bono
Montsent 2881
Yebra de Basa
Laspuña
Barruera
Llavorsi
Cabdella
Bernués
Hostal de Ipiés
Sierra Ferrera
Laspaules
Llessui
Boltaña
La Torre de Cabdella
Ainsa
Campo
Sort
Gállego
Rasal
Caldearenas
Pont de Suert
Malpas
Tierrantona
Torre la Ribera
Embalse de Escales
Embalse de Mediano
Gerri de la Sal
Loarre
CASTILLO DE LOARRE
Arcusa
Senterada
Els Cas
Nueno
La Puebla de Roda
Sierra de Guara
SANTUARIO S. COSME
Pobla de Segur
Igries
Bárcabo
Embalse de el Grado
Emb. de Talarn-Tremp
Esquedas
Graus
Castilgaleu
Aguas
Naval
Laguarres
Tremp
Boixols
Alquézar
Puente de Montañana
Huesca
Embalse de Barasona
Figols
Isona
Embalse de la Sotonera
El Grado
Tolva
Sietamo
Angües
Abiego
Benabarre
Embalse de Canelles
Serra del Montsec
Monflorite
Emb. de Terradets
Pozán de Vero
Estadilla
Blecua
Barbastro
Peralta de la Sal
Novales
Fonz
Ager
Estopiñán
Azanúy-Alins
Baells
Camporrells
Embalse Camarasa
La Ser
Grañén
Berbegal
Ilche
Alberuela de Tubo
Selgua
San Esteban de Litera
Pont
Castillonroy
Artesa de Segre
Ballerias
Monzón
Alcampell
El Tormillo
Binefar
Camarasa
Tamarite de Litera
Robres
Poleñino
Castelló de Farfaña
Alfarrás
Alcubierre
Sariñena
La Masadera
Binaced
Montgai
Agramunt
Leciñena
Esplús
Almenar
Balaguer
Berclaire d'Urgell
Lanaja
Alguaire
Termens
Sierra de Alcubierre
Sena
Alcolea de Cinca
Albalate de Cinca
Linyola
La Fulioala
Almacelles
Roselló
Farlete
Pallaruelo de Monegros
Belver de Cinca
Bellvis
Anglesola
Monegrillo
Lleida
Bell-lloc d'Urgell
Mollerussa
Bellpuig d'Urgell
Castejón de Monegros
Ballobar
Zaidin
Alcarraz
Torregrosa

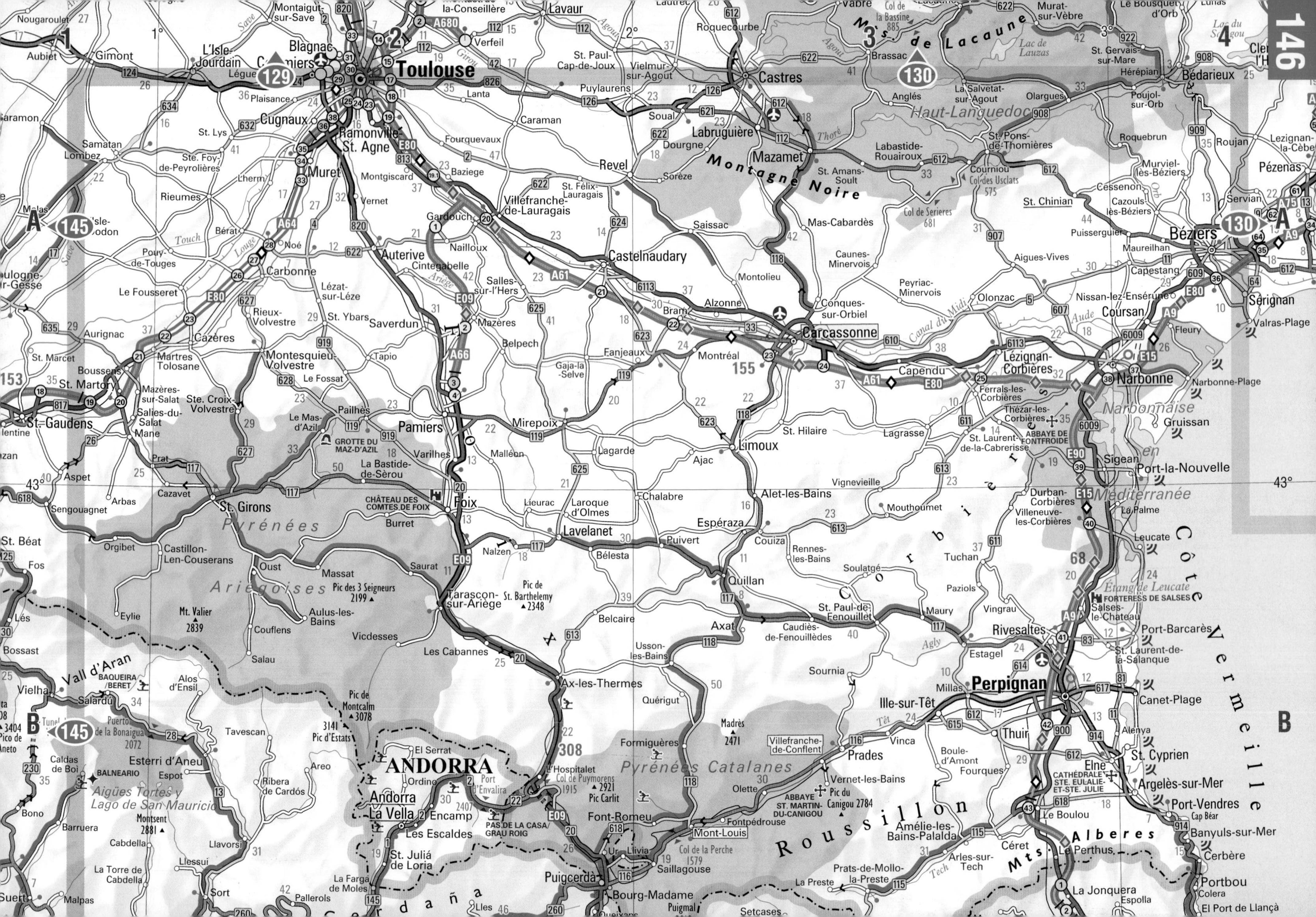
Toulouse
Blagnac
Colomiers
L'Isle-Jourdain
Gimont
Aubiet
Samatan
Lombez
Muret
Ramonville-St. Agne
Cugnaux
Plaisance
St. Lys
Rieumes
Carbonne
Noé
Cazères
Martres Tolosane
St. Martory
St. Gaudens
Aspet
Aurignac
Boussens
Salies-du-Salat
Mane
St. Girons
Castillon-en-Couserans
Massat
Oust
Aulus-les-Bains
Seix
Mt. Valier 2839
Pic de Montcalm 3078
Auterive
Cintegabelle
Saverdun
Pamiers
Foix
Varilhes
Tarascon-sur-Ariège
Ax-les-Thermes
Lavelanet
Mirepoix
Belpech
Castelnaudary
Villefranche-de-Lauragais
Revel
Puylaurens
Lavaur
Verfeil
Caraman
Lanta
St. Félix-Lauragais
Castres
Mazamet
Labruguière
Dourgne
Sorèze
Montagne Noire
Carcassonne
Alzonne
Bram
Montréal
Limoux
Quillan
Espéraza
Couiza
Alet-les-Bains
Chalabre
Puivert
Bélesta
Lagrasse
Capendu
Lézignan-Corbières
Narbonne
Coursan
Béziers
Sérignan
Pézenas
Bédarieux
St. Pons-de-Thomières
St. Chinian
Olargues
Capestang
Gruissan
Narbonne-Plage
Sigean
Port-la-Nouvelle
Leucate
Étang de Leucate
Salses-le-Château
Port-Barcarès
Rivesaltes
Perpignan
Canet-Plage
St. Cyprien
Argelès-sur-Mer
Port-Vendres
Banyuls-sur-Mer
Cerbère
Portbou
Elne
Thuir
Ille-sur-Têt
Prades
Vernet-les-Bains
Villefranche-de-Conflent
Olette
Mont-Louis
Font-Romeu
Saillagouse
Bourg-Madame
Puigcerdà
Llívia
Céret
Le Boulou
Le Perthus
Amélie-les-Bains-Palalda
Arles-sur-Tech
Prats-de-Mollo-la-Preste
La Jonquera
Côte Vermeille
Roussillon
Corbières
Pyrénées Catalanes
Mts. Albères
Mts. de Lacaune
Haut-Languedoc
Pyrénées Ariégeoises
Méditerranée
ANDORRA
Andorra la Vella
Les Escaldes
Encamp
Ordino
St. Juliá de Loria
Pas de la Casa
Vall d'Aran
Vielha
Esterri d'Aneu
Sort
Cerdaña
Fortress de Salses
Abbaye de Fontfroide
Abbaye St. Martin-du-Canigou
Pic du Canigou 2784
Château des Comtes de Foix
Grotte du Maz-d'Azil

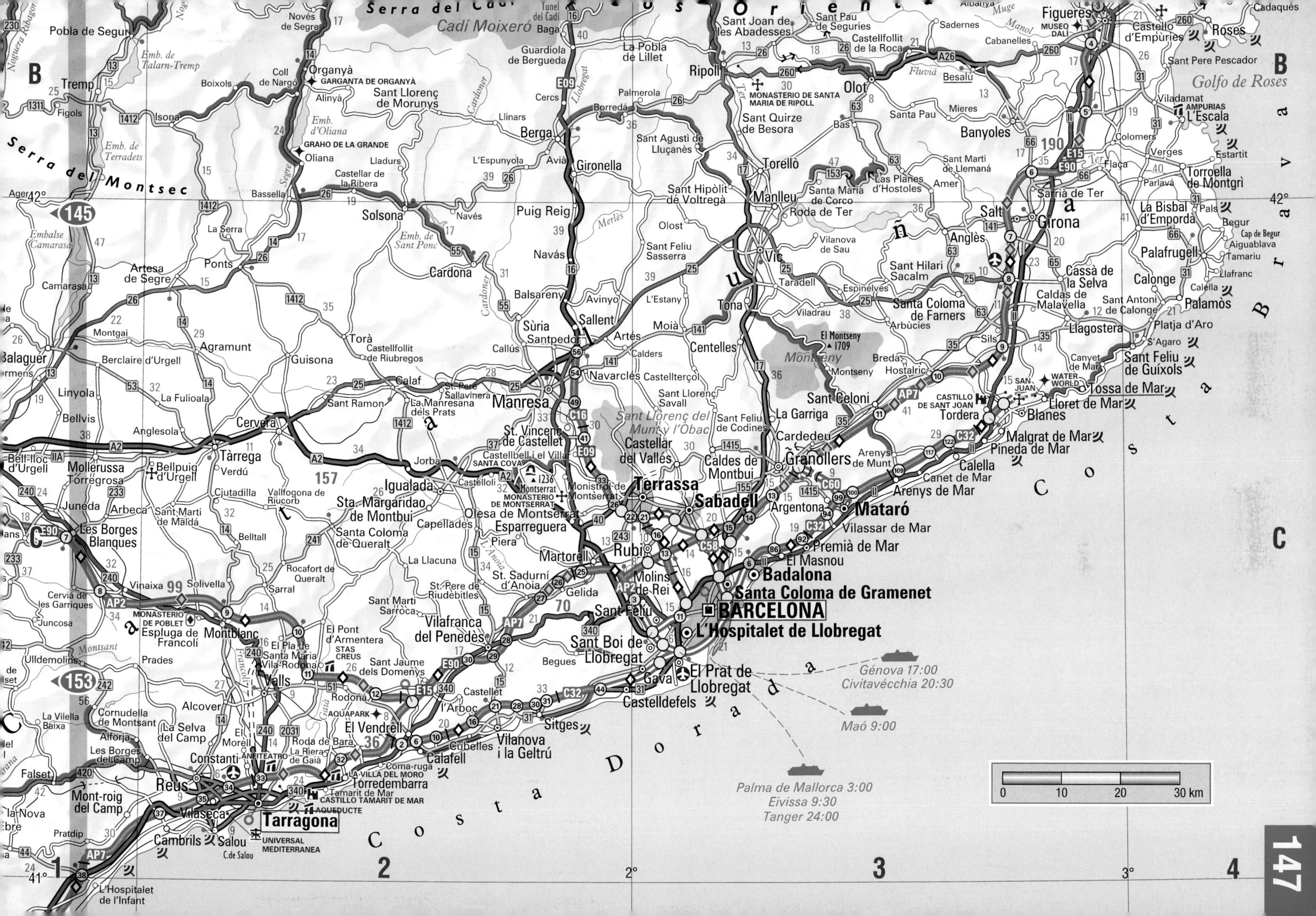
Golfo de Roses
Costa Brava
Costa Daurada
Serra del Cadí
Serra del Montsec
Cadí Moixeró
BARCELONA
L'Hospitalet de Llobregat
Santa Coloma de Gramenet
Badalona
Mataró
Sabadell
Terrassa
Girona
Figueres
Tarragona
Manresa
Vic
Granollers
Reus
Salou
Sitges
Vilanova i la Geltrú
Vilafranca del Penedès
Igualada
Blanes
Lloret de Mar
Tossa de Mar
Palamós
Palafrugell
Olot
Ripoll
Berga
Solsona
Cardona
Tàrrega
Cervera
Valls
El Vendrell
Calafell
Cambrils
Castelldefels
El Prat de Llobregat
Sant Boi de Llobregat
Rubí
Martorell
Arenys de Mar
Calella
Malgrat de Mar
Pineda de Mar
Sant Feliu de Guíxols
La Bisbal d'Empordà
Torroella de Montgrí
L'Escala
Roses
Castelló d'Empúries
Banyoles
Montseny
Gènova 17:00
Civitavècchia 20:30
Maó 9:00
Palma de Mallorca 3:00
Eivissa 9:30
Tanger 24:00
0 10 20 30 km
1° 2° 3° 41° 42°
B C 1 2 3 4

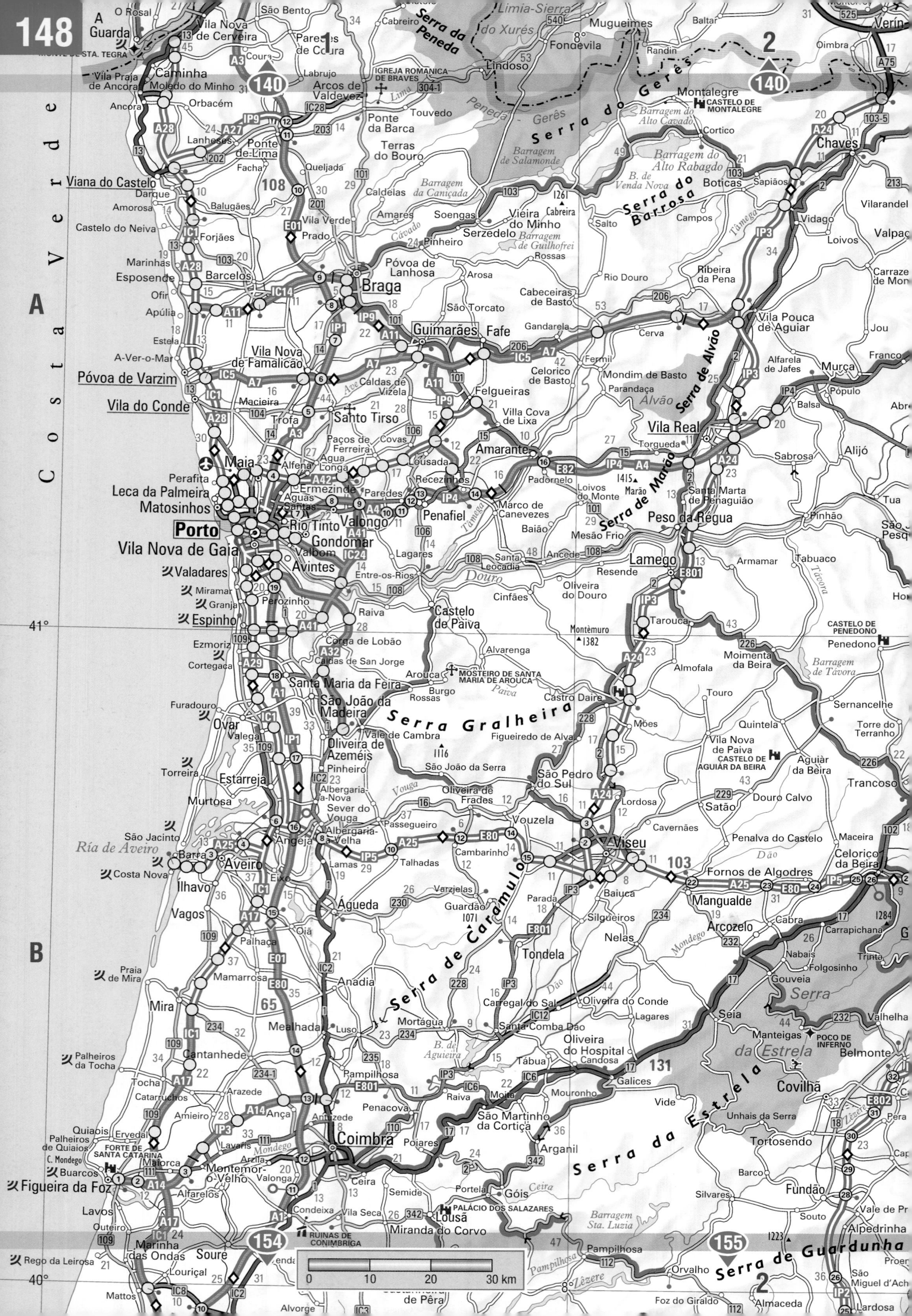

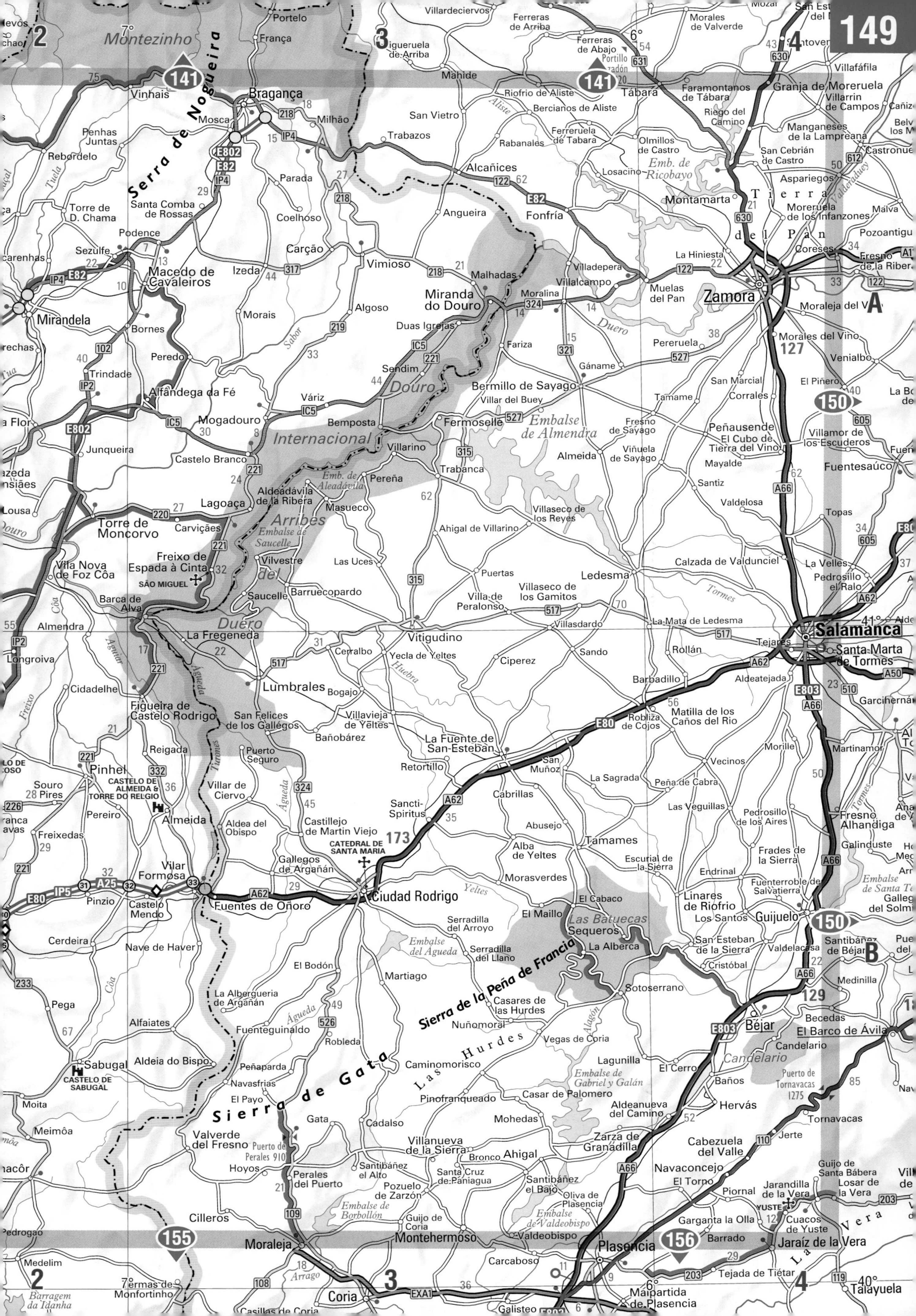

Montezinho
Serra de Nogueira
Portelo
França
Vinhais
Bragança
Mosca
Milhão
Penhas Juntas
Rebordelo
Torre de D. Chama
Santa Comba de Rossas
Parada
Coelhoso
Podence
Sezulfe
Macedo de Cavaleiros
Izeda
Carção
Vimioso
Mirandela
Bornes
Morais
Algoso
Miranda do Douro
Duas Igrejas
Peredo
Trindade
Alfândega da Fé
Mogadouro
Váriz
Sendim
Bemposta
Douro Internacional
Junqueira
Castelo Branco
Lagoaça
Aldeadávila de la Ribera
Emb. de Aleadávila
Pereña
Masueco
Torre de Moncorvo
Carviçães
Arribes del Duero
Embalse de Saucelle
Freixo de Espada à Cinta
SÃO MIGUEL
Vila Nova de Foz Côa
Vilvestre
Saucelle
Barruecopardo
Barca de Alva
Almendra
La Fregeneda
Longroiva
Cidadelhe
Figueira de Castelo Rodrigo
Lumbrales
Bogajo
San Felices de los Gallegos
Villavieja de Yeltes
Bañobárez
Reigada
Puerto Seguro
Pinhel
Souro Pires
CASTELO DE ALMEIDA & TORRE DO RELGIO
Pereiro
Almeida
Villar de Ciervo
Aldea del Obispo
Freixedas
Vilar Formosa
Castelo Mendo
Pinzio
Fuentes de Oñoro
Cerdeira
Nave de Haver
Gallegos de Argañán
Castillejo de Martin Viejo
CATEDRAL DE SANTA MARIA
Ciudad Rodrigo
Sancti-Spiritus
Retortillo
La Fuente de San-Esteban
Villardeciervos
Ferreras de Arriba
Ferreras de Abajo
Figueruela de Arriba
Mahide
Riofrio de Aliste
Bercianos de Aliste
San Vietro
Trabazos
Rabanales
Ferreruela de Tabara
Alcañices
Angueira
Fonfría
Malhadas
Moralina
Villadepera
Villalcampo
Fariza
Gáname
Bermillo de Sayago
Villar del Buey
Fermoselle
Embalse de Almendra
Villarino
Trabanca
Fresno de Sayago
Viñuela de Sayago
Almeida
Villaseco de los Reyes
Ahigal de Villarino
Las Uces
Puertas
Villa de Peralonso
Villaseco de los Gamitos
Ledesma
Vitigudino
Cerralbo
Yecla de Yeltes
Ciperez
Villasdardo
Sando
Morales de Valverde
Tábara
Faramontanos de Tábara
Riego del Camino
Olmillos de Castro
Losacino
Emb. de Ricobayo
Montamarta
Tierra del Pan
La Hiniesta
Muelas del Pan
Zamora
Pereruela
Duero
San Marcial
Tamame
Corrales
Peñausende
El Cubo de Tierra del Vino
Mayalde
Santiz
Valdelosa
Calzada de Valdunciel
La Mata de Ledesma
Tormes
Salamanca
Tejares
Santa Marta de Tormes
Rollán
Barbadillo
Aldeatejada
Matilla de los Caños del Rio
Robliza de Cojos
San Muñoz
Vecinos
Morille
La Sagrada
Peña de Cabra
Cabrillas
Las Veguillas
Pedrosillo de los Aires
Abusejo
Tamames
Alba de Yeltes
Escurial de la Sierra
Frades de la Sierra
Morasverdes
Endrinal
Fuenterroble de Salvatierra
Linares de Riofrio
Los Santos
Guijuelo
El Cabaco
El Maillo
Las Batuecas
Sequeros
La Alberca
San Esteban de la Sierra
Valdelacasa
Cristóbal
Serradilla del Arroyo
Serradilla del Llano
Embalse del Águeda
El Bodón
Martiago
Sierra de la Peña de Francia
Sotoserrano
Casares de las Hurdes
Nuñomoral
Vegas de Coria
Las Hurdes
Béjar
Candelario
Villafáfila
Granja de Moreruela
Villarrin de Campos
Manganeses de la Lampreana
San Cebrián de Castro
Castronuevo
Aspariegos
Moreruela de los Infanzones
Malva
Pozoantiguo
Coreses
Fresno de la Ribera
Moraleja del Vino
Morales del Vino
Venialbo
El Piñero
Villamor de los Escuderos
Fuentesaúco
Topas
La Velles
Pedrosillo el Ralo
Garcihernández
Martinamor
Fresno Alhandiga
Galinduste
Embalse de Santa Teresa
Santibáñez de Béjar
Medinilla
Becedas
El Barco de Ávila
Puerto de Tornavacas 1275
Tornavacas
Jerte
Cabezuela del Valle
Navaconcejo
El Torno
Piornal
Jarandilla de la Vera
Guijo de Santa Bábera
Losar de la Vera
YUSTE
Cuacos de Yuste
La Vera
Jaraíz de la Vera
Garganta la Olla
Barrado
Tejada de Tiétar
Talayuela
Hervás
Baños
El Cerro
Lagunilla
Embalse de Gabriel y Galán
Aldeanueva del Camino
Zarza de Granadilla
Casar de Palomero
Caminomorisco
Pinofranqueado
Mohedas
Ahigal
Villanueva de la Sierra
Santa Cruz de Paniagua
Santibáñez el Bajo
Oliva de Plasencia
Embalse de Valdeobispo
Valdeobispo
Plasencia
Carcaboso
Malpartida de Plasencia
Galisteo
Montehermoso
Guijo de Coria
Embalse de Borbollón
Pozuelo de Zarzón
Santibáñez el Alto
Cadalso
Gata
Sierra de Gata
Perales del Puerto
Puerto de Perales 910
Hoyos
Valverde del Fresno
El Payo
Navasfrías
Peñaparda
Fuenteguinaldo
Robleda
La Albergueria de Argañán
Alfaiates
Pega
Sabugal
CASTELO DE SABUGAL
Aldeia do Bispo
Moita
Meimôa
Cilleros
Moraleja
Coria
Casillas de Coria
Arrago
Termas de Monfortinho
Medelim
Barragem da Idanha
Pedrogão
Penamacor
141
150
155
156
127
129
173
2
3
4
A
B

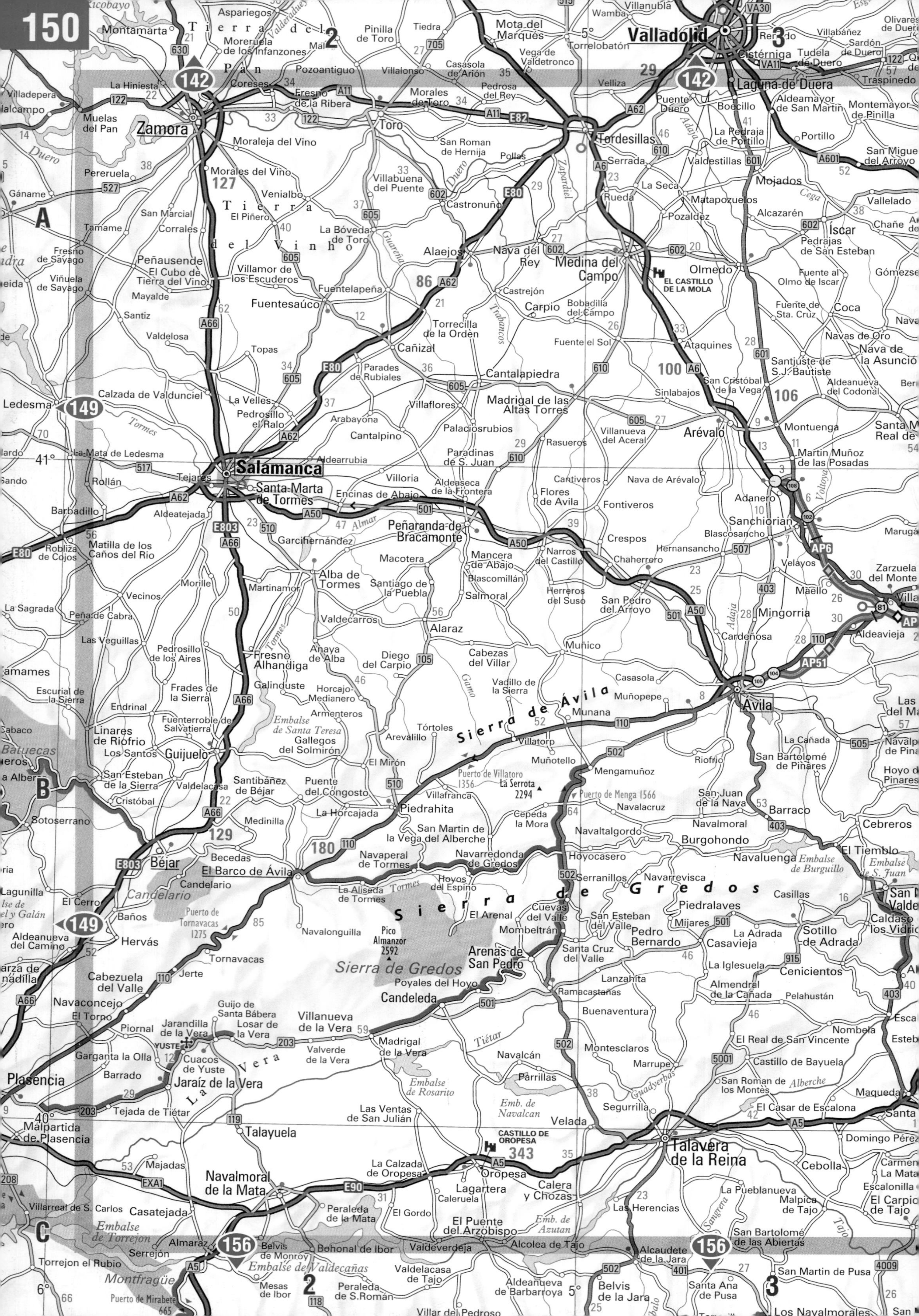
Montamarta
Aspariegos
Tierra del Pan
Moreruela de los Infanzones
Pinilla de Toro
Tiedra
Mota del Marqués
Wamba
Villanubla
Valladolid
Villabáñez
Olivares de Duero
Vega de Valdetronco
Torrelobatón
Cistérniga
Tudela de Duero
Sardón de Duero
Pozoantiguo
Villalonso
Casasola de Arión
La Hiniesta
Coreses
Fresno de la Ribera
Morales de Toro
Pedrosa del Rey
Velliza
Laguna de Duera
Traspinedo
Villadepera
Muelas del Pan
Zamora
Toro
Puente Duero
Boecillo
Aldeamayor de San Martín
Montemayor de Pinilla
Moraleja del Vino
San Roman de Hernija
Pollos
Tordesillas
La Pedraja de Portillo
Portillo
San Miguel del Arroyo
Duero
Pereruela
Morales del Vino
Villabuena del Puente
Serrada
Valdestillas
Mojados
Gáname
Venialbo
Castronuño
Zapardiel
Rueda
La Seca
Matapozuelos
Cega
Vallelado
Tierra del Vinho
San Marcial
El Piñero
Corrales
Pozaldez
Alcazarén
Chañe
Tamame
La Bóveda de Toro
Íscar
Pedrajas de San Esteban
Fresno de Sayago
Peñausende
El Cubo de Tierra del Vino
Alaejos
Nava del Rey
Medina del Campo
Olmedo
Gómezserracín
Viñuela de Sayago
Villamor de los Escuderos
EL CASTILLO DE LA MOLA
Fuente al Olmo de Iscar
Mayalde
Fuentelapeña
Castrejón
Fuentesaúco
Carpio
Bobadilla del Campo
Fuente de Sta. Cruz
Coca
Santiz
Torrecilla de la Orden
Trabancos
Guareña
Valdelosa
Fuente el Sol
Ataquines
Navas de Oro
Nava de la Asunción
Topas
Cañizal
Parades de Rubiales
Cantalapiedra
Santjuste de S.J. Bautiste
San Cristóbal de la Vega
Aldeanueva del Codonal
Ledesma
Calzada de Valdunciel
La Velles
Pedrosillo el Ralo
Villaflores
Madrigal de las Altas Torres
Sinlabajos
Montuenga
Santa María Real de Nieva
Tormes
Arabayona
Cantalpino
Palaciosrubios
Villanueva del Aceral
Arévalo
Martin Muñoz de las Posadas
La Mata de Ledesma
Paradinas de S. Juan
Rasueros
Aldearrubia
Salamanca
Rollán
Tejares
Villoria
Aldeaseca de la Frontera
Cantiveros
Nava de Arévalo
Voltoya
Santa Marta de Tormes
Encinas de Abajo
Flores de Avila
Fontiveros
Adanero
Barbadillo
Aldeatejada
Almar
Peñaranda de Bracamonte
Sanchiorian
Blascosancho
Maruganda
Matilla de los Caños del Rio
Robliza de Cojos
Garcihernández
Crespos
Hernansancho
Macotera
Mancera de Abajo
Narros del Castillo
Chaherrero
Velayos
Zarzuela del Monte
Alba de Tormes
Santiago de la Puebla
Blascomillán
Herreros del Suso
Maello
Morille
Martinamor
Salmoral
San Pedro del Arroyo
Mingorria
Vecinos
La Sagrada
Peña de Cabra
Valdecarros
Alaraz
Adaja
Aldeavieja
Cardeñosa
Las Veguillas
Pedrosillo de los Aires
Fresno Alhandiga
Anaya de Alba
Diego del Carpio
Cabezas del Villar
Muñico
Tamames
Frades de la Sierra
Galinduste
Horcajo-Medianero
Gamo
Vadillo de la Sierra
Casasola
Muñopepe
Escurial de la Sierra
Endrinal
Fuenterroble de Salvatierra
Embalse de Santa Teresa
Armenteros
Sierra de Ávila
Munana
Ávila
Las Navas del Marqués
Cabaco
Linares de Riofrio
Los Santos
Guijuelo
Gallegos del Solmirón
Arevalillo
Tórtoles
Villatorp
Muñotello
La Cañada
Navalperal de Pinares
Batuecas
San Esteban de la Sierra
Cristóbal
Santibáñez de Béjar
Valdelacasa
Puente del Congosto
El Mirón
Puerto de Villatoro 1356
La Serrota 2294
Puerto de Menga 1566
Mengamuñoz
Riofrío
San Bartolomé de Pinares
Hoyo de Pinares
Sotoserrano
Medinilla
La Horcajada
Piedrahita
Villafranca
Cepeda la Mora
Navalacruz
San Juan de la Nava
Barraco
Cebreros
Béjar
Becedas
San Martin de la Vega del Alberche
Navaltalgordo
Navalmoral
Burgohondo
El Tiemblo
Candelario
El Barco de Ávila
Navaperal de Tormes
Navarredonda de Gredos
Hoyocasero
Navaluenga
Embalse de Burguillo
Embalse de S. Juan
Lagunilla
El Cerro
La Aliseda de Tormes
Hoyos del Espino
Serranillos
Navarrevisca
Sierra de Gredos
Casillas
San Martín de Valdeiglesias
Baños
Puerto de Tornavacas 1275
El Arenal
Cuevas del Valle
San Esteban del Valle
Piedralaves
Caldas de los Vidrios
Aldeanueva del Camino
Hervás
Navalonguilla
Pico Almanzor 2592
Mombeltrán
Pedro Bernardo
Mijares
La Adrada
Sotillo de Adrada
Tornavacas
Arenas de San Pedro
Santa Cruz del Valle
Casavieja
La Iglesuela
Cenicientos
Cabezuela del Valle
Jerte
Poyales del Hoyo
Lanzahita
Almendral de la Cañada
Pelahustán
Navaconcejo
Candeleda
Ramacastañas
El Torno
Guijo de Santa Bábera
Piornal
Jarandilla de la Vera
Losar de la Vera
Villanueva de la Vera
Buenaventura
Escalona
YUSTE
Madrigal de la Vera
Tiétar
Montesclaros
Nombela
El Real de San Vincente
Garganta la Olla
Cuacos de Yuste
Valverde de la Vera
Navalcán
Marrupe
Castillo de Bayuela
Barrado
La Vera
Parrillas
Plasencia
Jaraíz de la Vera
Embalse de Rosarito
Guadyerbas
San Roman de los Montes
Alberche
Maqueda
Tejada de Tiétar
Emb. de Navalcan
Segurrilla
El Casar de Escalona
Malpartida de Plasencia
Talayuela
Las Ventas de San Julián
Velada
CASTILLO DE OROPESA
Talavera de la Reina
Domingo Pérez
Majadas
La Calzada de Oropesa
Oropesa
Cebolla
Carmena
La Mata
Navalmoral de la Mata
Lagartera
Calera y Chozas
La Pueblanueva
Escalonilla
Villarreal de S. Carlos
Casatejada
Peraleda de la Mata
Caleruela
El Gordo
Las Herencias
Malpica de Tajo
El Carpio de Tajo
Embalse de Torrejon
El Puente del Arzobispo
Emb. de Azutan
Sangrera
Tajo
Serrejón
Almaraz
Belvis de Monroy
Bohonal de Ibor
Valdeverdeja
Alcolea de Tajo
Alcaudete de la Jara
San Bartolomé de las Abiertas
Torrejon el Rubio
Embalse de Valdecañas
Valdelacasa de Tajo
San Martin de Pusa
Montfragüe
Mesas de Ibor
Peraleda de S.Román
Aldeanueva de Barbarroya
Belvis de la Jara
Santa Ana de Pusa
Puerto de Mirabete 665
Villar del Pedroso
Los Navalmorales
142
149
156
127
86
100
106
129
180
343
A
B
C
2
3
5°
6°
40°
41°

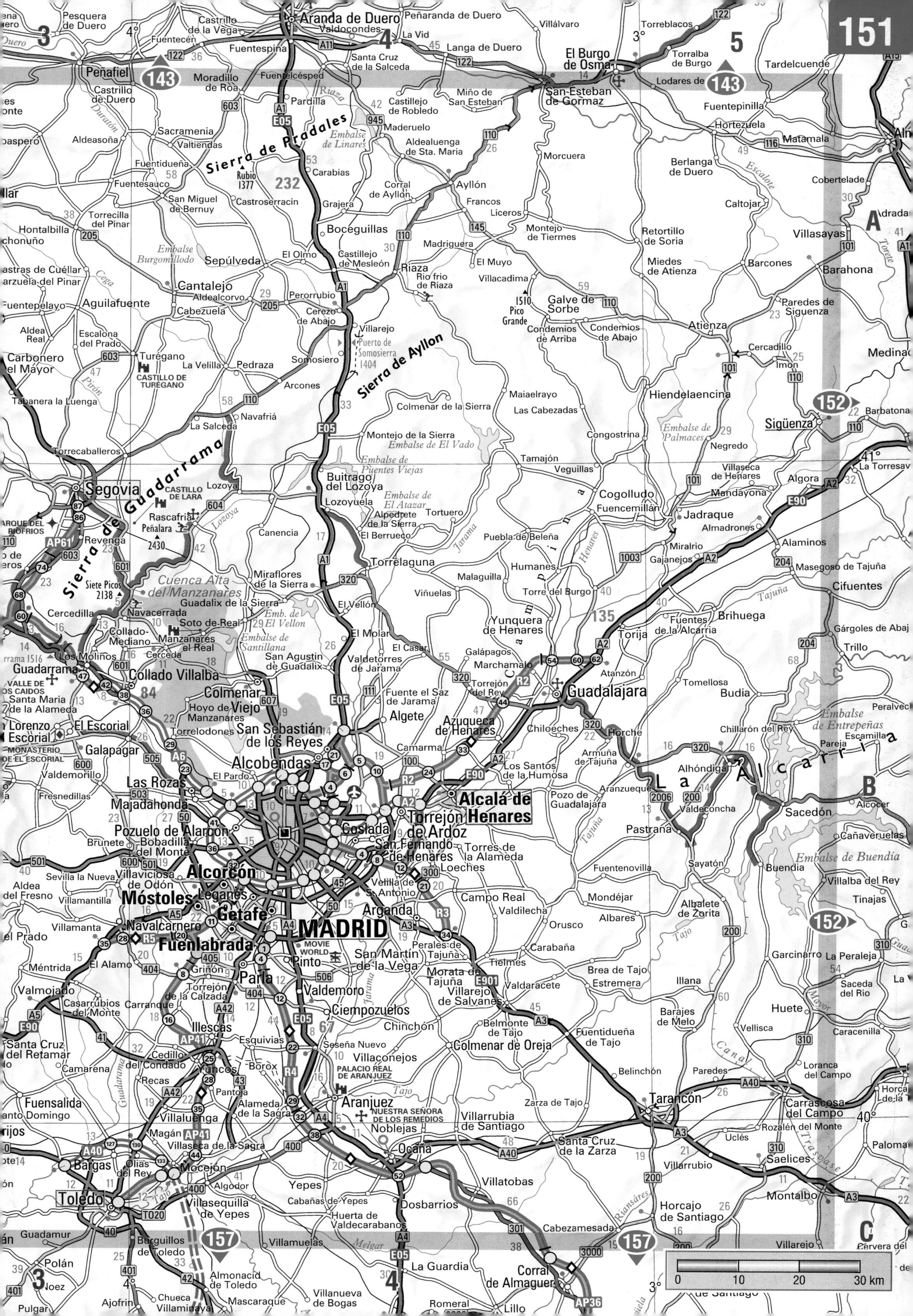
Aranda de Duero
Peñaranda de Duero
Pesquera de Duero
Castrillo de la Vega
Valdocondes
Villálvaro
Torreblacos
Torralba de Burgo
La Vid
Langa de Duero
El Burgo de Osma
Fuentecén
Fuentespina
Santa Cruz de la Salceda
Peñafiel
Moradillo de Roa
Fuentelcésped
Lodares de Osma
Tardelcuende
Castrillo de Duero
Pardilla
Castillejo de Robledo
Miño de San Esteban
San Esteban de Gormaz
Fuentepinilla
Sacramenia
Valtiendas
Sierra de Pradales
Maderuelo
Embalse de Linares
Aldealuenga de Sta. Maria
Hortezuela
Matamala
Aldeasoña
Fuentidueña
Rubio 1377
Carabias
Morcuera
Berlanga de Duero
Fuentesauco
San Miguel de Bernuy
Castroserracin
Corral de Ayllón
Ayllón
Cobertelade
Grajera
Francos
Liceros
Caltojar
Torrecilla del Pinar
Hontalbilla
Boceguillas
Montejo de Tiermes
Retortillo de Soria
Villasayas
Embalse Burgomillodo
Sepúlveda
El Olmo
Castillejo de Mesleón
Madriguera
El Muyo
Miedes de Atienza
Barcones
Barahona
Riaza
Rio frio de Riaza
Villacadima
Cantalejo
Aldealcorvo
Perorrubio
Cabezuela
Aguilafuente
Fuentepelayo
Cerezo de Abajo
1510 Pico Grande
Galve de Sorbe
Condemios de Arriba
Condemios de Abajo
Paredes de Siguenza
Atienza
Aldea Real
Escalona del Prado
Villarejo
Puerto de Somosierra 1404
Carbonero el Mayor
Turégano
Castillo de Turegano
La Velilla
Pedraza
Somosierra
Sierra de Ayllon
Cercadillo
Imon
Medinaceli
Tabanera la Luenga
Arcones
Maiaelrayo
Las Cabezadas
Hiendelaencina
Navafriá
La Salceda
Colmenar de la Sierra
Montejo de la Sierra
Embalse de El Vado
Sierra de Guadarrama
Congostrina
Embalse de Palmaces
Negredo
Sigüenza
Barbatona
Torrecaballeros
Embalse de Puentes Viejas
Tamajón
Veguillas
Villaseca de Henares
Algora
La Torresavi
Segovia
Castillo de Lara
Lozoya
Buitrago del Lozoya
Lozoyuela
Embalse de El Atazar
Cogolludo
Fuencemillán
Mandayona
Rascafria
Peñalara 2430
Alpedrete de la Sierra
Tortuero
Jadraque
Almadrones
Revenga
Canencia
El Berrueco
Puebla de Beleña
Miralrio
Gajanejos
Alaminos
Masegoso de Tajuña
Torrelaguna
Humanes
Cuenca Alta del Manzanares
Siete Picos 2138
Miraflores de la Sierra
Malaguilla
Torre del Burgo
Cifuentes
Guadalix de la Sierra
Viñuelas
Cercedilla
Navacerrada
El Vellón
Soto de Real
Embalse de El Vellon
Fuentes de la Alcarria
Brihuega
Gárgoles de Abajo
Yunquera de Henares
Collado-Mediano
Manzanares el Real
El Molar
Torija
Trillo
Embalse de Santillana
Cerceda
El Casar
Los Molinos
San Agustín de Guadalix
Valdetorres de Jarama
Galápagos
Marchamalo
Guadarrama
Valle de los Caidos
Collado Villalba
Torrejón del Rey
Guadalajara
Atanzón
Tomellosa
Santa María de la Alameda
Colmenar Viejo
Hoyo de Manzanares
Fuente el Saz de Jarama
Budia
Peralveche
Algete
Azuqueca de Henares
San Lorenzo de El Escorial
El Escorial
Torrelodones
San Sebastián de los Reyes
Chiloeches
Horche
Chillarón del Rey
Embalse de Entrepeñas
Escamilla
Monasterio de El Escorial
Galapagar
Camarma
Armuña de Tajuña
Pareja
Alcobendas
Los Santos de la Humosa
Alhóndiga
Valdemorillo
El Pardo
Las Rozas
Alcalá de Henares
Aranzueque
La Alcarria
Fresnedillas
Majadahonda
Torrejón de Ardoz
Pozo de Guadalajara
Valdeconcha
Sacedón
Alcocer
Pozuelo de Alarcón
Coslada
Pastrana
Brunete
Boadilla del Monte
San Fernando de Henares
Torres de la Alameda
Cañaveruelas
Sayatón
Embalse de Buendía
Sevilla la Nueva
Villaviciosa de Odón
Alcorcón
Loeches
Fuentenovilla
Buendia
Aldea del Fresno
Móstoles
Leganés
Velilla de S. Antonio
Campo Real
Mondéjar
Villalba del Rey
Villamantilla
Getafe
Valdilecha
Albalate de Zorita
Tinajas
Villamanta
Navalcarnero
MADRID
Arganda
Orusco
Albares
Fuenlabrada
Movie World
Perales de Tajuña
Carabaña
Méntrida
El Alamo
Pinto
San Martin de la Vega
Tielmes
Garcinarro
La Peraleja
Griñon
Parla
Morata de Tajuña
Brea de Tajo
Sacedo del Rio
Valmojado
Torrejón de la Calzada
Valdemoro
Villarejo de Salvanés
Valdaracete
Estremera
Illana
Casarrubios del Monte
Carranque
Ciempozuelos
Huete
Illescas
Chinchón
Belmonte de Tajo
Barajes de Melo
Vellisca
Caracenilla
Santa Cruz del Retamar
Esquivias
Seseña Nuevo
Colmenar de Oreja
Fuentidueña de Tajo
Cedillo del Condado
Villaconejos
Camarena
Yuncos
Borox
Palacio Real de Aranjuez
Belinchón
Paredes
Loranca del Campo
Recas
Pantoja
Aranjuez
Fuensalida
Alameda de la Sagra
Nuestra Señora de los Remedios
Villarrubia de Santiago
Zarza de Tajo
Tarancón
Carrascosa del Campo
Horcajo de la Sierra
Villaluenga
Magán
Noblejas
Rozalén del Monte
Uclés
Villaseca de la Sagra
Ocaña
Santa Cruz de la Zarza
Paloma
Bargas
Olias del Rey
Mocejón
Villarrubio
Saelices
Algodor
Yepes
Villatobas
Toledo
Villasequilla de Yepes
Cabañas de Yepes
Dosbarrios
Montalbo
Huerta de Valdecarabanos
Horcajo de Santiago
Guadamur
Burguillos de Toledo
Villamuelas
Cabezamesada
Villarejo
Cervera del Llano
Polán
Almonacid de Toledo
La Guardia
Corral de Almaguer
Chueca
Mascaraque
Villanueva de Bogas
Ajofrin
Villaminaya
Romeral
Lillo
Pulgar
0 10 20 30 km

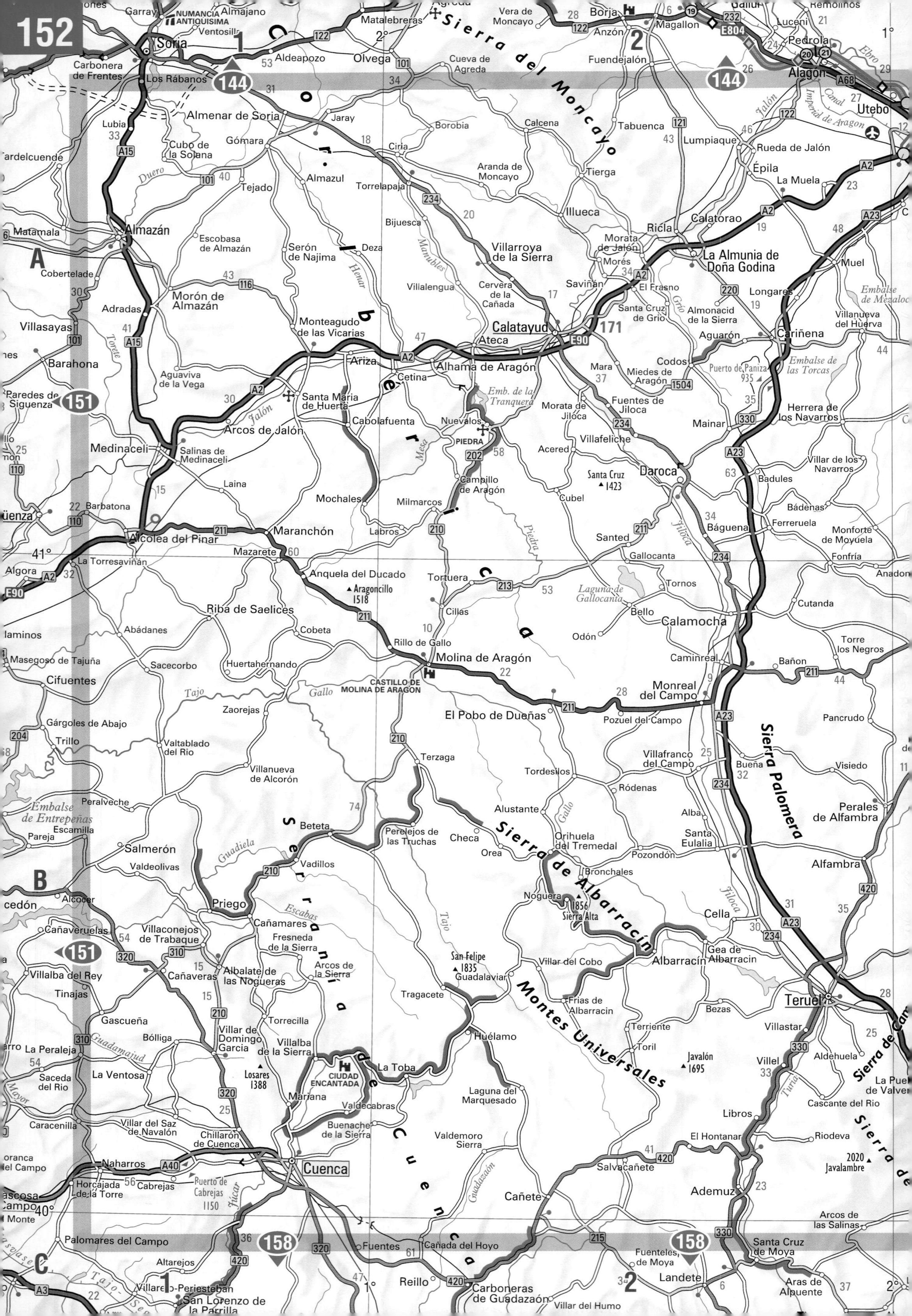
Soria
Garray
NUMANCIA
ANTIQUISIMA
Almajano
Ventosilla
Matalebreras
Sierra del Moncayo
Vera de Moncayo
Borja
Magallon
Anzón
Fuendejalón
Luceni
Pedrola
Alagón
Remolinos
Ebro
Utebo
Canal Imperial de Aragon
Carbonera de Frentes
Los Rábanos
Aldeapozo
Olvega
Cueva de Agreda
Almenar de Soria
Jaray
Borobia
Calcena
Tabuenca
Lumpiaque
Rueda de Jalón
Lubia
Gómara
Cirla
Aranda de Moncayo
Tierga
Épila
La Muela
Cardelcuende
Cubo de la Solana
Duero
Tejado
Almazul
Torrelapaja
Illueca
Calatorao
Almazán
Matamala
Escobasa de Almazán
Serón de Najima
Deza
Bijuesca
Villarroya de la Sierra
Ricla
Morata de Jalón
Morés
La Almunia de Doña Godina
Muel
A
Cobertelade
Morón de Almazán
Adradas
Villalengua
Cervera de la Cañada
Saviñán
El Frasno
Santa Cruz de Grio
Almonacid de la Sierra
Longares
Embalse de Mezalocha
Villanueva del Huerva
Villasayas
Barahona
Monteagudo de las Vicarias
Calatayud
Ateca
Cariñena
Aguarón
Ariza
Cetina
Alhama de Aragón
Codos
Puerto de Paniza 935
Embalse de las Torcas
Paredes de Siguenza
Aguaviva de la Vega
Santa María de Huerta
Jalón
Emb. de la Tranquera
Mara
Miedes de Aragón
Fuentes de Jiloca
Morata de Jiloca
Herrera de los Navarros
Arcos de Jalón
Cabolafuenta
Nuevalos
PIEDRA
Mainar
Medinaceli
Salinas de Medinaceli
Villafeliche
Acered
Daroca
Villar de los Navarros
Laina
Campillo de Aragón
Santa Cruz 1423
Badules
Mochales
Milmarcos
Cubel
Bádenas
Barbatona
Sigüenza
Alcolea del Pinar
Maranchón
Labros
Santed
Báguena
Ferreruela
Monforte de Moyuela
Mazarete
Gallocanta
Fonfría
Algora
La Torresaviñán
Anquela del Ducado
Aragoncillo 1518
Tortuera
Tornos
Anadón
Laguna de Gallocanta
Cutanda
Riba de Saelices
Cillas
Bello
Calamocha
Abádanes
Cobeta
Odón
laminos
Rillo de Gallo
Torre los Negros
Masegoso de Tajuña
Sacecorbo
Huertahernando
Molina de Aragón
Caminreal
Bañon
Cifuentes
CASTILLO DE MOLINA DE ARAGON
Tajo
Gallo
Monreal del Campo
Zaorejas
El Pobo de Dueñas
Pozuel del Campo
Pancrudo
Gárgoles de Abajo
Trillo
Valtablado del Rio
Terzaga
Villafranco del Campo
Bueña
Visiedo
Villanueva de Alcorón
Tordesilos
Ródenas
Sierra Palomera
Peralveche
Alustante
Perales de Alfambra
Embalse de Entrepeñas
Escamilla
Pareja
Serranía de Cuenca
Beteta
Perelejos de las Truchas
Checa
Sierra de Albarracín
Orihuela del Tremedal
Alba
Santa Eulalia
Salmerón
Orea
Pozondón
Alfambra
Valdeolivas
Guadiela
Vadillos
Bronchales
B
Alcocer
Noguera
1856 Sierra Alta
Escabas
Priego
Cella
Cañamares
Cañaveruelas
Villaconejos de Trabaque
Fresneda de la Sierra
Gea de Albarracin
Albarracín
Villalba del Rey
Cañaveras
Albalate de las Nogueras
Arcos de la Sierra
San Felipe 1835
Guadalaviar
Villar del Cobo
Tinajas
Montes Universales
Tragacete
Frias de Albarracin
Teruel
Gascueña
Bezas
Torrecilla
Bólliga
Villar de Domingo Garcia
Villalba de la Sierra
Huélamo
Terriente
Villastar
La Peraleja
Guadamajud
Toril
Saceda del Rio
La Ventosa
Losares 1388
CIUDAD ENCANTADA
La Toba
Javalón 1695
Aldehuela
Villel
Mayor
Mariana
Laguna del Marquesado
Sierra de Javalambre
La Puebla de Valverde
Cascante del Rio
Valdecabras
Caracenilla
Villar del Saz de Navalón
Chillarón de Cuenca
Buenache de la Sierra
Valdemoro Sierra
Libros
Riodeva
Naharros
Cuenca
Cabrejas
Puerto de Cabrejas 1150
Salvacañete
El Hontanar
2020 Javalambre
Horcajada de la Torre
Júcar
Cañete
Guadazaón
Ademuz
Montalbo
Monte
Palomares del Campo
Fuentes
Cañada del Hoyo
Arcos de las Salinas
Fuenteleal de Moya
Santa Cruz de Moya
Altarejos
Reillo
Landete
Villar de Olalla
Villarejo-Periesteban
San Lorenzo de la Parrilla
Carboneras de Guadazaón
Villar del Humo
Aras de Alpuente
C
Tajo-Segura
41°
40°
1°
2°
E804
E90
A2
A3
A15
A23
A40
A68
144
151
158
171

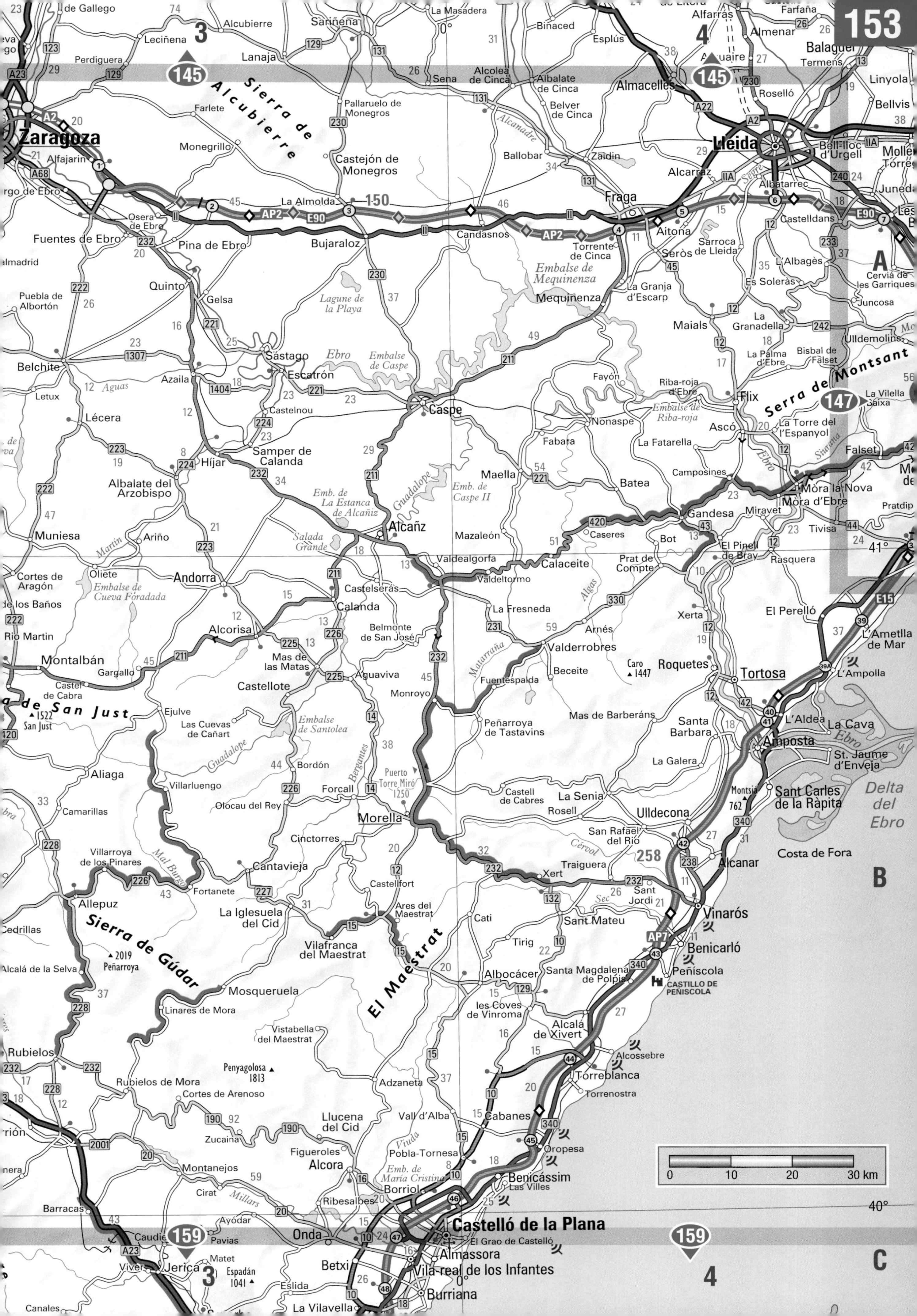
Zaragoza
Lleida
Sierra de Alcubierre
Leciñena
Alcubierre
Sariñena
Lanaja
Perdiguera
Farlete
Monegrillo
Castejón de Monegros
Pallaruelo de Monegros
Alfajarín
La Almolda
Bujaraloz
Candasnos
Fraga
Alcarràz
Almacelles
Binaced
Esplús
Alcolea de Cinca
Albalate de Cinca
Belver de Cinca
Ballobar
Zaidín
Sena
Alfarràs
Almenar
Balaguer
Termens
Linyola
Bellvis
Bell-lloc d'Urgell
Mollerussa
Albatàrrec
Rosselló
Juneda
Castelldans
Aitona
Torrente de Cinca
Seròs
Sarroca de Lleida
L'Albagès
Es Soleràs
Cervià de les Garrigues
Juncosa
Embalse de Mequinenza
Mequinenza
La Granja d'Escarp
Maials
La Granadella
Ulldemolins
Osera de Ebro
Fuentes de Ebro
Pina de Ebro
Quinto
Gelsa
Puebla de Albortón
Belchite
Sástago
Escatrón
Azaila
Letux
Lécera
Castelnou
Samper de Calanda
Híjar
Albalate del Arzobispo
Lagune de la Playa
Embalse de Caspe
Ebro
Caspe
Fayón
Riba-roja d'Ebre
Flix
Serra de Montsant
La Palma d'Ebre
Bisbal de Falset
La Vilella Baixa
Embalse de Riba-roja
Nonaspe
Ascó
La Torre de l'Espanyol
Fabara
La Fatarella
Falset
Maella
Batea
Camposines
Mora la Nova
Mora d'Ebre
Gandesa
Miravet
Tivisa
Pratdip
Emb. de La Estanca de Alcañiz
Emb. de Caspe II
Alcañiz
Mazaleón
Caseres
Bot
El Pinell de Bray
Rasquera
Muniesa
Ariño
Salada Grande
Valdealgorfa
Calaceite
Prat de Compte
Valdeltormo
Oliete
Cortes de Aragón
Embalse de Cueva Foradada
Andorra
Castelserás
Calanda
La Fresneda
Arnés
Xerta
El Perelló
L'Ametlla de Mar
Belmonte de San José
Alcorisa
Mas de las Matas
Valderrobres
Beceite
Caro 1447
Roquetes
Tortosa
L'Ampolla
Montalbán
Gargallo
Aguaviva
Castellote
Monroyo
Fuentespalda
Castel de Cabra
Sierra de San Just
San Just
Ejulve
Las Cuevas de Cañart
Embalse de Santolea
Peñarroya de Tastavins
Mas de Barberáns
Santa Barbara
L'Aldea
La Cava
Amposta
St. Jaume d'Enveja
La Galera
Aliaga
Bordón
Villarluengo
Puerto Torre Miró 1250
Forcall
Olocau del Rey
Camarillas
Castell de Cabres
La Senia
Rosell
Montsià 762
Sant Carles de la Ràpita
Delta del Ebro
Morella
Ulldecona
San Rafael del Río
Cinctorres
Costa de Fora
Villarroya de los Pinares
Cantavieja
Traiguera
Alcanar
Xert
Fortanete
Allepuz
Castellfort
Sant Jordi
Vinarós
Ares del Maestrat
Sant Mateu
Cati
La Iglesuela del Cid
Sierra de Gúdar
Cedrillas
2019 Peñarroya
Alcalá de la Selva
Vilafranca del Maestrat
El Maestrat
Tirig
Benicarló
Peñíscola
Castillo de Peñíscola
Albocácer
Santa Magdalena de Polpís
Mosqueruela
Linares de Mora
les Coves de Vinroma
Alcalá de Xivert
Vistabella del Maestrat
Alcossebre
Rubielos
Penyagolosa 1813
Torreblanca
Torrenostra
Rubielos de Mora
Adzaneta
Cortes de Arenoso
Cabanes
Llucena del Cid
Vall d'Alba
Zucaina
Oropesa
Pobla-Tornesa
Figueroles
Alcora
Emb. de María Cristina
Montanejos
Benicàssim
Las Villes
Borriol
Cirat
Ribesalbes
Barracas
Ayódar
Castelló de la Plana
El Grao de Castelló
Caudiel
Pavias
Onda
Almassora
Vila-real de los Infantes
Viver
Jerica
Matet
Espadán 1041
Betxi
Eslida
Burriana
Canales
La Vilavella
0 10 20 30 km
40°
41°
A
B
C
3
4
145
147
159
258

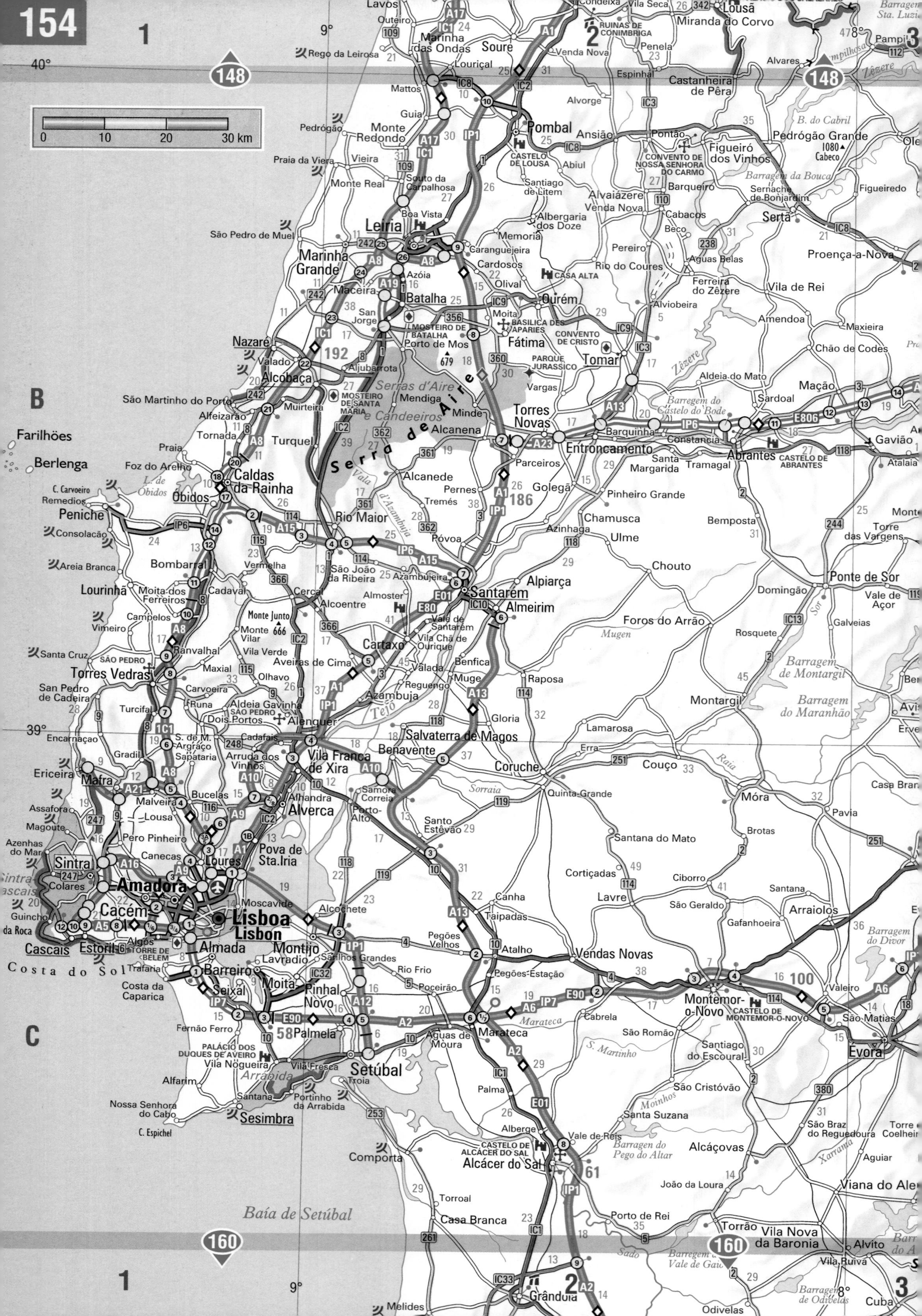

Leiria
Pombal
Marinha Grande
Nazaré
Alcobaça
Batalha
Fátima
Ourém
Tomar
Torres Novas
Entroncamento
Abrantes
Caldas da Rainha
Óbidos
Peniche
Berlenga
Farilhões
Rio Maior
Santarém
Almeirim
Cartaxo
Torres Vedras
Alenquer
Vila Franca de Xira
Benavente
Coruche
Mafra
Ericeira
Sintra
Amadora
Cacém
Lisboa
Lisbon
Cascais
Estoril
Almada
Barreiro
Montijo
Seixal
Moita
Palmela
Setúbal
Sesimbra
Montemor-o-Novo
Évora
Vendas Novas
Alcácer do Sal
Grândola
Serra de Aire
Baía de Setúbal
Costa do Sol
0 10 20 30 km

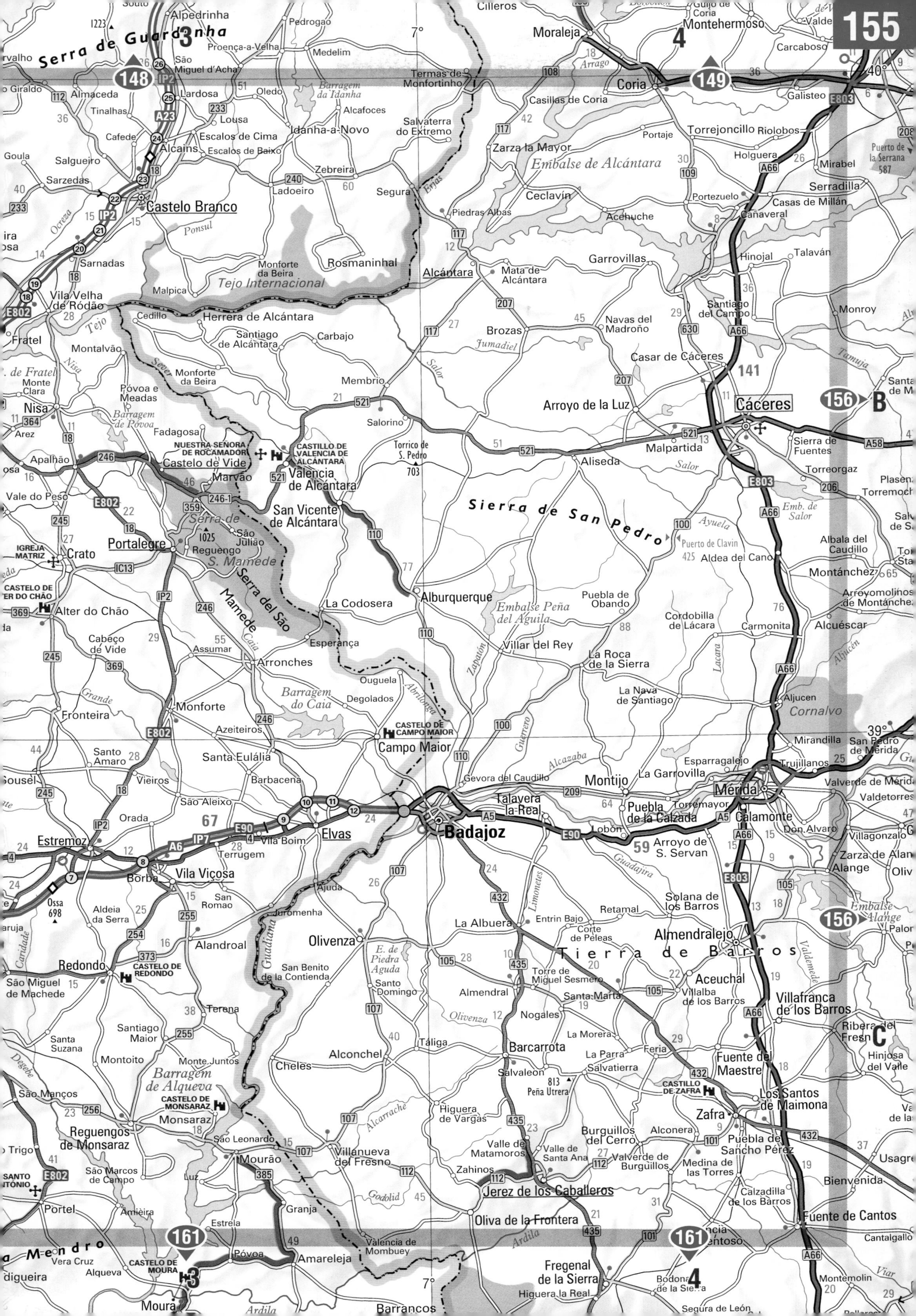

Alpedrinha
Serra de Guardunha
Pedrogão
Cilleros
Moraleja
Montehermoso
Carcaboso
Proença-a-Velha
Medelim
São Miguel d'Acha
Termas de Monfortinho
Coria
Galisteo
Almaceda
Lardosa
Oledo
Barragem da Idanha
Casillas de Coria
Tinalhas
Alcafoces
Salvaterra do Extremo
Torrejoncillo
Riolobos
Lousa
Idanha-a-Novo
Zarza la Mayor
Portaje
Cafede
Escalos de Cima
Escalos de Baixo
Alcains
Embalse de Alcántara
Holguera
Mirabel
Puerto de la Serrana 587
Goula
Salgueiro
Zebreira
Sarzedas
Ladoeiro
Segura
Erjas
Ceclavín
Serradilla
Castelo Branco
Ocreza
Piedras Albas
Portezuelo
Casas de Millán
Cañaveral
Acehuche
Ponsul
Rosmaninhal
Garrovillas
Hinojal
Talaván
Sarnadas
Monforte da Beira
Alcántara
Mata de Alcántara
Tejo Internacional
Vila Velha de Ródão
Malpica
Santiago del Campo
Monroy
Cedillo
Herrera de Alcántara
Brozas
Navas del Madroño
Fratel
Tejo
Santiago de Alcántara
Carbajo
Jumadiel
Montalvão
Sever
Casar de Cáceres
Nisa
Monte Clara
Póvoa e Meadas
Membrio
Salor
Arroyo de la Luz
Cáceres
Barragem de Póvoa
Salorino
Arez
Fadagosa
Nuestra Señora de Rocamador
Castillo de Valencia de Alcántara
Torrico de S. Pedro 703
Malpartida
Sierra de Fuentes
Apalhão
Castelo de Vide
Marvão
Valencia de Alcántara
Aliseda
Torreorgaz
Vale do Peso
San Vicente de Alcántara
Sierra de San Pedro
Emb. de Salor
Serra de São Julião 1025
Reguengo
Portalegre
Crato
Igreja Matriz
Ayuela
Puerto de Clavín 425
Aldea del Cano
Albala del Caudillo
Montánchez
S. Mamede
Serra del São Mamede
Castelo de Alter do Chão
Alter do Chão
La Codosera
Alburquerque
Embalse Peña del Águila
Puebla de Obando
Cordobilla de Lácara
Carmonita
Arroyomolinos de Montánchez
Alcuéscar
Cabeço de Vide
Assumar
Esperança
Villar del Rey
Zapatón
La Roca de la Sierra
Lácara
Arronches
Ouguela
Abrilongo
Caia
Barragem do Caia
Degolados
La Nava de Santiago
Aljucen
Cornalvo
Fronteira
Monforte
Grande
Azeiteiros
Castelo de Campo Maior
Campo Maior
Guerrero
Mirandilla
San Pedro de Mérida
Santo Amaro
Santa Eulália
Alcazaba
Esparragalejo
Sousel
Vieiros
Barbacena
Gevora del Caudillo
Montijo
La Garrovilla
Trujillanos
Valverde de Mérida
Mérida
Valdetorres
São Aleixo
Talavera la Real
Puebla de la Calzada
Torremayor
Calamonte
Don Alvaro
Orada
Elvas
Badajoz
Lobón
Arroyo de S. Servan
Villagonzalo
Estremoz
Vila Boim
Terrugem
Guadajira
Zarza de Alange
Alange
Borba
Vila Viçosa
Ossa 698
San Romao
Ajuda
Juromenha
Solana de los Barros
Retamal
Limonetes
Embalse Alange
Aldeia da Serra
La Albuera
Entrin Bajo
Corte de Peleas
Almendralejo
Alandroal
Olivenza
E. de Piedra Aguda
Tierra de Barros
Redondo
Castelo de Redondo
San Benito de la Contienda
Guadiana
Torre de Miguel Sesmero
Aceuchal
Villalba de los Barros
Villafranca de los Barros
São Miguel de Machede
Santo Domingo
Almendral
Santa Marta
Nogales
Terena
Olivenza
Santiago Maior
Santa Suzana
La Morera
Ribera del Fresno
Montoito
Monte Juntos
Alconchel
Táliga
Barcarrota
La Parra
Feria
Fuente del Maestre
Hinojosa del Valle
Barragem de Alqueva
Cheles
Salvaleón
813 Peña Utrera
Salvatierra
Castillo de Zafra
Los Santos de Maimona
São Manços
Castelo de Monsaraz
Monsaraz
Higuera de Vargas
Zafra
Reguengos de Monsaraz
São Leonardo
Alcarrache
Valle de Matamoros
Burguillos del Cerro
Alconera
Puebla de Sancho Pérez
Usagre
Mourão
Villanueva del Fresno
Valle de Santa Ana
Valverde de Burguillos
Medina de las Torres
São Marcos de Campo
Luz
Zahinos
Jerez de los Caballeros
Bienvenida
Santo António
Godolid
Calzadilla de los Barros
Portel
Amieira
Granja
Oliva de la Frontera
Fuente de Cantos
Estrela
Ardila
Cantalgallo
Mendro
Vera Cruz
Castelo de Moura
Póvoa
Amareleja
Valencia de Mombuey
Fregenal de la Sierra
Bodonal de la Sierra
Montemolín
Vidigueira
Alqueva
Moura
Barrancos
Higuera la Real
Segura de León
Viar
148
149
156
161
141
67
59
3
4
B
C
7°
39°
40°

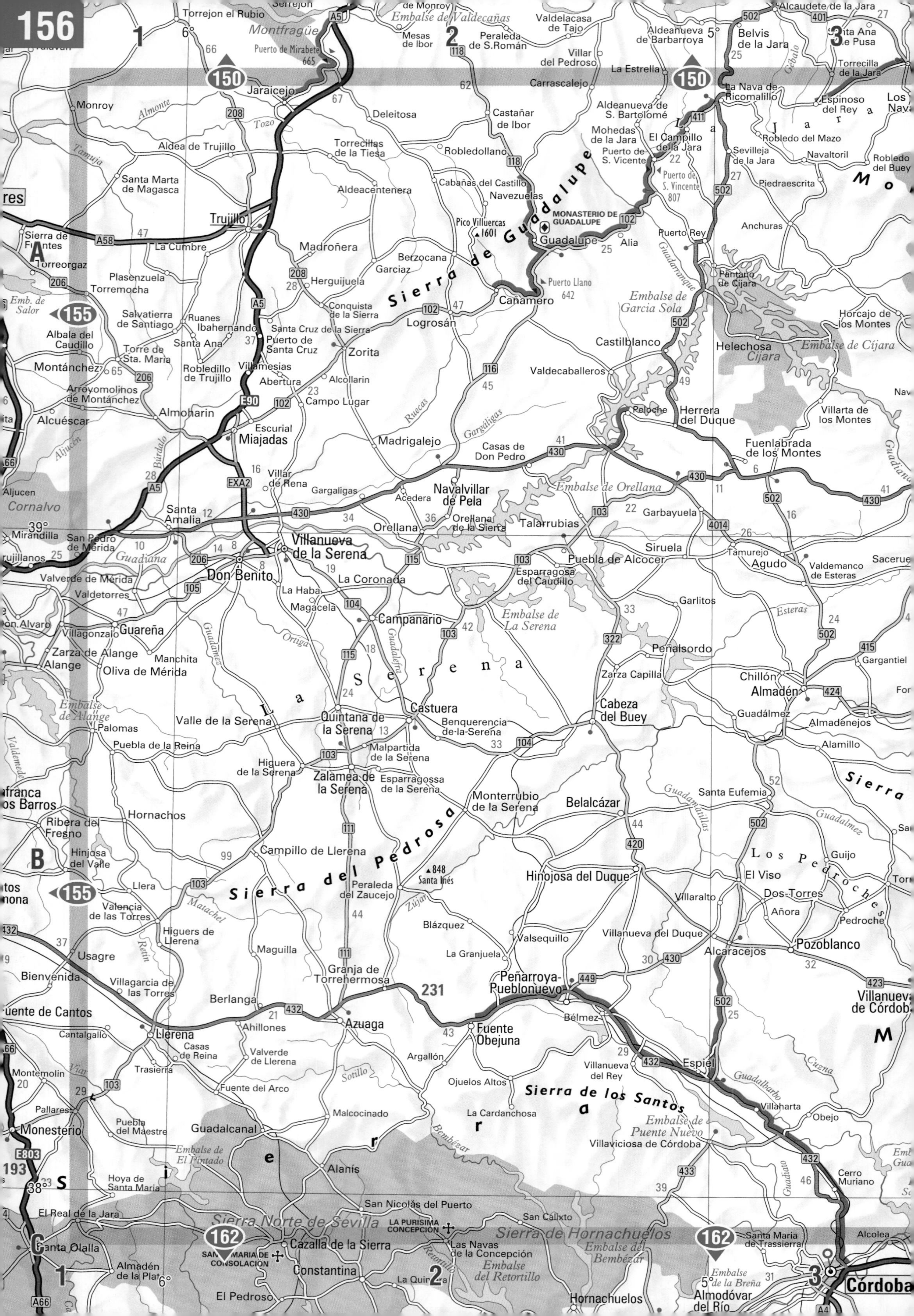
Torrejon el Rubio
Montfragüe
Puerto de Mirabete 665
Embalse de Valdecañas
Mesas de Ibor
Peraleda de S.Román
Valdelacasa de Tajo
Villar del Pedroso
Aldeanueva de Barbarroya
Alcaudete de la Jara
Belvis de la Jara
Torrecilla de la Jara
La Estrella
Carrascalejo
Jaraicejo
Monroy
Almonte
Tozo
Deleitosa
Castañar de Ibor
Aldeanueva de S. Bartolomé
La Nava de Ricomalillo
Espinoso del Rey
Aldea de Trujillo
Torrecillas de la Tiesa
Robledollano
Mohedas de la Jara
El Campillo de la Jara
Puerto de S. Vicente
Sevilleja de la Jara
Navaltoril
Robledo del Mazo
Robledo del Buey
Tamuja
Santa Marta de Magasca
Aldeacentenera
Cabañas del Castillo
Navezuelas
Puerto de S. Vincente 807
Piedraescrita
Trujillo
Pico Villuercas 1601
MONASTERIO DE GUADALUPE
Sierra de Guadalupe
Guadalupe
Alía
Puerto Rey
Anchuras
Sierra de Fuentes
La Cumbre
Madroñera
Berzocana
Garciaz
Torreorgaz
Plasenzuela
Torremocha
Herguijuela
Puerto Llano 642
Cañamero
Pantano de Cijara
Emb. de Salor
Salvatierra de Santiago
Ruanes
Ibahernando
Conquista de la Sierra
Santa Cruz de la Sierra
Logrosán
Embalse de García Sola
Horcajo de los Montes
Albala del Caudillo
Santa Ana
Puerto de Santa Cruz
Zorita
Castilblanco
Helechosa
Embalse de Cijara
Cijara
Torre de Sta. María
Montánchez
Robledillo de Trujillo
Villamesias
Abertura
Alcollarín
Valdecaballeros
Arroyomolinos de Montánchez
Campo Lugar
Ruecas
Peloche
Herrera del Duque
Villarta de los Montes
Almoharín
Escurial
Miajadas
Alcuéscar
Madrigalejo
Gargáligas
Casas de Don Pedro
Fuenlabrada de los Montes
Aljucén
Búrdalo
Villar de Rena
Gargaligas
Acedera
Navalvillar de Pela
Embalse de Orellana
Garbayuela
Aljucen
Cornalvo
Santa Amalia
Orellana
Orellana de la Sierra
Talarrubias
39°
Mirandilla
San Pedro de Mérida
Villanueva de la Serena
Siruela
Tamurejo
Agudo
Valdemanco de Esteras
Sacerue
Guadiana
Don Benito
Puebla de Alcocer
Esparragosa del Caudillo
Valverde de Mérida
Valdetorres
La Coronada
La Haba
Magacela
Garlitos
Campanario
Embalse de La Serena
Esteras
Guareña
Villagonzalo
Ortiga
Guadalefra
Zarza de Alange
Alange
Manchita
Oliva de Mérida
Peñalsordo
La Serena
Zarza Capilla
Chillón
Almadén
Gargantiel
Embalse de Alange
Castuera
Cabeza del Buey
Guadálmez
Almadenejos
Palomas
Valle de la Serena
Quintana de la Serena
Benquerencia de la Serena
Alamillo
Puebla de la Reina
Malpartida de la Serena
Higuera de la Serena
Zalamea de la Serena
Esparragossa de la Serena
Santa Eufemia
Sierra
Hornachos
Ribera del Fresno
Monterrubio de la Serena
Belalcázar
Guadamatillas
Guadalmez
Hinojosa del Valle
Campillo de Llerena
Sierra del Pedrosa
Los Pedroches
Guijo
Santa Inés 848
Peraleda del Zaucejo
Hinojosa del Duque
El Viso
Llera
Villaralto
Dos Torres
Añora
Pedroche
Valencia de las Torres
Matachel
Zújar
Higuers de Llerena
Blázquez
Valsequillo
Villanueva del Duque
Alcaracejos
Pozoblanco
Usagre
Maguilla
Retín
La Granjuela
Bienvenida
Villagarcia de las Torres
Granja de Torrehermosa
Peñarroya-Pueblonuevo
Villanueva de Córdoba
Berlanga
Fuente de Cantos
Ahillones
Azuaga
Fuente Obejuna
Bélmez
Cantalgallo
Llerena
Casas de Reina
Valverde de Llerena
Argallón
Villanueva del Rey
Espiel
Cuzna
Montemolín
Viar
Trasierra
Sotillo
Ojuelos Altos
Sierra de los Santos
Guadalbarbo
Fuente del Arco
Pallares
Puebla del Maestre
Malcocinado
La Cardanchosa
Villaharta
Obejo
Monesterio
Guadalcanal
Bembézar
Embalse de Puente Nuevo
Villaviciosa de Córdoba
Embalse de El Pintado
Alanís
Guadiato
Cerro Muriano
Hoya de Santa María
38°
San Nicolás del Puerto
San Calixto
El Real de la Jara
Sierra Norte de Sevilla
LA PURISIMA CONCEPCIÓN
Sierra de Hornachuelos
Santa Maria de Trassierra
Alcolea
Santa Olalla
SANTA MARIA DE CONSOLACIÓN
Cazalla de la Sierra
Las Navas de la Concepción
Embalse del Bembézar
Almadén de la Plata
Constantina
Retortillo
Embalse del Retortillo
La Quintera
Embalse de la Breña
Almodóvar del Río
Córdoba
El Pedroso
Hornachuelos
A5
A58
A66
E90
EXA2
E803
A4
150
155
162
193
231

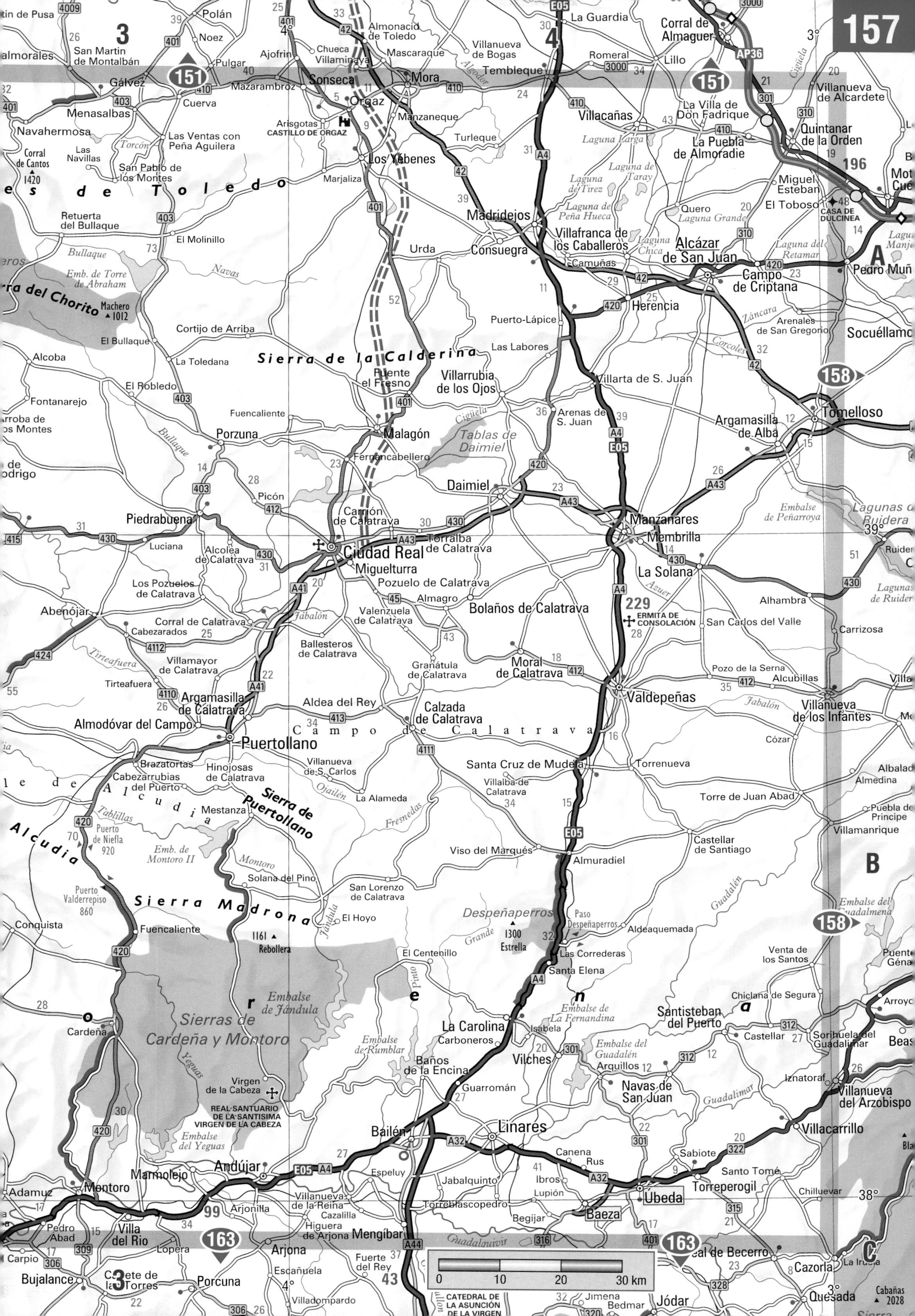
Polán
San Martín de Montalbán
Gálvez
Menasalbas
Navahermosa
Corral de Cantos 1420
Las Navillas
San Pablo de los Montes
Las Ventas con Peña Aguilera
Montes de Toledo
Retuerta del Bullaque
El Molinillo
Emb. de Torre de Abraham
Sierra del Chorito
Machero 1012
Cortijo de Arriba
El Bullaque
Alcoba
La Toledana
El Robledo
Fontanarejo
Porzuna
Fuencaliente
Piedrabuena
Picón
Luciana
Alcolea de Calatrava
Los Pozuelos de Calatrava
Abenójar
Corral de Calatrava
Cabezarados
Villamayor de Calatrava
Tirteafuera
Argamasilla de Calatrava
Almodóvar del Campo
Puertollano
Brazatortas
Cabezarrubias del Puerto
Hinojosas de Calatrava
Mestanza
Valle de Alcudia
Sierra de Puertollano
Puerto de Niefla 920
Emb. de Montoro II
Solana del Pino
Puerto Valderrepiso 860
Sierra Madrona
Conquista
Fuencaliente
1161 Rebollera
Sierra Morena
Embalse de Jándula
Sierras de Cardeña y Montoro
Cardeña
Virgen de la Cabeza
REAL SANTUARIO DE LA SANTÍSIMA VIRGEN DE LA CABEZA
Embalse del Yeguas
Marmolejo
Andújar
Montoro
Adamuz
Pedro Abad
Villa del Río
Carpio
Bujalance
Cañete de las Torres
Porcuna
Lopera
Arjona
Arjonilla
Escañuela
Villanueva de la Reina
Cazalilla
Higuera de Arjona
Mengíbar
Fuerte del Rey
Villadompardo
Ajofrín
Chueca
Villaminaya
Almonacid de Toledo
Mascaraque
Pulgar
Noez
Mazarambroz
Sonseca
Cuerva
Orgaz
Arisgotas
CASTILLO DE ORGAZ
Mora
Manzaneque
Los Yébenes
Marjaliza
Turleque
Villanueva de Bogas
Tembleque
La Guardia
Madridejos
Consuegra
Urda
Sierra de la Calderina
Fuente el Fresno
Villarrubia de los Ojos
Malagón
Fernancaballero
Tablas de Daimiel
Daimiel
Carrión de Calatrava
Ciudad Real
Torralba de Calatrava
Miguelturra
Pozuelo de Calatrava
Almagro
Valenzuela de Calatrava
Ballesteros de Calatrava
Bolaños de Calatrava
Granátula de Calatrava
Moral de Calatrava
Aldea del Rey
Calzada de Calatrava
Campo de Calatrava
Villanueva de San Carlos
La Alameda
Santa Cruz de Mudela
Villalba de Calatrava
Viso del Marqués
San Lorenzo de Calatrava
El Hoyo
Despeñaperros
1300 Estrella
Paso Despeñaperros
El Centenillo
Las Correderas
Santa Elena
Almuradiel
Embalse de La Fernandina
La Carolina
Carboneros
Isabela
Embalse de Rumblar
Baños de la Encina
Guarromán
Vilches
Bailén
Linares
Espeluy
Jabalquinto
Torreblascopedro
Begíjar
Baeza
Lupión
Ibros
Canena
Rus
Úbeda
Jimena
Bedmar
Jódar
CATEDRAL DE LA ASUNCIÓN DE LA VIRGEN
Villacañas
Laguna Larga
Laguna de Tirez
Laguna de Taray
Laguna de Peña Hueca
Villafranca de los Caballeros
Camuñas
Laguna Chica
Puerto-Lápice
Las Labores
Herencia
Arenas de S. Juan
Villarta de S. Juan
Manzanares
Membrilla
La Solana
ERMITA DE CONSOLACIÓN
San Carlos del Valle
Valdepeñas
Pozo de la Serna
Alcubillas
Torrenueva
Torre de Juan Abad
Castellar de Santiago
Aldeaquemada
Corral de Almaguer
Lillo
Romeral
La Villa de Don Fadrique
La Puebla de Almoradiel
Quintanar de la Orden
Villanueva de Alcardete
Miguel Esteban
Quero
Laguna Grande
El Toboso
CASA DE DULCINEA
Alcázar de San Juan
Laguna del Retamar
Campo de Criptana
Pedro Muñoz
Arenales de San Gregorio
Socuéllamos
Tomelloso
Argamasilla de Alba
Embalse de Peñarroya
Lagunas de Ruidera
Alhambra
Carrizosa
Villanueva de los Infantes
Cózar
Almedina
Puebla del Príncipe
Villamanrique
Embalse del Guadalmena
Venta de los Santos
Chiclana de Segura
Santisteban del Puerto
Castellar
Sorihuela del Guadalimar
Embalse del Guadalén
Arquillos
Navas de San Juan
Iznatoraf
Villanueva del Arzobispo
Villacarrillo
Sabiote
Santo Tomé
Torreperogil
Chilluevar
Cazorla
La Iruela
Quesada
Cabañas 2028
Huelma de Becerro
0 10 20 30 km

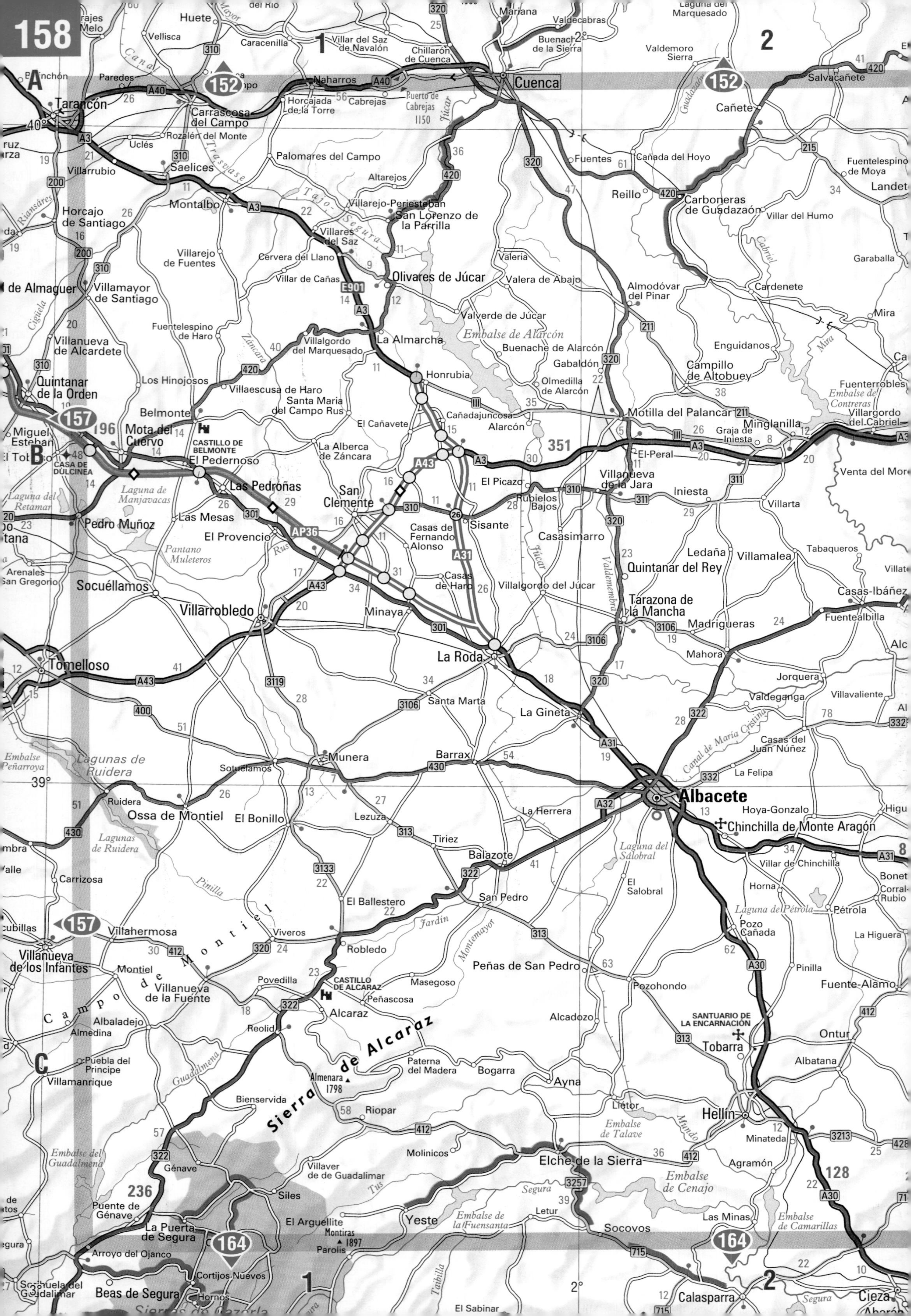
Huete
Vellisca
Caracenilla
Villar del Saz de Navalón
Chillarón de Cuenca
Mariana
Valdecabras
Buenache de la Sierra
Valdemoro Sierra
Salvacañete
Naharros
Cuenca
Puerto de Cabrejas 1150
Paredes
Tarancón
Horcajada de la Torre
Cabrejas
Carrascosa del Campo
Cañete
Rozalén del Monte
Uclés
Fuentes
Cañada del Hoyo
Fuentelespino de Moya
Villarrubio
Saelices
Palomares del Campo
Altarejos
Reillo
Carboneras de Guadazaón
Villar del Humo
Landete
Horcajo de Santiago
Montalbo
Villarejo-Periesteban
San Lorenzo de la Parrilla
Villares del Saz
Villarejo de Fuentes
Cervera del Llano
Villar de Cañas
Olivares de Júcar
Valeria
Valera de Abajo
Almodóvar del Pinar
Cardenete
Garaballa
de Almaguer
Villamayor de Santiago
Valverde de Júcar
Mira
Fuentelespino de Haro
Villanueva de Alcardete
Villalgordo del Marquesado
La Almarcha
Embalse de Alarcón
Buenache de Alarcón
Enguidanos
Gabaldón
Campillo de Altobuey
Quintanar de la Orden
Los Hinojosos
Villaescusa de Haro
Santa María del Campo Rus
Honrubia
Olmedilla de Alarcón
Fuenterrobles
Embalse de Contreras
Belmonte
Cañadajuncosa
Alarcón
Motilla del Palancar
Minglanilla
Villargordo del Cabriel
Miguel Esteban
Mota del Cuervo
Castillo de Belmonte
El Cañavete
Graja de Iniesta
El Toboso
Casa de Dulcinea
El Pedernoso
La Alberca de Záncara
El Peral
Venta del Moro
Laguna de Manjavacas
Las Pedroñas
San Clemente
El Picazo
Villanueva de la Jara
Iniesta
Laguna del Retamar
Las Mesas
Rubielos Bajos
Villarta
Pedro Muñoz
El Provencio
Casas de Fernando Alonso
Sisante
Casasimarro
Pantano Muleteros
Ledaña
Villamalea
Tabaqueros
Arenales San Gregorio
Casas de Haro
Villalgordo del Júcar
Quintanar del Rey
Socuéllamos
Casas-Ibáñez
Villarrobledo
Minaya
Tarazona de la Mancha
Madrigueras
Fuentealbilla
La Roda
Mahora
Tomelloso
Jorquera
Santa Marta
La Gineta
Valdeganga
Villavaliente
Embalse Peñarroya
Lagunas de Ruidera
Sotuélamos
Munera
Barrax
Casas del Juan Núñez
Canal de María Cristina
La Felipa
Ruidera
Ossa de Montiel
El Bonillo
Lezuza
La Herrera
Albacete
Hoya-Gonzalo
Chinchilla de Monte Aragón
Tiriez
Balazote
Laguna del Salobral
Villar de Chinchilla
Carrizosa
El Salobral
Horna
San Pedro
El Ballestero
Laguna de Pétrola
Pétrola
Villahermosa
Viveros
Jardín
Pozo Cañada
La Higuera
Villanueva de los Infantes
Robledo
Montiel
Campo de Montiel
Villanueva de la Fuente
Peñas de San Pedro
Pinilla
Povedilla
Masegoso
Pozohondo
Fuente-Álamo
Castillo de Alcaraz
Peñascosa
Albaladejo
Almedina
Alcaraz
Alcadozo
Santuario de la Encarnación
Reolid
Ontur
Tobarra
Puebla del Príncipe
Villamanrique
Sierra de Alcaraz
Paterna del Madera
Bogarra
Albatana
Ayna
Almenara 1798
Bienservida
Riopar
Liétor
Hellín
Embalse de Talave
Minateda
Embalse del Guadalmena
Molinicos
Elche de la Sierra
Agramón
Génave
Villaverde de Guadalimar
Embalse de Cenajo
Puente de Génave
Siles
La Puerta de Segura
El Arguellite
Yeste
Embalse de la Fuensanta
Letur
Socovos
Las Minas
Embalse de Camarillas
Montiras 1897
Parolis
Arroyo del Ojanco
Cortijos Nuevos
Beas de Segura
Hornos
Calasparra
El Sabinar
Cieza

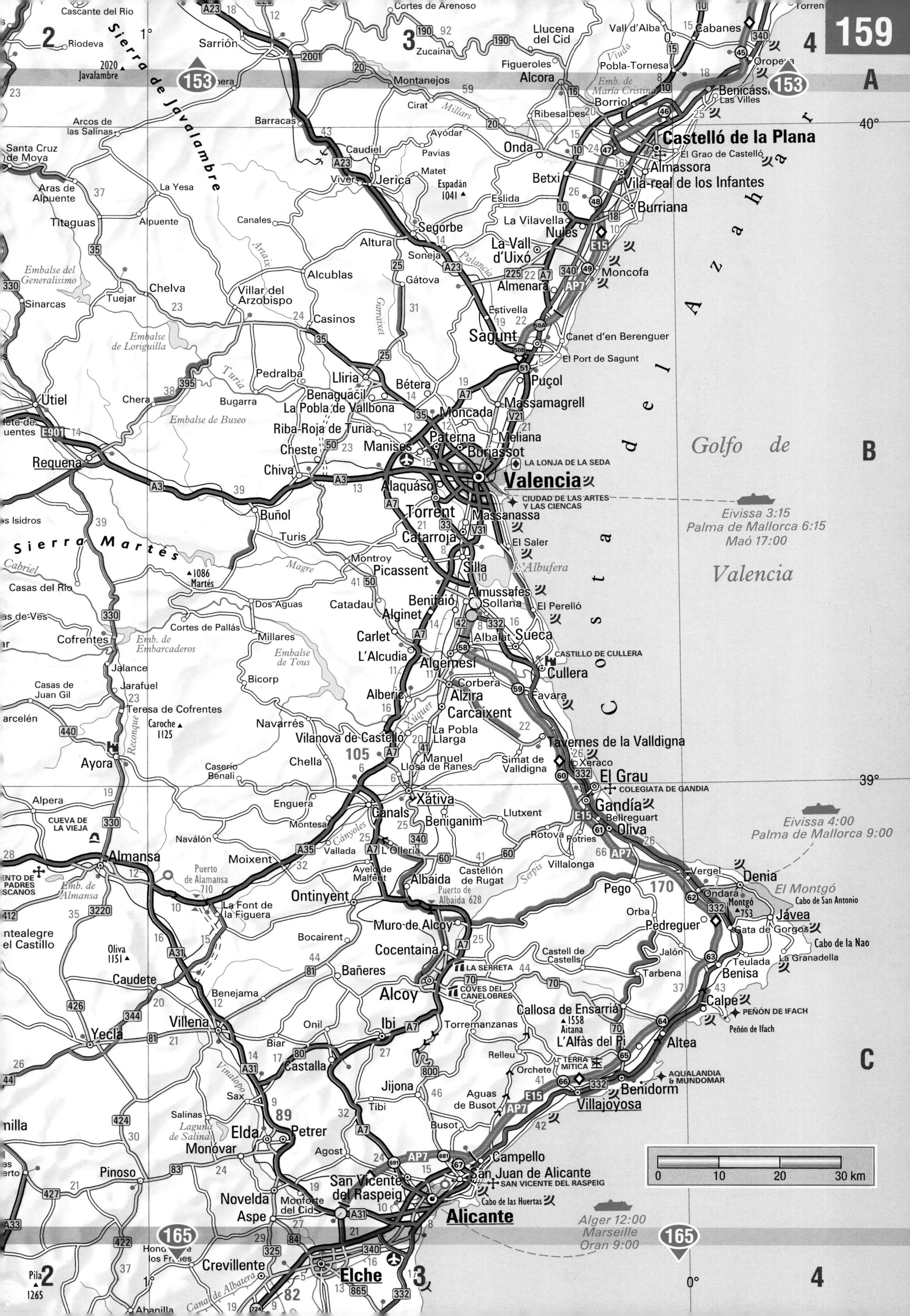
Sierra de Javalambre
Javalambre 2020
Cascante del Rio
Riodeva
Sarrión
Cortes de Arenoso
Zucaina
Llucena del Cid
Vall d'Alba
Cabanes
Oropesa
Figueroles
Alcora
Pobla-Tornesa
Emb. de María Cristina
Benicàssim
Las Villes
Montanejos
Cirat
Millars
Ribesalbes
Borriol
Barracas
Arcos de las Salinas
Santa Cruz de Moya
Ayódar
Caudiel
Pavias
Onda
Castelló de la Plana
El Grao de Castelló
Almassora
Vila-real de los Infantes
Betxi
Burriana
Aras de Alpuente
La Yesa
Matet
Viver
Jerica
Espadán 1041
Eslida
Titaguas
Alpuente
Canales
Segorbe
La Vilavella
Nules
Moncofa
Altura
Soneja
La Vall d'Uixó
Almenara
Palancia
Embalse del Generalisimo
Sinarcas
Tuejar
Chelva
Villar del Arzobispo
Alcublas
Gátova
Garraixet
Estivella
Casinos
Sagunt
Canet d'en Berenguer
El Port de Sagunt
Embalse de Loriguilla
Turia
Pedralba
Llíria
Bétera
Puçol
Útiel
Chera
Bugarra
Benaguacil
La Pobla de Vallbona
Moncada
Massamagrell
Embalse de Buseo
Riba-Roja de Turia
Paterna
Meliana
Requena
Cheste
Manises
Burjassot
LA LONJA DE LA SEDA
Chiva
Alaquàs
Valencia
CIUDAD DE LAS ARTES Y LAS CIENCIAS
Buñol
Torrent
Massanassa
Sierra Martés
Turis
Catarroja
El Saler
Montroy
Picassent
Silla
L'Albufera
Magre
Cabriel
Casas del Rio
Martés 1086
Almussafes
Dos Aguas
Catadau
Benifaió
Sollana
El Perelló
Alginet
Cofrentes
Cortes de Pallás
Millares
Carlet
Albalat
Sueca
Emb. de Embarcaderos
Embalse de Tous
L'Alcudia
Algemesí
CASTILLO DE CULLERA
Cullera
Jalance
Bicorp
Casas de Juan Gil
Jarafuel
Alberic
Corbera
Alzira
Favara
Teresa de Cofrentes
Carcaixent
Caroche 1125
Navarrés
Xúquer
La Pobla Llarga
Tavernes de la Valldigna
Vilanova de Castelló
Ayora
Chella
Manuel
Llosa de Ranes
Simat de Valldigna
Xeraco
Caserío Benali
El Grau
COLEGIATA DE GANDIA
Alpera
Enguera
Xàtiva
Gandía
Bellreguart
Canals
Llutxent
Oliva
CUEVA DE LA VIEJA
Montesa
Beniganim
Rotova
Potries
Navalón
Almansa
Moixent
Vallada
Cànyoles
L'Olleria
Ayelo de Malferit
Albaida
Castellón de Rugat
Villalonga
Vergel
Denia
Emb. de Almansa
Puerto de Alamansa 710
Ontinyent
Puerto de Albaida 628
Serpis
Pego
Ondara
El Montgó
Montgó 753
Cabo de San Antonio
La Font de la Figuera
Orba
Pedreguer
Jávea
Gata de Gorgos
Muro de Alcoy
Bocairent
Cabo de la Nao
Oliva 1151
Cocentaina
Castell de Castells
Jalón
Teulada
La Granadella
LA SERRETA
Bañeres
Tarbena
Benisa
Caudete
COVES DEL CANELOBRES
Alcoy
Benejama
Calpe
PEÑON DE IFACH
Peñón de Ifach
Callosa de Ensarriá
Villena
Onil
Ibi
Torremanzanas
Aitana 1558
Yecla
L'Alfàs del Pi
Altea
Biar
Castalla
Relleu
TERRA MITICA
Orchete
AQUALANDIA & MUNDOMAR
Benidorm
Jijona
Vinalopó
Sax
Villajoyosa
Aguas de Busot
Tibi
Salinas
Laguna de Salinas
Elda
Petrer
Busot
Monóvar
Agost
Campello
Pinoso
San Juan de Alicante
SAN VICENTE DEL RASPEIG
San Vicente del Raspeig
Cabo de las Huertas
Novelda
Monforte del Cid
Aspe
Alicante
Hondón de los Frailes
Crevillente
Elche
Pila 1265
Abanilla
Canal de Albatera
Golfo de Valencia
Costa del Azahar
Eivissa 3:15
Palma de Mallorca 6:15
Maó 17:00
Eivissa 4:00
Palma de Mallorca 9:00
Alger 12:00
Marseille
Oran 9:00
40°
39°
0°
1°
0 10 20 30 km
A
B
C
2
3
4
153
165

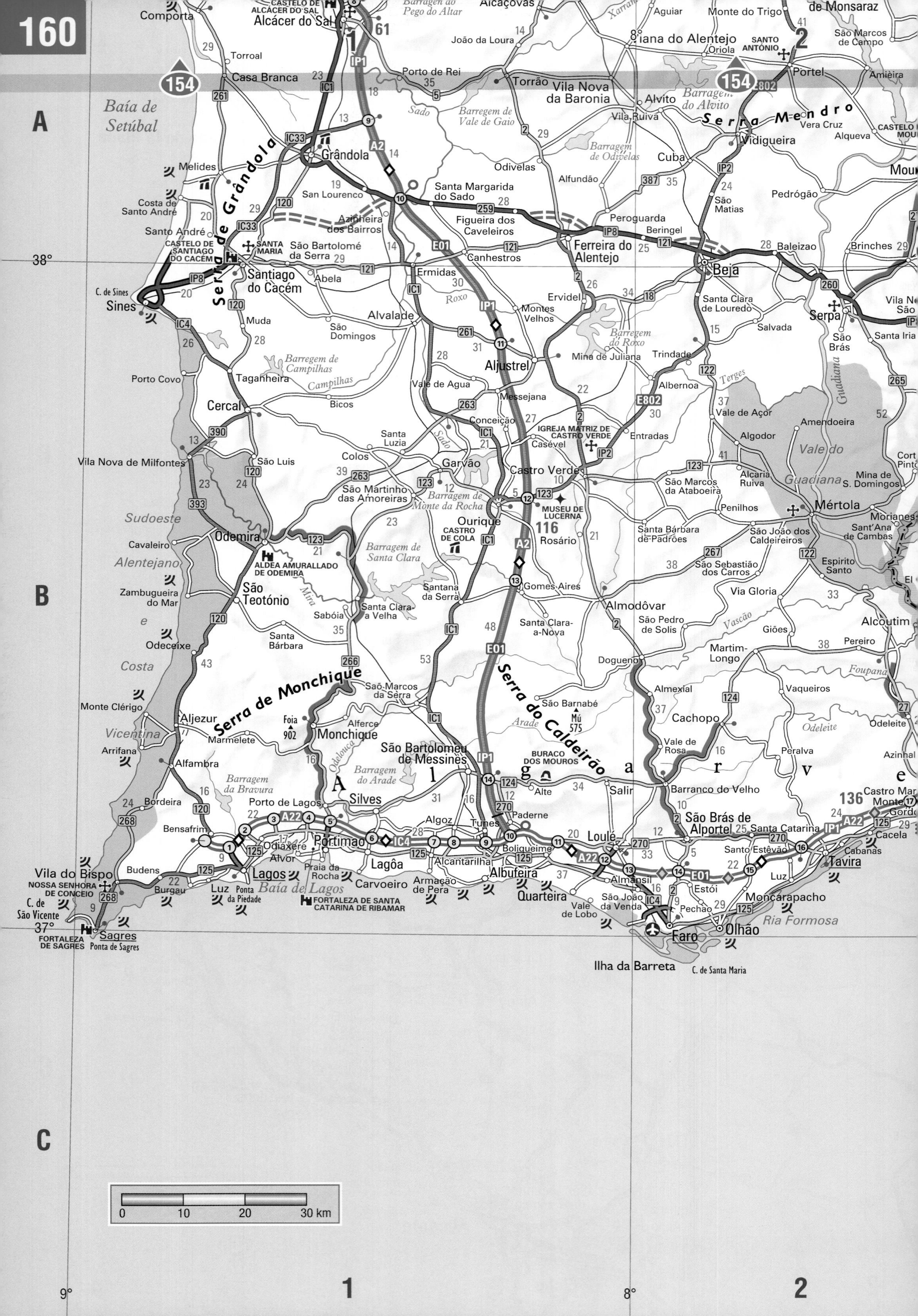
154
A
B
C
1
2
Baía de Setúbal
Comporta
Alcácer do Sal
Castelo de Alcácer do Sal
Barragem do Pego do Altar
Alcáçovas
Aguiar
Monte do Trigo
de Monsaraz
São Marcos de Campo
Torroal
João da Loura
Viana do Alentejo
Oriola
Santo António
Portel
Amieira
Casa Branca
Porto de Rei
Torrão
Vila Nova da Baronia
Alvito
Barragem do Alvito
Sado
Barragem de Vale de Gaio
Vila Ruiva
Serra Mendro
Vera Cruz
Alqueva
Castelo Mou
Serra de Grândola
Grândola
Vidigueira
Barragem de Odivelas
Cuba
Melides
Odivelas
Alfundão
Costa de Santo André
San Lourenco
Santa Margarida do Sado
Pedrógão
São Matias
Azinheira dos Bairros
Figueira dos Caveleiros
Peroguarda
Beringel
Santo André
Castelo de Santiago do Cacém
Santa Maria
São Bartolomé da Serra
Canhestros
Ferreira do Alentejo
Baleizao
Brinches
38°
Santiago do Cacém
Abela
Ermidas
Beja
C. de Sines
Sines
Roxo
Montes Velhos
Ervidel
Santa Clara de Louredo
Serpa
Vila Nova de São Bento
Muda
Alvalade
São Domingos
Barregem do Roxo
Salvada
São Brás
Santa Iria
Barregem de Campilhas
Aljustrel
Mina de Juliana
Trindade
Porto Covo
Taganheira
Campilhas
Vale de Agua
Albernoa
Terges
Guadiana
Cercal
Bicos
Messejana
Vale de Açor
Santa Luzia
Conceição
Igreja Matriz de Castro Verde
Entradas
Amendoeira
Casével
Algodor
Vale do Guadiana
Vila Nova de Milfontes
São Luis
Colos
Garvão
Castro Verde
São Marcos da Ataboeira
Alcaria Ruiva
Mina de S. Domingos
São Martinho das Amoreiras
Barragem de Monte da Rocha
Museu de Lucerna
Mértola
Sudoeste
Ourique
Penilhos
Morianes
Sant'Ana de Cambas
Castro de Cola
Rosário
Santa Bárbara de Padrões
São João dos Caldeireiros
Cavaleiro
Odemira
Alentejano
Aldea Amurallado de Odemira
Barragem de Santa Clara
São Sebastião dos Carros
Espirito Santo
Zambugueira do Mar
São Teotónio
Mira
Santana da Serra
Gomes Aires
Via Gloria
Sabóia
Santa Clara-a-Velha
Almodôvar
São Pedro de Solis
Vascão
Alcoutim
Odeceixe
Santa Bárbara
Santa Clara-a-Nova
Gióes
Pereiro
Costa
Martim-Longo
Dogueno
Foupana
Serra de Monchique
São Marcos da Serra
Serra do Caldeirão
Almexial
Vaqueiros
Monte Clérigo
São Barnabé
Aljezur
Foia 902
Alferce
Mú 575
Arade
Cachopo
Odeleite
Vicentina
Marmelete
Monchique
Vale de Rosa
Arrifana
São Bartolomeu de Messines
Peralva
Azinhal
Alfambra
Buraco dos Mouros
Barragem do Arade
Barragem da Bravura
Algarve
Alte
Salir
Barranco do Velho
Castro Marim
Monte Gordo
Bordeira
Porto de Lagos
Silves
Paderne
São Brás de Alportel
Santa Catarina
Cacela
Bensafrim
Algoz
Tunes
Loulé
Cabanas
Odiáxere
Portimao
Boliqueime
Santo Estêvão
Tavira
Alvor
Alcantarilha
Vila do Bispo
Budens
Lagos
Praia da Rocha
Lagôa
Albufeira
Almansil
Luz
Nossa Senhora de Conceio
Burgau
Ponta da Piedade
Baía de Lagos
Carvoeiro
Armação de Pera
Quarteira
Estói
Moncarapacho
C. de São Vicente
Fortaleza de Santa Catarina de Ribamar
Vale de Lobo
São João da Venda
Pechao
Ria Formosa
37°
Sagres
Fortaleza de Sagres
Ponta de Sagres
Faro
Olhão
Ilha da Barreta
C. de Santa Maria
0
10
20
30 km
9°
8°

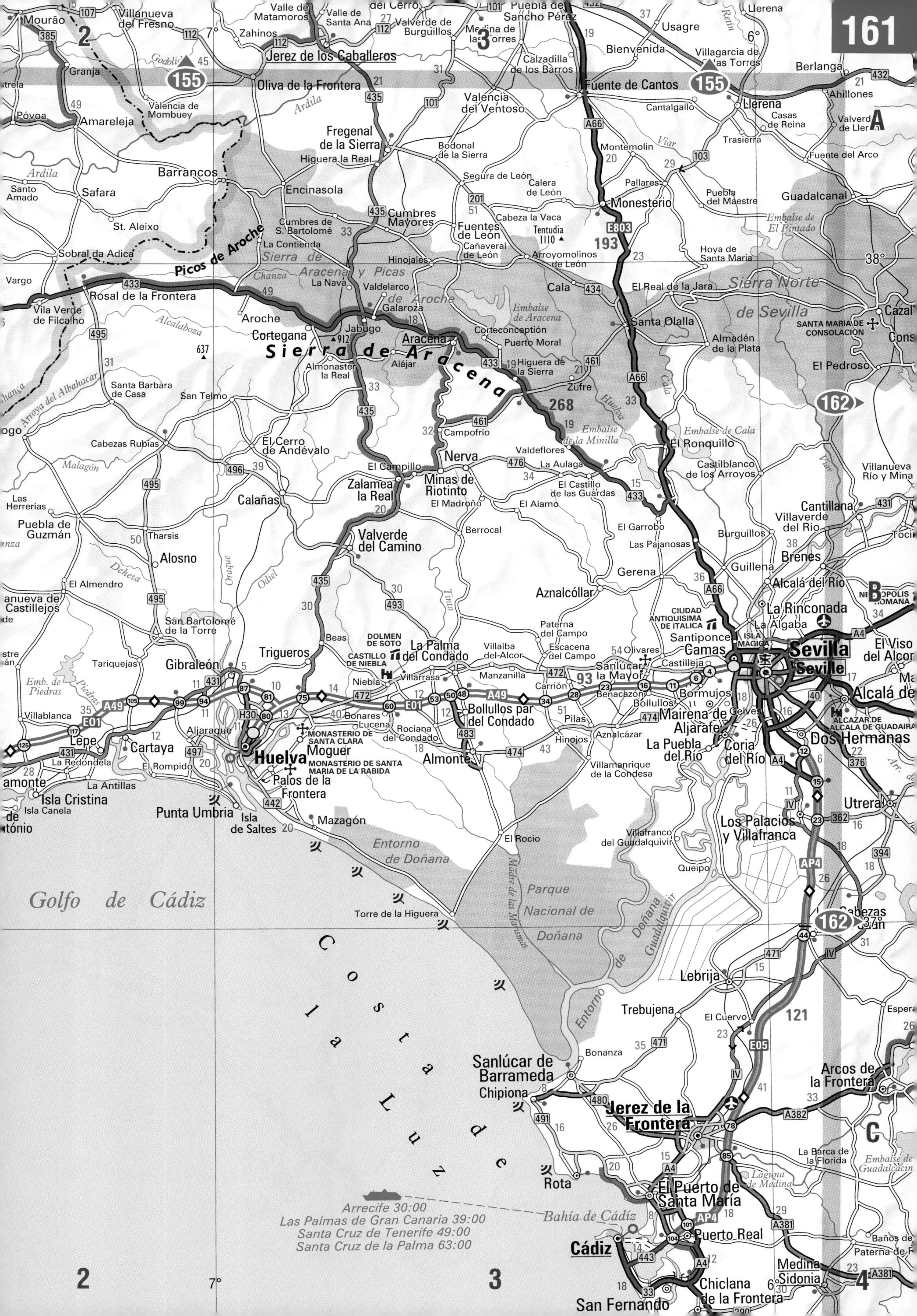
Jerez de los Caballeros
Oliva de la Frontera
Fuente de Cantos
Llerena
Fregenal de la Sierra
Barrancos
Encinasola
Cumbres Mayores
Monesterio
Sierra de Aracena y Picas de Aroche
Picos de Aroche
Rosal de la Frontera
Aroche
Cortegana
Jabugo
Aracena
Sierra de Aracena
Santa Olalla
Sierra Norte de Sevilla
Cazalla
El Pedroso
Nerva
Minas de Riotinto
Zalamea la Real
Valverde del Camino
Calañas
Alosno
Aznalcóllar
Gerena
Trigueros
La Palma del Condado
Gibraleón
Niebla
Sanlúcar la Mayor
Sevilla
Seville
Alcalá de Guadaira
Dos Hermanas
Mairena de Aljarafe
Coria del Río
La Puebla del Río
Huelva
Moguer
Palos de la Frontera
Lepe
Cartaya
Isla Cristina
Punta Umbría
Almonte
Bollullos par del Condado
Mazagón
El Rocío
Parque Nacional de Doñana
Entorno de Doñana
Golfo de Cádiz
Costa de la Luz
Utrera
Los Palacios y Villafranca
Lebrija
Trebujena
Sanlúcar de Barrameda
Chipiona
Jerez de la Frontera
Arcos de la Frontera
Rota
El Puerto de Santa María
Puerto Real
Cádiz
Bahía de Cádiz
Chiclana de la Frontera
San Fernando
Medina Sidonia
Arrecife 30:00
Las Palmas de Gran Canaria 39:00
Santa Cruz de Tenerife 49:00
Santa Cruz de la Palma 63:00

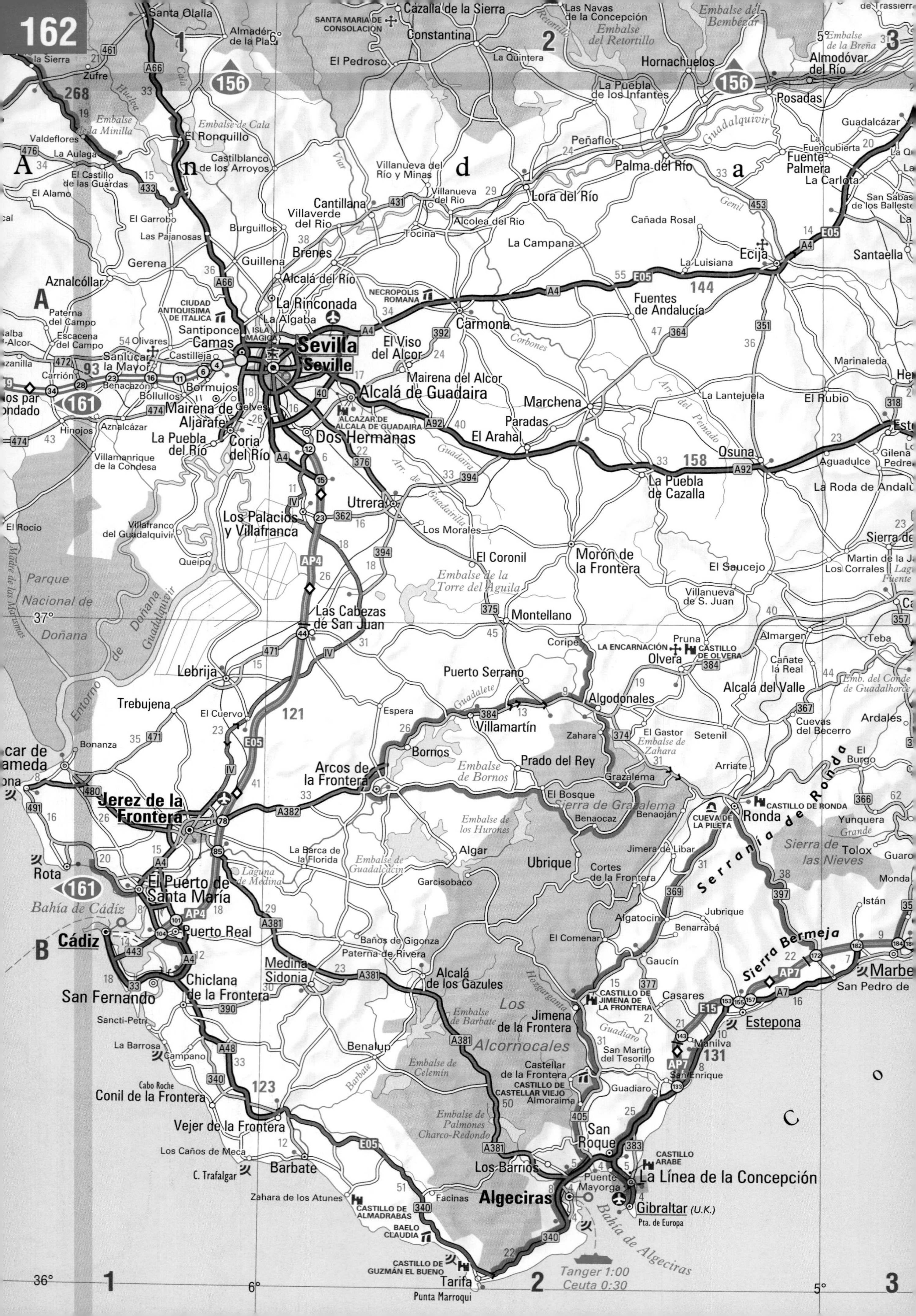

Santa Olalla
Almadén de la Plata
Cazalla de la Sierra
Constantina
El Pedroso
Las Navas de la Concepción
Embalse del Retortillo
Embalse del Bembézar
La Quintera
Hornachuelos
Almodóvar del Río
Embalse de la Breña
Posadas
La Puebla de los Infantes
Zufre
Embalse de la Minilla
Embalse de Cala
El Ronquillo
Valdeflores
La Aulaga
Castilblanco de los Arroyos
El Castillo de las Guardas
El Alamo
El Garrobo
Las Pajanosas
Gerena
Burguillos
Guillena
Villanueva del Río y Minas
Villanueva del Río
Cantillana
Villaverde del Río
Brenes
Tocina
Alcolea del Río
Lora del Río
Peñaflor
Palma del Río
Guadalcázar
La Fuencubierta
Fuente Palmera
La Carlota
San Sebastián de los Ballesteros
Cañada Rosal
La Campana
La Luisiana
Ecija
Santaella
Aznalcóllar
Alcalá del Río
La Rinconada
La Algaba
Ciudad Antiquísima de Itálica
Necropolis Romana
Carmona
Fuentes de Andalucía
Paterna del Campo
Escacena del Campo
Olivares
Santiponce
Isla Mágica
Camas
Sevilla
Seville
El Viso del Alcor
Sanlúcar la Mayor
Castilleja
Carrión
Benacazón
Bollullos
Bormujos
Mairena de Aljarafe
Gelves
Mairena del Alcor
Alcalá de Guadaira
Alcazar de Alcalá de Guadaira
Marchena
La Lantejuela
El Rubio
Marinaleda
Hinojos
Aznalcázar
La Puebla del Río
Coria del Río
Dos Hermanas
El Arahal
Paradas
Osuna
Villamanrique de la Condesa
La Puebla de Cazalla
Aguadulce
Gilena
La Roda de Andalucía
Utrera
Los Palacios y Villafranca
Los Morales
El Rocio
Villafranco del Guadalquivir
Queipo
El Coronil
Morón de la Frontera
El Saucejo
Martín de la Jara
Los Corrales
Sierra de Yeguas
Parque Nacional de Doñana
Entorno de Doñana
Embalse de la Torre del Aguila
Villanueva de S. Juan
Las Cabezas de San Juan
Montellano
Almargen
Teba
Coripe
La Encarnación
Pruna
Castillo de Olvera
Olvera
Cañete la Real
Lebrija
Puerto Serrano
Alcalá del Valle
Emb. del Conde de Guadalhorce
Trebujena
El Cuervo
Espera
Algodonales
Villamartín
Zahara
El Gastor
Embalse de Zahara
Setenil
Cuevas del Becerro
Ardales
Bonanza
Sanlúcar de Barrameda
Chipiona
Bornos
Embalse de Bornos
Prado del Rey
Arcos de la Frontera
Grazalema
Arriate
El Burgo
Jerez de la Frontera
El Bosque
Sierra de Grazalema
Benaocaz
Benaoján
Cueva de la Pileta
Ronda
Castillo de Ronda
Serranía de Ronda
Yunquera
Embalse de los Hurones
Rota
La Barca de la Florida
Embalse de Guadalcacín
Algar
Ubrique
Jimera de Líbar
Cortes de la Frontera
Sierra de las Nieves
Tolox
El Puerto de Santa María
Laguna de Medina
Garcisobaco
Bahía de Cádiz
Puerto Real
Cádiz
Algatocín
Jubrique
Benarrabá
Istán
Baños de Gigonza
Paterna de Rivera
El Comenar
Sierra Bermeja
Medina Sidonia
Alcalá de los Gazules
Gaucín
Marbella
San Pedro de Alcántara
San Fernando
Chiclana de la Frontera
Los Alcornocales
Castillo de Jimena de la Frontera
Jimena de la Frontera
Casares
Estepona
Sancti-Petri
Embalse de Barbate
La Barrosa
Campano
Benalup
Embalse de Celemín
Guadiaro
San Martín del Tesorillo
Manilva
San Enrique
Cabo Roche
Conil de la Frontera
Castellar de la Frontera
Castillo de Castellar Viejo
Almoraima
Embalse de Palmones
Charco-Redondo
Vejer de la Frontera
San Roque
Los Caños de Meca
C. Trafalgar
Barbate
Los Barrios
Castillo Arabe
La Línea de la Concepción
Puente Mayorga
Zahara de los Atunes
Castillo de Almadrabas
Facinas
Algeciras
Gibraltar (U.K.)
Pta. de Europa
Baelo Claudia
Bahía de Algeciras
Castillo de Guzmán el Bueno
Tarifa
Tanger 1:00
Ceuta 0:30
Punta Marroquí

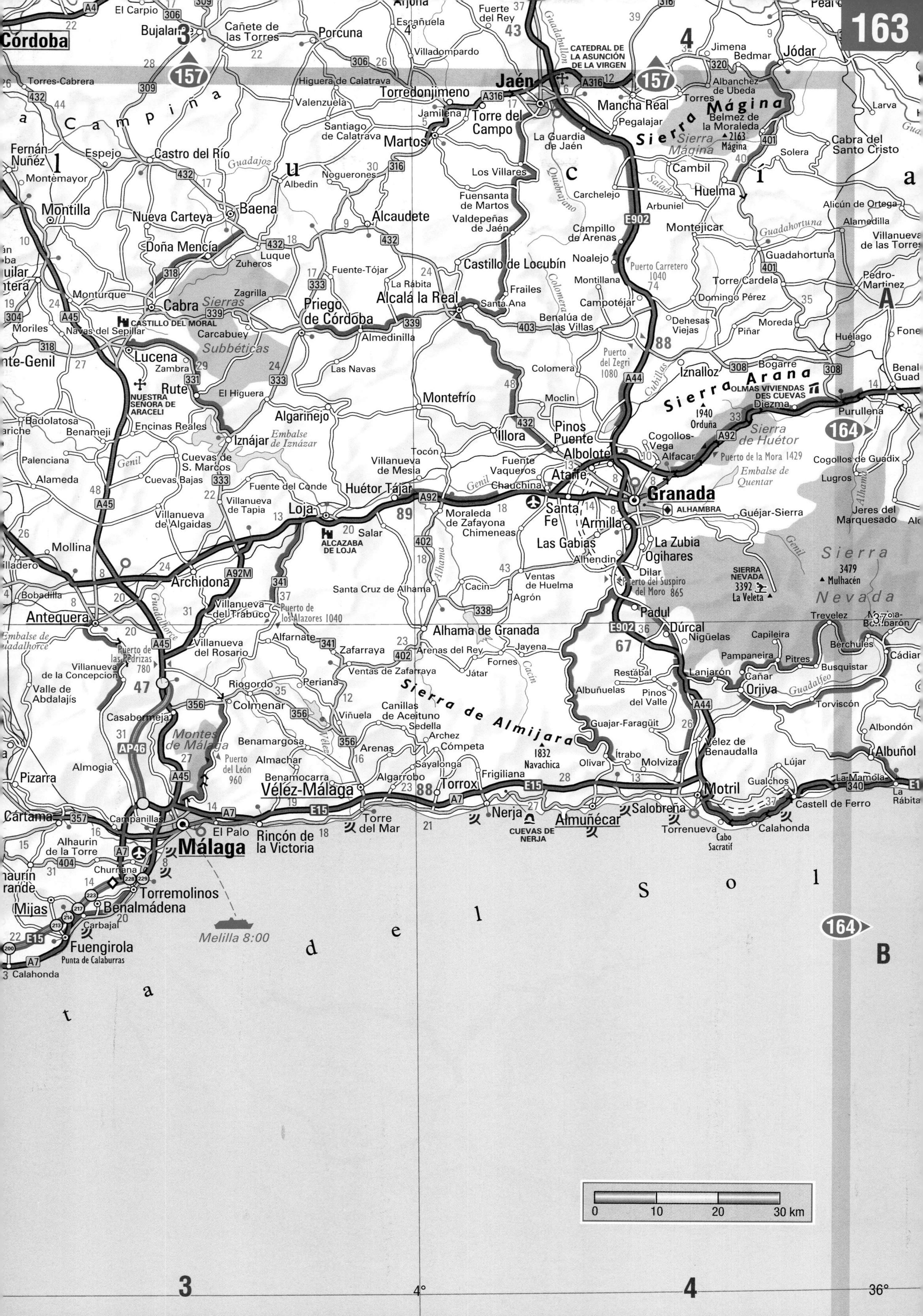

Córdoba
El Carpio
Bujalance
Cañete de las Torres
Porcuna
Arjona
Escañuela
Fuerte del Rey
Villardompardo
Higuera de Calatrava
Torredonjimeno
Jaén
CATEDRAL DE LA ASUNCIÓN DE LA VIRGEN
Jimena
Bedmar
Jódar
Albanchez de Ubeda
Torres
Mancha Real
Pegalajar
Sierra Mágina
Belmez de la Moraleda
Mágina
Cabra del Santo Cristo
Larva
Solera
Torres-Cabrera
Campiña
Valenzuela
Jamilena
Torre del Campo
La Guardia de Jaén
Santiago de Calatrava
Martos
Fernán Núñez
Espejo
Castro del Río
Montemayor
Noguerones
Albedín
Los Villares
Cambil
Huelma
Montilla
Nueva Carteya
Baena
Alcaudete
Fuensanta de Martos
Valdepeñas de Jaén
Carchelejo
Arbuniel
Alicún de Ortega
Alamedilla
Villanueva de las Torres
Campillo de Arenas
Montejícar
Doña Mencía
Luque
Zuheros
Castillo de Locubín
Noalejo
Puerto Carretero 1040
Guadahortuna
Fuente-Tójar
La Rábita
Montillana
Torre Cardela
Pedro-Martínez
Monturque
Cabra
Zagrilla
Priego de Córdoba
Alcalá la Real
Frailes
Santa Ana
Campotéjar
Domingo Pérez
CASTILLO DEL MORAL
Sierras Subbéticas
Moriles
Navas del Sepillar
Carcabuey
Almedinilla
Benalúa de las Villas
Dehesas Viejas
Moreda
Piñar
Huélago
Lucena
Zambra
Puente-Genil
Las Navas
Colomera
Puerto del Zegri 1080
Iznalloz
Bogarre
Sierra Arana
Rute
NUESTRA SEÑORA DE ARACELI
El Higuera
Montefrío
Moclín
OLMAS VIVIENDAS DES CUEVAS
Diezma
Purullena
Badolatosa
Benamejí
Encinas Reales
Algarinejo
1940 Orduña
Illora
Pinos Puente
Cogollos-Vega
Sierra de Huétor
Iznájar
Embalse de Iznázar
Tocón
Albolote
Alfacar
Puerto de la Mora 1429
Cogollos de Guadix
Palenciana
Cuevas de S. Marcos
Villanueva de Mesía
Fuente Vaqueros
Atarfe
Embalse de Quentar
Lugros
Alameda
Cuevas Bajas
Fuente del Conde
Huétor Tájar
Chauchina
Granada
Villanueva de Tapia
Loja
Salar
Moraleda de Zafayona
Santa Fe
Armilla
ALHAMBRA
Güéjar-Sierra
Jeres del Marquesado
Villanueva de Algaidas
ALCAZABA DE LOJA
Chimeneas
Las Gabias
La Zubia
Ogíhares
Mollina
Alhendín
Sierra Nevada
3479 Mulhacén
Dílar
Puerto del Suspiro del Moro 865
3392 La Veleta
Archidona
Santa Cruz de Alhama
Cacín
Ventas de Huelma
Agrón
Bobadilla
Antequera
Villanueva del Trabuco
Puerto de los Alazores 1040
Padul
Alhama de Granada
Dúrcal
Nigüelas
Capileira
Trevelez
Bérchules
Cádiar
Villanueva del Rosario
Alfarnate
Zafarraya
Arenas del Rey
Jayena
Fornes
Puerto de las Pedrizas 780
Villanueva de la Concepción
Ventas de Zafarraya
Játar
Restábal
Pampaneira
Pitres
Lanjarón
Cáñar
Busquistar
Valle de Abdalajís
Riogordo
Periana
Sierra de Almijara
Albuñuelas
Pinos del Valle
Orjiva
Colmenar
Torviscón
Casabermeja
Viñuela
Canillas de Aceituno
Sedella
Guajar-Faragüit
Montes de Málaga
Benamargosa
Archez
Cómpeta
Vélez de Benaudalla
Albondón
Arenas
1832 Navachica
Ítrabo
Albuñol
Almogía
Almachar
Puerto del León 960
Sayalonga
Olivar
Molvízar
Lújar
Pizarra
Benamocarra
Algarrobo
Frigiliana
Vélez-Málaga
Torrox
Motril
Gualchos
La Mamola
Cártama
Campanillas
Torre del Mar
Nerja
Almuñécar
Salobreña
Castell de Ferro
La Rábita
Alhaurín de la Torre
El Palo
Rincón de la Victoria
CUEVAS DE NERJA
Torrenueva
Cabo Sacratif
Calahonda
Málaga
Churriana
Torremolinos
Mijas
Benalmádena
Carbajal
Fuengirola
Punta de Calaburras
Calahonda
Melilla 8:00
Costa del Sol
0
10
20
30 km

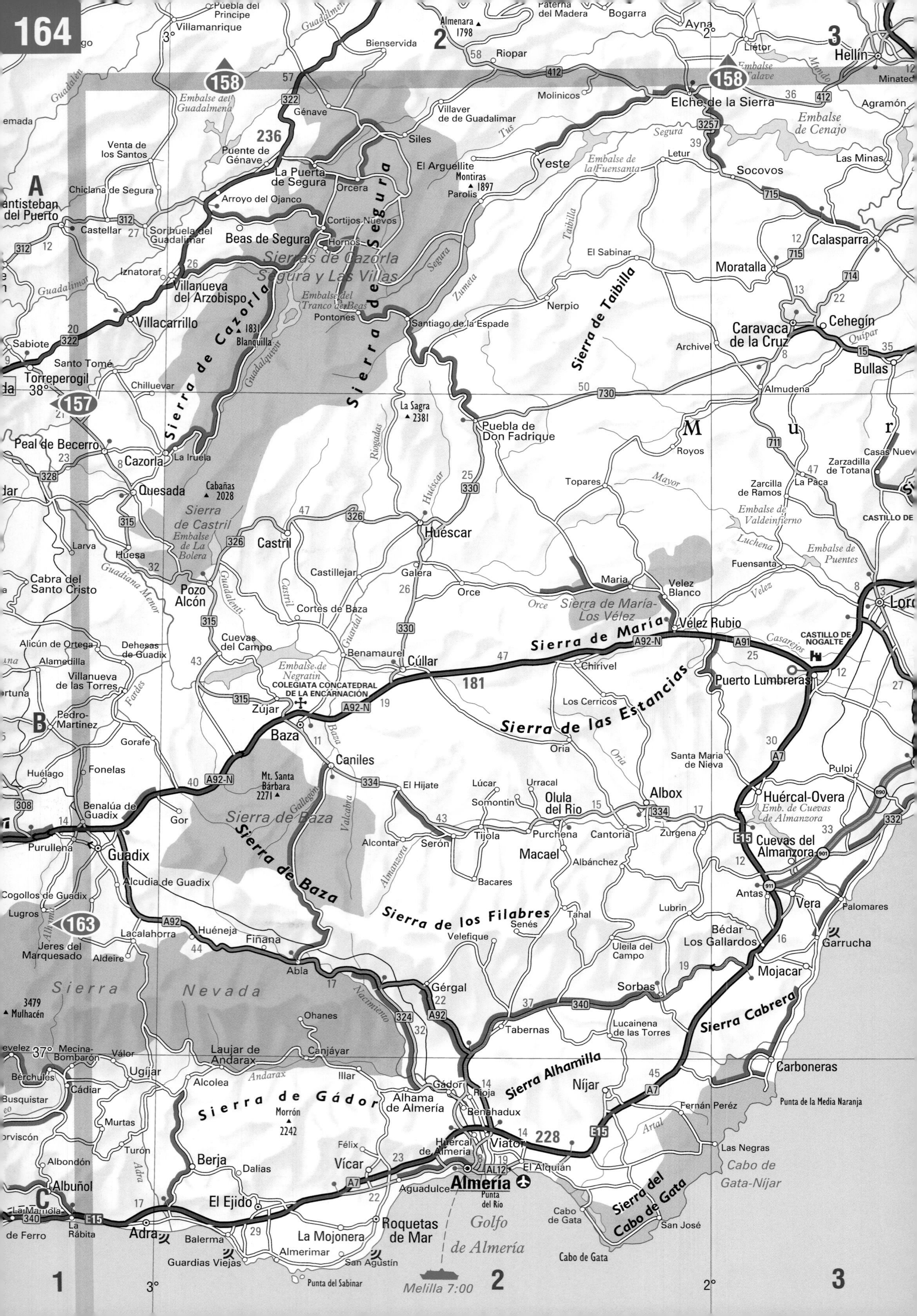
Puebla del Principe
Villamanrique
Almenara 1798
Paterna del Madera
Bogarra
Ayna
Hellín
Bienservida
Riopar
Liétor
Minateda
158
Embalse del Guadalmena
Génave
Villaver de de Guadalimar
Molinicos
Elche de la Sierra
Agramón
Embalse de Cenajo
Venta de los Santos
236
Puente de Génave
Siles
Yeste
Letur
Embalse de la Fuensanta
Las Minas
Socovos
La Puerta de Segura
El Arguellite
Montiras 1897
Parolis
Chiclana de Segura
Orcera
Santisteban del Puerto
Arroyo del Ojanco
Cortijos Nuevos
Castellar
Sorihuela del Guadalimar
Beas de Segura
Hornos
Calasparra
Sierras de Cazorla Segura y Las Villas
El Sabinar
Moratalla
Iznatoraf
Villanueva del Arzobispo
Embalse del Tranco de Beas
Pontones
Nerpio
Villacarrillo
Blanquilla 1831
Santiago de la Espade
Sierra de Taibilla
Caravaca de la Cruz
Cehegín
Sabiote
Archivel
Bullas
Santo Tomé
Torreperogil
Sierra de Cazorla
Sierra de Segura
Chilluevar
Almudena
157
La Sagra 2381
Puebla de Don Fadrique
Murcia
Peal de Becerro
Cazorla
La Iruela
Royos
Casas Nuevas
Zarzadilla de Totana
Quesada
Cabañas 2028
Topares
Zarcilla de Ramos
La Paca
Sierra de Castril
Embalse de La Bolera
Castril
Huéscar
Embalse de Valdeinfierno
CASTILLO DE
Larva
Huesa
Castillejar
Galera
Fuensanta
Embalse de Puentes
Cabra del Santo Cristo
Pozo Alcón
Cortes de Baza
Orce
Maria
Velez Blanco
Sierra de María-Los Vélez
Lorca
Vélez Rubio
Sierra de María
Alicún de Ortega
Dehesas de Guadix
Cuevas del Campo
CASTILLO DE NOGALTE
Alamedilla
Villanueva de las Torres
Benamaurel
Cúllar
Chirivel
Embalse de Negratín
COLEGIATA CONCATEDRAL DE LA ENCARNACIÓN
181
Puerto Lumbreras
Zújar
Los Cerricos
Pedro-Martinez
Baza
Sierra de las Estancias
Gorafe
Oria
Caniles
Santa Maria de Nieva
Fonelas
Huélago
Mt. Santa Bárbara 2271
Lúcar
Urracal
Pulpi
El Hijate
Somontin
Olula del Rio
Albox
Huércal-Overa
Emb. de Cuevas de Almanzora
Benalúa de Guadix
Gor
Sierra de Baza
Tíjola
Purchena
Cantoria
Zurgena
Purullena
Guadix
Alcontar
Serón
Macael
Albánchez
Cuevas del Almanzora
Alcudia de Guadix
Bacares
Cogollos de Guadix
Antas
Vera
Palomares
Lugros
163
Sierra de los Filabres
Tahal
Lubrín
Lacalahorra
Huéneja
Senés
Bédar
Jeres del Marquesado
Aldeire
Fiñana
Velefique
Los Gallardos
Garrucha
Uleila del Campo
Abla
Mojacar
Sierra Nevada
Gérgal
Sorbas
3479 Mulhacén
Ohanes
Tabernas
Lucainena de las Torres
Sierra Cabrera
Trevelez
Mecina-Bombarón
Válor
Laujar de Andarax
Canjáyar
Ugíjar
Illar
Sierra Alhamilla
Carboneras
Bérchules
Alcolea
Gádor
Níjar
Cádiar
Sierra de Gádor
Alhama de Almería
Rioja
Busquistar
Morrón 2242
Benahadux
Fernán Peréz
Punta de la Media Naranja
Murtas
Sorvicón
228
Turón
Félix
Huércal de Almería
Viator
Las Negras
Albondón
Berja
Dalias
Vícar
El Alquián
Cabo de Gata-Níjar
Albuñol
Almería
Aguadulce
Punta del Río
Sierra del Cabo de Gata
La Mamola
La Rábita
de Ferro
Adra
El Ejido
Roquetas de Mar
Golfo de Almería
Cabo de Gata
San José
Balerma
La Mojonera
Almerimar
Guardias Viejas
San Agustín
Punta del Sabinar
Melilla 7:00
A
B
C
1
2
3
3°
2°
38°
37°

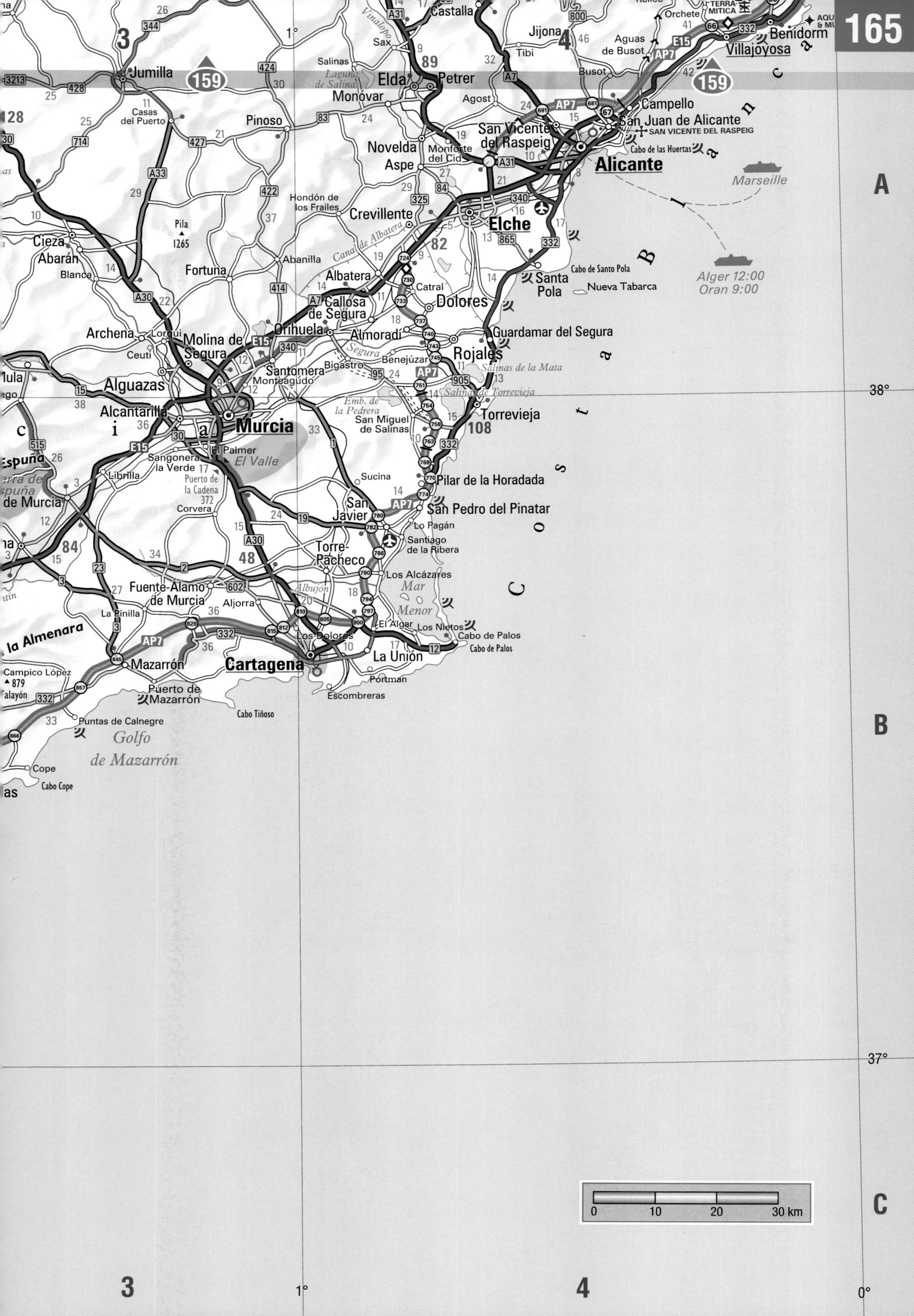

Jumilla
Casas del Puerto
Pinoso
Salinas
Laguna de Salinas
Elda
Petrer
Monóvar
Castalla
Sax
Jijona
Tibi
Aguas de Busot
Busot
Orchete
Benidorm
Villajoyosa
Agost
Campello
San Juan de Alicante
SAN VICENTE DEL RASPEIG
San Vicente del Raspeig
Novelda
Monforte del Cid
Aspe
Cabo de las Huertas
Alicante
Marseille
Hondón de los Frailes
Crevillente
Elche
Canal de Albatera
Pila
1265
Cieza
Abarán
Blanca
Fortuna
Abanilla
Albatera
Catral
Dolores
Callosa de Segura
Cabo de Santo Pola
Santa Pola
Nueva Tabarca
Alger 12:00
Oran 9:00
Archena
Lorquí
Ceuti
Molina de Segura
Orihuela
Almoradí
Guardamar del Segura
Segura
Bigastro
Benejúzar
Rojales
Salinas de la Mata
Salinas de Torrevieja
Santomera
Monteagudo
Alguazas
Alcantarilla
Murcia
Emb. de la Pedrera
San Miguel de Salinas
Torrevieja
Palmer
Sangonera la Verde
El Valle
Puerto de la Cadena
372
Librilla
Corvera
Sucina
Pilar de la Horadada
San Javier
San Pedro del Pinatar
Lo Pagán
Santiago de la Ribera
Torre-Pacheco
Los Alcázares
Mar Menor
Fuente-Álamo de Murcia
Albujón
Aljorra
La Pinilla
El Algar
Los Nietos
Cabo de Palos
la Almenara
Mazarrón
Cartagena
Los Dolores
La Unión
Portman
Escombreras
Campico López
879
Puerto de Mazarrón
Cabo Tiñoso
Puntas de Calnegre
Golfo de Mazarrón
Cope
Cabo Cope
Costa Blanca
38°
37°
1°
0°
A
B
C
3
4
0
10
20
30 km

1 2

A

40°

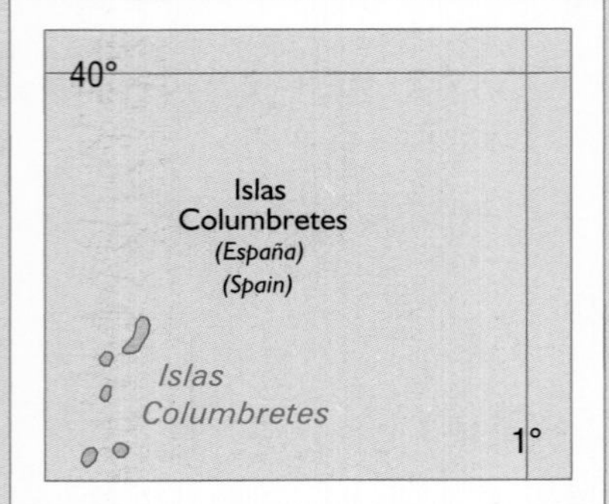

Islas
Columbretes
(España)
(Spain)

*Islas
Columbretes*

40°

1°

ISLAS
BALEARES

BALEARIC
ISLANDS

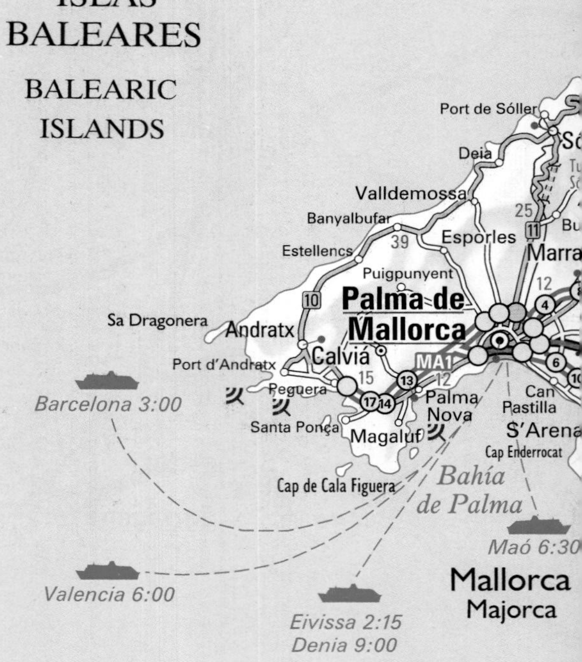

Port de Sóller

Deia

So

Tu
So

Valldemossa

Banyalbufar

Marra

Esporles

11

Estellencs

39

25

Puigpunyent

12

Sa Dragonera

10

**Palma de
Mallorca**

Andratx

Port d'Andratx

Calviá

MA1

4

6

15

13

12

Barcelona 3:00

Peguera

Palma
Nova

Can
Pastilla

17 14

Santa Ponça

Magaluf

S'Arena

Cap Enderrocat

Cap de Cala Figuera

*Bahía
de Palma*

Maó 6:30

Valencia 6:00

Mallorca
Majorca

*Eivissa 2:15
Denia 9:00*

B

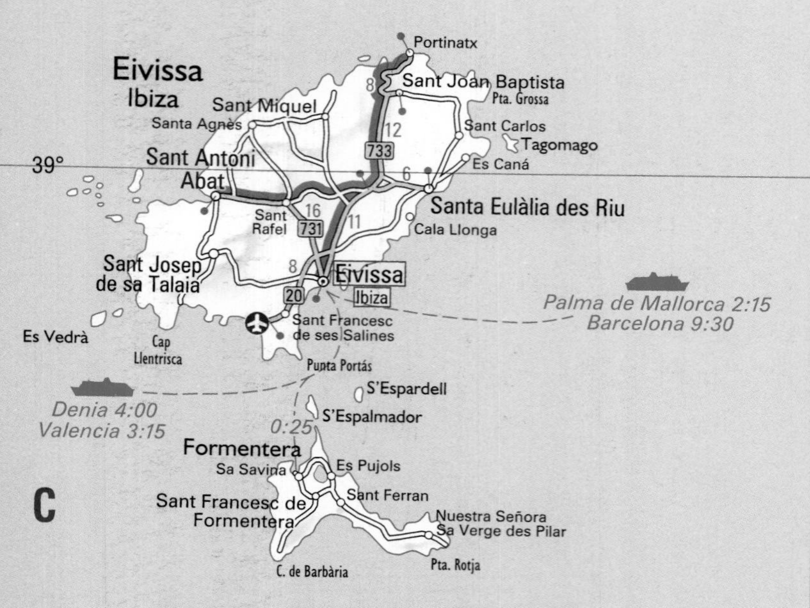

Portinatx

Eivissa
Ibiza

Sant Joan Baptista

Sant Miquel

Pta. Grossa

Santa Agnès

8

Sant Carlos

12

Tagomago

**Sant Antoni
Abat**

733

6

Es Caná

39°

Santa Eulàlia des Riu

Sant
Rafel

16

731

11

Cala Llonga

**Sant Josep
de sa Talaia**

8

Eivissa

20

Ibiza

*Palma de Mallorca 2:15
Barcelona 9:30*

Es Vedrà

Cap
Llentrisca

Sant Francesc
de ses Salines

Punta Portás

*Denia 4:00
Valencia 3:15*

S'Espardell

S'Espalmador

0:25

Formentera

Es Pujols

Sa Savina

Sant Ferran

C

**Sant Francesc de
Formentera**

Nuestra Señora
Sa Verge des Pilar

C. de Barbària

Pta. Rotja

1 2

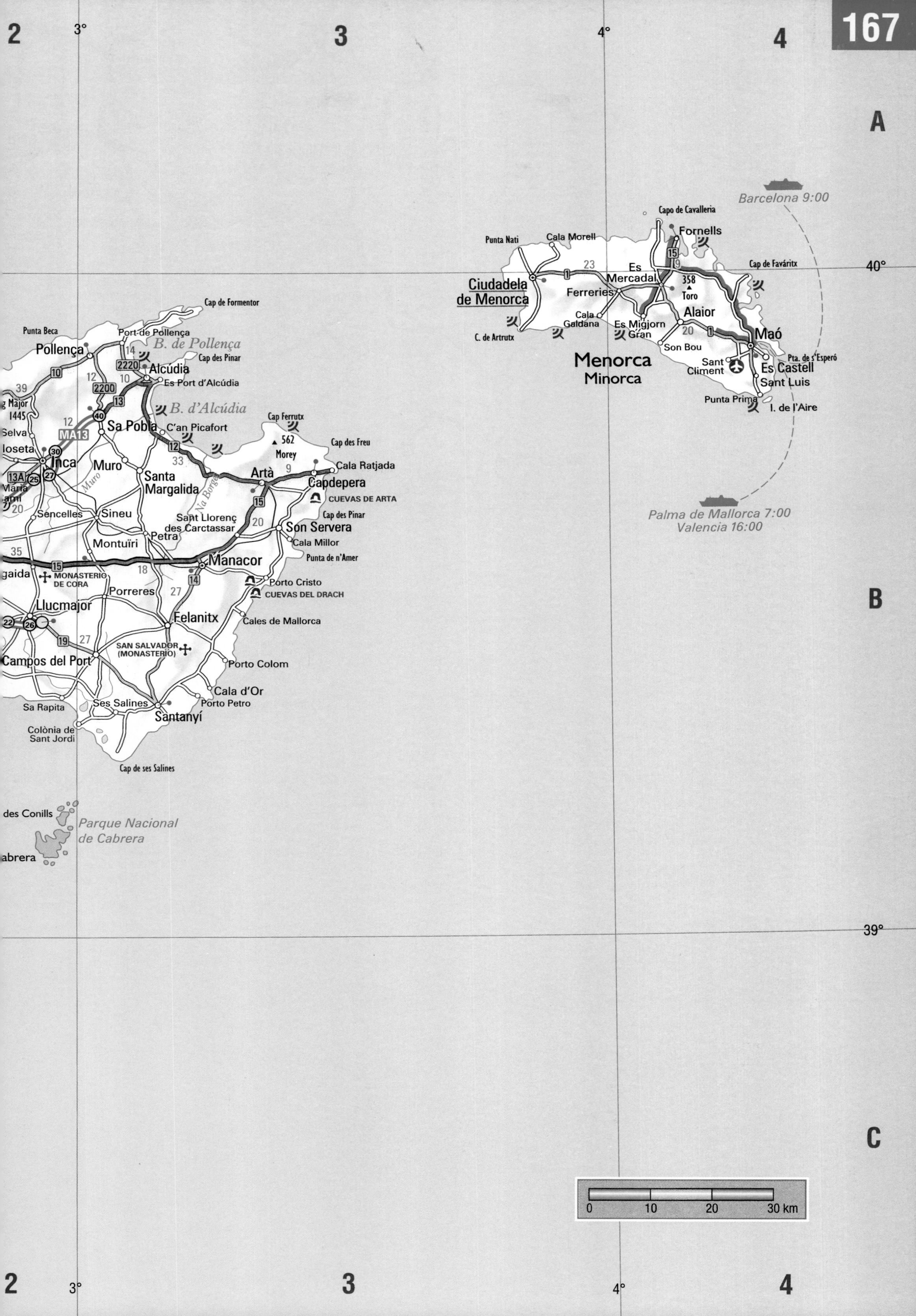

2   3°   3   4°   4

A

Barcelona 9:00

Capo de Cavalleria

Punta Nati   Cala Morell   Fornells
                                        15
                                        9
Ciudadela   23   Es   40°
de Menorca   Ferreries   Mercadal   358
                                        Toro
C. de Artrutx   Cala   Es Migjorn   Alaior
               Galdana   Gran   20   1   Maó
                              Son Bou   Pta. de s'Esperó
Menorca   Sant   Es Castell
Minorca   Climent   Sant Luis
          Punta Prima   I. de l'Aire

Cap de Formentor
Punta Beca   Port de Pollença
Pollença   14   B. de Pollença
     10   2220   Cap des Pinar
     12   10   Alcúdia
     2200   Es Port d'Alcúdia
g Major   13   B. d'Alcúdia   Cap Ferrutx
1445   12   40   Sa Pobla   C'an Picafort
Selva   MA13   562
loseta   30   12   Morey   Cap des Freu
30   Inca   33   Muro   Artà   Cala Ratjada
13A   27   Santa   9
Maria   25   Margalida   Capdepera
20   Sencelles   Sineu   Sant Llorenç   CUEVAS DE ARTA
               des Carctassar   Cap des Pinar
          Montuïri   Petra   15   Son Servera
35   18   20   Cala Millor
15   gaida   MONASTERIO   Manacor   Punta de n'Amer
          DE CORA   14
     Porreres   27   Porto Cristo
Llucmajor   CUEVAS DEL DRACH
22   26   Felanitx   Cales de Mallorca
19   27   SAN SALVADOR
Campos del Port   (MONASTERIO)   Porto Colom
     Sa Rapita   Ses Salines   Cala d'Or
Colònia de   Santanyí   Porto Petro
Sant Jordi
          Cap de ses Salines

des Conills
          Parque Nacional
          de Cabrera
abrera

B

Palma de Mallorca 7:00
Valencia 16:00

39°

C

0   10   20   30 km

2   3°   3   4°   4

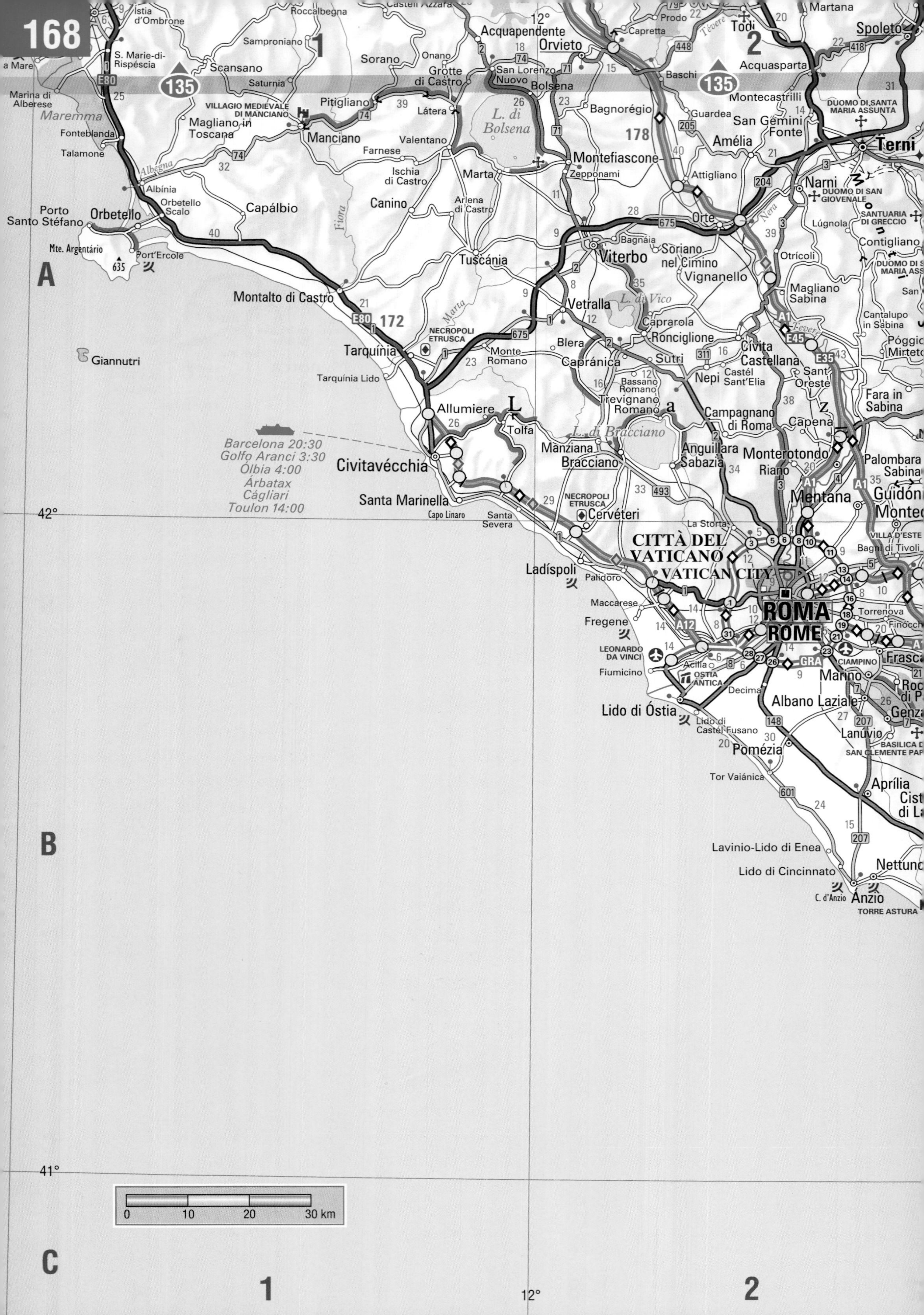
Ístia d'Ombrone
Roccalbegna
Castell Azzara
12°
Acquapendente
Orvieto
Prodo
Todi
Martana
Spoleto
Capretta
Tévere
a Mare
S. Marie-di-Rispéscia
Semproniano
1
2
Sorano
Onano
Grotte di Castro
San Lorenzo Nuovo
Baschi
Acquasparta
Scansano
135
Saturnia
Bolsena
Montecastrilli
Marina di Alberese
Maremma
VILLAGIO MEDIEVALE DI MANCIANO
Pitigliano
Látera
L. di Bolsena
Bagnorégio
Guardea
San Gémini Fonte
DUOMO DI SANTA MARIA ASSUNTA
Terni
Fonteblanda
Magliano in Toscana
Manciano
Valentano
178
Amélia
Talamone
Farnese
Montefiascone
Albegna
Ischia di Castro
Marta
Zepponami
Attigliano
Narni
Albínia
Orbetello Scalo
DUOMO DI SAN GIOVENALE
Porto Santo Stéfano
Orbetello
Capálbio
Canino
Arlena di Castro
Orte
Nera
SANTUARIA DI GRECCIO
Lúgnola
Mte. Argentário
635
Port'Ercole
Fiora
Tuscánia
Bagnáia
Viterbo
Soriano nel Cimino
Contigliano
Otrícoli
Vignanello
A
Montalto di Castro
Vetralla
L. di Vico
Magliano Sabina
172
Marta
Caprarola
Ronciglione
Cantalupo in Sabina
NECROPOLI ETRUSCA
Tarquínia
Monte Romano
Blera
Capránica
Sutri
Cívita Castellana
Póggio Mirteto
Giannutri
Tarquínia Lido
Bassano Romano
Nepi
Castél Sant'Elia
Sant'Oreste
Trevignano Romano
Fara in Sabina
Allumiere
Tolfa
Campagnano di Roma
Capena
L. di Bracciano
Barcelona 20:30
Golfo Aranci 3:30
Ólbia 4:00
Árbatax
Cágliari
Toulon 14:00
Civitavécchia
Manziana
Bracciano
Anguillara Sabazia
Monterotondo
Riano
Palombara Sabina
Santa Marinella
NECROPOLI ETRUSCA
Cervéteri
Mentana
Guidónia
42°
Capo Linaro
Santa Severa
La Storta
VILLA D'ESTE
Bagni di Tivoli
CITTÀ DEL VATICANO
VATICAN CITY
Ladíspoli
Palidoro
Maccarese
ROMA
ROME
Torrenova
Fregene
LEONARDO DA VINCI
Acilia
CIAMPINO
Fiumicino
OSTIA ANTICA
Marino
Decima
Albano Laziale
Lido di Óstia
Lido di Castél Fusano
Lanúvio
Pomézia
BASILICA DI SAN CLEMENTE PAPA
Tor Vaiánica
Aprília
B
Lavinio-Lido di Enea
Lido di Cincinnato
Nettuno
C. d'Anzio
Anzio
TORRE ASTURA
41°
0
10
20
30 km
C
1
12°
2

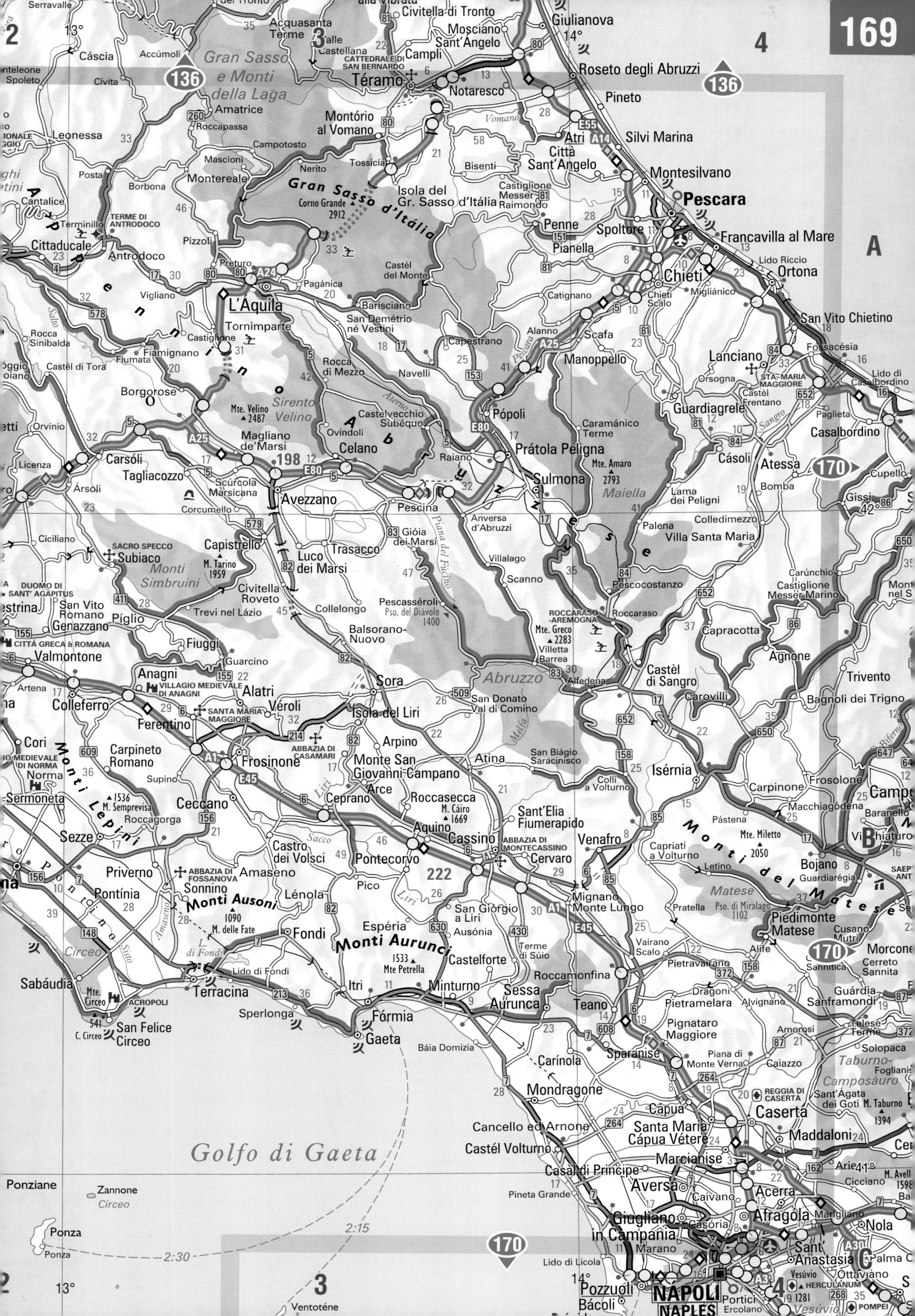
Gran Sasso e Monti della Laga
Gran Sasso d'Itália
Corno Grande 2912
Appennino Abruzzese
Téramo
Giulianova
Roseto degli Abruzzi
Pineto
Silvi Marina
Atri
Montesilvano
Pescara
Francavilla al Mare
Chieti
Ortona
San Vito Chietino
Lanciano
Fossacésia
Guardiagrele
Casalbordino
Vasto
Cupello
Gissi
Atessa
Cásoli
Civitella di Tronto
Mosciano Sant'Angelo
Campli
Notaresco
Montório al Vomano
Isola del Gr. Sasso d'Itália
Città Sant'Angelo
Penne
Spoltore
Pianella
Castél del Monte
Amatrice
Leonessa
Cáscia
Accúmoli
Acquasanta Terme
Valle Castellana
Campotosto
Montereale
Cantalice
Cittaducale
Antrodoco
Rieti
L'Áquila
Tornimparte
Pagánica
Barisciano
San Demétrio né Vestini
Capestrano
Navelli
Rocca di Mezzo
Pópoli
Scafa
Manoppello
Caramánico Terme
Mte. Amaro 2793
Maiella
Sulmona
Prátola Peligna
Raiano
Castelvecchio Subéquo
Celano
Mte. Velino 2487
Sirento Velino
Magliano de'Marsi
Avezzano
Tagliacozzo
Carsóli
Árcoli
Pescina
Gióia dei Marsi
Trasacco
Luco dei Marsi
Capistrello
M. Tarino 1959
Monti Simbruini
Subiaco
Sacro Speco
Civitella Roveto
Trevi nel Lázio
Collelongo
Pescasséroli
Pso. del Diávolo 1400
Balsorano-Nuovo
Anversa d'Abruzzi
Villalago
Scanno
Roccaraso
Mte. Greco 2283
Villetta Barrea
Alfedena
Pescocostanzo
Palena
Villa Santa Maria
Castiglione Messer Marino
Capracotta
Agnone
Trivento
Castél di Sangro
Abruzzo
Sora
San Donato Val di Comino
Isola del Liri
Arpino
Atina
San Biágio Saracinisco
Iśernia
Colli a Volturno
Carpinone
Frosolone
Campobasso
Bojano
Mte. Miletto 2050
Monti del Matese
Matese
Piedimonte Matese
Morcone
Venafro
Mignano Monte Lungo
Vairano Scalo
Pietravairano
Teano
Sessa Aurunca
Roccamonfina
Castelforte
Minturno
Cassino
Abbazia di Montecassino
Cervaro
Sant'Elia Fiumerapido
Aquino
Roccasecca
M. Cáiro 1669
Pontecorvo
Ceprano
Arce
Monte San Giovanni Campano
Frosinone
Véroli
Abbazia di Casamari
Alatri
Ferentino
Fiuggi
Anagni
Colleferro
Valmontone
Genazzano
Palestrina
Cori
Monti Lepini
Carpineto Romano
Norma
Sermoneta
Sezze
Priverno
Abbazia di Fossanova
Sonnino
Amaseno
Ceccano
Castro dei Volsci
Pico
Lénola
Monti Ausoni
M. delle Fate 1090
Fondi
Espéria
Monti Aurunci
Mte Petrella 1533
Itri
Fórmia
Gaeta
Sperlonga
Terracina
Lido di Fondi
Sabáudia
Circeo
San Felice Circeo
Mte. Circeo 541
Pontínia
Golfo di Gaeta
Báia Domizia
Mondragone
Carínola
Sparanise
Cápua
Caserta
Maddaloni
Santa Maria Cápua Vétere
Castél Volturno
Cancello ed Arnone
Marcianise
Aversa
Acerra
Afragola
Giugliano in Campania
Nola
Sant'Anastasia
Ottaviano
Napoli
Naples
Pozzuoli
Bácoli
Portici
Ercolano
Vesúvio 1281
Pompei
Herculanum
Ponza
Zannone
Ventoténe
Isernia
2:15
2:30
136
170
198
222
A14
A24
A25
A1
E80
E45
13°
14°
2
3
4
A
B
C

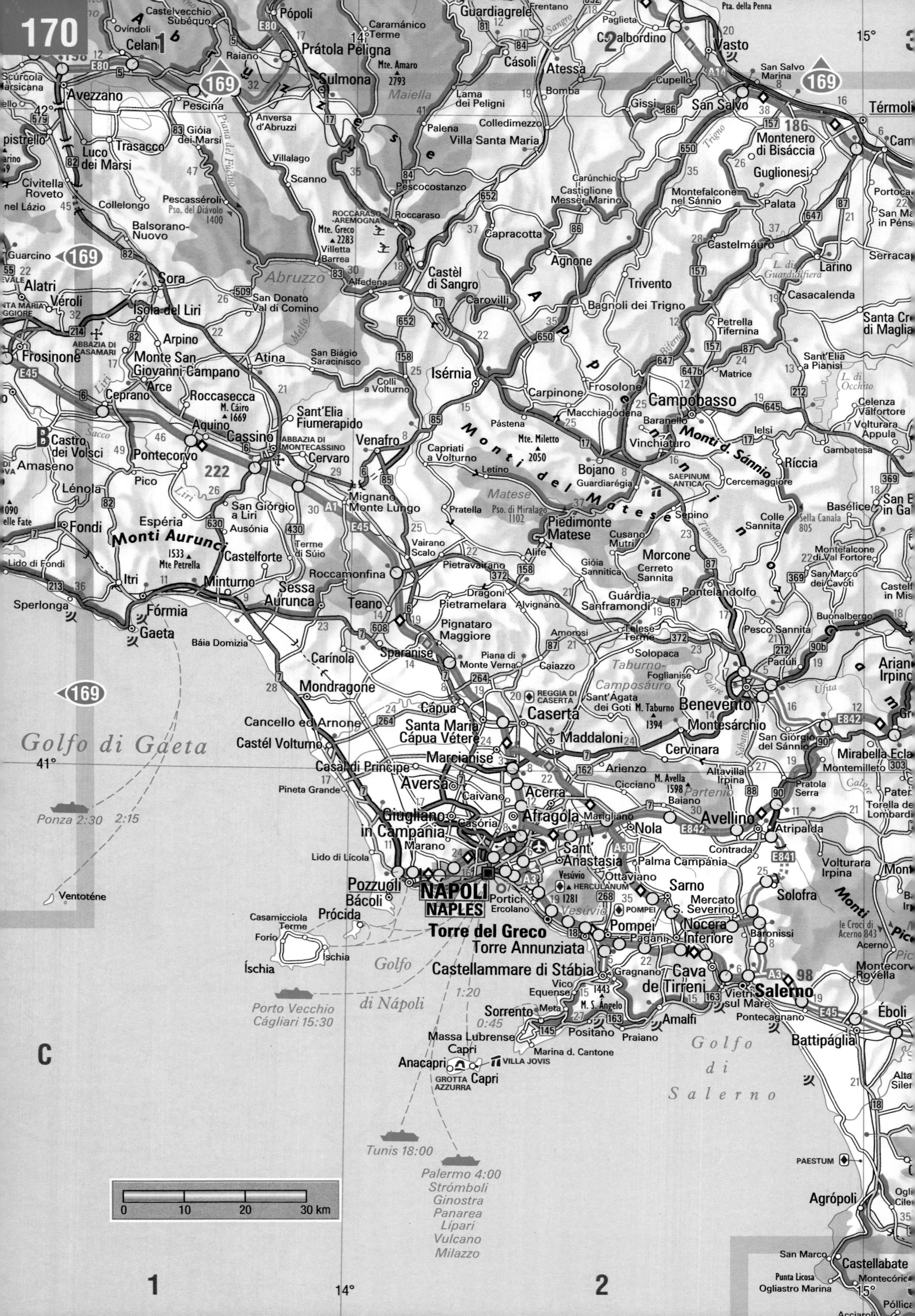
Castelvecchio Subèquo
Ovindoli
Celano
Pópoli
Caramánico Terme
Guardiagrele
Frentano
Paglieta
Pta. della Penna
San Salvo Marina
Vasto
15°
Avezzano
Raiano
Prátola Peligna
Sulmona
Mte. Amaro 2793
Maiella
Cásoli
Atessa
Casalbordino
Cupello
169
Scúrcola Marsicana
42°
Pescina
Anversa d'Abruzzi
Lama dei Peligni
Bomba
Gissi
San Salvo
Térmoli
Palena
Colledimezzo
Villa Santa Maria
Montenero di Bisáccia
Luco dei Marsi
Trasacco
Gióia dei Marsi
Piana del Fucino
Villalago
Scanno
Pescocostanzo
Guglionesi
Civitella Roveto
Collelongo
Pescasséroli
Pso. del Diávolo 1400
Carúnchio
Castiglione Messer Marino
Montefalcone nel Sánnio
Palata
San Martino in Pénsilis
Roccaraso-Aremogna
Roccaraso
Mte. Greco 2283
Balsorano-Nuovo
Capracotta
Villetta Barrea
Castelmáuro
Guarcino
Agnone
L. di Guardialfiera
Larino
Serracapriola
Alatri
Sora
Abruzzo
Alfedena
Castèl di Sangro
Trivento
Véroli
Isola del Liri
San Donato Val di Comino
Carovilli
Casacalenda
Bagnoli del Trigno
Santa Croce di Magliano
Abbazia di Casamari
Arpino
Frosinone
Monte San Giovanni Campano
Atina
San Biágio Saracinisco
Petrella Tifernina
Sant'Elia a Pianisi
Isérnia
Matrice
L. di Occhito
Arce
Colli a Volturno
Ceprano
Roccasecca
Carpinone
Frosolone
Campobasso
Celenza Valfortore
M. Cáiro 1669
Sant'Elia Fiumerapido
Pástena
Macchiagódena
Baranello
Volturara Áppula
Castro dei Volsci
Aquino
Cassino
Abbazia di Montecassino
Venafro
Mte. Miletto 2050
Vinchiaturo
Monti d. Sánnio
Iélsi
Pontecorvo
Cervaro
Capriati a Volturno
Ríccia
Gambatesa
Amaseno
Letino
Bojano
Guardiarégia
Saepinum Antica
Cercemaggiore
Lénola
Pico
Mignano Monte Lungo
Matese
Monti del Matese
222
San Giórgio a Liri
Pratella
Pso. di Miralago 1102
Sepino
Colle Sannita
Basélice
Fondi
Espéria
Ausónia
Piedimonte Matese
Cusano Mutri
Sella Canala 805
Monti Aurunci
Vairano Scalo
Alife
Morcone
Montefalcone di Val Fortore
Terme di Súio
1533 Mte Petrella
Castelforte
Pietravairano
Gióia Sannitica
Cerreto Sannita
San Marco dei Cavoti
Lido di Fondi
Roccamonfina
Itri
Minturno
Sessa Aurunca
Teano
Dragoni
Pietramelara
Alvignano
Guárdia Sanframondi
Pontelandolfo
Sperlonga
Fórmia
Gaeta
Pignataro Maggiore
Amorosi
Telese Terme
Pesca Sannita
Buonalbergo
Báia Domizia
Carínola
Sparanise
Piana di Monte Verna
Caiazzo
Solopaca
Taburno-Camposáuro
Foglianise
Paduli
Ariano Irpino
Mondragone
Reggia di Caserta
Sant'Ágata dei Goti
M. Taburno 1394
Benevento
Cápua
Caserta
Montesárchio
Cancello ed Arnone
Santa Maria Cápua Vétere
Maddaloni
San Giórgio del Sánnio
Mirabella Eclano
Golfo di Gaeta
Castél Volturno
Cervinara
41°
Marcianise
Casal di Principe
Arienzo
Altavilla Irpina
Montemiletto
Aversa
Cicciano
M. Avella 1598
Partenio
Pratola Serra
Pineta Grande
Caivano
Acerra
Baiano
Giugliano in Campania
Casória
Afragola
Marigliano
Nola
Avellino
Atripalda
Torella dei Lombardi
Ponza 2:30
2:15
Marano
Sant'Anastasia
Contrada
Lido di Lícola
Palma Campánia
Volturara Irpina
Pozzuoli
Napoli
Naples
Vesúvio 1281
Herculaneum
Ottaviano
Sarno
Solofra
Bácoli
Portici
Ercolano
Pompei
Mercato S. Severino
Ventoténe
Prócida
Casamicciola Terme
Torre del Greco
Nocera Inferiore
Baronissi
le Croci di Acerno 843
Acerno
Forío
Torre Annunziata
Pagani
Íschia
Golfo
Castellammare di Stábia
Gragnano
Cava de' Tirreni
Montecorvino Rovella
Vico Equense
1443
M. S. Ángelo
Porto Vecchio
Cágliari 15:30
di Nápoli
1:20
Sorrento
Meta
Positano
Vietri sul Mare
Salerno
Pontecagnano
Éboli
0:45
Amalfi
Massa Lubrense
Praiano
Golfo di Salerno
Battipáglia
C
Capri
Marina d. Cantone
Anacapri
Villa Jovis
Grotta Azzurra
Tunis 18:00
Paestum
Palermo 4:00
Strómboli
Ginostra
Panarea
Lípari
Vulcano
Milazzo
Agrópoli
0
10
20
30 km
San Marco
Castellabate
Punta Licosa
Ogliastro Marina
1
14°
2

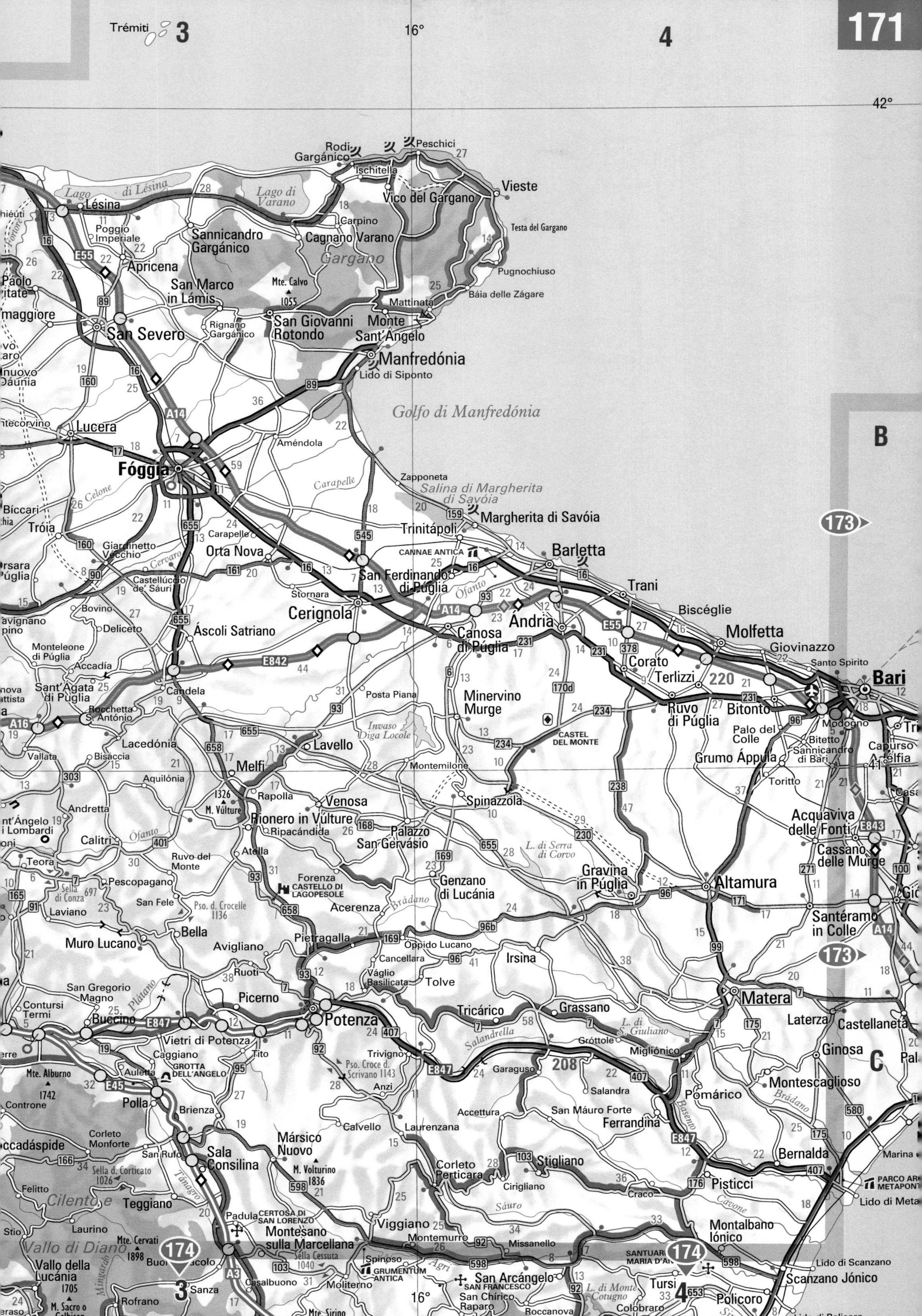
Trémiti
3
16°
4
42°
Rodi Gargánico
Peschici
Ischitella
Vieste
Lago di Lésina
Lago di Varano
Lésina
Vico del Gargano
Carpino
Testa del Gargano
Poggio Imperiale
Sannicandro Gargánico
Cagnano Varano
Gargano
Apricena
Pugnochiuso
San Marco in Lámis
Mte. Calvo 1055
Báia delle Zágare
Mattinata
San Severo
Rignano Gargánico
San Giovanni Rotondo
Monte Sant'Angelo
Manfredónia
Lido di Siponto
Golfo di Manfredónia
B
Lucera
Améndola
Fóggia
Zapponeta
Carapelle
Salina di Margherita di Savóia
Margherita di Savóia
Bíccari
Tróia
Trinitápoli
Carapelle
173
Orta Nova
Giardinetto Vecchio
Cervaro
CANNAE ANTICA
Barletta
San Ferdinando di Púglia
Castellúccio de' Sáuri
Stornara
Ófanto
Trani
Cerignola
Bovino
Ándria
Bisceglie
Deliceto
Canosa di Púglia
Molfetta
Áscoli Satriano
Giovinazzo
Monteleone di Púglia
Accadía
Santo Spirito
Corato
Bari
Sant'Ágata di Púglia
Terlizzi
Candela
Posta Piana
Minervino Murge
Rocchetta S. António
Ruvo di Púglia
Bitonto
Modugno
Invaso Diga Locone
Palo del Colle
Bitetto
Lacedónia
Lavello
CASTEL DEL MONTE
Capurso
Vallata
Bisáccia
Sannicandro di Bari
Grumo Áppula
Melfi
Montemilone
Aquilónia
Toritto
Rapolla
Spinazzola
Venosa
Andretta
M. Vúlture
Rionero in Vúlture
Acquaviva delle Fonti
Ripacándida
Palazzo San Gervásio
L. di Serra di Corvo
Cassano delle Murge
Calitri
Ófanto
Atella
Teora
Ruvo del Monte
Gravina in Púglia
Altamura
Pescopagano
Forenza
CASTELLO DI LAGOPESOLE
Genzano di Lucánia
Sella di Conza 697
San Fele
Pso. d. Crocelle 1136
Acerenza
Bradano
Santéramo in Colle
Laviano
Bella
Muro Lucano
Avigliano
Pietragalla
Óppido Lucano
Irsina
Cancellara
Ruoti
Váglio Basilicata
Tolve
173
San Gregorio Magno
Plátano
Contursi Terme
Picerno
Matera
Buccino
Potenza
Tricárico
Grassano
Laterza
Castellaneta
Vietri di Potenza
L. di S. Giuliano
Salandrella
Gróttole
Migliónico
Ginosa
Caggiano
Tito
Trivigno
C
Mte. Alburno 1742
Auletta
GROTTA DELL'ANGELO
Pso. Croce d. Scrivano 1143
Garaguso
Montescaglioso
Anzi
Salandra
Pomárico
Bradano
Controne
Polla
Brienza
Accettura
San Máuro Forte
Ferrandina
Basento
Calvello
Laurenzana
Corleto Monforte
Mársico Nuovo
San Rufo
Sala Consilina
Sella d. Corticato 1026
M. Volturino 1836
Stigliano
Bernalda
Marina
Corleto Perticara
Cirigliano
Pisticci
PARCO AR. METAPONT.
Felitto
Cilento e
Teggiano
Tánagro
Craco
Cavone
Lido di Meta
Sáuro
Stio
Laurino
Padula
CERTOSA DI SAN LORENZO
Montesano sulla Marcellana
Viggiano
Montalbano Iónico
Vallo di Diano
Mte. Cervati 1898
174
Montemurro
Missanello
Vallo della Lucánia 1705
Spinoso
Sella Cessuta 1040
GRUMENTUM ANTICA
SANTUARIO MARIA D'A.
174
Lido di Scanzano
Agri
San Arcángelo
SAN FRANCESCO
Scanzano Jónico
Sanza
Casalbuono
Moliterno
San Chírico Raparo
L. di Monte Cotugno
Tursi
M. Sacro o Gelbison
Rofrano
Mte. Sirino
Roccanova
Colobraro
Policoro
Sinni
Lido di Policoro

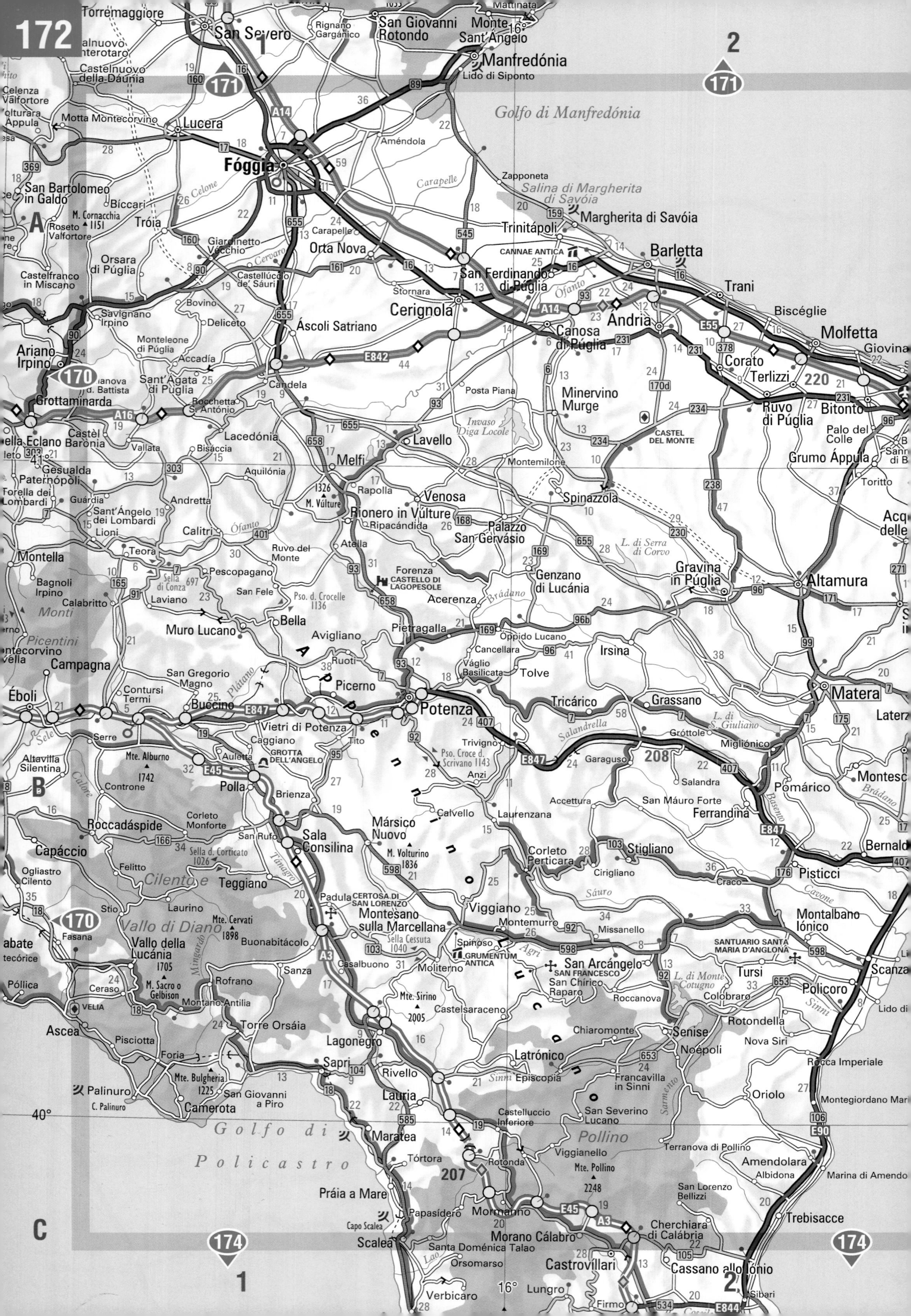

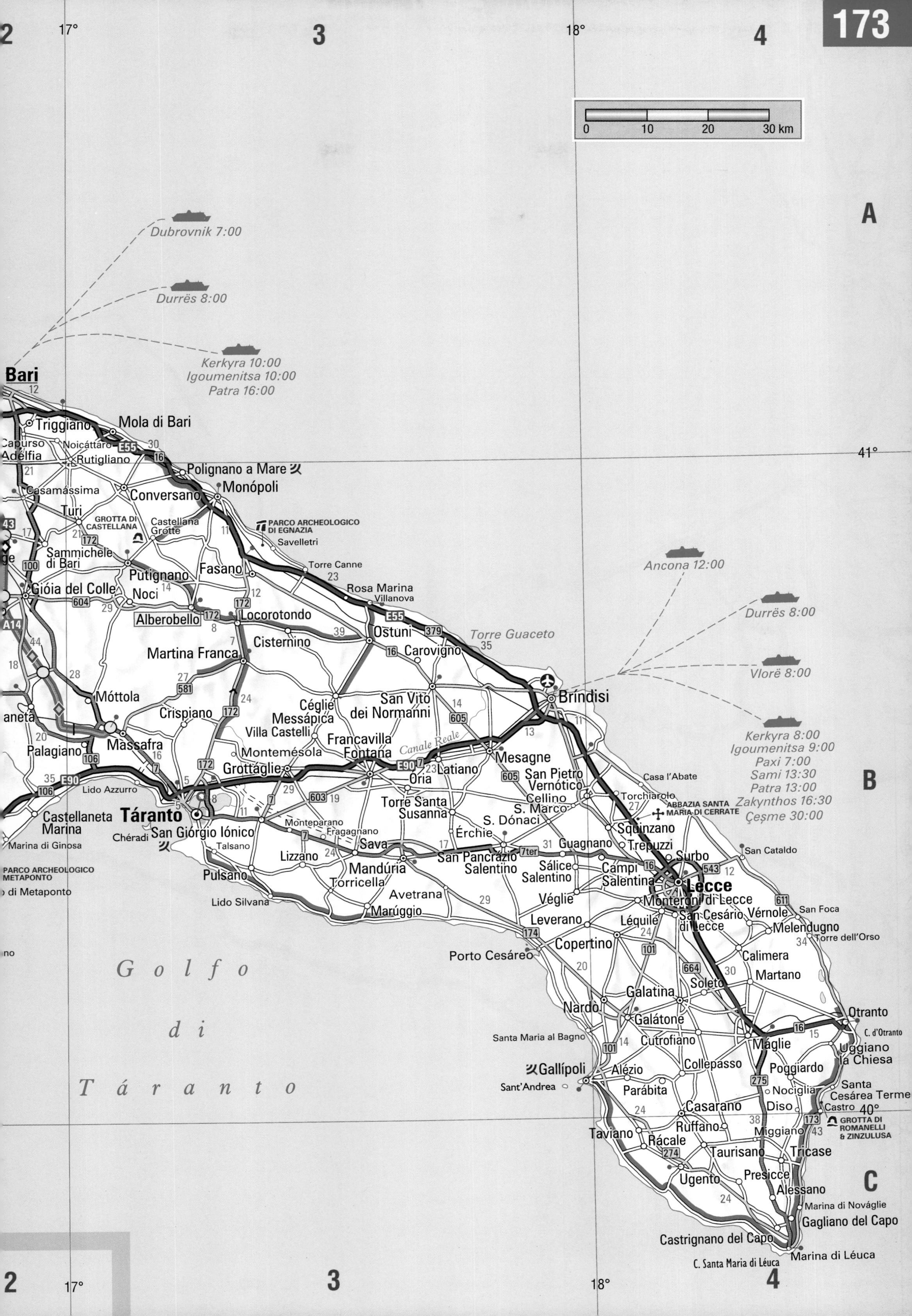

0 10 20 30 km
Dubrovnik 7:00
Durrës 8:00
Kerkyra 10:00
Igoumenitsa 10:00
Patra 16:00
Ancona 12:00
Durrës 8:00
Vlorë 8:00
Kerkyra 8:00
Igoumenitsa 9:00
Paxi 7:00
Sami 13:30
Patra 13:00
Zakynthos 16:30
Çeşme 30:00
Bari
Triggiano
Mola di Bari
Noicáttaro
Rutigliano
Adélfia
Casamássima
Conversano
Polignano a Mare
Monópoli
Turi
GROTTA DI CASTELLANA
Castellana Grotte
PARCO ARCHEOLOGICO DI EGNAZIA
Savelletri
Sammichele di Bari
Putignano
Fasano
Torre Canne
Gióia del Colle
Noci
Rosa Marina
Villanova
Alberobello
Locorotondo
Ostuni
Torre Guaceto
Martina Franca
Cisternino
Carovigno
Móttola
Crispiano
Céglie Messápica
San Vito dei Normanni
Bríndisi
Palagiano
Massafra
Villa Castelli
Francavilla Fontana
Canale Reale
Montemésola
Mesagne
Grottaglie
Latiano
Oria
San Pietro Vernótico
Casa l'Abate
Lido Azzurro
Castellaneta Marina
Táranto
Chéradi
San Giórgio Iónico
Torre Santa Susanna
Cellino
S. Marco
Torchiarolo
ABBAZIA SANTA MARIA DI CERRATE
S. Dónaci
Squinzano
Marina di Ginosa
Monteparano
Fragagnano
Érchie
Trepuzzi
Talsano
Lizzano
Sava
San Pancrazio Salentino
Guagnano
Surbo
San Cataldo
PARCO ARCHEOLOGICO METAPONTO
Pulsano
Mandúria
Sálice Salentino
Campi Salentina
Lecce
Torricella
Avetrana
Véglie
Monteroni di Lecce
Lido Silvana
Marúggio
Leverano
Léquile
San Cesário di Lecce
Vérnole
San Foca
Melendugno
Torre dell'Orso
Golfo di Táranto
Porto Cesáreo
Copertino
Calimera
Martano
Soleto
Galatina
Nardò
Galátone
Otranto
C. d'Otranto
Santa Maria al Bagno
Cutrofiano
Maglie
Uggiano la Chiesa
Gallípoli
Alézio
Collepasso
Poggiardo
Sant'Andrea
Parábita
Nociglia
Santa Cesárea Terme
Castro
Diso
Casarano
GROTTA DI ROMANELLI & ZINZULUSA
Taviano
Ruffano
Miggiano
Rácale
Taurisano
Tricase
Ugento
Presicce
Alessano
Marina di Nováglie
Gagliano del Capo
Castrignano del Capo
Marina di Léuca
C. Santa Maria di Léuca

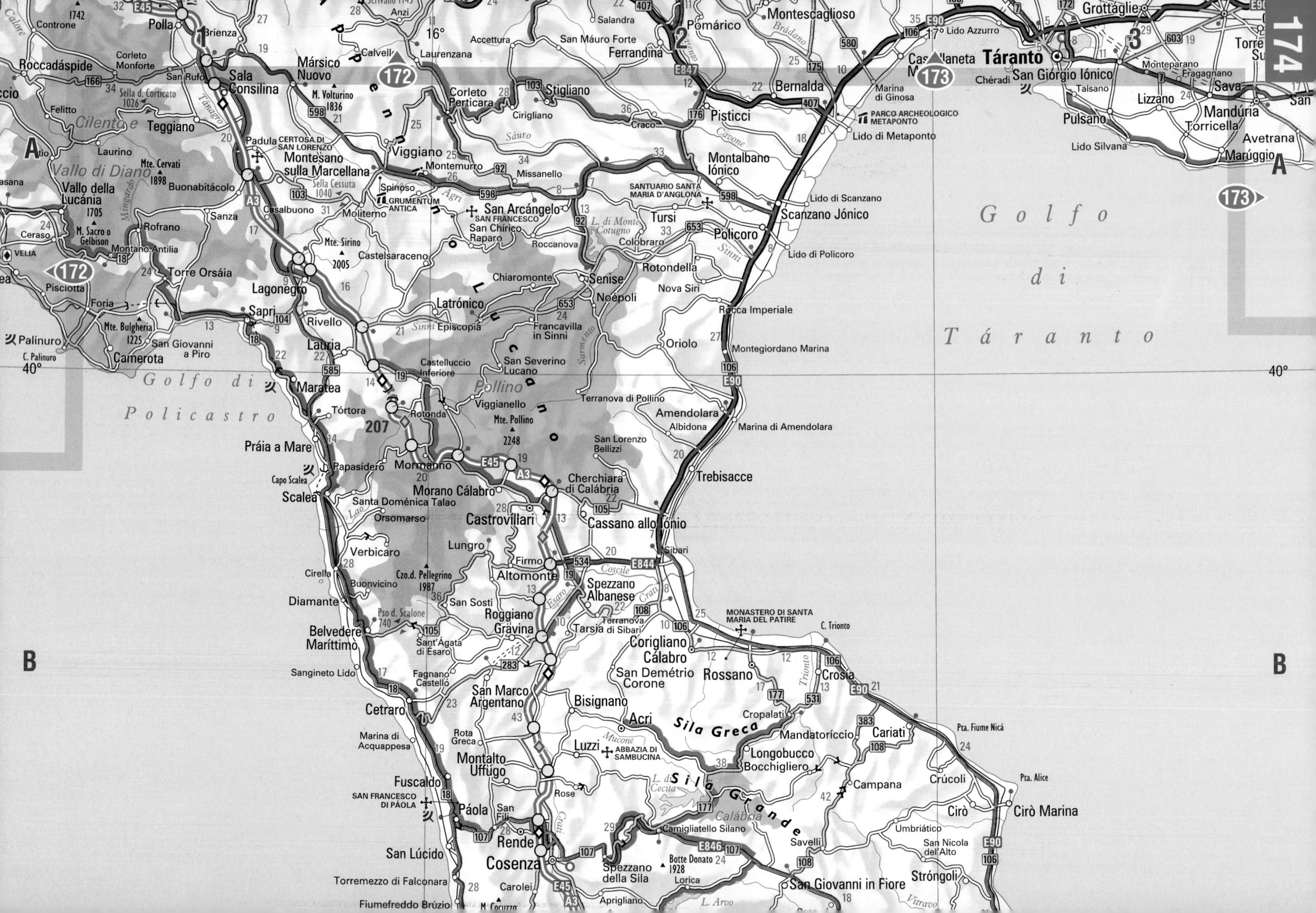
Golfo di Táranto
Golfo di Policastro
Táranto
San Giórgio Iónico
Grottáglie
Manduria
Sava
Lizzano
Pulsano
Torricella
Avetrana
Marúggio
Lido Silvana
Castellaneta
Lido Azzurro
Montescaglioso
Pomárico
Bernalda
Pisticci
Marina di Ginosa
PARCO ARCHEOLOGICO METAPONTO
Lido di Metaponto
Lido di Scanzano
Scanzano Jónico
Policoro
Lido di Policoro
Montalbano Iónico
Tursi
SANTUARIO SANTA MARIA D'ANGLONA
Rotondella
Nova Siri
Rocca Imperiale
Oriolo
Montegiordano Marina
Amendolara
Albidona
Marina di Amendolara
Trebisacce
Cassano allo Iónio
Sibari
Corigliano Cálabro
Rossano
San Demétrio Corone
MONASTERO DI SANTA MARIA DEL PATIRE
C. Trionto
Crosia
Cariati
Mandatoríccio
Cropalati
Longobucco
Bocchigliero
Campana
Crúcoli
Cirò
Cirò Marina
Pta. Fiume Nicá
Pta. Alice
Umbriático
San Nicola dell'Alto
Stróngoli
Savelli
San Giovanni in Fiore
Sila Greca
Sila Grande
Camigliatello Silano
Spezzano della Sila
Botte Donato 1928
Lorica
Aprigliano
Cosenza
Rende
Carolei
Páola
San Lúcido
SAN FRANCESCO DI PÁOLA
Fuscaldo
Marina di Acquappesa
Cetraro
Sangineto Lido
Belvedere Maríttimo
Diamante
Cirella
Buonvicino
Verbicaro
Orsomarso
Santa Doménica Talao
Scalea
Capo Scalea
Práia a Mare
Papasídero
Tórtora
Maratea
Sapri
Lagonegro
Rivello
Lauria
Castelluccio Inferiore
Rotonda
Mormanno
Morano Cálabro
Castrovillari
Mte. Pollino 2248
Pollino
Viggianello
San Severino Lucano
Francavilla in Sinni
Latrónico
Episcopia
Chiaromonte
Senise
Noépoli
Terranova di Pollino
San Lorenzo Bellizzi
Cerchiara di Calábria
Lungro
Firmo
Altomonte
Spezzano Albanese
Terranova
Tarsia di Sibari
San Sosti
Roggiano Gravina
Sant'Ágata di Ésaro
Fagnano Castello
San Marco Argentano
Bisignano
Acri
Luzzi
ABBAZIA DI SAMBUCINA
Rose
Montalto Uffugo
Rota Greca
San Fili
Torremezzo di Falconara
Fiumefreddo Brúzio
Czo.d. Pellegrino 1987
Pso d. Scalone 740
Castelsaraceno
Mte. Sirino 2005
Moliterno
Spinoso
GRUMENTUM ANTICA
San Arcángelo
SAN FRANCESCO
San Chírico Raparo
Roccanova
Colobraro
L. di Monte Cotugno
Missanello
Montemurro
Viggiano
Montesano sulla Marcellana
Padula
CERTOSA DI SAN LORENZO
Sella Cessuta 1040
Casalbuono
Buonabitácolo
Sanza
Rofrano
Montano Antilia
Torre Orsáia
San Giovanni a Piro
Camerota
Mte. Bulgheria 1225
Foria
Pisciotta
Palinuro
C. Palinuro
VELIA
Ceraso
M. Sacro o Gelbison 1705
Vallo della Lucánia
Vallo di Diano
Mte. Cervati 1898
Laurino
Cilento e
Teggiano
Sella d. Corticato 1026
Felitto
Roccadáspide
Corleto Monforte
Controne
San Rufo
Sala Consilina
Polla
Brienza
Mársico Nuovo
M. Volturino 1836
Calvello
Laurenzana
Anzi
Accettura
Corleto Perticara
Cirigliano
Stigliano
San Máuro Forte
Salandra
Ferrandina
Craco
Appennino Lucano
E45
A3
E90
E847
E844
E846
207
172
173

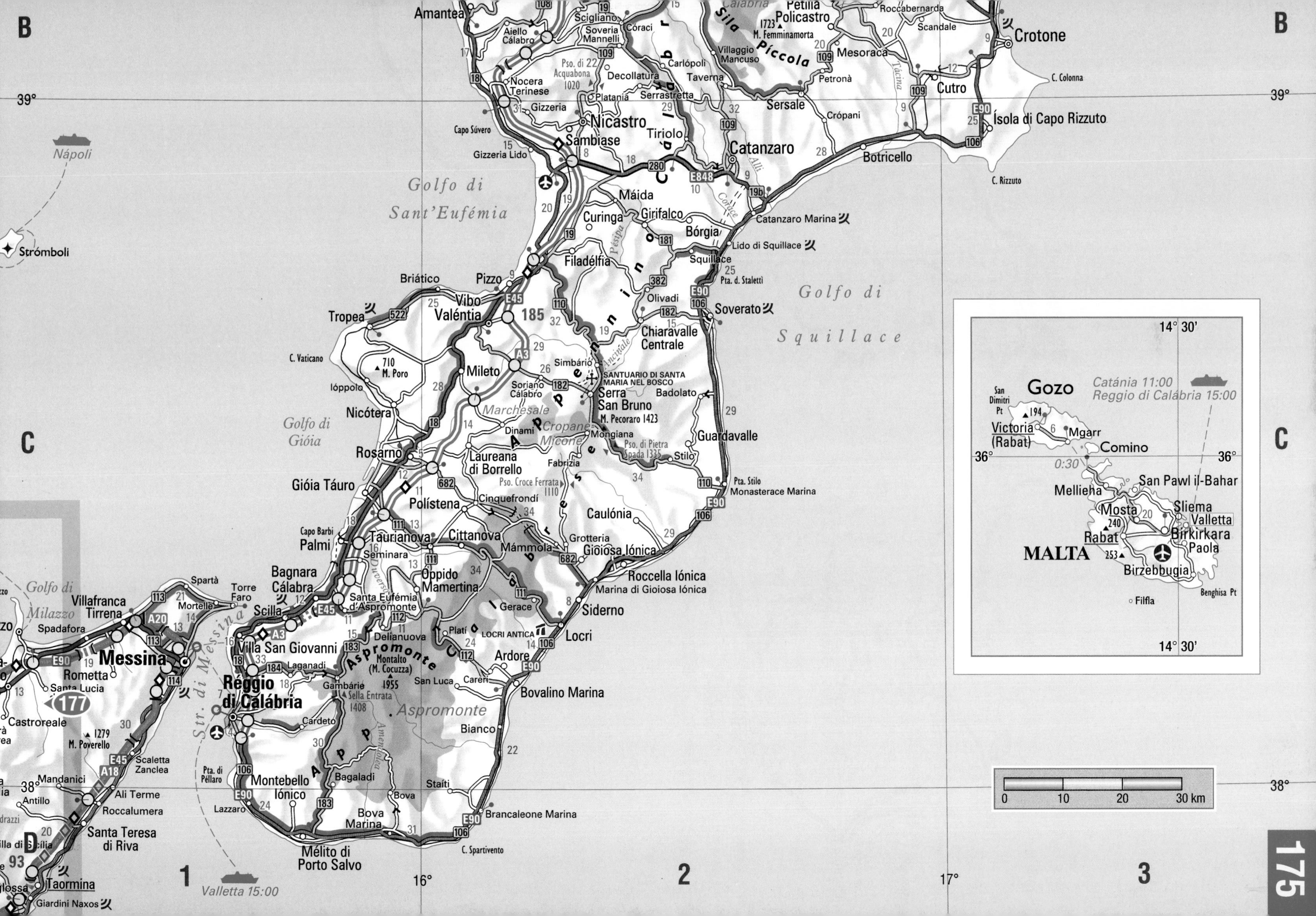

B

39°

C

38°

Catánia 11:00
Reggio di Calábria 15:00

14° 30'

36°

Gozo

14° 30'

San
Dimitri
Pt

Victoria
(Rabat)

36°

Mgarr

194

6

0:30

Comino

San Pawl il-Bahar

Mellieha

Mosta

Sliema

Valletta

Birkirkara

Rabat

Paola

Benghia Pt

Birzebbugia

240

253

Filfla

MALTA

17°

30 km

20

10

0

2

3

C. Colonna

Crotone

Isola di Capo Rizzuto

C. Rizzuto

9

E90

106

25

106

Scandale

Roccabernarda

Mesoraca

Cutro

109

Petilia
Policastro

1723

20

M. Femminamorta

20

Tácina

109

Botricello

Petronà

9

Cropani

28

Sersale

Villaggio
Mancuso

Sila
Piccola

Carlópoli

Taverna

32

Catanzaro Marina

Catanzaro

9

Alli

109

Golfo di

Squillace

Golfo di
Squillace

Córace

E848

10

Girifalco

Bórgia

Squillace

Pta. di Staletti

Lido di Squillace

25

E90

106

Soverato

Guardavalle

Pta. Stilo

Monasterace Marina

Amantea

108

Aiello
Cálabro

17

Nocera
Terinese

Pso. di
Acquabona
1020

Gizzeria

Gizzeria Lido

15

Capo Suvero

Golfo di

Sant'Eufémia

Golfo di
Sant'Eufémia

Pizzo

9

Vibo
Valéntia

25

Briático

C. Vaticano

Tropea

Ióppolo

M. Poro
710

522

28

Nicótera

Rosarno

Golfo di
Gióia

Golfo di
Gióia

Gióia Táuro

Capo Barbi

Palmi

Bagnara
Cálabra

Torre
Faro

Spartà

Sparta

Mortelle

Scilla

21

14

13

Villa San Giovanni

Laganadi

A3

18

33

184

18

Reggio di Calábria

Pta. di Pellaro

Lazzaro

Villafranca
Tirrena

Rometta

Spadafora

19

Santa Lucia

M. Poverello
1279

Castroreale

M. Mandanici

Antillo

20

Messina

Ali Terme

Roccalumera

Santa Teresa
di Riva

Scaletta
Zanclea

Giardini Naxos

Taormina

93

Nápoli

Strómboli

B

C

D

1

Valletta 15:00

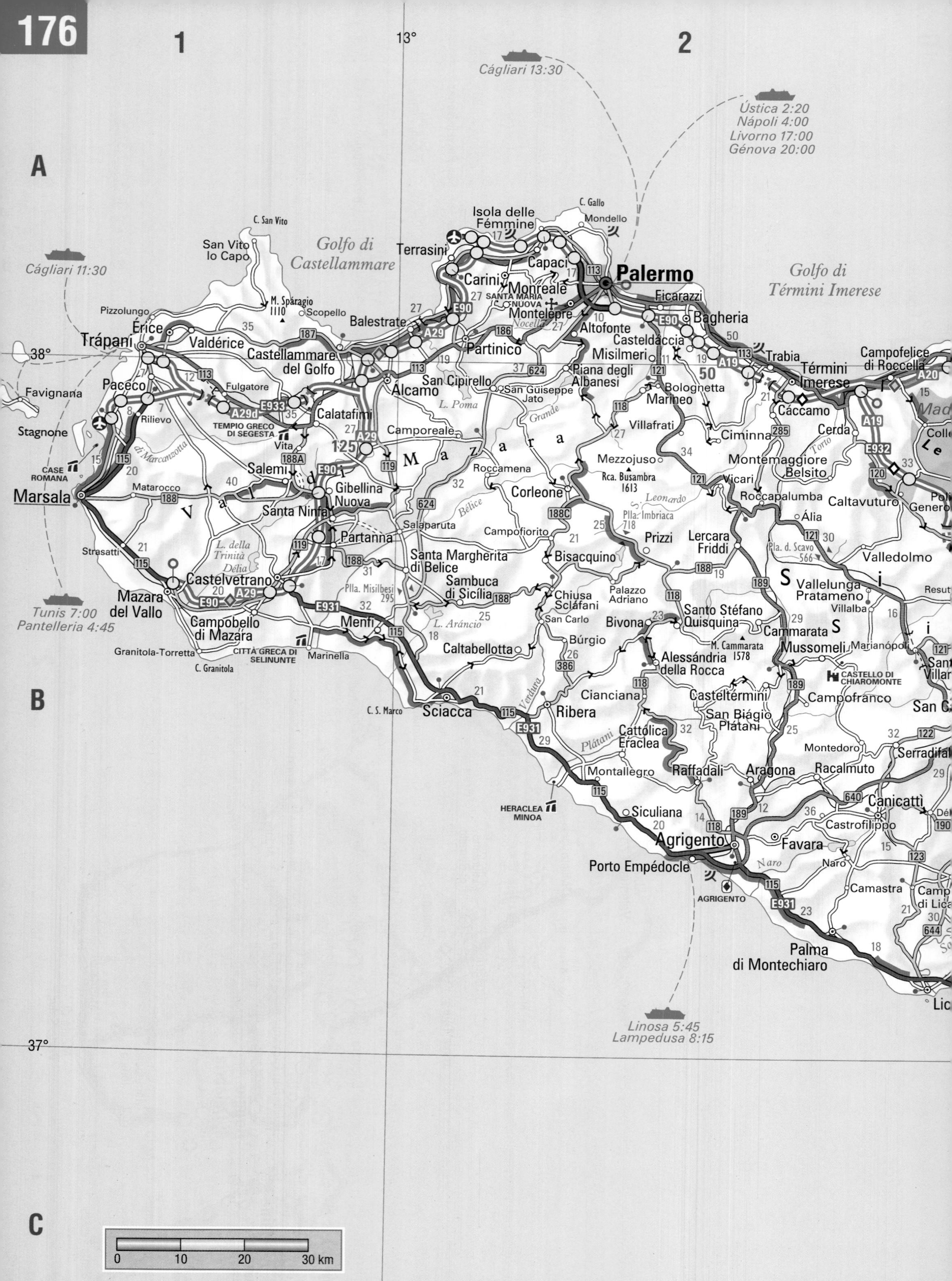
1
13°
2
Cágliari 13:30
Ústica 2:20
Nápoli 4:00
Livorno 17:00
Génova 20:00
A
C. Gallo
Isola delle Fémmine
Mondello
C. San Vito
San Vito lo Capo
Golfo di Castellammare
Terrasini
Capaci
Palermo
Golfo di Términi Imerese
Cágliari 11:30
Carini
Monreale
M. Spáragio 1110
Scopello
Santa Maria Nuova
Montelepre
Ficarazzi
Bagheria
Pizzolungo
Érice
Balestrate
Altofonte
Casteldáccia
Trápani
Valdérice
Partinico
Misilmeri
Trabia
Campofelice di Roccella
38°
Castellammare del Golfo
Piana degli Albanesi
Términi Imerese
Favignana
Paceco
Fulgatore
Álcamo
San Cipirello
San Giuseppe Jato
Bolognetta
Marineo
Cáccamo
Rilievo
Calatafimi
L. Poma
Stagnone
Tempio Greco di Segesta
Vita
Camporeale
Villafrati
Cerda
Ciminna
Case Romana
Salemi
Mazara
Mezzojuso
Montemaggiore Belsito
Roccamena
Rca. Busambra 1613
Marsala
Matarocco
Gibellina Nuova
Corleone
Vicari
Roccapalumba
Caltavuturo
Santa Ninfa
Plla. Imbriaca 718
Ália
Salaparuta
Campofiorito
Prizzi
Lercara Friddi
Strasatti
L. della Trinità Délia
Partanna
Santa Margherita di Belice
Bisacquino
Pla. d. Scavo 566
Valledolmo
Castelvetrano
Sambuca di Sicília
Chiusa Sclafani
Palazzo Adriano
Vallelunga Pratameno
Mazara del Vallo
Pllа. Misilbesi 295
Villalba
Tunis 7:00
Pantelleria 4:45
Campobello di Mazara
Menfi
L. Aráncio
San Carlo
Bivona
Santo Stéfano Quisquina
Cammarata
Granitola-Torretta
C. Granitola
Città Greca di Selinunte
Marinella
Caltabellotta
Búrgio
M. Cammarata 1578
Mussomeli
Marianópoli
Alessándria della Rocca
Castello di Chiaromonte
B
C. S. Marco
Sciacca
Ribera
Cianciana
Casteltérmini
Campofranco
San Biágio Plátani
Plátani
Cattólica Eraclea
Montedoro
Serradifal
Montallegro
Raffadali
Aragona
Racalmuto
Canicattì
Heraclea Minoa
Siculiana
Castrofilippo
Agrigento
Favara
Porto Empédocle
Naro
Camastra
Palma di Montechiaro
Linosa 5:45
Lampedusa 8:15
37°
C
0
10
20
30 km
1
13°
2

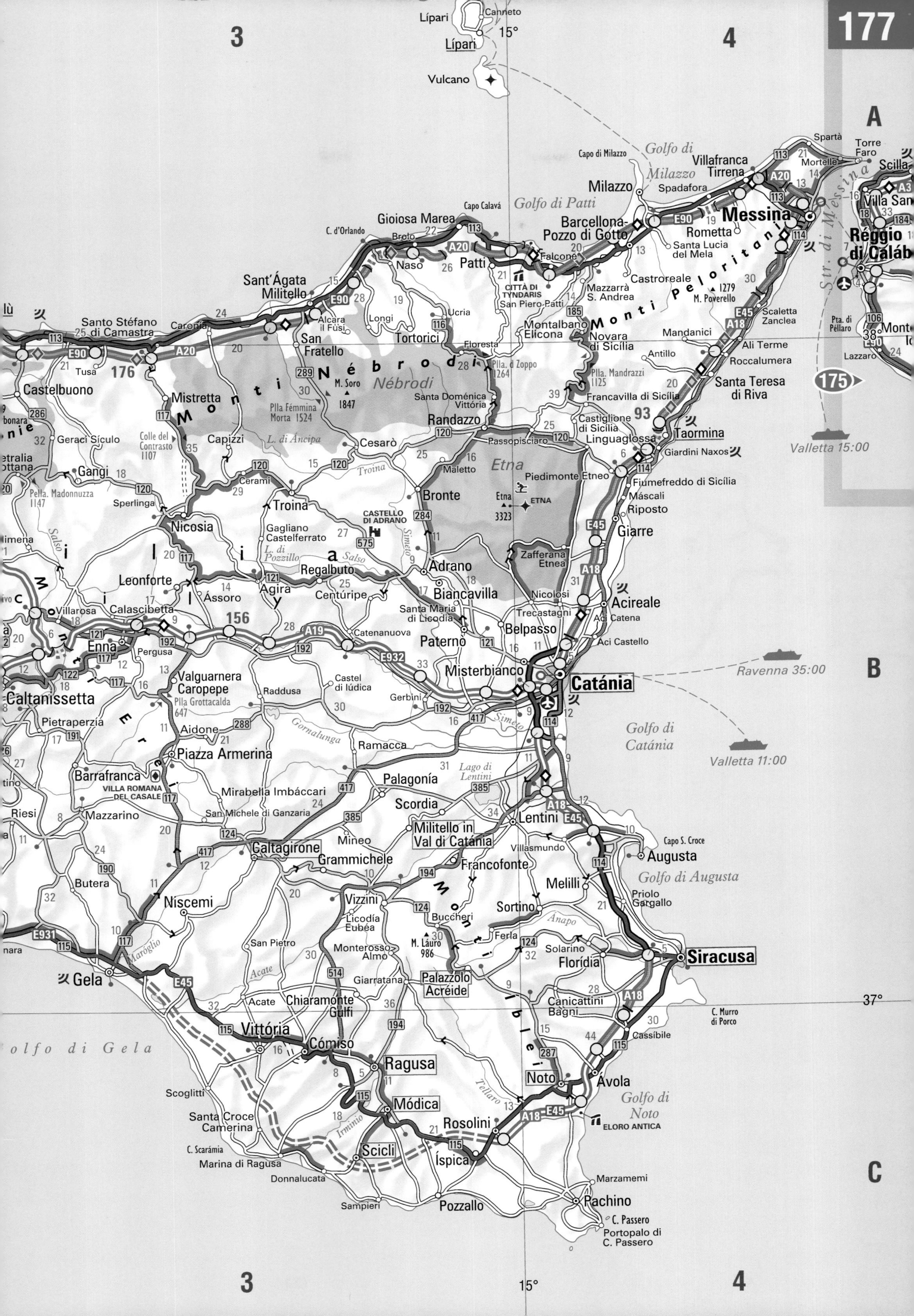

A   B

1   4

Génova
Porto-Vécchio
180

Civitavécchia 3:30
Génova 10:00
Livorno 10:00
Civitavécchia 4:00
Arbatax

Génova
Livorno 9:00
La Spézia 5:30

Bonifácio
C. Pertusato
île. de Cavallo
Bouches de Bonifácio

Museo Nazionale del Compendio Garibaldino di Caprera
Maddalena della Maddalena
Arcipélago
Caprera
Costa Smeralda

Santa Teresa Gallura
C. Testa
la Maddalena
Palau
Pto. Cervo
Porto Cervo
C. Ferro
San Pantaleo
Arzachena
San Pietro
Golfo Aranci
C. Figari
G. di Ólbia
Ólbia

Asinara
La Reale
Pta. Capara
Stintino
Fornelli
C. del Falcone
Asinara

Marseille 14:15
Toulon 9:30
180

Propriano 3:30
Génova 10:00

Golfo dell'Asinara

Pozzo San Nicola
Argentiera
C. dell'Argentiera
Palmádula
Santa Maria la Palma
M. Forte 464
Tramariglio
Grotta di Nettuno
Capo Cáccia
Alghero

Castelsardo
Valledória
Sédini
Castello di Casteldória
Perfugas
Martis
Chiaramonti

Porto Tórres
Platamona Lido
Sorso
Sénnori
Ósilo
Nulvi
Sássari
Ossi
Usini
Codrongianos
Olmedo
Ittiri
Villanova Monteleone
M. Minerva 644

Luogosanto
Sant'Antonio-di-Gallura
Calangiánus
Tempio Pausánia
M. Limbara 1359
Berchidda
Óschiri

Agius
Trinità d'Agultu
Valledória
la Tariante 676
Luras
Aggentu
Coghinas
L. del Coghinas

Tula
Ozieri
Pattada
Foresta di Búrgos
M. Rasu 1259
Bono
Orotelli
Bottidda
Ottana

Monti di Alà
Bitti
Buddusò
Nule
Osidda
Orune

Ploaghe
Ardara
Bonnánaro
Thiesi
Bonórva
Torralba
Mores
Ittireddu
Bonnánaro
Pozzomaggiore
Romana
Padria
Pádria

Budoni
Tanaunella
Posada
La Caletta
Siniscóla
C. Comino
C. Coda Cavallo
Tavolara
Molara
Straulas
Torpè
Posada
Monte Albo
Monti Remule

Lode
Lula
Orune
Núoro
Oliena
Orgósolo
Galtelli
Irgoli
Dorgali
Orosei
C. Cómino
Cala Gonone
Grotta di Bue Marino
Golfo di Orosei
Golfo Orosei e del Gennargentu
Urzulei
Flumineddu
Mamoiada
Orani
Gavoi
Fonni
Ovodda
Olzai
Ottana
Sárdara
Silanus
Bolótana
Sédilo
Ghilarza
Borore
Dualchi
Lei
L. Omodeo
Macomer
Sindia
Suni
Santu Lussurgiu
M. Urtigu 1050
Bonárcado
Cúglieri
Tresnuraghes
Bosa
Montresta
Temo
Capo Marargiu
Santa Caterina di Pittinuri
Nuraghe Losa
132
118

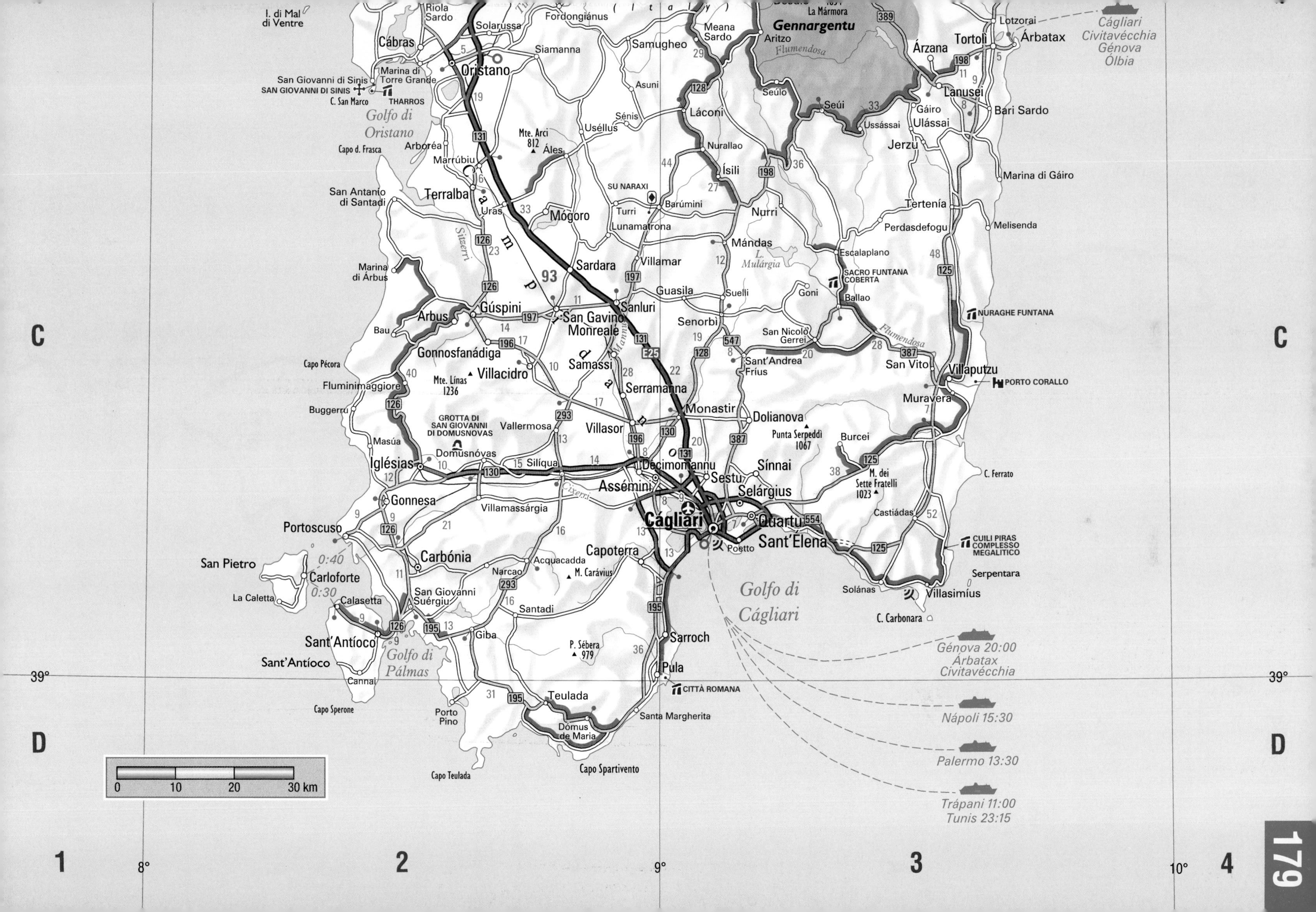

C 4 10° D

39° 39°

Cagliari

Golfo di Cágliari

Génova 20:00
Arbatax
Civitavécchia

Nápoli 15:30

Palermo 13:30

Trápani 11:00
Tunis 23:15

Lotzorai
Árbatax
Tortolì
Árzana
Lanusei
Bari Sardo
Marina di Gáiro
Melisenda
NURAGHE FUNTANA
PORTO CORALLO
Villaputzu
Muravera
C. Ferrato
CUILI PIRAS
COMPLESSO MEGALITICO
Serpentara
Villasimius
C. Carbonara
Solánas
Castíadas
M. dei Sette Fratelli 1023
Burcei
Sant'Elena
Quartu 554
Pirri
Poetto
Selárgius
Sinnai
Sestu
CITTÀ ROMANA
Sarroch
Pula
Santa Margherita
Capo Spartivento
Teulada
Dómus de Maria
P. Sébera 919
M. Carávius
Capoterra
Santadi
Giba
Narcao
293
Villamassárgia
Villaperúccio
Carbónia
San Giovanni Suérgiu
Giba
Porto Pino
Golfo di Pálmas
Calasetta
Camai
Sant'Antíoco
Sant'Antíoco
Capo Sperone
La Caletta
San Pietro
Carloforte
Portoscuso
Gonnesa
Iglésias
Masúa
Buggerru
Fluminimaggiore
Capo Pécora
Marina di Arbus
Bau
San António di Santadi
Arboréa
Terralba
Gonnosfanádiga
Arbus
Mte. Linas 1236
GROTTA DI SAN GIOVANNI DI DOMUSNÓVAS
Domusnóvas
Siliqua
Vallermosa
Villacidro
Gúspini
Uras
Marrúbiu
Mógoro
Ales
Mte. Arci 812
Sardara
Sanluri
San Gavino Monreale
Samassi
Serramanna
Villasor
Decimomannu
Assémini
Uta
Monastir
Ussana
Dolianova
Sant'Andrea Frius
San Nicolò Gerrei
Ballao
Goni
San Vito
Tertenia
Perdasdefogu
SACRO FUNTANA COBERTA
Escalaplano
Nurri
Mándas
Suelli
Guasila
Senorbì
Barúmini
SU NARAXI
Láconi
Isili
Nurallao
Gáiro
Ulássai
Ussássai
Seùi
Seùlo
Aritzo
Gennargentu
La Mármora
Meana Sardo
Samugheo
Asuni
Sénis
Uséllus
Fordongiánus
Siamanna
Solarussa
Oristano
Cábras
Riola Sardo
Marina di Torre Grande
THARROS
San Giovanni di Sinis
SAN GIOVANNI DI SINIS
C. San Marco
Capo d. Frasca
I. di Mal di Ventre
Golfo di Oristano
Sitzerri
Turri
Lunamatrona
Villamar
Villanovaforru
Gesturi

Meana Sardo

Golfo di Cágliari

0 10 20 30 km

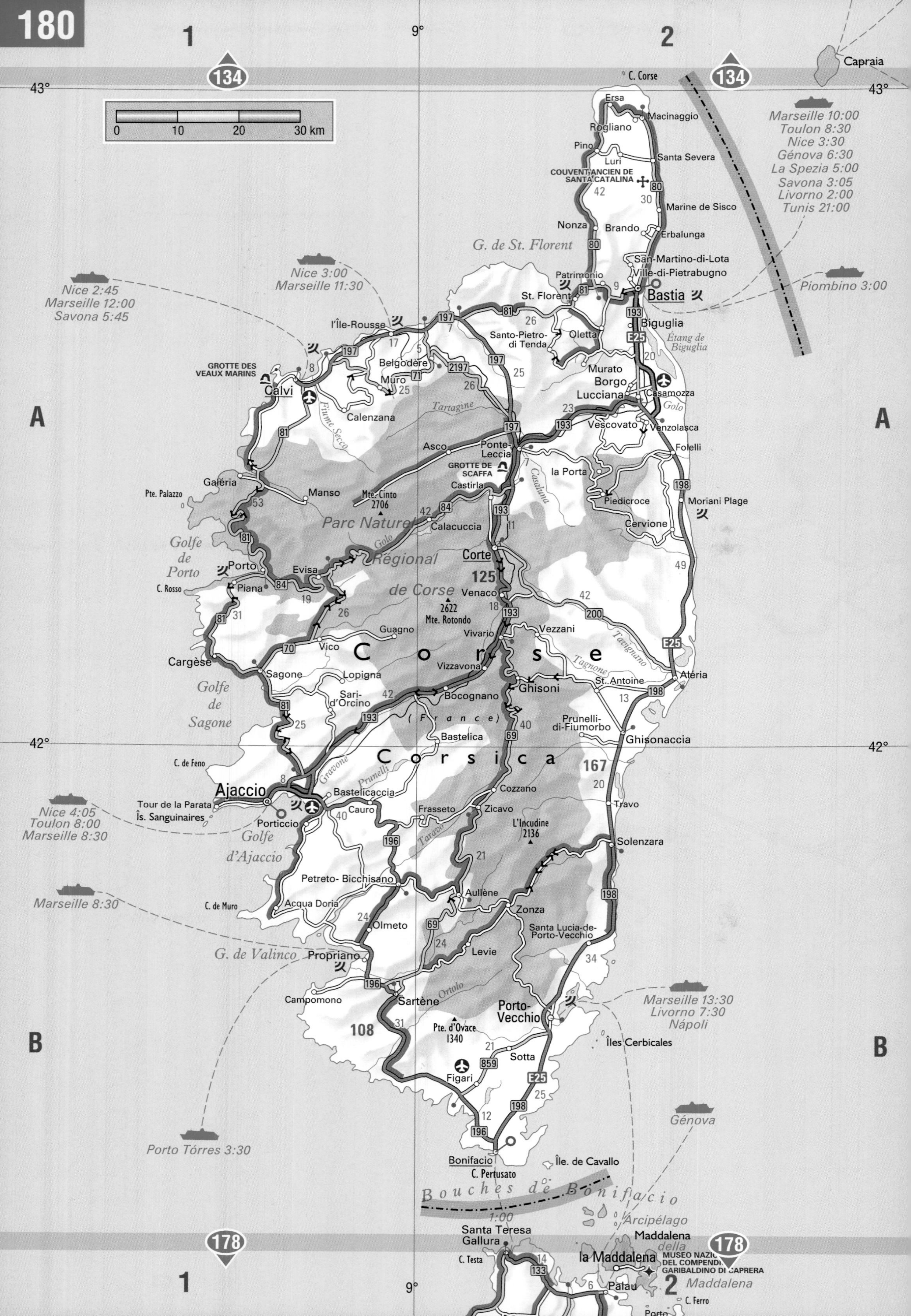
Corse
Corsica
(France)
Parc Naturel Régional de Corse
Bastia
Ajaccio
Corte
Calvi
Porto-Vecchio
Bonifacio
Sartène
Propriano
Bouches de Bonifacio
G. de St. Florent
Golfe de Porto
Golfe de Sagone
Golfe d'Ajaccio
G. de Valinco
Marseille 10:00
Toulon 8:30
Nice 3:30
Génova 6:30
La Spezia 5:00
Savona 3:05
Livorno 2:00
Tunis 21:00
Piombino 3:00
Nice 2:45
Marseille 12:00
Savona 5:45
Nice 3:00
Marseille 11:30
Nice 4:05
Toulon 8:00
Marseille 8:30
Marseille 8:30
Porto Tórres 3:30
Marseille 13:30
Livorno 7:30
Nápoli
Génova
Capraia
Mte. Cinto 2706
Mte. Rotondo 2622
L'Incudine 2136
Pte. d'Ovace 1340
Arcipélago della Maddalena
la Maddalena
Santa Teresa Gallura
Palau
0 10 20 30 km

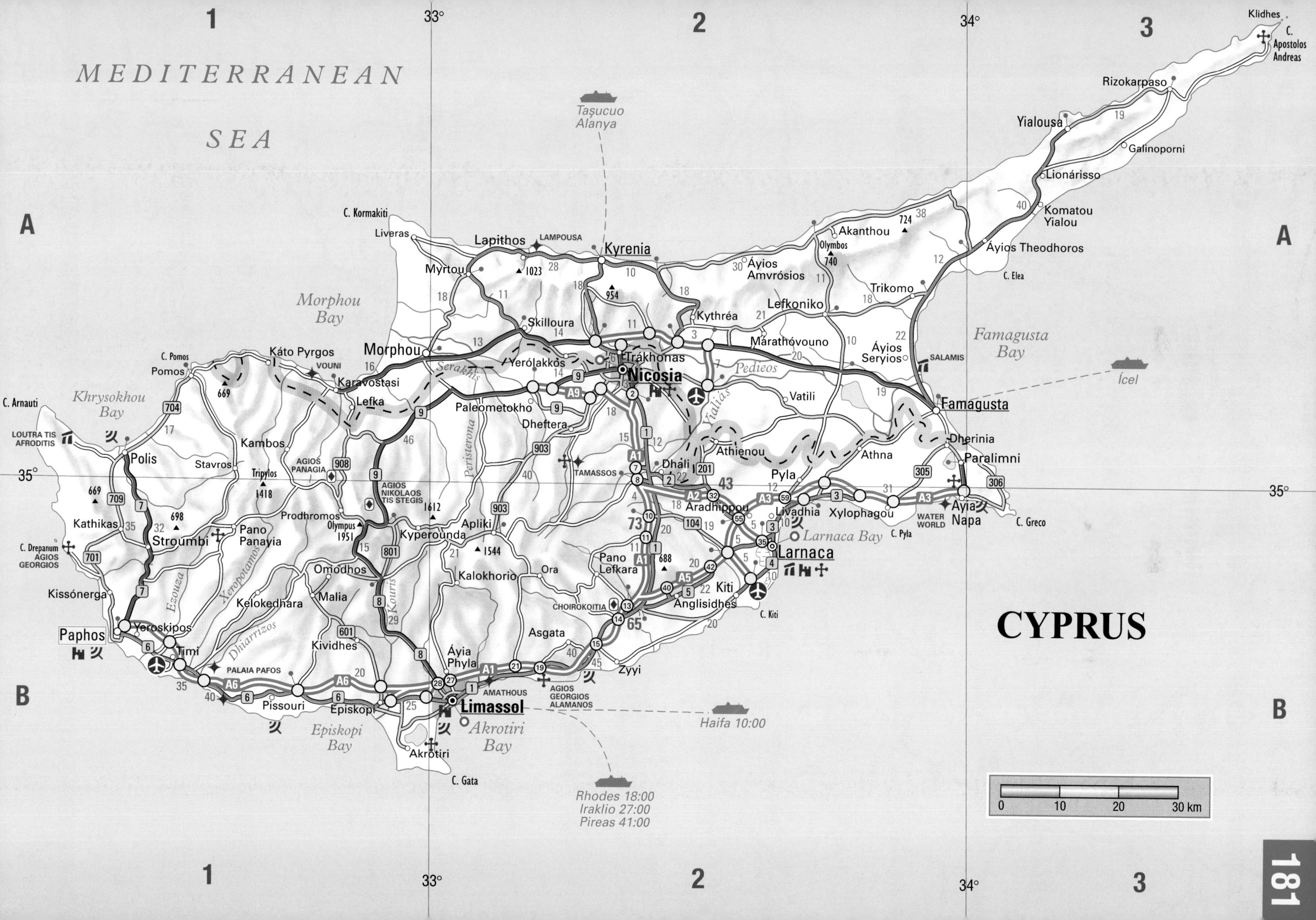
CYPRUS
MEDITERRANEAN
SEA
Morphou Bay
Khrysokhou Bay
Famagusta Bay
Larnaca Bay
Akrotiri Bay
Episkopi Bay
Kyrenia
Nicosia
Famagusta
Larnaca
Limassol
Paphos
Morphou
Lapithos
LAMPOUSA
Myrtou
Liveras
C. Kormakiti
Skilloura
Trakhonas
Yerólakkos
Paleometokho
Dheftera
Kythréa
Lefkoniko
Marathóvouno
Áyios Amvrósios
Akanthou
Olymbos
Trikomo
Áyios Seryios
SALAMIS
Vatili
Athienou
Athna
Dherinia
Paralimni
Ayia Napa
WATER WORLD
C. Greco
C. Pyla
Xylophagou
Livadhia
Pyla
Aradhippou
Dhali
TAMASSOS
Kiti
C. Kiti
Anglisidhes
Pano Lefkara
CHOIROKOITIA
Asgata
Zyyi
AGIOS GEORGIOS ALAMANOS
AMATHOUS
Áyia Phyla
Kalokhorio
Ora
Apliki
Kyperounda
AGIOS NIKOLAOS TIS STEGIS
Olympus
Prodhromos
Omodhos
Malia
Kivides
Kelokedhara
Pissouri
Episkopi
Akrotiri
C. Gata
PALAIA PAFOS
Timi
Yeroskipos
Kissónerga
C. Drepanum
AGIOS GEORGIOS
Kathikas
Stroumbi
Pano Panayia
Tripylos
Stavros
Kambos
AGIOS PANAGIA
Polis
LOUTRA TIS AFRODITIS
C. Arnauti
Pomos
C. Pomos
Káto Pyrgos
VOUNI
Karavostasi
Lefka
Rizokarpaso
Yialousa
Galinoporni
Lionárisso
Komatou Yialou
Áyios Theodhoros
C. Elea
Klidhes
C. Apostolos Andreas
Pedieos
Yialias
Serakhis
Peristerona
Kouris
Xeropotamos
Ezouza
Dhiarrizos
Taşucuo
Alanya
Içel
Haifa 10:00
Rhodes 18:00
Iraklio 27:00
Pireas 41:00
0
10
20
30 km
A
B
1
2
3
33°
34°
35°

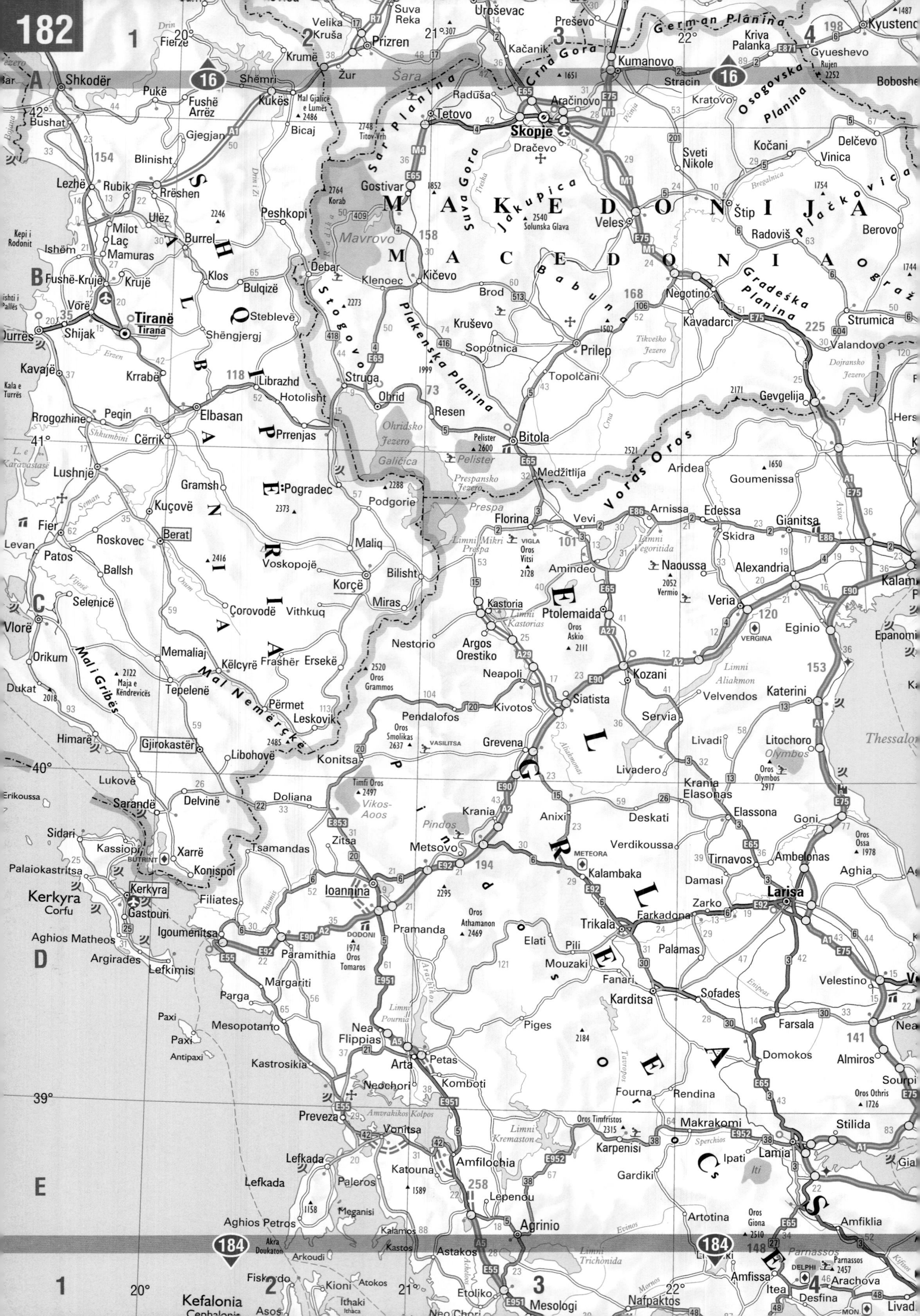

SHQIPËRIA
ALBANIA
MAKEDONIJA
MACEDONIA
ELLAS
GREECE
Shkodër
Pukë
Fushë Arrëz
Kukës
Shëmri
Mal Gjalicë e Lumës
Bushat
Gjegjan
Bicaj
Blinisht
Lezhë
Rubik
Rrëshen
Milot
Laç
Mamuras
Ulëz
Burrel
Peshkopi
Kepi i Rodonit
Ishëm
Fushë-Krujë
Krujë
Klos
Bulqizë
Vorë
Durrës
Shijak
Tiranë
Tirana
Steblevë
Shëngjergj
Kavajë
Kala e Turrës
Krrabë
Librazhd
Hotolisht
Rrogozhinë
Peqin
Elbasan
Prrenjas
Cërrik
Shkumbini
Lushnjë
Gramsh
Pogradec
Fier
Levan
Patos
Roskovec
Kuçovë
Berat
Ballsh
Vjosë
Osum
Selenicë
Vlorë
Çorovodë
Vithkuq
Orikum
Mali Gribës
Memaliaj
Këlcyrë
Frashër
Ersekë
Maja e Këndrevicës
Tepelenë
Mal Nemërçkë
Dukat
Përmet
Leskovik
Himarë
Gjirokastër
Libohovë
Lukovë
Erikoussa
Sarandë
Delvinë
Sidari
Kassiopi
Xarrë
Butrint
Konispol
Palaiokastritsa
Kerkyra
Corfu
Gastouri
Aghios Matheos
Argirades
Lefkimis
Drin
Fierzë
Velika Kruša
Suva Reka
Prizren
Krumë
Žur
Šara
Uroševac
Kačanik
Preševo
Crna Gora
Kumanovo
German Planina
Kriva Palanka
Gyueshevo
Kyustendil
Rujen
Stracin
Boboshevo
Osogovska Planina
Kratovo
Šar Planina
Raduša
Tetovo
Titov Vrh
Aračinovo
Skopje
Dračevo
Suva Gora
Jakupica
Solunska Glava
Treska
Pčinja
Sveti Nikole
Kočani
Delčevo
Vinica
Bregalnica
Gostivar
Korab
Mavrovo
Radika
Veles
Štip
Plačkovica
Radoviš
Berovo
Debar
Kičevo
Klenoec
Stogovo
Plakenska Planina
Babuna
Negotino
Kavadarci
Gradeška Planina
Ogražden
Strumica
Brod
Kruševo
Sopotnica
Prilep
Tikveško Jezero
Valandovo
Dojransko Jezero
Struga
Ohrid
Resen
Topolčani
Gevgelija
Ohridsko Jezero
Galičica
Pelister
Bitola
Voras Oros
Aridea
Goumenissa
Prespansko Jezero
Medžitlija
Podgorie
Prespa
Florina
Vevi
Arnissa
Edessa
Gianitsa
Axios
Skidra
Maliq
Bilisht
Voskopojë
Korçë
Miras
Limni Mikri Prespa
Vigla
Oros Vitsi
Limni Vegoritida
Amindeo
Naoussa
Vermio
Alexandria
Kastoria
Limni Kastorias
Ptolemaida
Veria
Vergina
Eginio
Epanomi
Kalamaria
Nestorio
Argos Orestiko
Oros Askio
Kozani
Limni Aliakmon
Neapoli
Siatista
Velvendos
Katerini
Oros Grammos
Pendalofos
Kivotos
Servia
Livadi
Litochoro
Thessaloniki
Oros Smolikas
Vasilitsa
Grevena
Olymbos
Oros Olymbos
Konitsa
Livadero
Krania Elassonas
Timfi Oros
Vikos-Aoos
Aliakmonas
Doliana
Deskati
Elassona
Goni
Kranja
Anixi
Oros Ossa
Pindos
Tsamandas
Zitsa
Metsovo
Verdikoussa
Tirnavos
Ambelonas
Meteora
Kalambaka
Aghia
Ioannina
Filiates
Damasi
Thiamis
Larisa
Zarko
Farkadona
Trikala
Igoumenitsa
Pramanda
Dodoni
Oros Athamanon
Elati
Pili
Palamas
Paramithia
Oros Tomaros
Mouzaki
Fanari
Velestino
Volos
Margariti
Karditsa
Sofades
Enipeas
Parga
Arachthos
Limni Pournia
Paxi
Antipaxi
Mesopotamo
Piges
Farsala
Nea Anchialos
Nea Flippias
Almiros
Domokos
Kastrosikia
Arta
Petas
Tavropos
Oros Othris
Sourpi
Neochori
Komboti
Fourna
Rendina
Preveza
Amvrakikos Kolpos
Vonitsa
Limni Kremaston
Oros Timfristos
Karpenisi
Makrakomi
Sperchios
Stilida
Lamia
Lefkada
Paleros
Katouna
Amfilochia
Gardiki
Ipati
Iti
Lepenou
Meganisi
Aghios Petros
Artotina
Oros Giona
Agrinio
Amfiklia
Kalamos
Kastos
Astakos
Evinos
Akra Doukaton
Arkoudi
Limni Trichonida
Parnassos
Delphi
Acheloos
Amfissa
Itea
Arachova
Fiskardo
Kioni
Atokos
Ithaki
Ithaca
Kefalonia
Cephalonia
Asos
Etoliko
Mesologi
Mornos
Nafpaktos
Desfina
Livadia
Kifisos
Neo Chori
Galaxidi

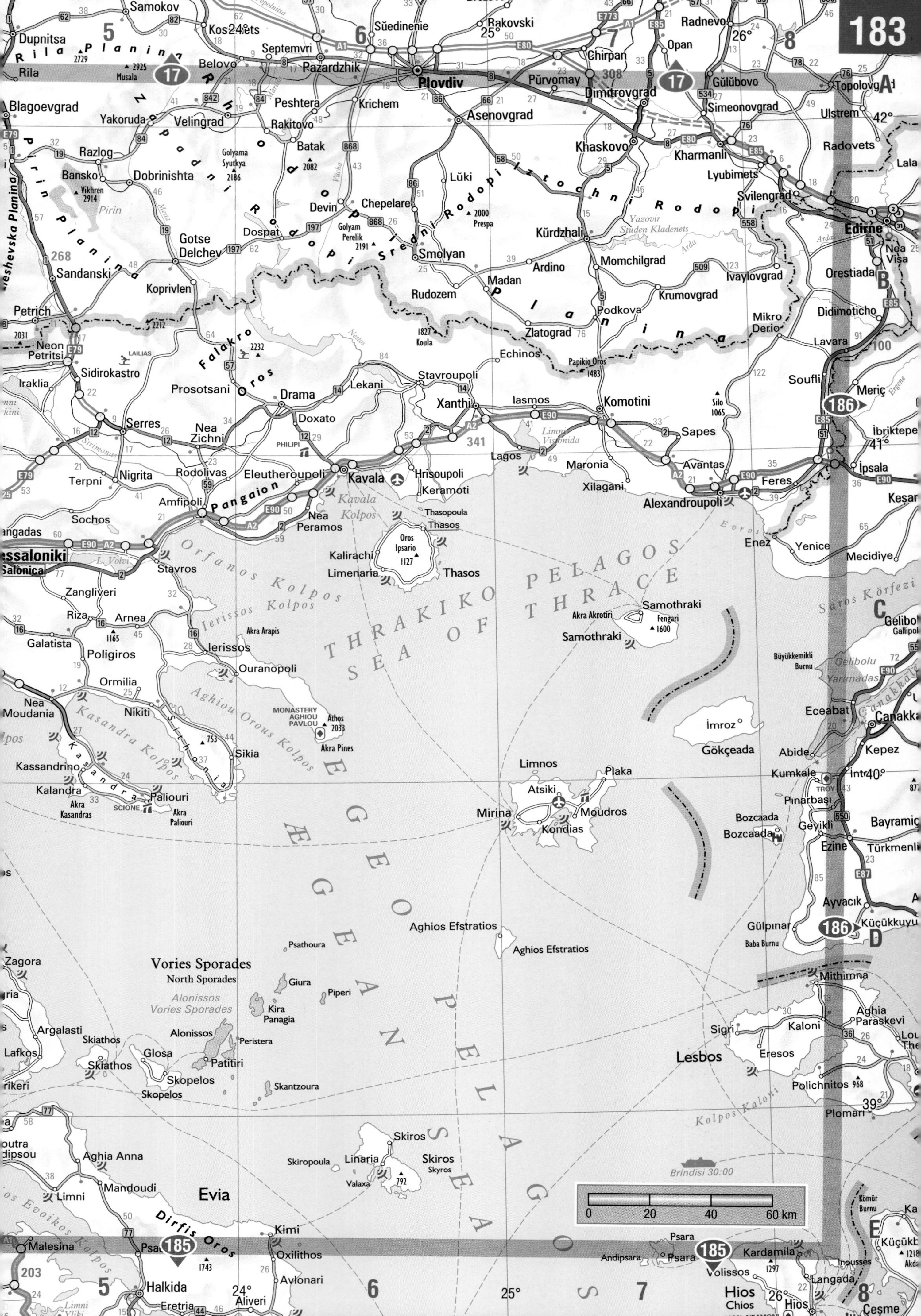
Samokov
Dupnitsa
Kostenets
Rila Planina
Rila
Musala
2925
Belovo
Septemvri
Pazardzhik
Sŭedinenie
Rakovski
Plovdiv
Radnevo
Opan
Chirpan
Pŭrvomay
Dimitrovgrad
Gŭlŭbovo
Topolovgrad
Simeonovgrad
Ulstrem
Blagoevgrad
Yakoruda
Velingrad
Peshtera
Krichem
Asenovgrad
Rakitovo
Batak
Khaskovo
Kharmanli
Radovets
Lala
Razlog
Bansko
Vikhren
2914
Dobrinishta
Golyama Syutkya
2186
Zapadni Rodopi
Rhodope
Pirin
Pirin Planina
Lŭki
Lyubimets
Svilengrad
Devin
Chepelare
Golyam Perelik
2191
Iztochni Rodopi
Sredni Rodopi
2000
Prespa
Gotse Delchev
Dospat
Smolyan
Kŭrdzhali
Yazovir Studen Kladenets
Arda
Edirne
Nea Visa
Sandanski
Koprivlen
Ardino
Momchilgrad
Ivaylovgrad
Orestiada
Madan
Rudozem
Krumovgrad
Podkova
Planina
Didimoticho
Mikro Derio
Petrich
Zlatograd
Neon Petritsi
Falakro Oros
2232
1827
Koula
Echinos
Papikio Oros
1483
Lavara
Sidirokastro
Iraklia
Prosotsani
Drama
Lekani
Stavroupoli
Xanthi
Iasmos
Komotini
Silo
1065
Soufli
Meriç
Ergene
İbriktepe
Serres
Nea Zichni
Doxato
Philipi
Limni Vistonida
Sapes
Strimonas
Terpni
Nigrita
Rodolivas
Eleutheroupoli
Kavala
Hrisoupoli
Keramoti
Lagos
Maronia
Xilagani
Avantas
Feres
İpsala
Keşan
Amfipoli
Pangaion
Kavala Kolpos
Nea Peramos
Thasopoula
Thasos
Alexandroupoli
Sochos
Evros
Enez
Yenice
Mecidiye
Thessaloniki
Salonica
L. Volvi
Stavros
Oros Ipsario
1127
Kalirachi
Limenaria
Orfanos Kolpos
THRAKIKO PELAGOS
SEA OF THRACE
Zangliveri
Riza
Arnea
1165
Galatista
Poligiros
Ierissos Kolpos
Akra Arapis
Ierissos
Ouranopoli
Samothraki
Akra Akrotiri
Fengari
1600
Saros Körfezi
Gelibolu
Gallipoli
Büyükkemikli Burnu
Gelibolu Yarımadası
Ormilia
Nea Moudania
Nikiti
Sithonia
Aghiou Orous Kolpos
Monastery Aghiou Pavlou
Athos
2033
Akra Pines
Eceabat
Çanakkale
İmroz
Gökçeada
Kepez
Abide
Kasandra Kolpos
Kassandrino
Kasandra
753
Sikia
Limnos
Plaka
Kumkale
Troy
Kalandra
Akra Kasandras
Scione
Paliouri
Akra Paliouri
Atsiki
Mirina
Moudros
Kondias
Pınarbaşı
Bozcaada
Geyikli
Bayramiç
Ezine
Türkmenli
AEGEAN SEA
AIGAIO PELAGOS
Ayvacık
Küçükkuyu
Gülpınar
Baba Burnu
Aghios Efstratios
Psathoura
Vories Sporades
North Sporades
Alonissos Vories Sporades
Giura
Piperi
Kira Panagia
Mithimna
Zagora
Argalasti
Skiathos
Alonissos
Peristera
Glosa
Patitiri
Skopelos
Skantzoura
Sigri
Kaloni
Aghia Paraskevi
Lafkos
Eresos
Lesbos
Polichnitos
968
Plomari
Kolpos Kaloni
Loutra Edipsou
Aghia Anna
Skiros
Skiropoula
Linaria
Skyros
Valaxa
792
Brindisi 30:00
0
20
40
60 km
Mandoudi
Limni
Evia
Evoikos Kolpos
Dirfis Oros
Kimi
Oxilithos
1743
Malesina
Psachna
Halkida
Avlonari
Aliveri
Eretria
Limni Yliki
Psara
Andipsara
Kardamila
1297
Volissos
Inousses
Langada
Hios
Chios
Çeşme
Kömür Burnu
Küçükbahçe
Karaburun
24°
25°
26°
39°
40°
41°
42°
5
6
7
8
A
B
C
D
E
17
185
186

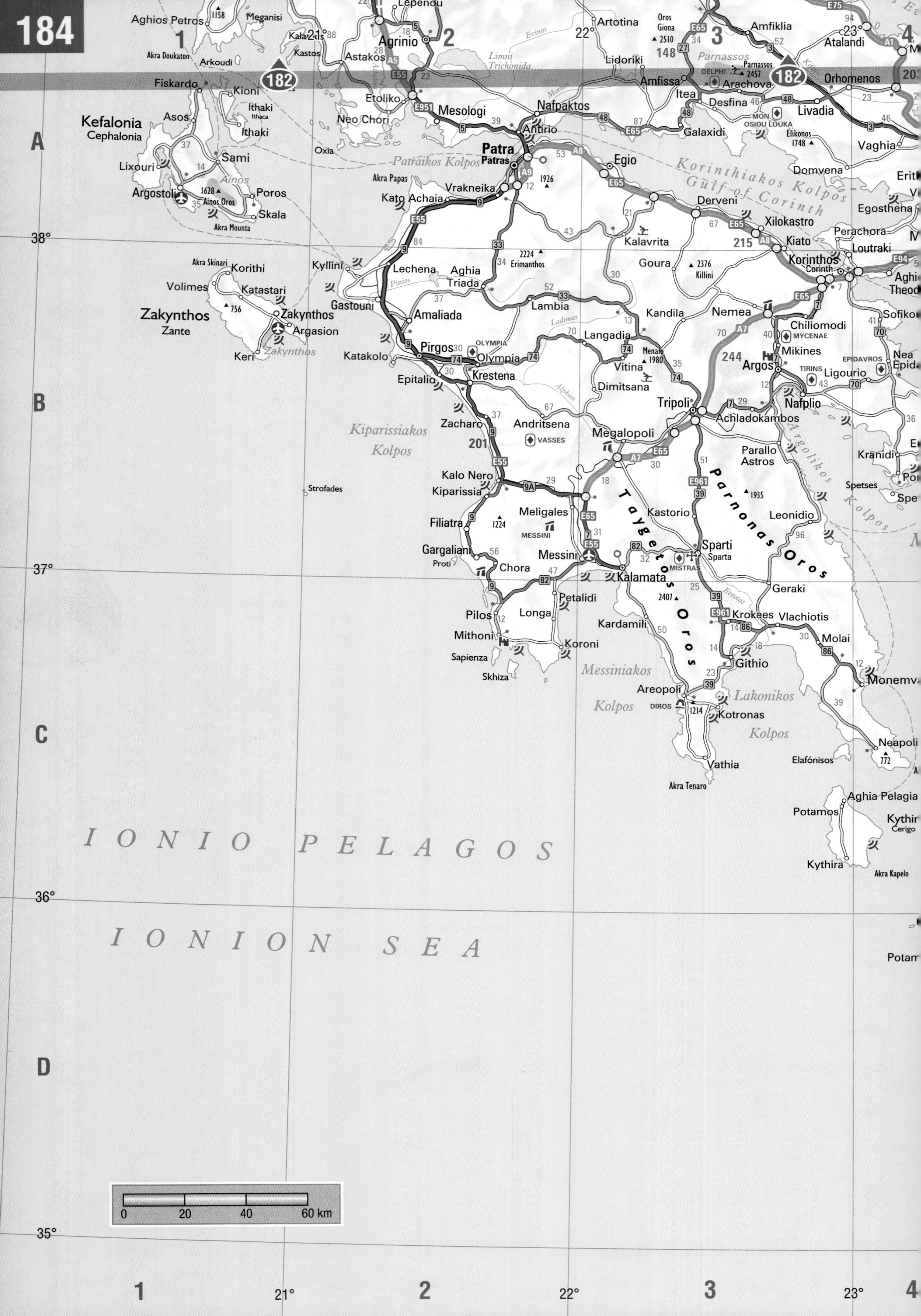
Aghios Petros
Meganisi
Akra Doukaton
Arkoudi
Kastos
Astakos
Agrinio
Lepenou
Artotina
Oros Giona
Amfiklia
Atalandi
Lidoriki
Parnassos
Delphi
Arachova
Orhomenos
Fiskardo
Kioni
Ithaki
Ithaca
Etoliko
Mesologi
Nafpaktos
Amfissa
Itea
Desfina
Livadia
Limni Trichonida
Kefalonia
Cephalonia
Asos
Neo Chori
Antirio
Galaxidi
Mon. Osiou Louka
Elikonos
Vaghia
Oxia
Patra
Patras
Sami
Lixouri
Patraikos Kolpos
Egio
Korinthiakos Kolpos
Gulf of Corinth
Domvena
Ainos
Akra Papas
Argostoli
Ainos Oros
Poros
Vrakneika
Kato Achaia
Derveni
Egosthena
Skala
Akra Mounta
Xilokastro
Perachora
Kalavrita
Kiato
Loutraki
Akra Skinari
Korithi
Kyllini
Lechena
Aghia Triada
Erimanthos
Goura
Killini
Korinthos
Corinth
Volimes
Katastari
Pinios
Gastouni
Lambia
Zakynthos
Zante
Amaliada
Kandila
Nemea
Sofiko
Argasion
Ladonas
Langadia
Chiliomodi
Mycenae
Keri
Katakolo
Pirgos
Olympia
Menalo
Mikines
Vitina
Argos
Tirins
Ligourio
Epidavros
Epitalio
Krestena
Dimitsana
Alphios
Tripoli
Nafplio
Zacharo
Andritsena
Achladokambos
Kiparissiakos Kolpos
Vasses
Megalopoli
Argolikos Kolpos
Parallo Astros
Kranidi
Kalo Nero
Kiparissia
Strofades
Spetses
Parnonas Oros
Taygetos Oros
Kastorio
Meligales
Messini
Leonidio
Filiatra
Gargaliani
Proti
Chora
Sparti
Sparta
Mistras
Kalamata
Geraki
Petalidi
Evrotas
Pilos
Longa
Kardamili
Krokees
Vlachiotis
Mithoni
Molai
Sapienza
Koroni
Githio
Skhiza
Messiniakos Kolpos
Monemvasia
Areopoli
Lakonikos Kolpos
Diros
Kotronas
Neapoli
Vathia
Elafonisos
Akra Tenaro
Aghia Pelagia
Potamos
Kythira
Cerigo
Akra Kapelo
IONIO PELAGOS
IONION SEA
0 20 40 60 km
38°
37°
36°
35°
21°
22°
23°
A
B
C
D
1
2
3
4

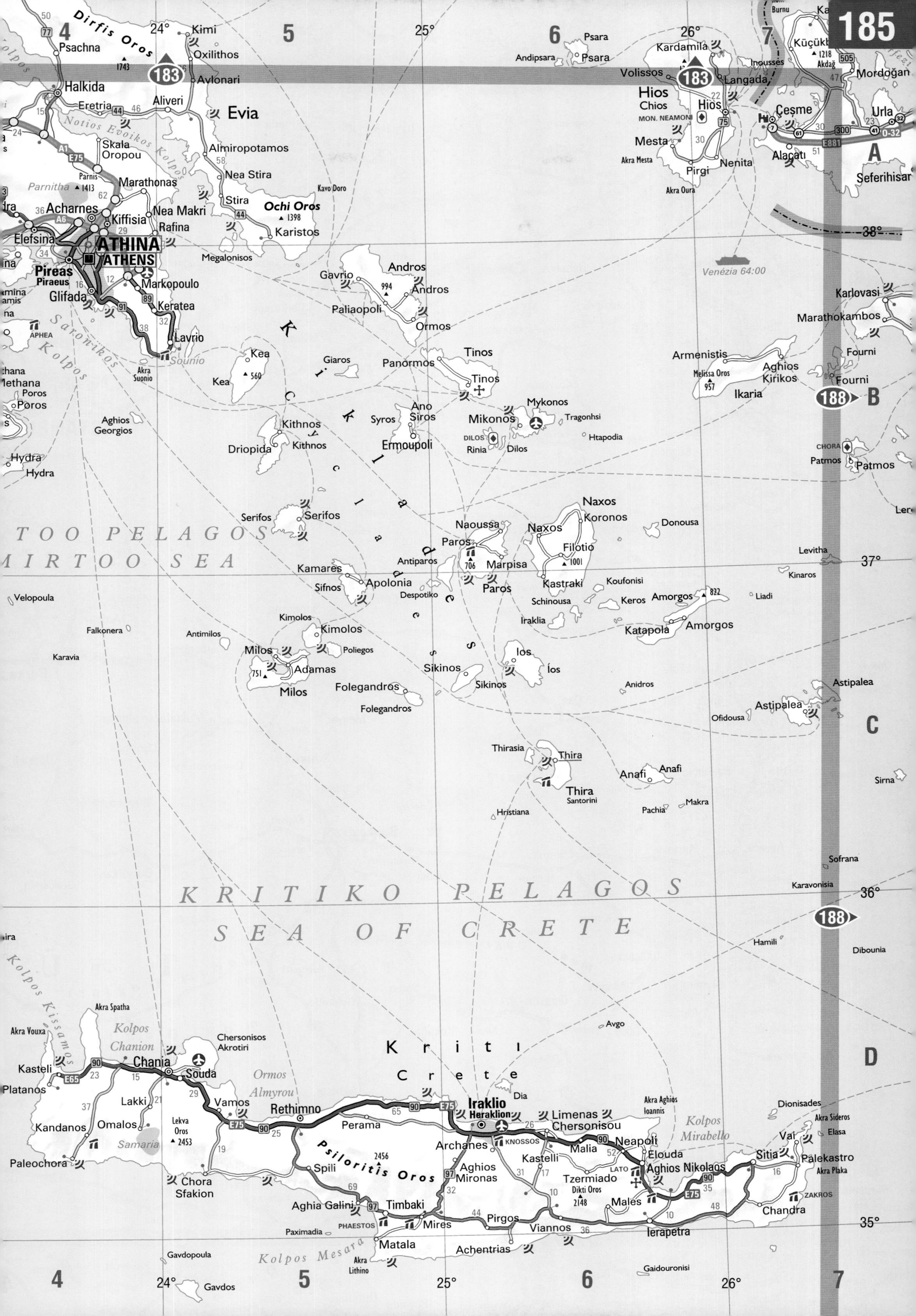
Dirfis Oros
Psachna
Kimi
Oxilithos
Avlonari
Halkida
Eretria
Aliveri
Evia
Notios Evoikos Kolpos
Skala Oropou
Almiropotamos
Nea Stira
Parnitha
Marathonas
Stira
Ochi Oros
Acharnes
Kiffisia
Nea Makri
Rafina
Karistos
Elefsina
ATHINA
ATHENS
Megalonisos
Pireas
Piraeus
Markopoulo
Glifada
Keratea
Saronikos Kolpos
Lavrio
Sounio
Akra Sounio
Kea
Poros
Aghios Georgios
Kithnos
Driopida
Hydra
Serifos
Kamares
Sifnos
Apolonia
Kimolos
Milos
Adamas
Antimilos
Falkonera
Karavia
Velopoula
MIRTOO PELAGOS
MIRTOO SEA
Andros
Gavrio
Paliaopoli
Ormos
Giaros
Panormos
Tinos
Syros
Ano Siros
Ermoupoli
Mikonos
Mykonos
Dilos
Rinia
Tragonhsi
Htapodia
Kiklades
Cyclades
Naoussa
Paros
Antiparos
Despotiko
Marpisa
Naxos
Koronos
Filotio
Kastraki
Donousa
Koufonisi
Schinousa
Keros
Iraklia
Amorgos
Katapola
Poliegos
Folegandros
Sikinos
Ios
Anidros
Thirasia
Thira
Santorini
Anafi
Pachia
Makra
Hristiana
Astipalea
Ofidousa
Levitha
Kinaros
Liadi
Psara
Andipsara
Kardamila
Volissos
Hios
Chios
MON. NEAMONI
Langada
Inousses
Mesta
Akra Mesta
Pirgi
Nenita
Akra Oura
Venézia 64:00
Burnu
Küçükbahçe
Akdağ
Mordoğan
Çeşme
Urla
Alaçatı
Seferihisar
Karlovasi
Marathokambos
Armenistis
Melissa Oros
Ikaria
Aghios Kirikos
Fourni
CHORA
Patmos
Sirna
Sofrana
Karavonisia
Hamili
Dibounia
KRITIKO PELAGOS
SEA OF CRETE
Kolpos Kissamos
Akra Spatha
Akra Vouxa
Kolpos Chanion
Chersonisos Akrotiri
Kasteli
Chania
Souda
Platanos
Vamos
Lakki
Rethimno
Ormos Almyrou
Kandanos
Omalos
Lekva Oros
Samaria
Paleochora
Chora Sfakion
Psiloritis Oros
Spili
Perama
Aghia Galini
Timbaki
Mires
PHAESTOS
Paximadia
Matala
Kolpos Mesara
Akra Lithino
Gavdopoula
Gavdos
Kriti
Crete
Dia
Iraklio
Heraklion
Archanes
Aghios Mironas
KNOSSOS
Limenas Chersonisou
Malia
Kastelli
Tzermiado
Dikti Oros
Pirgos
Achentrias
Viannos
Neapoli
Elounda
Aghios Nikolaos
LATO
Kolpos Mirabello
Akra Aghios Ioannis
Males
Ierapetra
Gaidouronisi
Sitia
Dionisades
Akra Sideros
Elasa
Vai
Palekastro
Akra Plaka
ZAKROS
Chandra
Avgo

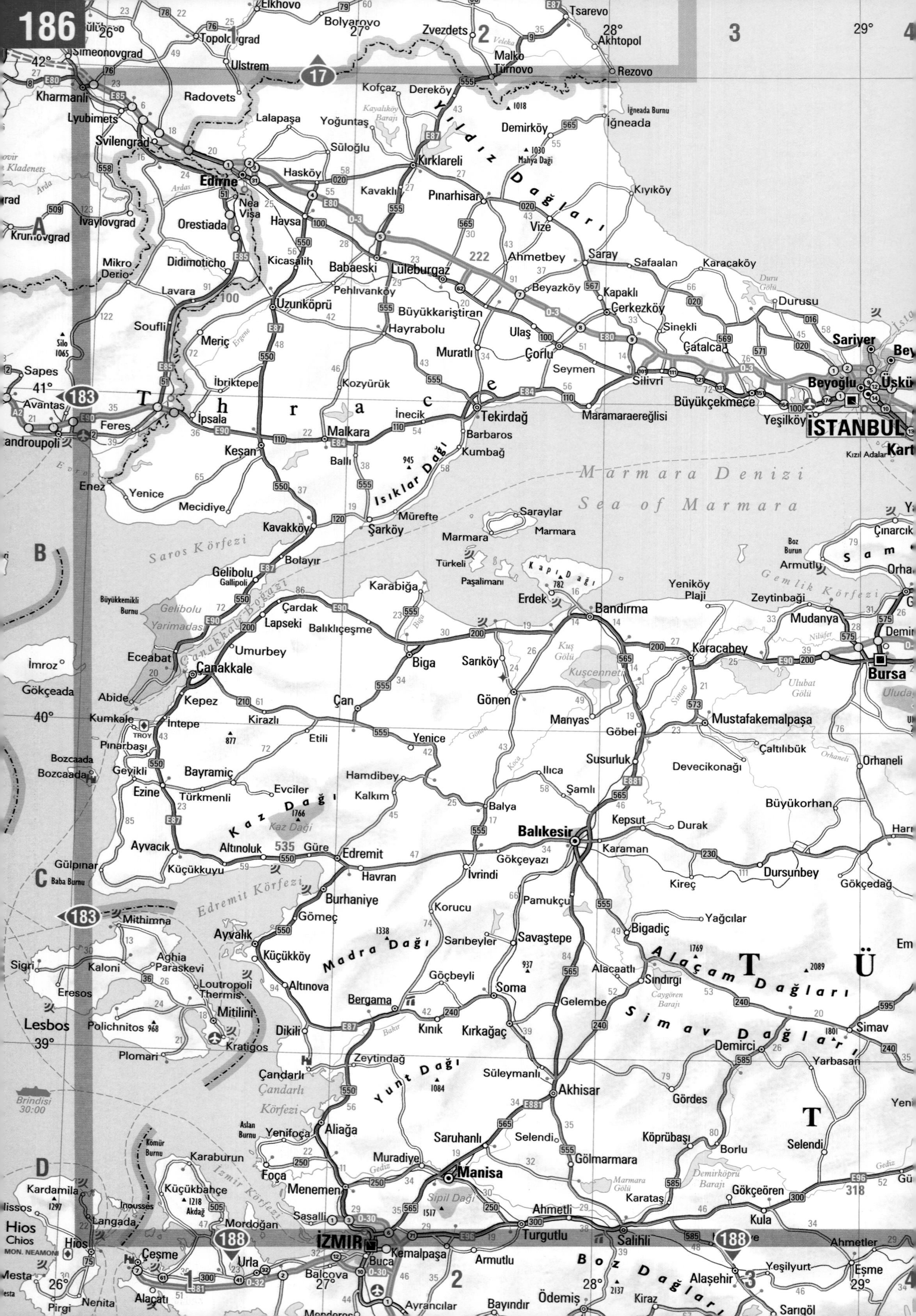

Elkhovo
Bolyarovo
Zvezdets
Tsarevo
Akhtopol
Malko Türnovo
Rezovo
Topolovgrad
Simeonovgrad
Ulstrem
Kharmanli
Radovets
Lyubimets
Svilengrad
Kofçaz
Dereköy
Lalapaşa
Yoğuntaş
Demirköy
İğneada
İğneada Burnu
Süloğlu
Kırklareli
Mahya Dağı
Edirne
Hasköy
Kavaklı
Pınarhisar
Kıyıköy
Nea Visa
Havsa
Orestiada
Ivaylovgrad
Krumovgrad
Vize
Yıldız Dağları
Mikro Derio
Didimoticho
Kicasalih
Babaeski
Lüleburgaz
Ahmetbey
Saray
Safaalan
Karacaköy
Lavara
Pehlivanköy
Beyazköy
Kapaklı
Uzunköprü
Büyükkarıştıran
Çerkezköy
Durusu
Soufli
Hayrabolu
Sinekli
Meriç
Ulaş
Çatalca
Sarıyer
Muratlı
Çorlu
Silo
Sapes
Kozyürük
Seymen
Silivri
Beyoğlu
İbriktepe
Büyükçekmece
Avantas
Thrace
İnecik
Tekirdağ
Maramaraereğlisi
Yeşilköy
İSTANBUL
İpsala
Feres
Malkara
Barbaros
Alexandroupoli
Keşan
Kumbağ
Kızıl Adalar
Ballı
Işıklar Dağı
Marmara Denizi
Sea of Marmara
Enez
Yenice
Mecidiye
Saraylar
Mürefte
Kavakköy
Şarköy
Marmara
Saros Körfezi
Bolayır
Türkeli
Kapı Dağı
Boz Burun
Armutlu
Gelibolu
Gallipoli
Paşalimanı
Karabiğa
Yeniköy Plaji
Gemlik Körfezi
Büyükkemikli Burnu
Gelibolu Yarimadası
Çardak
Lapseki
Balıklıçeşme
Erdek
Bandırma
Zeytinbaği
Mudanya
Çanakkale Boğazi
Umurbey
Karacabey
İmroz
Eceabat
Çanakkale
Biga
Sarıköy
Kuş Gölü
Kuşcenneti
Bursa
Gökçeada
Abide
Kepez
Çan
Gönen
Ulubat Gölü
Kumkale
TROY
İntepe
Kirazlı
Manyas
Mustafakemalpaşa
Pınarbaşı
Etili
Yenice
Göbel
Çaltılıbük
Bozcaada
Geyikli
Bayramiç
Hamdibey
Ilıca
Susurluk
Devecikonağı
Orhaneli
Ezine
Türkmenli
Evciler
Kalkım
Şamlı
Kaz Dağı
Balya
Büyükorhan
Kepsut
Durak
Ayvacık
Altınoluk
Güre
Edremit
Balıkesir
Karaman
Gülpınar
Küçükkuyu
Gökçeyazı
Baba Burnu
Havran
İvrindi
Dursunbey
Kireç
Gökçedağ
Edremit Körfezi
Burhaniye
Pamukçu
Korucu
Mithimna
Gömeç
Yağcılar
Ayvalık
Madra Dağı
Savaştepe
Sarıbeyler
Bigadiç
Aghia Paraskevi
Küçükköy
Sigri
Kaloni
Alaçam Dağları
Alacaatlı
Sındırgı
Eresos
Lesbos
Loutropoli Thermis
Mitilini
Altınova
Göçbeyli
Soma
Bergama
Gelembe
Caygören Barajı
Simav Dağları
Polichnitos
Kınık
Kırkağaç
Simav
Dikili
Kratigos
Demirci
Plomari
Zeytindağ
Yunt Dağı
Yarbasan
Çandarlı
Çandarlı Körfezi
Süleymanlı
Akhisar
Gördes
Brindisi 30:00
Aslan Burnu
Yenifoça
Aliağa
Saruhanlı
Selendi
Köprübaşı
Borlu
Kömür Burnu
Karaburun
İzmir Körfezi
Muradiye
Manisa
Gölmarmara
Demirköprü Barajı
Kardamila
Küçükbahçe
Akdağ
Foça
Menemen
Marmara Gölü
Karataş
Gökçeören
Inousses
Langada
Mordoğan
Sasalli
Sipil Dağı
Ahmetli
Kula
Hios
Chios
MON. NEAMONI
Çeşme
İZMİR
Kemalpaşa
Turgutlu
Salihli
Ahmetler
Urla
Buca
Armutlu
Boz Dağları
Yeşilyurt
Eşme
Mesta
Balçova
Alaşehir
Pirgi
Nenita
Alaçatı
Ayrancılar
Bayındır
Ödemiş
Kiraz
Sarıgöl
Menderes

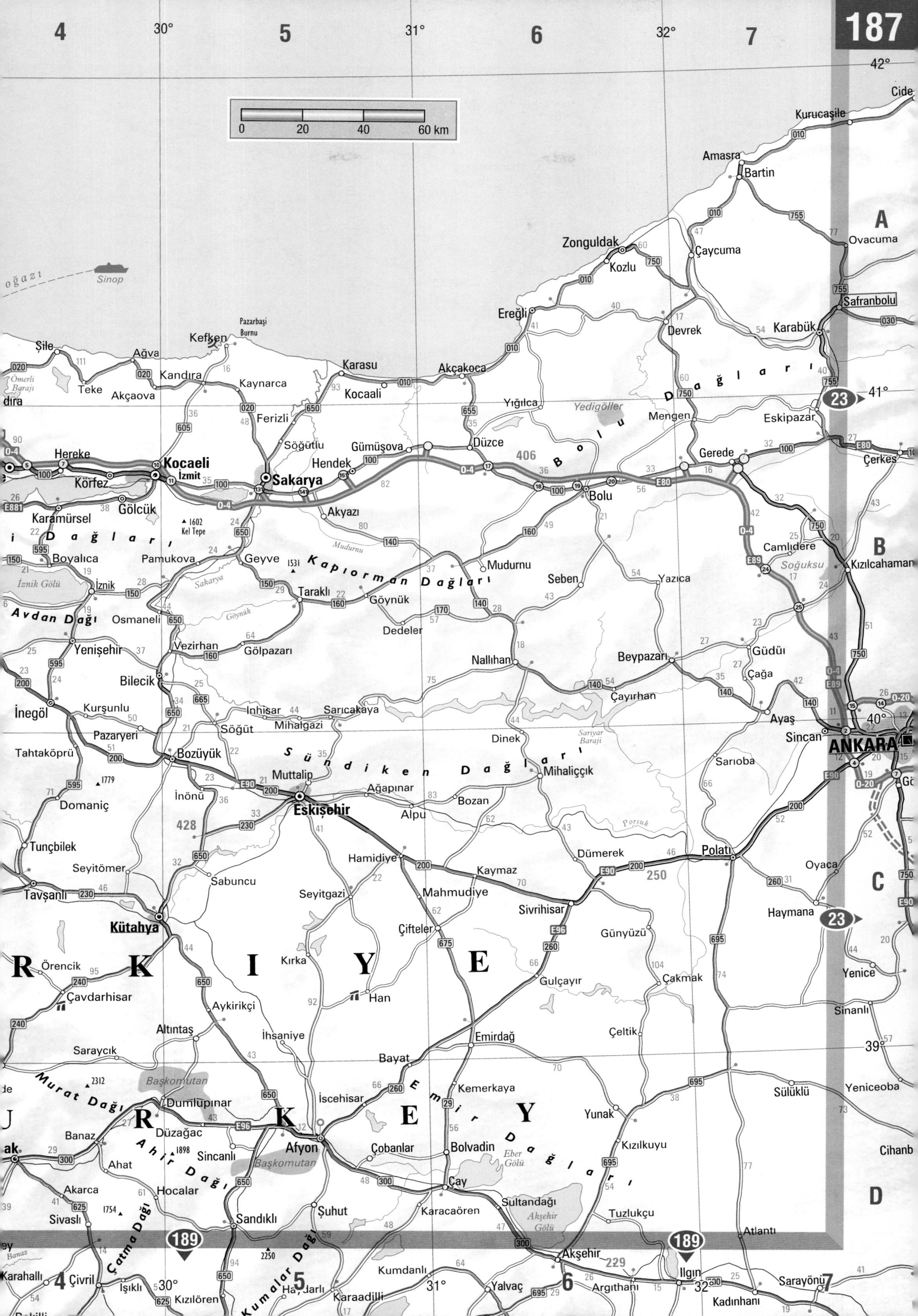

4
5
6
7
30°
31°
32°
42°
41°
40°
39°
A
B
C
D
0
20
40
60 km
Sinop
Cide
Kurucaşile
Amasra
Bartin
Ovacuma
Zonguldak
Kozlu
Çaycuma
Safranbolu
Ereğli
Devrek
Karabük
Kefken
Pazarbaşi Burnu
Şile
Ağva
Kandıra
Teke
Akçaova
Karasu
Kaynarca
Kocaali
Akçakoca
Yığılca
Yedigöller
Mengen
Eskipazar
Ferizli
Söğütlu
Gümüşova
Düzce
Hendek
Gerede
Çerkeş
Hereke
Kocaeli
İzmit
Körfez
Sakarya
Bolu
Gölcük
Karamürsel
Akyazı
Kel Tepe
Mudurnu
Bolu Dağları
Camlıdere
Soğuksu
Kızılcahaman
Boyalıca
Pamukova
Geyve
Kapiorman Dağları
Seben
Yazıca
İznik
İznik Gölü
Taraklı
Göynük
Avdan Dağı
Osmaneli
Dedeler
Yenişehir
Vezirhan
Gölpazarı
Nallıhan
Beypazarı
Güdül
Çağa
Bilecik
Çayırhan
İnegöl
Kurşunlu
İnhisar
Sarıcakaya
Ayaş
Mihalgazi
Söğüt
Sincan
ANKARA
Pazaryeri
Dinek
Sarıyar Baraji
Tahtaköprü
Bozüyük
Sündiken Dağları
Sarıoba
Mihalıççık
Muttalip
Domaniç
Ağapınar
İnönü
Eskişehir
Bozan
Alpu
Porsuk
Tunçbilek
Dümerek
Polatlı
Hamidiye
Seyitömer
Kaymaz
Oyaca
Tavşanlı
Sabuncu
Seyitgazi
Mahmudiye
Sivrihisar
Haymana
Kütahya
Çifteler
Günyüzü
Örencik
Kırka
Gulçayır
Çakmak
Yenice
Çavdarhisar
Han
Aykirikçi
Sinanlı
Altıntaş
İhsaniye
Emirdağ
Çeltik
Saraycık
Bayat
Murat Dağı
Başkomutan
Kemerkaya
Sülüklü
Yeniceoba
Dumlupınar
İscehisar
Emir Dağları
Yunak
Banaz
Düzağaç
Sincanlı
Afyon
Çobanlar
Bolvadin
Eber Gölü
Kızılkuyu
Cihanbeyli
Ahat
Ahir Dağı
Akarca
Hocalar
Çay
Sultandağı
Sivaslı
Şuhut
Karacaören
Tuzlukçu
Sandıklı
Akşehir Gölü
Atlantı
Çatma Dağı
Kumalar Dağı
Akşehir
Ilgın
Karahallı
Çivril
Işıklı
Kızılören
Kumdanlı
Karaadilli
Yalvaç
Argıthani
Sarayönü
Kadınhanı
189
23
TÜRKİYE

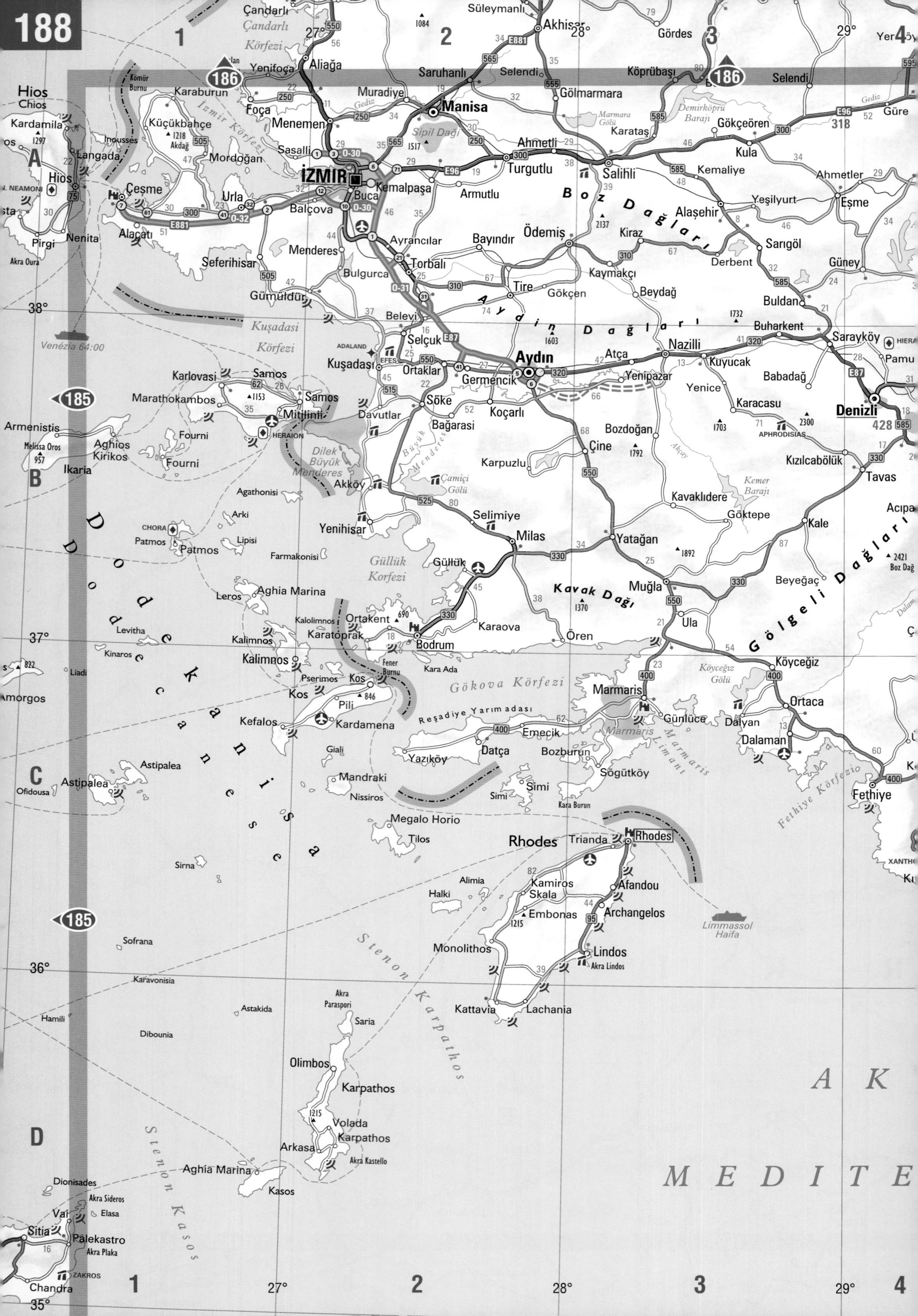
Çandarlı
Çandarlı Körfezi
Aliağa
Yenifoça
Karaburun
Foça
Menemen
Küçükbahçe
Küçükbahçe
Mordoğan
Sasalli
İZMIR
İzmir Körfezi
Çeşme
Urla
Balçova
Buca
Kemalpaşa
Alaçatı
Seferihisar
Menderes
Gümüldür
Süleymanlı
Akhisar
Gördes
Saruhanlı
Selendi
Köprübaşı
Muradiye
Manisa
Gölmarmara
Karataş
Gökçeören
Kula
Güre
Ahmetli
Turgutlu
Salihli
Kemaliye
Ahmetler
Armutlu
Boz Dağları
Alaşehir
Yeşilyurt
Eşme
Ödemiş
Kiraz
Sarıgöl
Bayındır
Ayrancılar
Torbalı
Bulgurca
Kaymakçı
Derbent
Güney
Tire
Gökçen
Beydağ
Buldan
Belevi
Aydın Dağları
Buharkent
Sarayköy
Selçuk
Kuşadası Körfezi
Kuşadası
Ortaklar
Germencik
Aydın
Atça
Nazilli
Kuyucak
Pamu
Babadağ
Yenipazar
Yenice
Denizli
Karacasu
Söke
Koçarlı
Davutlar
Bağarasi
Bozdoğan
Çine
Kızılcabölük
Tavas
Dilek Büyük Menderes
Karpuzlu
Çamiçi Gölü
Akköy
Kavaklıdere
Kemer Barajı
Göktepe
Acıpa
Kale
Yenihisar
Selimiye
Milas
Yatağan
Güllük Körfezi
Güllük
Kavak Dağı
Muğla
Beyeğaç
Gölgeli Dağları
Boz Dağ
Karaova
Ula
Ortakent
Karatoprak
Bodrum
Ören
Köyceğiz
Köyceğiz Gölü
Kara Ada
Gökova Körfezi
Marmaris
Reşadiye Yarımadası
Günlüce
Dalyan
Ortaca
Dalaman
Emecik
Datça
Yazıköy
Bozburun
Marmaris Limanı
Söğütköy
Simi
Fethiye Körfezi
Fethiye
Hios
Chios
Kardamila
Langada
Inousses
Hios
Pirgi
Nenita
Akra Oura
Venézia 64:00
Karlovasi
Samos
Marathokambos
Samos
Mitilinii
Heraion
Armenistis
Melissa Oros
Aghios Kirikos
Ikaria
Fourni
Fourni
Agathonisi
Arki
Chora
Patmos
Patmos
Lipisi
Farmakonisi
Dodekanisa
Dodecanese
Leros
Aghia Marina
Kalolimnos
Levitha
Kalimnos
Kalimnos
Kinaros
Liadi
Amorgos
Pserimos
Kos
Fener Burnu
Kos
Pili
Kefalos
Kardamena
Giali
Astipalea
Astipalea
Ofidousa
Mandraki
Nissiros
Megalo Horio
Tilos
Kara Burun
Rhodes
Trianda
Rhodes
Sirna
Alimia
Halki
Kamiros Skala
Afandou
Embonas
Archangelos
Limmassol Haifa
Sofrana
Monolithos
Lindos
Akra Lindos
Stenon Karpathos
Karavonisia
Kattavia
Lachania
Astakida
Akra Paraspori
Saria
Hamili
Dibounia
Olimbos
Karpathos
Volada
Karpathos
Arkasa
Akra Kastello
Aghia Marina
Kasos
Stenon Kasos
Dionisades
Akra Sideros
Vai
Elasa
Sitia
Palekastro
Akra Plaka
Zakros
Chandra
A K
M E D I T E

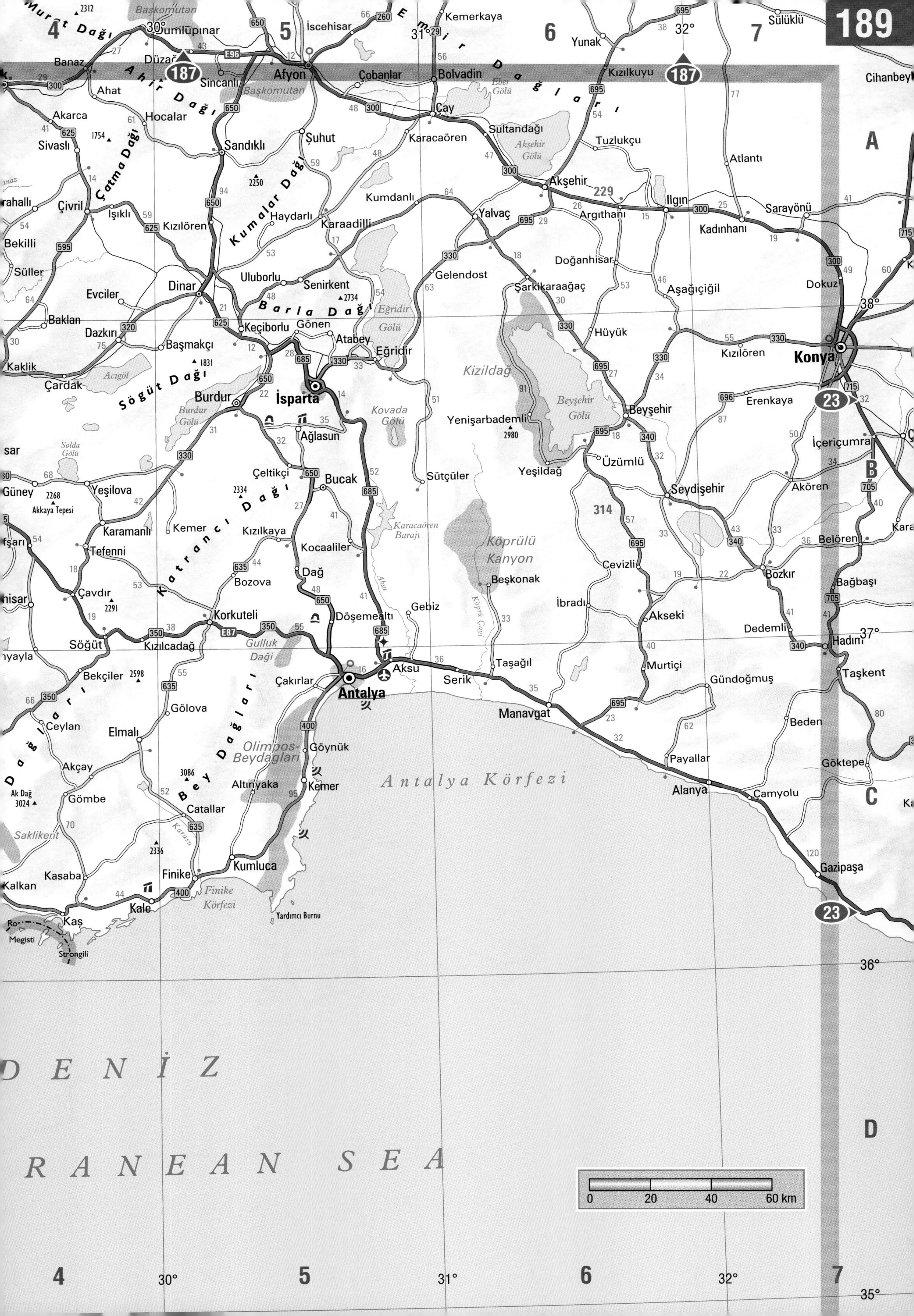
Afyon
Bolvadin
Çay
Şuhut
Sandıklı
Dinar
Akşehir
Ilgın
Kadınhanı
Sarayönü
Konya
Yalvaç
Gelendost
Şarkikaraağaç
Beyşehir
Beyşehir Gölü
Eğridir
Eğridir Gölü
Isparta
Burdur
Burdur Gölü
Acıgöl
Keçiborlu
Ağlasun
Bucak
Seydişehir
Köprülü Kanyon
Beşkonak
Korkuteli
Antalya
Aksu
Serik
Manavgat
Akseki
Alanya
Gazipaşa
Kemer
Kumluca
Finike
Elmalı
Kaş
Kale
Olimpos-Beydağları
Antalya Körfezi
Finike Körfezi
Yardımcı Burnu
Megisti
Strongili
Sultandağı
Akşehir Gölü
Eber Gölü
Tuzlukçu
Atlantı
Doğanhisar
Hüyük
Aşağıçiğil
Bozkır
Hadım
Taşkent
Murtiçi
İbradı
Gündoğmuş
Payallar
Çamyolu
Göktepe
Beden
Dedemli
Bağbaşı
Belören
Akören
İçeriçumra
Erenkaya
Kızılören
Dokuz
Cihanbey
Sülüklü
Yunak
Kızılkuyu
Kemerkaya
İscehisar
Çobanlar
Sincanlı
Dumlupınar
Banaz
Düzağaç
Ahat
Akarca
Sivaslı
Hocalar
Çivril
Işıklı
Kızılören
Bekilli
Süller
Evciler
Baklan
Dazkırı
Çardak
Kaklik
Başmakçı
Uluborlu
Senirkent
Gönen
Atabey
Kumdanlı
Karaadilli
Haydarlı
Karacaören
Kızıldağ
Yenişarbademli
Yeşildağ
Üzümlü
Sütçüler
Kovada Gölü
Karacaören Barajı
Çeltikçi
Kızılkaya
Kocaaliler
Dağ
Bozova
Döşemealtı
Gebiz
Taşağıl
Çakırlar
Göynük
Altınyaka
Catallar
Kemer
Karamanlı
Tefenni
Yeşilova
Güney
Çavdır
Söğüt
Kızılcadağ
Bekçiler
Gölova
Ceylan
Akçay
Gömbe
Saklikent
Kasaba
Kalkan
Cevizli
Murat Dağı
Ahır Dağı
Emir Dağları
Çatma Dağı
Kumalar Dağı
Barla Dağı
Söğüt Dağı
Katrancı Dağı
Bey Dağları
Akdağ
Akkaya Tepesi
Gulluk Dağı
Başkomutan
Solda Gölü
DENİZ
MEDITERRANEAN SEA
0 20 40 60 km
30° 31° 32° 35° 36° 37° 38°
4 5 6 7
A B C D

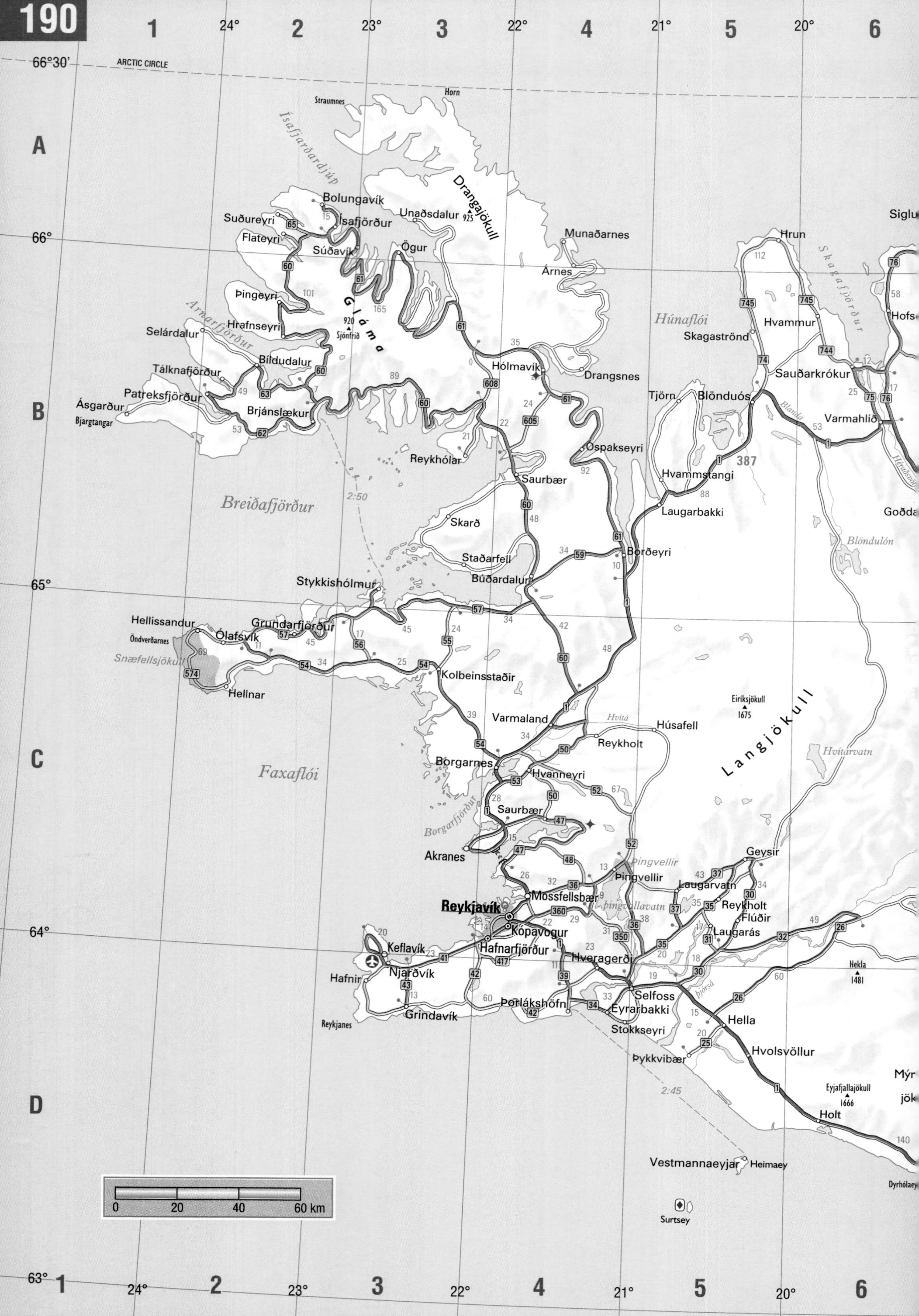
1
2
3
4
5
6
A
B
C
D
24°
23°
22°
21°
20°
66°30'
66°
65°
64°
63°
ARCTIC CIRCLE
Straumnes
Horn
Ísafjarðardjúp
Drangajökull
925
Bolungavík
Ísafjörður
Unaðsdalur
Suðureyri
Flateyri
Súðavík
Ögur
Munaðarnes
Árnes
Þingeyri
Glámа
920
Sjónfríð
Arnarfjörður
Hrafnseyri
Selárdalur
Bíldudalur
Tálknafjörður
Patreksfjörður
Ásgarður
Bjargtangar
Brjánslækur
Hólmavík
Drangsnes
Reykhólar
Breiðafjörður
Saurbær
Skarð
Staðarfell
Búðardalur
Borðeyri
Ospakseyri
Húnaflói
Skagaströnd
Hrun
Skagafjörður
Hvammur
Sauðarkrókur
Tjörn
Blönduós
Blanda
Varmahlíð
Hvammstangi
387
Laugarbakki
Blöndulón
Goðda
Sigl
Hofs
Stykkishólmur
Hellissandur
Öndverðarnes
Ólafsvík
Grundarfjörður
Snæfellsjökull
Hellnar
Kolbeinsstaðir
Varmaland
Hvítá
Húsafell
Reykholt
Eiríksjökull
1675
Langjökull
Hvítárvatn
Faxaflói
Borgarnes
Hvanneyri
Borgarfjörður
Saurbær
Akranes
Þingvellir
Geysir
Laugarvatn
Reykjavík
Mossfellsbær
Þingvallavatn
Reykholt
Flúðir
Laugarás
Kópavogur
Hafnarfjörður
Keflavík
Njarðvík
Hafnir
Hveragerði
Selfoss
Eyrarbakki
Stokkseyri
Þjórsá
Hella
Hekla
1481
Grindavík
Reykjanes
Þorlákshöfn
Þykkvibær
Hvolsvöllur
Eyjafjallajökull
1666
Mýr
jök
Holt
Vestmannaeyjar
Heimaey
Dyrhólaey
Surtsey
2:50
2:45
0
20
40
60 km

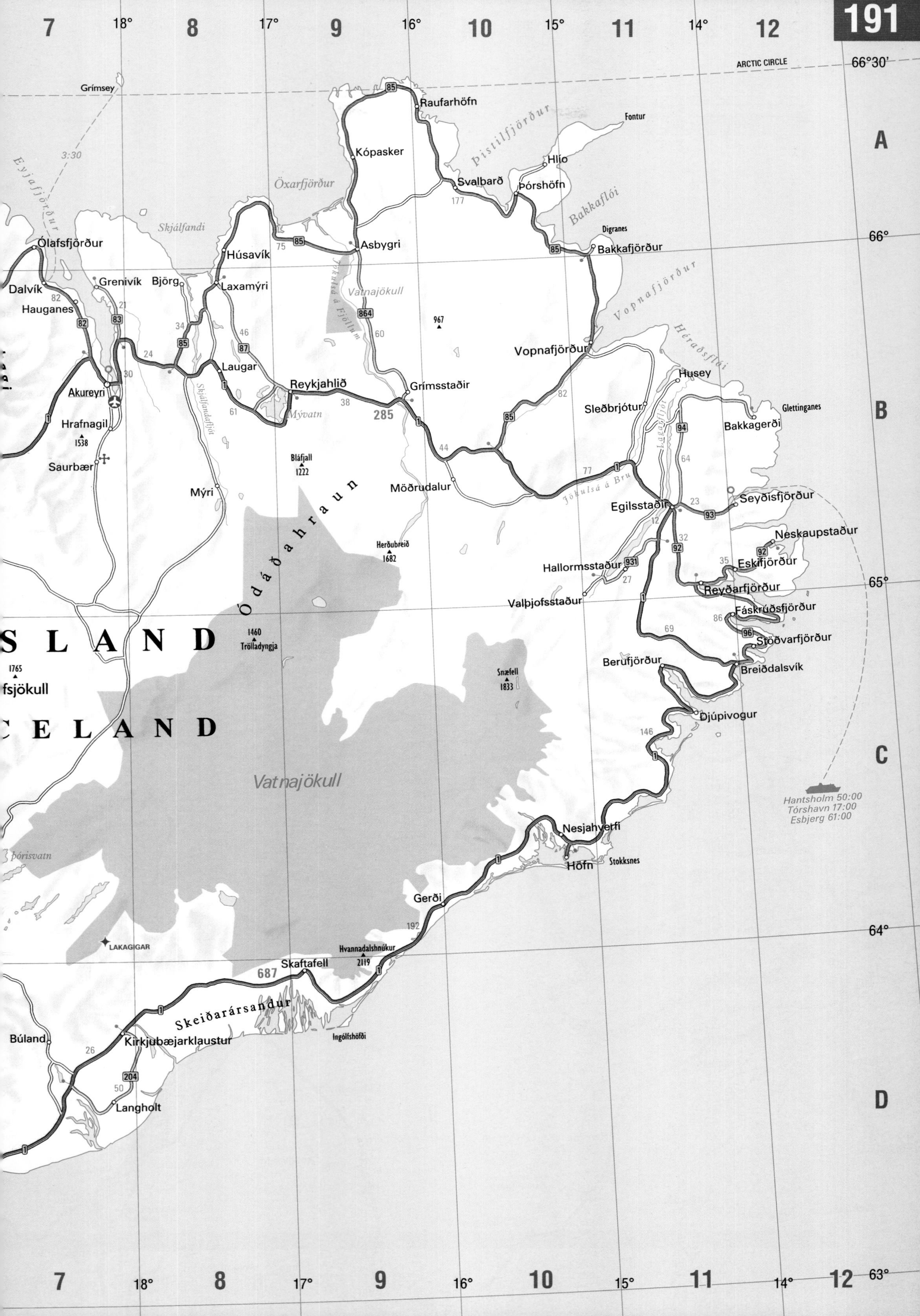

ARCTIC CIRCLE
66°30'
Grímsey
3:30
Raufarhöfn
Fontur
Kópasker
Pistilfjörður
Hlíð
Svalbarð
Þórshöfn
Öxarfjörður
Skjálfandi
Eyjafjörður
Bakkaflói
Digranes
Ólafsfjörður
Húsavík
Asbygri
Bakkafjörður
Dalvík
Grenivík
Björg
Laxamýri
Hauganes
Vatnajökull
Vopnafjörður
967
Héraðsflói
Akureyri
Laugar
Reykjahlíð
Grímsstaðir
Húsey
Mývatn
Sleðbrjótur
Glettinganes
Hrafnagil
1538
Bakkagerði
Saurbær
Bláfjall
1222
Möðrudalur
Mýri
Ódáðahraun
Jökulsá á Brú
Egilsstaðir
Seyðisfjörður
Neskaupstaður
Herðubreið
1682
Eskifjörður
Hallormsstaður
Reyðarfjörður
Valþjofsstaður
Fáskrúðsfjörður
SLAND
1460
Trölladyngja
Stöðvarfjörður
1765
fsjökull
Berufjörður
Breiðdalsvík
Snæfell
1833
CELAND
Djúpivogur
Vatnajökull
Hantsholm 50:00
Tórshavn 17:00
Esbjerg 61:00
Nesjahverfi
Þórisvatn
Höfn
Stokksnes
Gerði
LAKAGIGAR
Hvannadalshnúkur
2119
Skaftafell
687
Skeiðarársandur
Búland
Kirkjubæjarklaustur
Ingólfshöfði
Langholt
7
8
9
10
11
12
18°
17°
16°
15°
14°
66°
65°
64°
63°
A
B
C
D

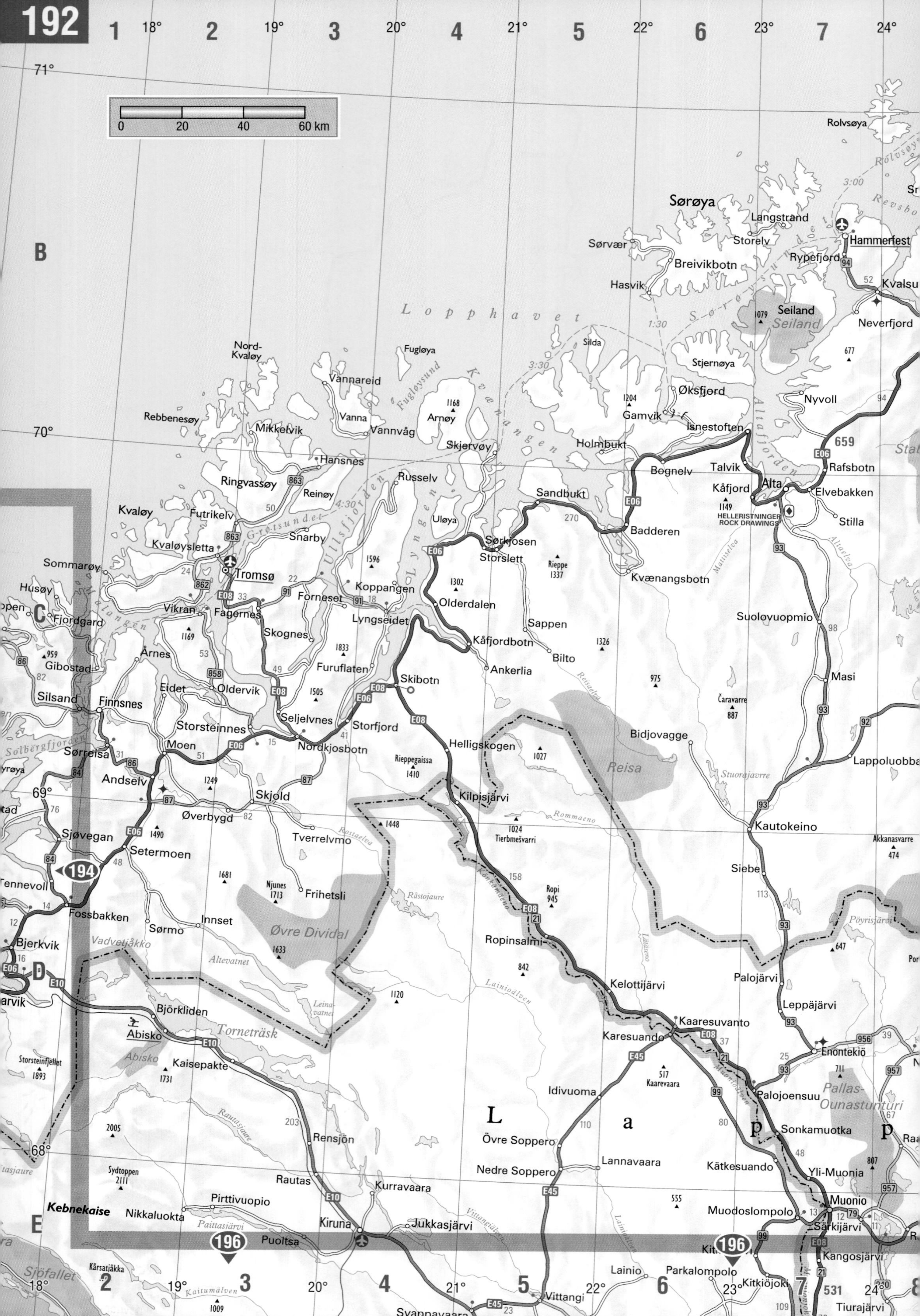
1
2
3
4
5
6
7
18°
19°
20°
21°
22°
23°
24°
71°
70°
69°
68°
B
C
D
E
0
20
40
60 km
Rolvsøya
Sørøya
Langstrand
Storelv
Hammerfest
Sørvær
Breivikbotn
Rypefjord
Hasvik
Kvalsu
Seiland
Neverfjord
Lopphavet
Sørøysundet
1:30
3:30
3:00
4:30
Silda
Stjernøya
Nord-Kvaløy
Fugløya
Vannareid
Fugløysund
Kvænangen
Øksfjord
Nyvoll
Rebbenesøy
Mikkelvik
Vanna
Vannvåg
Arnøy
Skjervøy
Gamvik
Isnestoften
Altafjorden
Holmbukt
659
Hansnes
Ringvassøy
Reinøy
Russelv
Bognelv
Talvik
Alta
Rafsbotn
Kåfjord
Elvebakken
Sandbukt
Kvaløy
Futrikelv
Uløya
HELLERISTNINGER ROCK DRAWINGS
Stilla
Grøtsundet
Snarby
Ullsfjorden
Lyngen
Badderen
Kvaløysletta
Sørkjosen
Storslett
Sommarøy
Tromsø
Rieppe 1337
Kvænangsbotn
Husøy
Malangen
Koppangen
Forneset
Olderdalen
Fjordgard
Vikran
Fagernes
Lyngseidet
Suolovuopmio
Sappen
Skognes
Kåfjordbotn
Bilto
Gibostad
Årnes
Furuflaten
Ankerlia
Masi
Skibotn
Eidet
Oldervik
Silsand
Finnsnes
Čaravarre 887
Seljelvnes
Storsteinnes
Storfjord
Bidjovagge
Nordkjosbotn
Helligskogen
Sølbergfjorden
Sørreisa
Moen
Rieppegaissa 1410
Reisa
Lappoluobba
Andselv
Stuorajavrre
Skjold
Kilpisjärvi
Øverbygd
Rommaeno
Tverrelvmo
1024 Tierbmešvarri
Kautokeino
Sjøvegan
Akkanasvarre 474
Setermoen
Siebe
Tennevoll
Njunes 1713
Frihetsli
Råstojaure
Ropi 945
Fossbakken
Innset
Sørmo
Øvre Dividal
Ropinsalmi
Pöyrisjärvi
Bjerkvik
Vadvetjåkko
Altevatnet
Lainioälven
Palojärvi
Kelottijärvi
Leinavatnet
Leppäjärvi
Narvik
Björkliden
Kaaresuvanto
Karesuando
Abisko
Torneträsk
Enontekiö
Storsteinfjellet 1893
Kaisepakte
517 Kaarevaara
Palojoensuu
Pallas-Ounastunturi
Idivuoma
Rautasjaure
Muonionjoki
L
a
p
p
Rensjön
Övre Soppero
Sonkamuotka
Lannavaara
Nedre Soppero
Kätkesuando
Yli-Muonia
Sydtoppen 2111
Rautas
Kurravaara
Pirttivuopio
Muonio
Kebnekaise
Nikkaluokta
Muodoslompolo
Paittasjärvi
Kiruna
Jukkasjärvi
Vittangiälven
Särkijärvi
Puoltsa
Kangosjärvi
Sjöfallet
Kårsatjäkka
Kaitumälven
Lainio
Parkalompolo
Kitkiöjoki
Vittangi
Tiurajärvi
Svappavaara
194
196
E06
E08
E10
E45

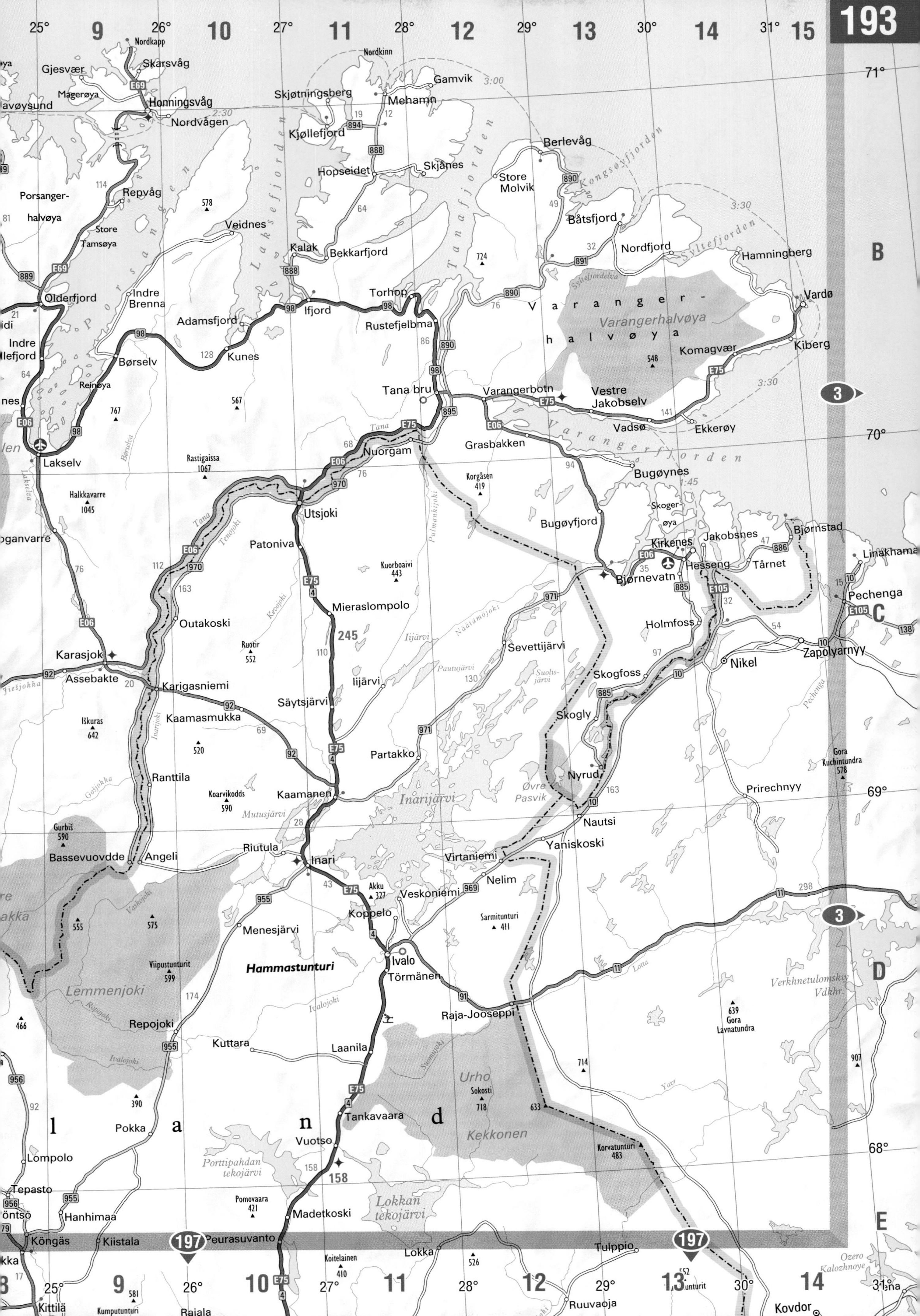
Nordkapp
Skarsvåg
Gjesvær
Magerøya
Honningsvåg
Nordvågen
Repvåg
Porsanger-
halvøya
Store
Tamsøya
Olderfjord
Indre
Brenna
Lakselv
Karasjok
Assebakte
Nordkinn
Gamvik
Mehamn
Skjøtningsberg
Kjøllefjord
Hopseidet
Skjånes
Veidnes
Kalak
Bekkarfjord
Adamsfjord
Ifjord
Kunes
Børselv
Torhop
Rustefjelbma
Tana bru
Berlevåg
Store
Molvik
Båtsfjord
Nordfjord
Hamningberg
Vardø
Kiberg
Komagvær
Varanger-
halvøya
Varangerhalvøya
Varangerbotn
Vestre
Jakobselv
Vadsø
Ekkerøy
Grasbakken
Varangerfjorden
Bugøynes
Bugøyfjord
Kirkenes
Jakobsnes
Bjørnstad
Tårnet
Hesseng
Bjørnevatn
Pechenga
Holmfoss
Zapolyarnyy
Nikel
Skogfoss
Skogly
Nyrud
Nautsi
Yaniskoski
Prirechnyy
Nuorgam
Utsjoki
Patoniva
Mieraslompolo
Outakoski
Karigasniemi
Kaamasmukka
Säytsjärvi
Iijärvi
Sevettijärvi
Partakko
Kaamanen
Ranttila
Inarijärvi
Riutula
Inari
Angeli
Bassevuovdde
Virtaniemi
Nelim
Veskoniemi
Koppelo
Menesjärvi
Ivalo
Törmänen
Hammastunturi
Raja-Jooseppi
Lemmenjoki
Repojoki
Kuttara
Laanila
Urho
Kekkonen
Tankavaara
Vuotso
Pokka
Lompolo
Tepasto
Hanhimaa
Könkäs
Kiistala
Peurasuvanto
Madetkoski
Lokkan tekojärvi
Porttipahdan tekojärvi
Lokka
Tulppio
Korvatunturi
Kittilä
Rajala
Ruuvaoja
Kovdor
Verkhnetulomskiy Vdkhr.

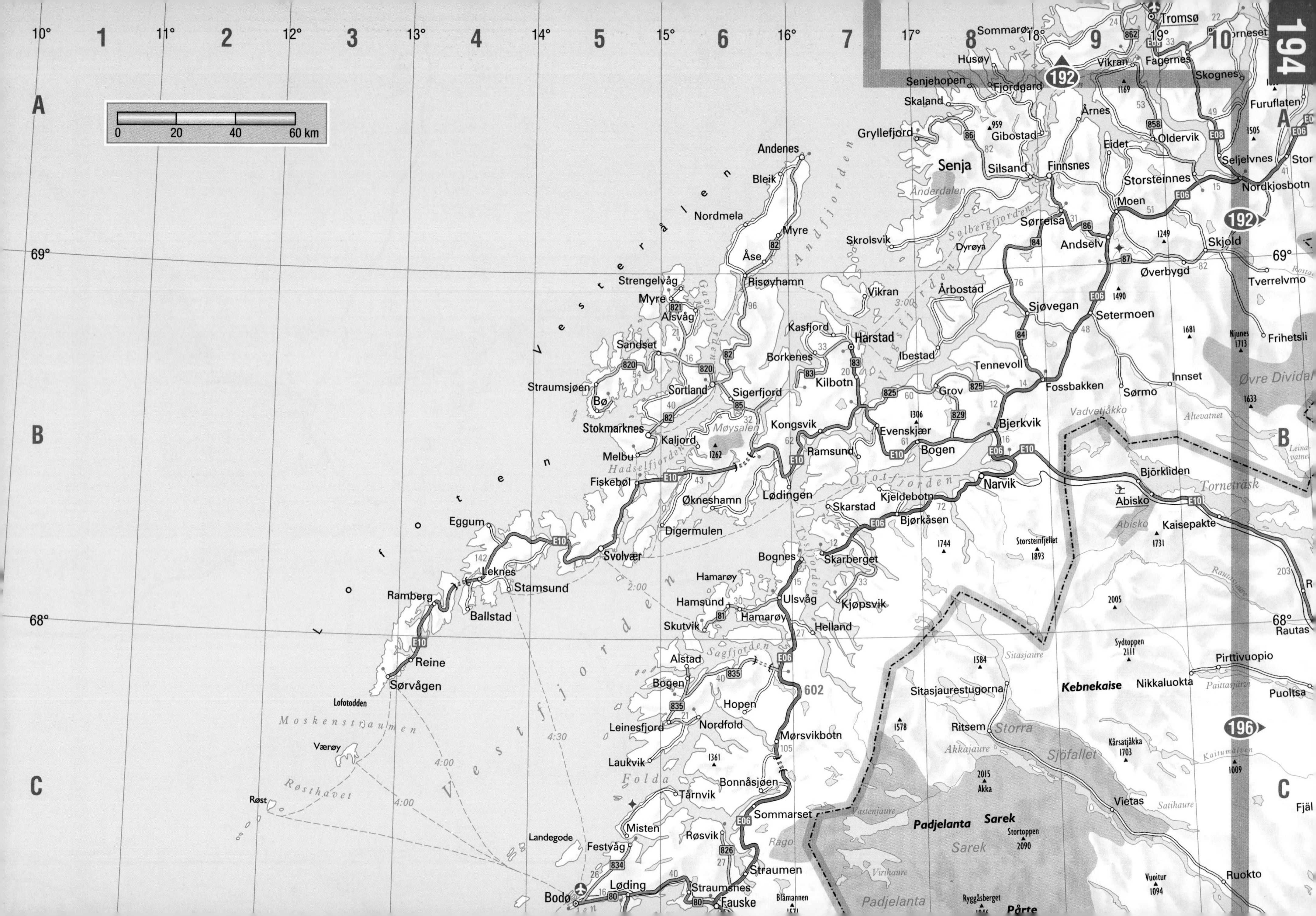

Vesterålen
Lofoten
Andfjorden
Vestfjorden
Moskenstraumen
Røsthavet
Andenes
Bleik
Nordmela
Myre
Åse
Risøyhamn
Strengelvåg
Alsvåg
Sandset
Straumsjøen
Bø
Sortland
Sigerfjord
Stokmarknes
Kaljord
Melbu
Fiskebøl
Kongsvik
Kasfjord
Harstad
Borkenes
Kilbotn
Ibestad
Vikran
Årbostad
Skrolsvik
Senja
Gryllefjord
Skaland
Senjehopen
Husøy
Fjordgard
Gibostad
Silsand
Finnsnes
Sørreisa
Andselv
Moen
Tromsø
Fagernes
Skognes
Oldervik
Storsteinnes
Nordkjosbotn
Seljelvnes
Furuflaten
Skjold
Øverbygd
Tverrelvmo
Frihetsli
Sjøvegan
Setermoen
Tennevoll
Fossbakken
Sørmo
Innset
Grov
Evenskjær
Bogen
Bjerkvik
Ramsund
Lødingen
Narvik
Kjeldebotn
Skarstad
Bjørkåsen
Bjørkliden
Abisko
Kaisepakte
Torneträsk
Øvre Dividal
Eggum
Svolvær
Økneshamn
Digermulen
Leknes
Stamsund
Ramberg
Ballstad
Reine
Sørvågen
Lofotodden
Værøy
Røst
Bognes
Skarberget
Kjøpsvik
Hamarøy
Hamsund
Ulsvåg
Skutvik
Helland
Alstad
Bogen
Hopen
Leinesfjord
Nordfold
Mørsvikbotn
Laukvik
Bonnåsjøen
Tårnvik
Sommarset
Misten
Røsvik
Landegode
Festvåg
Straumen
Løding
Straumsnes
Bodø
Fauske
Sitasjaurestugorna
Ritsem
Stora Sjöfallet
Kebnekaise
Nikkaluokta
Pirttivuopio
Puoltsa
Rautas
Vietas
Ruokto
Padjelanta
Sarek
0 20 40 60 km

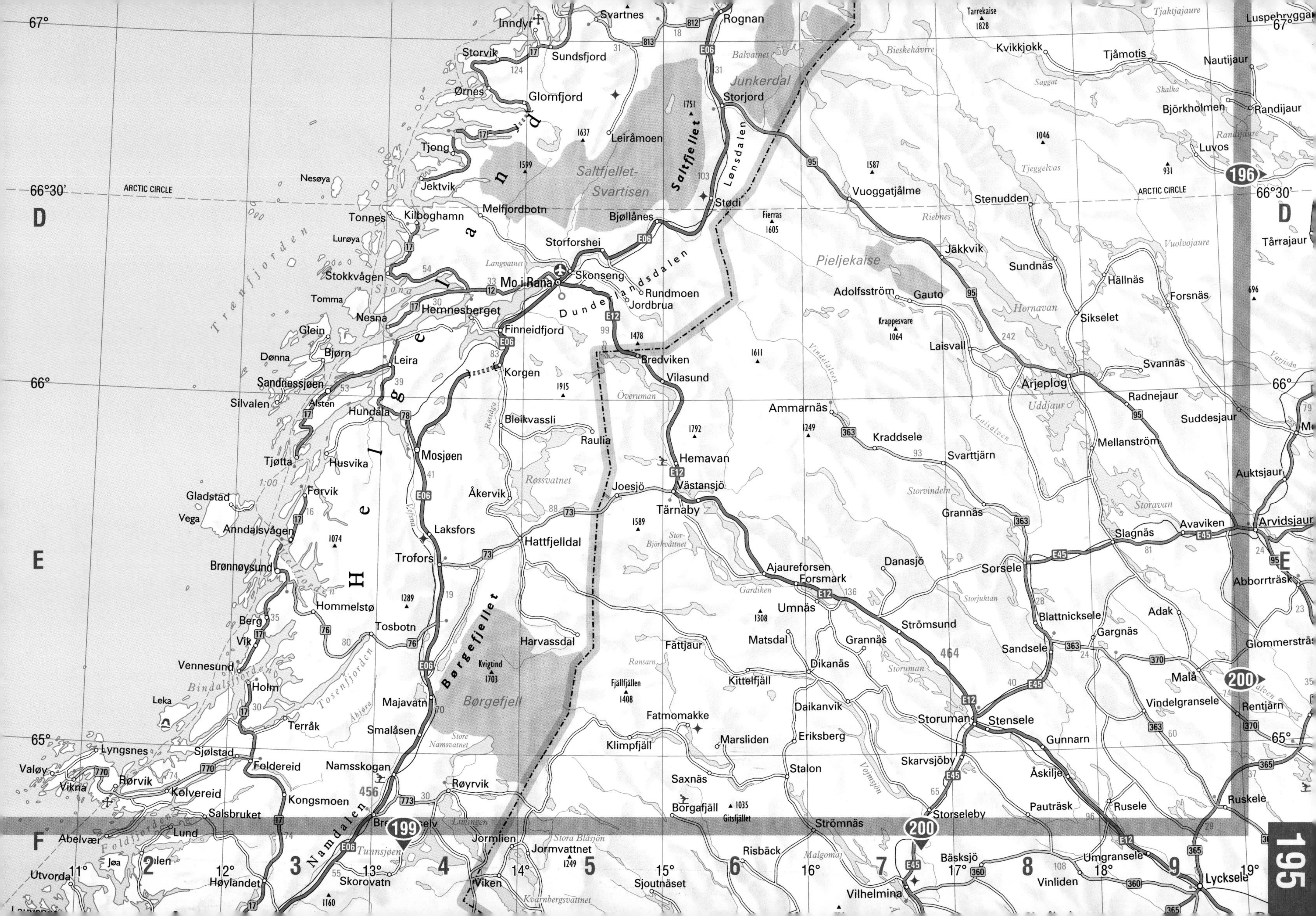

Mo i Rana
Mosjøen
Brønnøysund
Sandnessjøen
Hattfjelldal
Trofors
Nesna
Korgen
Hemnesberget
Finneidfjord
Storforshei
Skonseng
Bjøllånes
Storjord
Rognan
Ørnes
Glomfjord
Inndyr
Sundsfjord
Svartnes
Saltfjellet
Saltfjellet-Svartisen
Lønsdalen
Stødi
Junkerdal
Børgefjell
Børgefjellet
Namsskogan
Majavatn
Smalåsen
Foldereid
Kongsmoen
Salsbruket
Kolvereid
Rørvik
Vikna
Abelvær
Høylandet
Terråk
Holm
Vennesund
Vik
Berg
Hommelstø
Tosbotn
Vega
Gladstad
Anndalsvågen
Tjøtta
Forvik
Husvika
Hundåla
Leira
Stokkvågen
Tonnes
Kilboghamn
Jektvik
Tjong
Melfjordbotn
Storvik
Arjeplog
Jäkkvik
Laisvall
Adolfsström
Gauto
Vuoggatjålme
Sorsele
Stensele
Storuman
Tärnaby
Hemavan
Joesjö
Ammarnäs
Kraddsele
Slagnäs
Arvidsjaur
Malå
Lycksele
Vilhelmina
Dikanäs
Saxnäs
Klimpfjäll
Fatmomakke
Borgafjäll
Kittelfjäll
Risbäck
Strömnäs
Kvikkjokk
Tjåmotis
Björkholmen
Nautijaur
Randijaur
Luvos
Forsnäs
Sikselet
Hällnäs
Svannäs
Radnejaur
Suddesjaur
Auktsjaur
Avaviken
Mellanström
Stenudden
Sundnäs
Blattnicksele
Gargnäs
Adak
Vindelgransele
Rusele
Umgransele
Gunnarn
Åskilje
Pauträsk
Vinliden
Bäsksjö
Storseleby
Skarvsjöby
Grannäs
Strömsund
Danasjö
Svartjärn
Forsmark
Umnäs
Ajaureforsen
Matsdal
Fättjaur
Vilasund
Bredviken
Västansjö
Raulia
Bleikvassli
Rundmoen
Jordbrua
Harvassdal
Laksfors
Åkervik
Røyrvik
Jormlien
Jormvattnet
Viken
Sjoutnäset
Stalon
Eriksberg
Daikanvik
Marsliden
Pieljekaise
Namdalen
Dunderlandsdalen
Helgeland
Trænfjorden
Vefsna
Bindalsfjorden
Tosenfjorden
Lurøya
Nesøya
Tomma
Dønna
Glein
Bjørn
Alsten
Silvalen
Leka
Jøa
Lund
Sjølstad
Lyngsnes
Valøy
Utvorda
Lyngsnes
Skorovatn
Abborrträsk
Glommersträsk
Rentjärn
Ruskele
Tårrajaur
Luspebryggan
ARCTIC CIRCLE
E06
E12
E45
95
363
17
73
76
66°30'
66°
65°
67°
D
E
F
11°
12°
13°
14°
15°
16°
17°
18°
19°
196
199
200

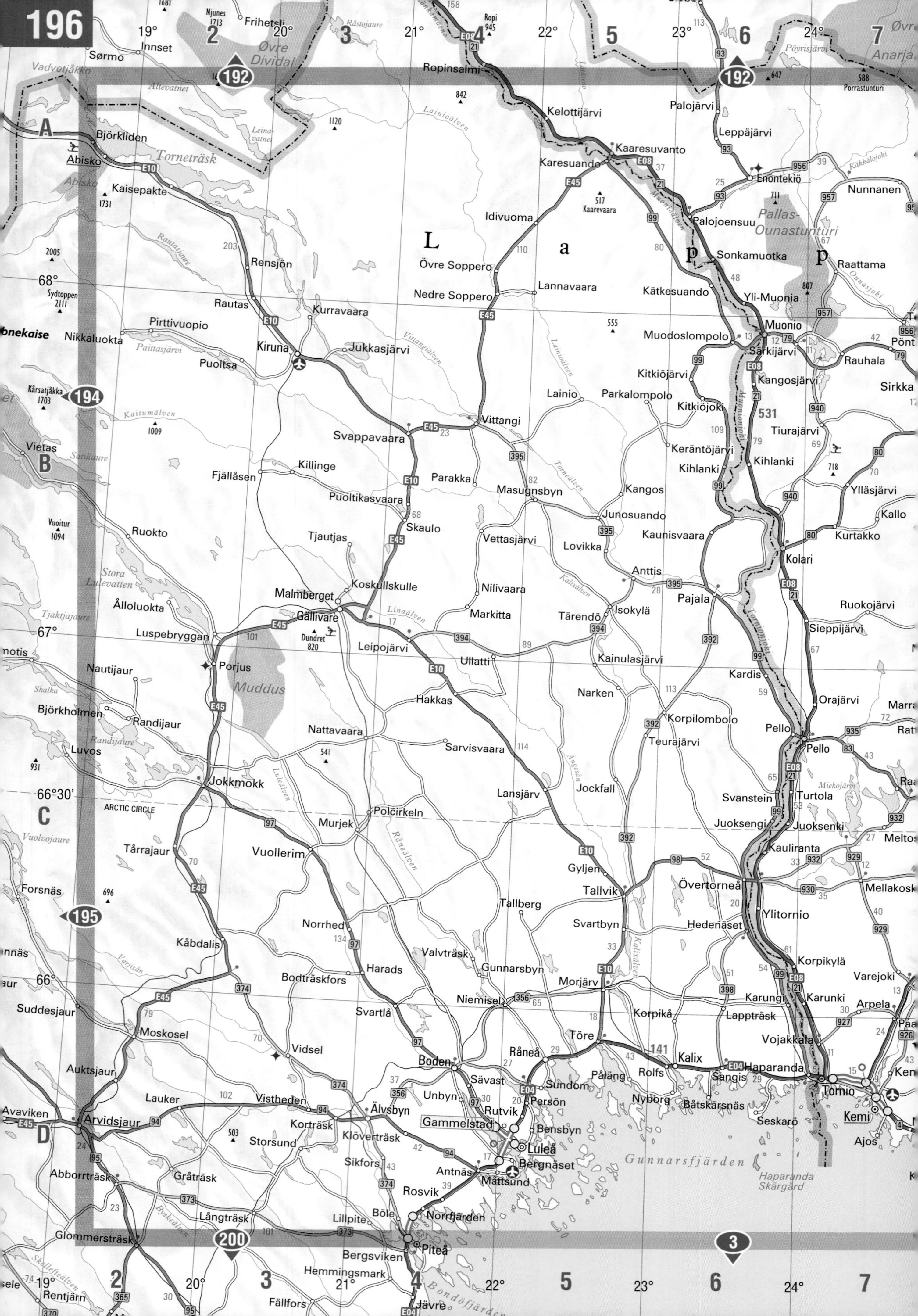
192
194
195
200
3
L a p p
Abisko
Björkliden
Torneträsk
Kaisepakte
Rensjön
Rautas
Kiruna
Kurravaara
Jukkasjärvi
Pirttivuopio
Nikkaluokta
Puoltsa
Kebnekaise
Kårsatjåkka
Vietas
Svappavaara
Killinge
Fjällåsen
Puoltikasvaara
Skaulo
Tjautjas
Koskullskulle
Malmberget
Gällivare
Dundret
Ruokto
Stora Lulevatten
Ålloluokta
Luspebryggan
Porjus
Muddus
Nautijaur
Björkholmen
Randijaur
Luvos
Jokkmokk
ARCTIC CIRCLE
66°30'
Tårrajaur
Forsnäs
Kåbdalis
Suddesjaur
Moskosel
Auktsjaur
Arvidsjaur
Avaviken
Lauker
Abborrträsk
Gråträsk
Långträsk
Glommersträsk
Rentjärn
Vuollerim
Murjek
Polcirkeln
Nattavaara
Sarvisvaara
Hakkas
Leipojärvi
Ullatti
Norrhed
Harads
Bodträskfors
Svartlå
Vidsel
Boden
Sävast
Unbyn
Vistheden
Älvsbyn
Korträsk
Storsund
Klöverträsk
Sikfors
Antnäs
Rosvik
Böle
Lillpite
Norrfjärden
Piteå
Bergsviken
Hemmingsmark
Fällfors
Jävre
Gammelstad
Luleå
Bergnäset
Mattsund
Rutvik
Persön
Bensbyn
Sundom
Råneå
Niemisel
Gunnarsbyn
Valvträsk
Tallberg
Töre
Morjärv
Svartbyn
Tallvik
Gyljen
Lansjärv
Jockfall
Korpilombolo
Teurajärvi
Narken
Kainulasjärvi
Tärendö
Isokylä
Markitta
Nilivaara
Vettasjärvi
Masugnsbyn
Parakka
Vittangi
Lainio
Parkalompolo
Övre Soppero
Nedre Soppero
Lannavaara
Idivuoma
Karesuando
Kaaresuvanto
Kelottijärvi
Ropinsalmi
Palojärvi
Leppäjärvi
Enontekiö
Palojoensuu
Pallas-Ounastunturi
Sonkamuotka
Kätkesuando
Yli-Muonia
Muonio
Muodoslompolo
Särkijärvi
Kitkiöjärvi
Kitkiöjoki
Kangosjärvi
Keräntöjärvi
Kihlanki
Kangos
Junosuando
Lovikka
Kaunisvaara
Anttis
Pajala
Kardis
Pello
Svanstein
Turtola
Juoksengi
Juoksenki
Kauliranta
Övertorneå
Ylitornio
Hedenäset
Korpikylä
Karungi
Karunki
Lappträsk
Korpikå
Vojakkala
Kalix
Rolfs
Pålänge
Nyborg
Båtskärsnäs
Sangis
Haparanda
Tornio
Kemi
Seskarö
Ajos
Gunnarsfjärden
Haparanda Skärgård
Kolari
Kurtakko
Kallo
Ylläsjärvi
Tiurajärvi
Sieppijärvi
Ruokojärvi
Orajärvi
Mellakoski
Varejoki
Arpela
Nunnanen
Raattama
Rauhala
Sirkka
Sørmo
Innset
Frihetsli
Øvre Dividal

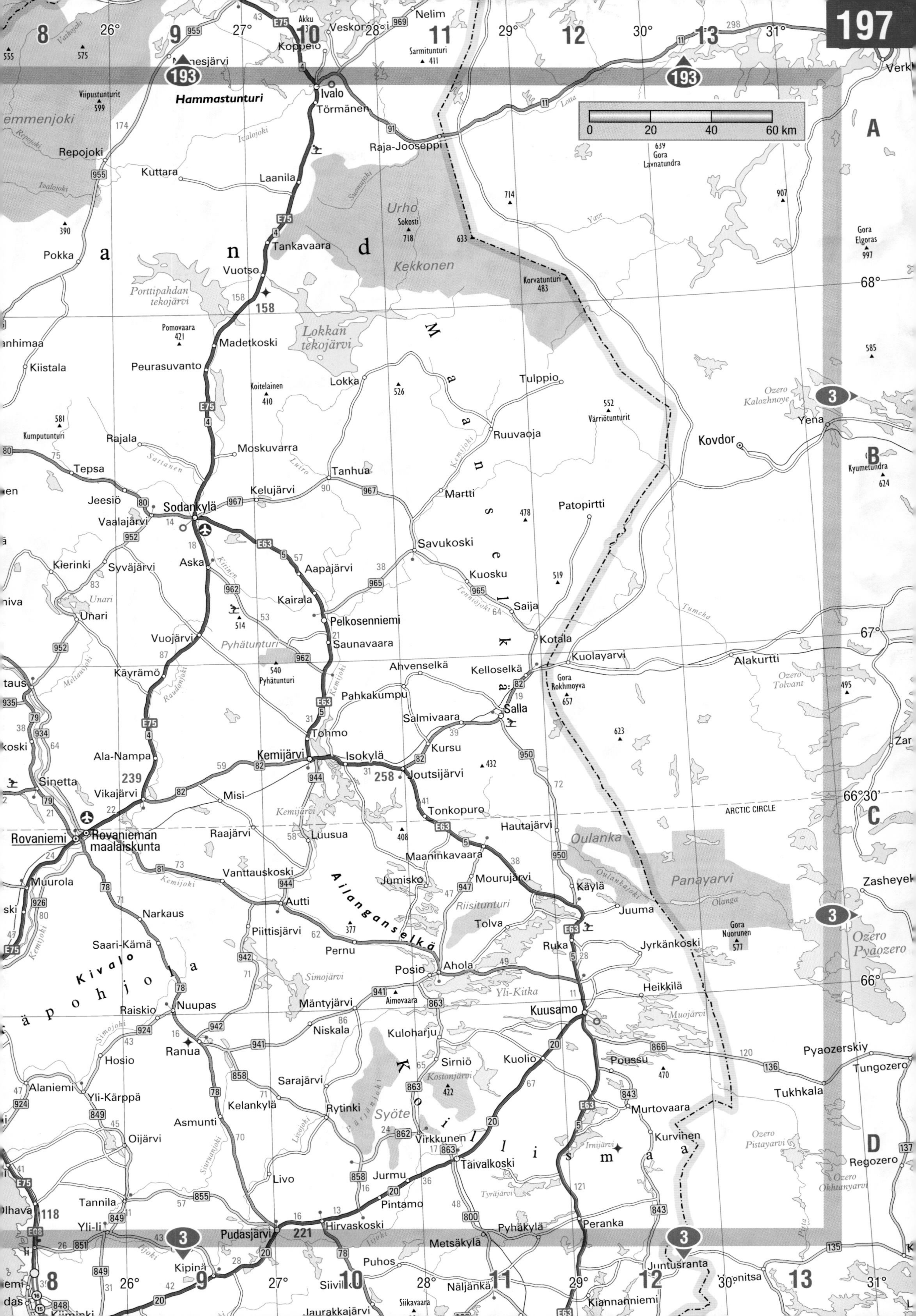

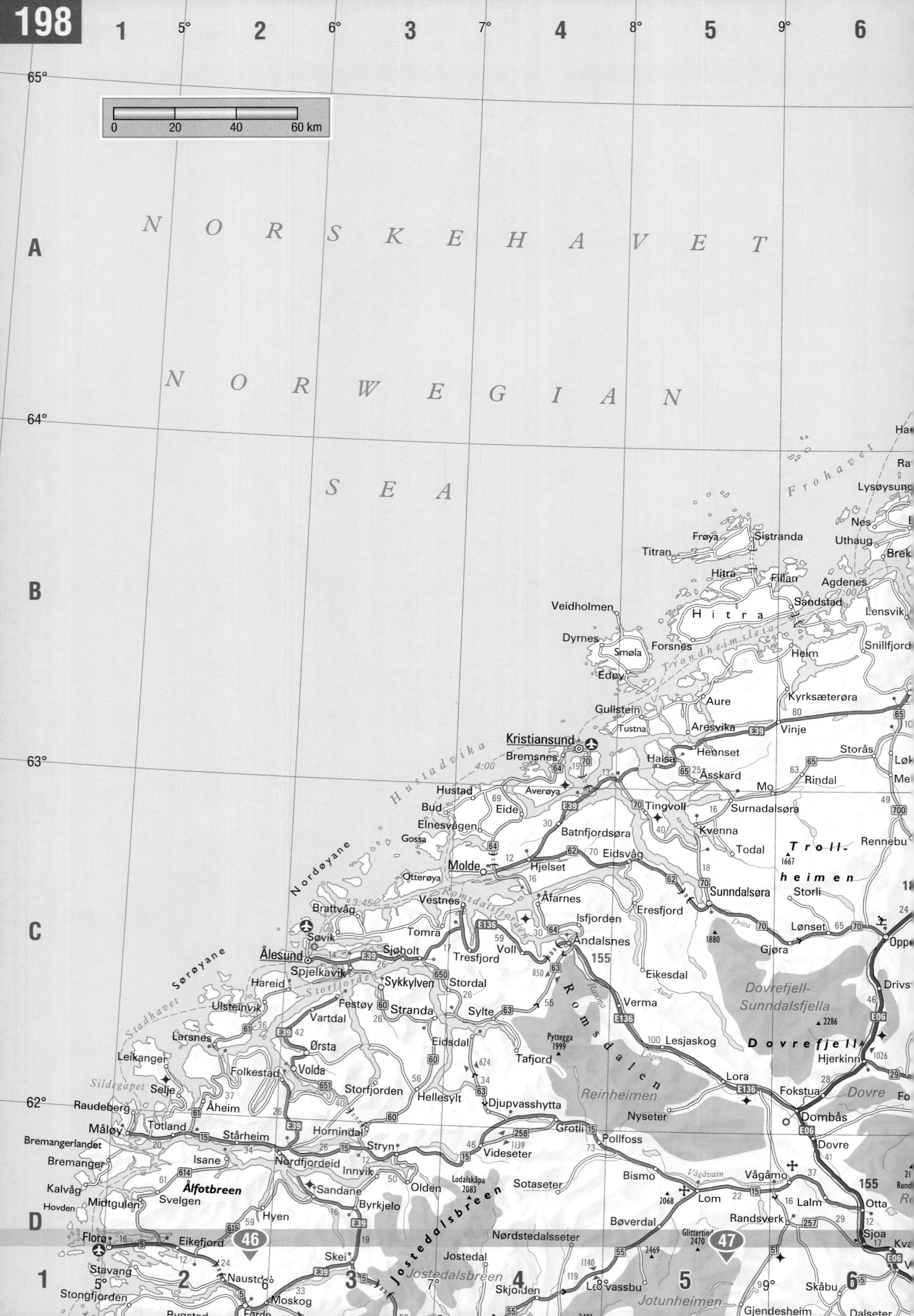
1
2
3
4
5
6
5°
6°
7°
8°
9°
65°
64°
63°
62°
A
B
C
D
0
20
40
60 km
N O R S K E H A V E T
N O R W E G I A N
S E A
Frohavet
Lysøysund
Nes
Uthaug
Brek
Frøya
Sistranda
Titran
Hitra
Fillan
Agdenes
Sandstad
Lensvik
Veidholmen
Dyrnes
Smøla
Forsnes
Heim
Snillfjord
Trondheimsleia
Edøy
Aure
Kyrksæterøra
Gullstein
Tustna
Aresvika
Vinje
Kristiansund
Bremsnes
Halsa
Hennset
Storås
Hustadvika
Hustad
Averøya
Åsskard
Rindal
Bud
Eide
Tingvoll
Surnadalsøra
Elnesvågen
Batnfjordsøra
Kvenna
Gossa
Nordøyane
Molde
Hjelset
Eidsvåg
Todal
Trollheimen
Rennebu
Otterøya
Sunndalsøra
Storli
Brattvåg
Vestnes
Romsdalsfjorden
Åfarnes
Eresfjord
Søvik
Tomra
Isfjorden
Driva
Lønset
Ålesund
Sjøholt
Andalsnes
Gjøra
Spjelkavik
Tresfjord
Voll
Sørøyane
Hareid
Sykkylven
Stordal
Eikesdal
Storfjorden
Dovrefjell-Sunndalsfjella
Ulsteinvik
Festøy
Stranda
Sylte
Verma
Vartdal
Romsdalen
Rauma
Larsnes
Ørsta
Eidsdal
Pyttegga 1999
Lesjaskog
Dovrefjell
Leikanger
Volda
Tafjord
Hjerkinn
Folkestad
Sildegapet
Selje
Storfjorden
Hellesylt
Lora
Fokstua
Dovre
Raudeberg
Åheim
Djupvasshytta
Reinheimen
Nyseter
Dombås
Måløy
Totland
Stårheim
Hornindal
Grotli
Pollfoss
Bremangerlandet
Stryn
Videseter
Isane
Bremanger
Nordfjordeid
Innvik
Bismo
Vågåvatn
Vågåmo
Kalvåg
Ålfotbreen
Sandane
Olden
Lodalskåpa 2083
Sotaseter
Hovden
Midtgulen
Svelgen
Byrkjelo
Jostedalsbreen
Lom
Lalm
Otta
Hyen
Bøverdal
Randsverk
Florø
Eikefjord
Nordstedalsseter
Glittertind 2470
Sjoa
Stavang
Skei
Jostedal
Stongfjorden
Naustdal
Jostedalsbreen
Leirvassbu
Skåbu
Bygstad
Førde
Moskog
Skjolden
Jotunheimen
Gjendesheim
Dalseter
Stadhavet
Dovre
Drivs
Opp
Løk
Me
Ra
Ha
Fo
46
47
155

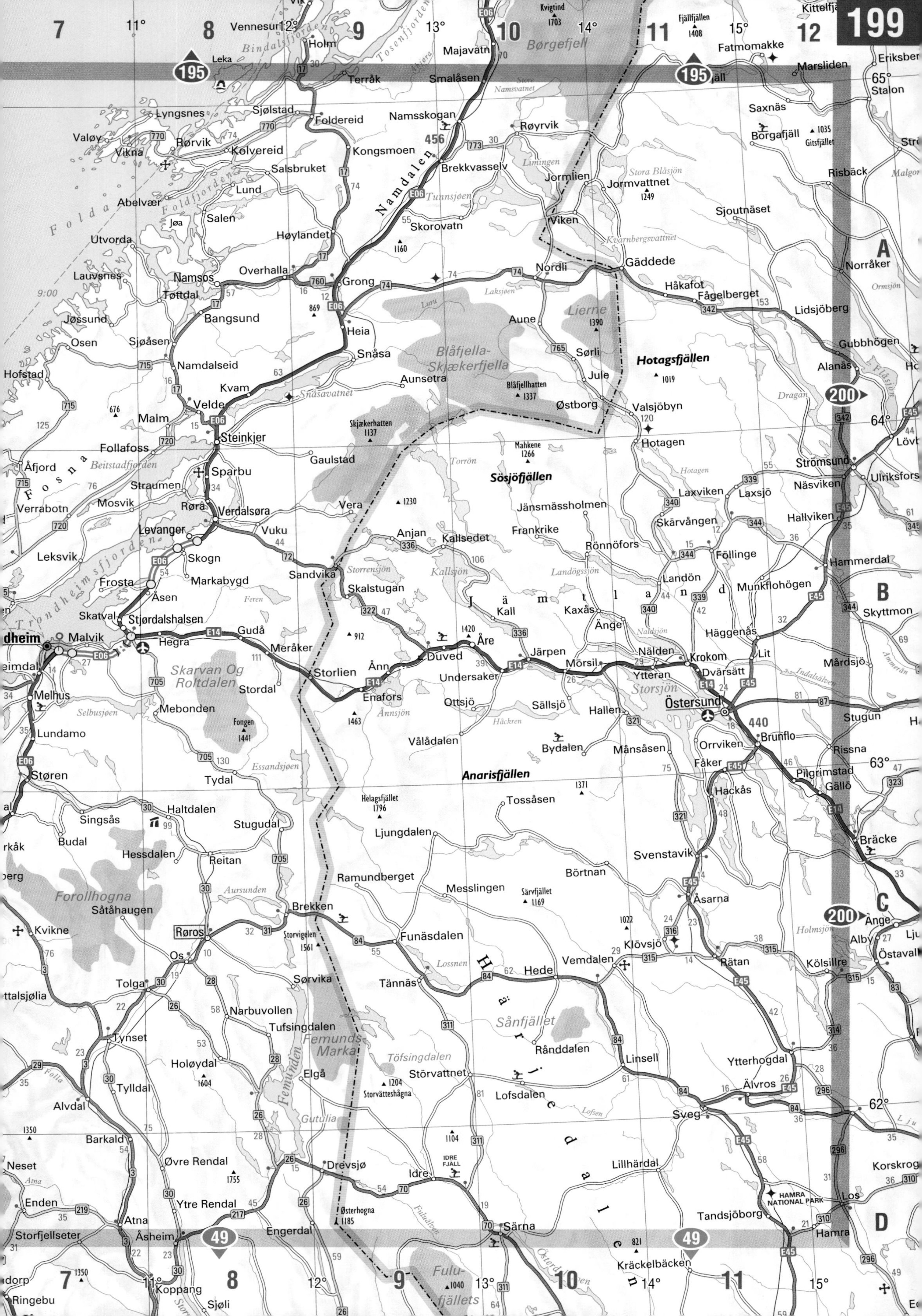

199
7
11°
8
Vennesund
12°
Bindalsfjorden
Holm
9
Tosenfjorden
13°
E06
10
Kvigtind 1703
14°
11
Fjällfjällen 1408
15°
12
Kittelfjäll
Majavatn
Børgefjell
Fatmomakke
Marsliden
Eriksberg
195
Leka
Terråk
Smalåsen
Namsvatnet
65°
Stalon
Lyngsnes
Sjølstad
Foldereid
Namsskogan
Røyrvik
Saxnäs
Valøy
770
Rørvik
Vikna
Kolvereid
Kongsmoen
456
773
Borgafjäll
1035 Gitsfjället
Salsbruket
Namdalen
Brekkvasselv
Limingen
Stora Blåsjön
Risbäck
Malgomaj
Lund
Jormlien
Jormvattnet
1249
Folda
Foldfjorden
Abelvær
Tunnsjøen
Jøa
Salen
Skorovatn
Viken
Sjoutnäset
Utvorda
Høylandet
1160
Kvarnbergsvattnet
A
Namsos
Overhalla
Grong
Nordli
Gäddede
Norråker
Lauvsnes
Tøttdal
Laksjøen
Håkafot
Fågelberget
Ormsjön
Bangsund
869
Luru
Lierne
1390
Lidsjöberg
Jøssund
Heia
Aune
Osen
Sjøåsen
Snåsa
Blåfjella-Skjækerfjella
Sørli
Hotagsfjällen
Gubbhögen
Namdalseid
Jule
Alanäs
Hofstad
Kvam
Aunsetra
1019
Flåsjön
Velde
Snåsavatnet
Blåfjellhatten 1337
Østborg
Dragan
200
Malm
Valsjöbyn
676
Skjækerhatten 1137
64°
Steinkjer
Hotagen
Lövberga
Follafoss
Mahkene 1266
Strömsund
Åfjord
Beitstadfjorden
Gaulstad
Torrön
Ulriksfors
Fosna
Sparbu
Sösjöfjällen
Näsviken
Straumen
Laxviken
Laxsjö
Verrabotn
Mosvik
Røra
Vera
1230
Jänsmässholmen
Verdalsøra
Hallviken
Levanger
Vuku
Skärvången
Leksvik
Skogn
Anjan
Kallsedet
Frankrike
Trondheimsfjorden
Rönnöfors
Föllinge
Hammerdal
Markabygd
Sandvika
Storrensjön
Kallsjön
Landögssjön
Landön
Frosta
Skalstugan
Jämtland
Munkflohögen
B
Åsen
Feren
Kaxås
Skyttmon
Skatval
Stjørdalshalsen
Kall
Änge
Trondheim
Malvik
Hegra
Gudå
Meråker
912
1420
Åre
Häggenås
Mårdsjö
Heimdal
Duved
Järpen
Nälden
Krokom
Lit
Skarvan Og Roltdalen
Storlien
Ånn
Undersaker
Mörsil
Ytteran
Dvärsätt
Indalsälven
Stordal
Storsjön
Enafors
Ottsjö
Sällsjö
Hallen
Östersund
Stugun
Melhus
Mebonden
Selbusjøen
1463
Ånnsjön
Håckren
440
Fongen 1441
Vålådalen
Bydalen
Månsåsen
Brunflo
Lundamo
Orrviken
Rissna
Fåker
63°
Støren
Essandsjøen
Tydal
Anarisfjällen
1371
Pilgrimstad
Gällö
Hackås
Singsås
Haltdalen
Tossåsen
Helagsfjället 1796
Stugudal
Ljungdalen
Budal
Bräcke
Hessdalen
Reitan
Svenstavik
Börtnan
Ramundberget
Messlingen
Särvfjället 1169
Aursunden
Forollhogna
Såtåhaugen
Åsarna
C
Brekken
Kvikne
1022
Ånge
Røros
Storvigelen 1561
Funäsdalen
Klövsjö
Holmsjön
Os
Alby
Östavall
Lossnen
Vemdalen
Rätan
Kölsillre
Tolga
Sørvika
Tännäs
Hede
Narbuvollen
Härjedalen
Tufsingdalen
Sånfjället
Tynset
Femundsmarka
Rånddalen
Holøydal
1604
Töfsingdalen
Linsell
Ytterhogdal
Elgå
Störvattnet
Tylldal
1204 Storvätteshågna
Lofsdalen
Älvros
Alvdal
Femunden
Sveg
62°
Gutulia
Lofsen
Ljusnan
1350
Barkald
1104
Neset
Øvre Rendal
1755
Drevsjø
IDRE FJÄLL
Lillhärdal
Korskrogen
Atna
Idre
HAMRA NATIONAL PARK
Los
Enden
Ytre Rendal
Østerhogna 1185
Fulufjället
Tandsjöborg
D
Storfjellseter
Atna
Åsheim
49
Engerdal
Särna
Hamra
821
Kräckelbäcken
Österdalälven
Fulufjällets
1040
Koppang
Stor-Elvdal
Sjøli
Ringebu
12°
13°
14°
15°

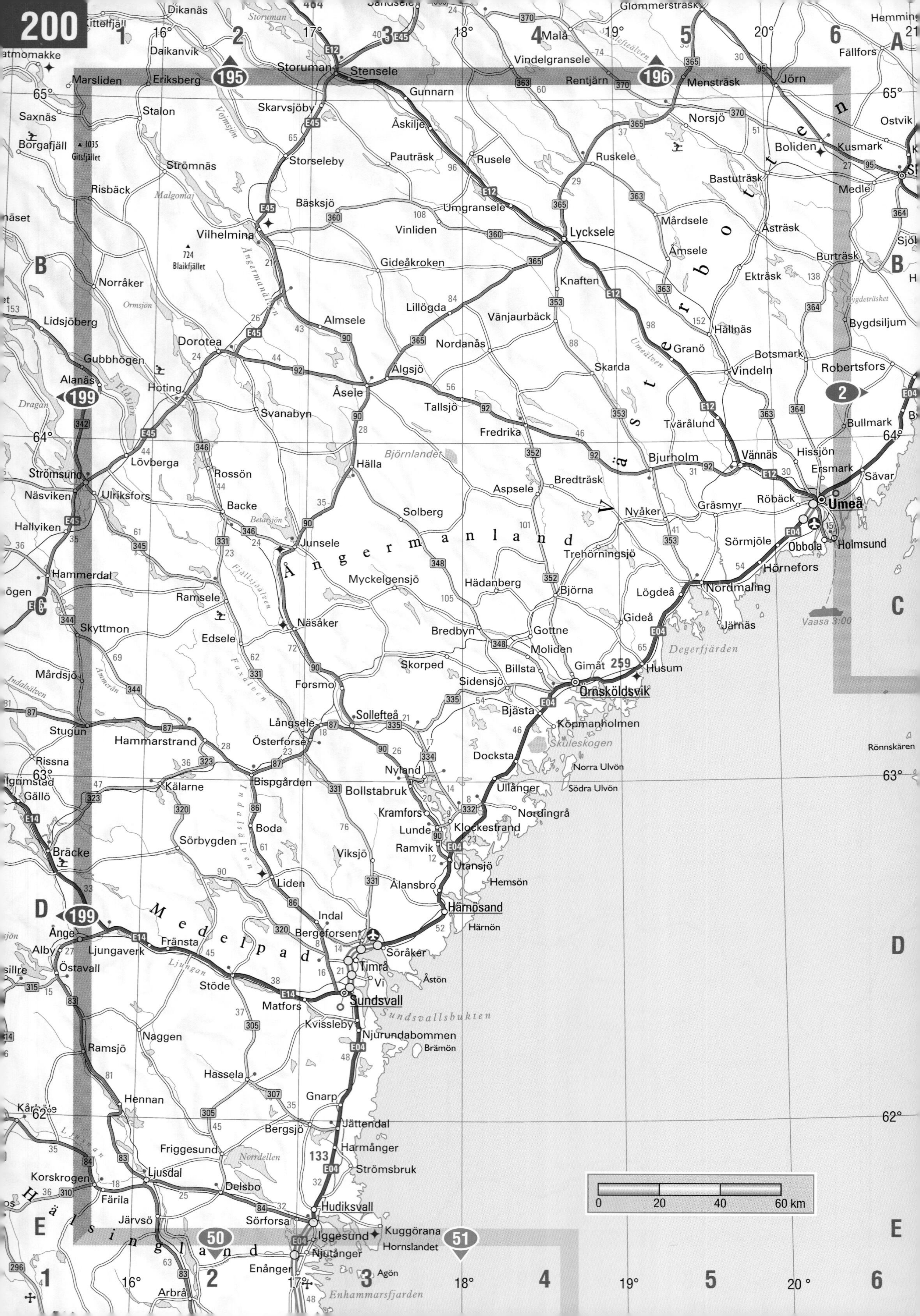
195
196
199
2
50
51
Storuman
Stensele
Gunnarn
Skarvsjöby
Åskilje
Marsliden
Eriksberg
Stalon
Saxnäs
Borgafjäll
1035 Gitsfjället
Strömnäs
Risbäck
Malgomaj
Storseleby
Pauträsk
Rusele
Bäsksjö
Umgransele
Vinliden
Vilhelmina
724 Blaikfjället
Gideåkroken
Lycksele
Norråker
Lillögda
Vänjaurbäck
Knaften
Lidsjöberg
Almsele
Dorotea
Nordanås
Gubbhögen
Alanäs
Hoting
Ålgsjö
Åsele
Tallsjö
Svanabyn
Fredrika
Björnlandet
Hälla
Lövberga
Strömsund
Rossön
Näsviken
Ulriksfors
Backe
Solberg
Aspsele
Bredträsk
Hallviken
Junsele
Hammerdal
Ramsele
Myckelgensjö
Hädanberg
Skyttmon
Edsele
Näsåker
Bredbyn
Gottne
Moliden
Mårdsjö
Skorped
Billsta
Gimåt
Husum
Forsmo
Sidensjö
Örnsköldsvik
Bjästa
Långsele
Sollefteå
Stugun
Hammarstrand
Österforse
Köpmanholmen
Skuleskogen
Dockstad
Rissna
Nyland
Norra Ulvön
Södra Ulvön
Gällö
Kälarne
Bispgården
Bollstabruk
Ullånger
Nordingrå
Kramfors
Lunde
Klockestrand
Boda
Sörbygden
Ramvik
Viksjö
Bräcke
Utansjö
Hemsön
Liden
Ålansbro
Härnösand
Härnön
Indal
Ånge
Bergeforsen
Fränsta
Ljungaverk
Söråker
Alby
Östavall
Timrå
Åstön
Stöde
Vi
Sundsvall
Matfors
Kvissleby
Sundsvallsbukten
Njurundabommen
Brämön
Naggen
Ramsjö
Hassela
Hennan
Gnarp
Jättendal
Bergsjö
Harmånger
Friggesund
Norrdellen
Strömsbruk
Ljusdal
Korskrogen
Delsbo
Färila
Hudiksvall
Järvsö
Sörforsa
Iggesund
Kuggörana
Hornslandet
Njutånger
Enånger
Agön
Enhammarsfjärden
Arbrå
Malå
Vindelgransele
Rentjärn
Mensträsk
Jörn
Norsjö
Boliden
Kusmark
Ruskele
Bastuträsk
Medle
Mårdsele
Åsträsk
Åmsele
Burträsk
Ekträsk
Hällnäs
Bygdsiljum
Granö
Botsmark
Vindeln
Robertsforts
Skarda
Tvärålund
Bullmark
Vännäs
Hissjön
Bjurholm
Ersmark
Sävar
Röbäck
Umeå
Nyåker
Gräsmyr
Sörmjöle
Obbola
Holmsund
Trehörningsjö
Hörnefors
Björna
Lögdeå
Nordmaling
Gideå
Järnäs
Vaasa 3:00
Degerfjärden
Rönnskären
Fällfors
Ostvik
Västerbotten
Ångermanland
Medelpad
Hälsingland
16°
17°
18°
19°
20°
65°
64°
63°
62°
0 20 40 60 km

City plans • Plans de villes
Stadtpläne • Piante di città

Motorway	Autoroute	Autobahn	Autostrada
Major through route	Route principale majeure	Hauptstrecke	Strada di grande communicazione
Through route	Route principale	Schnellstrasse	Strada d'importanza regionale
Secondary road	Route secondaire		
Dual carriageway	Chaussées séparées	Nebenstrasse	Strada d'interesse locale
Other road	Autre route	Zweispurig Schnellstrasse	Strada a carreggiate doppie
Tunnel	Tunnel	Nebenstrecke	Altra strada
Limited access / pedestrian road	Rue réglementée / rue piétonne	Tunnel	Galleria stradale
One-way street	Sens unique	Beschränkter Zugang/ Fussgängerzone	Strada pedonale / a accesso limitato
Parking	Parc de stationnement	Einbahnstrasse	Senso unico
Motorway number	Numéro d'autoroute	Parkplatz	Parcheggio
National road number	Numéro de route nationale	Autobahnnummer	Numero di autostrada
European road number	Numéro de route européenne	Nationalstrassen-nummer	Numero di strada nazionale
Destination	Destination	Europäische Strassennummer	Numero di strada europea
Car ferry	Bac passant les autos	Ziel	Destinazione
Railway	Chemin de fer	Autofähre	Traghetto automobili
Rail/bus station	Gare / gare routière	Eisenbahn	Ferrovia
Underground, metro station	Station de métro	Bahnhof / Busstation	Stazione ferrovia / pullman
Cable car	Téléférique	U-Bahnstation	Metropolitano
Abbey, cathedral	Abbaye, cathédrale	Drahtseilbahn	Funivia
Church of interest	Église intéressante	Abtei, Kloster, Kathedrale	Abbazia, duomo
Synagogue	Synagogue	Interessante Kirche	Chiesa da vedere
Hospital	Hôpital	Synagoge	Sinagoga
Police station	Police	Krankenhaus	Ospedale
Post office	Bureau de poste	Polizeiwache	Polizia
Tourist information	Office de tourisme	Postamt	Ufficio postale
Place of interest	Autre curiosité	Informationsbüro	Ufficio informazioni turistiche
		Sonstige Sehenswürdigkeit	Luogo da vedere

Approach maps • Agglomérations
Carte régionale • Regionalkarte

Toll motorway – with motorway number	Autoroute à péage – avec numéro d'autoroute	Gebührenpflichtige Autobahn – mit Autobahnnummer	Autostrada a pedaggio – con numero
Toll-free motorway – with European road number	Autoroute – avec numéro de route européenne	Gebührenfreie Autobahn – Europäische Strassennummer	Autostrada – con numero di strada europea
Pre-pay motorway – vignette required	Autoroute – 'vignette'	Autobahn – 'vignette'	Autostrada – 'vignette'
Motorway services	Aire de service	Autobahnservice	Area di servizio autostradale
Motorway junction full access, restricted access	Échangeur d'autoroute – accès libre, accès reglementé	Autobahnkreuz – voller/begrenzter Zugang	Raccordi autostradali – completo/parziali
Under construction	En construction	Im Bau	In construzione
Tunnel	Tunnel	Tunnel	Galleria stradale
Major route dual carriageway single carriageway	Route principale chausées séparées chausée sans séparation	Hauptstrecke – zweispurige Schnellstrasse	Strada di grande communicazione carreggiata doppia carreggiata unica
Secondary route dual carriageway single carriageway	Route secondaire chausées séparées chausée sans séparation	Nebenstrasse – zweispurige Schnellstrasse	Strada d'interesse locale – carreggiata doppia carreggiata unica
Other road	Autre route	Nebenstrecke	Altra strada
Car ferry	Bac passant les autos	Autofähre	Traghetto automobili
Destination	Destination	Ziel GIRONA	Destinazione
Railway	Chemin de fer	Eisenbahn	Ferrovia
Railway station	Gare	Hauptbahnhof	Stazione ferrovia
Height – in metres	Altitude – en mètres	Höhe – über dem Meeresspiegel	Altezza in metri
Airport	Aéroport principal	Flughafen	Aeroporto
Airfield	Autre aéroport	Flugplatz	Aerodromo/ campo d'aviazione
City plan coverage area	Région de plan de ville	Vom Stadtplan abgedecktes Gebiet	Area della pianta della città

Alicante

0 — km — 0.5

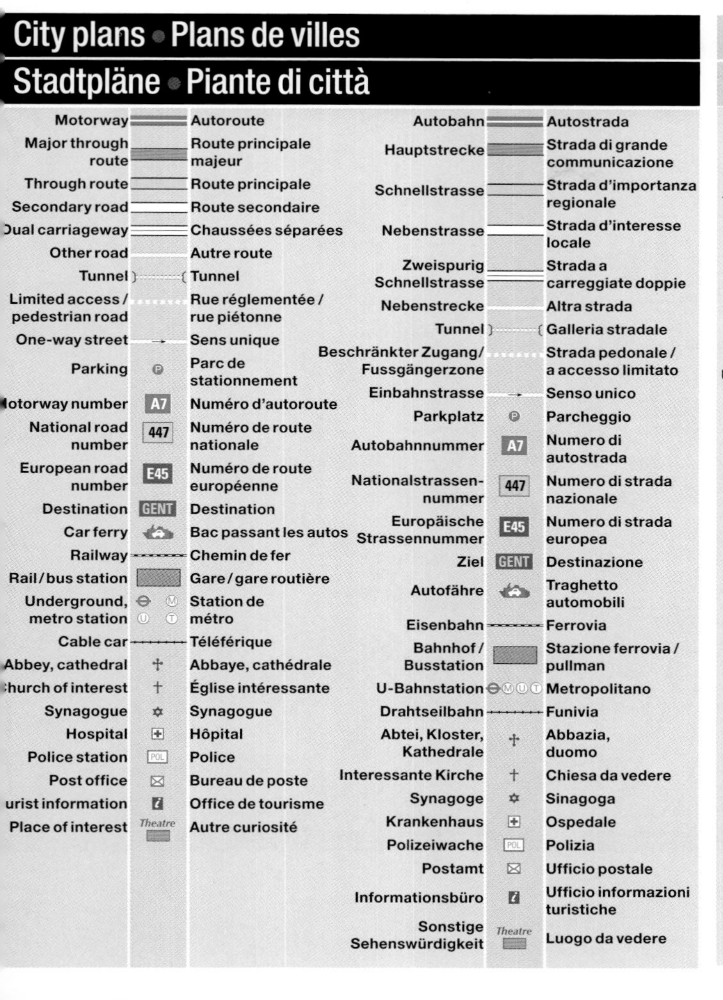
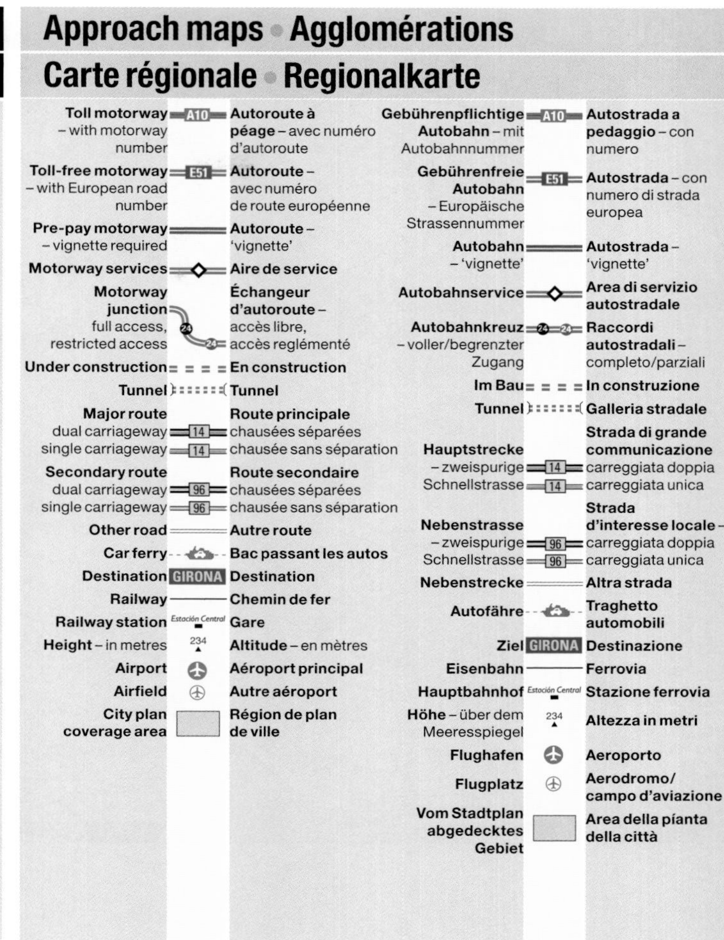

Antwerpen Antwerp

0 — km — 1

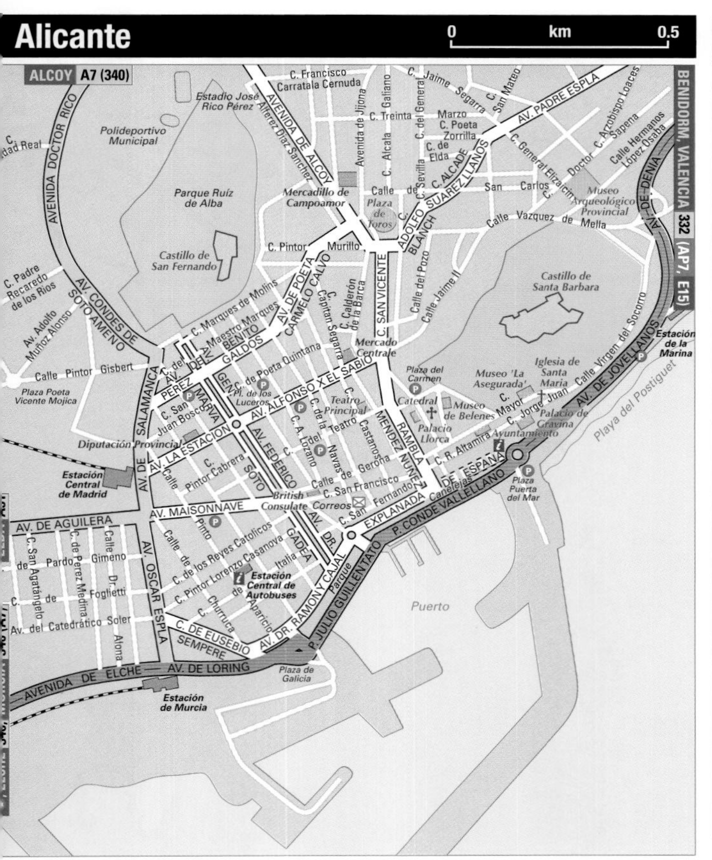
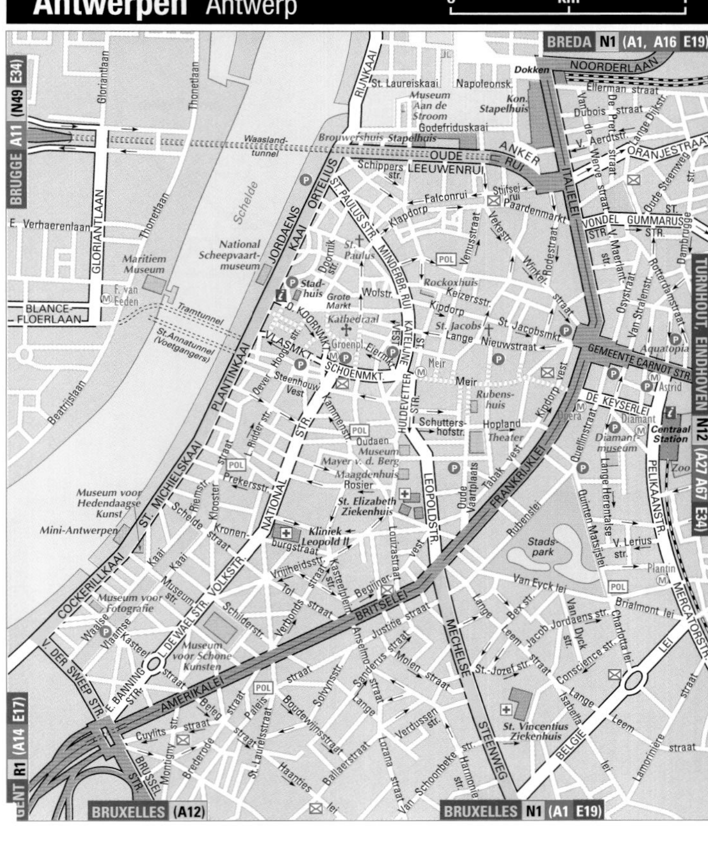

Amsterdam

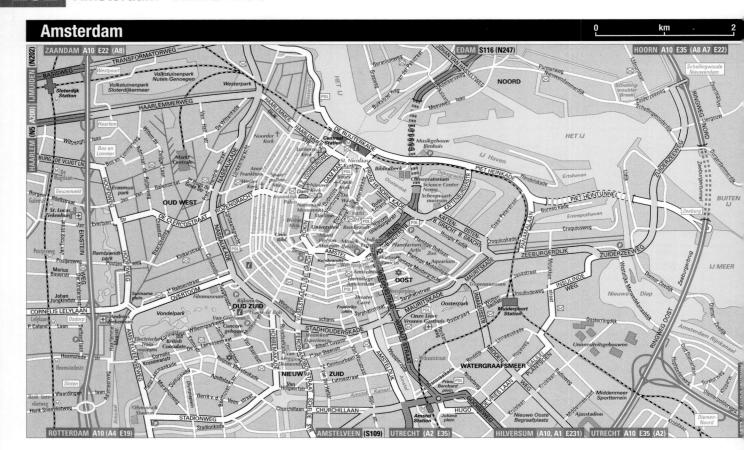

Amsterdam

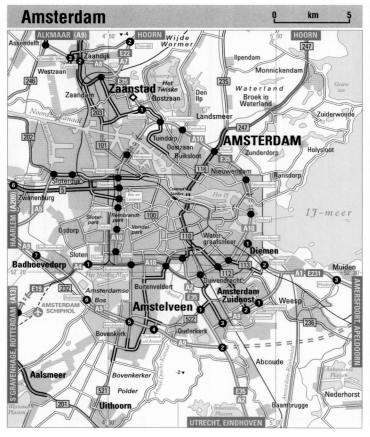

Athina Athens

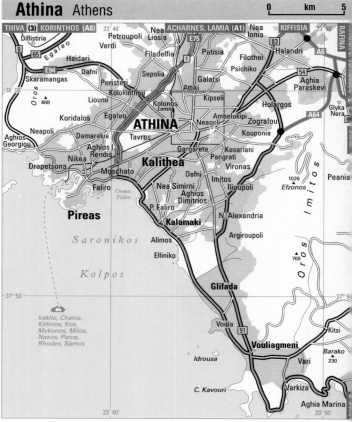

Athina Athens

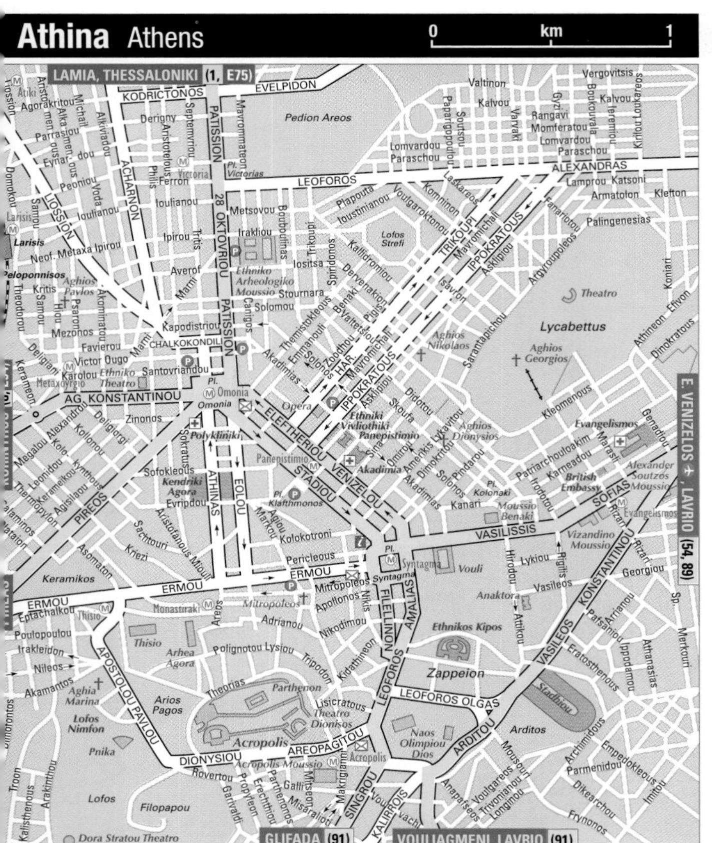
0 km 1
LAMIA, THESSALONIKI (1, E75)
EVELPIDON
KODRIGTONOS
Pedion Areos
PATISSION
ACHARNON
LIOSSION
ALEXANDRAS
LEOFOROS
28 OKTOVRIOU
Larisis
Peloponnisos
Lycabettus
Theatro
Aghios Georgios
CHALKOKONDILI
Omonia
AG. KONSTANTINOU
PIREOS
STADIOU
ELEFTHERIOU VENIZELOU
ATHINAS
EOLOU
VASILISSIS SOFIAS
Evangelismos
British Embassy
Keramikos
ERMOU
Syntagma
Vouli
Ethnikos Kipos
Zappeion
Stadion
LEOFOROS OLGAS
Ardittos
Parthenon
Acropolis
Arios Pagos
Filopapou
Lofos
Dora Stratou Theatro
AREOPAGITOU
DIONYSIOU
VASILEOS KONSTANTINOU
E. VENIZELOS LAVRIO (54, 89)
GLIFADA (91)
VOULIAGMENI, LAVRIO (91)

Basel

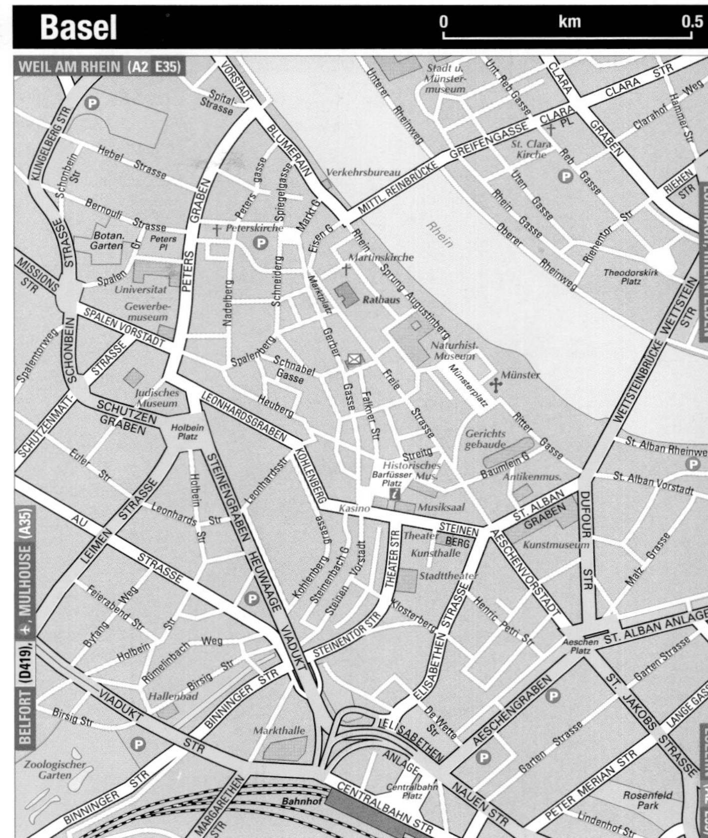
0 km 0.5
WEIL AM RHEIN (A2 E35)
LÖRRACH, RHEINFELDEN
Rhein
MITTLERE BRÜCKE
Verkehrsbureau
GREIFENGASSE
CLARA STR
St. Clara Kirche
Theodorskirch Platz
WETTSTEINBRÜCKE
Botan. Garten
Peterskirche
Martinskirche
Rathaus
Universität
Gewerbe-museum
Naturhist. Museum
Münster
SPALEN VORSTADT
SCHÜTZENGRABEN
Jüdisches Museum
LEONHARDSGRABEN
Historisches Museum
Kunstmuseum
Antikenmus.
ST. ALBAN GRABEN
DUFOUR STR
Musiksaal
Kasino
Theater
Kunsthalle
Stadttheater
STEINEN BERG
AESCHENVORSTADT
ST. ALBAN ANLAGE
Aeschen Platz
ELISABETHEN STR
HEUWAAGE VIADUKT
STEINENTOR STR
Markthalle
Bahnhof
CENTRALBAHN STR
Centralbahn Platz
AESCHENGRABEN
ST. JAKOBS STRASSE
PETER MERIAN STR
Rosenfeld Park
Zoologischer Garten
BINNINGER STR
Hallenbad
BELFORT (D419), MULHOUSE (A35)
LUZERN (A2 E35)

Barcelona

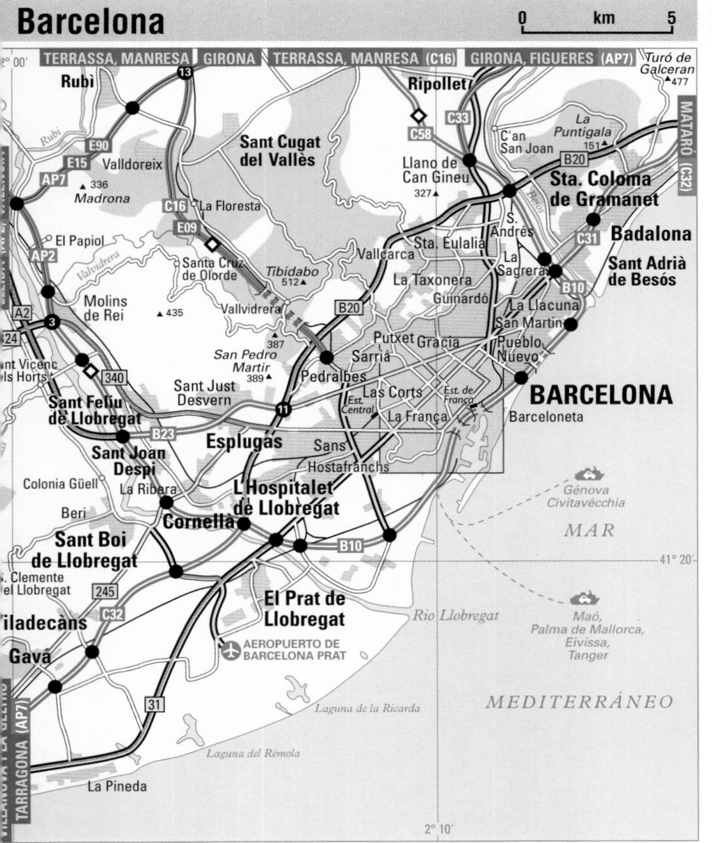
0 km 5
TERRASSA, MANRESA
GIRONA
TERRASSA, MANRESA (C16)
GIRONA, FIGUERES (AP7)
MATARÓ (C32)
Turó de Galceran
Rubí
Ripollet
Sant Cugat del Vallès
Valldoreix
Madrona
La Floresta
Llano de Can Gineu
C'an San Joan
La Puntigala
Sta. Coloma de Gramanet
Badalona
Sant Adrià de Besós
El Papiol
Santa Cruz de Olorde
Tibidabo
Molins de Rei
Vallvidrera
Vallcarca
Sta. Eulalia
La Taxonera
Guinardó
S. Andrés
La Sagrera
La Llacuna
San Martin
Pueblo Nuevo
Putxet
Gracia
Sarriá
Pedralbes
San Pedro Martir
Sant Just Desvern
Sant Feliu de Llobregat
Sant Joan Despí
Esplugas
Las Corts
La França
Sans
Hostafranchs
BARCELONA
Barceloneta
Colonia Güell
La Ribera
Beri
L'Hospitalet de Llobregat
Cornellà
Sant Boi de Llobregat
Sant Clemente del Llobregat
Viladecans
Gavà
El Prat de Llobregat
AEROPUERTO DE BARCELONA PRAT
Río Llobregat
Génova Civitavécchia
MAR
Maó, Palma de Mallorca, Eivissa, Tanger
MEDITERRÁNEO
Laguna de la Ricarda
Laguna del Remola
La Pineda
TARRAGONA (AP7)

Barcelona

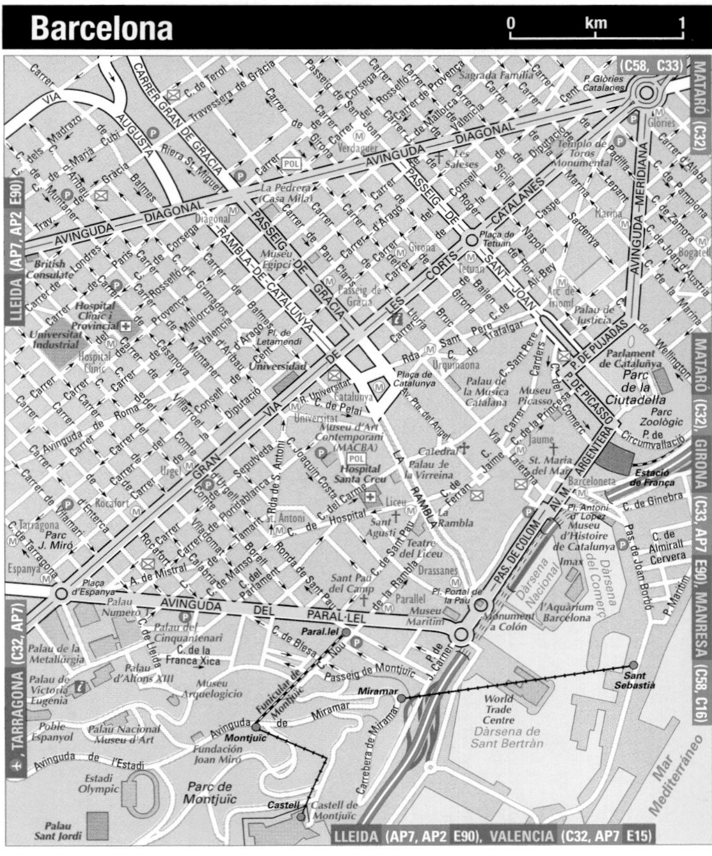
0 km 1
(C58, C33)
MATARÓ (C32)
AVINGUDA DIAGONAL
Sagrada Família
Pl. Glòries Catalanes
Temple de la Sagrada Família
AVINGUDA MERIDIANA
Plaça de Toros Monumental
La Pedrera (Casa Milà)
PASSEIG DE GRÀCIA
RAMBLA DE CATALUNYA
GRAN VIA DE LES CORTS CATALANES
Plaça de Tetuan
British Consulate
Hospital Clínic i Provincial
Universitat Industrial
Universitat
Museu Egipci
Pl. de Catalunya
Plaça de Catalunya
Palau de la Música Catalana
Museu Picasso
Parc de la Ciutadella
Parc Zoològic
Museu d'Art Contemporani (MACBA)
Catedral
Palau de la Virreina
LA RAMBLA
Gran Teatre del Liceu
Drassanes
Barceloneta
Estació de França
Museu d'Història de Catalunya
Imax
L'Aquàrium Barcelona
Monument a Colón
PAS DE COLOM
Darsena Nacional
Dàrsena del Comerç
Parc J. Miró
Plaça d'Espanya
AVINGUDA DEL PARAL·LEL
Palau Nacional Museu d'Art
Fundación Joan Miró
Parc de Montjuïc
Estadi Olympic
Palau Sant Jordi
Castell de Montjuïc
Poble Espanyol
World Trade Centre
Dàrsena de Sant Bertrán
Sant Sebastià
Miramar
Mar Mediterráneo
LLEIDA (AP7, AP2 E90)
TARRAGONA (C32, AP7)
LLEIDA (AP7, AP2 E90), VALENCIA (C32, AP7 E15)
MATARÓ (C32), GIRONA (C33, AP7 E90), MANRESA (C58, C16)

Berlin

0 km 5

HAMBURG (A24), ROSTOCK (A24, A19)
ORANIENBURG, SASSNITZ (96)
HAMBURG (A24, A29)
SZCZECIN (A6)
NAUEN, KYRITZ
BRANDENBURG
MAGDEBURG (A10, A2), LEIPZIG (A10, A9)
DRESDEN (A13, E55)

BERLIN

Berlin

0 km 1

ORANIENBURG 96 E251
ORANIENBURG (96 E251)
BERNAU
NAUEN 2 5
POTSDAM (A100 A115 E51 1)
POTSDAM 1 (A103)
LUCKAU 96
BERLIN-BRANDENBURG 17

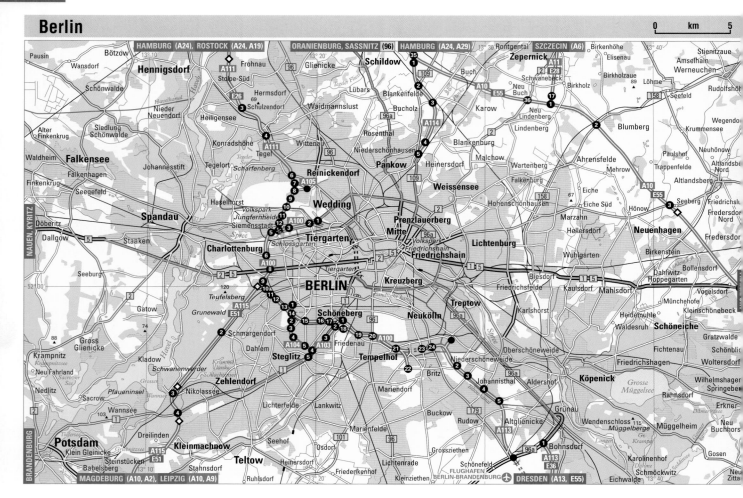

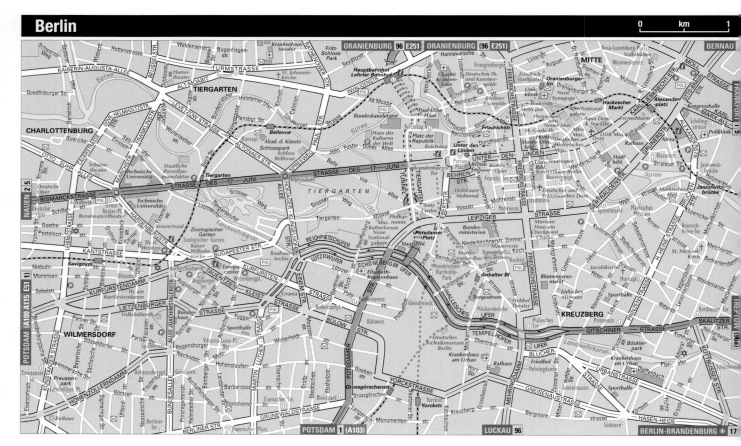

Beograd Belgrade

0 km 1

Bruxelles Brussels

0 km 5

Bordeaux

0 km 5

Bordeaux

0 km 1

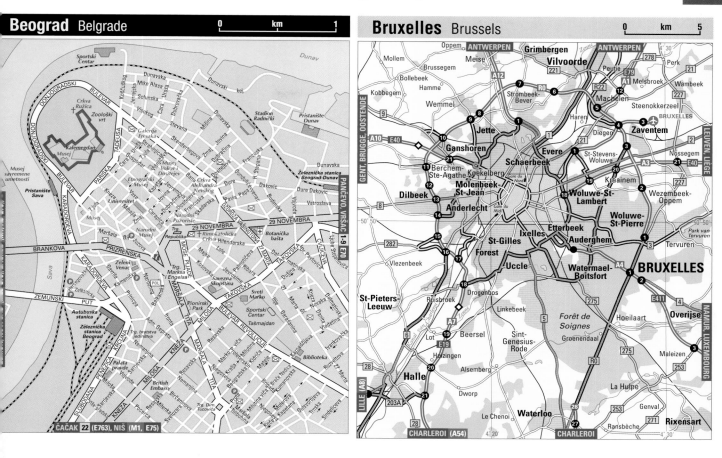

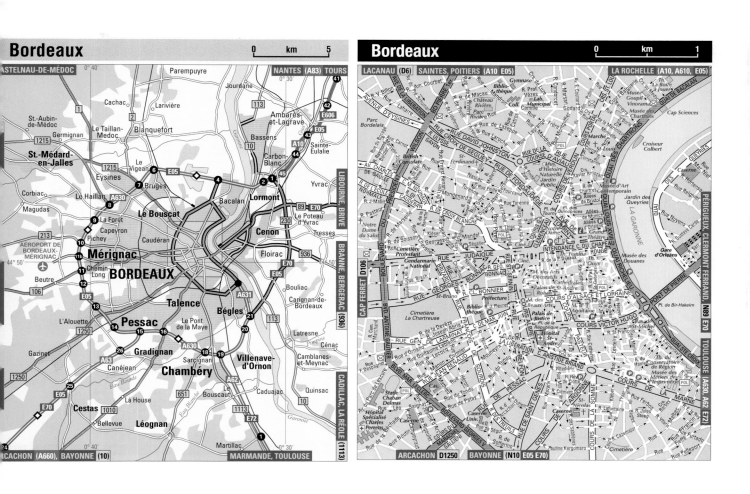

Bruxelles Brussels

0 km 1

GENT, OOSTENDE (A10 E40) · ANTWERPEN (A12) · MECHELEN N1 · ANTWERPEN (A1) · BRUXELLES NATIONAL (A201) · NINOVE N8 · MONS N6 · CHARLEROI N5 · NAMUR (A4 E411)

ANDERLECHT · ST.-JOSSE · ETTERBEEK · IXELLES · ST-GILLES

Gare du Nord · Gare Centrale · Gare du Midi (Eurostar) · Gare du Quartier Léopold · Bourse · Cathédrale St-Michel · Palais Royal · Palais de Justice · Parc de Bruxelles · Parc Léopold · Cinquantenaire · Jardin Botanique

Budapest

0 km 5

VÁC · VÁC · Fót · Mogyoród · MISKOLC, NYÍREGYHÁZA, DEBRECEN (M35) · ESZTERGOM (111) · GYŐR, WIEN (A4) · DUNAÚJVÁROS, SZÉKESFEHÉRVÁR (M7) · KECSKEMÉT, SZEGED · SZOLNOK

Üröm · Bekásmegyer · Káposztásmegyer · Sikátorpuszta · Rómaifürdő · Újpest · Rákospalota · Széphalom · Pesthidegkút · Óbuda · Pestújhely · Csömör · Hűvösvölgy · Angyalföld · Újpalota · Árpádföld · Rákosszentmihály · Cinkota · Virányos · Buda · Zugló · Sashalom · Zugliget · Mátyásföld · Pest · Józsefváros · Rákosliget · Gazdagrét · Ferencváros · Kőbánya · Rákoskert · Budaörs · Sasad · Kelenföld · Erzsébet-Telep · Rákoskeresztúr · Rákoshegy · BUDAPEST · Kispest · Pesterzsébet · Pestlőrinc · BUDAPEST FERIHEGY · Budafok · Budatétény · Csepel · Erd · Pestimre · Háros · Soroksár · Csillagtelep · Vecsés · Gyál · Halásztelek · Duna

Budapest

0 km 1

ESZTERGOM 11 · VÁC 2, ZVOLEN (66) E77 · GYŐR (M1 E60 E75), SZÉKESFEHÉRVÁR (M7 E66 E71) · PÉCS (6 E73) · PÉCS (6 E73) · BAJA 51

Margitsziget · MARGIT HÍD · SZENT ISTVÁN KÖRÚT · Nyugati Pályaudvar · Batthyány Tér · Országház · Déli Pályaudvar · Budavári palota · SZÉCHENYI LÁNCHÍD · ERZSÉBET HÍD · SZABADSÁG HÍD · Gellért-hegy · Citadella · ANDRÁSSY ÚT · Keleti · DUNA

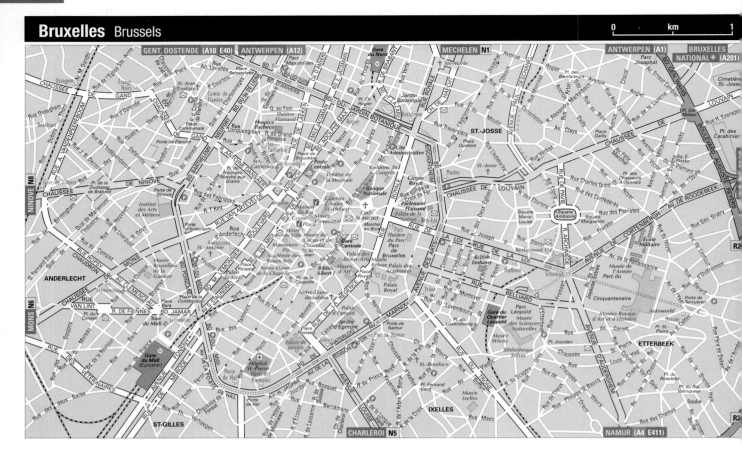

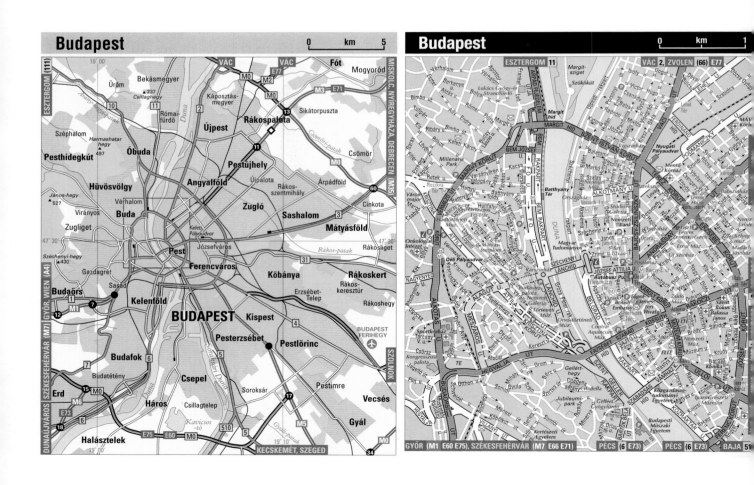

Dublin

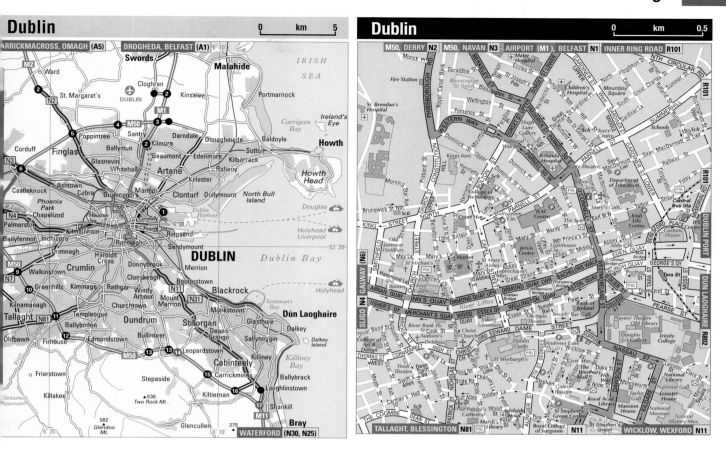

Dublin

Düsseldorf

Edinburgh

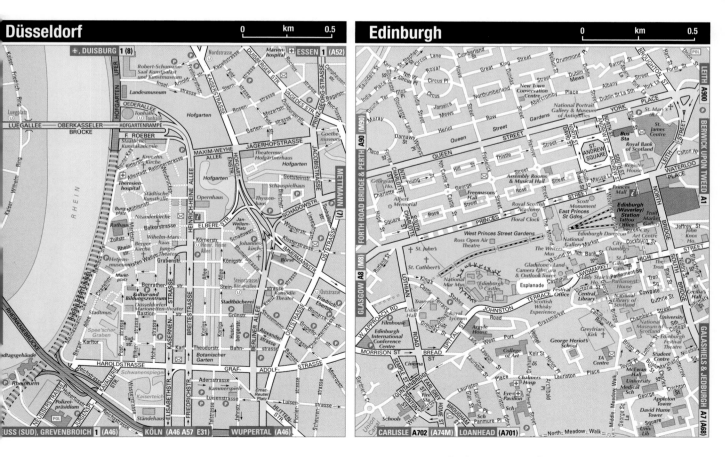

For Cologne and Copenhagen see page 212

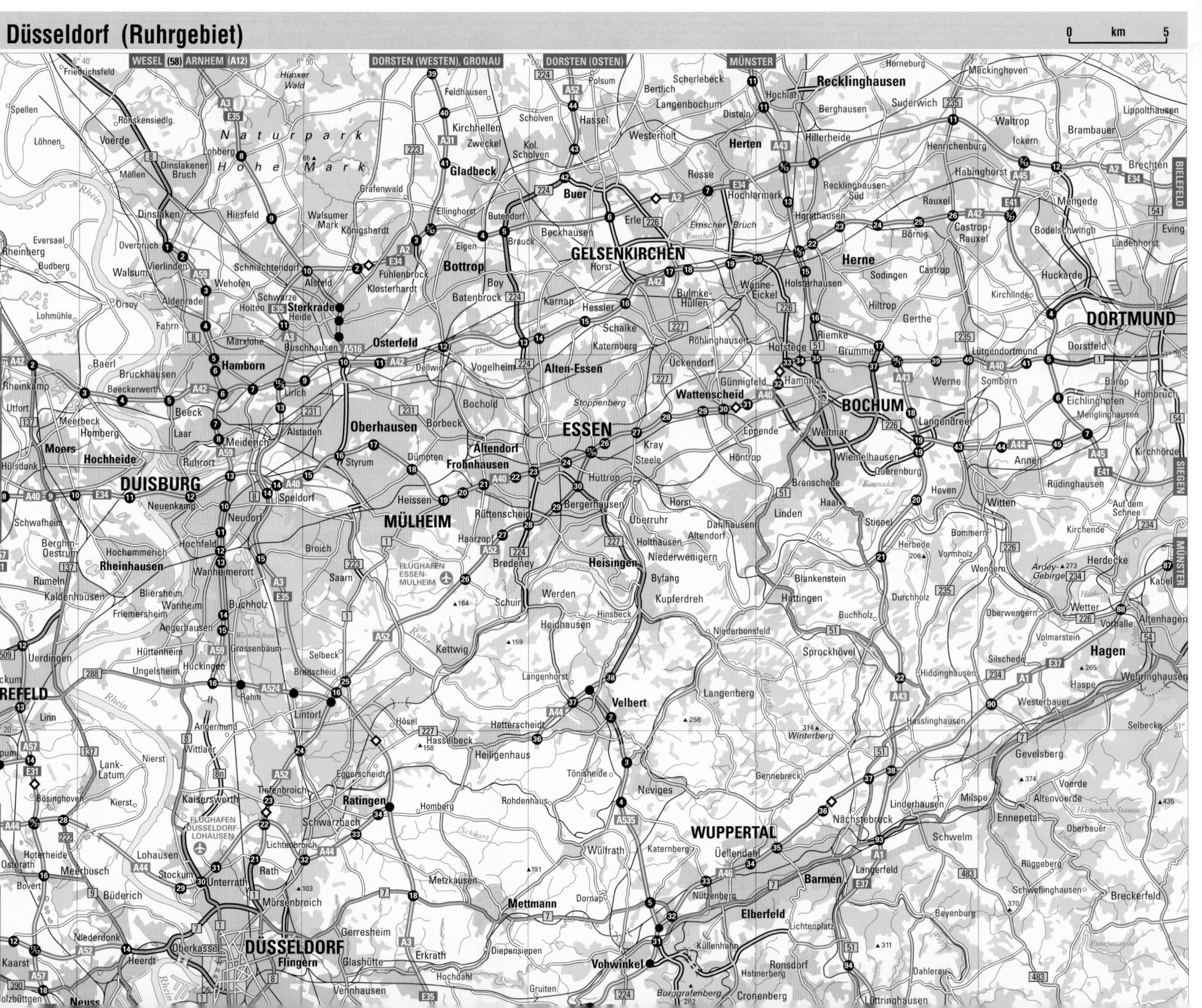
Düsseldorf (Ruhrgebiet)
DORTMUND
BOCHUM
ESSEN
GELSENKIRCHEN
DUISBURG
DÜSSELDORF
WUPPERTAL
KREFELD
MÜLHEIM
Oberhausen
Hagen
Herne
Recklinghausen
Herten
Bottrop
Gladbeck
Buer
Wattenscheid
Witten
Moers
Velbert
Ratingen
Mettmann
Neuss
Elberfeld
Barmen
Sterkrade
Osterfeld
Hamborn
Rheinhausen
Heisingen
Altendorf
Alten-Essen
Vohwinkel
Hochheide
FLUGHAFEN ESSEN-MÜLHEIM
FLUGHAFEN DÜSSELDORF-LOHAUSEN
BIELEFELD
SIEGEN
MÜNSTER
WESEL
ARNHEM
DORSTEN (WESTEN), GRONAU
DORSTEN (OSTEN)
RHEINBERG
EINDHOVEN
VENLO
MÖNCHEN GLADBACH

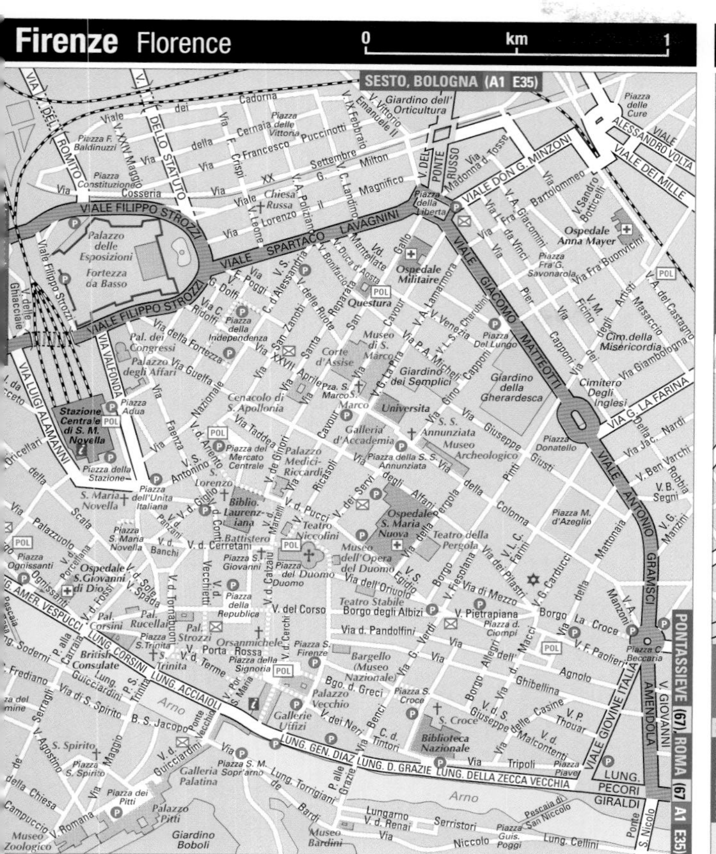

Firenze Florence

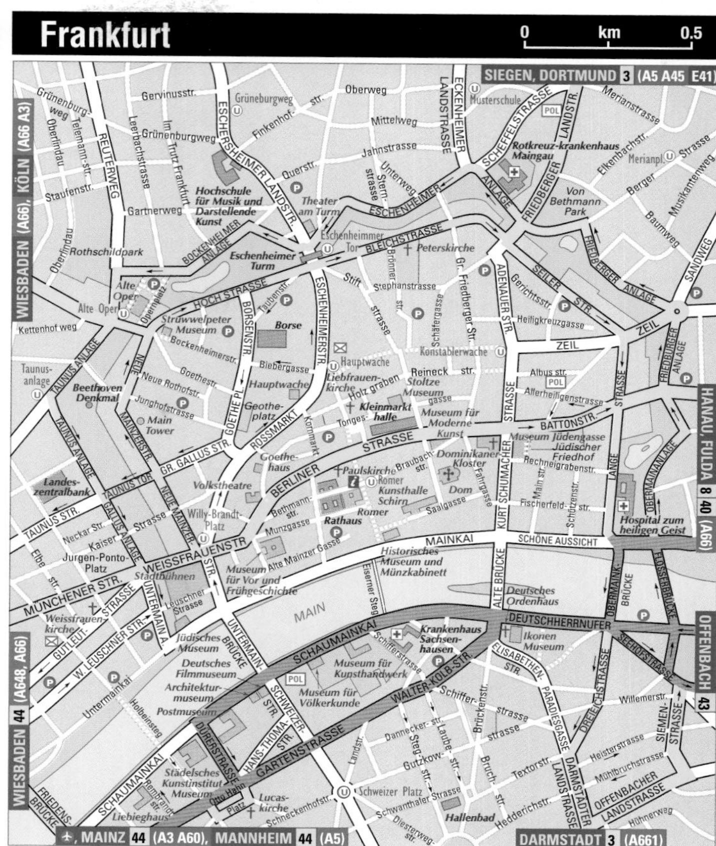

Frankfurt

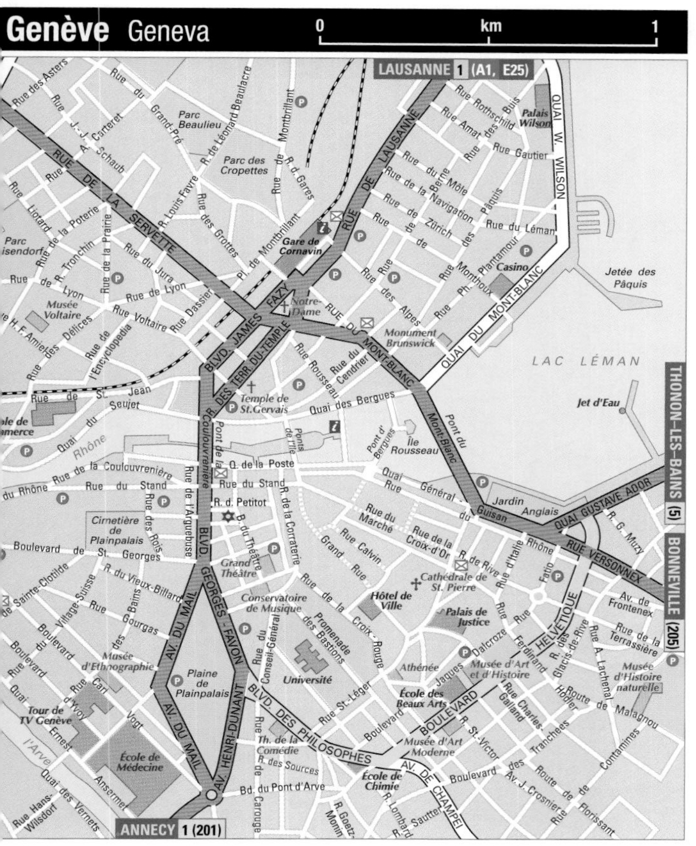

Genève Geneva

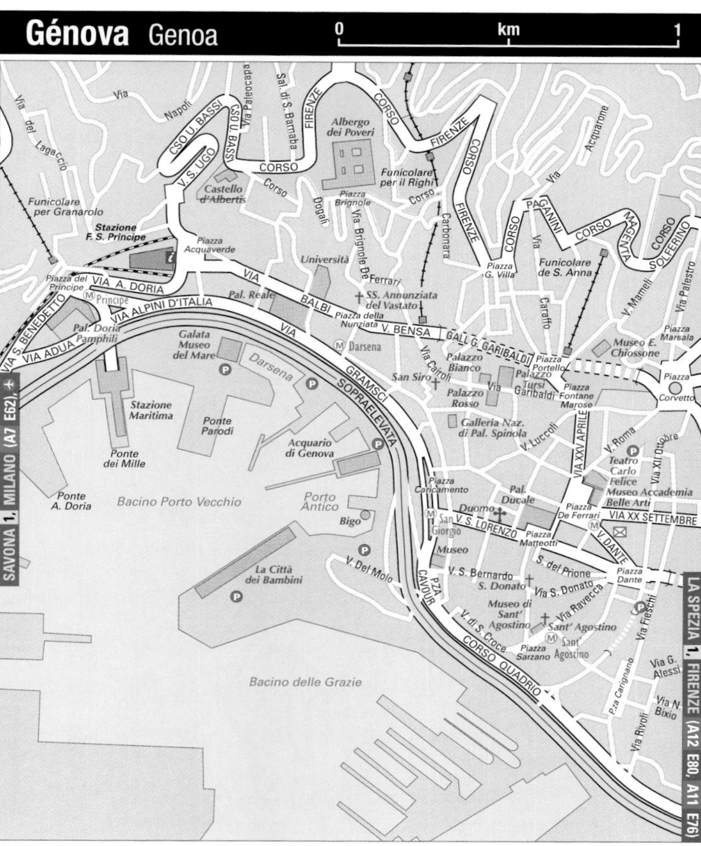

Génova Genoa

Granada

0 km 0.5

SEVILLA (A92) · JAÉN (A44 E902) · MOTRIL (A44 E902)

ALBAICAN · ALHAMBRA · Catedral · Palacio Arzobispal · Palacio Madraza · Ayuntamiento · Capitanía General · Diputación · Palacio de Carlos V · Palacio Real · Torre Bermejas · Puerta de las Granadas · Casa de los Tiros · Museo Arqueológico · Palacio de Zafra · Real Chancillería · Hospital San Juan de Dios · Jardín Botánico · Campo del Príncipe · Museo de Falla

Cuesta de Alhacaba · Gran Vía de Colón · Calle Reyes Católicos · Carrera del Darro · Paseo de Padre Manjón · Cuesta de Gomérez · Paseo de la Alhambra · Calle Ángel Ganivet · Calle San Matías · Acera del Casino · Carrera del Genil · Calle de Molinos · Cuesta del Caidero · Calle San Antón · Camino Nuevo de San Nicolás · Calle de San Juan de los Reyes

Göteborg Gothenburg

0 km 1

UDDEVALLA (E06) · TROLLHÄTTAN E6 · VARBERG (158 E06 E20)

GÖTA ÄLV · Lundbyhamnen · Frihamnen · LUNDBYVASSEN · GULLBERGSVASS · HEDEN · HAGA · VASA-STADEN · LORENSBERG · Centralstationen · Göteborgs Operan · Rådhuset · Börsen · Domkyrkan · British Consulate · Gamla Ullevi · Bussterminal · Skansparken · Universitet · Vasaparken · Stora Teatern · Haga Kyrkan · Skolmuseet · Handels Institut · Lilla Torget · Stortorget · Ullevigatan · Skeppsbron · Götaleden · Sjöfarten · Nya Allén · Södra Allégatan · Parkgatan · Kungsgatan · Östra Hamngatan · Vasagatan · Aschebergsgatan · Viktor Rydbergsgatan

Hamburg

0 km 5

NEUMÜNSTER, KIEL (A215) · ITZEHOE, HEIDE · ELMSHORN · BERLIN · LÜBECK · LAUENBURG (5) · HANNOVER, BREMEN (A1) · LÜNEBURG (A250)

HAMBURG · Pinneberg · Halstenbeck · Schenefeld · Osdorf · Blankenese · Altona · St. Pauli · Harburg · Wilhelmsburg · Finkenwerder · Norderstedt · Langenhorn · Poppenbüttel · Fuhlsbüttel · Barmbek · Wandsbek · Eimsbüttel · Harvestehude · Uhlenhorst · Hamm · Horn · Billstedt · Bergedorf · Veddel · Moorburg · Neugraben-Fischbek · Neu Wulmstorf · Flughafen Hamburg · Elbe

Hamburg

0 km 1

KIEL 447 (A7, E45 A215) · FLUGHAFEN HAMBURG 433 · ITZEHOE 4/5 (A23) · BREMEN (A7 A1, E22) · WEDEL 4 (431)

Universität · Planten un Blomen · Congress-Centrum-Hamburg · Dammtor · Hamburg Messe · Alte Botanischer Garten · Staatsoper Hamburg · Binnenalster · Aussenalster · Rathaus · Börse · Jungfernstieg · Hauptbahnhof · St. Petri · St. Jacobi · Speicherstadt · Deichtorhallen · Museum für Hamburgische Geschichte · Bismarck Denkmal · Landungsbrücken · Museumsschiff Rickmer Rickmers · Museumsschiff Cap San Diego · Binnenhafen · British Consulate · Kennedybrücke · Lombardsbrücke · Ludwig-Erhard-Strasse · Willy-Brandt-Strasse · Mönckebergstrasse · Holstenwall · Glacischaussee · Esplanade · Steinstrasse · Elbe

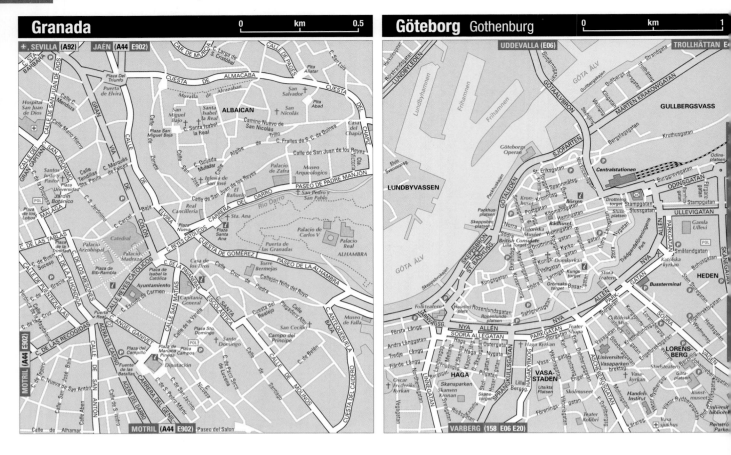

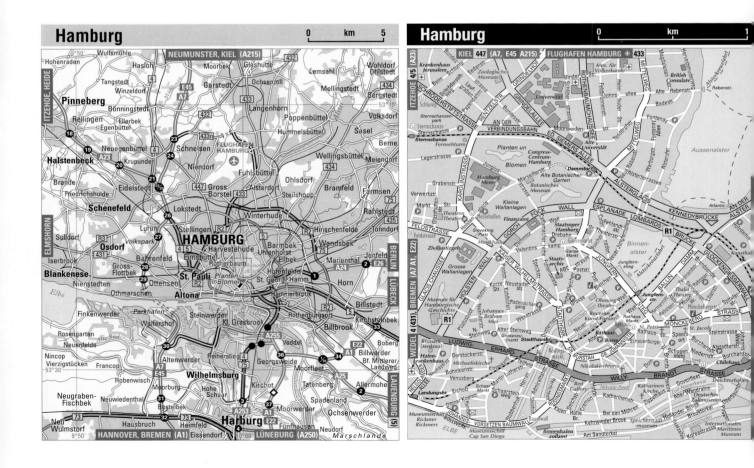

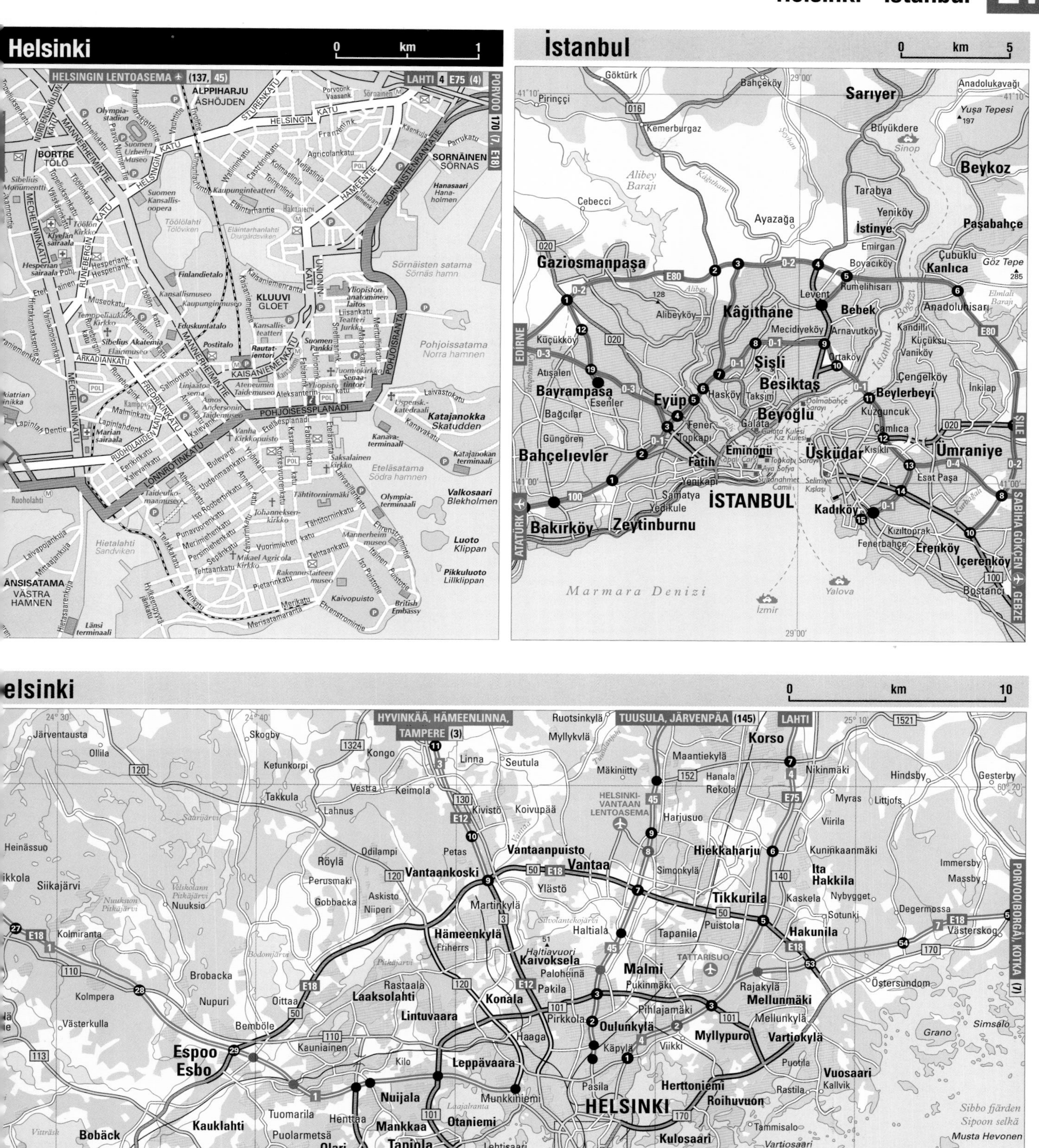
Helsinki
0 km 1
HELSINGIN LENTOASEMA (137, 45)
LAHTI 4 E75 (4)
PORVOO 170 (7, E18)
ALPPIHARJU ÅSHÖJDEN
BORTRE TÖLÖ
SÖRNÄINEN SÖRNÄS
KLUUVI GLOET
POHJOISESPLANADI
Sörnäisten satama Sörnäs hamn
Pohjoissatama Norra hamnen
Katajanokka Skatudden
Eteläsatama Södra hamnen
Hietalahti Sandviken
ÄNSISATAMA VÄSTRA HAMNEN
Länsi terminaali
Luoto Klippan
Pikkuluoto Lillklippan
Valkosaari Blekholmen
İstanbul
0 km 5
Sarıyer
Beykoz
Gaziosmanpaşa
Kâğıthane
Şişli
Beşiktaş
Bayrampaşa
Eyüp
Beyoğlu
Üsküdar
Ümraniye
Bahçelıevler
Fatih
İSTANBUL
Bakırköy
Zeytinburnu
Kadıköy
Erenköy
Içerenköy
Marmara Denizi
EDIRNE
ATATÜRK
ŞILE
SABIHA GÖKÇEN GEBZE
Helsinki
0 km 10
HYVINKÄÄ, HÄMEENLINNA, TAMPERE (3)
TUUSULA, JÄRVENPÄÄ (145)
LAHTI
PORVOO/BORGÅ, KOTKA (7)
HELSINKI-VANTAAN LENTOASEMA
Korso
Vantaa
Vantaankoski
Tikkurila
Hakunila
Malmi
Espoo Esbo
Leppävaara
HELSINKI
Tapiola
Otaniemi
Kauklahti
Bobäck
Kirkkonummi Kyrkslätt
Vuosaari
Lauttasaari
Nokkala
Westend

København Copenhagen

0 km 5

Köln Cologne

0 km 1

København Copenhagen

0 km 1

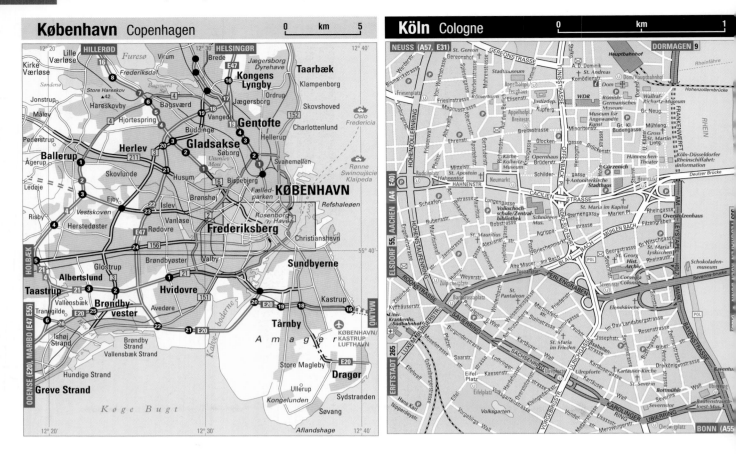

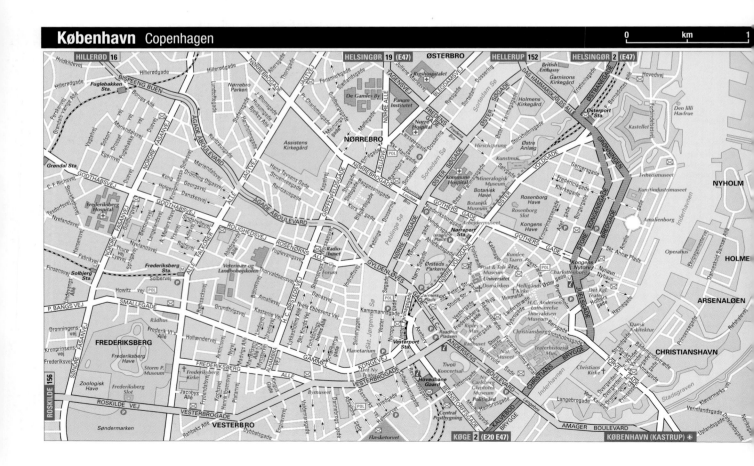

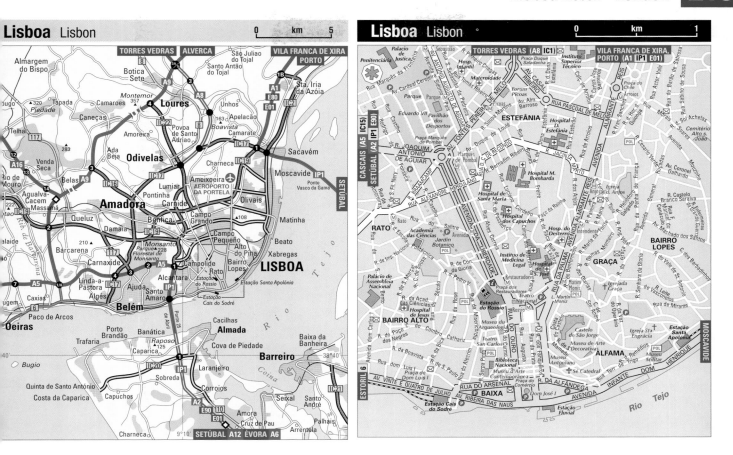

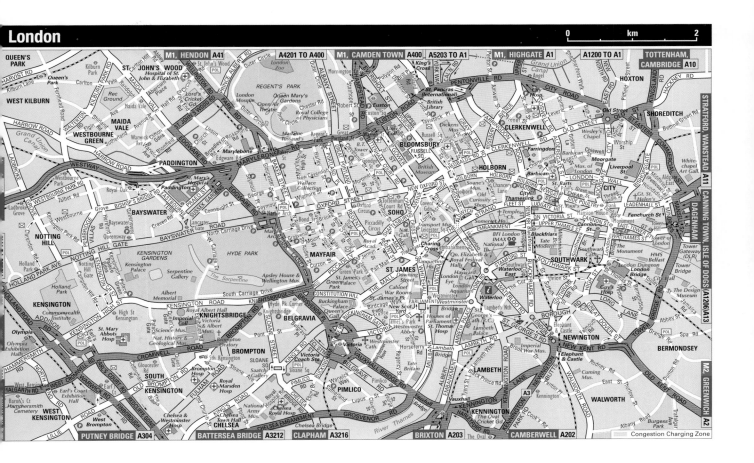

London

0 km

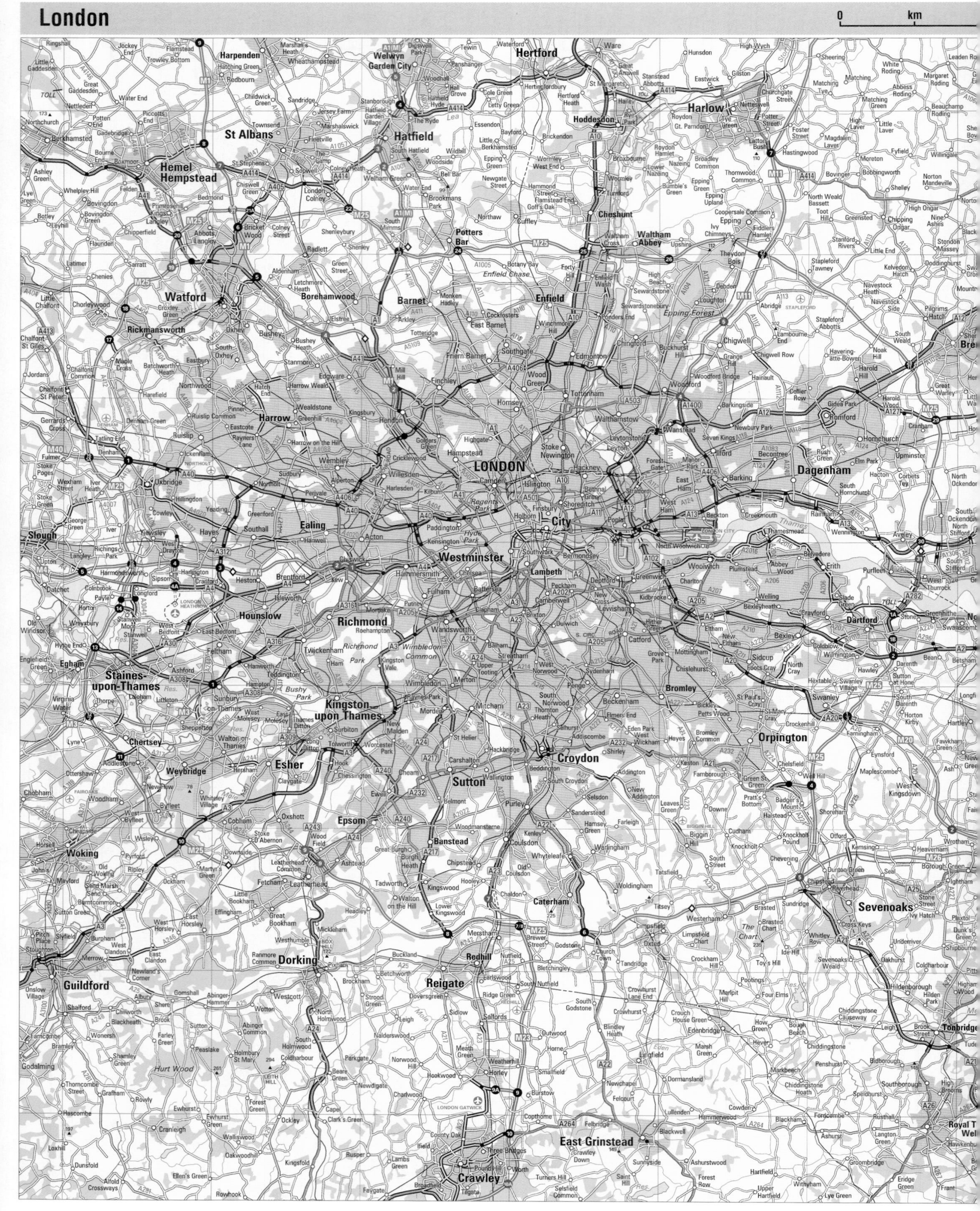
Harpenden
Welwyn Garden City
Hertford
Harlow
Hoddesdon
St Albans
Hatfield
Hemel Hempstead
Cheshunt
Waltham Abbey
Potters Bar
Watford
Borehamwood
Barnet
Enfield
Rickmansworth
Harrow
LONDON
Dagenham
Uxbridge
Slough
Ealing
City
Westminster
Lambeth
Hounslow
Richmond
Dartford
Egham
Staines-upon-Thames
Kingston upon Thames
Bromley
Chertsey
Esher
Croydon
Orpington
Weybridge
Sutton
Woking
Epsom
Banstead
Caterham
Sevenoaks
Dorking
Redhill
Guildford
Reigate
Tonbridge
East Grinstead
Crawley
LONDON HEATHROW
LONDON CITY
LONDON GATWICK

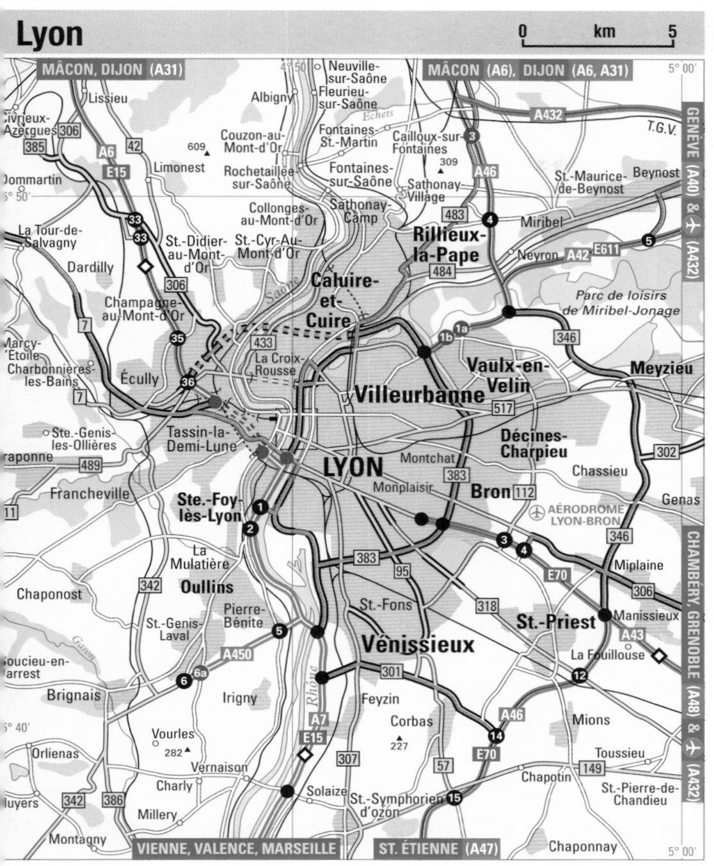
Lyon
0 km 5
MÂCON, DIJON (A31)
MÂCON (A6), DIJON (A6, A31)
GENEVE (A40) & ✈ (A432)
CHAMBÉRY, GRENOBLE (A48) & ✈ (A432)
VIENNE, VALENCE, MARSEILLE
ST. ÉTIENNE (A47)
Lissieu
Albigny
Neuville-sur-Saône
Fleurieu-sur-Saône
Couzon-au-Mont-d'Or
Fontaines-St.-Martin
Cailloux-sur-Fontaines
Limonest
Rochetaillée-sur-Saône
Fontaines-sur-Saône
Sathonay-Village
Sathonay-Camp
St.-Maurice-de-Beynost
Beynost
Collonges-au-Mont-d'Or
La Tour-de-Salvagny
Dardilly
St.-Didier-au-Mont-d'Or
St.-Cyr-Au-Mont-d'Or
Rillieux-la-Pape
Miribel
Neyron
Caluire-et-Cuire
Parc de loisirs de Miribel-Jonage
Champagne-au-Mont-d'Or
Écully
La Croix-Rousse
Villeurbanne
Vaulx-en-Velin
Meyzieu
Tassin-la-Demi-Lune
Ste.-Genis-les-Ollières
LYON
Montchat
Décines-Charpieu
Chassieu
Francheville
Ste.-Foy-lès-Lyon
Monplaisir
Bron
AÉRODROME LYON-BRON
Genas
La Mulatière
Oullins
Chaponost
Pierre-Bénite
St.-Fons
Miplaine
St.-Genis-Laval
Vénissieux
St.-Priest
Manissieux
La Fouillouse
Brignais
Irigny
Feyzin
Corbas
Mions
Vourles
Vernaison
Charly
Millery
Solaize
St.-Symphorien-d'ozon
Toussieu
Chapotin
St.-Pierre-de-Chandieu
Montagny
Chaponnay
Orlienas
Rhône
Saône
T.G.V.
5° 00'

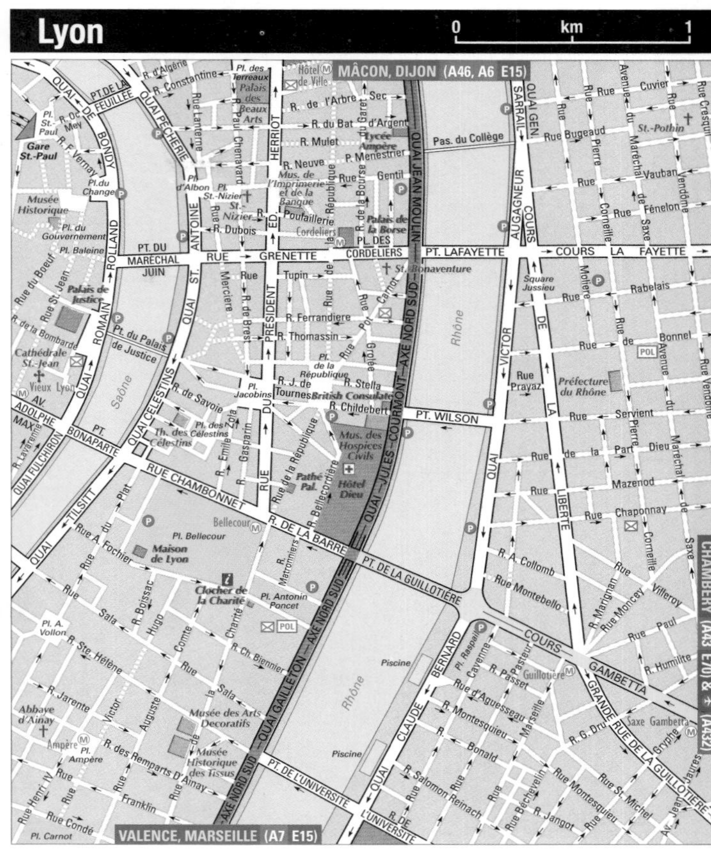
Lyon
0 km 1
MÂCON, DIJON (A46, A6 E15)
CHAMBÉRY (A43 E70) & ✈ (A432)
VALENCE, MARSEILLE (A7 E15)
QUAI DE BONDY
QUAI PECHERIE
Rue Constantine
Pl. des Terreaux
Hôtel de Ville
Palais des Beaux Arts
R. de l'Arbre Sec
R. du Bat d'Argent
R. Mulet
Lycée Ampère
R. Neuve
Mus. de l'Imprimerie et de la Banque
Palais de la Bourse
PL. DES CORDELIERS
QUAI JEAN MOULIN
Pas. du Collège
QUAI GÉN. SARRAIL
COURS AUGAGNEUR
Rue Bugeaud
Rue Cuvier
Rue Vauban
Rue Fénelon
Gare St.-Paul
Musée Historique
Pl. du Gouvernement
PT. DU MARÉCHAL JUIN
RUE GRENETTE
PT. LAFAYETTE
COURS LA FAYETTE
QUAI ROMAIN ROLLAND
QUAI ST. ANTOINE
PRESIDENT EDOUARD HERRIOT
Palais de Justice
Cathédrale St.-Jean
R. Ferrandière
R. Thomassin
R. Stella
Rue Rabelais
Rue Bonnel
Préfecture du Rhône
QUAI VICTOR AUGAGNEUR
Rhône
Saône
QUAI FULCHIRON
QUAI DES CELESTINS
Th. des Célestins
Pl. des Jacobins
R. de la République
British Consulate
R. Childebert
Mus. des Hospices Civils
Hôtel Dieu
PT. WILSON
Rue Servient
Rue Mazenod
PT. BONAPARTE
RUE CHAMBONNET
R. DE LA BARRE
Bellecour
Pl. Bellecour
Maison de Lyon
Clocher de la Charité
Pl. Antonin Poncet
PT. DE LA GUILLOTIÈRE
QUAI DE LA LIBERTE
Rue Montebello
R. A. Collomb
Square Jussieu
Rue Sala
Rue Auguste Comte
Rue Victor Hugo
Musée des Arts Decoratifs
Musée Historique des Tissus
Abbaye d'Ainay
Ampère
Rue des Remparts d'Ainay
Rue Franklin
QUAI CLAUDE BERNARD
Piscine
COURS GAMBETTA
GRANDE RUE DE LA GUILLOTIÈRE
QUAI GAILLETON
PT. DE L'UNIVERSITÉ
Pl. Carnot

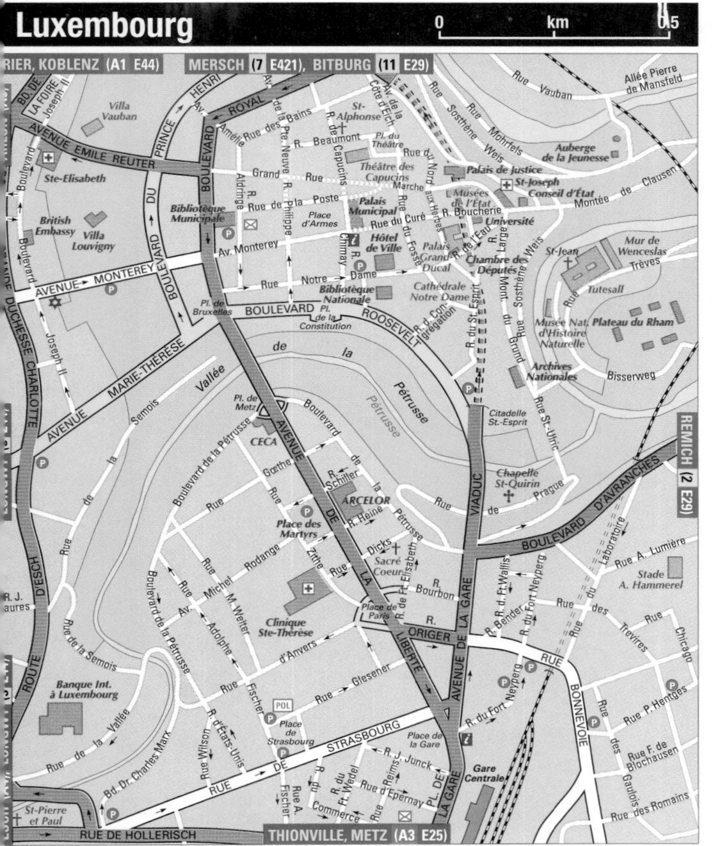
Luxembourg
0 km 0.5
MERSCH (7 E421), BITBURG (11 E29)
REMICH (2 E29)
THIONVILLE, METZ (A3 E25)
AVENUE EMILE REUTER
Ste-Elisabeth
Villa Vauban
British Embassy
Villa Louvigny
BOULEVARD ROYAL
BOULEVARD PRINCE HENRI
AVENUE MONTEREY
BOULEVARD ROOSEVELT
Bibliothèque Municipale
Palais Municipal
Hôtel de Ville
Place d'Armes
Théâtre des Capucins
Palais de Justice
St-Joseph Conseil d'État
Auberge de la Jeunesse
Université
Palais Grand Ducal
Chambre des Députés
Cathédrale Notre Dame
Bibliothèque Nationale
Musée Nat. d'Histoire Naturelle
Plateau du Rham
Archives Nationales
Bisserweg
Citadelle St.-Esprit
Pétrusse
CECA
ARCELOR
Place des Martyrs
Clinique Ste-Thérèse
Banque Int. à Luxembourg
AVENUE MARIE-THÉRÈSE
BOULEVARD D'AVRANCHES
AVENUE DE LA GARE
AVENUE DE LA LIBERTÉ
VIADUC
Chapelle St-Quirin
Place de Paris
Place de Strasbourg
Place de la Gare
Gare Centrale
RUE DE STRASBOURG
RUE DE HOLLERISCH
BOULEVARD CHARLOTTE
ROUTE D'ESCH
St-Pierre et Paul
Stade A. Hammerel

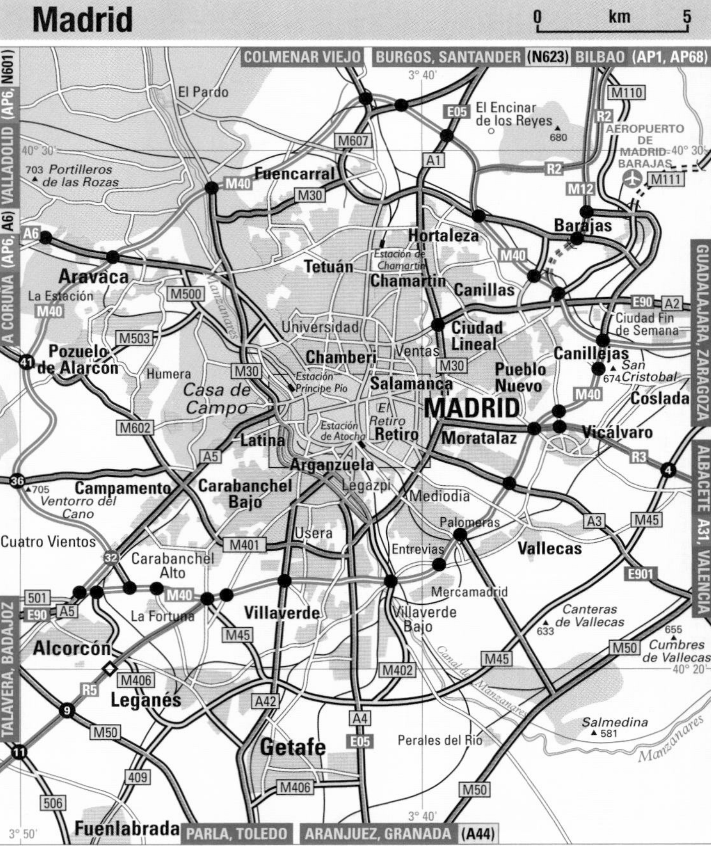
Madrid
0 km 5
COLMENAR VIEJO
BURGOS, SANTANDER (N623)
BILBAO (AP1, AP68)
VALLADOLID (AP6, N601)
A CORUÑA (AP6, A6)
GUADALAJARA, ZARAGOZA
ALBACETE A31 VALENCIA
TALAVERA, BADAJOZ
PARLA, TOLEDO
ARANJUEZ, GRANADA (A44)
El Pardo
El Encinar de los Reyes
AEROPUERTO DE MADRID-BARAJAS
703 Portilleros de las Rozas
Fuencarral
Hortaleza
Barajas
Aravaca
La Estación
Tetuán
Chamartín
Canillas
Ciudad Fin de Semana
Pozuelo de Alarcón
Universidad
Ciudad Lineal
Chamberí
Ventas
Canillejas
Humera
Pueblo Nuevo
San Cristobal
Casa de Campo
Salamanca
MADRID
Coslada
Retiro
Moratalaz
Vicálvaro
Latina
Arganzuela
Campamento
Carabanchel Bajo
Legazpi
Mediodia
Ventorro del Cano
Palomeras
Cuatro Vientos
Usera
Entrevias
Vallecas
Carabanchel Alto
Mercamadrid
La Fortuna
Villaverde
Villaverde Bajo
Canteras de Vallecas
Alcorcón
Cumbres de Vallecas
Leganés
Salmedina
Getafe
Perales del Rio
Fuenlabrada
Manzanares
3° 40'
3° 50'
40° 20'
40° 30'

Madrid

0 km 1

ARÉVALO (A6, A6)
COLMENAR (M607)
BURGOS (AI E05)
(A2, E90) ALCALÁ
A CORUÑA M30 (AP6, A6)
TALAVERA DE LA REINA A5 E90
TOLEDO M30 (A42)
TOLEDO A42
ARANJUEZ A4 E05
ARANJUEZ M30 (A4)

Málaga

0 km 0,5

CÓRDOBA A45
MOTRIL, ALMERÍA (A7 E15)
CÁRTAMA (357)
TORREMOLINOS, MARBELLA (AP15 E15)

Marseille Marseilles

0 km 0,5

MARTIGUES, A55 LYON (A7)
LYON, A7 E714 AIX-EN-PROVENCE (A51 E712)
TOULON (A50), BRIGNOLES (A50, N560)

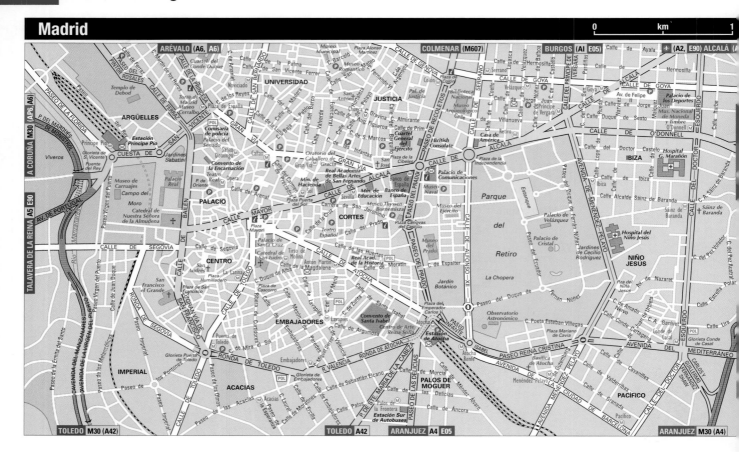

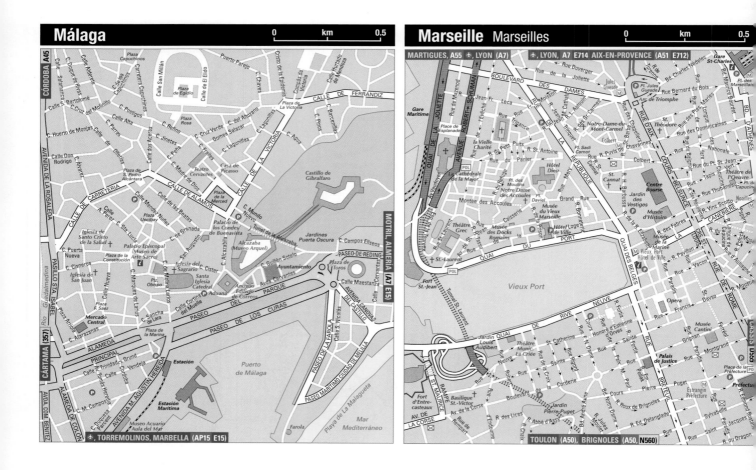

Milano

0 km 5

MALPENSA, VARESE · COMO, ZÜRICH (A2) · LECCO · LECCO (342d) · BÉRGAMO, BRÉSCIA · GÉNOVA, NICE (A10) · PARMA, BOLOGNA

Milano Milan

0 km 1

MALPENSA, VARESE (A8) · VARESE 233 · COMO 35 MONZA (36) · BÉRGAMO 11 (525) · LINATE, BRÉSCIA (11) · ABBIATEGRASSO 494 · GÉNOVA (A7 E62) · PAVIA 35 · LODI 9 PARMA (A51, A1)

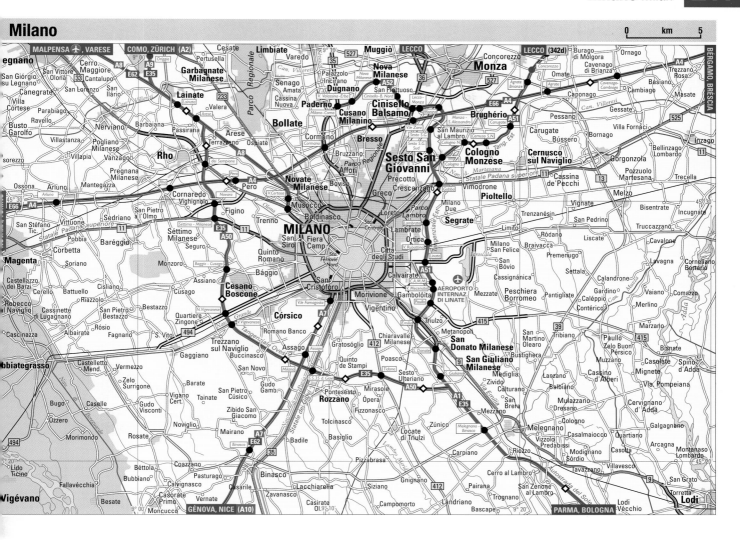

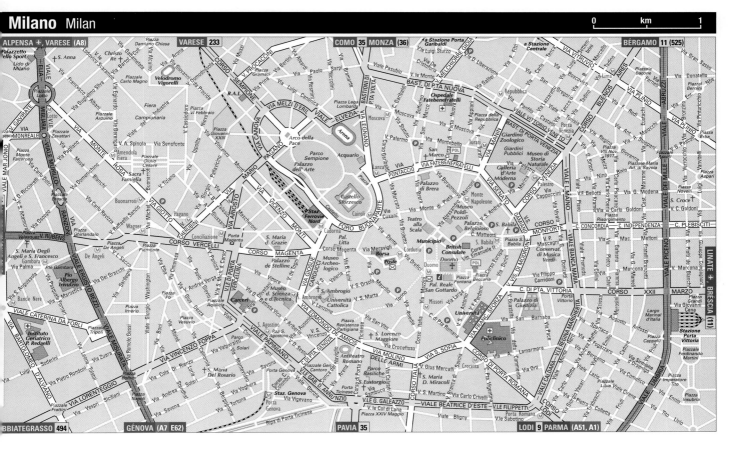

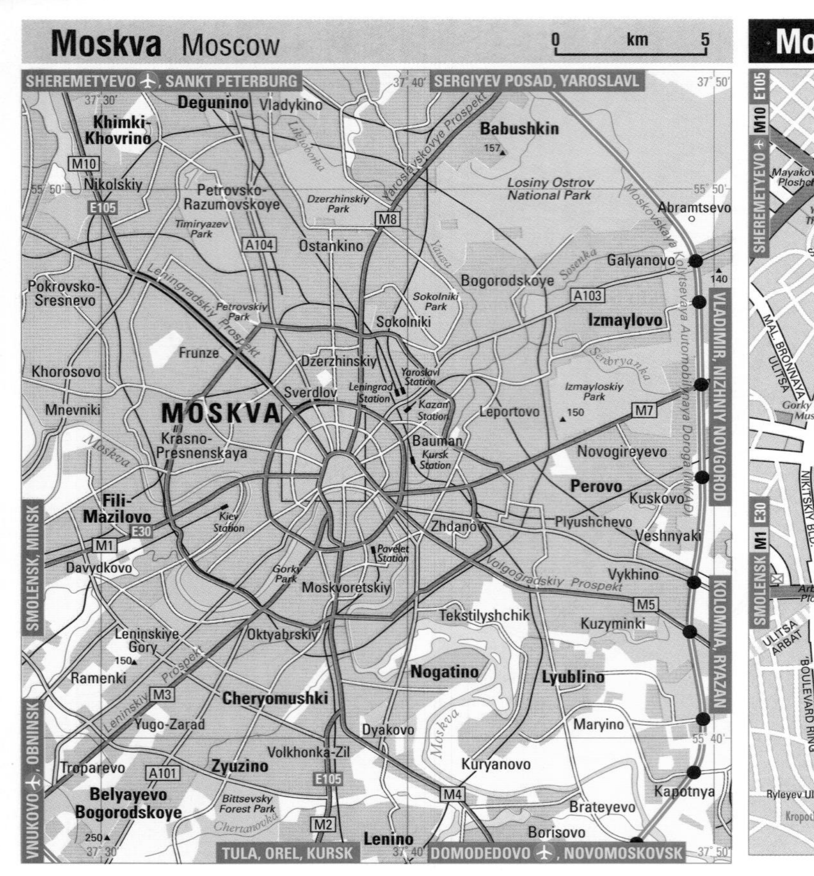

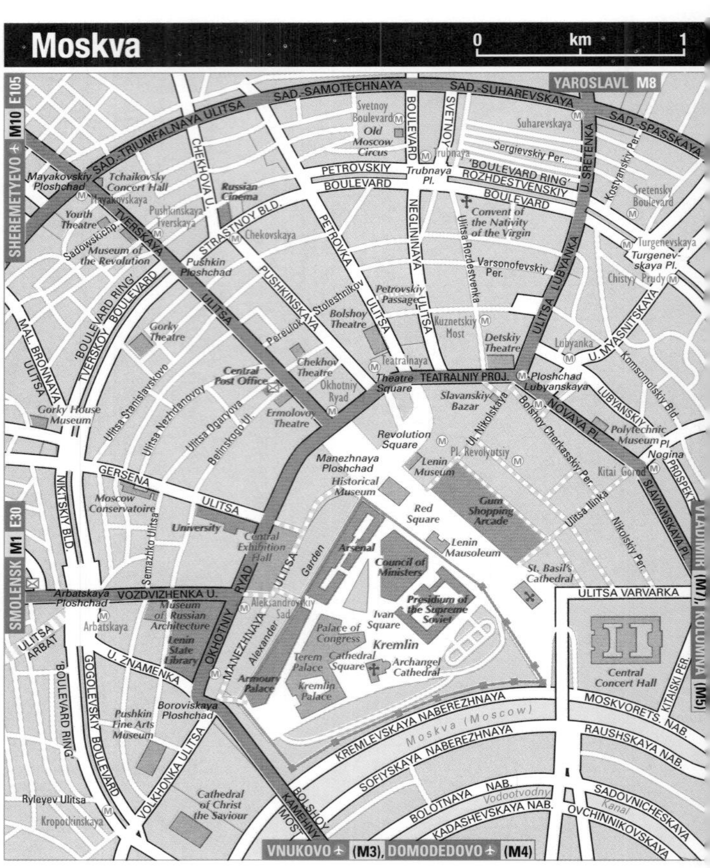

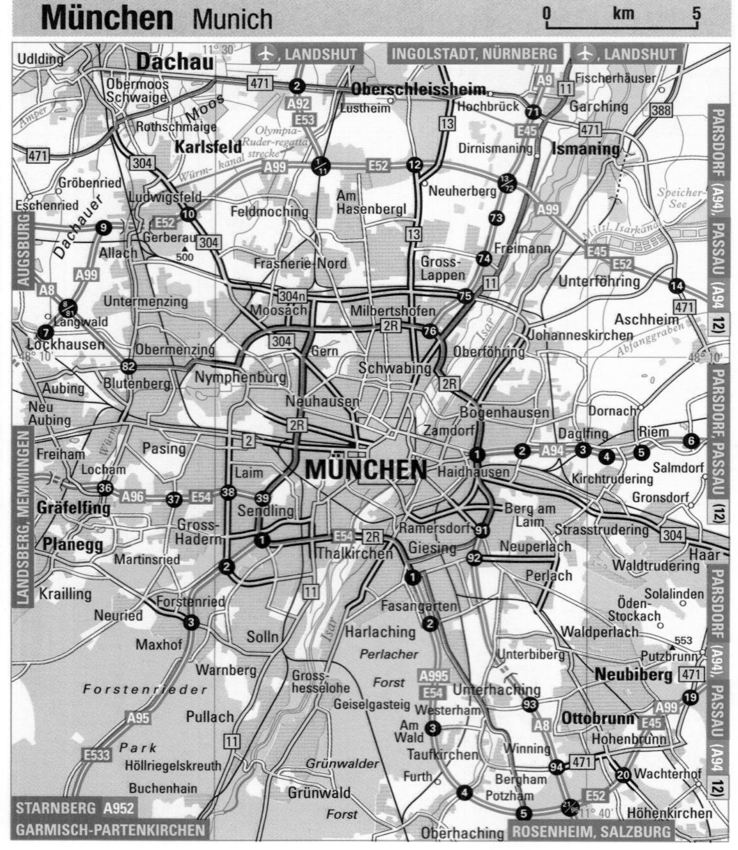

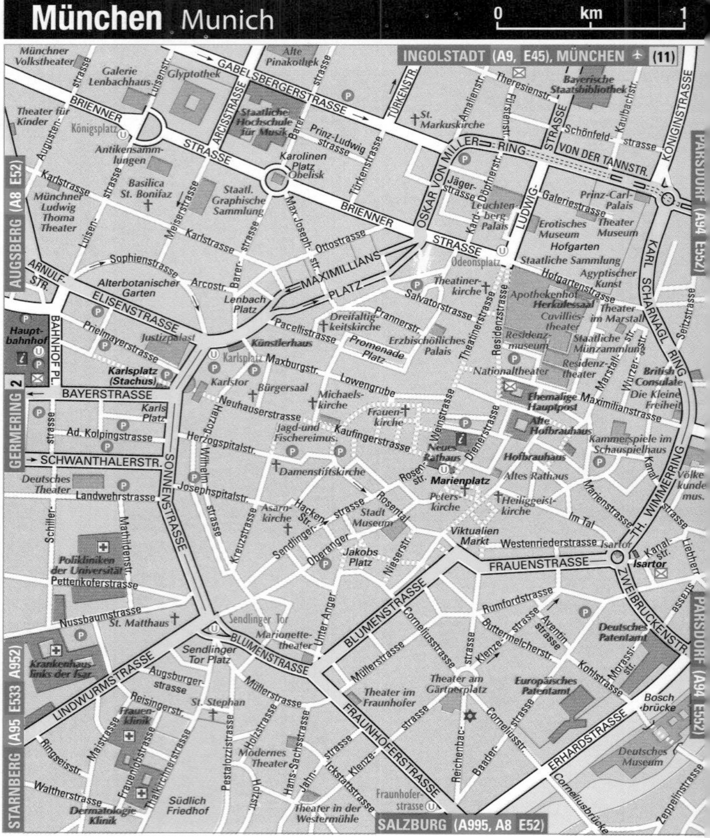

Nápoli Naples

0 km 5
CASERTA, ROMA
AVELLINO, ANDRIA (A14)
SALERNO, POTENZA (E847)
Aversa
Succivo
Cesa
Lusciano
Caivano
Gaudello
Pontedei Cani
Sant' Antimo
Crispano
Cardito
Acerra
Giugliano in Campania
Casandrino
Grumo Nevano
Frattamaggiore
Villaricca
Melito di Nápoli
Afragola
Arzano
Casalnuovo di Nápoli
Marigliano
Brusciano
Castello di Cisterna
Mugnano di Nápoli
Casavatore
Casória
Pomigliano d'Arco
Licignano di Nápoli
Tavernanova
Chiaiano
Secondigliano
S. Pietro a Patierno
Aeroporto Capodichino
Marianella
Miano
Capodimonte
Bosco di Capodimonte
Romani
Mad. d. Arco
Somma Vesuviana
Volla
Ottocalli
Caravita
Sant' Anastasia
Camaldoli
Poggioreale
Cércola
Vasto
Ponticelli
Trócchia
Póllena
Antignano
Vómero
Soccavo
Massa di Somma
San Sebastiano al Vesúvio
Mte. Somma 1132
Barra
San Giórgio a Cremano
Santa Lúcia
Mergellina
NÁPOLI
S. Giovanni a Tedúccio
S. Vito
Vesúvio
Vesuvius
1281
Posillipo
Pórtici
Ercolano
Corόglio
Marechiaro
C. Di Posíllipo
di Nisida
Capri Sorrento
Lava Nuova
Golfo di Nápoli
Torre del Greco
Prócida Ischia
Leopardi
Porto Vecchio, Cágliari, Palermo, Strómboli, Ginostra, Panarea, Lipari, Vulcano, Milazzo, Tunis
Torre Annunziata
14° 20'
40° 50'

Nápoli Naples

0 km 1
MARANO DI NÁPOLI
CAPODICHINO
ROMA (A1, E45)
POMPEI, SALERNO (A3)
PORTICI (18)
POZZUOLI
Museo Archeologico Nazionale
Accademia di Belle Arti
Castel Capuano
Stazione Centrale
Policlinico
Santa Maria Maggiore
Ospedale dei Pellegrini
Spirito Santo
Stazione Cumana
Palazzo Filomarino
Archivio di Stato
Università
Palazzo Gravina
Borsa
Posta e Telegrafo
Municipio
Stazione Funicolare
Castel Nuovo
Gall. Umberto I
Palazzo Reale
Teatro San Carlo
Piazza del Plebiscito
S. Francesco di Paola
Piazza dei Martiri
Piazza Vittoria
Le Crocelle Chiatamone
Stazione Marittima
Porto Beverello
Capri, Sorrento, Ischia, Prócida
Porto Vecchio, Cágliari, Isole Eólie, Milazzo, Palermo, Tunis
Molo di San Vincenzo
Bacino del Piliero
Molo Angioino
Calata Villa del Popolo
Capitaneria di Porto
Ospedale Loreto Mare
VIA TOLEDO
CORSO UMBERTO I
VIA NUOVA MARINA
VIA A. DEPRETIS
VIA CRISTOFORO COLOMBO
VIA PARTENOPE
VIA NAZARIO SAURO
VIA A. F. ACTON
CORSO V. EMANUELE
VIA FORIA
CORSO GARIBALDI
VIA DUOMO
VIA MEDINA

Oslo

0 km 5
BERGEN
GJØVIK, LILLEHAMMER
JESSHEIM, OSLO GARDERMOEN, HAMAR
MMEN, TORP, KRISTIANSAND
ASKIM, KARLSTAD
MOSS, RYGGE, FREDRIKSTAD
Nordmarka
Utvika
Bruløkka
Slakteren
Sørkedalen
Turter
Sandermosen
Slattum
Glosli
Nittedal
Skedsmo-Korset
Skytta
Homledal
Tryvannshøgda 531
Maridalen
Maridalsvatnet
By
Holmenkollen
Romas
Hvam
Kjeller
Sollihøgda
Holsfjorden
Kjelsås
Gorud
Vestli
Skjetten
Lillestrøm
Stovner
Bærums Verk
Ila
Røa
Ris
Ullevål
Rødtvet
Strømmen
Rud
Øverskogen
Rustad
Lijordet
Ullern
OSLO
RING 2
RING 3
Sinsen
Høybråten
Smestad
Rykkinn
Haslum
Skøyen
Alna
Skui
Kolsås
Lørenskog
Toverud
Stabekk
Lysaker
Tøyen
Bærum
Høvik
Bryn
Sylling
Tanum
Bygdøy
Hovedøya
Ryen
Sandvika
Lindøya
Oppsal
Losby
Rælingen
Tronstad
Slependen
Snarøya
Fornebu
Bekkelaget
Bøler
Rustan
Nesøya
Frederikshavn, Helsingborg, København, Kiel
Nesoddtangen
Ormøya
Lambertseter
Hvalstad
Nesbru
Østøya
Malmøya
Nordstrand
Østmarkkapellet
Brønnøya
Oksval
Ljabru
Asker
Flaskebekk
Skoklefall
Hauketo
Skullerud
Sørsdal
Helvik
Konglungen
Klemetsrud
Lierskogen
Oslofjorden
Bunnefjorden
Ingierstrand
Sandbakken
Tonekollen 368
Blakstad
Torvik
Tranby
Dikemark
Kolbotn
Rausjø
Liertoppen
Nesodden
Krokhol
Vollen
Fjellstrand
Bomansvik
Siggerud
Bjerkås
Gjersjøen
Heggedal
Svestad
Granerud
Svartskog
Myrvoll
Bru
Reistad
Slemmestad
Blylaget
Oppegård
Nærsnes
10° 20'
10° 30'
10° 40'
10° 50'
11° 00'
60° 00'
59° 50'

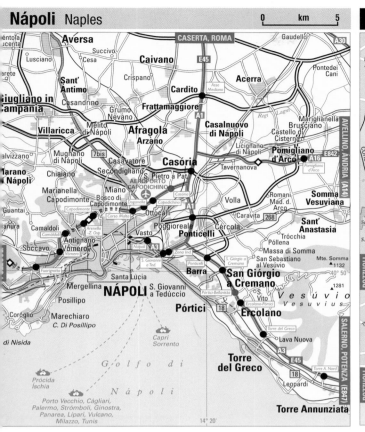

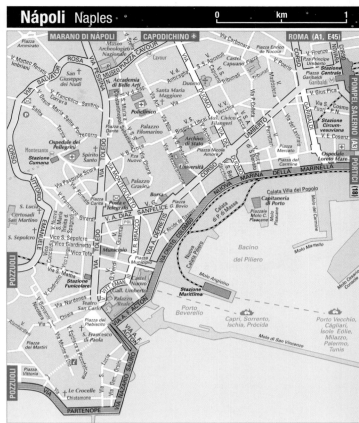

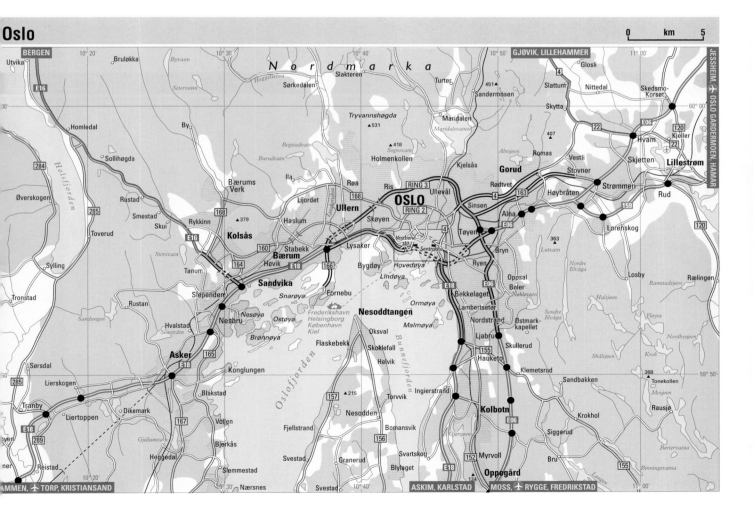

Oslo

0 km 0,5

RING 2

RING 2/3, RØA 168

LILLESTRØM 4 (22

OSLO ✈ 4 (22, E6

DRAMMEN, TORP ✈ E18

KARLSTAD E18, RYGGE ✈ E18, FREDRIKSTAD E18 (E06)

Paris

0 km 1

BOULEVARD PÉRIPHÉRIQUE

ARGENTEUIL (909)

ROUEN D14 A15

✈ CHARLES DE GAULLE, LILLE (A1, E15 E19)

ST-GERMAIN-EN-LAYE N13 (A14)

ROUEN (A13 E05)

VERSAILLES 910

✈ ORLY (A6), LE MANS (A10 A11 E50)

REIMS (A4 E50)

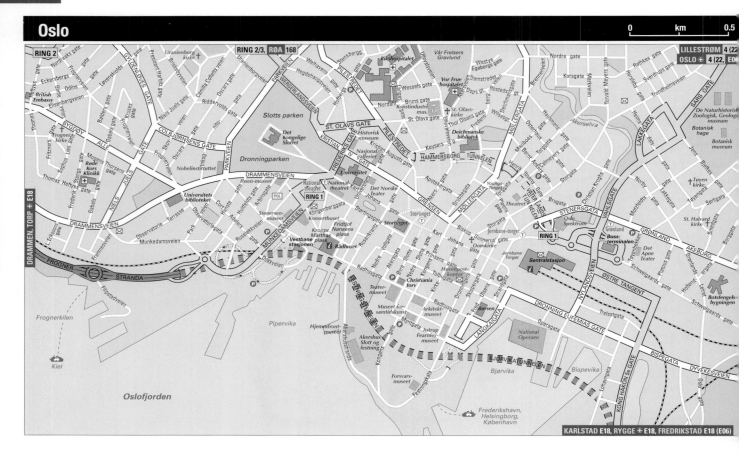

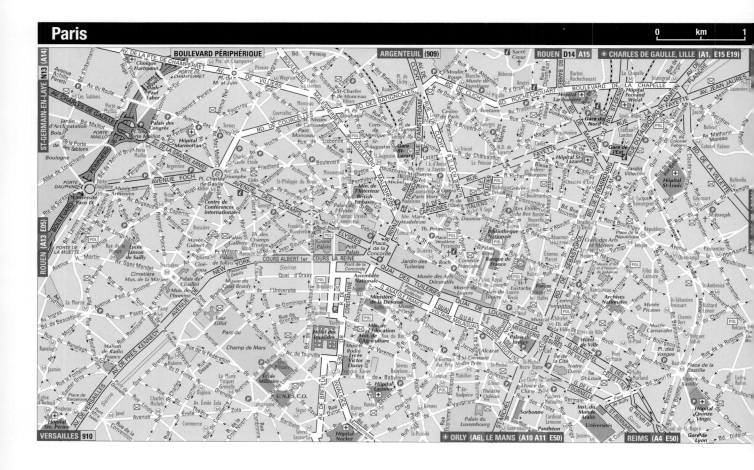

Paris

0 km 5

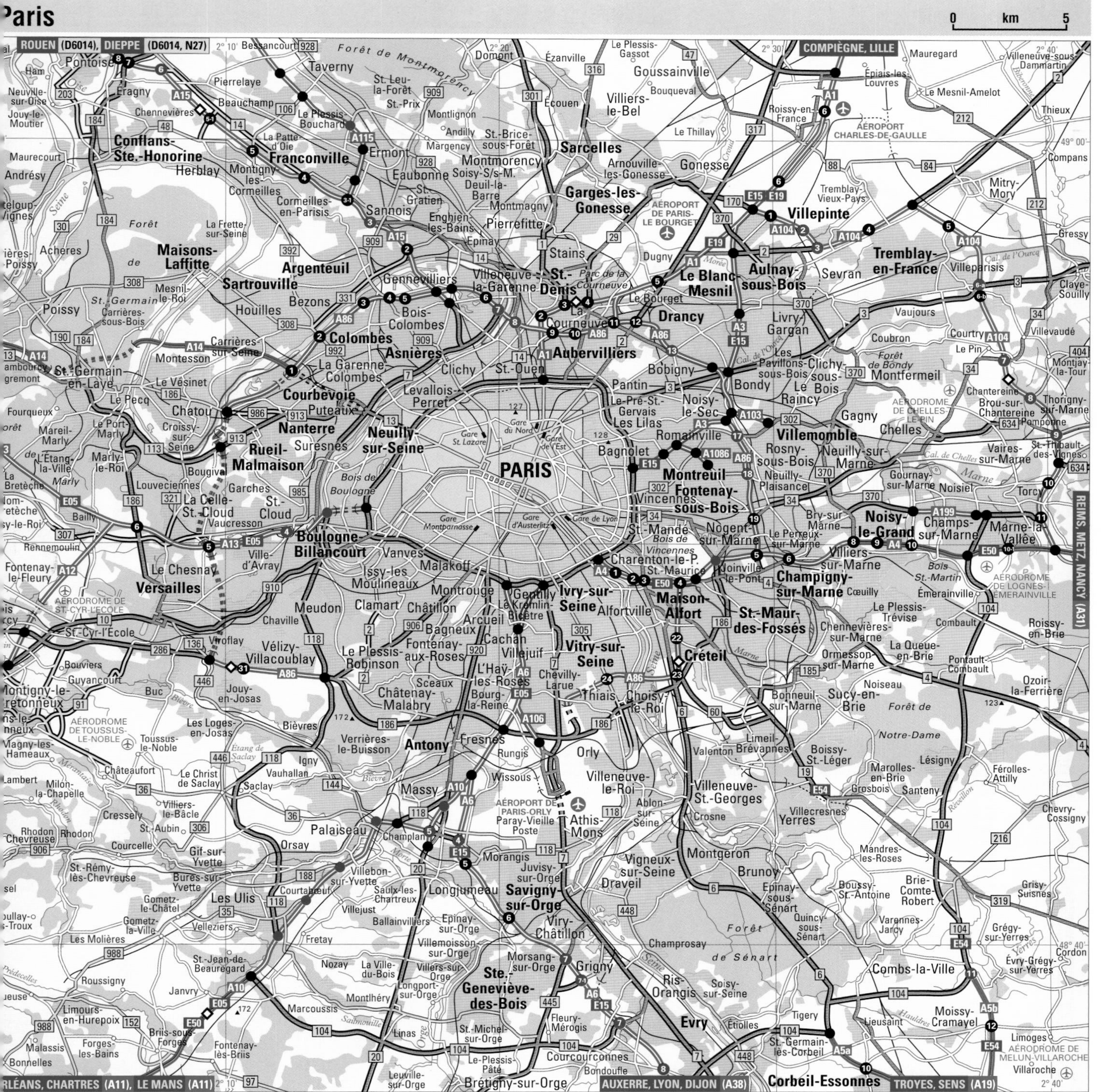
ROUEN (D6014), DIEPPE (D6014, N27)
COMPIÈGNE, LILLE
REIMS, METZ, NANCY (A31)
ORLÉANS, CHARTRES (A11), LE MANS (A11)
AUXERRE, LYON, DIJON (A38)
TROYES, SENS (A19)
PARIS
Pontoise
Taverny
Forêt de Montmorency
Domont
Écouen
Goussainville
Roissy-en-France
AÉROPORT CHARLES-DE-GAULLE
Mauregard
Villeneuve-sous-Dammartin
Le Mesnil-Amelot
Thieux
Compans
Mitry-Mory
Conflans-Ste.-Honorine
Franconville
Herblay
Ermont
Eaubonne
Montmorency
Sarcelles
Villiers-le-Bel
Gonesse
Garges-lès-Gonesse
AÉROPORT DE PARIS-LE BOURGET
Villepinte
Tremblay-en-France
Aulnay-sous-Bois
Sevran
Le Blanc-Mesnil
Maisons-Laffitte
Argenteuil
Sartrouville
Sannois
Pierrefitte
Stains
Dugny
Villeparisis
Claye-Souilly
Poissy
Houilles
Bezons
Gennevilliers
Villeneuve-la-Garenne
St.-Denis
La Courneuve
Le Bourget
Drancy
Livry-Gargan
Vaujours
Coubron
Courtry
St.-Germain-en-Laye
Carrières-sur-Seine
Colombes
Asnières
Bois-Colombes
La Garenne-Colombes
Clichy
St.-Ouen
Aubervilliers
Bobigny
Pavillons-sous-Bois
Clichy-sous-Bois
Montfermeil
Le Vésinet
Chatou
Le Pecq
Courbevoie
Puteaux
Nanterre
Levallois-Perret
Neuilly-sur-Seine
Pantin
Le Pré-St.-Gervais
Les Lilas
Noisy-le-Sec
Bondy
Le Raincy
Villemomble
Gagny
Chelles
Rueil-Malmaison
Suresnes
Bougival
Marly-le-Roi
Garches
St.-Cloud
La Celle-St.-Cloud
Vaucresson
Bagnolet
Romainville
Montreuil
Fontenay-sous-Bois
Rosny-sous-Bois
Neuilly-sur-Marne
Neuilly-Plaisance
Vincennes
St.-Mandé
Nogent-sur-Marne
Le Perreux-sur-Marne
Bry-sur-Marne
Noisy-le-Grand
Champs-sur-Marne
Marne-la-Vallée
Torcy
Boulogne-Billancourt
Vanves
Issy-les-Moulineaux
Malakoff
Montrouge
Gentilly
Le Kremlin-Bicêtre
Ivry-sur-Seine
Charenton-le-P.
St.-Maurice
Joinville-le-Pont
Champigny-sur-Marne
Villiers-sur-Marne
Maison-Alfort
Alfortville
St.-Maur-des-Fossés
Versailles
Le Chesnay
Ville-d'Avray
Meudon
Clamart
Châtillon
Bagneux
Arcueil
Cachan
Villejuif
Vitry-sur-Seine
Créteil
Chennevières-sur-Marne
Ormesson-sur-Marne
Sucy-en-Brie
Roissy-en-Brie
St.-Cyr-l'École
Viroflay
Vélizy-Villacoublay
Le Plessis-Robinson
Fontenay-aux-Roses
Sceaux
L'Haÿ-les-Roses
Chevilly-Larue
Thiais
Choisy-le-Roi
Bonneuil-sur-Marne
Montigny-le-Bretonneux
Guyancourt
Buc
Jouy-en-Josas
Bièvres
Châtenay-Malabry
Bourg-la-Reine
Antony
Fresnes
Rungis
Orly
Villeneuve-le-Roi
Valenton
Limeil-Brévannes
Boissy-St.-Léger
Ozoir-la-Ferrière
Forêt de Notre-Dame
Massy
Palaiseau
Wissous
AÉROPORT DE PARIS-ORLY
Paray-Vieille-Poste
Athis-Mons
Ablon-sur-Seine
Villeneuve-St.-Georges
Crosne
Yerres
Villecresnes
Orsay
Gif-sur-Yvette
Chevreuse
Les Ulis
Longjumeau
Morangis
Juvisy-sur-Orge
Savigny-sur-Orge
Vigneux-sur-Seine
Draveil
Montgeron
Brunoy
Epinay-sous-Sénart
Brie-Comte-Robert
Viry-Châtillon
Grigny
Ste.-Geneviève-des-Bois
Ris-Orangis
Forêt de Sénart
Combs-la-Ville
Evry
Moissy-Cramayel
Marcoussis
Montlhéry
Linas
Limours-en-Hurepoix
St.-Germain-lès-Corbeil
Corbeil-Essonnes
Brétigny-sur-Orge
Courcouronnes
AÉRODROME DE MELUN-VILLAROCHE

Praha Prague

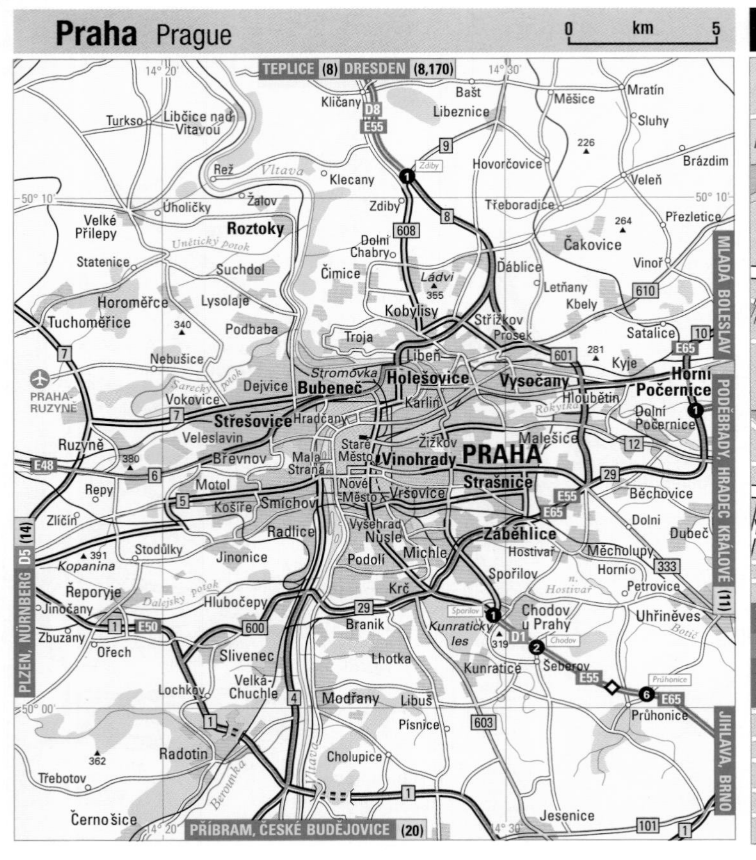

Praha · Prague

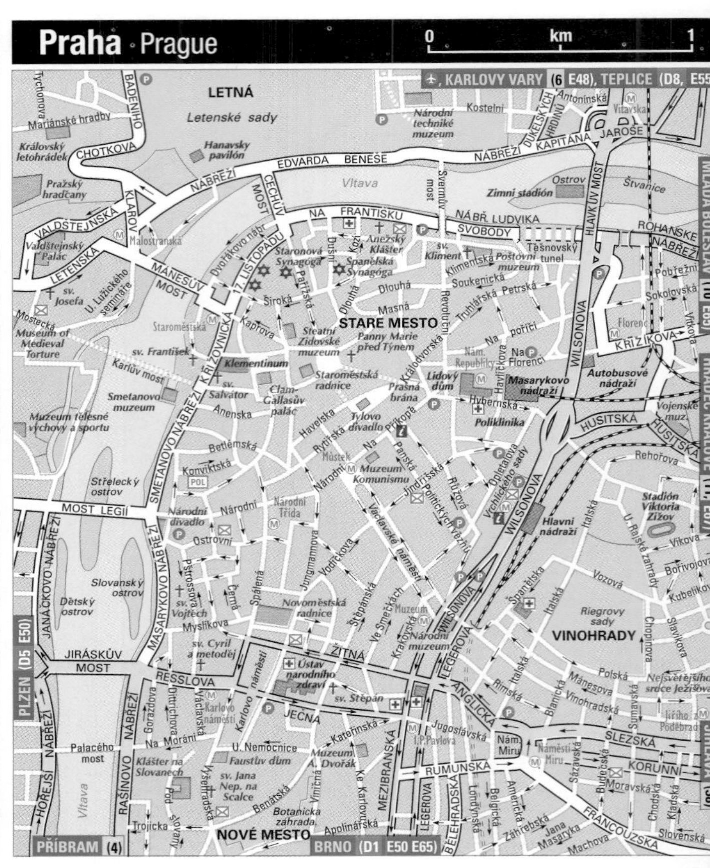

Rotterdam

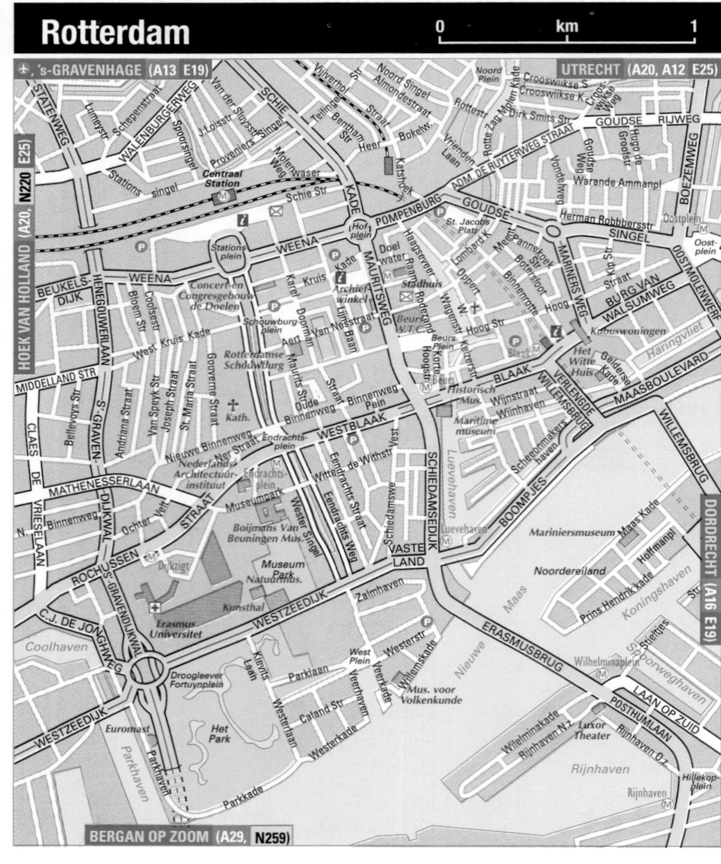

Sankt-Peterburg St Petersburg

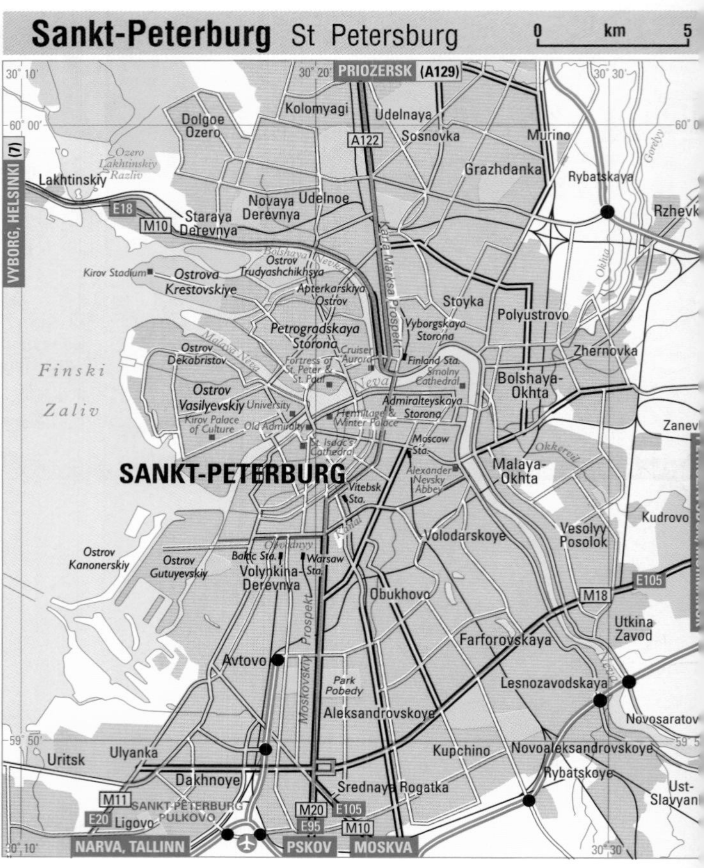

Stockholm

0 km 5

VÄSTERÅS, ÖREBRO
ARLANDA, UPPSALA
NORRTÄLJE, KAPPELSKÄR
Kallhäll
Kungsängen
Jakobsberg
Häggvik
Edsberg
Skarpäng
Täby
Viggbyholm
Svinningeudd
Sollentuna
Tureberg
Enebyberg
Helenelund
Roslags-Näsby
Näsbypark
Näsby
Rydbohölm
Österskär
Resarö
Barkarby
Järfälla
Akalla
Husby
Kista
Danderyd
Djursholm
Stora Värtan
Södersby
Frösvik
Uteke
Ellboda
Vaxholm
Skarpö
Munsö
Kungsberga
Vantholmen
Färentuna
Hilleshög
Ricksattra
Spånga
Rinkeby
Ursvik
Ulriksdal
Mörby
Stocksund
Sticklinge udde
Bosön
Mariehamn
Langnas
Turku
Helsinki
Tallinn
Riga
Klaipeda
Ekeby
Degerby
Sånga
Nälsta
Hässelby
Flysta
Sundbyberg
Vällingby
Bromma Flygplats
Bromma
Solna
Haga
Lidingö
Gåshaga
Älvvik
Koviksudde
Käppala
Kummelnäs
Björkö
Svartsjölandet
Stenhamra
Ängby
Norrmalm
Östermalm
STOCKHOLM
Brevik
Ormingelandet
Skå
Lovö
Drottningholm
Nockeby
Alvik
Ålsten
Kungsholmen
Essingen
Djurgården
Orminge
Gustavsberg
Kärsön
Nacka
Björknäs
Rasta
Lovön
Fågelön
Södermalm
Skuru
Saltsjö-Duvnäs
Eknäs
Boo
STAVSNÄS
Rastaborg
Ekerön
Kungshatt
Hägersten
Mälarhöjden
Årsta
Hammarby
Hästhagen
Fisksätra
Igelboda
Farstalandet
Närsta
Sätra
Gällstao
Kaggeholm
Ekerö
Skärholmen
Brännkyrka
Enskede
Stureby
Älvsjö
Tallkrogen
Skarpnäck
Kolarängen
Saltsjöbaden
Ingarölandet
Vällinge
Segeltorp
Kungens kurva
Värby
Snättringe
Örby
Älgö
Slagsta
Masmo
Stuvsta
Sköndal
Älta
Tyresö Strand
Fittja
Alby
Fagersjö
Farsta
Bollmora
Glömsta
Bergaholm
Botkyrka
Huddinge
Holmgård
St. Magelungen
Trångsund
Trollbäcken
Gimmersta
Krusboda
Tyresö
Ritorp
Katrineberg
Balingsnäs
Ågesta
Kumla
Salem
Balingsta
Brevik
Salemstaden
Länna
Drevviken
Gudö
Södertälje
Östertälje
Tumba
Tullinge
Gladökvarn
Vidja
Vendalsö
Rönninge
Eklundshov
Orlångsvik
Vega
Lyckebyn
NYKÖPING, NORRKÖPING
NYNÄSHAMN

Stockholm

0 km 1

VÄSTERÅS (E04, E18)
UPPSALA (E04), NORRTÄLJE E04, (E18)
LIDINGÖ E20 227
Karlbergs Slott
Karlberg
Observatorielunden
Vasaparken
Sankt Eriksplan
Humlegården
Kungliga Biblioteket
Karlbergssjön
STADSHAGEN
Sabbatsbergs sjukhus
Läns Museum
Johanneskyrkan
Strindbergs-museum
Hologram-museum
Karlaplan
ÖSTERMALM
Barnklinik
KLARASTRANDSLEDEN
NORRMALM
Norra Bantorget
Vasateatern
Hötorget
KUNGSGATAN
Stora teatern
Sankt Eriks sjukhus
Konserthuset
Hallwylska museet
H. Eleonora kyrka
Historiska museet
Armé museum
Sankt Görans sjukhus
FLEMINGGATAN
Oscarsteatern
Central-postkont.
Stadsteatern
Kulturhuset
Berzelii Park
Dramatiske teatern
Thorildsplan
DROTTNINGHOLMSVÄGEN
KUNGSHOLMEN
Kronobergsparken
Polishuset
City Terminalen
Stockholm Central
Klara kyrka
Kungsträdgården
Karl XII Torg
Nybroviken
Ladugårdslandsviken
Nordiska museet
Rålambshovs sjukhus
Rådhuset
Medelhavsmuseet
Operan
Norrström
Junibacken
Vasamuseet
Rålambshovsparken
Friluftsteater
Stadshuset
Riksdagshuset
Riksdagens ledamothus
Helgeandsholmen
Medeltidsmuseum
Nationalmuseum
Östasiatiska museet
MARIEBERG
Kungliga Slottet
Livrustkammaren
Kungliga Myntkabinettet
SKEPPSHOLMEN
Moderna museet
RIDDARHOLMEN
Högsta domstolen
Storkyrkan
Arkitekturmuseum
Riddarholmskyrkan
GAMLA STAN
Postmus.
Tyska kyrkan
Strömmen
Riddarfjärden
Mälaren
Saltsjön
Kastellholmen
LÅNGHOLMEN
Friluftsteater
Långholmskanalen
SÖDERMALM
Slussen
NYNÄSHAMN 73 (73)
GUSTAVSBERG 222 (222)

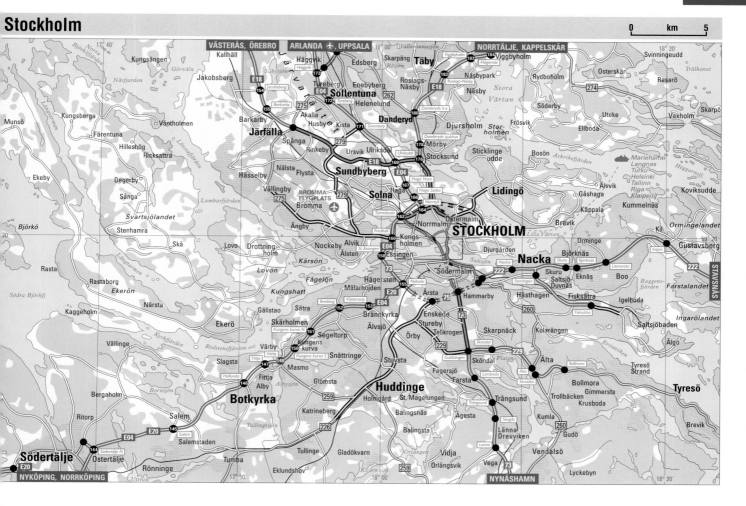

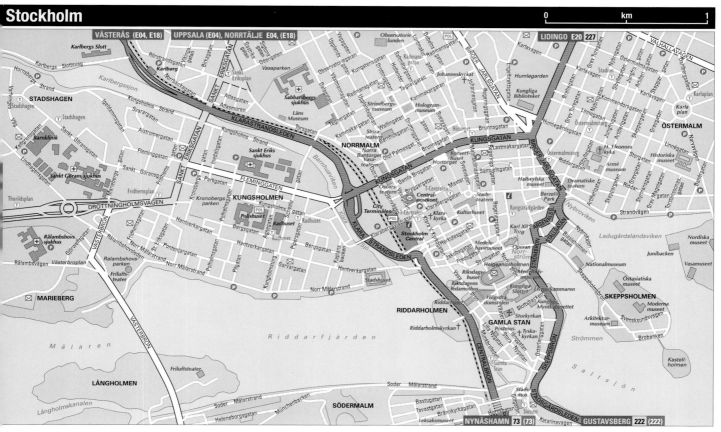

Torino Turin

0 km 5

Bertesseno
Mte. Colombano 658
Moncolombone
Niquidetto
Grange
Rossignoli
Robassomero
Malanghero
AEROPORTO DI CASELLE
Volpiano
AOSTA
NOVARA, MILANO
Torassi
Castell
Truc di Miola
S. Giacomo
Caselle Tor.
Léini
Rivera
Chivasso
Verol
Mte. Arpone 1600
Mte. Lera 1371
la Cassa
Parco Regionale La Mándria
Brandizzo
Mompellato
Castello
Rivasacco
Val della Torre
Givoletto
Montelera
Rubbianetta
Bórgaro Torinese
Fornacino
Cimena
S. Genésio
Castagneto Po
S. Raffaele
S. Sebastiano da Po
Rubiana
Mte. Curt 1325
Verna
S. Gillio
Mándria
Cast. S. Cristina
Villaretto
Piana di S. Raffaele
Brione
Druento
Venaria
Settimo Torinese
Bussolini Gassinese
Casalborgone
Laghi di Caselette
Grange
Mte. Musinè 1150
Villár Dora
Almese
Rivera
Savonera
Tangenziale Nord
Ababadia di Stura
Gássino Torinese
Rivalba
Castiglione Torinese
Caselette
S. Pancrazio
SUSA, GRENOBLE (A43, A41)
Gránglia
Drubáglio
Cast. di Camerletto
Pianezza
Alpignano
Lucento
Barca
Bertolla
Barca
S. Martino
Bardassano
Sciolze
S. Ambrógio di Torino
Dora Riparia
Parco M. Carrara
S. Máuro Tor
Rivodora
Cordova
Cinzano
Avigliana
Collegno
Regina Margherita
Superga
Roccati
Vernone
Buttigliere Alta
Rosta
Rívoli
TORINO
Po
Pavarolo
Moncucco Torinese
Molino
L. Grande
Meana
Mongreno
Reáglie
Baldissero Tor.
Montaldo Tor.
Avuglione
Sala
Rivata
Reano
Corbiglia
Grugliasco
Parco del Valentino
S. Margherita
Marentino
Mombello d'Torino
Giaveno
L. Piccolo
Tetti Neirotti
l'Éremo
Pino Torinese
Paiere
Trana
Roncáglia
Villarbasse
Gérbido
Andezeno
Arignano
S. Bernardino
Villa
Rivalta di Torino
S. Vito
Colle d. Maddalena
Cipresso
Moranda
Sangano
Doirone
Tangenziale Sud
Lingotto
Bausone
Dalmassi
Bruino
Beinasco
Mirafiori
Cavoretto
Castelvécchio
Pecetto Tor.
S. Felice
Chieri
Buttigliera d'Asti
S. Giovanni
Pratovigero
Sangone
S. Pietro
S. Giovanni
Orbassano
Borgaretto
Stupiniġi
Moncalieri
Mad. d. Scala
Mte. S. Giórgio 837
Nichelino
Oviglia
Burdini
Allivellatori
Montegrosso
Piossasco
Piazza
Parco Naturale di Stupingi
Testone
Trofarello
Valle Saúglio
Riva presso Chieri
Cumiana
Cascina Parpáglia
Tagliaferro
Pallera
Mago
Costa
Chisola
Tetti Rolle
Cambiano
Terraz
Paschero
Valdichiesa
Bianchi
Pessione
Tavernette
Volvera
Candiolo
la Loggia
Sántena
Cast. di S. Salva
Villanova d'Asti
Vinovo
Tetti Sapini
Tetti Giro
Frossasco
PINEROLO
None
Brassi
SAVONA
CÚNEO (20)
Marocchi
Banna
Corvéglia

Venézia Venice

0 km 0.5

MESTRE, PÁDOVA (A4 E70)

Stazione FF. SS. S. Lucia
Fondamenta S. Lucia
Degli Scalzi
Ponte d. Scalzi
Riva di Biasio
Campo C. S. Degola
Campo S. Stae
S. Stae
Ca' Pesaro
Ca' d'Oro
Strada Nuova
R. Terrà Barba Fruttarol
Fondamenta Nuove
Canal Grande
Lista dei Bari
C. Lunga
C. Bergami
Rio Marin
Ruga Vecchia
Campo S. Giac. dell'Orio
Palazzo Corner d. Regina
Campo S. Apostoli
Chiara
Fond. S. Chiara
Palazzo Papadopoli
Cllo. Stroppe
Campo Pescheria
Ca' da Mosto
Sal. S. Canciano
Santa Maria dei Miracoli
Ospedale Civile
S. Maria della Pianta
S. Giovanni e Paolo
Campo S. Andrea
Sant' Andrea
Giardino Papadopoli
Fabbriche Nuove di Rialto
Teatro Malibran
Autorimessa
Piazzale Roma
Fond. S. Andrea
Campo S. Polo
Ponte di Rialto
Poste Telegafi
Campo S. Bartolomeo
Campo S. Maria Formosa
Campo S. Lorenzo
Scuola di S. Giorgio degli Schiavoni
S. Maria dei Frari
Campo dei Frari
Palazzo Bernardo
Pal. Papadopoli
Campo S. Salvador
San Salvador
S. Maria Formosa
San Lorenzo
Fond. delle Burchielle
Rio Terra dei Pensieri
Canale di S. Maria Maggiore
Sal. S. Pantalon
Casa Goldoni
Municipio
Teatro Goldoni
Campo S. Luca
Campo S. Zulian
C. Lion
Ex Chiesa di S. Maria Maggiore
Fond. Rizzi
San Pantalon
Campo S. Pantlon
Palazzo Barbarigo
Palazzo Corner Spinelli
Campo Manin
San Marco (Basilica)
S. Zaccaria
Palazzo Mocenigo
Ca' Foscari
Palazzo Grassi
Campo S. Angelo
Museo Civico Correr
Piazza San Marco
Ponte dei Sospiri
S. Maria della Visitazione
Riva degli Schiavoni
Fond. S. Marta
Rio Terra dei Secchi
Scuola dei Carmini
Campo S. Margherita
Carmini
Rio Terrà della Scoazzera
Ca' Rezzonico
San Stefano
Teatro La Fenice
Campo S. Moise
Giardini ex Reali
Molo
Palazzo Ducale
San Nicolò dei Mendicoli
Angelo Raffaele
Campo A. Raffaele
Campo S. Sebastiano
S. Sebastiano
Campo S. Barnaba
Campo Francesco Morosini
Campo Maurizio
Campo S. M. Zobenigo
Palazzo Giustinian
Bacino di San Marco
Canale di San Marco
Ospedale G. B. Giustinian
Campo S. Vidal
Palazzo Cavalli
Prefettura
Campo Traghetto
Sal. S. Basegio
Stazione Marittima
Galleria Accademia
Pte. Accademia
Palazzo Contarini Dal Zaffo
Palazzo Dario
Palazzo Dogana di Mare
Punta della Dogana
Canal Grande
San Trovaso
Campo S. Trovaso
Collezione P. Guggenheim
S. Maria della Salute
Isola di San Giorgio Maggiore
Fond. Zattere Ponte Lungo
Gesuati
Campo S. Agnese
F. Zorzi
R. Terrà S. Vio
Campo San Giorgio
Canale della Giudecca
Fond. Zattere dei Gesuiti
Fond. Zattere Spirito Santo
Fond. Zattere ai Saloni
San Giorgio Maggiore
Fondamenta Beata Giuliana di Collalto

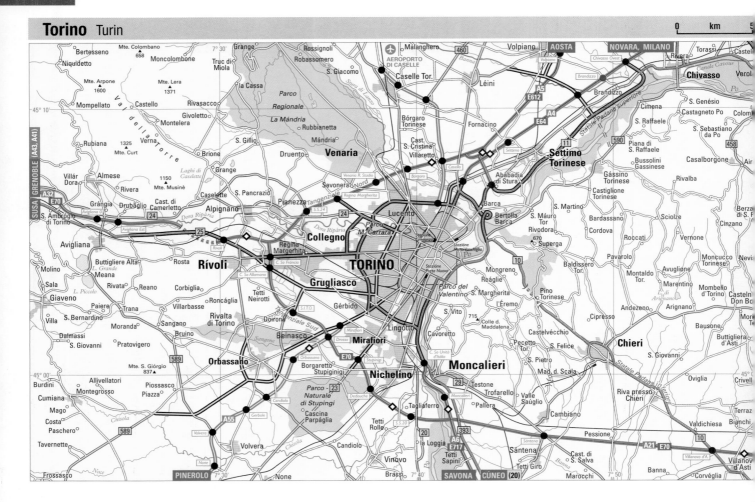

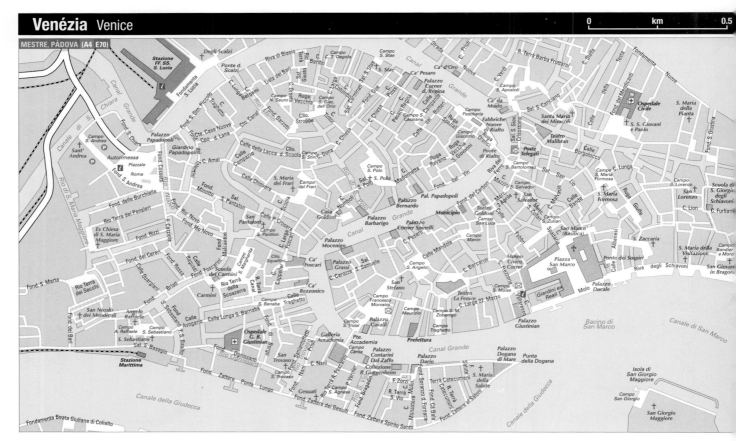

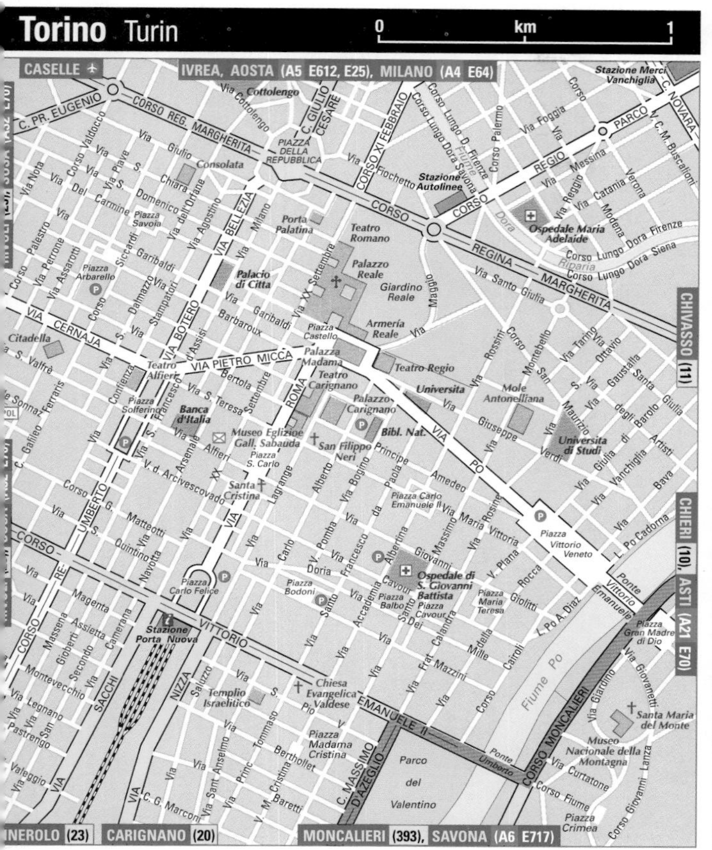

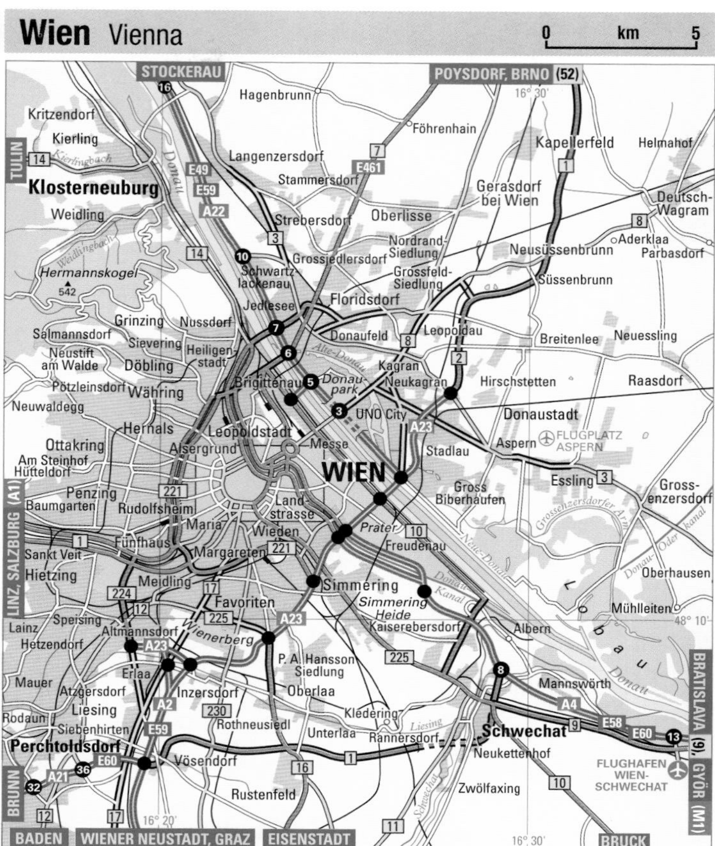

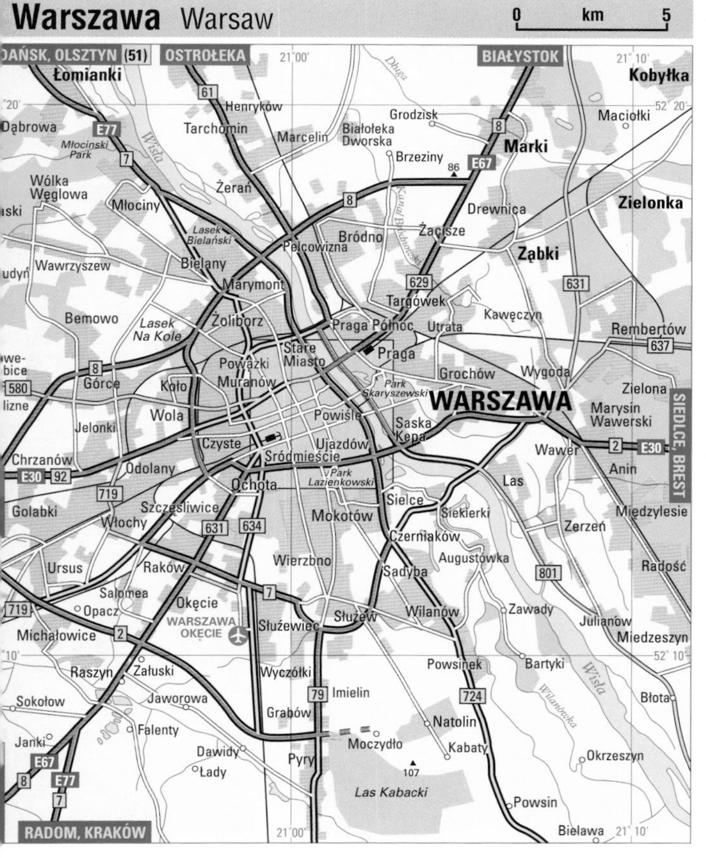

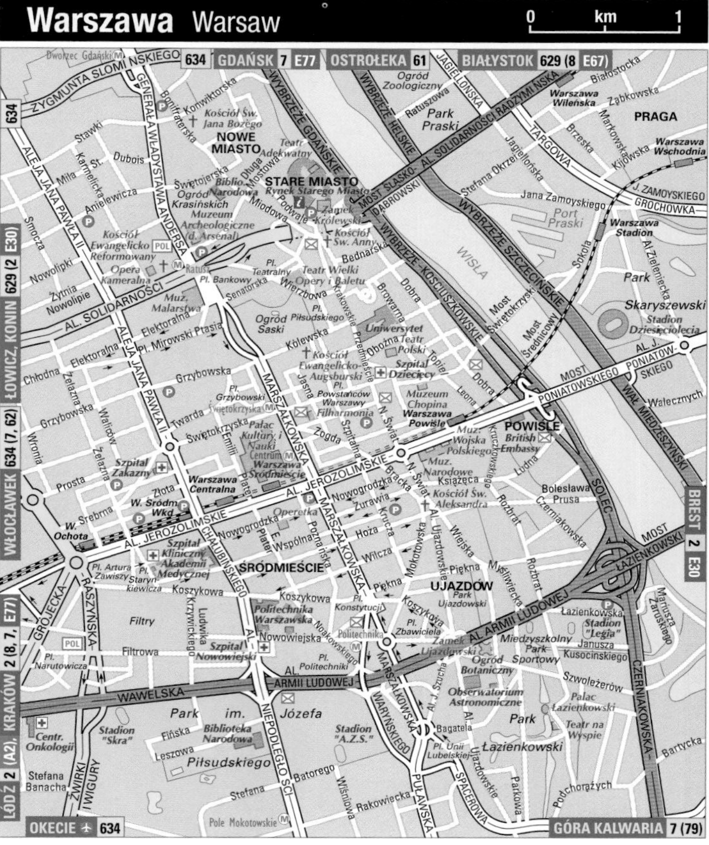

Wien Vienna

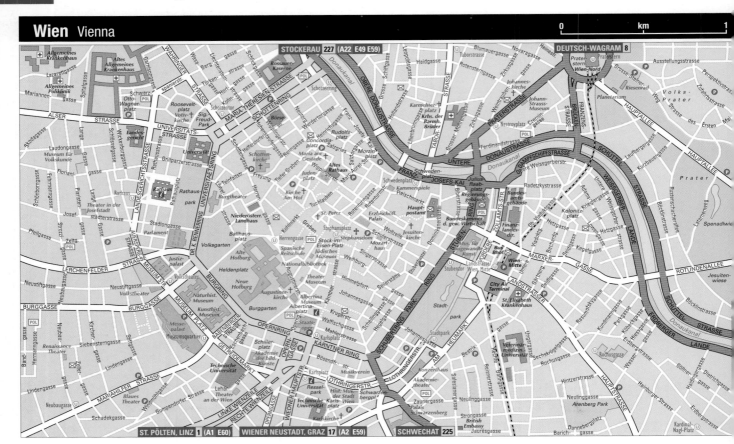

0   km   1

STOCKERAU 227 (A22 E49 E59)   DEUTSCH-WAGRAM 8

ST. PÖLTEN, LINZ 1 (A1 E60)   WIENER NEUSTADT, GRAZ 17 (A2 E59)   SCHWECHAT 225

Zagreb   ## Zürich

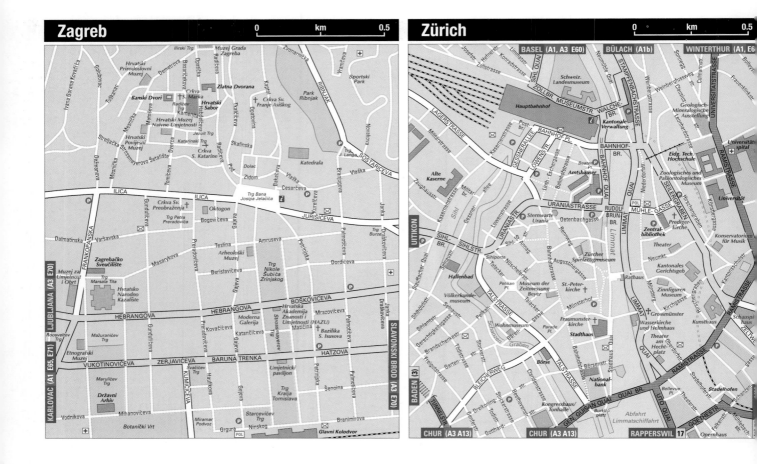

Zagreb:
0   km   0.5

Zürich:
0   km   0.5

	GB	F	D	I
A	Austria	Autriche	Österreich	Austria
AL	Albania	Albanie	Albanien	Albania
AND	Andorra	Andorre	Andorra	Andorra
B	Belgium	Belgique	Belgien	Belgio
BG	Bulgaria	Bulgarie	Bulgarien	Bulgaria
BIH	Bosnia-Herzegovin	Bosnia-Herzegovine	Bosnien-Herzegowina	Bosnia-Herzogovina
BY	Belarus	Belarus	Weissrussland	Bielorussia
CH	Switzerland	Suisse	Schweiz	Svizzera
CY	Cyprus	Chypre	Zypern	Cipro
CZ	Czech Republic	République Tchèque	Tschechische Republik	Repubblica Ceca
D	Germany	Allemagne	Deutschland	Germania
DK	Denmark	Danemark	Dänemark	Danimarca
E	Spain	Espagne	Spanien	Spagna
EST	Estonia	Estonie	Estland	Estonia
F	France	France	Frankreich	Francia
FIN	Finland	Finlande	Finnland	Finlandia
FL	Liechtenstein	Liechtenstein	Liechtenstein	Liechtenstein
FO	Faeroe Islands	Îles Féroé	Färoër-Inseln	Isole Faroe
GB	United Kingdom	Royaume Uni	Grossbritannien und Nordirland	Regno Unito
GBZ	Gibraltar	Gibraltar	Gibraltar	Gibilterra
GR	Greece	Grèce	Greichenland	Grecia
H	Hungary	Hongrie	Ungarn	Ungheria
HR	Croatia	Croatie	Kroatien	Croazia
I	Italy	Italie	Italien	Italia
IRL	Ireland	Irlande	Irland	Irlanda
IS	Iceland	Islande	Island	Islanda
KOS	Kosovo	Kosovo	Kosovo	Kosovo
L	Luxembourg	Luxembourg	Luxemburg	Lussemburgo
LT	Lithuania	Lituanie	Litauen	Lituania
LV	Latvia	Lettonie	Lettland	Lettonia
M	Malta	Malte	Malta	Malta
MC	Monaco	Monaco	Monaco	Monaco
MD	Moldova	Moldavie	Moldawien	Moldavia
MK	Macedonia	Macédoine	Makedonien	Macedonia
MNE	Montenegro	Monténégro	Montenegro	Montenegro
N	Norway	Norvège	Norwegen	Norvegia
NL	Netherlands	Pays-Bas	Niederlande	Paesi Bassi
P	Portugal	Portugal	Portugal	Portogallo
PL	Poland	Pologne	Polen	Polonia
RO	Romania	Roumanie	Rumanien	Romania
RSM	San Marino	Saint-Marin	San Marino	San Marino
RUS	Russia	Russie	Russland	Russia
S	Sweden	Suède	Schweden	Svezia
SK	Slovak Republic	République Slovaque	Slowak Republik	Repubblica Slovacca
SLO	Slovenia	Slovénie	Slowenien	Slovenia
SRB	Serbia	Serbie	Serbien	Serbia
TR	Turkey	Turquie	Türkei	Turchia
UA	Ukraine	Ukraine	Ukraine	Ucraina

A

Aabenraa DK 64 A2
Aabybro DK 58 A2
Aach D 107 B4
Aachen D 80 B2
Aalborg DK 58 A2
Aalen D 94 C2
Aalestrup DK 58 B2
Aalsmeer NL 70 B1
Aalst B 79 B4
Aalten NL 71 C3
Alter B 79 A3
Äänekoski FIN 8 A4
Aapajärvi FIN 197 B10
Ağapınar TR 187 C5
Aarau CH 106 B3
Aarberg CH 106 B2
Aarburg CH 106 B2
Aardenburg NL 79 A3
Aars DK 58 B2
Aarschot B 79 B4
Aarup DK 59 C3
Aba H 112 B2
Abádanes E 152 B1
Abades E 151 B3
Abadin E 141 A3
Abádszalók H 113 B4
Abaliget H 125 A4
Abana TR 23 A8
A Baña E 140 B2
Abanilla E 165 A3
Abano Terme I 121 B4
Abarán E 165 A3
Abasár H 113 B4
Abbadia San Salvatore I 135 C4
Abbaue D 74 A2
Abbehausen D 72 A1
Abbekäs S 66 A2
Abbeville F 90 A1
Abbey IRL 28 A3
Abbeydorney IRL 29 B2
Abbeyfeale IRL 29 B2
Abbeyleix IRL 30 B1
Abbey Town GB 36 B3
Abbiategrasso I 120 B1
Abborrträsk S 196 D2
Abbots Bromley GB 40 C2
Abbotsbury GB 43 B4
Abda H 111 B4
Abejar E 143 C4
Abela P 160 B1
Abelvær N 199 A8
Abenberg D 94 B2
Abenójar E 157 B3
Abensberg D 95 C3
Aberaeron GB 39 B2
Abercarn GB 39 C3
Aberchirder GB 33 D4
Aberdare GB 39 C3
Aberdaron GB 38 B2
Aberdeen GB 33 D4
Aberdulais GB 39 C3
Aberdyfi GB 39 B2
Aberfeldy GB 35 B4
Aberffraw GB 38 A2
Aberfoyle GB 34 B3
Abergavenny GB 39 C3
Abergele GB 38 A3
Abergynolwyn GB 38 B3
Aberporth GB 39 B2
Abersoch GB 38 B2
Abertillery GB 39 C3
Abertura E 156 A2
Aberystwyth GB 39 B2
Abetone I 135 A3
Abfaltersbach A 109 C3
Abide
  Çanakkale TR 186 B1
  Kütahya TR 187 D4
Abiego E 145 B3
Abild DK 64 B1
Abingdon GB 44 B2
Abington GB 36 A3
Abisko S 194 B9
Abiul P 154 B2
Abla E 164 B2
Ablis F 90 C1
A Bola E 140 B3
Abondance F 118 A3
Abony H 113 B4
Aboyne GB 33 D4
Abrantes P 154 B2
Abreiro P 148 A2
Abreschviller F 92 C3
Abrest F 117 A3
Abriès F 119 C3
Abrud RO 17 B5
Absdorf A 97 C3
Abtenau A 109 B4
Abtsgmünd D 94 C1
Abusejo E 149 B3
Åby
  Kronoberg S 62 A2
  Östergötland S 56 B2
Åbyggeby S 51 B4
Åbytorp S 55 A6
A Cañiza E 140 B2
A Capela E 140 A2
Acate I 177 B3
Accadía I 171 B3
Accéglio I 132 A2
Accettura I 172 B2
Acciaroli I 170 C3
Accous F 145 A3
Accrington GB 40 B1
Accúmoli I 169 A3
Acedera E 156 A2
Acehuche E 155 B4
Acered E 152 A2
Acerenza I 172 B1
Acerno I 170 C3
Acerra I 170 C2
Aceuchal E 155 C4
Acharacle GB 34 B2
Acharnes GR 185 A4
Achavanich GB 32 C3
Achene B 79 B5
Achenkirch A 108 B2
Achensee A 108 B2
Achenthal A 108 B2
Achentrias GR 185 E6
Achern D 93 C4
Acheux-en-Amienois F 90 A2
Achiltibuie GB 32 C1
Achim D 72 A2
Achladokambos GR 184 B3
Achnasheen GB 32 D1
Achnashellach GB 32 D1
Achosnich GB 34 B1
Aci Castello I 177 B4
Aci Catena I 177 B4
Acilia I 168 B2
Acıpayam TR 189 B4
Acireale I 177 B4
Acle GB 41 C5
A Coruña E 140 A2
Acquacadda I 179 C2
Acqua Doria F 180 B1
Acquanegra sul Chiese I 121 B3
Acquapendente I 168 A1
Acquasanta Terme I 136 C2
Acquasparta I 168 A2
Acquaviva I 135 B4
Acquaviva delle Fonti I 171 C4
Acquaviva Picena I 136 C2
Acquigny F 89 A5
Ácqui Terme I 119 C5
Acri I 174 B2
Acs H 112 B2
Acsa H 112 B3
Ácsteszér H 112 B1
Acy-en-Multien F 90 B2
Ada SRB 126 B2
Adak S 195 E9
Ådalsbruk N 48 B3
Adamas GR 185 C5
Adamsfjord N 193 B10
Adamuz E 157 B3
Adana TR 23 C8
Ádánd H 112 C2
Adanero E 150 B3
Adare IRL 29 B3
Adaševci SRB 125 B5
Adeanueva de Ebro E 144 B2
Adelboden CH 106 C2
Adelebsen D 82 A1
Adélfia I 173 A2
Adelmannsfelden D 94 C2
Adelsheim D 94 B1
Adelsö S 57 A3
Ademuz E 152 B2
Adenau D 80 B2
Adendorf D 72 A3
Adinkerke B 78 A2
Adjud RO 17 B7
Adliswil CH 107 B3
Admont A 110 B1
Ådneram N 52 A2
Adolfsström S 195 D7
Adony H 112 B2
Adorf
  Hessen D 81 A4
  Sachsen D 83 B4
Adra E 164 C1
Adradas E 152 A1
Adrall E 147 B2
Adrano I 177 B3
Ádria I 121 B5
Adrigole IRL 29 C2
Adwick le Street GB 40 B2
Adzaneta E 153 B3
Aesch CH 106 B2
A Estrada E 140 B2
Afandou GR 188 C3
Åfarnes N 198 C4
Affing D 94 C2
Affoltern CH 106 B3
Affric Lodge GB 32 D1
Åfjord N 199 B7
Aflenz Kurort A 110 B2
A Fonsagrada E 141 A3
Afragóla I 170 C2
Afritz A 109 C4
Afyon TR 187 D5
Ágasegyháza H 112 C3
Agay F 132 B2
Agazzano I 120 C2
Agde F 130 B2
Agdenes N 198 B6
Agen F 129 B3
Ager E 145 C4
Agerbæk DK 59 C1
Agerskov DK 64 A2
Agger DK 58 B1
Aggersund DK 58 A2
Ággius I 178 B3
Aggsbach Dorf A 97 C3
Aggsbach Markt A 97 C3
Aggtelek H 99 C4
Aghalee GB 27 B4
Aghia GR 182 D4
Aghia Anna GR 183 E5
Aghia Galini GR 185 D5
Aghia Marina GR 188 D1
Aghia Paraskevi GR 186 C1
Aghia Pelagia GR 184 C3
Aghia Triada GR 184 B2
Aghiokambos GR 182 D4
Aghios Efstratios GR 183 D6
Aghios Kirikos GR 185 B7
Aghios Matheos GR 182 D1
Aghios Mironas GR 185 D6
Aghios Nikolaos GR 185 D6
Aghios Petros GR 182 E2
Aghio Theodori GR 184 B4
Agiči BIH 124 C2
Agira I 177 B3
Aglientu I 178 A3
Agnières F 118 C2
Agno CH 120 B1
Agnone I 170 B2
Agolada E 140 B2
Agon Coutainville F 88 A2
Ágordo I 121 A5
Agost E 165 A4
Agramón E 158 C2
Agramunt E 147 C2
Agreda E 144 C2
Agria GR 183 D5
Agrigento I 176 B2
Agrinio GR 182 E3
Agrón E 163 A4
Agrópoli I 170 C2
Aguadulce
  Almería E 164 C2
  Sevilla E 162 A3
Agualada E 140 A2
Agua Longa P 148 A1
A Guarda E 140 C2
Aguarón E 152 A2
Aguas E 145 B3
Aguas Belas P 154 B2
Aguas de Busot E 159 C3
Aguas de Moura P 154 C2
Águas Frias P 148 A2
Aguas Santas P 148 A1
Aguaviva E 153 B3
Aguaviva de la Vega E 152 A1
A Gudiña E 141 B3
Agudo E 156 B3
Águeda P 148 B1
Aguessac F 130 A2
Agugliano I 136 B2
Aguiar P 154 C3
Aguiàr da Beira P 148 B2
Aguilafuente E 151 A3
Aguilar de Campóo E 142 B2
Aguilar de la Frontera E 163 A3
Aguilas E 164 B3
Agunnaryd S 60 C4
Ahat TR 187 D4
Ahaus D 71 B3
Åheim N 198 C2
Ahigal E 149 B3
Ahigal de Villarino E 149 A3
Ahillones E 156 B2
Ahlbeck
  Mecklenburg-Vorpommern D 66 C3
  Mecklenburg-Vorpommern D 74 A3
Ahlen D 81 A3
Ahlhorn D 71 B5
Ahmetbey TR 186 A2
Ahmetler TR 188 A4
Ahmetli TR 188 A2
Ahoghill GB 27 B4
Ahola FIN 197 C11
Ahrensbök D 65 B3
Ahrensburg D 72 A3
Ahrenshoop D 66 B1
Ahun F 116 A2
Åhus S 63 C2
Ahvenselkä FIN 197 C11
Aibar E 144 B2
Aich D 95 C4
Aicha D 96 C1
Aichach D 94 C3
Aidone I 177 B3
Aiello Cálabro I 175 B2
Aigen im Mühlkreis A 96 C1
Aigle CH 119 A3
Aignan F 128 C3
Aignay-le-Duc F 104 B3
Aigre F 115 C4
Aigrefeuille-d'Aunis F 114 B3
Aigrefeuille-sur-Maine F 101 B4
Aiguablava E 147 C4
Aiguebelle F 118 B3
Aigueperse F 116 A3
Aigues-Mortes F 131 B3
Aigues-Vives F 130 B1
Aiguilles F 119 C3
Aiguillon F 129 B3
Aigurande F 103 C3
Ailefroide F 118 C3
Aillant-sur-Tholon F 104 B2
Ailly-sur-Noye F 90 B2
Ailly-sur-Somme F 90 B2
Aimargues F 131 B3
Aime F 118 B3

Aab–Aku

Ainaži LV 8 D4
Ainet A 109 C3
Ainhoa F 144 A2
Ainsa E 145 B4
Airaines F 90 B1
Aird GB 34 B2
Aird Asaig Tairbeart GB 31 B2
Airdrie GB 35 C4
Aire-sur-l'Adour F 128 C2
Aire-sur-la-Lys F 78 B2
Airole I 133 B3
Airolo CH 107 C3
Airvault F 102 C1
Aisey-sur-Seine F 104 B3
Aïssey F 105 B5
Aisy-sur-Armançon F 104 B3
Aiterhofen D 95 C4
Aith
  Orkney GB 33 B4
  Shetland GB 33 A5
Aitona E 153 A4
Aitrach D 107 B5
Aiud RO 17 B5
Aix-en-Othe F 104 A2
Aix-en-Provence F 131 B4
Aixe-sur-Vienne F 115 C5
Aix-les-Bains F 118 B2
Aizenay F 114 B2
Aizkraukle LV 8 D4
Aizpute LV 8 D2
Ajac F 146 A3
Ajaccio F 180 B1
Ajain F 116 A1
Ajaureforsen S 195 E6
Ajdovščina SLO 122 B2
Ajka H 111 B4
Ajo E 143 A3
Ajofrin E 157 A4
Ajos FIN 196 D7
Ajuda P 155 C3
Akanthou CY 181 A2
Akarca TR 189 A4
Akasztó H 112 C3
Akçakoca TR 187 A6
Akçaova TR 187 A4
Akçay TR 189 C4
Aken D 83 A4
Åkerby S 51 B4
Åkernes N 52 B3
Åkersberga S 57 A4
Åkers styckebruk S 56 A3
Åkervik N 195 E4
Akhisar TR 186 D2
Åkirkeby DK 67 A3
Akköy TR 188 B2
Akkrum NL 70 A2
Akören TR 189 B7
Åkra N 52 A2
Akranes IS 190 C3
Åkrehamn N 52 A1
Akrotiri CY 181 B1
Aksaray TR 23 B8
Akşehir TR 189 A6
Akseki TR 189 B6
Aksla N 46 A3
Aksu TR 189 C5
Aktsyabrski BY 13 B8
Akureyri IS 191 B7

Åkvåg N 53 B5
Akyazı TR 187 B5
Ål N 47 B5
Ala I 121 B4
Alaca TR 23 A8
Alacaatlı TR 186 C3
Alaçam TR 23 A8
Alaçatı TR 188 A1
Alàdei Sardi I 178 B3
Ala di Stura I 119 B4
Alaejos E 150 A2
Alagna Valsésia I 119 B4
Alagón E 144 C2
Alaior E 167 B4
Alájar E 161 B3
Alakurtti RUS 197 C13
Alakylä FIN 196 B7
Alameda E 163 A3
Alameda de la Sagra E 151 B4
Alamedilla E 163 A4
Alamillo E 156 B3
Alaminos E 151 B5
Ala-Nampa FIN 197 C9
Alanäs S 199 A12
Alandroal P 155 C3
Alange E 156 B1
Alaniemi FIN 197 D8
Alanís E 156 B2
Alanno I 169 A3
Ålansbro S 200 D3
Alanya TR 189 C7
Alap H 112 C2
Alaquáso E 159 B3
Alaraz E 150 B2
Alarcón E 158 B1
Alar del Rey E 142 B2
Alaró E 167 B2
Alaşehir TR 188 A3
Alássio I 133 A4
Ağlasun TR 189 B5
Alatoz E 158 B2
Alatri I 169 B3
Alavus FIN 8 A3
Alba
E 152 B2
I 119 C5
Alba Adriática I 136 C2
Albacete E 158 C2
Alba de Tormes E 150 B2
Alba de Yeltes E 149 B3
Albaida E 159 C3
Alba-Iulia RO 17 B5
Albæk DK 58 A3
Albaladejo E 158 C1
Albala del Caudillo E 156 A1
Albalat E 159 B3
Albalate de Cinca E 145 C4
Albalate del Arzobispo E 153 A3
Albalate de las Nogueras E 152 B1
Albalete de Zorita E 151 B5
Alban F 130 B1
Albánchez E 164 B2
Albanchez de Ubeda E 163 A4
Albano Laziale I 168 B2
Albanyà E 147 B3
Albaredo d'Adige I 121 B4
Albares E 151 B4
Albarracín E 152 B2
Albatana E 158 C2
Albatarrec E 153 A4
Albatera E 165 A4
Albbruck D 106 B3
Albedin E 163 A3
Albelda de Iregua E 143 B4
Albenga I 133 A4
Albens F 118 B2
Ålberga
Södermanland S 56 A2
Södermanland S 56 B2
Albergaria-a-Nova P 148 B1
Albergaria-a-Velha P 148 B1
Albergaria dos Doze P 154 B2
Alberge P 154 C2
Alberic E 159 B3
Albernoa P 160 B2
Alberobello I 173 B3
Alberoni I 122 B1
Albersdorf D 64 B2
Albersloh D 81 A3
Albert F 90 A2
Albertirsa H 112 B3
Albertville F 118 B3
Alberuela de Tubo E 145 C3
Albi F 130 B1
Albidona I 174 B2
Albínia I 168 A1
Albino I 120 B2
Albinshof D 66 C2
Albires E 142 B1
Albisola Marina I 133 A4
Albocácer E 153 B4
Albolote E 163 A4
Albondón E 164 C1
Alborea E 158 B2
Albox E 164 B2
Albrechtice nad Vitavou CZ 96 B2
Albstadt D 107 A4
Albufeira P 160 B1
Albuñol E 164 C1
Albuñuelas E 163 B4
Alburquerque E 155 B3
Alby
Öland S 63 B4
Västernorrland S 200 D1
Alcácer do Sal P 154 C2
Alcáçovas P 154 C2
Alcadozo E 158 C2
Alcafoces P 155 B3
Alcains P 155 B3
Alcaláde Guadaira E 162 A2
Alcaláde Gurrea E 144 B3
Alcaláde Henares E 151 B4
Alcaláde la Selva E 153 B3
Alcalá del Júcar E 158 B2
Alcaláde los Gazules E 162 B2
Alcalá del Rio E 162 A2
Alcalá del Valle E 162 B2
Alcaláde Xivert E 153 B4
Alcalála Real E 163 A4
Álcamo I 176 B1
Alcampell E 145 C4
Alcanadre E 144 B1
Alcanar E 153 B4
Alcanede P 154 B2
Alcanena P 154 B2
Alcañices E 149 A3
Alcántara E 155 B4
Alcantarilha P 160 B1
Alcantarilla E 165 B3
Alcañiz E 153 A3
Alcaracejos E 156 B3
Alcara il Fusi I 177 A3
Alcaraz E 158 C1
Alcaria Ruiva P 160 B2
Alcarraz E 153 A4
Alcaudete E 163 A3
Alcaudete de la Jara E 150 C3
Alcázar de San Juan E 157 A4
Alcazarén E 150 A3
Alcester GB 44 A2
Alcoba E 157 A3
Alcobaça P 154 B1
Alcobendas E 151 B4
Alcocer E 151 B5
Alcochete P 154 C2
Alcoentre P 154 B2
Alcolea
Almería E 164 C2
Córdoba E 156 C3
Alcolea de Calatrava E 157 B3
Alcolea de Cinca E 145 C4
Alcolea del Pinar E 152 A1
Alcolea del Rio E 162 A2
Alcolea de Tajo E 150 C2
Alcollarin E 156 A2
Alconchel E 155 C3
Alconera E 155 C4
Alcontar E 164 B2
Alcora E 153 B3
Alcorcón E 151 B4
Alcorisa E 153 B3
Alcossebre E 153 B4
Alcoutim P 160 B2
Alcover E 147 C2
Alcoy E 159 C3
Alcsútdoboz H 112 B2
Alcubierre E 145 C3
Alcubilla de Avellaneda E 143 C3
Alcubilla de Nogales E 141 B5
Alcubillas E 157 B4
Alcublas E 159 B3
Alcúdia E 167 B3
Alcudia de Guadix E 164 B1
Alcuéscar E 155 B4
Aldbrough GB 41 B3
Aldeacentenera E 156 A2
Aldeadávila de la Ribera E 149 A3
Aldea del Cano E 155 B4
Aldea del Fresno E 151 B3
Aldea del Obispo E 149 B3
Aldea del Rey E 157 B4
Aldea de Trujillo E 156 A2
Aldealcorvo E 151 A4
Aldealuenga de Santa Maria E 151 A4
Aldeamayor de San Martin E 150 A3
Aldeanueva de Barbarroya E 150 C2
Aldeanueva del Camino E 149 B4
Aldeanueva del Codonal E 150 A3
Aldeanueva de San Bartolomé E 156 A2
Aldeapozo E 144 C1
Aldeaquemada E 157 B4
Aldea Real E 151 A3
Aldearrubia E 150 A2
Aldeaseca de la Frontera E 150 B2
Aldeasoña E 151 A3
Aldeatejada E 150 B2
Aldeavieja E 150 B3
Aldeburgh GB 45 A5
Aldehuela E 152 B2
Aldehuela de Calatañazor E 143 C4
Aldeia da Serra P 155 C3
Aldeia do Bispo P 149 B3
Aldeia do Mato P 154 B2
Aldeia Gavinha P 154 B1
Aldeire E 164 B1
Aldenhoven D 80 B2
Aldersbach D 95 C5
Aldershot GB 44 B3
Aldudes F 144 A2
Åled S 60 C2
Aledo E 165 B3
Alegria E 143 B4
Aleksandrovac SRB 127 C3
Aleksandrów Kujawski PL 76 B3
Aleksandrów Łódźki PL 86 A3
Aleksa Šantić SRB 126 B1
Ålem S 62 B4
Alençon F 89 B4
Alenquer P 154 B1
Alenya F 146 B3
Aléria F 180 A2
Alès F 131 A3
Áles I 179 C2
Alessándria I 120 C1
Alessándria della Rocca I 176 B2
Alessano I 173 C4
Ålesund N 198 C3
Alet-les-Bains F 146 B3
Alexandria
GB 34 C3
GR 182 C4
RO 17 D6
Alexandroupoli GR 183 C7
Aleyrac F 131 A3
Alézio I 173 B4
Alfacar E 163 A4
Alfaiates P 149 B3
Alfajarin E 153 A3
Alfambra
E 152 B2
P 160 B1
Alfândega da Fé P 149 A3
Alfarela de Jafes P 148 A2
Alfarelos P 148 B1
Alfarim P 154 C1
Alfarnate E 163 B3
Alfaro E 144 B2
Alfarrás E 145 C4
Alfaz del Pi E 159 C3
Alfedena I 169 B4
Alfeizarão P 154 B1
Alfeld
Bayern D 95 B3
Niedersachsen D 72 C2
Alfena P 148 A1
Alferce P 160 B1
Alfhausen D 71 B4
Alfonsine I 135 A5
Alford
Aberdeenshire GB 33 D4
Lincolnshire GB 41 B4
Alforja E 147 C1
Alfoz E 141 A3
Alfreton GB 40 B2
Alfta S 50 A3
Alfundão P 160 A1
Algaida E 167 B2
Algar E 162 B2
Älgarås S 55 B5
Ålgård N 52 B1
Algarinejo E 163 A3
Algarrobo E 163 B3
Algatocin E 162 B2
Algeciras E 162 B2
Algemesí E 159 B3
Algés P 154 C1
Algete E 151 B4
Alghero I 178 B2
Älghult S 62 A3
Alginet E 159 B3
Algodonales E 162 B2
Algodor
E 151 C4
P 160 B2
Algora E 151 B5
Algoso P 149 A3
Algoz P 160 B1
Älgsjö S 200 B3
Alguaire E 145 C4
Alguazas E 165 A3
Algutsrum S 63 B4
Algyö H 126 A2
Alhama de Almería E 164 C2
Alhama de Aragón E 152 A2
Alhama de Granada E 163 B4
Alhama de Murcia E 165 B3
Alhambra E 157 B4
Alhandra P 154 C1
Alhaurin de la Torre E 163 B3
Alhaurin el Grande E 163 B3
Alhendin E 163 A4
Alhóndiga E 151 B5
Alia E 156 A2
Ália I 176 B2
Aliağa TR 186 D1
Aliaga E 153 B3
Alibunar SRB 127 B2
Alicante E 165 A4
Alicún de Ortega E 164 B1
Alife I 170 B2
Alija del Infantado E 141 B5
Alijó P 148 A2
Alimena I 177 B3
Alingsås S 60 B2
Alinyà E 147 B2
Aliseda E 155 B4
Ali Terme I 177 A4
Aliveri GR 185 A5
Alixan F 117 C5
Aljaraque E 161 B2
Aljezur P 160 B1
Aljorra E 165 B3
Aljubarrota P 154 B2
Aljucen E 155 B4
Aljustrel P 160 B1
Alken B 79 B5
Alkmaar NL 70 B1
Alkoven A 96 C2
Allaines F 103 A3
Allaire F 101 B3
Allanche F 116 B2
Alland A 111 A3
Allariz E 140 B3
Allassac F 129 A4
Allauch F 131 B4
Alleen N 52 B3
Allègre F 117 B3
Allemont F 118 B3
Allendale Town GB 37 B4
Allendorf D 81 B4
Allentsteig A 97 C3
Allepuz E 153 B3
Allersberg D 95 B3
Allershausen D 95 C3
Alles E 142 A2
Allevard F 118 B3
Allgunnen S 62 A3
Allihies IRL 29 C1
Allingåbro DK 58 B3
Allmannsdorf D 107 B4
Allo E 144 B1
Alloa GB 35 B4
Allogny F 103 B4
Ålloluokta S 196 B2
Allones
Eure et Loire F 90 C1
Maine-et-Loire F 102 B2
Allonnes F 102 B2
Allons F 128 B2
Allos F 132 A2
Allstedt D 82 A3
Alltwalis GB 39 C2
Allumiere I 168 A1
Almaceda P 155 B3
Almacelles E 145 C4
Almachar E 163 B3
Almada P 154 C1
Almadén E 156 B3
Almadén de la Plata E 161 B3
Almadenejos E 156 B3
Almadrones E 151 B5
Almagro E 157 B4
Almajano E 144 C1
Almansa E 159 C2
Almansil P 160 B1
Almanza E 142 B1
Almaraz E 150 C2
Almargen E 162 B2
Almarza E 143 C4
Almásfüzitő H 112 B2
Almassora E 159 B3
Almazán E 152 A1
Almazul E 152 A1
Alme D 81 A4
Almedina E 158 C1
Almedinilla E 163 A3
Almeida
E 149 A3
P 149 B3
Almeirim P 154 B2
Almelo NL 71 B3
Almenar E 145 C4
Almenara E 159 B3
Almenar de Soria E 152 A1
Almendra P 149 B2
Almendral E 155 C4
Almendral de la Cañada E 150 B3
Almendralejo E 155 C4
Almenno San Bartolomeo I 120 B2
Almere NL 70 B2
Almería E 164 C2
Almerimar E 164 C2
Almese I 119 B4
Almexial P 160 B2
Älmhult S 63 B2
Almiropotamos GR 185 A5
Almiros GR 182 D4
Almodôvar P 160 B1
Almodóvar del Campo E 157 B3
Almodóvar del Pinar E 158 B2
Almodóvar del Río E 162 A2
Almofala P 148 B2
Almogia E 163 B3
Almoharin E 156 A1
Almonacid de la Sierra E 152 A2
Almonacid de Toledo E 157 A4
Almonaster la Real E 161 B3
Almondsbury GB 43 A4
Almonte E 161 B3
Almoradí E 165 A4
Almoraima E 162 B2
Almorox E 150 B3
Almoster P 154 B2
Almsele S 200 B3
Älmsta S 51 C5
Almudena E 164 A3
Almudévar E 145 B3
Almuñécar E 163 B4
Almunge S 51 C5
Almuradiel E 157 B4
Almussafes E 159 B3
Almvik S 62 A4
Alness GB 32 D2
Alnmouth GB 37 A5
Alnwick GB 37 A5
Åloppe S 51 C4
Álora E 163 B3
Alos d'Ensil E 146 B2
Alosno E 161 B2
Alozaina E 162 B3
Alpbach A 108 B2
Alpedrete de la Sierra E 151 B4
Alpedrinha P 148 B2
Alpen D 80 A2
Alpera E 159 C2
Alphen aan de Rijn NL 70 B1
Alpiarça P 154 B2
Alpignano I 119 B4
Alpirsbach D 93 C4
Alpu TR 187 C5
Alpuente E 159 B2
Alqueva P 160 A2
Alquézar E 145 B4
Als DK 58 B3
Alsasua E 144 B1
Alsdorf D 80 B2
Alselv DK 59 C1
Alsfeld D 81 B5
Alsike S 57 A3
Alskog S 57 C4
Alsleben D 83 A3
Alsónémedi H 112 B3
Alsótold H 112 B3
Alsóújlak H 111 B3
Alstad N 194 C6
Alstätte D 71 B3
Alsterbro S 62 B3
Alstermo S 62 B3
Alston GB 37 B4
Alsvåg N 194 B6
Alsvik N 194 C5
Alta N 192 C7
Älta S 57 A4
Altamura I 172 B2
Altarejos E 158 B1
Altaussee A 109 B4
Altavilla Irpina I 170 B2
Altavilla Silentina I 170 C3
Altdöbern D 84 A2
Altdorf
CH 107 C3
D 95 C4
Altdorf bei Nürnberg D 95 B3
Alte P 160 B1
Altea E 159 C3
Altedo I 121 C4
Altena D 81 A3
Altenau D 82 A2
Altenberg D 84 B1
Altenberge D 71 B4
Altenbruch D 64 C1
Altenburg D 83 B4
Altenfelden A 96 C1
Altengronau D 82 B1
Altenheim D 93 C3
Altenhundem D 81 A4
Altenkirchen
Mecklenburg-Vorpommern D 66 B2
Radom D 81 B3
Altenkunstadt D 82 B3
Altenmarkt
A 110 B1
D 109 A3
Altenmarkt im Pongall A 109 B4
Altensteig D 93 C4
Altentreptow D 74 A2
Altenwalde D 64 C1
Alten-weddingen D 73 B4
Alter do Chão P 155 B3
Altfraunhofen D 95 C4
Altheim
A 109 A4
D 94 B1
Althofen A 110 C1
Altınoluk TR 186 C1
Altınova TR 186 C1
Altıntaş TR 187 C5
Altınyaka TR 189 C5
Altınyayla TR 189 B4
Altkirch F 106 B2
Altlandsberg D 74 B2
Altlewin D 74 B3
Altmannstein D 95 C3
Altmorschen D 82 A1
Altmunster A 109 B4
Altnaharra GB 32 C2
Alto Campoó E 142 A2
Altofonte I 176 A2
Altomonte I 174 B2
Alton
Hampshire GB 44 B3
Staffordshire GB 40 C2
Altopáscio I 135 B3
Altötting D 109 A3
Altreichenau D 96 C1
Alt Ruppin D 74 B1
Altshausen D 107 B4
Altstätten CH 107 B4
Altura E 159 B3
Altusried D 107 B5
Alūksne LV 8 D5
Alunda S 51 B5
Alustante E 152 B2
Alva GB 35 B4
Alvaiázere P 154 B2
Alvalade P 160 B1
Älvängen S 60 B2
Alvarenga P 148 B1
Alvares P 154 A2
Alvdal N 199 C7
Älvdalen S 49 A6
Alverca P 154 C1
Alversund N 46 B2
Alvesta S 62 B2
Alvignac F 129 B4
Alvignano I 170 B2
Ålvik N 46 B3
Alvik S 50 B1
Alvimare F 89 A4
Alviobeira P 154 B2
Alvito P 160 A2
Älvkarleby S 51 B4
Älvkarleöbruk S 51 B4
Alvor P 160 B1
Alvorge P 154 B2
Alvøy N 46 B2
Älvros S 199 C11
Alvsbacka S 55 A4
Älvsbyn S 196 D4
Älvsered S 60 B2
Alwernia PL 86 B3
Alwinton GB 37 A4
Alyth GB 35 B4
Alytus LT 13 A6
Alzénau D 93 A5
Alzey D 93 B4
Alzira E 159 B3
Alzonne F 146 A3
Amadora P 154 C1
Åmål S 55 A3
Amalfi I 170 C2
Amaliada GR 184 B2
Amance F 105 B5
Amancey F 105 B5
Amándola I 136 C2
Amantea I 175 B2
Amarante P 148 A1
Amareleja P 161 A2
Amares P 148 A1
Amaseno I 169 B3
Amasra TR 187 A7
Amatrice I 169 A3
Amay B 79 B5
Ambarnyy RUS 3 D13
Ambazac F 115 C5
Ambelonas GR 182 D4
Amberg D 95 B3
Ambérieu-en-Bugey F 118 B2
Ambérieux-en-Dombes F 117 A4
Ambert F 117 B3
Ambés F 128 A2
Ambjörby S 49 B5
Ambjörnarp S 60 B3
Amble GB 37 A5
Ambleside GB 36 B4
Ambleteuse F 78 B1
Amboise F 102 B2
Ambrières-les-Vallées F 88 B3
Amden CH 107 B4
Amel B 80 B2
Amélia I 168 A2
Amélie-les-Bains-Palalda F 146 B3
Amelinghausen D 72 A3
Amendoa P 154 B2
Amendoeira P 160 B2
Améndola I 171 B3
Amendolara I 174 B2
Amer E 147 B3
A Merca E 140 B3
Amerongen NL 70 B2
Amersfoort NL 70 B2
Amersham GB 44 B3
Ames E 140 B2
Amesbury GB 44 B2
Amfiklia GR 182 E4
Amfilochia GR 182 E3
Amfipoli GR 183 C5
Amfissa GR 184 A3
Amièira P 155 C3

Amieira P 154 B3
Amieiro P 148 B1
Amiens F 90 B2
Amindeo GR 182 C3
Åminne S 60 B3
Åmli N 53 B4
Amlwch GB 38 A2
Ammanford GB 39 C3
Ammarnäs S 195 E7
Åmmeberg S 55 B5
Amorbach D 94 B1
Amorebieta E 143 A4
Amorgos GR 185 C6
Amorosa P 148 A1
Amorosi I 170 B2
Åmot
Buskerud N 48 C1
Telemark N 53 A3
S 50 B3
Åmotfors S 54 A3
Åmotsdal N 53 A4
Amou F 128 C2
Ampezzo I 122 A1
Ampfing D 95 C4
Ampflwang A 109 A4
Amplepuis F 117 B4
Amposta E 153 B4
Ampthill GB 44 A3
Ampudia E 142 C2
Ampuero E 143 A3
Amriswil CH 107 B4
Åmsele S 200 B5
Amstelveen NL 70 B1
Amsterdam NL 70 B1
Amstetten A 110 A1
Amtzell D 107 B4
Amulree GB 35 B4
Amurrio E 143 A4
Amusco E 142 B2
Anacapri I 170 C2
Anadia P 148 B1
Anadon E 152 B2
Anafi GR 185 C6
Anagni I 169 B3
Anamur TR 23 C7
Ananyiv UA 17 B8
Anascaul IRL 29 B1
Ånäset S 2 D7
Åna-Sira N 52 B2
Anastażewo PL 76 B3
Anaya de Alba E 150 B2
Ança P 148 B1
Ancaster GB 40 C3
Ancede P 148 A1
Ancenis F 101 B4
Ancerville F 91 C5
Anchuras E 156 A3
Ancona I 136 B2
Ancora P 148 A1
Ancrum GB 35 C5
Ancy-le-Franc F 104 B3
Andalo I 121 A3
Åndalsnes N 198 C4
Andance F 117 B4
Andau A 111 B4
Andebu N 53 A6
Andeer CH 107 C4
Andelfingen CH 107 B3
Andelot-Blanchville F 105 A4
Andelot-en-Montagne F 105 C4
Andenes N 194 A7
Andenne B 79 B5
Anderlues B 79 B4
Andermatt CH 107 C3
Andernach D 80 B3
Andernos-les-Bains F 128 B1
Anderslöv S 66 A2
Anderstorp S 60 B3
Andijk NL 70 B2
Andoain E 144 A1
Andocs H 112 C1
Andolsheim F 106 A2
Andorra E 153 B3
Andorra La Vella AND 146 B2
Andosilla E 144 B2
Andover GB 44 B2
Andratx E 166 B2
Andreapol RUS 9 D8
Andreas GB 36 B2
Andréspol PL 86 A3
Andrest F 145 A4
Andretta I 172 B1
Andrezieux-Bouthéon F 117 B4
Ándria I 171 B4
Andrijevica MNE 16 D3
Andritsena GR 184 B2
Andros GR 185 B5
Andrychów PL 99 B3
Andselv N 194 A9
Andújar E 157 B3
Anduze F 131 A2
Åneby N 48 B2
Aneby S 62 A2
Añes E 143 A3
Anet F 90 C1
Anfo I 121 B3
Ang S 62 A2
Anga S 57 C4
Angaïs F 145 A3
Änge S 199 B11
Ånge S 200 D1
Angeja P 148 B1
Ängelholm S 61 C2
Angeli FIN 193 D9
Ängelsberg S 50 C3
Anger A 110 B2
Angera I 120 B1
Angermünde D 74 A3
Angern A 97 C4
Angers F 102 B1
Angerville F 90 C2
Anghiari I 135 B5
Angle GB 39 C1
Anglès E 147 C3
Anglés F 130 B1
Angles F 114 B2
Anglesola E 147 C2
Angles sur l'Anglin F 115 B4
Anglet F 128 C1
Anglisidhes CY 181 B2
Anglure F 91 C3
Angoulême F 115 C4
Angoulins F 114 B2
Angsö S 56 A2
Angueira P 149 A3
Angües E 145 B3
Anguiano E 143 B4
Anguillara Sabazia I 168 A2
Anguillara Véneta I 121 B4
Anhée B 79 B4
Anholt DK 60 C1
Aniane F 130 B2
Aniche F 78 B3
Ånimskog S 54 B3
Anina RO 16 C4
Anixi GR 182 D3
Anizy-le-Château F 91 B3
Anjalankoski FIN 8 B5
Anjan S 199 B9
Ankara TR 187 C7
Ankaran SLO 122 B2
Ankarsrum S 62 A4
Ankerlia N 192 C4
Anklam D 66 C2
Ankum D 71 B4
Anlauftal A 109 B4
Anlezy F 104 C2
Ånn S 199 B9
Annaberg A 110 B2
Annaberg-Buchholz D 83 B5
Annaberg im Lammertal A 109 B4
Annaburg D 83 A5
Annahütte D 84 A1
Annalong GB 27 B5
Annan GB 36 B3
Anndalsvågen N 195 E3
Anneberg
Halland S 60 B2
Jönköping S 62 A2
Annecy F 118 B3
Annelund S 60 B3
Annemasse F 118 A3
Annenskiy Most RUS 9 B10
Annerstad S 60 C3
Annestown IRL 30 B1
Annevoie-Rouillon B 79 B4
Annonay F 117 B4
Annot F 132 B2
Annweiler D 93 B3
Ano Poroia GR 183 B5
Añora E 156 B3
Ano Siros GR 185 B5
Anould F 106 A1
Anquela del Ducado E 152 B1
Anröchte D 81 A4
Ans DK 59 B2
Ansager DK 59 C1
Ansbach D 94 B2
Anse F 117 B4
Anseroeul B 79 B3
Ansfelden A 110 A1
Ansião P 154 B2
Ansó E 144 B3
Ansoain E 144 B2
Anstruther GB 35 B5
Antalya TR 189 C5
Antas E 164 B3
Antegnate I 120 B2
Antequera E 163 A3
Anterselva di Mezzo I 108 C3
Antibes F 132 B3
Antigüedad E 142 C2
Antillo I 177 B4
Antirio GR 184 A2
Antnäs S 196 D4
An t-Ob GB 31 B1
Antoing B 79 B3
Antonin PL 86 A1
Antrain F 88 B2
Antrim GB 27 B4
Antrodoco I 169 A3
Antronapiana I 119 A5
Anttis S 196 B5
Antuzede P 148 B1
Antwerp = Antwerpen B 79 A4
Antwerpen = Antwerp B 79 A4
Anversa d'Abruzzi I 169 B3
Anvin F 78 B2
Anzat-le-Luguet F 116 B3
Anzi I 172 B1
Ánzio I 168 B2
Anzola d'Emilia I 135 A4
Anzón E 144 C2
Aoiz E 144 B2
Aosta I 119 B4
Apalhão P 155 B3
Apátfalva H 126 A2
Apatin SRB 125 B5
Apatity RUS 3 C13
Apc H 112 B3
Apécchio I 136 B1
Apeldoorn NL 70 B2
Apen D 71 A4
Apenburg D 73 B4
Apensen D 72 A2
A Peroxa E 140 B3
Apiro I 136 B2
Apliki CY 181 B2
Apolda D 82 A3
Apolonia GR 185 C5
A Pontenova E 141 A3
Apostag H 112 C2
Äppelbo S 49 B6
Appennino I 136 C2
Appenzell CH 107 B4
Appiano I 108 C2
Appingedam NL 71 A3
Appleby-in-Westmorland GB 37 B4
Applecross GB 31 B3
Appledore GB 42 A2
Appoigny F 104 B2
Apremont-la-Forêt F 92 C1
Aprica I 120 A3
Apricena I 171 B3
Aprigliano I 174 B2
Aprília I 168 B2
Apt F 131 B4
Apúlia P 148 A1
Aquiléia I 122 B2
Aquilónia I 172 B1
Aquino I 169 B3
Ar S 57 C4
Arabayona E 150 A2
Arabba I 108 C2
Araç TR 23 A7
Aracena E 161 B3
Arachova GR 184 A3
Aračinovo MK 182 A3
Arad RO 126 A3
Aradac SRB 126 B2
Aradhippou CY 181 B2
Aragnouet F 145 B4
Aragona I 176 B2
Aramits F 144 A3
Aramon F 131 B3
Aranda de Duero E 143 C3
Aranda de Moncayo E 152 A2
Arandjelovac SRB 127 C2
Aranjuez E 151 B4
Arantzazu E 143 B4
Aranzueque E 151 B4
Aras de Alpuente E 159 B2
Arauzo de Miel E 143 C3
Arazede P 148 B1
Arbas F 145 B4
Árbatax I 179 C3
Arbeca E 147 C1
Arberg D 94 B2
Arbesbach A 96 C2
Arboga S 56 A1
Arbois F 105 C4
Arbon CH 107 B4
Arboréa I 179 C2
Arbório I 119 B5
Årbostad N 194 B8
Arbrå S 50 A3
Arbroath GB 35 B5
Arbùcies E 147 C3
Arbuniel E 163 A4
Arbus I 179 C2
Arcachon F 128 B1
Arce I 169 B3
Arcen NL 80 A2
Arc-en-Barrois F 105 B3
Arces-Dilo F 104 A2
Arc-et-Senans F 105 B4
Arcévia I 136 B1
Arcey F 106 B1
Archanes GR 185 D6
Archangelos GR 188 C3
Archena E 165 A3
Archez E 163 B4
Archiac F 115 C3
Archidona E 163 A3
Archiestown GB 32 D3
Archivel E 164 A3
Arcidosso I 135 C4
Arcille I 135 C4
Arcis-sur-Aube F 91 C4
Arc-lès-Gray F 105 B4
Arco I 121 B3
Arcones E 151 A4
Arcos E 143 B3
Arcos de Jalón E 152 A1
Arcos de la Frontera E 162 B2
Arcos de la Sierra E 152 B1
Arcos de las Salinas E 159 B2
Arcos de Valdevez P 148 A1
Arcozelo P 148 B2
Arc-sur-Tille F 105 B4
Arcusa E 145 B4
Arcy-sur-Cure F 104 B2
Ardagh IRL 29 B2
Årdal N 52 A2
Ardala S 55 B4
Ardales E 162 B3
Årdalstangen N 47 A4
Ardara
I 178 B2
IRL 26 B2
Ardarroch GB 31 B3
Ardbeg GB 34 C1
Ardcharnich GB 32 D1
Ardchyle GB 34 B3
Ardee IRL 27 C4
Arden DK 58 B2
Ardentes F 103 C3
Ardenza I 134 B3
Ardersier GB 32 D2
Ardes F 116 B3
Ardessie GB 32 D1
Ardez CH 107 C5
Ardfert IRL 29 B2
Ardgay GB 32 D2
Ardglass GB 27 B5
Ardgroom IRL 29 C2
Ardhasig GB 31 B2
Ardino BG 183 B7
Ardisa E 144 B3
Ardkearagh IRL 29 C1
Ardlui GB 34 B3
Ardlussa GB 34 B2
Ardón E 142 B1
Ardooie B 78 B3
Ardore I 175 C2
Ardre S 57 C4
Ardres F 78 B1
Ardrishaig GB 34 B2
Ardrossan GB 34 C3
Are N 52 A1
Åre S 199 B10
Areia Branca P 154 B1
Aremark N 54 A2
Arenales de San Gregorio E 157 A4
Arenas E 163 B3
Arenas de Iguña E 142 A2
Arenas del Rey E 163 B4
Arenas de San Juan E 157 A4
Arenas de San Pedro E 150 B2
Arendal N 53 B4
Arendonk B 79 A5
Arengosse F 128 B2
Arentorp S 55 B3
Arenys de Mar E 147 C3
Arenys de Munt E 147 C3
Arenzano I 133 A4
Areo E 146 B2
Areopoli GR 184 C3
Ares E 140 A2
Arès F 128 B1
Ares del Maestrat E 153 B3
Aresvika N 198 B5
Arette F 144 A3
Aretxabaleta E 143 A4
Arevalillo E 150 B2
Arévalo E 150 A3
Arez P 155 B3
Arezzo I 135 B4
Arfeuilles F 117 A3
Argalasti GR 183 D5
Argallón E 156 B2
Argamasilla de Alba E 157 A4
Argamasilla de Calatrava E 157 B3
Arganda E 151 B4
Arganil P 148 B1
Argasion GR 184 B1
Argegno I 120 B2
Argelès-Gazost F 145 A3
Argelès-sur-Mer F 146 B4
Argenta I 121 C4
Argentan F 89 B3
Argentat F 116 B1
Argentera I 132 A2
Argenteuil F 90 C2
Argenthal D 93 B3
Argentiera I 178 B2
Argentona E 147 C3
Argenton-Château F 102 C1
Argenton-sur-Creuse F 103 C3
Argentré F 102 A1
Argentré-du-Plessis F 101 A4
Argent-sur-Sauldre F 103 B4
Argirades GR 182 D1
Argıthanı TR 189 A6
Argos GR 184 B3
Argos Orestiko GR 182 C3
Argostoli GR 184 A1
Argote E 143 B4
Arguedas E 144 B2
Argueil F 90 B1
Arholma S 51 C6
Århus DK 59 B3
Ariano Irpino I 170 B3
Ariano nel Polésine I 121 C5
Aribe E 144 B2
Aridea GR 182 C4
Arienzo I 170 B2
Arild S 61 C2
Arileod GB 34 B1
Arinagour GB 34 B1
Ariño E 153 A3
Arinthod F 118 A3
Arisaig GB 34 B2
Arisgotas E 157 A4
Aritzo I 179 C3
Ariza E 152 A1
Årjäng S 54 A3
Arjeplog S 195 D8
Arjona E 157 C3
Arjonilla E 157 C3
Arkasa GR 188 D2
Arkelstorp S 63 B2
Arklow IRL 30 B2
Arkösund S 56 B2
Ärla S 56 A2
Arlanc F 117 B3
Arlanzón E 143 B3
Arlebosc F 117 B4
Arlena di Castro I 168 A1
Arles F 131 B3
Arles-sur-Tech F 146 B3
Arló H 113 A4
Arlon B 92 B1
Armação de Pera P 160 B1
Armadale
Highland GB 31 B3
West Lothian GB 35 C4
Armagh GB 27 B4
Armamar P 148 A2
Armenistis GR 185 B7
Armeno I 119 B5
Armenteros E 150 B2
Armentières F 78 B2
Armilla E 163 A4
Armiñón E 143 B4
Armoy GB 27 A4
Armuña de Tajuña E 151 B4
Armutlu
Bursa TR 186 B3
İzmir TR 188 A2
Arnac-Pompadour F 115 C5
Arnafjord N 46 A3
Arnage F 102 B2
Arnas F 117 A4
Årnäs S 55 B4
Arnay-le-Duc F 104 B3
Arnborg DK 59 B2
Arnbruck D 95 B4
Arnea GR 183 C5
Arneberg
Hedmark N 48 A2
Hedmark N 49 B4
Arneburg D 73 B5
Arnedillo E 144 B1
Arnedo E 144 B1
Arneguy F 144 A2
Arnés E 153 B4
Árnes IS 190 A4
Årnes
Akershus N 48 B3
Troms N 194 A9
Arnfels A 110 C2
Arnhem NL 70 C2
Arnissa GR 182 C3
Arno S 56 B3
Arnold GB 40 B2
Arnoldstein A 109 C4
Arnsberg D 81 A4
Arnschwang D 95 B4
Arnsdorf D 84 A1
Årnset N 198 B6
Arnside GB 37 B4
Arnstadt D 82 B2
Arnstein D 94 B1
Arnstorf D 95 C4
Arnum DK 59 C1
Aroche E 161 B3
Ároktő H 113 B4
Arolla CH 119 A4
Arolsen D 81 A5
Arona I 119 B5
Åros N 54 A1
Arosa
CH 107 C4
P 148 A1
Ærøskøbing DK 65 B3
Årøsund DK 59 C2
Arouca P 148 B1
Årøysund N 54 A1
Arpajon F 90 C2
Arpajon-sur-Cère F 116 C2
Arpela FIN 196 C7
Arpino I 169 B3
Arquata del Tronto I 136 C2
Arques F 78 B2
Arques-la-Bataille F 89 A5
Arquillos E 157 B4
Arraia-Maeztu E 143 B4
Arraiolos P 154 C2
Arrancourt F 92 C2
Arras F 78 B2
Arrasate E 143 A4
Årre DK 59 C1
Arreau F 145 B4
Arredondo E 143 A3
Arrens-Marsous F 145 B3
Arriate E 162 B2
Arrifana P 160 B1
Arrigorriaga E 143 A4
Arriondas E 142 A1
Arroba de los Montes E 157 A3
Arrochar GB 34 B3
Arromanches-les-Bains F 88 A3
Arronches P 155 B3
Arroniz E 144 B1
Arrou F 103 A3
Arroya E 142 B2
Arroya de Cuéllar E 150 A3
Arroyal E 142 B2
Arroyo de la Luz E 155 B4
Arroyo del Ojanco E 164 A2
Arroyo de San Servan E 155 C4
Arroyomolinos de León E 161 A3
Arroyomolinos de Montánchez E 156 A1
Arruda dos Vinhos P 154 C1
Arsac F 128 B2
Ars-en-Ré F 114 B2
Arsiè I 121 B4
Arsiero I 121 B4
Årslev DK 59 C3
Ársoli I 169 A3
Ars-sur-Moselle F 92 B2
Årsunda S 50 B3
Artà E 167 B3
Arta GR 182 D3
Artajona E 144 B2
Artegna I 122 A2
Arteixo E 140 A2
Artemare F 118 B2
Arten I 121 A4
Artena I 169 B2
Artenay F 103 A3
Artern D 82 A3
Artés E 147 C2
Artesa de Segre E 147 C2
Arth CH 107 B3
Arthez-de-Béarn F 145 A3
Arthon-en-Retz F 101 B4
Arthurstown IRL 30 B2
Artieda E 144 B3
Artix F 145 A3
Artotina GR 182 E4
Artsyz UA 17 B8
Artziniega E 143 A3
A Rúa E 141 B3
Arudy F 145 A3
Arundel GB 44 C3
Arveyres F 128 B2
Arvidsjaur S 196 D2
Arvieux F 118 C3
Arvika S 54 A3
Åryd
Blekinge S 63 B3
Kronoberg S 62 B2
Arzachena I 178 A3
Arzacq-Arraziguet F 128 C2
Árzana I 179 C3
Arzano F 100 B2
Aržano HR 138 B2
Arzberg D 95 A4
Arzignano I 121 B4
Arzila P 148 B1
Arzl im Pitztal A 108 B1
Arzúa E 140 B2
As B 80 A1
Aš CZ 83 B4
Ås N 54 A1
Åsa S 60 B2
Asaa DK 58 A3
Aşağıçiğil TR 189 A6
Ašanja SRB 127 C2
Åsarna S 199 C11
Åsarøy N 52 A2
Åsarp S 55 B4
Asasp F 145 A3
Åsbro S 55 A6
Åsby S 60 B2
Asby S 62 A3
Asbygri IS 191 A9
Ascain F 144 A2
Ascea I 172 B1
Ascha D 95 B4
Aschach an der Donau A 96 C2
Aschaffenburg D 93 B5
Aschbach Markt A 110 A1
Ascheberg
Nordrhein-Westfalen D 81 A3
Schleswig-Holstein D 65 B3
Aschendorf D 71 A4
Aschersleben D 82 A3
Asciano I 135 B4
Ascó E 153 A4
Asco F 180 A2
Áscoli Piceno I 136 C2
Áscoli Satriano I 171 B3
Ascona CH 120 A1
Ascot GB 44 B3
Ascoux F 103 A4
Åse N 194 A6
Åseda S 62 A3
Åsele S 200 B3

Åsen
N 199 B8
S 49 A5
Asendorf D 72 B2
Asenovgrad BG 183 A6
Åsensbruk S 54 B3
Åseral N 52 B3
Asfeld F 91 B4
Åsgårdstrand N 54 A1
Ásgarður IS 190 B1
Asgate CY 181 B2
Ash
Kent GB 45 B5
Surrey GB 44 B3
Åshammar S 50 B3
Ashbourne
GB 40 B2
IRL 30 A2
Ashburton GB 43 B3
Ashby-de-la-Zouch
GB 40 C2
Ashchurch GB 44 B1
Åsheim N 199 D8
Ashford GB 45 B4
Ashington GB 37 A5
Ashley GB 38 B4
Ashmyany BY 13 A6
Ashton Under Lyne
GB 40 B1
Ashwell GB 44 A3
Asiago I 121 B4
Asipovichy BY 13 B8
Aska FIN 197 B9
Askam-in-Furness
GB 36 B3
Askeaton IRL 29 B3
Asker N 48 C2
Askersund S 55 B5
Åskilje S 200 B3
Askim N 54 A2
Askland N 53 B4
Äsköping S 56 A2
Askvoll N 46 A2
Åsljunga S 61 C3
Asmunti FIN 197 D9
Asnæs DK 61 D1
As Neves E 140 B2
As Nogais E 141 B3
Ásola I 120 B3
Asolo I 121 B4
Asos GR 184 A1
Asotthalom H 126 A1
Aspach A 109 A4
Aspang Markt A 111 B3
Aspariegos E 149 A4
Asparn an der Zaya
A 97 C4
Aspatria GB 36 B3
Aspberg S 55 A4
Aspe E 165 A4
Aspet F 145 A4
Äspö S 63 B3
As Pontes de García
Rodríguez E 140 A3
Aspres-sur-Buëch
F 132 A1
Aspsele S 200 C4
Assafora P 154 C1
Asse B 79 B4
Assebakte N 193 C9
Assel D 72 A2
Asselborn L 92 A1
Assémini I 179 C2
Assen NL 71 B3
Assenede B 79 A3
Assens
Aarhus Amt. DK 58 B3
Fyns Amt. DK 59 C2
Assesse B 79 B5
Assisi I 136 B1
Åsskard N 198 B5
Assling D 108 B3
Asso I 120 B2
Asson F 145 A3
Ássoro I 177 B3
Assumar P 155 B3
Åsta N 48 A3
Astaffort F 129 B3
Astakos GR 184 A2
Asten NL 80 A1
Asti I 119 C5
Astipalea GR 188 C1
Astorga E 141 B4
Åstorp S 61 C2
Åsträsk S 200 B5
Astudillo E 142 B2
Asuni I 179 C2
Asványráró H 111 B4
Aszód H 112 B3
Aszófő H 111 C4
Atabey TR 189 B5
Atalaia P 154 B3
Atalandi GR 182 E4
Atalho P 154 C2
Átány H 113 B4
Atanzón E 151 B4
Ataquines E 150 A3
Atarfe E 163 A4
Atça TR 188 B3
Ateca E 152 A2
A Teixeira E 141 B3
Atella I 172 B1
Atessa I 169 A4
Ath B 79 B3
Athboy IRL 30 A2
Athea IRL 29 B2
Athenry IRL 28 A3
Athens = Athina
GR 185 B4
Atherstone GB 40 C2
Athienou CY 181 A2
Athies F 90 B2
Athies-sous-Laon F 91 B3
Athina = Athens
GR 185 B4
Athleague IRL 28 A3
Athlone IRL 28 A4
Athna CY 181 A2
Athy IRL 30 B2
Atienza E 151 A5
Atina I 169 B3
Atkár H 113 B3
Atlantı TR 189 A7
Atna N 199 D7
Åtorp S 55 A5
Åtrå N 47 C5
Ätran S 60 B2
Atri I 169 A3
Atripalda I 170 C2
Atsiki GR 183 D7
Attendorn D 81 A3
Attichy F 90 B3
Attigliano I 168 A2
Attigny F 91 B4
Attleborough GB 41 C5
Åtvidaberg S 56 B1
Atzendorf D 73 C4
Au
Steiermark A 110 B2
Vorarlberg A 107 B4
Bayern D 95 C3
Bayern D 108 B2
Aub D 94 B2
Aubagne F 132 B1
Aubange B 92 B1
Aubel B 80 B1
Aubenas F 117 C4
Aubenton F 91 B4
Auberive F 105 B4
Aubeterre-sur-Dronne
F 128 A3
Aubiet F 129 C3
Aubigné F 115 B3
Aubigny F 114 B2
Aubigny-au-Bac F 78 B3
Aubigny-en-Artois F 78 B2
Aubigny-sur-Nère
F 103 B4
Aubin F 130 A1
Aubonne CH 105 C5
Aubrac F 116 C2
Aubusson F 116 B2
Auch F 129 C3
Auchencairn GB 36 B3
Auchinleck GB 36 A2
Auchterarder GB 35 B4
Auchtermuchty GB 35 B4
Auchtertyre GB 31 B3
Auchy-au-Bois F 78 B2
Audenge F 128 B1
Auderville F 88 A2
Audierne F 100 A1
Audincourt F 106 B1
Audlem GB 38 B4
Audruicq F 78 B2
Audun-le-Roman F 92 B1
Audun-le-Tiche F 92 B1
Aue
Nordrhein-Westfalen
D 81 A4
Sachsen D 83 B4
Auerbach
Bayern D 95 B3
Sachsen D 83 B4
Auffach A 108 B3
Augher GB 27 B3
Aughnacloy GB 27 B4
Aughrim IRL 30 B2
Augignac F 115 C4
Augsburg D 94 C2
Augusta I 177 B4
Augusten-borg DK 64 B2
Augustfehn D 71 A4
Augustów PL 12 B5
Aukrug D 64 B2
Auktsjaur S 196 D2
Auldearn GB 32 D3
Aulendorf D 107 B4
Auletta I 172 B1
Aulla I 134 A2
Aullène F 180 B2
Aulnay F 115 B3
Aulnoye-Aymeries
F 79 B3
Ault F 90 A1
Aultbea GB 31 B3
Aulum DK 59 B1
Aulus-les-Bains F 146 B2
Auma D 83 B3
Aumale F 90 B1
Aumetz F 92 B1
Aumont-Aubrac F 116 C3
Aunay-en-Bazois F 104 B2
Aunay-sur-Odon F 88 A3
Aune N 199 A10
Auneau F 90 C1
Auneuil F 90 B1
Auning DK 58 B3
Aunsetra N 199 A9
Aups F 132 B2
Aura D 82 B1
Auray F 100 B3
Aurdal N 47 B6
Aure N 198 B5
Aurich D 71 A4
Aurignac F 145 A4
Aurillac F 116 C2
Auriol F 132 B1
Auritz-Burguette E 144 B2
Aurlandsvangen N 47 B4
Auronzo di Cadore
I 109 C3
Auros F 128 B2
Auroux F 117 C3
Aurskog N 48 C3
Aursmoen N 48 C3
Ausónia I 169 B3
Ausservillgraton A 109 C3
Austad N 52 B3
Austbygda N 47 B5
Aústis I 178 B3
Austmarka N 49 B4
Austre Moland N 53 B4
Austre Vikebygd N 52 A1
Austrheim N 46 B1
Auterive F 146 A2
Autheuil-Authouillet
F 89 A5
Authon F 132 A2
Authon-du-Perche
F 102 A2
Autol E 144 B2
Autreville F 92 C1
Autrey-lès-Gray F 105 B4
Autti FIN 197 C10
Autun F 104 C3
Auty-le-Châtel F 103 B4
Auvelais B 79 B4
Auvillar F 129 B3
Auxerre F 104 B2
Auxi-le-Château F 78 B2
Auxon F 104 A2
Auxonne F 105 B4
Auxy F 104 C3
Auzances F 116 A2
Auzon F 117 B3
Ağva TR 187 A4
Availles-Limouzine
F 115 B4
Avaldsnes N 52 A1
Avallon F 104 B2
Avantas GR 183 C7
Avaviken S 195 E9
Avebury GB 44 B2
A Veiga E 141 B3
Aveiras de Cima P 154 B2
Aveiro P 148 B1
Avelgem B 79 B3
Avellino I 170 C2
Avenches CH 106 C2
A-Ver-o-Mar P 148 A1
Aversa I 170 C2
Avesnes-le-Comte F 78 B2
Avesnes-sur-Helpe
F 91 A3
Avesta S 50 B3
Avetrana I 173 B3
Avezzano I 169 A3
Avià E 147 B2
Aviano I 122 A1
Aviemore GB 32 D3
Avigliana I 119 B4
Avigliano I 172 B1
Avignon F 131 B3
Ávila E 150 B3
Avilés E 141 A5
Avilley F 105 B5
Avintes P 148 A1
Avinyo E 147 C2
Àvio I 121 B3
Avioth F 92 B1
Avis P 154 B3
Avize F 91 C4
Avlonari GR 185 A5
Ávola I 177 C4
Avon F 90 C2
Avonmouth GB 43 A4
Avord F 103 B4
Avranches F 88 B2
Avril F 92 B1
Avrillé F 102 B1
Avtovac BIH 139 B4
Awans B 79 B5
Axams A 108 B2
Axat F 146 B3
Axbridge GB 43 A4
Axel NL 79 A3
Ax-les-Thermes F 146 B2
Axmarby S 51 B4
Axmarsbruk S 51 A4
Axminster GB 43 B3
Axvall S 55 B4
Ay F 91 B4
Aya E 144 A1
Ayamonte E 161 B2
Ayancık TR 23 A8
Ayaş TR 187 B7
Aydın TR 188 B2
Ayelo de Malferit E 159 C3
Ayer CH 119 A4
Ayerbe E 144 B3
Ayette F 78 B2
Ayia Napa CY 181 B2
Áyia Phyla CY 181 B2
Áyios Amvrósios
CY 181 A2
Áyios Seryios CY 181 A2
Áyios Theodhoros
CY 181 A3
Aykirikçi TR 187 C5
Aylesbury GB 44 B3
Ayllón E 151 A4
Aylsham GB 41 C5
Ayna E 158 C1
Ayódar E 159 B3
Ayora E 159 B2
Ayr GB 36 A2
Ayrancı TR 23 C7
Ayrancılar TR 188 A2
Ayron F 115 B4
Aysgarth GB 37 B4
Ayton GB 35 C5
Aytos BG 17 D7
Ayvacık TR 186 C1
Ayvalık TR 186 C1
Aywaille B 80 B1
Azaila E 153 A3
Azambuja P 154 B2
Azambujeira P 154 B2
Azanja SRB 127 C2
Azannes-et-
Soumazannes F 92 B1
Azanúy-Alins E 145 C4
Azaruja P 155 C3
Azay-le-Ferron F 115 B5
Azay-le-Rideau F 102 B2
Azcoitia E 143 A4
Azé F 117 A4
Azeiteiros P 155 B3
Azenhas do Mar P 154 C1
Azinhaga P 154 B2
Azinhal P 160 B2
Azinheira dos Bairros
P 160 A1
Aznalcázar E 161 B3
Aznalcóllar E 161 B3
Azóia P 154 B2
Azpeitia E 144 A1
Azuaga E 156 B2
Azuara E 153 A3
Azuqueca de Henares
E 151 B4
Azur F 128 C1
Azzano Décimo I 122 B1

B

Baad A 107 B5
Baamonde E 140 A3
Baar CH 107 B3
Bağarasi TR 188 B2
Baarle-Nassau B 79 A4
Baarn NL 70 B2
Babadağ TR 188 B3
Babadag RO 17 C8
Babaeski TR 186 A2
Babayevo RUS 9 C9
Babenhausen
Bayern D 107 A5
Hessen D 93 B4
Babiak PL 76 B3
Babice PL 86 B3
Babigoszcz PL 75 A3
Babimost PL 75 B4
Babina Greda HR 125 B4
Babócsa H 124 A3
Bábolma H 112 B1
Baborów PL 86 B1
Baboszewo PL 77 B5
Babót H 111 B4
Babruysk BY 13 B8
Babsk PL 87 A4
Bac GB 31 A2
Bač SRB 125 B5
Bacares E 164 B2
Bacău RO 17 B7
Baccarat F 92 C2
Bacharach D 93 A3
Backa S 50 B2
Bačka Palanka
SRB 126 B1
Backaryd S 63 B3
Bačka Topola SRB 126 B1
Backe S 200 C2
Bäckebo S 62 B4
Bäckefors S 54 B3
Bäckhammar S 55 A5
Bački Breg SRB 125 B4
Bački-Brestovac
SRB 126 B1
Bački Monoštor
SRB 125 B4
Bački Petrovac
SRB 126 B1
Bački Sokolac
SRB 126 B1
Backnang D 94 C1
Bačko Gradište
SRB 126 B2
Bačko Novo Selo
SRB 125 B5
Bačko Petrovo Selo
SRB 126 B2
Bácoli I 170 C2
Bacqueville-en-Caux
F 89 A5
Bácsalmás H 126 A1
Bácsbokod H 125 A5
Bad Abbach D 95 C4
Badacsonytomaj H 111 C4
Bad Aibling D 108 B3
Badajoz E 155 C4
Badalona E 147 C3
Badalucco I 133 B3
Bad Aussee A 109 B4
Bad Bederkesa D 72 A1
Bad Bentheim D 71 B4
Bad Bergzabern D 93 B3
Bad Berka D 82 B3
Bad Berleburg D 81 A4
Bad Berneck D 95 A3
Bad Bevensen D 73 A3
Bad Bibra D 82 A3
Bad Birnbach D 95 C5
Bad Blankenburg D 82 B3
Bad Bleiberg A 109 C4
Bad Brambach D 83 B4
Bad Bramstedt D 64 C2
Bad Breisig D 80 B3
Bad Brückenau D 82 B1
Bad Buchau D 107 A4
Bad Camberg D 81 B4
Badderen N 192 C6
Bad Doberan D 65 B4
Bad Driburg D 81 A5
Bad Düben D 83 A4
Bad Dürkheim D 93 B4
Bad Dürrenberg D 83 A4
Bad Dürrheim D 107 A3
Bad Elster D 83 B4
Bad Ems D 81 B3
Baden
A 111 A3
CH 106 B3
Bádenas E 152 A2
Baden-Baden D 93 C4
Bad Endorf D 109 B3
Badenweiler D 106 B2
Baderna HR 122 B2
Bad Essen D 71 B5
Bad Fischau A 111 B3
Bad Frankenhausen
D 82 A3
Bad Freienwalde D 74 B3
Bad Friedrichshall
D 93 B5
Bad Füssing D 96 C1
Bad Gandersheim D 82 A2
Bad Gastein A 109 B4
Bad Gleichenberg
A 110 C2
Bad Goisern A 109 B4
Bad Gottleuba D 84 B1
Bad Grund D 82 A2
Bad Hall A 110 A1
Bad Harzburg D 82 A2
Bad Herrenalb D 93 C4
Bad Hersfeld D 82 B1
Bad Hofgastein A 109 B4
Bad Homburg D 81 B4
Bad Honnef D 80 B3
Bad Hönningen D 80 B3
Badia Calavena I 121 B4
Badia Polésine I 121 B4
Badia Prátáglia I 135 B4
Badia Tedalda I 135 B5
Bad Iburg D 71 B5
Bad Innerlaterns A 107 B4
Bad Ischl A 109 B4
Bad Karlshafen D 81 A5
Bad Kemmeriboden
CH 106 C2
Bądki PL 69 B3
Bad Kissingen D 82 B2
Bad Kleinen D 65 C4
Bad Kohlgrub D 108 B2
Bad König D 93 B5
Bad Königshofen D 82 B2
Bad Köstritz D 83 B4
Badkowo PL 76 B3
Bad Kreuzen A 110 A1
Bad Kreuznach D 93 B3
Bad Krozingen D 106 B2
Bad Laasphe D 81 B4
Bad Langensalza D 82 A2
Bad Lauchstädt D 83 A3
Bad Lausick D 83 A4
Bad Lauterberg D 82 A2
Bad Leonfelden A 96 C2
Bad Liebenwerda D 83 A5
Bad Liebenzell D 93 C4
Bad Lippspringe D 81 A4
Badljevina HR 124 B3
Bad Meinberg D 81 A4
Bad Mergentheim D 94 B1
Bad Mitterndorf A 109 B4
Bad Münder D 72 B2
Bad Münstereifel D 80 B2
Bad Muskau D 84 A2
Bad Nauheim D 81 B4
Bad Nenndorf D 72 B2
Bad Neuenahr-Ahrweiler
D 80 B3
Bad Neustadt D 82 B2
Bad Oeynhausen D 72 B1
Badolato I 175 C2
Badolatosa E 163 A3
Bad Oldesloe D 65 C3
Badonviller F 92 C2
Bad Orb D 81 B5
Badovinci SRB 127 C1
Bad Peterstal D 93 C4
Bad Pyrmont D 72 C2
Bad Radkersburg
A 110 C2
Bad Ragaz CH 107 C4
Bad Rappenau D 93 B5
Bad Reichenhall D 109 B3
Bad Saarow-Pieskow
D 74 B3
Bad Sachsa D 82 A2
Bad Säckingen D 106 B2
Bad Salzdetfurth D 72 B3
Bad Salzig D 81 B3
Bad Salzuflen D 72 B1
Bad Salzungen D 82 B2
Bad Sankt Leonhard
A 110 C1
Bad Sassendorf D 81 A4
Bad Schandau D 84 B2
Bad Schmiedeberg
D 83 A4
Bad Schönborn D 93 B4
Bad Schussenried
D 107 A4
Bad Schwalbach D 81 B4
Bad Schwartau D 65 C3
Bad Segeberg D 64 C3
Bad Soden D 81 B4
Bad Soden-Salmünster
D 81 B5
Bad Sooden-Allendorf
D 82 A1
Bad Sulza D 83 A3
Bad Sülze D 66 B1
Bad Tatzmannsdorf
A 111 B3
Bad Tennstedt D 82 A2
Bad Tölz D 108 B2
Badules E 152 A2
Bad Urach D 94 C1
Bad Vellach A 110 C1
Bad Vilbel D 81 B4
Bad Vöslau A 111 B3
Bad Waldsee D 107 B4
Bad Wiessee D 108 B2
Bad Wildungen D 81 A5
Bad Wilsnack D 73 B4
Bad Windsheim D 94 B2
Bad Wörishafen D 108 A1
Bad Wurzach D 107 B4
Bad Zwesten D 81 A5
Bad Zwischenahn D 71 A5
Baells E 145 C4
Baena E 163 A3
Baesweiler D 80 B2
Baeza E 157 C4
Baflo NL 71 A3
Baga E 147 B2
Bagaladi I 175 C1
Bagenkop DK 65 B3
Baggetorp S 56 A2
Bagh a Chaisteil GB 31 C1
Bagheria I 176 A2
Bagn N 47 B6
Bagnacavallo I 135 A4
Bagnáia I 168 A2
Bagnara Cálabra I 175 C1
Bagnasco I 133 A4
Bagnères-de-Bigorre
F 145 A4
Bagnères-de-Luchon
F 145 B4
Bagni del Másino I 120 A2
Bagni di Lucca I 134 A3
Bagni di Rabbi I 121 A3
Bagni di Tívoli I 168 B2
Bagno di Romagna
I 135 B4
Bagnoles-de-l'Orne
F 89 B3
Bagnoli dei Trigno
I 170 B2
Bagnoli di Sopra I 121 B4
Bagnoli Irpino I 170 C3
Bagnolo Mella I 120 B3
Bagnols-en-Forêt
F 132 B2
Bagnols-sur-Cèze
F 131 A3
Bagnorégio I 168 A2
Bagolino I 121 B3
Bagrationovsk RUS 12 A4
Bagrdan SRB 127 C3
Báguena E 152 A2
Bahabón de Esgueva
E 143 C3
Bahillo E 142 B2
Báia delle Zágare
I 171 B4
Báia Domizia I 169 B3
Baia Mare RO 17 B5
Baiano I 170 C2
Baião P 148 A1
Baiersbronn D 93 C4
Baiersdorf D 94 B3
Baignes-Ste Radegonde
F 115 C3
Baigneux-les-Juifs
F 104 B3
Baildon GB 40 B2
Bailén E 157 B4
Băileşti RO 17 C5
Baileux B 91 A4
Bailieborough IRL 27 C4
Bailleul F 78 B2
Baillonville B 79 B5
Bailó E 144 B3
Bain-de-Bretagne
F 101 B4
Bains F 117 B3
Bains-les-Bains F 105 A5
Bainton GB 40 B3
Baio E 140 A2
Baiona E 140 B2
Bais F 89 B3
Baiso I 134 A3
Baiuca P 148 B2
Baja H 125 A4
Bajánsenye H 111 C3
Bajina Bašta SRB 127 D1
Bajmok SRB 126 B1
Bajna H 112 B2
Bajovo Polje MNE 139 B4

Bajša SRB 126 B1
Bak H 111 C3
Bakar HR 123 B3
Bakewell GB 40 B2
Bakio E 143 A4
Bakka N 47 C6
Bakkafjörður IS 191 A11
Bakkagerði IS 191 B12
Bække DK 59 C2
Bakken N 48 B3
Baklan TR 189 B4
Bækmarksbro DK 58 B1
Bakonybél H 111 B4
Bakonycsernye H 112 B2
Bakonyjákó H 111 B4
Bakonyszentkirály H 111 B4
Bakonyszombathely H 112 B1
Bakov nad Jizerou CZ 84 B2
Bąkowiec PL 87 A5
Baks H 113 C4
Baksa H 125 B4
Bakum D 71 B5
Bala GB 38 B3
Bâlâ TR 23 B7
Balaguer E 145 C4
Balassagyarmat H 112 A3
Balástya H 113 C4
Balatonakali H 111 C4
Balatonalmádi H 112 B2
Balatonboglár H 111 C4
Balatonbozsok H 112 C2
Balatonederics H 111 C4
Balatonfenyves H 111 C4
Balatonföldvár H 112 C1
Balatonfüred H 112 C1
Balatonfűzfő H 112 B2
Balatonkenese H 112 B2
Balatonkiliti H 112 C2
Balatonlelle H 111 C4
Balatonszabadi H 112 C2
Balatonszemes H 111 C4
Balatonszentgyörgy H 111 C4
Balazote E 158 C1
Balbeggie GB 35 B4
Balbigny F 117 B4
Balboa E 141 B4
Balbriggan IRL 30 A2
Balchik BG 17 D8
Balçova TR 188 A2
Baldock GB 44 B3
Bale HR 122 B2
Baleira E 141 A3
Baleizao P 160 A2
Balen B 79 A5
Balerma E 164 C2
Balestrand N 46 A3
Balestrate I 176 A2
Balfour GB 33 B4
Bälganet S 63 B3
Balıkesir TR 186 C2
Balıklıçeşme TR 186 B2
Bälinge S 51 C4
Balingen D 107 A3
Balingsta S 56 A3
Balintore GB 32 D3
Balizac F 128 B2
Balk NL 70 B2
Balkbrug NL 71 B3
Balla IRL 28 A2
Ballachulish GB 34 B2
Ballaghaderreen IRL 26 C2
Ballancourt-sur-Essonne F 90 C2
Ballantrae GB 36 A2
Ballao I 179 C3
Ballasalla GB 36 B2
Ballater GB 32 D3
Ballen DK 59 C3
Ballenstedt D 82 A3
Ballerias E 145 C3
Balleroy F 88 A3
Ballerup DK 61 D2
Ballesteros de Calatrava E 157 B4
Ballı TR 186 B2
Ballina IRL 26 B1
Ballinalack IRL 30 A1
Ballinamore IRL 26 B3
Ballinascarty IRL 29 C3
Ballinasloe IRL 28 A3
Ballindine IRL 28 A3
Balling DK 58 B1
Ballingarry
Limerick IRL 29 B3
Tipperary IRL 30 B1
Ballingeary IRL 29 C2
Ballinhassig IRL 29 C3
Ballinluig GB 35 B4
Ballino I 121 B3
Ballinrobe IRL 28 A2
Ballinskelligs IRL 29 C1
Ballinspittle IRL 29 C3
Ballintra IRL 26 B2
Ballivor IRL 30 A2
Ballobar E 153 A4
Ballon
F 102 A2
IRL 30 B2
Ballószög H 112 C3
Ballsh AL 182 C1
Ballstad N 194 B4
Ballum DK 64 A1
Ballybay IRL 27 B4
Ballybofey IRL 26 B3
Ballybunion IRL 29 B2
Ballycanew IRL 30 B2
Ballycarry GB 27 B5
Ballycastle
GB 27 A4
IRL 26 B1
Ballyclare GB 27 B5
Ballyconneely IRL 28 A1
Ballycotton IRL 29 C3
Ballycroy IRL 26 B1
Ballydehob IRL 29 C2
Ballyferriter IRL 29 B1
Ballygawley GB 27 B3
Ballygowan GB 27 B5
Ballyhaunis IRL 28 A3
Ballyheige IRL 29 B2
Ballyjamesduff IRL 27 C3
Ballylanders IRL 29 B3
Ballylynan IRL 30 B1
Ballymahon IRL 28 A4
Ballymena GB 27 B4
Ballymoe IRL 28 A3
Ballymoney GB 27 A4
Ballymore IRL 28 A4
Ballymote IRL 26 B2
Ballynacorra IRL 29 C3
Ballynagore IRL 30 A1
Ballynahinch GB 27 B5
Ballynure GB 27 B5
Ballyragget IRL 30 B1
Ballysadare IRL 26 B2
Ballyshannon IRL 26 B2
Ballyvaghan IRL 28 A2
Ballyvourney IRL 29 C2
Ballywalter GB 27 B5
Balmaclellan GB 36 A2
Balmaseda E 143 A3
Balmazújváros H 113 B5
Balme I 119 B4
Balmedie GB 33 D4
Balmuccia I 119 B5
Balna-paling GB 32 D2
Balneario de Panticosa E 145 B3
Balotaszállás H 126 A1
Balsa P 148 A2
Balsareny E 147 C2
Balsorano-Nuovo I 169 B3
Bålsta S 57 A3
Balsthal CH 106 B2
Balta UA 17 A8
Baltanás E 142 C2
Baltar E 140 C3
Baltasound GB 33 A6
Bălţi MD 17 B7
Baltimore IRL 29 C2
Baltinglass IRL 30 B2
Baltiysk RUS 69 A4
Baltów PL 87 A5
Balugães P 148 A1
Bælum DK 58 B3
Balve D 81 A3
Balvi LV 8 D5
Balvicar GB 34 B2
Balya TR 186 C2
Balzo I 136 C2
Bamberg D 94 B2
Bamburgh GB 37 A5
Banatska Palanka SRB 127 C3
Banatski Brestovac SRB 127 C2
Banatski Despotovac SRB 126 B2
Banatski Dvor SRB 126 B2
Banatski-Karlovac SRB 127 B3
Banatsko Arandjelovo SRB 126 A2
Banatsko-Novo Selo SRB 127 C2
Banaz TR 187 D4
Banbridge GB 27 B4
Banbury GB 44 A2
Banchory GB 33 D4
Bande
B 79 B5
E 140 B3
Bandholm DK 65 B4
Bandırma TR 186 B2
Bandol F 132 B1
Bandon IRL 29 C3
Bañeres E 159 C3
Banff GB 33 D4
Bangor
F 100 B2
Down GB 27 B5
Gwynedd GB 38 A2
IRL 26 B1
Bangsund N 199 A8
Banie PL 74 A3
Banja Koviljača SRB 127 C1
Banjaloka SLO 123 B3
Banja Luka BIH 124 C3
Banjani SRB 127 C1
Banja Vručica BIH 125 C3
Banka SK 98 C1
Bankekind S 56 B1
Bankend GB 36 A3
Bankeryd S 62 A2
Bankfoot GB 35 B4
Banloc RO 126 B3
Bannalec F 100 B2
Bannes F 91 C3
Bannockburn GB 35 B4
Bañobárez E 149 B3
Bañon E 152 B2
Banon F 132 A1
Baños E 149 B4
Baños de Gigonza E 162 B2
Baños de la Encina E 157 B4
Baños de Molgas E 140 B3
Baños de Rio Tobia E 143 B4
Baños de Valdearados E 143 C3
Bánov CZ 98 C1
Banova Jaruga HR 124 B2
Bánovce nad Bebravou SK 98 C2
Banovići BIH 139 A4
Banovići Selo BIH 139 A4
Bánréve H 99 C4
Bansin D 66 C3
Banská Belá SK 98 C2
Banská Bystrica SK 99 C3
Banská Štiavnica SK 98 C2
Bansko BG 183 B5
Banstead GB 44 B3
Banteer IRL 29 B3
Bantheville F 91 B5
Bantry IRL 29 C2
Bantzenheim F 106 B2
Banyalbufar E 166 B2
Banyoles E 147 B3
Banyuls-sur-Mer F 146 B4
Bapaume F 90 A2
Bar
MNE 16 D3
UA 13 D7
Barabhas GB 31 A2
Barači BIH 138 A2
Baracs H 112 C2
Baracska H 112 B2
Barahona E 151 A5
Barajes de Melo E 151 B5
Barakaldo E 143 A4
Baralla E 141 B3
Barañain E 144 B2
Baranavichy BY 13 B7
Báránd H 113 B5
Baranda SRB 127 B2
Baranello I 170 B2
Baranów Sandomierski PL 87 B5
Baraqueville F 130 A1
Barasoain E 144 B2
Barbacena P 155 C3
Barbadás E 140 B3
Barbadillo E 149 B4
Barbadillo de Herreros E 143 B3
Barbadillo del Mercado E 143 B3
Barbadillo del Pez E 143 B3
Barban HR 123 B3
Barbarano Vicento I 121 B4
Barbariga HR 122 C2
Barbaros TR 186 B2
Barbastro E 145 B4
Barbate E 162 B2
Barbatona E 152 A1
Barbâtre F 114 B1
Barbazan F 145 A4
Barbeitos E 141 A3
Barbentane F 131 B3
Barberino di Mugello I 135 A4
Barbezieux-St Hilaire F 115 C3
Barbonne-Fayel F 91 C3
Barbotan-les-Thermes F 128 C2
Barby D 73 C4
Bárcabo E 145 B4
Barca de Alva P 149 A3
Barcarrota E 155 C4
Barcellona-Pozzo di Gotto I 177 A4
Barcelona E 147 C3
Barcelonette F 132 A2
Barcelos P 148 A1
Bárcena del Monasterio E 141 A4
Barcena de Pie de Concha E 142 A2
Barchfeld D 82 B2
Barcin PL 76 B2
Barcino PL 68 A1
Bárcis I 122 A1
Barco P 148 B2
Barcones E 151 A5
Barcs H 124 B3
Barcus F 144 A3
Bardejov SK 12 D4
Bårdesø DK 59 C3
Bardi I 120 C2
Bardney GB 40 B3
Bardo PL 85 B4
Bardolino I 121 B3
Bardonécchia I 118 B3
Bardoňovo SK 112 A2
Barèges F 145 B4
Barenstein D 83 B5
Barentin F 89 A4
Barenton F 88 B3
Barevo BIH 138 A3
Barfleur F 88 A2
Barga I 134 A3
Bargas E 151 C3
Barge I 119 C4
Bargemon F 132 B2
Barghe I 120 B3
Bargoed GB 39 C3
Bargrennan GB 36 A2
Bargteheide D 64 C3
Barham GB 45 B5
Bari I 173 A2
Barič Draga HR 137 A4
Barilović HR 123 B4
Bari Sardo I 179 C3
Barisciano I 169 A3
Barjac F 131 A3
Barjols F 132 B1
Barjon F 105 B3
Bårkåker N 54 A1
Barkald N 199 D7
Barkowo
Dolnośląskie PL 85 A4
Pomorskie PL 68 B2
Bârlad RO 17 B7
Bar-le-Duc F 91 C5
Barles F 132 A2
Barletta I 171 B4
Barlinek PL 75 B4
Barmouth GB 38 B2
Barmstedt D 64 C2
Barnard Castle GB 37 B5
Barnarp S 62 A2
Bärnau D 95 B4
Bärnbach A 110 B2
Barneberg D 73 B4
Barnenitz D 74 B1
Barnet GB 44 B3
Barnetby le Wold GB 40 B3
Barneveld NL 70 B2
Barneville-Carteret F 88 A2
Barnoldswick GB 40 B1
Barnowko PL 75 B3
Barnsley GB 40 B2
Barnstädt D 83 A3
Barnstaple GB 42 A2
Barnstorf D 72 B1
Barntrup D 72 C2
Baron F 90 B2
Baronissi I 170 C2
Barqueiro P 154 B2
Barquinha P 154 B2
Barr
F 93 C3
GB 36 A2
Barra P 148 B1
Barracas E 159 A3
Barraco E 150 B3
Barrado E 150 B2
Barrafranca I 177 B3
Barranco do Velho P 160 B2
Barrancos P 161 A3
Barrax E 158 B1
Barrbaar D 94 C2
Barre-des-Cevennes F 130 A2
Barreiro P 154 C1
Barreiros E 141 A3
Barrême F 132 B2
Barret-le-Bas F 132 A1
Barrhead GB 34 C3
Barrhill GB 36 A2
Barrio de Nuesra Señora E 142 B1
Barrowford GB 40 B1
Barrow-in-Furness GB 36 B3
Barrow upon Humber GB 40 B3
Barruecopardo E 149 A3
Barruelo de Santullán E 142 B2
Barruera E 145 B4
Barry GB 39 C3
Bårse DK 65 A4
Barsinghausen D 72 B2
Barssel D 71 A4
Bar-sur-Aube F 104 A3
Bar-sur-Seine F 104 A3
Barth D 66 B1
Bartholomä D 94 C1
Bartin TR 187 A7
Barton upon Humber GB 40 B3
Barúmini I 179 C2
Baruth D 74 B2
Barvaux B 80 B1
Barver D 72 B1
Barwałd PL 99 B3
Barwice PL 68 B1
Barysaw BY 13 A8
Barzana E 141 A5
Bârzava RO 16 B4
Bárzio I 120 B2
Bas E 147 B3
Bašaid SRB 126 B2
Basaluzzo I 120 C1
Basarabeasca MD 17 B8
Basauri E 143 A4
Baschi I 168 A2
Baschurch GB 38 B4
Basconcillos del Tozo E 143 B3
Bascones de Ojeda E 142 B2
Basécles B 79 B3
Basel CH 106 B2
Basélice I 170 B2
Basildon GB 45 B4
Basingstoke GB 44 B2
Baška
CZ 98 B2
HR 123 C3
Baška Voda HR 138 B2
Bäsksjö S 200 B3
Baslow GB 40 B2
Başmakçı TR 189 B5
Basovizza I 122 B2
Bassacutena I 178 A3
Bassano del Grappa I 121 B4
Bassano Romano I 168 A2
Bassecourt CH 106 B2
Bassella E 147 B2
Bassevuovdde N 193 D9
Bassou F 104 B2
Bassoues F 128 C3
Bassum D 72 B1
Båstad S 61 C2
Bastardo I 136 C1
Bastelica F 180 A2
Bastelicaccia F 180 B1
Bastia
F 180 A2
I 136 B1
Bastogne B 92 A1
Baston GB 40 C3
Bastuträsk S 200 B6
Bata H 125 A4
Batajnica SRB 127 C2
Batak BG 183 B6
Batalha P 154 B2
Bátaszék H 125 A4
Batea E 153 A4
Batelov CZ 97 B3
Bath GB 43 A4
Bathgate GB 35 C4
Batida H 126 A2
Batignano I 135 C4
Batina HR 125 B4
Bátka SK 99 C4
Batković BIH 125 C5
Batley GB 40 B2
Batnfjordsøra N 198 C4
Batočina SRB 127 C3
Bátonyterenye H 113 B3
Batrina HR 125 B3
Båtsfjord N 193 B13
Båtskärsnäs S 196 D6
Battaglia Terme I 121 B4
Bätterkinden CH 106 B2
Battice B 80 B1
Battipáglia I 170 C2
Battle GB 45 C4
Battonya H 126 A3
Batuša SRB 127 C3
Bátya H 112 C2
Bau I 179 C2
Baud F 100 B2
Baudour B 79 B3
Baugé F 102 B1
Baugy F 103 B4
Bauma CH 107 B3
Baume-les-Dames F 105 B5
Baumholder D 93 B3
Baunatal D 81 A5
Baunei I 178 B3
Bauska LV 8 D4
Bautzen D 84 A2
Bavanište SRB 127 C2
Bavay F 79 B3
Bavilliers F 106 B1
Bavorov CZ 96 B2
Bawdsey GB 45 A5
Bawinkel D 71 B4
Bawtry GB 40 B2
Bayat TR 187 D5
Bayel F 105 A3
Bayeux F 88 A3
Bayındır TR 188 A2
Bayon F 92 C2
Bayonne F 128 C1
Bayons F 132 A2
Bayramiç TR 186 C1
Bayreuth D 95 B3
Bayrischzell D 108 B3
Baza E 164 B2
Bazas F 128 B2
Baziege F 146 A2
Bazoches-les-Gallerandes F 103 A4
Bazoches-sur-Hoëne F 89 B4
Bazzano I 135 A4
Beaconsfield GB 44 B3
Beade E 140 B2
Beadnell GB 37 A5
Beaminster GB 43 B4
Bearsden GB 34 C3
Beas E 161 B3
Beasain E 144 A1
Beas de Segura E 164 A2
Beattock GB 36 A3
Beaubery F 117 A4
Beaucaire F 131 B3
Beaufort
F 118 B3
IRL 29 B2
Beaufort-en Vallée F 102 B1
Beaugency F 103 B3
Beaujeu
Alpes-de-Haute-Provence F 132 A2
Rhône F 117 A4
Beaulac F 128 B2
Beaulieu
F 103 B4
GB 44 C2
Beaulieu-sous-la-Roche F 114 B2
Beaulieu-sur-Dordogne F 129 B4
Beaulieu-sur-Mer F 133 B3
Beaulon F 104 C2
Beauly GB 32 D2
Beaumaris GB 38 A2
Beaumesnil F 89 A4
Beaumetz-lès-Loges F 78 B2
Beaumont
B 79 B4
F 129 B3
Beaumont-de-Lomagne F 129 C3
Beaumont-du-Gâtinais F 103 A4
Beaumont-en-Argonne F 91 B5
Beaumont-Hague F 88 A2
Beaumont-la-Ronce F 102 B2
Beaumont-le-Roger F 89 A4
Beaumont-sur-Oise F 90 B2
Beaumont-sur-Sarthe F 102 A2
Beaune F 105 B3
Beaune-la-Rolande F 103 A4
Beaupréau F 101 B5
Beauraing B 91 A4
Beaurepaire F 117 B5
Beaurepaire-en-Bresse F 105 C4
Beaurières F 132 A1
Beauvais F 90 B2
Beauval F 90 A2
Beauville F 129 B3
Beauvoir-sur-Mer F 114 B1
Beauvoir-sur-Niort F 114 B3
Beba Veche RO 126 A2
Bebertal D 73 B4
Bebington GB 38 A3
Bebra D 82 B1
Bebrina HR 125 B3
Beccles GB 45 A5
Becedas E 150 B2
Beceite E 153 B4
Bečej SRB 126 B2
Becerreá E 141 B3
Becerril de Campos E 142 B2
Bécherel F 101 A4
Bechhofen D 94 B2
Bechyně CZ 96 B2
Becilla de Valderaduey E 142 B1
Beckfoot GB 36 B3
Beckingham GB 40 B3
Beckum D 81 A4
Beco P 154 B2
Bécon-les-Granits F 102 B1
Bečov nad Teplou CZ 83 B4
Becsehely H 111 C3
Bedale GB 37 B5
Bedames E 143 A3
Bédar E 164 B3
Bédarieux F 130 B2
Bédarrides F 131 A3
Bedburg D 80 B2
Beddgelert GB 38 A2
Beddingestrand S 66 A2
Bédée F 101 A4
Bedegkér H 112 C2
Beden TR 189 C7
Bedford GB 44 A3
Będków PL 87 A3
Bedlington GB 37 A5
Bedlno PL 77 B4
Bedmar E 163 A4
Bédoin F 131 A4
Bedónia I 134 A2
Bedretto CH 107 C3
Bedsted DK 58 B1
Bedum NL 71 A3
Bedwas GB 39 C3
Bedworth GB 40 C2
Będzin PL 86 B3
Beekbergen NL 70 B2
Beek en Donk NL 80 A1
Beelen D 71 C5
Beelitz D 74 B1
Beer GB 43 B3
Beerfelde D 74 B3
Beerfelden D 93 B4
Beernem B 78 A3
Beeskow D 74 B3
Beetsterzwaag NL 70 A3
Beetzendorf D 73 B4
Beflelay CH 106 B2
Begaljica SRB 127 C2
Bégard F 100 A2

Begejci SRB 126 B2
Begijar E 157 C4
Begijnendijk B 79 A4
Begndal N 48 B1
Begues E 147 C2
Beguildy GB 39 B3
Begur E 147 C4
Beho B 80 B1
Behringen D 82 A2
Beilen NL 71 B3
Beilngries D 95 B3
Beine-Nauroy F 91 B4
Beinwil CH 106 B3
Beiseförth D 82 A1
Beith GB 34 C3
Beitostølen N 47 A5
Beiuş RO 16 B5
Beja P 160 A2
Béjar E 149 B4
Bekçiler TR 189 C4
Békés H 113 C5
Békéscsaba H 113 C5
Bekilli TR 189 A4
Bekkarfjord N 193 B11
Bela SK 98 B2
Bélâbre F 115 B5
Bela Crkva SRB 127 C3
Belalcázar E 156 B2
Belánad Radbuzou
CZ 95 B4
Belanovica SRB 127 C2
Bélapátfalva H 113 A4
Bělápod Bezdězem
CZ 84 B2
Belcaire F 146 B2
Bełchatów PL 86 A3
Belchite E 153 A3
Bělčice CZ 96 B1
Belcoo GB 26 B3
Belecke D 81 A4
Beled H 111 B4
Belej HR 123 C3
Beleño E 142 A1
Bélesta F 146 B2
Belevi TR 188 A2
Belfast GB 27 B5
Belford GB 37 A5
Belfort F 106 B1
Belgentier F 132 B1
Belgern D 83 A5
Belgioioso I 120 B2
Belgodère F 180 A2
Belgooly IRL 29 C3
Belgrade = Beograd
SRB 127 C2
Belhade F 128 B2
Belica HR 124 A2
Beli Manastir HR 125 B4
Belin-Bèliet F 128 B2
Belinchón E 151 B4
Belišće HR 125 B4
Bělkovice-Lašťany
CZ 98 B1
Bella I 172 B1
Bellac F 115 B5
Bellágio I 120 B2
Bellananagh IRL 27 C3
Bellano I 120 A2
Bellária I 136 A1
Bellavary IRL 26 C1
Belleau F 90 B3
Belleek GB 26 B2
Bellegarde
Gard F 131 B3
Loiret F 103 B4
Bellegarde-en-Diois
F 132 A1
Bellegarde-en-Marche
F 116 B2
Bellegarde-sur-Valserine
F 118 A2
Belle-Isle-en-Terre
F 100 A2
Bellême F 89 B4
Bellenaves F 116 A3
Bellentre F 118 B3
Bellevaux F 118 A3
Bellevesvre F 105 C4
Belleville F 117 A4
Belleville-sur-Vie F 114 B2
Bellevue-la-Montagne
F 117 B3
Belley F 118 B2
Bellheim D 93 B4
Bellinge DK 59 C3
Bellingham GB 37 A4
Bellinzago Novarese
I 120 B1
Bellinzona CH 120 A2
Bell-lloc d'Urgell E 153 A4
Bello E 152 B2
Bellpuig d'Urgell E 147 C2
Bellreguart E 159 C3
Bellsbank GB 36 A2
Belltall E 147 C2
Belluno I 121 A5
Bellver de Cerdanya
E 146 B2
Bellvis E 147 C1
Bélmez E 156 B2
Belmez de la Moraleda
E 163 A4
Belmont GB 33 A6
Belmont-de-la-Loire
F 117 A4
Belmonte
Asturias E 141 A4
Cuenca E 158 B1
P 148 B2
Belmonte de San José
E 153 B3
Belmonte de Tajo
E 151 B4
Belmont-sur-Rance
F 130 B1
Belmullet IRL 26 B1
Belobreşca RO 127 C3
Beloeil B 79 B3
Belogradchik BG 16 D5
Belokorovichi UA 13 C8
Belorado E 143 B3
Belotič SRB 127 C1
Bělotín CZ 98 B1
Belovo BG 183 A6
Belozersk RUS 9 C10
Belp CH 106 C2
Belpasso I 177 B3
Belpech F 146 A2
Belper GB 40 B2
Belsay GB 37 A5
Belsk Duzy PL 87 A4
Beltinci SLO 111 C3
Beltra IRL 26 C1
Belturbet IRL 27 B3
Beluša SK 98 B2
Belvedere Maríttimo
I 174 B1
Belver de Cinca E 153 A4
Belver de los Montes
E 142 C1
Belvès F 129 B3
Belvezet F 130 A2
Belvis de la Jara E 150 C3
Belvis de Monroy
E 150 C2
Belyy RUS 9 E8
Belz F 100 B2
Bełżec PL 13 C5
Belzig D 73 B5
Bembibre E 141 B4
Bembridge GB 44 C2
Bemmel NL 80 A1
Bemposta
Bragança P 149 A3
Santarém P 154 B2
Benabarre E 145 B4
Benacazón E 161 B3
Benaguacil E 159 B3
Benahadux E 164 C2
Benalmádena E 163 B3
Benalúa de Guadix
E 164 B1
Benalúa de las Villas
E 163 A4
Benalup E 162 B2
Benamargosa E 163 B3
Benamaurel E 164 B2
Benameji E 163 A3
Benamocarra E 163 B3
Benaocaz E 162 B2
Benaoján E 162 B2
Benarrabá E 162 B2
Benasque E 145 B4
Benátky nad Jizerou
CZ 84 B2
Benavente
E 142 B1
P 154 C2
Benavides de Órbigo
E 141 B5
Benavila P 154 B3
Bendorf D 81 B3
Benedikt SLO 110 C2
Benejama E 159 C3
Benejúzar E 165 A4
Benešov CZ 96 B2
Bénestroff F 92 C2
Benet F 114 B3
Bene Vagienna I 133 A3
Bénévent-l'Abbaye
F 116 A1
Benevento I 170 B2
Benfeld F 93 C3
Benfica P 154 B2
Bengtsfors S 54 A3
Bengtsheden S 50 B2
Beničanci HR 125 B4
Benicarló E 153 B4
Benicássim E 153 B4
Benidorm E 159 C3
Benifaió E 159 B3
Beniganim E 159 C3
Benington GB 41 B4
Benisa E 159 C4
Benkovac HR 137 A4
Benllech GB 38 A2
Benneckenstein D 82 A2
Bénodet F 100 B1
Benquerencia de la
Serena E 156 B2
Bensafrim P 160 B1
Bensbyn S 196 D5
Bensdorf D 73 B5
Benshausen D 82 B2
Bensheim D 93 B4
Bentley GB 44 B3
Bentwisch D 65 B5
Beočin SRB 126 B1
Beograd = Belgrade
SRB 127 C2
Beragh GB 27 B3
Beranga E 143 A3
Berat AL 182 C1
Bérat F 146 A2
Beratzhausen D 95 B3
Bérbaltavár H 111 B3
Berbegal E 145 C3
Berbenno di Valtellina
I 120 A2
Berberana E 143 B3
Bercedo E 143 A3
Bercel H 112 B3
Bercenay-le-Hayer
F 91 C3
Berceto I 134 A2
Berchem B 79 B3
Berchidda I 178 B3
Berching D 95 B3
Berchtesgaden D 109 B4
Bérchules E 163 B4
Bercianos de Aliste
E 149 A3
Berck F 78 B1
Berclaire d'Urgell
E 147 C1
Berdoias E 140 A1
Berducedo E 141 A4
Berdún E 144 B3
Berdychiv UA 13 D8
Bere Alston GB 42 B2
Bereguardo I 120 B2
Berehommen N 53 A3
Berehove UA 16 A5
Berek BIH 124 B3
Beremend H 125 B4
Bere Regis GB 43 B4
Berestechko UA 13 C6
Berettyóújfalu H 113 B5
Berezhany UA 13 D6
Berezivka UA 17 B9
Berezna UA 13 C9
Berg
D 95 B3
N 195 E3
S 56 B2
Berga
Sachsen-Anhalt D 82 A3
Thüringen D 83 B4
E 147 B2
S 62 A4
Bergama TR 186 C2
Bérgamo I 120 B2
Bergara E 143 A4
Bergby S 51 B4
Berge
Brandenburg D 74 B1
Niedersachsen D 71 B4
Telemark N 53 A4
Telemark N 53 A4
Bergeforsen S 200 D3
Bergen
Mecklenburg-Vorpommern D 66 B2
Niedersachsen D 72 B2
Niedersachsen D 73 B3
N 46 B2
NL 70 B1
Bergen op Zoom NL 79 A4
Bergerac F 129 B3
Bergères-lés-Vertus
F 91 C4
Bergeyk NL 79 A5
Berghausen D 93 C4
Bergheim D 80 B2
Berghem S 60 B2
Berg im Gau D 95 C3
Bergisch Gladbach
D 80 B3
Bergkamen D 81 A3
Bergkvara S 63 B4
Berglern D 95 C3
Bergnäset S 196 D5
Bergneustadt D 81 A3
Bergsäng S 49 B5
Bergshamra S 57 A4
Bergsjö S 200 E3
Bergs slussar S 56 B1
Bergsviken S 196 D4
Bergtheim D 94 B2
Bergues F 78 B2
Bergum NL 70 A2
Bergün Bravuogn
CH 107 C4
Bergwitz D 83 A4
Berhida H 112 B2
Beringel P 160 A2
Beringen B 79 A5
Berja E 164 C2
Berkåk N 199 C7
Berkeley GB 43 A4
Berkenthin D 65 C3
Berkhamsted GB 44 B3
Berkheim D 107 A5
Berkhof D 72 B2
Berkovići BIH 139 B4
Berkovitsa BG 17 D5
Berlanga E 156 B2
Berlanga de Duero
E 151 A5
Berlevåg N 193 B13
Berlikum NL 70 A2
Berlin D 74 B2
Berlstedt D 82 A3
Bermeo E 143 A4
Bermillo de Sayago
E 149 A3
Bern CH 106 C2
Bernalda I 174 A2
Bernardos E 150 A3
Bernartice
Jihočeský CZ 96 B2
Bernartice
Východočeský CZ 85 B3
Bernau
Baden-Württemberg
D 106 B3
Bayern D 109 B3
Brandenburg D 74 B2
Bernaville F 90 A2
Bernay F 89 A4
Bernburg D 83 A3
Berndorf A 111 B3
Berne D 72 A1
Bernecebarati H 112 A2
Bernhardsthal A 97 C4
Bernkastel-Kues D 92 B3
Bernolakovo SK 111 A4
Bernsdorf D 84 A2
Bernstadt D 84 A2
Bernstein A 111 B3
Bernués E 145 B3
Beromünster CH 106 B3
Beroun CZ 96 B2
Berovo MK 182 B4
Berre-l'Etang F 131 B4
Berriedale GB 32 C3
Berriew GB 39 B3
Berrocal E 161 B3
Bersenbrück D 71 B4
Bershad' UA 13 D8
Berthåga S 51 C4
Berthelming F 92 C2
Bertincourt F 90 A2
Bertinoro I 135 A5
Bertogne B 92 A1
Bertrix B 91 B5
Berufjörður IS 191 C11
Berville-sur-Mer F 89 A4
Berwick-upon-Tweed
GB 37 A4
Berzasca RO 16 C4
Berzence H 124 A3
Berzocana E 156 A2
Besalú E 147 B3
Besançon F 105 B5
Besenfeld D 93 C4
Besenyötelek H 113 B4
Besenyszög H 113 B4
Beshenkovichi BY 13 A8
Besigheim D 93 C5
Běšiny CZ 96 B1
Beška SRB 126 B2
Beşkonak TR 189 B6
Besle F 101 B4
Besnyö H 112 B2
Bessais-le-Fromental
F 103 C4
Bessan F 130 B2
Besse-en-Chandesse
F 116 B2
Bessèges F 131 A3
Bessé-sur-Braye F 102 B2
Bessines-sur-Gartempe
F 115 B5
Best NL 79 A5
Bestorp S 56 B1
Betanzos E 140 A2
Betelu E 144 A2
Bétera E 159 B3
Beteta E 152 B1
Béthenville F 91 B4
Bethesda GB 38 A2
Béthune F 78 B2
Beton-Bazoches F 90 C3
Bettembourg L 92 B2
Betterdorf L 92 B2
Bettna S 56 B2
Béttola I 120 C2
Bettona I 136 B1
Bettyhill GB 32 C2
Betws-y-Coed GB 38 A3
Betxi E 159 B3
Betz F 90 B2
Betzdorf D 81 B3
Beuil F 132 A2
Beulah GB 39 B3
Beuzeville F 89 A4
Bevagna I 136 C1
Bevens-bruk S 56 A1
Beveren B 79 A4
Beverley GB 40 B3
Bevern D 81 A5
Beverstedt D 72 A1
Beverungen D 81 A5
Beverwijk NL 70 B1
Bex CH 119 A4
Bexhill GB 45 C4
Beyazköy TR 186 A2
Beychevelle F 128 A2
Beydağ TR 188 A3
Beyeğaç TR 188 B3
Beykoz TR 186 A4
Beynat F 129 A4
Beyoğlu TR 186 A4
Beypazarı TR 187 B6
Beyşehir TR 189 B6
Bezas E 152 B2
Bezau A 107 B4
Bezdan SRB 125 B4
Bèze F 105 B4
Bezenet F 116 A2
Bezhetsk RUS 9 D10
Béziers F 130 B2
Bezzecca I 121 B3
Biadki PL 85 A5
Biała
Łódzkie PL 77 C4
Opolskie PL 85 B5
Białaczów PL 87 A4
Biała Podlaska PL 13 B5
Biała Rawska PL 87 A4
Biale Błota PL 76 A2
Białobłoty PL 76 B2
Białobrzegi PL 87 A4
Białogard PL 67 C4
Bialośliwie PL 76 A2
Białowąs PL 68 B1
Biały Bór PL 68 B1
Białystok PL 13 B5
Biancavilla I 177 B3
Bianco I 175 C2
Biandrate I 119 B5
Biar E 159 C3
Biarritz F 144 A2
Bias F 128 B1
Biasca CH 120 A1
Biatorbágy H 112 B2
Bibbiena I 135 B4
Bibbona I 134 B3
Biberach
Baden-Württemberg
D 93 C4
Baden-Württemberg
D 107 A4
Bibinje HR 137 A4
Bibione I 122 B2
Biblis D 93 B4
Bibury GB 44 B2
Bicaj AL 182 B2
Biccari I 171 B3
Bicester GB 44 B2
Bichl D 108 B2
Bichlbach A 108 B1
Bicorp E 159 B3
Bicos P 160 B1
Bicske H 112 B2
Bidache F 128 C1
Bidart F 144 A2
Biddinghuizen NL 70 B2
Biddulph GB 40 B1
Bideford GB 42 A2
Bidford-on-Avon
GB 44 A2
Bidjovagge N 192 C6
Bie S 56 A2
Bieber D 81 B5
Biebersdorf D 74 C2
Biedenkopf D 81 B4
Biel
CH 106 B2
E 144 B3
Bielany Wroclawskie
PL 85 A4
Bielawa PL 85 B4
Bielawy PL 77 B4
Bielefeld D 72 B1
Biella I 119 B5
Bielsa E 145 B4
Bielsk PL 77 B4
Bielsko-Biała PL 99 B3
Bielsk Podlaski PL 13 B5
Bienenbuttel D 72 A3
Bieniow PL 84 A3
Bienservida E 158 C1
Bienvenida E 156 B1
Bierdzany PL 86 B2
Bierné F 102 B1
Biersted DK 58 A2
Bierun PL 86 B3
Bierutów PL 85 A5
Bierwart B 79 B5
Bierzwina PL 75 A4
Bierzwnik PL 75 A4
Biescas E 145 B3
Biesenthal D 74 B2
Biesiekierz PL 67 B5
Bietigheim-Bissingen
D 93 C5
Bièvre B 91 B5
Bieżuń PL 77 B4
Biga TR 186 B2
Bigadiç TR 186 C3
Biganos F 128 B2
Bigas P 148 B2
Bigastro E 165 A4
Bigbury GB 42 B3
Biggar GB 36 A3
Biggin Hill GB 45 B4
Biggleswade GB 44 A3
Bignasco CH 119 A5
Biguglia F 180 A2
Bihać BIH 124 C1
Biharnagybajom H 113 B5
Bijeljani BIH 139 B4
Bijeljina BIH 125 C5
Bijuesca E 152 A2
Bilaj HR 137 A4
Bila Tserkva UA 13 D9
Bilbao E 143 A4
Bilcza PL 87 B4
Bildudalur IS 190 B2
Bileća BIH 139 C4
Bilecik TR 187 B4
Biled RO 126 B2
Biłgoraj PL 12 C5
Bilhorod-Dnistrovskyy
UA 17 B9
Bilina CZ 84 B1
Bilisht AL 182 C2
Bilje HR 125 B4
Billdal S 60 B1
Billerbeck D 71 C4
Billericay GB 45 B4
Billesholm S 61 C2
Billingborough GB 40 C3
Billinge S 61 D3
Billingham GB 37 B5
Billinghay GB 41 B3
Billingsfors S 54 B3
Billingshurst GB 44 B3
Billom F 116 B3
Billsta S 200 C4
Billund DK 59 C2
Bílovec CZ 98 B2
Bilstein D 81 A4
Bilthoven NL 70 B2
Bilto N 192 C5
Bilzen B 80 B1
Bíňa SK 112 B2
Binaced E 145 C4
Binasco I 120 B2
Binbrook GB 41 B3
Binche B 79 B4
Bindlach D 95 B3
Bindslev DK 58 A3
Binefar E 145 C4
Bingen D 93 B3
Bingham GB 40 C3
Bingley GB 40 B2
Bingsjö S 50 A2
Binic F 100 A3
Binz D 66 B2
Biograd na Moru
HR 137 B4
Bionaz I 119 B4
Bioska SRB 127 D1
Birda RO 126 B3
Birdlip GB 44 B1
Biri N 48 B2
Birkeland N 53 B4
Birkenfeld
Baden-Württemberg
D 93 C4
Rheinland-Pfalz D 92 B3
Birkenhead GB 38 A3
Birkerød DK 61 D2
Birkfeld A 110 B2
Birkirkara M 175 C3
Birmingham GB 40 C2
Birr IRL 28 A4
Birresborn D 80 B2
Birstein D 81 B5
Biržai LT 8 D4
Birzebbugia M 175 C3
Bisáccia I 172 A1
Bisacquino I 176 B2
Bisbal de Falset E 153 A4
Biscarosse F 128 B1
Biscarosse Plage
F 128 B1
Biscarrués E 144 B3
Biscéglie I 171 B4
Bischheim F 93 C3
Bischofsheim D 82 B1
Bischofshofen A 109 B4
Bischofswerda D 84 A2
Bischofswiesen D 109 B3
Bischofszell CH 107 B4
Bischwiller F 93 C3
Bisenti I 169 A3
Bishop Auckland
GB 37 B5
Bishop's Castle GB 39 B4
Bishops Lydeard
GB 43 A3
Bishop's Stortford
GB 45 B4
Bishop's Waltham
GB 44 C2
Bisignano I 174 B2
Bisingen D 93 C4
Biskupice-Oławskie
PL 85 A5
Biskupiec PL 69 B4
Bismark D 73 B4
Bismo N 198 D5
Bispgården S 200 C2
Bispingen D 72 A2
Bissen L 92 B2
Bissendorf D 71 B5
Bisserup DK 65 A4
Bistango I 119 C5
Bistarac Donje BIH 139 A4
Bistrica BIH 124 C3
Bistrica ob Sotli
SLO 123 A4
Bistriţa RO 17 B6
Bitburg D 92 B2
Bitche F 93 B3
Bitetto I 171 B4
Bitola MK 182 B3
Bitonto I 171 B4
Bitschwiller F 106 B2
Bitterfeld D 83 A4
Bitti I 178 B3
Biville-sur-Mer F 89 A5
Bivona I 176 B2
Biwer L 92 B2
Bizeljsko SLO 123 A4
Bizovac HR 125 B4
Bjåen N 52 A3
Bjärnum S 61 C3
Bjärred S 61 D3
Bjästa S 200 C4
Bjelland
Vest-Agder N 52 B2
Vest-Agder N 52 B3
Bjelovar HR 124 B2
Bjerkreim N 52 B2
Bjerkvik N 194 B8
Bjerreby DK 65 B3
Bjerregrav DK 58 B2
Bjerringbro DK 59 B2
Bjøberg N 47 B5
Bjøllånes N 195 D5

Bjö–Bov 235

Björbo S 50 B1
Bjordal N 46 A2
Björg IS 191 B8
Bjørkåsen N 194 B7
Björke
Gävleborg S 51 B4
Östergötland S 56 B1
Bjørkelangen N 48 C3
Björketorp S 60 B2
Björkholmen S 196 C2
Björkliden S 194 B9
Björklinge S 51 B4
Björko S 51 C6
Björkö S 60 B1
Björköby S 62 A2
Björkvik S 56 B2
Bjørn N 195 D3
Björna S 200 C4
Björneborg S 55 A5
Björnerod S 54 A2
Bjørnevatn N 193 C13
Björnlunda S 56 A3
Bjørnstad N 193 C14
Björsäter S 56 B2
Bjurberget S 49 B4
Bjurholm S 200 C5
Bjursås S 50 B2
Bjurtjärn S 55 A5
Bjuv S 61 C2
Blachownia PL 86 B2
Blackburn GB 38 A4
Blackpool GB 38 A3
Blackstad S 62 A4
Blackwater IRL 30 B2
Blackwaterfoot GB 34 C2
Blacy F 91 C4
Bladåker S 51 B5
Blaenau Ffestiniog
GB 38 B3
Blaenavon GB 39 C3
Blaengarw GB 39 C3
Blagaj
BIH 124 B2
BIH 139 B3
Blagdon GB 43 A4
Blagnac F 129 C4
Blagoevgrad BG 183 A5
Blaichach D 107 B5
Blain F 101 B4
Blainville-sur-l'Eau
F 92 C2
Blair Atholl GB 35 B4
Blairgowrie GB 35 B4
Blajan F 145 A4
Blakeney GB 39 C4
Blakstad N 53 B4
Blâmont F 92 C2
Blanca E 165 A3
Blancos E 140 C3
Blandford Forum
GB 43 B4
Blanes E 147 C3
Blangy-sur-Bresle F 90 B1
Blankaholm S 62 A4
Blankenberge B 78 A3
Blankenburg D 82 A2
Blankenfelde D 74 B2
Blankenhain D 82 B3
Blankenheim D 80 B2
Blanquefort F 128 B2
Blansko CZ 97 B4
Blanzac F 115 C4
Blanzy F 104 C3
Blaricum NL 70 B2
Blarney IRL 29 C3
Blascomillán E 150 B2
Blascosancho E 150 B3
Błaszki PL 86 A2
Blatná CZ 96 B1
Blatné SK 111 A4
Blatnice CZ 98 C1
Blatnika BIH 139 A3
Blato HR 138 C2
Blato na Cetini HR 138 B2
Blatten CH 119 A4
Blattnicksele S 195 E8
Blatzheim D 80 B2
Blaubeuren D 94 C1
Blaufelden D 94 B1
Blaustein D 94 C1
Blaydon GB 37 B5
Blaye F 128 A2
Blaye-les-Mines F 130 A1
Blázquez E 156 B2
Bleckede D 73 A3
Blecua E 145 B3
Bled SLO 123 A3
Bleiburg A 110 C1
Bleichenbach D 81 B5
Bleicherode D 82 A2
Bleik N 194 A6
Bleikvassli N 195 E4
Bléneau F 104 B1
Blentarp S 61 D3
Blera I 168 A2
Blérancourt F 90 B3
Bléré F 102 B2
Blesle F 116 B3
Blessington IRL 30 A2
Blet F 103 C4
Bletchley GB 44 B3
Bletterans F 105 C4
Blidö S 57 A4
Blidsberg S 60 B3
Blieskastel D 92 B3
Bligny-sur-Ouche
F 104 B3
Blikstorp S 55 B5
Blinisht AL 182 B1
Blinja HR 124 B2
Blizanówek PL 76 C3
Bliżyn PL 87 A4
Blois F 103 B3
Blokhus DK 58 A2
Blokzijl NL 70 B2
Blombacka S 55 A4
Blomberg D 72 C2
Blomskog S 54 A3
Blomstermåla S 62 B4
Blomvåg N 46 B1
Blönduós IS 190 B5
Błonie PL 77 B5
Blonville-sur-Mer F 89 A4
Blötberget S 50 B2
Blovice CZ 96 B1
Bloxham GB 44 A2
Blšany CZ 83 B5
Bludenz A 107 B4
Bludov CZ 97 B4
Blumberg D 107 B3
Blyberg S 49 A6
Blyth
Northumberland
GB 37 A5
Nottinghamshire
GB 40 B2
Blyth Bridge GB 35 C4
Blythburgh GB 45 A5
Blythe Bridge GB 40 C1
Bø
Nordland N 194 B5
Telemark N 53 A5
Boal E 141 A4
Boan MNE 139 C5
Boario Terme I 120 B3
Boat of Garten GB 32 D3
Boa Vista P 154 B2
Boğazkale TR 23 A8
Boğazlıyan TR 23 B8
Boba H 111 B4
Bobadilla
Logroño E 143 B4
Málaga E 163 A3
Bobadilla del Campo
E 150 A2
Bobadilla del Monte
E 151 B4
Bóbbio I 120 C2
Bóbbio Pellice I 119 C4
Bobigny F 90 C2
Bobingen D 94 C2
Böblingen D 93 C5
Bobolice PL 68 B1
Boboras E 140 B2
Boboshevo BG 182 A4
Bobowa PL 99 B4
Bobrová CZ 97 B4
Bobrovitsa UA 13 C9
Bobrowice PL 75 C4
Bobrówko PL 75 B4
Boca de Huérgano
E 142 B2
Bocairent E 159 C3
Bočar SRB 126 B2
Bocchigliero I 174 B2
Boceguillas E 151 A4
Bochnia PL 99 B4
Bocholt
B 80 A1
D 80 A2
Bochov CZ 83 B5
Bochum D 80 A3
Bockara S 62 A4
Bockenem D 72 B3
Bockfliess A 97 C4
Bockhorn D 71 A5
Bočna SLO 123 A3
Bocognano F 180 A2
Boconád H 113 B4
Bőcs H 113 A4
Boczów PL 75 B3
Boda S 50 A2
Böda S 62 A5
Boda
Stockholm S 51 B5
Värmland S 55 A4
Västernorrland S 200 D2
Bodafors S 62 A2
Boda Glasbruk S 63 B3
Bodajk H 112 B2
Boddam
Aberdeenshire
GB 33 D5
Shetland GB 33 B5
Boddin D 73 A4
Bödefeld-Freiheit D 81 A4
Boden S 196 D4
Bodenmais D 95 B5
Bodenteich D 73 B3
Bodenwerder D 72 C2
Bodiam GB 45 B4
Bodinnick GB 42 B2
Bodio CH 120 A1
Bodjani SRB 125 B5
Bodmin GB 42 B2
Bodø N 194 C5
Bodonal de la Sierra
E 161 A3
Bodrum TR 188 B2
Bodstedt D 66 B1
Bodträskfors S 196 C3
Bodzanów PL 77 B5
Bodzanowice PL 86 B2
Bodzechów PL 87 B5
Bodzentyn PL 87 B4
Boecillo E 150 A3
Boëge F 118 A3
Boën F 117 B3
Bogács H 113 B4
Bogadmindszent H 125 B4
Bogajo E 149 B3
Bogarra E 158 C1
Bogarre E 163 A4
Bogatić SRB 127 C1
Bogatynia PL 84 B2
Bogda RO 126 B3
Bogdaniec PL 75 B4
Boge S 57 C4
Bogen
D 95 C4
Nordland N 194 B7
Nordland N 194 C6
S 49 B4
Bogense DK 59 C3
Bognanco Fonti I 119 A5
Bognelv N 192 B6
Bognes N 194 B7
Bogno CH 120 A2
Bognor Regis GB 44 C3
Bogoria PL 87 B5
Bograngen S 49 B4
Boguchwaly PL 69 B5
Bogumiłowice PL 86 A3
Boguslav UA 13 D9
Boguszów-Gorce
PL 85 B4
Bogyiszló H 112 C2
Bohain-en-Vermandois
F 91 B3
Böheimkirchen A 110 A2
Bohinjska Bistrica
SLO 122 A2
Böhlen D 83 A4
Böhmenkirch D 94 C1
Bohmte D 71 B5
Bohonal de Ibor E 150 C2
Böhönye H 124 A3
Bohumin CZ 98 B2
Boiro E 140 B2
Bois-d'Amont F 105 C5
Boisseron F 131 B3
Boitzenburg D 74 A2
Boixols E 147 B2
Boizenburg D 73 A3
Bojadła PL 75 C4
Bojano I 170 B2
Bojanowo PL 85 A4
Bøjden DK 64 A3
Bojkovice CZ 98 B1
Bojná SK 98 C2
Bojnice SK 98 C2
Boka SRB 126 B2
Böklund D 64 B2
Bokod H 112 B2
Böksholm S 62 A2
Boksitogorsk RUS 9 C8
Bol HR 138 B2
Bolaños de Calatrava
E 157 B4
Bolayır TR 186 B1
Bolbec F 89 A4
Bölcske H 112 C2
Bolderslev DK 64 B2
Boldog H 112 B3
Boldva H 113 A4
Böle S 196 D4
Bolea E 145 B3
Bolekhiv UA 13 D5
Bolesławiec PL 84 A3
Boleszkowice PL 74 B3
Bolewice PL 75 B5
Bólgheri I 134 B3
Bolhrad UA 17 C8
Boliden S 200 B6
Bolimów PL 77 B5
Boliqueime P 160 B1
Boljevci SRB 127 C2
Boljkovci SRB 127 C2
Bolków PL 85 B4
Bollebygd S 60 B2
Bollène F 131 A3
Bólliga E 152 B1
Bollnäs S 50 A3
Bollstabruk S 200 D3
Bollullos E 161 B3
Bollullos par del
Condado E 161 B3
Bologna I 135 A4
Bologne F 105 A4
Bolognetta I 176 B2
Bolognola I 136 C2
Bologoye RUS 9 D9
Bolótana I 178 B2
Bolsena I 168 A1
Bolshaya Vradiyevka
UA 17 B9
Bolsover GB 40 B2
Bolstad S 54 B3
Bolsward NL 70 A2
Boltaña E 145 B4
Boltenhagen D 65 C4
Boltigen CH 106 C2
Bolton GB 38 A4
Bolu TR 187 B6
Bolungavík IS 190 A2
Bolvadin TR 187 D6
Bóly H 125 B4
Bolzaneto I 133 A4
Bolzano I 108 C2
Bomba I 169 A4
Bombarral P 154 B1
Bömenzien D 73 B4
Bomlitz D 72 B2
Bømlo N 52 A1
Bøn N 48 B3
Bona F 104 B2
Bonaduz CH 107 C4
Bonanza E 161 C3
Boñar E 142 B1
Bonarbridge GB 32 D2
Bonárcado I 178 B2
Bonares E 161 B3
Bonäs S 50 A1
Bonassola I 134 A2
Bonawe GB 34 B2
Bondal N 53 A4
Bondeno I 121 C4
Bondorf D 93 C4
Bondstorp S 60 B3
Bon-Encontre F 129 B3
Bo'ness GB 35 B4
Bonete E 158 C2
Bonifacio F 180 B2
Bonigen CH 106 C2
Bonin PL 67 B5
Bonn D 80 B3
Bonnánaro I 178 B2
Bonnåsjøen N 194 C6
Bonnat F 116 A1
Bonndorf D 106 B3
Bonnétable F 102 A2
Bonnétage F 106 B1
Bonneuil-les-Eaux F 90 B2
Bonneuil-Matours
F 115 B4
Bonneval F 103 A3
Bonneval-sur-Arc
F 119 B4
Bonneville F 118 A3
Bonnières-sur-Seine
F 90 B1
Bonnieux F 131 B4
Bönnigheim D 93 B5
Bonnyrigg GB 35 C4
Bonny-sur-Loire F 103 B4
Bono
E 145 B4
I 178 B3
Bonorva I 178 B2
Bønsnes N 48 B2
Bonyhád H 125 A4
Boom B 79 A4
Boos F 89 A5
Boostedt D 64 B3
Bootle
Cumbria GB 36 B3
Merseyside GB 38 A3
Bopfingen D 94 C2
Boppard D 81 B3
Boqueixón E 140 B2
Bor
CZ 95 B4
S 62 A2
SRB 16 C5
TR 23 C8
Boran-sur-Oise F 90 B2
Borås S 60 B2
Borba P 155 C3
Borbona I 169 A3
Borča SRB 127 C2
Borci BIH 139 B4
Borculo NL 71 B3
Bordány H 126 A1
Bordeaux F 128 B2
Bordeira P 160 B1
Bordesholm D 64 B3
Borðeyri IS 190 B4
Bordighera I 133 B3
Bording DK 59 B2
Bordón E 153 B3
Bore I 120 C2
Borehamwood GB 44 B3
Borek Strzeliński PL 85 B5
Borek Wielkopolski
PL 76 C2
Boreland GB 36 A3
Borello I 135 A5
Borensberg S 56 B1
Borgafjäll S 199 A12
Borgarnes IS 190 C4
Borgentreich D 81 A5
Börger D 71 B4
Borger NL 71 B3
Borggård S 56 B1
Borghamn S 55 B5
Borghetta di Vara I 134 A2
Borghetto d'Arróscia
I 133 A3
Borghetto Santo Spirito
I 133 A4
Borgholm S 62 B4
Borghorst D 71 B4
Bórgia I 175 C2
Borgloon B 79 B5
Børglum DK 58 A2
Borgo F 180 A2
Borgo alla Collina I 135 B4
Borgo a Mozzano I 134 B3
Borgoforte I 121 B3
Borgofranco d'Ivrea
I 119 B4
Borgomanero I 119 B5
Borgomasino I 119 B4
Borgonovo Val Tidone
I 120 B2
Borgo Pace I 135 B5
Borgorose I 169 A3
Borgo San Dalmazzo
I 133 A3
Borgo San Lorenzo
I 135 B4
Borgosésia I 119 B5
Borgo Val di Taro I 134 A2
Borgo Valsugana I 121 A4
Borgo Vercelli I 119 B5
Borgstena S 60 B3
Borgue GB 36 B2
Borgund N 47 A4
Borgvik S 55 A3
Borja E 144 C2
Bork D 80 A3
Borken D 80 A2
Borkenes N 194 B7
Børkop DK 59 C2
Borkowice PL 87 A4
Borkowo PL 77 B5
Borkum D 71 A3
Borlänge S 50 B2
Borlu TR 186 D3
Bormes-les-Mimosas
F 132 B2
Bórmio I 107 C5
Bormujos E 161 B3
Borna D 83 A4
Borne NL 71 B3
Bornes P 149 A2
Borne Sulinowo PL 68 B1
Bornheim D 80 B2
Bornhöved D 64 B3
Börnicke D 74 B1
Bornos E 162 B2
Borobia E 152 A2
Borodino RUS 9 E9
Borohrádek CZ 85 B4
Boronów PL 86 B2
Bórore I 178 B2
Borosźow PL 86 B2
Borota H 126 A1
Boroughbridge GB 40 A2
Borovany CZ 96 C2
Borovichi RUS 9 C8
Borovnica SLO 123 B3
Borovo HR 125 B4
Borovsk RUS 9 E10
Borovy CZ 96 B1
Borowa PL 85 A5
Borox E 151 B4
Borrby S 66 A3
Borre
DK 65 B5
N 54 A1
Borredá E 147 B2
Borrenes E 141 B4
Borriol E 159 A3
Borris
DK 59 C1
IRL 30 B2
Borris-in-Ossory
IRL 28 B4
Borrisokane IRL 28 B3
Borrisoleigh IRL 28 B4
Borrowdale GB 36 B3
Børrud N 49 C4
Borşa RO 17 B6
Borsdorf D 83 A4
Børselv N 193 B9
Borsfa H 111 C3
Borský Mikuláš SK 98 C1
Borsodivánka H 113 B4
Borsodnádasd H 113 A4
Börte N 53 A3
Borth GB 39 B2
Bort-les-Orgues F 116 B2
Börtnan S 199 C10
Børtnes N 47 B6
Boruja Kościelne
PL 75 B5
Borup DK 61 D1
Boryslav UA 13 D5
Boryspil UA 13 C9
Boryszyn PL 75 B4
Borzęciczki PL 85 A5
Borzęcin PL 77 B5
Borzonasca I 134 A2
Borzyszkowy PL 68 A2
Borzytuchom PL 68 A2
Bosa I 178 B2
Bošáca SK 98 C1
Bosanci HR 123 B4
Bosanska Dubica
BIH 124 B2
Bosanska Gradiška
BIH 124 B3
Bosanska Kostajnica
BIH 124 B2
Bosanska Krupa
BIH 124 C2
Bosanski Brod BIH 125 B3
Bosanski Novi BIH 124 B2
Bosanski Petrovac
BIH 124 C2
Bosanski Šamac
BIH 125 B4
Bosansko Grahovo
BIH 138 A2
Bošany SK 98 C2
Bösárkány H 111 B4
Bosau D 65 B3
Bósca H 112 C3
Boscastle GB 42 B2
Bosco I 120 C1
Bosco Chiesanuova
I 121 B4
Bösdorf D 65 B3
Bösel D 71 A4
Bosham GB 44 C3
Bösingfeld D 72 B2
Bosjön S 49 C5
Boskoop NL 70 B1
Boskovice CZ 97 B4
Bošnjaci HR 125 B4
Bošnjane SRB 127 D3
Bossast E 145 B4
Bossolasco I 133 A4
Boštanj SLO 123 A4
Boston GB 41 C3
Bostrak N 53 A4
Böszénfa H 125 A3
Bot E 153 A4
Botajica BIH 125 C4
Bøte By DK 65 B4
Bothel GB 36 B3
Boticas P 148 A2
Botilsäter S 55 A4
Botngård N 198 B6
Botoš SRB 126 B2
Botoşani RO 17 B7
Botricello I 175 C2
Botsmark S 200 B6
Bottendorf D 81 A4
Bottesford GB 40 C3
Bottnaryd S 60 B3
Bottrop D 80 A2
Botunje SRB 127 C3
Bötzingen D 106 A2
Bouaye F 101 B4
Bouça P 149 A2
Boucau F 128 C1
Bouchain F 78 B3
Bouchoir F 90 B2
Boudreville F 105 B3
Boudry CH 106 C1
Bouesse F 103 C3
Bouguenais F 101 B4
Bouhy F 104 B2
Bouillargues F 131 B3
Bouillon B 91 B5
Bouilly F 104 A2
Bouin F 114 B2
Boulay-Moselle F 92 B2
Boulazac F 129 A3
Boule-d'Amont F 146 B3
Bouligny F 92 B1
Boulogne-sur-Gesse
F 145 A4
Boulogne-sur-Mer F 78 B1
Bouloire F 102 B2
Bouquemaison F 78 B2
Bourbon-Lancy F 104 C2
Bourbon-l'Archambault
F 104 C2
Bourbonne-les-Bains
F 105 B4
Bourbourg F 78 B2
Bourbriac F 100 A2
Bourcefranc-le-Chapus
F 114 C2
Bourdeaux F 131 A4
Bouresse F 115 B4
Bourg F 128 A2
Bourg-Achard F 89 A4
Bourganeuf F 116 B1
Bourg-Argental F 117 B4
Bourg-de-Péage F 117 B5
Bourg-de-Thizy F 117 A4
Bourg-de-Visa F 129 B3
Bourg-en-Bresse F 118 A2
Bourges F 103 B4
Bourg-et-Comin F 91 B3
Bourg-Lastic F 116 B2
Bourg-Madame F 146 B2
Bourgneuf-en-Retz
F 114 A2
Bourgogne F 91 B4
Bourgoin-Jallieu F 118 B2
Bourg-St Andéol F 131 A3
Bourg-St Maurice
F 119 B3
Bourgtheroulde F 89 A4
Bourgueil F 102 B2
Bourmont F 105 A4
Bourne GB 40 C3
Bournemouth GB 43 B5
Bourneville F 89 A4
Bournezeau F 114 B2
Bourran F 129 B3
Bourret F 129 C4
Bourron-Marlotte F 90 C2
Bourton-on-The-Water
GB 44 B2
Boussac F 116 A2
Boussens F 145 A4
Boutersem B 79 B4
Bouttencourt F 90 B1
Bouvières F 131 A4
Bouvron F 101 B4
Bouxwiller F 93 C3
Bouzas E 140 B2
Bouzonville F 92 B2
Bova I 175 D1
Bovalino Marina I 175 C2
Bovallstrand S 54 B2
Bova Marina I 175 D1
Bovec SLO 122 A2
Bóveda E 141 B3
Bóvegno I 120 B3
Bovenau D 64 B2
Bovenden D 82 A1
Bøverdal N 198 D5
Boves F 90 B2
Bóves I 133 A3
Bovey Tracey GB 43 B3
Bovino I 171 B3
Bøvlingbjerg DK 58 B1
Bovolenta I 121 B4

Bovolone I 121 B4
Bowes GB 37 B5
Bowmore GB 34 C1
Bowness-on-Windermere GB 36 B4
Box GB 43 A4
Boxberg
Baden-Württemberg D 94 B1
Sachsen D 84 A2
Boxholm S 55 B6
Boxmeer NL 80 A1
Boxtel NL 79 A5
Boyabat TR 23 A8
Boyalıca TR 187 B4
Boyle IRL 26 C2
Bozan TR 187 C6
Božava HR 137 A3
Bozburun TR 188 C3
Bozcaada TR 186 C1
Bozdoğan TR 188 B3
Bożepole Wielkie PL 68 A2
Boževac SRB 127 C3
Božice CZ 97 C4
Boži Dar CZ 83 B4
Bozkır TR 189 B7
Bozouls F 130 A1
Bozova TR 189 B5
Bozüyük TR 187 C5
Bózzolo I 121 B3
Bra I 119 C4
Braås S 62 A3
Brabrand DK 59 B3
Bracadale GB 31 B2
Bracciano I 168 A2
Bracieux F 103 B3
Bräcke S 199 C12
Brackenheim D 93 B5
Brackley GB 44 A2
Bracklin IRL 27 C4
Bracknell GB 44 B3
Brackwede D 72 C1
Braco GB 35 B4
Brad RO 16 B5
Bradford GB 40 B2
Bradford on Avon GB 43 A4
Bradina BIH 139 B4
Brådland N 52 B2
Brædstrup DK 59 C2
Brae GB 33 A5
Braemar GB 32 D3
Braemore GB 32 D1
Braga P 148 A1
Bragança P 149 A3
Brăila RO 17 C7
Braine F 91 B3
Braine-le-Comte B 79 B4
Braintree GB 45 B4
Braives B 79 B5
Brake D 72 A1
Brakel
B 79 B3
D 81 A5
Bräkne-Hoby S 63 B3
Brålanda S 54 B3
Bralin PL 86 A1
Brallo di Pregola I 120 C2
Bram F 146 A3
Bramafan F 132 B2
Bramberg am Wildkogel A 109 B3
Bramdrupdam DK 59 C2
Bramming DK 59 C1
Brampton GB 37 B4
Bramsche D 71 B4
Branca I 136 B1
Brancaleone Marina I 175 D2
Brancaster GB 41 C4
Brand
Nieder Östereich A 96 C3
Vorarlberg A 107 B4
Brandbu N 48 B2
Brande DK 59 C2
Brande-Hornerkirchen D 64 C2
Brandenberg A 108 B2
Brandenburg D 73 B5
Brand-Erbisdorf D 83 B5
Brandis D 83 A4
Brando F 180 A2
Brandomil E 140 A2
Brandon GB 45 A4
Brandshagen D 66 B2
Brandval N 49 B4
Brandýs nad Labem CZ 84 B2
Branice PL 98 A1
Braničevo SRB 127 C3
Braniewo PL 69 A4
Branik SLO 122 B2
Brankovina SRB 127 C1
Branky CZ 98 B1
Branne F 128 B2
Brannenburg-Degerndorf D 108 B3
Brantôme F 115 C4
Branzi I 120 A2
Bras d'Asse F 132 B2
Braskereidfoss N 48 B3
Braslaw BY 13 A7
Braşov RO 17 C6
Brasparts F 100 A2
Brassac F 130 B1
Brassac-les-Mines F 116 B3
Brasschaat B 79 A4
Brastad S 54 B2
Břasy CZ 96 B1
Brąszewice PL 86 A2
Bratislava SK 111 A4
Brattfors S 55 A5
Brattvåg N 198 C3
Bratunac BIH 127 C1
Braubach D 81 B3
Braunau A 95 C5
Braunfels D 81 B4
Braunlage D 82 A2
Braunsbedra D 83 A3
Braunschweig D 73 B3
Bray IRL 30 A2
Bray Dunes F 78 A2
Bray-sur-Seine F 90 C3
Bray-sur-Somme F 90 B2
Brazatortas E 157 B3
Brazey-en-Plaine F 105 B4
Brbinj HR 137 A4
Brčko BIH 125 C4
Brdani SRB 127 D2
Brdów PL 76 B3
Brea de Tajo E 151 B4
Brécey F 88 B2
Brechen D 81 B4
Brechin GB 35 B5
Brecht B 79 A4
Brecketfeld D 80 A3
Břeclav CZ 97 C4
Brecon GB 39 C3
Brécy F 103 B4
Breda
E 147 C3
NL 79 A4
Bredaryd S 60 B3
Bredbyn S 200 C4
Breddin D 73 B5
Bredebro DK 64 A1
Bredelar D 81 A4
Bredenfelde D 74 A2
Bredsjö S 50 C1
Bredstedt D 64 B1
Bredsten DK 59 C2
Bredträsk S 200 C4
Bredviken S 195 D5
Bree B 80 A1
Bregana HR 123 B4
Breganze I 121 B4
Bregenz A 107 B4
Bréhal F 88 B2
Brehna D 83 A4
Breiðdalsvík IS 191 C11
Breidenbach F 93 B3
Breil-sur-Roya F 133 B3
Breisach D 106 A2
Breitenbach
CH 106 B2
D 81 B5
Breitenberg D 96 C1
Breitenfelde D 73 A3
Breitengussbach D 94 B2
Breivikbotn N 192 B6
Brejning DK 59 C2
Brekke N 46 A2
Brekken N 199 C8
Brekkestø N 53 B4
Brekkvasselv N 199 A10
Brekstad N 198 B6
Breland N 53 B3
Bremanger N 198 D1
Bremen D 72 A1
Bremerhaven D 72 A1
Bremervörde D 72 A2
Bremgarten CH 106 B3
Bremsnes N 198 B4
Brem-sur-Mer F 114 B2
Brenderup DK 59 C2
Brenes E 162 A2
Brengova SLO 110 C2
Brenna PL 98 B2
Breno I 120 B3
Brénod F 118 A2
Brensbach D 93 B4
Brentwood GB 45 B4
Brescello I 121 C3
Bréscia I 120 B3
Breskens NL 79 A3
Bresles F 90 B2
Bresnica SRB 127 D2
Bressana I 120 B2
Bressanone I 108 C2
Bressuire F 102 C1
Brest
BY 13 B5
F 100 A1
HR 122 B2
Brestač SRB 127 C1
Brestanica SLO 123 A4
Brestova HR 123 B3
Brestovac HR 125 B3
Bretenoux F 129 B4
Breteuil
Eure F 89 B4
Oise F 90 B2
Brétigny-sur-Orge F 90 C2
Bretten D 93 B4
Bretteville-sur-Laize F 89 A3
Brettheim D 94 B2
Breuil-Cervínia I 119 B4
Breukelen NL 70 B2
Brevik
N 53 A5
Stockholm S 57 A4
Västra Götaland S 55 B5
Breza BIH 139 A4
Brežice SLO 123 B4
Bréziers F 132 A2
Breznica HR 124 A2
Breznica Našička HR 125 B4
Březnice CZ 96 B1
Brezno SK 99 C3
Brezolles F 89 B5
Březovánad Svitavou CZ 97 B4
Brezovápod Bradlom SK 98 C1
Brezovica
SK 99 B4
SLO 123 A3
Brezovo Polje Selo BIH 125 C4
Briançon F 118 C3
Brianconnet F 132 B2
Briare F 103 B4
Briatexte F 129 C4
Briático I 175 C2
Briaucourt F 105 A4
Bribir HR 123 B3
Bricquebec F 88 A2
Bridgend
Argyll & Bute GB 34 C1
Bridgend GB 39 C3
Bridge of Cally GB 35 B4
Bridge of Don GB 33 D4
Bridge of Earn GB 35 B4
Bridge of Orchy GB 34 B3
Bridgnorth GB 39 B4
Bridgwater GB 43 A4
Břidličná CZ 98 B1
Bridlington GB 41 A3
Bridport GB 43 B4
Briec F 100 A1
Brie-Comte-Robert F 90 C2
Brienne-le-Château F 91 C4
Brienon-sur-Armançon F 104 B2
Brienz CH 106 C3
Brienza I 172 B1
Briesen D 74 B3
Brieskow Finkenheerd D 74 B3
Brietlingen D 72 A3
Brieva de Cameros E 143 B4
Briey F 92 B1
Brig CH 119 A5
Brigg GB 40 B3
Brighouse GB 40 B2
Brightlingsea GB 45 B5
Brighton GB 44 C3
Brignogan-Plage F 100 A1
Brignoles F 132 B2
Brigstock GB 40 C3
Brihuega E 151 B5
Brijuni HR 122 C2
Brillon-en-Barrois F 91 C5
Brilon D 81 A4
Brimnes N 46 B3
Brinches P 160 A2
Bríndisi I 173 B3
Brinje HR 123 B4
Brinon-sur-Beuvron F 104 B2
Brinon-sur-Sauldre F 103 B4
Brinyan GB 33 B3
Brión E 140 B2
Briones E 143 B4
Brionne F 89 A4
Brioude F 117 B3
Brioux-sur-Boutonne F 115 B3
Briouze F 89 B3
Briscous F 144 A2
Brisighella I 135 A4
Brissac-Quincé F 102 B1
Brissago CH 120 A1
Bristol GB 43 A4
Brive-la-Gaillarde F 129 A4
Briviesca E 143 B3
Brixham GB 43 B3
Brixlegg A 108 B2
Brjánslækur IS 190 B2
Brka BIH 125 C4
Brnaze HR 138 B2
Brněnec CZ 97 B4
Brno CZ 97 B4
Bro S 57 A3
Broadclyst GB 43 B3
Broadford
GB 31 B3
IRL 28 B3
Broad Haven GB 39 C1
Broadstairs GB 45 B5
Broadstone GB 43 B4
Broadway GB 44 A2
Broager DK 64 B2
Broaryd S 60 B3
Broby S 61 C4
Brobyværk DK 59 C3
Bročanac BIH 138 B3
Brocas F 128 B2
Brock D 71 B4
Brockel D 72 A2
Brockenhurst GB 44 C2
Broczyno PL 75 A5
Brod MK 182 B3
Brodalen S 54 B2
Broddbo S 50 C3
Brodek u Přerova CZ 98 B1
Broden-bach D 80 B3
Brodick GB 34 C2
Brod na Kupi HR 123 B3
Brodnica PL 69 B4
Brodnica Graniczna PL 68 A3
Brodowe Łąki PL 77 A6
Brody
Lubuskie PL 75 B4
Lubuskie PL 84 A2
Mazowieckie PL 77 B5
UA 13 C6
Broglie F 89 B4
Brójce PL 75 B4
Brokind S 56 B1
Brolo I 177 A3
Brome D 73 B3
Bromley GB 45 B4
Bromölla S 63 B2
Bromont-Lamothe F 116 B2
Brömsebro S 63 B3
Bromsgrove GB 44 A1
Bromyard GB 39 B4
Bronchales E 152 B2
Bronco E 149 B3
Brønderslev DK 58 A2
Broni I 120 B2
Brønnøysund N 195 E3
Brøns DK 59 C1
Bronte I 177 B3
Bronzani Mejdan BIH 124 C2
Bronzolo I 121 A4
Broons F 101 A3
Broquies F 130 A1
Brora GB 32 C3
Brørup DK 59 C2
Brösarp S 63 C2
Brossac F 115 C3
Brostrud N 47 B5
Brotas P 154 C2
Brötjärna S 50 B2
Broto E 145 B3
Brottby S 57 A4
Brøttum N 48 A2
Brou F 103 A3
Brouage F 114 C2
Brough GB 37 B4
Broughshane GB 27 B4
Broughton GB 35 C4
Broughton-in-Furness GB 36 B3
Broumov CZ 85 B4
Broût-Vernet F 116 A3
Brouvelieures F 106 A1
Brouwershaven NL 79 A3
Brovary UA 13 C9
Brovst DK 58 A2
Brownhills GB 40 C2
Brozas E 155 B4
Brozzo I 120 B3
Brtnice CZ 97 B3
Brtonigla HR 122 B2
Bruay-la-Buissière F 78 B2
Bruchhausen-Vilsen D 72 B2
Bruchsal D 93 B4
Bruck D 95 B4
Brück D 74 B1
Bruck an der Grossglocknerstrasse A 109 B3
Bruck an der Leitha A 111 A3
Bruck an der Mur A 110 B2
Brückl A 110 C1
Bruckmühl D 108 B2
Brue-Auriac F 132 B1
Brüel D 65 C4
Bruen CH 107 C3
Bruère-Allichamps F 103 C4
Bruff IRL 29 B3
Bruflat N 47 B6
Brugg CH 106 B3
Brugge B 78 A3
Brüggen D 80 A2
Brühl D 80 B2
Bruinisse NL 79 A4
Brûlon F 102 B1
Brumano I 120 B2
Brumath F 93 C3
Brummen NL 70 B3
Brumov-Bylnice CZ 98 B2
Brumunddal N 48 B2
Brunau D 73 B4
Brunehamel F 91 B4
Brünen D 80 A2
Brunete E 151 B3
Brunflo S 199 B11
Brunico I 108 C2
Brunkeberg N 53 A4
Brunn D 74 A2
Brunnen CH 107 C3
Brunsbüttel D 64 C2
Brunssum NL 80 B1
Bruntál CZ 98 B1
Brušane HR 137 A4
Brusasco I 119 B5
Brusio CH 120 A3
Brusno SK 99 C3
Brusque F 130 B1
Brussels = Bruxelles B 79 B4
Brusson I 119 B4
Brüssow D 74 A3
Brusy PL 68 B2
Bruton GB 43 A4
Bruvno HR 138 A1
Bruvoll N 48 B3
Bruxelles = Brussels B 79 B4
Bruyères F 106 A1
Bruz F 101 A4
Bruzaholm S 62 A3
Brwinów PL 77 B5
Brynamman GB 39 C3
Bryncrug GB 39 B2
Bryne N 52 B1
Brynmawr GB 39 C3
Bryrup DK 59 B2
Brzeg PL 85 B5
Brzeg Dolny PL 85 A4
Brześć Kujawski PL 76 B3
Brzesko PL 99 B4
Brzeszcze PL 99 B3
Brzezie PL 68 B1
Brzeziny
Łódzkie PL 87 A3
Wielkopolskie PL 86 A2
Brzeźnica PL 84 A3
Brzeźnica Nowa PL 86 A3
Brzeżno PL 75 A4
Brzotin SK 99 C4
Brzozie Lubawskie PL 69 B4
Bua S 60 B2
Buarcos P 148 B1
Buaveg N 52 A1
Bubbio I 119 C5
Bubry F 100 B2
Buca TR 188 A2
Bucak TR 189 B5
Bučany SK 98 C1
Buccheri I 177 B3
Buccino I 172 B1
Bucelas P 154 C1
Buch
Bayern D 94 C2
Bayern D 95 C4
Buchach UA 13 D6
Bucharest = Bucureşti RO 17 C7
Buchbach D 95 C4
Buchboden A 107 B4
Buchen D 94 B1
Büchen D 73 A3
Buchenberg D 107 B5
Buchères F 104 A3
Buchholz D 72 A2
Buchloe D 108 A1
Buchlovice CZ 98 B1
Buchlyvie GB 34 B3
Bucholz D 73 A5
Buchs CH 107 B4
Buchy F 89 A5
Bückeburg D 72 B2
Buckfastleigh GB 42 B3
Buckhaven GB 35 B4
Buckie GB 33 D4
Buckingham GB 44 A3
Buckley GB 38 A3
Bückwitz D 73 B5
Bučovice CZ 97 B5
Bucsa H 113 B5
Bucureşti = Bucharest RO 17 C7
Bucy-lés-Pierreport F 91 B3
Buczek PL 86 A3
Bud N 198 C3
Budakalasz H 112 B3
Budakeszi H 112 B2
Budal N 199 C7
Budaörs H 112 B2
Budapest H 112 B3
Búðardalur IS 190 B4
Budča SK 99 C3
Buddusò I 178 B3
Bude GB 42 B2
Budeč CZ 97 B3
Büdelsdorf D 64 B2
Budens P 160 B1
Budia E 151 B5
Budimlić-Japra BIH 124 C2
Büdingen D 81 B5
Budinščina HR 124 A2
Budišov CZ 98 B1
Budleigh Salterton GB 43 B3
Budmerice SK 98 C1
Budoni I 178 B3
Búdrio I 135 A4
Budva MNE 16 D3
Budyněnad Ohří CZ 84 B2
Budziszewice PL 87 A3
Budzyń PL 76 B1
Bue N 52 B1
Bueña E 152 B2
Buenache de Alarcón E 158 B1
Buenache de la Sierra E 152 B2
Buenaventura E 150 B3
Buenavista de Valdavia E 142 B2
Buendia E 151 B5
Bueu E 140 B2
Buezo E 143 B3
Bugac H 112 C3
Bugarra E 159 B3
Bugeat F 116 B1
Buggerru I 179 C2
Bugojno BIH 138 A3
Bugøyfjord N 193 C13
Bugøynes N 193 C13
Bugyi H 112 B3
Buharkent TR 188 B3
Bühl
Baden-Württemberg D 93 C4
Bayern D 107 B5
Bühlertal D 93 C4
Bühlertann D 94 B1
Buia I 122 A2
Builth Wells GB 39 B3
Buin N 47 B6
Buis-les-Baronnies F 131 A4
Buitenpost NL 70 A3
Buitrago del Lozoya E 151 B4
Bujalance E 157 C3
Bujaraloz E 153 A3
Buje HR 122 B2
Bujedo E 143 B3
Bük H 111 B3
Buk PL 75 B5
Bükkösd H 125 A3
Bükkzsérc H 113 B4
Bukovci SLO 124 A1
Bukowiec PL 75 B5
Bukowina Tatrzańska PL 99 B4
Bukownica PL 86 A2
Bukowno PL 86 B3
Bülach CH 107 B3
Búland IS 191 D7
Buldan TR 188 A3
Bulgnéville F 105 A4
Bulgurca TR 188 A2
Bülkau D 64 C1
Bulken N 46 B3
Bulkowo PL 77 B5
Bullas E 164 A3
Bulle CH 106 C2
Büllingen B 80 B2
Bullmark S 200 B6
Bulqizë AL 182 B2
Buna BIH 139 B3
Bunahowen IRL 26 B1
Bunbeg IRL 26 A2
Bunclody IRL 30 B2
Buncrana IRL 27 A3
Bunde D 71 A4
Bünde D 72 B1
Bundoran IRL 26 B2
Bunessan GB 34 B1
Bungay GB 45 A5
Bunge S 57 C5
Bunić HR 123 C4
Bunmahon IRL 30 B1
Bunnyconnellan IRL 26 B1
Buño E 140 A2
Buñol E 159 B3
Bunratty IRL 29 B3
Bunsbeek B 79 B4
Buñuel E 144 C2
Bunyola E 166 B2
Buonabitácolo I 172 B1
Buonalbergo I 170 B2
Buonconvento I 135 B4
Buonvicino I 174 B1
Burano I 122 B1
Burbach D 81 B4
Burcei I 179 C3
Burdons-sur-Rognon F 105 A4
Burdur TR 189 B5
Bureå S 2 D7
Burela E 141 A3
Büren D 81 A4
Büren an der Aare CH 106 B2
Burford GB 44 B2
Burg
Cottbus D 84 A2
Magdeburg D 73 B4
Schleswig-Holstein D 64 C2
Burgas BG 17 D7
Burgau
A 111 B3
D 94 C2
P 160 B1
Burg auf Fehmarn D 65 B4
Burgbernheim D 94 B2
Burgdorf
CH 106 B2
D 72 B3
Burgebrach D 94 B2
Bürgel D 83 B3
Burgess Hill GB 44 C3
Burghaslach D 94 B2
Burghausen D 109 A3
Burghead GB 32 D3
Burgheim D 94 C3
Burgh le Marsh GB 41 B4
Búrgio I 176 B2
Burgkirchen D 109 A3
Burgkunstadt D 82 B3
Burglengenfeld D 95 B4

Burgo P 148 B1
Burgoberbach D 94 B2
Burgohondo E 150 B3
Burgos E 143 B3
Burgsinn D 82 B1
Burgstädt D 83 B4
Burgstall D 73 B4
Burg Stargard D 74 A2
Burgsvik S 57 C4
Burgui E 144 B3
Burguillos E 162 A2
Burguillos del Cerro E 155 C4
Burguillos de Toledo E 151 C4
Burhaniye TR 186 C1
Burhave D 71 A5
Burie F 114 C3
Burjassot E 159 B3
Burk D 94 B2
Burkhardtsdorf D 83 B4
Burlada E 144 B2
Burladingen D 107 A4
Burlage D 71 A4
Burness GB 33 B4
Burnham GB 44 B3
Burnham Market GB 41 C4
Burnham-on-Crouch GB 45 B4
Burnham-on-Sea GB 43 A4
Burniston GB 40 A3
Burnley GB 40 B1
Burntisland GB 35 B4
Burón E 142 A1
Buronzo I 119 B5
Burovac SRB 127 C3
Burow D 74 A2
Burravoe GB 33 A5
Burrel AL 182 B2
Burret F 146 B2
Burriana E 159 B3
Burry Port GB 39 C2
Bürs A 107 B4
Bursa TR 186 B4
Burseryd S 60 B3
Bürstadt D 93 B4
Burton GB 37 B4
Burton Agnes GB 41 A3
Burton Bradstock GB 43 B4
Burton Latimer GB 44 A3
Burton upon Stather GB 40 B3
Burton upon Trent GB 40 C2
Burträsk S 200 B6
Burujón E 151 C3
Burwell GB 45 A4
Burwick GB 33 C4
Bury GB 40 B1
Bury St Edmunds GB 45 A4
Burzenin PL 86 A2
Busachi I 179 B2
Busalla I 134 A1
Busana I 134 A3
Busano I 119 B4
Busca I 133 A3
Busch D 73 B4
Buševec HR 124 B2
Bushat AL 182 B1
Bushey GB 44 B3
Bushmills GB 27 A4
Bušince SK 112 A3
Buskhyttan S 56 B2
Busko-Zdrój PL 87 B4
Busot E 159 C3
Busovača BIH 139 A3
Busquistar E 163 B4
Bussang F 106 B1
Busseto I 120 C3
Bussière-Badil F 115 C4
Bussière-Poitevine F 115 B4
Bussolengo I 121 B3
Bussoleno I 119 B4
Bussum NL 70 B2
Busto Arsízio I 120 B1
Büsum D 64 B1
Butera I 177 B3
Butgenbach B 80 B2
Butler's Bridge IRL 27 B3
Butryny PL 77 A5
Bütschwil CH 107 B4
Buttermere GB 36 B3
Buttevant IRL 29 B3
Buttle S 57 C4
Buttstädt D 82 A3
Butzbach D 81 B4
Bützfleth D 72 A2
Bützow D 65 C4
Buxières-les-Mines F 104 C1
Buxtehude D 72 A2
Buxton GB 40 B2
Buxy F 104 C3
Büyükçekmece TR 186 A3
Büyükkariştiran TR 186 A2
Büyükorhan TR 186 C3
Buzançais F 103 C3
Buzancy F 91 B4
Buzău RO 17 C7
Buzet HR 122 B2
Buziaş RO 126 B3
Buzsák H 111 C4
Buzy F 145 A3
By S 50 B3
Byala BG 17 D6
Byaroza BY 13 B6
Byczyna PL 86 A2
Bydalen S 199 B10
Bydgoszcz PL 76 A3
Bygdin N 47 A5
Bygdsiljum S 200 B6
Bygland N 53 B3
Byglandsfjord N 53 B3
Bygstad N 46 A2
Bykhaw BY 13 B9
Bykle N 52 A3
Bylderup-Bov DK 64 B2
Byrkjedal N 52 B2
Byrkjelo N 198 D3
Byrum DK 58 A3
Byšice CZ 84 B2
Byske S 2 D7
Býškovice CZ 98 B1
Bysław PL 76 A2
Bystré CZ 97 B4
Bystřice CZ 96 B2
Bystrice CZ 98 B2
Bystřice nad Pernštejnem CZ 97 B4
Bystřice pod Hostýnem CZ 98 B1
Bystrzyca Kłodzka PL 85 B4
Bytča SK 98 B2
Bytnica PL 75 B4
Bytom PL 86 B2
Bytom Odrzański PL 85 A3
Bytów PL 68 A2
Byxelkrok S 62 A5
Bzenec CZ 98 C1
Bzince SK 98 C1

C

Çağa TR 187 B7
Cabacos P 154 B2
Cabaj-Čápor SK 98 C2
Cabana E 140 A2
Cabanac-et-Villagrains F 128 B2
Cabañaquinta E 142 A1
Cabanas P 160 B2
Cabañas del Castillo E 156 A2
Cabañas de Yepes E 151 C4
Cabanelles E 147 B3
Cabanes E 153 B4
Cabanillas E 144 B2
Čabar HR 123 B3
Cabasse F 132 B2
Cabdella E 146 B2
Cabeceiras de Basto P 148 A1
Cabeço de Vide P 155 B3
Cabella Ligure I 120 C2
Cabeza del Buey E 156 B2
Cabeza la Vaca E 161 A3
Cabezamesada E 151 C4
Cabezarados E 157 B3
Cabezarrubias del Puerto E 157 B3
Cabezas del Villar E 150 B2
Cabezas Rubias E 161 B2
Cabezón E 142 C2
Cabezón de la Sal E 142 A2
Cabezón de Liébana E 142 A2
Cabezuela E 151 A4
Cabezuela del Valle E 149 B4
Cabo de Gata E 164 C2
Cabo de Palos E 165 B4
Cabolafuenta E 152 A1
Cabourg F 89 A3
Cabra
E 163 A3
P 148 B2
Cabrach GB 32 D3
Cabra del Santo Cristo E 163 A4
Cábras I 179 C2
Cabreiro P 140 C2
Cabreiros E 140 A3
Cabrejas E 152 B1
Cabrela P 154 C2
Cabrillas E 149 B3
Cabuna HR 125 B3
Cacabelos E 141 B4
Čačak SRB 127 D2
Cáccamo I 176 B2
Caccuri I 174 B2
Cacela P 160 B2
Cacém P 154 C1
Cáceres E 155 B4
Cachafeiro E 140 B2
Cachopo P 160 B2
Čachtice SK 98 C1
Cacin E 163 A4
Čačinci HR 125 B3
Cadafais P 154 C1
Cadalen F 129 C5
Cadalso E 149 B3
Cadaqués E 147 B4
Cadaval P 154 B1
Cadavedo E 141 A4
Čadavica BIH 138 A2
Čadca SK 98 B2
Cadéac F 145 B4
Cadelbosco di Sopra I 121 C3
Cadenazzo CH 120 A1
Cadenberge D 64 C2
Cadenet F 131 B4
Cadeuil F 114 C3
Cádiar E 164 C1
Cadillac F 128 B2
Cádiz E 162 B1
Čadjavica HR 125 B3
Cadouin F 129 B3
Cadours F 129 C4
Cadrete E 152 A3
Caen F 89 A3
Caerleon GB 39 C4
Caernarfon GB 38 A2
Caerphilly GB 39 C3
Caersws GB 39 B3
Cafede P 155 B3
Caggiano I 172 B1
Cagli I 136 B1
Cágliari I 179 C3
Čaglin HR 125 B3
Cagnano Varano I 171 B3
Cagnes-sur-Mer F 132 B3
Caher IRL 29 B4
Caherciveen IRL 29 C1
Caherdaniel IRL 29 C1
Cahors F 129 B4
Cahul MD 17 C8
Caiazzo I 170 B2
Caion E 140 A2
Cairndow GB 34 B3
Cairnryan GB 36 B1
Cairo Montenotte I 133 A4
Caister-on-Sea GB 41 C5
Caistor GB 41 B3
Caivano I 170 C2
Cajarc F 129 B4
Čajniče BIH 139 B5
Çakırlar TR 189 C5
Çakmak TR 187 C6
Čakovec HR 124 A2
Çal TR 189 A4
Cala E 161 B3
Calabritto I 172 B1
Calaceite E 153 B4
Calacuccia F 180 A2
Cala d'Or E 167 B3
Calaf E 147 C2
Calafat RO 17 C5
Calafell E 147 C2
Cala Galdana E 167 B3
Cala Gonone I 178 B3
Calahonda
Granada E 163 B4
Málaga E 163 B3
Calahorra E 144 B2
Calais F 78 B1
Cala Llonga E 166 C1
Calalzo di Cadore I 109 C3
Cala Millor E 167 B3
Calamocha E 152 B2
Calamonte E 155 C4
Cala Morell E 167 A3
Calanais GB 31 A2
Calañas E 161 B3
Calanda E 153 B3
Calangiánus I 178 B3
Călăraşi RO 17 C7
Cala Ratjada E 167 B3
Calascibetta I 177 B3
Calasetta I 179 C2
Calasparra E 164 A3
Calatafimi I 176 B1
Calatayud E 152 A2
Calatorao E 152 A2
Calau D 84 A1
Calbe D 73 C4
Calcena E 152 A2
Calcinelli I 136 B1
Calco I 120 B2
Caldarola I 136 B2
Caldaro sulla strada del Vino I 121 A4
Caldas da Rainha P 154 B1
Caldas de Bo i E 145 B4
Caldas de Malavella E 147 C3
Caldas de Reis E 140 B2
Caldas de San Jorge P 148 B1
Caldas de Vizela P 148 A1
Caldaso de los Vidrios E 150 B3
Caldbeck GB 36 B3
Caldearenas E 145 B3
Caldelas P 148 A1
Calders E 147 C2
Caldes de Montbui E 147 C3
Caldicot GB 39 C4
Caldirola I 120 C2
Caledon GB 27 B4
Calella
Barcelona E 147 C3
Girona E 147 C4
Calenzana F 180 A1
Calera de León E 161 A3
Calera y Chozas E 150 C3
Caleruega E 143 C3
Caleruela E 150 C2
Cales de Mallorca E 167 B3
Calestano I 134 A3
Calfsound GB 33 B4
Calgary GB 34 B1
Calimera I 173 B4
Calitri I 172 B1
Calizzano I 133 A4
Callac F 100 A2
Callan IRL 30 B1
Callander GB 35 B3
Callas F 132 B2
Calliano
Piemonte I 119 B5
Trentino Alto Adige I 121 B4
Callington GB 42 B2
Callosa de Ensarriá E 159 C3
Callosa de Segura E 165 A4
Callús E 147 C2
Čalma SRB 127 B1
Calmbach D 93 C4
Calne GB 43 A5
Calolziocorte I 120 B2
Calonge E 147 C4
Čalovec SK 112 B1
Calpe E 159 C4
Caltabellotta I 176 B2
Caltagirone I 177 B3
Caltanissetta I 177 B3
Caltavuturo I 176 B2
Çaltılıbük TR 186 C3
Caltojar E 151 A5
Caluire-et-Cuire F 117 B4
Caluso I 119 B4
Calvello I 172 B1
Calvi F 180 A1
Calviá E 166 B2
Calvinet F 116 C2
Calvisson F 131 B3
Calvörde D 73 B4
Calw D 93 C4
Calzada de Calatrava E 157 B4
Calzada de Valdunciel E 150 A2
Calzadilla de los Barros E 155 C4
Cam GB 43 A4
Camaiore I 134 B3
Camarasa E 145 C4
Camarena E 151 B3
Camarès F 130 B1
Camaret-sur-Aigues F 131 A3
Camaret-sur-Mer F 100 A1
Camarillas E 153 B3
Camariñas E 140 A1
Camarma E 151 B4
Camarzana de Tera E 141 B4
Camas E 162 A1
Camastra I 176 B2
Cambados E 140 B2
Cambarinho P 148 B1
Camberley GB 44 B3
Cambil E 163 A4
Cambligeu F 78 B2
Cambo-les-Bains F 144 A2
Camborne GB 42 B1
Cambrai F 78 B3
Cambre E 140 A2
Cambridge GB 45 A4
Cambrils E 147 C2
Cambs D 65 C4
Camburg D 83 A3
Camden GB 44 B3
Cameleño E 142 A2
Camelford GB 42 B2
Çameli TR 189 B4
Camelle E 140 A1
Camerano I 136 B2
Camerino I 136 B2
Camerota I 172 B1
Camigliatello Silano I 174 B2
Caminha P 148 A1
Caminomorisco E 149 B3
Caminreal E 152 B2
Camisano Vicentino I 121 B4
Camlıdere TR 187 B7
Cammarata I 176 B2
Camogli I 134 A2
Camors F 100 B3
Camp IRL 29 B2
Campagna I 172 B1
Campagnano di Roma I 168 A2
Campagnático I 135 C4
Campan F 145 A4
Campana I 174 B2
Campanario E 156 B2
Campanillas E 163 B3
Campano E 162 B1
Campaspero E 151 A3
Campbeltown GB 34 C2
Campello E 165 A4
Campelos P 154 B1
Campi Bisénzio I 135 B4
Campico López E 165 B3
Campíglia Maríttima I 134 B3
Campillo de Altobuey E 158 B2
Campillo de Aragón E 152 A2
Campillo de Arenas E 163 A4
Campillo de Llerena E 156 B2
Campillos E 162 A3
Câmpina RO 17 C6
Campi Salentina I 173 B4
Campli I 136 C2
Campo E 145 B4
Campobasso I 170 B2
Campobello di Licata I 176 B2
Campobello di Mazara I 176 B1
Campo da Feira E 140 A3
Campodársego I 121 B4
Campo de Bacerros E 141 B3
Campo de Caso E 142 A1
Campo de Criptana E 157 A4
Campodolcino I 120 A2
Campofelice di Roccella I 176 B2
Campofiorito I 176 B2
Campofórmido I 122 A2
Campofranco I 176 B2
Campofrio E 161 B3
Campogalliano I 121 C3
Campo Ligure I 133 A4
Campolongo I 109 C3
Campo Lugar E 156 A2
Campo Maior P 155 B3
Campomanes E 141 A5
Campomarino I 170 B3
Campo Molino I 133 A3
Campomono F 180 B1
Campo Real E 151 B4
Camporeale I 176 B2
Camporeggiano I 136 B1
Camporrells E 145 C4
Camporrobles E 158 B2
Campos P 148 A2
Camposa P 148 A1
Camposampiero I 121 B4
Camposanto I 121 C4
Campos del Port E 167 B3
Camposines E 153 A4
Campotéjar E 163 A4
Campotosto I 169 A3
Campo Túres I 108 C2
Camprodón E 147 B3
Campsegret F 129 B3
Camrose GB 39 C1
Camuñas E 157 A4
Çamyolu TR 189 C7
Çan TR 186 B2
Cana I 135 C4
Cañada del Hoyo E 158 B2
Cañadajuncosa E 158 B1
Cañada Rosal E 162 A2
Čanak HR 123 C4
Çanakkale TR 186 B1
Canale I 119 C4
Canales
Asturias E 141 B5
Castellón de la Plana E 159 B3
Canals E 159 C3
Canal San Bovo I 121 A4
Cañamares E 152 B1
Cañamero E 156 A2
Cañar E 163 B4
Cañate la Real E 162 B2
Cañaveral E 155 B4
Cañaveral de León E 161 A3
Cañaveras E 152 B1
Cañaveruelas E 151 B5
Canazei I 108 C2
Cancale F 88 B2
Cancellara I 172 B1
Cancello ed Arnone I 170 B2
Cancon F 129 B3
Canda E 141 B4
Candamil E 140 A3
Candanchu E 145 B3
Çandarlı TR 186 D1
Candas E 141 A5
Candasnos E 153 A4
Candé F 101 B4
Candela I 172 A1
Candelario E 150 B2
Candeleda E 150 B2
Cándia Lomellina I 120 B1
Candide Casamazzagno I 109 C3
Candin E 141 B4
Candosa P 148 B2
Canecas P 154 C1
Canelli I 119 C5
Canena E 157 B4
Canencia E 151 B4
Canero E 141 A4
Canet F 130 B2
Canet de Mar E 147 C3
Canet d'en Berenguer E 159 B3
Cañete E 158 A2
Cañete de las Torres E 163 A3
Canet-Plage F 146 B4
Canfranc E 145 B3
Cangas
Lugo E 141 A3
Pontevedra E 140 B2
Cangas de Narcea E 141 A4
Cangas de Onís E 142 A1
Canha P 154 C2
Canhestros P 160 A1
Canicattì I 176 B2
Canicattini Bagni I 177 B4
Canicosa de la Sierra E 143 C3
Caniles E 164 B2
Canillas de Aceituno E 163 B3
Canino I 168 A1
Canisy F 88 A2
Cañizal E 150 A2
Cañizo E 142 C1
Canjáyar E 164 C2
Çankırı TR 23 A7
Cannai I 179 C2
Cannara I 136 B1
Cánnero Riviera I 120 A1
Cannes F 132 B3
Canneto
Sicilia I 177 A3
Toscana I 135 B3
Canneto sull'Oglio I 120 B3
Cannich GB 32 D2
Cannóbio I 120 A1
Cannock GB 40 C1
Canonbie GB 36 A4
Canosa di Púglia I 171 B4
Can Pastilla E 166 B2
C'an Picafort E 167 B3
Cantalapiedra E 150 A2
Cantalejo E 151 A4
Cantalgallo E 161 A3
Cantalice I 169 A2
Cantalpino E 150 A2
Cantalupo in Sabina I 168 A2
Cantanhede P 148 B1
Cantavieja E 153 B3
Čantavir SRB 126 B1
Canterbury GB 45 B5
Cantiano I 136 B1
Cantillana E 162 A2
Cantiveros E 150 B3
Cantoria E 164 B2
Cantù I 120 B2
Canvey GB 45 B4
Cany-Barville F 89 A4
Canyet de Mar E 147 C3
Caol GB 34 B2
Cáorle I 122 B1
Caorso I 120 B2
Capáccio I 172 B1
Capaci I 176 A2
Capálbio I 168 A1
Capánnori I 134 B3
Caparde BIH 139 A4
Caparroso E 144 B2
Capbreton F 128 C1
Capdenac-Gare F 116 C2
Capdepera E 167 B3
Cap-de-Pin F 128 B2
Capel Curig GB 38 A3
Capellades E 147 C2
Capena I 168 A2
Capendu F 146 A3
Capestang F 130 B2
Capestrano I 169 A3
Cap Ferret F 128 B1
Capileira E 163 B4
Capinha P 148 B2
Ca'Pisani I 122 C1
Capistrello I 169 B3
Capizzi I 177 B3
Čaplje BIH 124 C2
Čapljina BIH 139 B3
Capo di Ponte I 120 A3
Caposile I 122 B1
Capoterra I 179 C2
Cappamore IRL 29 B3
Cappeln D 71 B5
Cappoquin IRL 29 B4
Capracotta I 169 B4
Capránica I 168 A2
Caprarola I 168 A2
Capretta I 135 C5
Capri I 170 C2
Capriati a Volturno I 170 B2
Caprino Veronese I 121 B3
Captieux F 128 B2
Cápua I 170 B2
Capurso I 173 A2
Capvern F 145 A4
Carabaña E 151 B4
Carabias E 151 A4
Caracal RO 17 C6
Caracenilla E 152 B1
Caráglio I 133 A3
Caraman F 146 A2
Caramánico Terme I 169 A4
Caranga E 141 A4
Caranguejeira P 154 B2
Caransebeş RO 16 C5
Carantec F 100 A2
Carapelle I 171 B3

Carasco I 134 A2
Carate Brianza I 120 B2
Caravaca de la Cruz E 164 A3
Caravàggio I 120 B2
Carbajal E 163 B3
Carbajo E 155 B3
Carballeda E 140 B3
Carballeda de Avia E 140 B2
Carballo E 140 A2
Carbis Bay GB 42 B1
Carbon-Blanc F 128 B2
Carbonera de Frentes E 143 C4
Carboneras E 164 C3
Carboneras de Guadazaón E 158 B2
Carbonero el Mayor E 151 A3
Carboneros E 157 B4
Carbónia I 179 C2
Carbonin I 108 C3
Carbonne F 146 A2
Carbost
Highland GB 31 B2
Highland GB 31 B2
Carcaboso E 149 B3
Carcabuey E 163 A3
Carcaixent E 159 B3
Carcans F 128 A1
Carcans-Plage F 128 A1
Carção P 149 A3
Carcar E 144 B2
Cárcare I 133 A4
Carcassonne F 146 A3
Carcastillo E 144 B2
Carcedo de Burgos E 143 B3
Carcelén E 159 B2
Carcès F 132 B2
Carchelejo E 163 A4
Çardak
Çanakkale TR 186 B1
Denizli TR 189 B4
Cardedeu E 147 C3
Cardeña E 157 B3
Cardenete E 158 B2
Cardeñosa E 150 B3
Cardeto I 175 C1
Cardiff GB 39 C3
Cardigan GB 39 B2
Cardona E 147 C2
Cardosos P 154 B2
Carei RO 16 B5
Carentan F 88 A2
Carentoir F 101 B3
Careri I 175 C2
Carevdar HR 124 A2
Cargèse F 180 A1
Carhaix-Plouguer F 100 A2
Caria P 148 B2
Cariati I 174 B2
Carignan F 91 B5
Carignano I 119 C4
Cariñena E 152 A2
Carini I 176 A2
Cariño E 140 A3
Carínola I 170 B1
Carisbrooke GB 44 C2
Carlabhagh GB 31 A2
Carlepont F 90 B3
Carlet E 159 B3
Carlingford IRL 27 B4
Carlisle GB 36 B4
Carloforte I 179 C2
Carlópoli I 175 B2
Carlow
D 65 C3
IRL 30 B2
Carlton GB 40 C2
Carluke GB 35 C4
Carmagnola I 119 C4
Carmarthen GB 39 C2
Carmaux F 130 A1
Carmena E 150 C3
Cármenes E 142 B1
Carmine I 133 A3
Carmona E 162 A2
Carmonita E 155 B4
Carmyllie GB 35 B5
Carnac F 100 B2
Carndonagh IRL 27 A3
Carnew IRL 30 B2
Carnforth GB 37 B4
Cárnia I 122 A2
Carnlough GB 27 B5
Carno GB 39 B3
Carnon Plage F 131 B2
Carnota E 140 B1
Carnoustie GB 35 B5
Carnwath GB 35 C4
Carolei I 174 B2
Carolinensiel D 71 A4
Carolles F 88 B2
Carona I 120 A2
Caronía I 177 A3
Carovigno I 173 B3
Carovilli I 170 B2
Carpaneto Piacentino I 120 C2
Carpegna I 135 B5
Carpenédolo I 121 B3
Carpentras F 131 A4
Carpi I 121 C3
Carpignano Sésia I 119 B5
Carpineti I 134 A3
Carpineto Romano I 169 B3
Cărpinis RO 126 B2
Carpino I 171 B3
Carpinone I 170 B2
Carpio E 150 A2
Carquefou F 101 B4
Carqueiranne F 132 B2
Carral E 140 A2
Carranque E 151 B4
Carrapichana P 148 B2
Carrara I 134 A3
Carraroe IRL 28 A2
Carrascalejo E 156 A2
Carrascosa del Campo E 151 B5
Carratraca E 162 B3
Carrazeda de Ansiães P 148 A2
Carrazedo de Montenegro P 148 A2
Carrbridge GB 32 D3
Carregal do Sal P 148 B1
Carreña E 142 A2
Carrick IRL 26 B2
Carrickart IRL 26 A3
Carrickfergus GB 27 B5
Carrickmacross IRL 27 C4
Carrick-on-Shannon IRL 26 C2
Carrick-on-Suir IRL 30 B1
Carrigallen IRL 27 C3
Carrión E 161 B3
Carrión de Calatrava E 157 A4
Carrión de los Condes E 142 B2
Carrizo de la Ribera E 141 B5
Carrizosa E 157 B5
Carro F 131 B4
Carrocera E 142 B1
Carros F 133 B3
Carrouge CH 106 C1
Carrouges F 89 B3
Carrù I 133 A3
Carryduff GB 27 B5
Carry-le-Rouet F 131 B4
Carsóli I 169 A3
Carsphairn GB 36 A2
Cartagena E 165 B4
Cártama E 163 B3
Cartaxo P 154 B2
Cartaya E 161 B2
Carteret F 88 A2
Cartes E 142 A2
Carúnchio I 170 B2
Carviçães P 149 A3
Carvin F 78 B2
Carvoeira P 154 B1
Carvoeiro P 160 B1
Casabermeja E 163 B3
Casa Branca
Portalegre P 154 C3
Setúbal P 154 C2
Casacalenda I 170 B2
Casa Castalda I 136 B1
Casaio E 141 B4
Casa l'Abate I 173 B4
Casalarreina E 143 B4
Casalbordino I 169 A4
Casalborgone I 119 B4
Casalbuono I 174 A1
Casalbuttano ed Uniti I 120 B2
Casàl di Principe I 170 B2
Casalécchio di Reno I 135 A4
Casale Monferrato I 119 B5
Casalina I 136 C1
Casalmaggiore I 121 C3
Casalnuovo Monterotaro I 170 B3
Casaloldo I 121 B3
Casalpusterlengo I 120 B2
Casamássima I 173 B2
Casamicciola Terme I 170 C1
Casamozza F 180 A2
Casarabonela E 162 B3
Casarano I 173 B4
Casar de Cáceres E 155 B4
Casar de Palomero E 149 B3
Casarejos E 143 C3
Casares E 162 B2
Casares de las Hurdes E 149 B3
Casariche E 163 A3
Casarrubios del Monte E 151 B3
Casas de Don Pedro E 156 A2
Casas de Fernando Alonso E 158 B1
Casas de Haro E 158 B1
Casas de Juan Gil E 159 B2
Casas del Juan Núñez E 158 B2
Casas del Puerto E 159 C2
Casas del Rio E 159 B2
Casas de Millán E 155 B4
Casas de Reina E 156 B2
Casas de Ves E 159 B2
Casas-Ibáñez E 158 B2
Casasimarro E 158 B1
Casas Nuevas E 164 B3
Casasola E 150 B3
Casasola de Arión E 150 A2
Casasuertes E 142 A2
Casatejada E 150 C2
Casavieja E 150 B3
Casazza I 120 B2
Cascais P 154 C1
Cascante E 144 C2
Cascante del Rio E 152 B2
Cáscia I 169 A3
Casciana Terme I 134 B3
Cáscina I 134 B3
Cáseda E 144 B2
Casekow D 74 A3
Casella I 134 A2
Caselle Torinese I 119 B4
Casemurate I 135 A5
Casenove I 136 C1
Caseres E 153 A4
Caserío Benali E 159 B3
Caserta I 170 B2
Casével P 160 B1
Cashel IRL 29 B4
Casillas E 150 B3
Casillas de Coria E 155 B4
Casina I 134 A3
Casinos E 159 B3
Čáslav CZ 97 B3
Cásola Valsénio I 135 A4
Cásole d'Elsa I 135 B4
Cásoli I 169 A4
Casória I 170 C2
Caspe E 153 A3
Cassàde la Selva E 147 C3
Cassagnas F 130 A2
Cassagnes-Bégonhès F 130 A1
Cassano allo Iónio I 174 B2
Cassano d'Adda I 120 B2
Cassano delle Murge I 171 C4
Cassano Magnago I 120 B1
Cassano Spinola I 120 C1
Cassel F 78 B2
Cassíbile I 177 C4
Cassine I 119 C5
Cassino I 169 B3
Cassis F 132 B1
Cassolnovo I 120 B1
Cassuéjouls F 116 C2
Častá SK 98 C1
Castagnaro I 121 B4
Castagneto Carducci I 134 B3
Castagnola CH 120 A1
Castalla E 159 C3
Castañar de Ibor E 156 A2
Castanheira de Pêra P 154 A2
Cástano Primo I 120 B1
Castasegna CH 120 A2
Castéggio I 120 B2
Casteição P 148 B2
Castejón E 144 B2
Castejón de Monegros E 153 A3
Castejón de Sos E 145 B4
Castejón de Valdejasa E 144 C3
Castèl Baronia I 172 A1
Castel Bolognese I 135 A4
Castelbuono I 177 B3
Casteldáccia I 176 A2
Castel d'Aiano I 135 A3
Castel d'Ario I 121 B3
Castel de Cabra E 153 B3
Casteldelfino I 132 A3
Castél del Monte I 169 A3
Castel del Piano I 135 C4
Castel di Iúdica I 177 B3
Castel di Rio I 135 A4
Castèl di Sangro I 169 B4
Castél di Tora I 169 A2
Castelfidardo I 136 B2
Castelfiorentino I 135 B3
Castelforte I 169 B3
Castelfranco Emília I 121 C4
Castelfranco in Miscano I 170 B3
Castelfranco Véneto I 121 B4
Castèl Frentano I 169 A4
Casteljaloux F 128 B3
Castellabate I 170 C2
Castellammare del Golfo I 176 A1
Castellammare di Stábia I 170 C2
Castellamonte I 119 B4
Castellana Grotte I 173 B3
Castellane F 132 B2
Castellaneta I 173 B2
Castellaneta Marina I 173 B2
Castellar E 157 B4
Castellarano I 135 A3
Castellar de la Frontera E 162 B2
Castellar de la Ribera E 147 B2
Castellar del Vallés E 147 C3
Castellar de Santiago E 157 B4
Castell Arquato I 120 C2
Castell'Azzara I 135 C4
Castellbell i Villar E 147 C2
Castelldans E 153 A4
Castell de Cabres E 153 B4
Castell de Castells E 159 C3
Castelldefels E 147 C2
Castell de Ferro E 163 B4
Castelleone I 120 B2
Castellet E 147 C2
Castelletto di Brenzone I 121 B3
Castellfollit de la Roca E 147 B3
Castellfollit de Riubregos E 147 C2
Castellfort E 153 B3
Castellina in Chianti I 135 B4
Castellina Marittima I 134 B3
Castellóde Farfaña E 145 C4
Castellóde la Plana E 159 B3
Castello d'Empùries E 147 B4
Castello di Fiemme I 121 A4
Castelloli E 147 C2
Castellón de Rugat E 159 C3
Castellote E 153 B3
Castello Tesino I 121 A4
Castellterçol E 147 C3
Castellúcchio I 121 B3
Castellúccio de'Sáuri I 171 B3
Castelluccio Inferiore I 174 B1
Castelmassa I 121 B4
Castelmáuro I 170 B2
Castelmoron-sur-Lot F 129 B3
Castelnaudary F 146 A2
Castelnau-de-Médoc F 128 A2
Castelnau-de-Montmirail F 129 C4
Castelnau-Magnoac F 145 A4
Castelnau-Montratier F 129 B4
Castelnou E 153 A3
Castelnovo ne'Monti I 134 A3
Castelnuovo Berardenga I 135 B4
Castelnuovo della Dáunia I 170 B3
Castelnuovo di Garfagnana I 134 A3
Castelnuovo di Val di Cécina I 135 B3
Castelnuovo Don Bosco I 119 B4
Castelnuovo Scrivia I 120 C1
Castelo Branco
Bragança P 149 A3
Castelo Branco P 155 B3
Castelo de Paiva P 148 A1
Castelo de Vide P 155 B3
Castelo do Neiva P 148 A1
Castelo Mendo P 149 B3
Castelraimondo I 136 B2
Castel San Gimignano I 135 B4
Castèl San Giovanni I 120 B2
Castèl San Pietro Terme I 135 A4
Castelsantángelo I 136 C2
Castél Sant'Elía I 168 A2
Castelsaraceno I 174 A1
Castelsardo I 178 B2
Castelsarrasin F 129 B4
Castelserás E 153 B3
Casteltérmini I 176 B2
Castelvecchio Subéquo I 169 A3
Castelvetrano I 176 B1
Castél Volturno I 170 B1
Castenédolo I 120 B3
Castets F 128 C1
Castiádas I 179 C3
Castiglioncello I 134 B3
Castiglione I 169 A3
Castiglione Chiavarese I 134 A2
Castiglione d'Adda I 120 B2
Castiglione dei Pepoli I 135 A4
Castiglione del Lago I 135 B5
Castiglione della Pescáia I 135 C3
Castiglione delle Stiviere I 121 B3
Castiglione di Sicília I 177 B4
Castiglione d'Órcia I 135 B4
Castiglione Messer Marino I 170 B2
Castiglione Messer Raimondo I 169 A3
Castiglion Fibocchi I 135 B4
Castiglion Fiorentino I 135 B4
Castilblanco E 156 A2
Castilblanco de los Arroyos E 161 B4
Castil de Peones E 143 B3
Castilfrio de la Sierra E 144 C1
Castilgaleu E 145 B4
Castilisar E 144 B2
Castilleja E 161 B3
Castillejar E 164 B2
Castillejo de Martin Viejo E 149 B3
Castillejo de Mesleón E 151 A4
Castillejo de Robledo E 151 A4
Castillo de Bayuela E 150 B3
Castillo de Locubín E 163 A4
Castillonès F 129 B3
Castillon-la-Bataille F 128 B2
Castillon-Len-Couserans F 146 B2
Castillonroy E 145 C4
Castilruiz E 144 C1
Castione CH 120 A2
Castions di Strada I 122 B2
Castirla F 180 A2
Castlebar IRL 28 A2
Castlebellingham IRL 27 C4
Castleblaney IRL 27 B4
Castlebridge IRL 30 B2
Castle Cary GB 43 A4
Castlecomer IRL 30 B1
Castlederg GB 27 B3
Castledermot IRL 30 B2
Castle Douglas GB 36 B3
Castleford GB 40 B2
Castleisland IRL 29 B2
Castlemaine IRL 29 B2
Castlemartyr IRL 29 C3
Castlepollard IRL 30 A1
Castlerea IRL 28 A3
Castleton GB 40 B2
Castletown
Highland GB 32 C3
Isle of Man GB 36 B2
Castletown Bearhaven IRL 29 C2
Castletownroche IRL 29 B3
Castlewellan GB 27 B5
Casto I 120 B3
Castrejón E 150 A2
Castrelo del Valle E 141 B3
Castres F 130 B1
Castricum NL 70 B1
Castries F 131 B2
Castrignano del Capo I 173 C4
Castril E 164 B2
Castrillo de Duero E 151 A4
Castrillo de la Vega E 143 C3
Castrillo de Onielo E 142 C2
Castro
E 142 A2
I 173 B4
Castrocabón E 141 B5
Castro-Caldelas E 141 B3
Castrocaro Terme I 135 A4
Castrocontrigo E 141 B4
Castro Daire P 148 B2
Castro dei Volsci I 169 B3
Castro del Río E 163 A3
Castro de Rey E 141 A3
Castrofilippo I 176 B2
Castrogonzaio E 142 B1
Castrojeriz E 142 B2
Castro Laboreiro P 140 B2
Castro Marim P 160 B2
Castromonte E 142 C1
Castromudarra E 142 B1
Castronuevo E 142 C1
Castronuño E 150 A2
Castropol E 141 A3
Castroreale I 177 A4
Castroserracin E 151 A4
Castro-Urdiales E 143 A3
Castroverde E 141 A3
Castro Verde P 160 B1
Castroverde de Campos E 142 C1
Castroverde de Cerrato E 142 C2
Castrovíllari I 174 B2
Castuera E 156 B2
Catadau E 159 B3
Cataéggio I 120 A2
Çatalca TR 186 A3
Catallar TR 189 C5
Çatalzeytin TR 23 A8
Catánia I 177 B4
Catanzaro I 175 C2
Catanzaro Marina I 175 C2
Catarroja E 159 B3
Catarruchos P 148 B1
Catcleugh GB 37 A4
Catenanuova I 177 B3
Caterham GB 44 B3
Cati E 153 B4
Čatići BIH 139 A4
Catignano I 169 A3
Catillon F 91 A3
Catoira E 140 B2
Caton GB 37 B4
Catral E 165 A4
Catterick GB 37 B5
Cattólica I 136 B1
Cattólica Eraclea I 176 B2
Catton GB 37 B4
Caudebec-en-Caux F 89 A4
Caudete E 159 C3
Caudete de las Fuentes E 159 B2
Caudiel E 159 B3
Caudiès-de-Fenouillèdes F 146 B3
Caudry F 91 A3
Caulkerbush GB 36 B3
Caulnes F 101 A3
Caulónia I 175 C2
Caumont-l'Evente F 88 A3
Caunes-Minervois F 146 A3
Cauro F 180 B1
Caussade F 129 B4
Causse-de-la-Selle F 130 B2
Cauterets F 145 B3
Cava de Tirreni I 170 C2
Cavaglia I 119 B5
Cavaillon F 131 B4
Cavalaire-sur-Mer F 132 B2
Cavaleiro P 160 B1
Cavalese I 121 A4
Cavallermaggiore I 119 C4
Cavallino I 122 B1
Cavan IRL 27 C3
Cavárzere I 121 B5
Çavdarhisar TR 187 C4
Çavdır TR 189 B4
Cavernães P 148 B2
Cavezzo I 121 C4
Cavignac F 128 A2
Čavle HR 123 B3
Cavo I 134 C3
Cavour I 119 C4
Cawdor GB 32 D3
Çay TR 187 D6
Çaycuma TR 187 A7
Cayeux-sur-Mer F 78 B1
Cayiralan TR 23 B8
Çayırhan TR 187 B6
Caylus F 129 B4
Cayres F 117 C3
Cazalilla E 157 C4
Cazalla de la Sierra E 156 C2
Cazals F 129 B4
Cazanuecos E 142 B1
Cazaubon F 128 C2
Cazaux F 128 B1
Cazavet F 146 A2
Cazères F 146 A2
Cazin BIH 124 C1
Çazis CH 107 C4
Čazma HR 124 B2
Cazo E 142 A1
Cazorla E 164 B2
Cazouls-lès-Béziers F 130 B2
Cea
León E 142 B1
Orense E 140 B3
Ceánuri E 143 A4
Ceauce F 88 B3
Cebolla E 150 C3
Čebovce SK 112 A3
Cebreros E 150 B3
Čečava BIH 125 C3
Ceccano I 169 B3
Cece H 112 C2
Cecenowo PL 68 A2
Čechtice CZ 96 B3
Čechtín CZ 97 B3
Cécina I 134 B3
Ceclavín E 155 B4
Cedégolo I 120 A3
Cedeira E 140 A2
Cedillo E 155 B3
Cedillo del Condado E 151 B4
Cedrillas E 153 B3
Cedynia PL 74 B3
Cée E 140 B1
Cefalù I 177 A3
Céggia I 122 B1
Cegléd H 113 B3

Ceglédbercel H 112 B3
Céglie Messápica I 173 B3
Cehegín E 164 A3
Ceilhes-et-Rocozels F 130 B2
Ceinos de Campos E 142 B1
Ceira P 148 B1
Čejč CZ 97 C4
Cekcyn PL 76 A3
Čela BIH 124 C2
Čelákovice CZ 84 B2
Celano I 169 A3
Celanova E 140 B3
Celbridge IRL 30 A2
Čelebič BIH 138 B2
Celenza Valfortore I 170 B2
Čelić BIH 125 C4
Čelinac BIH 124 C3
Celje SLO 123 A4
Cella E 152 B2
Celldömölk H 111 B4
Celle D 72 B3
Celle Ligure I 133 A4
Celles B 79 B4
Celles-sur-Belle F 115 B3
Cellino San Marco I 173 B3
Celorico da Beira P 148 B2
Celorico de Basto P 148 A1
Çeltik TR 187 C6
Çeltikçi TR 189 B5
Cemaes GB 38 A2
Cembra I 121 A4
Čemerno BIH 139 B4
Cenad RO 126 A2
Cencenighe Agordino I 121 A4
Cenei RO 126 B2
Ceneselli I 121 B4
Cenicero E 143 B4
Cenicientos E 150 B3
Censeau F 105 C5
Čenta SRB 126 B2
Centallo I 133 A3
Centelles E 147 C3
Cento I 121 C4
Centúripe I 177 B3
Cepeda la Mora E 150 B2
Cépet F 129 C4
Čepin HR 125 B4
Čepinski Martinci HR 125 B4
Cepovan SLO 122 A2
Ceprano I 169 B3
Čeralije HR 125 B3
Cerami I 177 B3
Cerano I 120 B1
Cérans Foulletourte F 102 B2
Ceraso I 172 B1
Cerbaia I 135 B4
Cerbère F 146 B4
Cercadillo E 151 A5
Cercal
Lisboa P 154 B1
Setúbal P 160 B1
Čerčany CZ 96 B2
Cerceda E 151 B4
Cercedilla E 151 B3
Cercemaggiore I 170 B2
Cercs E 147 B2
Cercy-la-Tour F 104 C2
Cerda I 176 B2
Cerdedo E 140 B2
Cerdeira P 149 B2
Cerdon F 103 B4
Cerea I 121 B4
Ceres
GB 35 B5
I 119 B4
Cerese I 121 B3
Ceresole-Reale I 119 B4
Cereste F 132 B1
Céret F 146 B3
Cerezo de Abajo E 151 A4
Cerezo de Riotirón E 143 B3
Cerfontaine B 79 B4
Cergy F 90 B2
Cerignola I 171 B3
Cérilly F 103 C4
Cerisiers F 104 A2
Cerizay F 114 B3
Çerkeş TR 23 A7
Çerkezköy TR 186 A3
Cerkije SLO 123 A3
Cerknica SLO 123 B3
Cerkno SLO 122 A2
Cerkwica PL 67 B4
Cerna HR 125 B4
Černá Hora CZ 97 B4
Cernavodă RO 17 C8
Cernay F 106 B2
Cerne Abbas GB 43 B4
Cernégula E 143 B3
Cernik HR 124 B3
Cernóbbio I 120 B2
Černošin CZ 95 B4
Cernovice CZ 96 B2
Cérons F 128 B2
Cerovlje HR 123 B3
Cerovo SK 99 C3
Cerqueto I 135 C5
Cerralbo E 149 B3
Cerreto d'Esi I 136 B1
Cerreto Sannita I 170 B2
Cerrigydrudion GB 38 A3
Cërrik AL 182 B1
Cerro Muriano E 156 B3
Certaldo I 135 B4
Certosa di Pésio I 133 A3
Cerva P 148 A2
Cervaro I 169 B3
Cervatos de la Cueza E 142 B2
Červena Řečice CZ 97 B3
Červená-Skala SK 99 C4
Červená Voda CZ 97 A4
Cerveny Kostelec CZ 85 B4
Cervera E 147 C2
Cervera de la Cañada E 152 A2
Cervera del Llano E 158 B1
Cervera del Río Alhama E 144 B2
Cervera de Pisuerga E 142 B2
Cervéteri I 168 B2
Cérvia I 135 A5
Cerviáde les Garriques E 147 C1
Cervignano del Friuli I 122 B2
Cervinara I 170 B2
Cervione F 180 A2
Cervo E 141 A3
Cervon F 104 B2
Cesana Torinese I 119 C3
Cesarica HR 137 A4
Cesarò I 177 B3
Cesena I 135 A5
Cesenático I 135 A5
Cēsis LV 8 D4
Česká Belá CZ 97 B3
Česká Kamenice CZ 84 B2
Česká Lípa CZ 84 B2
Česká Skalice CZ 85 B4
Česká Třebová CZ 97 B4
České Budějovice CZ 96 C2
České Velenice CZ 96 C2
Český Brod CZ 96 A2
Český Dub CZ 84 B2
Český Krumlov CZ 96 C2
Český Těšín CZ 98 B2
Čeśljeva Bara SRB 127 C3
Çeşme TR 188 A1
Cessenon F 130 B2
Cesson-Sévigné F 101 A4
Cestas F 128 B2
Čestobrodica SRB 127 D2
Cesuras E 140 A2
Cetina E 152 A2
Cetin Grad HR 123 B4
Cetinje MNE 16 D3
Cetraro I 174 B1
Ceuti E 165 A3
Ceva I 133 A4
Cevico de la Torre E 142 C2
Cevico Navero E 142 C2
Cevins F 118 B3
Cévio CH 119 A5
Cevizli TR 189 B6
Cewice PL 68 A2
Ceylan TR 189 C4
Ceyrat F 116 B3
Ceyzériat F 118 A2
Chaam NL 79 A4
Chabanais F 115 C4
Chabeuil F 117 C5
Chabielice PL 86 A3
Chablis F 104 B2
Châbons F 118 B2
Chabówka PL 99 B3
Chabreloche F 117 B3
Chabris F 103 B3
Chagford GB 42 B3
Chagny F 105 C3
Chagoda RUS 9 C9
Chaherrero E 150 B3
Chailland F 88 B3
Chaillé-les-Marais F 114 B2
Chailles F 103 B3
Chailley F 104 A2
Chalabre F 146 B3
Chalais F 128 A3
Chalamont F 118 B2
Châlette-sur-Loing F 103 A4
Chalindrey F 105 B4
Challacombe GB 42 A3
Challans F 114 B2
Challes-les-Eaux F 118 B2
Chalmazel F 117 B3
Chalmoux F 104 C2
Chalonnes-sur-Loire F 102 B1
Châlons-en-Champagne F 91 C4
Chalon-sur-Saône F 105 C3
Chalupy PL 69 A3
Châlus F 115 C4
Cham
CH 106 B3
D 95 B4
Chamberet F 116 B1
Chambéry F 118 B2
Chambilly F 117 A4
Chambley F 92 B1
Chambly F 90 B2
Chambois F 89 B4
Chambon-sur-Lac F 116 B2
Chambon-sur-Voueize F 116 A2
Chambord F 103 B3
Chamborigaud F 131 A2
Chamboulive F 116 B1
Chamerau D 95 B4
Chamonix-Mont Blanc F 119 B3
Chamoux-sur-Gelon F 118 B3
Champagnac-le-Vieux F 117 B3
Champagney F 106 B1
Champagnole F 105 C4
Champagny-Mouton F 115 B4
Champaubert F 91 C3
Champdeniers-St Denis F 114 B3
Champdieu F 117 B4
Champdôtre F 105 B4
Champeix F 116 B3
Champéry CH 119 A3
Champigne F 102 B1
Champignelles F 104 B2
Champigny-sur-Veude F 102 B2
Champlitte-et-le-Prelot F 105 B4
Champoluc I 119 B4
Champoly F 117 B3
Champorcher I 119 B4
Champrond-en-Gâtine F 89 B5
Champs-sur-Tarentaine F 116 B2
Champs-sur-Yonne F 104 B2
Champtoceaux F 101 B4
Chamrousse F 118 B2
Chamusca P 154 B2
Chanac F 130 A2
Chanaleilles F 117 C3
Chandler's Ford GB 44 C2
Chandra GR 185 D7
Chandrexa de Queixa E 141 B3
Chañe E 150 A3
Changy F 117 A3
Chania GR 185 D5
Channes F 104 B3
Chantada E 140 B3
Chantelle F 116 A3
Chantenay-St Imbert F 104 C2
Chanteuges F 117 B3
Chantilly F 90 B2
Chantonnay F 114 B2
Chão de Codes P 154 B2
Chaource F 104 A3
Chapa E 140 B2
Chapareillan F 118 B2
Chapel en le Frith GB 40 B2
Chapelle Royale F 103 A3
Chapelle-St Laurent F 102 C1
Charbonnat F 104 C3
Chard GB 43 B4
Charenton-du-Cher F 103 C4
Charlbury GB 44 B2
Charleroi B 79 B4
Charlestown
GB 42 B2
IRL 26 C2
Charlestown of Aberlour GB 32 D3
Charleville IRL 29 B3
Charleville-Mézières F 91 B4
Charlieu F 117 A4
Charlottenberg S 49 C4
Charlton Kings GB 44 B1
Charly F 90 C3
Charmes F 92 C2
Charmes-sur-Rhône F 117 C4
Charmey CH 106 C2
Charminster GB 43 B4
Charmont-en-Beauce F 103 A4
Charny F 104 B2
Charolles F 117 A4
Chârost F 103 C4
Charquemont F 106 B1
Charrin F 104 C2
Charroux F 115 B4
Chartres F 90 C1
Charzykow PL 68 B2
Chasseneuil-sur-Bonnieure F 115 C4
Chassigny F 105 B4
Château-Arnoux F 132 A2
Châteaubernard F 115 C3
Châteaubourg F 101 A4
Châteaubriant F 101 B4
Château-Chinon F 104 B2
Château-d'Oex CH 106 C2
Château-d'Olonne F 114 B2
Château-du-Loir F 102 B2
Châteaudun F 103 A3
Châteaugiron F 101 A4
Château-Gontier F 102 B1
Château-Landon F 103 A4
Château-la-Vallière F 102 B2
Château-l'Evêque F 129 A3
Châteaulin F 100 A1
Châteaumeillant F 103 C4
Châteauneuf
Nièvre F 104 B2
Saône-et-Loire F 117 A4
Châteauneuf-de-Randon F 117 C3
Châteauneuf-d'Ille-et-Vilaine F 88 B2
Châteauneuf-du-Faou F 100 A2
Châteauneuf-du-Pape F 131 A3
Châteauneuf-en-Thymerais F 89 B5
Châteauneuf la-Forêt F 116 B1
Châteauneuf-le-Rouge F 132 B1
Châteauneuf-sur-Charente F 115 C3
Châteauneuf-sur-Cher F 103 C4
Châteauneuf-sur-Loire F 103 B4
Châteauneuf-sur-Sarthe F 102 B1
Châteauponsac F 115 B5
Château-Porcien F 91 B4
Châteauredon F 132 A2
Châteaurenard
Bouches du Rhône F 131 B3
Loiret F 104 B1
Château-Renault F 102 B2
Châteauroux F 103 C3
Châteauroux-les-Alpes F 118 C3
Château-Salins F 92 C2
Château-Thierry F 91 B3
Châteauvillain F 105 A3
Châtel F 119 A3
Châtelaillon-Plage F 114 B2
Châtelaudren F 100 A3
Châtel-Censoir F 104 B2
Châtel-de-Neuvre F 116 A3
Châtelet B 79 B4
Châtelguyon F 116 B3
Châtellerault F 115 B4
Châtel-Montagne F 117 A3
Châtel-St Denis CH 106 C1
Châtel-sur-Moselle F 92 C2
Châtelus-Malvaleix F 116 A2
Châtenois F 105 A4
Châtenois-les-Forges F 106 B1
Chatham GB 45 B4
Châtillon I 119 B4
Châtillon-Coligny F 103 B4
Châtillon-en-Bazois F 104 B2
Châtillon-en-Diois F 118 C2
Châtillon-sur Chalaronne F 117 A4
Châtillon-sur-Indre F 103 C3
Châtillon-sur-Loire F 103 B4
Châtillon-sur-Marne F 91 B3
Châtillon-sur-Seine F 104 B3
Châtres F 91 C3
Chatteris GB 45 A4
Chatton GB 37 A5
Chauchina E 163 A4
Chaudes-Aigues F 116 C3
Chaudrey F 91 C4
Chauffailles F 117 A4
Chaulnes F 90 B2
Chaument Gistoux B 79 B4
Chaumergy F 105 C4
Chaumont F 105 A4
Chaumont-en-Vexin F 90 B1
Chaumont-Porcien F 91 B4
Chaumont-sur-Aire F 91 C5
Chaumont-sur-Loire F 103 B3
Chaunay F 115 B4
Chauny F 90 B3
Chaussin F 105 C4
Chauvigny F 115 B4
Chavagnes-en-Paillers F 114 B2
Chavanges F 91 C4
Chaves P 148 A2
Chavignon F 91 B3
Chazelles-sur-Lyon F 117 B4
Chazey-Bons F 118 B2
Cheadle
Greater Manchester GB 40 B1
Staffordshire GB 40 C2
Cheb CZ 83 B4
Chebsara RUS 9 C11
Checa E 152 B2
Chęciny PL 87 B4
Cheddar GB 43 A4
Cheddleton GB 40 B1
Chef-Boutonne F 115 B3
Cheles E 155 C3
Chella E 159 B3
Chelles F 90 C2
Chełm PL 13 C5
Chełmno
Kujawsko-Pomorskie PL 76 A3
Wielkopolskie PL 76 B3
Chelmsford GB 45 B4
Chelmuzhi RUS 9 A9
Chełmża PL 76 A3
Cheltenham GB 44 B1
Chelva E 159 B2
Chémery F 103 B3
Chemery-sur-Bar F 91 B4
Chemillé F 102 B1
Chemin F 105 C4
Chemnitz D 83 B4
Chénerailles F 116 A2
Cheniménil F 105 A5
Chenonceaux F 103 B3
Chenôve F 105 B3
Chepelare BG 183 B6
Chepstow GB 39 C4
Chera E 159 B3
Cherasco I 119 C4
Cherbonnières F 115 C3
Cherbourg F 88 A2
Cherchiara di Calábria I 174 B2
Cherepovets RUS 9 C10
Chernihiv UA 13 C9
Chernivtsi UA 17 A6
Chernobyl = Chornobyl UA 13 C9
Chernyakhovsk RUS 12 A4
Chéroy F 104 A1
Cherven BY 13 B8
Chervonohrad UA 13 C6
Cherykaw BY 13 B9
Chesham GB 44 B3
Cheshunt GB 44 B3
Chessy-lès-Pres F 104 A2
Cheste E 159 B3
Chester GB 38 A4
Chesterfield GB 40 B2
Chester-le-Street GB 37 B5
Chevagnes F 104 C2
Chevanceaux F 115 C3
Chevillon F 91 C5
Chevilly F 103 A3
Chew Magna GB 43 A4
Chézery-Forens F 118 A2
Chialamberto I 119 B4
Chiampo I 121 B4
Chianale I 119 C4
Chianciano Terme I 135 B4
Chiaramonte Gulfi I 177 B3
Chiaramonti I 178 B2
Chiaravalle I 136 B2
Chiaravalle Centrale I 175 C2
Chiaréggio I 120 A2
Chiari I 120 B2
Chiaromonte I 174 A2
Chiasso CH 120 B2
Chiávari I 134 A2
Chiavenna I 120 A2
Chiché F 102 C1
Chichester GB 44 C3
Chiclana de la Frontera E 162 B1
Chiclana de Segura E 164 A1
Chiddingfold GB 44 B3
Chieri I 119 B4
Chiesa in Valmalenco I 120 A2
Chieti I 169 A4
Chieti Scalo I 169 A4
Chiéuti I 171 B3
Chigwell GB 45 B4
Chiliomodi GR 184 B3
Chillarón de Cuenca E 152 B1
Chillarón del Rey E 151 B5
Chilleurs-aux-Bois F 103 A4
Chillón E 156 B3
Chilluevar E 164 B1
Chiloeches E 151 B4
Chimay B 91 A4
Chimeneas E 163 A4
Chinchilla de Monte Aragón E 158 C2
Chinchón E 151 B4
Chingford GB 45 B4
Chinon F 102 B2
Chióggia I 122 B1
Chiomonte I 119 B3
Chipiona E 161 C3
Chippenham GB 43 A4
Chipping Campden GB 44 A2
Chipping Norton GB 44 B2
Chipping Ongar GB 45 B4
Chipping Sodbury GB 43 A4
Chirac F 130 A2
Chirbury GB 39 B3
Chirens F 118 B2
Chirivel E 164 B2
Chirk GB 38 B3
Chirnside GB 35 C5
Chişinău = Khisinev MD 17 B8
Chişineu Criş RO 113 C5
Chissey-en-Morvan F 104 B3
Chiusa I 108 C2
Chiusa di Pésio I 133 A3
Chiusaforte I 122 A2
Chiusa Sclàfani I 176 B2
Chiusi I 135 B4
Chiva E 159 B3
Chivasso I 119 B4
Chlewiska PL 87 A4
Chludowo PL 75 B5
Chlumec nad Cidlinou CZ 84 B3
Chlum u Třeboně CZ 96 C2
Chmielnik PL 87 B4
Chobienia PL 85 A4
Chobienice PL 75 B4
Choceň CZ 97 A4
Choceń PL 77 B4
Chochołow PL 99 B3
Chocianów PL 85 A3
Chociw PL 86 A3
Chociwel PL 75 A4
Choczewo PL 68 A2
Chodaków PL 77 B5
Chodecz PL 77 B4
Chodov CZ 83 B4
Chodzież PL 75 B5
Chojna PL 74 B3
Chojnice PL 68 B2
Chojno
Kujawsko-Pomorskie PL 77 B4
Wielkopolskie PL 75 B5
Chojnów PL 85 A3
Cholet F 114 A3
Chomérac F 117 C4
Chomutov CZ 83 B5
Chop UA 12 D5
Chora GR 184 B2
Chora Sfakion GR 185 D5
Chorges F 132 A2
Chorley GB 38 A4
Chornobyl = Chernobyl UA 13 C9
Chortkiv UA 13 D6
Chorzele PL 77 A5
Chorzew PL 86 A2
Chorzów PL 86 B2
Choszczno PL 75 A4
Chotěboř CZ 97 B3
Chouilly F 91 B4
Chouto P 154 B2
Chouzy-sur-Cisse F 103 B3
Chozas de Abajo E 142 B1
Chrast CZ 97 B3
Chrást CZ 96 B1
Chrastava CZ 84 B2
Chřibská CZ 84 B2
Christchurch GB 44 C2
Christiansfeld DK 59 C2
Chroberz PL 87 B4
Chropyně CZ 98 B1
Chrudim CZ 97 B3
Chrzanów PL 86 B3
Chtelnica SK 98 C1
Chudovo RUS 9 C7
Chueca E 157 A4
Chulmleigh GB 42 B3
Chur CH 107 C4
Church Stretton GB 39 B4
Churriana E 163 B3
Churwalden CH 107 C4
Chvalšiny CZ 96 C2
Chwaszczyno PL 69 A3
Chynava CZ 96 A2
Chýnov CZ 96 B2
Ciacova RO 126 B3
Ciadîr-Lunga MD 17 B8
Ciadoncha E 143 B3
Cianciana I 176 B2
Ciano d'Enza I 134 A3
Ciążen PL 76 B2
Cibakhaza H 113 C4
Ciborro P 154 C2
Cicagna I 134 A2
Cicciano I 170 C2
Ciciliano I 169 B2
Cicognolo I 120 B3
Cidadelhe P 149 B2
Cide TR 23 A7
Cidones E 143 C4
Ciechanów
Dolnośląskie PL 85 A4
Mazowieckie PL 77 B5

Ciechocinek PL 76 B3
Ciełądz PL 87 A4
Ciemnik PL 75 A4
Ciempozuelos E 151 B4
Ciepielów PL 87 A5
Čierny Balog SK 99 C3
Cierp-Gaud F 145 B4
Cierpice PL 76 B3
Ciervana E 143 A3
Cierznie PL 68 B2
Cieslé PL 77 B5
Cieszyn PL 98 B2
Cieutat F 145 A4
Cieza E 165 A3
Cifer SK 98 C1
Çifteler TR 187 C6
Cifuentes E 151 B5
Cigales E 142 C2
Cigliano I 119 B5
Cihanbeyli TR 23 B7
Cillas E 152 B2
Cilleros E 149 B3
Cilleruelo de Arriba
E 143 C3
Cilleruelo de Bezana
E 143 B3
Cimalmotto CH 119 A5
Cimanes del Tejar
E 141 B5
Ciminna I 176 B2
Cimişlia MD 17 B8
Cimoláis I 122 A1
Cîmpulung RO 17 C6
Çınarcık TR 186 B4
Cinctorres E 153 B3
Cinderford GB 39 C4
Çine TR 188 B3
Činěves CZ 84 B3
Ciney B 79 B5
Cinfães P 148 A1
Cingia de Botti I 120 B3
Cingoli I 136 B2
Cinigiano I 135 C4
Cinobaňa SK 99 C3
Cinq-Mars-la-Pile F 102 B2
Cinquefrondí I 175 C2
Cintegabelle F 146 A2
Cintruénigo E 144 B2
Ciółkowo PL 77 B4
Ciperez E 149 B3
Cirat E 153 B3
Cirella I 174 B1
Cirencester GB 44 B2
Cirey-sur-Vezouze
F 92 C2
Ciria E 152 A2
Ciriè I 119 B4
Cirigliano I 174 A2
Cirò I 174 B3
Cirò Marina I 174 B3
Ciry-le-Noble F 104 C3
Cislău RO 17 C7
Cismon del Grappa
I 121 B4
Cisneros E 142 B2
Cissac-Médoc F 128 A2
Čista CZ 96 A1
Cisterna di Latina I 169 B2
Cistérniga E 150 A3
Cisternino I 173 B3
Cistierna E 142 B1
Čitluk BIH 139 B3
Cítov CZ 84 B2
Cittadella I 121 B4
Cittàdella Pieve I 135 C5
Cittàdel Vaticano =
Vatican City I 168 B2
Cittàdi Castello I 135 B5
Cittaducale I 169 A2
Cittanova I 175 C2
Città Sant'Angelo I 169 A4
Ciudadela de Menorca
E 167 B3
Ciudad Real E 157 B4
Ciudad Rodrigo E 149 B3
Cividale del Friuli I 122 A2
Cívita I 169 A3
Cívita Castellana I 168 A2
Civitanova Alta I 136 B2
Civitanova Marche
I 136 B2
Civitavécchia I 168 A1
Civitella di Romagna
I 135 A4
Civitella di Tronto I 136 C2
Civitella Roveto I 169 B3
Civray F 115 B4
Çivril TR 189 A4
Cizur Mayor E 144 B2
Cjutadilla E 147 C2
Clabhach GB 34 B1
Clachan GB 31 B2
Clachan na Luib GB 31 B1
Clacton-on-Sea GB 45 B5
Cladich GB 34 B2
Claggan GB 34 B2
Clairvaux-les-Lacs
F 105 C4
Clamecy F 104 B2
Claonaig GB 34 C2
Clarecastle IRL 28 B3
Claregalway IRL 28 A3
Claremorris IRL 28 A2
Clarinbridge IRL 28 A3
Clashmore
GB 32 D2
IRL 29 B4
Claudy GB 27 B3
Clausthal-Zellerfeld
D 82 A2
Cláut I 122 A1
Clay Cross GB 40 B2
Claye-Souilly F 90 C2
Cléder F 100 A1
Cleethorpes GB 41 B3
Clefmont F 105 A4
Cléguérec F 100 A2
Clelles F 118 C2
Clenze D 73 B3
Cleobury Mortimer
GB 39 B4
Cléon-d'Andran F 117 C4
Cléré-les-Pins F 102 B2
Clères F 89 A5
Clermont F 90 B2
Clermont-en-Argonne
F 91 B5
Clermont-Ferrand
F 116 B3
Clermont-l'Hérault
F 130 B2
Cerval F 105 B5
Clervaux L 92 A2
Cléry-St André F 103 B3
Cles I 121 A4
Clevedon GB 43 A4
Cleveleys GB 38 A3
Cley GB 41 C5
Clifden IRL 28 A1
Clifford GB 39 B3
Clisson F 101 B4
Clitheroe GB 40 B1
Clogh IRL 30 B1
Cloghan
Donegal IRL 26 B3
Offaly IRL 28 A4
Clogheen IRL 29 B4
Clogher GB 27 B3
Cloghjordan IRL 28 B3
Clohars-Carnoët F 100 B2
Clonakilty IRL 29 C3
Clonaslee IRL 30 A1
Clondalkin IRL 30 A2
Clones IRL 27 B3
Clonmany IRL 27 A3
Clonmel IRL 29 B4
Clonmellon IRL 30 A1
Clonord IRL 30 A1
Clonroche IRL 30 B2
Cloone IRL 26 C3
Cloppenburg D 71 B5
Closeburn GB 36 A3
Clough GB 27 B5
Clova GB 35 B4
Clovelly GB 42 B2
Clowne GB 40 B2
Cloyes-sur-le-Loir
F 103 B3
Cloyne IRL 29 C3
Cluis F 103 C3
Cluj-Napoca RO 17 B5
Clun GB 39 B3
Clunes GB 34 B3
Cluny F 117 A4
Cluses F 118 A3
Clusone I 120 B2
Clydach GB 39 C3
Clydebank GB 34 C3
Coachford IRL 29 C3
Coagh GB 27 B4
Coalisland GB 27 B4
Coalville GB 40 C2
Coaña E 141 A4
Çobanlar TR 187 D5
Cobas E 140 A2
Cobertelade E 151 A5
Cobeta E 152 B1
Cóbh IRL 29 C3
Cobreces E 142 A2
Coburg D 82 B2
Coca E 150 A3
Cocentaina E 159 C3
Cochem D 80 B3
Cockburnspath GB 35 C5
Cockermouth GB 36 B3
Codigoro I 121 C5
Codogno I 120 B2
Codos E 152 A2
Codróipo I 122 B1
Codrongianos I 178 B2
Coelhoso P 149 A3
Coesfeld D 71 C4
Coevorden NL 71 B3
Cofrentes E 159 B2
Cogeces del Monte
E 150 A3
Coggeshall GB 45 B4
Cognac F 115 C3
Cogne I 119 B4
Cognin F 118 B2
Cogolin F 132 B2
Cogollos de Guadix
E 164 B1
Cogollos-Vega E 163 A4
Cogolludo E 151 B4
Coimbra P 148 B1
Coín E 163 B3
Coirós E 140 A2
Čoka SRB 126 B2
Col SLO 123 B3
Colares P 154 C1
Cölbe D 81 B4
Colbitz D 73 B4
Colchester GB 45 B4
Coldingham GB 35 C5
Colditz D 83 A4
Coldstream GB 35 C5
Colebrooke GB 43 B3
Colera E 146 B4
Coleraine GB 27 A4
Colfiorito I 136 B1
Cólico I 120 A2
Coligny F 118 A2
Colindres E 143 A3
Collado-Mediano E 151 B3
Collado Villalba E 151 B4
Collagna I 134 A3
Collanzo E 142 A1
Collat F 117 B3
Coll de Nargó E 147 B2
Collécchio I 120 C3
Colledimezzo I 169 B4
Colle di Val d'Elsa
I 135 B4
Colleferro I 169 B3
Colle Isarco I 108 C2
Collelongo I 169 B3
Collepasso I 173 B4
Collepepe I 136 C1
Collesalvetti I 134 B3
Colle Sannita I 170 B2
Collesano I 176 B2
Colli a Volturno I 169 B4
Collin GB 36 A3
Collinée F 101 A3
Collingham
Nottinghamshire
GB 40 B2
West Yorkshire GB 40 B3
Collinghorst D 71 A4
Cóllio I 120 B3
Collobrières F 132 B2
Collon IRL 27 C4
Collooney IRL 26 B2
Colmar F 106 A2
Colmars F 132 A2
Colmenar E 163 B3
Colmenar de la Sierra
E 151 A4
Colmenar de Oreja
E 151 B4
Colmenar Viejo E 151 B4
Colmonel GB 36 A2
Colne GB 40 B1
Colobraro I 174 A2
Cologna Véneta I 121 B4
Cologne = Köln D 80 B2
Cologne F 129 C3
Cologne al Serio I 120 B2
Colombey-les-Belles
F 92 C1
Colombey-les-deux-
Églises F 105 A3
Colombres E 142 A2
Colomera E 163 A4
Colomers E 147 B3
Colomiers F 129 C4
Colònia de Sant Jordi
E 167 B3
Colorno I 120 C3
Colos P 160 B1
Cölpin D 74 A2
Colpy GB 33 D4
Colsterworth GB 40 C3
Coltishall GB 41 C5
Colunga E 142 A1
Colwell GB 37 A4
Colwyn Bay GB 38 A3
Colyford GB 43 B3
Comácchio I 121 C5
Coma-ruga E 147 C2
Combarros E 141 B4
Combeaufontaine
F 105 B4
Comber GB 27 B5
Comblain-au-Pont B 80 B1
Combloux F 118 B3
Combourg F 88 B2
Combronde F 116 B3
Comeglians I 109 C3
Comillas E 142 A2
Comines F 78 B3
Cómiso I 177 C3
Comloşu Mare RO 126 B2
Commensacq F 128 B2
Commentry F 116 A2
Commerau D 84 A2
Commercy F 92 C1
Como I 120 B2
Cómpeta E 163 B4
Compiègne F 90 B2
Comporta P 154 C2
Comps-sur-Artuby
F 132 B2
Comrat MD 17 B8
Comrie GB 35 B4
Comunanza I 136 C2
Cona
Emilia Romagna
I 121 C4
Veneto I 121 B5
Concarneau F 100 B2
Conceição P 160 B1
Conches-en-Ouche
F 89 B4
Concordia Sagittária
I 122 B1
Concordia sulla Sécchia
I 121 C3
Concots F 129 B4
Condat F 116 B2
Condé-en-Brie F 91 C3
Condeixa P 148 B1
Condemios de Abajo
E 151 A4
Condemios de Arriba
E 151 A4
Condé-sur-l'Escaut
F 79 B3
Conde-sur-Marne F 91 B4
Condé-sur-Noireau
F 88 B3
Condino I 121 B3
Condom F 129 C3
Condove I 119 B4
Condrieu F 117 B4
Conegliano I 122 B1
Conflans-sur-Lanterne
F 105 B5
Confolens F 115 B4
Conforto E 141 A3
Cong IRL 28 A2
Congleton GB 40 B1
Congosto E 141 B4
Congosto de Valdavia
E 142 B2
Congostrina E 151 A4
Conil de la Frontera
E 162 B1
Coningsby GB 41 B3
Coniston GB 36 B3
Conlie F 102 A1
Conliège F 105 C4
Conna IRL 29 B3
Connah's Quay GB 38 A3
Connantre F 91 C3
Connaugh IRL 28 B3
Connaux F 131 A3
Connel GB 34 B2
Connerré F 102 A2
Cononbridge GB 32 D2
Čonoplja SRB 126 B1
Conques F 116 C2
Conques-sur-Orbiel
F 146 A3
Conquista E 157 B3
Conquista de la Sierra
E 156 A2
Consándolo I 121 C4
Consélice I 135 A4
Conselve I 121 B4
Consenvoye F 91 B5
Consett GB 37 B5
Consolacão P 154 B1
Constancia P 154 B2
Constanco E 140 A2
Constanţa RO 17 C8
Constanti E 147 C2
Constantina E 162 A2
Consuegra E 157 A4
Consuma I 135 B4
Contarina I 122 B1
Contay F 90 B2
Conthey CH 119 A4
Contigliano I 168 A2
Contis-Plage F 128 B1
Contrada I 170 C2
Contres F 103 B3
Contrexéville F 105 A4
Controne I 172 B1
Contursi Termi I 172 B1
Conty F 90 B2
Conversano I 173 B3
Conwy GB 38 A3
Cookstown GB 27 B4
Coole F 91 C4
Coolgreany IRL 30 B2
Cooneen GB 27 B3
Cootehill IRL 27 B3
Cope E 165 B3
Copenhagen =
København DK 61 D2
Copertino I 173 B4
Copparo I 121 C4
Coppenbrugge D 72 B2
Corabia RO 17 D6
Córaci I 175 B2
Coralići BIH 124 C1
Corato I 171 B4
Coray F 100 A2
Corbeil-Essonnes F 90 C2
Corbeny F 91 B3
Corbera E 159 B3
Corbie F 90 B2
Corbigny F 104 B2
Corbion B 91 B4
Corbridge GB 37 B4
Corby GB 40 C3
Corconte E 143 A3
Corcubión E 140 B1
Corcumello I 169 A3
Cordenòns I 122 B1
Cordes-sur-Ciel F 129 B4
Córdoba E 156 C3
Cordobilla de Lácara
E 155 B4
Cordovado I 122 B1
Corella E 144 B2
Coreses E 150 A2
Corfe Castle GB 43 B4
Corga de Lobão P 148 B1
Cori I 169 B2
Coria E 155 B4
Coria del Río E 162 A1
Corigliano Cálabro
I 174 B2
Corinaldo I 136 B1
Corinth = Korinthos
GR 184 B3
Cório I 119 B4
Coripe E 162 B2
Cork IRL 29 C3
Corlay F 100 A2
Corleone I 176 B2
Corleto Monforte I 172 B1
Corleto Perticara I 174 A2
Çorlu TR 186 A2
Cormainville F 103 A3
Cormatin F 104 C3
Cormeilles F 89 A4
Cormery F 102 B2
Cormòns I 122 B2
Cormoz F 118 A2
Cornago E 144 B1
Cornberg D 82 A1
Cornellana E 141 A4
Corneşti MD 17 B8
Corníglio I 134 A3
Cornimont F 106 B1
Corniolo I 135 B4
Cornuda I 121 B5
Cornudella de Montsant
E 147 C1
Cornudilla E 143 B3
Cornus F 130 B2
Çorovodë AL 182 C2
Corpach GB 34 B2
Corps F 118 C2
Corps Nuds F 101 B4
Corral de Almaguer
E 157 A4
Corral de Ayllon E 151 A4
Corral de Calatrava
E 157 B3
Corrales E 149 A4
Corral-Rubio E 158 C2
Corran GB 34 B2
Corredoiras E 140 A2
Corréggio I 121 C3
Corrèze F 116 B1
Corridónia I 136 B2
Corris GB 38 B3
Corrubedo E 140 B1
Córsico I 120 B2
Corsock GB 36 A3
Corte F 180 A2
Corteconcepción E 161 B3
Corte de Peleas E 155 C4
Cortegaca P 148 B1
Cortegada E 140 B2
Cortegana E 161 B3
Cortemaggiore I 120 B2
Cortemilia I 133 A4
Corte Pinto P 160 B2
Cortes E 144 C2
Cortes de Aragón
E 153 B3
Cortes de Arenoso
E 153 B3
Cortes de Baza E 164 B2
Cortes de la Frontera
E 162 B2
Cortes de Pallás E 159 B3
Cortiçadas P 154 C2
Cortico P 148 A2
Cortijo de Arriba E 157 A3
Cortijos Nuevos E 164 A2
Cortina d'Ampezzo
I 108 C3
Corton GB 41 C5
Cortona I 135 B4
Coruche P 154 C2
Corullón E 141 B4
Çorum TR 23 A8
Corvara in Badia I 108 C2
Corvera E 165 B3
Corwen GB 38 B3
Cosenza I 174 B2
Cosham GB 44 C2
Coslada E 151 B4
Cosne-Cours-sur-Loire
F 104 B1
Cosne d'Allier F 103 C4
Cospeito E 140 A3
Cossato I 119 B5
Cossaye F 104 C2
Cossé-le-Vivien F 101 B5
Cossonay CH 105 C5
Costa da Caparica
P 154 C1
Costa de Santo André
P 160 A1
Costalpino I 135 B4
Costa Nova P 148 B1
Costaros F 117 C3
Costeşti RO 17 C6
Costigliole d'Asti I 119 C5
Costigliole Saluzzo
I 133 A3
Coswig
Sachsen D 83 A5
Sachsen-Anhalt D 83 A4
Cotherstone GB 37 B5
Cotronei I 175 B2
Cottbus D 84 A2
Cottenham GB 45 A4
Cottingham GB 40 B3
Coublanc F 105 B4
Couches F 104 C3
Couço P 154 C2
Coucouron F 117 C3
Coucy-le-Château-
Auffrique F 90 B3
Couëron F 101 B4
Couflens F 146 B2
Couhé F 115 B4
Couiza F 146 B3
Coulags GB 31 B3
Coulanges F 104 C2
Coulanges-la-Vineuse
F 104 B2
Coulanges-sur-Yonne
F 104 B2
Couleuvre F 104 C1
Coulmier-le-Sec F 104 B3
Coulommiers F 90 C3
Coulonges-sur-l'Autize
F 114 B3
Coulounieix-Chamiers
F 129 A3
Coulport GB 34 B3
Coupar Angus GB 35 B4
Coupéville F 91 C4
Couptrain F 89 B3
Coura P 140 C2
Courcelles B 79 B4
Courcelles-Chaussy
F 92 B2
Courchevel F 118 B3
Cour-Cheverny F 103 B3
Courcôme F 115 C4
Courçon F 114 B3
Cour-et-Buis F 117 B4
Courgenay CH 106 B2
Courmayeur I 119 B3
Courniou F 130 B1
Cournon-d'Auvergne
F 116 B3
Cournonterral F 130 B2
Courpière F 117 B3
Coursan F 130 B2
Courseulles-sur-Mer
F 89 A3
Cours-la-Ville F 117 A4
Courson-les-Carrières
F 104 B2
Courtalain F 103 A3
Courtenay F 104 A2
Courtomer F 89 B4
Courville
Eure-et-Loire F 89 B5
Marne F 91 B3
Coussac-Bonneval
F 115 C5
Coutances F 88 A2
Couterne F 89 B3
Coutras F 128 A2
Couvet CH 106 C1
Couvin B 91 A4
Couzon F 104 C2
Covadonga E 142 A1
Covaleda E 143 C4
Covarrubias E 143 B3
Covas P 148 A1
Cove GB 31 B3
Coventry GB 44 A2
Coverack GB 42 B1
Covigliáio I 135 A4
Covilhã P 148 B2
Cowbridge GB 39 C3
Cowdenbeath GB 35 B4
Cowes GB 44 C2
Cox F 129 C4
Cózar E 157 B4
Cozes F 114 C3
Cozzano F 180 B2
Craco I 174 A2
Cracow = Kraków
PL 99 A3
Craibstone GB 33 D4
Craighouse GB 34 C2
Craignure GB 34 B2
Crail GB 35 B5
Crailsheim D 94 B2
Craiova RO 17 C5
Cramlington GB 37 A5
Cranleigh GB 44 B3
Craon F 101 B5
Craonne F 91 B3
Craponne F 117 B4
Craponne-sur-Arzon
F 117 B3
Crathie GB 32 D3
Crato P 155 B3
Craughwell IRL 28 A3
Craven Arms GB 39 B4
Crawford GB 36 A3
Crawinkel D 82 B2
Crawley GB 44 B3
Creag Ghoraidh GB 31 B1
Crecente E 140 B2
Crèches-sur-Saône
F 117 A4
Crécy-en-Ponthieu
F 78 B1
Crécy-la-Chapelle F 90 C2
Crécy-sur-Serre F 91 B3
Crediton GB 43 B3
Creeslough IRL 26 A3
Creetown GB 36 B2
Creeve GB 27 B4
Creglingen D 94 B2
Creil F 90 B2
Creissels F 130 A2
Crema I 120 B2
Cremeaux F 117 B3
Crémenes E 142 B1
Crémieu F 118 B2
Cremlingen D 73 B3
Cremona I 120 B3
Creney F 91 C4
Črenšovci SLO 111 C3
Créon F 128 B2

Crepaja SRB 127 B2
Crépey F 92 C1
Crépy F 91 B3
Crépy-en-Valois F 90 B2
Cres HR 123 C3
Crescentino I 119 B5
Crespino I 121 C4
Crespos E 150 B3
Cressage GB 39 B4
Cressensac F 129 A4
Cressia F 105 C4
Crest F 117 C5
Cresta CH 107 C4
Créteil F 90 C2
Creully F 88 A3
Creussen D 95 B3
Creutzwald F 92 B2
Creuzburg D 82 A2
Crevalcore I 121 C4
Crèvecoeur-le-Grand
F 90 B2
Crevillente E 165 A4
Crévola d'Ossola I 119 A5
Crewe GB 38 A4
Crewkerne GB 43 B4
Criales E 143 B3
Crianlarich GB 34 B3
Criccieth GB 38 B2
Crickhowell GB 39 C3
Cricklade GB 44 B2
Crieff GB 35 B4
Criel-sur-Mer F 90 A1
Crikvenica HR 123 B3
Crillon F 90 B1
Crimmitschau D 83 B4
Crimond GB 33 D5
Crinitz D 84 A1
Cripán E 143 B4
Criquetot-l'Esneval
F 89 A4
Crispiano I 173 B3
Crissolo I 119 C4
Cristóbal E 149 B4
Crivitz D 73 A4
Črna SLO 110 C1
Crna Bara
Srbija SRB 127 C1
Vojvodina SRB 126 B2
Crnac HR 125 B3
Crnča SRB 127 C1
Crni Lug
BIH 138 A2
HR 123 B3
Črni Vrh SLO 123 B3
Crnjelovo Donje
BIH 125 C5
Črnomelj SLO 123 B4
Crocketford GB 36 A3
Crocq F 116 B2
Crodo I 119 A5
Croglin GB 37 B4
Crolly IRL 26 A2
Cromarty GB 32 D2
Cromer GB 41 C5
Cronat F 104 C2
Crookhaven IRL 29 C2
Crookstown IRL 29 C3
Croom IRL 29 B3
Cropalati I 174 B2
Crópani I 175 C2
Crosbost GB 31 A2
Crosby GB 38 A3
Crosía I 174 B2
Crossakiel IRL 27 C3
Cross-Hands GB 39 C2
Crosshaven IRL 29 C3
Crosshill GB 36 A2
Crossmolina IRL 26 B1
Crotone I 175 B3
Crottendorf D 83 B4
Crouy F 90 B3
Crowborough GB 45 B4
Crowland GB 41 C3
Crowthorne GB 44 B3
Croyde GB 42 A2
Croydon GB 44 B3
Crozon F 100 A1
Cruas F 117 C4
Cruceni RO 126 A3
Crúcoli I 174 B3
Cruden Bay GB 33 D5
Crudgington GB 38 B4
Cruis F 132 A1
Crumlin GB 27 B4
Cruseilles F 118 A3
Crusheen IRL 28 B3
Cruz de Incio E 141 B3
Črvenka SRB 126 B1
Črveny Kamen SK 98 B2
Csabacsüd H 113 C4
Csabrendek H 111 B4
Csákánydoroszló
H 111 C3
Csákvár H 112 B2
Csanádapáca H 113 C4
Csanádpalota H 126 A2
Csány H 113 B3
Csanytelek H 113 C4
Csapod H 111 B3
Császár H 112 B2
Császártöltés H 112 C3
Csávoly H 125 A5
Csemö H 113 B3
Csengöd H 112 C3
Csépa H 113 C4
Csepreg H 111 B3
Cserkeszölö H 113 C4
Csernely H 113 A4
Csesztreg H 111 C3
Csökmö H 113 B5
Csököly H 124 A3
Csokonyavisonta
H 124 A3
Csólyospálos H 113 C3
Csongrád H 113 C4
Csopak H 112 C1
Csorna H 111 B4
Csorvás H 113 C4
Csurgo H 124 A3
Cuacos de Yuste E 150 B2
Cualedro E 140 C3
Cuanca de Campos
E 142 B1
Cuba P 160 A2
Cubel E 152 A2
Cubelles E 147 C2
Cubillos E 143 C4
Cubillos del Sil E 141 B4
Cubjac F 129 A3
Cubo de la Solana
E 152 A1
Çubuk TR 23 A7
Cuckfield GB 44 B3
Cucuron F 131 B4
Cudillero E 141 A4
Cuéllar E 151 A3
Cuenca E 152 B1
Cuers F 132 B2
Cuerva E 157 A3
Cueva de Agreda
E 144 C2
Cuevas Bajas E 163 A3
Cuevas del Almanzora
E 164 B3
Cuevas del Becerro
E 162 B2
Cuevas del Campo
E 164 B2
Cuevas del Valle E 150 B2
Cuevas de San
Clemente E 143 B3
Cuevas de San Marcos
E 163 A3
Cuges-les-Pins F 132 B1
Cúglieri I 178 B2
Cugnaux F 129 C4
Cuijk NL 80 A1
Cuinzier F 117 A4
Cuiseaux F 105 C4
Cuisery F 105 C4
Culan F 103 C4
Culemborg NL 79 A5
Cúllar E 164 B2
Cullaville GB 27 B4
Cullera E 159 B3
Cullivoe GB 33 A5
Cullompton GB 43 B3
Cully CH 106 C1
Culoz F 118 B2
Cults GB 33 D4
Cumbernauld GB 35 C4
Cumbres de San
Bartolomé E 161 A3
Cumbres Mayores
E 161 A3
Cumiana I 119 C4
Čumić SRB 127 C2
Cumnock GB 36 A2
Çumra TR 23 C7
Cúneo I 133 A3
Çunlhat F 117 B3
Čunski HR 123 C3
Cuntis E 140 B2
Cuorgnè I 119 B4
Cupar GB 35 B4
Cupello I 170 A2
Cupra Maríttima I 136 B2
Cupramontana I 136 B2
Ćuprija SRB 127 D3
Curinga I 175 C2
Currelos E 140 B3
Currie GB 35 C4
Curtea de Argeş RO 17 C6
Curtici RO 126 A3
Curtis E 140 A2
Curtis Santa Eulalia
E 140 A2
Čurug SRB 126 B2
Cusano Mutri I 170 B2
Cushendall GB 27 A4
Cusset F 117 A3
Cussy-les-Forges
F 104 B3
Custines F 92 C2
Cutanda E 152 B2
Cutro I 175 B2
Cutrofiano I 173 B4
Cuts F 90 B3
Cuvilly F 90 B2
Cuxhaven D 64 C1
Cvikov CZ 84 B2
Cwmbran GB 39 C3
Cybinka PL 75 B3
Czacz PL 75 B5
Czajków PL 86 A2
Czaplinek PL 75 A5
Czarlin PL 69 A3
Czarna-Dąbrówka
PL 68 A2
Czarna Woda PL 68 B3
Czarnca PL 87 B3
Czarne PL 68 B1
Czarnków PL 75 B5
Czarnowo PL 76 A3
Czarnozyly PL 86 A2
Czarny Bór PL 85 B4
Czarny-Dunajec PL 99 B3
Czarny Las PL 86 A1
Czchow PL 99 B4
Czechowice-Dziedzice
PL 98 B2
Czempiń PL 75 B5
Czermno PL 87 A4
Czernichow PL 99 B3
Czerniejewo PL 76 B2
Czernikowo PL 76 B3
Czersk PL 68 B2
Czerwieńsk PL 75 B4
Czerwionka-Leszczyny
PL 86 B2
Częstochowa PL 86 B3
Czeszewo PL 76 B2
Człopa PL 75 A5
Człuchów PL 68 B2
Czołpino PL 68 A2

D

Dağ TR 189 B5
Daaden D 81 B3
Dabas H 112 B3
Dąbie PL 76 B3
Dąbki PL 67 B5
Dabo F 92 C3
Dabrowa PL 76 B2
Dąbrowa Górnicza
PL 86 B3
Dąbrowa Tarnowska
PL 87 B4
Dąbrowice PL 77 B4
Dabrowno PL 77 A5
Dachau D 108 A2
Dačice CZ 97 B3
Daday TR 23 A7
Dagali N 47 B5
Dägebüll D 64 B1
Dagmersellen CH 106 B2
Dahlen D 83 A4
Dahlenburg D 73 A3
Dahme D 83 A5
Dahn D 93 B3
Dähre D 73 B3
Daikanvik S 195 E7
Dail bho Dheas GB 31 A2
Dailly GB 36 A2
Daimiel E 157 A4
Daingean IRL 30 A1
Đakovica KOS 16 D4
Đakovo HR 125 B4
Dal
Akershus N 48 B3
Telemark N 47 C5
Dalaas A 107 B5
Dalabrog GB 31 B1
Dala-Floda S 50 B1
Dala-Husby S 50 B2
Dala-Järna S 50 B1
Dalaman TR 188 C3
Dalarö S 57 A4
Dalbeattie GB 36 B3
Dalby
DK 59 C3
Skåne S 61 D3
Uppsala S 57 A3
Värmland S 49 B4
Dale
Pembrokeshire
GB 39 C1
Shetland GB 33 A5
Hordaland N 46 B2
Sogn og Fjordane
N 46 A2
Dalen
Akershus N 48 C3
Telemark N 53 A4
Daleszyce PL 87 B4
Dalhalvaig GB 32 C3
Dalheim L 92 B2
Dalhem S 57 C4
Dalias E 164 C2
Dalj HR 125 B4
Dalkeith GB 35 C4
Dalkey IRL 30 A2
Dalmally GB 34 B3
Dalmellington GB 36 A2
Dalmose DK 65 A4
Daløy N 46 A1
Dalry
Dumfries & Galloway
GB 34 C3
North Ayrshire GB 36 A2
Dalrymple GB 36 A2
Dalseter N 47 A6
Dalsjöfors S 60 B3
Dalskog S 54 B3
Dals Långed S 54 B3
Dals Rostock S 54 B3
Dalston GB 36 B4
Dalstorp S 60 B3
Dalton-in-Furness
GB 36 B3
Daluis F 132 A2
Dalum
D 71 B4
S 60 B3
Dalvík IS 191 B7
Dalwhinnie GB 32 E2
Dalyan TR 188 C3
Damasi GR 182 D4
Damasławek PL 76 B2
Damazan F 129 B3
Damgan F 101 B3
Dammarie-les-Lys F 90 C2
Dammartin-en-Goële
F 90 B2
Damme D 71 B5
Damnica PL 68 A2
Dampierre F 105 B4
Dampierre-sur-Salon
F 105 B4
Damüls A 107 B4
Damville F 89 B5
Damvillers F 92 B1
Damwoude NL 70 A2
Danasjö S 195 E7
Danbury GB 45 B4
Dångebo S 63 B3
Dangers F 89 B5
Dangé-St Romain
F 102 C2
Dangeul F 89 B4
Danilovgrad MNE 16 D3
Danischenhagen D 64 B3
Daniszyn PL 85 A5
Danjoutin F 106 B1
Dannas S 60 B3
Dannemarie F 106 B2
Dannemora S 51 B4
Dannenberg D 73 A4
Dánszentmiklós H 112 B3
Dány H 112 B3
Daoulas F 100 A1
Darabani RO 17 A7
Darány H 125 B3
Darda HR 125 B4
Dardesheim D 73 C3
Darfeld D 71 B4
Darfo I 120 B3
Dargiń PL 68 A1
Dargun D 66 C1
Darlington GB 37 B5
Darłowo PL 68 A1
Darmstadt D 93 B4
Darney F 105 A5
Daroca E 152 A2
Darque P 148 A1
Darragh IRL 28 B2
Dartford GB 45 B4
Dartington GB 43 B3
Dartmouth GB 43 B3
Darton GB 40 B2
Daruvar HR 124 B3
Darvas H 113 B5
Darvel GB 36 A2
Darwen GB 38 A4
Dassel D 82 A1
Dassow D 65 C3
Datça TR 188 C2
Datteln D 80 A3
Dattenfeld D 81 B3
Daugard DK 59 C2
Daugavpils LV 8 E5
Daumeray F 102 B1
Daun D 80 B2
Daventry GB 44 A2
Davle CZ 96 B2
Davor HR 124 B3
Davos CH 107 C4
Davutlar TR 188 B2
Davyd Haradok BY 13 B7
Dawlish GB 43 B3
Dax F 128 C1
Dazkırı TR 189 B4
Deal GB 45 B5
Deauville F 89 A4
Deba E 143 A4
Debar MK 182 B2
Dębe PL 77 B5
Dębica PL 87 B5
Dębnica Kaszubska
PL 68 A2
Dębno PL 74 B3
Dębołęka PL 86 A2
Dębowa Łaka PL 69 B4
Debrc SRB 127 C1
Debrecen H 113 B5
Debrznica PL 75 B4
Debrzno PL 68 B2
Debstedt D 72 A1
Decazeville F 130 A1
Dechtice SK 98 C1
Decima I 168 B2
Decimomannu I 179 C2
Děčín CZ 84 B2
Decize F 104 C2
De Cocksdorp NL 70 A1
Decollatura I 175 B2
Decs H 125 A4
Deddington GB 44 B2
Dedeler TR 187 B5
Dedelow D 74 A2
Dedemli TR 189 B7
Dedemsvaart NL 71 B3
Dédestapolcsány
H 113 A4
Dedovichi RUS 9 D6
Deeping St Nicholas
GB 41 C3
Dég H 112 C2
Degaña E 141 B4
Degeberga S 61 D4
Degerby FIN 51 B7
Degerfors S 55 A5
Degerhamn S 63 B4
Degernes N 54 A2
Deggendorf D 95 C4
Deggingen D 94 C1
Dego I 133 A4
Degolados P 155 B3
De Haan B 78 A3
Dehesas de Guadix
E 164 B1
Dehesas Viejas E 163 A4
Deia E 166 B2
Deining D 95 B3
Deinze B 79 B3
Déiva Marina I 134 A2
Dej RO 17 B5
Deje S 55 A4
De Koog NL 70 A1
Delabole GB 42 B2
Delary S 61 C3
Delbrück D 81 A4
Delčevo MK 182 B4
Delden NL 71 B3
Deleitosa E 156 A2
Delekovec HR 124 A2
Delémont CH 106 B2
Delft NL 70 B1
Delfzijl NL 71 A3
Délia I 176 B2
Delianuova I 175 C1
Deliblato SRB 127 C3
Delice TR 23 B7
Deliceto I 171 B3
Delitzsch D 83 A4
Dellach A 109 C4
Delle F 106 B2
Delme F 92 C2
Delmen-horst D 72 A1
Delnice HR 123 B3
Delsbo S 200 E2
Delvin IRL 30 A1
Delvinë AL 182 D2
Demandice SK 112 A2
Demen D 73 A4
Demidov RUS 13 A9
Demigny F 105 C3
Demirci TR 186 C3
Demirköy TR 186 A2
Demirtaş TR 186 B4
Demmin D 66 C2
Demonte I 133 A3
Demyansk RUS 9 D8
Denain F 78 B3
Denbigh GB 38 A3
Den Burg NL 70 A1
Dender-monde B 79 A4
Denekamp NL 71 B4
Den Ham NL 71 B3
Den Helder NL 70 B1
Denholm GB 35 C5
Denia E 159 C4
Denizli TR 188 B4
Denkendorf D 95 C3
Denklingen D 81 B3
Denny GB 35 B4
Den Oever NL 70 B2
Denta RO 126 B3
Déols F 103 C3
De Panne B 78 A2
Derbent TR 188 A3
Derby GB 40 C2
Derecske H 113 B5
Dereköy TR 186 A2
Derenberg D 82 A2
Derinkuyu TR 23 B8
Dermbach D 82 B2
Dermulo I 121 A4
Deronje SRB 125 B5
Derrygonnelly GB 26 B3
Derrylin GB 27 B3
Derry/Londonderry
GB 27 B3
Dersingham GB 41 C4
Deruta I 136 C1
Dervaig GB 34 B1
Derval F 101 B4
Derveni GR 184 A3
Derventa BIH 125 C3
Dervock GB 27 A4
Desana I 119 B5
Descartes F 102 C2
Desenzano del Garda
I 121 B3
Deset N 48 A3
Deševa BIH 139 B4
Desfina GR 184 A3
Desimirovac SRB 127 C2
Désio I 120 B2
Deskati GR 182 D3
Deskle SLO 122 A2
Desná CZ 84 B3
Dešov CZ 97 C3
Despotovac SRB 127 C3
Despotovo SRB 126 B1
Dessau D 83 A4
Deštná CZ 96 B2
Destriana E 141 B4
Désulo I 179 B3
Desvres F 78 B1
Deszk H 126 A2
Deta RO 126 B3
Detmold D 72 C1
Dětřichov CZ 98 B1
Dettelbach D 94 B2
Dettingen
Baden-Württemberg
D 94 C1
Baden-Württemberg
D 107 B4
Dettwiller F 93 C3
Detva SK 99 C3
Deurne NL 80 A1
Deutschkreutz A 111 B3
Deutschlandsberg
A 110 C2
Deutsch Wagram
A 111 A3
Deva RO 16 C5
Dévaványa H 113 B4
Devecikonağı TR 186 C3
Devecser H 111 B4
Develi TR 23 B8
Deventer NL 70 B3
Devil's Bridge GB 39 B3
Devin BG 183 B6
Devinska Nova Ves
SK 111 A3
Devizes GB 43 A5
Devonport GB 42 B2
Devrek TR 187 A6
Devrekâni TR 23 A7
Đevrske HR 137 B4
De Wijk NL 71 B3
Dewsbury GB 40 B2
Deza E 152 A1
Dežanovac HR 124 B3
Dezzo I 120 B3
Dhali CY 181 A2
Dheftera CY 181 A2
Dherinia CY 181 A2
Diamante I 174 B1
Dianalund DK 61 D1
Diano d'Alba I 119 C5
Diano Marina I 133 B4
Dicomano I 135 B4
Didcot GB 44 B2
Didimoticho GR 186 A1
Die F 118 C2
Diebling F 92 B2
Dieburg D 93 B4
Diego del Carpio E 150 B2
Diekirch L 92 B2
Diélette F 88 A2
Diémoz F 118 B2
Dienten am Hochkönig
A 109 B3
Diepenbeck B 79 B5
Diepholz D 71 B5
Dieppe F 89 A5
Dierberg D 74 A1
Dierdorf D 81 B3
Dieren NL 70 B3
Dierhagen D 66 B1
Diesdorf D 73 B3
Diessen D 108 B2
Diest B 79 B5
Dietenheim D 94 C2
Dietfurt D 95 B3
Dietikon CH 106 B3
Dietzenbach D 93 A4
Dieue-sur-Meuse F 92 B1
Dieulefit F 131 A4
Dieulouard F 92 C2
Dieuze F 92 C2
Diever NL 71 B3
Diez D 81 B4
Diezma E 163 A4
Differdange L 92 B1
Digermulen N 194 B6
Dignac F 115 C4
Dignano I 122 A1
Digne-les-Bains F 132 A2
Digny F 89 B5
Digoin F 104 C2
Dijon F 105 B4
Dikanäs S 195 E7
Dikili TR 186 C1
Diksmuide B 78 A2
Dilar E 163 A4
Dillenburg D 81 B4
Dillingen
Bayern D 94 C2
Saarland D 92 B2
Dilsen B 80 A1
Dimaro I 121 A3
Dimitrovgrad BG 183 A7
Dimitsana GR 184 B3
Dinami I 175 C2
Dinan F 101 A3
Dinant B 79 B4
Dinar TR 189 A5
Dinard F 101 A3
Dinek TR 187 C6
Dingden D 80 A2
Dingelstädt D 82 A2
Dingle
IRL 29 B1
S 54 B2
Dingolfing D 95 C4
Dingtuna S 56 A2
Dingwall GB 32 D2
Dinkelsbühl D 94 B2
Dinkelscherben D 94 C2
Dinklage D 71 B5
Dinslaken D 80 A2
Dinxperlo NL 80 A2
Diö S 63 B2
Diósgyör H 113 A4
Diósjeno H 112 B3
Diou F 104 C2
Dippen GB 34 C2
Dipperz D 82 B1
Dippoldiswalde D 84 B1
Dirdal N 52 B2
Dirksland NL 79 A4
Dirlewang D 108 B1
Dischingen D 94 C2
Disentis CH 107 C3
Diso I 173 B4
Diss GB 45 A5

Dissen D 71 B5
Distington GB 36 B3
Ditzingen D 93 C5
Ditzum D 71 A4
Divača SLO 122 B2
Dives-sur-Mer F 89 A3
Divín SK 99 C3
Divion F 78 B2
Divišov CZ 96 B2
Divonne les Bains
F 118 A3
Dixmont F 104 A2
Dizy-le-Gros F 91 B4
Djúpivogur IS 191 C11
Djupvasshytta N 198 C4
Djura S 50 B1
Djurås S 50 B2
Djurmo S 50 B2
Djursdala S 62 A3
Dlouhá Loucka CZ 98 B1
Długowola PL 87 A5
Dmitrov RUS 9 D10
Dno RUS 9 D6
Doade E 141 B3
Doğanhisar TR 189 A6
Dobanovci SRB 127 C2
Dobbertin D 73 A5
Dobbiaco I 108 C3
Dobczyce PL 99 B4
Dobele LV 8 D3
Döbeln D 83 A5
Doberlug-Kirchhain
D 83 A5
Dobern D 84 A2
Dobersberg A 97 C3
Dobiegniew PL 75 B4
Dobieszyn PL 87 A5
Doboj BIH 125 C4
Dobošnica BIH 125 C4
Doboz H 113 C5
Dobrá CZ 98 B2
Dobra
Wielkopolskie PL 76 C3
Zachodnio-Pomorskie
PL 74 A3
Zachodnio-Pomorskie
PL 75 A4
Dobrá Niva SK 99 C3
Dobřany CZ 96 B1
Dobre PL 76 B3
Dobre Miasto PL 69 B5
Dobreta-Turnu-Severin
RO 16 C5
Dobri H 111 C3
Dobrica SRB 126 B2
Dobrich BG 17 D7
Dobrinishta BG 183 B5
Dobříš CZ 96 B2
Dobro E 143 B3
Dobrodzień PL 86 B2
Döbrököz H 112 C2
Dobromierz PL 85 B4
Dobrosołowo PL 76 B3
Dobroszyce PL 85 A5
Dobrovnik SLO 111 C3
Dobrush BY 13 B9
Dobruška CZ 85 B4
Dobrzany PL 75 A4
Dobrzen Wielki PL 86 B1
Dobrzyca
Wielkopolskie PL 75 A5
Wielkopolskie PL 85 A5
Zachodnio-Pomorskie
PL 67 B4
Dobrzyńnad Wisłą
PL 77 B4
Dobšiná SK 99 C4
Dobwalls GB 42 B2
Dochamps B 80 B1
Docking GB 41 C4
Docksta S 200 C4
Doddington GB 37 A4
Döderhult S 62 A4
Doesburg NL 70 B3
Doetinchem NL 71 C3
Dogliani I 133 A3
Dogueno P 160 B2
Doische B 91 A4
Dois Portos P 154 B1
Dojč SK 98 C1
Dokka N 48 B2
Dokkedal DK 58 B3
Dokkum NL 70 A2
Dokležovje SLO 111 C3
Doksy CZ 84 B2
Dokuz TR 189 A7
Dolancourt F 104 A3
Dolceácqua I 133 B3
Dol-de-Bretagne F 88 B2
Dole F 105 B4
Dølemo N 53 B4
Dolenja vas SLO 123 B3
Dolenjske Toplice
SLO 123 B4
Dolfor GB 39 B3
Dolgarrog GB 38 A3
Dolgellau GB 38 B3
Doliana GR 182 D2
Dolianova I 179 C3
Dolice PL 75 A4
Doljani HR 138 A2
Döllach im Mölltal
A 109 C3
Dolle D 73 B4
Dollnstein D 94 C3
Dollot F 104 A2
Döllstadt D 82 A2
Dolná Strehová SK 99 C3
Dolné Saliby SK 111 A4
Dolni Benešov CZ 98 B2
Dolni Bousov CZ 84 B3
Dolni Kounice CZ 97 B4
Dolni Kralovice CZ 97 B3
Dolni Újezd CZ 97 B4
Dolni Žandov CZ 95 A4
Dolný Kubín SK 99 B3
Dolo I 121 B5
Dolores E 165 A4
Dolovo SRB 127 C2
Dölsach A 109 C3
Dolsk PL 76 B2
Dolwyddelan GB 38 A3
Domaljevac BIH 125 B4
Domaniç TR 187 C4
Domaniža SK 98 B2
Domanovići BIH 139 B3
Domašov CZ 85 B5
Domaszék H 126 A1
Domaszków PL 85 B4
Domaszowice PL 86 A1
Domat-Ems CH 107 C4
Domažlice CZ 95 B4
Dombås N 198 C6
Dombasle-sur-Meurthe
F 92 C2
Dombegyház H 126 A3
Dombóvár H 112 C2
Domène F 118 B2
Domérat F 116 A2
Domfessel F 92 C3
Domfront F 88 B3
Domfront-en-
Champagne F 102 A2
Domingão P 154 B2
Domingo Pérez
Granada E 163 A4
Toledo E 150 C3
Dömitz D 73 A4
Dommartin F 91 C4
Dommartin-le-Franc
F 91 C4
Domme F 129 B4
Dommitzsch D 83 A4
Domodóssola I 119 A5
Domokos GR 182 D4
Domoszló H 113 B4
Dompaire F 105 A5
Dompierre-du-Chemin
F 88 B2
Dompierre-sur-Besbre
F 104 C2
Dompierre-sur-Mer
F 114 B2
Domrémy-la-Pucelle
F 92 C1
Dömsöd H 112 B3
Domsure F 118 A2
Dómus de Maria I 179 D2
Domusnóvas I 179 C2
Domvena GR 184 A3
Domžale SLO 123 A3
Donado E 141 B4
Donaghadee GB 27 B5
Don Alvaro E 155 C4
Doña Mencía E 163 A3
Donaueschingen D 106 B3
Donauwörth D 94 C2
Don Benito E 156 B2
Doncaster GB 40 B2
Donegal IRL 26 B2
Donestebe-Santesteban
E 144 A2
Donges F 101 B3
Dongo I 120 A2
Donington GB 41 C3
Doniños E 140 A2
Donja Bebrina HR 125 B4
Donja Brela HR 138 B2
Donja Dubica BIH 125 B4
Donja Dubrava HR 124 A2
Donja Kupčina HR 123 B4
Donja Šatornja
SRB 127 C2
Donja Stubica HR 124 B1
Donje Brišnik BIH 138 B3
Donje Stative HR 123 B4
Donji-Andrijevci
HR 125 B4
Donji Kazanci BIH 138 B2
Donji Koričáni BIH 138 A3
Donji Lapac HR 124 C1
Donji Malovan BIH 138 B3
Donji Miholjac HR 125 B4
Donji Mosti HR 124 A2
Donji Poloj HR 123 B4
Donji-Rujani BIH 138 B2
Donji Srb HR 138 A2
Donji Svilaj BIH 125 B4
Donji Tovarnik
SRB 127 C1
Donji Vakuf BIH 138 A3
Donnalucata I 177 C3
Donnemarie-Dontilly
F 90 C3
Donnersbach A 110 B1
Donnersbachwald
A 109 B5
Donnerskirchen A 111 B3
Donorático I 134 B3
Donostia-San Sebastián
E 144 A2
Donovaly SK 99 C3
Donzenac F 129 A4
Donzère F 131 A3
Donzy F 104 B2
Doonbeg IRL 29 B2
Doorn NL 70 B2
Dor E 140 A1
Dorchester GB 43 B4
Dørdal N 53 B5
Dordrecht NL 79 A4
Dörenthe D 71 B4
Dores GB 32 D2
Dorfen D 95 C4
Dorfgastein A 109 B4
Dorfmark D 72 B2
Dorf Mecklenburg D 65 C4
Dorgali I 178 B3
Dorking GB 44 B3
Dormagen D 80 A2
Dormánd H 113 B4
Dormans F 91 B3
Dornava SLO 124 A1
Dornbirn A 107 B4
Dornburg D 83 A3
Dorndorf D 82 B2
Dornecy F 104 B2
Dornes F 104 C2
Dornhan D 93 C4
Dornie GB 31 B3
Dornoch GB 32 D2
Dornum D 71 A4
Dorog H 112 B2
Dorohoi RO 17 B7
Dorotea S 200 B2
Dorotowo PL 69 B5
Dörpen D 71 B4
Dorsten D 80 A2
Dortan F 118 A2
Dortmund D 80 A3
Doruchów PL 86 A2
Dorum D 64 C1
Dörverden D 72 B2
Dörzbach D 94 B1
Dos Aguas E 159 B3
Dosbarrios E 151 C4
Döşemealtı TR 189 B5
Dos Hermanas E 162 A2
Dospat BG 183 B6
Dos-Torres E 156 B3
Dötlingen D 72 B1
Dottignies B 78 B3
Döttingen CH 106 B3
Douai F 78 B3
Douarnenez F 100 A1
Douchy F 104 B2
Douchy-les-Mines F 78 B3
Doucier F 105 C4
Doudeville F 89 A4
Doué-la-Fontaine
F 102 B1
Douglas
Isle of Man GB 36 B2
South Lanarkshire
GB 36 A3
Doulaincourt-Saucourt
F 91 C5
Doulevant-le-Château
F 91 C4
Doullens F 90 A2
Dounby GB 33 B3
Doune GB 35 B3
Dounreay GB 32 C3
Dour B 79 B3
Dourdan F 90 C2
Dourgne F 146 A3
Dournazac F 115 C4
Douro Calvo P 148 B2
Douvaine F 118 A3
Douvres-la-Délivrande
F 89 A3
Douzy F 91 B5
Dover GB 45 B5
Dovje SLO 109 C4
Dovre N 198 D6
Downham Market
GB 41 C4
Downhill GB 27 A4
Downpatrick GB 27 B5
Dowra IRL 26 B2
Doxato GR 183 B6
Doyet F 116 A2
Dozule F 89 A3
Drača SRB 127 C2
Dračevo
BIH 139 C4
MK 182 B3
Drachten NL 70 A3
Draga SLO 123 B3
Drăgăşani RO 17 C6
Dragatuš SLO 123 B4
Dragichyn BY 13 B6
Draginja SRB 127 C1
Dragocvet SRB 127 D3
Dragolovci BIH 125 C3
Dragoni I 170 B2
Dragør DK 61 D2
Dragotina HR 124 B2
Dragotinja BIH 124 B2
Dragozetići HR 123 B3
Draguignan F 132 B2
Drahnsdorf D 74 C2
Drahonice CZ 96 B2
Drahovce SK 98 C1
Drama GR 183 B6
Drammen N 54 A1
Drangedal N 53 A5
Drangsnes IS 190 B4
Dransfeld D 82 A1
Dranske D 66 B2
Draperstown GB 27 B4
Drassburg A 111 B3
Drávaszabolcs H 125 B4
Dravograd SLO 110 C2
Drawno PL 75 A4
Drawsko Pomorskie
PL 75 A4
Drayton GB 41 C5
Drązdżewo PL 77 A6
Draženov CZ 95 B4
Draževac SRB 127 C2
Dražice HR 123 B3
Drebkau D 84 A2
Dreieich D 93 A4
Dreisen D 93 B4
Drenovci HR 125 C4
Drensteinfurt D 81 A3
Dresden D 84 A1
Dretyń PL 68 A1
Dreux F 89 B5
Dřevohostice CZ 98 B1
Drevsjø N 199 D9
Drewitz D 73 B5
Drezdenko PL 75 B4
Drežnica HR 123 B4
Drežnik-Grad HR 123 C4
Drietona SK 98 C1
Driffield GB 40 A3
Drimnin GB 34 B2
Drimoleague IRL 29 C2
Dringenberg D 81 A5
Drinić BIH 138 A2
Drinjača BIH 139 A5
Drinovci BIH 138 B3
Driopida GR 185 B5
Drivstua N 198 C6
Drlače SRB 127 C1
Drnholec CZ 97 C4
Drniš HR 138 B2
Drnje HR 124 A2
Drnovice CZ 97 B4
Dro I 121 B3
Drøbak N 54 A1
Drobin PL 77 B5
Drochia MD 17 A7
Drochtersen D 64 C2
Drogheda IRL 30 A2
Drohobych UA 13 D5
Droitwich Spa GB 44 A1
Drołtowice PL 85 A5
Dromahair IRL 26 B2
Dromcolliher IRL 29 B3
Dromore
Down GB 27 B4
Tyrone GB 27 B3
Dromore West IRL 26 B2
Dronero I 133 A3
Dronfield GB 40 B2
Drongan GB 36 A2
Dronninglund DK 58 A3
Dronrijp NL 70 A2
Dronten NL 70 B2
Drosendorf A 97 C3
Drösing A 97 C4
Drottningholm S 57 A3
Droué F 103 A3
Drulingen F 92 C3
Drumbeg GB 32 C1
Drumcliff IRL 26 B2
Drumgask GB 32 D2
Drumkeeran IRL 26 B2
Drummore GB 36 B2
Drumnadrochit GB 32 D2
Drumquin GB 27 B3
Drumshanbo IRL 26 B2
Drumsna IRL 26 C2
Drunen NL 79 A5
Druskininkai LT 13 A5
Druten NL 80 A1
Druya BY 13 A7
Družetići SRB 127 C2
Drvar BIH 138 A2
Drvenik HR 138 B3
Drwalew PL 77 C6
Drymen GB 34 B3
Drynoch GB 31 B2
Drzewce PL 76 B2
Drzewiany PL 68 B1
Drzewica PL 87 A4
Dualchi I 178 B2
Duas Igrejas P 149 A3
Dub SRB 127 D1
Dubá CZ 84 B2
Dubăsari MD 17 B8
Duben D 74 C2
Dübendorf CH 107 B3
Dubi CZ 84 B1
Dubica HR 124 B2
Dublin IRL 30 A2
Dubna RUS 9 D10
Dubňany CZ 98 C1
Dubnica nad Váhom
SK 98 C2
Dubnik SK 112 B2
Dubno UA 13 C6
Dubodiel SK 98 C2
Dubona SRB 127 C2
Dubovac SRB 127 C3
Dubovic BIH 124 C2
Dubranec HR 124 B1
Dubrava HR 124 B2
Dubrave BIH 125 C4
Dubravica
HR 123 B4
SRB 127 C3
Dubrovnik HR 139 C4
Dubrovytsya UA 13 C7
Ducey F 88 B2
Duchcov CZ 84 B1
Ducherow D 74 A2
Dučina SRB 127 C2
Duclair F 89 A4
Dudar H 112 B1
Duddington GB 40 C3
Duderstadt D 82 A2
Dudeştii Vechi RO 126 A2
Dudley GB 40 C1
Dueñas E 142 C2
Duesund N 46 B2
Dueville I 121 B4
Duffel B 79 A4
Duffield GB 40 C2
Dufftown GB 32 D3
Duga Resa HR 123 B4
Dugi Rat HR 138 B2
Dugny-sur-Meuse F 92 B1
Dugopolje HR 138 B2
Dugo Selo HR 124 B2
Duino I 122 B2
Duisburg D 80 A2
Dukat AL 182 C1
Dukovany CZ 97 B4
Duleek IRL 30 A2
Dülken D 80 A2
Dülmen D 80 A3
Dulovo BG 17 D7
Dulpetorpet N 49 B4
Dulverton GB 43 A3
Dumbarton GB 34 C3
Dümerek TR 187 C6
Dumfries GB 36 A3
Dumlupınar TR 187 D4
Dümpelfeld D 80 B2
Dunaalmás H 112 B2
Dunabogdány H 112 B3
Dunafalva H 125 A4
Dunaföldvár H 112 C2
Dunaharaszti H 112 B3
Dunajská Streda
SK 111 B4
Dunakeszi H 112 B3
Dunakiliti H 111 B4
Dunakömlöd H 112 C2
Dunapataj H 112 C2
Dunaszekcső H 125 A4
Dunaszentgyorgy
H 112 C2
Dunatetétlen H 112 C3
Dunaújváros H 112 C2
Dunavecse H 112 C2
Dunbar GB 35 B5
Dunbeath GB 32 C3
Dunblane GB 35 B4
Dunboyne IRL 30 A2
Dundalk IRL 27 B4
Dundee GB 35 B5
Dundrennan GB 36 B3
Dundrum GB 27 B5
Dunfanaghy IRL 26 A3
Dunfermline GB 35 B4
Dungannon GB 27 B4
Dungarvan IRL 29 B4
Dungiven GB 27 B4
Dunglow IRL 26 B2
Dungourney IRL 29 C3
Duninowo PL 68 A1
Dunkeld GB 35 B4
Dunker S 56 A2
Dunkerque = Dunkirk
F 78 A2
Dunkineely IRL 26 B2
Dunkirk = Dunkerque
F 78 A2
Dun Laoghaire IRL 30 A2
Dunlavin IRL 30 A2
Dunleer IRL 27 C4
Dun-le-Palestel F 116 A1
Dun-les-Places F 104 B3
Dunlop GB 36 A2
Dunloy GB 27 A4
Dunmanway IRL 29 C2
Dunmore IRL 28 A3
Dunmore East IRL 30 B2
Dunmurry GB 27 B4
Dunnet GB 32 C3
Dunningen D 107 A3
Dunoon GB 34 C3
Duns GB 35 C5
Dunscore GB 36 A3
Dunsford GB 43 B3
Dunshaughlin IRL 30 A2
Dunstable GB 44 B3
Dunster GB 43 A3
Dun-sur-Auron F 103 C4
Dun-sur-Meuse F 91 B5
Dunvegan GB 31 B2
Duplek SLO 110 C2
Dupnitsa BG 17 D5
Durağan TR 23 A8
Durach D 107 B5
Durak TR 186 C3
Durana E 143 B4
Durance F 128 B3
Durango E 143 A4
Durankulak BG 17 D8
Duras F 128 B3
Durban-Corbières
F 146 B3
Dürbheim D 107 A3
Durbuy B 79 B5
Dúrcal E 163 B4
Đurdjenovac HR 125 B4
Đurdjevac HR 124 A3
Đurdjevik BIH 139 A4
Düren D 80 B2
Durham GB 37 B5
Đurinci SRB 127 C2
Durlach D 93 C4
Đurmanec HR 124 A1
Durness GB 32 C2
Dürnkrut A 97 C4
Dürrboden CH 107 C4
Dürrenboden CH 107 C3
Durrës AL 182 B1
Durrow IRL 30 B1
Durrus IRL 29 C2
Dursunbey TR 186 C3
Durtal F 102 B1
Durup DK 58 B1
Durusu TR 186 A3
Dusina BIH 139 B3
Dusnok H 112 C2
Dusocin PL 69 B3
Düsseldorf D 80 A2
Dusslingen D 93 C5
Duszniki PL 75 B5
Duszniki-Zdrój PL 85 B4
Dutovlje SLO 122 B2
Duvebo S 55 B5
Duved S 199 B9
Düzağac TR 187 D5
Düzce TR 187 B6
Dvärsätt S 199 B11
Dvor HR 124 B2
Dvorce CZ 98 B1
Dvorníky SK 98 C1
Dvory nad Žitavou
SK 112 B2
Dvůr Královénad Labem
CZ 85 B3
Dybvad DK 58 A3
Dyce GB 33 D4
Dygowo PL 67 B4
Dykehead GB 35 B4
Dymchurch GB 45 B5
Dymer UA 13 C9
Dyrnes N 198 B4
Dywity PL 69 B5
Džaniči BIH 139 B3
Dziadowa Kłoda PL 86 A1
Działdowo PL 77 A5
Działoszyce PL 87 B4
Działoszyn PL 86 A2
Dziemiany PL 68 A2
Dzierzążnia PL 77 B5
Dzierzgoń PL 69 B4
Dzierzgowo PL 77 A5
Dzierżoniów PL 85 B4
Dzisna BY 13 A8
Dziwnów PL 67 B3
Dźwierzuty PL 77 A5
Dzyarzhynsk BY 13 B7
Dzyatlava BY 13 B6

E

Ea E 143 A4
Eaglesfield GB 36 A3
Ealing GB 44 B3
Eardisley GB 39 B3
Earls Barton GB 44 A3
Earl Shilton GB 40 C2
Earlston GB 35 C5
Easington GB 41 B4
Easky IRL 26 B2
Eastbourne GB 45 C4
East Calder GB 35 C4
East Dereham GB 41 C4
Easter Skeld GB 33 A5
East Grinstead GB 45 B4
East Ilsley GB 44 B2
East Kilbride GB 36 A2
Eastleigh GB 44 C2
East Linton GB 35 C5
East Markham GB 40 B3
Easton GB 43 B4
East Wittering GB 44 C3
Eaton Socon GB 44 A3
Eaux-Bonnes F 145 B3
Eauze F 128 C3
Ebberup DK 59 C2
Ebbs A 108 B3
Ebbw Vale GB 39 C3
Ebeleben D 82 A2
Ebeltoft DK 59 B3
Ebene Reichenau
A 109 C4
Eben im Pongau A 109 B4
Ebensee A 109 B4
Ebensfeld D 94 A2
Eberbach D 93 B4
Ebergötzen D 82 A2
Ebermann-Stadt D 94 B3
Ebern D 82 B2
Eberndorf A 110 C1
Ebersbach D 84 A2
Ebersberg D 108 A2
Ebersdorf
Bayern D 82 B3
Niedersachsen D 72 A2
Eberstein A 110 C1
Eberswalde D 74 B2
Ebnat-Kappel CH 107 B4
Éboli I 170 C3
Ebrach D 94 B2
Ebreichsdorf A 111 B3
Ebreuil F 116 A3
Ebstorf D 72 A3
Ecclefechan GB 36 A3
Eccleshall GB 40 C1
Eceabat TR 186 B1
Echallens CH 106 C1
Echauri E 144 B2
Echinos GR 183 B7

Echiré F 114 B3
Échirolles F 118 B2
Echourgnac F 128 A3
Echt NL 80 A1
Echte D 82 A2
Echternach L 92 B2
Ecija E 162 A2
Ečka SRB 126 B2
Eckartsberga D 82 A3
Eckelshausen D 81 B4
Eckental D 94 B3
Eckernförde D 64 B2
Eckerö FIN 51 B6
Eckington GB 40 B2
Éclaron F 91 C4
Écommoy F 102 B2
Écouché F 89 B3
Ecouis F 90 B1
Ecséd H 113 B3
Ecsegfalva H 113 B4
Écueillé F 103 B3
Ed S 54 B2
Eda S 49 C4
Eda glasbruk S 49 C4
Edam NL 70 B2
Edane S 55 A3
Edderton GB 32 D2
Ede NL 70 B2
Edebäck S 49 B5
Edebo S 51 B5
Edelény H 99 C4
Edelschrott A 110 B2
Edemissen D 72 B3
Edenbridge GB 45 B4
Edenderry IRL 30 A1
Edenkoben D 93 B4
Edesheim D 93 B4
Edessa GR 182 C4
Edewecht D 71 A4
Edgeworthstown IRL 30 A1
Edinburgh GB 35 C4
Edineţ MD 17 A7
Edirne TR 186 A1
Edland N 52 A3
Edolo I 120 A3
Edøy N 198 B5
Edremit TR 186 C2
Edsbro S 51 C5
Edsbruk S 56 B2
Edsbyn S 50 A2
Edsele S 200 C2
Edsleskog S 54 A3
Edsvalla S 55 A4
Eekloo B 79 A3
Eemshaven NL 71 A3
Eerbeek NL 70 B3
Eersel NL 79 A5
Eferding A 96 C2
Effiat F 116 A3
Efteløt N 53 A5
Egeln D 73 C4
Eger H 113 B4
Egerbakta H 113 B4
Egernsund DK 64 B2
Egersund N 52 B2
Egerszólát H 113 B4
Egervár H 111 C3
Egg
A 107 B4
D 107 A5
Eggby S 55 B4
Eggedal N 47 B6
Eggenburg A 97 C3
Eggenfelden D 95 C4
Eggesin D 74 A3
Eggum N 194 B4
Egham GB 44 B3
Éghezée B 79 B4
Egiertowo PL 68 A3
Egilsstaðir IS 191 B11
Egina GR 185 B4
Eginio GR 182 C4
Egio GR 184 A3
Égletons F 116 B2
Egling D 108 B2
Eglinton GB 27 A3
Eglisau CH 107 B3
Égliseneuve-d'Entraigues F 116 B2
Eglofs D 107 B4
Egmond aan Zee NL 70 B1
Egna I 121 A4
Egosthena GR 184 A4
Egremont GB 36 B3
Egtved DK 59 C2
Eguilles F 131 B4
Eguilly-sous-Bois F 104 A3
Éguzon-Chantôme F 103 C3
Egyek H 113 B4
Egyházasrádóc H 111 B3
Ehekirchen D 94 C3
Ehingen D 94 C1
Ehra-Lessien D 73 B3
Ehrang D 92 B2
Ehrenfriedersdorf D 83 B4
Ehrenhain D 83 B4
Ehrenhausen A 110 C2
Ehringshausen D 81 B4
Ehrwald A 108 B1
Eibar E 143 A4
Eibelstadt D 94 B2
Eibenstock D 83 B4
Eibergen NL 71 B3
Eibiswald A 110 C2
Eichenbarleben D 73 B4
Eichendorf D 95 C4
Eichstätt D 95 C3
Eickelborn D 81 A4
Eide
Hordaland N 46 B3
Møre og Romsdal N 198 C4
Eidet N 194 A9
Eidfjord N 46 B4
Eidsberg N 54 A2
Eidsbugarden N 47 A5
Eidsdal N 198 C4
Eidsfoss N 53 A6
Eidskog N 49 B4
Eidsvåg
Hordaland N 46 B2
Møre og Romsdal N 198 C5
Eidsvoll N 48 B3
Eikefjord N 46 A2
Eikelandsosen N 46 B2
Eiken N 52 B3
Eikesdal N 198 C5
Eikstrand N 53 A5
Eilenburg D 83 A4
Eilsleben D 73 B4
Eina N 48 B2
Einbeck D 82 A1
Eindhoven NL 79 A5
Einsiedeln CH 107 B3
Einville-au-Jard F 92 C2
Eisenach D 82 B2
Eisenberg
Rheinland-Pfalz D 93 B4
Thüringen D 83 B3
Eisenerz A 110 B1
Eisenhüttenstadt D 74 B3
Eisenkappel A 110 C1
Eisenstadt A 111 B3
Eisentratten A 109 C4
Eisfeld D 82 B2
Eisleben D 82 A3
Eislingen D 94 C1
Eitensheim D 95 C3
Eiterfeld D 82 B1
Eitorf D 80 B3
Eivindvik N 46 B2
Eivissa = Ibiza E 166 C1
Eixo P 148 B1
Ejby DK 59 C2
Ejea de los Caballeros E 144 B2
Ejstrupholm DK 59 C2
Ejulve E 153 B3
Eke B 79 B3
Ekeby
Gotland S 57 C4
Skåne S 61 D2
Uppsala S 51 B5
Ekeby-Almby S 56 A1
Ekenäs S 55 B4
Ekenässjön S 62 A3
Ekerö S 57 A3
Eket S 61 C3
Eketorp S 63 B4
Ekevik S 56 B2
Ekkerøy N 193 B14
Ekshärad S 49 B5
Eksingedal N 46 B2
Eksjö S 62 A2
Eksta S 57 C4
Ekträsk S 200 B5
El Alamo
Madrid E 151 B4
Sevilla E 161 B3
El Algar E 165 B4
El Almendro E 161 B2
El Alquián E 164 C2
Élancourt F 90 C1
El Arahal E 162 A2
El Arenal E 150 B2
El Arguellite E 164 A2
Elassona GR 182 D4
El Astillero E 143 A3
Elati GR 182 D3
Żelazno PL 85 B4
El Ballestero E 158 C1
El Barco de Ávila E 150 B2
Elbasan AL 182 B2
El Berrón E 142 A1
El Berrueco E 151 B4
Elbeuf F 89 A4
Elbingerode D 82 A2
Elbląg PL 69 A4
El Bodón E 149 B3
El Bonillo E 158 C1
El Bosque E 162 B2
El Bullaque E 157 A3
Elburg NL 70 B2
El Burgo E 162 B3
El Burgo de Ebro E 153 A3
El Burgo de Osma E 151 A4
El Burgo Ranero E 142 B1
El Buste E 144 C2
El Cabaco E 149 B3
El Callejo E 143 A3
El Campillo E 161 B3
El Campillo de la Jara E 156 A2
El Cañavete E 158 B1
El Carpio E 157 C3
El Carpio de Tajo E 150 C3
El Casar E 151 B4
El Casar de Escalona E 150 B3
El Castillo de las Guardas E 161 B3
El Centenillo E 157 B4
El Cerro E 149 B4
El Cerro de Andévalo E 161 B3
Elche E 165 A4
Elche de la Sierra E 158 C1
Elchingen D 94 C2
El Comenar E 162 B2
El Coronil E 162 A2
El Crucero E 141 A4
El Cubo de Tierra del Vino E 149 A4
El Cuervo E 162 B1
Elda E 159 C3
Eldena D 73 A4
Eldingen D 72 B3
Elefsina GR 185 A4
El Ejido E 164 C2
Elek H 113 C5
Elemir SRB 126 B2
El Escorial E 151 B3
El Espinar E 151 B3
Eleutheroupoli GR 183 C6
El Frago E 144 B3
El Franco E 141 A4
El Frasno E 152 A2
Elgå N 199 C8
El Garrobo E 161 B3
El Gastor E 162 B2
Elgin GB 32 D3
Elgoibar E 143 A4
Elgol GB 31 B2
El Gordo E 150 C2
El Grado E 145 B4
El Granado E 161 B2
El Grao de Castelló E 159 B4
El Grau E 159 C3
Elgshøa N 49 A4
El Higuera E 163 A3
El Hijate E 164 B2
El Hontanar E 152 B2
El Hoyo E 157 B4
Elie GB 35 B5
Elizondo E 144 A2
Ełk PL 12 B5
Elkhovo BG 17 D7
Ellenberg D 94 B2
Ellesmere GB 38 B4
Ellesmere Port GB 38 A4
Ellezelles B 79 B3
Ellingen D 94 B2
Ellmau A 109 B3
Ellon GB 33 D4
Ellös S 54 B2
Ellrich D 82 A2
Ellwangen D 94 C2
Elm
CH 107 C4
D 72 A2
Elmadağ TR 23 B7
El Madroño E 161 B3
El Maillo E 149 B3
Elmalı TR 189 C4
El Masnou E 147 C3
El Mirón E 150 B2
El Molar E 151 B4
El Molinillo E 157 A3
El Morell E 147 C2
Elmshorn D 64 C2
Elmstein D 93 B3
El Muyo E 151 A4
Elne F 146 B3
Elnesvågen N 198 C4
El Olmo E 151 A4
Elorrio E 143 A4
Elöszállás H 112 C2
Elouda GR 185 D6
Éloyes F 105 A5
El Palo E 163 B3
El Pardo E 151 B4
El Payo E 149 B3
El Pedernoso E 158 B1
El Pedroso E 162 A2
El Peral E 158 B2
El Perelló
Tarragona E 153 B4
Valencia E 159 B3
Elphin GB 32 C1
El Picazo E 158 B1
El Pinell de Bray E 153 A4
El Piñero E 150 A2
El Pla de Santa Maria E 147 C2
El Pobo E 153 B3
El Pobo de Dueñas E 152 B2
El Pont d'Armentera E 147 C2
El Port de la Selva E 147 B4
El Port de Llançà E 146 B4
El Port de Sagunt E 159 B3
El Prat de Llobregat E 147 C3
El Provencio E 158 B1
El Puente E 143 A3
El Puente del Arzobispo E 150 C2
El Puerto E 141 A4
El Puerto de Santa María E 162 B1
El Real de la Jara E 161 B3
El Real de San Vincente E 150 B3
El Robledo E 157 A3
El Rocio E 161 B3
El Rompido E 161 B2
El Ronquillo E 161 B3
El Royo E 143 C4
El Rubio E 162 A3
El Sabinar E 164 A2
El Saler E 159 B3
El Salobral E 158 C2
El Saucejo E 162 A2
Els Castells E 147 B2
Elsdorf D 80 B2
Elsenfeld D 93 B5
El Serrat AND 146 B2
Elsfleth D 72 A1
Elspeet NL 70 B2
Elst NL 70 C2
Elstead GB 44 B3
Elster D 83 A4
Elsterberg D 83 B4
Elsterwerda D 83 A5
Elstra D 84 A2
El Temple E 144 C3
El Tiemblo E 150 B3
Eltmann D 94 B2
El Toboso E 157 A5
El Tormillo E 145 C3
El Torno E 149 B4
Eltville D 93 A4
El Valle de las Casas E 142 B1
Elvas P 155 C3
Elvebakken N 192 C7
El Vellón E 151 B4
Elven F 101 B3
El Vendrell E 147 C2
Elverum N 48 B3
El Villar de Arnedo E 144 B1
Elvington GB 40 B3
El Viso E 156 B3
El Viso del Alcor E 162 A2
Elxleben D 82 A2
Ely GB 45 A4
Elzach D 106 A3
Elze D 72 B2
Emådalen S 50 A1
Embleton GB 37 A5
Embonas GR 188 C2
Embrun F 132 A2
Embún E 144 B3
Emden D 71 A4
Emecik TR 188 C2
Emet TR 186 C4
Emirdağ TR 187 C6
Emlichheim D 71 B3
Emmaboda S 63 B3
Emmaljunga S 61 C3
Emmeloord NL 70 B2
Emmen
CH 106 B3
NL 71 B3
Emmendingen D 106 A2
Emmer-Compascuum NL 71 B4
Emmerich D 80 A2
Emmern D 72 B2
Emöd H 113 B4
Émpoli I 135 B3
Emsbüren D 71 B4
Emsdetten D 71 B4
Emsfors S 62 A4
Emskirchen D 94 B2
Emstek D 71 B5
Emsworth GB 44 C3
Emyvale IRL 27 B4
Enafors S 199 B9
Enånger S 51 A4
Encamp AND 146 B2
Encarnaçao P 154 C1
Encinas de Abajo E 150 B2
Encinas de Esgueva E 142 C2
Encinasola E 161 A3
Encinas Reales E 163 A3
Encio E 143 B3
Enciso E 144 B1
Enden N 199 D7
Endingen D 106 A2
Endrinal E 149 B4
Endröd H 113 C4
Enebakk N 54 A2
Eneryda S 63 B2
Enese H 111 B4
Enez TR 183 C8
Enfield IRL 30 A2
Eng A 108 B2
Engelberg CH 106 C3
Engelhartszell A 96 C1
Engelskirchen D 80 B3
Engen D 107 B3
Enger N 48 B2
Engerdal N 199 D8
Engerneset N 49 A4
Enge-sande D 64 B1
Engesvang DK 59 B2
Enghien B 79 B4
Engstingen D 94 C1
Engter D 71 B5
Enguera E 159 C3
Enguidanos E 158 B2
Enkenbach D 93 B3
Enkhuizen NL 70 B2
Enklinge FIN 51 B7
Enköping S 56 A3
Enna I 177 B3
Ennezat F 116 B3
Ennigerloh D 81 A4
Enningdal N 54 B2
Ennis IRL 28 B3
Enniscorthy IRL 30 B2
Enniskean IRL 29 C3
Enniskillen GB 27 B3
Ennistimon IRL 28 B2
Enns A 110 A1
Eno FIN 9 A7
Enontekiö FIN 196 A6
Ens NL 70 B2
Enschede NL 71 B3
Ensdorf D 95 B3
Ensisheim F 106 B2
Enstaberga S 56 B2
Enstone GB 44 B2
Entlebuch CH 106 B3
Entrácque I 133 A3
Entradas P 160 B1
Entrains-sur-Nohain F 104 B2
Entrambasaguas E 143 A3
Entrambasmestas E 143 A3
Entraygues-sur-Truyère F 116 C2
Entre-os-Rios P 148 A1
Entrevaux F 132 B2
Entrin Bajo E 155 C4
Entroncamento P 154 B2
Entzheim F 93 C3
Envermeu F 89 A5
Enviken S 50 B2
Enying H 112 C2
Enzingerboden A 109 B3
Enzklösterle D 93 C4
Épagny F 90 B3
Epalinges CH 106 C1
Epannes F 114 B3
Epanomi GR 182 C4
Epe
D 71 B4
NL 70 B2
Épernay F 91 B3
Épernon F 90 C1
Epfig F 93 C3
Epierre F 118 B3
Épila E 152 A2
Épinac F 104 C3
Épinal F 105 A5
Episcopia I 174 A2
Episkopi CY 181 B1
Epitalio GR 184 B2
Epoisses F 104 B3
Eppenbrunn D 93 B3
Eppendorf D 83 B5
Epping GB 45 B4
Eppingen D 93 B4
Epsom GB 44 B3
Epworth GB 40 B3
Eraclea I 122 B1
Eraclea Mare I 122 B1
Erba I 120 B2
Erbach
Baden-Württemberg D 94 C1
Hessen D 93 B4
Erbalunga F 180 A2
Erbendorf D 95 B4
Érchie I 173 B3
Ercolano I 170 C2
Ercsi H 112 B2
Érd H 112 B2
Erdek TR 186 B2
Erdemli TR 23 C8
Erdevik SRB 126 B1
Erding D 95 C3
Erdötelek H 113 B4
Erdut HR 125 B5
Erdweg D 95 C3
Ereğli
Konya TR 23 C8
Zonguldak TR 187 A6
Erenkaya TR 189 B7
Eresfjord N 198 C5
Eresos GR 183 D7
Eretria GR 185 A4
Erfde D 64 B2
Erfjord N 52 A2
Erfstadt D 80 B2
Erfurt D 82 B3
Ergli LV 8 D4
Ergoldsbach D 95 C4
Eriboll GB 32 C2
Érice I 176 A1
Ericeira P 154 C1
Eğridir TR 189 B5
Eriksberg S 195 E6
Eriksmåla S 62 B3
Eringsboda S 63 B3
Eriswil CH 106 B2
Erithres GR 185 A4
Erkelenz D 80 A2
Erkner D 74 B2
Erkrath D 80 A2
Erla E 144 B3
Erlangen D 94 B3
Erli I 133 A4
Erlsbach A 109 C3
Ermelo NL 70 B2
Ermenak TR 23 C7
Ermenonville F 90 B2
Ermezinde P 148 A1
Ermidas P 160 A1
Ermioni GR 184 B4
Ermoupoli GR 185 B5
Ermsleben D 82 A3
Erndtebrück D 81 B4
Ernée F 88 B3
Ernestinovo HR 125 B4
Ernstbrunn A 97 C4
Erolzheim D 107 A5
Erquelinnes B 79 B4
Erquy F 101 A3
Erra P 154 C2
Erratzu E 144 A2
Errindlev DK 65 B4
Erro E 144 B2
Ersa F 180 A2
Érsekcsanád H 125 A4
Ersekë AL 182 C2
Érsekvadkert H 112 B3
Ersmark S 200 C6
Erstein F 93 C3
Erstfeld CH 107 C3
Ertebølle DK 58 B2
Ertingen D 107 A4
Ervedal
Coimbra P 148 B1
Portalegre P 154 B3
Ervenik HR 138 A1
Ervidel P 160 B1
Ervy-le-Châtel F 104 A2
Erwitte D 81 A4
Erxleben D 73 B4
Erzsébet H 125 A4
Esbjerg DK 59 C1
Esbly F 90 C2
Escacena del Campo E 161 B3
Escairón E 140 B3
Escalada E 143 B3
Escalante E 143 A3
Escalaplano I 179 C3
Escalona E 150 B3
Escalona del Prado E 151 A3
Escalonilla E 150 C3
Escalos de Baixo P 155 B3
Escalos de Cima P 155 B3
Escamilla E 152 B1
Es Caná E 166 B1
Escañuela E 157 C3
Es Castell E 167 B4
Escatrón E 153 A3
Eschach D 107 B4
Eschau D 94 B1
Eschede D 72 B3
Eschenau D 95 B3
Eschenbach D 95 B3
Eschenz CH 107 B3
Eschershausen D 72 C2
Esch-sur-Alzette L 92 B1
Esch-sur-Sûre L 92 B1
Eschwege D 82 A2
Eschweiler D 80 B2
Escobasa de Almazán E 152 A1
Escoeuilles F 78 B1
Escombreras E 165 B4
Escos F 144 A2
Escource F 128 B1
Escragnolles F 132 B2
Escrick GB 40 B2
Escurial E 156 A2
Escurial de la Sierra E 149 B4
Esens D 71 A4
Esgos E 140 B3
Esher GB 44 B3
Eskdalemuir GB 36 A3
Eskifjörður IS 191 B12
Eskilhem S 57 C4
Eskilsäter S 55 B4
Eskilstrup DK 65 B4
Eskilstuna S 56 A2
Eskipazar TR 187 B7
Eskişehir TR 187 C5
Eslarn D 95 B4
Eslava E 144 B2
Eslida E 159 B3
Eslohe D 81 A4
Eslöv S 61 D3
Eşme TR 188 A3
Es Mercadal E 167 B4
Es Migjorn Gran E 167 B4
Espa N 48 B3
Espalion F 130 A1
Esparragalejo E 155 C4
Esparragosa del Caudillo E 156 B2
Esparragossa de la Serena E 156 B2
Esparreguera E 147 C2
Esparron F 132 B1
Espe N 46 B3
Espedal N 52 B2
Espejo
Alava E 143 B3
Córdoba E 163 A3
Espeland N 46 B2
Espelkamp D 72 B1
Espeluche F 131 A3
Espeluy E 157 B4
Espera E 162 B2
Esperança P 155 B3

Espéraza F 146 B3
Espéria I 169 B3
Espevær N 52 A1
Espiel E 156 B2
Espinama E 142 A2
Espiñaredo E 140 A3
Espinasses F 132 A2
Espinelves E 147 C3
Espinhal P 154 A2
Espinho P 148 A1
Espinilla E 142 A2
Espinosa de Cerrato E 143 C3
Espinosa de los Monteros E 143 A3
Espinoso del Rey E 156 A3
Espirito Santo P 160 B2
Espluga de Francolí E 147 C2
Esplús E 145 C4
Espolla E 146 B3
Espoo FIN 8 B4
Esporles E 166 B2
Es Port d'Alcúdia E 167 B3
Esposende P 148 A1
Espot E 146 B2
Es Pujols E 166 C1
Esquedas E 145 B3
Esquivias E 151 B4
Essay F 89 B4
Essen
B 79 A4
Niedersachsen D 71 B4
Nordrhein-Westfalen D 80 A3
Essenbach D 95 C4
Essertaux F 90 B2
Essingen D 94 C2
Esslingen D 94 C1
Es Solerãs E 153 A4
Essoyes F 104 A3
Estacas E 140 B2
Estadilla E 145 B4
Estagel F 146 B3
Estaires F 78 B2
Estang F 128 C2
Estarreja P 148 B1
Estartit E 147 B4
Estavayer-le-Lac CH 106 C1
Este I 121 B4
Esteiro E 140 A2
Estela P 148 A1
Estella E 144 B1
Estellencs E 166 B2
Estepa E 162 A3
Estépar E 143 B3
Estepona E 162 B2
Esternay F 91 C3
Esterri d'Aneu E 146 B2
Esterwegen D 71 B4
Estissac F 104 A2
Estivadas E 140 B3
Estivareilles F 116 A2
Estivella E 159 B3
Estói P 160 B2
Estopiñán E 145 C4
Estoril P 154 C1
Estoublon F 132 B2
Estrée-Blanche F 78 B2
Estrées-St Denis F 90 B2
Estrela P 155 C3
Estremera E 151 B4
Estremoz P 155 C3
Estuna S 51 C5
Esyres F 102 B2
Esztergom H 112 B2
Etables-sur-Mer F 100 A3
Étain F 92 B1
Étalans F 105 B5
Etalle B 92 B1
Étampes F 90 C2
Etang-sur-Arroux F 104 C3
Étaples F 78 B1
Etauliers F 128 A2
Etili TR 186 C1
Etna N 48 B1
Etne N 52 A1
Etoges F 91 C3
Etoliko GR 184 A2
Eton GB 44 B3
Etréaupont F 91 B3
Étréchy F 90 C2
Étrépagny F 90 B1
Étretat F 89 A4
Étroeungt F 91 A3
Étroubles I 119 B4
Ettal D 108 B2
Ettelbruck L 92 B2
Etten NL 79 A4
Ettenheim D 106 A2
Ettington GB 44 A2
Ettlingen D 93 C4
Ettringen D 108 A1
Etuz F 105 B4
Etxarri-Aranatz E 144 B1
Etyek H 112 B2
Eu F 90 A1
Euerdorf D 82 B2
Eulate E 144 B1
Eupen B 80 B2
Europoort NL 79 A4
Euskirchen D 80 B2
Eutin D 65 B3
Evanger N 46 B3
Évaux-les-Bains F 116 A2
Evciler
Afyon TR 189 A4
Çanakkale TR 186 C1
Evenskjær N 194 B7
Evenstad N 48 A3
Evercreech GB 43 A4
Evergem B 79 A3
Everöd S 61 D4
Eversberg D 81 A4
Everswinkel D 71 C4
Evertsberg S 49 A5
Evesham GB 44 A2
Évian-les-Bains F 118 A3
Evisa F 180 A1
Evje N 53 B3
Evolène CH 119 A4
Évora P 154 C3
Evoramonte P 155 C3
Evran F 101 A4
Evrecy F 89 A3
Évreux F 89 A5
Évron F 102 A1
Évry F 90 C2
Ewell GB 44 B3
Ewersbach D 81 B4
Excideuil F 115 C5
Exeter GB 43 B3
Exmes F 89 B4
Exminster GB 43 B3
Exmouth GB 43 B3
Eydehamn N 53 B4
Eye
Peterborough GB 41 C3
Suffolk GB 45 A5
Eyemouth GB 35 C5
Eyguians F 132 A1
Eyguières F 131 B4
Eygurande F 116 B2
Eylie F 145 B4
Eymet F 129 B3
Eymoutiers F 116 B1
Eynsham GB 44 B2
Eyrarbakki IS 190 D4
Eystrup D 72 B2
Ezaro E 140 B1
Ezcaray E 143 B4
Ezcároz E 144 B2
Ezine TR 186 C1
Ezmoriz P 148 B1

F

Fabara E 153 A4
Fábbrico I 121 C3
Fåberg N 48 A2
Fabero E 141 B4
Fábiánsebestyén H 113 C4
Fåborg DK 64 A3
Fabrègues F 130 B2
Fabriano I 136 B1
Fabrizia I 175 C2
Facha P 148 A1
Facinas E 162 B2
Fačkov SK 98 B2
Fadagosa P 155 B3
Fadd H 112 C2
Faédis I 122 A2
Faenza I 135 A4
Fafe P 148 A1
Fagagna I 122 A2
Făgăras RO 17 C6
Fågelberget S 199 A11
Fågelfors S 62 A3
Fågelmara S 63 B3
Fågelsta S 55 B6
Fagerås S 55 A4
Fagerheim N 47 B4
Fagerhøy N 48 A1
Fagerhult S 62 A3
Fagerlund N 48 B2
Fagernes
Oppland N 47 B6
Troms N 192 C3
Fagersanna S 55 B5
Fagersta S 50 B2
Fåglavik S 55 B4
Fagnano Castello I 174 B2
Fagnières F 91 C4
Faido CH 107 C3
Fains-Véel F 91 C5
Fairford GB 44 B2
Fairlie GB 34 C3
Fajsz H 112 C2
Fakenham GB 41 C4
Fåker S 199 B11
Fakse DK 65 A5
Fakse Ladeplads DK 65 A5
Falaise F 89 B3
Falcade I 121 A4
Falcarragh IRL 26 A2
Falces E 144 B2
Fălciu RO 17 B8
Falconara I 177 B3
Falconara Maríttima I 136 B2
Falcone I 177 A4
Faldingworth GB 40 B3
Falerum S 56 B2
Fălești MD 17 B7
Falkenberg
Bayern D 95 B4
Falkenberg
Bayern D 95 C4
Brandenburg D 83 A5
S 60 C2
Falkensee D 74 B2
Falkenstein
Bayern D 95 B4
Sachsen D 83 B4
Falkenthal D 74 B2
Falkirk GB 35 B4
Falkland GB 35 B4
Falköping S 55 B4
Fall D 108 B2
Falla S 56 B1
Fallingbostel D 72 B2
Falmouth GB 42 B1
Falset E 147 C1
Fălticeni RO 17 B7
Falun S 50 B2
Famagusta CY 181 A2
Fammestad N 46 B2
Fana N 46 B2
Fanano I 135 A3
Fanari GR 182 D3
Fanjeaux F 146 A3
Fano I 136 B2
Fântânele RO 126 A3
Fara in Sabina I 168 A2
Faramontanos de Tábara E 149 A4
Fara Novarese I 119 B5
Farasdues E 144 B2
Fårbo S 62 A4
Fareham GB 44 C2
Färentuna S 57 A3
Färgelanda S 54 B2
Färila S 200 E1
Faringdon GB 44 B2
Faringe S 51 C5
Farini I 120 C2
Fariza E 149 A3
Färjestaden S 63 B4
Farkadona GR 182 D4
Farkasfa H 111 C3
Farlete E 153 A3
Färlöv S 61 C4
Farmos H 113 B3
Farnå SK 112 B2
Färnäs S 50 B1
Farnborough GB 44 B3
Farnese I 168 A1
Farnham GB 44 B3
Farnroda D 82 B2
Faro P 160 B2
Fåro S 57 C5
Fårösund S 57 C5
Farra d'Alpago I 122 A1
Farranfore IRL 29 B2
Farre DK 59 B2
Farsala GR 182 D4
Farsø DK 58 B2
Farsund N 52 B2
Farum DK 61 D2
Fårup DK 58 B2
Fasana I 172 B1
Fasano I 173 B3
Fáskrúðsfjörður IS 191 C11
Fassberg D 72 B3
Fastiv UA 13 C8
Fastnäs S 49 B5
Fátima P 154 B2
Fatmomakke S 195 E6
Fättjaur S 195 E6
Faucogney-et-la-Mer F 105 B5
Fauguerolles F 128 B3
Faulenrost D 74 A1
Faulquemont F 92 B2
Fauquembergues F 78 B2
Fauske N 194 C6
Fauville-en-Caux F 89 A4
Fauvillers B 92 B1
Fåvang N 48 A2
Favara
E 159 B3
I 176 B2
Faverges F 118 B3
Faverney F 105 B5
Faversham GB 45 B4
Favignana I 176 B1
Fawley GB 44 C2
Fay-aux-Loges F 103 B4
Fayence F 132 B2
Fayet F 130 B1
Fayl-Billot F 105 B4
Fayón E 153 A4
Fearn GB 32 D3
Fécamp F 89 A4
Feda N 52 B2
Fedje N 46 B1
Feeny GB 27 B3
Fegen S 60 B3
Fegyvernek H 113 B4
Fehrbellin D 74 B1
Fehring A 111 C3
Feichten A 108 B1
Feiring N 48 B3
Feistritz im Rosental A 110 C1
Feketić SRB 126 B1
Felanitx E 167 B3
Feld am See A 109 C4
Feldbach A 110 C2
Feldberg D 74 A2
Feldkirch A 107 B4
Feldkirchen in Kärnten A 109 C5
Feldkirchen-Westerham D 108 B2
Felgueiras P 148 A1
Felitto I 172 B1
Félix E 164 C2
Felixstowe GB 45 B5
Felizzano I 119 C5
Felletin F 116 B2
Fellingsbro S 56 A1
Felnac RO 126 A3
Felnémet H 113 B4
Felpéc H 111 B4
Fels am Wagram A 97 C3
Felsberg D 81 A5
Felsönyék H 112 C2
Felsöszentiván H 126 A1
Felsöszentmárton H 125 B3
Felsözsolca H 113 A4
Felsted DK 64 B2
Feltre I 121 A4
Femsjö S 60 C3
Fenagh IRL 26 B3
Fene E 140 A2
Fenestrelle I 119 B4
Fénétrange F 92 C3
Feneu F 102 B1
Fengersfors S 54 B3
Fenit IRL 29 B2
Fensmark DK 65 A4
Fenwick GB 36 A2
Feolin Ferry GB 34 C1
Ferbane IRL 28 A4
Ferdinandovac HR 124 A3
Ferdinandshof D 74 A2
Fère-Champenoise F 91 C3
Fère-en-Tardenois F 91 B3
Ferentillo I 168 A2
Ferentino I 169 B3
Feres GR 183 C8
Feria E 155 C4
Feričanci HR 125 B3
Ferizli TR 187 B5
Ferla I 177 B3
Ferlach A 110 C1
Ferleiten A 109 B3
Fermil P 148 A2
Fermo I 136 B2
Fermoselle E 149 A3
Fermoy IRL 29 B3
Fernancabellero E 157 A4
Fernán Nuñéz E 163 A3
Fernán Peréz E 164 C2
Fernão Ferro P 154 C1
Fernay-Voltaire F 118 A3
Ferndown GB 43 B5
Ferness GB 32 D3
Fernhurst GB 44 B3
Ferns IRL 30 B2
Ferpécle CH 119 A4
Ferrals-les-Corbières F 146 A3
Ferrandina I 172 B2
Ferrara I 121 C4
Ferrara di Monte Baldo I 121 B3
Ferreira E 141 A3
Ferreira do Alentejo P 160 A1
Ferreira do Zêzere P 154 B2
Ferreras de Abajo E 141 C4
Ferreras de Arriba E 141 C4
Ferreries E 167 B4
Ferreruela E 152 A2
Ferreruela de Tabara E 149 A3
Ferret CH 119 B4
Ferrette F 106 B2
Ferriere I 120 C2
Ferrière-la-Grande F 79 B3
Ferrières
Hautes-Pyrénées F 145 A3
Loiret F 103 A4
Oise F 90 B2
Ferrières-sur-Sichon F 117 A3
Ferrol E 140 A2
Ferryhill GB 37 B5
Fertörakos H 111 B3
Fertöszentmiklós H 111 B3
Ferwerd NL 70 A2
Festieux F 91 B3
Festøy N 198 C3
Festvåg N 194 C5
Fetești RO 17 C7
Fethard
Tipperary IRL 29 B4
Wexford IRL 30 B2
Fethiye TR 188 C4
Fetsund N 48 C3
Fettercairn GB 35 B5
Feucht D 95 B3
Feuchtwangen D 94 B2
Feudingen D 81 B4
Feuges F 91 C4
Feuquières F 90 B1
Feurs F 117 B4
Fevik N 53 B4
Ffestiniog GB 38 B3
Fiamignano I 169 A3
Fiano I 119 B4
Ficarazzi I 176 A2
Ficarolo I 121 C4
Fichtelberg D 95 A3
Ficulle I 135 C5
Fidenza I 120 C3
Fidjeland N 52 B2
Fieberbrunn A 109 B3
Fier AL 182 C1
Fiera di Primiero I 121 A4
Fiesch CH 119 A5
Fiesso Umbertiano I 121 C4
Figari F 180 B2
Figeac F 116 C2
Figeholm S 62 A4
Figgjo N 52 B1
Figline Valdarno I 135 B4
Figols E 145 B4
Figueira da Foz P 148 B1
Figueira de Castelo Rodrigo P 149 B3
Figueira dos Caveleiros P 160 A1
Figueiredo P 154 B3
Figueiredo de Alva P 148 B2
Figueiródos Vinhos P 154 B2
Figueres E 147 B3
Figueroles E 153 B3
Figueruela de Arriba E 141 C4
Filadélfia I 175 C2
Fil'akovo SK 99 C3
Filderstadt D 94 C1
Filey GB 41 A3
Filiaşi RO 17 C5
Filiates GR 182 D2
Filiatra GR 184 B2
Filipstad S 55 A5
Filisur CH 107 C4
Fillan N 198 B5
Filotio GR 185 B6
Filottrano I 136 B2
Filskov DK 59 C2
Filton GB 43 A4
Filtvet N 54 A1
Filzmoos A 109 B4
Finale Emília I 121 C4
Finale Lígure I 133 A4
Fiñana E 164 B2
Finby FIN 51 B7
Fincham GB 41 C4
Finchingfield GB 45 B4
Findhorn GB 32 D3
Findochty GB 33 D4
Finike TR 189 C5
Finkenberg A 108 B2
Finnea IRL 27 C3
Finneidfjord N 195 D4
Finnerödja S 55 B5
Finnskog N 49 B4
Finnsnes N 194 A9
Finntorp S 54 A3
Finócchio I 168 B2
Finsjö S 62 A4
Finsland N 52 B3
Finspång S 56 B1
Finsterwalde D 84 A1
Finsterwolde NL 71 A4
Finstown GB 33 B3
Fintona GB 27 B3
Fionnphort GB 34 B1
Fiorenzuola d'Arda I 120 C2
Firenze = Florence I 135 B4
Firenzuola I 135 A4
Firmi F 130 A1
Firminy F 117 B4
Firmo I 174 B2
Fischamend Markt A 111 A3
Fischbach
A 110 B2
D 93 B3
Fischbeck D 73 B5
Fischen D 107 B5
Fishbourne GB 44 C2
Fishguard GB 39 C2
Fiskardo GR 184 A1
Fiskebäckskil S 54 B2
Fiskebøl N 194 B5
Fismes F 91 B3
Fisterra E 140 B1
Fitero E 144 B2
Fitjar N 46 C2
Fiuggi I 169 B3
Fiumata I 169 A3
Fiumefreddo Brúzio I 174 B2
Fiumefreddo di Sicília I 177 B4
Fiumicino I 168 B2
Fivemiletown GB 27 B3
Fivizzano I 134 A3
Fjälkinge S 63 B2
Fjällåsen S 196 B3
Fjällbacka S 54 B2
Fjæra N 46 C3
Fjärdhundra S 56 A2
Fjellerup DK 58 B3
Fjerritslev DK 58 A2
Fjordgard N 194 A8
Fjugesta S 55 A5
Flå N 47 B6
Flåbygd N 53 A4
Flaça E 147 B3
Flace F 117 A4
Fladungen D 82 B2
Flaine F 118 A3
Flaka FIN 51 B7
Flåm N 46 B4
Flamatt CH 106 C2
Flamborough GB 41 A3
Flammersfeld D 81 B3
Flassans-sur-Issole F 132 B2
Flatdal N 53 A4
Flatebø N 46 B3
Flateby N 48 C3
Flateland N 52 A3
Flateyri IS 190 A2
Flatøydegard N 47 B6
Flatråker N 46 C2
Flattach A 109 C4
Flatvarp S 62 A4
Flauenskjold DK 58 A3
Flavigny-sur-Moselle F 92 C2
Flavy-le-Martel F 90 B3
Flawil CH 107 B4
Flayosc F 132 B2
Flechtingen D 73 B4
Fleckeby D 64 B2
Fleet GB 44 B3
Fleetmark D 73 B4
Fleetwood GB 38 A3
Flehingen D 93 B4
Flekke N 46 A2
Flekkefjord N 52 B2
Flen S 56 A2
Flensburg D 64 B2
Fleringe S 57 C4
Flerohopp S 62 B3
Flers F 88 B3
Flesberg N 47 C6
Fleurance F 129 C3
Fleuré F 115 B4
Fleurier CH 105 C5
Fleurus B 79 B4
Fleury
Hérault F 130 B2
Yonne F 104 B2
Fleury-les-Aubrais F 103 B3
Fleury-sur-Andelle F 89 A5
Fleury-sur-Orne F 89 A3
Flieden D 81 B5
Flimby GB 36 B3
Flims CH 107 C4
Flines-lèz-Raches F 78 B3
Flint GB 38 A3
Flirey F 92 C1
Flirsch A 108 B1
Flisa N 49 B4
Flisby S 62 A2
Fliseryd S 62 A4
Flix E 153 A4
Flixecourt F 90 A2
Flize F 91 B4
Flobecq B 79 B3
Floby S 55 B4
Floda S 60 B2
Flodden GB 37 A4
Flogny-la-Chapelle F 104 B2
Flöha D 83 B5
Flonheim D 93 B4
Florac F 130 A2
Floreffe B 79 B4
Florence = Firenze I 135 B4
Florennes B 79 B4
Florensac F 130 B2
Florentin F 129 C5
Florenville B 91 B5
Flores de Avila E 150 B2
Floresta I 177 B3
Florești MD 17 B8
Florídia I 177 B4
Florina GR 182 C3
Florø N 46 A2
Flörsheim D 93 A4
Floss D 95 B4
Fluberg N 48 B2
Flúðir IS 190 C5
Flühli CH 106 C3
Flumet F 118 B3
Fluminimaggiore I 179 C2
Flums CH 107 B4
Flyeryd S 63 B3
Flygsfors S 62 B3
Foča BIH 139 B4
Foça TR 186 D1
Fochabers GB 32 D3
Focşani RO 17 C7
Foel GB 38 B3
Foeni RO 126 B2
Fogdö S 56 A2
Fóggia I 171 B3
Foglianise I 170 B2
Föglö FIN 51 B7
Fohnsdorf A 110 B1
Foiano della Chiana I 135 B4
Foix F 146 B2
Fojnica
BIH 139 B3
BIH 139 B4
Fokstua N 198 C6
Földeák H 126 A2
Foldereid N 199 A9
Főldes H 113 B5

Fol–Gar 245

Folegandros GR 185 C5
Folelli F 180 A2
Folgaria I 121 B4
Folgosinho P 148 B2
Folgoso de la Ribera E 141 B4
Folgoso do Courel E 141 B3
Foligno I 136 C1
Folkärna S 50 B3
Folkestad N 198 C3
Folkestone GB 45 B5
Follafoss N 199 B8
Folldal N 198 C6
Follebu N 48 A2
Follina I 121 B5
Föllinge S 199 B11
Follónica I 135 C3
Fölsbyn S 54 A3
Foncebadón E 141 B4
Foncine-le-Bas F 105 C5
Fondevila E 140 C2
Fondi I 169 B3
Fondo I 121 A4
Fonelas E 164 B1
Fonfría
Teruel E 152 B2
Zamora E 149 A3
Fonn N 46 A3
Fonnes N 46 B1
Fonni I 178 B3
Fontaine F 91 C4
Fontainebleau F 90 C2
Fontaine de Vaucluse F 131 B4
Fontaine-Française F 105 B4
Fontaine-le-Dun F 89 A4
Fontan F 133 A3
Fontanarejo E 157 A3
Fontane I 133 A3
Fontanélice I 135 A4
Fontanières F 116 A2
Fontanosas E 157 B3
Fonteblanda I 168 A1
Fontenay-le-Comte F 114 B3
Fontenay-Trésigny F 90 C2
Fontevrault-l'Abbaye F 102 B2
Fontiveros E 150 B3
Fontoy F 92 B1
Fontpédrouse F 146 B3
Font-Romeu F 146 B3
Fontstown IRL 30 A2
Fonyód H 111 C4
Fonz E 145 B4
Fonzaso I 121 A4
Fóppolo I 120 A2
Föra S 62 A4
Forbach
D 93 C4
F 92 B2
Forcall E 153 B3
Forcalquier F 132 B1
Forcarei E 140 B2
Forchheim D 94 B3
Forchtenau A 111 B3
Forchtenberg D 94 B1
Ford GB 34 B2
Førde
Hordaland N 52 A1
Sogn og Fjordane N 46 A2
Förderstedt D 83 A3
Førdesfjorden N 52 A1
Fordham GB 45 A4
Fordingbridge GB 44 C2
Fordon PL 76 A3
Fordongiánus I 179 C2
Forenza I 172 B1
Foresta di Búrgos I 178 B2
Forfar GB 35 B5
Forges-les-Eaux F 90 B1
Foria I 172 B1
Forio I 170 C1
Forjães P 148 A1
Førland N 52 B3
Forlì I 135 A5
Forlimpopoli I 135 A5
Formazza I 119 A5
Formby GB 38 A3
Formerie F 90 B1
Fórmia I 169 B3
Formígine I 135 A3
Formigliana I 119 B5
Formiguères F 146 B3
Fornalutx E 166 B2
Fornåsa S 56 B1
Fornelli I 178 B2
Fornells E 167 A4
Fornelos de Montes E 140 B2
Fornes E 163 B4
Forneset N 192 C3
Forni Avoltri I 109 C3
Forni di Sopra I 122 A1
Forni di Sotto I 122 A1
Forno
Piemonte I 119 B4
Piemonte I 119 B5
Forno Alpi-Gráie I 119 B4
Forno di Zoldo I 121 A5
Fornos de Algodres P 148 B2
Fornovo di Taro I 120 C3
Foros do Arrão P 154 B2
Forráskút H 126 A1
Forres GB 32 D3
Forriolo E 140 B3
Fors S 50 B3
Forsand N 52 B2
Forsbacka S 51 B3
Forserum S 62 A2
Forshaga S 55 A4
Forsheda S 60 B3
Forsinain GB 32 C3
Førslev DK 65 A4
Förslöv S 61 C2
Forsmark
Uppsala S 51 B5
Västerbotten S 195 E6
Forsmo S 200 C3
Forsnäs S 195 D9
Forsnes N 198 B5
Forssa FIN 8 B3
Forssjöbruk S 56 B2
Forst D 84 A2
Forsvik S 55 B5
Fortanete E 153 B3
Fort Augustus GB 32 D2
Forte dei Marmi I 134 B3
Fortezza I 108 C2
Forth GB 35 C4
Fort-Mahon-Plage F 78 B1
Fortrie GB 33 D4
Fortrose GB 32 D2
Fortun N 47 A4
Fortuna E 165 A3
Fortuneswell GB 43 B4
Fort William GB 34 B2
Forvik N 195 E3
Fos F 145 B4
Fosdinovo I 134 A3
Foss N 47 B6
Fossacésia I 169 A4
Fossano I 133 A3
Fossato di Vico I 136 B1
Fossbakken N 194 B8
Fosse-la-Ville B 79 B4
Fossombrone I 136 B1
Fos-sur-Mer F 131 B3
Fot H 112 B3
Fouchères F 104 A3
Fouesnant F 100 B1
Foug F 92 C1
Fougères F 88 B2
Fougerolles F 105 B5
Foulain F 105 A4
Fountainhall GB 35 C5
Fouras F 114 C2
Fourchambault F 104 B2
Fourmies F 91 A4
Fourna GR 182 D3
Fournels F 116 C3
Fourni GR 188 B1
Fournols F 117 B3
Fourques F 146 B3
Fourquevaux F 146 A2
Fours F 104 C2
Fowey GB 42 B2
Foxdale GB 36 B2
Foxford IRL 26 C1
Foyers GB 32 D2
Foynes IRL 29 B2
Foz E 141 A3
Foza I 121 B4
Foz do Arelho P 154 B1
Foz do Giraldo P 155 B3
Frabosa Soprana I 133 A3
Frades de la Sierra E 149 B4
Fraga E 153 A4
Fragagnano I 173 B3
Frailes E 163 A4
Fraire B 79 B4
Fraize F 106 A1
Framlingham GB 45 A5
Frammersbach D 94 A1
Framnes N 54 A1
França P 141 C4
Francaltroff F 92 C2
Francavilla al Mare I 169 A4
Francavilla di Sicília I 177 B4
Francavilla Fontana I 173 B3
Francavilla in Sinni I 174 A2
Francescas F 129 B3
Franco P 148 A2
Francofonte I 177 B3
Francos E 151 A4
Frändefors S 54 B3
Franeker NL 70 A2
Frangy F 118 A2
Frankenau D 81 A4
Frankenberg
Hessen D 81 A4
Sachsen D 83 B5
Frankenburg A 109 A4
Frankenfels A 110 B2
Frankenmarkt A 109 B4
Frankenthal D 93 B4
Frankfurt
Brandenburg D 74 B3
Hessen D 81 B4
Frankrike S 199 B10
Fränsta S 200 D2
Františkovy Lázně CZ 83 B4
Franzburg D 66 B1
Frascati I 168 B2
Frasdorf D 109 B3
Fraserburgh GB 33 D4
Frashër AL 182 C2
Frasne F 105 C5
Frasnes-lez-Anvaing B 79 B3
Frasseto F 180 B2
Frastanz A 107 B4
Fratel P 155 B3
Fratta Todina I 135 C5
Frauenau D 96 C1
Frauenfeld CH 107 B3
Frauenkirchen A 111 B3
Frauenstein D 83 B5
Frauental A 110 C2
Frayssinet F 129 B4
Frayssinet-le-Gélat F 129 B4
Frechas P 149 A2
Frechen D 80 B2
Frechilla E 142 B2
Freckenhorst D 71 C4
Fredeburg D 81 A4
Fredelsloh D 82 A1
Fredeng N 48 B2
Fredensborg DK 61 D2
Fredericia DK 59 C2
Frederiks DK 59 B2
Frederikshavn DK 58 A3
Frederikssund DK 61 D2
Frederiksværk DK 61 D2
Fredrika S 200 B4
Fredriksberg S 50 B1
Fredriksdal S 62 A2
Fredrikstad N 54 A1
Fregenal de la Sierra E 161 A3
Fregene I 168 B2
Freiberg D 83 B5
Freiburg
Baden-Württemberg D 106 B2
Niedersachsen D 64 C2
Freienhagen D 81 A5
Freienhufen D 84 A1
Freiensteinau D 81 B5
Freihung D 95 B3
Freilassing D 109 B3
Freisen D 92 B3
Freising D 95 C3
Freistadt A 96 C2
Freital D 84 A1
Freixedas P 149 B2
Freixo de Espada à Cinta P 149 A3
Fréjus F 132 B2
Fremdingen D 94 C2
Frenštát pod Radhoštěm CZ 98 B2
Freren D 71 B4
Freshford IRL 30 B1
Freshwater GB 44 C2
Fresnay-sur-Sarthe F 89 B4
Fresneda de la Sierra E 152 B1
Fresneda de la Sierra Tiron E 143 B3
Fresnedillas E 151 B3
Fresnes-en-Woevre F 92 B1
Fresne-St Mamès F 105 B4
Fresno Alhandiga E 150 B2
Fresno de la Ribera E 150 A2
Fresno de la Vega E 142 B1
Fresno de Sayago E 149 A4
Fresnoy-Folny F 90 B1
Fresnoy-le-Grand F 91 B3
Fressenville F 90 A1
Fresvik N 46 A3
Fréteval F 103 B3
Fretigney F 105 B4
Freudenberg
Baden-Württemberg D 94 B1
Nordrhein-Westfalen D 81 B3
Freudenstadt D 93 C4
Freux B 92 B1
Frévent F 78 B2
Freyburg D 83 A3
Freyenstein D 73 A5
Freyming-Merlebach F 92 B2
Freystadt D 95 B3
Freyung D 96 C1
Frias de Albarracin E 152 B2
Fribourg CH 106 C2
Frick CH 106 B3
Fridafors S 63 B2
Fridaythorpe GB 40 A3
Friedberg
A 111 B3
Bayern D 94 C2
Hessen D 81 B4
Friedeburg D 71 A4
Friedewald D 82 B1
Friedland
Brandenburg D 74 B3
Mecklenburg-Vorpommern D 74 A2
Niedersachsen D 82 A1
Friedrichroda D 82 B2
Friedrichsdorf D 81 B4
Friedrichshafen D 107 B4
Friedrichskoog D 64 B1
Friedrichstadt D 64 B2
Friedrichswalde D 74 A2
Friesach A 110 C1
Friesack D 73 B5
Friesenheim D 93 C3
Friesoythe D 71 A4
Friggesund S 200 E2
Frigiliana E 163 B4
Frihetsli N 192 D3
Frillesås S 60 B2
Frinnaryd S 62 A2
Frinton-on-Sea GB 45 B5
Friockheim GB 35 B5
Friol E 140 A3
Fristad S 60 B2
Fritsla S 60 B2
Fritzlar D 81 A5
Frizington GB 36 B3
Frödinge S 62 A4
Froges F 118 B2
Frohburg D 83 A4
Frohnhausen D 81 B4
Frohnleiten A 110 B2
Froissy F 90 B2
Frombork PL 69 A4
Frome GB 43 A4
Frómista E 142 B2
Fröndenberg D 81 A3
Fronsac F 128 B2
Front I 119 B4
Fronteira P 155 B3
Frontenay-Rohan-Rohan F 114 B3
Frontenhausen D 95 C4
Frontignan F 130 B2
Fronton F 129 C4
Fröseke S 62 B3
Frosinone I 169 B3
Frosolone I 170 B2
Frosta N 199 B7
Frøstrup DK 58 A1
Frosunda S 57 A4
Frouard F 92 C2
Frövi S 56 A1
Frøyset N 46 B2
Fruges F 78 B2
Frutigen CH 106 C2
Frýdek-Místek CZ 98 B2
Frýdlant CZ 84 B3
Frydlant nad Ostravicí CZ 98 B2
Frygnowo PL 77 A5
Fryšták CZ 98 B1
Fucécchio I 135 B3
Fuencaliente
Ciudad Real E 157 A4
Ciudad Real E 157 B3
Fuencemillán E 151 B4
Fuendejalón E 144 C2
Fuengirola E 163 B3
Fuenlabrada E 151 B4
Fuenlabrada de los Montes E 156 A3
Fuensalida E 151 B3
Fuensanta E 164 B3
Fuensanta de Martos E 163 A4
Fuente-Álamo E 158 C2
Fuente-Álamo de Murcia E 165 B3
Fuentealbilla E 158 B2
Fuente al Olmo de Iscar E 150 A3
Fuentecén E 151 A4
Fuente Dé E 142 A2
Fuente de Cantos E 155 C4
Fuente del Arco E 156 B2
Fuente del Conde E 163 A3
Fuente del Maestre E 155 C4
Fuente de Santa Cruz E 150 A3
Fuente el Fresno E 157 A4
Fuente el Saz de Jarama E 151 B4
Fuente el Sol E 150 A3
Fuenteguinaldo E 149 B3
Fuentelapeña E 150 A2
Fuentelcésped E 151 A4
Fuentelespino de Haro E 158 B1
Fuentelespino de Moya E 158 B2
Fuentenovilla E 151 B4
Fuente Obejuna E 156 B2
Fuente Palmera E 162 A2
Fuentepelayo E 151 A3
Fuentepinilla E 151 A5
Fuenterroble de Salvatierra E 150 B2
Fuenterrobles E 158 B2
Fuentes E 158 B1
Fuentesauco E 151 A3
Fuentesaúco E 150 A2
Fuentes de Andalucía E 162 A2
Fuentes de Ebro E 153 A3
Fuentes de Jiloca E 152 A2
Fuentes de la Alcarria E 151 B5
Fuentes de León E 161 A3
Fuentes de Nava E 142 B2
Fuentes de Oñoro E 149 B3
Fuentes de Ropel E 142 B1
Fuentespalda E 153 B4
Fuentespina E 151 A4
Fuente-Tójar E 163 A3
Fuente Vaqueros E 163 A4
Fuentidueña E 151 A4
Fuentidueña de Tajo E 151 B4
Fuerte del Rey E 157 C4
Fügen A 108 B2
Fuglebjerg DK 65 A4
Fuglevik N 54 A1
Fuhrberg D 72 B2
Fulda D 82 B1
Fulgatore I 176 B1
Fully CH 119 A4
Fulnek CZ 98 B1
Fülöpszállás H 112 C3
Fulpmes A 108 B2
Fulunäs S 49 A5
Fumay F 91 B4
Fumel F 129 B3
Funäsdalen S 199 C9
Fundão P 148 B2
Funzie GB 33 A6
Furadouro P 148 B1
Fure N 46 A2
Fürstenau D 71 B4
Furstenau D 81 A5
Fürstenberg D 74 A2
Fürstenfeld A 111 B3
Fürstenfeldbruck D 108 A2
Fürstenstein D 96 C1
Fürstenwalde D 74 B3
Fürstenwerder D 74 A2
Fürstenzell D 96 C1
Furta H 113 B5
Fürth
Bayern D 94 B2
Hessen D 93 B4
Furth im Wald D 95 B4
Furtwangen D 106 A3
Furuby S 62 B3
Furudal S 50 A2
Furuflaten N 192 C4
Furulund S 61 D3
Furusjö S 60 B3
Fusa N 46 B2
Fuscaldo I 174 B2
Fusch an der Grossglocknerstrasse A 109 B3
Fushë Arrëz AL 182 A2
Fushë-Krujë AL 182 B1
Fusina I 122 B1
Fusio CH 107 C3
Füssen D 108 B1
Fustiñana E 144 B2
Futog SRB 126 B1
Futrikelv N 192 C3
Füzesabony H 113 B4
Füzesgyarmat H 113 B5
Fužine HR 123 B3
Fyllinge S 61 C2
Fynshav DK 64 B2
Fyresdal N 53 A4

G

Gaaldorf A 110 B1
Gabaldón E 158 B2
Gabarret F 128 C2
Gabčíkovo SK 111 B4
Gąbin PL 77 B4
Gabriac F 130 A1
Gabrovo BG 17 D6
Gaby I 119 B4
Gacé F 89 B4
Gacko BIH 139 B4
Gäddede S 199 A11
Gadebusch D 65 C4
Gadmen CH 106 C3
Gádor E 164 C2
Gádoros H 113 C4
Gael F 101 A3
Găeşti RO 17 C6
Gaeta I 169 B3
Gafanhoeira P 154 C2
Gaflenz A 110 B1
Gagarin RUS 9 E9
Gaggenau D 93 C4
Gagliano Castelferrato I 177 B3
Gagliano del Capo I 173 C4
Gagnet S 50 B2
Gaibanella I 121 C4
Gaildorf D 94 B1
Gaillac F 129 C4
Gaillefontaine F 90 B1
Gaillon F 89 A5
Gainsborough GB 40 B3
Gairloch GB 31 B3
Gairlochy GB 34 B3
Gáiro I 179 C3
Gaj
HR 124 B3
SRB 127 C3
Gaja-la-Selve F 146 A2
Gajanejos E 151 B5
Gajary SK 97 C4
Gajdobra SRB 126 B1
Galan F 145 A4
Galanta SK 111 A4
Galapagar E 151 B3
Galápagos E 151 B4
Galaroza E 161 B3
Galashiels GB 35 C5
Galatas GR 185 B4
Galaţi RO 17 C8
Galatina I 173 B4
Galatista GR 183 C5
Galátone I 173 B4
Galaxidi GR 184 A3
Galdakao E 143 A4
Galeata I 135 B4
Galende E 141 B4
Galera E 164 B2
Galéria F 180 A1
Galgamácsa H 112 B3
Galgate GB 38 A4
Galgon F 128 B2
Galices P 148 B2
Galinduste E 150 B2
Galinoporni CY 181 A3
Galisteo E 155 B4
Galków PL 87 A3
Gallarate I 120 B1
Gallardon F 90 C1
Gallegos de Argañán E 149 B3
Gallegos del Solmirón E 150 B2
Galleguillos de Campos E 142 B1
Galleno I 135 B3
Galliate I 120 B1
Gallicano I 134 A3
Gállio I 121 B4
Gallipoli = Gelibolu TR 186 B1
Gallípoli I 173 B3
Gällivare S 196 B3
Gallizien A 110 C1
Gallneukirchen A 96 C2
Gällö S 199 C12
Gallocanta E 152 B2
Gällstad S 60 B3
Gallur E 144 C2
Galmisdale GB 31 C2
Galmpton GB 43 B3
Galston GB 36 A2
Galta N 52 A1
Galtelli I 178 B3
Galten DK 59 B2
Galtür A 107 C5
Galve de Sorbe E 151 A4
Galveias P 154 B2
Gálvez E 157 A3
Galway IRL 28 A2
Gamaches F 90 B1
Gámbara I 120 B3
Gambárie I 175 C1
Gambassi Terme I 135 B3
Gambatesa I 170 B2
Gambolò I 120 B1
Gaming A 110 B2
Gamla Uppsala S 51 C4
Gamleby S 62 A4
Gamlingay GB 44 A3
Gammelgarn S 57 C4
Gammelstad S 196 D5
Gammertingen D 107 A4
Gams CH 107 B4
Gamvik
Finnmark N 192 B6
Finnmark N 193 A12
Gan F 145 A3
Gáname E 149 A3
Ganda di Martello I 108 C1
Gandarela P 148 A1
Ganddal N 52 B1
Ganderkesee D 72 A1
Gandesa E 153 A4
Gandía E 159 C3
Gandino I 120 B2
Gandrup DK 58 A3
Ganges F 130 B2
Gånghester S 60 B3
Gangi I 177 B3
Gangkofen D 95 C4
Gannat F 116 A3
Gannay-sur-Loire F 104 C2
Gänserdorf A 97 C4
Ganzlin D 73 A5
Gap F 132 A2
Gara H 125 A5
Garaballa E 158 B2
Garaguso I 172 B2
Garbayuela E 156 A2
Garbhallt GB 34 B2
Garbsen D 72 B2
Garching D 109 A3
Garciaz E 156 A2
Garcihernández E 150 B2
Garcillán E 151 B3
Garcinarro E 151 B5
Garcisobaco E 162 B2
Garda I 121 B3
Gardanne F 131 B4
Gärdås S 49 B5
Gårdby S 63 B4
Gardeja PL 69 B3
Gardelegen D 73 B4
Gardermoen N 48 B3
Gardiki GR 182 E3

Garding D 64 B1
Gardone Riviera I 121 B3
Gardone Val Trómpia I 120 B3
Gárdony H 112 B2
Gardouch F 146 A2
Gårdsjö S 55 B5
Gårdskär S 51 B4
Gards Köpinge S 63 C2
Garein F 128 B2
Garelochhead GB 34 B3
Garéoult F 132 B2
Garešnica HR 124 B2
Garéssio I 133 A4
Garforth GB 40 B2
Gargaliani GR 184 B2
Gargaligas E 156 A2
Gargallo E 153 B3
Garganta la Olla E 150 B2
Gargantiel E 156 B3
Gargellen A 107 C4
Gargilesse-Dampierre F 103 C3
Gargnano I 121 B3
Gargnäs S 195 E8
Gárgoles de Abajo E 152 B1
Gargrave GB 40 B1
Garitz D 73 C5
Garlasco I 120 B1
Garlieston GB 36 B2
Garlin F 128 C2
Garlitos E 156 B2
Garmisch-Partenkirchen D 108 B2
Garnat-sur-Engièvre F 104 C2
Garpenberg S 50 B3
Garphyttan S 55 A5
Garray E 143 C4
Garrel D 71 B5
Garriguella E 146 B4
Garrison GB 26 B2
Garrovillas E 155 B4
Garrucha E 164 B3
Gars-am-Kamp A 97 C3
Garsås S 50 B1
Garsdale Head GB 37 B4
Gärsnäs S 63 C2
Garstang GB 38 A4
Gartow D 73 A4
Gartz D 74 A3
Gærum DK 58 A3
Garvagh GB 27 B4
Garvão P 160 B1
Garve GB 32 D2
Garwolin PL 12 C4
Garz D 66 B2
Garzyn PL 85 A4
Gąsawa PL 76 B2
Gåsborn S 49 C6
Gaschurn A 107 C5
Gascueña E 152 B1
Gasny F 90 B1
Gąsocin PL 77 B5
Gastes F 128 B1
Gastouni GR 184 B2
Gastouri GR 182 D1
Gata
E 149 B3
HR 138 B2
Gata de Gorgos E 159 C4
Gătaia RO 126 B3
Gatchina RUS 9 C7
Gatehouse of Fleet GB 36 B2
Gátér H 113 C3
Gateshead GB 37 B5
Gátova E 159 B3
Gattendorf A 111 A3
Gatteo a Mare I 136 A1
Gattinara I 119 B5
Gattorna I 134 A2
Gaucín E 162 B2
Gaulstad N 199 B9
Gaupne N 47 A4
Gautefall N 53 A4
Gauting D 108 A2
Gauto S 195 D7
Gava E 147 C3
Gavardo I 121 B3
Gavarnie F 145 B3
Gávavencsello H 113 A5
Gavi I 120 C1
Gavião P 154 B3
Gavirate I 120 B1
Gävle S 51 B4
Gavoi I 178 B3
Gavorrano I 135 C3
Gavray F 88 B2
Gavrio GR 185 B5
Gävunda S 49 B6
Gaweinstal A 97 C4
Gaworzyce PL 85 A3
Gawroniec PL 75 A5
Gaydon GB 44 A2
Gayton GB 41 C4
Gazipaşa TR 189 C7
Gazoldo degli Ippoliti I 121 B3
Gazzuolo I 121 B3
Gbelce SK 112 B2
Gdańsk PL 69 A3
Gdinj HR 138 B2
Gdov RUS 8 C5
Gdów PL 99 B4
Gdynia PL 69 A3
Gea de Albarracin E 152 B2
Geary GB 31 B2
Géaudot F 91 C4
Geaune F 128 C2
Gebesee D 82 A2
Gebiz TR 189 B5
Gebze TR 187 B4
Géderlak H 112 C2
Gedern D 81 B5
Gedinne B 91 B4
Gediz TR 187 D4
Gèdre F 145 B4
Gedser DK 65 B4
Gedsted DK 58 B2
Geel B 79 A4
Geesthacht D 72 A3
Geetbets B 79 B5
Gefell D 83 B3
Gehrden D 72 B2
Gehren D 82 B3
Geilenkirchen D 80 B2
Geilo N 47 B5
Geinsheim D 93 B4
Geisa D 82 B1
Geiselhöring D 95 C4
Geiselwind D 94 B2
Geisenfeld D 95 C3
Geisenhausen D 95 C4
Geisenheim D 93 B4
Geising D 84 B1
Geisingen D 107 B3
Geislingen D 94 C1
Geistthal A 110 B2
Geiteryggshytta N 47 B4
Geithain D 83 A4
Geithus N 48 C1
Gela I 177 B3
Geldermalsen NL 79 A5
Geldern D 80 A2
Geldrop NL 80 A1
Geleen NL 80 B1
Gelembe TR 186 C2
Gelendost TR 189 A6
Gelibolu = Gallipoli TR 186 B1
Gelida E 147 C2
Gelnhausen D 81 B5
Gelnica SK 99 C4
Gelsa E 153 A3
Gelse H 111 C3
Gelsenkirchen D 80 A3
Gelsted DK 59 C2
Geltendorf D 108 A2
Gelterkinden CH 106 B2
Gelting D 64 B2
Gelu RO 126 A3
Gelves E 162 A1
Gembloux B 79 B4
Gemeaux F 105 B4
Gémenos F 132 B1
Gemerská Poloma SK 99 C4
Gemerská Ves SK 99 C4
Gemert NL 80 A1
Gemla S 62 B2
Gemlik TR 186 B4
Gemmenich B 80 B1
Gemona del Friuli I 122 A2
Gémozac F 114 C3
Gemund D 80 B2
Gemünden
Bayern D 94 A1
Hessen D 81 B4
Rheinland-Pfalz D 93 B3
Genappe B 79 B4
Génave E 164 A2
Genazzano I 169 B2
Gençay F 115 B4
Gencsapáti H 111 B3
Gendringen NL 80 A2
Genelard F 104 C3
Genemuiden NL 70 B3
Generalski Stol HR 123 B4
Geneva = Genève CH 118 A3
Genevad S 61 C3
Genève = Geneva CH 118 A3
Genevriéres F 105 B4
Gengenbach D 93 C4
Genillé F 103 B3
Genk B 80 B1
Genlis F 105 B4
Gennep NL 80 A1
Genner DK 64 A2
Gennes F 102 B1
Genoa = Génova I 134 A1
Genola I 133 A3
Génova = Genoa I 134 A1
Genowefa PL 76 B3
Gensingen D 93 B3
Gent = Ghent B 79 A3
Genthin D 73 B5
Gentioux F 116 B1
Genzano di Lucánia I 172 B2
Genzano di Roma I 168 B2
Georgenthal D 82 B2
Georgsmarienhütte D 71 B5
Gera D 83 B4
Geraards-bergen B 79 B3
Gerace I 175 C2
Geraci Sículo I 177 B3
Geraki GR 184 C3
Gérardmer F 106 A1
Geras A 97 C3
Gerbéviller F 92 C2
Gerbini I 177 B3
Gerbstedt D 83 A3
Gerði IS 191 C9
Gerede TR 187 B7
Gerena E 161 B3
Geretsried D 108 B2
Gérgal E 164 B2
Gergy F 105 C3
Gerindote E 150 C3
Gerjen H 112 C2
Gerlos A 108 B3
Germay F 92 C1
Germencik TR 188 B2
Germering D 108 A2
Germersheim D 93 B4
Gernika-Lumo E 143 A4
Gernrode D 82 A3
Gernsbach D 93 C4
Gernsheim D 93 B4
Geroda D 82 B1
Gerola Alta I 120 A2
Geroldsgrun D 83 B3
Gerolsbach D 95 C3
Gerolstein D 80 B2
Gerolzhofen D 94 B2
Gerovo HR 123 B3
Gerpinnes B 79 B4
Gerrards Cross GB 44 B3
Gerri de la Sal E 147 B2
Gersfeld D 82 B1
Gerstetten D 94 C2
Gersthofen D 94 C2
Gerstungen D 82 B2
Gerswalde D 74 A2
Gerzat F 116 B3
Gerze TR 23 A8
Gerzen D 95 C4
Gescher D 71 C4
Geseke D 81 A4
Geslau D 94 B2
Gespunsart F 91 B4
Gesté F 101 B4
Gestorf D 72 B2
Gesualda I 170 C3
Gesunda S 50 B1
Gesztely H 113 A4
Geta FIN 51 B6
Getafe E 151 B4
Getinge S 60 C2
Getxo E 143 A4
Geversdorf D 64 C2
Gevgelija MK 182 B4
Gevora del Caudillo E 155 C4
Gevrey-Chambertin F 105 B3
Gex F 118 A3
Gey D 80 B2
Geyikli TR 186 C1
Geysir IS 190 C5
Geyve TR 187 B5
Gföhl A 97 C3
Ghedi I 120 B3
Ghent = Gent B 79 A3
Gheorgheni RO 17 B6
Ghigo I 119 C4
Ghilarza I 178 B2
Ghisonaccia F 180 A2
Ghisoni F 180 A2
Gialtra GR 182 E4
Gianitsa GR 182 C4
Giardinetto Vécchio I 171 B3
Giardini Naxos I 177 B4
Giarratana I 177 B3
Giarre I 177 B4
Giat F 116 B2
Giaveno I 119 B4
Giazza I 121 B4
Giba I 179 C2
Gibellina Nuova I 176 B1
Gibostad N 194 A9
Gibraleón E 161 B3
Gibraltar GBZ 162 B2
Gic H 111 B4
Gideå S 200 C5
Gideåkroken S 200 B3
Gidle PL 86 B3
Giebelstadt D 94 B1
Gieboldehausen D 82 A2
Gielniów PL 87 A4
Gielow D 74 A1
Gien F 103 B4
Giengen D 94 C2
Giens F 132 B2
Giera RO 126 B2
Gieselwerder D 81 A5
Giessen D 81 B4
Gieten NL 71 A3
Giethoorn NL 70 B3
Giffaumont-Champaubert F 91 C4
Gifford GB 35 C5
Gifhorn D 73 B3
Gige H 125 A3
Gignac F 130 B2
Gijón = Xixón E 142 A1
Gilena E 162 A3
Gilford GB 27 B4
Gillberga S 55 A3
Gilleleje DK 61 C2
Gilley F 105 B5
Gilley-sur-Loire F 104 C2
Gillingham
Dorset GB 43 A4
Medway GB 45 B4
Gilocourt F 90 B2
Gilserberg D 81 B5
Gilsland GB 37 B4
Gilze NL 79 A4
Gimåt S 200 C4
Gimo S 51 B5
Gimont F 129 C3
Ginasservis F 132 B1
Gingelom B 79 B5
Gingst D 66 B2
Ginosa I 171 C4
Ginzling A 108 B2
Giões P 160 B2
Gióia dei Marsi I 169 B3
Gióia del Colle I 173 B2
Gióia Sannitica I 170 B2
Gióia Táuro I 175 C1
Gioiosa Iónica I 175 C2
Gioiosa Marea I 177 A3
Giosla GB 31 A2
Giovinazzo I 171 B4
Girifalco I 175 C2
Giromagny F 106 B1
Girona E 147 C3
Gironcourt-sur-Vraine F 92 C1
Gironella E 147 B2
Gironville-sous-les-Côtes F 92 C1
Girvan GB 36 A2
Gislaved S 60 B3
Gislev DK 59 C3
Gisors F 90 B1
Gissi I 170 A2
Gistad S 56 B1
Gistel B 78 A2
Gistrup DK 58 B3
Giswil CH 106 C3
Githio GR 184 C3
Giugliano in Campania I 170 C2
Giulianova I 136 C2
Giulvăz RO 126 B2
Giurgiu RO 17 D6
Give DK 59 C2
Givet F 91 A4
Givors F 117 B4
Givry
B 79 B4
F 104 C3
Givry-en-Argonne F 91 C4
Givskud DK 59 C2
Giżałki PL 76 B2
Gizeux F 102 B2
Giżycko PL 12 A4
Gizzeria I 175 C2
Gizzeria Lido I 175 C2
Gjedved DK 59 C2
Gjegjan AL 182 B2
Gjendesheim N 47 A5
Gjerde N 46 B3
Gjerlev DK 58 B3
Gjermundshamn N 46 B2
Gjerrild DK 58 B3
Gjerstad N 53 B5
Gjesås N 49 B4
Gjesvær N 193 A9
Gjirokastër AL 182 C2
Gjøfjell N 54 A1
Gjøl DK 58 A2
Gjøra N 198 C6
Gjøvik N 48 B2
Gladbeck D 80 A2
Gladenbach D 81 B4
Gladstad N 195 E2
Glamis GB 35 B4
Glamoč BIH 138 A2
Glamsbjerg DK 59 C3
Gland CH 105 C5
Glandorf D 71 B4
Glanegg A 110 C1
Glanshammar S 56 A1
Glarus CH 107 B4
Glasgow GB 35 C3
Glashütte
Bayern D 108 B2
Sachsen D 84 B1
Glastonbury GB 43 A4
Glatzau A 110 C2
Glauchau D 83 B4
Glava S 54 A3
Glavatičevo BIH 139 B4
Glavičice BIH 127 C1
Gŭlŭbovo BG 183 A7
Glein
A 110 B1
N 195 D3
Gleinstätten A 110 C2
Gleisdorf A 110 B2
Glenamoy IRL 26 B1
Glenarm GB 27 B5
Glenavy GB 27 B4
Glenbarr GB 34 C2
Glenbeigh IRL 29 B2
Glenbrittle GB 31 B2
Glencoe GB 34 B2
Glencolumbkille IRL 26 B2
Glendalough IRL 30 A2
Glenealy IRL 30 B2
Glenelg GB 31 B3
Glenfinnan GB 34 B2
Glengarriff IRL 29 C2
Glenluce GB 36 B2
Glennamaddy IRL 28 A3
Glenrothes GB 35 B4
Glenties IRL 26 B2
Glesborg DK 58 B3
Glesien D 83 A4
Gletsch CH 106 C3
Glewitz D 66 B1
Glifada GR 185 B4
Glimåkra S 63 B2
Glin IRL 29 B2
Glina HR 124 B2
Glinde D 72 A3
Glinojeck PL 77 B5
Glinsk IRL 28 A2
Gliwice PL 86 B2
Glödnitz A 109 C5
Gloggnitz A 110 B2
Głogoczów PL 99 B3
Glogonj SRB 127 C2
Glogovac SRB 127 C3
Głogów PL 85 A4
Głogówek PL 86 B1
Glomel F 100 A2
Glomfjord N 195 D4
Glommen S 60 C2
Glommersträsk S 196 D2
Glonn D 108 B2
Glorenza I 108 C1
Gloria P 154 B2
Glosa GR 183 D5
Glossop GB 40 B2
Gloucester GB 39 C4
Głowaczów PL 87 A5
Główczyce PL 68 A2
Glöwen D 73 B5
Głowno PL 77 C4
Gložan SRB 126 B1
Głubczyce PL 86 B1
Głuchołazy PL 85 B5
Głuchów PL 87 A4
Głuchowo PL 75 B5
Glücksburg D 64 B2
Glückstadt D 64 C2
Glumina BIH 139 A5
Glumsø DK 65 A4
Glušci SRB 127 C1
Glusk BY 13 B8
Głuszyca PL 85 B4
Glyngøre DK 58 B1
Glyn Neath GB 39 C3
Gmünd
Karnten A 109 C4
Nieder Östereich A 96 C2
Gmund D 108 B2
Gmunden A 109 B4
Gnarp S 200 D3
Gnarrenburg D 72 A2
Gnesau A 109 C4
Gnesta S 56 A3
Gnięchowice PL 85 A4
Gniew PL 69 B3
Gniewkowo PL 76 B3
Gniezno PL 76 B2
Gnoien D 66 C1
Gnojnice BIH 139 B3
Gnojno PL 87 B4
Gnosall GB 40 C1
Gnosjö S 60 B3
Göbel TR 186 B3
Göçbeyli TR 186 C2
Goch D 80 A2
Gochsheim D 94 A2
Göd H 112 B3
Godalming GB 44 B3
Godby FIN 51 B6
Goðdalir IS 190 B6
Goddelsheim D 81 A4
Gódega di Sant'Urbano I 122 B1
Godegård S 56 B1
Godelheim D 81 A5
Goderville F 89 A4
Godiasco I 120 C2
Godič SLO 123 A3
Godkowo PL 69 A4
Godmanchester GB 44 A3
Gödöllö H 112 B3
Gödre H 125 A3
Godshill GB 44 C2
Godzikowice PL 85 B5
Godziszewo PL 69 A3
Goes NL 79 A3
Goetzenbrück F 93 C3
Góglio I 119 A5
Gogolin PL 86 B2
Göhren D 66 B2
Goirle NL 79 A5
Góis P 148 B1
Góito I 121 B3
Goizueta E 144 A2
Gojna Gora SRB 127 D2
Gójsk PL 77 B4
Gökçedağ TR 186 C3
Gökçen TR 188 A2
Gökçeören TR 188 A3
Gökçeyazı TR 186 C2
Göktepe TR 188 B3
Gol N 47 B5
Gola
HR 124 A3
N 48 A1
Gołańcz PL 76 B2
Gölbaşı TR 23 B7
Gölby FIN 51 B6
Gölcük
Kocaeli TR 187 B4
Niğde TR 23 B8
Golčův Jenikov CZ 97 B3
Gołczewo PL 67 C3
Goldach CH 107 B4
Goldbach D 93 A5
Goldbeck D 73 B4
Goldberg D 73 A5
Goldelund D 64 B2
Goldenstedt D 72 B1
Gołębiewo PL 69 A3
Golegã P 154 B2
Goleniów PL 75 A3
Golfo Aranci I 178 B3
Gölhisar TR 189 B4
Golina PL 76 B3
Gölle H 112 C2
Göllersdorf A 97 C4
Golling an der Salzach A 109 B4
Gölmarmara TR 186 D2
Golnice PL 84 A3
Golnik SLO 123 A3
Gölova TR 189 C5
Gölpazarı TR 187 B5
Gols A 111 B3
Golspie GB 32 D3
Golssen D 74 C2
Golub-Dobrzyń PL 77 A4
Golubinci SRB 127 C2
Goluchów PL 86 A1
Golymin-Ośrodek PL 77 B5
Golzow D 73 B5
Gomagoi I 108 C1
Gómara E 152 A1
Gomaringen D 93 C5
Gömbe TR 189 C4
Gömeç TR 186 C1
Gomel = Homyel BY 13 B9
Gomes Aires P 160 B1
Gómezserracin E 150 A3
Gommern D 73 B4
Gomulin PL 86 A3
Gonäs S 50 B2
Goncelin F 118 B2
Gończyce PL 87 A5
Gondomar
E 140 B2
P 148 A1
Gondrecourt-le-Château F 92 C1
Gondrin F 128 C3
Gönen
Balıkesir TR 186 B2
İsparta TR 189 B5
Gonfaron F 132 B2
Goñi E 144 B2
Goni
GR 182 D4
I 179 C3
Gonnesa I 179 C2
Gonnosfanádiga I 179 C2
Gönyü H 111 B4
Gonzaga I 121 C3
Goodrich GB 39 C4
Goodwick GB 39 B1
Gooik B 79 B4
Goole GB 40 B3
Goor NL 71 B3
Göpfritz an der Wild A 97 C3
Goppenstein CH 119 A4
Göppingen D 94 C1
Gor E 164 B2
Góra
Dolnośląskie PL 85 A4
Mazowieckie PL 77 B5
Gorafe E 164 B1
Gorawino PL 67 C4
Goražde BIH 139 B4
Gőrbeháza H 113 B5
Gordaliza del Pino E 142 B1
Gördes TR 186 D3
Gørding DK 59 C1
Górdola CH 120 A1
Gordon GB 35 C5
Gordoncillo E 142 B1
Gorebridge GB 35 C4
Gorenja Vas SLO 123 A3
Gorenje Jelenje HR 123 B3
Gorey
GB 88 A1
IRL 30 B2
Gorgonzola I 120 B2
Gorica HR 137 A4
Gorican HR 124 A2
Gorinchem NL 79 A4
Goring GB 44 B2
Goritsy RUS 9 D10
Göritz D 74 A2
Gorízia I 122 B2
Górki PL 77 B4
Gorleben D 73 A4
Gorleston-on-sea GB 41 C5
Gørlev DK 61 D1
Görlitz D 84 A2
Górliz E 143 A4
Görmin D 66 C2
Górna Grupa PL 69 B3
Gorna Oryakhovitsa BG 17 D6
Gornja Gorevnica SRB 127 D2
Gornja Ploča HR 137 A4
Gornja Radgona SLO 110 C2
Gornja Sabanta SRB 127 D3
Gornja Trešnjevica SRB 127 C2

Gornja Tuzla BIH 125 C4
Gornje Polje MNE 139 C4
Gornje Ratkovo BIH 124 C2
Gornji Grad SLO 123 A3
Gornji Humac HR 138 B2
Gornji Jasenjani BIH 139 B3
Gornji Kamengrad BIH 124 C2
Gornji Kneginec HR 124 A2
Gornji Kosinj HR 123 C4
Gornji Milanovac SRB 127 C2
Gornji Podgradci BIH 124 B3
Gornji Ravno BIH 138 B3
Gornji Sjenicak HR 124 B1
Gornji Vakuf BIH 138 B3
Górno PL 87 B4
Görömböly H 113 A4
Górowo Iławeckie PL 69 A5
Gorran Haven GB 42 B2
Gorredijk NL 70 A3
Gorron F 88 B3
Gorseinon GB 39 C2
Gort IRL 28 A3
Gortin GB 27 B3
Görzke D 73 B5
Gorzkowice PL 86 A3
Górzno
Kujawsko-Pomorskie PL 77 A4
Zachodnio-Pomorskie PL 75 A4
Gorzów Śląski PL 86 A2
Gorzów Wielkopolski PL 75 B4
Górzyca PL 74 B3
Gorzyce PL 98 B2
Górzyn PL 84 A2
Gorzyń PL 75 B4
Gorzyno PL 68 A2
Gosaldo I 121 A4
Gosau A 109 B4
Gosberton GB 41 C3
Gościcino PL 68 A3
Gościęcin PL 86 B2
Gościm PL 75 B4
Gościno PL 67 B4
Gosdorf A 110 C2
Gosforth GB 36 B3
Goslar D 82 A2
Goslice PL 77 B4
Gospič HR 137 A4
Gosport GB 44 C2
Gössäter S 55 B4
Gossau CH 107 B4
Goss Ilsede D 72 B3
Gössnitz D 83 B4
Gössweinstein D 95 B3
Gostivar MK 182 B2
Gostkow PL 77 C4
Göstling an der Ybbs A 110 B1
Gostomia PL 75 A5
Gostycyn PL 76 A2
Gostyń PL 85 A5
Gostynin PL 77 B4
Goszczyn PL 87 A4
Göta S 54 B3
Göteborg = Gothenburg S 60 B1
Götene S 55 B4
Gotha D 82 B2
Gothem S 57 C4
Gothenburg = Göteborg S 60 B1
Gotse Delchev BG 183 B5
Gottersdorf D 95 C4
Göttingen D 82 A1
Gottne S 200 C4
Götzis A 107 B4
Gouarec F 100 A2
Gouda NL 70 B1
Goudhurst GB 45 B4
Goumenissa GR 182 C4
Goura GR 184 B3
Gourdon F 129 B4
Gourgançon F 91 C4
Gourin F 100 A2
Gournay-en-Bray F 90 B1
Gourock GB 34 C3
Gouveia P 148 B2
Gouvy B 80 B1
Gouzeacourt F 90 A3
Gouzon F 116 A2
Govedari HR 138 C3
Govérnolo I 121 B3
Gowarczów PL 87 A4
Gowerton GB 39 C2
Gowidlino PL 68 A2
Gowran IRL 30 B1
Goyatz D 74 B3
Göynük TR 187 B5
Antalya TR 189 C5
Gozdnica PL 84 A3
Gozdowo PL 77 B4
Gozee B 79 B4
Graal-Müritz D 65 B5
Grabenstätt D 109 B3
Grabhair GB 31 A2
Gråbo S 60 B2
Grabovac HR 138 B2
Grabovac SRB 127 C2
Grabovci SRB 127 C1
Grabow D 73 A4
Grabów PL 77 B4
Grabow nad Pilicą PL 87 A5
Grabów nad Prosną PL 86 A2
Grabowno PL 76 A2
Grabs CH 107 B4
Gračac HR 138 A1
Gračanica BIH 125 C4
Graçay F 103 B3
Grad SLO 111 C3
Gradac
BIH 139 C4
HR 138 B3
MNE 139 B5
Gradačac BIH 125 C4
Gradec HR 124 B2
Gradefes E 142 B1
Grades A 110 C1
Gradil P 154 C1
Gradina
HR 124 B3
MNE 139 B5
Gradisca d'Isonzo I 122 B2
Gradište HR 125 B4
Grado
E 141 A4
I 122 B2
Grafenau D 96 C1
Gräfenberg D 95 B3
Gräfenhainichen D 83 A4
Grafenschlag A 97 C3
Grafenstein A 110 C1
Gräfenthal D 82 B3
Grafentonna D 82 A2
Grafenwöhr D 95 B3
Grafing D 108 A2
Grafling D 95 C4
Gräfsnäs S 54 B3
Gragnano I 170 C2
Grahovo SLO 122 A2
Graiguenamanagh IRL 30 B2
Grain GB 45 B4
Grainau D 108 B2
Graja de Iniesta E 158 B2
Grajera E 151 A4
Gram DK 59 C2
Gramais A 108 B1
Gramat F 129 B4
Gramatneusiedl A 111 A3
Grambow D 74 A3
Grammichele I 177 B3
Gramsh AL 182 C2
Gramzow D 74 A3
Gran N 48 B2
Granada E 163 A4
Granard IRL 27 C3
Grañas E 140 A3
Granátula de Calatrava E 157 B4
Grancey-le-Château F 105 B4
Grandas de Salime E 141 A4
Grandcamp-Maisy F 88 A2
Grand-Champ F 100 B3
Grand Couronne F 89 A5
Grand-Fougeray F 101 B4
Grândola P 160 A1
Grandpré F 91 B4
Grandrieu
B 79 B4
F 117 C3
Grandson CH 106 C1
Grandvillars F 106 B1
Grandvilliers F 90 B1
Grañén E 145 C3
Grangärde S 50 B1
Grange IRL 26 B2
Grangemouth GB 35 B4
Grange-over-Sands GB 36 B4
Grängesberg S 50 B1
Granges-de Crouhens F 145 B4
Granges-sur-Vologne F 106 A1
Gräningen D 73 B5
Granitola-Torretta I 176 B1
Granja
Évora P 155 C3
Porto P 148 A1
Granja de Moreruela E 142 C1
Granja de Torrehermosa E 156 B2
Gränna S 55 B5
Grannäs
Västerbotten S 195 E7
Västerbotten S 195 E8
Granö S 200 B5
Granollers E 147 C3
Granowiec PL 85 A5
Granowo PL 75 B5
Gransee D 74 A2
Gransherad N 53 A5
Grantham GB 40 C3
Grantown-on-Spey GB 32 D3
Grantshouse GB 35 C5
Granville F 88 B2
Granvin N 46 B3
Grærup Strand DK 59 C1
Gräsås S 60 C2
Grasbakken N 193 B12
Grasberg D 72 A2
Grasmere GB 36 B3
Gräsmyr S 200 C5
Grasö S 51 B5
Grassano I 172 B2
Grassau D 109 B3
Grasse F 132 B2
Grassington GB 40 A2
Græsted DK 61 C2
Gråsten DK 64 B2
Grästorp S 54 B3
Gratkorn A 110 B2
Gråträsk S 196 D2
Gratwein A 110 B2
Graulhet F 129 C4
Graus E 145 B4
Grávalos E 144 B2
Gravberget N 49 B4
Grave NL 80 A1
Gravedona I 120 A2
Gravelines F 78 A2
Gravellona Toce I 119 B5
Gravendal S 50 B1
Gravens DK 59 C2
Gravesend GB 45 B4
Graveson F 131 B3
Gravina in Púglia I 172 B2
Gray F 105 B4
Grayrigg GB 37 B4
Grays GB 45 B4
Grayshott GB 44 B3
Graz A 110 B2
Grazalema E 162 B2
Grążawy PL 69 B4
Grazzano Visconti I 120 C2
Greåker N 54 A2
Great Dunmow GB 45 B4
Great Malvern GB 39 B4
Great Torrington GB 42 B2
Great Waltham GB 45 B4
Great Yarmouth GB 41 C5
Grebbestad S 54 B2
Grebenstein D 81 A5
Grębocice PL 85 A4
Grębocin PL 76 A3
Greding D 95 B3
Gredstedbro DK 59 C1
Greenhead GB 37 B4
Greenisland GB 27 B5
Greenlaw GB 35 C5
Greenock GB 34 C3
Greenway GB 39 C2
Greenwich GB 45 B4
Grefrath D 80 A2
Greifenburg A 109 C4
Greiffenberg D 74 A2
Greifswald D 66 B2
Grein A 110 A1
Greipstad N 53 B3
Greiz D 83 B4
Grenaa DK 58 B3
Grenade F 129 C4
Grenade-sur-l'Adour F 128 C2
Grenchen CH 106 B2
Grendi N 53 B3
Grenivík IS 191 B7
Grenoble F 118 B2
Gréoux-les-Bains F 132 B1
Gresenhorst D 66 B1
Gressoney-la-Trinité I 119 B4
Gressoney-St.-Jean I 119 B4
Gressthal D 82 B2
Gressvik N 54 A1
Gresten A 110 B2
Gretna GB 36 B3
Greussen D 82 A2
Greve in Chianti I 135 B4
Greven
Mecklenburg-Vorpommern D 73 A3
Nordrhein-Westfalen D 71 B4
Grevena GR 182 C3
Grevenbroich D 80 A2
Grevenbrück D 81 A4
Grevenmacher L 92 B2
Grevesmühlen D 65 C4
Grevestrand DK 61 D2
Grevie S 61 C2
Greystoke GB 36 B4
Greystones IRL 30 A2
Grez-Doiceau B 79 B4
Grèzec F 129 B4
Grez-en-Bouère F 102 B1
Grezzana I 121 B4
Grgar SLO 122 A2
Grgurevci SRB 127 B1
Gries A 108 B2
Griesbach D 96 C1
Griesheim D 93 B4
Gries in Sellrain A 108 B2
Grieskirchen A 109 A4
Griffen A 110 C1
Grignan F 131 A3
Grignano I 122 B2
Grigno I 121 A4
Grignols F 128 B2
Grignon F 118 B3
Grijota E 142 B2
Grijpskerk NL 71 A3
Grillby S 56 A3
Grimaud F 132 B2
Grimbergen B 79 B4
Grimma D 83 A4
Grimmen D 66 B2
Grimmialp CH 106 C2
Grimsås S 60 B3
Grimsby GB 41 B3
Grimslöv S 62 B2
Grímsstaðir IS 191 B9
Grimstad N 53 B4
Grimstorp S 62 A2
Grindavík IS 190 D3
Grindelwald CH 106 C3
Grindheim N 52 B3
Grindsted DK 59 C1
Griñón E 151 B4
Gripenberg S 62 A2
Gripsholm S 56 A3
Grisolles F 129 C4
Grisslehamn S 51 B5
Gritley GB 33 C4
Grizebeck GB 36 B3
Grndina BIH 124 C2
Gröbming A 109 B4
Gröbzig D 83 A3
Grocka SRB 127 C2
Gröditz D 83 A5
Gródki PL 77 A5
Grodków PL 85 B5
Grodziec PL 76 B3
Grodzisk Mazowiecki PL 77 B5
Groenlo NL 71 B3
Groesbeek NL 80 A1
Grohote HR 138 B2
Groitzsch D 83 A4
Groix F 100 B2
Grójec PL 77 C5
Grom PL 77 A5
Gromiljca BIH 139 B4
Grömitz D 65 B3
Gromnik PL 99 B4
Gromo I 120 B2
Gronau
Niedersachsen D 72 B2
Nordrhein-Westfalen D 71 B4
Grønbjerg DK 59 B1
Grönenbach D 107 B5
Grong N 199 A9
Grönhögen S 63 B4
Groningen
D 73 C4
NL 71 A3
Grønnestrand DK 58 A2
Grono CH 120 A2
Grönskåra S 62 A3
Grootegast NL 71 A3
Gropello Cairoli I 120 B1
Grorud N 48 C2
Grósio I 120 A3
Grošnica SRB 127 D2
Grossalmerode D 82 A1
Grossarl A 109 B4
Gross Beeren D 74 B2
Gross Berkel D 72 B2
Grossbodungen D 82 A2
Gross-botwar D 94 C1
Grossburgwedel D 72 B2
Grosschönau D 84 B2
Gross-Dölln D 74 A2
Grossenbrode D 65 B4
Grossenehrich D 82 A2
Grossengottern D 82 A2
Grossenhain D 83 A5
Grossenkneten D 71 B5
Grossenlüder D 81 B5
Grossensee D 72 A3
Grossenzersdorf A 111 A3
Grosseto I 135 C4
Gross-Gerau D 93 B4
Grossgerungs A 96 C2
Grossglobnitz A 97 C3
Grosshabersdorf D 94 B2
Grossharras A 97 C4
Grosshartmansdorf D 83 B5
Grosshöchstetten CH 106 C2
Gross Kreutz D 74 B1
Grosskrut A 97 C4
Gross Lafferde D 72 B3
Gross Leutheb D 74 B3
Grosslohra D 82 A2
Grossmehring D 95 C3
Gross Muckrow D 74 B3
Gross Oesingen D 72 B3
Grossostheim D 93 B5
Grosspertholz A 96 C2
Grosspetersdorf A 111 B3
Grosspostwitz D 84 A2
Grossraming A 110 B1
Grossräschen D 84 A2
Gross Reken D 80 A3
Grossrinderfeld D 94 B1
Grossröhrsdorf D 84 A2
Gross Sarau D 65 C3
Gross Särchen D 84 A2
Grossschirma D 83 B5
Gross Schönebeck D 74 B2
Grossschweinbarth A 97 C4
Grosssiegharts A 97 C3
Grosssölk A 109 B4
Gross Umstadt D 93 B4
Grosswarasdorf A 111 B3
Gross Warnow D 73 A4
Gross-Weikersdorf A 97 C3
Gross-Welle D 73 A5
Grosswilfersdorf A 110 B2
Gross Wokern D 65 C5
Grostenquin F 92 C2
Grosuplje SLO 123 B3
Grotli N 198 C4
Grötlingbo S 57 C4
Grottáglie I 173 B3
Grottaminarda I 170 B3
Grottammare I 136 C2
Grotte di Castro I 168 A1
Grotteria I 175 C2
Gróttole I 172 B2
Grouw NL 70 A2
Grov N 194 B8
Grova N 53 A4
Grove E 140 B2
Grua N 48 B2
Grube D 65 B4
Grubišno Polje HR 124 B3
Grude BIH 138 B3
Grudovo BG 17 D7
Grudusk PL 77 A5
Grudziądz PL 69 B3
Grue N 49 B4
Gruissan F 130 B2
Grullos E 141 A4
Grumo Áppula I 171 B4
Grums S 55 A4
Grünau im Almtal A 109 B4
Grünberg D 81 B4
Grünburg A 110 B1
Grundarfjörður IS 190 C2
Gründau D 81 B5
Gründelhardt D 94 B1
Grundforsen S 49 A4
Grundlsee A 109 B4
Grundsund S 54 B2
Grunewald D 84 A1
Grungedal N 53 A3
Grunow D 74 B3
Grünstadt D 93 B4
Gruvberget S 50 A3
Gruyères CH 106 C2
Gruža SRB 127 D2
Grybów PL 99 B4
Grycksbo S 50 B2
Gryfice PL 67 C4
Gryfino PL 74 A3
Gryfów Śląski PL 84 A3
Gryllefjord N 194 A8
Grymyr N 48 B2
Gryt S 56 B2
Grytgöl S 56 B1
Grythyttan S 55 A5
Grytnäs S 57 B3
Grzmiąca PL 68 B1
Grzybno PL 74 A3
Grzywna PL 76 A3
Gschnitz A 108 B2
Gschwend D 94 C1
Gstaad CH 106 C2
Gsteig CH 119 A4
Guadahortuna E 163 A4
Guadalajara E 151 B4
Guadalaviar E 152 B2
Guadalcanal E 156 B2
Guadalcázar E 162 A3
Guadalix de la Sierra E 151 B4
Guadálmez E 156 B3
Guadalupe E 156 A2
Guadamur E 151 C3
Guadarrama E 151 B3
Guadiaro E 162 B2
Guadix E 164 B1
Guagnano I 173 B3
Guagno F 180 A1
Guajar-Faragüit E 163 B4
Gualchos E 163 B4
Gualdo Tadino I 136 B1
Gualtieri I 121 C3
Guarcino I 169 B3
Guarda P 149 B2
Guardamar del Segura E 165 A4
Guardão P 148 B1
Guardavalle I 175 C2
Guardea I 168 A2
Guárdia I 172 B1
Guardiagrele I 169 A4
Guardiarégia I 170 B2
Guárdia Sanframondi I 170 B2
Guardias Viejas E 164 C2
Guardiola de Bergueda E 147 B2
Guardo E 142 B2
Guareña E 156 B1
Guaro E 162 B3
Guarromán E 157 B4
Guasila I 179 C3
Guastalla I 121 C3
Gubbhögen S 199 A12
Gúbbio I 136 B1
Guben D 74 C3
Gubin PL 74 C3
Gudå N 199 B8
Gudavac BIH 124 C2
Guddal N 46 A2
Güderup DK 64 B2
Gudhem S 55 B4
Gudhjem DK 67 A3
Gudovac HR 124 B2
Gudow D 73 A3
Güdül TR 187 B7
Gudvangen N 46 B3
Guebwiller F 106 B2
Guéjar-Sierra E 163 A4
Guéméné-Penfao F 101 B4
Guéméné-sur-Scorff F 100 A2
Güeñes E 143 A3
Guer F 101 B3
Guérande F 101 B3
Guéret F 116 A1
Guérigny F 104 B2
Guesa E 144 B2
Gueugnon F 104 C3
Guglionesi I 170 B2
Gühlen Glienicke D 74 A1
Guia P 154 B2
Guichen F 101 B4
Guidizzolo I 121 B3
Guidónia-Montecélio I 168 B2
Guiglia I 135 A3
Guignes F 90 C2
Guijo E 156 B3
Guijo de Coria E 149 B3
Guijo de Santa Bábera E 150 B2
Guijuelo E 150 B2
Guildford GB 44 B3
Guillaumes F 132 A2
Guillena E 162 A1
Guillestre F 118 C3
Guillos F 128 B2
Guilsfield GB 38 B3
Guilvinec F 100 B1
Guimarães P 148 A1
Guincho P 154 C1
Guînes F 78 B1
Guingamp F 100 A2
Guipavas F 100 A1
Guisborough GB 37 B5
Guiscard F 90 B3
Guiscriff F 100 A2
Guise F 91 B3
Guisona E 147 C2
Guitiriz E 140 A3
Guîtres F 128 A2
Gujan-Mestras F 128 B1
Gulbene LV 8 D5
Gulçayır TR 187 C6
Guldborg DK 65 B4
Gullabo S 63 B3
Gullane GB 35 B5
Gullbrå N 46 B3
Gullbrandstorp S 61 C2
Gulleråsen S 50 A2
Gullhaug N 53 A6
Gullringen S 62 A3
Gullspång S 55 B5
Gullstein N 198 B5
Güllük TR 188 B2
Gülnar TR 23 C7
Gülpınar TR 186 C1
Gülşehir TR 23 B8
Gulsvik N 48 B1
Gumiel de Hizán E 143 C3
Gummersbach D 81 A3
Gümüldür TR 188 A2
Gümüşhaciköy TR 23 A8
Gümüşova TR 187 B5
Gundelfingen D 94 C2
Gundel-fingen D 106 A2
Gundelsheim D 93 B5
Gunderschoffen F 93 C3
Gundertshausen A 109 A3
Gundinci HR 125 B4
Gündoğmuş TR 189 C7
Güney
Burdur TR 189 B4
Denizli TR 188 A4
Gunja HR 125 C4
Günlüce TR 188 C3
Gunnarn S 195 E8
Gunnarsbyn S 196 C4
Gunnarskog S 49 C4
Gunnebo S 62 A4
Gunnislake GB 42 B2
Günselsdorf A 111 B3
Guntersblum D 93 B4
Guntersdorf A 97 C4
Guntin E 140 B3
Günyüzü TR 187 C6
Günzburg D 94 C2
Gunzenhausen D 94 B2
Güre
Balıkesir TR 186 C1
Uşak TR 186 D4
Gurk A 110 C1
Gurrea de Gállego E 144 B3
Gürsu TR 186 B4
Gušće HR 124 B2
Gusev RUS 12 A5
Gúspini I 179 C2
Gusselby S 56 A1
Güssing A 111 B3
Gusswerk A 110 B2
Gustav Adolf S 49 B5
Gustavsberg S 57 A4
Gustavsfors S 54 A3
Güstrow D 65 C5
Gusum S 56 B2

Gutcher GB 33 A5
Gutenstein A 110 B2
Gütersloh D 81 A4
Guttannen CH 106 C3
Guttaring A 110 C1
Guttau D 84 A2
Güttingen CH 107 B4
Gützkow D 66 C2
Guzów PL 77 B5
Gvardeysk RUS 12 A4
Gvarv N 53 A5
Gvozd MNE 139 C5
Gvozdansko HR 124 B2
Gwda Wielka PL 68 B1
Gwennap GB 42 B1
Gy F 105 B4
Gyál H 112 B3
Gyarmat H 111 B4
Gyékényes H 124 A3
Gyé-sur-Seine F 104 A3
Gyljen S 196 C5
Gylling DK 59 C3
Gyoma H 113 C4
Gyömöre H 111 B4
Gyömrö H 112 B3
Gyón H 112 B3
Gyöngyfa H 125 B3
Gyöngyös H 113 B3
Gyöngyöspata H 113 B3
Gyönk H 112 C2
Györ H 111 B4
Györszemere H 111 B4
Gypsera CH 106 C2
Gysinge S 51 B3
Gyttorp S 55 A5
Gyula H 113 C5
Gyulafirátót H 112 B1
Gyulaj H 112 C2

H

Haacht B 79 B4
Haag
Nieder Östereich
A 110 A1
Ober Östereich A 109 A4
D 108 A3
Haaksbergen NL 71 B3
Haamstede NL 79 A3
Haan D 80 A3
Haapajärvi FIN 3 E9
Haapsalu EST 8 C3
Haarlem NL 70 B1
Habas F 128 C2
Habay B 92 B1
Habo S 62 A2
Håbol S 54 B3
Habry CZ 97 B3
Habsheim F 106 B2
Hachenburg D 81 B3
Hacıbektaş TR 23 B8
Hacılar TR 23 B8
Hacinas E 143 C3
Hackås S 199 C11
Hacketstown IRL 30 B2
Hackthorpe GB 37 B4
Hadamar D 81 B4
Hädanberg S 200 C4
Haddington GB 35 C5
Hadersdorf am Kamp
A 97 C3
Haderslev DK 59 C2
Haderup DK 59 B1
Hadım TR 23 C7
Hadleigh
Essex GB 45 B4
Suffolk GB 45 A4
Hadlow GB 45 B4
Hadmersleben D 73 B4
Hadsten DK 59 B3
Hadsund DK 58 B3
Hadžići BIH 139 B4
Hafnarfjörður IS 190 C4
Hafnir IS 190 D3
Hafslo N 47 A4
Haganj HR 124 B2
Hagby S 63 B4
Hage D 71 A4
Hægebostad N 52 B3
Hægeland N 53 B3
Hagen
Niedersachsen D 72 A1
Nordrhein-Westfalen
D 80 A3
Hagenbach D 93 B4
Hagenow D 73 A4
Hagetmau F 128 C2
Hagfors S 49 B5
Häggenås S 199 B11
Hagondange F 92 B2
Hagsta S 51 B4
Haguenau F 93 C3
Hahnbach D 95 B3
Hahnslätten D 81 B4
Hahót H 111 C3
Haiger D 81 B4
Haigerloch D 93 C4
Hailsham GB 45 C4
Hainburg A 111 A3
Hainfeld A 110 A2
Hainichen D 83 B5
Hajdúböszörmény
H 113 B5
Hajdučica SRB 126 B2
Hajdúdorogo H 113 B5
Hajdúnánás H 113 B5
Hajdúszoboszló H 113 B5
Hajnáčka SK 113 A3
Hajnówka PL 13 B5
Hajós H 112 C3
Håkafot S 199 A11
Hakkas S 196 C4
Håksberg S 50 B2
Halaszi H 111 B4
Halberstadt D 82 A3
Halberton GB 43 B3
Hald Ege DK 58 B2
Haldem D 71 B5
Halden N 54 A2
Haldensleben D 73 B4
Halenbeck D 73 A5
Halesowen GB 40 C1
Halesworth GB 45 A5
Halfing D 109 B3
Halhjem N 46 B2
Håliden S 49 B5
Halifax GB 40 B2
Häljelöt S 56 B2
Halkida GR 185 A4
Halkirk GB 32 C3
Hall S 57 C4
Hälla S 200 C3
Hallabro S 63 B3
Hällabrottet S 56 A1
Halland GB 45 C4
Hällaryd S 63 B2
Hallaryd S 61 C3
Hällberga S 56 A2
Hällbybrunn S 56 A2
Halle
B 79 B4
Nordrhein-Westfalen
D 72 B1
Sachsen-Anhalt D 83 A3
Hålleberga S 62 B3
Hällefors S 55 A5
Hälleforsnäs S 56 A2
Hallein A 109 B4
Hällekis S 55 B4
Hallen S 199 B11
Hållen S 51 B4
Hallenberg D 81 A4
Hällestad S 56 B1
Hällevadsholm S 54 B2
Hällevik S 63 B2
Hälleviksstrand S 54 B2
Hallingby N 48 B2
Hallingeberg S 62 A4
Hallingen N 47 B6
Hall in Tirol A 108 B2
Hällnäs S 195 D9
Hållnäs S 51 B4
Hällnäs S 200 B5
Hallormsstaður
IS 191 B11
Hallsberg S 56 A1
Hållsta S 56 A2
Hallstahammar S 56 A2
Hallstatt A 109 B4
Hallstavik S 51 B5
Halltorp S 63 B4
Halluin F 78 B3
Hallviken S 199 B12
Hallworthy GB 42 B2
Halmstad S 61 C2
Hals DK 58 A3
Halsa N 198 B5
Halstead GB 45 B4
Haltdalen N 199 C8
Haltern D 80 A3
Haltwhistle GB 37 B4
Halvarsgårdarna S 50 B2
Halver D 80 A3
Halvrimmen DK 58 A2
Ham F 90 B3
Hamar N 48 B3
Hamarhaug N 46 B2
Hamarøy N 194 B6
Hambach F 92 B3
Hambergen D 72 A1
Hambergsund S 54 B2
Hambledon GB 44 C2
Hambuhren D 72 B2
Hamburg D 72 A3
Hamdibey TR 186 C2
Hamdorf D 64 B2
Hämeenlinna FIN 8 B4
Hameln = Hamlin D 72 B2
Hamersleben D 73 B4
Hamidiye TR 187 C5
Hamilton GB 36 A2
Hamina FIN 8 B5
Hamlagrø N 46 B3
Hamlin = Hameln D 72 B2
Hamm D 81 A3
Hammar S 55 B5
Hammarland FIN 51 B6
Hammarö S 55 A4
Hammarstrand S 200 C2
Hamme B 79 A4
Hammel DK 59 B2
Hammelburg D 82 B1
Hammelspring D 74 A2
Hammenhög S 66 A3
Hammerdal S 199 B12
Hammerfest N 192 B7
Hammershøj DK 58 B2
Hammerum DK 59 B2
Hamminkeln D 80 A2
Hamnavoe GB 33 A5
Hamneda S 60 C3
Hamningberg N 193 B14
Hamoir B 80 B1
Hamont B 80 A1
Hámor H 113 A4
Hamra
Gävleborg S 199 D12
Gotland S 57 D4
Hamrångefjärden S 51 B4
Hamstreet GB 45 B4
Hamsund N 194 B6
Han TR 187 C5
Hanaskog S 61 C4
Hanau D 81 B4
Händelöp S 62 A4
Handlová SK 98 C2
Hanerau-Hademarschen
D 64 B2
Hånger S 60 B3
Hanhimaa FIN 197 B8
Hanken S 55 B5
Hankensbüttel D 73 B3
Han Knežica BIH 124 B2
Hanko FIN 8 C3
Hannover D 72 B2
Hannut B 79 B5
Han Pijesak BIH 139 A4
Hansnes N 192 C3
Hanstedt D 72 A3
Hanstholm DK 58 A1
Hantsavichy BY 13 B7
Hanušovice CZ 85 B4
Haparanda S 196 D7
Haradok BY 13 A8
Harads S 196 C4
Häradsbäck S 63 B2
Häradsbygden S 50 B2
Harbo S 51 B4
Harboør DK 58 B1
Harburg
Bayern D 94 C2
Hamburg D 72 A2
Hårby DK 59 C3
Harc H 112 C2
Hardegarijp NL 70 A2
Hardegsen D 82 A1
Hardelot Plage F 78 B1
Hardenbeck D 74 A2
Hardenberg NL 71 B3
Harderwijk NL 70 B2
Hardheim D 94 B1
Hardt D 106 A3
Hareid N 198 C3
Haren
D 71 B4
NL 71 A3
Harestua N 48 B2
Harfleur F 89 A4
Harg S 51 B5
Hargicourt F 90 B3
Hargnies F 91 A4
Hargshamn S 51 B5
Härja S 55 B4
Harkány H 125 B4
Härkeberga S 56 A3
Harkebrügge D 71 A4
Harlech GB 38 B2
Harleston GB 45 A5
Hårlev DK 65 A5
Harlingen NL 70 A2
Harlösa S 61 D3
Harlow GB 45 B4
Harmancık TR 186 C4
Harmånger S 200 E3
Härnevi S 56 A3
Härnösand S 200 D3
Haro E 143 B4
Haroldswick GB 33 A6
Háromfa H 124 A3
Haroué F 92 C2
Harpenden GB 44 B3
Harplinge S 60 C2
Harpstedt D 72 B1
Harrogate GB 40 A2
Harrow GB 44 B3
Härryda S 60 B2
Harsefeld D 72 A2
Harsewinkel D 71 C5
Hârşova 17 C7
Harstad N 194 B7
Harsum D 72 B2
Harsvik N 199 A7
Harta H 112 C3
Hartberg A 110 B2
Hartburn GB 37 A5
Hartennes F 90 B3
Hartest GB 45 A4
Hartha D 83 A4
Hartland GB 42 B2
Hartlepool GB 37 B5
Hartmanice CZ 96 B1
Hartmannsdorf A 110 B2
Harvassdal N 195 E5
Harwell GB 44 B2
Harwich GB 45 B5
Harzgerode D 82 A3
Häselgehr A 108 B1
Haselünne D 71 B4
Hasköy TR 186 A1
Haslach D 106 A3
Haslach an der Mühl
A 96 C2
Hasle DK 67 A3
Haslemere GB 44 B3
Haslev DK 65 A4
Hasloch D 94 B1
Hasparren F 144 A2
Hassela S 200 D2
Hasselfelde D 82 A2
Hasselfors S 55 A5
Hasselt
B 79 B5
NL 70 B3
Hassfurt D 94 A2
Hassleben D 74 A2
Hässleholm S 61 C3
Hasslö S 63 B3
Hassloch D 93 B4
Hästbo S 51 B4
Hastersboda FIN 51 B7
Hästholmen S 55 B5
Hastière-Lavaux B 79 B4
Hastigrow GB 32 C3
Hastings GB 45 C4
Hästveda S 61 C3
Hasvik N 192 B6
Hatfield
Hertfordshire GB 44 B3
South Yorkshire GB 40 B3
Hatherleigh GB 42 B2
Hathersage GB 40 B2
Hatlestrand N 46 B2
Hattem NL 70 B3
Hatten
D 71 A5
F 93 C3
Hattfjelldal N 195 E4
Hatting DK 59 C2
Hattingen D 80 A3
Hattstadt F 106 A2
Hattstedt D 64 B2
Hatvan H 112 B3
Hatvik N 46 B2
Hau D 80 A2
Haudainville F 92 B1
Hauganes IS 191 B7
Haugastøl N 47 B4
Hauge N 52 B2
Haugesund N 52 A1
Haughom N 52 B2
Haugsdal N 46 B2
Haugsdorf A 97 C4
Haukedal N 46 A3
Haukeland N 46 B2
Haukeligrend N 52 A3
Haukeliseter N 52 A3
Haukipudas FIN 3 D9
Haulerwijk NL 71 A3
Haunersdorf D 95 C4
Haus N 46 B2
Hausach D 106 A3
Hausham D 108 B2
Hausmannstätten
A 110 C2
Hausvik N 52 B2
Hautajärvi FIN 197 C12
Hautefort F 129 A4
Hauterives F 117 B5
Hauteville-Lompnès
F 118 B2
Haut-Fays B 91 A5
Hautmont F 79 B3
Hautrage B 79 B3
Hauzenberg D 96 C1
Havant GB 44 C3
Havdhem S 57 C4
Havdrup DK 61 D2
Havelange B 79 B5
Havelberg D 73 B5
Havelte NL 70 B3
Haverfordwest GB 39 C2
Haverhill GB 45 A4
Havering GB 45 B4
Håverud S 54 B3
Havířov CZ 98 B2
Havixbeck D 71 C4
Havlíčkův Brod CZ 97 B3
Havndal DK 58 B3
Havneby DK 64 A1
Havnebyen DK 61 D1
Havnsø DK 61 D1
Havøysund N 193 A8
Havran TR 186 C2
Havrebjerg DK 61 D1
Havsa TR 186 A1
Havstenssund S 54 B2
Havza TR 23 A8
Hawes GB 37 B4
Hawick GB 35 C5
Hawkhurst GB 45 B4
Hawkinge GB 45 B5
Haxey GB 40 B3
Hayange F 92 B2
Haydarlı TR 189 A5
Haydon Bridge GB 37 B4
Hayle GB 42 B1
Haymana TR 187 C7
Hay-on-Wye GB 39 B3
Hayrabolu TR 186 A2
Haysyn UA 13 D8
Hayvoron UA 13 D8
Haywards Heath GB 44 C3
Hazebrouck F 78 B2
Hazlov CZ 83 B4
Heacham GB 41 C4
Headcorn GB 45 B4
Headford IRL 28 A2
Heanor GB 40 B2
Héas F 145 B4
Heathfield GB 45 C4
Hebden Bridge GB 40 B1
Heberg S 60 C2
Heby S 51 C3
Hechingen D 93 C4
Hechlingen D 94 C2
Hecho E 144 B3
Hechtel B 79 A5
Hechthausen D 72 A2
Heckelberg D 74 B2
Heckington GB 41 C3
Hecklingen D 82 A3
Hed S 56 A1
Hedalen N 48 B1
Hedared S 60 B2
Heddal N 53 A5
Hédé F 101 A4
Hede S 199 C10
Hedekas S 54 B2
Hedemora S 50 B2
Hedenäset S 196 C6
Hedensted DK 59 C2
Hedersleben D 82 A3
Hedesunda S 51 B4
Hedge End GB 44 C2
Hedon GB 41 B3
Heede D 71 B4
Heek D 71 B4
Heemstede NL 70 B1
Heerde NL 70 B3
Heerenveen NL 70 B2
Heerhugowaard NL 70 B1
Heerlen NL 80 B1
Heeze NL 80 A1
Heggenes N 47 A6
Hegra N 199 B8
Hegyeshalom H 111 B4
Hegyközség H 111 B3
Heia N 199 A9
Heide D 64 B2
Heidelberg D 93 B4
Heiden D 80 A2
Heidenau D 84 B1
Heidenheim D 94 C2
Heidenreichstein A 97 C3
Heikendorf D 64 B3
Heikkilä FIN 197 C12
Heilam GB 32 C2
Heiland N 53 B4
Heilbad Heiligenstadt
D 82 A2
Heilbronn D 93 B5
Heiligenblut A 109 B3
Heiligendamn D 65 B4
Heiligendorf D 73 B3
Heiligengrabe D 73 A5
Heiligenhafen D 65 B3
Heiligenhaus D 80 A2
Heiligenkreuz A 111 C3
Heiligenstadt D 94 B3
Heiloo NL 70 B1
Heilsbronn D 94 B2
Heim N 198 B6
Heimburg D 82 A2
Heimdal N 199 B7
Heinerscheid L 92 A2
Heinersdorf D 74 B3
Heining D 96 C1
Heiningen D 94 C1
Heinola FIN 8 B5
Heinsberg D 80 A2
Heist-op-den-Berg
B 79 A4
Hejde S 57 C4
Hejdeby S 57 C4
Hejls DK 59 C2
Hejnice CZ 84 B3
Hel PL 69 A3
Helchteren B 79 A5
Heldburg D 82 B2
Heldrungen D 82 A3
Helechosa E 156 A3
Helensburgh GB 34 B3
Helfenberg A 96 C2
Helgen N 53 A5
Helgeroa N 53 B5
Hella
IS 190 D5
N 46 A3
Helland N 194 B7
Hellas S 55 B3
Helle N 52 B2
Helleland N 52 B2
Hellendoorn NL 71 B3
Hellenthal D 80 B2
Hellesøy N 46 B1
Hellesylt N 198 C3
Hellevoetsluis NL 79 A4
Helligskogen N 192 C4
Hellin E 158 C2
Hellissandur IS 190 C2
Hellnar IS 190 C2
Hellum DK 58 A3
Hellvi S 57 C4
Hellvik N 52 B1
Helm-brechts D 83 B3
Helmond NL 80 A1
Helmsdale GB 32 C3
Helmsley GB 37 B5
Helmstedt D 73 B3
Hel'pa SK 99 C3
Helsa D 82 A1
Helsby GB 38 A4
Helsingborg S 61 C2
Helsinge DK 61 C2
Helsingør DK 61 C2
Helsinki FIN 8 B4
Helston GB 42 B1
Hemau D 95 B3
Hemavan S 195 E6
Hemel Hempstead
GB 44 B3
Hemer D 81 A3
Héming F 92 C2
Hemmet DK 59 C1
Hemmingstedt D 64 B2
Hemmoor D 64 C2
Hemnes N 54 A2
Hemnesberget N 195 D4
Hemse S 57 C4
Hemsedal N 47 B5
Hemslingen D 72 A2
Hemsworth GB 40 B2
Hen N 48 B2
Henån S 54 B2
Hendaye F 144 A2
Hendek TR 187 B5
Hendungen D 82 B2
Henfield GB 44 C3
Hengelo
Gelderland NL 71 B3
Overijssel NL 71 B3
Hengersberg D 95 C5
Hengoed GB 39 C3
Hénin-Beaumont F 78 B2
Henley-on-Thames
GB 44 B3
Hennan S 200 D1
Henneberg D 82 B2
Hennebont F 100 B2
Henne Strand DK 59 C1
Hennigsdorf D 74 B2
Hennset N 198 B5
Hennstedt
Schleswig-Holstein
D 64 B2
Schleswig-Holstein
D 64 B2
Henrichemont F 103 B4
Henryków PL 85 B5
Henrykowo PL 69 A5
Hensås N 47 A5
Henstedt-Ulzburg D 64 C2
Heppenheim D 93 B4
Herad
Buskerud N 47 B6
Vest-Agder N 52 B2
Heradsbygd N 48 B3
Heraklion = Iraklio
GR 185 D6
Herálec CZ 97 B4
Herand N 46 B3
Herbault F 103 B3
Herbern D 81 A3
Herbertstown IRL 29 B3
Herbeumont B 91 B5
Herbignac F 101 B3
Herbisse F 91 C4
Herbitzheim F 92 B3
Herbolzheim D 106 A2
Herborn D 81 B4
Herbrechtingen D 94 C2
Herby PL 86 B2
Herceg-Novi MNE 16 D3
Hercegovać HR 124 B3
Hercegszántó H 125 B4
Herchen D 80 B3
Heréd H 112 B3
Hereford GB 39 B4
Herefoss N 53 B4
Hereke TR 187 B4
Herencia E 157 A4
Herend H 111 B4
Herent B 79 B4
Herentals B 79 A4
Hérépian F 130 B2
Herfølge DK 61 D2
Herford D 72 B1
Herguijuela E 156 A2
Héric F 101 B4
Héricourt F 106 B1
Héricourt-en-Caux
F 89 A4
Hérimoncourt F 106 B1
Heringsdorf D 65 B4
Herisau CH 107 B4
Hérisson F 103 C4
Herk-de-Stad B 79 B5
Herlufmagle DK 65 A4
Hermagor A 109 C4
Hermannsburg D 72 B3
Hermansverk N 46 A3
Heřmanův Městec
CZ 97 B3
Herment F 116 B2
Hermeskeil D 92 B2
Hermisende E 141 C4
Hermonville F 91 B3
Hermsdorf D 83 B3
Hernani E 144 A2
Hernansancho E 150 B3
Herne D 80 A3
Herne Bay GB 45 B5
Hernes N 48 B3
Herning DK 59 B1
Herøya N 53 A5
Herramelluri E 143 B3
Herräng S 51 B5
Herre N 53 A5
Herrenberg D 93 C4
Herrera E 162 A3
Herrera de Alcántara
E 155 B3
Herrera del Duque
E 156 A2
Herrera de los Navarros
E 152 A2
Herrera de Pisuerga
E 142 B2
Herreros del Suso
E 150 B2
Herrestad S 54 B2
Herrhamra S 57 B3
Herritslev DK 65 B4
Herrlisheim F 93 C3

Herrljunga S 55 B4
Herrnhut D 84 A2
Herrsching D 108 A2
Hersbruck D 95 B3
Hersby S 57 A4
Herscheid D 81 A3
Herselt B 79 A4
Herso GR 182 B4
Herstal B 80 B1
Herstmonceux GB . 45 C4
Herten D 80 A3
Hertford GB 44 B3
Hervás E 149 B4
Hervik N 52 A1
Herxheim D 93 B4
Herzberg
Brandenburg D 74 B1
Brandenburg D 83 A5
Niedersachsen D . . . 82 A2
Herzebrock D 81 A4
Herzfelde D 74 B2
Herzlake D 71 B4
Herzogenaurach D . 94 B2
Herzogenbuchsee
CH 106 B2
Herzogenburg A . . . 110 A2
Herzsprung D 73 A5
Hesby N 52 A1
Hesdin F 78 B2
Hesel D 71 A4
Heskestad N 52 B2
Hessdalen N 199 C8
Hesselager DK 65 A3
Hesseng N 193 C13
Hessisch Lichtenau
D 82 A1
Hessisch-Oldendorf
D 72 B2
Hestra S 60 B3
Heswall GB 38 A3
Hetlevik N 46 B2
Hettange-Grande F . 92 B2
Hetton-le-Hole GB . . 37 B5
Hettstedt D 82 A3
Heuchin F 78 B2
Heudicourt-sous-les-
Côtes F 92 C1
Heunezel F 105 A5
Heuqueville F 89 A4
Heves H 113 B4
Héviz H 111 C4
Hexham GB 37 B4
Heysham GB 36 B4
Heytesbury GB 43 A4
Hidas H 125 A4
Hieflau A 110 B1
Hiendelaencina E . 151 A5
Hiersac F 115 C4
High Bentham GB . . 37 B4
Highclere GB 44 B2
High Hesket GB 37 B4
Highley GB 39 B4
High Wycombe GB . 44 B3
Higuera de Arjona
E 157 C4
Higuera de Calatrava
E 163 A3
Higuera de la Serena
E 156 B2
Higuera de la Sierra
E 161 B3
Higuera de Vargas
E 155 C4
Higuera la Real E . 161 A3
Higuers de Llerena
E 156 B1
Higueruela E 158 C2
Híjar E 153 A3
Hilchenbach D 81 A4
Hildburghausen D . . 82 B2
Hilden D 80 A2
Hilders D 82 B1
Hildesheim D 72 B2
Hilgay GB 41 C4
Hillared S 60 B3
Hille D 72 B1
Hillegom NL 70 B1
Hillerød DK 61 D2
Hillerstorp S 60 B3
Hillesheim D 80 B2
Hillestad N 53 A6
Hillmersdorf D 83 A5
Hillsborough GB . . . 27 B4
Hillswick GB 33 A5
Hilpoltstein D 95 B3
Hiltpoltstein D 94 B3
Hilvarenbeek NL . . . 79 A5
Hilversum NL 70 B2
Himarë AL 182 C1
Himbergen D 73 A3
Himesháza H 125 A4
Himmelberg A 109 C5
Himmelpforten D . . . 72 A2
Himód H 111 B4
Hinckley GB 40 C2
Hindås S 60 B2
Hindelang D 108 B1
Hindelbank CH 106 B2
Hinderavåg N 52 A1
Hindhead GB 44 B3
Hinjosa del Valle E 156 B1
Hinnerup DK 59 B3
Hinneryd S 61 C3
Hinojal E 155 B4
Hinojales E 161 B3
Hinojos E 161 B3
Hinojosa del Duque
E 156 B2
Hinojosas de Calatrava
E 157 B3
Hinterhornbach A . 108 B1
Hinterriss A 108 B2
Hintersee
A 109 B4
D 74 A3
Hinterstoder A 110 B1
Hintertux A 108 B2
Hinterweidenthal D . 93 B3
Hinwil CH 107 B3
Hios GR 185 A7
Hippolytushoef NL . 70 B1
Hirschaid D 94 B2
Hirschau D 95 B3
Hirschfeld D 83 A5
Hirschhorn D 93 B4
Hirsingue F 106 B2
Hirson F 91 B4
Hirtshals DK 58 A2
Hirvaskoski FIN . . 197 D10
Hirzenhain D 81 B5
Hisarcık TR 186 C4
Hishult S 61 C3
Hissjön S 200 C6
Hitchin GB 44 B3
Hitra N 198 B5
Hittarp S 61 C2
Hittisau A 107 B4
Hittun N 46 A1
Hitzacker D 73 A4
Hjallerup DK 58 A3
Hjällstad S 49 B5
Hjältevad S 62 A3
Hjärnarp S 61 C2
Hjartdal N 53 A4
Hjellestad N 46 B2
Hjelmeland N 52 A2
Hjelset N 198 C4
Hjerkinn N 198 C6
Hjerm DK 58 B1
Hjerpsted DK 64 A1
Hjerting DK 59 C1
Hjo S 55 B5
Hjordkær DK 64 A2
Hjørring DK 58 A2
Hjorted S 62 A4
Hjortkvarn S 56 B1
Hjortnäs S 50 B1
Hjortsberga S 62 B2
Hjukse N 53 A5
Hjuksebø N 53 A5
Hjulsjö S 55 A5
Hliník nad Hronom
SK 98 C2
Hlinsko CZ 97 B3
Hlío IS 191 A10
Hlohovec SK 98 C1
Hlubokánad Vltavou
CZ 96 B2
Hlučín CZ 98 B2
Hlyboka UA 17 A6
Hlybokaye BY 13 A7
Hniezdne SK 99 B4
Hnilec SK 99 C4
Hnúšťa SK 99 C3
Hobol H 125 A3
Hobro DK 58 B2
Hobscheid L 92 B1
Hocalar TR 189 A4
Hochdonn D 64 B2
Hochdorf CH 106 B3
Hochfelden F 93 C3
Hochspeyer D 93 B3
Höchstadt D 94 B2
Höchstädt D 94 C2
Hochstenbach D . . . 81 B3
Höchst im Odenwald
D 93 B5
Höckendorf D 83 B5
Hockenheim D 93 B4
Hoddesdon GB 44 B3
Hodejov SK 99 C3
Hodenhagen D 72 B2
Hodkovice CZ 84 B3
Hódmezővásárhely
H 113 C4
Hodnet GB 38 B4
Hodonín CZ 98 C1
Hodslavice CZ 98 B2
Hoedekenskerke NL 79 A3
Hoegaarden B 79 B4
Hoek van Holland
NL 79 A4
Hoenderlo NL 70 B2
Hof
D 83 B3
N 53 A6
Hofbieber D 82 B1
Hoff GB 37 B4
Hofgeismar D 81 A5
Hofheim
Bayern D 82 B2
Hessen D 93 A4
Hofkirchen im Mühlkreis
A 96 C1
Höfn IS 191 C10
Hofors S 50 B3
Hofsós IS 190 B6
Hofstad N 199 A7
Höganäs S 61 C2
Högbo S 51 B3
Hogdal S 54 A2
Høgebru N 46 A4
Högfors S 50 C2
Högklint S 57 C4
Högsäter S 54 B3
Högsby S 62 A4
Högsjö S 56 A1
Hogstad S 55 B6
Högyész H 112 C2
Hohenau A 97 C4
Hohenberg A 110 B2
Hohenbucko D 83 A5
Hohenburg D 95 B3
Hohendorf D 66 B1
Hohenems A 107 B4
Hohenhameln D . . . 72 B3
Hohenhausen D 72 B1
Hohenkirchen D . . . 71 A4
Hohenlinden D . . . 108 A2
Hohenlockstedt D . . 64 C2
Hohenmölsen D . . . 83 A4
Hohennauen D 73 B5
Hohen Neuendorf D 74 B2
Hohenseeden D . . . 73 B5
Hohentauern A 110 B1
Hohentengen D . . . 106 B3
Hohenwepel D 81 A5
Hohenwestedt D . . . 64 B2
Hohenwutzen D 74 B3
Hohenzieritz D 74 A2
Hohn D 64 B2
Hohne D 72 B3
Hohnstorf D 73 A3
Højer DK 64 B1
Højslev Stby DK . . . 58 B2
Hok S 62 A2
Hökerum S 60 B3
Hökhuvud S 51 B5
Hokksund N 53 A5
Hökön S 63 B2
Hol N 47 B5
Hólar IS 190 B6
Holašovice CZ 96 C2
Holbæk
Aarhus Amt. DK 58 B3
Vestsjællands Amt.
DK 61 D1
Holbeach GB 41 C4
Holdenstedt D 73 B3
Holdhus N 46 B2
Holdorf D 71 B5
Holeby DK 65 B4
Hølen N 54 A1
Hølervasseter N . . . 47 B6
Holešov CZ 98 B1
Holguera E 155 B4
Holič SK 98 C1
Holice
CZ 97 A3
SK 111 B4
Höljes S 49 B4
Hollabrunn A 97 C4
Hollandstoun GB . . 33 B4
Høllen N 53 B3
Hollfeld D 95 B3
Hollókő H 112 B3
Hollstadt D 82 B2
Hollum NL 70 A2
Höllviksnäs S 66 A1
Holm N 195 E3
Hólmavík IS 190 B4
Holmbukt N 192 B5
Holmedal S 54 A2
Holmegil N 54 A2
Holmen N 48 B2
Holme-on-Spalding-
Moor GB 40 B3
Holmes Chapel GB . 38 A4
Holmestrand N 54 A1
Holmfirth GB 40 B2
Holmfoss N 193 C14
Holmsbu N 54 A1
Holmsjö S 63 B3
Holmsund S 200 C6
Holmsveden S 50 A3
Holmudden S 57 C5
Hölö S 57 A3
Holøydal N 199 C8
Holsbybrunn S 62 A3
Holseter N 48 A1
Holsljunga S 60 B2
Holstebro DK 59 B1
Holsted DK 59 C1
Holsworthy GB 42 B2
Holt
D 64 B2
Norfolk GB 41 C5
Wrexham GB 38 A4
IS 190 D6
N 53 B4
Holten NL 71 B3
Holtwick D 71 B4
Holum N 52 B3
Holwerd NL 70 A2
Holycross IRL 29 B4
Holyhead GB 38 A2
Holýšov CZ 95 B5
Holywell GB 38 A3
Holywood GB 27 B5
Holzdorf D 83 A5
Holzhausen D 72 B1
Holzheim D 94 C2
Holzkirchen D 108 B2
Holzminden D 81 A5
Holzthaleben D 82 A2
Homberg
Hessen D 81 A5
Hessen D 81 B5
Homburg D 93 B3
Hommelstø N 195 E3
Hommersåk N 52 B1
Homokmegy H . . . 112 C3
Homokszentgyörgy
H 124 A3
Homyel = Gomel BY 13 B9
Honaz TR 188 B4
Hondarribia E 144 A2
Hondón de los Frailes
E 165 A4
Hondschoote F 78 B2
Hönebach D 82 B1
Hønefoss N 48 B2
Honfleur F 89 A4
Høng DK 61 D1
Honiton GB 43 B3
Hönningen D 80 B2
Honningsvåg N . . . 193 B9
Hönö S 60 B1
Honrubia E 158 B1
Hontalbilla E 151 A3
Hontheim D 92 A2
Hontianske-Nemce
SK 98 C2
Hontoria de la Cantera
E 143 B3
Hontoria del Pinar
E 143 C3
Hontoria de Valdearados
E 143 C3
Hoofddorp NL 70 B1
Hoogerheide NL . . . 79 A4
Hoogeveen NL 71 B3
Hoogezand-Sappemeer
NL 71 A3
Hoogkarspel NL . . . 70 B2
Hoogkerk NL 71 A3
Hoogstede D 71 B3
Hoogstraten B 79 A4
Hook GB 44 B3
Hooksiel D 71 A5
Höör S 61 D3
Hoorn NL 70 B2
Hope GB 38 A3
Hopen N 194 C6
Hope under Dinmore
GB 39 B4
Hopfgarten A 108 B3
Hopfgarten in
Defereggen A . . . 109 C3
Hopseidet N 193 B11
Hopsten D 71 B4
Hoptrup DK 59 C2
Hora Svatého
Sebestiána CZ . . . 83 B5
Horaždóvice CZ . . . 96 B1
Horb am Neckar D . . 93 C4
Horbelev DK 65 B5
Hørby DK 58 A3
Hörby S 61 D3
Horcajada de la Torre
E 158 A1
Horcajo de los Montes
E 156 A3
Horcajo de Santiago
E 151 C4
Horcajo-Medianero
E 150 B2
Horche E 151 B4
Horda S 62 A2
Hordabø N 46 B1
Hordalia N 52 A2
Hordvik N 46 B2
Hořesedly CZ 83 B5
Horezu RO 17 C6
Horgen CH 107 B3
Horgoš SRB 126 A1
Horia RO 126 A3
Hořice CZ 84 B3
Horjul SLO 123 A3
Horka D 84 A2
Hörken S 50 B1
Horki BY 13 A9
Hörle S 60 B4
Horn
A 97 C3
D 81 A4
N 48 B2
S 62 A3
Horna E 158 C2
Hornachos E 156 B1
Hornachuelos E . . . 162 A2
Horná Mariková SK . 98 B2
Hornanes N 46 C2
Horná Streda SK . . . 98 C1
Horná Štrubna SK . . 98 C2
Horná Súča SK 98 C1
Hornbæk
Aarhus Amt. DK 58 B2
Frederiksværk DK . . 61 C2
Hornberg D 106 A3
Hornburg D 73 B3
Horncastle GB 41 B3
Horndal S 50 B3
Horndean GB 44 C2
Horne
Fyns Amt. DK 64 A3
Ribe Amt. DK 59 C1
Hörnebo S 55 B5
Horneburg D 72 A2
Hörnefors S 200 C5
Horní Bečva CZ 98 B2
Horni Benešov CZ . . 98 B1
Horni Cerekev CZ . . 97 B3
Horní Jiřetín CZ 83 B5
Horní Lomná CZ . . . 98 B2
Horni Maršov CZ . . . 85 B3
Hornindal N 198 D3
Hørning DK 59 B3
Hörningsholm S . . . 57 A3
Horní Planá CZ 96 C2
Horni Slavkov CZ . . 83 B4
Horni Vltavice CZ . . 96 C1
Hornnes N 53 B3
Horno D 84 A2
Hornos E 164 A2
Hornoy-le-Bourg F . 90 B1
Hornsea GB 41 B3
Hornsjø N 48 A2
Hornslet DK 59 B3
Hornstein A 111 B3
Hörnum D 64 B1
Hornum DK 58 B2
Horný Tisovník SK . 99 C3
Horodenka UA 13 D6
Horodnya UA 13 C9
Horodok
Khmelnytskyy UA . . 13 D7
Lviv UA 13 D5
Horokhiv UA 13 C6
Horovice CZ 96 B1
Horred S 60 B2
Hörröd S 61 D4
Hörsching A 110 A1
Horsens DK 59 C2
Horsham GB 44 B3
Hørsholm DK 61 D2
Horslunde DK 65 B4
Horšovský Týn CZ . 95 B4
Horst NL 80 A2
Horstel D 71 B4
Horsten D 71 A4
Horstmar D 71 B4
Hort H 113 B3
Horta P 148 A2
Horten N 54 A1
Hortezuela E 151 A5
Hortiguela E 143 B3
Hortobágy H 113 B5
Horton in Ribblesdale
GB 37 B4
Hørve DK 61 D1
Hörvik S 63 B2
Horwich GB 38 A4
Hosanger N 46 B2
Hösbach D 93 A5
Hosena D 84 A2
Hosenfeld D 81 B5
Hosingen L 92 A2
Hosio FIN 197 D8
Hospental CH 107 C3
Hospital IRL 29 B3
Hossegor F 128 C1
Hosszuhetény H . . 125 A4
Hostal de Ipiés E . . 145 B3
Hoštálkova CZ 98 B1
Hostalric E 147 C3
Hostens F 128 B2
Hostěradice CZ 97 C4
Hostinné CZ 85 B3
Hostomice CZ 96 B2
Hostouň CZ 95 B4
Hotagen S 199 B11
Hoting S 200 B2
Hotolisht AL 182 B2
Hotton B 79 B5
Houdain F 78 B2
Houdan F 90 C1
Houdelaincourt F . . 92 C1
Houeillès F 128 B3
Houffalize B 92 A1
Houghton-le-Spring
GB 37 B5
Houlberg DK 59 B2
Houlgate F 89 A3
Hounslow GB 44 B3
Hourtin F 128 A1
Hourtin-Plage F . . . 128 A1
Houthalen B 79 A5
Houyet B 79 B4
Hov
DK 59 C3
N 48 B2
Hova S 55 B5
Høvåg N 53 B4
Hovborg DK 59 C1
Hovda N 47 B6
Hovden N 52 A3
Hove GB 44 C3
Hovedgård DK 59 C2
Hovelhof D 81 A4
Hoven DK 59 C1
Hovet N 47 B5
Hovingham GB 40 A3
Hovmantorp S 62 B3
Hovsta S 56 A1
Howden GB 40 B3
Howe D 72 A3
Höxter D 81 A5
Hoya D 72 B2
Hoya de Santa Maria
E 161 B3
Hoya-Gonzalo E . . 158 C2
Høyanger N 46 A3
Hoyerswerda D 84 A2
Høyjord N 53 A6
Hoylake GB 38 A3
Høylandet N 199 A9
Hoym D 82 A3
Høymyr N 47 C6
Hoyocasero E 150 B3
Hoyo de Manzanares
E 151 B4
Hoyo de Pinares E 150 B3
Hoyos E 149 B3
Hoyos del Espino
E 150 B2
Hrabusiče SK 99 C4
Hradec Králové CZ . 85 B3
Hradec nad Moravicí
CZ 98 B1
Hrádek CZ 97 C4
Hrádek nad Nisou
CZ 84 B2
Hradište SK 98 C2
Hrafnagil IS 191 B7
Hrafnseyri IS 190 B2
Hranice
Severomoravsky
CZ 98 B1
Západočeský CZ . . . 83 B4
Hranovnica SK 99 C4
Hrasnica BIH 139 B4
Hrastnik SLO 123 A4
Hřensko CZ 84 B2
Hriňová SK 99 C3
Hrisoupoli GR 183 C6
Hrochov CZ 97 B4
Hrochův Tynec CZ . 97 B3
Hrodna BY 13 B5
Hrodzyanka BY 13 B8
Hronov CZ 85 B4
Hronský Beňadik
SK 98 C2
Hrotovice CZ 97 B4
Hrtkovci SRB 127 C1
Hrun IS 190 A5
Hrušov SK 112 A3
Hrušovany nad
Jevišovkou CZ . . . 97 C4
Hřuštin SK 99 B3
Hrvaćani BIH 124 C3
Hrvace HR 138 B2
Hrymayliv UA 13 D7
Huben A 109 C3
Hückel-hoven D . . . 80 A2
Hückeswagen D . . . 80 A3
Hucknall GB 40 B2
Hucqueliers F 78 B1
Huddersfield GB . . . 40 B2
Huddinge S 57 A3
Huddunge S 51 B3
Hude D 72 A1
Hudiksvall S 200 E3
Huélago E 163 A4
Huélamo E 152 B2
Huelgoat F 100 A2
Huelma E 163 A4
Huelva E 161 B3
Huéneja E 164 B2
Huércal de Almeria
E 164 C2
Huércal-Overa E . . 164 B3
Huerta de Abajo E . 143 B3
Huerta del Rey E . . 143 C3
Huerta de
Valdecarabanos
E 151 C4
Huertahernando E 152 B1
Huesa E 164 B1
Huesca E 145 B3
Huéscar E 164 B2
Huete E 151 B5
Huétor Tájar E 163 A3
Hüfingen D 106 B3
Hufthamar N 46 B2
Hugh Town GB 42 B1
Huglfing D 108 B2
Huissen NL 70 C2
Huittinen FIN 8 B3
Huizen NL 70 B2
Hulín CZ 98 B1
Hüls D 80 A2
Hulsig DK 58 A3
Hulst NL 79 A4
Hult S 62 A3
Hulta S 56 B2
Hulteby S 55 A5
Hulterstad S 63 B4
Hultsfred S 62 A3
Humanes E 151 B4
Humberston GB . . . 41 B3
Humble DK 65 B3
Humenné SK 12 D4
Humilladero E 163 A3
Humlebæk DK 61 D2
Humlum DK 58 B1
Hummelsta S 56 A2
Humpolec CZ 97 B3
Humshaugh GB 37 A4
Hundåla N 195 E3
Hundested DK 61 D1
Hundorp N 48 A1
Hundvåg N 52 A1
Hundvin N 46 B2
Hunedoara RO 17 C5
Hünfeld D 82 B1
Hungen D 81 B4
Hungerford GB 44 B2
Hunndalen N 48 B2
Hunnebostrand S . . 54 B2
Hunstanton GB 41 C4
Huntingdon GB 44 A3
Huntley GB 39 C4
Huntly GB 33 D4
Hünxe D 80 A2
Hurbanovo SK 112 B2
Hürbel D 107 A4
Hurdal N 48 B3
Hurezani RO 17 C5
Hurlford GB 36 A2
Hurstbourne Tarrant
GB 44 B2
Hurstpierpoint GB . . 44 C3
Hürth D 80 B2
Hurum N 47 A5

Hurup DK 58 B1
Húsafell IS 190 C5
Húsavík IS 191 A8
Husbands Bosworth GB 44 A2
Husby
D 64 B2
DK 59 B1
Husey IS 191 B11
Huşi RO 17 B8
Husina BIH 139 A4
Husinec CZ 96 B1
Husinish GB 31 B1
Huskvarna S 62 A2
Husnes N 46 C2
Husøy N 194 A8
Hustad N 198 C4
Hüsten D 81 A3
Hustopeče CZ 97 C4
Hustopeče nad Bečvou CZ 98 B1
Husum
D 64 B2
S 200 C5
Husvika N 195 E3
Huta PL 75 B5
Hutovo BIH 139 C3
Hüttenberg A 110 C1
Hüttlingen D 94 C2
Huttoft GB 41 B4
Hutton Cranswick GB 40 B3
Hüttschlag A 109 B4
Huttwil CH 106 B2
Huy B 79 B5
Hüyük TR 189 B6
Hval N 48 B2
Hvåle N 47 B6
Hvaler N 54 A2
Hvalpsund DK 58 B2
Hvammstangi IS 190 B5
Hvammur IS 190 B6
Hvanneyri IS 190 C4
Hvar HR 138 B2
Hvarnes N 53 A5
Hveragerði IS 190 D4
Hvidbjerg DK 58 B1
Hvide Sande DK 59 C1
Hvittingfoss N 53 A6
Hvolsvöllur IS 190 D5
Hybe SK 99 B3
Hycklinge S 62 A3
Hydra GR 185 B4
Hyen N 198 D2
Hyères F 132 B2
Hyéres Plage F 132 B2
Hylestad N 52 A3
Hylke DK 59 C2
Hyllestad N 46 A2
Hyllstofta S 61 C3
Hyltebruk S 60 B3
Hynnekleiv N 53 B4
Hythe
Hampshire GB 44 C2
Kent GB 45 B5
Hyvinkää FIN 8 B4

I

Iam RO 127 B3
Iaşi RO 17 B7
Iasmos GR 183 B7
Ibahernando E 156 A2
Ibarranguelua E 143 A4
Ibbenbüren D 71 B4
Ibeas de Juarros E 143 B3
Ibestad N 194 B8
Ibi E 159 C3
Ibiza = Eivissa E 166 C1
İbradı TR 189 B6
İbriktepe TR 186 A1
Ibros E 157 B4
Ibstock GB 40 C2
İçel TR 23 C8
Ichenhausen D 94 C2
Ichtegem B 78 A3
Ichtershausen D 82 B2
Idanha-a-Novo P 155 B3
Idar-Oberstein D 93 B3
Idd N 54 A2
Idiazábal E 144 B1
Idivuoma S 196 A4
Idkerberget S 50 B2
Idön S 51 B5
Idre S 199 D9
Idrija SLO 123 A3
Idritsa RUS 9 D6
Idstein D 81 B4
Idvor SRB 126 B2
Iecca Mare RO 126 B2
Ielsi I 170 B2
Ieper = Ypres B 78 B2
Ierapetra GR 185 D6
Ierissos GR 183 C5
Ifjord N 193 B11
Ig SLO 123 B3
Igal H 112 C1
Igea E 144 B1
Igea Marina I 136 A1
Igelfors S 56 B1
Igersheim D 94 B1
Iggesund S 200 E3
Iglesias E 143 B3
Iglésias I 179 C2
Igls A 108 B2
Igny-Comblizy F 91 B3
Igorre E 143 A4
Igoumenitsa GR 182 D2
Igries E 145 B3
Igualada E 147 C2
Igüeña E 141 B4
Iguerande F 117 A4
Iharosberény H 124 A3
Ihl'any SK 99 B4
Ihlienworth D 64 C1
Ihringen D 106 A2
Ihrlerstein D 95 C3
İhsaniye TR 187 C5
Ii FIN 197 D8
Iijärvi FIN 193 C11
Iisalmi FIN 3 E10
IJmuiden NL 70 B1
IJsselmuiden NL 70 B2
IJzendijke NL 79 A3
Ikast DK 59 B2
Ikervár H 111 B3
Ilandža SRB 126 B2
Ilanz CH 107 C4
Ilava SK 98 C2
Iława PL 69 B4
il Castagno I 135 B3
Ilche E 145 C4
Ilchester GB 43 B4
Ilfeld D 82 A2
Ilfracombe GB 42 A2
Ilgaz TR 23 A7
Ilgın TR 189 A6
Ílhavo P 148 B1
Ilica TR 186 C2
Ilidža BIH 139 B4
Ilijaš BIH 139 B4
Ilirska Bistrica SLO 123 B3
Ilkeston GB 40 C2
Ilkley GB 40 B2
Illana E 151 B5
Illano E 141 A4
Illar E 164 C2
Illas E 141 A5
Illats F 128 B2
Illertissen D 94 C2
Illescas E 151 B4
Ille-sur-Têt F 146 B3
Illfurth F 106 B2
Illichivsk UA 17 B9
Illiers-Combray F 89 B5
Illkirch-Graffenstaden F 93 C3
Illmersdorf D 74 C2
Illmitz A 111 B3
Íllora E 163 A4
Illueca E 152 A2
Ilmajoki FIN 8 A3
Ilmenau D 82 B2
Ilminster GB 43 B4
Ilok HR 126 B1
Ilomantsi FIN 9 A7
Iłow PL 77 B5
Iłowa PL 84 A3
Iłowo-Osada PL 77 A5
Ilsenburg D 82 A2
Ilshofen D 94 B1
Ilz A 110 B2
Iłża PL 87 A5
Imatra FIN 9 B6
Imielin PL 86 B3
Imingen N 47 B5
Immeln S 63 B2
Immenhausen D 81 A5
Immenstadt D 107 B5
Immingham GB 41 B3
Ímola I 135 A4
Imon E 151 A5
Imotski HR 138 B3
Impéria I 133 B4
Imphy F 104 C2
İmroz TR 183 C7
Imsland N 52 A1
Imst A 108 B1
Inagh IRL 28 B2
Inari FIN 193 D10
Inca E 167 B2
Inchnadamph GB 32 C2
Incinillas E 143 B3
Indal S 200 D3
Indjija SRB 127 B2
Indre Arna N 46 B2
Indre Billefjord N 193 B9
Indre Brenna N 193 B9
İğneada TR 186 A2
İnebolu TR 23 A7
İnecik TR 186 B2
İnegöl TR 187 B4
Inerthal CH 107 B3
Infiesto E 142 A1
Ingatorp S 62 A3
Ingedal N 54 A2
Ingelheim D 93 B4
Ingelmunster B 78 B3
Ingelstad S 62 B2
Ingleton GB 37 B4
Ingolfsland N 47 C5
Ingolstadt D 95 C3
Ingrandes
Maine-et-Loire F 101 B5
Vienne F 102 C2
Ingwiller F 93 C3
Inhisar TR 187 B5
Iniesta E 158 B2
Inishannon IRL 29 C3
Inishcrone IRL 26 B1
Inke H 124 A3
Inndyr N 195 C5
Innellan GB 34 C3
Innerleithen GB 35 C4
Innermessan GB 36 B2
Innertkirchen CH 106 C3
Innervillgraten A 109 C3
Innsbruck A 108 B2
Innset N 194 B9
Innvik N 198 D3
İnönü TR 187 C5
Inowłódz PL 87 A4
Inowrocław PL 76 B3
Ins CH 106 B2
Insch GB 33 D4
Insjön S 50 B2
Ińsko PL 75 A4
Instow GB 42 A2
İntepe TR 186 B1
Interlaken CH 106 C2
Intragna CH 120 A1
Introbio I 120 B2
Inverallochy GB 33 D5
Inveran
GB 32 D2
IRL 28 A2
Inveraray GB 34 B2
Inverbervie GB 35 B5
Invergarry GB 32 D2
Invergordon GB 32 D2
Invergowrie GB 35 B4
Inverkeilor GB 35 B5
Inverkeithing GB 35 B4
Invermoriston GB 32 D2
Inverness GB 32 D2
Inveruno I 120 B1
Inverurie GB 33 D4
Ioannina GR 182 D2
Iolanda di Savoia I 121 C4
Ion Corvin RO 17 C7
Ióppolo I 175 C1
Ios GR 185 C6
Ipati GR 182 E4
İpsala TR 186 B1
Ipswich GB 45 A5
Iraklia GR 183 B5
Iraklio = Heraklion GR 185 D6
Irdning A 110 B1
Iregszemcse H 112 C2
Irgoli I 178 B3
Irig SRB 127 B1
Ironbridge GB 39 B4
Irpin UA 13 C9
Irrel D 92 B2
Irsina I 172 B2
Irsta S 56 A2
Irthlingborough GB 44 A3
Iruela E 141 B4
Irún E 144 A2
Irurita E 144 A2
Irurzun E 144 B2
Irvine GB 36 A2
Irvinestown GB 27 B3
Isaba E 144 B3
Isabela E 157 B4
Ísafjörður IS 190 A2
Isane N 198 D2
Isaszeg H 112 B3
Isbister GB 33 A5
Íscar E 150 A3
İscehisar TR 187 D5
Ischgl A 107 B5
Íschia I 170 C1
Ischia di Castro I 168 A1
Ischitella I 171 B3
Isdes F 103 B4
Ise N 54 A2
Iseler I 119 A5
Iseltwald CH 106 C2
Isen D 108 A3
Isenbüttel D 73 B3
Iseo I 120 B3
Iserlohn D 81 A3
Isérnia I 170 B2
Isfjorden N 198 C4
Ishëm AL 182 B1
Isigny-sur-Mer F 88 A2
Işıklı TR 189 A4
Ísili I 179 C3
İskilip TR 23 A8
Isla Canela E 161 B2
Isla Cristina E 161 B2
Islares E 143 A3
Isleham GB 45 A4
Isle of Whithorn GB 36 B2
Ismaning D 108 A2
Isna P 154 B3
Isnestoften N 192 B6
Isny D 107 B5
Isoba E 142 A1
Isokylä
FIN 197 C10
S 196 B5
Isola F 132 A3
Isola d'Asti I 119 C5
Isola del Gran Sasso d'Itália I 169 A3
Ísola della Scala I 121 B4
Isola delle Fémmine I 176 A2
Ísola del Liri I 169 B3
Ísola di Capo Rizzuto I 175 C3
Isona E 147 B2
Ispagnac F 130 A2
Isparta TR 189 B5
Isperikh BG 17 D7
Íspica I 177 C3
Isselburg D 80 A2
Issigeac F 129 B3
Issogne I 119 B4
Issoire F 116 B3
Issoncourt F 91 C5
Issoudun F 103 C4
Issum D 80 A2
Is-sur-Tille F 105 B4
Issy-l'Evêque F 104 C2
Istán E 162 B3
İstanbul TR 186 A3
Istebna PL 98 B2
Ístia d'Ombrone I 135 C4
Istiea GR 183 E5
Istres F 131 B3
Istvándi H 125 A3
Itea GR 184 A3
Ithaki GR 184 A1
Itoiz E 144 B2
Ítrabo E 163 B4
Itri I 169 B3
Ittireddu I 178 B2
Íttiri I 178 B2
Itzehoe D 64 C2
Ivalo FIN 193 D11
Iván H 111 B3
Ivanava BY 13 B6
Ivančice CZ 97 B4
Ivančna Gorica SLO 123 B3
Iváncsa H 112 B2
Ivanec HR 124 A2
Ivanić Grad HR 124 B2
Ivanjska BIH 124 C3
Ivanka SK 98 C2
Ivankovo HR 125 B4
Ivano-Frankivsk UA 13 D6
Ivanovice na Hané CZ 98 B1
Ivanska HR 124 B2
Ivatsevichy BY 13 B6
Ivaylovgrad BG 183 B8
Iveland N 53 B3
Ivoz Ramet B 79 B5
Ivrea I 119 B4
İvrindi TR 186 C2
Ivry-en-Montagne F 104 B3
Ivry-la-Bataille F 90 C1
Ivybridge GB 42 B3
Iwaniska PL 87 B5
Iwiny PL 85 A3
Iwuy F 78 B3
Ixworth GB 45 A4
Izarra E 143 B4
Izbica Kujawska PL 76 B3
Izbište SRB 127 B3
Izeda P 149 A3
Izegem B 78 B3
Izernore F 118 A2
Izmayil UA 17 C8
İzmir TR 188 A2
İzmit = Kocaeli TR 187 B4
Iznájar E 163 A3
Iznalloz E 163 A4
Iznatoraf E 164 A1
İznik TR 187 B4
Izola SLO 122 B2
Izsák H 112 C3
Izsófalva H 99 C4
Izyaslav UA 13 C7

J

Jabalquinto E 157 B4
Jablanac HR 123 C3
Jablanica BIH 139 B3
Jablonec nad Jizerou CZ 84 B3
Jablonec nad Nisou CZ 84 B3
Jablonica SK 98 C1
Jablonka PL 99 B3
Jabłonna PL 77 B5
Jablonnénad Orlicí CZ 97 A4
Jablonne Podještědi CZ 84 B2
Jablonov nad Turňou SK 99 C4
Jabłonowo Pomorskie PL 69 B4
Jablúnka CZ 98 B1
Jablunkov CZ 98 B2
Jabučje SRB 127 C2
Jabugo E 161 B3
Jabuka SRB 127 C2
Jabukovac HR 124 B2
Jaca E 145 B3
Jáchymov CZ 83 B4
Jacobidrebber D 72 B1
Jade D 71 A5
Jäderfors S 50 B3
Jädraås S 50 B3
Jadraque E 151 B5
Jaén E 163 A4
Jagare BIH 124 C3
Jagel D 64 B2
Jagenbach A 96 C3
Jægerspris DK 61 D1
Jagodina SRB 127 D3
Jagodnjak HR 125 B4
Jagodzin PL 84 A3
Jagstheim D 94 B2
Jagstzell D 94 B2
Jahodna SK 111 A4
Jajce BIH 138 A3
Ják H 111 B3
Jakabszálbs H 112 C3
Jäkkvik S 195 D8
Jakobsnes N 193 C14
Jakovlje HR 124 B1
Jakšic HR 125 B3
Jakubany SK 99 B4
Jalance E 159 B2
Jalasjärvi FIN 8 A3
Jalhay B 80 B1
Jaligny-sur-Besbre F 117 A3
Jallais F 102 B1
Jalón E 159 C3
Jâlons F 91 C4
Jamena SRB 125 C5
Jamilena E 163 A4
Jämjö S 63 B3
Jamnička Kiselica HR 124 B1
Jamno PL 67 B5
Jamoigne B 92 B1
Jämsä FIN 8 B4
Jämshög S 63 B2
Jamu Mare RO 126 B3
Janakkala FIN 8 B4
Jandelsbrunn D 96 C1
Jänickendorf D 74 B2
Janikowo PL 76 B3
Janja BIH 125 C5
Janjina HR 138 C3
Janki
Łódzkie PL 86 A3
Mazowieckie PL 77 B5
Jankov CZ 96 B2
Jankowo Dolne PL 76 B2
Jánoshalma H 126 A1
Jánosháza H 111 B4
Jánoshida H 113 B4
Jánossomorja H 111 B4
Janovice nad Uhlavou CZ 96 B1
Janów PL 86 B3
Janowiec Wielkopolski PL 76 B2
Janowo PL 77 A5
Jänsmässholmen S 199 B10
Janville F 103 A3
Janzé F 101 B4
Jarabá SK 99 C3
Jaraczewo PL 76 C2
Jarafuel E 159 B2
Jaraicejo E 156 A2
Jaraíz de la Vera E 150 B2
Jarak SRB 127 C1
Jarandilla de la Vera E 150 B2
Jaray E 152 A1
Järbo S 50 B3
Jard-sur-Mer F 114 B2
Jaren N 48 B2
Jargeau F 103 B4
Jarkovac SRB 126 B2
Järlåsa S 51 C4
Jarmen D 66 C2
Järna S 57 A3
Jarnac F 115 C3
Järnäs S 200 C5
Järnforsen S 62 A3
Jarny F 92 B1
Jarocin PL 76 C2
Jaroměř CZ 85 B3
Jaroměřice nad Rokytnou CZ 97 B3
Jaroslav CZ 97 A4
Jaroslavice CZ 97 C4
Jarosław PL 12 C5
Jaroslawiec PL 68 A1
Jarošov nad Nežarkou CZ 96 B3
Järpås S 55 B3
Järpen S 199 B10
Jarrow GB 37 B5
Järso FIN 51 B6
Järvenpää FIN 8 B4
Jarvorník CZ 85 B4
Järvsö S 200 E2
Jarzé F 102 B1
Jaša Tomic SRB 126 B2
Jasenak HR 123 B4
Jasenica BIH 124 C2
Jasenice HR 137 A4
Jasenovac HR 124 B2
Jasenovo SRB 127 C3
Jasień PL 84 A3
Jasienica PL 84 A2
Jasło PL 12 D4
Jásova SK 112 B2
Jasseron F 118 A2
Jastarnia PL 69 A3
Jastrebarsko HR 123 B4
Jastrowie PL 68 B1
Jastrzębia-Góra PL 68 A3
Jastrzębie Zdrój PL 98 B2
Jászals-Lószentgyörgy H 113 B4
Jászapáti H 113 B4
Jászárokszállás H 113 B3
Jászberény H 113 B3
Jászdózsa H 113 B4
Jászfényszaru H 113 B3
Jászjákóhalma H 113 B4
Jászkarajenö H 113 B4
Jászkisér H 113 B4
Jászladány H 113 B4
Jászszentlászló H 113 C3
Jásztelek H 113 B4
Játar E 163 B4
Jättendal S 200 E3
Jatznick D 74 A2
Jaun CH 106 C2
Jausiers F 132 A2
Jávea E 159 C4
Jävenitz D 73 B4
Javerlhac F 115 C4
Javier E 144 B2
Javorani BIH 124 C3
Javorina SK 99 B4
Javron F 89 B3
Jawor PL 85 A4
Jaworzno PL 86 B3
Jaworzyna Śl. PL 85 B4
Jayena E 163 B4
Jażow PL 84 A2
Jebel RO 126 B3
Jebjerg DK 58 B2
Jedburgh GB 35 C5
Jedlinsk PL 87 A5
Jedlnia PL 87 A5
Jedlnia Letnisko PL 87 A5
Jednorożec PL 77 A6
Jedovnice CZ 97 B4
Jędrychow PL 69 B4
Jędrzejów PL 87 B4
Jedwabno PL 77 A5
Jeesiö FIN 197 B9
Jegłownik PL 69 A4
Jegun F 129 C3
Jēkabpils LV 8 D4
Jektevik N 46 C2
Jektvik N 195 D4
Jelcz-Laskowice PL 85 A5
Jelenec SK 98 C2
Jelenia Góra PL 85 B3
Jelgava LV 8 D3
Jelka SK 111 A4
Jelling DK 59 C2
Jels DK 59 C2
Jelsa
HR 138 B2
N 52 A2
Jelšava SK 99 C4
Jemgum D 71 A4
Jemnice CZ 97 B3
Jena D 82 B3
Jenaz CH 107 C4
Jenbach A 108 B2
Jenikow PL 75 A4
Jennersdorf A 111 C3
Jenny S 62 A4
Jerchel D 73 B4
Jeres del Marquesado E 164 B1
Jerez de la Frontera E 162 B1
Jerez de los Caballeros E 155 C4
Jerica E 159 B3
Jerichow D 73 B5
Jerka PL 75 B5
Jermenovci SRB 126 B3
Jerslev DK 58 A3
Jerte E 150 B2
Jerup DK 58 A3
Jerxheim D 73 B3
Jerzmanowice PL 87 B3
Jerzu I 179 C3
Jerzwałd PL 69 B4
Jesberg D 81 B5
Jesenice
Středočeský CZ 83 B5
Středočeský CZ 96 B2
SLO 109 C5
Jeseník CZ 85 B5
Jesenké SK 99 C4
Jesi I 136 B2
Jésolo I 122 B1
Jessen D 83 A4
Jessenitz D 73 A4
Jessheim N 48 B3
Jessnitz D 83 A4
Jesteburg D 72 A2
Jeumont F 79 B4
Jeven-stedt D 64 B2
Jever D 71 A4
Jevíčko CZ 97 B4
Jevišovice CZ 97 C3
Jevnaker N 48 B2
Jezerane HR 123 B4
Jezero
BIH 138 A3
HR 123 B4
Jezów PL 87 A3
Jičín CZ 84 B3
Jičíněves CZ 84 B3
Jihlava CZ 97 B3
Jijona E 159 C3
Jilemnice CZ 84 B3
Jílové CZ 84 B2
Jílovéu Prahy CZ 96 B2
Jimbolia RO 126 B2
Jimena E 163 A4
Jimena de la Frontera E 162 B2
Jimera de Libar E 162 B2
Jimramov CZ 97 B4
Jince CZ 96 B1
Jindřichovice CZ 83 B4
Jindřichův Hradec CZ 96 B3
Jirkov CZ 83 B5
Jistebnice CZ 96 B2
Joachimsthal D 74 B2
João da Loura P 154 C2

Jobbágyi H 112 B3
Jochberg A 109 B3
Jockfall S 196 C5
Jódar E 163 A4
Jodoigne B 79 B4
Joensuu FIN 9 A6
Joesjö S 195 E5
Joeuf F 92 B1
Jõgeva EST 8 C5
Johanngeorgenstadt D 83 B4
Johannishus S 63 B3
Johanniskirchen D 95 C4
Johansfors S 63 B3
John o'Groats GB 32 C3
Johnshaven GB 35 B5
Johnstone GB 34 C3
Johnstown IRL 30 B1
Jõhvi EST 8 C5
Joigny F 104 B2
Joinville F 91 C5
Jokkmokk S 196 C2
Jöllenbeck D 72 B1
Jomala FIN 51 B6
Jönåker S 56 B2
Jonava LT 13 A6
Jonchery-sur-Vesle F 91 B3
Jondal N 46 B3
Jondalen N 53 A5
Joniškis LT 8 D3
Jönköping S 62 A2
Jonkowo PL 69 B5
Jønnbu N 53 A5
Jonsberg S 56 B2
Jonsered S 60 B2
Jonstorp S 61 C2
Jonzac F 114 C3
Jorba E 147 C2
Jordanów PL 99 B3
Jordanowo PL 75 B4
Jordanów Ślaski PL 85 B4
Jordbro S 57 A4
Jordbrua N 195 D5
Jördenstorf D 66 C1
Jordet N 49 A4
Jordøse DK 59 C3
Jork D 72 A2
Jörlanda S 60 B1
Jormlien S 199 A10
Jormvattnet S 199 A11
Jörn S 200 A6
Jørpeland N 52 A2
Jorquera E 158 B2
Jošan HR 123 C4
Jošavka BIH 124 C3
Josipdol HR 123 B4
Josipovac HR 125 B4
Jössefors S 54 A3
Josselin F 101 B3
Jøssund N 199 A7
Jostedal N 47 A4
Jósvafő H 99 C4
Jou P 148 A2
Jouarre F 90 C3
Joué-lès-Tours F 102 B2
Joué-sur-Erdre F 101 B4
Joure NL 70 B2
Joutseno FIN 9 B6
Joutsijärvi FIN 197 C10
Joux-la-Ville F 104 B2
Jouy F 90 C1
Jouy-le-Châtel F 90 C3
Jouy-le-Potier F 103 B3
Joyeuse F 131 A3
Joze F 116 B3
Juankoski FIN 8 A6
Juan-les-Pins F 132 B3
Jübek D 64 B2
Jubera E 144 B1
Jubrique E 162 B2
Jüchsen D 82 B2
Judaberg N 52 A1
Judenburg A 110 B1
Juelsminde DK 59 C3
Jugon-les-Lacs F 101 A3
Juillac F 129 A4
Juillan F 145 A4
Juist D 71 A4
Jukkasjärvi S 196 B3
Jule N 199 A10
Julianadorp NL 70 B1
Julianstown IRL 30 A2
Jülich D 80 B2
Jullouville F 88 B2
Jumeaux F 117 B3
Jumièges F 89 A4
Jumilhac-le-Grand F 115 C5
Jumilla E 159 C2
Jumisko FIN 197 C11
Juncosa E 153 A4
Juneda E 147 C1
Jung S 55 B4
Jungingen D 93 C5
Junglingster L 92 B2
Juniville F 91 B4
Junosuando S 196 B5
Junqueira P 149 A2
Junsele S 200 C2
Juoksengi S 196 C6
Juoksenki FIN 196 C6
Juprelle B 80 B1
Jurata PL 69 A3
Jurbarkas LT 12 A5
Jurjevo HR 123 C3
Jūrmala LV 8 D3
Jurmu FIN 197 D10
Juromenha P 155 C3
Jursla S 56 B2
Jussac F 116 C2
Jussey F 105 B4
Jussy F 90 B3
Juta H 125 A3
Jüterbog D 74 C2
Juuka FIN 3 E11
Juuma FIN 197 C12
Juvigny-le-Terte F 88 B2
Juvigny-sous-Andaine F 89 B3
Juzennecourt F 105 A3
Jyderup DK 61 D1
Jyrkänkoski FIN 197 C12
Jyväskylä FIN 8 A4

K

Kaamanen FIN 193 C11
Kaamasmukka FIN 193 C10
Kaaresuvanto FIN 192 D6
Kaarssen D 73 A4
Kaatscheuvel NL 79 A5
Kaba H 113 B5
Kåbdalis S 196 C3
Kačarevo SRB 127 C2
Kács H 113 B4
Kadan CZ 83 B5
Kadarkút H 125 A3
Kadınhanı TR 189 A7
Kaduy RUS 9 C10
Kåfalla S 56 A1
Kåfjord N 192 C7
Kåfjordbotn N 192 C4
Kågeröd S 61 D3
Kahl D 93 A5
Kahla D 82 B3
Kainach bei Voitsberg A 110 B2
Kaindorf A 110 B2
Kainulasjärvi S 196 C5
Kairala FIN 197 B10
Kaisepakte S 192 D3
Kaisersesch D 80 B3
Kaiserslautern D 93 B3
Kaisheim D 94 C2
Kajaani FIN 3 D10
Kajárpéc H 111 B4
Kajdacs H 112 C2
Kakanj BIH 139 A4
Kakasd H 125 A4
Kaklik TR 189 B4
Kakolewo PL 85 A4
Kál H 113 B4
Kalajoki FIN 3 D8
Kalak N 193 B11
Kalamata GR 184 B3
Kalambaka GR 182 D3
Kalamria GR 182 C4
Kalandra GR 183 D5
Kälarne S 200 D2
Kalavrita GR 184 A3
Kalbe D 73 B4
Kalce SLO 123 B3
Káld H 111 B4
Kale
Antalya TR 189 C4
Denizli TR 188 B3
Kalecik TR 23 A7
Kalefeld D 82 A2
Kalesija BIH 139 A4
Kalety PL 86 B2
Kalevala RUS 3 D12
Kalhovd N 47 B5
Kali HR 137 A4
Kalimnos GR 188 C2
Kaliningrad RUS 69 A5
Kalinkavichy BY 13 B8
Kalinovac HR 124 A3
Kalinovik BIH 139 B4
Kalinovo SK 99 C3
Kalirachi GR 183 C6
Kaliska
Pomorskie PL 68 A3
Pomorskie PL 68 B3
Kalisko PL 86 A3
Kalisz PL 86 A2
Kalisz Pomorski PL 75 A4
Kaljord N 194 B6
Kalkan TR 189 C4
Kalkar D 80 A2
Kalkım TR 186 C2
Kall
D 80 B2
S 199 B10
Källby S 55 B4
Kållered S 60 B2
Kållerstad S 60 B3
Kallinge S 63 B3
Kallmünz D 95 B3
Kallo FIN 196 B7
Kallsedet S 199 B9
Källvik S 56 B3
Kalmar S 63 B4
Kalmthout B 79 A4
Kalná SK 112 A2
Kalocsa H 112 C2
Kalokhorio CY 181 B2
Kalo Nero GR 184 B2
Kaloni GR 186 C1
Káloz H 112 C2
Kals A 109 B3
Kalsdorf A 110 C2
Kaltbrunn CH 107 B4
Kaltenbach A 108 B2
Kaltenkirchen D 64 C2
Kaltennordheim D 82 B2
Kalundborg DK 61 D1
Kalush UA 13 D6
Kalv S 60 B3
Kalvåg N 198 D1
Kalvehave DK 65 A5
Kalwang A 110 B1
Kalwaria-Zebrzydowska PL 99 B3
Kalyazin RUS 9 D10
Kam H 111 B3
Kaman TR 23 B7
Kamares GR 185 C5
Kambos CY 181 A1
Kamen D 81 A3
Kamenice CZ 97 B3
Kamenice nad Lipou CZ 96 B3
Kameničná SK 112 B2
Kamenný Most SK 112 B2
Kamenny Ujezd CZ 96 C2
Kamenska HR 124 B3
Kamensko HR 138 B2
Kamenz D 84 A2
Kamičak BIH 124 C2
Kamień PL 87 A4
Kamieniec Zabk PL 85 B4
Kamienka SK 99 B4
Kamień Krajeński PL 76 A2
Kamienna Góra PL 85 B4
Kamień Pomorski PL 67 C3
Kamieńsk PL 86 A3
Kamiros Skala GR 188 C2
Kamnik SLO 123 A3
Kampen NL 70 B2
Kampinos PL 77 B5
Kamp-Lintfort D 80 A2
Kampor HR 123 C3
Kamyanets-Podil's'kyy UA 13 D7
Kamyanka-Buz'ka UA 13 C6
Kamýk nad Vltavou CZ 96 B2
Kanal SLO 122 A2
Kanalia GR 182 D4
Kandalaksha RUS 3 C13
Kandanos GR 185 D4
Kandel D 93 B4
Kandern D 106 B2
Kandersteg CH 106 C2
Kandila GR 184 B3
Kandıra TR 187 A5
Kandyty PL 69 A5
Kanfanar HR 122 B2
Kangasala FIN 8 B4
Kangos S 196 B5
Kangosjärvi FIN 196 B6
Kaniów PL 75 C3
Kanjiža SRB 126 A2
Kankaanpää FIN 8 B3
Kannus FIN 3 E8
Kanturk IRL 29 B3
Kapaklı TR 186 A2
Kapellen
A 110 B2
B 79 A4
Kapellskär S 57 A5
Kapfenberg A 110 B2
Kapfenstein A 110 C2
Kaplice CZ 96 C2
Kapljuh BIH 124 C2
Kápolna H 113 B4
Kápolnásnyék H 112 B2
Kaposfő H 125 A3
Kaposfüred H 125 A3
Kaposszekcsö H 125 A4
Kaposvár H 125 A3
Kapp N 48 B2
Kappel D 93 C3
Kappeln D 64 B2
Kappelshamn S 57 C4
Kappl A 107 B5
Kappstad S 55 A4
Kaprun A 109 B3
Kaptol HR 125 B3
Kapuvár H 111 B4
Karaadilli TR 189 A5
Karabiğa TR 186 B2
Karabük TR 187 A7
Karaburun TR 186 D1
Karacabey TR 186 B3
Karacaköy TR 186 A3
Karacaören TR 189 A5
Karacasu TR 188 B3
Karácsond H 113 B4
Karád H 112 C1
Karahallı TR 189 A4
Karaisali TR 23 C8
Karaman
Balıkesir TR 186 C3
Karaman TR 23 C7
Karamanlı TR 189 B4
Karamürsel TR 187 B4
Karan SRB 127 D1
Karancslapujto H 113 A3
Karaova TR 188 B2
Karapınar TR 23 C7
Karasjok N 193 C9
Karasu TR 187 A5
Karataş
Adana TR 23 C8
Manisa TR 188 A3
Karatoprak TR 188 B2
Karavostasi CY 181 A1
Karbenning S 50 B3
Kårberg S 55 B5
Kårböle S 199 D12
Karby
D 64 B2
DK 58 B1
Kårby S 62 A4
Karby S 57 A4
Karcag H 113 B4
Karczów PL 86 B1
Karczowiska PL 85 A4
Kardamena GR 188 C2
Kardamila GR 185 A7
Kardamili GR 184 C3
Kardašova Rečice CZ 96 B2
Kardis S 196 C6
Karditsa GR 182 D3
Kärdla EST 8 C3
Kardoskút H 113 C4
Karesuando S 192 D6
Kargı TR 23 A8
Kargopol RUS 9 B11
Kargowa PL 75 B4
Karigasniemi FIN 193 C9
Karise DK 65 A5
Karistos GR 185 A5
Karkkila FIN 8 B4
Karlholmsbruk S 51 B4
Karlino PL 67 B4
Karlobag HR 137 A4
Karlovac HR 123 B4
Karlovasi GR 188 B1
Karlovčic SRB 127 C2
Karlovice CZ 85 B5
Karlovo BG 17 D6
Karlovy Vary CZ 83 B4
Karłowice PL 86 B1
Karlsborg S 55 B5
Karlshamn S 63 B2
Karlshöfen D 72 A2
Karlshus N 54 A1
Karlskoga S 55 A5
Karlskrona S 63 B3
Karlsrud N 47 B5
Karlsruhe D 93 B4
Karlstad S 55 A4
Karlstadt D 94 B1
Karlstetten A 110 A2
Karlstift A 96 C2
Karlstorp S 62 A3
Karmacs H 111 C4
Karmin PL 85 A5
Kärna S 60 B1
Karnobat BG 17 D7
Karojba HR 122 B2
Karow D 73 A5
Karpacz PL 85 B3
Karpathos GR 188 D2
Karpenisi GR 182 E3
Karpuzlu TR 188 B2
Kärrbo S 56 A2
Karrebaeksminde DK 65 A4
Karshult S 60 B3
Karsin PL 68 B2
Kårsta S 57 A4
Karstädt D 73 A4
Kartal TR 186 B4
Kartitsch A 109 C3
Kartuzy PL 68 A3
Karungi S 196 C6
Karunki FIN 196 C7
Karup DK 59 B2
Karviná CZ 98 B2
Kås DK 58 A2
Kaş TR 189 C4
Kasaba TR 189 C4
Kašava CZ 98 B1
Kåseberga S 66 A3
Kasejovice CZ 96 B1
Kasfjord N 194 B7
Kashin RUS 9 D10
Kašina HR 124 B2
Kasina-Wielka PL 99 B4
Kaskinen FIN 8 A2
Kašperské Hory CZ 96 B1
Kassandrino GR 183 C5
Kassel D 81 A5
Kassiopi GR 182 D1
Kastamonu TR 23 A7
Kastav HR 123 B3
Kasteli GR 185 D4
Kastellaun D 93 A3
Kastelli GR 185 D6
Kaštel-Stari HR 138 B2
Kaštel Zegarski HR 138 A1
Kasterlee B 79 A4
Kastl D 95 B3
Kastlösa S 63 B4
Kastorf D 65 C3
Kastoria GR 182 C3
Kastorio GR 184 B3
Kastraki GR 185 C6
Kastrosikia GR 182 D2
Kastsyukovichy BY 13 B10
Kaszaper H 113 C4
Katakolo GR 184 B2
Katapola GR 185 C6
Katastari GR 184 B1
Katerbow D 74 B1
Katerini GR 182 C4
Kathikas CY 181 B1
Kätkesuando S 196 A6
Katlenburg-Lindau D 82 A2
Kato Achaia GR 184 A2
Káto Pyrgos CY 181 A1
Katouna GR 182 E3
Katovice CZ 96 B1
Katowice PL 86 B3
Katrineberg S 50 A3
Katrineholm S 56 B2
Kattarp S 61 C2
Kattavia GR 188 D2
Katthammarsvik S 57 C4
Kattilstorp S 55 B4
Katwijk NL 70 B1
Katymár H 125 A5
Kąty Wrocławskie PL 85 A4
Katzenelnbogen D 81 B3
Katzhütte D 82 B3
Kaub D 93 A3
Kaufbeuren D 108 B1
Kauhajoki FIN 8 A3
Kauhava FIN 8 A3
Kaukonen FIN 196 B7
Kauliranta FIN 196 C6
Kaulsdorf D 82 B3
Kaunas LT 13 A5
Kaunisvaara S 196 B6
Kaupanger N 47 A4
Kautokeino N 192 C7
Kautzen A 97 C3
Kavadarci MK 182 B4
Kavajë AL 182 B1
Kavakköy TR 186 B1
Kavaklı TR 186 A2
Kavaklıdere TR 188 B3
Kavala GR 183 C6
Kavarna BG 17 D8
Kävlinge S 61 D3
Kawcze PL 68 A1
Kaxås S 199 B10
Kaxholmen S 62 A2
Käylä FIN 197 C12
Kaymakçı TR 188 A3
Kaymaz TR 187 C6
Kaynarca TR 187 A5
Käyrämö FIN 197 C9
Kayseri TR 23 B8
Kaysersberg F 106 A2
Kazanlŭk BG 17 D6
Kazár H 113 A3
Kazimierza Wielka PL 87 B4
Kazincbarcika H 113 A4
Kaźmierz PL 75 B5
Kcynia PL 76 A2
Kdyně CZ 95 B5
Kea GR 185 B5
Keadew IRL 26 B2
Keady GB 27 B4
Kecel H 112 C3
Keçiborlu TR 189 B5
Kecskemét H 113 C3
Kėdainiai LT 13 A5
Kędzierzyn-Koźle PL 86 B2
Keel IRL 28 A1
Keenagh IRL 28 A4
Keerbergen B 79 A4
Kefalos GR 188 C1
Kefken TR 187 A5
Keflavík IS 190 C3
Kegworth GB 40 C2
Kehl D 93 C3
Kehrigk D 74 B2
Keighley GB 40 B2
Keila EST 8 C4
Keillmore GB 34 C2
Keiss GB 32 C3
Keith GB 33 D4
Kelankylä FIN 197 D10
Kelberg D 80 B2
Kelbra D 82 A3
Kelč CZ 98 B1
Kelchsau A 108 B3
Këlcyrë AL 182 C2
Keld GB 37 B4
Kelebia H 126 A1
Kelekçi TR 188 B4
Kelemér H 99 C4
Keles TR 186 C4
Kelheim D 95 C3
Kell D 92 B2
Kellas GB 32 D3
Kellinghusen D 64 C2
Kelloselkä FIN 197 C11
Kells
GB 27 B4
IRL 27 C4
Kelmis B 80 B2
Kelokedhara CY 181 B1
Kelottijärvi FIN 192 D6
Kelsall GB 38 A4
Kelso GB 35 C5
Kelsterbach D 93 A4
Keltneyburn GB 35 B3
Kelujärvi FIN 197 B10
Kemaliye TR 188 A3
Kemalpaşa TR 188 A2
Kematen A 108 B2
Kemberg D 83 A4
Kemer
Antalya TR 189 C5
Burdur TR 189 B5
Muğla TR 189 C4
Kemerkaya TR 187 D6
Kemeten A 111 B3
Kemi FIN 196 D7
Kemijärvi FIN 197 C10
Keminmaa FIN 196 D7
Kemnath D 95 B3
Kemnay GB 33 D4
Kemnitz
Brandenburg D 74 B1
Mecklenburg-Vorpommern D 66 B2
Kempen D 80 A2
Kempsey GB 39 B4
Kempten D 107 B5
Kemptthal CH 107 B3
Kendal GB 37 B4
Kenderes H 113 B4
Kengyel H 113 B4
Kenilworth GB 44 A2
Kenmare IRL 29 C2
Kenmore GB 35 B4
Kennacraig GB 34 C2
Kenyeri H 111 B4
Kenzingen D 106 A2
Kepez TR 186 B1
Kępice PL 68 A1
Kępno PL 86 A2
Kepsut TR 186 C3
Keramoti GR 183 C6
Keräntöjärvi S 196 B6
Keratea GR 185 B4
Kerava FIN 8 B4
Kerecsend H 113 B4
Kerekegyhaza H 112 C3
Kerepestarcsa H 112 B3
Keri GR 184 B1
Kérien F 100 A2
Kerkafalva H 111 C3
Kerken D 80 A2
Kerkrade NL 80 B2
Kerkyra GR 182 D1
Kerlouan F 100 A1
Kernascléden F 100 A2
Kernhof A 110 B2
Kerns CH 106 C3
Kerpen D 80 B2
Kerrysdale GB 31 B3
Kerta H 111 B4
Kerteminde DK 59 C3
Kerzers CH 106 C2
Keşan TR 186 B1
Kesgrave GB 45 A5
Kesh GB 26 B3
Keskin TR 23 B7
Kesselfall A 109 B3
Kestenga RUS 3 D12
Keswick GB 36 B3
Keszthely H 111 C4
Kétegyháza H 113 C5
Kéthely H 111 C4
Kętrzyn PL 12 A4
Kettering GB 44 A3
Kettlewell GB 40 A1
Kęty PL 99 B3
Ketzin D 74 B1
Keula D 82 A2
Keuruu FIN 8 A4
Kevelaer D 80 A2
Kevermes H 113 C5
Kevi SRB 126 B1
Keyingham GB 41 B3
Keynsham GB 43 A4
Kežmarok SK 99 B4
Kharmanli BG 183 B7
Khaskovo BG 183 B7
Khimki RUS 9 E10
Khisinev = Chişinău MD 17 B8
Khmelnik UA 13 D7
Khmelnytskyy UA 13 D7
Khodoriv UA 13 D6
Kholm RUS 9 D7
Khotyn UA 13 D7
Khoyniki BY 13 C8
Khust UA 17 A5
Khvoynaya RUS 9 C9
Kiato GR 184 A3
Kibæk DK 59 B1
Kiberg N 193 B14
Kicasalih TR 186 A1
Kičevo MK 182 B2
Kidderminster GB 39 B4
Kidlington GB 44 B2
Kidsgrove GB 40 B1
Kidwelly GB 39 C2
Kiefersfelden D 108 B3
Kiel D 64 B3
Kielce PL 87 B4
Kiełczygłów PL 86 A3
Kielder GB 37 A4
Kiełpino PL 68 A3
Kielpiny PL 77 A4
Kierinki FIN 197 B8
Kiernozia PL 77 B4
Kierspe D 81 A3
Kietrz PL 86 B2
Kietz D 74 B3
Kiev = Kyyiv UA 13 C9
Kiezmark PL 69 A3
Kiffisia GR 185 A4
Kifino Selo BIH 139 B4
Kihlanki
FIN 196 B6
S 196 B6
Kiistala FIN 197 B8
Kije PL 87 B4
Kijevo HR 138 B2
Kikallen N 46 B2
Kikinda SRB 126 B2

Kil
N 53 B5
Örebro S 55 A6
Värmland S 55 A4
Kila S 55 A3
Kilafors S 50 A3
Kilbaha IRL 29 B2
Kilbeggan IRL 30 A1
Kilberry GB 34 C2
Kilbirnie GB 34 C3
Kilboghamn N 195 D4
Kilbotn N 194 B7
Kilb Rabenstein A 110 A2
Kilchattan GB 34 C2
Kilchoan GB 34 B1
Kilcock IRL 30 A2
Kilconnell IRL 28 A3
Kilcormac IRL 28 A4
Kilcreggan GB 34 C3
Kilcullen IRL 30 A2
Kilcurry IRL 27 B4
Kildare IRL 30 A2
Kildinstroy RUS 3 B13
Kildonan GB 32 C3
Kildorrery IRL 29 B3
Kilegrend N 53 A4
Kilen N 53 A4
Kilgarvan IRL 29 C2
Kiliya UA 17 C8
Kilkee IRL 29 B2
Kilkeel GB 27 B4
Kilkelly IRL 26 C2
Kilkenny IRL 30 B1
Kilkieran IRL 28 A2
Kilkinlea IRL 29 B2
Kilkis GR 182 B4
Killadysert IRL 29 B2
Killala IRL 26 B1
Killaloe IRL 28 B3
Killarney IRL 29 B2
Killashandra IRL 27 B3
Killashee IRL 28 A4
Killearn GB 34 B3
Killeberg S 61 C4
Killeigh IRL 30 A1
Killenaule IRL 29 B4
Killimor IRL 28 A3
Killin GB 34 B3
Killinaboy IRL 28 B2
Killinge S 196 B3
Killinick IRL 30 B2
Killorglin IRL 29 B2
Killucan IRL 30 A1
Killybegs IRL 26 B2
Killyleagh GB 27 B5
Kilmacrenan IRL 26 A3
Kilmacthomas IRL 30 B1
Kilmaine IRL 28 A2
Kilmallock IRL 29 B3
Kilmarnock GB 36 A2
Kilmartin GB 34 B2
Kilmaurs GB 36 A2
Kilmeadan IRL 30 B1
Kilmeedy IRL 29 B3
Kilmelford GB 34 B2
Kilmore Quay IRL 30 B2
Kilmuir GB 32 D2
Kilnaleck IRL 27 C3
Kilninver GB 34 B2
Kilpisjärvi FIN 192 C4
Kilrea GB 27 B4
Kilrush IRL 29 B2
Kilsmo S 56 A1
Kilsyth GB 35 C3
Kiltoom IRL 28 A3
Kilwinning GB 36 A2
Kimasozero RUS 3 D12
Kimi GR 185 A5
Kimolos GR 185 C5
Kimovsk RUS 9 E10
Kimratshofen D 107 B5
Kimry RUS 9 D10
Kimstad S 56 B1
Kinbrace GB 32 C3
Kincardine GB 35 B4
Kincraig GB 32 D3
Kindberg A 110 B2
Kindelbruck D 82 A3
Kingarrow IRL 26 B2
Kingisepp RUS 9 C6
Kingsbridge GB 43 B3
Kingsclere GB 44 B2
Kingscourt IRL 27 C4
King's Lynn GB 41 C4
Kingsteignton GB 43 B3
Kingston
Greater London
GB 44 B3
Moray GB 32 D3
Kingston Bagpuize
GB 44 B2
Kingston upon Hull
GB 40 B3
Kingswear GB 43 B3
Kingswood GB 43 A4
Kington GB 39 B3
Kingussie GB 32 D2
Kınık
Antalya TR 188 C4
İzmir TR 186 C2
Kinloch
Highland GB 31 B2
Highland GB 32 C2
Kinlochbervie GB 32 C1
Kinlochewe GB 32 D1
Kinlochleven GB 34 B3
Kinlochmoidart GB 34 B2
Kinloch Rannoch
GB 35 B3
Kinloss GB 32 D3
Kinlough IRL 26 B2
Kinn N 48 B2
Kinna S 60 B2
Kinnared S 60 B3
Kinnarp S 55 B4
Kinnegad IRL 30 A1
Kinne-Kleva S 55 B4
Kinnitty IRL 28 A4
Kinrooi B 80 A1
Kinross GB 35 B4
Kinsale IRL 29 C3
Kinsarvik N 46 B3
Kintarvie GB 31 A2
Kintore GB 33 D4
Kinvarra IRL 28 A3
Kioni GR 184 A1
Kiparissia GR 184 B2
Kipfenburg D 95 C3
Kippen GB 35 B3
Kiraz TR 188 A3
Kirazlı TR 186 B1
Kirberg D 81 B4
Kirchbach in Steiermark
A 110 C2
Kirchberg
CH 106 B2
Baden-Württemberg
D 94 B1
Rheinland-Pfalz D 93 B3
Kirchberg am Wechsel
A 110 B2
Kirchberg an der Pielach
A 110 A2
Kirchberg in Tirol
A 109 B3
Kirchbichl A 108 B3
Kirchdorf
Bayern D 96 C1
Mecklenburg-
Vorpommern D 65 C4
Niedersachsen D 72 B1
Kirchdorf an der Krems
A 109 B5
Kirchdorf in Tirol A 109 B3
Kirchenlamitz D 83 B3
Kirchenthumbach D 95 B3
Kirchhain D 81 B4
Kirchheim
Baden-Württemberg
D 94 C1
Bayern D 108 A1
Hessen D 81 B5
Kirchheimbolanden
D 93 B4
Kirchhundem D 81 A4
Kirchlintein D 72 B2
Kirchschlag A 111 B3
Kirchweidach D 109 A3
Kirchzarten D 106 B2
Kircubbin GB 27 B5
Kireç TR 186 C3
Kırıkkale TR 23 B7
Kirillov RUS 9 C11
Kirishi RUS 9 C8
Kırka TR 187 C5
Kırkağaç TR 186 C2
Kirkbean GB 36 B3
Kirkbride GB 36 B3
Kirkby GB 38 A4
Kirkby Lonsdale GB 37 B4
Kirkby Malzeard GB 40 A2
Kirkbymoorside GB 37 B6
Kirkby Stephen GB 37 B4
Kirkcaldy GB 35 B4
Kirkcolm GB 36 B1
Kirkconnel GB 36 A2
Kirkcowan GB 36 B2
Kirkcudbright GB 36 B2
Kirkehamn N 52 B2
Kirke Hyllinge DK 61 D1
Kirkenær N 49 B4
Kirkenes N 193 C14
Kirkham GB 38 A4
Kirkintilloch GB 35 C3
Kirkjubæjarklaustur
IS 191 D7
Kirkkonummi FIN 8 B4
Kırklareli TR 186 A2
Kirkmichael GB 35 B4
Kirk Michael GB 36 B2
Kirkoswald GB 36 A2
Kirkpatrick Fleming
GB 36 A3
Kirkton of Glenisla
GB 35 B4
Kirkwall GB 33 C4
Kirkwhelpington GB 37 A5
Kirn D 93 B3
Kirovsk RUS 3 C13
Kirriemuir GB 35 B5
Kırşehir TR 23 B8
Kirton GB 41 C3
Kirton in Lindsey
GB 40 B3
Kirtorf D 81 B5
Kiruna S 196 B3
Kisa S 62 A3
Kisač SRB 126 B1
Kisbér H 112 B2
Kiseljak BIH 139 B4
Kisielice PL 69 B4
Kisköre H 113 B4
Kiskőrös H 112 C3
Kiskunfélegyháza
H 113 C3
Kiskunhalas H 112 C3
Kiskunlacháza H 112 B2
Kiskunmajsa H 113 C3
Kisláng H 112 C2
Kisslegg D 107 B4
Kissolt H 112 C3
Kissónerga CY 181 B1
Kist D 94 B1
Kistanje HR 138 B1
Kistelek H 113 C3
Kisterenye H 113 A3
Kisújszállás H 113 B4
Kisvárda H 16 A5
Kisvejke H 112 C2
Kiszkowo PL 76 B2
Kiszombor H 126 A2
Kitee FIN 9 A7
Kithnos GR 185 B5
Kiti CY 181 B2
Kitkiöjärvi S 196 B6
Kitkiöjoki S 196 B6
Kittelfjäll S 195 E6
Kittendorf D 74 A1
Kittilä FIN 196 B7
Kittlitz D 84 A2
Kittsee A 111 A4
Kitzbühel A 109 B3
Kitzingen D 94 B2
Kiuruvesi FIN 3 E10
Kivertsi UA 13 C6
Kividhes CY 181 B1
Kivik S 63 C2
Kivotos GR 182 C3
Kıyıköy TR 186 A3
Kızılcabölük TR 188 B4
Kızılcadağ TR 189 B4
Kızılcahamam TR 23 A7
Kızılırmak TR 23 A7
Kızılkaya TR 189 B5
Kızılkuyu TR 187 D6
Kızılören
Afyon TR 189 A5
Konya TR 189 B7
Kjeldebotn N 194 B7
Kjellerup DK 59 B2
Kjellmyra N 49 B4
Kjøllefjord N 193 B11
Kjopmannskjaer N 54 A1
Kjøpsvik N 194 B7
Kl'ačno SK 98 C2
Kladanj BIH 139 A4
Kläden D 73 B4
Klädesholmen S 60 B1
Kladnice HR 138 B2
Kladno CZ 84 B2
Kladruby CZ 95 B4
Klagenfurt A 110 C1
Klågerup S 61 D3
Klagstorp S 66 A2
Klaipėda LT 8 E2
Klaistow D 74 B1
Klaksvík FO 4 A3
Klana HR 123 B3
Klanac HR 123 C4
Klanjec HR 123 A4
Klardorf D 95 B4
Klarup DK 58 A3
Klašnice BIH 124 C3
Klässbol S 55 A3
Klášterec nad Ohří
CZ 83 B5
Kláštor pod Znievom
SK 98 C2
Klatovy CZ 96 B1
Klaus an der Pyhrnbahn
A 110 B1
Klazienaveen NL 71 B3
Kłecko PL 76 B2
Kleczew PL 76 B3
Klein Plasten D 74 A1
Klein Sankt Paul A 110 C1
Kleinsölk A 109 B4
Kleinzell A 110 B2
Klejtrup DK 58 B2
Klek SRB 126 B2
Klemensker DK 67 A3
Klenak SRB 127 C1
Klenci pod Cerchovem
CZ 95 B4
Klenica PL 75 C4
Klenje SRB 127 C1
Klenoec MK 182 B2
Klenovec SK 99 C3
Klenovica HR 123 B3
Klenovnik HR 124 A2
Kleppe N 52 B1
Kleppestø N 46 B2
Kleptow D 74 A2
Kleszewo PL 77 B6
Kleve D 80 A2
Klevshult S 60 B4
Klewki PL 77 A5
Kličevac SRB 127 C3
Kliening A 110 C1
Klietz D 73 B5
Klikuszowa PL 99 B3
Klimkovice CZ 98 B2
Klimontów PL 87 B5
Klimovichi BY 13 B9
Klimpfjäll S 195 E5
Klin RUS 9 D10
Klinča Sela HR 123 B4
Klingenbach A 111 B3
Klingenberg D 93 B5
Klingenmunster D 93 B4
Klingenthal D 83 B4
Klinken D 73 A4
Klintehamn S 57 C4
Kliny PL 87 A4
Kliplev DK 64 B2
Klippan S 61 C3
Klis HR 138 B2
Klitmøller DK 58 A1
Klitten S 49 A6
Klixbüll D 64 B1
Kljajićevo SRB 126 B1
Ključ BIH 138 A2
Klobouky CZ 97 C4
Kłobuck PL 86 B2
Klockestrand S 200 D3
Kłodawa
Lubuskie PL 75 B4
Wielkopolskie PL 76 B3
Kłodzko PL 85 B4
Kløfta N 48 B3
Klokkarvik N 46 B2
Klokkerholm DK 58 A3
Klokočov SK 98 B2
Kłomnice PL 86 B3
Klonowa PL 86 A2
Kloosterzande NL 79 A4
Kłopot PL 74 B3
Klos AL 182 B2
Kloštar Ivanić HR 124 B2
Kloster
D 66 B2
DK 59 B1
Klösterle A 107 B5
Klostermansfeld D 82 A3
Klosterneuburg A 97 C4
Klosters CH 107 C4
Kloten CH 107 B3
Klötze D 73 B4
Klöverträsk S 196 D4
Klövsjö S 199 C11
Kluczbork PL 86 B2
Kluczewo PL 75 A5
Kluisbergen B 79 B3
Klundert NL 79 A4
Klutz D 65 C4
Klwów PL 87 A4
Klyetsk BY 13 B7
Knaben N 52 B2
Knaften S 200 B4
Knapstad N 54 A2
Knäred S 61 C3
Knaresborough GB 40 A2
Knarvik N 46 B2
Knebel DK 59 B3
Knebworth GB 44 B3
Knesebeck D 73 B3
Knesselare B 78 A3
Knežak SLO 123 B3
Kneževi Vinogradi
HR 125 B4
Kneževo HR 125 B4
Knić SRB 127 D2
Knighton GB 39 B3
Knin HR 138 A2
Knislinge S 61 C4
Knittelfeld A 110 B1
Knivsta S 57 A3
Knock IRL 28 A3
Knocktopher IRL 30 B1
Knokke-Heist B 78 A3
Knowle GB 44 A2
Knurów PL 86 B2
Knutby S 51 C5
Knutsford GB 38 A4
Kobarid SLO 122 A2
København =
Copenhagen DK 61 D2
Kobenz A 110 B1
Kobersdorf A 111 B3
Kobiernice PL 99 B3
Kobierzyce PL 85 B4
Kobilje SLO 111 C3
Kobiór PL 86 B2
Koblenz
CH 106 B3
D 81 B3
Kobryn BY 13 B6
Kobylanka PL 75 A3
Kobylin PL 85 A5
Kobylniki PL 77 B5
Kocaali TR 187 A5
Kocaaliler TR 189 B5
Kocaeli = İzmit TR 187 B4
Kočani MK 182 B4
Koçarlı TR 188 B2
Koceljevo SRB 127 C1
Kočerin BIH 138 B3
Kočevje SLO 123 B3
Kočevska Reka
SLO 123 B3
Kochel am see D 108 B2
Kocs H 112 B2
Kocsér H 113 B3
Kocsola H 112 C2
Koczala PL 68 B2
Kodal N 53 A6
Kode S 60 B1
Kodersdorf D 84 A2
Kodrab PL 86 A3
Koekelare B 78 A2
Kofçaz TR 186 A2
Köflach A 110 B2
Køge DK 61 D2
Kohlberg D 95 B4
Kohtla-Järve EST 8 C5
Köinge S 60 B2
Kojetín CZ 98 B1
Kökar FIN 51 C7
Kokava SK 99 C3
Kokkola FIN 3 E8
Kokori BIH 124 C3
Kokoski PL 69 A3
Koksijde B 78 A2
Kola
BIH 124 C3
RUS 3 B13
Köla S 54 A3
Kołacin PL 87 A3
Kolari FIN 196 B6
Kolárovo SK 112 B1
Kolašin MNE 16 D3
Kolbäck S 56 A2
Kolbacz PL 75 A3
Kolbeinsstaðir IS 190 C3
Kolbermoor D 108 B3
Kolbnitz A 109 C4
Kolbotn N 54 A1
Kolbu N 48 B2
Kolby Kås DK 59 C3
Kolczewo PL 67 C3
Kolczyglowy PL 68 A2
Kolding DK 59 C2
Kölesd H 112 C2
Kolgrov N 46 A1
Kolín CZ 97 A3
Kolind DK 59 B3
Kolinec CZ 96 B1
Koljane HR 138 B2
Kølkær DK 59 B2
Kölleda D 82 A3
Kollum NL 70 A3
Köln = Cologne D 80 B2
Koło PL 76 B3
Kołobrzeg PL 67 B4
Kolochau D 83 A5
Kolomyya UA 13 D6
Kolonowskie PL 86 B2
Koloveč CZ 95 B5
Kolpino RUS 9 C7
Kolrep D 73 A5
Kölsillre S 199 C12
Kolsko PL 75 C4
Kolsva S 56 A1
Kolta SK 112 A2
Kolunič BIH 138 A2
Koluszki PL 87 A3
Kolut SRB 125 B4
Kolvereid N 199 A8
Kølvrå DK 59 B2
Komadi H 113 B5
Komagvær N 193 B14
Komarica BIH 125 C3
Komárno SK 112 B2
Komárom H 112 B2
Komatou Yialou
CY 181 A3
Komboti GR 182 D3
Komen SLO 122 B2
Komin HR 138 B3
Komiža HR 138 B2
Komjáti H 99 C4
Komjatice SK 112 A2
Komletinci HR 125 B4
Komló H 125 A4
Kömlo H 113 B4
Komoča SK 112 B2
Komorniki PL 75 B5
Komorzno PL 86 A2
Komotini GR 183 B7
Konak SRB 126 B2
Konakovo RUS 9 D10
Konarzyny PL 68 B2
Kondias GR 183 D7
Kondopaga RUS 9 A9
Kondorfa H 111 C3
Kondoros H 113 C4
Konevo RUS 9 A11
Køng DK 65 A4
Konga S 63 B3
Köngäs FIN 196 B7
Kongerslev DK 58 B3
Kongsberg N 53 A5
Kongshamn N 53 B4
Kongsmark DK 64 A1
Kongsmoen N 199 A9
Kongsvik N 194 B7
Kongsvinger N 48 B3
Konice CZ 97 B4
Konie PL 77 C5
Koniecpol PL 86 B3
Königsberg D 82 B2
Königsbronn D 94 C2
Königsbrück D 84 A1
Königsbrunn D 94 C2
Konigsdorf D 108 B2
Königsee D 82 B3
Königshorst D 74 B1
Königslutter D 73 B3
Königssee D 109 B3
Königstein
Hessen D 81 B4
Sachsen D 84 B2
Königstetten A 97 C4
Königswartha D 84 A2
Konigswiesen A 96 C2
Königswinter D 80 B3
Königs Wusterhausen
D 74 B2
Konin PL 76 B3
Konispol AL 182 D2
Konitsa GR 182 C2
Köniz CH 106 C2
Konjevići BIH 139 A5
Konjevrate HR 138 B2
Konjic BIH 139 B3
Konjščina HR 124 A2
Könnern D 83 A3
Konnerud N 53 A6
Konopiska PL 86 B2
Konotop PL 75 C4
Końskie PL 87 A4
Konsmo N 52 B3
Konstancin-Jeziorna
PL 77 B6
Konstantynów Łódźki
PL 86 A3
Konstanz D 107 B4
Kontich B 79 A4
Kontiolahti FIN 9 A6
Konya TR 189 B7
Konz D 92 B2
Kópasker IS 191 A9
Kópavogur IS 190 C4
Kopčany SK 98 C1
Koper SLO 122 B2
Kopervik N 52 A1
Kópháza H 111 B3
Kopice PL 85 B5
Kopidlno CZ 84 B3
Köping S 56 A1
Köpingebro S 66 A2
Köpingsvik S 62 B4
Köpmanholmen S 200 C4
Koppang N 48 A3
Koppangen N 192 C4
Kopparberg S 50 C1
Koppelo FIN 193 D11
Koppom S 54 A3
Koprivlen BG 183 B5
Koprivna BIH 125 C4
Koprivnica HR 124 A2
Kopřivnice CZ 98 B2
Köprübaşı TR 186 D3
Koprzywnica PL 87 B5
Kopstal L 92 B2
Kopychyntsi UA 13 D6
Kopytkowo PL 69 B3
Korbach D 81 A4
Körbecke D 81 A4
Korçë AL 182 C2
Korčula HR 138 C3
Korczyców PL 75 B3
Korenita SRB 127 C1
Korets UA 13 C7
Korfantów PL 85 B5
Körfez TR 187 B4
Korgen N 195 D4
Korinth DK 64 A3
Korinthos = Corinth
GR 184 B3
Korita
BIH 138 A2
HR 139 C3
Korithi GR 184 B1
Korkuteli TR 189 B5
Körmend H 111 B3
Korne PL 68 A2
Korneuburg A 97 C4
Kornevo RUS 69 A5
Kórnik PL 76 B2
Kornsjø N 54 B2
Környe H 112 B2
Koromačno HR 123 C3
Koroni GR 184 C2
Koronos GR 185 B6
Koronowo PL 76 A2
Körösladány H 113 C5
Köröstarcsa H 113 C5
Korosten UA 13 C8
Korostyshev UA 13 C8
Korpikå S 196 D6
Korpikylä FIN 196 C6
Korpilombolo S 196 C6
Korsberga
Jönköping S 62 A3
Skaraborg S 55 B5
Korshavn N 54 A1
Korskrogen S 200 E1
Korsnäs S 50 B2
Korsør DK 65 A4
Korsun
Shevchenkovskiy
UA 13 D9
Korträsk S 196 D3
Kortrijk B 78 B3
Korucu TR 186 C2
Koryčany CZ 98 B1
Korzeńsko PL 85 A4
Korzybie PL 68 A1
Kos GR 188 C2
Kosakowo PL 69 A3
Kosanica MNE 139 B5
Kösching D 95 C3
Kościan PL 75 B5
Kościelec PL 76 B3
Kościerzyna PL 68 A2
Koserow D 66 B2
Košetice CZ 97 B3
Košice SK 12 D4
Kosjerić SRB 127 D1
Koška HR 125 B4
Koskullskulle S 196 B3
Kosovska Mitrovica
KOS 16 D4
Kosta S 62 B3
Kostajnica HR 124 B2
Kostajnik SRB 127 C1
Kostanjevica SLO 123 B4
Kostelec nad Černými
Lesy CZ 96 B2
Kostelec na Hané
CZ 97 B5
Kostice CZ 84 B1
Kostkowo PL 68 A3
Kostojevići SRB 127 C1

Kostolac SRB 127 C3
Kostomłoty PL 85 A4
Kostopil UA 13 C7
Kostów PL 86 A2
Kostrzyn
Lubuskie PL 74 B3
Wielkopolskie PL 76 B2
Koszalin PL 67 B5
Koszęcin PL 86 B2
Kőszeg H 111 B3
Koszwaly PL 69 A3
Koszyce PL 87 B4
Kot SLO 123 B4
Kotala FIN 197 B11
Kötelek H 113 B4
Köthen D 83 A3
Kotka FIN 8 B5
Kotomierz PL 76 A3
Kotor MNE 16 D3
Kotoriba HR 124 A2
Kotorsko BIH 125 C4
Kotor Varoš BIH 124 C3
Kotovsk UA 17 B8
Kotronas GR 184 C3
Kötschach A 109 C3
Kötzting D 95 B4
Koudum NL 70 B2
Kouřim CZ 96 A2
Kout na Šumave CZ 95 B5
Kouvola FIN 8 B5
Kovačevac SRB 127 C2
Kovačica SRB 126 B2
Kovdor RUS 197 B13
Kovel' UA 13 C6
Kovilj SRB 126 B2
Kovin SRB 127 C2
Kowal PL 77 B4
Kowalewo Pomorskie
PL 69 B3
Kowalów PL 75 B3
Kowary PL 85 B3
Köyceğiz TR 188 C3
Kozani GR 182 C3
Kozarac
BIH 124 C2
HR 124 B1
Kozárovce SK 98 C2
Kozelets UA 13 C9
Kozica HR 138 B3
Koziegłowy PL 86 B3
Kozienice PL 87 A5
Kozina SLO 122 B2
Kozje SLO 123 A4
Kozlu TR 187 A6
Kozluk BIH 139 A5
Koźmin PL 85 A5
Koźminek PL 86 A2
Kozolupy CZ 96 B1
Kożuchów PL 84 A3
Kožuhe BIH 125 C4
Kozyatyn UA 13 D8
Kozyürük TR 186 A1
Kräckelbräken S 49 A6
Krackow D 74 A3
Kraddsele S 195 E7
Krąg PL 68 A1
Kragenæs DK 65 B4
Kragerø N 53 B5
Krągi PL 68 B1
Kragujevac SRB 127 C2
Kraiburg D 109 A3
Krajenka PL 68 B1
Krajišnik SRB 126 B2
Krajková CZ 83 B4
Krajné SK 98 C1
Krajnik Dolny PL 74 A3
Krakača BIH 124 B1
Kräklingbo S 57 C4
Kraków = Cracow
PL 99 A3
Krakow am See D 73 A5
Králíky CZ 85 B4
Kraljevica HR 123 B3
Kraljevo SRB 16 D4
Kral'ovany SK 99 B3
Kráľov Brod SK 111 A4
Kralovice CZ 96 B1
Kralupy nad Vltavou
CZ 84 B2
Králův Dvůr CZ 96 B2
Kramfors S 200 D3
Kramsach A 108 B2
Kramsk PL 76 B3
Krämvik N 53 A4
Kranenburg D 80 A2
Krania GR 182 D3
Krania Elasonas
GR 182 D4
Kranichfeld D 82 B3
Kranidi GR 184 B4
Kranj SLO 123 A3
Kranjska Gora
SLO 109 C4
Krapanj HR 138 B1
Krapina HR 124 A1
Krapje HR 124 B2
Krapkowice PL 86 B1
Kraselov CZ 96 B1
Krašić HR 123 B4
Krāslava LV 8 E5
Kraslice CZ 83 B4
Krasna PL 87 A4
Krasna Lipa CZ 84 B2
Krasne PL 77 B5
Kraśnik PL 12 C5
Krašnja SLO 123 A3
Krásno SK 98 B2
Krásnohorské Podhradie SK 99 C4
Krasno Polje HR 123 C4
Krasnozavodsk
RUS 9 D11
Krasnystaw PL 13 C5
Krasnyy RUS 13 A9
Krasnyy Kholm
RUS 9 C10
Krasocin PL 87 B4
Kraszewice PL 86 A2
Kraszkowice PL 86 A2
Kratigos GR 186 C1
Kratovo MK 182 A4
Kraubath A 110 B1
Krausnick D 74 B2
Krautheim D 94 B1
Kravaře CZ 84 B2
Kraváre CZ 98 B2
Kravarsko HR 124 B2
Kraznějov CZ 96 B1
Krčedin SRB 126 B2
Kŭrdzhali BG 183 B7
Krefeld D 80 A2
Kregme DK 61 D2
Krembz D 73 A4
Kremenets UA 13 C6
Kremmen D 74 B2
Kremna SRB 127 D1
Kremnica SK 98 C2
Krempe D 64 C2
Krems A 97 C3
Kremsbrücke A 109 C4
Kremsmünster A 110 A1
Křemže CZ 96 C2
Křenov CZ 97 B4
Krepa PL 76 C3
Krępa Krajeńska PL 75 A5
Krepsko PL 68 B1
Kreševo BIH 139 B4
Kressbronn D 107 B4
Krestena GR 184 B2
Kretinga LT 8 E2
Krettsy RUS 9 C8
Kreuth D 108 B2
Kreuzau D 80 B2
Kreuzlingen CH 107 B4
Kreuztal D 81 B3
Krewelin D 74 B2
Krezluk BIH 138 A3
Krichem BG 183 A6
Krieglach A 110 B2
Kriegsfeld D 93 B3
Kriens CH 106 B3
Krimml A 108 B3
Krimpen aan de IJssel
NL 79 A4
Křinec CZ 84 B3
Kristdala S 62 A4
Kristiansand N 53 B4
Kristianstad S 61 C4
Kristiansund N 198 B4
Kristiinankaupunki
FIN 8 A2
Kristinefors S 49 B4
Kristinehamn S 55 A5
Kriváň SK 99 C3
Kriva Palanka MK 182 A4
Křivoklát CZ 96 A1
Križ HR 124 B2
Křižanov CZ 97 B4
Križevci HR 124 A2
Krk HR 123 B3
Krka SLO 123 B3
Krnjača SRB 127 C2
Krnjak HR 123 B4
Krnjeuša BIH 124 C2
Krnjevo SRB 127 C3
Krnov CZ 98 A1
Krobia PL 85 A4
Kroczyce PL 86 B3
Krøderen N 48 B1
Krokees GR 184 C3
Krokek S 56 B2
Krokom S 199 B11
Krokowa PL 68 A3
Krokstad-elva N 53 A5
Kroksund N 54 A2
Kroměříž CZ 98 B1
Krommenie NL 70 B1
Krompachy SK 99 C4
Kronach D 82 B3
Kronshagen D 64 B3
Kronshtadt RUS 9 C6
Kröpelin D 65 B4
Kropp D 64 B2
Kroppenstedt D 73 C4
Kropstädt D 74 C1
Krościenko nad Dunajcem PL 99 B4
Kröslin D 66 B2
Krośnice PL 85 A5
Krośniewice PL 77 B4
Krosno PL 12 D4
Krosno Odrzańskie
PL 75 B4
Krostitz D 83 A4
Krotoszyn PL 85 A5
Krottendorf A 110 B2
Krouna CZ 97 B4
Krowiarki PL 86 B2
Krrabë AL 182 B1
Kršan HR 123 B3
Krško SLO 123 B4
Krstac MNE 139 B4
Krstur SRB 126 A2
Křtiny CZ 97 B4
Kruft D 80 B3
Kruishoutem B 79 B3
Krujë AL 182 B1
Krulyewshchyna BY 13 A7
Krumbach
A 111 B3
D 94 C2
Krumovgrad BG 183 B7
Krün D 108 B2
Krupá CZ 84 B1
Krupa na Vrbasu
BIH 124 C3
Krupanj SRB 127 C1
Krupina SK 99 C3
Krupka CZ 84 B1
Krupki BY 13 A8
Kruså DK 64 B2
Krušćica BIH 139 A3
Kruševac SRB 16 D4
Kruševo MK 182 B3
Kruszwica PL 76 B3
Kruszyn PL 77 B4
Krychaw BY 13 B9
Krynica PL 99 B4
Krynica Morska PL 69 A4
Krzęcin PL 75 A4
Krzelów PL 85 A4
Krzepice PL 86 B2
Krzepielów PL 85 A4
Krzeszowice PL 86 B3
Krzeszyce PL 75 B4
Krzynowlaga Mała
PL 77 A5
Krzywiń PL 75 C5
Krzyżanowice PL 98 B2
Krzyżowa PL 99 B3
Krzyż Wielkopolski
PL 75 B5
Ksiaz Wielkopolski
PL 87 B4
Książ Wielkopolski
PL 76 B2
Kętbowiec PL 75 A5
Kübekháza H 126 A2
Küblis CH 107 C4
Kuchary PL 86 A1
Kuchl A 109 B4
Kucice PL 77 B5
Kuciste HR 138 C3
Kuçovë AL 182 C1
Küçükbahçe TR 188 A1
Küçükköy TR 186 C1
Küçükkuyu TR 186 C1
Kucura SRB 126 B1
Kuczbork-Osada PL 77 A5
Kuddby S 56 B2
Kudowa-Zdrój PL 85 B4
Kufstein A 108 B3
Kuggeboda S 63 B3
Kuggörana S 200 E3
Kühbach D 95 C3
Kuhmo FIN 3 D11
Kuhmoinen FIN 8 B4
Kuhnsdorf A 110 C1
Kuhstedt D 72 A1
Kuinre NL 70 B2
Kuivaniemi FIN 197 D8
Kuivastu EST 8 C3
Kukës AL 182 A2
Kuklin PL 77 A5
Kukljica HR 137 A4
Kukujevci SRB 127 B1
Kula
Srbija SRB 127 C3
Vojvodina SRB 126 B1
TR 188 A3
Kuldīga LV 8 D2
Kulen Vakuf BIH 124 C2
Kulina BIH 125 C4
Kullstedt D 82 A2
Kulmain D 95 B3
Kulmbach D 82 B3
Kuloharju FIN 197 D11
Kulu TR 23 B7
Kumachevo RUS 69 A5
Kumafşarı TR 189 B4
Kumane SRB 126 B2
Kumanovo MK 182 A3
Kumbağ TR 186 B2
Kumdanlı TR 189 A5
Kumkale TR 186 C1
Kumla S 56 A1
Kumlakyrkby S 50 C3
Kumlinge FIN 51 B7
Kumluca TR 189 C5
Kumrovec HR 123 A4
Kunadacs H 112 C3
Kunágota H 113 C5
Kunbaja H 126 A1
Kunda EST 8 C5
Kundl A 108 B2
Kunes N 193 B10
Kunfehértó H 126 A1
Kungälv S 60 B1
Kungsängen S 57 A3
Kungsäter S 60 B2
Kungsbacka S 60 B2
Kungsgården S 50 B3
Kungshamn S 54 B2
Kungs-Husby S 56 A3
Kungsör S 56 A2
Kunhegyes H 113 B4
Kunmadaras H 113 B4
Kunovice CZ 98 B1
Kunów PL 87 B5
Kunowo
Wielkopolskie PL 76 C2
Zachodnio-Pomorskie
PL 74 A3
Kunštát CZ 97 B4
Kunszállás H 113 C3
Kunszentmárton
H 113 C4
Kunszentmiklós H 112 B3
Kunžak CZ 97 B3
Künzelsau D 94 B1
Kuolayarvi RUS 197 C12
Kuolio FIN 197 D11
Kuopio FIN 8 A5
Kuosku FIN 197 B11
Kup
H 111 B4
PL 86 B1
Kupferzell D 94 B1
Kupinec HR 123 B4
Kupinečki Kraljevac
HR 124 B1
Kupinovo SRB 127 C2
Kupirovo HR 138 A2
Kupjak HR 123 B3
Kuppenheim D 93 C4
Kupres BIH 138 B3
Küps D 82 B3
Kurd H 112 C2
Küre TR 23 A7
Kuressaare EST 8 C3
Kurikka FIN 8 A3
Kuřim CZ 97 B4
Kuřivody CZ 84 B2
Kurki PL 77 A5
Kurort Oberwiesenthal
D 83 B4
Kurort Schmalkalden
D 82 B2
Kurort Stolberg D 82 A2
Kurort Wippra D 82 A3
Kurów PL 12 C5
Kurowice PL 86 A3
Kurravaara S 196 B3
Kursu FIN 197 C11
Kurşunlu
Bursa TR 187 B4
Çankırı TR 23 A7
Kurtakko FIN 196 B7
Kürten D 80 A3
Kurucaşile TR 187 A7
Kurvinen FIN 197 D12
Kurzelów PL 87 B3
Kusadak SRB 127 C2
Kuşadası TR 188 B2
Kusel D 93 B3
Kusey D 73 B4
Küsnacht CH 106 B3
Kütahya TR 187 C4
Kutenholz D 72 A2
Kutina HR 124 B2
Kutjevo HR 125 B3
Kutná Hora CZ 97 B3
Kutno PL 77 B4
Kuttara FIN 193 D10
Küttingen CH 106 B3
Kúty SK 98 C1
Kuusamo FIN 197 D12
Kuusankoski FIN 8 B5
Kuvshinovo RUS 9 D9
Kuyucak TR 188 B3
Kuzmin SRB 127 B1
Kuźnia Raciborska
PL 86 B2
Kuźnica Czarnkowska
PL 75 B5
Kuźnica Żelichowska
PL 75 B5
Kvaløysletta N 192 C2
Kvalsund N 192 B7
Kvam
Nord-Trøndelag
N 199 A8
Oppland N 198 D6
Kvamsøy N 46 A3
Kvænangsbotn N 192 C6
Kvanndal N 46 B3
Kvänum S 55 B4
Kværndrup DK 59 C3
Kvås N 52 B3
Kvasice CZ 98 B1
Kvelde N 53 A5
Kvenna N 198 C5
Kvernaland N 52 B1
Kvibille S 60 C2
Kvicksund S 56 A2
Kvidinge S 61 C3
Kvikkjokk S 195 D8
Kvikne
Hedmark N 199 C7
Oppland N 47 A6
Kvilda CZ 96 B1
Kville S 54 B2
Kvillsfors S 62 A3
Kvinesdal N 52 B2
Kvinlog N 52 B2
Kvinnherad N 46 C3
Kvissel DK 58 A3
Kvissleby S 200 D3
Kviteseid N 53 A4
Kvitsøy N 52 A1
Kwakowo PL 68 A2
Kwidzyn PL 69 B3
Kwilcz PL 75 B5
Kyjov CZ 98 C1
Kyleakin GB 31 B3
Kyle of Lochalsh
GB 31 B3
Kylerhea GB 31 B3
Kylestrome GB 32 C1
Kyllburg D 92 A2
Kyllini GR 184 B2
Kynšperk nad Ohří
CZ 83 B4
Kyperounda CY 181 B1
Kyrenia CY 181 A2
Kyritz D 73 B5
Kyrkesund S 60 A1
Kyrkhult S 63 B2
Kyrksæterøra N 198 B6
Kysucké Nové Mesto
SK 98 B2
Kythira GR 184 C3
Kythréa CY 181 A2
Kyustendil BG 16 D5
Kyyiv = Kiev UA 13 C9
Kyyjärvi FIN 8 A4

L

Laa an der Thaya A 97 C4
La Adrada E 150 B3
Laage D 65 C5
La Alameda E 157 B4
La Alberca E 149 B3
La Alberca de Záncara
E 158 B1
La Albergueria de Argañán E 149 B3
La Albuera E 155 C4
La Aldea del Portillo del Busto E 143 B3
La Algaba E 162 A1
La Aliseda de Tormes
E 150 B2
La Almarcha E 158 B1
La Almolda E 153 A3
La Almunia de Doña Godina E 152 A2
Laanila FIN 193 D11
La Antillas E 161 B2
La Arena E 141 A4
Laatzen D 72 B2
La Aulaga E 161 B3
La Balme-de-Sillingy
F 118 B3
Laban IRL 28 A3
La Bañeza E 141 B5
La Barca de la Florida
E 162 B2
La Barre-de-Monts
F 114 B1
La Barre-en-Ouche
F 89 B4
La Barrosa E 162 B1
La Barthe-de-Neste
F 145 A4
La Bassée F 78 B2
La Bastide-de-Sèrou
F 146 A2
La Bastide-des-Jourdans F 132 B1
Labastide-Murat F 129 B4
La Bastide-Puylaurent
F 117 C3
Labastide-Rouairoux
F 130 B1
Labastide-St Pierre
F 129 C4
La Bathie F 118 B3
Lábatlan H 112 B2
La Baule-Escoublac
F 101 B3
La Bazoche-Gouet
F 102 A2
La Bégude-de-Mazenc
F 131 A3
Labenne F 128 C1
La Bernerie-en-Retz
F 114 A1
Labin HR 123 B3
La Bisbal d'Empordà
E 147 C4
Łabiszyn PL 76 B2
Lablachère F 131 A3
Lábod H 124 A3
Laboe D 64 B3
La Boissière F 89 A4
Labouheyre F 128 B2
La Bourboule F 116 B2
La Bóveda de Toro
E 150 A2
Łabowa PL 99 B4
La Brède F 128 B2
La Bresse F 106 A1
La Bridoire F 118 B2
La Brillanne F 132 B1
Labrit F 128 B2
Labros E 152 A2
La Bruffière F 114 A2
Labruguière F 130 B1
Labrujo P 148 A1
L'Absie F 114 B3
La Bussière F 103 B4
Laç AL 182 B1
La Caillère F 114 B3
Lacalahorra E 164 B1
La Caletta
Cágliari I 179 C2
Núoro I 178 B3
La Calmette F 131 B3
La Calzada de Oropesa
E 150 C2
La Campana E 162 A2
La Cañada E 150 B3
Lacanau F 128 B1
Lacanau-Océan F 128 A1
Lacanche F 104 B3
La Canourgue F 130 A2
La Capelle F 91 B3
Lacapelle-Marival
F 129 B4
Laćarak SRB 127 B1
La Cardanchosa E 156 B2
La Caridad E 141 A4
La Carlota E 162 A3
La Carolina E 157 B4
Lacaune F 130 B1
La Cava E 153 B4
La Cavalerie F 130 A2
Laceby GB 41 B3
Lacedónia I 172 A1
La Celle-en-Moravan
F 104 B3
La Celle-St Avant
F 102 B2
La Cerca E 143 B3
Láces I 108 C1
La Chaise-Dieu F 117 B3
La Chaize-Giraud
F 114 B2
La Chaize-le-Vicomte
F 114 B2
La Chambre F 118 B3
Lachania GR 188 D2
La Chapelaude F 116 A2
La Chapelle-d'Angillon
F 103 B4
La Chapelle-en-Aalgaudémar F 118 C3
La Chapelle-en-Vercors
F 118 C2
La Chapelle-Glain
F 101 B4
La Chapelle-la-Reine
F 90 C2
La Chapelle-Laurent
F 116 B3
La Chapelle-St Luc
F 91 C4
La Chapelle-sur-Erdre
F 101 B4
La Chapelle-Vicomtesse
F 103 B3
La Charce F 132 A1
La Charité-sur-Loire
F 104 B2
La Chartre-sur-le-Loir
F 102 B2
La Châtaigneraie
F 114 B3
La Châtre F 103 C3
La Chaussée-sur-Marne
F 91 C4
La Chaux-de-Fonds
CH 106 B1
Lachen CH 107 B3
Lachendorf D 72 B3
La Cheppe F 91 B4
La Chèze F 101 A3
Lachowice PL 99 B3
La Ciotat F 132 B1
Łąck PL 77 B4
Läckeby S 62 B4
Läckö S 55 B4
La Clayette F 117 A4
La Clusaz F 118 B3
Lacock GB 43 A4
La Codosera E 155 B3
La Concha E 143 A3
La Condamine-Châtelard F 132 A2
Láconi I 179 C3
La Contienda E 161 A3
La Coquille F 115 C4
La Coronada E 156 B2
La Côte-St André
F 118 B2
La Cotinière F 114 C2
La Courtine F 116 B2
Lacq F 145 A3
La Crau F 132 B2
La Crèche F 115 B3
La Croix F 102 B2
Lacroix-Barrez F 116 C2
Lacroix-St Ouen F 90 B2
Lacroix-sur-Meuse
F 92 C1
La Croix-Valmer F 132 B2
La Cumbre E 156 A2
Łącznik PL 86 B1
Lad H 125 A3
Ladbergen D 71 B4
Lądek-Zdrój PL 85 B4
Ladelund D 64 B2
Ladendorf A 97 C4
Ladignac-le-Long
F 115 C5
Ladíspoli I 168 B2
Ladoeiro P 155 B3
Ladon F 103 B4
La Douze F 129 A3
Ladushkin RUS 69 A5
Ladybank GB 35 B4
Laer D 71 B4
La Espina E 141 A4
La Estrella E 156 A2
La Farga de Moles
E 146 B2
La Fatarella E 153 A4
La Felipa E 158 B2
La Fère F 90 B3
La Ferrière
Indre-et-Loire F 102 B2

La Ferrière
Vendée F 114 B2
La Ferrière-en-Parthenay F 115 B3
La-Ferté-Alais F 90 C2
La Ferté-Bernard F 102 A2
La Ferté-Frênel F 89 B4
La Ferté-Gaucher F 90 C3
La Ferté-Imbault F 103 B3
La Ferté-Macé F 89 B3
La Ferté-Milon F 90 B3
La Ferté-sous-Jouarre F 90 C3
La Ferté-St-Aubin F 103 B3
La Ferté-St-Cyr F 103 B3
La Ferté-Vidame F 89 B4
La Ferté Villeneuil F 103 B3
La Feuillie F 90 B1
Lafkos GR 183 D5
La Flèche F 102 B1
La Flotte F 114 B2
Lafnitz A 111 B3
La Font de la Figuera E 159 C3
La Fouillade F 130 A1
Lafrançaise F 129 B4
La Fregeneda E 149 B3
La Fresneda E 153 B4
La Fuencubierta E 162 A3
La Fuente de San Esteban E 149 B3
La Fulioala E 147 C2
La Gacilly F 101 B3
La Galera E 153 B4
Lagan S 60 C3
Laganadi I 175 C1
Lagarde F 146 A2
La Garde-Freinet F 132 B2
Lagares
Coimbra P 148 B2
Porto P 148 A1
La Garnache F 114 B2
Lagaro I 135 A4
La Garriga E 147 C3
La Garrovilla E 155 C4
Lagartera E 150 C2
La Gaubretière F 114 B2
Lågbol S 51 B5
Lage D 72 C1
Lägerdorf D 64 C2
Lagg GB 34 C2
Laggan GB 32 D2
Laggartorp S 55 A5
Łagiewniki PL 85 B4
La Gineta E 158 B1
Láglio I 120 B2
Lagnieu F 118 B2
Lagny-sur-Marne F 90 C2
Lago
Calabria I 175 B2
Veneto I 121 B5
Lagôa P 160 B1
Lagoaça P 149 A3
Lagonegro I 174 A1
Lagos
GR 183 B7
P 160 B1
Lagosanto I 121 C5
Łagów
Lubuskie PL 75 B4
Świętokrzyskie PL 87 B5
La Granadella
Alicante E 159 C4
Lleida E 153 A4
La Grand-Combe F 131 A3
La Grande-Croix F 117 B4
La Grande-Motte F 131 B3
La Granja d'Escarp E 153 A4
La Granjuela E 156 B2
Lagrasse F 146 A3
La Grave F 118 B3
La Gravelle F 101 A4
Laguardia E 143 B4
La Guardia E 151 C4
La Guardia de Jaén E 163 A4
Laguarres E 145 B4
Laguenne F 116 B1
Laguépie F 129 B4
La Guerche-de-Bretagne F 101 B4
La Guerche-sur-l'Aubois F 104 C1
La Guérinière F 114 B1
Laguiole F 116 C2
Laguna de Duera E 150 A3
Laguna del Marquesado E 152 B2
Laguna de Negrillos E 142 B1
Lagundo I 108 C2
Lagunilla E 149 B3
La Haba E 156 B2
Laharie F 128 B1
La Haye-du-Puits F 88 A2
La Haye-Pesnel F 88 B2
Lahden D 71 B4
La Herlière F 78 B2
La Hermida E 142 A2
La Herrera E 158 C1
Laheycourt F 91 C5
La Higuera E 158 C2
La Hiniesta E 149 A4
Lahnstein D 81 B3
Laholm S 61 C3
La Horcajada E 150 B2
La Horra E 143 C3
Lahr D 93 C3
Lahti FIN 8 B4
La Hulpe B 79 B4
La Hutte F 89 B4
Laichingen D 94 C1
L'Aigle F 89 B4
La Iglesuela E 150 B3
La Iglesuela del Cid E 153 B3
Laignes F 104 B3
Laiguéglia I 133 B4
L'Aiguillon-sur-Mer F 114 B2
Laimbach am Ostrong A 97 C3
Laina E 152 A1
Lainio S 196 B5
Lairg GB 32 C2
La Iruela E 164 B2
Laissac F 130 A1
Laisvall S 195 D8
Láives I 121 A4
La Javie F 132 A2
Lajkovac SRB 127 C2
La Jonchère-St Maurice F 116 A1
La Jonquera E 146 B3
Lajoskomárom H 112 C2
Lajosmizse H 112 B3
Lak H 99 C4
Lakenheath GB 45 A4
Lakitelek H 113 C4
Lakki GR 185 D4
Lakolk DK 64 A1
Łąkorz PL 69 B4
Lakšárska Nová Ves SK 98 C1
Lakselv N 193 B8
Laksfors N 195 E4
Laktaši BIH 124 C3
La Lantejuela E 162 A2
Lalapaşa TR 186 A1
L'Albagès E 153 A4
Lalbenque F 129 B4
L'Alcudia E 159 B3
L'Aldea E 153 B4
Lalín E 140 B2
Lalinde F 129 B3
La Línea de la Concepción E 162 B2
Lalizolle F 116 A3
La Llacuna E 147 C2
Lalley F 118 C2
Lalling D 95 C5
Lalm N 198 D6
La Londe-les-Maures F 132 B2
La Loupe F 89 B5
La Louvière B 79 B4
L'Alpe-d'Huez F 118 B3
La Luisiana E 162 A2
Laluque F 128 C1
Lam D 95 B5
La Machine F 104 C2
la Maddalena I 178 A3
Lama dei Peligni I 169 A4
Lamadrid E 142 A2
Lamagistére F 129 B3
La Mailleraye-sur-Seine F 89 A4
La Malène F 130 A2
Lama Mocogno I 135 A3
La Mamola E 163 B4
La Manresana dels Prats E 147 C2
Lamarche F 105 A4
Lamarche-sur-Saône F 105 B4
Lamargelle F 105 B3
Lamarosa P 154 B2
Lamarque F 128 A2
Lamas P 148 B1
La Masadera E 145 C3
Lamas de Moaro P 140 B2
Lamastre F 117 C4
La Mata E 150 C3
La Mata de Ledesma E 149 A4
La Mata de Monteagudo E 142 B1
Lambach A 109 A4
Lamballe F 101 A3
Lamberhurst GB 45 B4
Lambesc F 131 B4
Lambia GR 184 B2
Lambley GB 37 B4
Lambourn GB 44 B2
Lamego P 148 A2
La Meilleraye-de-Bretagne F 101 B4
La Ménitré F 102 B1
L'Ametlla de Mar E 153 B4
Lamia GR 182 E4
Lammhult S 62 A2
La Mojonera E 164 C2
La Mole F 132 B2
La Molina E 147 B2
La Monnerie-le-Montel F 117 B3
La Morera E 155 C4
La Mothe-Achard F 114 B2
Lamothe-Cassel F 129 B4
Lamothe-Montravel F 128 B3
La Mothe-St Héray F 115 B3
Lamotte-Beuvron F 103 B4
La Motte-Chalançon F 131 A4
La Motte-du-Caire F 132 A2
La Motte-Servolex F 118 B2
Lampertheim D 93 B4
Lampeter GB 39 B2
L'Ampolla E 153 B4
Lamprechtshausen A 109 B3
Lamsfeld D 74 C3
Lamspringe D 72 C3
Lamstedt D 72 A2
La Mudarra E 142 C2
La Muela E 152 A2
La Mure F 118 C2
Lamure-sur-Azergues F 117 A4
Lana I 108 C2
Lanaja E 145 C3
Lanarce F 117 C3
Lanark GB 36 A3
La Nava E 161 B3
La Nava de Ricomalillo E 156 A3
La Nava de Santiago E 155 B4
Lancaster GB 37 B4
Lanchester GB 37 B5
Lanciano I 169 A4
Lancing GB 44 C3
Lançon-Provence F 131 B4
Lancova Vas SLO 124 A1
Landau
Bayern D 95 C4
Rheinland-Pfalz D 93 B4
Landeck A 108 B1
Landen B 79 B5
Landerneau F 100 A1
Landeryd S 60 B3
Landesbergen D 72 B2
Landete E 158 B2
Landévant F 100 B2
Landévennec F 100 A1
Landivisiau F 100 A1
Landivy F 88 B2
Landl A 108 B3
Landön S 199 B11
Landos F 117 C3
Landouzy-le-Ville F 91 B4
Landquart CH 107 C4
Landrecies F 91 A3
Landreville F 104 A3
Landriano I 120 B2
Landsberg D 108 A1
Lands-berg D 83 A4
Landsbro S 62 A3
Landscheid D 92 B2
Landshut D 95 C4
Landskrona S 61 D2
Landstuhl D 93 B3
Lanesborough IRL 28 A4
Lanester F 100 B2
Lanestosa E 143 A3
La Neuve-Lyre F 89 B4
La Neuveville CH 106 B2
Langå DK 59 B2
Langada GR 185 A7
Langadas GR 183 C5
Langa de Duero E 151 A4
Langadia GR 184 B3
Langangen N 53 A5
Långared S 60 A2
Långaröd S 61 D3
Långaryd S 60 B3
Långås S 60 C2
Långasjö S 63 B3
Langau A 97 C3
Langeac F 117 B3
Langeais F 102 B2
Langedijk NL 70 B1
Langeln D 73 C3
Langelsheim D 72 C3
Langemark-Poelkapelle B 78 B2
Langen
Hessen D 93 B4
Niedersachsen D 72 A1
Langenau D 94 C2
Langenberg D 81 A4
Langenbruck CH 106 B2
Langenburg D 94 B1
Längenfeld A 108 B1
Langenfeld D 80 A2
Langenhorn D 64 B1
Langenlois A 97 C3
Langenlonsheim D 93 B3
Langennaudorf D 83 A5
Langenneufnach D 94 C2
Langenthal CH 106 B2
Langenzenn D 94 B2
Langeoog D 71 A4
Langeskov DK 59 C3
Langesund N 53 A5
Langewiesen D 82 B2
Långflon S 49 A4
Langförden D 71 B5
Langhagen D 73 A5
Länghem S 60 B3
Langhirano I 120 C3
Langholm GB 36 A4
Langholt IS 191 D7
Långlöt S 62 B4
Langnau CH 106 C2
Langø DK 65 B4
Langogne F 117 C3
Langon F 128 B2
Langquaid D 95 C4
Långrådna S 56 B2
Langreo E 142 A1
Langres F 105 B4
Långsele S 200 C3
Långserud S 54 A3
Langset N 48 B3
Långshyttan S 50 B3
Langstrand N 192 B7
Långträsk S 196 D3
Langueux F 101 A3
Languidic F 100 B2
Längvik S 57 A4
Langwarden D 71 A5
Langwathby GB 37 B4
Langwedel D 72 B2
Langweid D 94 C2
Langwies CH 107 C4
Lanheses P 148 A1
Lanięta PL 77 B4
Lanildut F 100 A1
Lanjarón E 163 B4
Lanmeur F 100 A2
Lanna
Jönköping S 60 B3
Örebro S 55 A5
Lännaholm S 51 C4
Lannavaara S 196 A4
Lannéanou F 100 A2
Lannemezan F 145 A4
Lanneuville-sur-Meuse F 91 B5
Lannilis F 100 A1
Lannion F 100 A2
La Nocle-Maulaix F 104 C2
Lanouaille F 115 C5
Lansjärv S 196 C5
Lanškroun CZ 97 B4
Lanslebourg-Mont-Cenis F 119 B3
Lanta F 129 C4
Lantadilla E 142 B2
Lanton F 128 B1
Lantosque F 133 B3
La Nuez de Arriba E 143 B3
Lanusei I 179 C3
Lanúvio I 168 B2
Lanvollon F 100 A3
Lánycsók H 125 A4
Lanz D 73 A4
Lanza E 140 A2
Lanzada E 140 B2
Lanzahita E 150 B3
Lanžhot CZ 97 C4
Lanzo Torinese I 119 B4
Laole SRB 127 C3
Laon F 91 B3
Laons F 89 B5
La Paca E 164 B3
La Pacaudière F 117 A3
Lapalisse F 117 A3
La Palma d'Ebre E 153 A4
La Palma del Condado E 161 B3
La Palme F 146 B4
La Palmyre F 114 C2
La Parra E 155 C4
Łapczyna Wola PL 87 B3
La Pedraja de Portillo E 150 A3
La Peraleja E 152 B1
La Petit-Pierre F 93 C3
Lapeyrade F 128 B2
Lapeyrouse F 116 A2
Lapford GB 42 B3
La Pinilla E 165 B3
Lapithos CY 181 A2
La Plagne F 118 B3
La Plaza E 141 A4
Laplume F 129 B3
La Pobla de Lillet E 147 B2
La Pobla de Vallbona E 159 B3
La Pobla Llarga E 159 B3
La Pola de Gordón E 142 B1
la Porta F 180 A2
La Pouëze F 102 B1
Lapoutroie F 106 A2
La Póveda de Soria E 143 B4
Lapovo SRB 127 C3
Läppe S 56 A1
Lappeenranta FIN 8 B6
Lappoluobbal N 192 C7
Lappträsk S 196 C6
La Preste F 146 B3
La Primaube F 130 A1
Lapseki TR 186 B1
Lapua FIN 8 A3
La Puebla de Almoradie E 157 A4
La Puebla de Cazalla E 162 A2
La Puebla de los Infantes E 162 A2
La Puebla del Río E 162 A1
La Puebla de Montalbán E 150 C3
La Puebla de Roda E 145 B4
La Puebla de Valdavia E 142 B2
La Puebla de Valverde E 152 B3
La Pueblanueva E 150 C3
La Puerta de Segura E 164 A2
La Punt CH 107 C4
L'Àquila I 169 A3
La Quintana E 162 A3
La Quintera E 162 A2
La Rábita
Granada E 164 C1
Jaén E 163 A3
Laracha E 140 A2
Laragh IRL 30 A2
Laragne-Montéglin F 132 A1
La Rambla E 163 A3
l'Arboç E 147 C2
L'Arbresle F 117 B4
Lärbro S 57 C4
Larceveau F 144 A2
Larche
Alpes-de-Haute-Provence F 132 A2
Corrèze F 129 A4
Lårdal N 53 A4
Lærdalsøyri N 47 A4
Lardosa P 155 B3
La Reale I 178 A2
Laredo E 143 A3
La Redondela E 161 B2
La Réole F 128 B2
Largentière F 131 A3
L'Argentière-la-Bessée F 118 C3
Largs GB 34 C3
Lari I 134 B3
La Riera E 141 A4
La Riera de Gaià E 147 C2
La Rinconada E 162 A1
Lariño E 140 B1
Larino I 170 B2
Larisa GR 182 D4
La Rivière-Thibouville F 89 A4
Larkhall GB 36 A3
Larkollen N 54 A1
Larmor-Plage F 100 B2
Larnaca CY 181 B2
Larne GB 27 B5
La Robla E 142 B1
La Roca de la Sierra E 155 B4
La Roche CH 106 C2
La Rochebeaucourt-Argentine F 115 C4
La Roche-Bernard F 101 B3
La Roche-Canillac F 116 B1
La Roche-Chalais F 128 A3
La Roche Derrien F 100 A2
La Roche-des-Arnauds F 132 A1
La Roche-en-Ardenne B 80 B1
La Roche-en-Brénil F 104 B3
La Rochefoucauld F 115 C4
La Roche-Guyon F 90 B1
La Rochelle F 114 B2
La Roche-Posay F 115 B4
La Roche-sur-Foron F 118 A3
La Roche-sur-Yon F 114 B2
Larochette L 92 B2
La Rochette F 131 A4
La Roda
Albacete E 158 B1
Oviedo E 141 A4
La Roda de Andalucía E 162 A3
Laroquebrou F 116 C2
La Roquebrussanne F 132 B1
Laroque d'Olmes F 146 B2
La Roque-Gageac F 129 B4
La Roque-Ste Marguerite F 130 A2
Laroque-Timbaut F 129 B3
Larouco E 141 B3
Larraga E 144 B2
Larrau F 144 A3
Larrazet F 129 C4
Larsnes N 198 C2
La Rubia E 143 C4
Laruns F 145 A3
Larva E 164 B1
Larvik N 53 A6
La Sagrada E 149 B3
La Salceda E 151 A4
Lasalle F 131 A2
La Salle F 118 C3
la Salute di Livenza I 122 B1
La Salvetat-Peyralés F 130 A1
La Salvetat-sur-Agout F 130 B1
Las Arenas E 142 A2
La Sarraz CH 105 C5
Lasarte E 144 A1
Låsby DK 59 B2
Las Cabezadas E 151 A4
Las Cabezas de San Juan E 162 B2
Las Correderas E 157 B4
Las Cuevas de Cañart E 153 B3
La Seca E 150 A3
La Selva del Camp E 147 C2
La Senia E 153 B4
La Serra E 147 C2
La Seu d'Urgell E 146 B2
La Seyne-sur-Mer F 132 B1
Las Gabias E 163 A4
Las Herencias E 150 C3
Las Herrerias E 161 B2
Łasin PL 69 B4
Lask PL 86 A3
Laska PL 68 B2
Łaskarzow PL 87 A5
Laško SLO 123 A4
Laskowice PL 76 A3
Las Labores E 157 A4
Las Mesas E 158 B1
Las Minas E 164 A3
Las Navas E 163 A3
Las Navas de la Concepción E 156 C2
Las Navas del Marqués E 150 B3
Las Navillas E 157 A3
Las Negras E 164 C3
La Solana E 157 B4
La Souterraine F 116 A1
Las Pajanosas E 161 B3
Laspaules E 145 B4
Las Pedroñas E 158 B1
La Spézia I 134 A2
Las Planes d'Hostoles E 147 B3
Laspuña E 145 B4
Las Rozas
Cantabria E 142 B2
Madrid E 151 B4
Lassan D 66 C2
Lassay-les-Châteaux F 89 B3
Lasseube F 145 A3
Lassigny F 90 B2
La Storta I 168 B2
Lastovo HR 138 C2
Lastras de Cuéllar E 151 A3
Lästringe S 56 B3
Lastrup D 71 B4
Las Uces E 149 A3
La Suze-sur-Sarthe F 102 B2
Las Veguillas E 149 B4
Las Ventas con Peña Aguilera E 157 A3
Las Ventas de San Julián E 150 B2
Las Villes E 153 B4
Latasa E 144 B2
Látera I 168 A1
Laterza I 171 C4
La Teste F 128 B1
Lathen D 71 B4
Latheron GB 32 C3
La Thuile I 119 B3
Latiano I 173 B3
Latina I 169 B2
Latisana I 122 B2
Látky SK 99 C3
La Toba E 152 B2
La Toledana E 157 A3
La Torre de Cabdella E 146 B1
La Torre de Esteban Hambrán E 151 B3
La Torre del l'Espanyol E 153 A4
La Torresaviñán E 152 B1
La Tour d'Aigues F 132 B1
La Tour de Peilz CH 106 C1
La Tour-du-Pin F 118 B2
La Tranche-sur-Mer F 114 B2
La Tremblade F 114 C2
La Trimouille F 115 B5
La Trinité F 100 B2
La Trinité-Porhoët F 101 A3
Latrónico I 174 A2
Latronquière F 116 C2
Latterbach CH 106 C2
La Turballe F 101 B3
Laubach D 81 B4
Laubert F 117 C3
Laucha D 83 A3
Lauchhammer D 84 A1
Lauchheim D 94 C2
Lauda-Königshofen D 94 B1
Laudal N 52 B3
Lauder GB 35 C5
Lauenau D 72 B2
Lauenburg D 73 A3
Lauf D 95 B3

Laufach D 94 A1
Laufen
CH 106 B2
D 109 B3
Lauffen D 93 B5
Laugar IS 191 B8
Laugarás IS 190 C5
Laugarbakki IS 190 B5
Laugarvatn IS 190 C5
Laugharne GB 39 C2
Lauingen D 94 C2
Laujar de Andarax
E 164 C2
Laukaa FIN 8 A4
Lauker S 196 D2
Laukvik N 194 C5
La Uña E 142 A1
Launceston GB 42 B2
La Unión E 165 B4
Launois-sur-Vence
F 91 B4
Laupheim D 94 C1
Lauragh IRL 29 C2
Laureana di Borrello
I 175 C2
Laurencekirk GB 35 B5
Laurencetown IRL 28 A3
Laurenzana I 172 B1
Lauria I 174 A1
Laurière F 116 A1
Laurieston GB 36 B2
Laurino I 172 B1
Lausanne CH 106 C1
Laussonne F 117 C4
Lauta D 84 A2
Lautenthal D 82 A2
Lauterach A 107 B4
Lauterbach D 81 B5
Lauterbrunnen CH 106 C2
Lauterecken D 93 B3
Lauterhofen D 95 B3
Lautrec F 130 B1
Lauvsnes N 199 A7
Lauvvlk N 52 B2
Lauzerte F 129 B4
Lauzès F 129 B4
Lauzun F 129 B3
Lavagna I 134 A2
Laval F 102 A1
La Vall d'Uixó E 159 B3
Lavamünd A 110 C1
Lavara GR 186 A1
Lavardac F 129 B3
Lavaris P 148 B1
Lavarone I 121 B4
Lavau F 104 B1
Lavaur F 129 C4
La Vecilla de Curueño
E 142 B1
La Vega
Asturias E 141 A5
Asturias E 142 A1
Cantabria E 142 A2
Lavelanet F 146 B2
La Velilla E 151 A4
La Velles E 150 A2
Lavello I 172 A1
Lavelsloh D 72 B1
Lavenham GB 45 A4
Laveno I 120 B1
La Ventosa E 152 B1
Lavezzola I 135 A4
Laviano I 172 B1
La Victoria E 162 A3
La Vid E 151 A4
Lavik N 46 A2
La Vilavella E 159 B3
La Vilella Baixa E 147 C1
La Villa de Don Fadrique
E 157 A4
Lavilledieu F 131 A3
La Villedieu F 115 B3
La Ville Dieu-du-Temple
F 129 B4
Lavinio-Lido di Enea
I 168 B2
Lav is I 121 A4
Lavit F 129 C3
Lavoncourt F 105 B4
Lavos P 148 B1
La Voulte-sur-Rhône
F 117 C4
Lavoûte-Chilhac F 117 B3
Lavradio P 154 C1
Lavre P 154 C2
Lavrio GR 185 B5
La Wantzenau F 93 C3
Lawers GB 35 B3
Ławy PL 75 B3
Laxå S 55 B5
Laxamýri IS 191 B8
Laxe E 140 A2
Laxey GB 36 B2
Laxford Bridge GB 32 C1
Laxhall S 55 B4
Laxsjö S 199 B11
Laxtjarn S 49 B6
Laxvik S 61 C2
Laxviken S 199 B11
La Yesa E 159 B3
Laza E 141 B3
Lazarevac SRB 127 C2
Lazarevo SRB 126 B2
Lazise I 121 B3
Łaziska Grn. PL 86 B2
Lazkao E 144 A1
Lázně Bělohrad CZ 84 B3
Lázně Bohdaneč
CZ 97 A3
Lázně Kynžvart CZ 95 A4
Lazonby GB 37 B4
La Zubia E 163 A4
Łazy PL 67 B5
Lazzaro I 175 D1
Lea GB 40 B3
Leadburn GB 35 C4
Leadhills GB 36 A3
Leap IRL 29 C2
Leatherhead GB 44 B3
Łeba PL 68 A2
Lebach D 92 B2
Le Barp F 128 B2
Le Bar-sur-Loup F 132 B2
Le Béage F 117 C4
Le Beausset F 132 B1
Lebekke B 79 A4
Lébény H 111 B4
Le Bessat F 117 B4
Le Blanc F 115 B5
Le Bleymard F 130 A2
Łebno PL 68 A3
Leboreiro E 140 B3
Lębork PL 68 A2
Le Boullay-Mivoye
F 89 B5
Le Boulou F 146 B3
Le Bourg F 129 B4
Le Bourg-d'Oisans
F 118 B3
Le Bourget-du-Lac
F 118 B2
Le Bourgneuf-la-Forêt
F 101 A5
Le Bousquet d'Orb
F 130 B2
Le Brassus CH 105 C5
Le Breuil F 117 A3
Le Breuil-en-Auge F 89 A4
Lebrija E 162 B1
Lebring A 110 C2
Le Brusquet F 132 A2
Le Bry CH 106 C2
Le Bugue F 129 B3
Le Buisson F 129 B3
Lebus D 74 B3
Lebusa D 83 A5
Leca da Palmeira
P 148 A1
Le Caloy F 128 C2
Le Cap d'Agde F 130 B2
Le Cateau Cambrésis
F 91 A3
Le Caylar F 130 B2
Le Cayrol F 116 C2
Lecce I 173 B4
Lecco I 120 B2
Lécera E 153 A3
Lećevica HR 138 B2
Lech A 107 B5
Le Chambon-
Feugerolles F 117 B4
Le Chambon-sur-Lignon
F 117 B4
Le Château d'Oléron
F 114 C2
Le Châtelard F 118 B3
Le Châtelet F 103 C4
Le Chatelet-en-Brie
F 90 C2
Lechbruck D 108 B1
Lechena GR 184 B2
Le Chesne F 91 B4
Le Cheylard F 117 C4
Lechlade GB 44 B2
Lechovice CZ 97 C4
Leciñena E 145 C3
Leck D 64 B1
Le Collet-de-Deze
F 131 A2
Le Conquet F 100 A1
Le Creusot F 104 C3
Le Croisic F 101 B3
Le Crotoy F 78 B1
Lectoure F 129 C3
Łęczyca
Łódzkie PL 77 B4
Zachodnio-Pomorskie
PL 75 A4
Ledaña E 158 B2
Ledbury GB 39 B4
Lede B 79 B3
Ledečnad Sazavou
CZ 97 B3
Ledenice CZ 96 C2
Le Deschaux F 105 C4
Ledesma E 149 A3
Lédignan F 131 B3
Lédigos E 142 B2
Ledmore GB 32 C2
Lednice CZ 97 C4
Lednicke-Rovné SK 98 B2
Le Donjon F 117 A3
Le Dorat F 115 B5
Lędyczek PL 68 B1
Lędziny PL 86 B3
Leeds GB 40 B2
Leek
GB 40 B1
NL 71 A3
Leenaun IRL 28 A2
Leens NL 71 A3
Leer D 71 A4
Leerdam NL 79 A5
Leerhafe D 71 A4
Leese D 72 B2
Leeuwarden NL 70 A2
Leezen D 64 C3
Le Faou F 100 A1
Le Faoüet F 100 A2
Lefka CY 181 A1
Lefkada GR 182 E2
Lefkimis GR 182 D2
Lefkoniko CY 181 A2
Le Folgoet F 100 A1
Le Fossat F 146 A2
Le Fousseret F 146 A2
Le Fugeret F 132 A2
Leganés E 151 B4
Legau D 107 B5
Le Gault-Soigny F 91 C3
Legbąd PL 68 B2
Legé F 114 B2
Lège-Cap-Ferret F 128 B1
Legionowo PL 77 B5
Léglise B 92 B1
Legnago I 121 B4
Legnano I 120 B1
Legnaro I 121 B4
Legnica PL 85 A4
Łęgowo PL 69 A3
Legrad HR 124 A2
Le Grand-Bornand
F 118 B3
Le-Grand-Bourg F 116 A1
Le Grand-Lucé F 102 B2
Le Grand-Pressigny
F 102 C2
Le Grand-Quevilly F 89 A5
Le Grau-du-Roi F 131 B3
Léguevin F 129 C4
Legutiano E 143 B4
Le Havre F 89 A4
Lehesten D 82 B3
Lehnice SK 111 A4
Lehnin D 74 B1
Le Hohwald F 93 C3
Le Houga F 128 C2
Lehrberg D 94 B2
Lehre D 73 B3
Lehrte D 72 B2
Lehsen D 73 A4
Leibnitz A 110 C2
Leicester GB 40 C2
Leiden NL 70 B1
Leidschendam NL 70 B1
Leigh GB 38 A4
Leighlinbridge IRL 30 B2
Leighton Buzzard
GB 44 B3
Leignon B 79 B5
Leikanger N 198 C2
Leimen D 93 B4
Leinefelde D 82 A2
Leinesfjord N 194 C6
Leintwardine GB 39 B4
Leipojärvi S 196 B4
Leipzig D 83 A4
Leira
Nordland N 195 D4
Oppland N 47 B6
Leirámoen N 195 D5
Leiria P 154 B2
Leirvassbu N 47 A5
Leirvik
Hordaland N 52 A1
Sogn og Fjordane
N 46 A2
Leisach A 109 C3
Leisnig D 83 A4
Leiston GB 45 A5
Leitholm GB 35 C5
Leitrim IRL 26 C2
Leitza E 144 A2
Leitzkau D 73 B4
Lejkowo PL 68 A1
Lekani GR 183 B6
Łękawa PL 86 A3
Łekawica PL 99 B3
Lekeitio E 143 A4
Lekenik HR 124 B2
Lekeryd S 62 A2
Leknes N 194 B4
Łęknica PL 84 A2
Leksand S 50 B1
Leksvik N 199 B7
Lekunberri E 144 A2
Lekvattnet S 49 B4
Le Lardin-St Lazare
F 129 A4
Le Lauzet-Ubaye F 132 A2
Le Lavandou F 132 B2
Le Lion-d'Angers
F 102 B1
Lelkowo PL 69 A5
Le Locle CH 106 B1
Le Loroux-Bottereau
F 101 B4
Le Louroux-Béconnais
F 101 B5
Lelów PL 86 B3
Le Luc F 132 B2
Le Lude F 102 B2
Lelystad NL 70 B2
Lem
Ringkøbing DK 59 B1
Viborg Amt. DK 58 B1
Le Malzieu-Ville F 116 C3
Le Mans F 102 A2
Le Mas-d'Azil F 146 A2
Le Massegros F 130 A2
Le Mayet-de-Montagne
F 117 A3
Le May-sur-Evre F 101 B5
Lembach F 93 B3
Lemberg F 93 B3
Lembèye F 145 A3
Lemelerveld NL 71 B3
Le Mêle-sur-Sarthe
F 89 B4
Le Ménil F 105 A5
Le Merlerault F 89 B4
Le Mesnil-sur-Oger
F 91 C4
Lemförde D 71 B5
Lemgo D 72 B1
Le Miroir F 105 C4
Lemland FIN 51 B7
Lemmer NL 70 B2
Le Molay-Littry F 88 A3
Le Monastier-sur-
Gazeille F 117 C3
Le Monêtier-les-Bains
F 118 C3
Le Mont-Dore F 116 B2
Le Montet F 116 A3
Le Mont-St Michel F 88 B2
Lempdes F 116 B3
Le Muret F 128 B2
Le Muy F 132 B2
Lemvig DK 58 B1
Lemwerder D 72 A1
Lena N 48 B2
Lenart SLO 110 C2
Lenartovce SK 99 C4
Lenauheim RO 126 B2
Lencloître F 102 C2
Lend A 109 B4
Lendalfoot GB 36 A2
Lendava SLO 111 C3
Lendery RUS 3 E12
Lendinara I 121 B4
Lendorf A 109 C4
Lendum DK 58 A3
Le Neubourg F 89 A4
Lengefeld D 83 B5
Lengerich
Niedersachsen D 71 B4
Nordrhein-Westfalen
D 71 B4
Lenggries D 108 B2
Lengyeltóti H 111 C4
Lenhovda S 62 B3
Lenk CH 106 C2
Lennartsfors S 54 A2
Lennestadt D 81 A4
Lennoxtown GB 35 C3
Leno I 120 B3
Lénola I 169 B3
Le Nouvion-en-
Thiérache F 91 A3
Lens
B 79 B3
F 78 B2
Lensahn D 65 B3
Lens Lestang F 117 B5
Lensvik N 198 B6
Lentellais E 141 B3
Lentföhrden D 64 C2
Lenti H 111 C3
Lentini I 177 B3
Lenungshammar S 54 A3
Lenzburg CH 106 B3
Lenzen D 73 A4
Lenzerheide CH 107 C4
Leoben A 110 B2
Leogang A 109 B3
Leominster GB 39 B4
León E 142 B1
Léon F 128 C1
Leonberg D 93 C5
Léoncel F 118 C2
Leonding A 96 C2
Leonessa I 169 A2
Leonforte I 177 B3
Leonidio GR 184 B3
Leopoldsburg B 79 A5
Leopoldsdorf im
Marchfeld A 111 A3
Leopoldshagen D 74 A2
Leova MD 17 B8
Le Palais F 100 B2
Le Parcq F 78 B2
Lepe E 161 B2
Le Péage-de-Roussillon
F 117 B4
Le Pellerin F 101 B4
Lepenou GR 182 E3
Le Perthus F 146 B3
Le Pertuis F 117 B4
Le Petit-Bornand F 118 B3
Lephin GB 31 B2
L'Epine F 132 A1
Le Poët F 132 A1
Lepoglava HR 124 A2
Le Poirè-sur-Vie F 114 B2
Le Pont CH 105 C5
Le Pont-de-Montvert
F 130 A2
Le Porge F 128 B1
Le Porge-Océan F 128 B1
Le Portel F 78 B1
Le Pouldu F 100 B2
Le Pouliguen F 101 B3
Leppäjärvi FIN 192 D7
Leppävirta FIN 8 A5
Leppin D 73 B4
le Prese I 120 A3
Lepsény H 112 C2
Le Puy-en-Velay F 117 B3
Le Puy-Ste Réparade
F 131 B4
Le Quesnoy F 79 B3
Léquile I 173 B4
Le Rayol F 132 B2
Lercara Friddi I 176 B2
Lerdal S 54 B2
Leré F 103 B4
Lérici I 134 A2
Lerin E 144 B2
Lerma E 143 B3
Lerm-et-Musset F 128 B2
Lermoos A 108 B1
Le Roeulx B 79 B4
Le Rouget F 116 C2
Lérouville F 92 C1
Le Rozier F 130 A2
Lerum S 60 B2
Le Russey F 106 B1
Lervik N 54 A1
Lerwick GB 33 A5
Lés E 145 B4
Les Abrets F 118 B2
Les Aix-d'Angillon
F 103 B4
Lesaka E 144 A2
Les Ancizes-Comps
F 116 B2
Les Andelys F 90 B1
Les Arcs
Savoie F 119 B3
Var F 132 B2
Les-Aubiers F 102 C1
Les Baux-de-Provence
F 131 B3
Les Bézards F 103 B4
Les Bois CH 106 B1
Les Bordes F 103 B4
Les Borges Blanques
E 147 C1
Les Borges del Camp
E 147 C2
Les Brunettes F 104 C2
Lesbury GB 37 A5
Les Cabannes F 146 B2
L'Escala E 147 B4
Lescar F 145 A3
L'Escarène F 133 B3
Lesce SLO 123 A3
Lescheraines F 118 B3
Lesconil F 100 B1
Les Contamines-
Montjoie F 118 B3
les Coves de Vinroma
E 153 B4
Les Déserts F 118 B2
Les Deux-Alpes F 118 C3
Les Diablerets CH 119 A4
Lesdins F 90 B3
Les Echelles F 118 B2
Le Sel-de-Bretagne
F 101 B4
Le Sentier CH 105 C5
Les Escaldes AND 146 B2
Les Essarts F 114 B2
Les Estables F 117 C4
Les Eyzies-de-Tayac
F 129 B4
Les Gets F 118 A3
Les Grandes-Ventes
F 89 A5
Les Haudères CH 119 A4
Les Herbiers F 114 B2
Les Hôpitaux-Neufs
F 105 C5
Lesično SLO 123 A4
Lésina I 171 B3
Lesjaskog N 198 C5
Lesjöfors S 49 C6
Leskovac SRB 16 D4
Leskova Dolina
SLO 123 B3
Leskovec
CZ 98 B1
SLO 123 B4
Leskovice CZ 97 B3
Leskovik AL 182 C2
Leslie GB 35 B4
Les Lucs-sur-Boulogne
F 114 B2
Les Mages F 131 A3
Lesmahagow GB 36 A3
Les Mazures F 91 B4
Les Mées F 132 A1
Lesmont F 91 C4
Les Mureaux F 90 C1
Leśna PL 84 A3
Lesneven F 100 A1
Leśnica PL 86 B2
Lešnica SRB 127 C1
Leśniów Wielkoplski
PL 75 C4
Lesnoye RUS 9 C9
Les Omergues F 132 A1
Les Ormes-sur-Voulzie
F 90 C3
Les Orres F 132 A2
Le Souquet F 128 C1
Lesparre-Médoc F 128 A2
l'Espérance F 91 B3
l'Esperou F 130 A2
Les Pieux F 88 A2
Lesponne F 145 A4
Les Ponts-de-Cé F 102 B1
Les Ponts-de-Martel
CH 106 C1
Les Praz F 119 B3
L'Espunyola E 147 B2
Les Riceys F 104 B3
Les Roches F 117 B4
Les Rosaires F 101 A3
Les Rosiers F 102 B1
Les Rousses F 105 C5
Les Sables-d'Olonne
F 114 B2
Lessach A 109 B4
Lessay F 88 A2
Lessebo S 62 B3
Les Settons F 104 B3
Lessines B 79 B3
L'Estany E 147 C3
Les Ternes F 116 B2
Lesterps F 115 B4
Les Thilliers en-Vexin
F 90 B1
Les Touches F 101 B4
Les Trois Moûtiers
F 102 B2
Les Vans F 131 A3
Les Verrières CH 105 C5
Les Vignes F 130 A2
Leswalt GB 36 B1
Leszno
Mazowieckie PL 77 B5
Wielkopolskie PL 85 A4
Leszno Górne PL 84 A3
Letchworth GB 44 B3
Le Teil F 131 A3
Le Teilleul F 88 B3
Le Temple-de-Bretagne
F 101 B4
Letenye H 111 C3
Le Theil F 89 B4
Le Thillot F 106 B1
Letino I 170 B2
Letohrad CZ 97 A4
Le Touquet-Paris-Plage
F 78 B1
Le Touvet F 118 B2
Letovice CZ 97 B4
Le Translay F 90 B1
Le Tréport F 90 A1
Letschin D 74 B3
Letterfrack IRL 28 A2
Letterkenny IRL 26 B3
Lettermacaward IRL 26 B2
Lettoch GB 32 D3
Letur E 164 A2
Letux E 153 A3
Letzlingen D 73 B4
Leucate F 146 B4
Leuchars GB 35 B5
Leuglay F 105 B3
Leuk CH 119 A4
Leukerbad CH 119 A4
Leumrabhagh GB 31 A2
Leuna D 83 A4
Leusden NL 70 B2
Leutenberg D 82 B3
Leuterschach D 108 B1
Leutershausen D 94 B2
Leutkirch D 107 B5
Leuven B 79 B4
Leuze-en-Hainaut B 79 B3
Le Val F 132 B2
Le Val-André F 101 A3
Le Val-d'Ajol F 105 B5
Levan AL 182 C1
Levanger N 199 B8
Levanjska Varoš
HR 125 B4
Lévanto I 134 A2
Levaré F 88 B3
Levata I 120 B3
Leveld N 47 B5
Leven
East Yorkshire
GB 41 B3
Fife GB 35 B5
Leverano I 173 B3
Le Verdon-sur-Mer
F 114 C2
Leverkusen D 80 A2
Levern D 72 B1
Le Vernet F 132 A2
Levet F 103 C4
Levice SK 112 A2
Lévico Terme I 121 A4
Levie F 180 B2
Levier F 105 C5
Le Vigan F 130 B2
Lévignen F 90 B2
le Ville I 135 B5
Levinovac HR 124 B3
Le Vivier-sur-Mer F 88 B2
Levoča SK 99 B4
Levroux F 103 C3
Lewes GB 45 C4
Lewin Brzeski PL 85 B5
Lewisham GB 44 B3
Leyburn GB 37 B5
Leyland GB 38 A4
Leysdown-on-Sea
GB 45 B4
Leysin CH 119 A4
Lezajsk PL 12 C5
Lézardrieux F 100 A2
Lézat-sur-Léze F 146 A2
Lezay F 115 B3
Lezhë AL 182 B1
Lézignan-Corbières
F 130 B1
Lezignan-la-Cèbe
F 130 B2
Ležimir SRB 126 B1

Lézinnes F 104 B3
Lezoux F 117 B3
Lezuza E 158 C1
Lhenice CZ 96 C2
Lherm F 146 A2
Lhommaizé F 115 B4
L'Hospitalet F 146 B2
L'Hospitalet de l'Infant E 147 D1
L'Hospitalet de Llobregat E 147 C3
L'Hospitalet-du-Larzac F 130 B2
Lhuître F 91 C4
Liancourt F 90 B2
Liart F 91 B4
Liatorp S 63 B2
Liatrie GB 32 D2
Libáň CZ 84 B3
Libceves CZ 84 B1
Liběchov CZ 84 B2
Liber E 141 B3
Liberec CZ 84 B3
Libiąż PL 86 B3
Libina CZ 98 B1
Libochovice CZ 84 B2
Libohovë AL 182 C2
Libourne F 128 B2
Libramont B 92 B1
Librazhd AL 182 B2
Librilla E 165 B3
Libros E 152 B2
Licata I 176 B2
Licciana Nardi I 134 A3
Licenza I 169 A2
Liceros E 151 A4
Lich D 81 B4
Lichères-près-Aigremont F 104 B2
Lichfield GB 40 C2
Lichtenau
A 97 C3
D 81 A4
Lichtenberg D 83 B3
Lichtenfels D 82 B3
Lichtensteig CH 107 B4
Lichtenstein D 83 B4
Lichtenvoorde NL 71 C3
Lichtervelde B 78 A3
Lička Jesenica HR 123 B4
Lickershamn S 57 C4
Lički Osik HR 123 C4
Ličko Lešce HR 123 C4
Licodía Eubéa I 177 B3
Licques F 78 B1
Lida BY 13 B6
Lidar N 47 A6
Lidečko CZ 98 B2
Liden S 200 D2
Lidhult S 60 C3
Lidköping S 55 B4
Lido I 122 B1
Lido Azzurro I 173 B3
Lido degli Estensi I 122 C1
Lido degli Scacchi I 122 C1
Lido della Nazioni I 122 C1
Lido di Camaiore I 134 B3
Lido di Casalbordino I 169 A4
Lido di Castél Fusano I 168 B2
Lido di Cincinnato I 168 B2
Lido di Classe I 135 A5
Lido di Fermo I 136 B2
Lido di Fondi I 169 B3
Lido di Jésolo I 122 B1
Lido di Lícola I 170 C2
Lido di Metaponto I 174 A2
Lido di Óstia I 168 B2
Lido di Policoro I 174 A2
Lido di Pomposa I 122 C1
Lido di Savio I 135 A5
Lido di Scanzano I 174 A2
Lido di Siponto I 171 B3
Lido di Squillace I 175 C2
Lido di Volano I 122 C1
Lido Riccio I 169 A4
Lidoriki GR 184 A3
Lido Silvana I 173 B3
Lidsjöberg S 199 A12
Lidzbark PL 77 A4
Lidzbark Warmiński PL 69 A5
Liebenau
A 96 C2
D 72 B2
Liebenwalde D 74 B2
Lieberose D 74 C3
Liebling RO 126 B3
Lieboch A 110 C2
Liège B 80 B1
Lieksa FIN 3 E12
Lienen D 71 B4
Lienz A 109 C3
Liepāja LV 8 D2
Lier B 79 A4
Lierbyen N 54 A1
Liernais F 104 B3
Liesing A 109 C3
Liestal CH 106 B2
Liétor E 158 C2
Lieurac F 146 B2
Lieurey F 89 A4
Liévin F 78 B2
Liezen A 110 B1
Liffol-le-Grand F 92 C1
Lifford IRL 27 B3
Liffré F 101 A4
Ligardes F 129 B3
Lignano Sabbiadoro I 122 B2
Ligne F 101 B4
Lignières F 103 C4
Ligny-en-Barrois F 92 C1
Ligny-le-Châtel F 104 B2
Ligoła Polska PL 85 A5
Ligourio GR 184 B4
Ligowo PL 77 B4
Ligueil F 102 B2
Likavka SK 99 B3
Likenäs S 49 B5
Likhoslavl RUS 9 D9
Lild Strand DK 58 A1
L'Île-Bouchard F 102 B2
l'Île-Rousse F 180 A1
Lilienfeld A 110 A2
Lilienthal D 72 A1
Lilla Edet S 54 B3
Lilla Tjärby S 61 C3
Lille
B 79 A4
F 78 B3
Lillebonne F 89 A4
Lillehammer N 48 A2
Lillerød DK 61 D2
Lillers F 78 B2
Lillesand N 53 B4
Lillestrøm N 48 C3
Lillhärdal S 199 D11
Lillkyrka S 56 A3
Lillo E 157 A4
Lillögda S 200 B3
Lillpite S 196 D4
Lima S 49 B5
Limanowa PL 99 B4
Limassol CY 181 B2
Limavady GB 27 A4
Limbach-Oberfrohna D 83 B4
Limbaži LV 8 D4
Limbourg B 80 B1
Limburg D 81 B4
Lime DK 58 B3
Limedsforsen S 49 B5
Limenaria GR 183 C6
Limenas Chersonisou GR 185 D6
Limerick IRL 29 B3
Limes I 121 B3
Liméсу F 89 A4
Limmared S 60 B3
Limni GR 183 E5
Limoges F 115 C5
Limogne-en-Quercy F 129 B4
Limoise F 104 C2
Limone Piemonte I 133 A3
Limone sul Garda I 121 B3
Limons F 117 B3
Limours F 90 C2
Limoux F 146 A3
Linares E 157 B4
Linares de Mora E 153 B3
Linares de Riofrio E 149 B4
Linaria GR 183 E6
Linas de Broto E 145 B3
Lincoln GB 40 B3
Lind DK 59 B1
Lindås N 46 B2
Lindau D 107 B4
Lindberget N 48 A3
Lindelse DK 65 B3
Lindenberg D 74 B3
Lindenberg im Allgäu D 107 B4
Lindern D 71 B4
Linderöd S 61 D3
Lindesberg S 56 A1
Lindesnäs S 50 B1
Lindesnes N 52 C3
Lindholmen S 57 A4
Lindknud DK 59 C2
Lindlar D 80 A3
Lindö S 56 B2
Lindome S 60 B2
Lindos GR 188 C3
Lindoso P 148 A1
Lindow D 74 B1
Lindsdal S 62 B4
Lindshammar S 62 A3
Lindstedt D 73 B4
Lindved DK 59 C2
Líně CZ 96 B1
Lingbo S 50 A3
Lingen D 71 B4
Linghed S 50 B2
Linghem S 56 B1
Linguaglossa I 177 B4
Linia PL 68 A2
Linie PL 74 A3
Liniewo PL 68 A3
Linkenheim D 93 B4
Linköping S 56 B1
Linksness GB 33 C3
Linlithgow GB 35 C4
Linneryd S 63 B3
Linnes Hammarby S 51 C4
Linnich D 80 B2
Linsell S 199 C10
Linslade GB 44 B3
Linthal CH 107 C4
Linyola E 147 C1
Linz
A 96 C2
D 80 B3
Liomseter N 47 A6
Lionárisso CY 181 A3
Lioni I 172 B1
Lion-sur-Mer F 89 A3
Lipany SK 99 B4
Lipar SRB 126 B1
Lípari I 177 A3
Lipcani MD 17 A7
Liperi FIN 9 A6
Liphook GB 44 B3
Lipiany PL 75 A3
Lipik HR 124 B3
Lipka PL 68 B2
Lipki Wielkie PL 75 B4
Lipnica PL 68 B2
Lipnica Murowana PL 99 B4
Lipnik PL 87 B5
Lipník nad Bečvou CZ 98 B1
Lipno
Kujawsko-Pomorskie PL 77 B4
Łódzkie PL 86 A2
Liposthey F 128 B2
Lipovac HR 125 B5
Lipovec CZ 97 B4
Lipovets UA 13 D8
Lipovljani HR 124 B2
Lipowiec PL 77 A6
Lipowina PL 69 A4
Lippborg D 81 A4
Lippó H 125 B4
Lippoldsberg D 81 A5
Lippstadt D 81 A4
Lipsko PL 87 A5
Liptál CZ 98 B1
Liptovská-Lúžna SK 99 C3
Liptovská Osada SK 99 C3
Liptovská-Teplička SK 99 C4
Liptovský Hrádok SK 99 B3
Liptovský Milkuláš SK 99 B3
Lipusz PL 68 A2
Lipůvka CZ 97 B4
Liré F 101 B4
Lisac BIH 139 A3
Lisbellaw GB 27 B3
Lisboa = Lisbon P 154 C1
Lisbon = Lisboa P 154 C1
Lisburn GB 27 B4
Liscannor IRL 28 B2
Lisdoonvarna IRL 28 A2
Lisewo PL 69 B3
Lisia Góra PL 87 B5
Lisięcice PL 86 B1
Lisieux F 89 A4
Lisjö S 56 A2
Liskeard GB 42 B2
L'Isle CH 105 C5
L'Isle-Adam F 90 B2
L'Isle-de-Noé F 129 C3
L'Isle-en-Dodon F 145 A4
L'Isle-Jourdain
Gers F 129 C4
Vienne F 115 B4
L'Isle-sur-la-Sorgue F 131 B4
L'Isle-sur-le Doubs F 105 B5
L'Isle-sur-Serein F 104 B3
Lisle-sur-Tarn F 129 C4
Lismore IRL 29 B4
Lisnaskea GB 27 B3
Lišov CZ 96 B2
Lisów
Lubuskie PL 74 B3
Śląskie PL 86 B2
Lisse NL 70 B1
Lissycasey IRL 28 B2
List D 64 A1
Listerby S 63 B3
Listowel IRL 29 B2
Listrac-Médoc F 128 A2
Liszki PL 99 A3
Liszkowo PL 76 A2
Lit S 199 B11
Litava SK 99 C3
Litcham GB 41 C4
Lit-et-Mixe F 128 B1
Litija SLO 123 A3
Litke H 112 A3
Litlabø N 52 A1
Litochoro GR 182 C4
Litoměřice CZ 84 B2
Litomyšl CZ 97 B4
Litovel CZ 98 B1
Litschau A 96 C3
Littlehampton GB 44 C3
Littleport GB 45 A4
Littleton IRL 29 B4
Little Walsingham GB 41 C4
Litvinov CZ 83 B5
Livadero GR 182 C3
Livadhia CY 181 B2
Livadi GR 182 C4
Livadia GR 184 A3
Livarot F 89 B4
Liveras CY 181 A1
Livernon F 129 B4
Liverovici MNE 139 C5
Liverpool GB 38 A4
Livigno I 107 C5
Livingston GB 35 C4
Livno BIH 138 B2
Livo FIN 197 D9
Livold SLO 123 B3
Livorno I 134 B3
Livorno Ferraris I 119 B5
Livron-sur-Drôme F 117 C4
Livry-Louvercy F 91 B4
Lixheim F 92 C3
Lixouri GR 184 A1
Lizard GB 42 C1
Lizy-sur-Ourcq F 90 B3
Lizzano I 173 B3
Lizzano in Belvedere I 135 A3
Ljig SRB 127 C2
Ljørdalen N 49 A4
Ljosland N 52 B3
Ljubija BIH 124 C2
Ljubinje BIH 139 C4
Ljubljana SLO 123 A3
Ljubno ob Savinji SLO 123 A3
Ljubovija SRB 127 C1
Ljubuški BIH 138 B3
Ljugarn S 57 C4
Ljung S 60 B3
Ljunga S 56 B2
Ljungaverk S 200 D2
Ljungby S 60 C3
Ljungbyhed S 61 C3
Ljungbyholm S 63 B4
Ljungdalen S 199 C9
Ljungsarp S 60 B3
Ljungsbro S 56 B1
Ljungskile S 54 B2
Ljusdal S 200 E2
Ljusfallshammar S 56 B1
Ljusne S 51 A4
Ljusterö S 57 A4
Ljutomer SLO 111 C3
Lŭki BG 183 B6
Lladurs E 147 B2
Llafranc E 147 C4
Llagostera E 147 C3
Llanaelhaiarn GB 38 B2
Llanarth GB 39 B2
Llanbedr GB 38 B2
Llanbedrog GB 38 B2
Llanberis GB 38 A2
Llanbister GB 39 B3
Llanbrynmair GB 39 B3
Llançà E 146 B4
Llandeilo GB 39 C3
Llandissilio GB 39 C2
Llandovery GB 39 C3
Llandrillo GB 38 B3
Llandrindod Wells GB 39 B3
Llandudec F 100 A1
Llandudno GB 38 A3
Llandysul GB 39 B2
Llanelli GB 39 C2
Llanerchymedd GB 38 A2
Llanes E 142 A2
Llanfair Caereinion GB 38 B3
Llanfairfechan GB 38 A3
Llanfyllin GB 38 B3
Llangadog GB 39 C3
Llangefni GB 38 A2
Llangollen GB 38 B3
Llangrannog GB 39 B2
Llangurig GB 39 B3
Llanidloes GB 39 B3
Llanilar GB 39 B2
Llanrhystud GB 39 B2
Llanrwst GB 38 A3
Llansannan GB 38 A3
Llansawel GB 39 B2
Llanstephan GB 39 C2
Llanteno E 143 A3
Llanthony GB 39 C3
Llantrisant GB 39 C3
Llantwit-Major GB 39 C3
Llanuwchllyn GB 38 B3
Llanwddyn GB 38 B3
Llanwrda GB 39 C3
Llanwrtyd Wells GB 39 B3
Llanybydder GB 39 B2
Llanymynech GB 38 B3
Llavorsi E 146 B2
Lleida E 153 A4
Llera E 156 B1
Llerena E 156 B1
Lles E 146 B2
Llessui E 146 B2
Llinars E 147 B2
Lliria E 159 B3
Llivia E 146 B2
Llodio E 143 A4
Lloret de Mar E 147 C3
Llosa de Ranes E 159 B3
Lloseta E 167 B2
Llucena del Cid E 153 B3
Llucmajor E 167 B2
Llutxent E 159 C3
Llwyngwril GB 38 B2
Llyswen GB 39 B3
Lnáře CZ 96 B1
Lniano PL 76 A3
Loanhead GB 35 C4
Loano I 133 A4
Loarre E 145 B3
Löbau D 84 A2
Löbejün D 83 A3
Löberöd S 61 D3
Łobez PL 75 A4
Löbnitz D 66 B1
Lobón E 155 C4
Loburg D 73 B5
Łobżenica PL 76 A2
Locana I 119 B4
Locarno CH 120 A1
Loccum D 72 B2
Loče SLO 123 A4
Lochailort GB 34 B2
Lochaline GB 34 B2
Lochans GB 36 B1
Locharbriggs GB 36 A3
Lochau A 107 B4
Loch Baghasdail GB 31 B1
Lochcarron GB 31 B3
Lochearnhead GB 34 B3
Lochem NL 71 B3
Loches F 102 B2
Lochgelly GB 35 B4
Lochgilphead GB 34 B2
Lochgoilhead GB 34 B3
Lochinver GB 32 C1
Loch nam Madadh GB 31 B1
Lochranza GB 34 C2
Ločika SRB 127 D3
Lockenhaus A 111 B3
Lockerbie GB 36 A3
Löcknitz D 74 A3
Locmaria F 100 B2
Locmariaquer F 100 B3
Locminé F 100 B3
Locorotondo I 173 B3
Locquirec F 100 A2
Locri I 175 C2
Locronan F 100 A1
Loctudy F 100 B1
Lodares de Osma E 151 A5
Lodé I 178 B3
Lodeinoye Pole RUS 9 B8
Lodève F 130 B2
Lodi I 120 B2
Løding N 194 C5
Lødingen N 194 B6
Lodosa E 144 B1
Lödöse S 54 B3
Łódź PL 86 A3
Loeches E 151 B4
Løfallstrand N 46 B3
Lofer A 109 B3
Lofsdalen S 199 C10
Loftahammar S 62 A4
Lofthus N 46 B3
Loftus GB 37 B6
Loga N 52 B2
Logatec SLO 123 B3
Lögdeå S 200 C5
Lograto I 120 B3
Logroño E 143 B4
Logrosán E 156 A2
Løgstør DK 58 B2
Løgumgårde DK 64 A1
Løgumkloster DK 64 A1
Lohals DK 65 A3
Lohiniva FIN 197 B8
Lohja FIN 8 B4
Löhlbach D 81 A4
Lohmen
Mecklenburg-Vorpommern D 65 C5
Sachsen D 84 B2
Löhnberg D 81 B4
Lohne D 71 B5
Löhne D 72 B1
Lohr D 94 B1
Lohra D 81 B4
Lohsa D 84 A2
Loiano I 135 A4
Loimaa FIN 8 B3
Lóiri I 178 B3
Loitz D 66 C2
Loivos P 148 A2
Loivos do Monte P 148 A2
Loja E 163 A3
Lojanice SRB 127 C1
Lojsta S 57 C4
Løjt Kirkeby DK 64 A2
Lok SK 112 A2
Lokca SK 99 B3
Løken N 54 A2
Lokeren B 79 A3
Loket CZ 83 B4
Lokka FIN 197 B10
Løkken
DK 58 A2
N 198 B6
Loknya RUS 9 D7
Lökösháza H 113 C5
Lokve SRB 126 B3
Lollar D 81 B4
L'Olleria E 159 C3
Lölling-Graben A 110 C1
Lom
BG 17 D5
N 198 D5
Lom SK 99 C3
Lombez F 146 A1
Lomello I 120 B1
Łomianki PL 77 B5
Lomma S 61 D3
Lommaryd S 62 A2
Lommatzsch D 83 A5
Lommel B 79 A5
Lommersum D 80 B2
Lomnice CZ 97 B4
Lomnice nad Lužnici CZ 96 B2
Lomnice-nad Popelkou CZ 84 B3
Lompolo FIN 196 A7
Łomza PL 12 B5
Lönashult S 63 B2
Lønborg DK 59 C1
Londerzeel B 79 A4
Londinières F 89 A5
London GB 44 B3
Lonevåg N 46 B2
Longa GR 184 C2
Longare I 121 B4
Longares E 152 A2
Longarone I 122 A1
Longastrino I 135 A5
Long Bennington GB 40 C3
Longbenton GB 37 A5
Longchamp-sur-Aujon F 105 A3
Longchaumois F 118 A2
Long Eaton GB 40 C2
Longeau F 105 B4
Longecourt-en-Plaine F 105 B4
Longeville-les-St Avold F 92 B2
Longeville-sur-Mer F 114 B2
Longford IRL 28 A4
Longframlington GB 37 A5
Longhope GB 33 C3
Longhorsley GB 37 A5
Longhoughton GB 37 A5
Longi I 177 A3
Long Melford GB 45 A4
Longny-au-Perche F 89 B4
Longobucco I 174 B2
Long Preston GB 40 A1
Longré F 115 B3
Longridge GB 38 A4
Longroiva P 149 B2
Long Sutton GB 41 C4
Longtown
Cumbria GB 36 A4
Herefordshire GB 39 C4
Longueau F 90 B2
Longué-Jumelles F 102 B1
Longuyon F 92 B1
Longvic F 105 B4
Longvilly B 92 A1
Longwy F 92 B1
Lonigo I 121 B4
Löningen D 71 B4
Lonja HR 124 B2
Lönneberga S 62 A3
Lönsboda S 63 B2
Lønset N 198 C6
Lons-le-Saunier F 105 C4
Lønstrup DK 58 A2
Looe GB 42 B2
Loone-Plage F 78 A2
Loon op Zand NL 79 A5
Loosdorf A 110 A2
Lo Pagán E 165 B4
Lopar HR 123 C3
Lopare BIH 125 C4
Lopera E 157 C3
Lopigna F 180 A1
Loppersum NL 71 A3
Łopuszna PL 99 B4
Łopuszno PL 87 B4
Lor F 91 B4
Lora N 198 C5
Lora de Estepa E 162 A3
Lora del Río E 162 A2
Loranca del Campo E 151 B5
Lörby S 63 B2
Lorca E 164 B3
Lorch D 93 A3
Lørenfallet N 48 B3
Lørenskog N 48 C2
Loreo I 122 B1
Loreto I 136 B2
Lorgues F 132 B2
Lorica I 174 B2
Lorient F 100 B2
Lorignac F 114 C3
Lörinci H 112 B3
Loriol-sur-Drôme F 117 C4
Lormes F 104 B2
Loro Ciuffenna I 135 B4
Lorqui E 165 A3
Lörrach D 106 B2
Lorrez-le-Bocage F 103 A4
Lorris F 103 B4
Lorup D 71 B4
Łoś PL 77 C5
Los S 199 D12
Losacino E 149 A3

Los Alcázares E 165 B4
Los Arcos E 144 B1
Losar de la Vera E 150 B2
Los Barios de Luna E 141 B5
Los Barrios E 162 B2
Los Caños de Meca E 162 B1
Los Cerricos E 164 B2
Los Corrales E 162 A3
Los Corrales de Buelna E 142 A2
Los Dolores E 165 B3
Losenstein A 110 B1
Los Gallardos E 164 B3
Losheim
Nordrhein-Westfalen D 80 B2
Saarland D 92 B2
Los Hinojosos E 158 B1
Los Isidros E 159 B2
Los Molinos E 151 B3
Los Morales E 162 A2
Los Navalmorales E 156 A3
Los Navalucillos E 156 A3
Losne F 105 B4
Los Nietos E 165 B4
Løsning DK 59 C2
Los Palacios y Villafranca E 162 A2
Los Pozuelos de Calatrava E 157 B3
Los Rábanos E 143 C4
Los Santos E 149 B4
Los Santos de la Humosa E 151 B4
Los Santos de Maimona E 155 C4
Lossburg D 93 C4
Losse F 128 B2
Losser NL 71 B4
Lossiemouth GB 32 D3
Lössnitz D 83 B4
Loštice CZ 97 B4
Los Tijos E 142 A2
Lostwithiel GB 42 B2
Los Villares E 163 A4
Los Yébenes E 157 A4
Løten N 48 B3
Lotorp S 56 B1
Lottefors S 50 A3
Löttorp S 62 A5
Lotyń PL 68 B1
Lotzorai I 179 C3
Louargat F 100 A2
Loudéac F 101 A3
Loudun F 102 B2
Loué F 102 B1
Loughborough GB 40 C2
Loughbrickland GB 27 B4
Loughrea IRL 28 A3
Louhans F 105 C4
Louisburgh IRL 28 A2
Loukhi RUS 3 C13
Loulay F 114 B3
Loulé P 160 B1
Louny CZ 84 B1
Lourdes F 145 A3
Lourenzá E 141 A3
Loures P 154 C1
Loures-Barousse F 145 A4
Louriçal P 154 A2
Lourinhã P 154 B1
Lourmarin F 131 B4
Loury F 103 B4
Lousa
Bragança P 149 A2
Castelo Branco P 155 B3
Lousã P 148 B1
Lousa P 154 C1
Lousada
E 140 B3
P 148 A1
Louth GB 41 B3
Loutra Edipsou GR 183 E5
Loutraki GR 184 B3
Loutropoli Thermis GR 186 C1
Louverné F 102 A1
Louvie-Juzon F 145 A3
Louviers F 89 A5
Louvigné-du-Désert F 88 B2
Louvois F 91 B4
Lova I 121 B5
Lovasberény H 112 B2
Lövåsen S 49 C5
Lovászpatona H 111 B4
Lövberga S 200 C1
Lovech BG 17 D6
Lövenich D 80 A2
Lóvere I 120 B3
Lövestad S 61 D3
Loviisa FIN 8 B5
Lovikka S 196 B5
Lovinobaňa SK 99 C3
Loviste HR 138 B3
Lovke HR 123 B3
Lovnäs S 49 A5
Lövö H 111 B3
Lovosice CZ 84 B2
Lovozero RUS 3 C14
Lovran HR 123 B3
Lovreć HR 138 B2
Lovrenc na Pohorju SLO 110 C2
Lovrin RO 126 B2
Lövstabruk S 51 B4
Löwenberg D 74 B2
Löwenstein D 94 B1
Lowestoft GB 41 C5
Lowick GB 37 A5
Łowicz PL 77 B4
Loxstedt D 72 A1
Loyew BY 13 C9
Lož SLO 123 B3
Loza CZ 96 B1
Łozina PL 85 A5
Loznica SRB 127 C1
Lozničko Polje SRB 127 C1
Lozorno SK 111 A4
Lozovik SRB 127 C3
Lozoya E 151 B4
Lozoyuela E 151 B4
Lozzo di Cadore I 109 C3
Luanco E 141 A5
Luarca E 141 A4
Lubaczów PL 13 C5
Lubań PL 84 A3
Lubanie PL 76 B3
Lubanów PL 86 A3
Lubars D 73 B5
Lubasz PL 75 B5
Lubawa PL 69 B4
Lubawka PL 85 B4
Lübbecke D 72 B1
Lübben D 74 C2
Lübbenau D 84 A1
Lubczyna PL 74 A3
Lübeck D 65 C3
Lubenec CZ 83 B5
Lubersac F 115 C5
Lübesse D 73 A4
Lubia E 152 A1
Lubian E 141 B4
Lubiatowo PL 75 A4
Lubichowo PL 69 B3
Lubicz Dolny PL 76 A3
Lubień PL 99 B3
Lubienia PL 87 A5
Lubień Kujawski PL 77 B4
Lubieszewo PL 75 A4
Lubin
Dolnośląskie PL 85 A4
Zachodnio-Pomorskie PL 67 C3
Lublin PL 12 C5
Lubliniec PL 86 B2
Lubmin D 66 B2
Lubniewice PL 75 B4
Lubochnia PL 87 A4
Lubomierz
Dolnośląskie PL 84 A3
Małopolskie PL 99 B4
Lubomino PL 69 A5
Luboń PL 76 B1
L'ubotín SK 99 B4
Lubowidz PL 77 A4
Łubowo
Wielkopolskie PL 76 B2
Zachodnio-Pomorskie PL 68 B1
Lubraniec PL 76 B3
Lubrin E 164 B2
Lubrza PL 85 B5
Lubsko PL 84 A2
Lübtheen D 73 A4
Lubuczewo PL 68 A2
Luby CZ 83 B4
Lübz D 73 A5
Luc F 117 C3
Lucainena de las Torres E 164 B2
Lucan IRL 30 A2
Lučani SRB 127 D2
Lúcar E 164 B2
Luçay-le-Mâle F 103 B3
Lucca I 134 B3
Lucciana F 180 A2
Lucé F 90 C1
Luče SLO 123 A3
Lucena
Córdoba E 163 A3
Huelva E 161 B3
Lucenay-les-Aix F 104 C2
Lucenay-l'Evéque F 104 B3
Luc-en-Diois F 118 C2
Lučenec SK 99 C3
Luceni E 144 C2
Lucens CH 106 C1
Lucera I 171 B3
Luceram F 133 B3
Lüchow D 73 B4
Luciana E 157 B3
Lucignano I 135 B4
Lucija SLO 122 B2
Lucka D 83 A4
Luckau D 84 A1
Luckenwalde D 74 B2
Lückstedt D 73 B4
Luco dei Marsi I 169 B3
Luçon F 114 B2
Luc-sur-Mer F 89 A3
Ludanice SK 98 C2
Ludbreg HR 124 A2
Lüdenscheid D 81 A3
Lüderitz D 73 B4
Lüdersdorf D 65 C3
Ludgershall GB 44 B2
Ludgo S 56 B3
Lüdinghausen D 80 A3
Ludlow GB 39 B4
Ludomy PL 75 B5
Ludvika S 50 B2
Ludweiler Warndt D 92 B2
Ludwigsburg D 94 C1
Ludwigsfelde D 74 B2
Ludwigshafen D 93 B4
Ludwigslust D 73 A4
Ludwigsstadt D 82 B3
Ludza LV 8 D5
Luesia E 144 B2
Luftkurort Arendsee D 73 B4
Lug
BIH 139 C4
HR 125 B4
Luga RUS 9 C6
Lugagnano Val d'Arda I 120 C2
Lugano CH 120 A1
Lugau D 83 B4
Lugnas S 55 B4
Lúgnola I 168 A2
Lugny F 105 C3
Lugo
E 140 A3
I 135 A4
Lugoj RO 16 C4
Lugones E 141 A5
Lugros E 163 A4
Luhačovice CZ 98 B1
Luhe D 95 B4
Luino I 120 B1
Luintra E 140 B3
Lújar E 163 B4
Luka nad Jihlavou CZ 97 B3
Lukavac BIH 125 C4
Lukavika BIH 125 C4
Lukovë AL 182 D1
Lukovica SLO 123 A3
Lukovit BG 17 D6
Lukovo HR 123 C3
Lukovo Šugorje HR 137 A4
Łuków PL 12 C5
Łukowice Brzeskie PL 85 B5
Luksefjell N 53 A5
Łukta PL 69 B5
Lula I 178 B3
Luleå S 196 D5
Lüleburgaz TR 186 A2
Lumbarda HR 138 C3
Lumbier E 144 B2
Lumbrales E 149 B3
Lumbreras E 143 B4
Lumbres F 78 B2
Lummelunda S 57 C4
Lummen B 79 B5
Lumparland FIN 51 B7
Lumpiaque E 152 A2
Lumsås DK 61 D1
Lumsden GB 33 D4
Lumsheden S 50 B3
Lun HR 123 C3
Luna E 144 B3
Lunamatrona I 179 C2
Lunano I 136 B1
Lunas F 130 B2
Lund
N 199 A8
Skåne S 61 D3
Västra Götaland S 54 A3
Lundamo N 199 B7
Lunde
DK 59 C1
Sogn og Fjordane N 46 A3
Sogn og Fjordane N 46 A3
Telemark N 53 A5
S 200 D3
Lundebyvollen N 49 B4
Lunden D 64 B2
Lunderseter N 49 B4
Lunderskov DK 59 C2
Lundsberg S 55 A5
Lüneburg D 72 A3
Lunel F 131 B3
Lünen D 81 A3
Lunéville F 92 C2
Lungern CH 106 C3
Lungro I 174 B2
Luninyets BY 13 B7
Lünne D 71 B4
Lunner N 48 B2
Lunteren NL 70 B2
Lunz am See A 110 B2
Luogosanto I 178 A3
Łupawa PL 68 A2
Lupión E 157 B4
Lupoglav HR 123 B3
Luppa D 83 A4
Luque E 163 A3
Lurago d'Erba I 120 B2
Lúras I 178 B3
Lurcy-Lévis F 104 C1
Lure F 105 B5
Lurgan GB 27 B4
Luri F 180 A2
Lury-sur-Arnon F 103 B4
Lušci Palanka BIH 124 C2
Lusévera I 122 A2
Lushnjë AL 182 C1
Lusignan F 115 B4
Lusigny-sur-Barse F 104 A3
Lusnić BIH 138 B2
Luso P 148 B1
Lusówko PL 75 B5
Luspebryggan S 196 B2
Luss GB 34 B3
Lussac F 128 B2
Lussac-les-Châteaux F 115 B4
Lussac-les-Eglises F 115 B5
Lussan F 131 A3
Lüssow D 65 C5
Lustenau A 107 B4
Luštěnice CZ 84 B2
Luster N 47 A4
Lutago I 108 C2
Lutherstadt Wittenberg D 83 A4
Lütjenburg D 65 B3
Lutnes N 49 A4
Lutocin PL 77 B4
Lutomiersk PL 86 A3
Luton GB 44 B3
Lutry CH 106 C1
Lutsk UA 13 C6
Lutter am Barenberge D 72 C3
Lutterworth GB 40 C2
Lututów PL 86 A2
Lützen D 83 A4
Lutzow D 73 A4
Luusua FIN 197 C10
Luvos S 196 C1
Luxembourg L 92 B2
Luxeuil-les-Bains F 105 B5
Luxey F 128 B2
Luz
Évora P 155 C3
Faro P 160 B1
Faro P 160 B2
Luzarches F 90 B2
Luže CZ 97 B4
Luzech F 129 B4
Luzern CH 106 B3
Luzino PL 68 A3
Luz-St Sauveur F 145 B3
Luzy F 104 C2
Luzzi I 174 B2
L'viv UA 13 D6
Lwówek PL 75 B5
Lwówek Śląski PL 84 A3
Lyakhavichy BY 13 B7
Lybster GB 32 C3
Lychen D 74 A2
Lychkova RUS 9 D8
Lyckeby S 63 B3
Lycksele S 200 B4
Lydd GB 45 C4
Lydford GB 42 B2
Lydney GB 39 C4
Lyepyel BY 13 A8
Lygna N 48 B2
Lykkja N 47 B5
Lykling N 52 A1
Lyme Regis GB 43 B4
Lymington GB 44 C2
Lympne GB 45 B5
Lyndhurst GB 44 C2
Lyneham GB 43 A5
Lyness GB 33 C3
Lyngdal
Buskerud N 47 C6
Vest-Agder N 52 B3
Lyngør N 53 B5
Lyngsa DK 58 A3
Lyngseidet N 192 C4
Lyngsnes N 199 A8
Lynmouth GB 42 A3
Lynton GB 42 A3
Lyntupy BY 13 A7
Lyon F 117 B4
Lyons-la-Forêt F 90 B1
Lyozna BY 13 A9
Lyrestad S 55 B5
Lysánad Labem CZ 84 B2
Lysápod Makytou SK 98 B2
Lysebotn N 52 A2
Lysekil S 54 B2
Lysice CZ 97 B4
Lysomice PL 76 A3
Lysøysund N 198 B6
Lyss CH 106 B2
Lystrup DK 59 B3
Lysvik S 49 B5
Łyszkowice PL 77 C4
Lytham St Anne's GB 38 A3
Lyuban RUS 9 C7
Lyubertsy RUS 9 E10
Lyubimets BG 183 B8
Lyuboml' UA 13 C6
Lyubytino RUS 9 C8

M

Maaninkavaara FIN 197 C11
Maarheeze NL 80 A1
Maaseik B 80 A1
Maastricht NL 80 B1
Mablethorpe GB 41 B4
Mably F 117 A4
Macael E 164 B2
Maçanet de Cabrenys E 146 B3
Mação P 154 B2
Macau F 128 A2
Maccagno-Agra I 120 A1
Maccarese I 168 B2
Macchiagódena I 170 B2
Macclesfield GB 40 B1
Macduff GB 33 D4
Maceda E 140 B3
Macedo de Cavaleiros P 149 A3
Maceira
Guarda P 148 B2
Leiria P 154 B2
Macelj HR 124 A1
Macerata I 136 B2
Macerata Féltria I 136 B1
Machault F 91 B4
Machecoul F 114 B2
Mchowo PL 77 A5
Machrihanish GB 34 C2
Machynlleth GB 39 B3
Macieira P 148 A1
Maciejowice PL 87 A5
Macinaggio F 180 A2
Mackenrode D 82 A2
Mačkovci SLO 111 C3
Macomer I 178 B2
Macon B 91 A4
Mâcon F 117 A4
Macotera E 150 B2
Macroom IRL 29 C3
Macugnaga I 119 B4
Madan BG 183 B6
Madängsholm S 55 B4
Madaras H 126 A1
Maddaloni I 170 B2
Made NL 79 A4
Madeley GB 38 B4
Maderuelo E 151 A4
Madetkoski FIN 197 B9
Madley GB 39 B4
Madocsa H 112 C2
Madona LV 8 D5
Madonna di Campíglio I 121 A3
Madrid E 151 B4
Madridejos E 157 A4
Madrigal de las Altas Torres E 150 A2
Madrigal de la Vera E 150 B2
Madrigalejo E 156 A2
Madrigalejo de Monte E 143 B3
Madriguera E 151 A4
Madrigueras E 158 B2
Madroñera E 156 A2
Maël-Carhaix F 100 A2
Maella E 153 A4
Maello E 150 B3
Maesteg GB 39 C3
Mafra P 154 C1
Magacela E 156 B2
Magallon E 144 C2
Magaluf E 166 B2
Magán E 151 C4
Magaña E 144 C1
Magasa I 121 B3
Magaz E 142 C2
Magdeburg D 73 B4
Magenta I 120 B1
Magescq F 128 C1
Maghera GB 27 B4
Magherafelt GB 27 B4
Maghull GB 38 A4
Magione I 135 B5
Maglaj BIH 125 C4
Maglehem S 63 C2
Magliano de'Marsi I 169 A3
Magliano in Toscana I 168 A1
Magliano Sabina I 168 A2
Maglić SRB 126 B1
Máglie I 173 B4
Maglód H 112 B3
Magnac-Bourg F 115 C5
Magnac-Laval F 115 B5
Magnieres F 92 C2
Magnor N 49 C4
Magnuszew PL 87 A5
Magny-Cours F 104 C2
Magny-en-Vexin F 90 B1
Mágocs H 125 A4
Magoute P 154 C1
Maguilla E 156 B2
Maguiresbridge GB 27 B3
Magyarbóly H 125 B4
Magyarkeszi H 112 C2
Magyarszék H 125 A4
Mahide E 141 C4
Mahilyow BY 13 B9
Mahmudiye TR 187 C5
Mahora E 158 B2
Mahovo HR 124 B2
Mähring D 95 B4
Maia
E 144 A2
P 148 A1
Maiaelrayo E 151 A4
Maials E 153 A4
Maîche F 106 B1
Màida I 175 C2
Maiden Bradley GB 43 A4
Maidenhead GB 44 B3
Maiden Newton GB 43 B4
Maidstone GB 45 B4
Maienfeld CH 107 B4
Maignelay Montigny F 90 B2
Maijanen FIN 197 B8
Maillezais F 114 B3
Mailly-le-Camp F 91 C4
Mailly-le-Château F 104 B2
Mainar E 152 A2
Mainbernheim D 94 B2
Mainburg D 95 C3
Mainhardt D 94 B1
Maintal D 81 B4
Maintenon F 90 C1
Mainvilliers F 90 C1
Mainz D 93 A4
Maiorca P 148 B1
Mairena de Aljarafe E 162 A1
Mairena del Alcor E 162 A2
Maisach D 108 A2
Maishofen A 109 B3
Maison-Rouge F 90 C3
Maissau A 97 C3
Maisse F 90 C2
Maizières-lès-Vic F 92 C2
Maja HR 124 B2
Majadahonda E 151 B4
Majadas E 150 C2
Majavatn N 195 E4
Majs H 125 B4
Majšperk SLO 123 A4
Makarska HR 138 B3
Makkum NL 70 A2
Maklár H 113 B4
Makó H 126 A2
Makoszyce PL 85 B5
Makov SK 98 B2
Mąkowarsko PL 76 A2
Maków Mazowiecki PL 77 B6
Maków Podhalański PL 99 B3
Makrakomi GR 182 E4
Maksniemi FIN 196 D7
Malå S 195 E9
Mala Bosna SRB 126 A1
Malacky SK 97 C5
Maladzyechna BY 13 A7
Málaga E 163 B3
Malagón E 157 A4
Malaguilla E 151 B4
Malahide IRL 30 A2
Mala Kladuša BIH 124 B1
Mala Krsna SRB 127 C3
Malalbergo I 121 C4
Malá Lehota SK 98 C2
Malanów PL 76 C3
Mala Pijace SRB 126 A1
Mala Subotica HR 124 A2
Malaucène F 131 A4
Malaunay F 89 A5
Malaya Vishera RUS 9 C8
Malborghetto I 109 C4
Malbork PL 69 A4
Malborn D 92 B2
Malbuisson F 105 C5
Malcésine I 121 B3
Malchin D 74 A1
Malching D 96 C1
Malchow D 73 A5
Malcocinado E 156 B2
Malczyce PL 85 A4
Maldegem B 79 A3
Maldon GB 45 B4
Małdyty PL 69 B4
Malè I 121 A3
Malemort F 129 A4
Malente D 65 B3
Målerås S 62 B3
Males GR 185 D6
Malesherbes F 90 C2
Malesina GR 183 E5
Malestroit F 101 B3
Maletto I 177 B3
Malexander S 56 B1
Malgrat de Mar E 147 C3
Malhadas P 149 A3
Malia
CY 181 B1
GR 185 D6
Malicorne-sur-Sarthe F 102 B1
Malijai F 132 A2
Malildjoš SRB 126 B1
Målilla S 62 A3
Mali Lošinj HR 137 A3
Malin IRL 27 A3
Málinec SK 99 C3
Malingsbo S 50 C2
Maliniec PL 76 B3
Malinska HR 123 B3
Maliq AL 182 C2
Maljevac HR 123 B4
Malkara TR 186 B1
Małki PL 69 B4
Malko Tŭrnovo BG 17 D7
Mallaig GB 34 A2
Mallaranny IRL 28 A2
Mallemort F 131 B4
Mallén E 144 C2
Malléon F 146 A2

258 Mal–Med

Mallersdorf-Pfaffenberg D 95 C4
Málles Venosta I 108 C1
Malling DK 59 B3
Mallnitz A 109 C4
Mallow IRL 29 B3
Mallwyd GB 38 B3
Malm N 199 A8
Malmbäck S 62 A2
Malmberget S 196 B3
Malmby S 56 A3
Malmédy B 80 B2
Malmesbury GB 43 A4
Malmköping S 56 A2
Malmö S 61 D3
Malmon S 54 B2
Malmslätt S 56 B1
Malnate I 120 B1
Malo I 121 B4
Małogoszcz PL 87 B4
Maloja CH 120 A2
Małomice PL 84 A3
Måløy N 198 D2
Malpartida E 155 B4
Malpartida de la Serena E 156 B2
Malpartida de Plasencia E 150 C1
Malpas
E 145 B4
GB 38 A4
Malpica P 155 B3
Malpica de Bergantiños E 140 A2
Malpica de Tajo E 150 C3
Malsch D 93 C4
Malšice CZ 96 B2
Malta A 109 C4
Maltat F 104 C2
Maltby GB 40 B2
Malung S 49 B5
Malungsfors S 49 B5
Maluszów PL 75 B4
Maluszyn PL 87 B3
Malva E 142 C1
Malvaglia CH 120 A1
Malveira P 154 C1
Malvik N 199 B7
Malyn UA 13 C8
Mamarrosa P 148 B1
Mamer L 92 B2
Mamers F 89 B4
Mamirolle F 105 B5
Mammendorf D 108 A2
Mámmola I 175 C2
Mamoiada I 178 B3
Mamonovo RUS 69 A4
Mamuras AL 182 B1
Maňa SK 112 A2
Manacor E 167 B3
Manavgat TR 189 C6
Mancera de Abajo E 150 B2
Mancha Real E 163 A4
Manchester GB 40 B1
Manching D 95 C3
Manchita E 156 B1
Manciano I 168 A1
Manciet F 128 C3
Mandal N 52 B3
Mandanici I 177 A4
Mándas I 179 C3
Mandatoriccio I 174 B2
Mandayona E 151 B5
Mandelieu-la-Napoule F 132 B2
Mandello del Lário I 120 B2
Mandelsloh D 72 B2
Manderfeld B 80 B2
Manderscheid D 80 B2
Mandino Selo BIH 138 B3
Mandoudi GR 183 E5
Mandra GR 185 A4
Mandraki GR 188 C2
Mandúria I 173 B3
Mane
Alpes-de-Haute-Provence F 132 B1
Haute-Garonne F 145 A4
Manérbio I 120 B3
Mañeru E 144 B2
Manetin CZ 96 B1
Manfredónia I 171 B3
Mangalia RO 17 D8
Manganeses de la Lampreana E 149 A4
Manganeses de la Polvorosa E 141 B5
Mangen N 48 C3
Manger N 46 B2
Mangiennes F 92 B1
Mangotsfield GB 43 A4
Mångsbodarna S 49 A5
Mangualde P 148 B2
Maniago I 122 A1
Manilva E 162 B2
Manisa TR 186 D2
Manises E 159 B3
Mank A 110 A2
Månkarbo S 51 B4
Manlleu E 147 C3
Manna DK 58 A2
Männedorf CH 107 B3
Mannersdorf am Leithagebirge A 111 B3
Mannheim D 93 B4
Manningtree GB 45 B5
Manoppello I 169 A4
Manorbier GB 39 C2
Manorhamilton IRL 26 B2
Manosque F 132 B1
Manowo PL 67 B5
Manresa E 147 C2
Månsarp S 62 A2
Månsåsen S 199 B11
Manschnow D 74 B3
Mansfeld D 82 A3
Mansfield GB 40 B2
Mansilla de Burgos E 143 B3
Mansilla de las Mulas E 142 B1
Manskog S 55 A3
Mansle F 115 C4
Manso F 180 A1
Manteigas P 148 B2
Mantel D 95 B4
Mantes-la-Jolie F 90 C1
Mantes-la-Ville F 90 C1
Manthelan F 102 B2
Mantorp S 56 B1
Mántova I 121 B3
Mänttä FIN 8 A4
Mäntyjärvi FIN 197 C10
Manuel E 159 B3
Manyas TR 186 B2
Manzanal de Arriba E 141 B4
Manzanares E 157 A4
Manzanares el Real E 151 B4
Manzaneda
León E 141 B4
Orense E 141 B3
Manzanedo E 143 B3
Manzaneque E 157 A4
Manzanera E 153 B3
Manzanilla E 161 B3
Manzat F 116 B2
Manziana I 168 A2
Manziat F 117 A4
Maó E 167 B4
Maoča BIH 125 C4
Maqueda E 150 B3
Mara E 152 A2
Maramaraereğlisi TR 186 B2
Maraña E 142 A1
Maranchón E 152 A1
Maranello I 135 A3
Marano I 170 C2
Marano Lagunare I 122 B2
Marans F 114 B2
Maratea I 174 B1
Marateca P 154 C2
Marathokambos GR 188 B1
Marathonas GR 185 A4
Marathóvouno CY 181 A2
Marazion GB 42 B1
Marbach
Baden-Württemberg D 94 C1
Hessen D 82 B1
F 92 C2
Marbäck S 60 B3
Mårbacka S 55 A4
Marbella E 162 B3
Marboz F 118 A2
Marburg D 81 B4
Marcali H 111 C4
Marčana HR 122 C2
Marcaria I 121 B3
Marcelová SK 112 B2
Marcenat F 116 B2
March GB 41 C4
Marchamalo E 151 B4
Marchaux F 105 B5
Marche-en-Famenne B 79 B5
Marchegg A 111 A3
Marchena E 162 A2
Marchenoir F 103 B3
Marcheprime F 128 B2
Marciac F 128 C3
Marciana Marina I 134 C3
Marcianise I 170 B2
Marcigny F 117 A4
Marcilla E 144 B2
Marcillac-la-Croisille F 116 B2
Marcillac-Vallon F 130 A1
Marcillat-en-Combraille F 116 A2
Marcille-sur-Seine F 91 C3
Marcilloles F 118 B2
Marcilly-le-Hayer F 91 C3
Marcinkowice PL 75 A5
Marciszów PL 85 B4
Marck F 78 B1
Marckolsheim F 106 A2
Marco de Canevezes P 148 A1
Mårdsele S 200 B5
Mårdsjö S 200 C1
Mareham le Fen GB 41 B3
Marek S 62 A3
Marennes F 114 C2
Maresquel F 78 B1
Mareuil F 115 C4
Mareuil-en-Brie F 91 C3
Mareuil-sur-Arnon F 103 C4
Mareuil-sur-Lay F 114 B2
Mareuil-sur-Ourcq F 90 B3
Margam GB 39 C3
Margariti GR 182 D2
Margate GB 45 B5
Margaux F 128 A2
Margerie-Hancourt F 91 C4
Margès F 117 B5
Margherita di Savóia I 171 B4
Margita SRB 126 B3
Margone I 119 B4
Margonin PL 76 B2
Marguerittes F 131 B3
Margut F 91 B5
Maria E 164 B2
Mariager DK 58 B2
Mariana E 152 B1
Maria Neustift A 110 B1
Mariannelund S 62 A3
Marianópoli I 176 B2
Mariánské Lázně CZ 95 B4
Mariapfarr A 109 B4
Maria Saal A 110 C1
Mariazell A 110 B2
Maribo DK 65 B4
Maribor SLO 110 C2
Marieberg S 56 A1
Mariefred S 56 A3
Mariehamn FIN 51 B6
Marieholm S 61 D3
Mariembourg B 91 A4
Marienbaum D 80 A2
Marienberg D 83 B5
Marienheide D 81 A3
Mariental D 73 B3
Mariestad S 55 B4
Marieux F 90 A2
Marigliano I 170 C2
Marignane F 131 B4
Marigny
Jura F 105 C4
Manche F 88 A2
Marigny-le-Châtel F 91 C3
Marija Bistrica HR 124 A2
Marijampolė LT 13 A5
Marín E 140 B2
Marina HR 138 B2
Marina del Cantone I 170 C2
Marina di Acquappesa I 174 B1
Marina di Alberese I 168 A1
Marina di Amendolara I 174 B2
Marina di Árbus I 179 C2
Marina di Campo I 134 C3
Marina di Carrara I 134 A3
Marina di Castagneto-Donorático I 134 B3
Marina di Cécina I 134 B3
Marina di Gáiro I 179 C3
Marina di Ginosa I 173 B2
Marina di Gioiosa Iónica I 175 C2
Marina di Grosseto I 135 C3
Marina di Léuca I 173 C4
Marina di Massa I 134 A3
Marina di Nováglie I 173 C4
Marina di Pisa I 134 B3
Marina di Ragusa I 177 C3
Marina di Ravenna I 135 A5
Marina di Torre Grande I 179 C2
Marinaleda E 162 A3
Marina Romea I 135 A5
Marine de Sisco F 180 A2
Marinella I 176 B1
Marinella di Sarzana I 134 A3
Marineo I 176 B2
Marines F 90 B1
Maringues F 116 B3
Marinha das Ondas P 154 A2
Marinha Grande P 154 B2
Marinhas P 148 A1
Marino I 168 B2
Marjaliza E 157 A4
Markabygd N 199 B8
Markaryd S 61 C3
Markdorf D 107 B4
Markelo NL 71 B3
Market Deeping GB 40 C3
Market Drayton GB 38 B4
Market Harborough GB 40 C3
Markethill GB 27 B4
Market Rasen GB 40 B3
Market Warsop GB 40 B2
Market Weighton GB 40 B3
Markgröningen D 93 C5
Markhausen D 71 B4
Marki PL 77 B6
Markina-Xemein E 143 A4
Markinch GB 35 B4
Märkische Buchholz D 74 B2
Markitta S 196 B4
Markkleeberg D 83 A4
Marklohe D 72 B2
Marknesse NL 70 B2
Markneukirchen D 83 B4
Markopoulo GR 185 B4
Markovac
Srbija SRB 127 C3
Vojvodina SRB 126 B3
Markowice PL 86 B2
Markranstädt D 83 A4
Marksuhl D 82 B2
Markt Allhau A 111 B3
Markt Bibart D 94 B2
Marktbreit D 94 B2
Markt Erlbach D 94 B2
Markt-heidenfeld D 94 B1
Markt Indersdorf D 95 C3
Marktl D 95 C4
Marktleuthen D 83 B3
Marktoberdorf D 108 B1
Marktredwitz D 95 A4
Markt Rettenbach D 108 B1
Markt Schwaben D 108 A2
Markt-Übelbach A 110 B2
Markusica HR 125 B4
Markušovce SK 99 C4
Marl D 80 A3
Marlborough
Devon GB 42 B3
Wiltshire GB 44 B2
Marle F 91 B3
Marlieux F 117 A5
Marlow
D 66 B1
GB 44 B3
Marma S 51 B4
Marmagne F 104 C3
Marmande F 128 B3
Marmara TR 186 B2
Marmaris TR 188 C3
Marmelete P 160 B1
Marmolejo E 157 B3
Marmoutier F 93 C3
Marnay F 105 B4
Marne D 64 C2
Marnheim D 93 B4
Marnitz D 73 A4
Maroldsweisach D 82 B2
Marolles-les-Braults F 89 B4
Maromme F 89 A5
Marone I 120 B3
Maronia GR 183 C7
Maroslele H 126 A2
Maróstica I 121 B4
Marotta I 136 B2
Marpisa GR 185 B6
Marquion F 78 B3
Marquise F 78 B1
Marradi I 135 A4
Marrasjärvi FIN 197 C8
Marraskoski FIN 197 C8
Marratxi E 166 B2
Marrúbiu I 179 C2
Marrum NL 70 A2
Marrupe E 150 B3
Marsac F 129 C5
Marsac-en-Livradois F 117 B3
Marságlia I 120 C2
Marsala I 176 B1
Marsberg D 81 A4
Marsciano I 135 C5
Marseillan F 130 B2
Marseille = Marseilles F 131 B4
Marseille en Beauvaisis F 90 B1
Marseilles = Marseille F 131 B4
Mársico Nuovo I 172 B1
Marske-by-the-Sea GB 37 B5
Mars-la-Tours F 92 B1
Marsliden S 195 E6
Marson F 91 C4
Märsta S 57 A3
Marstal DK 65 B3
Marstrand S 60 B1
Marta I 168 A1
Martano I 173 B4
Martel F 129 B4
Martelange B 92 B1
Martfeld D 72 B2
Martfű H 113 B4
Martham GB 41 C5
Marthon F 115 C4
Martiago E 149 B3
Martigné-Briand F 102 B1
Martigné-Ferchaud F 101 B4
Martigne-sur-Mayenne F 102 A1
Martigny CH 119 A4
Martigny-les-Bains F 105 A4
Martigues F 131 B4
Martim-Longo P 160 B2
Martin SK 98 B2
Martina CH 108 C1
Martina Franca I 173 B3
Martinamor E 150 B2
Martin de la Jara E 162 A3
Martinengo I 120 B2
Martin Muñoz de las Posadas E 150 A3
Martinsberg A 97 C3
Martinšćica HR 123 C3
Martinshöhe D 93 B3
Martinsicuro I 136 C2
Martinszell D 107 B5
Mártis I 178 B2
Martofte DK 59 C3
Martonvásár H 112 B2
Martorell E 147 C2
Martos E 163 A4
Martres Tolosane F 146 A1
Martti FIN 197 B11
Marugán E 150 B3
Marúggio I 173 B3
Marvão P 155 B3
Marvejols F 130 A2
Marville F 92 B1
Marwałd PL 77 A4
Marykirk GB 35 B5
Marypark GB 32 D3
Maryport GB 36 B3
Marytavy GB 42 B2
Marzabotto I 135 A4
Marzahna D 74 C1
Marzahne D 73 B5
Marzamemi I 177 C4
Marzocca I 136 B2
Masa E 143 B3
Mas-Cabardès F 146 A3
Máscali I 177 B4
Mascaraque E 157 A4
Mascarenhas P 149 A2
Mascioni I 169 A3
Mas de Barberáns E 153 B4
Mas de las Matas E 153 B3
Masegoso E 158 C1
Masegoso de Tajuña E 151 B5
Masera I 119 A5
Masevaux F 106 B1
Masfjorden N 46 B2
Masham GB 37 B5
Masi N 192 C7
Maside E 140 B2
Maslacq F 144 A3
Maslinica HR 138 B2
Maşloc RO 126 B3
Maslovare BIH 138 A3
Masone I 133 A4
Massa I 134 A3
Massa Fiscáglia I 121 C5
Massafra I 173 B3
Massa Lombarda I 135 A4
Massa Lubrense I 170 C2
Massamagrell E 159 B3
Massa Maríttima I 135 B3
Massa Martana I 136 C1
Massanassa E 159 B3
Massarosa I 134 B3
Massat F 146 B2
Massay F 103 B3
Massbach D 82 B2
Masseret F 116 B1
Masseube F 145 A4
Massiac F 116 B3
Massignac F 115 C4
Massing D 95 C4
Massmechelen B 80 B1
Masterud N 49 B4
Mästocka S 61 C3
Masty BY 13 B6
Masúa I 179 C2
Masueco E 149 A3
Masugnsbyn S 196 B5
Mašun SLO 123 B3
Maszewo
Lubuskie PL 75 B3
Zachodnio-Pomorskie PL 75 A4
Mata de Alcántara E 155 B4
Matala GR 185 E5
Matalebreras E 144 C1
Matallana de Torio E 142 B1
Matamala E 151 A5
Mataporquera E 142 B2
Matapozuelos E 150 A3
Mataró E 147 C3
Matarocco I 176 B1
Matélica I 136 B2
Matera I 172 B2
Mátészalka H 16 B5
Matet E 159 B3
Matfors S 200 D3
Matha F 115 C3
Mathay F 106 B1
Matignon F 101 A3
Matilla de los Caños del Rio E 149 B4
Matlock GB 40 B2
Matosinhos P 148 A1
Matour F 117 A4
Mátrafüred H 113 B3
Mátraterenye H 113 A3
Matre
Hordaland N 46 B2
Hordaland N 52 A1
Matrei am Brenner A 108 B2
Matrei in Osttirol A 109 B3
Matrice I 170 B2
Matsdal S 195 E6
Mattarello I 121 A4
Mattersburg A 111 B3
Mattighofen A 109 A4
Mattinata I 171 B4
Mattos P 154 B2
Mattsee A 109 B4
Mattsmyra S 50 A2
Måttsund S 196 D5
Matulji HR 123 B3
Maubert-Fontaine F 91 B4
Maubeuge F 79 B3
Maubourguet F 145 A4
Mauchline GB 36 A2
Maud GB 33 D4
Mauer-kirchen A 109 A4
Mauern D 95 C3
Mauguio F 131 B3
Maulbronn D 93 C4
Maule F 90 C1
Mauléon F 114 B3
Mauléon-Barousse F 145 B4
Mauléon-Licharre F 144 A3
Maulévrier F 114 A3
Maum IRL 28 A2
Maurach A 108 B2
Maure-de-Bretagne F 101 B4
Maureilhan F 130 B2
Măureni RO 126 B3
Mauriac F 116 B2
Mauron F 101 A3
Maurs F 116 C2
Maury F 146 B3
Maussane-les-Alpilles F 131 B3
Mautern A 97 C3
Mauterndorf A 109 B4
Mautern im Steiermark A 110 B1
Mauthausen A 110 A1
Mauthen A 109 C3
Mauvezin F 129 C3
Mauzé-sur-le-Mignon F 114 B3
Maxent F 101 B3
Maxey-sur-Vaise F 92 C1
Maxial P 154 B1
Maxieira P 154 B2
Maxwellheugh GB 35 C5
Mayalde E 149 A4
Maybole GB 36 A2
Mayen D 80 B3
Mayenne F 88 B3
Mayet F 102 B2
Maylough IRL 28 A3
Mayorga E 142 B1
Mayres F 117 C4
Mayrhofen A 108 B2
Mazagón E 161 B3
Mazaleón E 153 A4
Mazamet F 130 B1
Mazan F 131 A4
Mazara del Vallo I 176 B1
Mazarambroz E 157 A3
Mazarete E 152 B1
Mazaricos E 140 B2
Mazarrón E 165 B3
Mažeikiai LT 8 D3
Mazères F 146 A2
Mazères-sur-Salat F 145 A4
Mazières-en-Gâtine F 115 B3
Mazin HR 138 A1
Mazuelo E 143 B3
Mazyr BY 13 B8
Mazzarino I 177 B3
Mazzarrà Sant'Andrea I 177 A4
Mazzo di Valtellina I 120 A3
Mdzewo PL 77 B5
Mealabost GB 31 A2
Mealhada P 148 B1
Méan B 79 B5
Meana Sardo I 179 C3
Meaulne F 103 C4
Meaux F 90 C2
Mebonden N 199 B8
Mecerreyes E 143 B3
Mechelen B 79 A4
Mechernich D 80 B2
Mechnica PL 86 B2
Mechowo PL 67 C4
Mechterstädt D 82 B2
Mecidiye TR 186 B1
Mecikal PL 68 B2
Mecina-Bombarón E 164 C1
Mecitözü TR 23 A8
Meckenbeuren D 107 B4
Meckenheim
Rheinland-Pfalz D 80 B3
Rheinland-Pfalz D 93 B4
Meckesheim D 93 B4
Mecseknádasd H 125 A4
Meda
I 120 B2
P 149 B2
Medak HR 137 A4
Mede I 120 B1
Medebach D 81 A4
Medelim P 155 A3
Medemblik NL 70 B2
Medena Selista BIH 138 A2
Medesano I 120 C3
Medevi S 55 B5
Medgidia RO 17 C8

Medgyesháza H 113 C5
Medhamn S 55 A4
Mediaş RO 17 B6
Medicina I 135 A4
Medinaceli E 152 A1
Medina de las Torres E 155 C4
Medina del Campo E 150 A3
Medina de Pomar E 143 B3
Medina de Rioseco E 142 C1
Medina Sidonia E 162 B2
Medinilla E 150 B2
Medja SRB 126 B2
Medjedja BIH 139 B5
Medulin HR 122 C2
Meduno I 122 A1
Medveda SRB 127 C3
Medvedov SK 111 B4
Medvezhyegorsk RUS 9 A9
Medvide HR 137 A4
Medvode SLO 123 A3
Medzev SK 99 C4
Medžitlija MK 182 C3
Meerane D 83 B4
Meerle B 79 A4
Meersburg D 107 B4
Meeuwen B 79 A5
Megalo Horio GR 188 C2
Megalopoli GR 184 B3
Megara GR 185 A4
Megève F 118 B3
Meggenhofen A 109 A4
Megra RUS 9 B10
Megyaszó H 113 A5
Mehamn N 193 A11
Mehedeby S 51 B4
Méhkerék H 113 C5
Mehun-sur-Yèvre F 103 B4
Meigle GB 35 B4
Meijel NL 80 A1
Meilen CH 107 B3
Meilhan F 128 C2
Meimôa P 149 B2
Meina I 119 B5
Meine D 73 B3
Meinersen D 72 B3
Meinerzhagen D 81 A3
Meiningen D 82 B2
Meira E 141 A3
Meiringen CH 106 C3
Meisenheim D 93 B3
Meissen D 83 A5
Meitingen D 94 C2
Meix-devant-Virton B 92 B1
Męka PL 86 A2
Meka Gruda BIH 139 B4
Mel I 121 A5
Melbu N 194 B5
Melč CZ 98 B1
Meldal N 198 B6
Méldola I 135 A5
Meldorf D 64 B2
Melegnano I 120 B2
Melenci SRB 126 B2
Melendugno I 173 B4
Melfi I 172 B1
Melfjordbotn N 195 D4
Melgaço P 140 B2
Melgar de Arriba E 142 B1
Melgar de Fernamental E 142 B2
Melgar de Yuso E 142 B2
Melhus N 199 B7
Meliana E 159 B3
Melide
CH 120 B1
E 140 B2
Melides P 160 A1
Meligales GR 184 B2
Melilli I 177 B4
Melinovac HR 124 C1
Melisenda I 179 C3
Melisey F 105 B5
Mélito di Porto Salvo I 175 D1
Melk A 110 A2
Melksham GB 43 A4
Mellakoski FIN 196 C7
Mellanström S 195 E9
Mellbystrand S 61 C2
Melle
B 79 A3
D 71 B5
F 115 B3
Mellendorf D 72 B2
Mellerud S 54 B3
Mellieha M 175 C3
Mellösa S 56 A2
Mellrichstadt D 82 B2
Mělnické Vtelno CZ 84 B2
Mělník CZ 84 B2
Melón E 140 B2
Melrose GB 35 C5
Mels CH 107 B4
Melsungen D 82 A1
Meltaus FIN 197 C8
Meltham GB 40 B2
Melton Mowbray GB 40 C3
Meltosjärvi FIN 196 C7
Melun F 90 C2
Melvaig GB 31 B3
Melvich GB 32 C3
Mélykút H 126 A1
Melzo I 120 B2
Memaliaj AL 182 C1
Membrilla E 157 B4
Membrio E 155 B3
Memer F 129 B4
Memmelsdorf D 94 B2
Memmingen D 107 B5
Memoria P 154 B2
Menággio I 120 A2
Menai Bridge GB 38 A2
Menasalbas E 157 A3
Menat F 116 A2
Mendavia E 144 B1
Mendaza E 144 B1
Mende F 130 A2
Menden D 81 A3
Menderes TR 188 A2
Mendig D 80 B3
Mendiga P 154 B2
Mendrisio CH 120 B1
Ménéac F 101 A3
Menemen TR 188 A2
Menen B 78 B3
Menesjärvi FIN 193 D10
Menetou-Salon F 103 B4
Menfi I 176 B1
Ménfőcsanak H 111 B4
Mengamuñoz E 150 B3
Mengen
D 107 A4
TR 187 B7
Mengeš SLO 123 A3
Mengibar E 157 C4
Mengkofen D 95 C4
Menou F 104 B2
Mens F 118 C2
Menslage D 71 B4
Mensträsk S 200 A5
Mentana I 168 A2
Menton F 133 B3
Méntrida E 151 B3
Méobecq F 115 B5
Méounes-les-Montrieux F 132 B1
Meppel NL 70 B3
Meppen D 71 B4
Mequinenza E 153 A4
Mer F 103 B3
Mera
Coruña E 140 A2
Coruña E 140 A3
Meråker N 199 B8
Merano I 108 C2
Merate I 120 B2
Mercadillo E 143 A3
Mercatale I 135 B5
Mercatino Conca I 136 B1
Mercato San Severino I 170 C2
Mercato Saraceno I 135 B5
Merching D 108 A1
Merchtem B 79 B4
Merdrignac F 101 A3
Merdžanići BIH 139 B3
Meré E 142 A2
Mere GB 43 A4
Meréville F 90 C2
Merfeld D 80 A3
Méribel F 118 B3
Méribel Motraret F 118 B3
Meriç TR 186 A1
Mérida E 155 C4
Mérignac F 128 B2
Měřín CZ 97 B3
Mering D 94 C2
Merkendorf D 94 B2
Merklin CZ 96 B1
Merksplas B 79 A4
Merlånna S 56 A2
Merlimont Plage F 78 B1
Mern DK 65 A5
Mernye H 111 C4
Mersch L 92 B2
Merseburg D 83 A3
Mers-les-Bains F 90 A1
Merthyr Tydfil GB 39 C3
Mertingen D 94 C2
Mértola P 160 B2
Méru F 90 B2
Merufe P 140 B2
Mervans F 105 C4
Merville F 78 B2
Méry-sur-Seine F 91 C3
Merzen D 71 B4
Merzifon TR 23 A8
Merzig D 92 B2
Mesagne I 173 B3
Mesão Frio P 148 A2
Mesas de Ibor E 156 A2
Meschede D 81 A4
Meschers-sur-Gironde F 114 C3
Meslay-du-Maine F 102 B1
Mesna N 48 A2
Mesnalien N 48 A2
Mesocco CH 120 A2
Mésola I 122 C1
Mesologi GR 184 A2
Mesopotamo GR 182 D2
Mesoraca I 175 B2
Messac F 101 B4
Messancy B 92 B1
Messdorf D 73 B4
Messei F 88 B3
Messejana P 160 B1
Messelt N 48 A3
Messina I 177 A4
Messingen D 71 B4
Messini GR 184 B3
Messkirch D 107 B4
Messlingen S 199 C9
Messtetten D 107 A3
Mesta GR 185 A6
Mestanza E 157 B3
Městec Králové CZ 84 B3
Mestlin D 73 A4
Město Albrechtice CZ 85 B5
Město Libavá CZ 98 B1
Město Touškov CZ 96 B1
Mestre I 122 B1
Mesvres F 104 C3
Mesztegnyő H 111 C4
Meta I 170 C2
Metajna HR 137 A4
Metelen D 71 B4
Methana GR 185 B4
Methlick GB 33 D4
Methven GB 35 B4
Methwold GB 41 C4
Metković HR 139 B3
Metlika SLO 123 B4
Metnitz A 110 C1
Metsäkylä FIN 197 D11
Metslawier NL 70 A3
Metsovo GR 182 D3
Metten D 95 C4
Mettendorf D 92 B2
Mettet B 79 B4
Mettingen D 71 B4
Mettlach D 92 B2
Mettlen CH 106 C2
Mettmann D 80 A2
Metz F 92 B2
Metzervisse F 92 B2
Metzingen D 94 C1
Meulan F 90 B1
Meung-sur-Loire F 103 B3
Meuselwitz D 83 A4
Meuzac F 115 C5
Mevagissey GB 42 B2
Mexborough GB 40 B2
Meximieux F 118 B2
Mey GB 32 C3
Meyenburg D 73 A5
Meyerhöfen D 71 B5
Meylan F 118 B2
Meymac F 116 B2
Meyrargues F 132 B1
Meyrueis F 130 A2
Meyssac F 129 A4
Meysse F 117 C4
Meyzieu F 117 B4
Mèze F 130 B2
Mézériat F 117 A5
Mežica SLO 110 C1
Mézidon-Canon F 89 A3
Mézières-en-Brenne F 115 B5
Mézières-sur-Issoire F 115 B4
Mézilhac F 117 C4
Mézilles F 104 B2
Mézin F 128 B3
Mezőberény H 113 C5
Mezőcsát H 113 B4
Mezöfalva H 112 C2
Mezőhegyes H 126 A2
Mezökeresztes H 113 B4
Mezőkomárom H 112 C2
Mezőkövácsháza H 113 C4
Mezőkövesd H 113 B4
Mezőörs H 111 B4
Mézos F 128 B1
Mezőszilas H 112 C2
Mezőtúr H 113 B4
Mezquita de Jarque E 153 B3
Mezzano
Emilia Romagna I 135 A5
Trentino Alto Adige I 121 A4
Mezzojuso I 176 B2
Mezzoldo I 120 A2
Mezzolombardo I 121 A4
Mgarr M 175 C3
Miajadas E 156 A2
Miały PL 75 B5
Mianowice PL 68 A2
Miasteczko Krajeńskie PL 76 A2
Miasteczko Sł. PL 86 B2
Miastko PL 68 A1
Michalovce SK 12 D4
Michałowice PL 87 B3
Michelau D 94 B2
Michelbach D 94 B2
Micheldorf A 110 B1
Michelhausen A 110 A2
Michelsneukirchen D 95 B4
Michelstadt D 93 B5
Michendorf D 74 B2
Michurin BG 17 D7
Mickleover GB 40 C2
Midbea GB 33 B4
Middelburg NL 79 A3
Middelfart DK 59 C2
Middelharnis NL 79 A4
Middelkerke B 78 A2
Middelstum NL 71 A3
Middlesbrough GB 37 B5
Middleton Cheney GB 44 A2
Middleton-in-Teesdale GB 37 B4
Middletown GB 27 B4
Middlewich GB 38 A4
Middlezoy GB 43 A4
Midhurst GB 44 C3
Midleton IRL 29 C3
Midlum D 64 C1
Midsomer Norton GB 43 A4
Midtgulen N 198 D2
Midtskogberget N 49 A4
Midwolda NL 71 A4
Mid Yell GB 33 A5
Miechów PL 87 B4
Miedes de Aragón E 152 A2
Miedes de Atienza E 151 A4
Międzybodzie Bielskie PL 99 B3
Międzybórz PL 85 A5
Międzychód PL 75 B4
Międzylesie PL 85 B4
Międzyrzec Podlaski PL 12 C5
Międzyrzecz PL 75 B4
Międzywodzie PL 67 B3
Międzyzdroje PL 67 C3
Miejska Górka PL 85 A4
Miélan F 145 A4
Mielec PL 87 B5
Mielęcin PL 75 A3
Mielno
Warmińsko-Mazurskie PL 77 A5
Zachodnio-Pomorskie PL 67 B5
Miengo E 143 A3
Mieraslompolo FIN 193 C11
Miercurea Ciuc RO 17 B6
Mieres
Asturias E 141 A5
Girona E 147 B3
Mieroszów PL 85 B4
Mierzyn PL 86 A3
Miesau D 93 B3
Miesbach D 108 B2
Mieścisko PL 76 B2
Mieste D 73 B4
Miesterhorst D 73 B4
Mieszków PL 76 B2
Mieszkowice PL 74 B3
Mietków PL 85 B4
Migennes F 104 B2
Miggiano I 173 C4
Migliánico I 169 A4
Migliarino I 121 C4
Migliónico I 172 B2
Mignano Monte Lungo I 169 B3
Migné F 115 B5
Miguel Esteban E 157 A4
Miguelturra E 157 B4
Mihajlovac SRB 127 C2
Miháld H 111 C4
Mihalgazi TR 187 B5
Mihaliççık TR 187 C6
Mihályi H 111 B4
Mihla D 82 A2
Mihohnić HR 123 B3
Miholjsko HR 123 B4
Mihovljan HR 124 A1
Mijares E 150 B3
Mijas E 163 B3
Mike H 124 A3
Mikines GR 184 B3
Mikkeli FIN 8 B5
Mikkelvik N 192 B3
Mikleuš HR 125 B3
Mikołajki Pomorskie PL 69 B4
Mikołów PL 86 B2
Mikonos GR 185 B6
Mikorzyn PL 86 A2
Mikro Derio GR 183 B8
Mikstat PL 86 A1
Mikulášovice CZ 84 B2
Mikulov CZ 97 C4
Mikulovice CZ 85 B5
Milagro E 144 B2
Miłakowo PL 69 A5
Milan = Milano I 120 B2
Miland N 47 C5
Milano = Milan I 120 B2
Milano Marittima I 135 A5
Milas TR 188 B2
Milazzo I 177 A4
Mildenhall GB 45 A4
Milejewo PL 69 A4
Milelín CZ 85 B3
Miletić SRB 125 B5
Miletićevo SRB 126 B3
Mileto I 175 C2
Milevsko CZ 96 B2
Milford IRL 26 A3
Milford Haven GB 39 C1
Milford on Sea GB 44 C2
Milhão P 149 A3
Milići BIH 139 A5
Miličin CZ 96 B2
Milicz PL 85 A5
Milín CZ 96 B2
Militello in Val di Catánia I 177 B3
Miljevina BIH 139 B4
Milkowice PL 85 A4
Millançay F 103 B3
Millares E 159 B3
Millas F 146 B3
Millau F 130 A2
Millesimo I 133 A4
Millevaches F 116 B2
Millom GB 36 B3
Millport GB 34 C3
Millstatt A 109 C4
Millstreet
Cork IRL 29 B2
Waterford IRL 29 B4
Milltown
Galway IRL 28 A3
Kerry IRL 29 B1
Milltown Malbay IRL 28 B2
Milly-la-Forêt F 90 C2
Milmarcos E 152 A2
Milmersdorf D 74 A2
Milna HR 138 B2
Milnthorpe GB 37 B4
Milogórze PL 69 A5
Miłomłyn PL 69 B4
Milos GR 185 C5
Miloševo SRB 127 C3
Miłosław PL 76 B2
Milot AL 182 B1
Milówka PL 99 B3
Miltach D 95 B4
Miltenberg D 94 B1
Milton Keynes GB 44 A3
Miltzow D 66 B2
Milverton GB 43 A3
Milzyn PL 76 B3
Mimice HR 138 B2
Mimizan F 128 B1
Mimizan-Plage F 128 B1
Mimoň CZ 84 B2
Mina de Juliana P 160 B1
Mina de São Domingos P 160 B2
Minas de Riotinto E 161 B3
Minateda E 158 C2
Minaya E 158 B1
Minde P 154 B2
Mindelheim D 108 A1
Mindelstetten D 95 C3
Minden D 72 B1
Mindszent H 113 C4
Minehead GB 43 A3
Mineo I 177 B3
Minerbe I 121 B4
Minérbio I 121 C4
Minervino Murge I 171 B4
Minglanilla E 158 B2
Mingorria E 150 B3
Minnesund N 48 B3
Miño E 140 A2
Miño de San Esteban E 151 A4
Minsen D 71 A4
Minsk BY 13 B7
Mińsk Mazowiecki PL 12 B4
Minsterley GB 39 B4
Mintlaw GB 33 D4
Minturno I 169 B3
Mionica
BIH 125 C4
SRB 127 C2
Mios F 128 B2
Mira
E 158 B2
I 121 B5
P 148 B1
Mirabel E 155 B4
Mirabel-aux-Baronnies F 131 A4
Mirabella Eclano I 170 B3
Mirabella Imbáccari I 177 B3
Mirabello I 121 C4
Miradoux F 129 B3
Miraflores de la Sierra E 151 B4
Miralrio E 151 B5
Miramar P 148 A1
Miramare I 136 A1
Miramas F 131 B3
Mirambeau F 114 C3
Miramont-de-Guyenne F 129 B3
Miranda de Arga E 144 B2
Miranda de Ebro E 143 B4
Miranda do Corvo P 148 B1
Miranda do Douro P 149 A3
Mirande F 129 C3
Mirandela P 149 A2
Mirandilla E 155 C4
Mirándola I 121 C4
Miranje HR 137 A4
Mirano I 121 B5
Miras AL 182 C2
Miravet E 153 A4
Miré F 102 B1
Mirebeau F 102 C2
Mirebeau-sur-Bèze F 105 B4
Mirecourt F 105 A5
Mirepoix F 146 A2
Mires GR 185 D5
Miribel F 117 B4
Miričina BIH 125 C4
Mirina GR 183 D7
Mirna SLO 123 B4
Miroslav CZ 97 C4
Mirosławice PL 85 B4
Mirosławiec PL 75 A5
Mirošov CZ 96 B1
Mirotice CZ 96 B2
Mirovice CZ 96 B2
Mirow D 74 A1
Mirsk PL 84 B3
Mirzec PL 87 A5
Misi FIN 197 C9
Misilmeri I 176 A2
Miske H 112 C3
Miskolc H 113 A4
Mislinja SLO 110 C2
Missanello I 174 A2
Missillac F 101 B3
Mistelbach
A 97 C4
D 95 B3
Misten N 194 C5
Misterbianco I 177 B4
Misterhult S 62 A4
Mistretta I 177 B3
Misurina I 109 C3
Mitchelstown IRL 29 B3
Mithimna GR 186 C1
Mithoni GR 184 C2
Mitilini GR 186 C1
Mitilinii GR 188 B1
Mittelberg
Tirol A 108 C1
Vorarlberg A 107 B5
Mittenwald D 108 B2
Mittenwalde D 74 B2
Mitterback A 110 B2
Mitterdorf im Mürztal A 110 B2
Mitter-Kleinarl A 109 B4
Mittersheim F 92 C2
Mittersill A 109 B3
Mitterskirchen D 95 C4
Mitterteich D 95 B4
Mitton F 128 B2
Mittweida D 83 B4
Mitwitz D 82 B3
Mizhhir'ya UA 13 D5
Mjällby S 63 B2
Mjåvatn N 53 B4
Mjöbäck S 60 B2
Mjölby S 56 B1
Mjølfjell N 46 B3
Mjøndalen N 53 A6
Mjørlund N 48 B2
Mladá Boleslav CZ 84 B2
Mladá Vožice CZ 96 B2
Mladé Buky CZ 85 B3
Mladenovac SRB 127 C2
Mladenovo SRB 126 B1
Mladikovine BIH 139 A3
Mława PL 77 A5
Mlinište BIH 138 A2
Młodzieszyn PL 77 B5
Mlogoszyn PL 77 B4
Młynary PL 69 A4
Mnichóvice CZ 96 B2
Mnichovo Hradiště CZ 84 B2
Mniów PL 87 A4
Mnisek nad Hnilcom SK 99 C4
Mníšek pod Brdy CZ 96 B2
Mniszek PL 87 A4
Mniszków PL 87 A4
Mo
Hedmark N 48 B3
Hordaland N 46 B2
Møre og Romsdal N 198 C5
Telemark N 53 A3
Gävleborg S 51 A3
Västra Götaland S 54 B2
Moaña E 140 B2
Moate IRL 28 A4
Mocejón E 151 C4
Močenok SK 111 A4
Mochales E 152 A1
Mochowo PL 77 B4
Mochy PL 75 B5
Mockern D 73 B4
Mockfjärd S 50 B1
Möckmühl D 94 B1
Mockrehna D 83 A4
Moclin E 163 A4
Mocsa H 112 B2
Mőcsény H 125 A4
Modane F 118 B3
Modbury GB 42 B3
Módena I 121 C3
Módica I 177 C3
Modigliana I 135 A4
Modlin PL 77 B5
Mödling A 111 A3
Modliszewice PL 87 A4
Modliszewko PL 76 B2
Modogno I 171 B4
Modra SK 98 C1
Modran BIH 125 C3
Modriča BIH 125 C4
Möðrudalur IS 191 B10
Modrý Kamen SK 99 C3
Moëlan-sur-Mer F 100 B2
Moelfre GB 38 A2

Moelv N 48 B2
Moen N 194 A9
Moena I 121 A4
Moerbeke B 79 A3
Moers D 80 A2
Móes P 148 B2
Moffat GB 36 A3
Mogadouro P 149 A3
Mogata S 56 B2
Móggio Udinese I 122 A2
Mogielnica PL 87 A4
Mogilany PL 99 B3
Mogilno PL 76 B2
Mogliano I 136 B2
Mogliano Véneto I 122 B1
Mogor E 140 B2
Mógoro I 179 C2
Moguer E 161 B3
Mohács H 125 B4
Moheda S 62 A2
Mohedas E 149 B3
Mohedas de la Jara
E 156 A2
Mohelnice CZ 97 B4
Mohill IRL 26 C3
Möhlin CH 106 B2
Moholm S 55 B5
Mohorn D 83 A5
Mohyliv-Podil's'kyy
UA 13 D7
Moi N 52 B2
Moià E 147 C3
Móie I 136 B2
Moimenta da Beira
P 148 B2
Mo i Rana N 195 D5
Moirans F 118 B2
Moirans-en-Montagne
F 118 A2
Moisaküla EST 8 C4
Moisdon-la-Rivière
F 101 B4
Moissac F 129 B4
Moita
Coimbra P 148 B1
Guarda P 149 B2
Santarém P 154 B2
Setúbal P 154 C1
Moita dos Ferreiros
P 154 B1
Moixent E 159 C3
Mojacar E 164 B3
Mojados E 150 A3
Mojmírovce SK 112 A2
Mojtin SK 98 C2
Möklinta S 50 B3
Mokošica HR 139 C4
Mokronog SLO 123 B4
Mokro Polje HR 138 A2
Mokrzyska PL 99 A4
Møkster N 46 B2
Mol
B 79 A5
SRB 126 B2
Mola di Bari I 173 A3
Molai GR 184 C3
Molare I 133 A4
Molaretto I 119 B4
Molas F 145 A4
Molassano I 134 A1
Molbergen D 71 B4
Mold GB 38 A3
Molde N 198 C4
Møldrup DK 58 B2
Moledo do Minho
P 148 A1
Molfetta I 171 B4
Molfsee D 64 B3
Moliden S 200 C4
Molières F 129 B4
Molina de Aragón
E 152 B2
Molina de Segura
E 165 A3
Molinar E 143 A3
Molinaseca E 141 B4
Molinella I 121 C4
Molinet F 104 C2
Molinicos E 158 C1
Molini di Tures I 108 C2
Molinos de Duero
E 143 C4
Molins de Rei E 147 C3
Moliterno I 174 A1
Molkom S 55 A4
Möllbrücke A 109 C4
Mölle S 61 C2
Molledo E 142 A2
Möllenbeck D 74 A2
Mollerussa E 147 C1
Mollet de Perelada
E 146 B3
Mollina E 163 A3
Mölln D 73 A3
Molló E 146 B3
Mollösund S 54 B2
Mölltorp S 55 B5
Mölnbo S 56 A3
Mölndal S 60 B2
Mölnlycke S 60 B2
Molompize F 116 B3
Moloy F 105 B3
Molsheim F 93 C3
Moltzow D 73 A5
Molve HR 124 A3
Molveno I 121 A3
Molvizar E 163 B4
Molzbichl A 109 C4
Mombaróccio I 136 B1
Mombeltrán E 150 B2
Mombris D 93 A5
Mombuey E 141 B4
Momchilgrad BG 183 B7
Mommark DK 64 B3
Momo I 119 B5
Monaghan IRL 27 B4
Monar Lodge GB 32 D2
Monasterace Marina
I 175 C2
Monasterevin IRL 30 A1
Monasterio de Rodilla
E 143 B3
Monastir I 179 C3
Monbahus F 129 B3
Monbazillac F 129 B3
Moncada E 159 B3
Moncalieri I 119 B4
Moncalvo I 119 B5
Monção P 140 B2
Moncarapacho P 160 B2
Moncel-sur-Seille F 92 C2
Monchegorsk RUS 3 C13
Mönchengladbach =
Munchen-Gladbach
D 80 A2
Mónchio della Corti
I 134 A3
Monchique P 160 B1
Monclar-de-Quercy
F 129 C4
Moncofa E 159 B3
Moncontour F 101 A3
Moncoutant F 114 B3
Monda E 162 B3
Mondariz E 140 B2
Mondavio I 136 B1
Mondéjar E 151 B4
Mondello I 176 A2
Mondim de Basto
P 148 A2
Mondolfo I 136 B2
Mondoñedo E 141 A3
Mondorf-les-Bains L 92 B2
Mondoubleau F 102 B2
Mondovì I 133 A3
Mondragon F 131 A3
Mondragone I 170 B1
Mondsee A 109 B4
Monéglia I 134 A2
Monegrillo E 153 A3
Monein F 145 A3
Monemvasia GR 184 C4
Mónesi I 133 A3
Monesiglio I 133 A4
Monesterio E 161 A3
Monestier-de-Clermont
F 118 C2
Monestiés F 130 A1
Monéteau F 104 B2
Moneygall IRL 28 B4
Moneymore GB 27 B4
Monfalcone I 122 B2
Monfero E 140 A2
Monflanquin F 129 B3
Monflorite E 145 B3
Monforte P 155 B3
Monforte da Beira
E 155 B3
P 155 B3
Monforte d'Alba I 133 A3
Monforte del Cid E 165 A4
Monforte de Lemos
E 140 B3
Monforte de Moyuela
E 152 A2
Monghidoro I 135 A4
Mongiana I 175 C2
Monguelfo I 108 C3
Monheim D 94 C2
Moniaive GB 36 A3
Monifieth GB 35 B5
Monikie GB 35 B5
Monistrol-d'Allier
F 117 C3
Monistrol de Montserrat
E 147 C2
Monistrol-sur-Loire
F 117 B4
Mönkebude D 74 A2
Monkton GB 36 A2
Monmouth GB 39 C4
Monnaie F 102 B2
Monnerville F 90 C2
Monnickendam NL 70 B2
Monolithos GR 188 C2
Monópoli I 173 B3
Monor H 112 B3
Monóvar E 159 C3
Monpazier F 129 B3
Monreal
D 80 B3
E 144 B2
Monreal del Campo
E 152 B2
Monreale I 176 A2
Monroy E 155 B4
Monroyo E 153 B3
Mons B 79 B3
Monsaraz P 155 C3
Monschau D 80 B2
Monségur F 128 B3
Monsélice I 121 B4
Mønshaug N 46 B3
Monster NL 70 B1
Mönsterås S 62 A4
Monsummano Terme
I 135 B3
Montabaur D 81 B3
Montafia I 119 C5
Montagnac F 130 B2
Montagnana I 121 B4
Montaigu F 114 B2
Montaigu-de-Quercy
F 129 B4
Montaiguët-en-Forez
F 117 A3
Montaigut F 116 A2
Montaigut-sur-Save
F 129 C4
Montainville F 90 C1
Montalbán E 153 B3
Montalbán de Córdoba
E 163 A3
Montalbano Elicona
I 177 A4
Montalbano Iónico
I 174 A2
Montalbo E 158 B1
Montalcino I 135 B4
Montaldo di Cósola
I 120 C2
Montalegre P 148 A2
Montalieu-Vercieu
F 118 B2
Montalivet-les-Bains
F 114 C2
Montallegro I 176 B2
Montalto delle Marche
I 136 C2
Montalto di Castro
I 168 A1
Montalto Pavese I 120 C2
Montalto Uffugo I 174 B2
Montalvão P 155 B3
Montamarta E 149 A4
Montana BG 17 D5
Montana-Vermala
CH 119 A4
Montánchez E 156 A1
Montanejos E 153 B3
Montano Antilia I 172 B1
Montans F 129 C4
Montargil P 154 B2
Montargis F 103 B4
Montastruc-la-
Conseillère F 129 C4
Montauban F 129 B4
Montauban-de-Bretagne
F 101 A3
Montbard F 104 B3
Montbarrey F 105 B4
Montbazens F 130 A1
Montbazon F 102 B2
Montbéliard F 106 B1
Montbenoit F 105 C5
Montbeugny F 104 C2
Montblanc E 147 C2
Montbozon F 105 B5
Montbrison F 117 B4
Montbron F 115 C4
Montbrun-les-Bains
F 131 A4
Montceau-les-Mines
F 104 C3
Montcenis F 104 C3
Montchanin F 104 C3
Montcornet F 91 B4
Montcuq F 129 B4
Montdardier F 130 B2
Mont-de-Marsan F 128 C2
Montdidier F 90 B2
Monteagudo E 165 A3
Monteagudo de las
Vicarias E 152 A1
Montealegre E 142 C2
Montealegre del Castillo
E 159 C2
Montebello Iónico
I 175 D1
Montebello Vicentino
I 121 B4
Montebelluna I 121 B5
Montebourg F 88 A2
Montebruno I 134 A2
Monte-Carlo MC 133 B3
Montecarotto I 136 B2
Montecassiano I 136 B2
Montecastrilli I 168 A2
Montecatini Terme
I 135 B3
Montécchio I 136 B1
Montécchio Emilia
I 121 C3
Montécchio Maggiore
I 121 B4
Montech F 129 C4
Montechiaro d'Asti
I 119 B5
Monte Clara P 155 B3
Monte Clérigo P 160 B1
Montecórice I 170 C2
Montecorvino Rovella
I 170 C2
Monte da Pedra P 155 B3
Monte de Goula P 155 B3
Montederramo E 141 B3
Montedoro I 176 B2
Monte do Trigo P 155 C3
Montefalco I 136 C1
Montefalcone di Val
Fortore I 170 B3
Montefalcone nel
Sánnio I 170 B2
Montefano I 136 B2
Montefiascone I 168 A2
Montefiorino I 134 A3
Montefortino I 136 C2
Montefranco I 168 A2
Montefrío E 163 A4
Montegiordano Marina
I 174 A2
Montegiórgio I 136 B2
Monte Gordo P 160 B2
Montegranaro I 136 B2
Montehermoso E 149 B3
Montejicar E 163 A4
Montejo de la Sierra
E 151 A4
Montejo de Tiermes
E 151 A4
Monte Juntos P 155 C3
Montel-de-Gelat F 116 B2
Monteleone di Púglia
I 171 B3
Monteleone di Spoleto
I 169 A2
Monteleone d'Orvieto
I 135 C5
Montelepre I 176 A2
Montelibretti I 168 A2
Montelier F 117 C5
Montélimar F 131 A3
Montella
E 146 B2
I 170 C3
Montellano E 162 A2
Montelupo Fiorentino
I 135 B4
Montemaggiore Belsito
I 176 B2
Montemagno I 119 C5
Montemayor E 163 A3
Montemayor de Pinilla
E 150 A3
Montemésola I 173 B3
Montemilleto I 170 B2
Montemilone I 172 A1
Montemolin E 161 A3
Montemónaco I 136 C2
Montemor-o-Novo
P 154 C2
Montemor-o-Velho
P 148 B1
Montemurro I 174 A1
Montendre F 128 A2
Montenegro de Cameros
E 143 B4
Montenero di Bisáccia
I 170 B2
Monteneuf F 101 B3
Monteparano I 173 B3
Montepescali I 135 C4
Montepiano I 135 A4
Monte Porzio I 136 B2
Montepulciano I 135 B4
Monte Real P 154 B2
Montereale I 169 A3
Montereale Valcellina
I 122 A1
Montereau-Faut-Yonne
F 90 C2
Monte Redondo P 154 B2
Monterénzio I 135 A4
Monte Romano I 168 A1
Monteroni d'Arbia
I 135 B4
Monteroni di Lecce
I 173 B4
Monterosso al Mare
I 134 A2
Monterosso Almo I 177 B3
Monterosso Grana
I 133 A3
Monterotondo I 168 A2
Monterotondo Maríttimo
I 135 B3
Monterrey E 141 C3
Monterroso E 140 B3
Monterrubio de la
Serena E 156 B2
Monterubbiano I 136 B2
Montesa E 159 C3
Montesalgueiro E 140 A2
Monte San Giovanni
Campano I 169 B3
Montesano sulla
Marcellana I 174 A1
Monte San Savino
I 135 B4
Monte Sant'Angelo
I 171 B3
Montesárchio I 170 B2
Montescaglioso I 171 C4
Montesclaros E 150 B3
Montesilvano I 169 A4
Montespértoli I 135 B4
Montesquieu-Volvestre
F 146 A2
Montesquiou F 129 C3
Montestruc-sur-Gers
F 129 C3
Montes Velhos P 160 B1
Montevarchi I 135 B4
Montéveglio I 135 A4
Monte Vilar P 154 B1
Montfaucon F 101 B4
Montfaucon-d'Argonne
F 91 B5
Montfaucon-en-Velay
F 117 B4
Montferrat
Isère F 118 B2
Var F 132 B2
Montfort-en-Chalosse
F 128 C2
Montfort-l'Amaury F 90 C1
Montfort-le-Gesnois
F 102 A2
Montfort-sur-Meu
F 101 A4
Montfort-sur-Risle F 89 A4
Montgai E 147 C1
Montgaillard F 145 A4
Montgenèvre F 118 C3
Montgiscard F 146 A2
Montgomery GB 39 B3
Montguyon F 128 A2
Monthermé F 91 B4
Monthey CH 119 A3
Monthois F 91 B4
Monthureux-sur-Saône
F 105 A4
Monti I 178 B3
Monticelli d'Ongina
I 120 B2
Montichiari I 120 B3
Monticiano I 135 B4
Montiel E 158 C1
Montier-en-Der F 91 C4
Montieri I 135 B4
Montiglio I 119 B5
Montignac F 129 A4
Montigny-le-Roi F 105 B4
Montigny-lès-Metz
F 92 B2
Montigny-sur-Aube
F 105 B3
Montijo
E 155 C4
P 154 C2
Montilla E 163 A3
Montillana E 163 A4
Montilly F 104 C2
Montivilliers F 89 A4
Montjaux F 130 A1
Montjean-sur-Loire
F 102 B1
Montlhéry F 90 C2
Montlieu-la-Garde
F 128 A2
Mont-Louis F 146 B3
Montlouis-sur-Loire
F 102 B2
Montluçon F 116 A2
Montluel F 117 B5
Montmarault F 116 A2
Montmartin-sur-Mer
F 88 B2
Montmédy F 92 B1
Montmélian F 118 B3
Montmeyan F 132 B2
Montmeyran F 117 C4
Montmirail
Marne F 91 C3
Sarthe F 102 A2
Montmiral F 118 B2
Montmirat F 131 B3
Montmirey-le-Château
F 105 B4
Montmoreau-St Cybard
F 115 C4
Montmorency F 90 C2
Montmorillon F 115 B4
Montmort-Lucy F 91 C3
Montoir-de-Bretagne
F 101 B3
Montoire-sur-le-Loir
F 102 B2
Montoito P 155 C3
Montolieu F 146 A3
Montório al Vomano
I 169 A3
Montoro E 157 B3
Montpellier F 131 B2
Montpezat-de-Quercy
F 129 B4
Montpezat-sous-Bouzon
F 117 C4
Montpon-Ménestérol
F 128 A3
Montpont-en-Bresse
F 105 C4
Montréal
Aude F 146 A3
Gers F 128 C3
Montredon-Labessonnié
F 130 B1
Montréjeau F 145 A4
Montrésor F 103 B3
Montresta I 178 B2
Montret F 105 C4
Montreuil
Pas de Calais F 78 B1
Seine St Denis F 90 C2
Montreuil-aux-Lions
F 90 B3
Montreuil-Bellay F 102 B1
Montreux CH 106 C1
Montrevault F 101 B4
Montrevel-en-Bresse
F 118 A2
Montrichard F 103 B3
Montricoux F 129 B4
Mont-roig del Camp
E 147 C1
Montrond-les-Bains
F 117 B4
Montrose GB 35 B5
Montroy E 159 B3
Montsalvy F 116 C2
Montsauche-les-Settons
F 104 B3
Montseny E 147 C3
Montsoreau F 102 B2
Mont-sous-Vaudrey
F 105 C4
Monts-sur-Guesnes
F 102 C2
Mont-St Aignan F 89 A5
Mont-St Vincent F 104 C3
Montsûrs F 102 A1
Montuenga E 150 A3
Montuïri E 167 B3
Monturque E 163 A3
Monza I 120 B2
Monzón E 145 C4
Monzón de Campos
E 142 B2
Moorbad Lobenstein
D 83 B3
Moordorf D 71 A4
Moorslede B 78 B3
Moos D 107 B3
Moosburg D 95 C3
Moosburg im Kärnten
A 110 C1
Mór H 112 B2
Mora E 157 A4
Móra P 154 C2
Mora S 50 A1
Moraby S 50 B2
Mòra d'Ebre E 153 A4
Mora de Rubielos
E 153 B3
Moradillo de Roa E 151 A4
Morąg PL 69 B4
Mórahalom H 126 A1
Moraime E 140 A1
Morais P 149 A3
Mòra la Nova E 153 A4
Moral de Calatrava
E 157 B4
Moraleda de Zafayona
E 163 A4
Moraleja E 149 B3
Moraleja del Vino
E 150 A2
Morales del Vino E 150 A2
Morales de Toro E 150 A2
Morales de Valverde
E 141 C5
Moralina E 149 A3
Morano Cálabro I 174 B2
Mörarp S 61 C2
Morasverdes E 149 B3
Morata de Jalón E 152 A2
Morata de Jiloca E 152 A2
Morata de Tajuña
E 151 B4
Moratalla E 164 A3
Moravče SLO 123 A3
Moravec CZ 97 B4
Moravița RO 126 B3
Morávka CZ 98 B2
Moravská Třebová
CZ 97 B4
Moravské Budějovice
CZ 97 B3
Moravské Lieskové
SK 98 C1
Moravske Toplice
SLO 111 C3
Moravský-Beroun
CZ 98 B1
Moravský Krumlov
CZ 97 B4
Moravský Svätý Ján
SK 98 C1
Morawica PL 87 B4
Morawin PL 86 A2
Morbach D 92 B3
Morbegno I 120 A2
Morbier F 105 C5
Mörbisch am See
A 111 B3
Mörbylånga S 63 B4
Morcenx F 128 B2
Morciano di Romagna
I 136 B1
Morcone I 170 B2
Morcuera E 151 A4
Mordelles F 101 A4
Mordoğan TR 188 A1
Moréac F 100 B3
Morebattle GB 35 C5
Morecambe GB 36 B4
Moreda
Granada E 163 A4
Oviedo E 142 A1
Morée F 103 B3
Moreles de Rey E 141 B5
Morella E 153 B3
Moreruela de los
Infanzones E 149 A4
Morés E 152 A2
Móres I 178 B2
Morestel F 118 B2
Moretonhampstead
GB 43 B3
Moreton-in-Marsh
GB 44 B2
Moret-sur-Loing F 90 C2
Moretta I 119 C4

Moreuil F 90 B2
Morez F 105 C5
Mörfelden D 93 B4
Morgat F 100 A1
Morges CH 105 C5
Morgex I 119 B4
Morgongåva S 51 C3
Morhange F 92 C2
Morhet B 92 B1
Mori I 121 B3
Morialmé B 79 B4
Morianes P 160 B2
Moriani Plage F 180 A2
Mórichida H 111 B4
Moriles E 163 A3
Morille E 150 B2
Moringen D 82 A1
Morjärv S 196 C5
Morkarla S 51 B4
Mørke DK 59 B3
Mørkøv DK 61 D1
Morkovice-Slížany CZ 98 B1
Morlaàs F 145 A3
Morlaix F 100 A2
Morley F 91 C5
Mörlunda S 62 A3
Mormanno I 174 B1
Mormant F 90 C2
Mornant F 117 B4
Mornay-Berry F 103 B4
Morón de Almazán E 152 A1
Morón de la Frontera E 162 A2
Morović SRB 125 B5
Morozzo I 133 A3
Morpeth GB 37 A5
Morphou CY 181 A1
Mörrum S 63 B2
Morsbach D 81 B3
Mörsch D 93 C4
Mörsil S 199 B10
Morsum D 64 B1
Mørsvikbotn N 194 C6
Mortagne-au-Perche F 89 B4
Mortagne-sur-Gironde F 114 C3
Mortagne-sur-Sèvre F 114 B3
Mortágua P 148 B1
Mortain F 88 B3
Mortara I 120 B1
Morteau F 105 B5
Mortegliano I 122 B2
Mortelle I 177 A4
Mortemart F 115 B4
Mortimer's Cross GB 39 B4
Mortrée F 89 B4
Mörtschach A 109 C3
Mortsel B 79 A4
Morud DK 59 C3
Morwenstow GB 42 B2
Moryń PL 74 B3
Morzeszczyn PL 69 B3
Morzewo PL 69 B4
Morzine F 118 A3
Mosbach D 93 B5
Mosbjerg DK 58 A3
Mosby N 53 B3
Mosca P 149 A3
Moscavide P 154 C1
Moščenica HR 124 B2
Mošćenice HR 123 B3
Moščenicka Draga HR 123 B3
Mosciano Sant'Ángelo I 136 C2
Mościsko PL 85 B4
Moscow = Moskva RUS 9 E10
Mosina PL 75 B5
Mosjøen N 195 E4
Moskog N 46 A3
Moskorzew PL 87 B3
Moskosel S 196 D2
Moskuvarra FIN 197 B9
Moskva = Moscow RUS 9 E10
Moslavina Podravska HR 125 B3
Moșnița Nouă RO 126 B3
Moso in Passíria I 108 C2
Mosonmagyaróvár H 111 B4
Mošorin SRB 126 B2
Mošovce SK 98 C2
Mosqueruela E 153 B3
Moss N 54 A1
Mossfellsbær IS 190 C4
Mössingen D 93 C5
Møsstrand N 47 C5
Most CZ 83 B5
Mosta M 175 C3
Mostar BIH 139 B3
Mosterhamn N 52 A1
Mostki PL 75 B4
Most na Soči SLO 122 A2
Móstoles E 151 B4
Mostová SK 111 A4
Mostowo PL 68 A1
Mostuéjouls F 130 A2
Mosty PL 75 A3
Mostys'ka UA 13 D5
Mosvik N 199 B7
Mota del Cuervo E 158 B1
Mota del Marqués E 150 A2
Motala S 55 B6
Motherwell GB 35 C4
Möthlow D 74 B1
Motilla del Palancar E 158 B2
Motnik SLO 123 A3
Motovun HR 122 B2
Motril E 163 B4
Motta I 121 B4
Motta di Livenza I 122 B1
Motta Montecorvino I 170 B3
Motta Visconti I 120 B1
Mottisfont GB 44 B2
Móttola I 173 B3
Mou DK 58 B3
Mouchard F 105 C4
Moudon CH 106 C1
Moudros GR 183 D7
Mougins F 132 B2
Mouilleron en-Pareds F 114 B3
Mouliherne F 102 B2
Moulinet F 133 B3
Moulins F 104 C2
Moulins-Engilbert F 104 C2
Moulins-la-Marche F 89 B4
Moulismes F 115 B4
Moult F 89 A3
Mountain Ash GB 39 C3
Mount Bellew Bridge IRL 28 A3
Mountfield GB 27 B3
Mountmellick IRL 30 A1
Mountrath IRL 30 A1
Mountsorrel GB 40 C2
Moura P 160 A2
Mourão P 155 C3
Mourenx F 145 A3
Mouriés F 131 B3
Mourmelon-le-Grand F 91 B4
Mouronho P 148 B1
Mourujärvi FIN 197 C11
Mouscron B 78 B3
Mousehole GB 42 B1
Moussac F 131 B3
Moussey F 92 C2
Mousteru F 100 A2
Moustey F 128 B2
Moustiers-Ste Marie F 132 B2
Mouthe F 105 C5
Mouthier-Haute-Pierre F 105 B5
Mouthoumet F 146 B3
Moutier CH 106 B2
Moûtiers F 118 B3
Moutiers-les-Mauxfaits F 114 B2
Mouy F 90 B2
Mouzaki GR 182 D3
Mouzon F 91 B5
Møvik N 46 B2
Moville IRL 27 A3
Moy
Highland GB 32 D2
Tyrone GB 27 B4
Moycullen IRL 28 A2
Moyenmoutier F 92 C2
Moyenvic F 92 C2
Mózar E 141 C5
Mozhaysk RUS 9 E10
Mozirje SLO 123 A3
Mözs H 112 C2
Mozzanica I 120 B2
Mramorak SRB 127 C2
Mrčajevci SRB 127 D2
Mrkonjić Grad BIH 138 A3
Mrkopalj HR 123 B3
Mrocza PL 76 A2
Mroczeń PL 86 A1
Mroczno PL 69 B4
Mrzezyno PL 67 B4
Mšec CZ 84 B1
Mšeno CZ 84 B2
Mstów PL 86 B3
Mstsislaw BY 13 A9
Mszana Dolna PL 99 B4
Mszczonów PL 77 C5
Muć HR 138 B2
Múccia I 136 B2
Much D 80 B3
Mücheln D 83 A3
Much Marcle GB 39 C4
Muchów PL 85 A4
Much Wenlock GB 39 B4
Mucientes E 142 C2
Muckross IRL 29 B2
Mucur TR 23 B8
Muda P 160 B1
Mudanya TR 186 B3
Mudau D 93 B5
Müden D 72 B3
Mudersbach D 81 B3
Mudurnu TR 187 B6
Muel E 152 A2
Muelas del Pan E 149 A4
Muess D 73 A4
Muff IRL 27 A3
Mugardos E 140 A2
Muge P 154 B2
Mügeln
Sachsen D 83 A5
Sachsen-Anhalt D 83 A5
Múggia I 122 B2
Mugnano I 135 B5
Mugron F 128 C2
Mugueimes E 140 C3
Muhi H 113 B4
Mühlacker D 93 C4
Mühlbach am Hochkönig A 109 B4
Mühlberg
Brandenburg D 83 A5
Thüringen D 82 B2
Mühldorf
A 109 C4
D 95 C4
Muhleberg CH 106 C2
Mühleim D 107 A3
Muhlen-Eichsen D 65 C4
Mühlhausen
Bayern D 94 B2
Thüringen D 82 A2
Mühltroff D 83 B3
Muhos FIN 3 D10
Muhr A 109 B4
Muine Bheag IRL 30 B2
Muirkirk GB 36 A2
Muir of Ord GB 32 D2
Muirteira P 154 B1
Mukacheve UA 12 D5
Muker GB 37 B4
Mula E 165 A3
Muğla TR 188 B3
Mulben GB 32 D3
Mulegns CH 107 C4
Mules I 108 C2
Mülheim D 80 A2
Mulhouse F 106 B2
Muljava SLO 123 B3
Mullanys Cross IRL 26 B2
Müllheim D 106 B2
Mullhyttan S 55 A5
Mullinavat IRL 30 B1
Mullingar IRL 30 A1
Mullion GB 42 B1
Müllrose D 74 B3
Mullsjö S 60 B3
Mulseryd S 60 B3
Munaðarnes IS 190 A4
Munana E 150 B2
Muñás E 141 A4
Münchberg D 83 B3
Müncheberg D 74 B3
München = Munich D 108 A2
Munchen-Gladbach = Mönchengladbach D 80 A2
Münchhausen D 81 B4
Mundaka E 143 A4
Münden D 82 A1
Munderfing A 109 A4
Munderkingen D 107 A4
Mundesley GB 41 C5
Munera E 158 B1
Mungia E 143 A4
Munich = München D 108 A2
Muñico E 150 B2
Muniesa E 153 A3
Munka-Ljungby S 61 C2
Munkebo DK 59 C3
Munkedal S 54 B2
Munkflohögen S 199 B11
Munkfors S 49 C5
Munktorp S 56 A2
Münnerstadt D 82 B2
Muñopepe E 150 B3
Muñotello E 150 B2
Münsingen
CH 106 C2
D 94 C1
Munsö S 57 A3
Münster
CH 106 C3
Hessen D 93 B4
Munster D 72 B3
Münster D 71 C4
Munster F 106 A2
Muntibar E 143 A4
Münzkirchen A 96 C1
Muodoslompolo S 196 B6
Muonio FIN 196 B6
Muotathal CH 107 C3
Muradiye TR 186 D2
Murakeresztúr H 124 A2
Murán SK 99 C4
Murano I 122 B1
Muras E 140 A3
Murat F 116 B2
Muratlı TR 186 A2
Murato F 180 A2
Murat-sur-Vèbre F 130 B1
Murau A 109 B5
Muravera I 179 C3
Murazzano I 133 A4
Murça P 148 A2
Murchante E 144 B2
Murchin D 66 C2
Murcia E 165 B3
Murczyn PL 76 B2
Mur-de-Barrez F 116 C2
Mur-de-Bretagne F 100 A2
Mur-de-Sologne F 103 B3
Mureck A 110 C2
Mürefte TR 186 B2
Muret F 146 A2
Murg CH 107 B4
Murguia E 143 B4
Muri CH 106 B3
Murias de Paredes E 141 B4
Muriedas E 143 A3
Muriel Viejo E 143 C4
Murillo de Rio Leza E 143 B4
Murillo el Fruto E 144 B2
Murjek S 196 C3
Murlaggan GB 34 B2
Murmansk RUS 3 B13
Murmashi RUS 3 B13
Murnau D 108 B2
Muro
E 167 B3
F 180 A1
Muro de Alcoy E 159 C3
Murol F 116 B2
Muro Lucano I 172 B1
Muron F 114 B3
Muros E 140 B1
Muros de Nalón E 141 A4
Murowana Goślina PL 76 B2
Mürren CH 106 C2
Murrhardt D 94 C1
Murska Sobota SLO 111 C3
Mursko Središce HR 111 C3
Murtas E 164 C1
Murten CH 106 C2
Murter HR 137 B4
Murtiçi TR 189 C6
Murtosa P 148 B1
Murtovaara FIN 197 D12
Murvica HR 137 A4
Murviel-lès-Béziers F 130 B2
Mürzsteg A 110 B2
Murzynowo PL 75 B4
Mürzzuschlag A 110 B2
Musculdy F 144 A3
Muskö S 57 A4
Mušov CZ 97 C4
Musselburgh GB 35 C4
Musselkanaal NL 71 B4
Mussidan F 129 A3
Mussomeli I 176 B2
Musson B 92 B1
Mussy-sur-Seine F 104 B3
Mustafakemalpaşa TR 186 B3
Muszaki PL 77 A5
Muszyna PL 99 B4
Mut TR 23 C7
Muta SLO 110 C2
Muthill GB 35 B4
Mutné SK 99 B3
Mutriku E 143 A4
Muttalip TR 187 C5
Mutterbergalm A 108 B2
Muurola FIN 197 C8
Muxía E 140 A1
Muxilka-Ugarte E 143 A4
Muzillac F 101 B3
Mužla SK 112 B2
Muzzano del Turgnano I 122 B2
Mybster GB 32 C3
Myckelgensjö S 200 C3
Myennes F 104 B1
Myjava SK 98 C1
Myking N 46 B2
Mykland N 53 B4
Myra N 53 B5
Myrdal N 46 B4
Myre
Nordland N 194 A6
Nordland N 194 B6
Myresjö S 62 A2
Mýri IS 191 B8
Myrtou CY 181 A2
Mysen N 54 A2
Mysłakowice PL 85 B3
Myślenice PL 99 B3
Myślibórz PL 75 B3
Mysłowice PL 86 B3
Myszków PL 86 B3
Mytishchi RUS 9 E10
Mýtna SK 99 C3
Mýtne Ludany SK 112 A2
Mýto CZ 96 B1

N

Nå N 46 B3
Naaldwijk NL 79 A4
Naantali FIN 8 B2
Naas IRL 30 A2
Nabais P 148 B2
Nabbelund S 62 A5
Nabburg D 95 B4
Načeradec CZ 96 B2
Náchod CZ 85 B4
Nacław PL 68 A1
Nadarzyce PL 75 A5
Nadarzyn PL 77 B5
Nádasd H 111 C3
Nădlac RO 126 A2
Nádudvar H 113 B5
Nadvirna UA 13 D6
Näfels CH 107 B4
Nafpaktos GR 184 A2
Nafplio GR 184 B3
Nagel D 95 B3
Nagele NL 70 B2
Naggen S 200 D2
Nagłowice PL 87 B4
Nagold D 93 C4
Nagore E 144 B2
Nagyatád H 124 A3
Nagybajom H 124 A3
Nagybaracska H 125 A4
Nagybátony H 113 B3
Nagyberény H 112 C2
Nagybörzsöny H 112 B2
Nagycenk H 111 B3
Nagycserkesz H 113 B5
Nagydorog H 112 C2
Nagyfüged H 113 B4
Nagyhersány H 125 B4
Nagyigmánd H 112 B2
Nagyiván H 113 B4
Nagykanizsa H 111 C3
Nagykáta H 113 B3
Nagykonyi H 112 C2
Nagykörös H 113 B3
Nagykörü H 113 B4
Nagylóc H 112 A3
Nagymágocs H 113 C4
Nagymányok H 125 A4
Nagymaros H 112 B2
Nagyoroszi H 112 A3
Nagyrábé H 113 B5
Nagyréde H 113 B3
Nagyszékely H 112 C2
Nagyszénás H 113 C4
Nagyszokoly H 112 C2
Nagytöke H 113 C4
Nagyvázsony H 111 C4
Nagyvenyim H 112 C2
Naharros E 152 B1
Nahe D 64 C3
Naila D 83 B3
Nailloux F 146 A2
Nailsworth GB 43 A4
Naintré F 115 B4
Nairn GB 32 D3
Najac F 129 B4
Nájera E 143 B4
Nak H 112 C2
Nakksjø N 53 A5
Nakło nad Notecią PL 76 A2
Nakskov DK 65 B4
Nalda E 143 B4
Nälden S 199 B11
Nálepkovo SK 99 C4
Nalliers F 114 B2
Nallıhan TR 187 B6
Nalzen F 146 B2
Nalžouské Hory CZ 96 B1
Namdalseid N 199 A8
Náměšť nad Oslavou CZ 97 B4
Námestovo SK 99 B3
Namnå N 49 B4
Namsos N 199 A8
Namsskogan N 199 A10
Namur B 79 B4
Namysłów PL 86 A1
Nançay F 103 B4
Nanclares de la Oca E 143 B4
Nancy F 92 C2
Nangis F 90 C3
Nannestad N 48 B3
Nant F 130 A2
Nanterre F 90 C2
Nantes F 101 B4
Nanteuil-le-Haudouin F 90 B2
Nantiat F 115 B5
Nantua F 118 A2
Nantwich GB 38 A4
Naoussa
Cyclades GR 185 B6
Imathia GR 182 C4
Napajedla CZ 98 B1
Napiwoda PL 77 A5
Naples = Nápoli I 170 C2
Nápoli = Naples I 170 C2
Nar S 57 C4
Nara N 46 A1
Naraval E 141 A4
Narberth GB 39 C2
Nærbø N 52 B1
Narbonne F 130 B1
Narbonne-Plage F 130 B2
Narbuvollen N 199 C8
Narcao I 179 C2
Nardò I 173 B4
Narkaus FIN 197 C9
Narken S 196 C5
Narmo N 48 B3
Narni I 168 A2
Naro I 176 B2
Naro Fominsk RUS 9 E10
Narón E 140 A2
Narros del Castillo E 150 B2
Narta HR 124 B2
Naruszewo PL 77 B5
Narva EST 8 C6
Narvik N 194 B8
Narzole I 133 A3
Näs FIN 51 B7
Nås S 50 B1
Näs S 57 C4
Näsåker S 200 C2
Năsăud RO 17 B6
Nasavrky CZ 97 B3
Nasbinals F 116 C3
Næsbjerg DK 59 C1
Näshull S 62 A3
Našice HR 125 B4
Nasielsk PL 77 B5
Naso I 177 A3
Nassau D 81 B3
Nassenfels D 95 C3
Nassenheide D 74 B2
Nassereith A 108 B1
Nässjö S 62 A2
Nastätten D 81 B3
Næstved DK 65 A4
Näsum S 63 B2
Näsviken S 199 B12
Natalinci SRB 127 C2
Naters CH 119 A5
Nater-Stetten D 108 A2
Nattavaara S 196 C3
Natters A 108 B2
Nattheim D 94 C2
Nättraby S 63 B3
Naturno I 108 C1
Naucelle F 130 A1
Nauders A 108 C1
Nauen D 74 B1
Naul IRL 30 A2
Naumburg D 83 A3
Naundorf D 83 B5
Naunhof D 83 A4
Naustdal N 46 A2
Nautijaur S 196 C2
Nautsi RUS 193 D13
Nava E 142 A1
Navacerrada E 151 B3
Navaconcejo E 149 B4
Nava de Arévalo E 150 B3
Nava de la Asunción E 150 A3
Nava del Rey E 150 A2
Navafriá E 151 A4
Navahermosa E 157 A3
Navahrudak BY 13 B6
Naval E 145 B4
Navalacruz E 150 B3
Navalcán E 150 B2
Navalcarnero E 151 B3
Navaleno E 143 C3
Navalmanzano E 151 A3
Navalmoral E 150 B3
Navalmoral de la Mata E 150 C2
Naválón E 159 C3
Navalonguilla E 150 B2
Navalperal de Pinares E 150 B3
Navalpino E 157 A3
Navaltalgordo E 150 B3
Navaltoril E 156 A3
Navaluenga E 150 B3
Navalvillar de Pela E 156 A2
Navan IRL 30 A2
Navaperal de Tormes E 150 B2
Navapolatsk BY 13 A8
Navarclés E 147 C2
Navarredonda de Gredos E 150 B2
Navarrenx F 144 A3
Navarrés E 159 B3
Navarrete E 143 B4
Navarrevisca E 150 B3
Navás E 147 C2
Navascués E 144 B2
Navas del Madroño E 155 B4
Navas del Rey E 151 B3
Navas del Sepillar E 163 A3
Navas de Oro E 150 A3
Navas de San Juan E 157 B4
Navasfrias E 149 B3
Nave I 120 B3
Nave de Haver P 149 B3
Nävekvarn S 56 B2
Navelli I 169 A3
Navenby GB 40 B3
Näverkärret S 56 A1
Naverstad S 54 B2
Navés E 147 C2
Navezuelas E 156 A2
Navia E 141 A4
Navia de Suarna E 141 B4
Navilly F 105 C4
Năvodari RO 17 C8
Naxos GR 185 B6
Nay F 145 A3
Nazaré P 154 B1
Nazarje SLO 123 A3
Nazilli TR 188 B3
Nazza D 82 A2
Nea Anchialos GR 182 D4
Nea Epidavros GR 184 B4
Nea Flippias GR 182 D2
Nea Kalikratia GR 183 C5
Nea Makri GR 185 A4
Nea Moudania GR 183 C5
Neap GB 33 A5
Nea Peramos GR 183 C6
Neapoli
Kozani GR 182 C3
Kriti GR 185 D6
Lakonia GR 184 C4
Nea Stira GR 185 A5

Neath GB 39 C3
Nea Visa GR 186 A1
Nea Zichni GR 183 B5
Nebljusi HR 124 C1
Neblo SLO 122 A2
Nebolchy RUS 9 C8
Nebra D 82 A3
Nebreda E 143 C3
Nechanice CZ 84 B3
Neckargemünd D 93 B4
Neckarsulm D 94 B1
Neda E 140 A2
Neded SK 112 A1
Nedelišće HR 124 A2
Nederweert NL 80 A1
Nedreberg N 48 B3
Nedre Gärdsjö S 50 B2
Nedre Soppero S 196 A4
Nedstrand N 52 A1
Nedvědice CZ 97 B4
Nędza PL 86 B2
Neede NL 71 B3
Needham Market GB 45 A5
Needingworth GB 44 A3
Neermoor D 71 A4
Neeroeteren B 80 A1
Neerpelt B 79 A5
Neesen D 72 B1
Neetze D 73 A3
Nefyn GB 38 B2
Negotin SRB 16 C5
Negotino MK 182 B4
Negrar I 121 B3
Negredo E 151 A5
Negreira E 140 B2
Nègrepelisse F 129 B4
Negru Vodă RO 17 D8
Negueira de Muñiz E 141 A4
Neheim D 81 A3
Neila E 143 B4
Néive I 119 C5
Nejdek CZ 83 B4
Nekla PL 76 B2
Neksø DK 67 A4
Nelas P 148 B2
Nelaug N 53 B4
Nelidovo RUS 9 D8
Nelim FIN 193 D12
Nellingen D 94 C1
Nelson GB 40 B1
Neman RUS 12 A5
Nemea GR 184 B3
Nemesgörzsöny H 111 B4
Nemeskér H 111 B3
Nemesnádudvar H 125 A5
Nemesszalók H 111 B4
Németkér H 112 C2
Nemours F 103 A4
Nemška Loka SLO 123 B4
Nemšová SK 98 C2
Nenagh IRL 28 B3
Nenince SK 112 A3
Nenita GR 185 A7
Nenzing A 107 B4
Neochori GR 182 D3
Neo Chori GR 184 A2
Neon Petritsi GR 183 B5
Nepi I 168 A2
Nepomuk CZ 96 B1
Nérac F 129 B3
Neratovice CZ 84 B2
Nerchau D 83 A4
Néré F 115 C3
Neresheim D 94 C2
Nereto I 136 C2
Nerezine HR 123 C3
Nerežišća HR 138 B2
Neringa LT 12 A4
Néris-les Bains F 116 A2
Nerito I 169 A3
Nerja E 163 B4
Néronde F 117 B4
Nérondes F 103 C4
Nerpio E 164 A2
Nersingen D 94 C2
Nerva E 161 B3
Nervesa della Battáglia I 121 B5
Nervi I 134 A2
Nes
Buskerud N 48 B1
Hedmark N 48 B2
NL 70 A2
Sogn og Fjordane N 46 A3
Sør-Trøndelag N 198 B6
Nesbyen N 47 B6
Neset N 199 D7
Nesflaten N 52 A2
Nesjahverfi IS 191 C10
Neskaupstaður IS 191 B12
Nesland N 53 A3
Neslandsvatn N 53 B5
Nesle F 90 B2
Nesna N 195 D4
Nesoddtangen N 48 C2
Nesovice CZ 98 B1
Nesselwang D 108 B1
Nesslau CH 107 B4
Nessmersiel D 71 A4
Nesso I 120 B2
Nesterov UA 13 C5
Nestorio GR 182 C3
Nesttun N 46 B2
Nesvady SK 112 B2
Nesvatnstemmen N 53 B4
Nether Stowey GB 43 A3
Netland N 52 B2
Netolice CZ 96 B2
Netphen D 81 B4
Netstal CH 107 B4
Nettancourt F 91 C4
Nettetal D 80 A2
Nettlingen D 72 B3
Nettuno I 168 B2
Neualbenreuth D 95 B4
Neubeckum D 81 A4
Neubrandenburg D 74 A2
Neubruchhausen D 72 B1
Neubukow D 65 B4
Neuburg D 94 C3
Neuchâtel CH 106 C1
Neu Darchau D 73 A3
Neudau A 111 B3
Neudietendorf D 82 B2
Neudorf D 93 B4
Neuenbürg D 93 C4
Neuenburg D 71 A4
Neuendorf D 66 B2
Neuenhagen D 74 B2
Neuenhaus D 71 B3
Neuenkirchen
Niedersachsen D 71 B5
Niedersachsen D 72 A2
Nordrhein-Westfalen D 71 B4
Nordrhein-Westfalen D 81 B3
Neuenrade D 81 A3
Neuenwalde D 64 C1
Neuerburg D 92 A2
Neufahrn
Bayern D 95 C3
Bayern D 95 C4
Neuf-Brisach F 106 A2
Neufchâteau
B 92 B1
F 92 C1
Neufchâtel-en-Bray F 90 B1
Neufchâtel-sur-Aisne F 91 B4
Neuflize F 91 B4
Neugersdorf D 84 B2
Neuhardenberg D 74 B3
Neuharlingersiel D 71 A4
Neuhaus
Bayern D 95 B3
Bayern D 96 C1
Niedersachsen D 64 C2
Niedersachsen D 73 A3
Niedersachsen D 81 A5
Neuhaus a Rennweg D 82 B3
Neuhausen
CH 107 B3
D 83 B5
Neuhausen ob Eck D 107 B3
Neuhof
Bayern D 94 B2
Hessen D 82 B1
Neuhofen an der Krems A 110 A1
Neuillé-Pont-Pierre F 102 B2
Neuilly-en-Thelle F 90 B2
Neuilly-le-Réal F 104 C2
Neuilly-l'Évêque F 105 B4
Neuilly-St Front F 90 B3
Neu-Isenburg D 93 A4
Neukalen D 66 C1
Neu Kaliss D 73 A4
Neukirch D 84 A2
Neukirchen
A 109 A4
Hessen D 81 B5
Schleswig-Holstein D 64 B1
Neukirchen am Grossvenediger A 109 B3
Neukirchen bei Heiligen Blut D 95 B4
Neukloster D 65 C4
Neulengbach A 110 A2
Neulise F 117 B4
Neu Lübbenau D 74 B2
Neum BIH 139 C3
Neumagen D 92 B2
Neumarkt D 95 B3
Neumarkt am Wallersee A 109 B4
Neumarkt im Hausruckkreis A 109 A4
Neumarkt im Mühlkreis A 96 C2
Neumarkt im Steiermark A 110 B1
Neumarkt Sankt Veit D 95 C4
Neumünster D 64 B2
Neunburg vorm Wald D 95 B4
Neung-sur-Beuvron F 103 B3
Neunkirch
Luzern CH 106 B3
Schaffhausen CH 107 B3
Neunkirchen
A 111 B3
Neunkirchen
Nordrhein-Westfalen D 80 B3
Saarland D 92 B3
Neunkirchen am Brand D 94 B3
Neuötting D 95 C4
Neupetershain D 84 A2
Neuravensburg D 107 B4
Neureut D 93 B4
Neuruppin D 74 B1
Neusäss D 94 C2
Neusiedl A 111 B3
Neuss D 80 A2
Neussargues-Moissac F 116 B2
Neustadt
Bayern D 94 B2
Bayern D 95 B4
Bayern D 95 C3
Brandenburg D 73 B5
Hessen D 81 B5
Niedersachsen D 72 B2
Rheinland-Pfalz D 93 B4
Sachsen D 84 A2
Schleswig-Holstein D 65 B3
Thüringen D 82 B3
Thüringen D 83 B3
Neustadt-Glewe D 73 A4
Neustift im Stubaital A 108 B2
Neustrelitz D 74 A2
Neutal A 111 B3
Neutrebbin D 74 B3
Neu-Ulm D 94 C2
Neuves-Maisons F 92 C2
Neuvic
Corrèze F 116 B2
Dordogne F 129 A3
Neuville-aux-Bois F 103 A4
Neuville-de-Poitou F 115 B4
Neuville-les-Dames F 117 A5
Neuville-sur-Saône F 117 B4
Neuvy-le-Roi F 102 B2
Neuvy-Santour F 104 A2
Neuvy-St Sépulchre F 103 C3
Neuvy-sur-Barangeon F 103 B4
Neuwied D 80 B3
Neuzelle D 74 B3
Névache F 118 B3
Neveklov CZ 96 B2
Nevel RUS 9 D6
Neverfjord N 192 B7
Nevers F 104 C2
Nevesinje BIH 139 B4
Névez F 100 B2
Nevlunghavn N 53 B5
Nevşehir TR 23 B8
New Abbey GB 36 B3
New Aberdour GB 33 D4
New Alresford GB 44 B2
Newark-on-Trent GB 40 B3
Newbiggin-by-the-Sea GB 37 A5
Newbliss IRL 27 B3
Newborough GB 38 A2
Newbridge IRL 30 A2
Newbridge on Wye GB 39 B3
Newburgh
Aberdeenshire GB 33 D4
Fife GB 35 B4
Newbury GB 44 B2
Newby Bridge GB 36 B4
Newcastle GB 27 B5
Newcastle Emlyn GB 39 B2
Newcastleton GB 37 A4
Newcastle-under-Lyme GB 40 B1
Newcastle upon Tyne GB 37 B5
Newcastle West IRL 29 B2
Newchurch GB 39 B3
New Costessey GB 41 C5
New Cumnock GB 36 A2
Newent GB 39 C4
New Galloway GB 36 A2
Newham GB 45 B4
Newhaven GB 45 C4
Newington GB 45 B5
Newinn IRL 29 B4
Newlyn GB 42 B1
Newmachar GB 33 D4
Newmarket
Suffolk GB 45 A4
Western Isles GB 31 A2
IRL 29 B3
Newmarket-on-Fergus IRL 28 B3
New Mills GB 40 B2
New Milton GB 44 C2
New Pitsligo GB 33 D4
Newport
Isle of Wight GB 44 C2
Newport GB 39 C4
Pembrokeshire GB 39 B2
Telford & Wrekin GB 38 B4
Newport
Mayo IRL 28 A2
Tipperary IRL 29 B3
Newport-on-Tay GB 35 B5
Newport Pagnell GB 44 A3
Newquay GB 42 B1
New Quay GB 39 B2
New Radnor GB 39 B3
New Romney GB 45 C4
New Ross IRL 30 B2
Newry GB 27 B4
New Scone GB 35 B4
Newton Abbot GB 43 B3
Newton Arlosh GB 36 B3
Newton Aycliffe GB 37 B5
Newton Ferrers GB 42 B2
Newtonhill GB 33 D4
Newtonmore GB 32 D2
Newton Stewart GB 36 B2
Newtown
Herefordshire GB 39 B4
Powys GB 39 B3
Newtownabbey GB 27 B5
Newtownards GB 27 B5
Newtownbutler GB 27 B3
Newtown Cunningham IRL 27 B3
Newtown Hamilton GB 27 B4
Newtownmountkennedy IRL 30 A2
Newtown St Boswells GB 35 C5
Newtown Sands IRL 29 B2
Newtownstewart GB 27 B3
Nexon F 115 C5
Neyland GB 39 C2
Nibbiano I 120 C2
Nibe DK 58 B2
Nicastro I 175 C2
Niccone I 135 B5
Nice F 133 B3
Nickelsdorf A 111 B4
Nicolosi I 177 B4
Nicosia
CY 181 A2
I 177 B3
Nicótera I 175 C1
Nidda D 81 B5
Niğde TR 23 C8
Nidzica PL 77 A5
Niebla E 161 B3
Nieborów PL 77 B5
Niebüll D 64 B1
Niechanowo PL 76 B2
Niechorze PL 67 B4
Niedalino PL 67 B5
Niederaula D 82 B1
Niederbipp CH 106 B2
Niederbronn-les-Bains F 93 C3
Niederfischbach D 81 B3
Niedergörsdorf D 74 C1
Niederkrüchten D 80 A2
Niederndorf A 108 B3
Nieder-Olm D 93 B4
Niedersachswerfen D 82 A2
Niederstetten D 94 B1
Niederurnen CH 107 B4
Niederwölz A 110 B1
Niedoradz PL 85 A3
Niedzica PL 99 B4
Niegosławice PL 85 A3
Nieheim D 81 A5
Niemcza PL 85 B4
Niemegk D 74 B1
Niemisel S 196 C5
Niemodlin PL 85 B5
Nienburg
Niedersachsen D 72 B2
Sachsen-Anhalt D 83 A3
Niepołomice PL 99 A4
Nierstein D 93 B4
Niesky D 84 A2
Niestronno PL 76 B2
Nieświń PL 87 A4
Nieszawa PL 76 B3
Nieul-le-Dolent F 114 B2
Nieul-sur-Mer F 114 B2
Nieuw-Amsterdam NL 71 B3
Nieuw-Buinen NL 71 B3
Nieuwegein NL 70 B2
Nieuwe Niedorp NL 70 B1
Nieuwe-Pekela NL 71 A3
Nieuwerkerken B 79 B5
Nieuwe-schans NL 71 A4
Nieuwolda NL 71 A3
Nieuwpoort B 78 A2
Nieuw-Weerdinge NL 71 B3
Nigrita GR 183 C5
Nigüelas E 163 B4
Nijar E 164 C2
Nijemci HR 125 B5
Nijkerk NL 70 B2
Nijlen B 79 A4
Nijmegen NL 80 A1
Nijverdal NL 71 B3
Nikel RUS 193 C14
Nikinci SRB 127 C1
Nikiti GR 183 C5
Nikitsch A 111 B3
Nikkaluokta S 196 B2
Nikla H 111 C4
Niklasdorf A 110 B2
Nikšić MNE 139 C4
Nilivaara S 196 B4
Nîmes F 131 B3
Nimis I 122 A2
Nimtofte DK 58 B3
Nin HR 137 A4
Nindorf D 64 B2
Ninemilehouse IRL 30 B1
Ninove B 79 B4
Niort F 114 B3
Niš SRB 16 D4
Nisa P 155 B3
Niscemi I 177 B3
Niskala FIN 197 D10
Nissafors S 60 B3
Nissan-lez-Ensérune F 130 B2
Nissedal N 53 A4
Nissumby DK 58 B1
Nisterud N 53 A5
Niton GB 44 C2
Nitra SK 98 C2
Nitrianske-Pravno SK 98 C2
Nitrianske Rudno SK 98 C2
Nitry F 104 B2
Nittedal N 48 B2
Nittenau D 95 B4
Nittendorf D 95 B3
Nivala FIN 3 E9
Nivelles B 79 B4
Nivnice CZ 98 C1
Nižná SK 99 B3
Nižná Boca SK 99 C3
Nižne Repaše SK 99 B4
Nizza Monferrato I 119 C5
Njarðvík IS 190 D3
Njegůsevo SRB 126 B1
Njivice HR 123 B3
Njurundabommen S 200 D3
Njutånger S 200 E3
Noailles F 90 B2
Noain E 144 B2
Noale I 121 B5
Noalejo E 163 A4
Noblejas E 151 C4
Noceda E 141 B4
Nocera Inferiore I 170 C2
Nocera Terinese I 175 B2
Nocera Umbra I 136 B1
Noceto I 120 C3
Noci I 173 B3
Nociglia I 173 B4
Nodeland N 53 B3
Nödinge S 60 B2
Nods F 105 B5
Noé F 146 A2
Noépoli I 174 A2
Noeux-les-Mines F 78 B2
Noez E 157 A3
Nogales E 155 C4
Nogara I 121 B4
Nogarejas E 141 B4
Nogaro F 128 C2
Nogent F 105 A4
Nogent l'Artaud F 90 C3
Nogent-le-Roi F 90 C1
Nogent-le-Rotrou F 89 B4
Nogent-sur-Seine F 91 C3
Nogent-sur-Vernisson F 103 B4
Nogersund S 63 B2
Noguera E 152 B2
Noguerones E 163 A3
Nohfelden D 92 B3
Nohn D 80 B2
Noia E 140 B2
Noicáttaro I 173 A2
Noirétable F 117 B3
Noirmoutier-en-l'Île F 114 A1
Noja E 143 A3
Nojewo PL 75 B5
Nokia FIN 8 B3
Nol S 60 B2
Nola I 170 C2
Nolay F 104 C3
Noli I 133 A4
Nolnyra S 51 B4
Nombela E 150 B3
Nomeny F 92 C2
Nomexy F 92 C2
Nonancourt F 89 B5
Nonant-le-Pin F 89 B4
Nonántola I 121 C4
Nonaspe E 153 A4
None I 119 C4
Nontron F 115 C4
Nonza F 180 A2
Noordhorn NL 71 A3
Noordwijk NL 70 B1
Noordwijkerhout NL 70 B1
Noordwolde NL 70 B3
Noppikoski S 50 A1
Nora S 55 A6
Nørager DK 58 B2
Norberg S 50 B2
Norboda S 51 B5
Nórcia I 136 C2
Nordagutu N 53 A5
Nordanås S 200 B4
Nordausques F 78 B2
Nordborg DK 64 A2
Nordby
Aarhus Amt. DK 59 C3
Ribe Amt. DK 59 C1
Norddeich D 71 A4
Norddorf D 64 B1
Norden D 71 A4
Nordenham D 72 A1
Norderhov N 48 B2
Norderney D 71 A4
Norderstapel D 64 B2
Norderstedt D 64 C3
Nordfjord N 193 B14
Nordfjordeid N 198 D3
Nordfold N 194 C6
Nordhalben D 82 B3
Nordhausen D 82 A2
Nordheim vor der Rhön D 82 B2
Nordholz D 64 C1
Nordhorn D 71 B4
Nordingrå S 200 D4
Nordkjosbotn N 192 C3
Nordli N 199 A10
Nördlingen D 94 C2
Nordmaling S 200 C5
Nordmark S 49 C6
Nordmela N 194 A6
Nord-Odal N 48 B3
Nordre Osen N 48 A3
Nordsinni N 48 B1
Nørdstedalsseter N 198 D4
Nordstemmen D 72 B2
Nordvågen N 193 B10
Nordwalde D 71 B4
Noreña E 142 A1
Noresund N 48 B1
Norg NL 71 A3
Norheimsund N 46 B3
Norie S 63 B2
Norma I 169 B2
Nornäs S 49 A5
Norrahammar S 62 A2
Norråker S 200 B1
Norrala S 51 A3
Norra Vi S 62 A3
Nørre Aaby DK 59 C2
Nørre Alslev DK 65 B4
Nørre Lyndelse DK 59 C3
Nørre Nebel DK 59 C1
Norrent-Fontes F 78 B2
Nørre Snede DK 59 C2
Nørresundby DK 58 A2
Nørre Vorupør DK 58 B1
Norrfjärden S 196 D4
Norrhed S 196 C3
Norrhult Klavreström S 62 A3
Norrköping S 56 B2
Norrskedika S 51 B5
Norrsundet S 51 B4
Norrtälje S 57 A4
Nors DK 58 A1
Norsbron S 55 A4
Norsholm S 56 B1
Norsjö S 200 B5
Nörten-Hardenberg D 82 A1
Northallerton GB 37 B5
Northampton GB 44 A3
North Berwick GB 35 B5
North Charlton GB 37 A5
Northeim D 82 A2
Northfleet GB 45 B4
North Frodingham GB 40 B3
North Kessock GB 32 D2
Northleach GB 44 B2
North Molton GB 42 A3
North Petherton GB 43 A3
Northpunds GB 33 B5
North Somercotes GB 41 B4
North Tawton GB 42 B3
North Thoresby GB 41 B3
North Walsham GB 41 C5
Northwich GB 38 A4
Norton GB 40 A3
Nortorf D 64 B2
Nort-sur-Erdre F 101 B4
Nörvenich D 80 B2
Norwich GB 41 C5
Norwick GB 33 A6
Nøsen N 47 B5
Nossa Senhora do Cabo P 154 C1
Nossebro S 55 B3
Nössemark S 54 A2
Nossen D 83 A5
Notaresco I 169 A3
Noto I 177 C4
Notodden N 53 A5
Nottingham GB 40 C2
Nottuln D 71 C4
Nouan-le-Fuzelier F 103 B4
Nouans-les-Fontaines F 103 B3
Nougaroulet F 129 C3
Nouvion F 78 B1
Nouzonville F 91 B4
Nova H 111 C3
Nová Baňa SK 98 C2
Nová Bystrica SK 99 B3
Nová Bystřice CZ 97 B3
Nova Crnja SRB 126 B2
Novafeltria I 135 B5
Nova Gorica SLO 122 B2
Nova Gradiška HR 124 B3
Nováky SK 98 C2
Novalaise F 118 B2
Novales E 145 B3

Nov–Orb 263

Nova Levante I 108 C2
Novalja HR 137 A3
Nová Paka CZ 84 B3
Nova Pazova SRB 127 C2
Nová Pec CZ 96 C1
Novara I 120 B1
Novara di Sicília I 177 A4
Nova Siri I 174 A2
Novate Mezzola I 120 A2
Nova Topola BIH 124 B3
Novaya Ladoga RUS 9 B8
Nova Zagora BG 17 D6
Nové Hrady CZ 96 C2
Novelda E 165 A4
Novellara I 121 C3
Nové Město SK 98 C1
Nové Město nad Metují CZ 85 B4
Nové Město na Moravě CZ 97 B4
Nové Město pod Smrkem CZ 84 B3
Nové Mitrovice CZ 96 B1
Noventa di Piave I 122 B1
Noventa Vicentina I 121 B4
Novés E 151 B3
Noves F 131 B3
Nové Sady SK 98 C1
Novés de Segre E 147 B2
Nové Strašeci CZ 84 B1
Nové Zámky SK 112 B2
Novgorod RUS 9 C7
Novi Bečej SRB 126 B2
Novi di Módena I 121 C3
Novigrad
Istarska HR 122 B2
Zadarsko-Kninska HR 137 A4
Novigrad Podravski HR 124 A2
Novi Kneževac SRB 126 A2
Novi Lígure I 120 C1
Noville B 92 A1
Novi Marof HR 124 A2
Novion-Porcien F 91 B4
Novi Pazar
BG 17 D7
SRB 16 D4
Novi Sad SRB 126 B1
Novi Slankamen SRB 126 B2
Novi Travnik BIH 139 A3
Novi Vinodolski HR 123 B3
Novohrad-Volynskyy UA 13 C7
Novo Mesto SLO 123 B4
Novo Miloševo SRB 126 B2
Novorzhev RUS 9 D6
Novo Selo BIH 125 B3
Novoselytsya UA 17 A7
Novosokolniki RUS 9 D6
Novoveská Huta SK 99 C4
Novovolynsk UA 13 C6
Novska HR 124 B2
Nový Bor CZ 84 B2
Nový Bydžov CZ 84 B3
Novy-Chevrières F 91 B4
Nowy Dwór Mazowiecki PL 77 B5
Nový-Hrozenkov CZ 98 B2
Nový Jičín CZ 98 B2
Novy Knin CZ 96 B2
Nowa Cerekwia PL 86 B1
Nowa Dęba PL 87 B5
Nowa Karczma PL 68 A3
Nowa Kościoł PL 85 A3
Nowa Ruda PL 85 B4
Nowa Słupia PL 87 B5
Nowa Sól PL 85 A3
Nowa Wieś PL 69 B4
Nowa-Wieś Wielka PL 76 B3
Nowe PL 69 B3
Nowe Brzesko PL 87 B4
Nowe Grudze PL 77 B4
Nowe Kiejkuty PL 77 A6
Nowe Miasteczko PL 85 A3
Nowe Miasto
Mazowieckie PL 77 B5
Mazowieckie PL 87 A4
Nowe Miasto Lubawskie PL 69 B4
Nowe Miasto nad Wartą PL 76 B2
Nowe Skalmierzyce PL 86 A2
Nowe Warpno PL 74 A3
Nowica PL 69 A4
Nowogard PL 75 A4
Nowogród Bobrzanski PL 84 A3
Nowogrodziec PL 84 A3
Nowosolna PL 86 A3
Nowy Dwór Gdański PL 69 A4
Nowy Korczyn PL 87 B4
Nowy Sącz PL 99 B4
Nowy Staw PL 69 A4
Nowy Targ PL 99 B4
Nowy Tomyśl PL 75 B5
Nowy Wiśnicz PL 99 B4
Noyalo F 101 B3
Noyal-Pontivy F 100 A3
Noyant F 102 B2
Noyelles-sur-Mer F 78 B1
Noyen-sur-Sarthe F 102 B1
Noyers F 104 B2
Noyers-sur-Cher F 103 B3
Noyers-sur-Jabron F 132 A1
Noyon F 90 B2
Nozay F 101 B4
Nuaillé F 102 B1
Nuaillé-d'Aunis F 114 B3
Nuars F 104 B2
Nubledo E 141 A5
Nuéno E 145 B3
Nuestra Señora Sa Verge des Pilar E 166 C1
Nueva E 142 A2
Nueva Carteya E 163 A3
Nuevalos E 152 A2
Nuits F 104 B3
Nuits-St Georges F 105 B3
Nule I 178 B3
Nules E 159 B3
Nulvi I 178 B2
Numana I 136 B2
Numansdorp NL 79 A4
Nümbrecht D 81 B3
Nunchritz D 83 A5
Nuneaton GB 40 C2
Nunnanen FIN 196 A7
N Unnaryd S 60 B3
Nuñomoral E 149 B3
Nunspeet NL 70 B2
Nuorgam FIN 193 B11
Núoro I 178 B3
Nurallao I 179 C3
Nuremberg = Nürnberg D 94 B3
Nurmes FIN 3 E11
Nürnberg = Nuremberg D 94 B3
Nurri I 179 C3
Nürtingen D 94 C1
Nus I 119 B4
Nusnäs S 50 B1
Nusplingen D 107 A3
Nuštar HR 125 B4
Nuupas FIN 197 C9
Nyåker S 200 C5
Nyáregyháza H 112 B3
Nyarlörinc H 113 C3
Nyasvizh BY 13 B7
Nybble S 55 A5
Nybergsund N 49 A4
Nybøl DK 64 B2
Nyborg
DK 59 C3
S 196 D6
Nybro S 62 B3
Nybster GB 32 C3
Nyby DK 65 B5
Nye S 62 A3
Nyékládháza H 113 B4
Nyergesujfalu H 112 B2
Nyhammar S 50 B1
Nyhyttan S 55 A5
Nyirád H 111 B4
Nyirbátor H 16 B5
Nyíregyháza H 16 B4
Nyker DK 67 A3
Nykil S 56 B1
Nykirke N 48 B2
Nykøbing
Falster DK 65 B4
Vestsjællands Amt. DK 61 D1
Nykøbing Mors DK 58 B1
Nyköping S 56 B3
Nykroppa S 55 A5
Nykvarn S 56 A3
Nykyrke S 55 B5
Nyland S 200 C3
Nylars DK 67 A3
Nymburk CZ 84 B3
Nynäshamn S 57 B3
Nyon CH 118 A3
Nyons F 131 A4
Nýřany CZ 96 B1
Nýrsko CZ 95 B5
Nyrud N 193 C13
Nysa PL 85 B5
Nysäter S 55 A3
Nyseter N 198 C5
Nyskoga S 49 B4
Nysted DK 65 B4
Nystrand N 53 A5
Nyúl H 111 B4
Nyvoll N 192 B7

O

Oadby GB 40 C2
Oakengates GB 38 B4
Oakham GB 40 C3
Oanes N 52 B2
Obalj BIH 139 B4
Oban GB 34 B2
O Barco E 141 B4
Obbola S 200 C6
Obdach A 110 B1
Obejo E 156 B3
Oberammergau D 108 B2
Oberasbach D 94 B2
Oberau D 108 B2
Oberaudorf D 108 B3
Oberbruck F 106 B1
Oberdiessbach CH 106 C2
Oberdorf CH 106 B2
Oberdrauburg A 109 C3
Oberelsbach D 82 B2
Obere Stanz A 110 B2
Ober Grafendorf A 110 A2
Obergünzburg D 108 B1
Obergurgl A 108 C2
Oberhausen D 80 A2
Oberhof D 82 B2
Oberkirch D 93 C4
Oberkirchen D 81 A4
Oberkochen D 94 C2
Obermassfeld-Grimmenthal D 82 B2
Ober-Morlen D 81 B4
Obermünchen D 95 C3
Obernai F 93 C3
Obernberg A 96 C1
Obernburg D 93 B5
Oberndorf D 93 C4
Oberndorf bei Salzburg A 109 B3
Obernkirchen D 72 B2
Oberort A 110 B2
Oberpullendorf A 111 B3
Oberriet CH 107 B4
Oberröblingen D 82 A3
Oberrot D 94 B1
Oberstaufen D 107 B5
Oberstdorf D 107 B5
Obertauern A 109 B4
Obertilliach A 109 C3
Obertraubling D 95 C4
Obertraun A 109 B4
Obertrubach D 95 B3
Obertrum A 109 B4
Oberursel D 81 B4
Obervellach A 109 C4
Oberviechtach D 95 B4
Oberwart A 111 B3
Oberwesel D 93 A3
Oberwinter D 80 B3
Oberwölzstadt A 110 B1
Oberzell D 96 C1
Obice PL 87 B4
Óbidos P 154 B1
Obing D 109 B3
Objat F 129 A4
Objazda PL 68 A2
Öblarn A 109 B5
Obninsk RUS 9 E10
O Bolo E 141 B3
Oborniki PL 75 B5
Oborniki Śląskie PL 85 A4
Obornjača SRB 126 B1
Obrenovac SRB 127 C2
Obrež SRB 127 C1
Obrigheim D 93 B5
Obrov SLO 123 B3
Obrovac
HR 137 A4
SRB 126 B1
Obrovac Sinjski HR 138 B2
Obruk TR 23 B7
Obrzycko PL 75 B5
Obudovac BIH 125 C4
Ocaña E 151 C4
O Carballiño E 140 B2
Occhiobello I 121 C4
Occimiano I 119 B5
Očevlja BIH 139 A4
Ochagavía E 144 B2
Ochiltree GB 36 A2
Ochla PL 84 A3
Ochotnica-Dolna PL 99 B4
Ochotnica-Górna PL 99 B4
Ochsenfurt D 94 B2
Ochsenhausen D 107 A4
Ochtendung D 80 B3
Ochtrup D 71 B4
Ocieka PL 87 B5
Ockelbo S 50 B3
Öckerö S 60 B1
Ocniţa MD 17 A7
O Corgo E 141 B3
Očová SK 99 C3
Ócsa H 112 B3
Öcseny H 125 A4
Öcsöd H 113 C4
Octeville F 88 A2
Ocypel PL 69 B3
Ödåkra S 61 C2
Odby DK 58 B1
Odda N 46 B3
Odder DK 59 C3
Ödeborg S 54 B2
Odeceixe P 160 B1
Odechów PL 87 A5
Odeleite P 160 B2
Odemira P 160 B1
Ödemiş TR 188 A2
Odensbacken S 56 A1
Odense DK 59 C3
Odensjö
Jönköping S 62 A2
Kronoberg S 60 C3
Oderberg D 74 B3
Oderzo I 122 B1
Odesa = Odessa UA 17 B9
Ödeshög S 55 B5
Odessa = Odesa UA 17 B9
Odiáxere P 160 B1
Odie GB 33 B4
Odiham GB 44 B3
Odintsovo RUS 9 E10
Odivelas P 160 A1
Odolanów PL 85 A5
Odón E 152 B2
Odorheiu Secuiesc RO 17 B6
Odrowaz PL 87 A4
Odry CZ 98 B1
Odrzywół PL 87 A4
Ødsted DK 59 C2
Odžaci SRB 126 B1
Odžak BIH 125 B4
Oebisfelde D 73 B3
Oederan D 83 B5
Oeding D 71 C3
Oegstgeest NL 70 B1
Oelde D 81 A4
Oelsnitz D 83 B4
Oer-Erkenschwick D 80 A3
Oerlinghausen D 72 C1
Oettingen D 94 C2
Oetz A 108 B1
Oeventrop D 81 A4
Offanengo I 120 B2
Offenbach D 81 B4
Offenburg D 93 C3
Offida I 136 C2
Offingen D 94 C2
Offranville F 89 A5
Ofir P 148 A1
Ofte N 53 A4
Ofterschwang D 107 B5
Oggiono I 120 B2
Ogihares E 163 A4
Ogliastro Cilento I 170 C3
Ogliastro Marina I 170 C2
Ogmore-by-Sea GB 39 C3
Ogna N 52 B1
Ogre LV 8 D4
Ogrodzieniec PL 86 B3
Ogulin HR 123 B4
Ögur IS 190 A3
Ohanes E 164 B2
Ohey B 79 B5
Ohlstadt D 108 B2
Ohrdorf D 73 B3
Ohrdruf D 82 B2
Ohrid MK 182 B2
Öhringen D 94 B1
Oia E 140 B2
Oiã P 148 B1
Oiartzun E 144 A2
Oijärvi FIN 197 D8
Oilgate IRL 30 B2
Oimbra E 148 A2
Oiselay-et-Grachoux F 105 B4
Oisemont F 90 B1
Oisterwijk NL 79 A5
Öja S 57 C4
Öje S 49 B5
Ojén E 162 B3
Ojrzeń PL 77 B5
Ojuelos Altos E 156 B2
Okalewo PL 77 A4
Okány H 113 C5
Okehampton GB 42 B2
Oklaj HR 138 B2
Økneshamn N 194 B6
Okoč SK 111 B4
Okoličné SK 99 B3
Okonek PL 68 B1
Okonin PL 69 B3
Okřisky CZ 97 B3
Oksa PL 87 B4
Oksbøl DK 59 C1
Oksby DK 59 C1
Øksfjord N 192 B6
Øksna N 48 B3
Okučani HR 124 B3
Okulovka RUS 9 C8
Ólafsfjörður IS 191 A7
Ólafsvík IS 190 C2
ÖLagnö S 57 A4
Olagüe E 144 B2
Oland N 53 B4
Olargues F 130 B1
Oława PL 85 B5
Olazagutia E 144 B1
Olbernhau D 83 B5
Ólbia I 178 B3
Olching D 108 A2
Oldbury GB 43 A4
Oldcastle IRL 27 C3
Old Deer GB 33 D4
Oldeberkoop NL 70 B3
Oldeboorn NL 70 A2
Olden N 198 D3
Oldenbrok D 71 A5
Oldenburg
Niedersachsen D 71 A5
Schleswig-Holstein D 65 B3
Oldenzaal NL 71 B3
Olderdalen N 192 C4
Olderfjord N 193 B9
Oldersum D 71 A4
Oldervik N 192 C2
Oldham GB 40 B1
Oldisleben D 82 A3
Oldmeldrum GB 33 D4
Olea E 142 B2
Oleby S 49 B5
Olechów PL 87 A5
Oledo P 155 B3
Oléggio I 120 B1
Oleiros
Coruña E 140 A2
Oleiros
Coruña E 140 B1
P 154 B3
Oleksandriya UA 13 C7
Olen B 79 A4
Ølen N 52 A1
Olenegorsk RUS 3 B13
Olenino RUS 9 D8
Olesa de Montserrat E 147 C2
Oleśnica PL 85 A5
Olešnice CZ 97 B4
Olesno PL 86 B2
Oletta F 180 A2
Olette F 146 B3
Olevsk UA 13 C7
Olfen D 80 A3
Olgiate Comasco I 120 B1
Olginate I 120 B2
Ølgod DK 59 C1
Olgrinmore GB 32 C3
Olhão P 160 B2
Olhava FIN 197 D8
Olhavo P 154 B1
Oliana E 147 B2
Olias del Rey E 151 C4
Oliena I 178 B3
Oliete E 153 B3
Olimbos GR 188 D2
Olite E 144 B2
Oliva E 159 C3
Oliva de la Frontera E 155 C4
Oliva de Mérida E 156 B1
Oliva de Plasencia E 149 B3
Olivadi I 175 C2
Olival P 154 B2
Olivar E 163 B4
Olivares E 161 B3
Olivares de Duero E 142 C2
Olivares de Júcar E 158 B1
Oliveira de Azeméis P 148 B1
Oliveira de Frades P 148 B1
Oliveira do Conde P 148 B2
Oliveira do Douro P 148 A1
Oliveira do Hospital P 148 B2
Olivenza E 155 C3
Olivet F 103 B3
Olivone CH 107 C3
Öljehult S 63 B3
Olkusz PL 86 B3
Ollerton GB 40 B2
Ollerup DK 65 A3
Olliergues F 117 B3
Ölmbrotorp S 56 A1
Ölme S 55 A4
Olmedilla de Alarcón E 158 B1
Olmedillo de Roa E 143 C3
Olmedo
E 150 A3
I 178 B2
Olmeto F 180 B1
Olmillos de Castro E 149 A3
Olmos de Ojeda E 142 B2
Olney GB 44 A3
Olobok PL 86 A2
Olocau del Rey E 153 B3
Olofström S 63 B2
Olomouc CZ 98 B1
Olonets RUS 9 B8
Olonne-sur-Mer F 114 B2
Olonzac F 130 B1
Oloron-Ste Marie F 145 A3
Olost E 147 C3
Olot E 147 B3
Olovo BIH 139 A4
Olpe D 81 A3
Olsberg D 81 A4
Olsene B 79 B3
Olserud S 55 A4
Olshammar S 55 B5
Olshanka UA 13 D9
Olszanica PL 85 A3
Olsztyn
Śląskie PL 86 B3
Warmińsko-Mazurskie PL 69 B5
Olsztynek PL 77 A5
Olszyna PL 84 A3
Olszyny PL 77 A6
Oltedal N 52 B2
Olten CH 106 B2
Olteniţa RO 17 C7
Olula del Rio E 164 B2
Ølve N 46 B2
Olvega E 144 C2
Olvera E 162 B2
Olympia GR 184 B2
Olzai I 178 B3
Omagh GB 27 B3
Omalos GR 185 D4
Omegna I 119 B5
Omiš HR 138 B2
Omišalj HR 123 B3
Ommen NL 71 B3
Omodhos CY 181 B1
Omoljica SRB 127 C2
On B 79 B5
Oña E 143 B3
Onano I 168 A1
O Näsberg S 49 B5
Oñati E 143 A4
Onda E 159 B3
Ondara E 159 C4
Ondarroa E 143 A4
Onesse-et-Laharie F 128 B1
Oneşti RO 17 B7
Onhaye B 79 B4
Onich GB 34 B2
Onil E 159 C3
Onis E 142 A2
Önnestad S 61 C4
Onsala S 60 B2
Ontinyent E 159 C3
Ontur E 158 C2
Onzain F 103 B3
Onzonilla E 142 B1
Oostburg NL 79 A3
Oostende B 78 A2
Oosterend NL 70 A2
Oosterhout NL 79 A4
Oosterwolde NL 71 B3
Oosterzele B 79 B3
Oosthuizen NL 70 B2
Oostkamp B 78 A3
Oostmalle B 79 A4
Oost-Vlieland NL 70 A2
Oostvoorne NL 79 A4
Ootmarsum NL 71 B3
Opalenica PL 75 B5
O Páramo E 140 B3
Opařany CZ 96 B2
Opatija HR 123 B3
Opatów
Śląskie PL 86 B2
Świętokrzyskie PL 87 B5
Wielkopolskie PL 86 A2
Opatówek PL 86 A2
Opatowiec PL 87 B4
Opava CZ 98 B1
O Pedrouzo E 140 B2
Opeinde NL 70 A3
Oper Thalkirchdorf D 107 B5
Opglabbeerk B 80 A1
Opicina I 122 B2
O Pino E 140 B2
Oplotnica SLO 123 A4
Opmeer NL 70 B1
Opochka RUS 9 D6
Opočno CZ 85 B4
Opoczno PL 87 A4
Opole PL 86 B1
Oporów PL 77 B4
O Porriño E 140 B2
Opovo SRB 127 B2
Oppach D 84 A2
Oppdal N 198 C6
Oppeby
Östergötland S 56 B1
Södermanland S 56 B2
Oppedal N 46 A2
Oppegård N 54 A1
Oppenau D 93 C4
Oppenberg A 110 B1
Oppenheim D 93 B4
Óppido Lucano I 172 B1
Óppido Mamertina I 175 C1
Opponitz A 110 B1
Oppstad N 48 B3
Oprtalj HR 122 B2
Opsaheden S 49 B5
Ópusztaszer H 113 C4
Opuzen HR 138 B3
Ora
CY 181 B2
I 121 A4
Orada P 155 C3
Oradea RO 16 B4
Oradour-sur-Glane F 115 C5
Oradour-sur-Vayres F 115 C4
Oragonja SLO 122 B2
Orah BIH 139 C4
Orahova BIH 138 A3
Orahovica HR 125 B3
Orahovo BIH 124 B3
Oraison F 132 B1
Orajärvi FIN 196 C7
Orange F 131 A3
Orani I 178 B3
Oranienbaum D 83 A4
Oranienburg D 74 B2
Oranmore IRL 28 A3
Orašac SRB 127 C2
Orašje BIH 125 B4
Oravská Lesná SK 99 B3
Oravská Polhora SK 99 B3
Oravské Veselé SK 99 B3
Oravsky-Podzámok SK 99 B3
Orba E 159 C3
Orbacém P 148 A1
Orbais F 91 C3
Ørbæk DK 59 C3
Orbassano I 119 B4
Orbe CH 105 C5
Orbec F 89 A4

Orbetello I 168 A1
Orbetello Scalo I 168 A1
Orbigny F 103 B3
Ørby DK 59 B3
Örbyhus S 51 B4
Orce E 164 B2
Orcera E 164 A2
Orchamps-Vennes F 105 B5
Orches F 102 C2
Orchete E 159 C3
Orchies F 78 B3
Orchowo PL 76 B3
Orcières F 118 C3
Ordes E 140 A2
Ordhead GB 33 D4
Ordino AND 146 B2
Ordizia E 144 A1
Orduña E 143 B4
Ore S 50 A2
Orea E 152 B2
Orebić HR 138 C3
Örebro S 56 A1
Öregcsertő H 112 C3
Öregrund S 51 B5
Orehoved DK 65 B4
Orellana E 156 A2
Orellana de la Sierra E 156 A2
Ören TR 188 B2
Örencik TR 187 C4
Orestiada GR 186 A1
Organyà E 147 B2
Orgaz E 157 A4
Orgelet F 105 C4
Ørgenvika N 48 B1
Orgères-en-Beauce F 103 A3
Orgibet F 145 B4
Orgnac-l'Aven F 131 A3
Orgon F 131 B4
Orgósolo I 178 B3
Orhaneli TR 186 C3
Orhangazi TR 187 B4
Orhei MD 17 B8
Orhomenos GR 184 A3
Oria E 164 B2
Ória I 173 B3
Origny-Ste Benoite F 91 B3
Orihuela E 165 A4
Orihuela del Tremedal E 152 B2
Orikum AL 182 C1
Oriola P 154 C3
Oriolo I 174 A2
Oriovac HR 125 B3
Orissaare EST 8 C3
Oristano I 179 C2
Öriszentpéter H 111 C3
Ørje N 54 A2
Orjiva E 163 B4
Orkanger N 198 B6
Örkelljunga S 61 C3
Örkény H 112 B3
Orlamünde D 82 B3
Orléans F 103 B3
Orlová CZ 98 B2
Orlovat SRB 126 B2
Ormea I 133 A3
Ormelet N 54 A1
Ormemyr N 53 A5
Ormilia GR 183 C5
Ormos GR 185 B5
Ormož SLO 124 A2
Ormskirk GB 38 A4
Ornans F 105 B5
Ornäs S 50 B2
Ørnes N 195 D4
Orneta PL 69 A5
Ørnhøj DK 59 B1
Ornö S 57 A4
Örnsköldsvik S 200 C4
Orolik HR 125 B4
Orom SRB 126 B1
Oron-la-Ville CH 106 C1
Oronsko PL 87 A4
Oropa I 119 B4
Oropesa
Castellón de la Plana E 153 B4
Toledo E 150 C2
O Rosal E 140 C2
Orosei I 178 B3
Orosháza H 113 C4
Oroslavje HR 124 B1
Oroszlány H 112 B2
Oroszlo H 125 A4
Orotelli I 178 B3
Orozko E 143 A4
Orphir GB 33 C3
Orpington GB 45 B4
Orreaga-Roncesvalles E 144 A2
Orrefors S 62 B3
Orrviken S 199 B11
Orsa S 50 A1
Orsara di Púglia I 171 B3
Orsay F 90 C2
Orscholz D 92 B2
Orsennes F 103 C3
Orserum S 55 B5
Orsha BY 13 A9
Orsières CH 119 A4
Örsjö S 63 B3
Ørslev DK 65 A4
Örslösa S 55 B3
Orsogna I 169 A4
Orsomarso I 174 B1
Orşova RO 16 C5
Ørsta N 198 C3
Ørsted DK 58 B3
Örsundsbro S 56 A3
Ortaca TR 188 C3
Ortakent TR 188 B2
Ortaklar TR 188 B2
Ortaköy TR 23 B8
Orta Nova I 171 B3
Orte I 168 A2
Ortenburg D 96 C1
Orth A 111 A3
Orthez F 128 C2
Ortigueira E 140 A3
Ortilla E 145 B3
Ortisei I 108 C2
Orţişoara RO 126 B3
Ortnevik N 46 A3
Orton GB 37 B4
Ortona I 169 A4
Ortrand D 84 A1
Orubica HR 124 B3
Ørum DK 58 B2
Orune I 178 B3
Orusco E 151 B4
Orvalho P 155 A3
Orvault F 101 B4
Ørvella N 53 A5
Orvieto I 168 A2
Orvínio I 169 A2
Oryakhovo BG 17 D5
Orzesze PL 86 B2
Orzinuovi I 120 B2
Orzivécchi I 120 B2
Orzyny PL 77 A6
Os
Hedmark N 48 B3
Hedmark N 199 C8
Osann-Monzel D 92 B2
Osbruk S 62 A2
Øsby DK 59 C2
Osby S 61 C3
Oščadnica SK 98 B2
Oschatz D 83 A5
Oschersleben D 73 B4
Óschiri I 178 B3
Osciłowo PL 77 B5
Osdorf D 64 B3
Osečina SRB 127 C1
Osečná CZ 84 B2
Oseja de Sajambre E 142 A1
Osek CZ 84 B1
Osen N 199 A7
Osera de Ebro E 153 A3
Osidda I 178 B3
Osie PL 69 B3
Osieczna
Pomorskie PL 68 B3
Wielkopolskie PL 75 C5
Osieczno PL 75 A4
Osiek
Kujawsko-Pomorskie PL 76 B3
Kujawsko-Pomorskie PL 77 A4
Pomorskie PL 69 B3
Świętokrzyskie PL 87 B5
Osiek nad Notecią PL 76 A2
Osielsko PL 76 A3
Osijek HR 125 B4
Osilnica SLO 123 B3
Ósilo I 178 B2
Ósimo I 136 B2
Osinja BIH 125 C3
Osintorf BY 13 A9
Osipaonica SRB 127 C3
Osjaków PL 86 A2
Oskamull GB 34 B1
Oskarshamn S 62 A4
Oskarström S 60 C2
Oslany SK 98 C2
Oslavany CZ 97 B4
Ošlje HR 139 C3
Oslo N 48 C2
Øsløs DK 58 A1
Osmancık TR 23 A8
Osmaneli TR 187 B4
Ösmo S 57 B3
Osmolin PL 77 B4
Osnabrück D 71 B5
Ośno Lubuskie PL 75 B3
Osoblaha CZ 85 B5
Osor HR 123 C3
Osorno E 142 B2
Øsoyra N 46 A2
Osøyro N 46 B2
Óspakseyri IS 190 B4
Os Peares E 140 B3
Ospedaletti I 133 B3
Ospitaletto I 120 B3
Oss NL 80 A1
Ossa de Montiel E 158 C1
Ossi I 178 B2
Ossjøen N 47 B5
Ossun F 145 A3
Ostanå S 61 C4
Ostanvik S 50 A2
Ostashkov RUS 9 D8
Östavall S 200 D1
Ostbevern D 71 B4
Østborg N 199 A10
Østby N 49 A4
Osted DK 61 D1
Ostenfeld D 64 B2
Oster UA 13 C9
Øster Assels DK 58 B1
Osterburg D 73 B4
Osterburken D 94 B1
Österbybruk S 51 B4
Osterbyhavn DK 58 A4
Österbymo S 62 A3
Ostercappeln D 71 B5
Österfärnebo S 51 B3
Osterfeld D 83 A3
Österforse S 200 C3
Osterhever D 64 B1
Osterhofen D 95 C5
Osterholz-Scharmbeck D 72 A1
Øster Hornum DK 58 B2
Øster Hurup DK 58 B3
Østerild DK 58 A1
Øster Jølby DK 58 B1
Österlövsta S 51 B4
Øster-marie DK 67 A4
Ostermiething A 109 A3
Osterode am Harz D 82 A2
Ostersiel D 64 B1
Östersund S 199 B11
Øster Tørslev DK 58 B3
Östervåla S 51 B4
Östervallskog S 54 A2
Øster Vrå DK 58 A3
Osterwieck D 73 C3
Osterzell D 108 B1
Ostffyasszonyfa H 111 B4
Östfora S 51 C4
Östhammar S 51 B5
Ostheim F 106 A2
Ostheim vor der Rhön D 82 B2
Osthofen D 93 B4
Ostiano I 120 B3
Ostíglia I 121 B4
Ostiz E 144 B2
Östmark S 49 B4
Östnor S 50 A1
Ostojićevo SRB 126 B2
Ostra I 136 B2
Östra Amtervik S 55 A4
Östraby S 61 D3
Ostrach D 107 B4
Östra Husby S 56 B2
Östra Ljungby S 61 C3
Östra Ryd S 56 B2
Ostrau D 83 A5
Ostrava CZ 98 B2
Østre Halsen N 53 A6
Ostrhauderfehn D 71 A4
Ostritz D 84 A2
Ostróda PL 69 B4
Ostroh UA 13 C7
Ostrołęka PL 12 B4
Ostropole PL 68 B1
Ostroróg PL 75 B5
Ostrošovac BIH 124 C1
Ostrov
CZ 83 B4
RUS 8 D6
Ostrov nad Oslavou CZ 97 B3
Ostrówek PL 86 A2
Ostrowiec PL 68 A1
Ostrowiec-Świętokrzyski PL 87 B5
Ostrowite PL 77 A4
Ostrów Mazowiecka PL 12 B4
Ostrowo PL 76 B3
Ostrów Wielkopolski PL 86 A1
Ostrožac BIH 139 B3
Ostrzeszów PL 86 A1
Ostseebad Kühlungsborn D 65 B4
Ostuni I 173 B3
Osuna E 162 A2
Osvětimany CZ 98 B1
Oswestry GB 38 B3
Oświęcim PL 86 B3
Osztopán H 111 C4
Oteiza E 144 B2
Otelec RO 126 B2
Oteo E 143 A3
Oterbekk N 54 A1
Otero de Herreros E 151 B3
Otero de O Bodas E 141 C4
Othem S 57 C4
Otley GB 40 B2
Otmuchów PL 85 B5
Otočac HR 123 C4
Otok
Splitsko-Dalmatinska HR 138 B2
Vukovarsko-Srijemska HR 125 B4
Otoka BIH 124 C2
Otranto I 173 B4
Otrić HR 138 A2
Otrícoli I 168 A2
Otrokovice CZ 98 B1
Otta N 198 D6
Ottana I 178 B3
Ottaviano I 170 C2
Ottenby S 63 B4
Ottendorf-Okrilla D 84 A1
Ottenhöfen D 93 C4
Ottenschlag A 97 C3
Ottensheim A 96 C2
Otterbach D 93 B3
Otterbäcken S 55 B5
Otterberg D 93 B3
Otterburn GB 37 A4
Otter Ferry GB 34 B2
Otterndorf D 64 C1
Ottersburg D 72 A2
Ottersweier D 93 C4
Otterup DK 59 C3
Ottery St Mary GB 43 B3
Ottignies B 79 B4
Ottmarsheim F 106 B2
Ottobeuren D 107 B5
Öttömös H 126 A1
Ottone I 120 C2
Ottsjö S 199 B10
Ottweiler D 92 B3
Otveşti RO 126 B3
Ötvöskónyi H 124 A3
Otwock PL 12 B4
Ouanne F 104 B2
Ouarville F 90 C1
Oucques F 103 B3
Oud-Beijerland NL 79 A4
Ouddorp NL 79 A3
Oudemirdum NL 70 B2
Oudenaarde B 79 B3
Oudenbosch NL 79 A4
Oudenburg B 78 A3
Oude-Pekela NL 71 A4
Oude-Tonge NL 79 A4
Oudewater NL 70 B1
Oud Gastel NL 79 A4
Oudon F 101 B4
Oughterard IRL 28 A2
Ouguela P 155 B3
Ouistreham F 89 A3
Oulainen FIN 3 D9
Oulchy-le-Château F 91 B3
Oullins F 117 B4
Oulmes F 114 B3
Oulton GB 41 C5
Oulton Broad GB 41 C5
Oulu FIN 3 D9
Oulx I 119 B3
Oundle GB 40 C3
Ouranopoli GR 183 C6
Ourém P 154 B2
Ourense E 140 B3
Ourique P 160 B1
Ourol E 140 A3
Ouroux-en-Morvan F 104 B2
Ousdale GB 32 C3
Oust F 146 B2
Outakoski FIN 193 C10
Outeiro P 148 B1
Outeiro de Rei E 140 A3
Outes E 140 B2
Outokumpu FIN 9 A6
Outreau F 78 B1
Outwell GB 41 C4
Ouzouer-le-Marché F 103 B3
Ouzouer-sur-Loire F 103 B4
Ovada I 133 A4
Ovar P 148 B1
Ove DK 58 B2
Ovelgönne D 72 A1
Overath D 80 B3
Overbister GB 33 B4
Øverbygd N 192 D3
Overdinkel NL 71 B4
Överenhörna S 56 A3
Overhalla N 199 A8
Overijse B 79 B4
Over-jerstal DK 59 C2
Overlade DK 58 B2
Överlida S 60 B2
Överö FIN 51 B7
Overpelt B 79 A5
Overton GB 38 B4
Övertorneå S 196 C6
Överum S 62 A4
Ovidiopol UA 17 B9
Oviedo E 141 A5
Oviglio I 119 C5
Ovíndoli I 169 A3
Ovodda I 178 B3
Øvre Årdal N 47 A4
Øvrebygd N 52 B2
Øvre Rendal N 199 D8
Øvre Sirdal N 52 B2
Övre Soppero S 196 A4
Övre Ullerud S 55 A4
Ovruch UA 13 C8
Ovtrup DK 59 C1
Owińska PL 76 B1
Oxaback S 60 B2
Oxberg S 49 A6
Oxelösund S 56 B3
Oxenholme GB 37 B4
Oxford GB 44 B2
Oxie S 61 D3
Oxilithos GR 185 A5
Oxted GB 45 B4
Oyaca TR 187 C7
Øye N 47 A5
Øyenkilen N 54 A1
Øyer N 48 A2
Øyeren N 49 B4
Oyfiell N 53 A4
Øygärdslia N 53 B4
Oykel Bridge GB 32 D2
Øymark N 54 A2
Oyonnax F 118 A2
Øyslebø N 52 B3
Øystese N 46 B3
Oyten D 72 A2
Øyuvsbu N 52 A3
Ozaeta E 143 B4
Ozalj HR 123 B4
Ożarów PL 87 B5
Ożarów Maz PL 77 B5
Ožbalt SLO 110 C2
Ózd H 113 A4
Ožďany SK 99 C3
Ozieri I 178 B3
Ozimek PL 86 B2
Ozimica BIH 139 A4
Ozora H 112 C2
Ozorków PL 77 C4
Ozzano Monferrato I 119 B5

P

Paakkola FIN 196 D7
Paal B 79 A5
Pabianice PL 86 A3
Pacanów PL 87 B5
Paceco I 176 B1
Pachino I 177 C4
Pačir SRB 126 B1
Pack A 110 B2
Paços de Ferreira P 148 A1
Pacov CZ 96 B3
Pacsa H 111 C4
Pacy-sur-Eure F 89 A5
Paczków PL 85 B5
Padany RUS 3 E13
Padborg DK 64 B2
Padej SRB 126 B2
Padene HR 138 A2
Paderborn D 81 A4
Paderne P 160 B1
Padiham GB 40 B1
Padina SRB 126 B2
Padinska Skela SRB 127 C2
Padornelo P 148 A1
Pádova I 121 B4
Padragkút H 111 B4
Padria I 178 B2
Padrón E 140 B2
Padru I 178 B3
Padstow GB 42 B2
Padul E 163 A4
Padula I 172 B1
Paduli I 170 B2
Paesana I 119 C4
Paese I 121 B5
Pag HR 137 A4
Pagani I 170 C2
Pagánica I 169 A3
Pagánico I 135 C4
Pagl ieta I 169 A4
Pagny-sur-Moselle F 92 C2
Páhi H 112 C3
Pahkakumpu FIN 197 C11
Pahl D 108 B2
Paide EST 8 C4
Paignton GB 43 B3
Pailhès F 146 A2
Paimboeuf F 101 B3
Paimpol F 100 A2
Paimpont F 101 A3
Painswick GB 43 A4
Painten D 95 C3
Paisley GB 34 C3
Pajala S 196 B6
Pajares E 141 A5
Pajares de los Oteros E 142 B1
Pajęczno PL 86 A2
Páka H 111 C3
Pakość PL 76 B3
Pakosławice PL 85 B5
Pakoštane HR 137 B4
Pakrac HR 124 B3
Paks H 112 C2
Palacios de la Sierra E 143 C3
Palaciòs de la Valduerna E 141 B5
Palacios del Sil E 141 B4
Palacios de Sanabria E 141 B4
Palaciosrubios E 150 A2
Palafrugell E 147 C4
Palagiano I 173 B3
Palagonia I 177 B3
Paláia I 135 B3
Palaiokastritsa GR 182 D1
Palaiseau F 90 C2
Palamas GR 182 D4
Palamós E 147 C4
Påläng S 196 D5
Palanga LT 8 E2
Palanzano I 134 A3
Palárikovo SK 112 A2
Palas de Rei E 140 B3
Palata I 170 B2
Palau I 178 A3
Palavas-les-Flots F 131 B2
Palazuelos de la Sierra E 143 B3
Palazzo Adriano I 176 B2
Palazzo del Pero I 135 B4
Palazzolo Acréide I 177 B3
Palazzolo sull Oglio I 120 B2
Palazzo San Gervásio I 172 B1
Palazzuolo sul Senio I 135 A4
Paldiski EST 8 C4
Pale BIH 139 B4
Palekastro GR 185 D7
Palena I 169 B4
Palencia E 142 B2
Palenciana E 163 A3
Paleochora GR 185 D4
Paleometokho CY 181 A2
Palermo I 176 A2
Paleros GR 182 E2
Palestrina I 169 B2
Pálfa H 112 C2
Palfau A 110 B1
Palhaça P 148 B1
Palheiros da Tocha P 148 B1
Palheiros de Quiaios P 148 B1
Paliaopoli GR 185 B5
Palić SRB 126 A1
Palidoro I 168 B2
Palinuro I 172 B1
Paliouri GR 183 D5
Paliseul B 91 B5
Pallanza I 119 B5
Pallares E 161 A3
Pallaruelo de Monegros E 153 A3
Pallas Green IRL 29 B3
Pallerols E 146 B2
Palling D 109 A3
Palluau F 114 B2
Palma P 154 C2
Palma Campània I 170 C2
Palma del Río E 162 A2
Palma de Mallorca E 166 B2
Palma di Montechiaro I 176 B2
Palmádula I 178 B2
Palmanova I 122 B2
Palma Nova E 166 B2
Palmela P 154 C2
Palmerola E 147 B3
Palmi I 175 C1
Pálmonostora H 113 C3
Palo del Colle I 171 B4
Palojärvi FIN 192 D7
Palojoensuu FIN 196 A6
Palomares E 164 B3
Palomares del Campo E 158 B1
Palomas E 156 B1
Palombara Sabina I 168 A2
Palos de la Frontera E 161 B3
Palotabozsok H 125 A4
Palotás H 112 B3
Pals E 147 C4
Pålsboda S 56 A1
Paluzza I 109 C4
Pamhagen A 111 B3
Pamiers F 146 A2
Pamiętowo PL 76 A2
Pampaneira E 163 B4
Pamparato I 133 A3
Pampilhosa
Aveiro P 148 B1
Coimbra P 148 B2
Pampliega E 143 B3
Pamplona E 144 B2
Pampow D 73 A4
Pamukçu TR 186 C2
Pamukkale TR 188 B4
Pamukova TR 187 B5
Panagyurishte BG 17 D6
Pancalieri I 119 C4
Pančevo SRB 127 C2
Pancey F 91 C5
Pancorvo E 143 B3
Pancrudo E 152 B2
Pandino I 120 B2
Pandrup DK 58 A2
Panenský-Týnec CZ 84 B1
Panes E 142 A2
Panevėžys LT 8 E4
Pangbourne GB 44 B2
Panissières F 117 B4
Panki PL 86 B2
Pannes F 103 A4
Panningen NL 80 A1
Pannonhalma H 111 B4
Pano Lefkara CY 181 B2
Pano Panayia CY 181 B1
Panormos GR 185 B6
Panschwitz-Kuckau D 84 A2
Pansdorf D 65 C3
Pantano de Cíjara E 156 A3
Panticosa E 145 B3
Pantín E 140 A2
Pantoja E 151 B4
Pantón E 140 B3
Panxon E 140 B2
Páola I 174 B2
Paola M 175 C3
Pápa H 111 B4

Papasídero I . . . 174 B1
Pápateszér H . . . 111 B4
Papenburg D . . . 71 A4
Paphos CY . . . 181 B1
Pappenheim D . . . 94 C2
Paprotnia PL . . . 77 B5
Parábita I . . . 173 B4
Paraćin SRB . . . 127 D3
Parád H . . . 113 B4
Parada
Bragança P . . . 149 A3
Viseu P . . . 148 B1
Paradas E . . . 162 A2
Paradela E . . . 140 B3
Parades de Rubiales
E . . . 150 A2
Paradinas de San Juan
E . . . 150 B2
Paradiso di Cevadale
I . . . 108 C1
Paradyż PL . . . 87 A4
Parainen FIN . . . 8 B3
Parakhino Paddubye
RUS . . . 9 C8
Parakka S . . . 196 B4
Paralimni CY . . . 181 A2
Parallo Astros GR . 184 B3
Paramé F . . . 88 B2
Paramithia GR . . . 182 D2
Páramo E . . . 141 A4
Páramo del Sil E . . 141 B4
Parandaça P . . . 148 A2
Paravadella E . . . 141 A3
Paray-le-Monial F . 104 C3
Parceiros P . . . 154 B2
Parcey F . . . 105 B4
Parchim D . . . 73 A4
Parciaki PL . . . 77 A6
Parcice PL . . . 86 A2
Pardilla E . . . 151 A4
Pardubice CZ . . . 97 A3
Paredes
E . . . 151 B5
P . . . 148 A1
Paredes de Coura
P . . . 140 C2
Paredes de Nava E 142 B2
Paredes de Siguenza
E . . . 151 A5
Pareja E . . . 151 B5
Parennes F . . . 102 A1
Parenti I . . . 175 B2
Parentis-en-Born F 128 B1
Parey D . . . 73 B4
Parfino RUS . . . 9 D7
Parga GR . . . 182 D2
Pargny-sur-Saulx F. 91 C4
Pari-Gagné F . . . 117 A4
Parigné-l'Évêque
F . . . 102 B2
Parikkala FIN . . . 9 B6
Paris F . . . 90 C2
Parisot F . . . 129 B4
Parkalompolo S . . 196 B5
Parkano FIN . . . 8 A3
Parknasilla IRL . . . 29 C2
Parla E . . . 151 B4
Parlavá E . . . 147 B4
Parma I . . . 120 C3
Parndorf A . . . 111 B3
Párnica SK . . . 99 B3
Parnu EST . . . 8 C4
Parolis E . . . 164 A2
Paros GR . . . 185 B6
Parrillas E . . . 150 B2
Parsberg D . . . 95 B3
Parstein D . . . 74 B3
Partakko FIN . . . 193 C11
Partanna I . . . 176 B1
Parthenay F . . . 102 C1
Partinico I . . . 176 A2
Partizani SRB . . . 127 C2
Partizánske SK . . . 98 C2
Partney GB . . . 41 B4
Påryd S . . . 63 B3
Parzymiechy PL . . . 86 A2
Paşcani RO . . . 17 B7
Pasewalk D . . . 74 A2
Pašina Voda MNE . 139 B5
Påskallavik S . . . 62 A4
Pasłęk PL . . . 69 A4
Pašman HR . . . 137 B4
Passage East IRL . . 30 B2
Passail A . . . 110 B2
Passais F . . . 88 B3
Passau D . . . 96 C1
Passegueiro P . . . 148 B1
Passignano sul
Trasimeno I . . . 135 B5
Passo di Tréia I . . . 136 B2
Passopisciaro I . . . 177 B4
Passow D . . . 74 A3
Passy F . . . 118 B3
Pastavy BY . . . 13 A7
Pástena I . . . 170 B2
Pastrana E . . . 151 B5
Pastrengo I . . . 121 B3
Pasym PL . . . 77 A5
Pásztó H . . . 113 B3
Pata SK . . . 98 C1
Patay F . . . 103 A3
Pateley Bridge GB . . 40 A2
Paterek PL . . . 76 A2
Paterna E . . . 159 B3
Paterna del Campo
E . . . 161 B3
Paterna del Madera
E . . . 158 C1
Paterna de Rivera
E . . . 162 B2
Paternion A . . . 109 C4
Paternò I . . . 177 B3
Paternópoli I . . . 170 C3
Patersdorf D . . . 95 B4
Paterswolde NL . . . 71 A3
Patitiri GR . . . 183 D5
Patmos GR . . . 188 B1
Patna GB . . . 36 A2
Pątnow PL . . . 76 B3
Patoniva FIN . . . 193 C11
Patopirtti FIN . . . 197 B12
Patos AL . . . 182 C1
Patra = Patras GR . 184 A2
Patras = Patra GR . 184 A2
Patreksfjörður IS . . 190 B2
Patrickswell IRL . . . 29 B3
Patrimonio F . . . 180 A2
Patrington GB . . . 41 B3
Pattada I . . . 178 B3
Pattensen
Niedersachsen D . . 72 A3
Niedersachsen D . . 72 B2
Patterdale GB . . . 36 B4
Patti I . . . 177 A3
Páty H . . . 112 B2
Pau F . . . 145 A3
Pauillac F . . . 128 A2
Paularo I . . . 109 C4
Paulhaguet F . . . 117 B3
Paulhan F . . . 130 B2
Paulilátino I . . . 178 B2
Paulistrom S . . . 62 A3
Paullo I . . . 120 B2
Paulstown IRL . . . 30 B1
Pausa D . . . 83 B3
Pauträsk S . . . 200 B3
Pavia
I . . . 120 B2
P . . . 154 C2
Pavias E . . . 159 B3
Pavilly F . . . 89 A4
Pāvilosta LV . . . 8 D2
Pavullo nel Frignano
I . . . 135 A3
Pawłowice PL . . . 86 A1
Pawlowice PL . . . 98 B2
Paxi GR . . . 182 D2
Payallar TR . . . 189 C6
Payerne CH . . . 106 C1
Paymogo E . . . 161 B2
Payrac F . . . 129 B4
Pazardzhik BG . . . 183 A6
Pazaryeri TR . . . 187 B4
Pazin HR . . . 122 B2
Paziols F . . . 146 B3
Pčelić HR . . . 124 B3
Peal de Becerro E . 164 B1
Peasmarsh GB . . . 45 C4
Peć KOS . . . 16 D4
Péccioli I . . . 135 B3
Pécel H . . . 112 B3
Pechao P . . . 160 B2
Pechenga RUS . . . 3 B12
Pechenizhyn UA . . . 13 D6
Pecica RO . . . 126 A3
Pećinci SRB . . . 127 C1
Pecka SRB . . . 127 C1
Peckelsheim D . . . 81 A5
Pečory RUS . . . 8 D5
Pécs H . . . 125 A4
Pécsvárad H . . . 125 A4
Peczniew PL . . . 86 A2
Pedaso I . . . 136 B2
Pedavena I . . . 121 A4
Pedérobba I . . . 121 B4
Pedersker DK . . . 67 A3
Pedescala I . . . 121 B4
Pedrafita E . . . 141 B3
Pedrajas de San
Esteban E . . . 150 A3
Pedralba E . . . 159 B3
Pedralba de la Praderia
E . . . 141 B4
Pedraza E . . . 151 A4
Pedreguer E . . . 159 C4
Pedrera E . . . 162 A3
Pedro Abad E . . . 157 C3
Pedro Bernardo E . 150 B3
Pedroche E . . . 156 B3
Pedrógão P . . . 160 A2
Pedrogao P . . . 149 B2
Pedrógão P . . . 154 B2
Pedrógão Grande
P . . . 154 B2
Pedrola E . . . 144 C2
Pedro-Martinez E . 164 B1
Pedro Muñoz E . . . 158 B1
Pedrosa del Rey E 150 A2
Pedrosa del Rio Urbel
E . . . 143 B3
Pedrosa de Tobalina
E . . . 143 B3
Pedrosillo de los Aires
E . . . 150 B2
Pedrosillo el Ralo
E . . . 150 A2
Pędzewo PL . . . 76 A3
Peebles GB . . . 35 C4
Peel GB . . . 36 B2
Peenemünde D . . . 66 B2
Peer B . . . 79 A5
Pega P . . . 149 B2
Pegalajar E . . . 163 A4
Pegau D . . . 83 A4
Peggau A . . . 110 B2
Pegli I . . . 133 A4
Pegnitz D . . . 95 B3
Pego E . . . 159 C3
Pegões-Estação P. 154 C2
Pegões Velhos P . . 154 C2
Pęgów PL . . . 85 A4
Pegswood GB . . . 37 A5
Peguera E . . . 166 B2
Pehlivanköy TR . . . 186 A1
Peine D . . . 72 B3
Peisey-Nancroix F . 118 B3
Peissenberg D . . . 108 B2
Peiting D . . . 108 B1
Peitz D . . . 84 A2
Péjo I . . . 121 A3
Pelagićevo BIH . . . 125 C4
Pelahustán E . . . 150 B3
Pełczyce PL . . . 75 A4
Pelhřimov CZ . . . 97 B3
Pélissanne F . . . 131 B4
Pelkosenniemi
FIN . . . 197 B10
Pellegrino Parmense
I . . . 120 C2
Pellegrue F . . . 128 B3
Pellérd H . . . 125 A4
Pellestrina I . . . 122 B1
Pellevoisin F . . . 103 C3
Pellizzano I . . . 121 A3
Pello
FIN . . . 196 C7
S . . . 196 C6
Peloche E . . . 156 A2
Pelplin PL . . . 69 B3
Pelussin F . . . 117 B4
Pély H . . . 113 B4
Pembroke GB . . . 39 C2
Pembroke Dock GB 39 C2
Peñacerrada E . . . 143 B4
Penacova P . . . 148 B1
Peña de Cabra E . . 149 B4
Peñafiel E . . . 151 A3
Penafiel P . . . 148 A1
Peñaflor E . . . 162 A2
Peñalba de Santiago
E . . . 141 B4
Peñalsordo E . . . 156 B2
Penalva do Castelo
P . . . 148 B2
Penamacôr P . . . 149 B2
Peñaparda E . . . 149 B3
Peñaranda de
Bracamonte E . . 150 B2
Peñaranda de Duero
E . . . 143 C3
Peñarroya de Tastavins
E . . . 153 B4
Peñarroya-Pueblonuevo
E . . . 156 B2
Peñarrubla E . . . 141 B3
Penarth GB . . . 39 C3
Peñascosa E . . . 158 C1
Peñas de San Pedro
E . . . 158 C2
Peñausende E . . . 149 A4
Penc H . . . 112 B3
Pencoed GB . . . 39 C3
Pendalofos GR . . . 182 C3
Pendeen GB . . . 42 B1
Pendine GB . . . 39 C2
Pendueles E . . . 142 A2
Penedono P . . . 148 B2
Penela P . . . 154 A2
Pénestin F . . . 101 B3
Penhas Juntas P . . 149 A2
Peniche P . . . 154 B1
Penicuik GB . . . 35 C4
Penig D . . . 83 B4
Penilhos P . . . 160 B2
Peñíscola E . . . 153 B4
Penistone GB . . . 40 B2
Penkridge GB . . . 40 C1
Penkun D . . . 74 A3
Penmarch F . . . 100 B1
Pennabilli I . . . 135 B5
Penne I . . . 169 A3
Penne-d'Agenais F 129 B3
Pennes I . . . 108 C2
Pennyghael GB . . . 34 B1
Peno RUS . . . 9 D8
Penpont GB . . . 36 A3
Penrhyndeudraeth
GB . . . 38 B2
Penrith GB . . . 37 B4
Penryn GB . . . 42 B1
Pentraeth GB . . . 38 A2
Penybontfawr GB . . 38 B3
Penygroes
Carmarthenshire
GB . . . 39 C2
Gwynedd GB . . . 38 A2
Penzance GB . . . 42 B1
Penzberg D . . . 108 B2
Penzlin D . . . 74 A2
Pepinster B . . . 80 B1
Peqin AL . . . 182 B1
Pér H . . . 111 B4
Pera Boa P . . . 148 B2
Perachora GR . . . 184 A3
Perafita P . . . 148 A1
Peraleda de la Mata
E . . . 150 C2
Peraleda del Zaucejo
E . . . 156 B2
Peraleda de San Román
E . . . 156 A2
Perales de Alfambra
E . . . 152 B2
Perales del Puerto
E . . . 149 B3
Perales de Tajuña
E . . . 151 B4
Peralta E . . . 144 B2
Peralta de la Sal E . 145 C4
Peralva P . . . 160 B2
Peralveche E . . . 152 B1
Perama GR . . . 185 D5
Peranka FIN . . . 197 D12
Perbál H . . . 112 B2
Perchtoldsdorf A . . 111 A3
Percy F . . . 88 B2
Perdasdefogu I . . . 179 C3
Perdiguera E . . . 145 C3
Peredo P . . . 149 A3
Peregu Mare RO . . 126 A2
Pereiro
Faro P . . . 160 B2
Guarda P . . . 149 B2
Santarém P . . . 154 B2
Pereiro de Aguiar
E . . . 140 B3
Perelada E . . . 147 B4
Perelejos de las Truchas
E . . . 152 B2
Pereña E . . . 149 A3
Pereruela E . . . 149 A4
Pérfugas I . . . 178 B2
Perg A . . . 110 A1
Pérgine Valsugana
I . . . 121 A4
Pérgola I . . . 136 B1
Pergusa I . . . 177 B3
Periam RO . . . 126 A2
Periana E . . . 163 B3
Périers F . . . 88 A2
Périgueux F . . . 129 A3
Perino I . . . 120 C2
Perjasica HR . . . 123 B4
Perkáta H . . . 112 B2
Perković HR . . . 138 B2
Perleberg D . . . 73 A4
Perlez SRB . . . 126 B2
Përmet AL . . . 182 C2
Pernarec CZ . . . 95 B5
Pernek SK . . . 98 C1
Pernes P . . . 154 B2
Pernes-les-Fontaines
F . . . 131 A4
Pernik BG . . . 17 D5
Pernink CZ . . . 83 B4
Pernitz A . . . 110 B2
Pernu FIN . . . 197 C10
Peroguarda P . . . 160 A1
Pérols F . . . 131 B2
Péronne F . . . 90 B2
Péronnes B . . . 79 B4
Pero Pinheiro P . . . 154 C1
Perorrubio E . . . 151 A4
Perosa Argentina I 119 C4
Perozinho P . . . 148 A1
Perpignan F . . . 146 B3
Perranporth GB . . . 42 B1
Perranzabuloe GB . . 42 B1
Perrecy-les-Forges
F . . . 104 C3
Perrero I . . . 119 C4
Perrignier F . . . 118 A3
Perros-Guirec F . . 100 A2
Persan F . . . 90 B2
Persberg S . . . 55 A5
Persenbeug A . . . 110 A2
Pershore GB . . . 44 A1
Persön S . . . 196 D5
Perstorp S . . . 61 C3
Perth GB . . . 35 B4
Pertisau A . . . 108 B2
Pertoča SLO . . . 111 C3
Pertuis F . . . 131 B4
Perućac SRB . . . 127 D1
Perúgia I . . . 136 B1
Perušić HR . . . 123 C4
Péruwelz B . . . 79 B3
Pervomaysk UA . . . 13 D9
Perwez B . . . 79 B4
Pesadas de Burgos
E . . . 143 B3
Pesaguero E . . . 142 A2
Pésaro I . . . 136 B1
Pescantina I . . . 121 B3
Pescara I . . . 169 A4
Pescasséroli I . . . 169 B3
Peschici I . . . 171 B4
Peschiera del Garda
I . . . 121 B3
Péscia I . . . 135 B3
Pescina I . . . 169 A3
Pescocostanzo I . . 169 B4
Pescopagano I . . . 172 B1
Pesco Sannita I . . . 170 B2
Peshkopi AL . . . 182 B2
Peshtera BG . . . 183 A6
Pesmes F . . . 105 B4
Pesnica SLO . . . 110 C2
Peso da Régua P . . 148 A2
Pesquera de Duero
E . . . 142 C2
Pessac F . . . 128 B2
Pestovo RUS . . . 9 C9
Petäjäskoski FIN . . 197 C8
Petalidi GR . . . 184 C2
Pétange L . . . 92 B1
Petas GR . . . 182 D3
Peteranec HR . . . 124 A2
Peterborough GB . . 41 C3
Peterculter GB . . . 33 D4
Peterhead GB . . . 33 D5
Peterlee GB . . . 37 B5
Petersfield GB . . . 44 B3
Petershagen
Brandenburg D . . . 74 B2
Brandenburg D . . . 74 B3
Nordrhein-Westfalen
D . . . 72 B1
Petershausen D . . . 95 C3
Peterswell IRL . . . 28 A3
Pétervására H . . . 113 A4
Petília Policastro I . 175 B2
Petín E . . . 141 B3
Pětipsy CZ . . . 83 B5
Petkus D . . . 74 C2
Petlovac HR . . . 125 B4
Petlovača SRB . . . 127 C1
Petőfiszallás H . . . 113 C3
Petra E . . . 167 B3
Petralia Sottana I . . 177 B3
Petrčane HR . . . 137 A4
Petrella Tifernina I . 170 B2
Petrer E . . . 159 C3
Petreto-Bicchisano
F . . . 180 B1
Petrich BG . . . 183 B5
Petrijevci HR . . . 125 B4
Petrinja HR . . . 124 B2
Petrodvorets RUS . . 9 C6
Pétrola E . . . 158 C2
Petronà I . . . 175 B2
Petronell A . . . 111 A3
Petroşani RO . . . 17 C5
Petrovac SRB . . . 127 C3
Petrovaradin SRB . 126 B1
Petrovice
BIH . . . 139 A4
CZ . . . 84 B1
Petrovo RUS . . . 69 A5
Petrozavodsk RUS . . 9 B9
Pettenbach A . . . 109 B5
Pettigo IRL . . . 26 B3
Petworth GB . . . 44 C3
Peuerbach A . . . 96 C1
Peuntenansa E . . . 142 A2
Peurasuvanto FIN . 197 B9
Pevensey Bay GB . . 45 C4
Peveragno I . . . 133 A3
Pewsey GB . . . 44 B2
Pewsum D . . . 71 A4
Peyrat-le-Château
F . . . 116 B1
Peyrehorade F . . . 128 C1
Peyriac-Minervois
F . . . 146 A3
Peyrins F . . . 117 B5
Peyrissac F . . . 116 B1
Peyrolles-en-Provence
F . . . 132 B1
Peyruis F . . . 132 A1
Pézarches F . . . 90 C2
Pézenas F . . . 130 B2
Pezinok SK . . . 111 A4
Pezuls F . . . 129 B3
Pfaffenhausen D . . 108 A1
Pfaffenhofen
Bayern D . . . 94 C2
Bayern D . . . 95 C3
Pfaffenhoffen F . . . 93 C3
Pfäffikon CH . . . 107 B3
Pfarrkirchen D . . . 95 C4
Pfeffenhausen D . . . 95 C3
Pfetterhouse F . . . 106 B2
Pforzheim D . . . 93 C4
Pfreimd D . . . 95 B4
Pfronten D . . . 108 B1
Pfullendorf D . . . 107 B4
Pfullingen D . . . 94 C1
Pfunds A . . . 108 C1
Pfungstadt D . . . 93 B4
Pfyn CH . . . 107 B3
Phalsbourg F . . . 92 C3
Philippeville B . . . 79 B4
Philippsreut D . . . 96 C1
Philippsthal D . . . 82 B1
Piacenza I . . . 120 B2
Piacenza d'Adige I 121 B4
Piádena I . . . 120 B3
Piana F . . . 180 A1
Piana Crixia I . . . 133 A4
Piana degli Albanesi
I . . . 176 B2
Piana di Monte Verna
I . . . 170 B2
Piancastagnáio I . . 135 C4
Piandelagotti I . . . 134 A3
Pianella
Abruzzi I . . . 169 A4
Toscana I . . . 135 B4
Pianello Val Tidone
I . . . 120 C2
Pianoro I . . . 135 A4
Pians A . . . 108 B1
Pías E . . . 141 B4
Pias P . . . 160 A2
Piaseczno PL . . . 77 B6
Piasek PL . . . 74 B3
Piaski PL . . . 69 A4
Piastów PL . . . 77 B5
Piaszcyna PL . . . 68 A2
Piątek PL . . . 77 B4
Piatra Neamţ RO . . 17 B7
Piazza al Sérchio I . 134 A3
Piazza Armerina I . 177 B3
Piazza Brembana I 120 B2
Piazze I . . . 135 C4
Piazzola sul Brenta
I . . . 121 B4
Picassent E . . . 159 B3
Piccione I . . . 136 B1
Picerno I . . . 172 B1
Picher D . . . 73 A4
Pickering GB . . . 40 A3
Pico I . . . 169 B3
Picón E . . . 157 A3
Picquigny F . . . 90 B2
Piechowice PL . . . 84 B3
Piecnik PL . . . 75 A5
Piedicavallo I . . . 119 B4
Piedicroce F . . . 180 A2
Piedimonte Etneo I 177 B4
Piedimonte Matese
I . . . 170 B2
Piedimulera I . . . 119 A5
Piedipaterno I . . . 136 C1
Piedrabuena E . . . 157 A3
Piedraescrita E . . . 156 A3
Piedrafita E . . . 142 A1
Piedrahita E . . . 150 B2
Piedralaves E . . . 150 B3
Piedras Albas E . . . 155 B4
Piedras Blancas E . 141 A5
Piegaro I . . . 135 C5
Piekary Śl. PL . . . 86 B2
Piekoszów PL . . . 87 B4
Pieksämäki FIN . . . 8 A5
Pielenhofen D . . . 95 B3
Pielgrzymka PL . . . 85 A3
Pieniężno PL . . . 69 A5
Pieńsk PL . . . 84 A3
Pienza I . . . 135 B4
Piera E . . . 147 C2
Pieranie PL . . . 76 B3
Pierowall GB . . . 33 B4
Pierre-Buffière F . . 115 C5
Pierrecourt F . . . 105 B4
Pierre-de-Bresse F 105 C4
Pierrefeu-du-Var F 132 B2
Pierrefitte-Nestalas
F . . . 145 B3
Pierrefitte-sur-Aire
F . . . 92 C1
Pierrefonds F . . . 90 B2
Pierrefontaine-les-
Varans F . . . 105 B5
Pierrefort F . . . 116 C2
Pierrelatte F . . . 131 A3
Pierrepont
Aisne F . . . 91 B3
Meurthe-et-Moselle
F . . . 92 B1
Piesendorf A . . . 109 B3
Piešťany SK . . . 98 C1
Pieszkowo PL . . . 69 A5
Pieszyce PL . . . 85 B4
Pietarsaari FIN . . . 3 E8
Pietragalla I . . . 172 B1
Pietra Ligure I . . . 133 A4
Pietralunga I . . . 136 B1
Pietramelara I . . . 170 B2
Pietraperzía I . . . 177 B3
Pietrasanta I . . . 134 B3
Pietravairano I . . . 170 B2
Pieve del Cáiro I . . 120 B1
Pieve di Bono I . . . 121 B3
Pieve di Cadore I . . 122 A1
Pieve di Cento I . . . 121 C4
Pieve di Soligo I . . 121 B5
Pieve di Teco I . . . 133 A3
Pievepélago I . . . 134 A3
Pieve Santo Stefano
I . . . 135 B5
Pieve Torina I . . . 136 B2
Piges GR . . . 182 D3
Píglio I . . . 169 B3
Pigna I . . . 133 B3
Pignan F . . . 130 B2
Pignataro Maggiore
I . . . 170 B2
Piittisjärvi FIN . . . 197 C9
Pijnacker NL . . . 70 B1
Pikalevo RUS . . . 9 C9
Piła PL . . . 75 A5
Pilar de la Horadada
E . . . 165 B4
Pilas E . . . 161 B3
Pilastri I . . . 121 C4
Piława Górna PL . . . 85 B4
Piławki PL . . . 69 B4
Pilchowice PL . . . 86 B2
Pilea GR . . . 183 C5
Pilgrimstad S . . . 199 C12
Pili
Dodekanisa GR . . 188 C2
Trikala GR . . . 182 D3
Pilica PL . . . 86 B3
Pilis H . . . 112 B3
Piliscaba H . . . 112 B2
Pilisszántó H . . . 112 B2
Pilisvörösvár H . . . 112 B2
Pilos GR . . . 184 C2
Pilsting D . . . 95 C4
Pilszcz PL . . . 98 A1
Pilterud N . . . 48 C2
Pilu RO . . . 113 C5
Pina de Ebro E . . . 153 A3
Piñar E . . . 163 A4
Pınarbaşı TR . . . 186 C1
Pınarhisar TR . . . 186 A2
Pinas F . . . 145 A4
Pincehely H . . . 112 C2
Pinchbeck GB . . . 41 C3
Pińczów PL . . . 87 B4

Pineda de la Sierra E 143 B3
Pineda de Mar E 147 C3
Pinerella I 135 A5
Pinerolo I 119 C4
Pineta Grande I 170 C1
Pineto I 169 A4
Piney F 91 C4
Pinggau A 111 B3
Pinhal Novo P 154 C2
Pinhão P 148 A2
Pinheiro
Aveiro P 148 A1
Aveiro P 148 B1
Pinheiro Grande P 154 B2
Pinhel P 149 B2
Pinhoe GB 43 B3
Pinilla E 158 C2
Pinilla de Toro E 150 A2
Pinkafeld A 111 B3
Pinneberg D 72 A2
Pinnow D 74 C3
Pino F 180 A2
Pino del Rio E 142 B2
Pino de Val E 140 B2
Pinofranqueado E 149 B3
Pinols F 117 B3
Piñor E 140 B2
Pinos del Valle E 163 B4
Pinoso E 159 C2
Pinos Puente E 163 A4
Pinsk BY 13 B7
Pintamo FIN 197 D10
Pinto E 151 B4
Pinzano al Tagliamento I 122 A1
Pinzio P 149 B2
Pinzolo I 121 A3
Pióbbico I 136 B1
Piombino I 134 C3
Pionki PL 87 A5
Pionsat F 116 A2
Pióraco I 136 B1
Piornal E 150 B2
Piotrkowice PL 87 B4
Piotrków-Kujawski PL 76 B3
Piotrków Trybunalski PL 86 A3
Piotrowo PL 75 B5
Piove di Sacco I 121 B5
Piovene I 121 B4
Piperskärr S 62 A4
Pipriac F 101 B4
Piraeus = Pireas GR 185 B4
Piran SLO 122 B2
Pireas = Piraeus GR 185 B4
Piré-sur-Seiche F 101 A4
Pirgi GR 185 A6
Pirgos
Ilia GR 184 B2
Kriti GR 185 D6
Piriac-sur-Mer F 101 B3
Piringsdorf A 111 B3
Pirmasens D 93 B3
Pirna D 84 B1
Pirnmill GB 34 C2
Pirot SRB 16 D5
Pirovac HR 137 B4
Pirttivuopio S 196 B2
Pisa I 134 B3
Pisany F 114 C3
Pisarovina HR 124 B1
Pischelsdorf in der Steiermark A 110 B2
Pişchia RO 126 B3
Pisciotta I 172 B1
Písek CZ 96 B2
Pisogne I 120 B3
Pissos F 128 B2
Pissouri CY 181 B1
Pisticci I 174 A2
Pistóia I 135 B3
Piteå S 196 D4
Piteşti RO 17 C6
Pithiviers F 103 A4
Pitigliano I 168 A1
Pitkyaranta RUS 9 B7
Pitlochry GB 35 B4
Pitomača HR 124 B3
Pitres E 163 B4
Pittentrail GB 32 D2
Pitvaros H 126 A2
Pivka SLO 123 B3
Pivnice SRB 126 B1
Piwniczna PL 99 B4
Pizarra E 163 B3
Pizzano I 121 A3
Pizzighettone I 120 B2
Pizzo I 175 C2
Pízzoli I 169 A3
Pizzolungo I 176 A1
Pjätteryd S 61 C4
Plabennec F 100 A1
Placencia E 143 A4
Plaffeien CH 106 C2
Plaisance
Gers F 128 C3
Haute-Garonne F 129 C4
Tarn F 130 B1
Plaka GR 183 D7
Plan E 145 B4
Planá CZ 95 B4
Planánad Lužnici CZ 96 B2
Plaňany CZ 96 A3
Planchez F 104 B3
Plancoët F 101 A3
Plancy-l'Abbaye F 91 C3
Plan-de-Baix F 118 C2
Plandište SRB 126 B3
Plan-d'Orgon F 131 B3
Plánice CZ 96 B1
Planina
SLO 123 A4
SLO 123 B3
Plankenfels D 95 B3
Plasencia E 149 B3
Plasenzuela E 156 A1
Plaški HR 123 B4
Plassen
Buskerud N 47 B4
Hedmark N 49 A4
Plášťovce SK 112 A3
Plasy CZ 96 B1
Platamona Lido I 178 B2
Platania I 175 B2
Platanos GR 185 D4
Platí I 175 C2
Platičevo SRB 127 C1
Platja d'Aro E 147 C4
Plattling D 95 C4
Plau D 73 A5
Plaue
Brandenburg D 73 B5
Thüringen D 82 B2
Plauen D 83 B4
Plavecký Mikuláš SK 98 C1
Plavinas LV 8 D4
Plavna SRB 125 B5
Plavnica SK 99 B4
Plavno HR 138 A2
Playben F 100 A2
Pléaux F 116 B2
Pleine-Fourgères F 88 B2
Pleinfeld D 94 B2
Pleinting D 95 C5
Plélan-le-Grand F 101 B3
Plémet F 101 A3
Pléneuf-Val-André F 101 A3
Plentzia E 143 A4
Plérin F 101 A3
Plešivec SK 99 C4
Plessa D 83 A5
Plessé F 101 B4
Plestin-les-Grèves F 100 A2
Pleszew PL 76 C2
Pleternica HR 125 B3
Plettenberg D 81 A3
Pleubian F 100 A2
Pleumartin F 115 B4
Pleumeur-Bodou F 100 A2
Pleurs F 91 C3
Pleven BG 17 D6
Plevnik-Drienové SK 98 B2
Pleyber-Christ F 100 A2
Pliego E 165 B3
Pliešovce SK 99 C3
Plitvička Jezera HR 123 C4
Plitvički Ljeskovac HR 123 C4
Ploaghe I 178 B2
Ploče HR 138 B3
Plochingen D 94 C1
Płock PL 77 B4
Ploemeur F 100 B2
Ploërmel F 101 B3
Ploeuc-sur-Lie F 101 A3
Plogastel St Germain F 100 B1
Plogoff F 100 A1
Ploieşti RO 17 C7
Plomari GR 186 D1
Plombières-les-Bains F 105 B5
Plomin HR 123 B3
Plön D 65 B3
Plonéour-Lanvern F 100 B1
Płonia PL 74 A3
Płoniawy PL 77 B6
Płońsk PL 77 B5
Płoskinia PL 69 A4
Plössberg D 95 B4
Płoty PL 67 C4
Plouagat F 100 A2
Plouaret F 100 A2
Plouarzel F 100 A1
Plouay F 100 B2
Ploubalay F 101 A3
Ploubazlanec F 100 A2
Ploudalmézeau F 100 A1
Ploudiry F 100 A1
Plouescat F 100 A1
Plouézec F 100 A3
Plougasnou F 100 A2
Plougastel-Daoulas F 100 A1
Plougonven F 100 A2
Plougonver F 100 A2
Plougrescant F 100 A2
Plouguenast F 101 A3
Plouguerneau F 100 A1
Plouha F 100 A3
Plouhinec F 100 A1
Plouigneau F 100 A2
Ploumanach F 100 A2
Plounévez-Quintin F 100 A2
Plouray F 100 A2
Plouzévédé F 100 A1
Plovdiv BG 183 A6
Plozévet F 100 B1
Plumbridge GB 27 B3
Pluméliau F 100 B3
Plumlov CZ 97 B5
Plungė LT 8 E2
Pluty PL 69 A5
Pluvigner F 100 B3
Plužine
BIH 139 B4
MNE 139 B4
Płuznica PL 69 B3
Plymouth GB 42 B2
Plymstock GB 42 B2
Płytnica PL 68 B1
Plyusa RUS 9 C6
Plzeň CZ 96 B1
Pniewy PL 75 B5
Pobes E 143 B4
Poběžovice CZ 95 B4
Pobiedziska PL 76 B2
Pobierowo PL 67 B3
Pobla de Segur E 145 B4
Pobladura del Valle E 142 B1
Pobla-Tornesa E 153 B4
Pobra de Trives E 141 B3
Pobra do Brollón E 141 B3
Pobra do Caramiñal E 140 B2
Pobudje BIH 139 A5
Počátky CZ 97 B3
Poceirão P 154 C2
Pöchlarn A 110 A2
Pociecha PL 87 A4
Pockau D 83 B5
Pocking D 96 C1
Pocklington GB 40 B3
Podbořany CZ 83 B5
Podbrdo SLO 122 A2
Podbrezová SK 99 C3
Podčetrtek SLO 123 A4
Poddębice PL 76 C3
Poděbrady CZ 84 B3
Podence P 149 A3
Podensac F 128 B2
Podenzano I 120 C2
Podersdorf am See A 111 B3
Podgaje PL 68 B1
Podgora HR 138 B3
Podgóra PL 87 A5
Podgorač HR 125 B4
Podgorica MNE 16 D3
Podgorie AL 182 C2
Podgrad SLO 123 B3
Podhájska SK 112 A2
Podkova BG 183 B7
Podlapača HR 123 C4
Podlejki PL 69 B5
Podlužany SK 98 C2
Podnovlje BIH 125 C4
Podolie SK 98 C1
Podolínec SK 99 B4
Podolsk RUS 9 E10
Podporozhy RUS 9 B9
Podromanija BIH 139 B4
Podturen HR 111 C3
Podvín CZ 97 C4
Podwilk PL 99 B3
Poetto I 179 C3
Poggendorf D 66 B2
Poggiardo I 173 B4
Poggibonsi I 135 B4
Póggio a Caiano I 135 B4
Poggio Imperiale I 171 B3
Póggio Mirteto I 168 A2
Póggio Moiano I 169 A2
Póggio Renatico I 121 C4
Póggio Rusco I 121 C4
Pöggstall A 97 C3
Pogny F 91 C4
Pogorzela PL 85 A5
Pogorzelice PL 68 A2
Pogradec AL 182 C2
Pogrodzie PL 69 A4
Pohorelá SK 99 C4
Pohořelice CZ 97 C4
Pohronská Polhora SK 99 C3
Poiares P 148 B1
Poio E 140 B2
Poirino I 119 C4
Poisson F 117 A4
Poissons F 91 C5
Poissy F 90 C2
Poitiers F 115 B4
Poix-de-Picardie F 90 B1
Poix-Terron F 91 B4
Pokka FIN 197 A8
Pokój PL 86 B1
Pokupsko HR 124 B1
Pol E 141 A3
Pola RUS 9 D7
Pol a Charra GB 31 B1
Pola de Allande E 141 A4
Pola de Laviana E 142 A1
Pola de Lena E 141 A5
Pola de Siero E 142 A1
Pola de Somiedo E 141 A4
Polaincourt-et-Clairefontaine F 105 B5
Połajewo PL 75 B5
Polán E 151 C3
Polanica-Zdrój PL 85 B4
Połaniec PL 87 B5
Polanów PL 68 A1
Polatı TR 187 C7
Polatsk BY 13 A8
Polch D 80 B3
Polcirkeln S 196 C4
Pólczno PL 68 A2
Połczyn-Zdrój PL 67 C5
Polegate GB 45 C4
Poleñino E 145 C3
Polesella I 121 C4
Polessk RUS 12 A4
Polgár H 113 B5
Polgárdi H 112 B2
Polhov Gradec SLO 123 A3
Police PL 74 A3
Police nad Metují CZ 85 B4
Polichnitos GR 186 C1
Polička CZ 97 B4
Poličnik HR 137 A4
Policoro I 174 A2
Policzna PL 87 A5
Poligiros GR 183 C5
Polignano a Mare I 173 B3
Poligny F 105 C4
Polis CY 181 A1
Polístena I 175 C2
Polizzi Generosa I 176 B3
Poljana SRB 127 C3
Poljanák HR 123 C4
Poljčane SLO 123 A4
Polje BIH 125 C3
Poljice
BIH 138 A2
BIH 139 A4
Polkowice PL 85 A4
Polla I 172 B1
Pollas E 150 A2
Pöllau A 110 B2
Polleben D 82 A3
Pollença E 167 B3
Pollenfeld D 95 C3
Pollfoss N 198 D4
Póllica I 170 C3
Polminhac F 116 C2
Polná CZ 97 B3
Polna RUS 8 C6
Polne PL 75 A5
Polomka SK 99 C3
Polonne UA 13 C7
Polperro GB 42 B2
Polruan GB 42 B2
Pöls A 110 B1
Polska Cerekiew PL 86 B2
Poltár SK 99 C3
Põltsamaa EST 8 C4
Polyarny RUS 3 B13
Polyarnyye Zori RUS 3 C13
Polzela SLO 123 A4
Pomarance I 135 B3
Pomarez F 128 C2
Pomárico I 172 B2
Pomáz H 112 B3
Pombal P 154 B2
Pomeroy GB 27 B4
Pomézia I 168 B2
Pommard F 105 B3
Pommelsbrunn D 95 B3
Pomonte I 134 C3
Pomorie BG 17 D7
Pomos CY 181 A1
Pompei I 170 C2
Pompey F 92 C2
Pomposa I 122 C1
Poncin F 118 A2
Pondorf D 95 C3
Ponferrada E 141 B4
Poniec PL 85 A4
Ponikva SLO 123 A4
Poniky SK 99 C3
Pons F 114 C3
Ponsacco I 134 B3
Pont I 119 B4
Pont-a-Celles B 79 B4
Pontacq F 145 A3
Pontailler-sur-Saône F 105 B4
Pont-a-Marcq F 78 B3
Pont-à-Mousson F 92 C2
Pontão P 154 B2
Pontardawe GB 39 C3
Pontarddulais GB 39 C2
Pontarion F 116 B1
Pontarlier F 105 C5
Pontassieve I 135 B4
Pontaubault F 88 B2
Pont-Audemer F 89 A4
Pontaumur F 116 B2
Pont-Aven F 100 B2
Pont Canavese I 119 B4
Pontcharra F 118 B3
Pontcharra-sur-Turdine F 117 B4
Pontchâteau F 101 B3
Pont-Croix F 100 A1
Pont-d'Ain F 118 A2
Pont-de-Beauvoisin F 118 B2
Pont-de-Buis-lès-Quimerch F 100 A1
Pont-de-Chéruy F 118 B2
Pont de Dore F 117 B3
Pont-de-Labeaume F 117 C4
Pont-de-l'Arche F 89 A5
Pont de Molins E 147 B3
Pont-de-Roide F 106 B1
Pont-de-Salars F 130 A1
Pont-d'Espagne F 145 B3
Pont de Suert E 145 B4
Pont-de-Vaux F 117 A4
Pont-de-Veyle F 117 A4
Pont d'Ouilly F 89 B3
Pont-du-Château F 116 B3
Pont-du-Navoy F 105 C4
Ponte a Moriano I 134 B3
Ponte Arche I 121 A3
Ponteareas E 140 B2
Pontebba I 109 C4
Ponte Cáffaro I 121 B3
Pontecagnano I 170 C2
Ponte-Caldelas E 140 B2
Ponteceso E 140 A2
Pontecesures E 140 B2
Pontecorvo I 169 B3
Ponte da Barca P 148 A1
Pontedássio I 133 B4
Pontedécimo I 133 A4
Ponte de Lima P 148 A1
Ponte dell'Ólio I 120 C2
Pontedera I 134 B3
Ponte de Sor P 154 B2
Pontedeume E 140 A2
Ponte di Barbarano I 121 B4
Ponte di Legno I 121 A3
Ponte di Nava I 133 A3
Ponte di Piave I 122 B1
Ponte Felcino I 136 B1
Pontefract GB 40 B2
Ponte Gardena I 108 C2
Ponteginori I 135 B3
Pontelagoscuro I 121 C4
Ponteland GB 37 A5
Pontelandolfo I 170 B2
Ponte-Leccia F 180 A2
Pontelongo I 121 B5
Ponte nelle Alpi I 122 A1
Pont-en-Royans F 118 B2
Pontenure I 120 C2
Pontenx-les-Forges F 128 B1
Ponterwyd GB 39 B3
Ponte San Giovanni I 136 B1
Ponte San Pietro I 120 B2
Pontevedra E 140 B2
Pontevico I 120 B3
Pont Farcy F 88 B2
Pontfaverger-Moronvillers F 91 B4
Pontgibaud F 116 B2
Ponticino I 135 B4
Pontigny F 104 B2
Pontijou F 103 B3
Pontínia I 169 B3
Pontinvrea I 133 A4
Pontivy F 100 A3
Pont-l'Abbé F 100 B1
Pont-l'Évêque F 89 A4
Pontlevoy F 103 B3
Pontoise F 90 B2
Pontones E 164 A2
Pontonx-sur-l'Abour F 128 C2
Pontoon IRL 26 C1
Pontorson F 88 B2
Pontrémoli I 134 A2
Pont-Remy F 90 A1
Pontresina CH 107 C4
Pontrhydfendigaid GB 39 B3
Pontrieux F 100 A2
Ponts E 147 C2
Ponts-aux-Dames F 90 C2
Pont Scorff F 100 B2
Pöntsö FIN 196 B7
Pont-Ste Maxence F 90 B2
Pont-St Esprit F 131 A3
Pont-St Mamet F 129 B3
Pont-St Martin
F 101 B4
I 119 B4
Pont-St Vincent F 92 C2
Pont-sur-Yonne F 104 A2
Pontvallain F 102 B2
Pontypool GB 39 C3
Pontypridd GB 39 C3
Ponza I 169 C2
Poo E 142 A2
Poole GB 43 B5
Poolewe GB 31 B3
Poperinge B 78 B2
Pópoli I 169 A3
Popovac SRB 127 D3
Popovača HR 124 B2
Popow PL 77 B4
Poppel B 79 A5
Poppenhausen
Bayern D 82 B2
Hessen D 82 B1
Poppi I 135 B4
Poprad SK 99 B4
Popučke SRB 127 C1
Pópulo P 148 A2
Populónia I 134 C3
Pörböly H 125 A4
Porcuna E 163 A3
Pordenone I 122 B1
Pordic F 100 A3
Poręba PL 86 B3
Poreč HR 122 B2
Pori FIN 8 B2
Porjus S 196 C2
Porkhov RUS 9 D6
Porlezza I 120 A2
Porlock GB 43 A3
Pörnbach D 95 C3
Pornic F 101 B3
Pornichet F 101 B3
Porodin SRB 127 C3
Poronin PL 99 B3
Poros
Attiki GR 185 B4
Kefalonia GR 184 A1
Poroszló H 113 B4
Porozina HR 123 B3
Porquerolles F 132 C2
Porrentruy CH 106 B2
Porreres E 167 B3
Porretta Terme I 135 A3
Porsgrunn N 53 A5
Porspoder F 100 A1
Port-a-Binson F 91 B3
Portacloy IRL 26 B1
Portadown GB 27 B4
Portaferry GB 27 B5
Portaje E 155 B4
Portalegre P 155 B3
Portarlington IRL 30 A1
Port Askaig GB 34 C1
Portavadie GB 34 C2
Portavogie GB 27 B5
Portbail F 88 A2
Port Bannatyne GB 34 C2
Port-Barcarès F 146 B4
Portbou E 146 B4
Port-Camargue F 131 B3
Port Charlotte GB 34 C1
Port d'Andratx E 166 B2
Port-de-Bouc F 131 B3
Port-de-Lanne F 128 C1
Port de Pollença E 167 B3
Port-des-Barques F 114 C2
Port de Sóller E 166 B2
Portegrandi I 122 B1
Portel P 155 C3
Portela P 148 B1
Port Ellen GB 34 C1
Portelo P 141 C4
Portemouro E 140 B2
Port-en-Bessin F 88 A3
Port'Ercole I 168 A1
Port Erin GB 36 B2
Portes-lès-Valence F 117 C4
Portets F 128 B2
Port Eynon GB 39 C2
Portezuelo E 155 B4
Port Glasgow GB 34 C3
Portglenone GB 27 B4
Porthcawl GB 39 C3
Port Henderson GB 31 B3
Porthleven GB 42 B1
Porthmadog GB 38 B2
Porticcio F 180 B1
Portici I 170 C2
Portico di Romagna I 135 A4
Portilla de la Reina E 142 A2
Portillo E 150 A3
Portimao P 160 B1
Portinatx E 166 B1
Portinho da Arrabida P 154 C1
Port Isaac GB 42 B2
Portishead GB 43 A4
Port-Joinville F 114 B1
Portknockie GB 33 D4
Port-la-Nouvelle F 130 B2
Portlaoise IRL 30 A1
Portlethen GB 33 D4
Port Logan GB 36 B2
Port Louis F 100 B2
Portmagne IRL 29 C1
Portmahomack GB 32 D3
Portman E 165 B4
Port Manech F 100 B2
Portnacroish GB 34 B2
Portnahaven GB 34 C1
Port Nan Giuran GB 31 A2
Port-Navalo F 100 B3
Port Nis GB 31 A2
Porto
F 180 A1
P 148 A1
Porto-Alto P 154 C2
Porto Azzurro I 134 C3
Portocannone I 170 B3
Porto Cerésio I 120 B1
Porto Cervo I 178 A3
Porto Cesáreo I 173 B3
Porto Colom E 167 B3
Porto Covo P 160 B1
Porto Cristo E 167 B3
Porto d'Áscoli I 136 C2
Porto de Lagos P 160 B1
Porto de Mos P 154 B2
Porto de Rei P 154 C2
Porto do Son E 140 B2
Porto Empédocle I 176 B2
Portoferráio I 134 C3
Portofino I 134 A2
Porto Garibaldi I 122 C1
Portogruaro I 122 B1

Portokhelion GR . . . 184 B4
Portomaggiore I . . . 121 C4
Portomarin E . . . 140 B3
Porton GB . . . 44 B2
Portonovo E . . . 140 B2
Portopalo di Capo
Passero I . . . 177 C4
Porto Petro E . . . 167 B3
Porto Pino I . . . 179 D2
Porto Potenza Picena
I . . . 136 B2
Portør N . . . 53 B5
Porto Recanati I . . . 136 B2
Porto San Giórgio
I . . . 136 B2
Porto Sant'Elpídio
I . . . 136 B2
Porto Santo Stéfano
I . . . 168 A1
Portoscuso I . . . 179 C2
Porto Tolle I . . . 122 C1
Porto Tórres I . . . 178 B2
Porto-Vecchio F . . . 180 B2
Portovénere I . . . 134 A2
Portpatrick GB . . . 36 B1
Portreath GB . . . 42 B1
Portree GB . . . 31 B2
Portroe IRL . . . 28 B3
Portrush GB . . . 27 A4
Port St Mary GB . . . 36 B2
Portsall F . . . 100 A1
Portsmouth GB . . . 44 C2
Portsoy GB . . . 33 D4
Port-Ste Marie F . . . 129 B3
Portstewart GB . . . 27 A4
Port-St-Louis-du-Rhône
F . . . 131 B3
Port-sur-Saône F . . . 105 B5
Port Talbot GB . . . 39 C3
Portugalete E . . . 143 A4
Portumna IRL . . . 28 A3
Port-Vendres F . . . 146 B4
Port William GB . . . 36 B2
Porvoo FIN . . . 8 B4
Porzuna E . . . 157 A3
Posada
Oviedo E . . . 141 A5
Oviedo E . . . 142 A2
I . . . 178 B3
Posada de Valdeón
E . . . 142 A2
Posadas E . . . 162 A2
Poschiavo CH . . . 120 A3
Posedarje HR . . . 137 A4
Posio FIN . . . 197 C11
Positano I . . . 170 C2
Possagno I . . . 121 B4
Posseck D . . . 83 B4
Possesse F . . . 91 C4
Pössneck D . . . 83 B3
Posta I . . . 169 A3
Postal I . . . 108 C2
Posta Piana I . . . 172 A1
Postbauer-Heng D . . . 95 B3
Posterholt NL . . . 80 A2
Postioma I . . . 121 B5
Postira HR . . . 138 B2
Postojna SLO . . . 123 B3
Postoloprty CZ . . . 84 B1
Postomino PL . . . 68 A1
Posušje BIH . . . 138 B3
Potamos
Attiki GR . . . 184 C3
Attiki GR . . . 184 D4
Potegowo PL . . . 68 A2
Potenza I . . . 172 B1
Potenza Picena I . . . 136 B2
Potes E . . . 142 A2
Potigny F . . . 89 B3
Potočari BIH . . . 127 C1
Potoci
BIH . . . 138 A2
BIH . . . 139 B3
Potony H . . . 125 B3
Potries E . . . 159 C3
Potsdam D . . . 74 B2
Potštát CZ . . . 98 B1
Pottenbrunn A . . . 110 A2
Pottendorf A . . . 111 B3
Pottenstein
A . . . 111 B3
D . . . 95 B3
Potters Bar GB . . . 44 B3
Pöttmes D . . . 94 C3
Pöttsching A . . . 111 B3
Potworów PL . . . 87 A4
Pouancé F . . . 101 B4
Pougues-les-Eaux
F . . . 104 B2
Pouilly-en-Auxois
F . . . 104 B3
Pouilly-sous Charlieu
F . . . 117 A4
Pouilly-sur-Loire F 104 B1
Poujol-sur-Orb F . . . 130 B2
Poullaouen F . . . 100 A2
Poulton-le-Fylde GB 38 A4
Poundstock GB . . . 42 B2
Pourcy F . . . 91 B3
Pourrain F . . . 104 B2
Poussu FIN . . . 197 D12
Pouyastruc F . . . 145 A4
Pouy-de-Touges F. 146 A2
Pouzauges F . . . 114 B3
Pova de Santa Iria
P . . . 154 C1
Považská Bystrica
SK . . . 98 B2
Povedilla E . . . 158 C1
Povenets RUS . . . 9 A9
Povlja HR . . . 138 B2
Povljana HR . . . 137 A4
Póvoa
Beja P . . . 161 A2
Santarém P . . . 154 B2
Póvoa de Lanhosa
P . . . 148 A1
Póvoa de Varzim
P . . . 148 A1
Póvoa e Meadas P. 155 B3
Powidz PL . . . 76 B2
Poyales del Hoyo
E . . . 150 B2
Poynton GB . . . 40 B1
Poyntz Pass GB . . . 27 B4
Poysdorf A . . . 97 C4
Poza de la Sal E . . . 143 B3
Pozaldez E . . . 150 A3
Pozán de Vero E . . . 145 B4
Pozanti TR . . . 23 C8
Požarevac SRB . . . 127 C3
Požega
HR . . . 125 B3
SRB . . . 127 D2
Poznań PL . . . 76 B1
Pozo Alcón E . . . 164 B2
Pozoantiguo E . . . 150 A2
Pozoblanco E . . . 156 B3
Pozo Cañada E . . . 158 C2
Pozo de Guadalajara
E . . . 151 B4
Pozo de la Serna E 157 B4
Pozohondo E . . . 158 C2
Pozondón E . . . 152 B2
Poźrzadło Wielkie
PL . . . 75 A4
Pozuel del Campo
E . . . 152 B2
Pozuelo de Alarcón
E . . . 151 B4
Pozuelo de Calatrava
E . . . 157 B4
Pozuelo del Páramo
E . . . 142 B1
Pozuelo de Zarzón
E . . . 149 B3
Pozzallo I . . . 177 C3
Pozzomaggiore I . . . 178 B2
Pozzo San Nicola I 178 B2
Pozzuoli I . . . 170 C2
Pozzuolo I . . . 135 B4
Prabuty PL . . . 69 B4
Prača BIH . . . 139 B4
Prachatice CZ . . . 96 B1
Prada E . . . 141 B3
Pradelle F . . . 118 C2
Pradelles F . . . 117 C3
Prades
E . . . 147 C1
F . . . 146 B3
Pradła PL . . . 86 B3
Prado
E . . . 142 A1
P . . . 148 A1
Prado del Rey E . . . 162 B2
Pradoluengo E . . . 143 B3
Pragelato I . . . 119 B3
Pragersko SLO . . . 123 A4
Prägraten A . . . 109 B3
Prague = Praha CZ . 84 B2
Praha = Prague CZ . 84 B2
Prahecq F . . . 115 B3
Praia P . . . 154 B1
Práia a Mare I . . . 174 B1
Praia da Rocha P . . . 160 B1
Praia da Viera P . . . 154 B2
Praia de Mira P . . . 148 B1
Praiano I . . . 170 C2
Pralboino I . . . 120 B3
Pralognan-la-Vanoise
F . . . 118 B3
Pramanda GR . . . 182 D3
Pranjani SRB . . . 127 C2
Prapatnica HR . . . 138 B2
Præstø DK . . . 65 A5
Praszka PL . . . 86 A2
Prat F . . . 146 A1
Prata I . . . 135 B3
Prata di Pordenone
I . . . 122 B1
Pratau D . . . 83 A4
Prat de Compte E . 153 B4
Pratdip E . . . 147 C1
Pratella I . . . 170 B2
Prato I . . . 135 B4
Prátola Peligna I . . . 169 A3
Pratola Serra I . . . 170 C2
Prats-de-Mollo-la-Preste
F . . . 146 B3
Prauthoy F . . . 105 B4
Pravia E . . . 141 A4
Praxmar A . . . 108 B2
Prayssac F . . . 129 B4
Prazzo I . . . 132 A3
Prebold SLO . . . 123 A4
Préchac F . . . 128 B2
Précy-sur-Thil F . . . 104 B3
Predáppio I . . . 135 A4
Predazzo I . . . 121 A4
Předin CZ . . . 97 B3
Preding A . . . 110 C2
Predjame SLO . . . 123 B3
Predlitz A . . . 109 B4
Predmeja SLO . . . 122 B2
Predoi I . . . 108 B3
Pré-en-Pail F . . . 89 B3
Prees GB . . . 38 B4
Preetz D . . . 64 B3
Préfailles F . . . 101 B3
Pregarten A . . . 96 C2
Pregrada HR . . . 123 A4
Preignan F . . . 129 C3
Preiļi LV . . . 8 D5
Preitenegg A . . . 110 C1
Prekaja BIH . . . 138 A2
Preko HR . . . 137 A4
Preljina SRB . . . 127 D2
Prelog HR . . . 124 A2
Prelošćica HR . . . 124 B2
Přelouč CZ . . . 97 A3
Prem SLO . . . 123 B3
Premantura HR . . . 122 C2
Prémery F . . . 104 B2
Prémia I . . . 119 A5
Premiàde Mar E . . . 147 C3
Premnitz D . . . 73 B5
Prémont F . . . 91 A3
Prenzlau D . . . 74 A2
Preodac BIH . . . 138 A2
Přerov CZ . . . 98 B1
Prerow D . . . 66 B1
Presencio E . . . 143 B3
Presicce I . . . 173 C4
Presly F . . . 103 B4
Prešov SK . . . 12 D4
Pressac F . . . 115 B4
Pressath D . . . 95 B3
Pressbaum A . . . 111 A3
Prestatyn GB . . . 38 A3
Prestebakke N . . . 54 B2
Presteigne GB . . . 39 B3
Přeštice CZ . . . 96 B1
Preston
Lancashire GB . . . 38 A4
Scottish Borders
GB . . . 35 C5
Prestonpans GB . . . 35 C5
Prestwick GB . . . 36 A2
Prettin D . . . 83 A4
Preturo I . . . 169 A3
Pretzchendorf D . . . 83 B5
Pretzier D . . . 73 B4
Pretzsch D . . . 83 A4
Preuilly-sur-Claise
F . . . 115 B4
Prevalje SLO . . . 110 C1
Prevenchères F . . . 131 A2
Préveranges F . . . 116 A2
Preveza GR . . . 182 E2
Prevršac HR . . . 124 B2
Prezid HR . . . 123 B3
Priaranza del Bierzo
E . . . 141 B4
Priay F . . . 118 A2
Pribeta SK . . . 112 B2
Priboj
BIH . . . 125 C4
SRB . . . 16 D3
Přibor CZ . . . 98 B2
Příbram CZ . . . 96 B2
Pribylina SK . . . 99 B3
Přibyslav CZ . . . 97 B3
Pričević SRB . . . 127 C1
Pridjel BIH . . . 125 C4
Priego E . . . 152 B1
Priego de Córdoba
E . . . 163 A3
Priekule LV . . . 8 D2
Prien D . . . 109 B3
Prienai LT . . . 13 A5
Prievidza SK . . . 98 C2
Prigradica HR . . . 138 C2
Prigrevica SRB . . . 125 B5
Prijeboj HR . . . 123 C4
Prijedor BIH . . . 124 C2
Prijepolje SRB . . . 16 D3
Prilep MK . . . 182 B3
Priluka BIH . . . 138 B2
Primda CZ . . . 95 B4
Primel-Trégastel F 100 A2
Primišje HR . . . 123 B4
Primorsk
Kaliningrad RUS . . . 69 A5
Severo-Zapadnyy
RUS . . . 9 B6
Primošten HR . . . 138 B1
Primstal D . . . 92 B2
Princes Risborough
GB . . . 44 B3
Princetown GB . . . 42 B2
Principina a Mare I 135 C4
Priolo Gargallo I . . . 177 B4
Prioro E . . . 142 B2
Priozersk RUS . . . 9 B7
Prirechnyy RUS . 193 C14
Prisoje BIH . . . 138 B3
Priština KOS . . . 16 D4
Pritzerbe D . . . 73 B5
Pritzier D . . . 73 A4
Pritzwalk D . . . 73 A5
Privas F . . . 117 C4
Priverno I . . . 169 B3
Privlaka
Vukovarsko-Srijemska
HR . . . 125 B4
Zadarska HR . . . 137 A4
Prizna HR . . . 123 C3
Prizren KOS . . . 16 D4
Prizzi I . . . 176 B2
Prnjavor
BIH . . . 125 C3
HR . . . 124 B1
SRB . . . 127 C1
Proaza E . . . 141 A4
Probstzella D . . . 82 B3
Probus GB . . . 42 B2
Prócchio I . . . 134 C3
Prochowice PL . . . 85 A4
Prócida I . . . 170 C2
Prodhromos CY . . . 181 B1
Prodo I . . . 135 C5
Proença-a-Nova P . 154 B3
Proença-a-Velha P 155 A3
Profondeville B . . . 79 B4
Prokuplje SRB . . . 16 D4
Propriano F . . . 180 B1
Prosec CZ . . . 97 B4
Prösen D . . . 83 A5
Prosenjakovci
SLO . . . 111 C3
Prosotsani GR . . . 183 B5
Prostějov CZ . . . 98 B1
Prószków PL . . . 86 B1
Proszowice PL . . . 87 B4
Protić BIH . . . 138 A2
Protivanov CZ . . . 97 B4
Protivín CZ . . . 96 B2
Prötzel D . . . 74 B2
Provins F . . . 90 C3
Prozor BIH . . . 139 B3
Prrenjas AL . . . 182 B2
Prudhoe GB . . . 37 B5
Prudnik PL . . . 85 B5
Pruggern A . . . 109 B4
Prügy H . . . 113 A5
Prüm D . . . 80 B2
Pruna E . . . 162 B2
Prunelli-di-Fiumorbo
F . . . 180 A2
Prunetta I . . . 135 A3
Pruniers F . . . 103 C4
Prusice PL . . . 85 A4
Pruské SK . . . 98 B2
Pruszce PL . . . 76 A3
Pruszcz Gdański PL 69 A3
Pruszków PL . . . 77 B5
Prutz A . . . 108 B1
Prüzen D . . . 65 C5
Pruzhany BY . . . 13 B6
Pružina SK . . . 98 B2
Pŭrvomay BG . . . 183 A7
Pryzlęg PL . . . 75 B4
Przasnysz PL . . . 77 A5
Przechlewo PL . . . 68 B2
Przecław PL . . . 87 B5
Przedbórz PL . . . 87 A3
Przedecz PL . . . 76 B3
Przejęslav PL . . . 84 A3
Przemków PL . . . 85 A3
Przemocze PL . . . 75 A3
Przemyśl PL . . . 12 D5
Przerąb PL . . . 87 A3
Przewodnik PL . . . 69 B3
Przewodowo Parcele
PL . . . 77 B5
Przewóz PL . . . 84 A2
Przezmark PL . . . 69 B4
Przodkowo PL . . . 68 A3
Przybiernów PL . . . 75 A3
Przyborowice PL . . . 77 B5
Przybyszew PL . . . 87 A4
Przybyszów PL . . . 86 A3
Przylęg PL . . . 75 B4
Przysucha PL . . . 87 A4
Przytóczna PL . . . 75 B4
Przytyk PL . . . 87 A4
Przywidz PL . . . 68 A3
Psachna GR . . . 185 A4
Psara GR . . . 185 A6
Psary PL . . . 76 C3
Pskov RUS . . . 8 D6
Pszczew PL . . . 75 B4
Pszczółki PL . . . 69 A3
Pszczyna PL . . . 98 B2
Pszów PL . . . 86 B2
Pteleos GR . . . 182 D4
Ptolemaida GR . . . 182 C3
Ptuj SLO . . . 124 A1
Ptusza PL . . . 68 B1
Puch A . . . 109 B4
Puchberg am
Schneeberg A . . . 110 B2
Puchevillers F . . . 90 A2
Puchheim D . . . 108 A2
Púchov SK . . . 98 B2
Pučišća HR . . . 138 B2
Puck PL . . . 69 A3
Puçol E . . . 159 B3
Puconci SLO . . . 111 C3
Pudasjärvi FIN . . . 197 D10
Puderbach D . . . 81 B3
Pudozh RUS . . . 9 B10
Puebla de Albortón
E . . . 153 A3
Puebla de Alcocer
E . . . 156 B2
Puebla de Beleña
E . . . 151 B4
Puebla de Don Fadrique
E . . . 164 B2
Puebla de Don Rodrigo
E . . . 156 A3
Puebla de Guzmán
E . . . 161 B2
Puebla de la Calzada
E . . . 155 C4
Puebla de la Reina
E . . . 156 B1
Puebla de Lillo E . . . 142 A1
Puebla del Maestre
E . . . 161 A3
Puebla del Principe
E . . . 158 C1
Puebla de Obando
E . . . 155 B4
Puebla de Sanabria
E . . . 141 B4
Puebla de Sancho Pérez
E . . . 155 C4
Puente Almuhey E 142 B2
Puente de Domingo
Flórez E . . . 141 B4
Puente de Génave
E . . . 164 A2
Puente del Congosto
E . . . 150 B2
Puente de Montañana
E . . . 145 B4
Puente Duero E . . . 150 A3
Puente-Genil E . . . 162 A3
Puente la Reina E . 144 B2
Puente la Reina de Jaca
E . . . 144 B3
Puentelarra E . . . 143 B3
Puente Mayorga E. 162 B2
Puente Viesgo E . . . 143 A3
Puertas
Asturias E . . . 142 A2
Salamanca E . . . 149 A3
Puerto de Mazarrón
E . . . 165 B3
Puerto de Santa Cruz
E . . . 156 A2
Puerto de San Vicente
E . . . 156 A2
Puerto-Lápice E . . . 157 A4
Puertollano E . . . 157 B3
Puerto Lumbreras
E . . . 164 B3
Puerto Moral E . . . 161 B3
Puerto Real E . . . 162 B1
Puerto Rey E . . . 156 A2
Puerto Seguro E . . . 149 B3
Puerto Serrano E . 162 B2
Puget-Sur-Argens
F . . . 132 B2
Puget-Théniers F . 132 B2
Puget-ville F . . . 132 B2
Pugnochiuso I . . . 171 B4
Puigcerdà E . . . 146 B2
Puigpunyent E . . . 166 B2
Puig Reig E . . . 147 C2
Puillon F . . . 128 C2
Puimichel F . . . 132 B2
Puimoisson F . . . 132 B2
Puiseaux F . . . 103 A4
Puisieux F . . . 90 A2
Puisserguier F . . . 130 B2
Puivert F . . . 146 B3
Pujols F . . . 128 B2
Pukanec SK . . . 98 C2
Pukavik S . . . 63 B2
Pukë AL . . . 182 A1
Pula
HR . . . 122 C2
I . . . 179 C2
Puławy PL . . . 12 C4
Pulborough GB . . . 44 C3
Pulfero I . . . 122 A2
Pulgar E . . . 157 A3
Pulheim D . . . 80 A2
Pulkau A . . . 97 C3
Pulpi E . . . 164 B3
Pulsano I . . . 173 B3
Pulsnitz D . . . 84 A2
Pułtusk PL . . . 77 B6
Pumpsaint GB . . . 39 B3
Punat HR . . . 123 B3
Punta Marina I . . . 135 A5
Punta Prima E . . . 167 B4
Punta Sabbioni I . . . 122 B1
Puntas de Calnegre
E . . . 165 B3
Punta Umbria E . . . 161 B3
Puolanka FIN . . . 3 D10
Puoltikasvaara S . . . 196 B4
Puoltsa S . . . 196 B2
Puračić BIH . . . 125 C4
Purbach am Neusiedler
See A . . . 111 B3
Purchena E . . . 164 B2
Purfleet GB . . . 45 B4
Purgstall A . . . 110 A2
Purkersdorf A . . . 111 A3
Purmerend NL . . . 70 B1
Purullena E . . . 164 B1
Pushkin RUS . . . 9 C7
Pushkino RUS . . . 9 D10
Püspökladány H . . . 113 B5
Pusté Ulany SK . . . 111 A4
Pustoshka RUS . . . 9 D6
Puszcza Mariańska
PL . . . 77 C5
Puszczykowo PL . . . 76 B1
Pusztamagyaród
H . . . 111 C3
Pusztamonostor H . 113 B3
Pusztaszabolcs H . 112 B2
Pusztavám H . . . 112 B2
Putanges-Pont-Ecrepin
F . . . 89 B3
Putbus D . . . 66 B2
Putignano I . . . 173 B3
Putlitz D . . . 73 A5
Putnok H . . . 99 C4
Putte B . . . 79 A4
Puttelange-aux-Lacs
F . . . 92 B2
Putten NL . . . 70 B2
Puttgarden D . . . 65 B4
Püttlingen D . . . 92 B2
Putzu Idu I . . . 179 B2
Puy-Guillaume F . . . 117 B3
Puylaroque F . . . 129 B4
Puylaurens F . . . 146 A3
Puy-l'Évêque F . . . 129 B4
Puymirol F . . . 129 B3
Puyôo F . . . 128 C2
Puyrolland F . . . 114 B3
Pwllheli GB . . . 38 B2
Pyetrikaw BY . . . 13 B8
Pyhäjärvi FIN . . . 3 E9
Pyhäkylä FIN . . . 197 D11
Pyla CY . . . 181 A2
Pyla-sur-Mer F . . . 128 B1
Pyrzyce PL . . . 75 A3
Pysely CZ . . . 96 B2
Pyskowice PL . . . 86 B2
Pytalovo RUS . . . 8 D5
Pyzdry PL . . . 76 B2

Q

Quakenbrück D . . . 71 B4
Quargnento I . . . 119 C5
Quarré-les-Tombes
F . . . 104 B2
Quarteira P . . . 160 B1
Quartu Sant'Élena
I . . . 179 C3
Quatre-Champs F . . . 91 B4
Quedlinburg D . . . 82 A3
Queensferry
Edinburgh GB . . . 35 C4
Flintshire GB . . . 38 A3
Queige F . . . 118 B3
Queipo E . . . 161 B3
Queixans E . . . 146 B2
Quel E . . . 144 B1
Quelaines-St-Gault
F . . . 102 B1
Queljada P . . . 148 A1
Quemada E . . . 143 C3
Queralbs E . . . 147 B3
Quercianella I . . . 134 B3
Querfurt D . . . 82 A3
Quérigut F . . . 146 B3
Quero
E . . . 157 A4
I . . . 121 B4
Querqueville F . . . 88 A2
Quesada E . . . 164 B1
Questembert F . . . 101 B3
Quettehou F . . . 88 A2
Quevauvillers F . . . 90 B2
Quevy B . . . 79 B4
Quiaois P . . . 148 B1
Quiberon F . . . 100 B2
Quiberville F . . . 89 A4
Quickborn D . . . 64 C2
Quiévrain B . . . 79 B3
Quillan F . . . 146 B3
Quillebeuf F . . . 89 A4
Quimper F . . . 100 A1
Quimperlé F . . . 100 B2
Quincampoix F . . . 89 A5
Quincoces de Yuso
E . . . 143 B3
Quincy F . . . 103 B4
Quinéville F . . . 88 A2
Quingey F . . . 105 B4
Quinson F . . . 132 B2
Quinssaines F . . . 116 A2
Quinta-Grande P . . . 154 C2
Quintana de la Serena
E . . . 156 B2
Quintana del Castillo
E . . . 141 B4
Quintana del Marco
E . . . 141 B5
Quintana del Puenta
E . . . 142 B2
Quintana-Martin
Galindez E . . . 143 B3
Quintanaortuño E . 143 B3
Quintanapalla E . . . 143 B3
Quintanar de la Orden
E . . . 157 A4
Quintanar de la Sierra
E . . . 143 C3
Quintanar del Rey
E . . . 158 B2
Quintanilla de la Mata
E . . . 143 C3
Quintanilla del Coco
E . . . 143 C3
Quintanilla de Onésimo
E . . . 150 A3
Quintanilla de Somoza
E . . . 141 B4
Quintas de Valdelucio
E . . . 142 B2
Quintela P . . . 148 B2
Quintin F . . . 100 A3
Quinto E . . . 153 A3
Quinzano d'Oglio I 120 B3
Quiroga E . . . 141 B3
Quismondo E . . . 150 B3
Quissac F . . . 131 B2
Quistello I . . . 121 B3

R

Raab A 96 C1
Raabs an der Thaya A 97 C3
Raahe FIN 3 D9
Raajärvi FIN 197 C9
Raalte NL 71 B3
Raamsdonksveer NL 79 A4
Raanujarvi FIN 196 C7
Raattama FIN 196 A7
Rab HR 123 C3
Rabac HR 123 B3
Rábade E 140 A3
Rábafüzes H 111 C3
Rábahidvég H 111 B3
Rabanales E 149 A3
Rábapatona H 111 B4
Rabapordány H 111 B4
Rabastens F 129 C4
Rabastens-de-Bigorre F 145 A4
Rabat = Victoria M 175 C3
Rabat M 175 C3
Rabča SK 99 B3
Rabe SRB 126 A2
Rabi CZ 96 B1
Rabino PL 67 C4
Rabka PL 99 B3
Rabrovo SRB 127 C3
Rača SRB 127 C3
Rácale I 173 C4
Rácalmás H 112 B2
Racalmuto I 176 B2
Racconigi I 119 C4
Rače SLO 123 A4
Rachecourt-sur-Marne F 91 C5
Raciąż PL 77 B5
Racibórz PL 86 B2
Račinovci HR 125 C4
Ráckeve H 112 B2
Racławice PL 87 B4
Racławice Śląskie PL 86 B1
Racot PL 75 B5
Råda
Skaraborg S 55 B4
Värmland S 49 B5
Radalj SRB 127 C1
Rădăuţi RO 17 B6
Radda in Chianti I 135 B4
Raddusa I 177 B3
Radeberg D 84 A1
Radebeul D 84 A1
Radeburg D 84 A1
Radeče SLO 123 A4
Radekhiv UA 13 C6
Radenci SLO 111 C3
Radenthein A 109 C4
Radevormwald D 80 A3
Radicófani I 135 C4
Radicóndoli I 135 B4
Radišići BIH 138 B3
Radizel SLO 110 C2
Radków PL 85 B4
Radlje ob Dravi SLO 110 C2
Radłów PL 87 B4
Radmer an der Stube A 110 B1
Radnejaur S 195 E9
Radnice CZ 96 B1
Radohova BIH 138 A3
Radojevo SRB 126 B2
Radolfzell D 107 B3
Radom PL 87 A5
Radomice PL 77 B4
Radomin PL 77 A4
Radomsko PL 86 A3
Radomyshl UA 13 C8
Radomyśl Wielki PL 87 B5
Radošina SK 98 C1
Radošovce SK 98 C1
Radoszewice PL 86 A2
Radoszyce PL 87 A4
Radotin CZ 96 B2
Radovets BG 186 A1
Radoviš MK 182 B4
Radovljica SLO 123 A3
Radowo Wielkie PL 75 A4
Radstadt A 109 B4
Radstock GB 43 A4
Raduc HR 137 A4
Raduša MK 182 A3
Radviliškis LT 8 E3
Radzanów
Mazowieckie PL 77 B5
Mazowieckie PL 87 A4
Radziejów PL 76 B3
Radziejowice PL 77 B5
Radzovce SK 113 A3
Radzyń Chełmiński PL 69 B3
Raeren B 80 B2
Raesfeld D 80 A2
Raffadali I 176 B2
Rafina GR 185 A4
Rafsbotn N 192 B7
Ragachow BY 13 B9
Ragály H 99 C4
Rågeleje DK 61 C2
Raglan GB 39 C4
Ragnitz A 110 C2
Ragusa I 177 C3
Rahden D 72 B1
Råholt N 48 B3
Raiano I 169 A3
Raigada E 141 B3
Rain D 94 C2
Rainbach im Mühlkreis A 96 C2
Rainham GB 45 B4
Rairiz de Veiga E 140 B3
Raisdorf D 64 B3
Raisio FIN 8 B3
Raiskio FIN 197 D9
Raiva
Aveiro P 148 A1
Coimbra P 148 B1
Raja-Jooseppi FIN 193 D12
Rajala FIN 197 B9
Rajcza PL 99 B3
Rajec SK 98 B2
Rájec-Jestřebi CZ 97 B4
Rajecké Teplice SK 98 B2
Rajevo Selo HR 125 C4
Rajhrad CZ 97 B4
Rajić HR 124 B3
Rajka H 111 B4
Rakaca H 99 C4
Rakamaz H 113 A5
Rakek SLO 123 B3
Rakhiv UA 17 A6
Rakitna SLO 123 B3
Rakitovo BG 183 B6
Rakkestad N 54 A2
Rákóczifalva H 113 B4
Rakoniewice PL 75 B5
Rakoszyce PL 85 A4
Raková SK 98 B2
Rakovac BIH 125 B3
Rakovica HR 123 C4
Rakovník CZ 96 A1
Rakow D 66 B2
Raków PL 87 B5
Rakvere EST 8 C5
Ralja SRB 127 C2
Rälla S 62 B4
Ramacastañas E 150 B2
Ramacca I 177 B3
Ramales de la Victoria E 143 A3
Ramberg N 194 B4
Rambervillers F 92 C2
Rambouillet F 90 C1
Rambucourt F 92 C1
Ramdala S 63 B3
Ramerupt F 91 C4
Ramingstein A 109 B4
Ramirás E 140 B2
Ramiswil CH 106 B2
Ramkvilla S 62 A2
Ramme DK 58 B1
Rämmen S 49 B6
Ramnäs S 56 A2
Ramnes N 54 A1
Râmnicu Vâlcea RO 17 C6
Ramonville-St Agne F 129 C4
Rampside GB 36 B3
Ramsau D 109 B3
Ramsbeck D 81 A4
Ramsberg S 56 A1
Ramsele S 200 C2
Ramsey
Cambridgeshire GB 44 A3
Isle of Man GB 36 B2
Ramseycleuch GB 36 A3
Ramsgate GB 45 B5
Ramsjö S 200 D1
Ramstein-Meisenbach D 93 B3
Ramsund N 194 B7
Ramundberget S 199 C9
Ramvik S 200 D3
Ranalt A 108 B2
Rånäs S 51 C5
Rånåsfoss N 48 B3
Rance B 91 A4
Ránchio I 135 B5
Randaberg N 52 A1
Randalstown GB 27 B4
Randan F 117 A3
Randazzo I 177 B3
Rånddalen S 199 C10
Randegg A 110 A1
Randers DK 58 B3
Randijaur S 196 C2
Randin E 140 C3
Randsverk N 198 D6
Råneå S 196 D5
Rånes F 89 B3
Rångedala S 60 B3
Ranis D 82 B3
Rankweil A 107 B4
Rånnaväg S 60 B3
Ränneslöv S 61 C3
Rannoch Station GB 34 B3
Ranovac SRB 127 C3
Ransäter S 55 A4
Ransbach-Baumbach D 81 B3
Ransta S 56 A2
Ranttila FIN 193 C9
Ranua FIN 197 D9
Ranum DK 58 B2
Ranvalhal P 154 B1
Raon-l'Étape F 92 C2
Ráossi I 121 B4
Rapallo I 134 A2
Rapla EST 8 C4
Rapness GB 33 B4
Rapolano Terme I 135 B4
Rapolla I 172 B1
Raposa P 154 B2
Rapperswil CH 107 B3
Raša HR 123 B3
Rasal E 145 B3
Rascafria E 151 B4
Rasdorf D 82 B1
Raseiniai LT 13 A5
Rašica SLO 123 B3
Rasines E 143 A3
Rasquera E 153 A4
Rássina I 135 B4
Rastatt D 93 C4
Rastede D 71 A5
Rastenberg D 82 A3
Rastošnica BIH 125 C4
Rastovac MNE 139 C4
Rasueros E 150 A2
Rasy PL 86 A3
Raszków PL 86 A1
Rätan S 199 C11
Rateče SLO 109 C4
Ratekau D 65 C3
Ratež SLO 123 B4
Rathangan IRL 30 A2
Rathcoole IRL 30 A2
Rathcormack IRL 29 B3
Rathdrum IRL 30 B2
Rathebur D 74 A2
Rathenow D 73 B5
Rathfriland GB 27 B4
Rathkeale IRL 29 B3
Rathmelton IRL 27 A3
Rathmolyon IRL 30 A2
Rathmore IRL 29 B2
Rathmullan IRL 27 A3
Rathnew IRL 30 B2
Rathvilly IRL 30 B2
Ratibořské Hory CZ 96 B2
Ratingen D 80 A2
Ratková SK 99 C4
Ratkovo SRB 126 B1
Ratne UA 13 C6
Rattelsdorf D 94 A2
Ratten A 110 B2
Rattosjärvi FIN 196 C7
Rattray GB 35 B4
Rättvik S 50 B2
Ratvika N 199 B7
Ratzeburg D 65 C3
Rätzlingen D 73 B4
Raucourt-et-Flaba F 91 B4
Raudeberg N 198 D2
Raufarhöfn IS 191 A10
Raufoss N 48 B2
Rauhala FIN 196 B7
Rauland N 53 A4
Raulhac F 116 C2
Raulia N 195 E5
Rauma FIN 8 B2
Raundal N 46 B3
Raunds GB 44 A3
Rauris A 109 B4
Rautas S 196 B2
Rautavaara FIN 3 E11
Rauville-la-Bigot F 88 A2
Rauzan F 128 B2
Ravanusa I 176 B2
Rava-Rus'ka UA 13 C5
Ravča HR 138 B3
Ravels B 79 A4
Rävemåla S 63 B3
Ravenglass GB 36 B3
Ravenna I 135 A5
Ravensburg D 107 B4
Rävlanda S 60 B2
Ravna Gora HR 123 B3
Ravne na Koroškem SLO 110 C1
Ravnje SRB 127 C1
Ravno BIH 139 C3
Ravno Selo SRB 126 B1
Rawa Mazowiecka PL 87 A4
Rawicz PL 85 A4
Rawtenstall GB 40 B1
Rayleigh GB 45 B4
Ražana SRB 127 C1
Ražanac HR 137 A4
Razboj BIH 124 B3
Razes F 115 B5
Razgrad BG 17 D7
Razkrižie SLO 111 C3
Razlog BG 183 B5
Razo E 140 A2
Reading GB 44 B3
Réalmont F 130 B1
Rebais F 90 C3
Reboly RUS 3 E12
Rebordelo P 149 A2
Recanati I 136 B2
Recas E 151 B4
Recco I 134 A2
Recess IRL 28 A2
Recey-sur-Ource F 105 B3
Recezinhos P 148 A1
Rechnitz A 111 B3
Rechytsa BY 13 B9
Recke D 71 B4
Recklinghausen D 80 A3
Recoaro Terme I 121 B4
Recogne B 92 B1
Recoules-Prévinquières F 130 A1
Recsk H 113 B4
Recz PL 75 A4
Reda PL 69 A3
Redalen N 48 B2
Redange L 92 B1
Redcar GB 37 B5
Redditch GB 44 A2
Redefin D 73 A4
Redhill GB 44 B3
Redics H 111 C3
Redkino RUS 9 D10
Redland GB 33 B3
Redlin D 73 A5
Redon F 101 B3
Redondela E 140 B2
Redondo P 155 C3
Red Point GB 31 B3
Redruth GB 42 B1
Redzikowo PL 68 A2
Reepham GB 41 C5
Rees D 80 A2
Reeth GB 37 B5
Reetz D 73 A4
Reftele S 60 B3
Regalbuto I 177 B3
Regen D 95 C5
Regensburg D 95 B4
Regenstauf D 95 B4
Reggello I 135 B4
Réggio di Calábria I 175 C1
Reggiolo I 121 C3
Réggio nell'Emília I 121 C3
Reghin RO 17 B6
Régil E 144 A1
Regna S 56 B1
Regniéville F 92 C1
Regny F 117 B4
Rego da Leirosa P 154 A2
Regöly H 112 C2
Regueiro E 140 B2
Reguengo
Portalegre P 155 B3
Santarém P 154 B2
Reguengos de Monsaraz P 155 C3
Rehau D 83 B4
Rehburg D 72 B2
Rehden D 72 B1
Rehna D 65 C4
Reichelsheim D 93 B4
Reichelshofen D 94 B2
Reichenau A 110 B2
Reichenbach
Sachsen D 83 B4
Sachsen D 84 A2
Reichenfels A 110 B1
Reichensachsen D 82 A2
Reichertshofen D 95 C3
Reichshoffen F 93 C3
Reiden CH 106 B2
Reigada
E 141 A4
P 149 B3
Reigate GB 44 B3
Reillanne F 132 B1
Reillo E 158 B2
Reims F 91 B4
Reinach CH 106 B3
Reinbek D 72 A3
Reinberg D 66 B2
Reine N 194 C4
Reinfeld D 65 C3
Reinheim D 93 B4
Reinli N 47 B6
Reinosa E 142 A2
Reinstorf D 65 C4
Reinsvoll N 48 B2
Reisach A 109 C4
Reiss GB 32 C3
Reitan N 199 C8
Reit im Winkl D 109 B3
Rejmyre S 56 B1
Rekavice BIH 124 C3
Rekovac SRB 127 D3
Relleu E 159 C3
Rém H 125 A5
Remagen D 80 B3
Rémalard F 89 B4
Rembercourt-aux-Pots F 91 C5
Remedios P 154 B1
Remels D 71 A4
Remetea Mare RO 126 B3
Remich L 92 B2
Rémilly F 92 B2
Remiremont F 105 A5
Remolinos E 144 C2
Remoulins F 131 B3
Remscheid D 80 A3
Rémuzat F 131 A4
Rena N 48 A3
Renaison F 117 A3
Renazé F 101 B4
Renchen D 93 C4
Rencurel F 118 B2
Rende I 174 B2
Rendina GR 182 D3
Rendsburg D 64 B2
Renedo E 150 A3
Renens CH 105 C5
Renfrew GB 34 C3
Rengsjö S 50 A3
Reni UA 17 C8
Rennebu N 198 C6
Rennerod D 81 B4
Rennertshofen D 94 C3
Rennes F 101 A4
Rennes-les-Bains F 146 B3
Rennweg A 109 B4
Rens DK 64 B2
Rensjön S 196 A2
Rentería E 144 A2
Rentjärn S 200 A4
Répcelak H 111 B4
Repojoki FIN 193 D9
Repvåg N 193 B9
Requena E 159 B2
Réquista F 130 A1
Rerik D 65 B4
Resana I 121 B4
Resarö S 57 A4
Reschen = Résia I 108 C1
Resen MK 182 B3
Resende P 148 A2
Résia = Reschen I 108 C1
Reşiţa
RO 16 C4
RO 126 B3
Resko PL 67 C4
Resnik SRB 127 C2
Ressons-sur-Matz F 90 B2
Restábal E 163 B4
Resuttano I 177 B3
Retamal E 155 C4
Retford GB 40 B3
Rethel F 91 B4
Rethem D 72 B2
Rethimno GR 185 D5
Retie B 79 A5
Retiers F 101 B4
Retortillo E 149 B3
Retortillo de Soria E 151 A4
Retournac F 117 B4
Rétság H 112 B3
Rettenegg A 110 B2
Retuerta del Bullaque E 157 A3
Retz A 97 C3
Retzbach D 94 B1
Reuden D 73 B5
Reuilly F 103 B4
Reus E 147 C2
Reusel NL 79 A5
Reuterstadt Stavenhagen D 74 A1
Reuth D 95 B4
Reutlingen D 94 C1
Reutte A 108 B1
Reuver NL 80 A2
Revel F 146 A2
Revello I 119 C4
Revenga E 151 B3
Revest-du-Bion F 132 A1
Révfülöp H 111 C4
Revigny-sur-Ornain F 91 C4
Revin F 91 B4
Řevnice CZ 96 B2
Řevničov CZ 84 B1
Revo I 121 A4
Revsnes N 47 A4
Revúca SK 99 C4
Rewa PL 69 A3
Rewal PL 67 B4
Rexbo S 50 B2
Reyðarfjörður IS 191 B11
Reyero E 142 B1
Reykhólar IS 190 B3
Reykholt
Árnessýsla IS 190 C5
Borgarfjarðarsýsla IS 190 C4
Reykjahlið IS 191 B9
Reykjavík IS 190 C4
Rezé F 101 B4
Rēzekne LV 8 D5
Rezovo BG 17 E8
Rezzato I 120 B3
Rezzoáglio I 134 A2
Rhade D 72 A2
Rhaunen D 93 B3
Rhayader GB 39 B3
Rheda-Wiedenbrück D 81 A4
Rhede
Niedersachsen D 71 A4
Nordrhein-Westfalen D 80 A2
Rheinau D 93 C3
Rheinbach D 80 B2
Rheinberg D 80 A2
Rheine D 71 B4
Rheinfelden D 106 B2
Rheinsberg D 74 A1
Rhêmes-Notre-Dame I 119 B4
Rhenen NL 70 C2
Rhens D 81 B3
Rheydt D 80 A2
Rhiconich GB 32 C2
Rhinow D 73 B5
Rhiw GB 38 B2
Rho I 120 B2
Rhoden D 81 A5
Rhodes GR 188 C3
Rhondda GB 39 C3
Rhosllanerchrugog GB 38 A3
Rhosneigr GB 38 A2
Rhossili GB 39 C2
Rhubodach GB 34 C2
Rhuddlan GB 38 A3
Rhyl GB 38 A3
Rhynie GB 33 D4
Riala S 57 A4
Riallé F 101 B4
Riaño E 142 B1
Riano I 168 A2
Rians F 132 B1
Rianxo E 140 B2
Riaza E 151 A4
Riba E 143 A3
Ribadavia E 140 B2
Ribadeo E 141 A3
Riba de Saelices E 152 B1
Ribadesella E 142 A1
Ribaflecha E 143 B4
Ribaforada E 144 C2
Ribare SRB 127 C3
Riba-roja d'Ebre E 153 A4
Riba-Roja de Turia E 159 B3
Ribe DK 59 C1
Ribeauvillé F 106 A2
Ribécourt-Dreslincourt F 90 B2
Ribeira da Pena P 148 A2
Ribeira de Piquín E 141 A3
Ribemont F 91 B3
Ribera I 176 B2
Ribérac F 129 A3
Ribera de Cardós E 146 B2
Ribera del Fresno E 156 B1
Ribesalbes E 159 A3
Ribes de Freser E 147 B3
Ribiers F 132 A1
Ribnica
BIH 139 A4
SLO 123 B3
Ribnica na Potorju SLO 110 C2
Ribnik HR 123 B4
Rîbniţa MD 17 B8
Ribnitz-Damgarten D 66 B1
Ribolla I 135 C4
Řicany CZ 97 B4
Říčany CZ 96 B2
Riccia I 170 B2
Riccione I 136 A1
Ricco Del Golfo I 134 A2
Richebourg F 105 A4
Richelieu F 102 B2
Richisau CH 107 B3
Richmond
Greater London GB 44 B3
North Yorkshire GB 37 B5
Richtenberg D 66 B1
Richterswil CH 107 B3
Rickling D 64 B3
Rickmansworth GB 44 B3
Ricla E 152 A2
Riddarhyttan S 50 C2
Ridderkerk NL 79 A4
Riddes CH 119 A4
Ridjica SRB 125 B5
Riec-sur-Bélon F 100 B2
Ried A 109 A4
Riedenburg D 95 C3
Ried im Oberinntal A 108 B1
Riedlingen D 107 A4
Riedstadt D 93 B4
Riegersburg A 110 C2
Riego de la Vega E 141 B5
Riego del Camino E 149 A4
Riello E 141 B5
Riemst B 80 B1
Rienne B 91 B4
Riénsena E 142 A2
Riesa D 83 A5
Riese Pio X I 121 B4
Riesi I 177 B3
Riestedt D 82 A3
Rietberg D 81 A4
Rieti I 169 A2
Rietschen D 84 A2
Rieumes F 146 A2
Rieupeyroux F 130 A1
Rieux-Volvestre F 146 A2
Riez F 132 B2
Rīga LV 8 D4
Riggisberg CH 106 C2
Rignac F 130 A1
Rignano Gargánico I 171 B3
Rigolato I 109 C3
Rigside GB 36 A3
Rigutino I 135 B4
Riihimäki FIN 8 B4
Rijeka HR 123 B3
Rijen NL 79 A4
Rijkevorsel B 79 A4
Rijssen NL 71 B3
Rila BG 183 A5
Rilić BIH 138 B3
Rilievo I 176 B1
Rillé F 102 B2
Rillo de Gallo E 152 B2

Rimavská Baňa SK 99 C3
Rimavská Seč SK 99 C4
Rimavská Sobota SK 99 C4
Rimbo S 57 A4
Rimforsa S 56 B1
Rímini I 136 A1
Rîmnicu Sărat RO 17 C7
Rimogne F 91 B4
Rimpar D 94 B1
Rimske Toplice SLO 123 A4
Rincón de la Victoria E 163 B3
Rincón de Soto E 144 B2
Rindal N 198 B6
Rinde N 46 A3
Ringarum S 56 B2
Ringaskiddy IRL 29 C3
Ringe DK 59 C3
Ringebu N 48 A2
Ringkøbing DK 59 B1
Ringsaker N 48 B2
Ringsted DK 61 D1
Ringwood GB 44 C2
Rinkaby S 63 C2
Rinkabyholm S 63 B4
Rinlo E 141 A3
Rinn A 108 B2
Rinteln D 72 B2
Rio E 140 B3
Riobo E 140 B2
Riodeva E 152 B2
Rio do Coures P 154 B2
Rio Douro P 148 A2
Riofrio E 150 B3
Rio Frio P 154 C2
Riofrio de Aliste E 149 A3
Rio frio de Riaza E 151 A4
Riogordo E 163 B3
Rioja E 164 C2
Riola I 135 A4
Riola Sardo I 179 C2
Riolobos E 155 B4
Riom F 116 B3
Riomaggiore I 134 A2
Rio Maior P 154 B2
Rio Marina I 134 C3
Riom-ès-Montagnes F 116 B2
Rion-des-Landes F 128 C2
Rionegro del Puente E 141 B4
Rionero in Vúlture I 172 B1
Riopar E 158 C1
Riós E 141 C3
Rioseco E 142 A1
Rioseco de Tapia E 141 B5
Rio Tinto P 148 A1
Riotord F 117 B4
Riotorto E 141 A3
Rioz F 105 B5
Ripač BIH 124 C1
Ripacándida I 172 B1
Ripanj SRB 127 C2
Ripatransone I 136 C2
Ripley GB 40 B2
Ripoll E 147 B3
Ripon GB 40 A2
Riposto I 177 B4
Ripsa S 56 B2
Risan MNE 16 D3
Risbäck S 200 B1
Risca GB 39 C3
Rischenau D 81 A5
Riscle F 128 C2
Risebo S 56 B2
Risnes N 46 A2
Rišňovce SK 98 C1
Risør N 53 B5
Risøyhamn N 194 B6
Rissna S 199 B12
Ritsem S 194 C8
Ritterhude D 72 A1
Riutula FIN 193 D10
Riva del Garda I 121 B3
Riva Lígure I 133 B3
Rivanazzano I 120 C2
Rivarolo Canavese I 119 B4
Rivarolo Mantovano I 121 B3
Rive-de-Gier F 117 B4
Rivedoux-Plage F 114 B2
Rivello I 174 A1
Rivergaro I 120 C2
Rives F 118 B2
Rivesaltes F 146 B3
Rivignano I 122 B2
Rivne UA 13 C7
Rívoli I 119 B4
Rivolta d'Adda I 120 B2
Rixheim F 106 B2
Rixo S 54 B2
Riza GR 183 C5
Rizokarpaso CY 181 A3
Rjukan N 47 C5
Rø DK 67 A3
Rö S 57 A4
Roa
E 143 C3
N 48 B2
Roade GB 44 A3
Roager DK 59 C1
Roaldkvam N 52 A2
Roanne F 117 A4
Röbäck S 200 C6
Robakowo PL 69 B3
Róbbio I 120 B1
Röbel D 73 A5
Roberton GB 35 C5
Robertsfors S 200 B6
Robertville B 80 B2
Robin Hood's Bay GB 37 B6
Robleda E 149 B3
Robledillo de Trujillo E 156 A2
Robledo
Albacete E 158 C1
Orense E 141 B4
Robledo de Chavela E 151 B3
Robledo del Buey E 156 A3
Robledo del Mazo E 156 A3
Robledollano E 156 A2
Robles de la Valcueva E 142 B1
Robliza de Cojos E 149 B4
Robres E 145 C3
Robres del Castillo E 144 B1
Rocafort de Queralt E 147 C2
Rocamadour F 129 B4
Roccabernarda I 175 B2
Roccabianca I 120 B3
Roccadáspide I 172 B1
Rocca di Mezzo I 169 A3
Rocca di Papa I 168 B2
Roccagorga I 169 B3
Rocca Imperiale I 174 A2
Roccalbegna I 135 C4
Roccalumera I 177 B4
Roccamena I 176 B2
Roccamonfina I 170 B1
Roccanova I 174 A2
Roccapalumba I 176 B2
Roccapassa I 169 A3
Rocca Priora I 136 B2
Roccaraso I 169 B4
Rocca San Casciano I 135 A4
Roccasecca I 169 B3
Rocca Sinibalda I 169 A2
Roccastrada I 135 B4
Roccatederighi I 135 B4
Roccella Iónica I 175 C2
Rocchetta Sant'António I 172 A1
Rocester GB 40 C2
Rochdale GB 40 B1
Rochechouart F 115 C4
Rochefort
B 79 B5
F 114 C3
Rochefort-en-Terre F 101 B3
Rochefort-Montagne F 116 B2
Rochefort-sur-Nenon F 105 B4
Roche-lez-Beaupré F 105 B5
Rochemaure F 131 A3
Rocheservière F 114 B2
Rochester
Medway GB 45 B4
Northumberland GB 37 A4
Rochlitz D 83 A4
Rociana del Condado E 161 B3
Rockenhausen D 93 B3
Rockhammar S 56 A1
Rockneby S 62 B4
Ročko Polje HR 123 B3
Ročov CZ 84 B1
Rocroi F 91 B4
Rodach D 82 B2
Roda de Bara E 147 C2
Roda de Ter E 147 C3
Rodalben D 93 B3
Rødberg N 47 B5
Rødby DK 65 B4
Rødbyhavn DK 65 B4
Rødding
Sønderjyllands Amt. DK 59 C2
Viborg Amt. DK 58 B1
Rödeby S 63 B3
Rodeiro E 140 B3
Rødekro DK 64 A2
Roden NL 71 A3
Ródenas E 152 B2
Rodenkirchen D 72 A1
Rödental D 82 B3
Rödermark D 93 B4
Rodewisch D 83 B4
Rodez F 130 A1
Rodi Gargánico I 171 B3
Roding D 95 B4
Rödjebro S 51 B4
Rødkærsbro DK 59 B2
Rodolivas GR 183 C5
Rodoñá E 147 C2
Rødvig DK 65 A5
Roermond NL 80 A1
Roesbrugge B 78 B2
Roeschwoog F 93 C4
Roeselare B 78 B3
Roetgen D 80 B2
Roffiac F 116 B3
Röfors S 55 B5
Rofrano I 172 B1
Rogač HR 138 B2
Rogačica SRB 127 C1
Rogalinek PL 76 B1
Rogaška Slatina SLO 123 A4
Rogatec SLO 123 A4
Rogatica BIH 139 B5
Rogatyn UA 13 D6
Rogätz D 73 B4
Roggendorf D 65 C4
Roggiano Gravina I 174 B2
Roghadal GB 31 B2
Rogliano
F 180 A2
I 175 B2
Rognan N 195 C6
Rogne N 47 A6
Rognes F 131 B4
Rogny-les-7-Ecluses F 103 B4
Rogowo PL 76 B2
Rogoznica HR 138 B1
Rogoźnica PL 85 A4
Rogoźno PL 76 B1
Rohan F 101 A3
Röhlingen D 94 C2
Rohožnik SK 98 C1
Rohr D 82 B2
Rohrbach A 96 C1
Rohrbach-lès-Bitche F 92 B3
Rohrberg D 73 B4
Rohr im Gebirge A 110 B2
Röhrnbach D 96 C1
Roisel F 90 B3
Roja LV 8 D3
Rojales E 165 A4
Röjeråsen S 50 B1
Rojewo PL 76 B3
Rokiciny PL 87 A3
Rokietnica PL 75 B5
Rokiškis LT 8 E4
Rokitki PL 85 A3
Rokycany CZ 96 B1
Rolampont F 105 B4
Rold DK 58 B2
Røldal N 52 A2
Rolde NL 71 B3
Rolfs S 196 D6
Rollag N 47 B6
Rollán E 149 B4
Rolle CH 105 C5
Roma = Rome I 168 B2
Roma S 57 C4
Romagnano Sésia I 119 B5
Romagné F 88 B2
Romakloster S 57 C4
Roman RO 17 B7
Romana I 178 B2
Romanèche-Thorins F 117 A4
Romano di Lombardia I 120 B2
Romanshorn CH 107 B4
Romans-sur-Isère F 118 B2
Rombas F 92 B2
Rome = Roma I 168 B2
Romeán E 141 B3
Romenay F 105 C4
Romeral E 157 A4
Römerstein D 94 C1
Rometta I 177 A4
Romford GB 45 B4
Romhány H 112 B3
Römhild D 82 B2
Romilly-sur-Seine F 91 C3
Romont CH 106 C1
Romorantin-Lanthenay F 103 B3
Romrod D 81 B5
Romsey GB 44 C2
Rømskog N 54 A2
Rønbjerg DK 58 B1
Roncal E 144 B3
Ronce-les-Bains F 114 C2
Ronchamp F 106 B1
Ronchi dei Legionari I 122 B2
Ronciglione I 168 A2
Ronco Canavese I 119 B4
Ronco Scrivia I 120 C1
Ronda E 162 B2
Rønde DK 59 B3
Rone S 57 C4
Ronehamn S 57 C4
Rong N 46 B1
Rönnäng S 60 B1
Rønne DK 67 A3
Ronneburg D 83 B4
Ronneby S 63 B3
Rönneshytta S 55 B6
Rönninge S 57 A3
Rönnöfors S 199 B10
Rönö S 56 B2
Ronov nad Doubravou CZ 97 B3
Ronse B 79 B3
Roosendaal NL 79 A4
Roosky IRL 26 C3
Ropczyce PL 87 B5
Ropeid N 52 A2
Ropinsalmi FIN 192 D5
Ropuerelos del Páramo E 141 B5
Roquebillière F 133 A3
Roquebrun F 130 B2
Roquecourbe F 130 B1
Roquefort F 128 B2
Roquemaure F 131 A3
Roquesteron F 132 B3
Roquetas de Mar E 164 C2
Roquetes E 153 B4
Roquevaire F 132 B1
Røra N 199 B8
Rörbäcksnäs S 49 A4
Rørbæk DK 58 B2
Rore BIH 138 A2
Röro S 60 B1
Røros N 199 C8
Rorschach CH 107 B4
Rørvig DK 61 D1
Rørvik N 199 A8
Rörvik S 62 A2
Rosà I 121 B4
Rosal de la Frontera E 161 B2
Rosalina Mare I 122 B1
Rosa Marina I 173 B3
Rosans F 132 A1
Rosário P 160 B1
Rosarno I 175 C1
Rosbach D 81 B3
Rosche D 73 B3
Rościszewo PL 77 B4
Roscoff F 100 A2
Roscommon IRL 28 A3
Roscrea IRL 28 B4
Rosdorf D 82 A1
Rose I 174 B2
Rosegg A 109 C5
Rosehall GB 32 D2
Rosehearty GB 33 D4
Rosel GB 88 A1
Rosell E 153 B4
Roselló E 153 A4
Rosendal N 46 C3
Rosenfeld D 93 C4
Rosenfors S 62 A3
Rosenheim D 108 B3
Rosenow D 74 A2
Rosenthal D 81 A4
Rosersberg S 57 A3
Roses E 147 B4
Roseto degli Abruzzi I 169 A4
Roseto Valfortore I 170 B3
Rosheim F 93 C3
Rosia I 135 B4
Rosice CZ 97 B4
Rosières-en-Santerre F 90 B2
Rosignano Maríttimo I 134 B3
Rosignano Solvay I 134 B3
Roşiori-de-Vede RO 17 C6
Roskhill GB 31 B2
Roskilde DK 61 D2
Roskovec AL 182 C1
Röslau D 83 B3
Roslev DK 58 B1
Rosmaninhal P 155 B3
Rosnowo PL 67 B5
Rosolini I 177 C3
Rosova MNE 139 B5
Rosoy F 104 A2
Rosporden F 100 B2
Rosquete P 154 B2
Rosrath D 80 B3
Rossa CH 120 A2
Rossano I 174 B2
Rossas
Aveiro P 148 B1
Braga P 148 A1
Rossdorf D 82 B2
Rossett GB 38 A4
Rosshaupten D 108 B1
Rossiglione I 133 A4
Rossignol B 92 B1
Rossla D 82 A3
Rosslare IRL 30 B2
Rosslare Harbour IRL 30 B2
Rosslau D 83 A4
Rosslea GB 27 B3
Rossleben D 82 A3
Rossön S 200 C2
Ross-on-Wye GB 39 C4
Rossoszyca PL 86 A2
Rosswein D 83 A5
Röstånga S 61 C3
Roštár SK 99 C4
Rostock D 65 B5
Rostrenen F 100 A2
Røsvik N 194 C6
Rosvik S 196 D4
Rosyth GB 35 B4
Röszke H 126 A2
Rot S 49 A6
Rota E 161 C3
Rota Greca I 174 B2
Rot am See D 94 B2
Rotberget N 49 B4
Rotella I 136 C2
Rotenburg
Hessen D 82 B1
Niedersachsen D 72 A2
Roth
Bayern D 94 B3
Rheinland-Pfalz D 81 B3
Rothbury GB 37 A5
Rothemühl D 74 A2
Röthenbach D 95 B3
Rothenburg D 84 A2
Rothenburg ob der Tauber D 94 B2
Rothéneuf F 88 B2
Rothenklempenow D 74 A3
Rothenstein D 94 C3
Rotherham GB 40 B2
Rothes GB 32 D3
Rothesay GB 34 C2
Rothwell GB 44 A3
Rotnes N 48 B2
Rotonda I 174 B2
Rotondella I 174 A2
Rotova E 159 C3
Rott
Bayern D 108 B1
Bayern D 108 B3
Rottach-Egern D 108 B2
Röttenbach D 94 B3
Rottenbuch D 108 B1
Rottenburg
Baden-Württemberg D 93 C4
Bayern D 95 C4
Rottenmann A 110 B1
Rotterdam NL 79 A4
Rotthalmünster D 96 C1
Rottingdean GB 44 C3
Röttingen D 94 B1
Rottleberode D 82 A2
Rottne S 62 A2
Rottneros S 55 A4
Rottofreno I 120 B2
Rottweil D 107 A3
Rötz D 95 B4
Roubaix F 78 B3
Roudnice nad Labem CZ 84 B2
Roudouallec F 100 A2
Rouen F 89 A5
Rouffach F 106 B2
Rougé F 101 B4
Rougemont F 105 B5
Rougemont le-Château F 106 B1
Rouillac F 115 C3
Rouillé F 115 B4
Roujan F 130 B2
Roulans F 105 B5
Roundwood IRL 30 A2
Rousínov CZ 97 B4
Roussac F 115 B5
Roussennac F 130 A1
Rousses F 130 A2
Roussillon F 117 B4
Rouvroy-sur-Audry F 91 B4
Rouy F 104 B2
Rovanieman maalaiskunta FIN 197 C8
Rovaniemi FIN 197 C8
Rovato I 120 B2
Rovensko pod Troskami CZ 84 B3
Roverbella I 121 B3
Rovereto I 121 B4
Rövershagen D 65 B5
Roverud N 49 B4
Rovigo I 121 B4
Rovinj HR 122 B2
Rovišce HR 124 B2
Rów PL 74 B3
Rowy PL 68 A2
Royal Leamington Spa GB 44 A2
Royal Tunbridge Wells GB 45 B4
Royan F 114 C2
Royat F 116 B3
Roybon F 118 B2
Roybridge GB 34 B3
Roye F 90 B2
Royère-de-Vassivière F 116 B1
Røykenvik N 48 B2
Royos E 164 B2
Røyrvik N 199 A10
Royston GB 44 A3
Rozadas E 141 A4
Rozalén del Monte E 151 C5
Różańsko PL 75 B3
Rozay-en-Brie F 90 C2
Roždalovice CZ 84 B3
Rozdilna UA 17 B9
Rozental PL 69 B4
Rozhyshche UA 13 C6
Rožmitál pod Třemšínem CZ 96 B1
Rožňava SK 99 C4
Rožnov pod Radhoštěm CZ 98 B2
Rozoy-sur-Serre F 91 B4
Rozprza PL 86 A3
Roztoky CZ 84 B2
Rozvadov CZ 95 B4
Rozzano I 120 B2
Rrëshen AL 182 B1
Rrogozhine AL 182 B1
Ruanes E 156 A2
Rubbestadneset N 46 C2
Rubi E 147 C3
Rubiá E 141 B4
Rubiacedo de Abajo E 143 B3
Rubielos Bajos E 158 B1
Rubielos de Mora E 153 B3
Rubiera I 121 C3
Rubik AL 182 B1
Rucandio E 143 B3
Rud
Akershus N 48 B3
Buskerud N 48 B2
Ruda
PL 86 A2
S 62 A4
Rudabánya H 99 C4
Ruda Maleniecka PL 87 A4
Ruda Pilczycka PL 87 A4
Ruda Śl. PL 86 B2
Ruddervorde B 78 A3
Ruden A 110 C1
Rudersberg D 94 C1
Rudersdorf A 111 B3
Rüdersdorf D 74 B2
Ruderting D 96 C1
Rüdesheim D 93 B3
Rudkøbing DK 65 B3
Rudmanns A 97 C3
Rudna
CZ 96 A2
PL 85 A4
Rudnik SRB 127 C2
Rudniki
Opolskie PL 86 A2
Śląskie PL 86 B3
Rudno
Dolnośląskie PL 85 A4
Pomorskie PL 69 B3
Rudnya RUS 13 A9
Rudolstadt D 82 B3
Rudowica PL 84 A3
Rudozem BG 183 B6
Rudskoga S 55 A5
Rudston GB 40 A3
Ruds Vedby DK 61 D1
Rudy PL 86 B2
Rue F 78 B1
Rueda E 150 A3
Rueda de Jalón E 152 A2
Ruelle-sur-Touvre F 115 C4
Ruerrero E 143 B3
Ruffano I 173 C4
Ruffec F 115 B4
Rufina I 135 B4
Rugby GB 44 A2
Rugeley GB 40 C2
Ruggstrop S 62 B4
Rugles F 89 B4
Rugozero RUS 3 D13
Rühen D 73 B3
Ruhla D 82 B2
Ruhland D 84 A1
Ruhle D 71 B4
Ruhpolding D 109 B3
Ruhstorf D 96 C1
Ruidera E 158 C1
Ruillé-sur-le-Loir F 102 B2
Ruinen NL 71 B3
Ruiselede B 78 A3
Ruka FIN 197 C12
Rulles B 92 B1
Rülzheim D 93 B4
Rum H 111 B3
Ruma SRB 127 B1
Rumboci BIH 138 B3
Rumburk CZ 84 B2
Rumenka SRB 126 B1
Rumia PL 69 A3
Rumigny F 91 B4
Rumilly F 118 B2
Rumma S 56 B2
Rumney GB 39 C3
Rumont F 91 C5
Runa P 154 B1
Runcorn GB 38 A4
Rundmoen N 195 D5
Rungsted DK 61 D2
Runhällen S 51 B3
Runowo PL 69 A5
Ruokojärvi FIN 196 B7
Ruokolahti FIN 9 B6
Ruokto S 196 B2
Ruoms F 131 A3
Ruoti I 172 B1
Rupa HR 123 B3
Ruppichteroth D 80 B3
Rupt-sur-Moselle F 106 B1
Rus E 157 B4
Ruse BG 17 D7
Ruše SLO 110 C2
Rusele S 200 B4
Ruševo HR 125 B4
Rush IRL 30 A2
Rushden GB 44 A3
Rusiec PL 86 A2
Rusinowo
Zachodnio-Pomorskie PL 67 C4
Zachodnio-Pomorskie PL 75 A5
Ruskele S 200 B4
Ruski Krstur SRB 126 B1
Ruskington GB 40 B3
Rusovce SK 111 A4
Rüsselsheim D 93 B4

Russelv N 192 C4
Russi I 135 A5
Rust A 111 B3
Rustefjelbma N 193 B12
Rustrel F 131 B4
Ruszki PL 77 B5
Ruszów PL 84 A3
Rute E 163 A3
Rüthen D 81 A4
Rutherglen GB 35 C3
Ruthin GB 38 A3
Ruthven GB 32 D2
Ruthwell GB 36 B3
Rüti CH 107 B3
Rutigliano I 173 A3
Rutledal N 46 A2
Rutuna S 56 B3
Rutvik S 196 D5
Ruurlo NL 71 B3
Ruuvaoja FIN 197 B11
Ruvo del Monte I 172 B1
Ruvo di Púglia I 171 B4
Ruynes-en-Margeride F 116 C3
Ružic HR 138 B2
Ružomberok SK 99 B3
Ruzsa H 126 A1
Ry DK 59 B2
Rybany SK 98 C2
Rybina PL 69 A4
Rybnik PL 86 B2
Rychliki PL 69 B4
Rychlocice PL 86 A2
Rychnov nad Kněžnou CZ 85 B4
Rychnowo PL 77 A5
Rychtal PL 86 A1
Rychwał PL 76 B3
Ryczywół PL 87 A5
Ryczywól PL 75 B5
Ryd S 63 B2
Rydaholm S 62 B2
Rydal S 60 B2
Rydbo S 57 A4
Rydboholm S 60 B2
Ryde GB 44 C2
Rydöbruk S 60 C3
Rydsgård S 66 A2
Rydsnäs S 62 A3
Rydultowy PL 86 B2
Rydzyna PL 85 A4
Rye GB 45 C4
Rygge N 54 A1
Ryjewo PL 69 B3
Rykene N 53 B4
Rymań PL 67 C4
Rýmařov CZ 98 B1
Rynarzewo PL 76 A2
Ryomgård DK 59 B3
Rypefjord N 192 B7
Rypin PL 77 A4
Rysjedalsvika N 46 A2
Ryssby S 60 C4
Rytel PL 68 B2
Rytinki FIN 197 D10
Rytro PL 99 B4
Rywociny PL 77 A5
Rzeczenica PL 68 B2
Rzeczniów PL 87 A5
Rzeczyca PL 87 A4
Rzęgnowo PL 77 A5
Rzejowice PL 87 A3
Rzemień PL 87 B5
Rzepin PL 75 B3
Rzesznikowo PL 67 C4
Rzeszów PL 12 C4
Rzgów PL 86 A3
Rzhev RUS 9 D9

S

Saal
Bayern D 82 B2
Bayern D 95 C3
Saalbach A 109 B3
Saalburg D 83 B3
Saales F 92 C3
Saalfeld D 82 B3
Saalfelden am Steinernen Meer A 109 B3
Saanen CH 106 C2
Saarbrücken D 92 B2
Saarburg D 92 B2
Saarijärvi FIN 8 A4
Saari-Kämä FIN 197 C9
Saarlouis D 92 B2
Saas-Fee CH 119 A4
Šabac SRB 127 C1
Sabadell E 147 C3
Sabáudia I 169 B3
Sabbioneta I 121 C3
Sabero E 142 B1
Sabiñánigo E 145 B3
Sabiote E 157 B4
Sables-d'Or-les-Pins F 101 A3
Sablé-sur-Sarthe F 102 B1
Sabóia P 160 B1
Saborsko HR 123 B4
Sæbøvik N 52 A1
Sabres F 128 B2
Sabrosa P 148 A2
Sabugal P 149 B2
Sabuncu TR 187 C5
Sæby DK 58 A3
Săcălaz RO 126 B3
Sacecorbo E 152 B1
Saceda del Rio E 151 B5
Sacedón E 151 B5
Săcele RO 17 C6
Saceruela E 156 B3
Sachsenburg A 109 C4
Sachsenhagen D 72 B2
Sacile I 122 B1
Sacramenia E 151 A4
Sada E 140 A2
Sádaba E 144 B2
Saddell GB 34 C2
Sadernes E 147 B3
Sadki PL 76 A2
Sadkowice PL 87 A4
Sadlinki PL 69 B3
Sadów PL 75 B3
Sadská CZ 84 B2
Saelices E 151 C5
Saelices de Mayorga E 142 B1
Saerbeck D 71 B4
Saeul L 92 B1
Safaalan TR 186 A3
Safara P 161 A2
Säffle S 55 A3
Saffron Walden GB 45 A4
Safranbolu TR 187 A7
Säfsnäs S 50 B1
Şag RO 126 B3
Sagard D 66 B2
S'Agaro E 147 C4
Sågmyra S 50 B2
Sagone F 180 A1
Sagres P 160 C1
Ságújfalu H 113 A3
Sagunt E 159 B3
Sagvåg N 52 A1
Ságvár H 112 C2
Sagy F 105 C4
Sahagún E 142 B1
Šahy SK 112 A2
Saignelégier CH 106 B1
Saignes F 116 B2
Saija FIN 197 B11
Saillagouse F 146 B3
Saillans F 118 C2
Sains Richaumont F 91 B3
St Abb's GB 35 C5
St Affrique F 130 B1
St Agnan F 104 C2
St Agnant F 114 C3
St Agnes GB 42 B1
St Agrève F 117 B4
St Aignan F 103 B3
St Aignan-sur-Roë F 101 B4
St Albans GB 44 B3
St Alban-sur-Limagnole F 117 C3
St Amand-en-Puisaye F 104 B2
St Amand-les-Eaux F 79 B3
St Amand-Longpré F 103 B3
St Amand-Montrond F 103 C4
St Amans F 117 C3
St Amans-Soult F 130 B1
St Amant-Roche-Savine F 117 B3
St Amarin F 106 B1
St Ambroix F 131 A3
St Amé F 106 A1
St Amour F 118 A2
St André-de-Corcy F 117 B4
St André-de-Cubzac F 128 B2
St André-de-l'Eure F 89 B5
St André-de-Roquepertuis F 131 A3
St André-de-Sangonis F 130 B2
St Andre-de-Valborgne F 130 A2
St André-les-Alpes F 132 B2
St Andrews GB 35 B5
St Angel F 116 B2
St Anthème F 117 B3
St Antoine F 180 A2
St Antoine-de-Ficalba F 129 B3
St Antönien CH 107 C4
St Antonin-Noble-Val F 129 B4
St Août F 103 C3
St Armant-Tallende F 116 B3
St Arnoult F 90 C1
St Asaph GB 38 A3
St Astier F 129 A3
St Athan GB 39 C3
St Auban F 132 B2
St Aubin
CH 106 C1
F 105 B4
GB 88 A1
St Aubin-d'Aubigne F 101 A4
St Aubin-du-Cormier F 101 A4
St Aubin-sur-Aire F 92 C1
St Aubin-sur-Mer F 89 A3
St Aulaye F 128 A3
St Austell GB 42 B2
St Avit F 116 B2
St Avold F 92 B2
St Aygulf F 132 B2
St Bauzille-de-Putois F 130 B2
St Béat F 145 B4
St Beauzély F 130 A1
St Bees GB 36 B3
St Benim-d'Azy F 104 C2
St Benoît-du-Sault F 115 B5
St Benoit-en-Woëvre F 92 C1
St Berthevin F 102 A1
St Blaise-la-Roche F 92 C3
St Blazey GB 42 B2
St Blin F 105 A4
St Bonnet F 118 C3
St Bonnet Briance F 115 C5
St Bonnet-de-Joux F 104 C3
St Bonnet-le-Château F 117 B4
St Bonnet-le-Froid F 117 B4
St Brévin-les-Pins F 101 B3
St Briac-sur-Mer F 101 A3
St Brice-en-Coglès F 88 B2
St Brieuc F 101 A3
St Bris-le-Vineux F 104 B2
St Broladre F 88 B2
St Calais F 102 B2
St Cannat F 131 B4
St Cast-le-Guildo F 101 A3
St Céré F 129 B4
St Cergue CH 118 A3
St Cergues F 118 A3
St Cernin F 116 B2
St Chamant F 116 B1
St Chamas F 131 B4
St Chamond F 117 B4
St Chély-d'Apcher F 116 C3
St Chély-d'Aubrac F 116 C2
St Chinian F 130 B1
St Christol F 131 A4
St Christol-lès-Alès F 131 A3
St Christoly-Médoc F 114 C3
St Christophe-du-Ligneron F 114 B2
St Christophe-en-Brionnais F 117 A4
St Ciers-sur-Gironde F 128 A2
St Clair-sur-Epte F 90 B1
St Clar F 129 C3
St Claud F 115 C4
St Claude F 118 A2
St Clears GB 39 C2
St Columb Major GB 42 B2
St Come-d'Olt F 130 A1
St Cosme-en-Vairais F 89 B4
St Cyprien
Dordogne F 129 B4
Pyrenées-Orientales F 146 B4
St Cyr-sur-Loire F 102 B2
St Cyr-sur-Mer F 132 B1
St Cyr-sur-Methon F 117 A4
St David's GB 39 C1
St Denis F 90 C2
St Denis-d'Oléron F 114 B2
St Denis d'Orques F 102 A1
St Didier F 117 A4
St Didier-en-Velay F 117 B4
St Dié F 92 C2
St Dier-d'Auvergne F 117 B3
St Dizier F 91 C4
St Dizier-Leyrenne F 116 A1
St Dogmaels GB 39 B2
Ste Adresse F 89 A4
Ste Anne F 89 B4
Ste Anne-d'Auray F 100 B3
Ste Croix CH 105 C5
Ste Croix-Volvestre F 146 A2
Ste Engrâce F 144 A3
Ste Enimie F 130 A2
St Efflam F 100 A2
Ste Foy-de-Peyrolières F 146 A2
Ste Foy-la-Grande F 128 B3
Ste Foy l'Argentiere F 117 B4
Ste Gauburge-Ste Colombe F 89 B4
Ste Gemme la Plaine F 114 B2
Ste Geneviève F 90 B2
St Égrève F 118 B2
Ste Hélène F 128 B2
Ste Hélène-sur-Isère F 118 B3
Ste Hermine F 114 B2
Ste Jalle F 131 A4
Ste Livrade-sur-Lot F 129 B3
St Eloy-les-Mines F 116 A2
Ste Marie-aux-Mines F 106 A2
Ste Marie-du-Mont F 88 A2
Ste Maure-de-Touraine F 102 B2
Ste Maxime F 132 B2
Ste Ménéhould F 91 B4
Ste Mère-Église F 88 A2
St Emiland F 104 C3
St Émilion F 128 B2
St Enoder GB 42 B2
Sainteny F 88 A2
Ste Ode B 92 A1
Saintes F 114 C3
Ste Savine F 91 C4
Ste Sévère-sur-Indre F 103 C4
Ste Sigolène F 117 B4
St Esteben F 144 A2
St Estèphe F 128 A2
Ste Suzanne F 102 A1
St Étienne F 117 B4
St Etienne-de-Baigorry F 144 A2
St Étienne-de-Cuines F 118 B3
St Etienne-de-Fursac F 116 A1
St Etienne-de-Montluc F 101 B4
St Etienne-de-St Geoirs F 118 B2
St Étienne-de-Tinée F 132 A2
St Étienne-du-Bois F 118 A2
St Étienne-du-Rouvray F 89 A5
St Etienne-les-Orgues F 132 A1
Ste Tulle F 132 B1
St Fargeau F 104 B2
St Félicien F 117 B4
St Felix-de-Sorgues F 130 B1
St Félix-Lauragais F 146 A2
Saintfield GB 27 B5
St Fillans GB 35 B3
St Firmin F 118 C3
St Florent F 180 A2
St Florentin F 104 B2
St Florent-le-Vieil F 101 B4
St Florent-sur-Cher F 103 C4
St Flour F 116 B3
St Flovier F 103 C3
St Fort-sur-le-Né F 115 C3
St Fulgent F 114 B2
St Galmier F 117 B4
St Gaudens F 145 A4
St Gaultier F 115 B5
St Gély-du-Fesc F 130 B2
St Genest-Malifaux F 117 B4
St Gengoux-le-National F 104 C3
St Geniez F 132 A2
St Geniez-d'Olt F 130 A1
St Genis-de-Saintonge F 114 C3
St Genis-Pouilly F 118 A3
St Genix-sur-Guiers F 118 B2
St Georges Buttavent F 88 B3
St Georges-d'Aurac F 117 B3
St Georges-de-Commiers F 118 B2
St Georges-de-Didonne F 114 C3
St Georges-de-Luzençon F 130 A1
St Georges-de Mons F 116 B2
St Georges-de-Reneins F 117 A4
St Georges d'Oléron F 114 C2
St Georges-en-Couzan F 117 B3
St Georges-lès-Baillargeaux F 115 B4
St Georges-sur-Loire F 102 B1
St Georges-sur-Meuse B 79 B5
St Geours-de-Maremne F 128 C1
St Gérand-de-Vaux F 117 A3
St Gérand-le-Puy F 117 A3
St Germain F 105 B5
St Germain-Chassenay F 104 C2
St Germain-de-Calberte F 130 A2
St Germain-de-Confolens F 115 B4
St Germain-de-Joux F 118 A2
St Germain-des-Fossés F 117 A3
St Germain-du-Bois F 105 C4
St Germain-du-Plain F 105 C3
St Germain-du Puy F 103 B4
St Germain-en-Laye F 90 C2
St Germain-Laval F 117 B4
St Germain-Lembron F 116 B3
St Germain-les-Belles F 116 B1
St Germain-Lespinasse F 117 A3
St Germain-l'Herm F 117 B3
St Gervais-d'Auvergne F 116 A2
St Gervais-les-Bains F 118 B3
St Gervais-sur-Mare F 130 B2
St Gildas-de-Rhuys F 100 B3
St Gildas-des-Bois F 101 B3
St Gilles
Gard F 131 B3
Ille-et-Vilaine F 101 A4
St Gilles-Croix-de-Vie F 114 B2
St Gingolph F 119 A3
St Girons
Ariège F 146 B2
Landes F 128 C1
St Girons-Plage F 128 C1
St Gobain F 91 B3
St Gorgon-Main F 105 B5
St Guénolé F 100 B1
St Harmon GB 39 B3
St Helens GB 38 A4
St Helier GB 88 A1
St Herblain F 101 B4
St Hilaire
Allier F 104 C2
Aude F 146 A3
St Hilaire-de-Riez F 114 B2
St Hilaire-des-Loges F 114 B3
St Hilaire-de-Villefranche F 114 C3
St Hilaire-du-Harcouët F 88 B2
St Hilaire-du-Rosier F 118 B2
St Hippolyte
Aveyron F 116 C2
Doubs F 106 B1
St Hippolyte-du-Fort F 130 B2
St Honoré-les-Bains F 104 C2
St Hubert B 92 A1
St Imier CH 106 B2
St Issey GB 42 B2
St Ives
Cambridgeshire GB 44 A3
Cornwall GB 42 B1
St Izaire F 130 B1
St Jacques-de-la-Lande F 101 A4
St Jacut-de-la-Mer F 101 A3
St James F 88 B2
St Jaume d'Enveja E 153 B4
St Jean-Brévelay F 101 B3
St Jean-d'Angély F 114 C3
St Jean-de-Belleville F 118 B3
St Jean-de-Bournay F 118 B2
St Jean-de-Braye F 103 B3
St Jean-de-Côle F 115 C4
St Jean-de-Daye F 88 A2
St Jean de Losne F 105 B4
St Jean-de-Luz F 144 A2
St Jean-de-Maurienne F 118 B3
St Jean-de-Monts F 114 B1
St Jean-d'Illac F 128 B2
St Jean-du-Bruel F 130 A2
St Jean-du-Gard F 131 A2
St Jean-en-Royans F 118 B2
St Jean-la-Riviere F 133 B3
St Jean-Pied-de-Port F 144 A2
St Jean-Poutge F 129 C3
St Jeoire F 118 A3
St Joachim F 101 B3
St Johnstown IRL 27 B3
St Jorioz F 118 B3
St Joris Winge B 79 B4
St Jouin-de-Marnes F 102 C1
St Juéry F 130 B1
St Julien F 118 A2
St Julien-Chapteuil F 117 B4
St Julien-de-Vouvantes F 101 B4
St Julien-du-Sault F 104 A2
St Julien-du-Verdon F 132 B2
St Julien-en-Born F 128 B1
St Julien-en-Genevois F 118 A3
St Julien-l'Ars F 115 B4
St Julien la-Vêtre F 117 B3
St Julien-Mont-Denis F 118 B3
St Julien-sur-Reyssouze F 118 A2
St Junien F 115 C4
St Just
F 131 A3
GB 42 B1
St Just-en-Chaussée F 90 B2
St Just-en-Chevalet F 117 B3
St Justin F 128 C2
St Just-St Rambert F 117 B4
St Keverne GB 42 B1
St Lary-Soulan F 145 B4
St Laurent-d'Aigouze F 131 B3
St Laurent-de-Chamousset F 117 B4
St Laurent-de-Condel F 89 A3
St Laurent-de-la-Cabrerisse F 146 A3
St Laurent-de-la-Salanque F 146 B3
St Laurent-des-Autels F 101 B4
St Laurent-du-Pont F 118 B2
St Laurent-en-Caux F 89 A4
St Laurent-en-Grandvaux F 105 C4
St Laurent-Médoc F 128 A2
St Laurent-sur-Gorre F 115 C4
St Laurent-sur-Mer F 88 A3
St Laurent-sur-Sèvre F 114 B3
St Leger B 92 B1
St Léger-de-Vignes F 104 C2
St Léger-sous-Beuvray F 104 C3
St Léger-sur-Dheune F 104 C3
St Léonard-de-Noblat F 116 B1
St Leonards GB 45 C4
St Lô F 88 A2
St Lon-les-Mines F 128 C1
St Louis F 106 B2
St Loup F 117 A3
St Loup-de-la-Salle F 105 C3
St Loup-sur-Semouse F 105 B5
St Lunaire F 101 A3
St Lupicin F 118 A2
St Lyphard F 101 B3
St Lys F 146 A2
St Macaire F 128 B2
St Maclou F 89 A4
St Maixent-l'École F 115 B3
St Malo F 88 B1
St Mamet-la-Salvetat F 116 C2
St Mandrier-sur-Mer F 132 B1
St Marcel
Drôme F 117 C4
Saône-et-Loire F 105 C3
St Marcellin F 118 B2
St Marcellin sur Loire F 117 B4
St Marcet F 145 A4
St Mards-en-Othe F 104 A2
St Margaret's-at-Cliffe GB 45 B5
St Margaret's Hope GB 33 C4
St Mars-la-Jaille F 101 B4
St Martin-d'Ablois F 91 C3
St Martin-d'Auxigny F 103 B4
St Martin-de-Belleville F 118 B3

St Martin-de-Bossenay F 91 C3
St Martin-de-Crau F 131 B3
St Martin-de-Londres F 130 B2
St Martin-d'Entraunes F 132 A2
St Martin-de-Queyrières F 118 C3
St Martin-de-Ré F 114 B2
St Martin des Besaces F 88 A3
St Martin-d'Estreaux F 117 A3
St Martin-de-Valamas F 117 C4
St Martin-d'Hères F 118 B2
St Martin-du-Frêne F 118 A2
St Martin-en-Bresse F 105 C4
St Martin-en-Haut F 117 B4
St Martin-la-Méanne F 116 B1
St Martin-Osmonville F 90 B1
St Martin-sur-Ouanne F 104 B2
St Martin-Valmeroux F 116 B2
St Martin-Vésubie F 133 A3
St Martory F 145 A4
St Mary's GB 33 C4
St Mathieu F 115 C4
St Mathieu-de-Tréviers F 131 B2
St Maurice CH 119 A3
St Maurice-Navacelles F 130 B2
St Maurice-sur-Moselle F 106 B1
St Mawes GB 42 B1
St Maximin-la-Ste Baume F 132 B1
St Méard-de-Gurçon F 128 B3
St Médard-de-Guizières F 128 A2
St Médard-en-Jalles F 128 B2
St Méen-le-Grand F 101 A3
St Menges F 91 B4
St Merløse DK 61 D1
St Město CZ 85 B4
St M'Hervé F 101 A4
St Michel
Aisne F 91 B4
Gers F 145 A4
St Michel-Chef-Chef F 101 B3
St Michel-de-Castelnau F 128 B2
St Michel-de-Maurienne F 118 B3
St Michel-en-Grève F 100 A2
St Michel-enl'Herm F 114 B2
St Michel-Mont-Mercure F 114 B3
St Mihiel F 92 C1
St Monance GB 35 B5
St Montant F 131 A3
St Moritz CH 107 C4
St Nazaire F 101 B3
St Nazaire-en-Royans F 118 B2
St Nazaire-le-Désert F 131 A4
St Nectaire F 116 B2
St Neots GB 44 A3
St Nicolas-de-Port F 92 C2
St Nicolas-de-Redon F 101 B3
St Nicolas-du-Pélem F 100 A2
St Niklaas B 79 A4
St Omer F 78 B2
St Pair-sur-Mer F 88 B2
St Palais F 144 A2
St Palais-sur-Mer F 114 C2
St Pardoux-la-Rivière F 115 C4
St Paul-Cap-de-Joux F 129 C4
St Paul-de-Fenouillet F 146 B3
St Paul-de-Varax F 118 A2
St Paulien F 117 B3
St Paul-le-Jeune F 131 A3
St Paul-lès-Dax F 128 C1
St Paul-Trois-Châteaux F 131 A3
St Pé-de-Bigorre F 145 A3
St Pée-sur-Nivelle F 144 A2
St Péravy-la-Colombe F 103 B3
St Péray F 117 C4
St Père-en-Retz F 101 B3
St Peter Port GB 88 A1
St Petersburg = Sankt-Peterburg RUS 9 C7
St Philbert-de-Grand-Lieu F 114 A2
St Pierre F 130 B1
St Pierre-d'Albigny F 118 B3
St Pierre-d'Allevard F 118 B3
St Pierre-de-Chartreuse F 118 B2
St Pierre-de-Chignac F 129 A3
St Pierre-de-la-Fage F 130 B2
St Pierre-d'Entremont F 118 B2
St Pierre-d'Oléron F 114 C2
St Pierre-Eglise F 88 A2
St Pierre-en-Port F 89 A4
St Pierre-le-Moûtier F 104 C2
St Pierre Montlimart F 101 B4
St Pierre-Quiberon F 100 B2
St Pierre-sur-Dives F 89 A3
St Pierreville F 117 C4
St Pieters-Leeuw B 79 B4
St Plancard F 145 A4
St Poix F 101 B4
St Pol-de-Léon F 100 A2
St Polgues F 117 B3
St Pol-sur-Ternoise F 78 B2
St Pons-de-Thomières F 130 B1
St Porchaire F 114 C3
St Pourçain-sur-Sioule F 116 A3
St Priest F 117 B4
St Privat F 116 B2
St Quay-Portrieux F 100 A3
St Quentin F 90 B3
St Quentin-la-Poterie F 131 A3
St Quentin-les-Anges F 102 B1
St Rambert-d'Albon F 117 B4
St Rambert-en-Bugey F 118 B2
St Raphaël F 132 B2
St Rémy-de-Provence F 131 B3
St Rémy-du-Val F 89 B4
St Remy-en-Bouzemont F 91 C4
St Renan F 100 A1
St Révérien F 104 B2
St Riquier F 90 A1
St Romain-de-Colbosc F 89 A4
St Rome-de-Cernon F 130 A1
St Rome-de-Tarn F 130 A1
St Sadurní-d'Anoia E 147 C2
St Saëns F 89 A5
St Sampson GB 88 A1
St Samson-la-Poterie F 90 B1
St Saturnin-de-Lenne F 130 A2
St Saturnin-lès-Apt F 131 B4
St Sauflieu F 90 B2
St Saulge F 104 B2
St Sauveur
Finistère F 100 A2
Haute-Saône F 105 B5
St Sauveur-de-Montagut F 117 C4
St Sauveur-en-Puisaye F 104 B2
St Sauveur-en-Rue F 117 B4
St Sauveur-Lendelin F 88 A2
St Sauveur-le-Vicomte F 88 A2
St Sauveur-sur-Tinée F 132 A3
St Savin
Gironde F 128 A2
Vienne F 115 B4
St Savinien F 114 C3
St Savournin F 131 B4
St Seine-l'Abbaye F 105 B3
St Sernin-sur-Rance F 130 B1
St Sevan-sur-Mer F 88 B1
St Sever F 128 C2
St Sever-Calvados F 88 B2
St Sorlin-d'Arves F 118 B3
St Soupplets F 90 B2
St Sulpice F 129 C4
St Sulpice-Laurière F 116 A1
St Sulpice-les-Feuilles F 115 B5
St Symphorien F 128 B2
St Symphoriende-Lay F 117 B4
St Symphorien d'Ozon F 117 B4
St Symphoriensur-Coise F 117 B4
St Teath GB 42 B2
St Thégonnec F 100 A2
St Thiébault F 105 A4
St Trivier-de-Courtes F 118 A2
St Trivier sur-Moignans F 117 A4
St Trojan-les-Bains F 114 C2
St Tropez F 132 B2
St Truiden B 79 B5
St Vaast-la-Hougue F 88 A2
St Valérien F 104 A2
St Valery-en-Caux F 89 A4
St Valéry-sur-Somme F 78 B1
St Vallier
Drôme F 117 B4
Saône-et-Loire F 104 C3
St Vallier-de-Thiey F 132 B2
St Varent F 102 C1
St Vaury F 116 A1
St Venant F 78 B2
St Véran F 119 C3
St Vincent I 119 B4
St Vincent-de-Tyrosse F 128 C1
St Vit F 105 B4
St Vith B 80 B2
St Vivien-de-Médoc F 114 C2
St Yan F 117 A4
St Ybars F 146 A2
St Yorre F 117 A3
St Yrieix-la-Perche F 115 C5
Saissac F 146 A3
Saja E 142 A2
Sajan SRB 126 B2
Šajkaš SRB 126 B2
Sajókaza H 99 C4
Sajószentpéter H 113 A4
Sajóvámos H 113 A4
Sakarya TR 187 B5
Šakiai LT 13 A5
Sakskøbing DK 65 B4
Sakule SRB 126 B2
Sala S 50 C3
Šal'a SK 111 A4
Sala Baganza I 120 C3
Sala Consilina I 172 B1
Salakovac SRB 127 C3
Salamanca E 150 B2
Salamina GR 185 B4
Salandra I 172 B2
Salaparuta I 176 B1
Salar E 163 A3
Salardú E 145 B4
Salas E 141 A4
Salas de los Infantes E 143 B3
Salau F 146 B2
Salavaux CH 106 C2
Salbertrand I 119 B3
Salbohed S 50 C3
Salbris F 103 B4
Salbu N 46 A2
Salce E 141 B4
Salching D 95 C4
Salcombe GB 43 B3
Saldaña E 142 B2
Saldus LV 8 D3
Sale I 120 C1
Saleby S 55 B4
Salem D 107 B4
Salemi I 176 B1
Salen
Argyll & Bute GB 34 B2
Highland GB 34 B2
N 199 A8
Sälen S 49 A5
Salernes F 132 B2
Salerno I 170 C2
Salers F 116 B2
Salford GB 40 B1
Salgótarján H 113 A3
Salgueiro P 155 B3
Salhus N 46 B2
Sali HR 137 B4
Sálice Salentino I 173 B3
Salientes E 141 B4
Salies-de-Béarn F 144 A3
Salies-du-Salat F 145 A4
Salignac-Eyvigues F 129 B4
Saligney-sur-Roudon F 104 C2
Salihli TR 188 A3
Salihorsk BY 13 B7
Salinas
Alicante E 159 C3
Huesca E 145 B4
Salinas de Medinaceli E 152 A1
Salinas de Pisuerga E 142 B2
Salindres F 131 A3
Saline di Volterra I 135 B3
Salins-les-Bains F 105 C4
Salir P 160 B1
Salisbury GB 44 B2
Salla
A 110 B1
FIN 197 C11
Sallachy GB 32 C2
Sallanches F 118 B3
Sallent E 147 C2
Sallent de Gállego E 145 B3
Salles F 128 B2
Salles-Curan F 130 A1
Salles-sur-l'Hers F 146 A2
Sallins IRL 30 A2
Sällsjö S 199 B10
Salmerón E 152 B1
Salmiech F 130 A1
Salmivaara FIN 197 C11
Salmoral E 150 B2
Salo FIN 8 B3
Salò I 121 B3
Salobreña E 163 B4
Salon-de-Provence F 131 B4
Salonica = Thessaloniki GR 182 C4
Salonta RO 16 B4
Salorino E 155 B3
Salornay-sur-Guye F 104 C3
Salorno I 121 A4
Salou E 147 C2
Šalovci SLO 111 C3
Salsbruket N 199 A8
Salses-le-Chateau F 146 B3
Salsomaggiore Terme I 120 C2
Salt E 147 C3
Saltaire GB 40 B2
Saltara I 136 B1
Saltash GB 42 B2
Saltburn-by-the-Sea GB 37 B6
Saltcoats GB 34 C3
Saltfleet GB 41 B4
Salto P 148 A2
Saltrød N 53 B4
Saltsjöbaden S 57 A4
Saltvik
FIN 51 B7
S 62 A4
Saludécio I 136 B1
Salussola I 119 B5
Saluzzo I 119 C4
Salvacañete E 152 B2
Salvada P 160 B2
Salvagnac F 129 C4
Salvaleon E 155 C4
Salvaterra de Magos P 154 B2
Salvaterra do Extremo P 155 B4
Salvatierra
Avila E 143 B4
Badajoz E 155 C4
Salvatierra de Santiago E 156 A1
Salviac F 129 B4
Salzburg A 109 B4
Salzgitter D 72 B3
Salzgitter Bad D 72 B3
Salzhausen D 72 A3
Salzhemmendorf D 72 B2
Salzkotten D 81 A4
Salzmünde D 83 A3
Salzwedel D 73 B4
Samadet F 128 C2
Samandıra TR 186 B4
Samassi I 179 C2
Samatan F 146 A1
Sambiase I 175 C2
Sambir UA 13 D5
Samborowo PL 69 B4
Sambuca di Sicilia I 176 B2
Samedan CH 107 C4
Samer F 78 B1
Sami GR 184 A1
Şamlı TR 186 C2
Sammichele di Bari I 173 B2
Samnaun CH 107 C5
Samobor HR 123 B4
Samoëns F 118 A3
Samogneux F 92 B1
Samokov BG 17 D5
Samora Correia P 154 C2
Šamorín SK 111 A4
Samos
E 141 B3
GR 188 B1
Samoš SRB 126 B2
Samothraki GR 183 C7
Samper de Calanda E 153 A3
Sampéyre I 133 A3
Sampieri I 177 C3
Sampigny F 92 C1
Samplawa PL 69 B4
Samproniano I 168 A1
Samtens D 66 B2
Samugheo I 179 C2
San Adrián E 144 B2
San Agustín E 164 C2
San Agustin de Guadalix E 151 B4
Sanaigmore GB 34 C1
San Alberto I 135 A5
San Amaro E 140 B2
Sânandrei RO 126 B3
San Andrês del Rabanedo E 142 B1
San Antanio di Santadi I 179 C2
San Antolín de Ibias E 141 A4
San Arcángelo I 174 A2
Sanary-sur-Mer F 132 B1
San Asensio E 143 B4
San Bartoloméde las Abiertas E 150 C3
San Bartoloméde la Torre E 161 B2
San Bartoloméde Pinares E 150 B3
San Bartolomeo in Galdo I 170 B3
San Benedetto del Tronto I 136 C2
San Benedetto in Alpe I 135 B4
San Benedetto Po I 121 B3
San Benito E 156 B3
San Benito de la Contienda E 155 C3
San Biágio Plátani I 176 B2
San Biágio Saracinisco I 169 B3
San Bonifacio I 121 B4
San Calixto E 156 C2
San Cándido I 109 C3
San Carlo
CH 119 A5
I 176 B2
San Carlos del Valle E 157 B4
San Casciano dei Bagni I 135 C4
San Casciano in Val di Pesa I 135 B4
San Cataldo
Puglia I 173 B4
Sicilia I 176 B2
San Cebrián de Castro E 149 A4
Sancergues F 104 B1
Sancerre F 103 B4
San Cesário di Lecce I 173 B4
Sancey-le-Long F 105 B5
Sanchiorian E 150 B3
San Chírico Raparo I 174 A2
Sanchonuño E 151 A3
San Cibrao das Viñas E 140 B3
San Cipirello I 176 B2
San Ciprián E 141 A3
San Clemente E 158 B1
San Clodio E 141 B3
Sancoins F 104 C1
San Colombano al Lambro I 120 B2
San Costanzo I 136 B2
San Crisóbal de Entreviñas E 142 B1
San Cristóbal de la Polantera E 141 B5
San Cristóbal de la Vega E 150 A3
San Cristovo E 141 C3
Sancti-Petri E 162 B1
Sancti-Spiritus E 149 B3
Sand
Hedmark N 48 B3
Rogaland N 52 A2
Sanda S 57 C4
San Damiano d'Asti I 119 C5
San Damiano Macra I 133 A3
Sandane N 198 D3
San Daniele del Friuli I 122 A2
Sandanski BG 183 B5
Sandared S 60 B2
Sandarne S 51 A4
Sandau D 73 B5
Sandbach
D 96 C1
GB 38 A4
Sandbank GB 34 C3
Sandbanks GB 43 B5
Sandbukt N 192 C5
Sandby DK 65 B4
Sande
D 71 A5
Sogn og Fjordane N 46 A2
Vestfold N 54 A1
Sandefjord N 54 A1
Sandeid N 52 A1
San Demétrio Corone I 174 B2
San Demétrio né Vestini I 169 A3
Sandersleben D 82 A3
Sanderstølen N 47 B6
Sandes N 53 B3
Sandesneben D 65 C3
Sandhead GB 36 B2
Sandhem S 60 B3
Sandhorst D 71 A4
Sandhurst GB 44 B3
Sandıklı TR 189 A5
Sandillon F 103 B4
Sandl A 96 C2
Sandnes N 52 B1
Sandness GB 33 A5
Sandnessjøen N 195 D3
Sando E 149 B3
Sandomierz PL 87 B5
San Dónaci I 173 B3
San Donàdi Piave I 122 B1
San Donato Val di Comino I 169 B3
Sándorfalva H 126 A2
Sandown GB 44 C2
Sandøysund N 54 A1
Sandrigo I 121 B4
Sandsele S 195 E8
Sandset N 194 B5
Sandsjöfors S 62 A2
Sandstad N 198 B6
Sandvatn N 52 B2
Sandvig-Allinge DK 67 A3
Sandvika
Akershus N 48 C2
Hedmark N 48 B3
Nord-Trøndelag N 199 B9
Sandviken S 51 B3
Sandvikvåy N 46 C2
Sandwich GB 45 B5
Sandy GB 44 A3
San Emiliano E 141 B5
San Enrique E 162 B2
San Esteban E 141 A4
San Esteban de Gormaz E 151 A4
San Esteban de la Sierra E 149 B4
San Esteban de Litera E 145 C4
San Esteban del Molar E 142 C1
San Esteban del Valle E 150 B3
San Esteban de Valdueza E 141 B4
San Fele I 172 B1
San Felice Circeo I 169 B3
San Felices E 143 B3
San Felices de los Gallégos E 149 B3
San Felice sul Panaro I 121 C4
San Ferdinando di Púglia I 171 B4
San Fernando E 162 B1
San Fernando de Henares E 151 B4
San Fili I 174 B2
San Foca I 173 B4
San Fratello I 177 B3
Sangatte F 78 B1
San Gavino Monreale I 179 C2
San Gémini Fonte I 168 A2
Sangerhausen D 82 A3
San Germano Vercellese I 119 B5
San Giácomo
Trentino Alto Adige I 108 C2
Umbria I 136 C1
San Gimignano I 135 B4
San Ginésio I 136 B2
Sangineto Lido I 174 B1
San Giórgio a Liri I 169 B3
San Giorgio della Richinvelda I 122 A1
San Giórgio del Sánnio I 170 B2
San Giórgio di Lomellina I 120 B1
San Giórgio di Nogaro I 122 B2
San Giorgio di Piano I 121 C4
San Giórgio Iónico I 173 B3
San Giovanni a Piro I 172 B1
San Giovanni Bianco I 120 B2
San Giovanni di Sinis I 179 C2
San Giovanni in Croce I 120 B3
San Giovanni in Fiore I 174 B2
San Giovanni in Persiceto I 121 C4
San Giovanni Reatino I 169 A2
San Giovanni Rotondo I 171 B3
San Giovanni Suérgiu I 179 C2
San Giovanni Valdarno I 135 B4
Sangis S 196 D6
San Giuliano Terme I 134 B3
San Giustino I 135 B5
San Godenzo I 135 B4

Sangonera la Verde E 165 B3
San Gregorio Magno I 172 B1
Sangüesa E 144 B2
Sanguinet F 128 B1
San Guiseppe Jato I 176 B2
Sanica BIH 124 C2
Sanitz D 65 B5
San Javier E 165 B4
San Jorge P 154 B2
San José E 164 C2
San Juan E 143 B3
San Juan de Alicante E 165 A4
San Juan de la Nava E 150 B3
San Justo de la Vega E 141 B4
Sankt Aegyd am Neuwalde A 110 B2
Sankt Andrä A 110 C1
Sankt Andreasberg D 82 A2
Sankt Anna S 56 B2
Sankt Anna am Aigen A 110 C2
Sankt Anton am Arlberg A 107 B5
Sankt Anton an der Jessnitz A 110 B2
Sankt Augustin D 80 B3
Sankt Blasien D 106 B3
Sankt Englmar D 95 B4
Sankt Gallen A 110 B1, CH 107 B4
Sankt Gallenkirch A 107 B4
Sankt Georgen A 96 C2, D 106 A3
Sankt Georgen am Reith A 110 B1
Sankt Georgen ob Judenburg A 110 B1
Sankt Georgen ob Murau A 109 B5
Sankt Gilgen A 109 B4
Sankt Goar D 81 B3
Sankt Goarshausen D 81 B3
Sankt Ingbert D 92 B3
Sankt Jacob A 109 C5
Sankt Jakob in Defereggen A 109 C3
Sankt Johann am Tauern A 110 B1
Sankt Johann am Wesen A 109 A4
Sankt Johann im Pongau A 109 B4
Sankt Johann in Tirol A 109 B3
Sankt Katharein an der Laming A 110 B2
Sankt Kathrein am Hauenstein A 110 B2
Sankt Lambrecht A 110 B1
Sankt Leonhard am Forst A 110 A2
Sankt Leonhard im Pitztal A 108 B1
Sankt Lorenzen A 109 C3
Sankt Marein *Steiermark* A 110 B2, *Steiermark* A 110 B2
Sankt Margarethen im Lavanttal A 110 C1
Sankt Margrethen CH 107 B4
Sankt Michael A 110 B2
Sankt Michael im Burgenland A 111 B3
Sankt Michael im Lungau A 109 B4
Sankt Michaelisdonn D 64 C2
Sankt Niklaus CH 119 A4
Sankt Nikolai im Sölktal A 109 B5
Sankt Olof S 63 C2
Sankt Oswald D 96 C1
Sankt Paul A 110 C1, F 132 A2
Sankt Peter D 106 A3
Sankt Peter am Kammersberg A 110 B1
Sankt-Peterburg = St Petersburg RUS 9 C7
Sankt Peter-Ording D 64 B1
Sankt Pölten A 110 A2
Sankt Radegund A 110 B2
Sankt Ruprecht an der Raab A 110 B2
Sankt Salvator A 110 C1
Sankt Stefan A 110 C1
Sankt Stefan an der Gail A 109 C4
Sankt Stefan im Rosental A 110 C2
Sankt Valentin A 110 A1
Sankt Veit an der Glan A 110 C1
Sankt Veit an der Gölsen A 110 A2
Sankt Veit in Defereggen A 109 C3
Sankt Wendel D 92 B3
Sankt Wolfgang A 109 B4, D 108 A3
San Lazzaro di Sávena I 135 A4
San Leo I 135 B5
San Leonardo de Yagüe E 143 C3
San Leonardo in Passiria I 108 C2
San Lorenzo al Mare I 133 B3
San Lorenzo a Merse I 135 B4
San Lorenzo Bellizzi I 174 B2
San Lorenzo de Calatrava E 157 B4
San Lorenzo de El Escorial E 151 B3
San Lorenzo de la Parrilla E 158 B1
San Lorenzo di Sebato I 108 C2
San Lorenzo in Campo I 136 B1
San Lorenzo Nuovo I 168 A1
San Lourenco P 160 A1
San Luca I 175 C2
Sanlúcar de Barrameda E 161 C3
Sanlúcar de Guadiana E 160 B2
Sanlúcar la Mayor E 161 B3
San Lúcido I 174 B2
Sanluri I 179 C2
San Marcello I 136 B2
San Marcello Pistoiese I 135 A3
San Marcial E 149 A4
San Marco I 170 C2
San Marco Argentano I 174 B2
San Marco dei Cavoti I 170 B2
San Marco in Lámis I 171 B3
San Marino RSM 136 B1
San Martin de Castañeda E 141 B4
San Martín de la Vega E 151 B4
San Martin de la Vega del Alberche E 150 B2
San Martín del Tesorillo E 162 B2
San Martin de Luiña E 141 A4
San Martin de Montalbán E 157 A3
San Martin de Oscos E 141 A4
San Martin de Pusa E 150 C3
San Martin de Unx E 144 B2
San Martín de Valdeiglesias E 150 B3
San Martino di Campagna I 122 A1
San Martino di Castrozza I 121 A4
San-Martino-di-Lota F 180 A2
San Martino in Pénsilis I 170 B3
San Mateo de Gallego E 144 C3
San Máuro Forte I 172 B2
San Michele all'Adige I 121 A4
San Michele di Ganzaria I 177 B3
San Michele Mondov i I 133 A3
San Miguel de Aguayo E 142 A2
San Miguel de Bernuy E 151 A4
San Miguel del Arroyo E 150 A3
San Miguel de Salinas E 165 B4
Sânmihaiu Roman RO 126 B3
San Millán de la Cogolla E 143 B4
San Miniato I 135 B3
San Muñoz E 149 B3
Sänna S 55 B5
Sannazzaro de'Burgondi I 120 B1
Sanne D 73 B4
Sannicandro di Bari I 171 B4
Sannicandro Gargánico I 171 B3
San Nicola del'Alto I 174 B2
San Nicolás del Puerto E 156 C2
Sânnicolau Mare RO 126 A2
San Nicolò I 121 C4
San Nicolò Gerrei I 179 C3
Sannidal N 53 B5
Sanniki PL 77 B4
Sanok PL 12 D5
San Pablo de los Montes E 157 A3
San Pancrázio Salentino I 173 B3
San Pantaleo I 178 A3
San Páolo di Civitate I 171 B3
San Pawl il-Bahar M 175 C3
San Pedro *Albacete* E 158 C1, *Oviedo* E 141 A4
San Pedro de Alcántara E 162 B3
San Pedro de Cadeira P 154 B1
San Pedro de Ceque E 141 B4
San Pedro del Arroyo E 150 B3
San Pedro de Latarce E 142 C1
San Pedro del Pinatar E 165 B4
San Pedro del Romeral E 143 A3
San Pedro de Merida E 156 B1
San Pedro de Valderaduey E 142 B2
San Pedro Manrique E 144 B1
San Pellegrino Terme I 120 B2
San Piero a Sieve I 135 B4
San Piero in Bagno I 135 B4
San Piero Patti I 177 A3
San Pietro I 177 B3
San Pietro in Casale I 121 C4
San Pietro in Gu I 121 B4
San Pietro in Palazzi I 134 B3
San Pietro in Volta I 122 B1
San Pietro Vara I 134 A2
San Pietro Vernótico I 173 B3
San Polo d'Enza I 121 C3
Sanquhar GB 36 A3
San Quírico d'Órcia I 135 B4
San Rafael del Rio E 153 B4
San Remo I 133 B3
San Román de Cameros E 143 B4
San Roman de Hernija E 150 A2
San Román de la Cuba E 142 B2
San Roman de los Montes E 150 B3
San Romao P 155 C3
San Roque E 162 B2
San Roque de Riomera E 143 A3
San Rufo I 172 B1
San Sabastián de los Ballesteros E 162 A3
San Salvador de Cantamuda E 142 B2
San Salvo I 170 A2
San Salvo Marina I 170 A2
San Sebastián de los Reyes E 151 B4
San Sebastiano Curone I 120 C2
San Secondo Parmense I 120 C3
Sansepolcro I 135 B5
San Severino Marche I 136 B2
San Severino Lucano I 174 A2
San Severo I 171 B3
San Silvestre de Guzmán E 161 B2
Sanski Most BIH 124 C2
San Sosti I 174 B2
San Stéfano di Cadore I 109 C3
San Stino di Livenza I 122 B1
Santa Agnès E 166 B1
Santa Amalia E 156 A1
Santa Ana *Cáceres* E 156 A2, *Jaén* E 163 A4
Santa Ana de Pusa E 150 C3
Santa Barbara E 153 B4
Santa Bárbara P 160 B1
Santa Barbara de Casa E 161 B2
Santa Bárbara de Padrões P 160 B2
Santacara E 144 B2
Santa Catarina P 160 B2
Santa Caterina di Pittinuri I 178 B2
Santa Caterina Villarmosa I 177 B3
Santa Cesárea Terme I 173 B4
Santa Clara-a-Nova P 160 B1
Santa Clara-a-Velha P 160 B1
Santa Clara de Louredo P 160 B2
Santa Coloma de Farners E 147 C3
Santa Coloma de Gramenet E 147 C3
Santa Coloma de Queralt E 147 C2
Santa Colomba de Curueño E 142 B1
Santa Colomba de Somoza E 141 B4
Santa Comba E 140 A2
Santa Comba Dáo P 148 B1
Santa Comba de Rossas P 149 A3
Santa Cristina I 120 B2
Santa Cristina de la Polvorosa E 141 B5
Santa Croce Camerina I 177 C3
Santa Croce di Magliano I 170 B2
Santa Cruz E 140 A2, P 154 B1
Santa Cruz de Alhama E 163 A4
Santa Cruz de Campezo E 143 B4
Santa Cruz de Grio E 152 A2
Santa Cruz de la Salceda E 151 A4
Santa Cruz de la Sierra E 156 A2
Santa Cruz de la Zarza E 151 C4
Santa Cruz del Retamar E 151 B3
Santa Cruz del Valle E 150 B2
Santa Cruz de Moya E 159 B2
Santa Cruz de Mudela E 157 B4
Santa Cruz de Paniagua E 149 B3
Santadi I 179 C2
Santa Doménica Talao I 174 B1
Santa Doménica Vittória I 177 B3
Santa Elena E 157 B4
Santa Elena de Jamuz E 141 B5
Santaella E 162 A3
Santa Eufemia E 156 B3
Santa Eufémia d'Aspromonte I 175 C1
Santa Eulalia E 152 B2
Santa Eulália P 155 C3
Santa Eulalia de Oscos E 141 A3
Santa Eulàlia des Riu E 166 C1
Santa Fe E 163 A4
Santa Fiora I 135 C4
Sant'Ágata dei Goti I 170 B2
Sant'Ágata di Ésaro I 174 B1
Sant'Ágata di Puglia I 171 B3
Sant'Agata Feltria I 135 B5
Sant'Ágata Militello I 177 A3
Santa Gertrude I 108 C1
Santa Giustina I 121 A5
Sant Agust ide Lluçanès E 147 B3
Santa Iria P 160 B2
Santa Leocadia P 148 A1
Santa Lucia del Mela I 177 A4
Santa Lucia-de-Porto-Vecchio F 180 B2
Santa Luzia P 160 B1
Santa Maddalena Vallalta I 108 C3
Santa Magdalena de Polpis E 153 B4
Santa Margalida E 167 B3
Santa Margarida P 154 B2
Santa Margarida do Sado P 160 A1
Santa Margaridao de Montbui E 147 C2
Santa Margherita I 179 D2
Santa Margherita di Belice I 176 B2
Santa Margherita Ligure I 134 A2
Santa Maria CH 108 C1
Santa Maria E 144 B3
Santa Maria al Bagno I 173 B3
Santa Maria Cápua Vétere I 170 B2
Santa Maria da Feira P 148 B1
Santa Maria de Cayón E 143 A3
Santa Maria de Corco E 147 B3
Santa Maria de Huerta E 152 A1
Santa Maria de la Alameda E 151 B3
Santa Maria de las Hoyas E 143 C3
Santa Maria del Camí E 167 B2
Santa Maria del Campo E 143 B3
Santa Maria del Campo Rus E 158 B1
Santa Maria della Versa I 120 C2
Santa Maria del Páramo E 142 B1
Santa Maria del Taro I 134 A2
Santa Maria de Mercadillo E 143 C3
Santa Maria de Nieva E 164 B3
Santa Maria de Trassierra E 156 C3
Santa Maria di Licodia I 177 B3
Santa Maria-di-Rispéscia I 168 A1
Santa Maria la Palma I 178 B2
Santa María la Real de Nieva E 150 A3
Santa Maria Maggiore I 119 A5
Santa Maria Ribarredonda E 143 B3
Santa Marina del Rey E 141 B5
Santa Marinella I 168 A1
Santa Marta *Albacete* E 158 B1, *Badajoz* E 155 C4
Santa Marta de Magasca E 156 A1
Santa Marta de Penaguião P 148 A2
Santa Marta de Tormes E 150 B2
Santana *Évora* P 154 C2, *Setúbal* P 154 C1
Sântana RO 126 A3
Santana da Serra P 160 B1
Sant'Ana de Cambas P 160 B2
Santana do Mato P 154 C2
Sant'Anastasia I 170 C2
Santander E 143 A3
Sant'Andrea Frius I 179 C3
Sant'Ángelo dei Lombardi I 172 B1
Sant'Angelo in Vado I 136 B1
Sant'Angelo Lodigiano I 120 B2
Santa Ninfa I 176 B1
Sant'Antíoco I 179 C2
Sant Antoni Abat E 166 C1
Sant Antoni de Calonge E 147 C4
Sant'Antonio-di-Gallura I 178 B3
Santanyí E 167 B3
Santa Olalla *Huelva* E 161 B3, *Toledo* E 150 B3
Santa Pau E 147 B3
Santa Pola E 165 A4
Santa Ponça E 166 B2
Santarcángelo di Romagna I 136 A1
Santarém P 154 B2
Santa Severa F 180 A2, I 168 A1
Santa Severina I 175 B2
Santas Martas E 142 B1
Santa Sofia I 135 B4
Santa Suzana *Évora* P 155 C3, *Setúbal* P 154 C2
Santa Teresa di Riva I 177 B4
Santa Teresa Gallura I 178 A3
Santa Uxía E 140 B2
Santa Valburga I 108 C1
Santa Vittória in Matenano I 136 B2
Sant Boi de Llobregat E 147 C3
Sant Carles de la Ràpita E 153 B4
Sant Carlos E 166 B1
Sant'Caterina I 135 C4
Sant Celoni E 147 C3
Sant Climent E 167 B4
Santed E 152 A2
Sant'Egídio alla Vibrata I 136 C2
Sant'Elia a Pianisi I 170 B2
Sant'Elia Fiumerapido I 169 B3
Santelices E 143 A3
San Telmo E 161 B3
Sant'Elpídio a Mare I 136 B2
Santéramo in Colle I 171 C4
Santervas de la Vega E 142 B2
Sant Feliu E 147 C3
Sant Feliu de Codines E 147 C3
Sant Feliu de Guíxols E 147 C4
Sant Feliu Sasserra E 147 C3
Sant Ferran E 166 C1
Sant Francesc de Formentera E 166 C1
Sant Francesc de ses Salines E 166 C1
Santhià I 119 B5
Sant Hilari Sacalm E 147 C3
Sant Hipòlit de Voltregà E 147 B3
Santiago de Alcántara E 155 B3
Santiago de Calatrava E 163 A3
Santiago de Compostela E 140 B2
Santiago de la Espade E 164 A2
Santiago de la Puebla E 150 B2
Santiago de la Ribera E 165 B4
Santiago del Campo E 155 B4
Santiago de Litem P 154 B2
Santiago do Cacém P 160 B1
Santiago do Escoural P 154 C2
Santiago Maior P 155 C3
Santibáñez de Béjar E 150 B2
Santibáñez de la Peña E 142 B2
Santibáñez de Murias E 142 A1
Santibáñez de Vidriales E 141 B4
Santibáñez el Alto E 149 B3
Santibáñez el Bajo E 149 B3
Santillana E 142 A2
Santiponce E 162 A1
San Tirso de Abres E 141 A3
Santisteban del Puerto E 157 B4
Santiuste de San Juan Bautiste E 150 A3
Santiz E 149 A4
Sant Jaume dels Domenys E 147 C2
Sant Joan Baptista E 166 B1
Sant Joan de les Abadesses E 147 B3
Sant Jordi E 153 B4
Sant Josep de sa Talaia E 166 C1
Sant Juliáde Loria AND 146 B2
Sant'Ilario d'Enza I 121 C3
Sant Llorençde Morunys E 147 B2
Sant Llorençdes Carctassar E 167 B3
Sant Llorenç Savall E 147 C3
Sant Luis E 167 B4
Sant Mart ide Llemaná E 147 B3
Sant Marti de Maldá E 147 C2
Sant Marti Sarroca E 147 C2
Sant Mateu E 153 B4
Sant Miquel E 166 B1
Santo Aleixo P 161 A2
Santo Amado P 161 A2
Santo Amaro P 155 C3
Santo André P 160 A1
Santo Domingo E 155 C3
Santo Domingo de la Calzada E 143 B4
Santo Domingo de Silos E 143 C3
Santo Estêvão *Faro* P 160 B2, *Santarém* P 154 C2
Santok PL 75 B4

Santomera E 165 A3
Santoña E 143 A3
Santo-Pietro-di Tenda F 180 A2
Sant'Oreste I 168 A2
Santo Spirito I 171 B4
Santo Stefano d'Aveto I 134 A2
Santo Stéfano di Camastra I 177 A3
Santo Stefano di Magra I 134 A2
Santo Stéfano Quisquina I 176 B2
Santo Tirso P 148 A1
Santotis E 142 A2
Santo Tomé E 164 A1
Santovenia
Burgos E 143 B3
Zamora E 142 C1
Sant Pau de Seguries E 147 B3
Santpedor E 147 C2
Sant Pere de Riudebitlles E 147 C2
Sant Pere Pescador E 147 B4
Sant Pere Sallavinera E 147 C2
Sant Quirze de Besora E 147 B3
Sant Rafel E 166 C1
Sant Ramon E 147 C2
Santu Lussurgiu I 178 B2
Santutzi E 143 A3
Sant Vincençde Castellet E 147 C2
San Valentino alla Muta I 108 C1
San Venanzo I 135 C5
San Vicente de Alcántara E 155 B3
San Vicente de Arana E 144 B1
San Vicente de la Barquera E 142 A2
San Vicente de la Sonsierra E 143 B4
San Vicente de Toranzo E 143 A3
San Vietro E 149 A3
San Vigilio I 108 C2
San Vincente del Raspeig E 165 A4
San Vincenzo I 134 B3
San Vito I 179 C3
San Vito al Tagliamento I 122 B1
San Vito Chietino I 169 A4
San Vito dei Normanni I 173 B3
San Vito di Cadore I 108 C3
San Vito lo Capo I 176 A1
San Vito Romano I 169 B2
Sanxenxo E 140 B2
Sanza I 172 B1
São Aleixo P 155 C3
São Barnabé P 160 B1
São Bartoloméda Serra P 160 A1
São Bartolomeu de Messines P 160 B1
São Bento P 140 C2
São Brás P 160 B2
São Brás de Alportel P 160 B2
São Braz do Reguedoura P 154 C2
São Cristóvão P 154 C2
São Domingos P 160 B1
São Geraldo P 154 C2
São Jacinto P 148 B1
São João da Madeira P 148 B1
São João da Pesqueira P 148 A2
São João da Ribeira P 154 B2
São João da Serra P 148 B1
São João da Venda P 160 B2
São João dos Caldeireiros P 160 B2
São Julião P 155 B3
São Leonardo P 155 C3
São Luis P 160 B1
São Manços P 155 C3
São Marcos da Ataboeira P 160 B2
Saõ Marcos da Serra P 160 B1
São Marcos de Campo P 155 C3
São Martinho da Cortiça P 148 B1
São Martinho das Amoreiras P 160 B1
São Martinho do Porto P 154 B1
São Matias
Beja P 160 A2
Évora P 154 C2
São Miguel d'Acha P 155 A3
São Miguel de Machede P 155 C3
São Pedro da Torre P 140 C2
São Pedro de Muel P 154 B1
São Pedro de Solis P 160 B2
São Pedro do Sul P 148 B1
Saorge F 133 B3
São Romão P 154 C2
São Sebastião dos Carros P 160 B2
São Teotónio P 160 B1
São Torcato P 148 A1
Sapataria P 154 C1
Sapes GR 183 B7
Sapiãos P 148 A2
Sa Pobla E 167 B3
Sappada I 109 C3
Sappen N 192 C5
Sapri I 174 A1
Sarajärvi FIN 197 D10
Sarajevo BIH 139 B4
Saramon F 129 C3
Sarandë AL 182 D2
Saranovo SRB 127 C2
Saraorci SRB 127 C3
Sa Rapita E 167 B3
Saray TR 186 A2
Saraycık TR 187 C4
Sarayköy TR 188 B3
Saraylar TR 186 B2
Sarayönü TR 189 A7
Sarbia PL 75 B5
Sarbinowo
Zachodnio-Pomorskie PL 67 B4
Zachodnio-Pomorskie PL 74 B3
Sárbogárd H 112 C2
Sarcelles F 90 B2
Sarche I 121 A3
Sardara I 179 C2
Sardoal P 154 B2
Sardón de Duero E 150 A3
Sare F 144 A2
S'Arenal E 166 B2
Šarengrad HR 125 B5
Sarentino I 108 C2
Sarezzo I 120 B3
Sargans CH 107 B4
Sári H 112 B3
Sarıbeyler TR 186 C2
Sarıcakaya TR 187 B5
Sari-d'Orcino F 180 A1
Sarıgöl TR 188 A3
Sarıkaya TR 23 B8
Sarıköy TR 186 B2
Sarilhos Grandes P 154 C2
Sariñena E 145 C3
Sarıoba TR 187 C7
Sárisáp H 112 B2
Sariyer TR 186 A4
Sarkad H 113 C5
Sárkeresztes H 112 B2
Sárkeresztúr H 112 B2
Särkijärvi FIN 196 B6
Şarkikaraağaç TR 189 A6
Şarköy TR 186 B2
Sarlat-la-Canéda F 129 B4
Sarliac-sur-l'Isle F 129 A3
Sármellék H 111 C4
Särna S 199 D10
Sarnadas P 155 B3
Sarnano I 136 B2
Sarnen CH 106 C3
Sarnesfield GB 39 B4
Sárnico I 120 B2
Sarno I 170 C2
Sarnonico I 121 A4
Sarnow D 74 A2
Sarny UA 13 C7
Särö S 60 B1
Saronno I 120 B2
Sárosd H 112 B2
Šarovce SK 112 A2
Sarpoil F 117 B3
Sarpsborg N 54 A2
Sarracín E 143 B3
Sarral E 147 C2
Sarralbe F 92 B3
Sarrancolin F 145 B4
Sarras F 117 B4
Sarre I 119 B4
Sarreaus E 140 B3
Sarrebourg F 92 C3
Sarreguemines F 92 B3
Sárrétudvari H 113 B5
Sarre-Union F 92 C3
Sarria E 141 B3
Sarriàde Ter E 147 B3
Sarrión E 153 B3
Sarroca de Lleida E 153 A4
Sarroch I 179 C3
Sarron F 128 C2
Sársina I 135 B5
Særslev DK 59 C3
Sarstedt D 72 B2
Sárszentlőrinc H 112 C2
Sárszentmihaly H 112 B2
Sárszentmiklós H 112 C2
Sarteano I 135 C4
Sartène F 180 B1
Sartilly F 88 B2
Sartirana Lomellina I 120 B1
Saruhanlı TR 186 D2
Sárvár H 111 B3
Sarvisvaara S 196 C4
Sarzana I 134 A2
Sarzeau F 101 B3
Sarzedas P 155 B3
Sasalli TR 188 A1
Sasamón E 142 B2
Sa Savina E 166 C1
Sásd H 125 A4
Sasino PL 68 A2
Sássari I 178 B2
Sassello I 133 A4
Sassenberg D 71 C5
Sassetta I 134 B3
Sassnitz D 66 B2
Sassocorvaro I 136 B1
Sasso d'Ombrone I 135 C4
Sassoferrato I 136 B1
Sassoleone I 135 A4
Sasso Marconi I 135 A4
Sassuolo I 135 A3
Sástago E 153 A3
Šaštinske Stráže SK 98 C1
Sas van Gent NL 79 A3
Såtåhaugen N 199 C7
Satão P 148 B2
Såtenäs S 55 B3
Säter S 50 B2
Sätila S 60 B2
Satillieu F 117 B4
Satnica Đakovačka HR 125 B4
Sátoraljaújhely H 16 A4
Satow D 65 C4
Sätra-brunn S 50 C3
Sætre N 54 A1
Satrup D 64 B2
Satteins A 107 B4
Satu Mare RO 17 B5
Saturnia I 168 A1
Saucats F 128 B2
Saucelle E 149 A3
Sauda N 52 A2
Sauðarkrókur IS 190 B6
Saudasjøen N 52 A2
Sauerlach D 108 B2
Saugues F 117 C3
Sauherad N 53 A5
Saujon F 114 C3
Sauland N 53 A4
Saulces Monclin F 91 B4
Saulgau D 107 A4
Saulgrub D 108 B2
Saulieu F 104 B3
Saulnot F 106 B1
Sault F 131 A4
Sault-Brénaz F 118 B2
Sault-de-Navailles F 128 C2
Saulx F 105 B5
Saulxures-sur-Moselotte F 106 B1
Saulzais-le-Potier F 103 C4
Saumos F 128 B1
Saumur F 102 B1
Saunavaara FIN 197 B10
Saundersfoot GB 39 C2
Saurat F 146 B2
Saurbær
Borgarfjarðarsýsla IS 190 C4
Dalasýsla IS 190 B4
Eyjafjarðarsýsla IS 191 B7
Sáuris I 109 C3
Sausset-les-Pins F 131 B4
Sauteyrargues F 131 B2
Sauvagnat F 116 B2
Sauve F 131 B2
Sauveterre-de-Béarn F 144 A3
Sauveterre-de-Guyenne F 128 B2
Sauviat-sur-Vige F 116 B1
Sauxillanges F 117 B3
Sauzet
Drôme F 117 C4
Lot F 129 B4
Sauzé-Vaussais F 115 B4
Sauzon F 100 B2
Sava I 173 B3
Sävar S 200 C6
Sævareid N 46 B2
Savarsin RO 16 B5
Sävast S 196 D4
Savaştepe TR 186 C2
Savci SLO 111 C3
Säve S 60 B1
Savelletri I 173 B3
Savelli I 174 B2
Savenay F 101 B4
Saverdun F 146 A2
Saverne F 93 C3
Savières F 91 C3
Savigliano I 119 C4
Savignac-les-Eglises F 129 A3
Savignano Irpino I 171 B3
Savignano sul Rubicone I 136 A1
Savigny-sur-Braye F 102 B2
Saviñán E 152 A2
Savines-le-lac F 132 A2
Savino Selo SRB 126 B1
Savio I 135 A5
Sävja S 51 C4
Šavnik MNE 139 C5
Savognin CH 107 C4
Savona I 133 A4
Savonlinna FIN 9 B6
Savournon F 132 A1
Sævråsvåg N 46 B2
Sävsjö S 62 A2
Savsjön S 50 C1
Sävsjöström S 62 A3
Savudrija HR 122 B2
Savukoski FIN 197 B11
Sawbridgeworth GB 45 B4
Sawtry GB 44 A3
Sax E 159 C3
Saxdalen S 50 B1
Saxilby GB 40 B3
Saxmundham GB 45 A5
Saxnäs S 195 F6
Saxthorpe GB 41 C5
Sayalonga E 163 B3
Sayatón E 151 B5
Sayda D 83 B5
Säytsjärvi FIN 193 C11
Śazava CZ 97 B3
Sázava CZ 96 B2
Scaër F 100 A2
Scafa I 169 A4
Scalasaig GB 34 B1
Scalby GB 40 A3
Scalea I 174 B1
Scaletta Zanclea I 177 A4
Scalloway GB 33 A5
Scamblesby GB 41 B3
Scandale I 175 B2
Scandiano I 121 C3
Scandicci I 135 B4
Scandolara Ravara I 120 B3
Scanno I 169 B3
Scansano I 168 A1
Scanzano Jónico I 174 A2
Scarborough GB 40 A3
Scardovari I 122 C1
Scardoy GB 32 D2
Scarperia I 135 B4
Scarriff IRL 28 B3
Scey-sur-Saône et St Albin F 105 B4
Schachendorf A 111 B3
Schaffhausen CH 107 B3
Schafstädt D 83 A3
Schafstedt D 64 B2
Schäftlarn D 108 B2
Schagen NL 70 B1
Schalkau D 82 B3
Schangnau CH 106 C2
Schapbach D 93 C4
Scharbeutz D 65 B3
Schärding A 96 C1
Scharnitz A 108 B2
Scharrel D 71 A4
Schattendorf A 111 B3
Scheemda NL 71 A3
Scheessel D 72 A2
Schéggia I 136 B1
Scheibbs A 110 A2
Scheibenberg D 83 B4
Scheidegg D 107 B4
Scheifling A 110 B1
Scheinfeld D 94 B2
Schelklingen D 94 C1
Schenefeld
Schleswig-Holstein D 64 B2
Schleswig-Holstein D 72 A2
Schenklengsfeld D 82 B1
Scherfede D 81 A5
Schermbeck D 80 A2
Scherpenzeel NL 70 B2
Schesslitz D 94 B3
Scheveningen NL 70 B1
Schiedam NL 79 A4
Schieder-Schwalenberg D 72 C2
Schierling D 95 C4
Schiers CH 107 C4
Schildau D 83 A4
Schillingen D 92 B2
Schillingsfürst D 94 B2
Schilpário I 120 A3
Schiltach D 93 C4
Schiltigheim F 93 C3
Schio I 121 B4
Schirmeck F 92 C3
Schirnding D 83 B4
Schkeuditz D 83 A4
Schkölen D 83 A3
Schlabendorf D 84 A1
Schladen D 73 B3
Schladming A 109 B4
Schlangen D 81 A4
Schleiden D 80 B2
Schleiz D 83 B3
Schleswig D 64 B2
Schleusingen D 82 B2
Schlieben D 83 A5
Schliengen D 106 B2
Schliersee D 108 B2
Schlitz D 81 B5
Schloss Neuhans D 81 A4
Schlossvippach D 82 A3
Schlotheim D 82 A2
Schluchsee D 106 B3
Schlüchtern D 81 B5
Schmallenberg D 81 A4
Schmelz D 92 B2
Schmidmühlen D 95 B3
Schmiedeberg D 84 B1
Schmiedefeld D 82 B2
Schmirn A 108 B2
Schmölln
Brandenburg D 74 A3
Sachsen D 83 B4
Schnaittach D 95 B3
Schneeberg D 83 B4
Schneizlreuth D 109 B3
Schneverdingen D 72 A2
Schöder A 109 B5
Schoenburg B 80 B2
Schollene D 73 B5
Schöllkrippen D 81 B5
Schomberg D 107 A3
Schönach D 95 C4
Schönau
Baden-Württemberg D 106 B2
Bayern D 95 C4
Schönbeck D 74 A2
Schönberg
Bayern D 96 C1
Mecklenburg-Vorpommern D 65 C3
Schleswig-Holstein D 65 B3
Schönebeck D 73 B4
Schöneck D 83 B4
Schönecken- D 80 B2
Schönermark D 74 A2
Schönewalde D 83 A5
Schongau D 108 B1
Schöngrabern A 97 C4
Schönhagen D 81 A5
Schönhausen D 73 B5
Schöningen D 73 B3
Schönkirchen D 64 B3
Schönsee D 95 B4
Schöntal D 94 B1
Schönthal D 95 B4
Schonungen D 94 A2
Schönwalde D 65 B3
Schoondijke NL 79 A3
Schoonebeek NL 71 B3
Schoonhoven NL 79 A4
Schopfheim D 106 B2
Schöppenstedt D 73 B3
Schörfling A 109 B4
Schorndorf D 94 C1
Schortens D 71 A4
Schotten D 81 B5
Schramberg D 106 A3
Schraplau D 83 A3
Schrattenberg A 97 C4
Schrecksbach D 81 B5
Schrems A 96 C3
Schrobenhausen D 95 C3
Schröcken A 107 B5
Schrozberg D 94 B1
Schruns A 107 B4
Schüpfheim CH 106 C3
Schüttorf D 71 B4
Schwaan D 65 C5
Schwabach D 94 B3
Schwäbisch Gmünd D 94 C1
Schwäbisch Hall D 94 B1
Schwabmünchen D 108 A1
Schwadorf A 111 A3
Schwagstorf D 71 B4
Schwaigern D 93 B5
Schwalmstadt D 81 B5
Schwanberg A 110 C2
Schwanden CH 107 C4
Schwandorf D 95 B4
Schwanebeck D 73 C4
Schwanenstadt A 109 A4
Schwanewede D 72 A1
Schwanfeld D 94 B2
Schwangau D 108 B1
Schwarmstedt D 72 B2
Schwarza D 82 B2
Schwarzach im Pongau A 109 B4
Schwarzau im Gebirge A 110 B2
Schwarzenau A 97 C3
Schwarzenbach D 83 B3
Schwarzenbach am Wald D 83 B3
Schwarzenbek D 72 A3
Schwarzenberg D 83 B4
Schwarzenburg CH 106 C2
Schwarzenfeld D 95 B4
Schwarz-heide D 84 A1
Schwaz A 108 B2
Schwechat A 111 A3
Schwedt D 74 A3
Schwei D 71 A5
Schweich D 92 B2
Schweighausen D 106 A2
Schweinfurt D 94 A2
Schweinitz D 83 A5
Schweinrich D 74 A1
Schwelm D 80 A3
Schwemsal D 83 A4
Schwendt A 109 B3
Schwenningen D 107 A3
Schwepnitz D 84 A1
Schwerin D 73 A4
Schwerte D 81 A3
Schweskau D 73 B4
Schwetzingen D 93 B4
Schwyz CH 107 B3
Sciacca I 176 B2
Scicli I 177 C3
Ściechów PL 75 B3
Scigliano I 175 B2
Scilla I 175 C1
Ścinawa PL 85 A4
Scionzier F 118 A3
Scoglitti I 177 C3
Scole GB 45 A5
Sconser GB 31 B2
Scopello
Piemonte I 119 B5
Sicilia I 176 A1
Scordia I 177 B3
Scorzè I 121 B5
Scotch Corner GB 37 B5
Scotter GB 40 B3
Scourie GB 32 C1
Scousburgh GB 33 B5
Scrabster GB 32 C3
Screeb IRL 28 A2
Scremerston GB 37 A5
Scritto I 136 B1
Scunthorpe GB 40 B3
Scuol CH 107 C5
Scúrcola Marsicana I 169 A3
Seaford GB 45 C4
Seaham GB 37 B5
Seahouses GB 37 A5
Seascale GB 36 B3
Seaton GB 43 B3
Sebazac-Concourès F 130 A1
Seben TR 187 B6
Sebersdorf A 110 B2
Sebezh RUS 8 D6
Sebnitz D 84 B2
Seborga I 133 B3
Seby S 63 B4
Seč
Vychodočeský CZ 97 B3
Západočeský CZ 96 B1
Sečanj SRB 126 B2
Secemin PL 87 B3
Séchault F 91 B4
Seckau A 110 B1
Seclin F 78 B3
Secondigny F 114 B3
Seda P 155 B3
Sedan F 91 B4
Sedano E 143 B3
Sedbergh GB 37 B4
Sedella E 163 B3
Séderon F 131 A4
Sedgefield GB 37 B5
Sedico I 121 A5
Sédilo I 178 B2
Sédini I 178 B2
Sedlarica HR 124 B3
Sedlčany CZ 96 B2
Sedlec-Prčice CZ 96 B2
Sedlice CZ 96 B1
Sędziejowice PL 86 A3
Sędziszów PL 87 B4
Sędziszów Małapolski PL 87 B5
Seebach F 93 C3
Seeboden A 109 C4
Seefeld
Brandenburg D 74 B2
Niedersachsen D 71 A5
Seefeld in Tirol A 108 B2
Seeg D 108 B1
Seehausen
Sachsen-Anhalt D 73 B4
Sachsen-Anhalt D 73 B4
Seeheim-Jugenheim D 93 B4
Seelbach D 93 C3
Seelow D 74 B3
Seelze D 72 B2
Seerhausen D 83 A5
Sées F 89 B4
Seesen D 82 A2
Seeshaupt D 108 B2
Seewalchen A 109 B4
Seferihisar TR 188 A1
Sefkerin SRB 127 B2
Segård N 48 B2
Segerstad S 55 A4
Segesd H 124 A3
Seglinge FIN 51 B7
Segmon S 55 A4
Segonzac F 115 C3
Segorbe E 159 B3
Segovia E 151 B3
Segré F 101 B5
Segura
E 144 B1
P 155 B3
Segura de León E 161 A3
Segura de los Baños E 152 B3
Ségur-les-Villas F 116 B2
Segurrilla E 150 B3
Sehnde D 72 B2
Seia P 148 B2
Seiches-sur-le-Loir F 102 B1

Seifhennersdorf D 84 B2
Seignelay F 104 B2
Seijo E 140 C2
Seilhac F 116 B1
Seilles B 79 B5
Seim N 46 B2
Seinäjoki FIN 8 A3
Seissan F 145 A4
Seitenstetten Markt
A 110 A1
Seixal P 154 C1
Seiz A 110 B1
Seizthal A 110 B1
Sejerslev DK 58 B1
Seksna RUS 9 C11
Selárdalur IS 190 B1
Selárgius I 179 C3
Selb D 83 B4
Selby GB 40 B2
Selca HR 138 B2
Selce HR 123 B3
Selçuk TR 188 B2
Selde DK 58 B2
Selenča SRB 126 B1
Selendi
Manisa TR 186 D2
Manisa TR 186 D3
Selenicë AL 182 C1
Sélestat F 106 A2
Seleuš SRB 126 B2
Selevac SRB 127 C2
Selfoss IS 190 D5
Selgua E 145 C4
Selice SK 112 A1
Seligenstadt D 93 A4
Seligenthal D 82 B2
Selimiye TR 188 B2
Selizharovo RUS 9 D8
Selja S 50 A1
Selje N 198 C2
Seljelvnes N 192 C3
Seljord N 53 A4
Selkirk GB 35 C5
Sellano I 136 C1
Selles-St Denis F 103 B3
Selles-sur-Cher F 103 B3
Sellières F 105 C4
Sellin D 66 B2
Sellye H 125 B3
Selm D 80 A3
Selnica ob Dravi
SLO 110 C2
Selongey F 105 B4
Selonnet F 132 A2
Selow D 65 C4
Selsey GB 44 C3
Selsingen D 72 A2
Selters D 81 B3
Seltz F 93 C4
Selva E 167 B2
Selva di Cadore I 108 C3
Selva di Val Gardena
I 108 C2
Selvik
Sogn og Fjordane
N 46 A2
Vestfold N 54 A1
Selvino I 120 B2
Selyatyn UA 17 B6
Sem N 54 A1
Semeljci HR 125 B4
Semič SLO 123 B4
Semide
F 91 B4
P 148 B1
Semily CZ 84 B3
Seminara I 175 C1
Semlac RO 126 A2
Semlacu Mare RO 126 B3
Semmen-stedt D 73 B3
Šempeter SLO 123 A4
Semriach A 110 B2
Semur-en-Auxois
F 104 B3
Sena E 145 C3
Sena de Luna E 141 B5
Senarpont F 90 B1
Sénas F 131 B4
Senćanski Trešnjevac
SRB 126 B1
Sencelles E 167 B2
Senčur SLO 123 A3
Senden
Bayern D 94 C2
Nordrhein-Westfalen
D 80 A3
Sendenhorst D 81 A3
Sendim P 149 A3
Senec SK 111 A4
Seneffe B 79 B4
Séneghe I 178 B2
Senés E 164 B2
Senez F 132 B2
Senftenberg D 84 A1
Sengouagnet F 145 B4
Sengwarden D 71 A5
Senica SK 98 C1
Senice na Hané CZ 98 B1
Senigállia I 136 B2
Senirkent TR 189 A5
Sénis I 179 C2
Senise I 174 A2
Senj HR 123 C3
Senje SRB 127 D3
Senjehopen N 194 A8
Senjski Rudnik
SRB 127 D3
Senlis F 90 B2
Sennan S 60 C2
Sennecey-le-Grand
F 105 C3
Sennen GB 42 B1
Senno BY 13 A8
Sénnori I 178 B2
Sennwald CH 107 B4
Sennybridge GB 39 C3
Senohrad SK 99 C3
Senonches F 89 B5
Senones F 92 C2
Senorb i I 179 C3
Senovo SLO 123 A4
Senožeče SLO 123 B3
Senožeti SLO 123 A3
Sens F 104 A2
Sens-de-Bretagne
F 101 A4
Senta SRB 126 B2
Senterada E 145 B4
Sentilj SLO 110 C2
Šentjernej SLO 123 B4
Šentjur SLO 123 A4
Senumstad N 53 B4
Seoane E 141 B3
Seon CH 106 B3
Sépeaux F 104 B2
Sépey CH 119 A4
Sepino I 170 B2
Sępólno Krajeńskie
PL 76 A2
Seppenrade D 80 A3
Seppois F 106 B2
Septemvri BG 183 A6
Septeuil F 90 C1
Sepúlveda E 151 A4
Sequals I 122 A1
Sequeros E 149 B3
Seraincourt F 91 B4
Seraing B 80 B1
Seravezza I 134 B3
Sered' SK 98 C1
Seredka RUS 8 C6
Şereflikoçhisar TR 23 B7
Seregélyes H 112 B2
Seregno I 120 B2
Sérent F 101 B3
Serfaus A 108 B1
Sergiyev Posad
RUS 9 D11
Seriate I 120 B2
Sérifontaine F 90 B1
Serifos GR 185 B5
Sérignan F 130 B2
Serik TR 189 C6
Serina I 120 B2
Serinhisar TR 188 B4
Sermaises F 90 C2
Sermaize-les-Bains
F 91 C4
Sérmide I 121 C4
Sermoneta I 169 B2
Sernache de Bonjardim
P 154 B2
Sernancelhe P 148 B2
Serock PL 77 B6
Serón E 164 B2
Serón de Najima E 152 A1
Serooskerke NL 79 A3
Seròs E 153 A4
Serpa P 160 B2
Serracapriola I 171 B3
Serrada E 150 A3
Serra de Outes E 140 B2
Serradifalco I 176 B2
Serradilla E 155 B4
Serradilla del Arroyo
E 149 B3
Serradilla del Llano
E 149 B3
Serramanna I 179 C2
Serramazzoni I 135 A3
Serranillos E 150 B3
Serrapetrona I 136 B2
Serra San Bruno I 175 C2
Serra San Quírico I 136 B2
Serrastretta I 175 B2
Serravalle
Piemonte I 119 B5
Umbria I 136 C2
Serravalle di Chienti
I 136 B1
Serravalle Scrívia I 120 C1
Serre I 172 B1
Serrejón E 150 C2
Serres
F 132 A1
GR 183 B5
Serrières F 117 B4
Serrières-de-Briord
F 118 B2
Sersale I 175 B2
Sertã P 154 B2
Sertig Dörfli CH 107 C4
Servance F 106 B1
Serverette F 117 C3
Servia GR 182 C4
Servian F 130 B2
Serviers F 131 A3
Servigliano I 136 B2
Serzedelo P 148 A1
Seseña Nuevo E 151 B4
Sesimbra P 154 C1
Seskarö S 196 D6
Seskinore GB 27 B3
Sesma E 144 B1
Sessa Aurunca I 170 B1
Ses Salines E 167 B3
Sesta Godano I 134 A2
Šestanovac HR 138 B2
Sestao E 143 A4
Sestino I 135 B5
Sesto I 109 C3
Sesto Calende I 120 B1
Sesto Fiorentino I 135 B4
Séstola I 135 A3
Sesto San Giovanni
I 120 B2
Sestriere I 119 C3
Sestri Levante I 134 A2
Sestroretsk RUS 9 B7
Sestu I 179 C3
Sesvete HR 124 B2
Setcases E 146 B3
Sète F 130 B2
Setenil E 162 B2
Setermoen N 194 B9
Šetonje SRB 127 C3
Setskog N 54 A2
Settalsjølia N 199 C7
Séttimo Torinese I 119 B4
Settimo Vittone I 119 B4
Settle GB 40 A1
Setúbal P 154 C2
Seubersdort D 95 B3
Seúi I 179 C3
Seúlo I 179 C3
Seurre F 105 C4
Sevel DK 58 B1
Sevenoaks GB 45 B4
Sévérac-le-Château
F 130 A2
Sever do Vouga P 148 B1
Severin HR 123 B4
Severomorsk RUS 3 B13
Séveso I 120 B2
Ševětin CZ 96 B2
Sevettijärvi FIN 193 C12
Sévigny F 91 B4
Sevilla = Seville E 162 A2
Sevilla la Nueva E 151 B3
Seville = Sevilla E 162 A2
Sevilleja de la Jara
E 156 A3
Sevlievo BG 17 D6
Sevnica SLO 123 A4
Sevojno SRB 127 D1
Sevrier F 118 B3
Sexdrega S 60 B3
Seyches F 129 B3
Seyda D 83 A4
Seydişehir TR 189 B6
Seyðisfjörður IS 191 B12
Seyitgazi TR 187 C5
Seyitömer TR 187 C4
Seymen TR 186 A2
Seyne F 132 A2
Seynes F 131 A3
Seyssel F 118 B2
Sežana SLO 122 B2
Sézanne F 91 C3
Sezulfe P 149 A2
Sezze I 169 B3
Sfântu Gheorghe
RO 17 C6
Sforzacosta I 136 B2
Sgarasta Mhor GB 31 B1
's-Gravendeel NL 79 A4
's-Gravenhage = The
Hague NL 70 B1
's-Gravenzande NL 79 A4
Shaftesbury GB 43 A4
Shaldon GB 43 B3
Shalskiy RUS 9 B9
Shanagolden IRL 29 B2
Shanklin GB 44 C2
Shap GB 37 B4
Sharpness GB 43 A4
Shawbury GB 38 B4
's-Heerenberg NL 80 A2
Sheerness GB 45 B4
Sheffield GB 40 B2
Shefford GB 44 A3
Shëmri AL 182 A2
Shenfield GB 45 B4
Shëngjergj AL 182 B2
Shepetivka UA 13 C7
Shepshed GB 40 C2
Shepton Mallet GB 43 A4
Sherborne GB 43 B4
Shercock IRL 27 C4
Sheringham GB 41 C5
's-Hertogenbosch
NL 79 A5
Shiel Bridge GB 32 D1
Shieldaig GB 31 B3
Shijak AL 182 B1
Shillelagh IRL 30 B2
Shimsk RUS 9 C7
Shipston-on-Stour
GB 44 A2
Shklow BY 13 A9
Shkodër AL 182 A1
Shoeburyness GB 45 B4
Shoreham-by-Sea
GB 44 C3
Shotley Gate GB 45 B5
Shrewsbury GB 38 B4
Shugozero RUS 9 C9
Shumen BG 17 D7
Siabost GB 31 A2
Siamanna I 179 C2
Sianów PL 67 B5
Siatista GR 182 C3
Siauges-St Romain
F 117 B3
Šiauliai LT 8 E3
Sibari I 174 B2
Sibbhult S 63 B2
Šibenik HR 138 B1
Sibinj HR 125 B3
Sibiu RO 17 C6
Sibnica SRB 127 C2
Sibsey GB 41 B4
Siculiana I 176 B2
Šid SRB 125 B5
Sidari GR 182 D1
Siddeburen NL 71 A3
Sidensjö S 200 C4
Siderno I 175 C2
Sidirokastro GR 183 B5
Sidmouth GB 43 B3
Sidzina PL 99 B3
Siebe N 192 D7
Siebenlehn D 83 A5
Siedlce PL 12 B5
Siedlice PL 75 A4
Siedlinghausen D 81 A4
Siedlisko PL 75 B5
Siegburg D 80 B3
Siegen D 81 B4
Siegenburg D 95 C3
Sieghartskirchen A 111 A3
Siegsdorf D 109 B3
Siekierki PL 74 B3
Sielpia PL 87 A4
Siemiany PL 69 B4
Siena I 135 B4
Sieniawka PL 84 B2
Sienno PL 87 A5
Sieppijärvi FIN 196 B7
Sieradz PL 86 A2
Sieraków
Śląskie PL 86 B2
Wielkopolskie PL 75 B5
Sierakowice PL 68 A2
Sierck-les-Bains F 92 B2
Sierentz F 106 B2
Sierning A 110 A1
Sierpc PL 77 B4
Sierra de Fuentes
E 155 B4
Sierra de Luna E 144 B3
Sierra de Yeguas E 162 A3
Sierre CH 119 A4
Siestrzeń PL 77 B5
Sietamo E 145 B3
Siewierz PL 86 B3
Sigdal N 48 B1
Sigean F 130 B1
Sigerfjord N 194 B6
Sighetu-Marmatiei
RO 17 B5
Sighişoara RO 17 B6
Sigillo I 136 B1
Siglufjörður IS 191 A7
Sigmaringen D 107 A4
Signa I 135 B4
Signes F 132 B1
Signy-l'Abbaye F 91 B4
Signy-le-Petit F 91 B4
Sigogne F 115 C3
Sigri GR 183 D7
Sigtuna S 57 A3
Sigueiro E 140 B2
Sigüenza E 151 A5
Sigües E 144 B2
Sigulda LV 8 D4
Siilinjärvi FIN 8 A5
Sikenica SK 112 A2
Sikfors S 196 D4
Sikia GR 183 C5
Sikinos GR 185 C6
Sikkilsdalseter N 47 A6
Siklós H 125 B4
Sikórz PL 77 B4
Sikselet S 195 D8
Silandro I 108 C1
Silánus I 178 B2
Silbaš SRB 126 B1
Silbersted D 64 B2
Şile TR 187 A4
Siles E 164 A2
Silgueiros P 148 B2
Silifke TR 23 C7
Siliqua I 179 C2
Silistra BG 17 C7
Silivri TR 186 A3
Siljan N 53 A5
Siljansnäs S 50 B1
Silkeborg DK 59 B2
Silla E 159 B3
Sillamäe EST 8 C5
Silleda E 140 B2
Sillé-le-Guillaume
F 102 A1
Sillenstede D 71 A4
Sillerud S 54 A3
Sillian A 109 C3
Silloth GB 36 B3
Silno PL 68 B2
Silnowo PL 68 B1
Silo HR 123 B3
Sils E 147 C3
Silsand N 194 A8
Silte S 57 C4
Šilute LT 12 A4
Silvalen N 195 E3
Silvaplana CH 107 C4
Silvares P 148 B2
Silvberg S 50 B2
Silverdalen S 62 A3
Silvermines IRL 28 B3
Silverstone GB 44 A2
Silverton GB 43 B3
Silves P 160 B1
Silvi Marina I 169 A4
Simandre F 105 C3
Šimanovci SRB 127 C2
Simard F 105 C4
Simat de Valldigna
E 159 B3
Simav TR 186 C3
Simbach
Bayern D 95 C4
Bayern D 95 C5
Simbário I 175 C2
Simeonovgrad BG 183 A7
Simeria RO 17 C5
Simi GR 188 C2
Simićevo SRB 127 C3
Simitli BG 183 B5
Simlångsdalen S 60 C3
Simmerath D 80 B2
Simmerberg D 107 B4
Simmern D 93 B3
Šimonovce SK 99 C4
Simonsbath GB 43 A3
Simonstorp S 56 B2
Simontornya H 112 C2
Simplon CH 119 A5
Simrishamn S 63 C2
Sinaia RO 17 C6
Sinalunga I 135 B4
Sinarcas E 159 B2
Sincan TR 187 C7
Sincanlı TR 187 D5
Sindal DK 58 A3
Sindelfingen D 93 C5
Sindia I 178 B2
Sındırgı TR 186 C3
Sinekli TR 186 A3
Sines P 160 B1
Sinetta FIN 197 C8
Sineu E 167 B3
Singen D 107 B3
Singleton GB 44 C3
Singsås N 199 C7
Siniscóla I 178 B3
Sinj HR 138 B2
Sinlabajos E 150 A3
Sinn D 81 B4
Sinnai I 179 C3
Sinnes N 52 B2
Sinop TR 23 A8
Sins CH 106 B3
Sinsheim D 93 B4
Sint Annaland NL 79 A4
Sint Annaparochie
NL 70 A2
Sint Athonis NL 80 A1
Sint Nicolaasga NL 70 B2
Sint Oedenrode NL 79 A5
Sintra P 154 C1
Sinzheim D 93 C4
Sinzig D 80 B3
Siófok H 112 C2
Sion CH 119 A4
Sion Mills GB 27 B3
Siorac-en-Périgord
F 129 B3
Šipanska Luka HR 139 C3
Šipovo BIH 138 A3
Sira N 52 B2
Siracusa I 177 B4
Siret RO 17 B7
Sirevåg N 52 B1
Sirig SRB 126 B1
Sirkka FIN 196 B7
Sirmione I 121 B3
Sirniö FIN 197 D11
Sirok H 113 B4
Široké SK 99 C4
Široki Brijeg BIH 139 B3
Sirolo I 136 B2
Siruela E 156 B2
Sisak HR 124 B2
Sisante E 158 B1
Šišljavić HR 123 B4
Sissach CH 106 B2
Sissonne F 91 B3
Sistelo P 140 C2
Sisteron F 132 A1
Sistiana I 122 B2
Sistranda N 198 B5
Sitasjaurestugorna
S 194 C8
Sitges E 147 C2
Sitia GR 185 D7
Sittard NL 80 A1
Sittensen D 72 A2
Sittingbourne GB 45 B4
Sitzenroda D 83 A4
Sivac SRB 126 B1
Sivaslı TR 189 A4
Siverić HR 138 B2
Sivrihisar TR 187 C6
Sixt-Fer-á-Cheval
F 119 A3
Siziano I 120 B2
Sizun F 100 A1
Sjenica SRB 16 D3
Sjoa N 198 D6
Sjøåsen N 199 A8
Sjöbo S 61 D3
Sjøenden
Hedmark N 48 A3
Hedmark N 48 B3
Sjøholt N 198 C3
Sjøli N 48 A3
Sjølstad N 199 A9
Sjölunda S 56 A1
Sjømarken S 60 B2
Sjørring DK 58 B1
Sjötofta S 60 B3
Sjötorp S 55 B4
Sjoutnäset S 199 A11
Sjøvegan N 194 B8
Sjuntorp S 54 B3
Skåbu N 47 A6
Skafså N 53 A4
Skaftafell IS 191 D9
Skagaströnd IS 190 B5
Skagen DK 58 A3
Skagersvik S 55 B5
Skaiå N 53 B3
Skaidi N 193 B8
Skala GR 184 A1
Skała PL 87 B3
Skaland N 194 A8
Skala Oropou GR 185 A4
Skala-Podilska UA 13 D7
Skalat UA 13 D6
Skalbmierz PL 87 B4
Skålevik N 53 B4
Skalica SK 98 C1
Skalité SK 98 B2
Skällinge S 60 B2
Skalná CZ 83 B4
Skals DK 58 B2
Skælskør DK 65 A4
Skalstugan S 199 B9
Skanderborg DK 59 B2
Skånes-Fagerhult S 61 C3
Skåne-Tranås S 61 D3
Skånevik N 52 A1
Skänninge S 55 B6
Skanör med Falsterbo
S 66 A1
Skåpafors S 54 A3
Skąpe PL 75 B4
Skara S 55 B4
Skærbæk DK 64 A1
Skarberget N 194 B7
Skärblacka S 56 B1
Skarð IS 190 B3
Skarda S 200 B4
Skare N 46 C3
Skåre S 55 A4
Skärhamn S 60 B1
Skarnes N 48 B3
Skärplinge S 51 B4
Skarpnatö FIN 51 B6
Skarp Salling DK 58 B2
Skarrild DK 59 C1
Skarstad N 194 B7
Skärstad S 62 A2
Skarsvåg N 193 A9
Skarszewy PL 69 A3
Skårup DK 65 A3
Skärvången S 199 B11
Skarvsjöby S 195 F8
Skaryszew PL 87 A5
Skarżysko-Kamienna
PL 87 A4
Skarzysko Ksiazece
PL 87 A4
Skatøy N 53 B5
Skattkärr S 55 A4
Skattungbyn S 50 A1
Skatval N 199 B7
Skaulo S 196 B4
Skave DK 59 B1
Skawina PL 99 B3
Skebobruk S 51 C5
Skebokvarn S 56 A2
Skedala S 61 C2
Skedevi S 56 B1
Skedsmokorset N 48 B3
Skee S 54 B2
Skegness GB 41 B4
Skei N 46 A3
Skela SRB 127 C2
Skelani BIH 127 D1
Skellefteå S 2 D7
Skelleftehamn S 2 D7
Skelmersdale GB 38 A4
Skelmorlie GB 34 C3
Skelund DK 58 B3
Skender Vakuf BIH 138 A3
Skene S 60 B2
Skępe PL 77 B4
Skepplanda S 60 B2
Skeppshult S 60 B3
Skerries IRL 30 A2
Ski N 54 A1
Skiathos GR 183 D5
Skibbereen IRL 29 C2
Skibotn N 192 C4
Skidra GR 182 C4
Skien N 53 A5
Skierniewice PL 77 C5
Skillingaryd S 60 B4
Skillinge S 63 C2
Skillingmark S 49 C4
Skilloura CY 181 A2
Skinnardai S 57 A4
Skinnskatteberg S 50 C2
Skipmannvik N 195 C6
Skipness GB 34 C2
Skipsea GB 41 B3
Skipton GB 40 B1
Skiptvet N 54 A2
Skiros GR 183 E6
Skivarp S 66 A2
Skive DK 58 B2

Skjånes N 193 B12
Skjærhalden N 54 A2
Skjeberg N 54 A2
Skjeggedal N 46 B3
Skjeljanger N 46 B1
Skjeljavik N 46 C2
Skjern DK 59 C1
Skjervøy N 192 B4
Skjold
Rogaland N 52 A1
Troms N 192 C3
Skjoldastraumen N 52 A1
Skjolden N 47 A4
Skjønhaug N 54 A2
Skjøtningsberg N 193 A11
Škocjan SLO 123 B4
Skoczów PL 98 B2
Skodborg DK 59 C2
Škofja Loka SLO 123 A3
Škofljica SLO 123 B3
Skog S 51 A3
Skoganvarre N 193 C9
Skogen S 54 A3
Skogfoss N 193 C13
Skoghall S 55 A4
Skogly N 193 C13
Skogn N 199 B8
Skognes N 192 C3
Skogstorp
Halland S 60 C2
Södermanland S 56 A2
Skoki PL 76 B2
Skokloster S 57 A3
Sköldinge S 56 A2
Skole UA 13 D5
Skollenborg N 53 A5
Sköllersta S 56 A1
Skomlin PL 86 A2
Skonseng N 195 D5
Skopelos GR 183 D5
Skopje MK 182 A3
Skoppum N 54 A1
Skórcz PL 69 B3
Skorogoszcz PL 86 B1
Skoroszów PL 85 A5
Skorovatn N 199 A10
Skorped S 200 C3
Skørping DK 58 B2
Skotfoss N 53 A5
Skotniki PL 87 A3
Skotselv N 48 C1
Skotterud N 49 C4
Skottorp S 61 C2
Skovby DK 64 B2
Skövde S 55 B4
Skovsgård DK 58 A2
Skrad HR 123 B3
Skradin HR 138 B1
Skradnik HR 123 B4
Skråmestø N 46 B1
Škrdlovice CZ 97 B3
Skrea S 60 C2
Skreia N 48 B2
Skrolsvik N 194 A7
Skruv S 63 B3
Skrwilno PL 77 A4
Skrydstrup DK 59 C2
Skucani BIH 138 B2
Skudeneshavn N 52 A1
Skui N 48 C2
Skulsk PL 76 B3
Skultorp S 55 B4
Skultuna S 56 A2
Skuodas LT 8 D2
Skurup S 66 A2
Skute N 48 B2
Skuteč CZ 97 B3
Skutskär S 51 B4
Skutvik N 194 B6
Skvyra UA 13 D8
Skwierzyna PL 75 B4
Skýcov SK 98 C2
Skyllberg S 55 B5
Skyttmon S 200 C1
Skyttorp S 51 B4
Sládkovičovo SK 111 A4
Slagelse DK 61 D1
Slagharen NL 71 B3
Slagnäs S 195 E9
Slaidburn GB 40 B1
Slane IRL 30 A2
Slangerup DK 61 D2
Slano HR 139 C3
Slantsy RUS 8 C6
Slaný CZ 84 B2
Slap SLO 122 A2
Šlapanice CZ 97 B4
Slåstad N 48 B3
Slatina
BIH 139 B3
HR 125 B3
RO 17 C6
Slatiňany CZ 97 B3
Slatinice CZ 98 B1
Slättberg S 50 A1
Slattum N 48 C2
Slavičin CZ 98 B1
Slavkov CZ 98 C1
Slavkovica SRB 127 C2
Slavkov u Brna CZ 97 B4
Slavonice CZ 97 C3
Slavonski Brod HR 125 B4
Slavonski Kobas
HR 125 B3
Slavŏsovce SK 99 C4
Slavskoye RUS 69 A5
Slavuta UA 13 C7
Sława
Lubuskie PL 85 A4
Zachodnio-Pomorskie
PL 67 C4
Slawharad BY 13 B9
Sławków PL 86 B3
Sławno
Wielkopolskie PL 76 B2
Zachodnio-Pomorskie
PL 68 A1
Sławoborze PL 67 C4
Sl'ažany SK 98 C2
Sleaford GB 40 C3
Sleðbrjótur IS 191 B11
Sledmere GB 40 A3
Sleights GB 37 B6
Slemmestad N 54 A1
Ślesin PL 76 B3
Sliač SK 99 C3
Sliema M 175 C3
Sligo IRL 26 B2
Slite S 57 C4
Slitu N 54 A2
Sliven BG 17 D7
Śliwice PL 68 B3
Slobozia RO 17 C7
Slochteren NL 71 A3
Slöinge S 60 C2
Słomniki PL 87 B4
Slonim BY 13 B6
Słońsk PL 75 B3
Slootdorp NL 70 B1
Slottsbron S 55 A4
Slough GB 44 B3
Slövag N 46 B2
Slovenj Gradec
SLO 110 C2
Slovenska Bistrica
SLO 123 A4
Slovenská L'upča
SK 99 C3
Slovenská-Ves SK 99 B4
Slovenské Darmoty
SK 112 A3
Slovenske Konjice
SLO 123 A4
Słubice PL 74 B3
Sluderno I 108 C1
Sluis NL 78 A3
Šluknov CZ 84 A2
Slunj HR 123 B4
Słupca PL 76 B2
Słupia PL 87 A3
Słupiec PL 85 B4
Słupsk PL 68 A2
Slutsk BY 13 B7
Smålandsstenar S 60 B3
Smalåsen N 195 E4
Smardzewo PL 75 B4
Smarhon BY 13 A7
Šmarje SLO 123 A4
Šmarjeta SLO 123 B4
Šmartno SLO 123 A3
Smečno CZ 84 B2
Smedby S 63 B4
Smědec CZ 96 C2
Smederevo SRB 127 C2
Smederevska Palanka
SRB 127 C2
Smedjebacken S 50 B2
Smęgorzów PL 87 B5
Smeland N 53 B4
Smidary CZ 84 B3
Śmigiel PL 75 B5
Smilde NL 71 B3
Smiřice CZ 85 B3
Smithfield GB 36 B4
Šmitowo PL 75 A5
Smögen S 54 B2
Smogulec PL 76 A2
Smołdzino PL 68 A2
Smolenice SK 98 C1
Smolensk RUS 13 A10
Smolník SK 99 C4
Smolyan BG 183 B6
Smuka SLO 123 B3
Smygehamn S 66 A2
Smykow PL 87 A4
Snainton GB 40 A3
Snaith GB 40 B2
Snaptun DK 59 C3
Snarby N 192 C3
Snarum N 48 B1
Snåsa N 199 A9
Snedsted DK 58 B1
Sneek NL 70 A2
Sneem IRL 29 C2
Snejbjerg DK 59 B1
Snillfjord N 198 B6
Šnjegotina BIH 125 C3
Snøde DK 65 A3
Snøfjord N 193 B8
Snogebaek DK 67 A4
Snyatyn UA 13 D6
Soave I 121 B4
Sober E 140 B3
Sobernheim D 93 B3
Soběslav CZ 96 B2
Sobota
Dolnośląskie PL 85 A3
Łódzkie PL 77 B4
Sobotište SK 98 C1
Sobotka CZ 84 B3
Sobótka
Dolnośląskie PL 85 B4
Wielkopolskie PL 86 A1
Sobra HR 139 C3
Sobrado
Coruña E 140 A2
Lugo E 141 B3
Sobral da Adica P 161 A2
Sobral de Monte
Argraço P 154 C1
Sobreira Formosa
P 154 B3
Søby DK 64 B3
Soca SLO 122 A2
Sochaczew PL 77 B5
Sochos GR 183 C5
Socodor RO 113 C5
Socol RO 127 C3
Socovos E 164 A3
Socuéllamos E 158 B1
Sodankylä FIN 197 B9
Soderåkra S 63 B4
Söderala S 51 A3
Söderås S 50 B2
Söderbärke S 50 B2
Söderby-Karl S 51 C5
Söderfors S 51 B4
Söderhamn S 51 A4
Söderköping S 56 B2
Söderö S 56 B1
Södertälje S 57 A3
Södingberg A 110 B2
Södra Finnö S 56 B2
Södra Ny S 55 A4
Södra Råda S 55 A5
Södra Sandby S 61 D3
Södra Vi S 62 A3
Sodražica SLO 123 B3
Sodupe E 143 A3
Soengas P 148 A1
Soest
D 81 A4
NL 70 B2
Sofades GR 182 D4
Sofia = Sofiya BG 17 D5
Sofikon GR 184 B4
Sofiya = Sofia BG 17 D5
Şofronea RO 126 A3
Sögel D 71 B4
Sogliano al Rubicone
I 135 A5
Sogndalsfjøra N 46 A4
Søgne N 53 B3
Sögütköy TR 188 C3
Soham GB 45 A4
Sohland D 84 A2
Sohren D 93 B3
Soignies B 79 B4
Soissons F 90 B3
Söjtör H 111 C3
Sokal' UA 13 C6
Söke TR 188 B2
Sokna N 48 B1
Sokndal N 52 B2
Soknedal N 199 C7
Soko BIH 125 C4
Sokolac BIH 139 B4
Sokółka PL 13 B5
Sokolov CZ 83 B4
Sokołowo PL 76 B3
Sokołów Podlaski
PL 12 B5
Sola N 52 B1
Solana de los Barros
E 155 C4
Solana del Pino E 157 B3
Solánas I 179 C3
Solares E 143 A3
Solarino I 177 B4
Solarussa I 179 C2
Solas GB 31 B1
Solberg S 200 C3
Solberga S 62 A2
Solber-gelva N 53 A6
Solbjørg N 46 B2
Solčany SK 98 C2
Solčava SLO 123 A3
Solda I 108 C1
Sölden A 108 C2
Solec Kujawski PL 76 A3
Soleils F 132 B2
Solenzara F 180 B2
Solera E 163 A4
Solesmes F 79 B3
Soleto I 173 B4
Solgne F 92 C2
Solheim N 46 B2
Solheimsvik N 52 A2
Solignac F 115 C5
Solihull GB 44 A2
Solin HR 138 B2
Solingen D 80 A3
Solivella E 147 C2
Solkan SLO 122 B2
Söll A 108 B3
Sollana E 159 B3
Sollebrunn S 54 B3
Sollefteå S 200 C3
Sollenau A 111 B3
Sollen-tuna S 57 A3
Sóller E 166 B2
Sollerön S 50 B1
Søllested DK 65 B4
Solliès-Pont F 132 B2
Sollihøgda N 48 C2
Solnechnogorsk
RUS 9 D10
Solnice CZ 85 B4
Solofra I 170 C2
Solomiac F 129 C3
Solopaca I 170 B2
Solórzano E 143 A3
Solothurn CH 106 B2
Solre-le-Château F 79 B4
Solsona E 147 C2
Solsvik N 46 B1
Solt H 112 C3
Soltau D 72 B2
Soltsy RUS 9 C7
Soltszentimre H 112 C3
Soltvadkert H 112 C3
Solumsmoen N 48 C1
Solund N 46 A1
Solva GB 39 C1
Sölvesborg S 63 B2
Solymár H 112 B2
Soma TR 186 C2
Somain F 78 B3
Somberek H 125 A4
Sombernon F 104 B3
Sombor SRB 125 B5
Sombreffe B 79 B4
Someren NL 80 A1
Somero FIN 8 B3
Somersham GB 44 A3
Somerton GB 43 A4
Sominy PL 68 A2
Somma Lombardo
I 120 B1
Sommariva del Bosco
I 119 C4
Sommarøy N 192 C2
Sommarset N 194 C6
Sommatino I 176 B2
Sommeilles F 91 C4
Sommen S 55 B5
Sommepy-Tahure F 91 B4
Sömmerda D 82 A3
Sommerfeld D 74 B2
Sommersted DK 59 C2
Sommesous F 91 C4
Somme-Tourbe F 91 B4
Sommières F 131 B3
Sommières-du-Clain
F 115 B4
Somo E 143 A3
Somogyfajsz H 111 C4
Somogyjád H 111 C4
Somogysámson H 111 C4
Somogysárd H 125 A3
Somogyszil H 112 C2
Somogyszob H 124 A3
Somogyvár H 111 C4
Somontin E 164 B2
Somosiero E 151 A4
Somoskőújfalu H 113 A3
Sompolno PL 76 B3
Sompuis F 91 C4
Son N 54 A1
Son Bou E 167 B4
Sonceboz CH 106 B2
Soncillo E 143 B3
Soncino I 120 B2
Sóndalo I 120 A3
Søndeled N 53 B5
Sønder Bjert DK 59 C2
Sønderborg DK 64 B2
Sønderby DK 64 B2
Sønder Felding DK 59 C1
Sønderho DK 59 C1
Sønder Hygum DK 59 C1
Sønder Omme DK 59 C1
Sondershausen D 82 A2
Søndersø DK 59 C3
Søndervig DK 59 B1
Søndre Enningdal
Kappel N 54 B2
Sóndrio I 120 A2
Soneja E 159 B3
Son en Breugel NL 80 A1
Songe N 53 B5
Songeons F 90 B1
Sonkamuotka FIN 196 A6
Sonkovo RUS 9 D10
Sönnarslöv S 61 D4
Sonneberg D 82 B3
Sonnefeld D 82 B3
Sonnewalde D 84 A1
Sonnino I 169 B3
Sonogno CH 120 A1
Sonsbeck D 80 A2
Sonseca E 157 A4
Son Servera E 167 B3
Sønsterud N 49 B4
Sonstorp S 56 B1
Sonta SRB 125 B5
Sontheim D 94 C2
Sonthofen D 107 B5
Sontra D 82 A1
Sopelana E 143 A4
Sopje HR 125 B3
Šoporňa SK 111 A4
Sopot
PL 69 A3
SRB 127 C2
Sopotnica MK 182 B3
Sopron H 111 B3
Šor SRB 127 C1
Sora I 169 B3
Soragna I 120 C3
Söråker S 200 D3
Sorano I 168 A1
Sorbara I 121 C4
Sorbas E 164 B2
Sórbolo I 121 C3
Sörbygden S 200 D2
Sordal N 52 B3
Sordale GB 32 C3
Sore F 128 B2
Sörenberg CH 106 C3
Soresina I 120 B2
Sorèze F 146 A3
Sörforsa S 200 E3
Sorges F 115 C4
Sórgono I 179 B3
Sorgues F 131 A3
Sorgun TR 23 B8
Soria E 143 C4
Soriano Cálabro I 175 C2
Soriano nel Cimino
I 168 A2
Sorihuela del
Guadalimar E 164 A1
Sorisdale GB 34 B1
Sørkjosen N 192 C4
Sørli N 199 A10
Sormás H 111 C3
Sörmjöle S 200 C6
Sørmo N 194 B9
Sornac F 116 B2
Sorø DK 61 D1
Soroca MD 17 A8
Sørreisa N 194 A9
Sorrento I 170 C2
Sorsele S 195 E8
Sörsjön S 49 A5
Sorso I 178 B2
Sort E 146 B2
Sortavala RUS 9 B7
Sortino I 177 B4
Sortland N 194 B6
Sørum N 48 B2
Sørumsand N 48 C3
Sorunda S 57 A3
Sörup D 64 B2
Sørvågen N 194 C3
Sørvær N 192 B6
Sorvik S 50 B2
Sørvika N 199 C8
Sos F 128 B3
Sösdala S 61 C3
Sos del Rey Católico
E 144 B2
Sošice HR 123 B4
Sośnica PL 75 A5
Sośnicowice PL 86 B2
Sośno PL 76 A2
Sosnovyy Bor RUS 9 C6
Sosnowiec PL 86 B3
Sospel F 133 B3
Šoštanj SLO 123 A4
Sotaseter N 198 D4
Sotillo de Adrada
E 150 B3
Sotillo de la Ribera
E 143 C3
Sotin HR 125 B5
Sotkamo FIN 3 D11
Sotobañado y Priorato
E 142 B2
Soto de la Marina
E 143 A3
Soto del Barco E 141 A4
Soto de los Infantes
E 141 A4
Soto de Real E 151 B4
Soto de Ribera E 141 A5
Sotoserrano E 149 B3
Soto y Amío E 141 B5
Sotresgudo E 142 B2
Sotrondio E 142 A1
Sotta F 180 B2
Sottomarina I 122 B1
Sottrum D 72 A2
Sottunga FIN 51 B7
Sotuelamos E 158 B1
Souain F 91 B4
Soual F 146 A3
Soucy F 104 A2
Souda GR 185 D5
Soudron F 91 C4
Souesmes F 103 B4
Soufflenheim F 93 C3
Soufli GR 186 A1
Souillac F 129 B4
Souilly F 91 B5
Soulac-sur-Mer F 114 C2
Soulaines-Dhuys F 91 C4
Soulatgé F 146 B3
Soultz-Haut-Rhin F 106 B2
Soultz-sous-Forêts
F 93 C3
Soumagne B 80 B1
Soumoulou F 145 A3
Souppes-sur-Loing
F 103 A4
Souprosse F 128 C2
Sourdeval F 88 B3
Soure P 154 A2
Sournia F 146 B3
Souro Pires P 149 B2
Sourpi GR 182 D4
Sours F 90 C1
Sousceyrac F 116 C2
Sousel P 155 C3
Soustons F 128 C1
Söğüt
Bilecik TR 187 B5
Burdur TR 189 B4
Soutelo de Montes
E 140 B2
Southam GB 44 A2
Southampton GB 44 C2
Southborough GB 45 B4
South Brent GB 42 B3
South Cave GB 40 B3
Southend GB 34 C2
Southend-on-Sea
GB 45 B4
South Hayling GB 44 C3
South Molton GB 42 A3
South Ockendon
GB 45 B4
South Petherton GB 43 B4
Southport GB 38 A3
South Shields GB 37 B5
South Tawton GB 42 B3
Southwell GB 40 B3
Southwold GB 45 A5
South Woodham Ferrers
GB 45 B4
Söğütlu TR 187 B5
Souto P 148 B2
Soutochao E 141 C3
Souto da Carpalhosa
P 154 B2
Souvigny F 104 C2
Souzay-Champigny
F 102 B1
Soverato I 175 C2
Soveria Mannelli I 175 B2
Sövestad S 66 A2
Sovetsk RUS 12 A4
Sovići BIH 138 B3
Sovicille I 135 B4
Søvik N 198 C3
Sowerby GB 37 B5
Soyaux F 115 C4
Søyland N 52 B1
Spa B 80 B1
Spadafora I 177 A4
Spaichingen D 107 A3
Spakenburg NL 70 B2
Spalding GB 41 C3
Spálené Poříčí CZ 96 B1
Spalt D 94 B2
Spangenberg D 82 A1
Spangereid N 52 B3
Spantekow D 74 A2
Sparanise I 170 B2
Sparbu N 199 B8
Sparkær DK 58 B2
Sparkford GB 43 A4
Sparreholm S 56 A2
Sparta = Sparti GR 184 B3
Spartà I 177 A4
Sparti = Sparta GR 184 B3
Spean Bridge GB 34 B3
Speicher D 92 B2
Speichersdorf D 95 B3
Speke GB 38 A4
Spello I 136 C1
Spenge D 72 B1
Spennymoor GB 37 B5
Spentrup DK 58 B3
Sperenberg D 74 B2
Sperlinga I 177 B3
Sperlonga I 169 B3
Spetalen N 54 A1
Spetses GR 184 B4
Speyer D 93 B4
Spézet F 100 A2
Spezzano Albanese
I 174 B2
Spezzano della Sila
I 174 B2
Spiddle IRL 28 A2
Spiegelau D 96 C1
Spiekeroog D 71 A4
Spiez CH 106 C2
Spigno Monferrato
I 133 A4
Spijk NL 71 A3
Spijkenisse NL 79 A4
Spilamberto I 135 A4
Spili GR 185 D5
Spilimbergo I 122 A1
Spilsby GB 41 B4
Spinazzola I 172 B2
Spincourt F 92 B1
Spind N 52 B2
Spindleruv-Mlyn CZ 84 B3
Spinoso I 174 A1
Špišjć Bukovica
HR 124 B3
Spišská Belá SK 99 B4
Spišská Nová Ves
SK 99 C4
Spisská Stará Ves
SK 99 B4
Spišské-Hanušovce
SK 99 B4
Spišské Podhradie
SK 99 C4
Spišské Vlachy SK 99 C4
Spišský-Štvrtok SK 99 C4
Spital A 110 B1
Spital am Semmering
A 110 B2
Spittal an der Drau
A 109 C4
Spittle of Glenshee
GB 35 B4
Spitz A 97 C3
Spjald DK 59 B1
Spjærøy N 54 A1
Spjelkavik N 198 C3
Spjutsbygd S 63 B3
Split HR 138 B2
Splügen CH 107 C4
Spodsbjerg DK 65 B3
Spofforth GB 40 B2

Spohle D 71 A5
Spoleto I 136 C1
Spoltore I 169 A4
Spondigna I 108 C1
Sponvika N 54 A2
Spornitz D 73 A4
Spotorno I 133 A4
Spraitbach D 94 C1
Sprakensehl D 72 B3
Spręcowo PL 69 B5
Spremberg D 84 A2
Spresiano I 122 B1
Sprimont B 80 B1
Springe D 72 B2
Sproatley GB 41 B3
Spydeberg N 54 A2
Spytkowice PL 99 B3
Squillace I 175 C2
Squinzano I 173 B4
Sračinec HR 124 A2
Srbac BIH 124 B3
Srbobran SRB 126 B1
Srebrenica BIH 127 C1
Srebrenik BIH 125 C4
Središče SLO 124 A2
Śrem PL 76 B2
Sremska Mitrovica
SRB 127 C1
Sremski Karlovci
SRB 126 B1
Srní CZ 96 B1
Srnice Gornje BIH 125 C4
Śrock PL 86 A3
Środa Śląska PL 85 A4
Środa Wielkopolski
PL 76 B2
Srpska Crnja SRB 126 B2
Srpski Itebej SRB 126 B2
Srpski Miletić SRB 125 B5
Staatz A 97 C4
Stabbursnes N 193 B8
Staberdorf D 65 B4
Stabroek B 79 A4
Stachy CZ 96 B1
Staðarfell IS 190 B3
Stade D 72 A2
Staden B 78 B3
Stadl an der Mur A 109 B4
Stadskanaal NL 71 B3
Stadtallendorf D 81 B5
Stadthagen D 72 B2
Stadtilm D 82 B3
Stadtkyll D 80 B2
Stadtlauringen D 82 B2
Stadtlengsfeld D 82 B2
Stadtlohn D 71 C3
Stadtoldendorf D 82 A1
Stadtroda D 83 B3
Stadtsteinach D 82 B3
Stäfa CH 107 B3
Staffanstorp S 61 D3
Staffelstein D 82 B2
Staffin GB 31 B2
Stafford GB 40 C1
Stainach A 110 B1
Staindrop GB 37 B5
Staines-upon-Thames
GB 44 B3
Stainville F 91 C5
Stainz A 110 C2
Staithes GB 37 B6
Staíti I 175 D2
Stäket S 57 A3
Stakroge DK 59 C1
Štalcerji SLO 123 B3
Stalden CH 119 A4
Stalham GB 41 C5
Stalheim N 46 B3
Stallarholmen S 56 A3
Ställberg S 50 C1
Ställdalen S 50 C1
Stallhofen A 110 B2
Stalon S 195 F6
Stalowa Wola PL 12 C5
Stamford GB 40 C3
Stamford Bridge GB 40 B3
Stamnes N 46 B2
Stams A 108 B1
Stamsried D 95 B4
Stamsund N 194 B4
Stanford le Hope
GB 45 B4
Stånga S 57 C4
Stange N 48 B3
Stanghella I 121 B4
Stanhope GB 37 B4
Stanišić SRB 125 B5
Staňkov CZ 95 B5
Stankovci HR 137 B4
Stanley GB 37 B5
Stans CH 106 C3
Stansted Mountfitchet
GB 45 B4
Stanzach A 108 B1
Stapar SRB 125 B5
Staphorst NL 70 B3
Staplehurst GB 45 B4
Stąporków PL 87 A4
Stara Baška HR 123 C3
Starachowice PL 87 A5
Stara Fužina SLO 122 A2
Stara Kamienica PL 84 B3
Stara Kiszewa PL 68 B3
Stará L'ubovňa SK 99 B4
Stara Moravica
SRB 126 B1
Stara Novalja HR 137 A3
Stara Pazova SRB 127 C2
Stará Turá SK 98 C1
Staraya Russa RUS 9 D7
Stara Zagora BG 17 D6
Stärbsnäs S 51 C6
Starčevo SRB 127 C2
Stare Dłutowo PL 77 A4
Staré Hamry CZ 98 B2
Stare Jabłonki PL 69 B5
Staré Město CZ 98 B1
Stare Pole PL 69 A4
Stare Sedlo CZ 96 B2
Stare Strącze PL 85 A4
Stargard Szczeciński
PL 75 A4
Stårheim N 198 D2
Stari Banovci SRB 127 C2
Starigrad
Ličko-Senjska
HR 123 C3
Splitsko-Dalmatinska
HR 138 B2
Stari Gradac HR 124 B3
Starigrad-Paklenica
HR 137 A4
Stari Jankovci HR 125 B4
Stari Majdan BIH 124 C2
Stari-Mikanovci
HR 125 B4
Staritsa RUS 9 D9
Starkenbach A 108 B1
Starnberg D 108 B2
Starogard PL 75 A4
Starogard Gdański
PL 69 B3
Starokonstyantyniv
UA 13 D7
Staro Petrovo Selo
HR 124 B3
Staro Selo
HR 124 B1
SRB 127 C3
Stary Brzozów PL 77 B5
Stary Dzierzgoń PL 69 B4
Starý Hrozenkov
CZ 98 C1
Stary Jaroslaw PL 68 A1
Starý Plzenec CZ 96 B1
Stary Sącz PL 99 B4
Starý Smokovec SK 99 B4
Staryy Chartoriysk
UA 13 C6
Staškov SK 98 B2
Stassfurt D 82 A3
Staszów PL 87 B5
Stathelle N 53 A5
Staufen D 106 B2
Staunton GB 39 C4
Stavang N 46 A2
Stavanger N 52 B1
Stavåsnäs S 49 B4
Stavby S 51 B5
Staveley GB 40 B2
Stavelot B 80 B1
Stavenisse NL 79 A4
Stavern N 53 B6
Stavnäs S 55 A3
Stavoren NL 70 B2
Stavros
CY 181 A1
GR 183 C5
Stavroupoli GR 183 B6
Stavseng N 47 A6
Stavsiø N 48 B2
Stavsnäs S 57 A4
Stawiszyn PL 76 C3
Steane N 53 A4
Steblevë AL 182 B2
Stechelberg CH 106 C2
Štechovice CZ 96 B2
Stechow D 73 B5
Steckborn CH 107 B3
Stede Broek NL 70 B2
Steeg A 107 B5
Steenbergen NL 79 A4
Steenvoorde F 78 B2
Steenwijk NL 70 B3
Štefanje HR 124 B2
Steffisburg CH 106 C2
Stegaurach D 94 B2
Stege DK 65 B5
Stegelitz D 74 A2
Stegersbach A 111 B3
Stegna PL 69 A4
Steimbke D 72 B2
Stein GB 31 B2
Steinach
A 108 B2
Baden-Württemberg
D 106 A3
Bayern D 82 B2
Thüringen D 82 B3
Stein an Rhein CH 107 B3
Steinau
Bayern D 81 B5
Niedersachsen D 64 C1
Steinbeck D 74 B2
Steinberg am Rofan
A 108 B2
Steindorf A 109 C5
Steine N 46 B2
Steinen D 106 B2
Steinfeld
A 109 C4
D 71 B5
Steinfurt D 71 B4
Steingaden D 108 B1
Steinhagen D 72 B1
Steinheid D 82 B3
Steinheim
Bayern D 107 A5
Nordrhein-Westfalen
D 81 A5
Steinhöfel D 74 B3
Steinhorst D 72 B3
Steinigtwolmsdorf
D 84 A2
Steinkjer N 199 A8
Steinsholt N 53 A5
Stekene B 79 A4
Stelle D 72 A3
Stellendam NL 79 A4
Stenåsa S 63 B4
Stenay F 91 B5
Stenberga S 62 A3
Stendal D 73 B4
Stenhammar S 55 B4
Stenhamra S 57 A3
Stenhousemuir GB 35 B4
Stenlose DK 61 D2
Stensätra S 50 B3
Stensele S 195 E8
Stenstorp S 55 B4
Stenstrup DK 65 A3
Stenudden S 195 D8
Stenungsund S 54 B2
Štěpánov CZ 98 B1
Stephanskirchen D 108 B3
Stepnica PL 74 A3
Stepojevac SRB 127 C2
Stepping DK 59 C2
Sterbfritz D 82 B1
Sternberg D 65 C4
Šternberk CZ 98 B1
Sterup D 64 B2
Stes Maries-de-la-Mer
F 131 B3
Stęszew PL 75 B5
Štěti CZ 84 B2
Stevenage GB 44 B3
Stewarton GB 36 A2
Steyerburg D 72 B2
Steyning GB 44 C3
Steyr A 110 A1
Stężyca PL 68 A2
Stezzano I 120 B2
Stia I 135 B4
Stibb Cross GB 42 B2
Sticciano Scalo I 135 C4
Stidsvig S 61 C3
Stiens NL 70 A2
Stige DK 59 C3
Stigen S 54 B3
Stigliano I 174 A2
Stigtomta S 56 B2
Stilida GR 182 E4
Stilla N 192 C7
Stillington GB 40 A2
Stilo I 175 C2
Stintino I 178 B2
Stio I 172 B1
Štip MK 182 B4
Stira GR 185 A5
Stirling GB 35 B4
Štítnik SK 99 C4
Štíty CZ 97 B4
Stjärnhov S 56 A3
Stjärnsund S 50 B3
Stjørdalshalsen N 199 B7
Stobnica PL 87 A3
Stobno PL 75 A5
Stobreč HR 138 B2
Stochov CZ 84 B1
Stockach D 107 B4
Stöckalp CH 106 C3
Stockaryd S 62 A2
Stockbridge GB 44 B2
Stockerau A 97 C4
Stockheim D 82 B3
Stockholm S 57 A4
Stockport GB 40 B1
Stocksbridge GB 40 B2
Stockton-on-Tees
GB 37 B5
Stod CZ 96 B1
Stöde S 200 D2
Stødi N 195 D6
Stöðvarfjörður
IS 191 C12
Stoer GB 32 C1
Stoholm DK 58 B2
Stoke Ferry GB 41 C4
Stoke Fleming GB 43 B3
Stoke Mandeville
GB 44 B3
Stoke-on-Trent GB 40 B1
Stokesley GB 37 B5
Stokke N 54 A1
Stokkemarke DK 65 B4
Stokken N 53 B4
Stokkseyri IS 190 D4
Stokkvågen N 195 D4
Stokmarknes N 194 B5
Štoky CZ 97 B3
Stolac BIH 139 B3
Stølaholmen N 46 A3
Stolberg D 80 B2
Stolin BY 13 C7
Stollberg D 83 B4
Stöllet S 49 B5
Stollhamm D 71 A5
Stolno PL 76 A3
Stolpen D 84 A2
Stolzenau D 72 B2
Stompetoren NL 70 B1
Ston HR 139 C3
Stonařov CZ 97 B3
Stone GB 40 C1
Stonehaven GB 33 E4
Stonehouse GB 36 A3
Stongfjorden N 46 A2
Stonndalen N 47 B4
Stony Stratford GB 44 A3
Stopnica PL 87 B4
Storå S 56 A1
Storås N 198 B6
Storby FIN 51 B6
Stordal
Møre og Romsdal
N 198 C4
Nord-Trøndelag N 199 B8
Store GB 33 B4
Storebø N 46 B2
Storebro S 62 A3
Store Damme DK 65 B5
Store Heddinge DK 65 A5
Store Herrestad S 66 A2
Store Levene S 55 B3
Storelv N 192 B6
Store Molvik N 193 B12
Støren N 199 B7
Store Skedvi S 50 B2
Store Vika S 57 B3
Storfjellseter N 199 D7
Storfjord N 192 C3
Storfjorden N 198 C3
Storfors S 55 A5
Storforshei N 195 D5
Storhøliseter N 47 A6
Storjord N 195 D6
Storkow
Brandenburg D 74 B2
Mecklenburg-
Vorpommern D 74 A3
Storli N 198 C6
Storlien S 199 B9
Stornara I 171 B3
Stornoway GB 31 A2
Storo I 121 B3
Storozhynets UA 17 A6
Storrington GB 44 C3
Storseleby S 200 B2
Storsjön S 50 A3
Storslett N 192 C5
Storsteinnes N 192 C3
Storsund S 196 D3
Storuman S 195 E8
Störvattnet S 199 C9
Storvik
N 195 D4
S 50 B3
Storvreta S 51 C4
Štos SK 99 C4
Stössen D 83 A3
Stotel D 72 A1
Stötten D 108 B1
Stotternheim D 82 A3
Stouby DK 59 C2
Stourbridge GB 40 C1
Stourport-on-Severn
GB 39 B4
Støvring DK 58 B2
Stow GB 35 C5
Stowbtsy BY 13 B7
Stowmarket GB 45 A5
Stow-on-the-Wold
GB 44 B2
Straach D 73 C5
Strabane GB 27 B3
Strachan GB 33 D4
Strachur GB 34 B2
Stracin MK 182 A4
Strackholt D 71 A4
Stradbally IRL 29 B1
Stradella I 120 B2
Straelen D 80 A2
Stragari SRB 127 C2
Strakonice CZ 96 B1
Strålsnäs S 55 B6
Stralsund D 66 B2
Strand N 48 A3
Stranda N 198 C3
Strandby DK 58 A3
Strandebarm N 46 B3
Strandhill IRL 26 B2
Strandlykkja N 48 B3
Strandvik N 46 B2
Strangford GB 27 B5
Strängnäs S 56 A3
Strångsjö S 56 B2
Stráni CZ 98 C1
Stranice SLO 123 A4
Stranorlar IRL 26 B3
Stranraer GB 36 B1
Strasatti I 176 B1
Strasbourg F 93 C3
Strasburg D 74 A2
Strašice CZ 96 B1
Stråssa S 56 A1
Strassburg A 110 C1
Strass im Steiermark
A 110 C2
Strasskirchen D 95 C4
Strasswalchen A 109 B4
Stratford-upon-Avon
GB 44 A2
Strathaven GB 36 A2
Strathdon GB 32 D3
Strathkanaird GB 32 D1
Strathpeffer GB 32 D2
Strathy GB 32 C3
Strathyre GB 34 B3
Stratinska BIH 124 C2
Stratton GB 42 B2
Straubing D 95 C4
Straulas I 178 B3
Straume N 53 A5
Straumen
Nordland N 194 C6
Nord-Trøndelag N 199 B8
Straumsjøen N 194 B5
Straumsnes N 194 C6
Straupitz D 74 C3
Strausberg D 74 B2
Straussfurt D 82 A3
Strawczyn PL 87 B4
Straža
SLO 123 B4
SRB 127 C3
Stražnad Nezárkou
CZ 96 B2
Strážnice CZ 98 C1
Strážný CZ 96 C1
Stráž Pod Ralskem
CZ 84 B2
Štrbské Pleso SK 99 B4
Strečno SK 98 B2
Street GB 43 A4
Strehla D 83 A5
Strekov SK 112 B2
Strem A 111 B3
Stremska-Rača
SRB 127 C1
Strengberg A 110 A1
Strengelvåg N 194 B6
Stresa I 119 B5
Streufdorf D 82 B2
Strib DK 59 C2
Striberg S 55 A5
Stříbro CZ 95 B4
Strichen GB 33 D4
Strigno I 121 A4
Štrigova HR 111 C3
Strijen NL 79 A4
Strizivojna HR 125 B4
Strmica HR 138 A2
Strmilov CZ 97 B3
Ströhen D 72 B1
Strokestown IRL 28 A3
Stromberg
Nordrhein-Westfalen
D 81 A4
Rheinland-Pfalz D 93 B3
Stromeferry GB 31 B3
Strömnäs S 200 B2
Stromness GB 33 C3
Strömsberg S 51 B4
Strömsbruk S 200 E3
Strömsfors S 56 B2
Strömsnäsbruk S 61 C3
Strömstad S 54 B2
Strömsund
Jämtland S 199 B12
Västerbotten S 195 E7
Stronachlachar GB 34 B3
Stróngoli I 174 B3
Stronie Ślaskie PL 85 B4
Strontian GB 34 B2
Stroppiana I 119 B5
Stroud GB 43 A4
Stroumbi CY 181 B1
Stróża PL 99 B3
Strücklingen D 71 A4
Struer DK 58 B1
Struga MK 182 B2
Strugi Krasnyye RUS 9 C6
Strumica MK 182 B4
Strumien PL 98 B2
Struy GB 32 D2
Stružec HR 124 B2
Stryków PL 77 C4
Stryn N 198 D3
Stryy UA 13 D5
Strzałkowo PL 76 B2
Strzegocin PL 77 B5
Strzegom PL 85 B4
Strzegowo PL 77 B5
Strzelce PL 77 B4
Strzelce Krajeńskie
PL 75 B4
Strzelce Kurowo PL 75 B4
Strzelce Opolskie
PL 86 B2
Strzelin PL 85 B5
Strzelno PL 76 B3
Strzepcz PL 68 A3
Strzybnica PL 86 B2
Strzygi PL 77 A4
Stubbekøbing DK 65 B5
Stuben A 107 B5
Stubenberg A 110 B2
Stubline SRB 127 C2
Studená CZ 97 B3
Studenci HR 138 B3
Studenka CZ 98 B2
Studenzen A 110 B2
Studienka SK 98 C1
Studland GB 43 B5
Studley GB 44 A2
Studzienice PL 68 A2
Stuer D 73 A5
Stugudal N 199 C8
Stugun S 200 C1
Stuhr D 72 A1
Stukenbrock D 81 A4
Stülpe D 74 B2
Stupava SK 111 A4
Stupnik HR 124 B1
Stupsk PL 77 A5
Sturkö S 63 B3
Sturminster Newton
GB 43 B4
Štúrovo SK 112 B2
Sturton GB 40 B3
Stuttgart D 94 C1
Stvolny CZ 96 A1
Stykkishólmur IS 190 B3
Styri N 48 B3
Stysö S 60 B1
Suances E 142 A2
Subbiano I 135 B4
Subiaco I 169 B3
Subotica SRB 126 A1
Subotište SRB 127 C1
Sučany SK 98 B2
Suceava RO 17 B7
Sucha-Beskidzka
PL 99 B3
Suchacz PL 69 A4
Suchań PL 75 A4
Suchdol nad Lužnice
CZ 96 C2
Suchedniów PL 87 A4
Suchorze PL 68 A2
Suchteln D 80 A2
Sucina E 165 B4
Suckow D 73 A4
Sućuraj HR 138 B3
Súðavík IS 190 A3
Sudbury GB 45 A4
Suddesjaur S 195 E10
Suden D 64 B1
Süderbrarup D 64 B2
Süderlügum D 64 B1
Sudoměřice u Bechyně
CZ 96 B2
Sudovec HR 124 A2
Suðureyri IS 190 A2
Sueca E 159 B3
Suelli I 179 C3
Sugenheim D 94 B2
Sugères F 117 B3
Sugny B 91 B4
Suhl D 82 B2
Suhlendorf D 73 B3
Suhopolje HR 124 B3
Suho Polje BIH 125 C5
Şuhut TR 189 A5
Šuica BIH 138 B3
Suippes F 91 B4
Sukošan HR 137 A4
Sükösd H 125 A4
Suków PL 87 B4
Šul'a SK 99 C3
Suldalsosen N 52 A2
Suldrup DK 58 B2
Sulechów PL 75 B4
Sulęcin PL 75 B4
Sulęczyno PL 68 A2
Sulejów PL 87 A3
Süleymanlı TR 186 D2
Sulgen CH 107 B4
Sulibórz PL 75 A4
Sulina RO 17 C8
Sulingen D 72 B1
Suliszewo PL 75 A4
Sulitjelma N 195 C7
Sułkowice PL 99 B3
Süller TR 189 A4
Sully-sur-Loire F 103 B4
Sulmierzyce
Łódzkie PL 86 A3
Wielkopolskie PL 85 A5
Sulmona I 169 A3
Suloğlu TR 186 A1
Sułoszowa PL 87 B3
Sulów PL 85 A5
Sulsdorf D 65 B4
Sultandağı TR 189 A6
Sülüklü TR 187 D7
Suluova TR 23 A8
Sulvik S 54 A3
Sülysáp H 112 B3
Sülz D 93 C4
Sulzbach
Baden-Württemberg
D 94 B1
Baden-Württemberg
D 94 C1
Bayern D 93 B5
Saarland D 92 B3
Sulzbach-Rosenberg
D 95 B3
Sülze D 72 B3
Sulzfeld D 82 B2
Sumartin HR 138 B2
Sumburgh GB 33 B5
Sümeg H 111 C4
Sumiswald CH 106 B2
Šumná CZ 97 C3
Šumperk CZ 97 B4
Šumvald CZ 98 B1
Sunbilla E 144 A2
Sünching D 95 C4
Sund
FIN 51 B7
S 54 A2
Sundborn S 50 B2
Sundby DK 58 B1
Sunde N 46 C2
Sunde bru N 53 B5
Sunderland GB 37 B5
Sundern D 81 A4
Sundhultsbrunn S 62 A2
Sundnäs S 195 D8
Sundom S 196 D5
Sunds DK 59 B2

Sundsfjord N 195 D5
Sundsvall S 200 D3
Sungurlu TR 23 A8
Suni I 178 B2
Sunja HR 124 B2
Sunnansjö S 50 B1
Sunnaryd S 60 B3
Sunndalsøra N 198 C5
Sunne S 49 C5
Sunnemo S 49 C5
Sunnersberg S 55 B4
Suolovuopmio N 192 C7
Suomussalmi FIN 3 D11
Suoyarvi RUS 9 A8
Super Sauze F 132 A2
Supetar HR 138 B2
Supetarska Draga HR 123 C3
Supino I 169 B3
Šuplja Stijena MNE 139 B5
Surahammar S 56 A2
Šurany SK 112 A2
Surazh BY 13 A9
Surbo I 173 B4
Surčin SRB 127 C2
Surgères F 114 B3
Surhuisterveen NL 70 A3
Sùria E 147 C2
Surin F 115 B4
Surka N 48 B2
Surnadalsøra N 198 C5
Sursee CH 106 B3
Surte S 60 B2
Surwold D 71 B4
Sury-le-Comtal F 117 B4
Susa I 119 B4
Šušara SRB 127 C3
Susch CH 107 C5
Susegana I 122 B1
Süsel D 65 B3
Sušice CZ 96 B1
Šušnjevica HR 123 B3
Sussen D 94 C1
Susurluk TR 186 C3
Susz PL 69 B4
Sütçüler TR 189 B5
Sutivan HR 138 B2
Sutjeska SRB 126 B2
Sutri I 168 A2
Sutton GB 44 B3
Sutton Coldfield GB 40 C2
Sutton-in-Ashfield GB 40 B2
Sutton-on-Sea GB 41 B4
Sutton-on-Trent GB 40 B3
Sutton Scotney GB 44 B2
Sutton Valence GB 45 B4
Suvaja BIH 124 C2
Suvereto I 135 B3
Suwałki PL 12 A5
Suze-la-Rousse F 131 A3
Suzzara I 121 C3
Svabensverk S 50 A2
Svalbarð IS 191 A10
Svalöv S 61 D3
Svanabyn S 200 B2
Svanberga S 51 C5
Svaneke DK 67 A4
Svanesund S 54 B2
Svängsta S 63 B2
Svannäs S 195 D9
Svanskog S 54 A3
Svanstein S 196 C6
Svappavaara S 196 B4
Svärdsjö S 50 B2
Svarstad N 53 A5
Svartå S 55 A5
Svärta S 56 B3
Svartå S 55 A4
Svartbyn S 196 C5
Svärtinge S 56 B2
Svartlå S 196 D4
Svartnäs S 50 B3
Svartnes N 195 C5
Svarttjärn S 195 E7
Svatsum N 48 A1
Svätý Jur SK 111 A4
Svätý Peter SK 112 B2
Svedala S 61 D3
Sveg S 199 C11
Sveindal N 52 B3
Sveio N 52 A1
Svejbæk DK 59 B2
Svelgen N 198 D2
Svelvik N 54 A1
Svendborg DK 65 A3
Svene N 53 A5
Svenljunga S 60 B3
Svennevad S 56 A1
Svenstavik S 199 C11
Svenstrup DK 58 B2
Švermov CZ 84 B2
Sveti Ivan Zabno HR 124 B2
Sveti Ivan Zelina HR 124 B2
Sveti Nikole MK 182 B3
Sveti Rok HR 137 A4
Světla nad Sázavou CZ 97 B3
Svetlyy RUS 69 A5
Svetvinčenat HR 122 B2
Švica HR 123 C4
Svidník SK 12 D4
Švihov CZ 96 B1
Svilajnac SRB 127 C3
Svilengrad BG 183 B8
Svindal N 54 A2
Svinhult S 62 A3
Svinna SK 98 C2
Svinninge
DK 61 D1
S 57 A4
Sviritsa RUS 9 B8
Svishtov BG 17 D6
Svislach BY 13 B6
Svit SK 99 B4
Svitavy CZ 97 B4
Svodin SK 112 B2
Svolvær N 194 B5
Svortemyr N 46 A2
Svortland N 52 A1
Svratka CZ 97 B4
Svrčinovec SK 98 B2
Svullrya N 49 B4
Svyetlahorsk BY 13 B8
Swadlincote GB 40 C2
Swaffham GB 41 C4
Swanage GB 43 B5
Swanley GB 45 B4
Swanlinbar IRL 26 B3
Swansea GB 39 C3
Swarzędz PL 76 B2
Swatragh GB 27 B4
Świątki PL 69 B5
Świdnica
Dolnośląskie PL 85 B4
Lubuskie PL 84 A3
Świdnik PL 12 C5
Świdwin PL 67 C4
Świebodzice PL 85 B4
Świebodzin PL 75 B4
Świecie PL 76 A3
Świedziebnia PL 77 A4
Świeradów Zdrój PL 84 B3
Świerki PL 85 B4
Swierzawa PL 85 A3
Swierzno PL 67 C3
Święta PL 74 A3
Swieta Anna PL 86 B3
Świętno PL 75 B5
Swifterbant NL 70 B2
Swindon GB 44 B2
Swineshead GB 41 C3
Swinford IRL 26 C2
Świnoujście PL 66 C3
Swinton GB 35 C5
Swobnica PL 74 A3
Swords IRL 30 A2
Swornegacie PL 68 B2
Sya S 56 B1
Syasstroy RUS 9 B8
Sycewice PL 68 A1
Sychevka RUS 9 E9
Syców PL 86 A1
Sycowice PL 75 B4
Sydnes N 52 A1
Syfteland N 46 B2
Syke D 72 B1
Sykkylven N 198 C3
Sylling N 48 C2
Sylte N 198 C4
Symbister GB 33 A5
Symington GB 36 A3
Symonds Yat GB 39 C4
Sypniewo
Kujawsko-Pomorskie PL 76 A2
Wielkopolskie PL 68 B1
Syserum S 62 A4
Sysslebäck S 49 B4
Syväjärvi FIN 197 B8
Szabadbattyán H 112 B2
Szabadegyháza H 112 B2
Szabadszállás H 112 C3
Szadek PL 86 A2
Szajol H 113 B4
Szakály H 112 C2
Szakcs H 112 C2
Szakmár H 112 C3
Szalánta H 125 B4
Szałas PL 87 A4
Szalkszentmárton H 112 C3
Szalonna H 99 C4
Szamocin PL 76 A2
Szamotuły PL 75 B5
Szany H 111 B4
Szarvas H 113 C4
Szarvaskő H 113 B4
Szászvár H 125 A4
Százhalombatta H 112 B2
Szczawa PL 99 B4
Szczawnica PL 99 B4
Szczecin PL 74 A3
Szczecinek PL 68 B1
Szczekociny PL 87 B3
Szczerców PL 86 A3
Szczucin PL 87 B5
Szczuczarz PL 75 A5
Szczuki PL 77 B5
Szczurowa PL 87 B4
Szczyrk PL 99 B3
Szczytna PL 85 B4
Szczytno PL 77 A5
Szczyty PL 86 A2
Szécsény H 112 A3
Szederkény H 125 B4
Szedres H 112 C2
Szeged H 126 A2
Szeghalom H 113 B5
Szegvár H 113 C4
Székesfehérvár H 112 B2
Székkutas H 113 C4
Szekszárd H 125 A4
Szemplino Czarne PL 77 A5
Szemud PL 68 A3
Szendehely H 112 B3
Szendrö H 99 C4
Szentendre H 112 B3
Szentes H 113 C4
Szentgotthárd H 111 C3
Szentlászló H 125 A3
Szentlörinc H 125 A3
Szentmártonkáta H 113 B3
Szenyér H 111 C4
Szeremle H 125 A4
Szerencs H 113 A5
Szerep H 113 B5
Szigetszentmiklós H 112 B3
Szigetvár H 125 A3
Szikáncs H 126 A2
Szikszó H 113 A4
Szil H 111 B4
Szilvásvárad H 113 A4
Szklarska Poreba PL 84 B3
Szlichtyngowa PL 85 A4
Szob H 112 B2
Szolnok H 113 B4
Szombathely H 111 B3
Szorosad H 112 C2
Szpetal Graniczny PL 77 B4
Szprotawa PL 84 A3
Szreńsk PL 77 A5
Sztum PL 69 B4
Sztutowo PL 69 A4
Szubin PL 76 A2
Szücsi H 113 B3
Szulmierz PL 77 B5
Szulok H 124 A3
Szumanie PL 77 B4
Szwecja PL 75 A5
Szydłów
Łódzkie PL 86 A3
Świętokrzyskie PL 87 B5
Szydłowiec PL 87 A4
Szydlowo PL 77 A5
Szydłowo PL 75 A5
Szymanów PL 77 B5
Szynkielów PL 86 A2

T

Taastrup DK 61 D2
Tab H 112 C2
Tabanera la Luenga E 151 A3
Tabaqueros E 158 B2
Tábara E 149 A4
Tabenera de Cerrato E 142 B2
Taberg S 62 A2
Tabernas E 164 B2
Tabiano Bagni I 120 C3
Taboada E 140 B3
Taboadela E 140 B3
Tábor CZ 96 B2
Táborfalva H 112 B3
Taborište HR 124 B2
Tábua P 148 B1
Tabuaco P 148 A2
Tabuenca E 152 A2
Tabuyo del Monte E 141 B4
Täby S 57 A4
Tác H 112 B2
Tachov CZ 95 B4
Tadcaster GB 40 B2
Tadley GB 44 B2
Tafalla E 144 B2
Tafjord N 198 C4
Taganheira P 160 B1
Tågarp S 61 D2
Tággia I 133 B3
Tagliacozzo I 169 A3
Táglio di Po I 121 B5
Tagnon F 91 B4
Tahal E 164 B2
Tahitótfalu H 112 B3
Tahtaköprü TR 187 C4
Tailfingen D 107 A4
Taillis F 101 A4
Tain GB 32 D2
Tain-l'Hermitage F 117 B4
Taipadas P 154 C2
Taivalkoski FIN 197 D11
Takene S 55 A4
Takovo SRB 127 C2
Taksony H 112 B3
Tal E 140 B2
Talachyn BY 13 A8
Talamello I 135 B5
Talamone I 168 A1
Talant F 105 B3
Talarrubias E 156 A2
Talaván E 155 B4
Talavera de la Reina E 150 C3
Talavera la Real E 155 C4
Talayuela E 150 C2
Talayuelas E 159 B2
Talgarth GB 39 C3
Talgje N 52 A1
Talhadas P 148 B1
Táliga E 155 C3
Talizat F 116 B3
Tálknafjörður IS 190 B2
Talla I 135 B4
Talladale GB 31 B3
Tallaght IRL 30 A2
Tallard F 132 A2
Tällberg S 50 B1
Tallberg S 196 C5
Tallinn EST 8 C4
Talloires F 118 B3
Tallow IRL 29 B3
Tallsjö S 200 B4
Tallvik S 196 C5
Talmay F 105 B4
Talmont-St Hilaire F 114 B2
Talmont-sur-Gironde F 114 C3
Talne UA 13 D9
Talsano I 173 B3
Talsi LV 8 D3
Talvik N 192 B6
Talybont GB 39 B3
Tal-Y-Llyn GB 38 B3
Tamajón E 151 B4
Tamame E 149 A4
Tamames E 149 B3
Tamarit de Mar E 147 C2
Tamarite de Litera E 145 C4
Tamariu E 147 C4
Tamási H 112 C2
Tambach-Dietharz D 82 B2
Tameza E 141 A4
Tammisaari FIN 8 B3
Tampere FIN 8 B3
Tamsweg A 109 B4
Tamurejo E 156 B3
Tamworth GB 40 C2
Tana bru N 193 B12
Tañabueyes E 143 B3
Tanakajd H 111 B3
Tananger N 52 B1
Tanaunella I 178 B3
Tancarville F 89 A4
Tandsjöborg S 199 D11
Tånga S 61 C2
Tangelic H 112 C2
Tangen N 48 B3
Tangerhütte D 73 B4
Tangermünde D 73 B4
Tanhua FIN 197 B10
Taninges F 118 A3
Tankavaara FIN 197 A10
Tann D 82 B2
Tanna D 83 B3
Tannadice GB 35 B5
Tannåker S 60 C3
Tännäs S 199 C9
Tannay
Ardennes F 91 B4
Nièvre F 104 B2
Tannenbergsthal D 83 B4
Tännesberg D 95 B4
Tannheim A 108 B1
Tannila FIN 197 D8
Tanowo PL 74 A3
Tanum S 54 B2
Tanumshede S 54 B2
Tanus F 130 A1
Tanvald CZ 84 B3
Taormina I 177 B4
Tapa EST 8 C4
Tapfheim D 94 C2
Tapia de Casariego E 141 A4
Tapio F 146 A2
Tápióbicske H 112 B3
Tápiógyörgye H 113 B3
Tápióság H 112 B3
Tápiószecsö H 112 B3
Tápiószele H 113 B3
Tápiószentmárton H 113 B3
Tapolca H 111 C4
Tapolcafö H 111 B4
Tar HR 122 B2
Tarabo S 60 B2
Taradell E 147 C3
Taraklı TR 187 B5
Taramundi E 141 A3
Tarancón E 151 B4
Táranto I 173 B3
Tarare F 117 B4
Tarascon F 131 B3
Tarascon-sur-Ariège F 146 B2
Tarashcha UA 13 D9
Tarazona E 144 C2
Tarazona de la Mancha E 158 B2
Tarbena E 159 C3
Tarbert
GB 34 C2
IRL 29 B2
Tarbes F 145 A4
Tarbet GB 34 B3
Tarbolton GB 36 A2
Tarcento I 122 A2
Tarčin BIH 139 B4
Tarczyn PL 77 C5
Tardajos E 143 B3
Tardelcuende E 151 A5
Tardets-Sorholus F 144 A3
Tardienta E 145 C3
Tärendö S 196 B5
Targon F 128 B2
Târgovişte RO 17 C6
Târgu-Jiu RO 17 C5
Târgu Mureş RO 17 B6
Târgu Ocna RO 17 B7
Târgu Secuiesc RO 17 C7
Tarifa E 162 B2
Tariquejas E 161 B2
Tarján H 112 B2
Tárkany H 112 B2
Tarland GB 33 D4
Tarłów PL 87 A5
Tarm DK 59 C1
Tarmstedt D 72 A2
Tärnaby S 195 E6
Tarnalelesz H 113 A4
Tarnaörs H 113 B4
Târnăveni RO 17 B6
Tårnet N 193 C14
Tarnobrzeg PL 87 B5
Tarnos F 128 C1
Tarnów
Lubuskie PL 75 B3
Małopolskie PL 87 B4
Tarnowo Podgórne PL 75 B5
Tarnowskie Góry PL 86 B2
Tärnsjö S 51 B3
Tårnvik N 194 C6
Tarouca P 148 A2
Tarp D 64 B2
Tarquínia I 168 A1
Tarquínia Lido I 168 A1
Tarragona E 147 C2
Tårrajaur S 196 C2
Tàrrega E 147 C2
Tarrenz A 108 B1
Tårs
Nordjyllands DK 58 A3
Storstrøms DK 65 B4
Tarsia I 174 B2
Tarsus TR 23 C8
Tartas F 128 C2
Tartu EST 8 C5
Tarves GB 33 D4
Tarvísio I 109 C4
Taşağıl TR 189 C6
Täsch CH 119 A4
Taşköprü TR 23 A8
Tasov CZ 97 B4
Tasovčići BIH 139 B3
Taşucuo TR 23 C7
Tát H 112 B2
Tata H 112 B2
Tatabánya H 112 B2
Tataháza H 126 A1
Tatarbunary UA 17 C8
Tatárszentgyörgy H 112 B3
Tatranská-Lomnica SK 99 B4
Tau N 52 A1
Tauberbischofsheim D 94 B1
Taucha D 83 A4
Taufkirchen D 95 C4
Taufkirchen an der Pram A 96 C1
Taulé F 100 A2
Taulignan F 131 A3
Taulov DK 59 C2
Taunton GB 43 A3
Taunusstein D 81 B4
Tauragė LT 12 A5
Taurianova I 175 C2
Taurisano I 173 C4
Tauste E 144 C2
Tauves F 116 B2
Tavankut SRB 126 A1
Tavannes CH 106 B2
Tavarnelle val di Pesa I 135 B4
Tavas TR 188 B4
Tavaux F 105 B4
Tävelsås S 62 B2
Taverna I 175 B2
Taverne CH 120 A1
Tavernelle I 135 B5
Tavernes de la Valldigna E 159 B3
Tavérnola Bergamasca I 120 B3
Taverny F 90 B2
Tavescan E 146 B2
Taviano I 173 C4
Tavira P 160 B2
Tavistock GB 42 B2
Tavşanlı TR 187 C4
Tayinloan GB 34 C2
Taynuilt GB 34 B2
Tayport GB 35 B5
Tázlár H 112 C3
Tazones E 142 A1
Tczew PL 69 A3
Tczów PL 87 A5
Teangue GB 31 B3
Teano I 170 B2
Teba E 162 B3
Tebay GB 37 B4
Techendorf A 109 C4
Tecklenburg D 71 B4
Tecko-matorp S 61 D3
Tecuci RO 17 C7
Tefenni TR 189 B4
Tegelsmora S 51 B4
Tegernsee D 108 B2
Teggiano I 172 B1
Tegoleto I 135 B4
Teichel D 82 B3
Teignmouth GB 43 B3
Teillay F 101 B4
Teillet F 130 B1
Teisendorf D 109 B3
Teistungen D 82 A2
Teixeiro E 140 A2
Tejada de Tiétar E 150 B2
Tejado E 152 A1
Tejares E 150 B2
Tejn DK 67 A3
Teke TR 187 A4
Tekirdağ TR 186 B2
Tekovské-Lužany SK 112 A2
Telavåg N 46 B1
Telč CZ 97 B3
Telese Terme I 170 B2
Telford GB 38 B4
Telfs A 108 B2
Telgárt SK 99 C4
Telgte D 71 C4
Tellingstedt D 64 B2
Telšiai LT 8 E3
Telti I 178 B3
Teltow D 74 B2
Tembleque E 157 A4
Temelin CZ 96 B2
Temerin SRB 126 B1
Temiño E 143 B3
Témpio Pausânia I 178 B3
Templederry IRL 28 B3
Templemore IRL 28 B4
Temple Sowerby GB 37 B4
Templin D 74 A2
Temse B 79 A4
Tenay F 118 B2
Ten Boer NL 71 A3
Tenbury Wells GB 39 B4
Tenby GB 39 C2
Tence F 117 B4
Tende F 133 A3
Tenhult S 62 A2
Tenja HR 125 B4
Tenneville B 92 A1
Tennevoll N 194 B8
Tensta S 51 B4
Tenterden GB 45 B4
Teo E 140 B2
Teora I 172 B1
Tepasto FIN 196 B7
Tepelenë AL 182 C2
Teplá CZ 95 B4
Teplice CZ 84 B1
Teplička nad Váhom SK 98 B2
Tepsa FIN 197 B8
Tera E 143 C4
Téramo I 169 A3
Ter Apel NL 71 B4
Terborg NL 71 C3
Terchová SK 99 B3
Terebovlya UA 13 D6
Teremia Mare RO 126 B2
Terena P 155 C3
Teresa de Cofrentes E 159 B2
Terešov CZ 96 B1
Terezín CZ 84 B2
Terezino Polje HR 124 B3
Tergnier F 90 B3
Teriberka RUS 3 B14
Terlizzi I 171 B4
Termas de Monfortinho P 155 A4
Terme di Súio I 169 B3
Terme di Valdieri I 133 A3
Termens E 145 C4
Termes F 116 C3
Términi Imerese I 176 B2
Terminillo I 169 A2
Térmoli I 170 B3
Termonfeckin IRL 27 C4
Ternberg A 110 B1
Terndrup DK 58 B3
Terneuzen NL 79 A3
Terni I 168 A2
Ternitz A 111 B3
Ternopil UA 13 D6
Terpni GR 183 C5
Terracina I 169 B3
Terråk N 195 E3
Terralba I 179 C2
Terranova di Pollino I 174 B2
Terranova di Sibari I 174 B2
Terras do Bouro P 148 A1
Terrasini I 176 A2
Terrassa E 147 C3
Terrasson-la-Villedieu F 129 A4
Terrazos E 143 B3
Terriente E 152 B2
Terrugem P 155 C3
Terteniá I 179 C3
Teruel E 152 B2
Tervola FIN 196 C7
Tervuren B 79 B4
Terzaga E 152 B2
Tešanj BIH 125 C3
Tesáske-Mlyňany SK 98 C2
Teslić BIH 125 C3
Tessin D 66 B1

Tessy-sur-Vire F . . . 88 B2
Tét H 111 B4
Tetbury GB 43 A4
Teterchen F 92 B2
Teterow D 65 C5
Teteven BG 17 D6
Tetiyev UA 13 D8
Tetovo MK 182 A2
Tettau D 82 B3
Tettnang D 107 B4
Teublitz D 95 B4
Teuchern D 83 A4
Teulada
E 159 C4
I 179 D2
Teupitz D 74 B2
Teurajärvi S 196 C5
Teutschenthal D . . . 83 A3
Tevel H 112 C2
Teviothead GB 36 A4
Tewkesbury GB 39 C4
Thale D 82 A3
Thalfang D 92 B2
Thalgau A 109 B4
Thalkirch CH 107 C4
Thalmässing D 95 B3
Thalwil CH 107 B3
Thame GB 44 B3
Thann F 106 B2
Thannhausen D 94 C2
Thaon-les-Vosges
F 105 A5
Tharandt D 83 B5
Tharsis E 161 B2
Thasos GR 183 C6
Thatcham GB 44 B2
Thaxted GB 45 B4
Thayngen CH 107 B3
Theale GB 44 B2
The Barony GB 33 B3
Thebes = Thiva GR 185 A4
Theding-hausen D . 72 B2
Theessen D 73 B5
The Hague = 's-Gravenhage NL . . . 70 B1
Themar D 82 B2
The Mumbles GB . . . 39 C3
Thénezay F 102 C1
Thenon F 129 A4
Therouanne F 78 B2
Thessaloniki = Salonica
GR 182 C4
Thetford GB 45 A4
Theux B 80 B1
Thézar-les-Corbières
F 146 A3
Thèze F 145 A3
Thiberville F 89 A4
Thibie F 91 C4
Thiéblemont-Farémont
F 91 C4
Thiendorf D 84 A1
Thiene I 121 B4
Thierrens CH 106 C1
Thiers F 117 B3
Thiesi I 178 B2
Thiessow D 66 B2
Thiezac F 116 B2
Þingeyri IS 190 B2
Þingvellir IS 190 C4
Thionville F 92 B2
Thira GR 185 C6
Thiron-Gardais F . . . 89 B4
Thirsk GB 37 B5
Thisted DK 58 B1
Thiva = Thebes GR 185 A4
Thivars F 90 C1
Thiviers F 115 C4
Thizy F 117 A4
Tholen NL 79 A4
Tholey D 92 B3
Thomas Street IRL . 28 A3
Thomastown IRL . . . 30 B1
Thônes F 118 B3
Thonnance-les-Joinville
F 91 C5
Thonon-les-Bains
F 118 A3
Thorame-Basse F . 132 A2
Thorame-Haute F . 132 A2
Thorens-Glières F . 118 A3
Thorigny-sur-Oreuse
F 91 C3
Thörl A 110 B2
Þorlákshöfn IS . . . 190 D4
Thornaby on Tees
GB 37 B5
Thornbury GB 43 A4
Thorne GB 40 B3
Thornhill
Dumfries & Galloway
GB 36 A3
Stirling GB 35 B3
Thornthwaite GB . . . 36 B3
Thornton-le-Dale
GB 40 A3
Þórshöfn IS 191 A10
Thouarcé F 102 B1
Thouars F 102 C1
Thrapston GB 44 A3
Threlkeld GB 36 B3
Thrumster GB 32 C3
Thueyts F 117 C4
Thuin B 79 B4
Thuir F 146 B3
Thumau D 95 A3
Thun CH 106 C2
Thuret F 116 B3
Thurey F 105 C4
Thüringen A 107 B4
Thurins F 117 B4
Thürkow D 65 C5
Thurles IRL 29 B4
Thurmaston GB 40 C2
Thurø By DK 65 A3
Thursby GB 36 B3
Thurso GB 32 C3
Thury-Harcourt F . . 89 B3
Thusis CH 107 C4
Thyborøn DK 58 B1
Þykkvibær IS 190 D5
Thyregod DK 59 C2
Tibi E 159 C3
Tibro S 55 B5
Tidaholm S 55 B4
Tidan S 55 B5
Tidersrum S 62 A3
Tiedra E 150 A2
Tiefenbach D 95 B4
Tiefencastel CH . . . 107 C4
Tiefenort D 82 B2
Tiefensee D 74 B2
Tiel NL 79 A5
Tielmes E 151 B4
Tielt B 78 A3
Tienen B 79 B4
Tiengen D 106 B3
Tiercé F 102 B1
Tierga E 152 A2
Tiermas E 144 B2
Tierp S 51 B4
Tierrantona E 145 B4
Tighina MD 17 B8
Tighnabruaich GB . . 34 C2
Tignes F 119 B3
Tigy F 103 B4
Tihany H 112 C1
Tijnje NL 70 A2
Tijola E 164 B2
Tikhvin RUS 9 C8
Tilburg NL 79 A5
Til Châtel F 105 B4
Tilh F 128 C2
Tillac F 145 A4
Tillberga S 56 A2
Tille F 90 B2
Tillicoultry GB 35 B4
Tilloy Bellay F 91 B4
Tilly F 115 B5
Tilly-sur-Seulles F . . 88 A3
Tim DK 59 B1
Timau I 109 C4
Timbaki GR 185 D5
Timi CY 181 B1
Timişoara RO 126 B3
Timmele S 60 B3
Timmendorfer Strand
D 65 C3
Timmernabben S . . . 62 B4
Timmersdala S 55 B4
Timoleague IRL 29 C3
Timolin IRL 30 B2
Timrå S 200 D3
Timsfors S 61 C3
Timsgearraidh GB . . 31 A1
Tinajas E 152 B1
Tinalhas P 155 B3
Tinchebray F 88 B3
Tincques F 78 B2
Tineo E 141 A4
Tinglev DK 64 B2
Tingsryd S 63 B2
Tingstäde S 57 C4
Tingvoll N 198 C5
Tinlot B 79 B5
Tinnoset N 53 A5
Tinos GR 185 B6
Tintagel GB 42 B2
Tinténiac F 101 A4
Tintern GB 39 C4
Tintigny B 92 B1
Tione di Trento I . . 121 A3
Tipperary IRL 29 B3
Tiptree GB 45 B4
Tirana = Tiranë AL . 182 B1
Tiranë= Tirana AL . 182 B1
Tirano I 120 A3
Tiraspol MD 17 B8
Tire TR 188 A2
Tires I 108 C2
Tiriez E 158 C1
Tirig E 153 B4
Tiriolo I 175 C2
Tirnavos GR 182 D4
Tirrénia I 134 B3
Tirschenreuth D . . . 95 B4
Tirstrup DK 59 B3
Tirteafuera E 157 B3
Tisno HR 137 B4
Tišnov CZ 97 B4
Tisovec SK 99 C3
Tisselskog S 54 B3
Tistedal N 54 A2
Tistrup DK 59 C1
Tisvildeleje DK 61 C2
Tiszaalpár H 113 C3
Tiszabö H 113 B4
Tiszacsége H 113 B5
Tiszadorogma H . . . 113 B4
Tiszaföldvár H 113 C4
Tiszafüred H 113 B4
Tiszajenö H 113 B4
Tiszakécske H 113 C4
Tiszakeszi H 113 B4
Tiszakürt H 113 C4
Tiszalök H 113 A5
Tiszalúc H 113 A5
Tiszanána H 113 B4
Tiszaörs H 113 B4
Tiszaroff H 113 B4
Tiszasüly H 113 B4
Tiszasziget H 126 A2
Tiszaszőlős H 113 B4
Tiszaújváros H 113 B5
Tiszavasvári H 113 B5
Titaguas E 159 B2
Titel SRB 126 B2
Titisee-Neustadt D 106 B3
Tito I 172 B1
Titova Korenica
HR 123 C4
Titran N 198 B5
Tittling D 96 C1
Tittmoning D 109 A3
Titz D 80 A2
Tiurajärvi FIN 196 B7
Tived S 55 B5
Tiverton GB 43 B3
Tivisa E 153 A4
Tívoli I 168 B2
Tizsadob H 113 A5
Tjällmo S 56 B1
Tjåmotis S 195 D9
Tjæreborg DK 59 C1
Tjautjas S 196 B3
Tjøme N 54 A1
Tjong N 195 D4
Tjonnefoss N 53 B4
Tjörn IS 190 B5
Tjörnarp S 61 D3
Tjøtta N 195 E3
Tkon HR 137 B4
Tleń PL 68 B3
Tlmače SK 98 C2
Tłuchowo PL 77 B4
Tlumačov CZ 98 B1
Tóalmas H 112 B3
Toano I 134 A3
Toba D 82 A2
Tobarra E 158 C2
Tobercurry IRL 26 B2
Tobermore GB 27 B4
Tobermory GB 34 B1
Toberonochy GB . . . 34 B2
Tobha Mor GB 31 B1
Tobo S 51 B4
Tocane-St Apre F . 129 A3
Tocha P 148 B1
Tocina E 162 A2
Töcksfors S 54 A2
Tocón E 163 A4
Todal N 198 C5
Todi I 136 C1
Todmorden GB 40 B1
Todorici BIH 138 A3
Todtmoos D 106 B3
Todtnau D 106 B2
Toén E 140 B3
Tofta
Gotland S 57 C4
Skaraborg S 55 B4
Toftbyn S 50 B2
Tofte N 54 A1
Töftedal S 54 B2
Tofterup DK 59 C1
Toftlund DK 59 C2
Tófű H 125 A4
Tohmo FIN 197 C10
Tokaj H 113 A5
Tokarnia PL 87 B4
Tokary PL 76 C3
Tokod H 112 B2
Tököl H 112 B2
Tolastadh bho Thuath
GB 31 A2
Toledo E 151 C3
Tolentino I 136 B2
Tolfa I 168 A1
Tolg S 62 A2
Tolga N 199 C8
Tolkmicko PL 69 A4
Tollarp S 61 D3
Tollered S 60 B2
Tølløse DK 61 D1
Tolmachevo RUS . . . 9 C6
Tolmezzo I 122 A2
Tolmin SLO 122 A2
Tolna H 112 C2
Tolnanémedi H 112 C2
Tolob GB 33 B5
Tolosa
E 144 A1
P 155 B3
Tolox E 162 B3
Tolpuddle GB 43 B4
Tolva
E 145 B4
FIN 197 C11
Tolve I 172 B2
Tomar P 154 B2
Tomaševac SRB . . 126 B2
Tomašica BIH 124 C2
Tomášikovo SK 111 A4
Tomašouka BY 13 C5
Tomášovce SK 99 C3
Tomaszów Mazowiecki
PL 87 A4
Tomatin GB 32 D3
Tombeboeuf F 129 B3
Tomdoun GB 32 D1
Tomelilla S 66 A2
Tomellosa E 151 B5
Tomelloso E 157 A4
Tomiño E 140 C2
Tomintoul GB 32 D3
Tomislavgrad BIH . 138 B3
Tomisław PL 84 A3
Tomisławice PL 76 B3
Tomnavoulin GB . . . 32 D3
Tompa H 126 A1
Tompaládony H 111 B3
Tomra N 198 C3
Tomter N 54 A1
Tona E 147 C3
Tonara I 179 B3
Tonbridge GB 45 B4
Tondela P 148 B1
Tønder DK 64 B1
Tongeren B 79 B5
Tongue GB 32 C2
Tönisvorst D 80 A2
Tønjum N 47 A4
Tonkopuro FIN . . 197 C11
Tonnay-Boutonne
F 114 C3
Tonnay-Charente
F 114 C3
Tonneins F 129 B3
Tonnerre F 104 B2
Tonnes N 195 D4
Tönning D 64 B1
Tonsåsen N 47 B6
Tønsberg N 54 A1
Tonstad N 52 B2
Toomyvara IRL 28 B3
Toormore IRL 29 C2
Topares E 164 B2
Topas E 150 A2
Toplița RO 17 B6
Topola SRB 127 C2
Topolčani MK 182 B3
Topol'čany SK 98 C2
Topoľčianky SK . . . 98 C2
Topolje HR 124 B2
Topólka PL 76 B3
Topoľníky SK 111 B4
Topolovățu Mare
RO 126 B3
Toponár H 125 A3
Toporów PL 75 B4
Topsham GB 43 B3
Topusko HR 124 B1
Toques E 140 B3
Torà E 147 C2
Toral de los Guzmanes
E 142 B1
Toral de los Vados
E 141 B4
Torbalı TR 188 A2
Torbjörntorp S 55 B4
Torbole I 121 B3
Torchiarolo I 173 B4
Torcross GB 43 B3
Torcy-le-Petit F 89 A5
Torda SRB 126 B2
Tørdal N 53 A4
Tordehumos E 142 C1
Tordera E 147 C3
Tordesillas E 150 A2
Tordesilos E 152 B2
Töre S 196 D5
Töreboda S 55 B5
Toreby DK 65 B4
Torekov S 61 C2
Torella dei Lombardi
I 170 C3
Torellò E 147 B3
Toreno E 141 B4
Torfou F 114 A2
Torgau D 83 A5
Torgelow D 74 A3
Torgueda P 148 A2
Torhamn S 63 B3
Torhop N 193 B11
Torhout B 78 A3
Torigni-sur-Vire F . . 88 A3
Torija E 151 B4
Toril E 152 B2
Torino = Turin I . . . 119 B4
Toritto I 171 C4
Torkovichi RUS 9 C7
Torla E 145 B3
Tormac RO 126 B3
Törmänen FIN . . . 193 D11
Tormestorp S 61 C3
Tórmini I 121 B3
Tornada P 154 B1
Tornal'a SK 99 C4
Tornavacas E 150 B2
Tornby DK 58 A2
Tornesch D 72 A2
Torness GB 32 D2
Torniella I 135 B4
Tornimparte I 169 A3
Torning DK 59 B2
Tornio FIN 196 D7
Tornjoš SRB 126 B1
Tornos E 152 B2
Toro E 150 A2
Törökszentmiklós
H 113 B4
Toropets RUS 9 D7
Torpa S 61 C3
Torpè I 178 B3
Torphins GB 33 D4
Torpo N 47 B5
Torpoint GB 42 B2
Torpsbruk S 62 A2
Torquay GB 43 B3
Torquemada E 142 B2
Torralba de Burgo
E 151 A5
Torralba de Calatrava
E 157 A4
Torrão P 154 C2
Torre Annunziata I . 170 C2
Torreblacos E 143 C4
Torreblanca E 153 B4
Torreblascopedro
E 157 B4
Torrecaballeros E . 151 A3
Torrecampo E 156 B3
Torre Canne I 173 B3
Torre Cardela E . . . 163 A4
Torrecilla E 152 B1
Torrecilla de la Jara
E 156 A3
Torrecilla de la Orden
E 150 A2
Torrecilla del Pinar
E 151 A3
Torrecilla en Cameros
E 143 B4
Torrecillas de la Tiesa
E 156 A2
Torre das Vargens
P 154 B3
Torre de Coelheiros
P 154 C3
Torre de Dom Chama
P 149 A2
Torre de Juan Abad
E 157 B4
Torre de la Higuera
E 161 B3
Torre del Bierzo E . 141 B4
Torre del Burgo E . 151 B4
Torre del Campo E 163 A4
Torre del Greco I . . 170 C2
Torre del Lago Puccini
I 134 B3
Torre dell'Orso I . . 173 B4
Torre del Mar E . . . 163 B3
Torredembarra E . . 147 C2
Torre de Miguel
Sesmero E 155 C4
Torre de Moncorvo
P 149 A2
Torre de Santa Maria
E 156 A1
Torredonjimeno E . 163 A4
Torre do Terranho
P 148 B2
Torre Faro I 177 A4
Torregrosa E 147 C1
Torreira P 148 B1
Torrejoncillo E 155 B4
Torrejón de Ardoz
E 151 B4
Torrejón de la Calzada
E 151 B4
Torrejón del Rey E 151 B4
Torrejon el Rubio
E 156 A1
Torrelaguna E 151 B4
Torrelapaja E 152 A2
Torre la Ribera E . . 145 B4
Torrelavega E 142 A2
Torrelobatón E 150 A2
Torrelodones E . . . 151 B4
Torre los Negros E 152 B2
Torremaggiore I . . . 171 B3
Torremanzanas E . 159 C3
Torremayor E 155 C4
Torremezzo di Falconara
I 174 B2
Torremocha E 156 A1
Torremolinos E . . . 163 B3
Torrenieri I 135 B4
Torrenostra E 153 B4
Torrenova I 168 B2
Torrent E 159 B3
Torrente de Cinca
E 153 A4
Torrenueva
Ciudad Real E 157 B4
Granada E 163 B4
Torreorgaz E 155 B4
Torre Orsáia I 172 B1
Torre-Pacheco E . . 165 B4
Torre Péllice I 119 C4
Torreperogil E 157 B4
Torres E 163 A4
Torresandino E . . . 143 C3
Torre Santa Susanna
I 173 B3
Torres-Cabrera E . . 163 A3
Torres de la Alameda
E 151 B4
Torres Novas P . . . 154 B2
Torres Vedras P . . . 154 B1
Torrevieja E 165 B4
Torricella I 173 B3
Torri del Benaco I . 121 B3
Torridon GB 31 B3
Torriglia I 134 A2
Torrijos E 151 C3
Tørring DK 59 C2
Torrita di Siena I . . 135 B4
Torroal P 154 C2
Torroella de Montgr ì
E 147 B4
Torrox E 163 B4
Torrskog S 54 A3
Torsåker S 50 B3
Torsang S 50 B2
Torsås S 63 B4
Torsby S 49 B4
Torsetra N 48 B2
Torshälla S 56 A2
Tórshavn FO 4 A3
Torslanda S 60 B1
Torsminde DK 59 B1
Torsnes N 46 B3
Törtel H 113 B3
Tórtoles E 150 B2
Tórtoles de Esgueva
E 142 C2
Tortol ì I 179 C3
Tortona I 120 C1
Tórtora I 174 B1
Tortoreto Lido I . . . 136 C2
Tortorici I 177 A3
Tortosa E 153 B4
Tortosendo P 148 B2
Tortuera E 152 B2
Tortuero E 151 B4
Toruń PL 76 A3
Torup S 60 C3
Tor Vaiánica I 168 B2
Torver GB 36 B3
Tørvikbygde N 46 B3
Torviscón E 163 B4
Torzhok RUS 9 D9
Torzym PL 75 B4
Tosbotn N 195 E3
Toscelanor-Maderno
I 121 B3
Tosno RUS 9 C7
Tossa de Mar E . . . 147 C3
Tossåsen S 199 C10
Tosse F 128 C1
Tösse S 54 B3
Tossicía I 169 A3
Tostedt D 72 A2
Tosya TR 23 A8
Tószeg H 113 B4
Toszek PL 86 B2
Totana E 165 B3
Totebo S 62 A4
Tôtes F 89 A5
Tótkomlós H 113 C4
Totland N 198 D2
Tøtlandsvik N 52 A2
Totnes GB 43 B3
Tótszerdahely H . . 124 A2
Tøttdal N 199 A8
Totton GB 44 C2
Touça P 149 A2
Toucy F 104 B2
Toul F 92 C1
Toulon F 132 B1
Toulon-sur-Allier F 104 C2
Toulon-sur-Arroux
F 104 C3
Toulouse F 129 C4
Tourcoing F 78 B3
Tour de la Parata F 180 B1
Tourlaville F 88 A2
Tournai B 78 B3
Tournan-en-Brie F . . 90 C2
Tournay F 145 A4
Tournon-d'Agenais
F 129 B3
Tournon-St Martin
F 115 B4
Tournon-sur-Rhône
F 117 B4
Tournus F 105 C3
Touro
E 140 B2
P 148 B2
Tourouvre F 89 B4
Tourriers F 115 C4
Tours F 102 B2
Tourteron F 91 B4
Tourves F 132 B1
Toury F 103 A3
Touvedo P 148 A1
Touvois F 114 B2
Toužim CZ 83 B4
Tovačov CZ 98 B1
Tovariševo SRB . . . 126 B1
Tovarnik HR 125 B5
Tovdal N 53 B4
Towcester GB 44 A3
Town Yetholm GB . . 35 C5
Tråastølen N 47 B4
Trabada E 141 A3
Trabadelo E 141 B4
Trabanca E 149 A3
Trabazos E 149 A3
Traben-Trarbach D . 92 B3
Trabia I 176 B2
Tradate I 120 B1
Trädet S 60 B3
Trafaria P 154 C1
Tragacete E 152 B2
Tragwein A 96 C2
Traiguera E 153 B4
Trainel F 91 C3
Traisen A 110 A2
Traismauer A 97 C3
Traitsching D 95 B4
Trákhonas CY 181 A2
Tralee IRL 29 B2
Tramacastilla de Tena
E 145 B3
Tramagal P 154 B2
Tramariglio I 178 B2
Tramatza I 179 B2
Tramelan CH 106 B2
Tramonti di Sopra
I 122 A1
Tramore IRL 30 B1

Trampot F 92 C1
Trana I 119 B4
Tranås S 55 B5
Tranbjerg DK 59 B3
Tranby N 54 A1
Trancoso P 148 B2
Tranebjerg DK 59 C3
Tranekær DK 65 B3
Tranemo S 60 B3
Tranent GB 35 C5
Tranevåg N 52 B2
Trängslet S 49 A5
Tranhult S 60 B3
Trani I 171 B4
Trans-en-Provence F 132 B2
Transtrand S 49 A5
Tranum DK 58 A2
Tranvik S 57 A4
Trápani I 176 A1
Trappes F 90 C2
Traryd S 61 C3
Trasacco I 169 B3
Trasierra E 156 B1
Träslövsläge S 60 B2
Trasmiras E 140 B3
Traspinedo E 150 A3
Trate SLO 110 C2
Trauchgau D 108 B1
Traun A 110 A1
Traunreut D 109 B3
Traunstein D 109 B3
Traunwalchen D 109 B3
Trävad S 55 B4
Travemünde D 65 C3
Traversétolo I 120 C3
Travnik
BIH 139 A3
SLO 123 B3
Travo
F 180 B2
I 120 C2
Trawsfynydd GB 38 B3
Trbovlje SLO 123 A4
Trbušani SRB 127 D2
Treban F 116 A3
Třebařov CZ 97 B4
Trebatsch D 74 B3
Trebbin D 74 B2
Třebechovice pod Orebem CZ 85 B3
Trebel D 73 B4
Třebenice CZ 84 B1
Trébeurden F 100 A2
Třebíč CZ 97 B3
Trebinje BIH 139 C4
Trebisacce I 174 B2
Trebitz D 83 A4
Trebnje SLO 123 B4
Třeboň CZ 96 B2
Třebovice CZ 97 B4
Trebsen D 83 A4
Trebujena E 161 C3
Trecastagni I 177 B4
Trecate I 120 B1
Trecenta I 121 B4
Tredegar GB 39 C3
Tredózio I 135 A4
Treffen A 109 C4
Treffort F 118 A2
Treffurt D 82 A2
Trefnant GB 38 A3
Tregaron GB 39 B3
Trégastel-Plage F 100 A2
Tregnago I 121 B4
Tregony GB 42 B2
Tréguier F 100 A2
Trégunc F 100 B2
Treharris GB 39 C3
Trehörningsjö S 200 C4
Tréia I 136 B2
Treignac F 116 B1
Treignat F 116 A2
Treignes B 91 A4
Treis-Karden D 80 B3
Trekanten S 63 B4
Trélazé F 102 B1
Trelech GB 39 C2
Trélissac F 129 A3
Trelleborg S 66 A2
Trélon F 91 A4
Trélou-sur-Marne F 91 B3
Tremblay-le-Vicomte F 89 B5
Tremés P 154 B2
Tremezzo I 120 B2
Třemošná CZ 96 B1
Tremp E 145 B4
Trenčianska Stankovce SK 98 C1
Trenčianska Turná SK 98 C2
Trenčianske Teplá SK 98 C2
Trenčianske Teplice SK 98 C2
Trenčín SK 98 C2
Trendelburg D 81 A5
Trengereid N 46 B2
Trensacq F 128 B2
Trent D 66 B2
Trento I 121 A4
Treorchy GB 39 C3
Trept F 118 B2
Trepuzzi I 173 B4
Trescore Balneário I 120 B2
Tresenda I 120 A3
Tresfjord N 198 C4
Tresigallo I 121 C4
Trešnjevica SRB 127 D3
Tresnurághes I 178 B2
Trespaderne E 143 B3
Třešt CZ 97 B3
Trestina I 135 B5
Tretower GB 39 C3
Trets F 132 B1
Tretten N 48 A2
Treuchtlingen D 94 C2
Treuen D 83 B4
Treuenbrietzen D 74 B1
Treungen N 53 A4
Trevelez E 163 B4
Trevi I 136 C1
Treviana E 143 B3
Treviglio I 120 B2
Trevignano Romano I 168 A2
Trevi nel Lázio I 169 B3
Treviso I 122 B1
Trévoux F 117 B4
Treysa D 81 B5
Trézelles F 117 A3
Trezzo sull'Adda I 120 B2
Trhová Kamenice CZ 97 B3
Trhové Sviny CZ 96 C2
Triacastela E 141 B3
Triaize F 114 B2
Trianda GR 188 C3
Triaucourt-en-Argonne F 91 C5
Tribanj Kruščica HR 137 A4
Triberg D 106 A3
Tribsees D 66 B1
Tribuče SLO 123 B4
Tricárico I 172 B2
Tricase I 173 C4
Tricésimo I 122 A2
Trieben A 110 B1
Triebes D 83 B4
Triepkendorf D 74 A2
Trier D 92 B2
Trieste I 122 B2
Trie-sur-Baïse F 145 A4
Triggiano I 173 A2
Triglitz D 73 A5
Trignac F 101 B3
Trigueros E 161 B3
Trigueros del Valle E 142 C2
Trikala GR 182 D3
Trikeri GR 183 D5
Trikomo CY 181 A2
Trilj HR 138 B2
Trillo E 152 B1
Trilport F 90 C2
Trim IRL 30 A2
Trimdon GB 37 B5
Trindade
Beja P 160 B2
Bragança P 149 A2
Třinec CZ 98 B2
Tring GB 44 B3
Trinità d'Agultu I 178 B2
Trinitápoli I 171 B4
Trino I 119 B5
Trinta P 148 B2
Triora I 133 B3
Tripoli GR 184 B3
Triponzo I 136 C1
Triptis D 83 B3
Triste E 144 B3
Trittau D 72 A3
Trivento I 170 B2
Trivero I 119 B5
Trivigno I 172 B1
Trn BIH 124 C3
Trnava
HR 125 B4
SK 98 C1
Trnovec SK 112 A1
Trnovo BIH 139 B4
Trnovska vas SLO 110 C2
Troarn F 89 A3
Trochtelfingen D 94 C1
Trödje S 51 B4
Troense DK 65 A3
Trofa P 148 A1
Trofaiach A 110 B2
Trofors N 195 E4
Trogir HR 138 B2
Trøgstad N 54 A2
Tróia I 171 B3
Troia P 154 C2
Troina I 177 B3
Troisdorf D 80 B3
Trois-Ponts B 80 B1
Troisvierges L 92 A2
Trojane SLO 123 A3
Troldhede DK 59 C1
Trollhättan S 54 B3
Trolog BIH 138 B2
Tromello I 120 B1
Tromøy N 53 B4
Tromsø N 192 C3
Trondheim N 199 B7
Tronget F 116 A3
Trönninge S 61 C2
Trönningeby S 60 B2
Trönö S 51 A3
Tronzano-Vercellese I 119 B5
Trôo F 102 B2
Troon GB 36 A2
Tropea I 175 C1
Tropy Sztumskie PL 69 B4
Trosa S 57 B3
Trösken S 50 B3
Trosly-Breuil F 90 B3
Trossingen D 107 A3
Trostberg D 109 A3
Trouville-sur-Mer F 89 A4
Trowbridge GB 43 A4
Troyes F 104 A3
Trpanj HR 138 B3
Trpinja HR 125 B4
Tršće HR 123 B3
Tršice CZ 98 B1
Trstená SK 99 B3
Trstenci BIH 125 B3
Trsteno HR 139 C3
Trstice SK 111 A4
Trstin SK 98 C1
Trubia E 141 A5
Trubjela MNE 139 C4
Truchas E 141 B4
Trujillanos E 155 C4
Trujillo E 156 A2
Trumieje PL 69 B4
Trun
CH 107 C3
F 89 B4
Truro GB 42 B1
Trusetal D 82 B2
Truskavets' UA 13 D5
Trustrup DK 59 B3
Trutnov CZ 85 B3
Tryserum S 56 B2
Trysil N 49 A4
Tryszczyn PL 76 A2
Trzcianka PL 75 A5
Trzciel PL 75 B4
Trzcińsko Zdrój PL 74 B3
Trzebiatów PL 67 B4
Trzebiel PL 84 A2
Trzebielino PL 68 A2
Trzebień PL 84 A3
Trzebiez PL 74 A3
Trzebinia PL 86 B3
Trzebnica PL 85 A5
Trzebnice PL 85 A4
Trzeciewiec PL 76 A3
Trzemeszno PL 76 B2
Trzemeszno-Lubuskie PL 75 B4
Trzetrzewina PL 99 B4
Tržič SLO 123 A3
Tsamandas GR 182 D2
Tschagguns A 107 B4
Tschernitz D 84 A2
Tsebrykove UA 17 B9
Tsyelyakhany BY 13 B6
Tua P 148 A2
Tuam IRL 28 A3
Tubbergen NL 71 B3
Tubilla del Lago E 143 C3
Tübingen D 93 C5
Tubize B 79 B4
Tučapy CZ 96 B2
Tučepi HR 138 B3
Tuchan F 146 B3
Tüchen D 73 A5
Tuchola PL 76 A2
Tuchomie PL 68 A2
Tuchów PL 99 B5
Tuczno PL 75 A5
Tuddal N 53 A4
Tudela E 144 B2
Tudela de Duero E 150 A3
Tudweiliog GB 38 B2
Tuejar E 159 B2
Tuffé F 102 A2
Tufsingdalen N 199 C8
Tuhaň CZ 84 B2
Tui E 140 B2
Tukhkala RUS 197 D13
Tukums LV 8 D3
Tula I 178 B2
Tulcea RO 17 C8
Tul'chyn UA 13 D8
Tulette F 131 A3
Tuliszków PL 76 B3
Tulla IRL 28 B3
Tullamore IRL 30 A1
Tulle F 116 B1
Tullins F 118 B2
Tulln A 97 C4
Tullow IRL 30 B2
Tułowice PL 85 B5
Tulppio FIN 197 B12
Tulsk IRL 28 A3
Tumba S 57 A3
Tummel Bridge GB 35 B3
Tun S 55 B3
Tuna
Kalmar S 62 A4
Uppsala S 51 B5
Tuna Hästberg S 50 B2
Tunçbilek TR 187 C4
Tunes P 160 B1
Tungelsta S 57 A4
Tunnerstad S 55 B5
Tunnhovd N 47 B5
Tunstall GB 45 A5
Tuohikotti FIN 8 B5
Tuoro sul Trasimeno I 135 B5
Tupadły PL 76 B3
Tupanari BIH 139 A4
Tupik RUS 9 E8
Tuplice PL 84 A2
Tura H 112 B3
Turanj HR 137 B4
Turany SK 99 B3
Turbe BIH 139 A3
Turbenthal CH 107 B3
Turcia E 141 B5
Turčianske Teplice SK 98 C2
Turcifal P 154 B1
Turckheim F 106 A2
Turda RO 17 B5
Turégano E 151 A4
Turek PL 76 B3
Tŭrgovishte BG 17 D7
Turgutlu TR 188 A2
Turi I 173 B3
Turin = Torino I 119 B4
Turis E 159 B3
Türje H 111 C4
Turka UA 12 D5
Túrkeve H 113 B4
Türkheim D 108 A1
Türkmenli TR 186 C1
Turku FIN 8 B3
Turleque E 157 A4
Turňa nad Bodvou SK 99 C4
Turnberry GB 36 A2
Turnhout B 79 A4
Türnitz A 110 B2
Turnov CZ 84 B3
Turnu RO 126 A3
Turnu Măgurele RO 17 D6
Turón E 164 C1
Turoszów PL 84 B2
Turowo PL 77 A5
Turquel P 154 B1
Turri I 179 C2
Turries F 132 A2
Turriff GB 33 D4
Tursi I 174 A2
Turtmann CH 119 A4
Turtola FIN 196 C6
Turze PL 86 A1
Turzovka SK 98 B2
Tusa I 177 B3
Tuscánia I 168 A1
Tuse DK 61 D1
Tušilovic HR 123 B4
Tuszyn PL 86 A3
Tutow D 66 C2
Tutrakan BG 17 C7
Tuttlingen D 107 B3
Tutzing D 108 B2
Tuzla
BIH 125 C4
TR 23 C8
Tuzlukçu TR 189 A6
Tvååker S 60 B2
Tvärålund S 200 B5
Tvärskog S 63 B4
Tvedestrand N 53 B4
Tveit
Hordaland N 47 B4
Rogaland N 52 A2
Tver RUS 9 D9
Tverrelvmo N 192 D3
Tversted DK 58 A3
Tving S 63 B3
Tvrdošin SK 99 B3
Tvrdošovce SK 112 A2
Twardogóra PL 85 A5
Twatt GB 33 B3
Twello NL 70 B3
Twimberg A 110 C1
Twist D 71 B4
Twistringen D 72 B1
Tworóg PL 86 B2
Twyford
Hampshire GB 44 B2
Wokingham GB 44 B3
Tyachiv UA 17 A5
Tychówka PL 67 C5
Tychowo PL 67 C5
Tychy PL 86 B2
Tydal N 199 B8
Týec nad Labem CZ 97 A3
Tyfors S 49 B6
Tygelsjö S 61 D2
Tylldal N 199 C7
Tylstrup DK 58 A2
Tymbark PL 99 B4
Tymowa PL 99 B4
Tyndrum GB 34 B3
Týnec nad Sázavou CZ 96 B2
Tynemouth GB 37 A5
Tyngsjö S 49 B5
Týništěnad Orlicí CZ 85 B4
Týn nad Vltavou CZ 96 B2
Tynset N 199 C7
Tyresö S 57 A4
Tyringe S 61 C3
Tyrislöt S 56 B2
Tyristrand N 48 B2
Tyrrellspass IRL 30 A1
Tysnes N 46 B2
Tysse N 46 B2
Tyssebotn N 46 B2
Tyssedal N 46 B3
Tystberga S 56 B3
Tysvær N 52 A1
Tywyn GB 39 B2
Tzermiado GR 185 D6
Tzummarum NL 70 A2

U

Ub SRB 127 C2
Ubby DK 61 D1
Úbeda E 157 B4
Überlingen D 107 B4
Ubidea E 143 A4
Ubli HR 138 C2
Ubrique E 162 B2
Ucero E 143 C3
Uchaud F 131 B3
Üchte D 72 B1
Uckerath D 80 B3
Uckfield GB 45 C4
Ucklum S 54 B2
Uclés E 151 C5
Ucria I 177 A3
Udbina HR 137 A4
Uddebo S 60 B3
Uddeholm S 49 B5
Uddevalla S 54 B2
Uddheden S 49 C4
Uden NL 80 A1
Uder D 82 A2
Udiča SK 98 B2
Údine I 122 A2
Udvar H 125 B4
Ueckermünde D 74 A3
Uelsen D 71 B3
Uelzen D 73 B3
Uetendorf CH 106 C2
Uetersen D 72 A2
Uetze D 72 B3
Uffculme GB 43 B3
Uffenheim D 94 B2
Ugarana E 143 A4
Ugento I 173 C4
Ugerldse DK 61 D1
Uggerby DK 58 A3
Uggerslev DK 59 C3
Uggiano la Chiesa I 173 B4
Ugíjar E 164 C1
Ugine F 118 B3
Uglejevik BIH 125 C5
Uglenes N 46 B2
Uglich RUS 9 D11
Ugljane HR 138 B2
Ugod H 111 B4
Uherské Hradiště CZ 98 B1
Uherský Brod CZ 98 B1
Uherský Ostroh CZ 98 C1
Uhingen D 94 C1
Uhlířské-Janovice CZ 96 B3
Uhříněves CZ 96 A2
Uhyst D 84 A2
Uig GB 31 B2
Uitgeest NL 70 B1
Uithoorn NL 70 B1
Uithuizen NL 71 A3
Uithuizermeeden NL 71 A3
Uivar RO 126 B2
Ujazd
Łódzkie PL 87 A3
Opolskie PL 86 B2
Ujezd u Brna CZ 97 B4
Ujhartyán H 112 B3
Újkígyós H 113 C5
Ujpetre H 125 B4
Ujście PL 75 A5
Ujsolt H 112 C3
Újszász H 113 B4
Újszentmargita H 113 B5
Ujué E 144 B2
Ukanc SLO 122 A2
Ukmergė LT 13 A6
Ukna S 56 B2
Ula TR 188 B3
Ul'anka SK 99 C3
Ulaş TR 186 A2
Ulássai I 179 C3
Ulbjerg DK 58 B2
Ulbster GB 32 C3
Ulceby GB 40 B3
Ulcinj MNE 16 E3
Uldum DK 59 C2
Ulefoss N 53 A5
Uleila del Campo E 164 B2
Ulëz AL 182 B1
Ulfborg DK 59 B1
Uljma SRB 127 B3
Ullånger S 200 C4
Ullapool GB 32 D1
Ullared S 60 B2
Ullatti S 196 B4
Ullatun N 52 A2
Ulldecona E 153 B4
Ulldemolins E 147 C1
Ullerslev DK 59 C3
Ullervad S 55 B4
Üllés H 126 A1
Üllő H 112 B3
Ulm D 94 C1
Ulme P 154 B2
Ulmen D 80 B2
Ulnes N 47 B6
Ulog BIH 139 B4
Ulricehamn S 60 B3
Ulrichstein D 81 B5
Ulrika S 56 B1
Ulriksfors S 200 C1
Ulrum NL 71 A3
Ulsberg N 198 C6
Ulsta GB 33 A5
Ulsted DK 58 A3
Ulsteinvik N 198 C2
Ulstrup
Vestsjællands Amt. DK 59 C3
Viborg Amt. DK 59 B2
Ulsvåg N 194 B6
Ulubey TR 188 A4
Uluborlu TR 189 A5
Ulukışla TR 23 C8
Ulverston GB 36 B3
Ulvik N 46 B3
Umag HR 122 B2
Uman UA 13 D9
Umba RUS 3 C14
Umbértide I 135 B5
Umbriático I 174 B2
Umčari SRB 127 C2
Umeå S 200 C6
Umgransele S 200 B4
Umhausen A 108 B1
Umka SRB 127 C2
Umljanovic HR 138 B2
Umnäs S 195 E7
Umurbey TR 186 B1
Unaðsdalur IS 190 A3
Unapool GB 32 C1
Unari FIN 197 B8
Unbyn S 196 D4
Uncastillo E 144 B2
Undenäs S 55 B5
Undersaker S 199 B10
Undredal N 46 B4
Unešić HR 138 B2
Úněšov CZ 96 B1
Ungheni MD 17 B7
Unhais da Serra P 148 B2
Unhošt CZ 84 B2
Unichowo PL 68 A2
Uničov CZ 98 B1
Uniejów PL 76 C3
Unisław PL 76 A3
Unkel D 80 B3
Unken A 109 B3
Unna D 81 A3
Unnaryd S 60 C3
Unquera E 142 A2
Unterach A 109 B4
Unterägeri CH 107 B3
Unterammergau D 108 B2
Unterhaching D 108 A2
Unteriberg CH 107 B3
Unterkochen D 94 C2
Unter Langkampfen A 108 B3
Unterlaussa A 110 B1
Unterlüss D 72 B3
Untermünkheim D 94 B1
Unterschächen CH 107 C3
Unterschleissheim D 95 C3
Unterschwaningen D 94 B2
Untersiemau D 82 B2
Unter-steinbach D 94 B2
Unterweissenbach A 96 C2
Unterzell D 95 B4
Upavon GB 44 B2
Úpice CZ 85 B4
Upiłka PL 68 B2
Upphärad S 54 B3
Uppingham GB 40 C3
Upplands-Väsby S 57 A3
Uppsala S 51 C4
Uppsjøhytta N 48 A1
Upton-upon-Severn GB 39 B4
Ur F 146 B2
Uras I 179 C2
Uraz PL 85 A4
Urbánia I 136 B1
Urbino I 136 B1
Urçay F 103 C4
Urda E 157 A4
Urdax E 144 A2
Urdilde E 140 B2
Urdos F 145 B3
Urk NL 70 B2
Úrkút H 111 B4
Urla TR 188 A1
Urlingford IRL 30 B1
Urnäsch CH 107 B4
Urnes N 47 A4
Uroševac KOS 16 D4
Urracal E 164 B2
Urries E 144 B2
Urroz E 144 B2
Ursensollen D 95 B3
Urshult S 63 B2
Uršna Sela SLO 123 B4
Urszulewo PL 77 B4
Ury F 90 C2
Urziceni RO 17 C7
Urzulei I 178 B3
Usagre E 156 B1
Uşak TR 187 D4
Usedom D 66 C2
Useldange L 92 B1
Uséllus I 179 C2
Ushakovo RUS 69 A5
Usingen D 81 B4
Usini I 178 B2
Usk GB 39 C4
Uskedal N 46 C2

Üsküdar TR 186 A4
Uslar D 82 A1
Úsov CZ 97 B5
Usquert NL 71 A3
Ussássai I 179 C3
Ussé F 102 B2
Usséglio I 119 B4
Ussel
Cantal F 116 B2
Corrèze F 116 B2
Usson-du-Poitou F 115 B4
Usson-en-Forez F 117 B3
Usson-les-Bains F 146 B3
Ustaoset N 47 B5
Ustaritz F 144 A2
Uštěk CZ 84 B2
Uster CH 107 B3
Ústi CZ 98 B1
Ustikolina BIH 139 B4
Ústínad Labem CZ 84 B2
Ústínad Orlicí CZ 97 B4
Ustipračà BIH 139 B5
Ustka PL 68 A1
Ust Luga RUS 8 C6
Ustroń PL 98 B2
Ustronie Morskie PL 67 B4
Ustyuzhna RUS 9 C10
Uszód H 112 C2
Utåker N 52 A1
Utansjö S 200 D3
Utebo E 152 A3
Utena LT 13 A6
Utery CZ 95 B5
Uthaug N 198 B6
Utiel E 159 B2
Utne N 46 B3
Utö S 57 B4
Utrecht NL 70 B2
Utrera E 162 A2
Utrillas E 153 B3
Utsjoki FIN 193 C11
Utstein kloster N 52 A1
Uttendorf A 109 B3
Uttenweiler D 107 A4
Utterslev DK 65 B4
Uttoxeter GB 40 C2
Utvälinge S 61 C2
Utvorda N 199 A7
Uusikaarlepyy FIN 3 E8
Uusikaupunki FIN 8 B2
Uvaly CZ 96 A2
Uvdal N 47 B5
Uza F 128 B1
Uzdin SRB 126 B2
Uzdowo PL 77 A5
Uzein F 145 A3
Uzel F 100 A3
Uzerche F 116 B1
Uzès F 131 A3
Uzhhorod UA 12 D5
Uzhok UA 12 D5
Užice SRB 127 D1
Uznach CH 107 B3
Üzümlü
Konya TR 189 B6
Muğla TR 188 C4
Uzunköprü TR 186 A1

V

Vaalajärvi FIN 197 B9
Vaas F 102 B2
Vaasa FIN 8 A2
Vaasen NL 70 B2
Vabre F 130 B1
Vác H 112 B3
Vacha D 82 B2
Váchartyán H 112 B3
Väckelsång S 63 B2
Vacqueyras F 131 A3
Vad S 50 B2
Vada I 134 B3
Väddö S 51 C5
Väderstad S 55 B5
Vadheim N 46 A2
Vadillo de la Sierra
E 150 B2
Vadillos E 152 B1
Vadla N 52 A2
Vado I 135 A4
Vado Lígure I 133 A4
Vadsø N 193 B13
Vadstena S 55 B5
Vadum DK 58 A2
Vaduz FL 107 B4
Vafos N 53 B5
Vág H 111 B4
Vågåmo N 198 D6
Væggerløse DK 65 B4
Vaggeryd S 62 A2
Vaghia GR 184 A4
Vaglia I 135 B4
Váglio Basilicata I 172 B1
Vagney F 106 A1
Vagnhärad S 57 B3
Vagnsunda S 57 A4
Vagos P 148 B1
Vai GR 185 D7
Vaiano I 135 B4
Vaiges F 102 A1
Vaihingen D 93 C4
Vaillant F 105 B4
Vailly-sur-Aisne F 91 B3
Vailly-sur Sauldre
F 103 B4
Vairano Scalo I 170 B2
Vaison-la-Romaine
F 131 A4
Vaite F 105 B4
Väjern S 54 B2
Vajszló H 125 B3
Vaksdal N 46 B2
Vál H 112 B2
Valaam RUS 9 B7
Valada P 154 B2
Vålådalen S 199 B10
Valadares P 148 A1
Valado P 154 B1
Valandovo MK 182 B4
Valaská SK 99 C3
Valaská Belá SK 98 C2
Valaská Dubová SK 99 B3
Valašská Polanka
CZ 98 B1
Valašské Klobouky
CZ 98 B2
Valašské Meziříčí
CZ 98 B1
Valberg F 132 A2
Vålberg S 55 A4
Valbo S 51 B4
Valbom P 148 A1
Valbondione I 120 A3
Valbonnais F 118 C2
Valbuena de Duero
E 142 C2
Vălcani RO 126 B2
Valdagno I 121 B4
Valdahon F 105 B5
Valdaracete E 151 B4
Valday RUS 9 D8
Valdealgorfa E 153 B3
Valdecaballeros E 156 A2
Valdecabras E 152 B1
Valdecarros E 150 B2
Valdeconcha E 151 B5
Valdeflores E 161 B3
Valdefresno E 142 B1
Valdeganga E 158 B2
Valdelacasa E 150 B2
Valdelacasa de Tajo
E 156 A2
Valdelarco E 161 B3
Valdelosa E 149 A4
Valdeltormo E 153 B4
Valdelugeros E 142 B1
Valdemanco de Esteras
E 156 B3
Valdemarsvik S 56 B2
Valdemorillo E 151 B3
Valdemoro E 151 B4
Valdemoro Sierra
E 152 B2
Valdenoceda E 143 B3
Valdeobispo E 149 B3
Valdeolivas E 152 B1
Valdepeñas E 157 B4
Valdepeñas de Jaén
E 163 A4
Valdepiélago E 142 B1
Valdepolo E 142 B1
Valderas E 142 B1
Valdérice I 176 A1
Valderrobres E 153 B4
Valderrueda E 142 B2
Val de San Lorenzo
E 141 B4
Val de Santo Domingo
E 150 B3
Val d'Esquières F 132 B2
Valdestillas E 150 A3
Valdetorres E 156 B1
Valdetorres de Jarama
E 151 B4
Valdeverdeja E 150 C2
Valdevimbre E 142 B1
Valdieri I 133 A3
Valdilecha E 151 B4
Val-d'Isère F 119 B3
Valdobbiádene I 121 B4
Valdocondes E 143 C3
Valdoviño E 140 A2
Valea lui Mihai RO 16 B5
Vale de Açor
Beja P 160 B2
Portalegre P 154 B3
Vale de Agua P 160 B1
Vale de Cambra P 148 B1
Vale de Lobo P 160 B1
Vale de Prazeres P 148 B2
Vale de Reis P 154 C2
Vale de Rosa P 160 B2
Vale de Santarém
P 154 B2
Vale de Vargo P 160 B2
Vale do Peso P 155 B3
Valega P 148 B1
Valéggio sul Mincio
I 121 B3
Valeiro P 154 C2
Valença P 140 B2
Valençay F 103 B3
Valence
Charente F 115 C4
Drôme F 117 C4
Valence d'Agen F 129 B3
Valence d'Albigeois
F 130 A1
Valence-sur-Baise
F 129 C3
Valencia E 159 B3
Valencia de Alcántara
E 155 B3
Valencia de Don Juan
E 142 B1
Valencia de las Torres
E 156 B1
Valencia del Ventoso
E 161 A3
Valencia de Mombuey
E 161 A2
Valenciennes F 79 B3
Valensole F 132 B1
Valentano I 168 A1
Valentigney F 106 B1
Valentine F 145 A4
Valenza I 120 B1
Valenzuela E 163 A3
Valenzuela de Calatrava
E 157 B4
Våler
Hedmark N 48 B3
Østfold N 54 A1
Valera de Abajo E 158 B1
Valeria E 158 B1
Valestrand N 52 A1
Valestrandsfossen
N 46 B2
Valevåg N 52 A1
Valfabbrica I 136 B1
Valflaunes F 131 B2
Valga EST 8 D5
Valgorge F 131 A3
Valgrisenche I 119 B4
Valguarnera Caropepe
I 177 B3
Valhelhas P 148 B2
Valjevo SRB 127 C1
Valka LV 8 D4
Valkeakoski FIN 8 B4
Valkenburg NL 80 B1
Valkenswaard NL 79 A5
Valkó H 112 B3
Valla S 56 A2
Vallada E 159 C3
Vallado E 141 A4
Valladolid E 150 A3
Vallåkra S 61 D2
Vallata I 172 A1
Vallberga S 61 C3
Vall d'Alba E 153 B3
Valldemossa E 166 B2
Valle N 52 A3
Valle Castellana I 136 C2
Valle de Abdalajís
E 163 B3
Valle de Cabuérniga
E 142 A2
Valle de la Serena
E 156 B2
Valle de Matamoros
E 155 C4
Valle de Santa Ana
E 155 C4
Valledolmo I 176 B2
Valledoria I 178 B2
Vallelado E 150 A3
Vallelunga Pratameno
I 176 B2
Valle Mosso I 119 B5
Vallendar D 81 B3
Vallentuna S 57 A4
Valleräs S 49 B5
Valleraugue F 130 A2
Vallermosa I 179 C2
Vallet F 101 B4
Valletta M 175 C3
Valley GB 38 A2
Vallfogona de Riucorb
E 147 C2
Valli del Pasúbio I 121 B4
Vallo della Lucánia
I 172 B1
Valloire F 118 B3
Vallombrosa I 135 B4
Vallon-Pont-d'Arc
F 131 A3
Vallorbe CH 105 C5
Vallouise F 118 C3
Valls E 147 C2
Vallset N 48 B3
Vallsta S 50 A3
Vallstena S 57 C4
Valmadrid E 153 A3
Valmiera LV 8 D4
Valmojado E 151 B3
Valmont F 89 A4
Valmontone I 169 B2
Valö S 51 B5
Valognes F 88 A2
Valonga P 148 B1
Valongo P 148 A1
Válor E 164 C1
Valoria la Buena E 142 C2
Valøy N 199 A7
Valozhyn BY 13 A7
Valpaços P 148 A2
Valpelline I 119 B4
Valpiana I 135 B3
Valpovo HR 125 B4
Valras-Plage F 130 B2
Valréas F 131 A3
Vals CH 107 C4
Valsavarenche I 119 B4
Vålse DK 65 B4
Valsequillo E 156 B2
Valsjöbyn S 199 A11
Vals-les-Bains F 117 C4
Valsonne F 117 B4
Valstagna I 121 B4
Val-Suzon F 105 B3
Valtablado del Rio
E 152 B1
Valþjofsstaður IS 191 B11
Val Thorens F 118 B3
Valtice CZ 97 C4
Valtiendas E 151 A4
Valtierra E 144 B2
Valtopina I 136 B1
Valtorta I 120 B2
Valtournenche I 119 B4
Valverde E 144 C2
Valverde de Burguillos
E 155 C4
Valverde de Júcar
E 158 B1
Valverde de la Vera
E 150 B2
Valverde de la Virgen
E 142 B1
Valverde del Camino
E 161 B3
Valverde del Fresno
E 149 B3
Valverde de Llerena
E 156 B2
Valverde de Mérida
E 156 B1
Valvträsk S 196 C4
Vamberk CZ 85 B4
Vamdrup DK 59 C2
Våmhus S 50 A1
Vamlingbo S 57 D4
Vammala FIN 8 B3
Vamos GR 185 D5
Vámosmikola H 112 B2
Vámosszabadi H 111 B4
Vanault-les-Dames
F 91 C4
Vandel DK 59 C2
Vandenesse F 104 C2
Vandenesse-en-Auxois
F 104 B3
Vandóies I 108 C2
Väne-Åsaka S 54 B3
Vänersborg S 54 B3
Vänersnäs S 54 B3
Vang N 47 A5
Vänge S 51 C4
Vangsnes N 46 A3
Vänjaurbäck S 200 B4
Vännacka S 54 A3
Vannareid N 192 B3
Vännäs S 200 C5
Vannes F 101 B3
Vannsätter S 51 A3
Vannvåg N 192 B3
Vansbro S 49 B6
Vanse N 52 B2
Vantaa FIN 8 B4
Vanttauskoski FIN 197 C9
Vanviken N 199 B7
Vanyarc H 112 B3
Vaour F 129 B4
Vapnyarka UA 13 D8
Vaprio d'Adda I 120 B2
Vaqueiros P 160 B2
Vara S 55 B3
Varacieux F 118 B2
Varades F 101 B4
Varages F 132 B1
Varaldsøy N 46 B2
Varallo I 119 B5
Varangerbotn N 193 B12
Varano de'Melegari
I 120 C3
Varaždin HR 124 A2
Varaždinske Toplice
HR 124 A2
Varazze I 133 A4
Varberg S 60 B2
Vardal N 48 B2
Varde DK 59 C1
Vårdö FIN 51 B7
Vardø N 193 B15
Vardomb H 125 A4
Varejoki FIN 196 C7
Varel D 71 A5
Varėna LT 13 A6
Vårenes N 52 A1
Varengeville-sur-Mer
F 89 A4
Varenna I 120 A2
Varennes-en-Argonne
F 91 B5
Varennes-le-Grand
F 105 C3
Varennes-St Sauveur
F 105 C4
Varennes-sur-Allier
F 117 A3
Varennes-sur-Amance
F 105 B4
Vareš BIH 139 A4
Varese I 120 B1
Varese Ligure I 134 A2
Vârfurile RO 16 B5
Vårgårda S 60 A2
Vargas
E 143 A3
P 154 B2
Vargön S 54 B3
Varhaug N 52 B1
Variaş RO 126 A2
Variaşu Mic RO 126 A3
Varilhes F 146 A2
Varin SK 98 B2
Väring S 55 B4
Váriz P 149 A3
Varkaus FIN 8 A5
Varmahlíð IS 190 B6
Varmaland IS 190 C4
Värmlands Bro S 55 A4
Värmskog S 55 A3
Varna
BG 17 D7
SRB 127 C1
Värnamo S 60 B4
Varnhem S 55 B4
Varnsdorf CZ 84 B2
Värö S 60 B2
Varoška Rijeka
BIH 124 B2
Városlöd H 111 B4
Várpalota H 112 B2
Varreddes F 90 C2
Vars F 118 C3
Varsi I 120 C2
Varsseveld NL 71 C3
Vårsta S 57 A3
Vartdal N 198 C3
Vartofta S 55 B4
Vårvik S 54 A3
Várvölgy H 111 C4
Varzi I 120 C2
Varzjelas P 148 B1
Varzo I 119 A5
Varzy F 104 B2
Vasad H 112 B3
Väse S 55 A4
Vašica SRB 125 B5
Vasilevichi BY 13 B8
Väskinde S 57 C4
Vaskút H 125 A4
Vaslui RO 17 B7
Vassbotn N 53 B4
Vassenden N 47 A6
Vassieux-en-Vercors
F 118 C2
Vassmolösa S 63 B4
Vassy F 88 B3
Västansjö S 195 E6
Västanvik S 50 B1
Västerås S 56 A2
Västerby S 50 B2
Västerfärnebo S 50 C3
Västergarn S 57 C4
Västerhaninge S 57 A4
Västervik S 62 A4
Vasto I 170 A2
Västra Ämtervik S 55 A4
Västra-Bodarne S 60 B2
Västra Karup S 61 C2
Vasvár H 111 B3
Vasylkiv UA 13 C9
Vát H 111 B3
Vatan F 103 B3
Väte S 57 C4
Vathia GR 184 C3
Vatican City = Cittádel
Vaticano I 168 B2
Vatili CY 181 A2
Vatin SRB 126 B3
Vatland N 52 B3
Vatnar N 53 A5
Vatnås N 48 C1
Vatne N 53 B3
Vatnestrøm N 53 B4
Vätö S 51 C5
Vatra-Dornei RO 17 B6
Vatry F 91 C4
Vattholma S 51 B4
Vättis CH 107 C4
Vauchamps F 91 C3
Vauchassis F 104 A2
Vaucouleurs F 92 C1
Vaudoy-en-Brie F 90 C3
Vaulen N 52 B1
Vaulruz CH 106 C1
Vaulx Vraucourt F 90 A2
Vaumas F 104 C2
Vausseroux F 115 B3
Vauvenargues F 132 B1
Vauvert F 131 B3
Vauvillers F 105 B5
Vaux-sur-Sure B 92 B1
Vawkavysk BY 13 B6
Vaxholm S 57 A4
Växjö S 62 B2
Våxtorp S 61 C3
Vayrac F 129 B4
Važec SK 99 B3
Veberöd S 61 D3
Vechelde D 72 B3
Vechta D 71 B5
Vecinos E 149 B4
Vecsés H 112 B3
Vedavågen N 52 A1
Veddige S 60 B2
Vedersø DK 59 B1
Vedeseta I 120 B2
Vedevåg S 56 A1
Vedra E 140 B2
Vedum S 55 B3
Veendam NL 71 A3
Veenendaal NL 70 B2
Vega
Asturias E 142 A1
Asturias E 142 A1
Vega de Espinareda
E 141 B4
Vega de Infanzones
E 142 B1
Vegadeo E 141 A3
Vega de Pas E 143 A3
Vega de Valcarce
E 141 B4
Vega de Valdetronco
E 150 A2
Vegårshei N 53 B4
Vegas de Coria E 149 B3
Vegas del Condado
E 142 B1
Vegby S 60 B3
Vegger DK 58 B2
Veggli N 47 B6
Veghel NL 80 A1
Veglast D 66 B1
Véglie I 173 B3
Veguillas E 151 B4
Vegusdal N 53 B4
Veidholmen N 198 B4
Veidnes N 193 B10
Veikåker N 48 B1
Veinge S 61 C3
Vejbystrand S 61 C2
Vejen DK 59 C2
Vejer de la Frontera
E 162 B2
Vejle DK 59 C2
Vejprty CZ 83 B5
Velada E 150 B3
Vela Luka HR 138 C2
Velayos E 150 B3
Velbert D 80 A3
Velburg D 95 B3
Velde N 199 A8
Velden
Bayern D 95 B3
Bayern D 95 C4
Velden am Worther See
A 109 C5
Velefique E 164 B2
Velen D 80 A2
Velenje SLO 123 A4
Veles MK 182 B3
Velesevec HR 124 B2
Velešin CZ 96 C2
Velestino GR 182 D4
Velez Blanco E 164 B2
Vélez de Benaudalla
E 163 B4
Vélez-Málaga E 163 B3
Vélez Rubio E 164 B2
Veliiki Radinci
SRB 127 B1
Velika HR 125 B3
Velika Gorica HR 124 B2
Velika Grdevac HR 124 B3
Velika Greda SRB 126 B3
Velika Ilova BIH 125 C3
Velika Kladuša BIH 124 B1
Velika Kopanica
HR 125 B4
Velika Krsna SRB 127 C2
Velika Obarska
BIH 125 C5
Velika Pisanica HR 124 B3
Velika Plana SRB 127 C3
Velika Zdenci HR 124 B3
Velike Lašče SLO 123 B3
Velike Središte
SRB 126 B3
Veliki Gaj SRB 126 B3
Veliki Popović
SRB 127 C3
Velikiye Luki RUS 9 D7
Veliko Gradište
SRB 127 C3
Veliko Orašje SRB 127 C3
Veliko Selo SRB 127 C3
Veliko Tŭrnovo BG 17 D6
Velilla del Río Carrió
E 142 B2
Velilla de San Antonio
E 151 B4
Veli Lošinj HR 137 A3
Velingrad BG 183 A5
Velizh RUS 9 E7
Veljun HR 123 B4
Velká Bíteš CZ 97 B4
Velka Hled'scbe CZ 95 B4
Velká Lomnica SK 99 B4
Velkánad Veličkou
CZ 98 C1
Velké Bystřice CZ 98 B1
Velké Heraltice CZ 98 B1
Velké Karlovice CZ 98 B2
Vel'ke'Kostol'any
SK 98 C1
Vel'ké Leváre SK 97 C5
Velké Losiny CZ 98 A1
Velké Meziříčí CZ 97 B4
Velké Pavlovice CZ 97 C4
Vel'ké Rovné SK 98 B2
Vel'ké Uherce SK 98 C2
Vel'ké Zálužie SK 98 C1
Vel'ký Blahovo SK 99 C4
Velky Bor CZ 96 B1
Vel'ký Cetin SK 112 A2
Vel'ký Krtíš SK 112 A3
Vel'ký Meder SK 111 B4
Velky Ujezd CZ 98 B1
Vellahn D 73 A3
Vellberg D 94 B1
Velles F 103 C3
Velletri I 168 B2
Vellinge S 66 A2
Vellisca E 151 B5
Velliza E 150 A3
Vellmar D 81 A5
Velp NL 70 B2
Velten D 74 B2

Velvary CZ 84 B2
Velvendos GR 182 C4
Vemb DK 59 B1
Vemdalen S 199 C10
Veme N 48 B2
Véménd H 125 A4
Vemmedrup DK 61 D2
Vena S 62 A3
Venaco F 180 A2
Venafro I 169 B4
Venarey-les-Laumes F 104 B3
Venaría I 119 B4
Venasca I 133 A3
Venčane SRB 127 C2
Vence F 132 B3
Venda Nova
Coimbra P 154 A2
Leiria P 154 B2
Vendas Novas P 154 C2
Vendays-Montalivet F 114 C2
Vendel S 51 B4
Vendelso S 57 A4
Vendeuil F 91 B3
Vendeuvre-sur-Barse F 104 A3
Vendoeuvres F 115 B5
Vendôme F 103 B3
Venelles F 131 B4
Veness GB 33 B4
Venézia = Venice I 122 B1
Venialbo E 150 A2
Venice = Venézia I 122 B1
Vénissieux F 117 B4
Venjan S 49 B5
Venlo NL 80 A2
Vennesla N 53 B3
Vennesund N 195 E3
Vennezey F 92 C2
Venn Green GB 42 B2
Venosa I 172 B1
Venray NL 80 A1
Vent A 108 C1
Venta de Baños E 142 C2
Venta del Moro E 158 B2
Venta de los Santos E 157 B4
Venta las Ranas E 142 A1
Ventanueva E 141 A4
Ventas de Huelma E 163 A4
Ventas de Zafarraya E 163 B3
Ventavon F 132 A1
Ventimíglia I 133 B3
Ventnor GB 44 C2
Ventosa de la Sierra E 143 C4
Ventosilla E 143 C4
Ventspils LV 8 D2
Venturina I 134 B3
Venzolasca F 180 A2
Venzone I 122 A2
Vép H 111 B3
Vera
E 164 B3
N 199 B9
Vera Cruz P 160 A2
Vera de Bidasoa E 144 A2
Vera de Moncayo E 144 C2
Verbánia I 119 B5
Verberie F 90 B2
Verbicaro I 174 B1
Verbier CH 119 A4
Vercelli I 119 B5
Vercel-Villedieu-le-Camp F 105 B5
Verchen D 66 C1
Vercheny F 118 C2
Verclause F 131 A4
Verdalsøra N 199 B8
Verden D 72 B2
Verdens Ende N 54 A1
Verdikoussa GR 182 D3
Verdille F 115 C3
Verdú E 147 C2
Verdun F 92 B1
Verdun-sur-Garonne F 129 C4
Verdun-sur-le-Doubs F 105 C4
Veresegyház H 112 B3
Verfeil F 129 C4
Vergato I 135 A4
Vergel E 159 C4
Vergeletto CH 120 A1
Verges E 147 B4
Vergiate I 120 B1
Vergt F 129 A3
Veria GR 182 C4
Verín E 141 C3
Veringenstadt D 107 A4
Verl D 81 A4
Verma N 198 C5
Vermand F 90 B3
Vermelha P 154 B1
Vermenton F 104 B2
Vernago I 108 C1
Vernante I 133 A3
Vernantes F 102 B2
Vernár SK 99 C4
Vernasca I 120 C2
Vernayaz CH 119 A4
Vernazza I 134 A2
Vern-d'Anjou F 102 B1
Verneřice CZ 84 B2
Vernet F 146 A2
Vernet-les-Bains F 146 B3
Verneuil F 91 B3
Verneuil-sur-Avre F 89 B4
Vernier CH 118 A3
Vérnio I 135 A4
Vérnole I 173 B4
Vernon F 90 B1
Vernoux-en-Vivarais F 117 C4
Veróce H 112 B3
Verolanuova I 120 B3
Véroli I 169 B3
Verona I 121 B4
Verpelét H 113 B4
Verrabotn N 199 B7
Verrès I 119 B4
Verrey-sous-Salmaise F 104 B3
Verrières F 115 B4
Versailles F 90 C2
Versam CH 107 C4
Verseg H 112 B3
Versmold D 71 B5
Versoix CH 118 A3
Verteillac F 115 C4
Vértesacsa H 112 B2
Vertou F 101 B4
Vertus F 91 C3
Verviers B 80 B1
Vervins F 91 B3
Verwood GB 43 B5
Veryan GB 42 B2
Veržej SLO 111 C3
Verzuolo I 133 A3
Verzy F 91 B4
Vescovato F 180 A2
Vése H 124 A3
Veselínad Lužnicí CZ 96 B2
Veselínad Moravou CZ 98 C1
Veseliy BG 17 D7
Vésime I 119 C5
Veskoniemi FIN 193 D11
Vesoul F 105 B5
Vespolate I 120 B1
Vessigebro S 60 C2
Vestbygd N 52 B2
Vestenanova I 121 B4
Vester Husby S 56 B2
Vester Nebel DK 59 C2
Vesterøhavn DK 58 A3
Vester Torup DK 58 A2
Vester Vedsted DK 59 C1
Vestervig DK 58 B1
Vestfossen N 53 A5
Vestmannaeyjar IS 190 D5
Vestmarka N 48 C3
Vestnes N 198 C4
Vestone I 120 B3
Vestre Gausdal N 48 A2
Vestre Jakobselv N 193 B13
Vestre Slidre N 47 A5
Vesyegonsk RUS 9 C10
Veszprém H 112 B1
Veszprémvarsány H 112 B1
Vésztő H 113 C5
Vetlanda S 62 A3
Vetovo HR 125 B3
Vetralla I 168 A2
Větrný Jeníkov CZ 97 B3
Vétroz CH 119 A4
Vetschau D 84 A2
Vettasjärvi S 196 B4
Vetto I 134 A3
Vetulónia I 135 C3
Veules-les-Roses F 89 A4
Veulettes-sur-Mer F 89 A4
Veum N 53 A4
Veurne B 78 A2
Veverská Bítýška CZ 97 B4
Vevey CH 106 C1
Vevi GR 182 C3
Vevring N 46 A2
Vex CH 119 A4
Veynes F 132 A1
Veyre-Monton F 116 B3
Veyrier F 118 B3
Vézelay F 104 B2
Vézelise F 92 C2
Vézenobres F 131 A3
Vezins F 102 B1
Vézins-de-Lévézou F 130 A1
Vezirhan TR 187 B5
Vezirköprü TR 23 A8
Vezza di Óglio I 120 A3
Vezzani F 180 A2
Vezzano I 121 A4
Vezzano sul Cróstolo I 121 C3
Vi S 200 D3
Viadana I 121 C3
Via Gloria P 160 B2
Viana E 143 B4
Viana do Alentejo P 154 C2
Viana do Bolo E 141 B3
Viana do Castelo P 148 A1
Vianden L 92 B2
Viannos GR 185 D6
Viaréggio I 134 B3
Viator E 164 C2
Vibble S 57 C4
Viborg DK 58 B2
Vibo Valéntia I 175 C2
Vibraye F 102 A2
Vic E 147 C3
Vícar E 164 C2
Vicarello I 134 B3
Vicari I 176 B2
Vicchio I 135 B4
Vicdesses F 146 B2
Vic-en-Bigorre F 145 A4
Vicenza I 121 B4
Vic-Fézensac F 129 C3
Vichy F 117 A3
Vickan S 60 B2
Vickerstown GB 36 B3
Vic-le-Comte F 116 B3
Vico F 180 A1
Vico del Gargano I 171 B3
Vico Equense I 170 C2
Vicopisano I 134 B3
Vicosoprano CH 120 A2
Vicovaro I 169 A2
Vic-sur-Aisne F 90 B3
Vic-sur-Cère F 116 C2
Victoria = Rabat M 175 C3
Vidago P 148 A2
Vidauban F 132 B2
Vide P 148 B2
Videbæk DK 59 B1
Videm SLO 123 B3
Videseter N 198 D4
Vidigueira P 160 A2
Vidin BG 16 D5
Vidlin GB 33 A5
Vidsel S 196 D3
Vidzy BY 13 A7
Viechtach D 95 B4
Vieille-Brioude F 117 B3
Vieira P 154 B2
Vieira do Minho P 148 A1
Vieiros P 155 C3
Vielha E 145 B4
Vielle-Aure F 145 B4
Viellespesse F 116 B3
Viellevigne F 114 B2
Vielmur-sur-Agout F 130 B1
Vielsalm B 80 B1
Viels Maison F 91 C3
Vienenburg D 73 C3
Vienna = Wien A 111 A3
Vienne F 117 B4
Vieritz D 73 B5
Viernheim D 93 B4
Vierraden D 74 A3
Viersen D 80 A2
Vierville-sur-Mer F 88 A3
Vierzon F 103 B4
Vieselbach D 82 B3
Vieste I 171 B4
Vietas S 194 C9
Vieteren B 78 B2
Vietri di Potenza I 172 B1
Vietri sul Mare I 170 C2
Vieux-Boucau-les-Bains F 128 C1
Vif F 118 B2
Vig DK 61 D1
Vigásio I 121 B3
Vigaun A 109 B4
Vigeland N 52 B3
Vigeois F 116 B1
Vigévano I 120 B1
Viggianello I 174 B2
Viggiano I 174 A1
Vigliano I 169 A3
Vigmostad N 52 B3
Vignale I 119 B5
Vignanello I 168 A2
Vigneulles-lès-Hattonchâtel F 92 C1
Vignevieille F 146 B3
Vignola I 135 A4
Vignory F 105 A4
Vignoux-sur Barangeon F 103 B4
Vigo E 140 B2
Vigo di Fassa I 121 A4
Vigone I 119 C4
Vigrestad N 52 B1
Vihiers F 102 B1
Viitasaari FIN 8 A4
Vik IS 190 D6
Vik
Nordland N 195 E3
Rogaland N 52 B1
Sogn og Fjordane N 46 A3
S 63 C2
Vika S 50 B2
Vikajärvi FIN 197 C9
Vikane N 54 A1
Vikarbyn S 50 B2
Vike N 46 B2
Vikedal N 52 A1
Vikeland N 53 B3
Viken
Jämtland S 199 A10
Skåne S 61 C2
Viker N 48 B2
Vikersund N 48 C1
Vikeså N 52 B2
Vikevåg N 52 A1
Vikingstad S 56 B1
Vikmanshyttan S 50 B2
Vikna N 199 A7
Vikøy N 46 B3
Vikran
Troms N 192 C2
Troms N 194 B7
Viksjö S 200 D3
Viksøyri N 46 A3
Viksta S 51 B4
Vila Boim P 155 C3
Vila Chãde Ourique P 154 B2
Viladamat E 147 B4
Vila de Cruces E 140 B2
Vila de Rei P 154 B2
Vila do Bispo P 160 B1
Vila do Conde P 148 A1
Viladrau E 147 C3
Vila Flor P 149 A2
Vila Franca das Navas P 149 B2
Vilafranca del Maestrat E 153 B3
Vilafranca del Penedès E 147 C2
Vila Franca de Xira P 154 C1
Vila Fresca P 154 C1
Vilagarcía de Arousa E 140 B2
Vilajuiga E 147 B4
Vilamarin E 140 B3
Vilamartín de Valdeorras E 141 B3
Vila Nogueira P 154 C1
Vila Nova da Baronia P 154 C2
Vilanova de Castelló E 159 B3
Vila Nova de Cerveira P 140 C2
Vila Nova de Famalicão P 148 A1
Vila Nova de Foz Côa P 149 A2
Vila Nova de Gaia P 148 A1
Vila Nova de Milfontes P 160 B1
Vila Nova de Paiva P 148 B2
Vila Nova de São Bento P 161 B2
Vilanova de Sau E 147 C3
Vilanova i la Geltrú E 147 C2
Vilapedre E 140 A3
Vila Pouca de Aguiar P 148 A2
Vila Praja de Ancora P 148 A1
Vilarandelo P 148 A2
Vilar de Santos E 140 B3
Vilardevós E 141 C3
Vila Real P 148 A2
Vila-real de los Infantes E 159 B3
Vila Real de Santo António P 160 B2
Vilar Formosa P 149 B3
Vila-Rodona E 147 C2
Vila Ruiva P 160 A2
Vilasantar E 140 A2
Vilaseca E 147 C2
Vila Seca P 148 B1
Vilassar de Mar E 147 C3
Vilasund S 195 D5
Vila Velha de Ródão P 155 B3
Vila Verde
Braga P 148 A1
Lisboa P 154 B1
Vila Verde de Filcalho P 161 B2
Vila Viçosa P 155 C3
Vilches E 157 B4
Vildbjerg DK 59 B1
Vilémov CZ 97 B3
Vileyka BY 13 A7
Vilhelmina S 200 B2
Vilia GR 184 A4
Viljandi EST 8 C4
Villabáñez E 150 A3
Villablanca E 161 B2
Villablino E 141 B4
Villabona E 144 A1
Villabragima E 142 C1
Villabuena del Puente E 150 A2
Villacadima E 151 A4
Villacañas E 157 A4
Villacarriedo E 143 A3
Villacarrillo E 164 A1
Villa Castelli I 173 B3
Villacastín E 150 B3
Villach A 109 C4
Villacidro I 179 C2
Villaconejos E 151 B4
Villaconejos de Trabaque E 152 B1
Villa Cova de Lixa P 148 A1
Villada E 142 B2
Villadangos del Páramo E 141 B5
Villadecanes E 141 B4
Villa del Prado E 150 B3
Villa del Rio E 157 C3
Villadepera E 149 A3
Villa de Peralonso E 149 A3
Villa di Chiavenna I 120 A2
Villadiego E 142 B2
Villadompardo E 163 A3
Villadóssola I 119 A5
Villaeles de Valdavia E 142 B2
Villaescusa de Haro E 158 B1
Villafáfila E 142 C1
Villafeliche E 152 A2
Villaflores E 150 A2
Villafrades de Campos E 142 B2
Villafranca
Avila E 150 B2
Navarra E 144 B2
Villafranca de Córdoba E 157 C3
Villafranca del Bierzo E 141 B4
Villafranca de los Barros E 155 C4
Villafranca de los Caballeros E 157 A4
Villafranca di Verona I 121 B3
Villafranca in Lunigiana I 134 A2
Villafranca-Montes de Oca E 143 B3
Villafranca Tirrena I 177 A4
Villafranco del Campo E 152 B2
Villafranco del Guadalquivir E 161 B3
Villafrati I 176 B2
Villafrechós E 142 C1
Villafruela E 143 C3
Villagarcia de las Torres E 156 B1
Villaggio Mancuso I 175 B2
Villagonzalo E 156 B1
Villagotón E 141 B4
Villagrains F 128 B2
Villaharta E 156 B3
Villahermosa E 158 C1
Villaherreros E 142 B2
Villahoz E 143 B3
Villaines-la-Juhel F 89 B3
Villajoyosa E 159 C3
Villalago I 169 B3
Villalba
E 140 A3
I 176 B2
Villalba de Calatrava E 157 B4
Villalba de Guardo E 142 B2
Villalba del Alcor E 161 B3
Villalba de la Sierra E 152 B1
Villalba de los Alcores E 142 C2
Villalba de los Barros E 155 C4
Villalba del Rey E 151 B5
Villalcampo E 149 A3
Villalcázar de Sirga E 142 B2
Villalengua E 152 A2
Villalgordo del Júcar E 158 B1
Villalgordo del Marquesado E 158 B1
Villalmóndar E 143 B3
Villalón de Campos E 142 B1
Villalonga E 159 C3
Villalonso E 150 A2
Villalpando E 142 C1
Villaluenga E 151 B4
Villalumbroso E 142 B2
Villálvaro E 143 C3
Villamalea E 158 B2
Villamanán E 142 B1
Villamanín E 142 B1
Villamanrique E 157 B5
Villamanrique de la Condesa E 161 B3
Villamanta E 151 B3
Villamantilla E 151 B3
Villamar I 179 C2
Villamartín E 162 B2
Villamartín de Campos E 142 B2
Villamartín de Don Sancho E 142 B1
Villamassárgia I 179 C2
Villamayor E 142 A1
Villamayor de Calatrava E 157 B3
Villamayor de Campos E 142 C1
Villamayor de Santiago E 157 A5
Villamblard F 129 A3
Villamejil E 141 B4
Villamesias E 156 A2
Villaminaya E 157 A4
Villa Minozzo I 134 A3
Villamor de los Escuderos E 150 A2
Villamoronta E 142 B2
Villamuelas E 151 C4
Villamuriel de Cerrato E 142 C2
Villandraut F 128 B2
Villanova I 173 B3
Villanova d'Asti I 119 C4
Villanova del Battista I 171 B3
Villanova Mondovì I 133 A3
Villanova Monteleone I 178 B2
Villante E 143 B3
Villantério I 120 B2
Villanubla E 142 C2
Villanueva de Alcardete E 157 A4
Villanueva de Alcorón E 152 B1
Villanueva de Algaidas E 163 A3
Villanueva de Argaña E 143 B3
Villanueva de Bogas E 157 A4
Villanueva de Córdoba E 156 B3
Villanueva de Gállego E 144 C3
Villanueva del Aceral E 150 A3
Villanueva de la Concepcion E 163 B3
Villanueva de la Fuente E 158 C1
Villanueva de la Jara E 158 B2
Villanueva de la Reina E 157 B4
Villanueva del Arzobispo E 164 A2
Villanueva de la Serena E 156 B2
Villanueva de la Sierra E 149 B3
Villanueva de las Manzanas E 142 B1
Villanueva de las Peras E 141 C5
Villanueva de las Torres E 164 B1
Villanueva de la Vera E 150 B2
Villanueva del Campo E 142 C1
Villanueva del Duque E 156 B3
Villanueva del Fresno E 155 C3
Villanueva del Huerva E 152 A2
Villanueva de los Castillejos E 161 B2
Villanueva de los Infantes E 157 B5
Villanueva del Rey E 156 B2
Villanueva del Rio E 162 A2
Villanueva del Río y Minas E 162 A2
Villanueva del Rosario E 163 B3
Villanueva del Trabuco E 163 A3
Villanueva de Mesia E 163 A4
Villanueva de Nía E 142 B2
Villanueva de Oscos E 141 A4
Villanueva de San Carlos E 157 B4
Villanueva de San Juan E 162 A2
Villanueva de Tapia E 163 A3
Villanueva de Valdegovia E 143 B3
Villány H 125 B4
Villaputzu I 179 C3
Villaquejida E 142 B1
Villaquilambre E 142 B1
Villaquiran de los Infantes E 142 B2
Villaralto E 156 B3
Villarcayo E 143 B3
Villard-de-Lans F 118 B2
Villar de Barrio E 140 B3
Villar de Cañas E 158 B1
Villar de Chinchilla E 158 C2
Villar de Ciervo E 149 B3
Villardeciervos E 141 C4
Villar de Domingo Garcia E 152 B1
Villardefrades E 142 C1
Villar del Arzobispo E 159 B3
Villar del Buey E 149 A3
Villar del Cobo E 152 B2
Villar del Humo E 158 B2
Villar de los Navarros E 152 A2
Villar del Pedroso E 156 A2

Villar del Rey E 155 B4
Villar del Rio E 143 B4
Villar del Saz de Navalón E 152 B1
Villar de Rena E 156 A2
Villarejo E 151 A4
Villarejo de Fuentes E 158 B1
Villarejo de Orbigo E 141 B5
Villarejo de Salvanes E 151 B4
Villarejo-Periesteban E 158 B1
Villares del Saz E 158 B1
Villaretto I 119 B4
Villargordo del Cabriel E 158 B2
Villarino E 149 A3
Villarino de Conso E 141 B3
Villarluengo E 153 B3
Villarobe E 143 B3
Villarosa I 177 B3
Villar Perosa I 119 C4
Villarramiel E 142 B2
Villarrasa E 161 B3
Villarreal de San Carlos E 150 C1
Villarrin de Campos E 142 C1
Villarrobledo E 158 B1
Villarroya de la Sierra E 152 A2
Villarroya de los Pinares E 153 B3
Villarrubia de los Ojos E 157 A4
Villarrubia de Santiago E 151 C4
Villarrubio E 151 C5
Villars-les-Dombes F 117 A5
Villarta E 158 B2
Villarta de los Montes E 156 A3
Villarta de San Juan E 157 A4
Villasana de Mena E 143 A3
Villasandino E 142 B2
Villa San Giovanni I 175 C1
Villa Santa Maria I 169 B4
Villasante E 143 A3
Villa Santina I 122 A1
Villasarracino E 142 B2
Villasayas E 151 A5
Villasdardo E 149 A3
Villaseca de Henares E 151 B5
Villaseca de Laciana E 141 B4
Villaseca de la Sagra E 151 C4
Villaseco de los Gamitos E 149 A3
Villaseco de los Reyes E 149 A3
Villasequilla de Yepes E 151 C4
Villasimíus I 179 C3
Villasmundo I 177 B4
Villasor I 179 C2
Villastar E 152 B2
Villastellone I 119 C4
Villatobas E 151 C4
Villatorp E 150 B2
Villatoya E 158 B2
Villavaliente E 158 B2
Villavelayo E 143 B4
Villavella E 141 B3
Villaver de de Guadalimar E 158 C1
Villaverde del Rio E 162 A2
Villaviciosa E 142 A1
Villaviciosa de Córdoba E 156 B3
Villaviciosa de Odón E 151 B4
Villavieja de Yeltes E 149 B3
Villayón E 141 A4
Villé F 93 C3
Villebois-Lavalette F 115 C4
Villecerf F 90 C2
Villecomtal F 130 A1
Villedieu-les-Poêles F 88 B2
Villedieu-sur-Indre F 103 C3
Ville-di-Pietrabugno F 180 A2
Villedômain F 103 B3
Villefagnan F 115 B4
Villefontaine F 118 B2
Villefort F 131 A2
Villefranche-d'Albigeois F 130 B1
Villefranche-d'Allier F 116 A2
Villefranche-de-Lauragais F 146 A2
Villefranche-de-Lonchat F 128 B3
Villefranche-de-Panat F 130 A1
Villefranche-de-Rouergue F 130 A1
Villefranche-du-Périgord F 129 B4
Villefranche-sur-Cher F 103 B3
Villefranche-sur-Mer F 133 B3
Villefranche-sur-Saône F 117 A4
Villegenon F 103 B4
Villel E 152 B2
Villemaur-sur-Vanne F 104 A2
Villemontais F 117 B3
Villemur-sur-Tarn F 129 C4
Villena E 159 C3
Villenauxe-la-Grande F 91 C3
Villenave-d'Ornon F 128 B2
Villeneuve
CH 119 A3
F 129 B5
Villeneuve-d'Ascq F 78 B3
Villeneuve-de-Berg F 131 A3
Villeneuve-de-Marsan F 128 C2
Villeneuve-de-Rivière F 145 A4
Villeneuve-la-Guyard F 90 C3
Villeneuve-l'Archevêque F 104 A2
Villeneuve-le-Comte F 90 C2
Villeneuve-lès-Avignon F 131 B3
Villeneuve-les-Corbières F 146 B3
Villeneuve-St Georges F 90 C2
Villeneuve-sur-Allier F 104 C2
Villeneuve-sur-Lot F 129 B3
Villeneuve-sur-Yonne F 104 A2
Villeréal F 129 B3
Villerias E 142 C2
Villeromain F 103 B3
Villers-Bocage
Calvados F 88 A3
Somme F 90 B2
Villers-Bretonneux F 90 B2
Villers-Carbonnel F 90 B2
Villers-Cotterêts F 90 B3
Villersexel F 105 B5
Villers-Farlay F 105 C4
Villers-le-Gambon B 79 B4
Villers-le-Lac F 106 B1
Villers-sur-Mer F 89 A3
Villerupt F 92 B1
Villerville F 89 A4
Villeseneux F 91 C4
Ville-sous-la-Ferté F 105 A3
Ville-sur-Illon F 105 A5
Ville-sur-Tourbe F 91 B4
Villetrun F 103 B3
Villetta Barrea I 169 B3
Villeurbanne F 117 B4
Villeveyrac F 130 B2
Villevocance F 117 B4
Villiers-St Benoit F 104 B2
Villiers-St Georges F 91 C3
Villingen D 106 A3
Villmar D 81 B4
Villoldo E 142 B2
Villon F 104 B3
Villoria E 150 B2
Vilnes N 46 A1
Vilnius LT 13 A6
Vils
A 108 B1
DK 58 B1
Vilsbiburg D 95 C4
Vilseck D 95 B3
Vilshofen D 96 C1
Vilshult S 63 B2
Vilusi MNE 139 C4
Vilvestre E 149 A3
Vilvoorde B 79 B4
Vimeiro P 154 B1
Vimercate I 120 B2
Vimianzo E 140 A1
Vimieiro P 154 C3
Vimioso P 149 A3
Vimmerby S 62 A3
Vimoutiers F 89 B4
Vimperk CZ 96 B1
Vimy F 78 B2
Vinadi CH 108 C1
Vinadio I 133 A3
Vinaixa E 147 C1
Vinarós E 153 B4
Vinäs S 50 B1
Vinay F 118 B2
Vinberg S 60 C2
Vinca F 146 B3
Vinča SRB 127 C2
Vinchiaturo I 170 B2
Vinci I 135 B3
Vindeby DK 65 A3
Vindelgransele S 195 E9
Vindeln S 200 B5
Vinderup DK 58 B1
Vindsvik N 52 A2
Vinets F 91 C4
Vineuil F 103 B3
Vinga RO 126 A3
Vingåker S 56 A1
Vingnes N 48 A2
Vingrau F 146 B3
Vingrom N 48 A2
Vinhais P 149 A3
Vinica
HR 124 A2
MK 182 B4
SK 112 A3
SLO 123 B4
Viniegra de Arriba E 143 B4
Vinje
Hordaland N 46 B3
Sør-Trøndelag N 198 B6
Telemark N 53 A3
Vinkovci HR 125 B4
Vinliden S 200 B3
Vinninga S 55 B4
Vinnytsya UA 13 D8
Vinon F 103 B4
Vinon-sur-Verdon F 132 B1
Vinslöv S 61 C3
Vinstra N 48 A1
Vintjärn S 50 B3
Vintrosa S 55 A5
Viñuela E 163 B3
Viñuela de Sayago E 149 A4
Viñuelas E 151 B4
Vinuesa E 143 C4
Vinzelberg D 73 B4
Viöl D 64 B2
Viola I 133 A3
Violay F 117 B4
Vipava SLO 122 B2
Vipiteno I 108 C2
Vipperow D 74 A1
Vir
BIH 138 B3
HR 137 A4
Vira CH 120 A1
Vire F 88 B3
Vireda S 62 A2
Vireux F 91 A4
Virgen A 109 B3
Virgen de la Cabeza E 157 B3
Virginia IRL 27 C3
Virieu F 118 B2
Virieu-le-Grand F 118 B2
Virje HR 124 A2
Virkkunen FIN 197 D10
Virklund DK 59 B2
Virovitica HR 124 B3
Virsbo S 50 C3
Virserum S 62 A3
Virtaniemi FIN 193 D12
Virton B 92 B1
Virtsu EST 8 C3
Viry F 118 A3
Vis HR 138 B2
Visbek D 71 B5
Visby
DK 64 A1
S 57 C4
Visé B 80 B1
Višegrad BIH 139 B5
Viserba I 136 A1
Viseu P 148 B2
Visiedo E 152 B2
Viskafors S 60 B2
Visland N 52 B2
Vislanda S 62 B2
Visnes N 52 A1
Višnja Gora SLO 123 B3
Višnjan HR 122 B2
Višnové CZ 97 C4
Visnums-Kil S 55 A5
Viso del Marqués E 157 B4
Visoko
BIH 139 B4
SLO 123 A3
Visone I 119 C5
Visp CH 119 A4
Vissefjärda S 63 B3
Visselhövede D 72 B2
Vissenbjerg DK 59 C3
Visso I 136 C2
Vistabella del Maestrat E 153 B3
Vistheden S 196 D3
Vita I 176 B1
Vitanje SLO 123 A4
Vitebsk = Vitsyebsk BY 13 A9
Viterbo I 168 A2
Vitez BIH 139 A3
Vithkuq AL 182 C2
Vitigudino E 149 A3
Vitina
BIH 138 B3
GR 184 B3
Vitis A 97 C3
Vítkov CZ 98 B1
Vitoria-Gasteiz E 143 B4
Vitré F 101 A4
Vitrey-sur-Mance F 105 B4
Vitry-en-Artois F 78 B2
Vitry-le-François F 91 C4
Vitry-sur-Seine F 90 C2
Vitsand S 49 B4
Vitsyebsk = Vitebsk BY 13 A9
Vittangi S 196 B4
Vittaryd S 60 C3
Vitteaux F 104 B3
Vittel F 105 A4
Vittinge S 51 C4
Vittória I 177 C3
Vittório Véneto I 122 B1
Vittsjö S 61 C3
Viù I 119 B4
Viul N 48 B2
Vivario F 180 A2
Viveiro E 140 A3
Vivel del Rio Martin E 152 B3
Viver E 159 B3
Viverols F 117 B3
Viveros E 158 C1
Viviers F 131 A3
Vivonne F 115 B4
Vivy F 102 B1
Vize TR 186 A2
Vizille F 118 B2
Viziňada HR 122 B2
Viziru RO 17 C7
Vizovice CZ 98 B1
Vizvár H 124 A3
Vizzavona F 180 A2
Vizzini I 177 B3
Vlachiotis GR 184 C3
Vlachovice CZ 98 B1
Vlachovo SK 99 C4
Vláchovo Březi CZ 96 B1
Vladimirci SRB 127 C1
Vladimirovac SRB 127 B2
Vladislav CZ 97 B3
Vlagtwedde NL 71 A4
Vlajkovac SRB 127 B3
Vlasenica BIH 139 A4
Vlašim CZ 96 B2
Vlatkovići BIH 138 A3
Vledder NL 70 B3
Vlissingen NL 79 A3
Vlkolínec SK 99 B3
Vlorë AL 182 C1
Vlotho D 72 B1
Vnanje Gorice SLO 123 B3
Vobarno I 121 B3
Voćin HR 124 B3
Vöcklabruck A 109 A4
Vöcklamarkt A 109 B4
Vodanj SRB 127 C2
Voderady SK 98 C1
Vodice
Istarska HR 123 B3
Šibenska HR 137 B4
SLO 123 A3
Vodňany CZ 96 B2
Vodnjan HR 122 C2
Vodskov DK 58 A3
Voe GB 33 A5
Voerså DK 58 A3
Voghera I 120 C2
Vogogna I 119 A5
Vogošća BIH 139 B4
Vogué F 131 A3
Vohburg D 95 C3
Vohenstrauss D 95 B4
Vöhl D 81 A4
Vöhrenbach D 106 A3
Vöhringen D 94 C2
Void-Vacon F 92 C1
Voiron F 118 B2
Voise F 90 C1
Voisey F 105 B4
Voiteg RO 126 B3
Voiteur F 105 C4
Voitsberg A 110 B2
Vojakkala FIN 196 D7
Vojens DK 59 C2
Vojka SRB 127 C2
Vojlovica SRB 127 C2
Vojnić HR 123 B4
Vojnice SK 112 B2
Vojnik SLO 123 A4
Vojvoda Stepa SRB 126 B2
Volada GR 188 D2
Volargne I 121 B3
Volary CZ 96 C1
Volče SLO 122 A2
Volda N 198 C3
Volendam NL 70 B2
Volga RUS 9 C11
Volimes GR 184 B1
Volissos GR 185 A6
Volkach D 94 B2
Völkermarkt A 110 C1
Volkhov RUS 9 C8
Völklingen D 92 B2
Volkmarsen D 81 A5
Voll N 198 C4
Vollenhove NL 70 B2
Vollore-Montagne F 117 B3
Vollsjö S 61 D3
Volodymyr-Volyns'kyy UA 13 C6
Volokolamsk RUS 9 D9
Volos GR 182 D4
Volosovo RUS 9 C6
Volovets UA 13 D5
Voltággio I 120 C1
Volta Mantovana I 121 B3
Volterra I 135 B3
Voltri I 133 A4
Volturara Áppula I 170 B3
Volturara Irpina I 170 C2
Volvic F 116 B3
Volx F 132 B1
Volyně CZ 96 B1
Vonitsa GR 182 E2
Vönöck H 111 B4
Vonsild DK 59 C2
Voorschoten NL 70 B1
Vopnafjörður IS 191 B11
Vorau A 110 B2
Vorbasse DK 59 C2
Vorchdorf A 109 B4
Vorden
D 71 B5
NL 71 B3
Vordernberg A 110 B1
Vordingborg DK 65 A4
Vorë AL 182 B1
Voreppe F 118 B2
Vorey F 117 B3
Vorgod DK 59 B1
Vormsund N 48 B3
Võru EST 8 D5
Voskopojë AL 182 C2
Voss N 46 B3
Votice CZ 96 B2
Voué F 91 C4
Vouillé F 115 B4
Voulx F 90 C2
Voussac F 116 A3
Vouvray F 102 B2
Vouvry CH 119 A3
Vouzela P 148 B1
Vouziers F 91 B4
Voves F 103 A3
Voxna S 50 A2
Voy GB 33 B3
Voynitsa RUS 3 D12
Voznesenye RUS 9 B9
Vrå
DK 58 A2
S 60 C3
Vráble SK 98 C2
Vračenovići MNE 139 C4
Vračev Gaj SRB 127 C3
Vraćevsnica SRB 127 C2
Vrådal N 53 A4
Vrakneika GR 184 A2
Vrana HR 123 C3
Vranduk BIH 139 A3
Vrångö S 60 B1
Vrani RO 127 B3
Vranić SRB 127 C2
Vraniči BIH 139 B4
Vranja HR 123 B3
Vranjak BIH 125 C4
Vranje SRB 16 D4
Vranovice CZ 97 C4
Vranov nad Dyje CZ 97 C3
Vransko SLO 123 A3
Vrapčići BIH 139 B3
Vratimov CZ 98 B2
Vratsa BG 17 D5
Vrbanja HR 125 C4
Vrbanjci BIH 124 C3
Vrbas SRB 126 B1
Vrbaška BIH 124 B3
Vrbnik
Primorsko-Goranska HR 123 B3
Zadarsko-Kninska HR 138 A2
Vrbno pod Pradědem CZ 85 B5
Vrboska HR 138 B2
Vrbov SK 99 B4
Vrbovce SK 98 C1
Vrbové SK 98 C1
Vrbovec HR 124 B2
Vrbovski SRB 127 C2
Vrbovsko HR 123 B4
Vrchlabí CZ 84 B3
Vrčin SRB 127 C2
Vrdy CZ 97 B3
Vrebac HR 137 A4
Vreden D 71 B3
Vreoci SRB 127 C2
Vretstorp S 55 A5
Vrginmost HR 124 B1
Vrgorac HR 138 B3
Vrhnika SLO 123 B3
Vrhovine HR 123 C4
Vrhpolie SRB 127 C1
Vriezenveen NL 71 B3
Vrigne-aux-Bois F 91 B4
Vrigstad S 62 A2
Vrlika HR 138 B2
Vrnograč BIH 124 B1
Vron F 78 B1
Vroomshoop NL 71 B3
Vroutek CZ 83 B5
Vrpolje HR 125 B4
Vršac SRB 126 B3
Vrsar HR 122 B2
Vrsi HR 137 A4
Vrtoče BIH 124 C2
Vrútky SK 98 B2
Všeruby CZ 95 B4
Všestary CZ 85 B3
Vsetín CZ 98 B1
Vučkovica SRB 127 D2
Vught NL 79 A5
Vuillafans F 105 B5
Vukovar HR 125 B5
Vuku N 199 B8
Vulcan RO 17 C5
Vulcăneşti MD 17 C8
Vuoggatjålme S 195 D7
Vuojärvi FIN 197 B9
Vuolijoki FIN 3 D10
Vuollerim S 196 C3
Vuotso FIN 197 A10
Vuzenica SLO 110 C2
Vyartsilya RUS 9 A7
Vyborg RUS 9 B6
Výčapy CZ 97 B3
Výčapy-Opatovce SK 98 C2
Východna SK 99 B3
Vydrany SK 111 A4
Vyerkhnyadzvinsk BY 13 A7
Vyhne SK 98 C2
Vy-lès Lure F 105 B5
Vylkove UA 17 C8
Vynohradiv UA 17 A5
Vyshniy Volochek RUS 9 D9
Vyškov CZ 97 B5
Vysokánad Kysucou SK 98 B2
Vysoké Mýto CZ 97 B4
Vysokovsk RUS 9 D10
Vyšší Brod CZ 96 C2
Vytegra RUS 9 B10

W

Waabs D 64 B2
Waalwijk NL 79 A5
Waarschoot B 79 A3
Wabern D 81 A5
Wąbrzeźno PL 69 B3
Wąchock PL 87 A5
Wachow D 74 B1
Wachów PL 86 B2
Wächtersbach D 81 B5
Wackersdorf D 95 B4
Waddington GB 40 B3
Wadebridge GB 42 B2
Wadelsdorf D 84 A2
Wädenswil CH 107 B3
Wadern D 92 B2
Wadersloh D 81 A4
Wadlew PL 86 A3
Wadowice PL 99 B3
Wagenfeld D 72 B1
Wageningen NL 70 C2
Waghäusel D 93 B4
Waging D 109 B3
Wagrain A 109 B4
Wagrowiec PL 76 B2
Wahlsdorf D 74 C2
Wahlstedt D 64 C3
Wahrenholz D 73 B3
Waiblingen D 94 C1
Waidhaus D 95 B4
Waidhofen an der Thaya A 97 C3
Waidhofen an der Ybbs A 110 B1
Waimes B 80 B2
Wainfleet All Saints GB 41 B4
Waizenkirchen A 96 C1
Wakefield GB 40 B2
Wałbrzych PL 85 B4
Walchensee D 108 B2
Walchsee A 109 B3
Wałcz PL 75 A5
Wald CH 107 B3
Waldaschaff D 94 B1
Waldbach A 110 B2
Waldböckelheim D 93 B3
Waldbröl D 81 B3
Waldeck D 81 A5
Waldenburg D 83 B4
Waldfischbach-Burgalben D 93 B3
Waldheim D 83 A5
Waldkappel D 82 A1
Waldkirch D 106 A2
Waldkirchen D 96 C1
Waldkirchen am Wesen A 96 C1
Waldkraiburg D 109 A3
Wald-Michelbach D 93 B4
Waldmohr D 93 B3
Waldmünchen D 95 B4
Waldring A 109 B3
Waldsassen D 95 A4
Waldshut D 106 B3
Waldstatt CH 107 B4
Waldwisse F 92 B2
Walenstadt CH 107 B4
Walentynów PL 87 A5
Walichnowy PL 86 A2
Walincourt F 90 A3
Walkenried D 82 A2
Walkeringham GB 40 B3
Wallasey GB 38 A3
Walldürn D 94 B1
Wallenfells D 82 B3
Wallenhorst D 71 B5
Wallers F 78 B3
Wallersdorf D 95 C4
Wallerstein D 94 C2
Wallingford GB 44 B2

Wallitz D 74 A1
Walls GB 33 A5
Wallsbüll D 64 B2
Walmer GB 45 B5
Walsall GB 40 C2
Walshoutem B 79 B5
Walsrode D 72 B2
Waltenhofen D 107 B5
Waltershausen D 82 B2
Waltham Abbey GB 45 B4
Waltham on the Wolds
GB 40 C3
Walton-on-Thames
GB 44 B3
Walton-on-the-Naze
GB 45 B5
Wamba E 142 C2
Wanderup D 64 B2
Wandlitz D 74 B2
Wanfried D 82 A2
Wangen im Allgäu
D 107 B4
Wangerooge D 71 A4
Wangersen D 72 A2
Wängi CH 107 B3
Wanna D 64 C1
Wansford GB 40 C3
Wantage GB 44 B2
Wanzleben D 73 B4
Waplewo PL 77 A5
Wapnica PL 75 A4
Wapno PL 76 B2
Warburg D 81 A5
Wardenburg D 71 A5
Ware GB 44 B3
Waregem B 79 B3
Wareham GB 43 B4
Waremme B 79 B5
Waren D 74 A1
Warendorf D 71 C4
Warga NL 70 A2
Warin D 65 C4
Wark GB 37 A4
Warka PL 87 A5
Warkworth GB 37 A5
Warlubie PL 69 B3
Warminster GB 43 A4
Warnemünde D 65 B5
Warnow D 65 C4
Warnsveld NL 70 B3
Warrenpoint GB 27 B4
Warrington GB 38 A4
Warsaw = Warszawa
PL 77 B6
Warsingsfehn D 71 A4
Warsow D 73 A4
Warstein D 81 A4
Warszawa = Warsaw
PL 77 B6
Warta PL 86 A2
Wartberg A 110 B1
Warth A 107 B5
Warwick GB 44 A2
Warza D 82 B2
Wasbister GB 33 B3
Washington GB 37 B5
Wąsosz PL 85 A4
Wasselonne F 93 C3
Wassen CH 107 C3
Wassenaar NL 70 B1
Wasserauen CH 107 B4
Wasserburg D 108 A3
Wassertrüdingen D 94 B2
Wassy F 91 C4
Wasungen D 82 B2
Watchet GB 43 A3
Waterford IRL 30 B1
Watergrasshill IRL 29 B3
Waterloo B 79 B4
Waterville IRL 29 C1
Watford GB 44 B3
Wathlingen D 72 B3
Watten
F 78 B2
GB 32 C3
Wattens A 108 B2
Watton GB 41 C4
Wattwil CH 107 B4
Waunfawr GB 38 A2
Wavignies F 90 B2
Wavre B 79 B4
Wearhead GB 37 B4
Węchadłow PL 87 B4
Wedel D 72 A2
Wedemark D 72 B2
Weedon Bec GB 44 A2
Weener D 71 A4
Weert NL 80 A1
Weesp NL 70 B2
Weeze D 80 A2
Weferlingen D 73 B4
Wegeleben D 82 A3
Weggis CH 106 B3
Węgierska-Górka
PL 99 B3
Węgliniec PL 84 A3
Węgorzyno PL 75 A4
Węgrzynice PL 75 B4
Wegscheid D 96 C1
Wehdel D 72 A1
Wehr D 106 B2
Weibersbrunn D 94 B1
Weichering D 95 C3
Weida D 83 B4
Weiden D 95 B4
Weidenberg D 95 B3
Weidenhain D 83 A4
Weidenstetten D 94 C1
Weierbach D 93 B3
Weikersheim D 94 B1
Weil D 108 A1
Weil am Rhein D 106 B2
Weilburg D 81 B4
Weil der Stadt D 93 C4
Weilerswist D 80 B2
Weilheim
Baden-Württemberg
D 94 C1
Bayern D 108 B2
Weilmünster D 81 B4
Weiltensfeld A 110 C1
Weimar D 82 B3
Weinberg D 94 B2
Weinfelden CH 107 B4
Weingarten
Baden-Württemberg
D 93 B4
Baden-Württemberg
D 107 B4
Weinheim D 93 B4
Weinstadt D 94 C1
Weismain D 82 B3
Weissbriach A 109 C4
Weissenbach A 108 B1
Weissenberg D 84 A2
Weissenbrunn D 82 B3
Weissenburg D 94 B2
Weissenfels D 83 A3
Weissenhorn D 94 C2
Weissenkirchen A 97 C3
Weissensee D 82 A3
Weissenstadt D 83 B3
Weisskirchen im
Steiermark A 110 B1
Weisstannen CH 107 C4
Weisswasser D 84 A2
Weitendorf D 65 C5
Weitersfeld A 97 C3
Weitersfelden A 96 C2
Weitnau D 107 B5
Wéitra A 96 C2
Weiz A 110 B2
Wejherowo PL 68 A3
Welkenraedt B 80 B1
Wellaune D 83 A4
Wellin B 91 A5
Wellingborough GB 44 A3
Wellington
Somerset GB 43 B3
Telford & Wrekin
GB 38 B4
Wellingtonbridge
IRL 30 B2
Wells GB 43 A4
Wells-next-the-Sea
GB 41 C4
Wels A 109 A5
Welschenrohr CH 106 B2
Welshpool GB 38 B3
Welver D 81 A3
Welwyn Garden City
GB 44 B3
Welzheim D 94 C1
Welzow D 84 A2
Wem GB 38 B4
Wembury GB 42 B2
Wemding D 94 C2
Wenden D 81 B3
Wendisch Rietz D 74 B3
Wendlingen D 94 C1
Weng A 109 A4
Weng bei Admont
A 110 B1
Wengen CH 106 C2
Wenigzell A 110 B2
Wennigsen D 72 B2
Wenns A 108 B1
Wenzenbach D 95 B4
Weppersdorf A 111 B3
Werben D 73 B4
Werbig D 74 C2
Werdau D 83 B4
Werder D 74 B1
Werdohl D 81 A3
Werfen A 109 B4
Werkendam NL 79 A4
Werl D 81 A3
Werlte D 71 B4
Wermelskirchen D 80 A3
Wermsdorf D 83 A4
Wernberg Köblitz D 95 B4
Werne D 81 A3
Werneck D 94 B2
Werneuchen D 74 B2
Wernigerode D 82 A2
Wertach D 108 B1
Wertheim D 94 B1
Wertingen D 94 C2
Weseke D 80 A2
Wesel D 80 A2
Wesenberg D 74 A1
Wesendorf D 73 B3
Wesołowo PL 77 A5
Wesselburen D 64 B1
Wesseling D 80 B2
West Bridgford GB 40 C2
West Bromwich GB 40 C2
Westbury
Shropshire GB 38 B4
Wiltshire GB 43 A4
Westbury-on-Severn
GB 39 C4
Westendorf A 108 B3
Westensee D 64 B3
Westerbork NL 71 B3
Westerburg D 81 B3
Westerhaar NL 71 B3
Westerholt D 71 A4
Westerkappeln D 71 B4
Westerland D 64 B1
Westerlo B 79 A4
Westerstede D 71 A4
West Haddon GB 44 A2
Westheim D 94 B2
Westhill GB 33 D4
Westkapelle
B 78 A3
NL 79 A3
West Kilbride GB 34 C3
West Linton GB 35 C4
West Lulworth GB 43 B4
West Mersea GB 45 B4
Westminster GB 44 B3
Weston GB 40 C1
Weston-super-Mare
GB 43 A4
Westport IRL 28 A2
Westruther GB 35 C5
West-Terschelling
NL 70 A2
Westward Ho! GB 42 A2
West Woodburn GB 37 A4
Wetheral GB 37 B4
Wetherby GB 40 B2
Wetter
Hessen D 81 B4
Nordrhein-Westfalen
D 80 A3
Wetteren B 79 A3
Wettin D 83 A3
Wettringen D 71 B4
Wetzikon CH 107 B3
Wetzlar D 81 B4
Wewelsfleth D 64 C2
Wexford IRL 30 B2
Weybridge GB 44 B3
Weyerbusch D 81 B3
Weyer Markt A 110 B1
Weyersheim F 93 C3
Weyhe D 72 B1
Weyhill GB 44 B2
Weymouth GB 43 B4
Weyregg A 109 B4
Węzyska PL 75 B3
Whalton GB 37 A5
Whauphill GB 36 B2
Wheatley GB 44 B2
Whickham GB 37 B5
Whipsnade GB 44 B3
Whitburn GB 35 C4
Whitby GB 37 B6
Whitchurch
Hampshire GB 44 B2
Herefordshire GB 39 C4
Shropshire GB 38 B4
White Bridge GB 32 D2
Whitegate IRL 29 C3
Whitehaven GB 36 B3
Whitehead GB 27 B5
Whithorn GB 36 B2
Whitley Bay GB 37 A5
Whitstable GB 45 B5
Whittington GB 38 B4
Whittlesey GB 41 C3
Wiązów PL 85 B5
Wick GB 32 C3
Wickede D 81 A3
Wickford GB 45 B4
Wickham GB 44 C2
Wickham Market GB 45 A5
Wicklow IRL 30 B2
Wicko PL 68 A2
Widawa PL 86 A2
Widdrington GB 37 A5
Widecombe in the Moor
GB 42 B3
Widemouth GB 42 B2
Widnes GB 38 A4
Widuchowo PL 74 A3
Więcbork PL 76 A2
Wiefelstede D 71 A5
Wiehe D 82 A3
Wiehl D 81 B3
Wiek D 66 B2
Większyce PL 86 B1
Wielbark PL 77 A5
Wiele PL 68 B2
Wieleń PL 75 B5
Wielgie
Kujawsko-Pomorskie
PL 77 B4
Łódzkie PL 86 A2
Mazowieckie PL 87 A5
Wielgomłyny PL 87 A3
Wielichowo PL 75 B5
Wieliczka PL 99 B4
Wielka Łąka PL 76 A3
Wielowies PL 86 B2
Wieluń PL 86 A2
Wien = Vienna A 111 A3
Wiener Neustadt A 111 B3
Wiepke D 73 B4
Wierden NL 71 B3
Wieren D 73 B3
Wieruszów PL 86 A2
Wierzbica
Mazowieckie PL 77 B6
Mazowieckie PL 87 A5
Wierzbie PL 86 A2
Wierzbięcin PL 75 A4
Wierzchowo PL 75 A5
Wierzchucino PL 68 A3
Wierzchy PL 86 A2
Wies A 110 C2
Wiesau D 95 B4
Wiesbaden D 93 A4
Wieselburg A 110 A2
Wiesen CH 107 C4
Wiesenburg D 73 B5
Wiesenfelden D 95 B4
Wiesensteig D 94 C1
Wiesentheid D 94 B2
Wiesloch D 93 B4
Wiesmath A 111 B3
Wiesmoor D 71 A4
Wietmarschen D 71 B4
Wietze D 72 B2
Wigan GB 38 A4
Wiggen CH 106 C2
Wigston GB 40 C2
Wigton GB 36 B3
Wigtown GB 36 B2
Wijchen NL 80 A1
Wijhe NL 70 B3
Wijk bij Duurstede
NL 70 C2
Wil CH 107 B4
Wilamowice PL 99 B3
Wilczęta PL 69 A4
Wilczkowice PL 77 B4
Wilczna PL 76 B3
Wilczyn PL 76 B3
Wildalpen A 110 B1
Wildbad D 93 C4
Wildberg
Baden-Württemberg
D 93 C4
Brandenburg D 74 B1
Wildegg CH 106 B3
Wildendürnbach A 97 C4
Wildeshausen D 72 B1
Wildon A 110 C2
Wilfersdorf A 97 C4
Wilhelmsburg
A 110 A2
D 74 A2
Wilhelmsdorf D 107 B4
Wilhelmshaven D 71 A5
Wilków PL 77 B5
Willebadessen D 81 A5
Willebroek B 79 A4
Willgottheim F 93 C3
Willhermsdorf D 94 B2
Willich D 80 A2
Willingen D 81 A4
Willington GB 37 B5
Willisau CH 106 B3
Wilmslow GB 40 B1
Wilsdruff D 83 A5
Wilster D 64 C2
Wilsum D 71 B3
Wilton GB 44 B2
Wiltz L 92 B1
Wimborne Minster
GB 43 B5
Wimereux F 78 B1
Wimmenau F 93 C3
Wimmis CH 106 C2
Wincanton GB 43 A4
Winchcombe GB 44 B2
Winchelsea GB 45 C4
Winchester GB 44 B2
Windermere GB 36 B4
Windischeschenbach
D 95 B4
Windischgarsten A 110 B1
Windorf D 96 C1
Windsbach D 94 B2
Windsor GB 44 B3
Wingene B 78 A3
Wingham GB 45 B5
Winkleigh GB 42 B3
Winklern A 109 C3
Winnenden D 94 C1
Winnica PL 77 B5
Winnigstedt D 73 B3
Winnweiler D 93 B3
Winschoten NL 71 A4
Winsen
Niedersachsen D 72 A3
Niedersachsen D 72 B2
Winsford GB 38 A4
Wińsko PL 85 A4
Winslow GB 44 B3
Winsum
Friesland NL 70 A2
Groningen NL 71 A3
Winterberg D 81 A4
Winterfeld D 73 B4
Winterswijk NL 71 C3
Winterthur CH 107 B3
Wintzenheim F 106 A2
Winzer D 95 C5
Wipperdorf D 82 A2
Wipperfürth D 80 A3
Wirksworth GB 40 B2
Wisbech GB 41 C4
Wischhafen D 64 C2
Wishaw GB 35 C4
Wisła PL 98 B2
Wisła Wielka PL 98 B2
Wiślica PL 87 B4
Wismar D 65 C4
Wiśniewo PL 77 A5
Wiśniowa PL 99 B4
Wissant F 78 B1
Wissembourg F 93 B3
Wissen D 81 B3
Witanowice PL 99 B3
Witham GB 45 B4
Withern GB 41 B4
Withernsea GB 41 B4
Witkowo PL 76 B2
Witmarsum NL 70 A2
Witney GB 44 B2
Witnica PL 75 B3
Witonia PL 77 B4
Witry-les-Reims F 91 B4
Wittdün D 64 B1
Wittelsheim F 106 B2
Witten D 80 A3
Wittenberge D 73 A4
Wittenburg D 73 A4
Wittenheim F 106 B2
Wittichenau D 84 A2
Wittighausen D 94 B1
Wittingen D 73 B3
Wittislingen D 94 C2
Wittlich D 92 B2
Wittmannsdorf A 110 C2
Wittmund D 71 A4
Wittorf D 72 A2
Wittstock D 73 A5
Witzenhausen D 82 A1
Wiveliscombe GB 43 A3
Wivenhoe GB 45 B4
Władysławowo PL 69 A3
Wleń PL 84 A3
Włocławek PL 77 B4
Włodawa PL 13 C5
Włodzimierzów PL 87 A3
Włosień PL 84 A3
Włostow PL 87 B5
Włoszakowice PL 75 C5
Włoszczowa PL 87 B3
Wöbbelin D 73 A4
Woburn GB 44 B3
Wodzisław PL 87 B4
Wodzisław Śląski
PL 98 B2
Woerden NL 70 B1
Woerth F 93 C3
Wohlen CH 106 B3
Woippy F 92 B2
Wojcieszow PL 85 B3
Wojkowice Kościelne
PL 86 B3
Wojnicz PL 99 B4
Woking GB 44 B3
Wokingham GB 44 B3
Wola Jachowa PL 87 B4
Wola Niechcicka PL 86 A3
Wolbórz PL 87 A3
Wolbrom PL 87 B3
Wołczyn PL 86 A2
Woldegk D 74 A2
Wolfach D 93 C4
Wolfegg D 107 B4
Wolfen D 83 A4
Wolfenbüttel D 73 B3
Wolfersheim D 81 B4
Wolfhagen D 81 A5
Wolfratshausen D 108 B2
Wolfsberg A 110 C1
Wolfsburg D 73 B3
Wolf's Castle GB 39 C2
Wolfshagen D 74 A2
Wolfstein D 93 B3
Wolfurt A 107 B4
Wolgast D 66 B2
Wolhusen CH 106 B3
Wolin PL 67 C3
Wolka PL 87 A4
Wolkenstein D 83 B5
Wolkersdorf A 97 C4
Wöllersdorf A 111 B3
Wollin D 73 B5
Wöllstadt D 81 B4
Wolmirstedt D 73 B4
Wolnzach D 95 C3
Wołów PL 85 A4
Wolsztyn PL 75 B5
Wolvega NL 70 B2
Wolverhampton GB 40 C1
Wolverton GB 44 A3
Wombwell GB 40 B2
Woodbridge GB 45 A5
Woodhall Spa GB 41 B3
Woodstock GB 44 B2
Wookey Hole GB 43 A4
Wool GB 43 B4
Woolacombe GB 42 A2
Wooler GB 37 A4
Woolwich GB 45 B4
Wooperton GB 37 A5
Worb CH 106 C2
Worbis D 82 A2
Worcester GB 39 B4
Wördern A 97 C4
Wörgl A 108 B3
Workington GB 36 B3
Worksop GB 40 B2
Workum NL 70 B2
Wörlitz D 83 A4
Wormer NL 70 B1
Wormhout F 78 B2
Wormit GB 35 B5
Worms D 93 B4
Worpswede D 72 A1
Wörrstadt D 93 B4
Wörschach A 110 B1
Worsley GB 38 A4
Wörth
Bayern D 93 B5
Bayern D 95 B4
Bayern D 95 C4
Rheinland-Pfalz D 93 B4
Worthing GB 44 C3
Woudsend NL 70 B2
Woumen B 78 A2
Woźniki PL 86 B3
Wragby GB 41 B3
Wrangle GB 41 B4
Wręczyca Wlk. PL 86 B2
Wredenhagen D 73 A5
Wremen D 72 A1
Wrentham GB 45 A5
Wrexham GB 38 A3
Wriedel D 72 A3
Wriezen D 74 B3
Wrist D 64 C2
Wróblewo
Mazowieckie PL 77 B5
Wielkopolskie PL 75 B5
Wrocki PL 69 B4
Wrocław PL 85 A5
Wronki PL 75 B5
Wroxham GB 41 C5
Września PL 76 B2
Wrzosowo PL 67 B4
Wschowa PL 85 A4
Wulfen D 80 A3
Wülfen D 83 A3
Wulkau D 73 B5
Wünnenberg D 81 A4
Wünsdorf D 74 B2
Wunsiedel D 95 A4
Wunstorf D 72 B2
Wuppertal D 80 A3
Wurmannsquick D 95 C4
Würselen D 80 B2
Wurzbach D 82 B3
Würzburg D 94 B1
Wurzen D 83 A4
Wust D 74 B1
Wusterhausen D 73 B5
Wusterwitz D 73 B5
Wustrau-Altfriesack
D 74 B1
Wustrow D 66 B1
Wuustwezel B 79 A4
Wye GB 45 B4
Wyględów PL 87 A5
Wyk D 64 B1
Wykroty PL 84 A3
Wylye GB 43 A5
Wymiarki PL 84 A3
Wymondham GB 41 C5
Wyrzysk PL 76 A2
Wyśmierzyce PL 87 A4
Wysoka
Dolnośląskie PL 85 A3
Wielkopolskie PL 76 A2
Wyszanów PL 86 A2
Wyszogród PL 77 B5

X

Xanten D 80 A2
Xanthi GR 183 B6
Xarrë AL 182 D2
Xátiva E 159 C3
Xeraco E 159 B3
Xert E 153 B4
Xerta E 153 B4
Xertigny F 105 A5
Xilagani GR 183 C7
Xilokastro GR 184 A3
Xinzo de Limia E 140 B3
Xixón = Gijón E 142 A1
Xove E 140 A3
Xubia E 140 A2
Xunqueira de Ambia
E 140 B3
Xunqueira de
Espadañedo E 140 B3
Xylophagou CY 181 B2

Y

Yablanitsa BG 17 D6
Yağcılar TR 186 C3
Yahyalı TR 23 B8
Yakoruda BG 183 A5
Yalova TR 187 B4
Yalvaç TR 189 A6
Yambol BG 17 D7
Yampil UA 13 D8
Yaniskoski RUS 193 D12
Yantarnyy RUS 69 A4
Yarbasan TR 186 D3
Yarcombe GB 43 B3
Yaremcha UA 13 D6
Yarm GB 37 B5
Yarmouth GB 44 C2
Yarrow GB 35 C4
Yasinya UA 17 A6
Yatağan TR 188 B3
Yate GB 43 A4
Yatton GB 43 A4
Yavoriv UA 13 D5
Yaxley GB 41 C3
Yazıca TR 187 B6
Yazıköy TR 188 C2
Ybbs A 110 A2
Ybbsitz A 110 B1
Ydby DK 58 B1
Yddal N 46 B2
Ydes F 116 B2
Yealmpton GB 42 B3
Yebra de Basa E 145 B3
Yecla E 159 C2
Yecla de Yeltes E 149 B3

Yelsk BY 13 C8
Yelverton GB 42 B2
Yena RUS 197 B14
Yenice
Ankara TR 23 B7
Aydın TR 188 B3
Çanakkale TR 186 C2
Edirne TR 183 C8
Yenifoça TR 186 D1
Yenihisar TR 188 B2
Yeniköy TR 186 D4
Yeniköy Plaji TR 186 B3
Yenipazar TR 188 B3
Yenişarbademli TR 189 B6
Yenişehir TR 187 B4
Yenne F 118 B2
Yeovil GB 43 B4
Yepes E 151 C4
Yerköy TR 23 B8
Yerólakkos CY 181 A2
Yeroskipos CY 181 B1
Yerseke NL 79 A4
Yerville F 89 A4
Yeşildağ TR 189 B6
Yeşilhisar TR 23 B8
Yeşilköy TR 186 B3
Yeşilova TR 189 B4
Yeşilyurt TR 188 A3
Yeste E 164 A2
Yezerishche BY 9 E6
Y Felinheli GB 38 A2
Ygos-St Saturnin F 128 C2
Ygrande F 104 C1
Yialousa CY 181 A3
Yığılca TR 187 B6
Yli-Ii FIN 197 D8
Yli-Kärppä FIN 197 D8
Yli-Muonia FIN 196 A6
Ylitornio FIN 196 C6
Ylivieska FIN 3 D9
Ylläsjärvi FIN 196 B7
Ymonville F 103 A3
Yngsjö S 63 C2
York GB 40 B2
Youghal IRL 29 C4
Yoğuntaş TR 186 A2
Yozgat TR 23 B8
Yport F 89 A4
Ypres = Ieper B 78 B2
Yssingeaux F 117 B4
Ystad S 66 A2
Ystalyfera GB 39 C3
Ystebrød N 52 B1
Ystradgynlais GB 39 C3
Ytre Arna N 46 B2
Ytre Enebakk N 54 A2
Ytre Rendal N 199 D8
Ytteran S 199 B11
Ytterhogdal S 199 C11
Yttermalung S 49 B5
Yunak TR 187 D6
Yuncos E 151 B4
Yunquera E 162 B3
Yunquera de Henares
E 151 B4
Yushkozero RUS 3 D13
Yverdon-les-Bains
CH 106 C1
Yvetot F 89 A4
Yvignac F 101 A3
Yvoir B 79 B4
Yvonand CH 106 C1
Yxnerum S 56 B2
Yzeure F 104 C2

Z

Zaamslag NL 79 A3
Zaanstad NL 70 B1
Žabalj SRB 126 B2
Zabar H 113 A4
Žabari SRB 127 C3
Zabiče SLO 123 B3
Zabierzów PL 87 B3
Ząbki PL 77 B6
Ząbkowice Śląskie
PL 85 B4
Zablaće HR 138 B1
Žabljak MNE 139 B5
Žabno PL 87 B4
Zabok HR 124 A1
Žabokreky SK 98 C2
Zabor PL 75 C4
Žabowo PL 75 A4
Zabrdje BIH 125 C4
Zábřeh CZ 97 B4
Zabrežje SRB 127 C2
Ząbrowo PL 67 C4
Zabrze PL 86 B2
Zabrzeź PL 99 B4
Zacharo GR 184 B2
Zadar HR 137 A4
Zadzim PL 86 A2
Zafarraya E 163 B3
Zafferana Etnea I 177 B4
Zafra E 155 C4
Žaga SLO 122 A2
Zagajica SRB 127 C3
Żagań PL 84 A3
Zaglav HR 137 B4
Zaglavak SRB 127 D1
Zagnanśk PL 87 B4
Zagora GR 183 D5
Zagorc SLO 110 C2
Zagorićani BIH 138 B3
Zagorje SLO 123 A4
Zagórów PL 76 B2
Zagradje SRB 127 C2
Zagreb HR 124 B1
Zagrilla E 163 A3
Zagvozd HR 138 B3
Zagwiździe PL 86 B1
Zagyvarekas H 113 B4
Zagyvaróna H 113 A3
Zahara E 162 B2
Zahara de los Atunes
E 162 B2
Zahinos E 155 C4
Zahna D 83 A4
Záhoři CZ 96 B2
Zahrádka CZ 97 B3
Zahrensdorf D 73 A3
Zaidin E 153 A4
Zaječar SRB 16 D5
Zákamenné SK 99 B3
Zákány H 124 A2
Zákányszék H 126 A1
Zakliczyn PL 99 B4
Zakopane PL 99 B3
Zakroczym PL 77 B5
Zakrzew PL 87 A5
Zakrzewo PL 76 B3
Zakupy CZ 84 B2
Zakynthos GR 184 B1
Zalaapáti H 111 C4
Zalabaksa H 111 C3
Zalaegerszeg H 111 C3
Zalakomár H 111 C4
Zalakoppány H 111 C4
Zalalövő H 111 C3
Zalamea de la Serena
E 156 B2
Zalamea la Real E 161 B3
Zalaszentgrót H 111 C4
Zalaszentiván H 111 C3
Zalău RO 17 B5
Zalavár H 111 C4
Zalcsie PL 86 A3
Zaldibar E 143 A4
Žalec SLO 123 A4
Zalesie PL 77 A5
Zalewo PL 69 B4
Zalishchyky UA 13 D6
Zalla E 143 A3
Zaltbommel NL 79 A5
Zamárdi H 112 C1
Zamarte PL 68 B2
Zamberk CZ 85 B4
Zambra E 163 A3
Zambugueira do Mar
P 160 B1
Zámoly H 112 B2
Zamora E 149 A4
Zamość PL 13 C5
Zamoście PL 86 A3
Zams A 108 B1
Zandhoven B 79 A4
Žandov CZ 84 B2
Zandvoort NL 70 B1
Zangliveri GR 183 C5
Zánka H 111 C4
Zaorejas E 152 B1
Zaovine SRB 127 D1
Zapadnaya Dvina
RUS 9 D8
Zapfend D 94 A2
Zapole PL 86 A2
Zapolyarnyy RUS 193 C14
Zapponeta I 171 B3
Zaprešić HR 124 B1
Zaragoza E 153 A3
Zarasai LT 13 A7
Zarautz E 144 A1
Zarcilla de Ramos
E 164 B3
Zaręby PL 77 A6
Żarki PL 86 B3
Zarko GR 182 D4
Žarnovica SK 98 C2
Zarnow PL 87 A4
Zarnowiec PL 68 A3
Zarošice CZ 97 B4
Żarów PL 85 B4
Zarren B 78 A2
Zarrentin D 73 A3
Żary PL 84 A3
Zarza Capilla E 156 B2
Zarza de Alange E 156 B1
Zarza de Granadilla
E 149 B3
Zarza de Tajo E 151 B4
Zarzadilla de Totana
E 164 B3
Zarza la Mayor E 155 B4
Zarzuela del Monte
E 150 B3
Zarzuela del Pinar
E 151 A3
Zas E 140 A2
Zasavica SRB 127 C1
Zasieki PL 84 A2
Zásmuky CZ 96 B3
Žatec CZ 83 B5
Zaton HR 139 C4
Zatonie PL 84 A3
Zator PL 99 A3
Zauchwitz D 74 B2
Zavala BIH 139 C3
Zavalje BIH 124 C1
Zavattarello I 120 C2
Zavidovići BIH 139 A4
Zavlaka SRB 127 C1
Zawady PL 77 C5
Zawadzkie PL 86 B2
Zawdy PL 86 A2
Zawidów PL 84 A3
Zawidz PL 77 B4
Zawiercie PL 86 B3
Zawoja PL 99 B3
Zawonia PL 85 A5
Žažina HR 124 B2
Zázrivá SK 99 B3
Zbarazh UA 13 D6
Zbąszyń PL 75 B4
Zbąszynek PL 75 B4
Zbehy SK 98 C2
Zbiersk PL 76 C3
Zbiroh CZ 96 B1
Zblewo PL 69 B3
Zbójno PL 77 A4
Zbrachlin PL 76 A3
Zbraslav CZ 96 B2
Zbraslavice CZ 97 B3
Ždala HR 124 A3
Ždánice CZ 98 B1
Žďár nad Sázavou
CZ 97 B3
Zdbice PL 75 A5
Zdenci HR 125 B3
Ždiar SK 99 B4
Zdice CZ 96 B1
Zdirec nad Doubravou
CZ 97 B3
Zdolbuniv UA 13 C7
Zdounky CZ 98 B1
Ždrelo SRB 127 C3
Zduńska Wola PL 86 A2
Zduny
Łódzkie PL 77 B4
Wielkopolskie PL 85 A5
Żdżary PL 87 A4
Zdziechowice
Opolskie PL 86 A2
Wielkopolskie PL 76 B2
Zdziszowice PL 86 B2
Zeberio E 143 A4
Žebrák CZ 96 B1
Zebreira P 155 B3
Zebrzydowa PL 84 A3
Zechlin D 74 A1
Zechlinerhütte D 74 A1
Zederhaus A 109 B4
Žednik SRB 126 B1
Zeebrugge B 78 A3
Zegrze PL 77 B6
Zehdenick D 74 B2
Zehren D 83 A5
Zeil D 94 A2
Zeilarn D 95 C4
Zeist NL 70 B2
Zeithain D 83 A5
Zeitz D 83 A4
Želatava CZ 97 B3
Želazno PL 68 A2
Zele B 79 A4
Zelenoborskiy RUS 3 C13
Zelenogorsk RUS 9 B6
Zelenograd RUS 9 D10
Zelenogradsk RUS 12 A4
Železná Ruda CZ 96 B1
Železnice CZ 84 B3
Železnik SRB 127 C2
Zelezniki SLO 123 A3
Železny Brod CZ 84 B3
Zelhem NL 71 B3
Želiezovce SK 112 A2
Želkowo PL 68 A2
Zell
CH 106 B2
Baden-Württemberg
D 93 C4
Baden-Württemberg
D 106 B2
Rheinland-Pfalz D 92 A3
Zella-Mehlis D 82 B2
Zell am See A 109 B3
Zell am Ziller A 108 B2
Zell an der Pram A 96 C1
Zell bei Zellhof A 96 C2
Zellerndorf A 97 C3
Zellingen D 94 B1
Želovce SK 112 A3
Zelów PL 86 A3
Zeltweg A 110 B1
Zelzate B 79 A3
Zemberovce SK 98 C2
Zembrzyce PL 99 B3
Zemianske-Kostol'any
SK 98 C2
Zemitz D 66 C2
Zemné SK 112 B1
Zemst B 79 B4
Zemun SRB 127 C2
Zemunik Donji HR 137 A4
Zenica BIH 139 A3
Zennor GB 42 B1
Žepa BIH 139 B5
Žepče BIH 139 A4
Zepponami I 168 A2
Zerbst D 73 C5
Zerf D 92 B2
Zerind RO 113 C5
Żerków PL 76 B2
Zermatt CH 119 A4
Zernez CH 107 C5
Zerpen-schleuse D 74 B2
Zestoa E 144 A1
Zetel D 71 A4
Zeulenroda D 83 B3
Zeven D 72 A2
Zevenaar NL 70 C3
Zevenbergen NL 79 A4
Zévio I 121 B4
Zeytinbaği TR 186 B3
Zeytindağ TR 186 D2
Zgierz PL 86 A3
Zgorzelec PL 84 A3
Zgošča BIH 139 A4
Zhabinka BY 13 B6
Zharkovskiy RUS 9 E8
Zhashkiv UA 13 D9
Zhlobin BY 13 B9
Zhmerynka UA 13 D8
Zhodzina BY 13 A8
Zhytomyr UA 13 C8
Žiar nad Hronom
SK 98 C2
Zicavo F 180 B2
Zickhusen D 65 C4
Zidani Most SLO 123 A4
Ziddorf D 73 A5
Židlochovice CZ 97 B4
Ziębice PL 85 B5
Ziegendorf D 73 A4
Ziegenrück D 83 B3
Zieleniec
Dolnośląskie PL 85 B4
Warmińsko-Mazurskie
PL 77 A6
Zachodnio-Pomorskie
PL 75 A4
Zielona PL 77 A4
Zielona Góra PL 75 C4
Zieluń-Osada PL 77 A4
Ziemetshausen D 94 C2
Zierenberg D 81 A5
Zierikzee NL 79 A3
Ziersdorf A 97 C3
Zierzow D 73 A4
Ziesar D 73 B5
Ziesendorf D 65 C5
Ziethen D 74 B2
Žihle CZ 96 A1
Žilina SK 98 B2
Ziltendorf D 74 B3
Zimandu Nou RO 126 A3
Zimna Woda PL 77 A5
Zimnicea RO 17 D6
Zinal CH 119 A4
Zinasco I 120 B2
Zingst D 66 B1
Zinkgruvan S 55 B6
Žinkovy CZ 96 B1
Zinnowitz D 66 B2
Zirc H 112 B1
Žiri SLO 123 A3
Zirl A 108 B2
Zirndorf D 94 B2
Žirovnica SRB 127 C3
Žirovnice CZ 97 B3
Zisterdorf A 97 C4
Žitište SRB 126 B2
Zitsa GR 182 D2
Zittau D 84 B2
Živaja HR 124 B2
Živinice BIH 139 A4
Zlatar HR 124 A2
Zlatar Bistrica HR 124 A2
Zlate Hory CZ 85 B5
Zlaté Klasy SK 111 A4
Zlaté Moravce SK 98 C2
Zlatnána Ostrove
SK 112 B1
Zlatniky SK 98 C2
Zlatograd BG 183 B7
Žlebič SLO 123 B3
Zlín CZ 98 B1
Złocieniec PL 75 A5
Złoczew PL 86 A2
Zlonice CZ 84 B2
Złotniki Kujawskie
PL 76 B3
Złotoryja PL 85 A3
Złotów PL 68 B2
Złoty Stok PL 85 B4
Zlutice CZ 83 B5
Zmajevac BIH 124 C2
Zmajevo SRB 126 B1
Żmigród PL 85 A4
Zmijavci HR 138 B3
Žminj HR 122 B2
Żnin PL 76 B2
Znojmo CZ 97 C4
Zöblitz D 83 B5
Zocca I 135 A3
Zoetermeer NL 70 B1
Zofingen CH 106 B2
Zogno I 120 B2
Zohor SK 111 A3
Zolling D 95 C3
Zolochiv UA 13 D6
Zomba H 112 C2
Zomergem B 79 A3
Zoñán E 141 A3
Zonguldak TR 187 A6
Zonhoven B 79 B5
Zonza F 180 B2
Zörbig D 83 A4
Zorita E 156 A2
Żory PL 98 A2
Zossen D 74 B2
Zottegem B 79 B3
Zoutkamp NL 71 A3
Zovi Do BIH 139 B4
Zreče SLO 123 A4
Zrenjanin SRB 126 B2
Žrnovica HR 138 B2
Zručnad Sazavou
CZ 97 B3
Zsadány H 113 C5
Zsámbék H 112 B2
Zsámbok H 112 B3
Zsana H 126 A1
Zschopau D 83 B5
Zuberec SK 99 B3
Zubieta E 144 A2
Zubiri E 144 B2
Zubtsov RUS 9 D9
Zucaina E 153 B3
Zudar D 66 B2
Zuera E 144 C3
Zufre E 161 B3
Zug CH 107 B3
Zuheros E 163 A3
Zuidhorn NL 71 A3
Zuidlaren NL 71 A3
Zuidwolde NL 71 B3
Zújar E 164 B2
Žukowo PL 69 A3
Žuljana HR 138 C3
Žulová CZ 85 B5
Zülpich D 80 B2
Zumaia E 144 A1
Zumárraga E 143 A4
Zundert NL 79 A4
Županja HR 125 B4
Zurgena E 164 B2
Zürich CH 107 B3
Żuromin PL 77 A4
Zurzach CH 106 B3
Zusmarshausen D 94 C2
Zusow D 65 C4
Züssow D 66 C2
Žuta Lovka HR 123 C4
Zutphen NL 70 B3
Žužemberk SLO 123 B3
Zvenyhorodka UA 13 D9
Zvikovské Podhradi
CZ 96 B2
Zvolen SK 99 C3
Zvolenská Slatina
SK 99 C3
Zvornik BIH 139 A5
Zwartsluis NL 70 B3
Zweibrücken D 93 B3
Zweisimmen CH 106 C2
Zwettl A 97 C3
Zwettl an der Rodl
A 96 C2
Zwickau D 83 B4
Zwiefalten D 107 A4
Zwieryn PL 75 B4
Zwierzno PL 69 A4
Zwiesel D 96 B1
Zwieselstein A 108 C2
Zwoleń PL 87 A5
Zwolle NL 70 B3
Zwönitz D 83 B4
Żychlin PL 77 B4
Zydowo
Wielkopolskie PL 76 B2
Zachodnio-Pomorskie
PL 68 A1
Żyrardów PL 77 B5
Żytno PL 86 B3
Żywiec PL 99 B3
Zyyi CY 181 B2